The Oxford Handbook of Eating Disorders

OXFORD LIBRARY OF PSYCHOLOGY

Editor-in-Chief PETER E. NATHAN

The Oxford Handbook of Eating Disorders

Edited by

W. Stewart Agras

OXFORD
UNIVERSITY PRESS

2010

616,8
Ox 20

OXFORD
UNIVERSITY PRESS

Oxford University Press, Inc., publishes works that further Oxford University's
objective of excellence in research, scholarship, and education.

Oxford   New York
Auckland   Cape Town   Dar es Salaam   Hong Kong   Karachi
Kuala Lumpur   Madrid   Melbourne   Mexico City   Nairobi
New Delhi   Shanghai   Taipei   Toronto

With offices in
Argentina   Austria   Brazil   Chile   Czech Republic   France   Greece
Guatemala   Hungary   Italy   Japan   Poland   Portugal   Singapore
South Korea   Switzerland   Thailand   Turkey   Ukraine   Vietnam

Published by Oxford University Press, Inc.
198 Madison Avenue, New York, New York 10016
www.oup.com

Library of Congress Cataloging-in-Publication Data

The Oxford handbook of eating disorders / edited by W. Stewart Agras.
    p. ; cm. — (Oxford library of psychology)
 Includes bibliographical references and index.
 ISBN 978-0-19-537362-2 (alk. paper)
 1. Eating disorders. I. Agras, W. Stewart. II. Series: Oxford library of psychology.
 [DNLM: 1. Eating Disorders. WM 175 O98 2010]
 RC552.E18O94 2010
 616.85'26—dc22   2009038182

9 8 7 6 5 4 3 2 1
Printed in the United States of America on acid-free paper

126.00

SHORT CONTENTS

Oxford Library of Psychology   vii

About the Editor   ix

Contributors   xi

Contents   xv

Chapters   1–490

Index   491

OXFORD LIBRARY OF PSYCHOLOGY

The *Oxford Library of Psychology*, a landmark series of handbooks, is published by Oxford University Press, one of the world's oldest and most highly respected publishers, with a tradition of publishing significant books in psychology. The ambitious goal of the *Oxford Library of Psychology* is nothing less than to span a vibrant, wide-ranging field and, in so doing, to fill a clear market need.

Encompassing a comprehensive set of handbooks, organized hierarchically, the *Library* incorporates volumes at different levels, each designed to meet a distinct need. At one level are a set of handbooks designed broadly to survey the major subfields of psychology; at another are numerous handbooks that cover important current focal research and scholarly areas of psychology in depth and detail. Planned as a reflection of the dynamism of psychology, the *Library* will grow and expand as psychology itself develops, thereby highlighting significant new research that will impact on the field. Adding to its accessibility and ease of use, the *Library* will be published in print and, later on, electronically.

The *Library* surveys psychology's principal subfields with a set of handbooks that capture the current status and future prospects of those major subdisciplines. This initial set includes handbooks of social and personality psychology, clinical psychology, counseling psychology, school psychology, educational psychology, industrial and organizational psychology, cognitive psychology, cognitive neuroscience, methods and measurements, history, neuropsychology, personality assessment, developmental psychology, and more. Each handbook undertakes to review one of psychology's major subdisciplines with breadth, comprehensiveness, and exemplary scholarship. In addition to these broadly conceived volumes, the *Library* also includes a large number of handbooks designed to explore in depth more specialized areas of scholarship and research, such as stress, health and coping, anxiety and related disorders, cognitive development, or child and adolescent assessment. In contrast to the broad coverage of the subfield handbooks, each of these latter volumes focuses on an especially productive, more highly focused line of scholarship and research. Whether at the broadest or most specific level, however, all of the *Library* handbooks offer synthetic coverage that reviews and evaluates the relevant past and present research and anticipates research in the future. Each handbook in the *Library* includes introductory and concluding chapters written by its editor to provide a roadmap to the handbook's table of contents and to offer informed anticipations of significant future developments in that field.

An undertaking of this scope calls for handbook editors and chapter authors who are established scholars in the areas about which they write. Many of the nation's and world's most productive and best-respected psychologists have agreed to edit *Library* handbooks or write authoritative chapters in their areas of expertise.

For whom has the *Oxford Library of Psychology* been written? Because of its breadth, depth, and accessibility, the *Library* serves a diverse audience, including graduate students in psychology and their faculty mentors, scholars, researchers, and practitioners in psychology and related fields. Each will find in the *Library* the information they seek on the subfield or focal area of psychology in which they work or are interested.

Befitting its commitment to accessibility, each handbook includes a comprehensive index, as well as extensive references to help guide research. And because the *Library* was designed from its inception as an online as well as a print resource, its structure and contents will be readily and rationally searchable online. Further, once the *Library* is released online, the handbooks will be regularly and thoroughly updated.

In summary, the *Oxford Library of Psychology* will grow organically to provide a thoroughly informed perspective on the field of psychology, one that reflects both psychology's dynamism and its increasing interdisciplinarity. Once published electronically, the *Library* is also destined to become a uniquely valuable interactive tool, with extended search and browsing capabilities. As you begin to consult this handbook, we sincerely hope you will share our enthusiasm for the more than 500-year tradition of Oxford University Press for excellence, innovation, and quality, as exemplified by the *Oxford Library of Psychology*.

Peter E. Nathan
Editor-in-Chief
Oxford Library of Psychology

ABOUT THE EDITOR

W. Stewart Agras

Stewart Agras, M.D., is Professor Emeritus in the Department of Psychiatry and Behavioral Sciences at Stanford University. He was Editor of the *Journal of Applied Behavior Analysis* and the *Annals of Behavioral Medicine*. He has been working in the field of eating disorders for the past 25 years and continues to direct an active research program at Stanford.

CONTRIBUTORS

W. Stewart Agras
Department of Psychiatry and
Behavioral Sciences
Stanford University School of
Medicine
Stanford, CA

Kelly C. Allison
Department of Psychiatry
University of Pennsylvania School of
Medicine
Philadelphia, PA

Drew A. Anderson
Department of Psychology
University at Albany, SUNY
Albany, NY

Eunice Y. Chen
Department of Psychology
University of Chicago
Chicago, IL

Ross D. Crosby
Neuropsychiatric Research Institute
Department of Clinical Neuroscience
University of North Dakota School of
Medicine and Health Sciences
Fargo, ND

Scott J. Crow
Department of Psychiatry
University of Minnesota School of
Medicine
Minneapolis, MN

Angélica de M. Claudino
Department of Psychiatry
Federal University of São Paulo
São Paulo, Brazil

Myles S. Faith
Center for Weight and Eating
Disorders
University of Pennsylvania School of
Medicine
Philadelphia, PA

Alison E. Field
Division of Adolescent/Young Adult
Medicine
Children's Hospital Boston
Department of Epidemiology
Harvard School of Public Health
Boston, MA

Eike Fittig
Institut für Klinische Psychologie und
Psychotherapie
Technische Universität Dresden
Dresden, Germany

E. Leigh Gibson
Clinical and Health Psychology
Research Centre
Department of Psychology
Roehampton University
London, UK

Kathryn H. Gordon
Department of Psychology
North Dakota State University
Neuropsychiatric Research Institute
Fargo, ND

Anna I. Guerdjikova
Lindner Center of HOPE
Mason, OH
Department of Psychiatry
University of Cincinnati College of
Medicine
Cincinnati, OH

Katherine A. Halmi
Department of Psychiatry
Weill Cornell Medical College
Cornell University
White Plains, NY

Phillipa J. Hay
School of Medicine and Psychiatry
University of Western Sydney
Campbeltown, New South Wales,
James Cook University, Australia

Jill M. Holm-Denoma
Department of Psychology
University of Denver
Denver, CO

Corinna Jacobi
Institut für Klinische Psychologie und
Psychotherapie
Technische Universität Dresden
Dresden, Germany

Nuray O. Kanbur
Division of Adolescent Medicine
The Hospital for Sick Children
University of Toronto
Toronto, Ontario, Canada

Debra K. Katzman
Division of Adolescent Medicine
The Hospital for Sick Children
University of Toronto
Toronto, Ontario, Canada

Walter H. Kaye
Department of Psychiatry
University of California, San Diego
La Jolla, CA

Paul E. Keck, Jr.
Lindner Center of HOPE
Mason, OH
Department of Psychiatry
University of Cincinnati College of
Medicine
Cincinnati, OH

Pamela K. Keel
Department of Psychology
Florida State University
Tallahassee, FL

Nicole Kitos
Division of Adolescent/Young Adult
Medicine
Children's Hospital Boston and Harvard
Medical School
Boston, MA

Daniel le Grange
Department of Psychiatry and Behavioral
Neuroscience
University of Chicago
Chicago, IL

Michael P. Levine
Department of Psychology
Kenyon College
Gambier, OH

James Lock
Department of Psychiatry and
Behavioral Science
Stanford University School of
Medicine
Stanford, CA

Jennifer D. Lundgren
Department of Psychology
University of Missouri – Kansas City
Kansas City, MO

Susan L. McElroy
Lindner Center of HOPE
Mason, OH
Department of Psychiatry
University of Cincinnati College of
Medicine
Cincinnati, OH

James E. Mitchell
Neuropsychiatric Research Institute
Department of Clinical Neuroscience
University of North Dakota School of
Medicine and Health Sciences
Fargo, ND

Nicole Mori
Lindner Center of HOPE
Mason, OH
Department of Psychiatry
University of Cincinnati College of
Medicine
Cincinnati, OH

Andrea D. Murray
Department of Psychology
University at Albany, SUNY
Albany, NY

Peter Musiat
Section of Eating Disorders
Institute of Psychiatry
London, UK

Tyson Oberndorfer
Department of Psychiatry
University of California, San Diego
La Jolla, CA

Anne M. O'Melia
Lindner Center of HOPE
Mason, OH
Department of Psychiatry
University of Cincinnati College of
Medicine
Cincinnati, OH

Katherine Presnell
Department of Psychology
Southern Methodist University
Dallas, TX

Renee Rienecke Hoste
Department of Psychiatry and Behavioral
Neuroscience
University of Chicago
Chicago, IL

Debra Safer
Department of Psychiatry
Stanford University
Stanford, CA

Ulrike Schmidt
Section of Eating Disorders
Institute of Psychiatry
London, UK

Nicholas Smiley
University of Minnesota
Minneapolis, MN

Linda Smolak
Department of Psychology
Kenyon College
Gambier, OH

Meghan M. Sinton
Department of Psychiatry
Washington University School of
Medicine
St. Louis, MO

Cathleen M. Steinegger
Division of Adolescent Medicine
The Hospital for Sick Children
University of Toronto
Toronto, Ontario, Canada

Eric Stice
Oregon Research Institute
Eugene, OR

Marian Tanofsky-Kraff
Department of Medical and Clinical
Psychology
Uniformed Services University of the
Health Sciences
Unit on Growth and Obesity, Program in
Developmental Endocrinology and
Genetics

Eunice Kennedy Shriver National
Institute of Child Health and Human
Development
National Institutes of Health
Bethesda, MD

C. Barr Taylor
Department of Psychiatry
Stanford University School of Medicine
Stanford, CA

Claus Vögele
INSIDE Research Centre,
Université du Luxembourg,
Luxembourg

Tracey D. Wade
Department of Psychology
Flinders University
Adelaide, South Australia, Australia

Denise E. Wilfley
Departments of Psychiatry, Medicine,
Pediatrics, and Psychology
Washington University School of
Medicine
St. Louis, MO

G. Terence Wilson
Graduate School of Applied and
Professional Psychology
Rutgers University
Piscataway, NJ

Stephen A. Wonderlich
Department of Clinical Neuroscience
University of North Dakota School of
Medicine and Health Sciences
Neuropsychiatric Research Institute
Fargo, ND

CONTENTS

1. Introduction and Overview   1
   W. Stewart Agras

Part One • Phenomenology and Epidemiology

2. The Classification of Eating Disorders   9
   *Kathryn H. Gordon, Jill M. Holm-Denoma, Ross D. Crosby, and
        Stephen A. Wonderlich*
3. Epidemiology and Course of Eating Disorders   25
   Pamela K. Keel
4. Proposed Syndromes and the *Diagnostic and
   Statistical Manual V*   33
   Kelly C. Allison and Jennifer D. Lundgren
5. Controversies and Questions in Current Evaluation, Treatment, and
   Research Related to Child and Adolescent Eating Disorders   51
   James Lock

**Part Two • Approaches to Understanding the
        Eating Disorders**

6. Appetitive Regulation in Anorexia Nervosa and Bulimia Nervosa   75
   Walter H. Kaye and Tyson Oberndorfer
7. Genetic Influences on Eating and the Eating Disorders   103
   Tracey D. Wade
8. Psychosocial Risk Factors for Eating Disorders   123
   Corinna Jacobi and Eike Fittig
9. Development of Child Taste and Food Preferences:
   The Role of Exposure   137
   Myles S. Faith
10. Dieting and the Eating Disorders   148
    Eric Stice and Katherine Presnell
11. Mood, Emotions, and Eating Disorders   180
    Claus Vögele and E. Leigh Gibson
12. Eating and Weight Concerns in Eating Disorders   206
    Alison E. Field and Nicole Kitos
13. Cultural Influences on Body Image and the Eating Disorders   223
    Michael P. Levine and Linda Smolak

Part Three • Assessment and Comorbidities of the Eating Disorders

14. Psychological Assessment of the Eating Disorders   249
    Drew A. Anderson and Andrea D. Murray

15. Medical Comorbidities of Eating Disorders   259
    James E. Mitchell and Scott J. Crow

16. Medical Screening and Management of Eating Disorders in Adolescents   267
    Debra K. Katzman, Nuray O. Kanbur, and Cathleen M. Steinegger

17. Psychological Comorbidity of Eating Disorders   292
    Katherine A. Halmi

Part Four • Prevention and Treatment

18. Prevention: Current Status and Underlying Theory   307
    Meghan M. Sinton and C. Barr Taylor

19. Cognitive Behavioral Therapy for Eating Disorders   331
    G. Terence Wilson

20. Interpersonal Psychotherapy for the Treatment of Eating Disorders   348
    Marian Tanofsky-Kraff and Denise E. Wilfley

21. Family Therapy   373
    Daniel le Grange and Renee Rienecke Hoste

22. Self-Help and Stepped Care in Eating Disorders   386
    Peter Musiat and Ulrike Schmidt

23. Dialectical Behavior Therapy   402
    Eunice Y. Chen and Debra Safer

24. Pharmacotherapy of the Eating Disorders   417
    Susan L. McElroy, Anna I. Guerdjikova, Anne M. O'Melia, Nicole Mori, and Paul E. Keck, Jr.

25. Evidence-Based Treatment for the Eating Disorders   452
    Phillipa J. Hay and Angelica de M. Claudino

26. Costs and Cost-Effectiveness in Eating Disorders   480
    Scott J. Crow and Nicholas Smiley

27. Overview   486
    W. Stewart Agras

Index   491

CHAPTER 1

Introduction and Overview

W. Stewart Agras

Abstract

This chapter provides a brief introduction to and overview of the contents of the Handbook. Several issues are highlighted, including the history of eating disorders over the ages, diagnostic issues including the overlap of eating disorders and obesity, and the problem of eating disorders not otherwise specified (EDNOS). The relative neglect of eating disorders in childhood and adolescence is noted. Finally, progress toward building an evidence base for the treatment of eating disorders is considered.

Keywords: classification, diagnosis, eating disorders, history of, overview, treatment of

Introduction

This book is divided into four sections: Phenomenology and epidemiology of the eating disorders; approaches to understanding the disorders; assessment and comorbidities of the disorders; and prevention and treatment. The first section deals with classification and epidemiology of the disorders, considerations for revisions to the *Diagnostic and Statistical Manual of Mental Disorders* (Association, 2000) and a chapter on the somewhat neglected topic of eating disorders in childhood and adolescence. The second section describes research basic to understanding the eating disorders including biological, psychosocial risk, and cultural factors, as well as the effects of behaviors such as dieting and eating and weight concerns in the genesis of eating disorders. The third section describes assessment of eating disorders, medical and psychological comorbidities, and medical management. The final section deals with various treatment modalities that have been found successful including psychotherapeutic and psychopharmacologic approaches, an overview of evidence-based treatment for the eating disorders, and a consideration of the cost effectiveness of the existing treatments.

Systematic study of the eating disorders began in the last third of the 20th century, although anorexia nervosa had been described in the 19th century and various treatments for that disorder were tried, none of them particularly successful, during the next 100 years. Since the 1970s research into the eating disorders has grown exponentially. The first issue of the *International Journal of Eating Disorders*, the premier journal in the field, appeared in the fall of 1981, encouraging further research and other journals including *Eating Behaviors* and *Eating and Weight Disorders have now appeared*. As the field is now maturing, the purpose of this volume is to update the state of research in the various aforementioned areas.

Epidemiologic studies suggest that eating disorders are common and have, in the last few decades, increased in prevalence (Chapter 3). Anorexia nervosa (AN) is the least common, with a prevalence between 0.5% and 1.0%. The majority of cases begin in adolescence and occur predominantly in females. Bulimia nervosa (BN) has a prevalence between 1% and 2.0%, and binge eating disorder (BED) is even more frequent. However, the proportion of males with BED is greater than for the other eating disorders. Altogether the prevalence of the three major syndromes may reach 5% to 6% of the population at risk and if individuals with eating disorder not otherwise specified (EDNOS) who do not meet criteria for a full syndrome but are associated with significant impairment are included, the total prevalence of clinically significant eating disorders may reach 8% to 10% of the population at risk. In 2003 The World Health Organization (WHO) designated ED's as a priority disorder based on the high prevalence worldwide and the severity of the disorders (WHO, 2003)Recently, the Academy for Eating Disorders issued a position paper stating that "…anorexia nervosa and bulimia nervosa, along with their variants, are biologically based, serious mental illnesses…" (Klump, Bulik, Kaye, Treasure, & Tyson, 2009 p. 97). Moreover, the costs of treatment for these disorders are as high as for schizophrenia and other serious mental disorders (Striegel-Moore et al., 2007). Despite these data both in the U.S. and worldwide, eating disorders are sometimes considered as mild and relatively unimportant conditions (Klump et al., 2009). These attitudes tend to trivialize eating disorders and the problems of those suffering from them despite the facts that they are common, costly, disabling, and sometimes fatal.

Adding to the cost of treatment are the medical conditions comorbid with the eating disorders. Patients with AN, particularly adolescents (Chapter 15 and 16), are most likely to experience physiological instability, which may become life threatening and lead to a higher mortality rate than expected. Hence, careful medical monitoring of such patients is an essential component of care. Bulimia nervosa also has several medical comorbidities associated with the disorder (Chapter 15), although these do not appear to lead to an increased risk of death. However, monitoring of physiologic indices such as potassium levels, which may be lowered due to purging, is important. In addition, enhanced dental care is indicated because of the effects of ingestion of sweets and of acid in the mouth, from binge eating and self-induced vomiting, on gums and teeth. Binge eating disorder, as noted previously, is often associated with overweight and obesity and therefore shares the medical comorbidities of obesity. Hence adequate medical assessment and care are important for all the eating disorders.

History of the Eating Disorders

Whether the eating disorders have historical continuity has been much debated (Habermas, 2005; Keel & Klump, 2003). Unfortunately, the historical record does not always provide sufficiently detailed case descriptions to enable certain diagnosis. It is clear that self-starvation and self-induced vomiting, combined with religious preoccupations apparently driving these symptoms, were present in medieval times (Bynum, 1987; Harrison, 2003), as well as cases of binge eating, often on strange foods, which is probably why they were recorded. Opinion is divided as to whether such individuals would meet present-day diagnostic criteria for an eating disorder or whether true eating disorder syndromes emerged only in the 19th and 20th centuries when detailed case histories became available (Habermas, 2005). Given the biological underpinnings of the eating disorders, for example, heritability, two explanations come to mind: First, eating disorders such as AN and BN may have been present throughout the centuries but the historical record is insufficient to fully confirm this possibility. Second, cultural conditions changed at some point, interacting with the genetic component, to produce full-fledged eating disorder syndromes. One possible cultural change is dieting to alter weight and shape that became increasingly common in young women from the mid-19th century onward (Habermas, 2005).

Hence, there are good descriptions of AN beginning in the mid-19th century (Gull, 1874; Habermas, 1989) although BN was first described in detail much later (Russell, 1979) and BED is a provisional diagnosis in *DSM-IV*, although it is likely to be changed to a full disorder in *DSM-V*. Moreover, the impetus for research in BN was the increase in cases seen in North American clinics in the mid-1970s.

The relatively recent recognition of the eating disorders and their apparent recent increase in frequency means that research has lagged behind that of established fields such as depression and anxiety disorders. For example, research on treatment of BN began only in the late 1970s with both pharmacologic and psychotherapeutic studies (Fairburn, 1981; Pope & Hudson, 1982; Schneider & Agras, 1985; Wermuth, Davis, Hollister, & Stunkard, 1977).

The Eating Disorders: Boundary Problems

One problem in classifying the eating disorders is that the disorders tend to merge over time. For example, it is not uncommon for patients with AN to begin to binge eat and purge, thus meeting criteria for BN when they no longer meet weight criteria for AN. Indeed, about 25% of participants with BN in treatment trials had been diagnosed with AN in the past (Agras, Walsh, Fairburn, Wilson, & Kraemer, 2000a; Fairburn et al., 1995). Such individuals tend to have worse treatment outcomes than those who have not had past AN. To a lesser extent, there is crossover between BN and BED. When there is a shift between syndromes, the question arises: should the diagnosis change or should it remain in the previous diagnostic grouping? Although there is considerable controversy over this point, it would seem sensible to preserve the original diagnosis rather than assuming, as a diagnostic change does, that there has been recovery from one syndrome and development of a new one. More problematic again is the fact that the residual grouping EDNOS is the most common ED diagnosis (Fairburn et al., 2007). This group appears to be largely composed of subclinical variants of AN, BN, and BED together with more tentatively identified entities such as (self-induced) vomiting disorder and night eating syndrome. One view of EDNOS, based on longitudinal data, is that it is a way station between recovery on the one hand and relapse on the other (Agras, Crow, Mitchell, Halmi, & Bryson, 42, 565-570, 2009). Given the instability of the EDNOS category, it would seem preferable to keep the subclinical variants of AN, BN, and BED within their major diagnostic categories using a measure of impact on living rather than symptom severity to determine whether they should reach syndromal status. This would significantly reduce the EDNOS category, although it would not entirely solve the EDNOS problem (Fairburn & Cooper, 2007).

A further boundary problem is the relationship of the eating disorders to overweight and obesity. Hence, the boundary between BED and obesity is the most complex because a substantial proportion of those with BED are also overweight or obese. A recent family study helped to clarify the relationship between these two disorders (Hudson et al., 2006). The authors found an aggregation of BED within families, probably due to interacting genetic and environmental variables. In addition, relatives of those with BED had a markedly higher prevalence of severe obesity than relatives of those without BED. These findings suggest that BED is a familial disorder caused by factors distinct from those that cause obesity, and that these BED-specific family factors also increase the risk of severe obesity. Hence obesity may be conceptualized as an entity separate from BED although BED is a risk factor for the development of obesity, especially severe obesity.

Family and Genetic Studies

Family and twin studies suggest that the eating disorders are heritable, with familial and environmental factors specific to individuals within the family interacting with genetic factors to produce the disorders. The estimated contributions of genetic and environmental variables differ considerably from study to study; hence the relative contribution of genes and environment to the eating disorders is unclear. Whether or not genetic studies will provide useful leads for treatment is debatable given the complexity of eating and its disorders that militate against finding even a few genes that explain significant variance associated with these disorders (Chapter 7). At this point, few genetic studies have large enough sample sizes to ensure reliable findings, and many specific findings have not been replicated in further studies.

Risk Factors and Prevention of Eating Disorders

Risk factors can be ascertained, usually after preliminary studies finding associations either retrospectively or concurrently between a disorder and particular variables, in two main ways. First a risk factor can be identified from prospective studies. Second, a causal risk factor can be identified experimentally by altering the strength of the risk factor and ascertaining the effect of such alteration on the occurrence of the disorder or an important component of the disorder. AN is the most difficult ED to study because the incidence and prevalence of this disorder are relatively low, requiring very large-scale prospective population studies to identify risk factors. However, our knowledge of risk factors for BN and to a lesser extent for BED has developed mainly by means of prospective studies with a few experimental studies aimed at identifying causal risk factors (Stice, 2002).

Knowledge of risk factors is crucial to the development of effective prevention studies (Chapters 8 and 18). Among the factors that form the basis for a number of prevention studies in adolescents and young women are an elevated perceived pressure to be thin emanating from family, peers, and the media; internalization of the thin-ideal espoused for women by Western culture; and elevated body mass and body dissatisfaction. These risk factors have predicted eating pathology in a number of prospective studies. Although prevention studies are in a fairly early stage of development they comprise a promising research field. Importantly, many of these studies make use of media and the Internet to deliver the intervention, thus reducing cost and providing easy access to the programs.

Interestingly, there is little evidence that dieting is a risk factor for BN despite the fact that it is universally regarded as a risk factor. Stice (Chapter 10) suggests that a third variable elicited by dieting scales may be a risk factor although it is unclear what that factor might be.

Eating Disorders in Childhood and Adolescence

A neglected area of study is childhood and adolescent eating disturbances and disorders, despite the fact that the eating disorders tend to have an onset in early or late adolescence. Developmental differences from adults probably accounts for the fact that a diagnostic system developed for adults does not fit well for children and adolescents. In addition, compared with adults, remarkably little is known about the treatment of children and adolescents with eating disorders because so few studies have been done in this area. Moreover, it cannot always be assumed that treatments effective in adults will be effective in children and adolescents, again because of developmental differences from childhood to adolescence, and also because of the greater influence of the family, particularly from a therapeutic viewpoint. In addition, the potential for prevention and early detection and treatment of the eating disorders is probably greatest in childhood and adolescence. Early treatment in AN, for example, may well reduce the number of adults with the chronic variant of the disorder.

Treatment of the Eating Disorders

The relatively low prevalence of AN combined with the reluctance of many patients with the disorder to seek or follow through with treatment makes treatment research for this disorder difficult. Many of the controlled studies that have been completed have too small sample sizes to allow conclusions about the effectiveness of treatment to be made. Hence, at this time there are no first-line evidence-based pharmacological or psychotherapeutic treatments available for AN (Agras & Robinson, 2008). This is disappointing given the fact that of all the eating disorders AN has the longest history, even in modern times. The most promising treatment at this time is a family-based approach for adolescents first developed at the Maudsley Hospital in London,

UK (Lock, Agras, Bryson, & Kraemer, 2005; Russell, Szmukler, Dare, & Eisler, 1987). However, data of adequate sample size are not yet available comparing this treatment with either individual psychotherapy or another type of family therapy, although these studies are in progress.

The situation is somewhat better for BN with a number of well-designed studies comparing various treatments. Although only fluoxetine is FDA approved for use in BN most antidepressants have been shown to be effective in reducing binge eating and purging (Shapiro et al., 2007). However, cognitive-behavioral therapy (CBT) appears to be more effective than medication in comparative studies (Agras et al., 1992; Mitchell et al., 1990). Similarly, CBT is more effective than interpersonal therapy (IPT) at the end of treatment, but not at follow-up (Agras, Walsh, Fairburn, Wilson, & Kraemer, 2000b), with IPT apparently acting more slowly than CBT. Hence, CBT can be recommended as a first-line evidence-based therapy for BN with IPT or medication as secondary choices. More recently, guided self-help treatments based on CBT have been found effective in both adults and adolescents and may form the basis for a cost-effective first step in the treatment of BN followed by CBT if needed. Despite these developments, only about 25% to 35% of patients with BN who are treated with CBT will recover, and some 50% will be in remission. Hence, the search for more effective treatments or combinations of treatments for BN needs to continue.

Although BED has been recognized as an important disorder only relatively recently, considerable progress has been made in developing evidence-based treatments for this condition because effective treatments for BN have been adapted for BED. Both CBT and IPT have been shown to be effective for BED in well designed studies, with more than 60% of individuals recovering both at the end of treatment and at follow-up (Wilfley et al., 1993; Wilfley et al., 2002). Interestingly, IPT is as effective as CBT both at the end of treatment and at follow-up, and has lower dropout rates than CBT. However, neither CBT or IPT has much effect on weight, an important issue because the majority of patients with BED are overweight. Individuals who stop binge eating and who maintain abstinence from binge eating during follow-up will lose about 5 kg. Here, medications such as the antiepileptic drug topiramate and similar compounds may be useful because such medications have larger effects on weight than does CBT or IPT and also reduce binge eating (Brownley, Berkman, Sedway, Lohr, &

Bulik, 2007). Further research combining medication and psychotherapy is needed. Hence, CBT, IPT, and both antidepressants and antiepileptics can be regarded as evidence-based treatments for BED, with CBT and IPT as first-line treatments. More recently a large-scale study compared IPT, behavioral weight loss treatment (BWL) and guided self-help (CBTgsh) for BED (Wilson, Wilfley, Agras, & Bryson, In press). At the end of treatment there were no differences among the three groups in reducing binge eating. However, the BWL group lost more weight than the other two groups. At 1-year follow-up there were no differences between groups on binge eating reduction, weight losses, or psychopathology, but at the 2-year follow-up both IPT and CBTgsh were superior to BWL in reducing binge eating. The authors concluded that CBTgsh may be useful as a first step in the treatment of BED, with IPT or CBT being used for those who do not improve with guided self-help.

Overall, this book delineates the considerable progress made in understanding and treating the eating disorders while drawing attention to the various gaps in our knowledge with suggestions as to how to address them.

References

Agras, W. S., Crow, S., Mitchell, J. E., Halmi, K. A., & Bryson, S. (1992). A 4-year prospective study of eating disorder NOS compared with full eating disorder syndromes. *International Journal of Eating Disorders*.

Agras, W. S., & Robinson, A. H. (2008). Fory years of progress in the treatment of the eating disorders. *Nordic Journal of Psychiatry*, S47, 19–24.

Agras, W. S., Rossiter, E. M., Arnow, B., Schneider, J. A., Telch, C. F., Raeburn, S. D., et al. (1992). Pharmacologic and cognitive-behavioral treatment for bulimia nervosa: A controlled comparison. *American Journal of Psychiatry*, 149, 82–87.

Agras, W. S., Walsh, B. T., Fairburn, C. G., Wilson, G. T., & Kraemer, H. C. (2000a). Comparison of cognitive-behavioral therapy and interpersonal psychotherapy for bulimia nervosa. *Archives of General Psychiatry*, 57, 1302–1308.

Agras, W. S., Walsh, B. T., Fairburn, C. G., Wilson, G. T., & Kraemer, H. C. (2000b). A multicenter comparison of cognitive-behavioral therapy and interpersonal psychotherapy for bulimia nervosa. *Archives of General Psychiatry*, 57, 459–66.

Association, A. P. (2000). *Diagnostic and Statistical Manual of Mental Disorders:DSM-1V* (4th ed, text revision ed.). Washington, DC: American Psychiatric Association.

Brownley, K. A., Berkman, N. D., Sedway, J. A., Lohr, K. N., & Bulik, C. M. (2007). Binge eating disorder treatment: A systematic review of randomize controlled trials. *International Journal of Eating Disorders*, 40, 337–48.

Bynum, C. (1987). *Holy feast and holy fast: The religious significance of food to medieval women*. Berkeley: University of California.

Fairburn, C. G. (1981). A cognitive-behavioural approach in the management of bulimia. *Psychological Medicine*, 11, 707–711.

Fairburn, C. G., & Cooper, Z. (2007). Thinking afresh about the classification of eating disorders. *International Journal of Eating Disorders*, 40, S107–S110.

Fairburn, C. G., Cooper, Z., Bohn, K., O'Connor, M. E., Doll, H. A., & Palmer, R. L. (2007). The severity and status of eating disorder NOS for DSM-V. *Behaviour Research & Therapy*, 45, 1705–1715.

Fairburn, C. G., Norman, P. A., Welch, S. L., O'Connor, M. E., Doll, H. A., & Peveler, R. C. (1995). A prospective study of outcome in bulimia nervosa and the long-term effects of three psychological treatments. *Archives of General Psychiatry*, 52, 304–312.

Gull, W. W. (1874). Anorexia nervosa. *Transactions of the Clinical Society London*, 7, 22–28.

Habermas, T. (1989). The psychiatric history of anorexia nervosa and bulimia nervosa: Weight concerns and bulimic symptoms in early case reports. *International Journal of Eating Disorders*, 8, 259–73.

Habermas, T. (2005). On the uses of history in psychiatry: Diagnostic implications for anorexia nervosa. *International Journal of Eating Disorders*, 38, 167–82.

Harrison, K. (2003). *Saint Therese of Lisieux*. London: Weidenfels & Nicholson.

Hudson, J. I., Lalonde, J. K., Berry, J. M., Pindyck, L. J., Bulik, C. M., Crow, S., et al. (2006). Binge-eating disorder as a distinct familial phenotype in obese individuals. *Archives of General Psychiatry*, 63, 313–319.

Keel, P. K., & Klump, K. L. (2003). Are eating disorders culture-bound syndromes? Implications for conceptualizing their etiology. *Psychological Bulletine*, 129, 747–69.

Klump, K. L., Bulik, C. M., Kaye, W. H., Treasure, J., & Tyson, E. (2009). Academy for Eating Disorders position paper: Eating disorders are serious mental illnesses. *International Journal of Eating Disorders*, 42, 97–103.

Lock, J., Agras, W. S., Bryson, S., & Kraemer, H. C. (2005). A comparison of short- and long-term family therapy for adolescent anorexia nervosa. *Journal of the American Academy of Child & Adolescent Psychiatry*, 44, 632–39.

Mitchell, J. E., Pyle, R. L., D., E. E., Hatsukami, D., Pomeroy, C., & Zimmerman, R. (1990). A comparison study of antidepressants and structured intensive group psychotherapy in the treatment of bulimia nervosa. *Archives of General Psychiatry*, 47, 149–57.

Pope, H. G., & Hudson, J. I. (1982). Treatment of bulimia with antidepressants. *Psychopharmacology*, 78, 167–79.

Russell, G. F., Szmukler, G. I., Dare, C., & Eisler, I. (1987). An evaluation of family therapy in anorexia nervosa and bulimia nervosa. *Archives of General Psychiatry*, 44, 347–57.

Russell, G. F. M. (1979). Bulimia nervosa: An ominous variant of anorexia nervosa. *Psychological Medicine*, 9, 429–48.

Schneider, J. A., & Agras, W. S. (1985). A cognitive-behavioral group treatment of bulimia. *British Journal of Psychiatry*, 146, 66–69.

Shapiro, J. R., Berkman, N. D., Brownley, K. A., Sedway, J. A., Lohr, K. N., & Bulik, C. M. (2007). Bulimia nervosa treatment: A systematic review of randomized controlled trials. *International Journal of Eating Disorders*, 40, 321–36.

Stice, E. (2002). Risk and maintenance factors for eating pathology: A meta-analytic study. *Psychological Bulletin*, 128, 825–36.

Striegel-Moore, R. H., DeBar, L., Wilson, G. T., Dickerson, J., Rosselli, F., Perrin, N., et al. (2007). Health services use in eating disorders. *Psychological Medicine*, 38, 1465–74.

Wermuth, B. M., Davis, K. L., Hollister, L. E., & Stunkard, A. J. (1977). Phenytoin treatment of the binge-eating syndrome. *American Journal of Psychiatry, 134,* 1249–53.

WHO(2003). Caring for children and adolescents with mental disorders: Setting WHO directions. Geneva.

Wilfley, D. E., Agras, W. S., Telch, C. F., Rossiter, E. M., Schneider, J. A., Cole, A. B., et al. (1993). Group cognitive-behavioral therap and group interpersonal psychotherapy for the non-purging bulimic: A controlled comparison. *Journal of Consulting and Clinical Psychology, 61,* 296–305.

Wilfley, D. E., Welch, R. R., Stein, R. I., Spurrell, E. B., Cohen, L. R., Saelens, B. E., et al. (2002). A randomized comparison of group cognitive-behavioral therap and group interpersonal psychotherapy for the treatment of overweight individuals with binge-eating disorder. *Archives of General Psychiatry,* 713–21.

Wilson, G. T., Wilfley, D. E., Agras, W. S., & Bryson, S. (In press). Psychological treatments of binge eating disorder. *Archives of General Psychiatry.*

PART 1

Phenomenology and Epidemiology

The Classification of Eating Disorders

Kathryn H. Gordon, Jill M. Holm-Denoma, Ross D. Crosby, *and* Stephen A. Wonderlich

Abstract

The purpose of the chapter is to elucidate the key issues regarding the classification of eating disorders. To this end, a review of nosological research in the area of eating disorders is presented, with a particular focus on empirically based techniques such as taxometric and latent class analysis. This is followed by a section outlining areas of overlap between the current *Diagnostic and Statistical Manual of Mental Disorders – Fourth Edition, Text Revision* (DSM-IV-TR; American Psychiatric Association, 2000) eating disorder categories and their symptoms. Next, eating disorder classification models that are alternatives to the *DSM-IV-TR* are described and critically examined in light of available empirical data. Finally, areas of controversy and considerations for change in next version of the *DSM* (i.e., the applicability of *DSM* criteria to minority groups, children, males; the question of whether clinical categories should be differentiated from research categories) are discussed.

Keywords: classification, diagnostic models, eating disorders, latent class analyses, nosology, taxometrics

Introduction

Taxonomy (the science of classification) is often undervalued as a glorified form of filing—with each species in its folder, like a stamp in its prescribed place in an album; but taxonomy is a fundamental and dynamic science, dedicated to exploring the causes of relationships and similarities among organisms. Classifications are theories about the basis of natural order, not dull catalogues compiled only to avoid chaos (Gould, 1989, p. 98).

Sound classification systems are the cornerstone of scientific progress. The universal language of classification systems allows scientists to communicate in an efficient, standardized manner about variables in their discipline. This function of classification is extremely important, and makes it possible to construct a collective knowledge base on which scientists can build upon and advance the field. However, as Stephen Jay Gould articulates in the quote above, classification systems, at their best, are not merely arbitrary organization systems. Rather, they are like Mendeleev's periodic table of elements for the field of chemistry: theoretically driven, parsimonious, and instrumental for scientific growth.

Within the disciplines of psychiatry and psychology, one of the most commonly used classification systems for mental disorders is the *Diagnostic and Statistical Manual of Mental Disorders – Fourth Edition, Text Revision* [DSM-IV-TR; American Psychiatric Association (APA), 2000]. The broad objectives of this chapter are (1) to examine how well the *DSM-IV-TR* eating disorder classification system performs in terms of the qualities that Gould and others (e.g., Waller & Meehl, 1998) have articulated and (2) to illuminate pathways for improvements on the current system. The chapter begins with a brief description of the *DSM*'s current system for classifying eating disorders and a review of research on nosological issues. Next, the overlap between diagnostic entities is reviewed, and alternative diagnostic models for eating disorders are presented. Finally, the chapter concludes with suggestions for change and future directions.

The Current DSM Classification of Eating Disorders

The *DSM-IV-TR* consists of three main categories for eating disorders: anorexia nervosa (AN), bulimia nervosa (BN), and eating disorder not otherwise specified (EDNOS), which includes the provisional diagnostic category of binge eating disorder (BED; currently in the appendix of *DSM-IV-TR*). AN is diagnosed when an individual will not maintain a minimal healthy body weight, expresses intense fear about weight gain and/or fatness despite being underweight, and (for females) has amenorrhea. AN is divided into two subtypes: a *binge eating/purging type* for those who engage in binge eating (i.e., an episode wherein one experiences a sense of loss of control while eating and consumes an objectively large quantity of food) and/or purging (i.e., self-induced vomiting or laxative or diuretic use) and a *restricting type* for individuals who do not regularly engage in binge eating or purging behavior (APA, 2000).

BN is diagnosed when an individual regularly (i.e., at minimum, an average of two times per week for a three-month period) engages in binge eating and inappropriate compensatory behaviors (e.g., excessive exercising, purging). Similar to AN, BN consists of two subtypes: a *nonpurging type* for those who fast and/or excessively exercise as a means of weight control and a *purging type* for those who regularly engage in behaviors such as vomiting, and/or misuse of laxatives or diuretics as a means of weight control. BN can be diagnosed only if the individual does not meet criteria for AN (otherwise an AN diagnosis trumps the BN diagnosis), and AN and BN diagnoses both require that the individual's self-evaluation is unduly influenced by weight and shape (APA, 2000).

Finally, EDNOS is reserved for individuals deemed to have a clinically significant (i.e., distressing and impairing) eating disorder that does not meet criteria for AN or BN. One of the many presentations that fall into this broad, heterogeneous category, is BED, a disorder defined by repeated binge eating episodes (i.e., approximately once per week over a six-month period) and associated distress in the absence of inappropriate compensatory behaviors (APA, 2000).

Review of Research on Nosological Issues

The methods by which eating disorders are defined, classified, and distinguished are likely to have important implications for both the scientific and clinical eating disorder communities. The eating disorder diagnoses currently defined in the *DSM-IV-TR* were based jointly on clinical wisdom and empirical evidence available at the time of publication. However, the validity of these diagnoses and the criteria used to define them have not always received empirical support (see Wonderlich, Joiner, Keel, Williamson, & Crosby, 2007). Statistical approaches to the classification of eating disorders, such as latent class analysis (Lazarsfeld & Henry, 1968) and taxometric analysis (Waller & Meehl, 1998), provide empirically based alternatives to the *DSM* that may have greater scientific validity and clinical utility. These empirical approaches are considered in the text that follows.

Latent class analysis is designed to identify homogeneous subsets of cases (i.e., latent classes) using observed signs and symptoms based on the principle of conditional independence (Lazarsfeld & Henry, 1968). Specifically, classes are created in latent class analysis in such a way that, within each class, the signs and symptoms are statistically independent (i.e., uncorrelated). Latent class analysis is a statistical model-based approach that provides objective criteria for the determination of the optimal number of clusters, and provides a probability-based method for assigning individuals to classes. Latent class analysis requires the use of dichotomous indicator variables. A variant of latent class analysis, latent profile analysis, allows the use of categorical, ordinal, and continuous variables.

A number of studies have used latent class or latent profile analysis to classify individuals with eating disorder symptoms. Sullivan, Bulik, and Kendler (1998) used latent class analysis to classify 1,897 female Caucasian twins from the Virginia Twin Registry using bulimic symptoms obtained from a structured interview. They identified four latent classes including a relatively healthy class (infrequent binge eating and vomiting) and a class approximating *DSM-IV-TR* BN. Bulik, Sullivan, and Kendler (2000) conducted a second latent class analysis from the Virginia Twin Registry using nine eating disorder symptoms in 2,163 Caucasian female twins. Six latent classes were identified, with three resembling *DSM-IV-TR* eating disorder diagnoses (AN, BN, and BED) and three classes that were characterized by shape and/or weight concerns that did not reflect clinical eating disorders.

More recently, Keel et al. (2004) classified 1,179 individuals with clinically significant eating disorders from the Price Foundation multisite studies.

They reported a four-class solution supporting distinctions among the AN restricting type, AN binge eating/purging subtype, and BN. Striegel-Moore et al. (2005) applied latent class analysis to a nonclinical, more ethnically diverse sample of young Black ($n = 74$) and White ($n = 164$) women who met criteria for full-syndrome eating disorders, and identified three latent classes characterized as purgers (50%), bingers (41%), and binge-purgers (9%).

Newer studies used these procedures in large population-based samples that included fewer eating disordered participants. For example, Wade, Crosby, and Martin (2006) used latent profile analysis to classify 1,002 Australian twins from a community sample. Five latent classes were identified, including one class that contained most women with eating disorders, including women with BED, AN (both restricting and binge eating/purging types), BN (purging and nonpurging types), and purging disorder (repeatedly engaging in purging behavior in the absence of binge eating behavior; Keel Haedt, & Edler, 2005b). Meanwhile, Duncan et al. (2007) identified five latent classes in a large ($n = 3,723$) general population community sample of American twins. One class represented clinically significant eating disorders, with other classes reflecting less clinically significant eating or weight concerns (e.g., dieting, weight concern, low weight gain) or nonaffected individuals. Finally, in a large ($n = 2,028$) community sample of young Portuguese women, Pinheiro, Bulik, Sullivan, and Machado (2008) identified four latent classes using the Eating Disorders Examination-Questionnaire (Fairburn & Beglin, 1994). These classes included a healthy class, a binge eating class resembling BED, a purging class, and class closely resembling BN.

Two other recent studies conducted latent profile analyses on clinical samples. Eddy and colleagues (2009) used latent profile analysis to classify 687 individuals seeking treatment for eating disorders using cognitive and behavioral symptom data. They identified five latent classes closely resembling *DSM-IV-TR* eating disorder classifications. One unique feature of this paper was the validation of latent classes using psychological comorbidity and functioning, medical morbidity, and treatment utilization. Finally, Mitchell et al. (2007) conducted latent profile analyses on cases of EDNOS to determine what classes may comprise this category. Five classes were identified including two representing subsyndromal levels of restricting AN and BN.

In summarizing the literature involving latent class analysis and eating disorders, most studies have found classes resembling BN, BED, and purging disorder (a variant of EDNOS). While the purging subtype of BN has emerged as distinct from a latent group resembling BED in several studies, it is unclear whether these findings would extend to comparisons involving the nonpurging subtype of BN, which has not emerged as distinct from the purging subtype of BN.

One of the advantages of latent class analysis is its ability to determine the optimal number and composition of homogeneous groups. However, a noted weakness of latent class analysis is the tendency for latent class analysis occasionally to produce spurious classes that represent different points along a continuum of severity (Uebersax, 1999). Taxometric analyses were specifically designed to address the question of whether two apparently separate classes represent categorically distinct entities (taxa) or superficially different manifestations of a single underlying condition (Waldman & Lilienfeld, 2001). Taxometric analysis, like latent class analysis, examines the associations between observed measures. However, unlike latent class analysis, taxometric analysis specifies a priori the number of groups (two). In taxometric analysis, indicators are selected to serve as proxies of group membership. If group membership is based on a dimensional distinction along an underlying continuum, then the strength of associations between any two indicators of group membership will remain constant across the range of a third indicator. In contrast, if the distinction between groups is truly qualitative, then the strength of associations will be lowest when examined separately in each distinct group and highest when examined in a mixed sample containing individuals from each group (Gordon, Holm-Denoma, Smith, Fink, & Joiner, 2007).

Four taxometric studies of eating disorders have been published to date. Gleaves, Lowe, Green, Cororve, and Williams (2000a) performed a series of seven analyses comparing different diagnostic subgroups. They found that individuals with BN did not appear to be qualitatively different from those with the binge eating/purging type of AN. In contrast, individuals with the restricting type of AN were found to be distinct from individuals with disorders involving binge eating or purging, but not distinct from those without eating disorders. A second taxometric study by this group used a mixed sample of college undergraduates and eating disorder patients, and provided additional evidence that BN is best conceptualized as a distinct disorder

(Gleaves, Lowe, Snow, Green, & Murphy-Eberenz, 2000b).

In a third taxometric study, Williamson et al. (2002) used measures of all *DSM-IV-TR* eating disorder symptom criteria obtained from clinical interviews. Their sample included eating disorder patients, nonclinical college students, and obese individuals. Their results provided further support for BN as a discrete entity, and for restricting AN as a point along a continuum that includes normality. Finally, Tylka and Subich (2003) conducted a taxometric study using psychological and sociocultural (as opposed to behavioral) indicators of eating disorders. In contrast to previous studies, they found no evidence of the qualitative nature of disorders involving binge eating and purging.

In summary, three of four taxometric analyses have supported a categorical distinction between BN and normality and two studies have suggested that AN binge eating/purging type might fall within the same category as BN. Thus, existing taxometric studies have tended to support a single "bulimic taxon" that is categorically distinct from normality.

To our knowledge, only one eating disorder study to date (currently under review) has used both latent class analysis and taxometric analysis. Keel, et al. (under review) used *DSM-IV-TR* eating disorder symptoms assessed by structured clinical interview in a latent profile analysis to identify five latent classes. Latent Group 1 (*n* = 137) was free of eating disorder symptoms/diagnoses. Latent Group 2 (*n* = 113) included a mixture of eating disorder symptoms and syndromes. Latent Group 3 (*n* = 123) was characterized by binge eating and compensatory behaviors and included subjects with BN purging and nonpurging subtype. Latent Group 4 (*n* = 110) was characterized by purging without binge eating and included subjects with AN binge eating/purging subtype and purging disorder. Latent Group 5 (*n* = 45) was characterized by binge eating, obesity, and relative absence of compensatory behaviors and included subjects with BED. Pairwise taxometric analyses were then performed to compare these latent classes. Results supported categorical distinctions between normality (Latent Group 1) and all eating disorder groups as well as categorical distinctions between some, but not all, eating disorder groups. Specifically, the mixed group (Latent Group 2) appeared to have a taxonic relationship with the purging disorder/AN group and BED group, suggesting that the members of the mixed group are qualitatively different from those without eating disorders and from those with eating

disorders defined primarily by the presence of binge eating or purging.

Overlap Between Diagnostic Entities

The previous section consisted of a review of research on nosological issues and eating disorders, while the current section discusses areas of overlap between the diagnostic categories. At a basic level, there is some overlap in the actual diagnostic criteria of AN and BN. Specifically, both diagnoses are made only if the criterion for "self-evaluation is unduly influenced by body shape and weight" is met (APA, 2000). This criterion is not currently included for the diagnosis of BED. However, Grilo et al. (2008) argue for its use as a diagnostic specifier for BED, based on findings that BED participants with clinical levels of overvaluation of weight/shape reported significantly higher levels of eating pathology and depression symptoms than BED participants with subclinical levels of overvaluation of weight and shape. It is interesting to note that these group differences (based on levels of overvaluation of weight and shape) emerged despite a lack of differences in body mass index and binge eating frequency between the two BED groups.

Overlap Between Eating Disorder Diagnoses on External Validators

In addition to criterion overlap, there is substantial evidence that there are not differences between the *DSM-IV-TR* diagnostic classes on a host of external validators. For example, a variety of studies have indicated that there is substantial diagnostic crossover between the eating disorder diagnoses and the eating disorder diagnosis subtypes (Eddy et al., 2002; Keel, Dorer, Franko, Jackson, & Herzog, 2005a; Tozzi et al., 2005). Family history studies have also failed to find that eating disorder diagnoses "breed true," as there has been cross-transmission of diagnoses in family members of both AN and BN probands (Strober, Freeman, Lamper, Diamond, & Kaye, 2000). In addition, all of the major eating disorder diagnoses are characterized by a frequently shared comorbidity profile. AN, BN, and BED all show high levels of mood disorders, substance use disorders, anxiety disorders, and personality disorders (Hudson, Hiripi, Pope, & Kessler, 2007; Johnson, Spitzer, & Williams, 2001; Wonderlich & Mitchell, 1997). Similarly, eating disorder classes are not distinguishable in terms of impaired interpersonal functioning (Gonzales, 2001; Hsu et al., 2002). At a biological level, there are also significant amounts of overlap in comparisons of various aspects of neurotransmitter functioning. For example, there is a series of studies that indicate that subjects with AN and BN show disturbances in neurotransmitter functioning, most often reduced activity of the 5-hydroxytryptamine (5-HT, serotonin) neurotransmission system (Jimerson, Lesem, Kaye, & Brewerton, 1992; Tauscher et al., 2001; Weizman, Carmi, Tyano, Apter, & Rehavi, 1986).

However, it is important to recognize that the current *DSM-IV-TR* eating disorder diagnoses provide some degree of discriminant validity on clinical outcome measures. It would appear as though AN is distinguished from the other eating disorders in terms of mortality rates (Fichter & Quadflieg, 2007; Keel et al., 2003) and likelihood of remission or recovery (Fichter & Quadflieg, 2007; Herzog et al., 1993). It is unclear if these diagnostic classes show differential treatment response because no study has currently been conducted that exposed all three eating disorder diagnoses to the same treatment agent. However, the literature implies that AN may be more treatment resistant than BN and BED (Fichter & Quadflieg, 2007). Thus, eating disorder diagnoses, as defined in the *DSM-IV-TR*, appear to lack discriminant validity on a number of variables. Nonetheless, there are important clinical validators that have been supported in comparisons of *DSM* classes and that are of vital importance to practicing clinicians.

Alternative Diagnostic Models

In response to the aforementioned concerns about the existing *DSM-IV-TR* eating disorder classification system, some researchers have proposed alternative diagnostic systems. Two of the proposed alternative models are described in this section. In addition, a critical review of each proposed classification system is provided.

Three-Dimensional Model

After examining the results of a series of taxometric studies (Gleaves et al., 2000b; Williamson et al., 2002), Williamson, Gleaves, and Stewart (2005) proposed the empirically based Three-Dimensional Model (TDM) of eating disorders. The TDM hypothesizes that three main factors underlie all disordered eating presentations. The first factor, binge eating, is considered to be taxonic (i.e., individuals either engage in binge eating or they do not), whereas the other two factors, drive for thinness and fear of fatness/inappropriate compensatory behaviors, are viewed as dimensional. Williamson et al. (2005) have conceptualized how each of the existing *DSM-IV-TR*

eating disorders and obesity would fill the TDM's space when all three factors are simultaneously considered (Fig. 2.1).

The diagnostic system proposed by the TDM differs from that of the *DSM-IV-TR* in several important ways. First, it posits that eating behaviors with a binge eating component (e.g., BN, BED, and the binge eating/purging type of AN) are qualitatively distinct from those without a binge eating component (e.g., the restricting type of AN, obesity, and normal eating). Second, the two *DSM-IV-TR* subtypes of BN are qualitatively similar according to the TDM, but differ according to where they fall on the fear of fatness/compensatory behavior dimension. Specifically, those with the purging type of BN have more intense fear of fatness than those with the nonpurging type of BN. Moreover, individuals with the binge eating/purging type of AN are posited to be qualitatively similar to those with both purging and nonpurging types of BN, but to differ quantitatively in their relatively higher levels of drive for thinness. Third, according to this model, BED is qualitatively similar to other disorders that have a binge eating component, but quantitatively different from them because it is defined by relatively lower levels of fear of fatness and drive for thinness. Finally, only one variant of AN exists according to the TDM: AN, restricting type.

One could imagine that a classification system stemming from the TDM would have two primary eating disorder categories: eating disorders accompanied by binge eating and eating disorders without a binge eating component. Within the binge eating category, individuals would be plotted on the dimensions of drive for thinness and fear of fatness. As described in the preceding text, those who had the highest levels of drive for thinness would have a syndrome that is like the *DSM-IV-TR*'s AN, binge eating/purging diagnosis, whereas those with relatively lower levels of drive for thinness would have syndromes that were similar to BED and both subtypes of BN. In addition, those with syndromes like the *DSM-IV-TR*'s BED, nonpurging BN, and purging BN, respectively, would have increasingly high levels of fear of fatness. Within the non–binge eating category, individuals with high levels of fear of fatness and drive for thinness would be considered to have a restrictive anorexic syndrome, whereas those with relatively lower levels of both factors would be considered obese or normal. Within both of the diagnostic categories proposed by the TDM (i.e., eating disorders accompanied by binge eating, and eating disorders without a binge eating component),

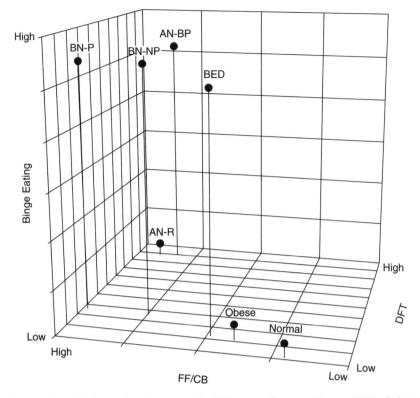

Fig. 2.1 Three-dimensional model of eating disorders proposed by Williamson, Gleaves, and Stewart. BN-P = bulimia nervosa, purging type; BN-NP = bulimia nervosa, nonpurging type; AN-R = anorexia nervosa, restricting type; AN-BP = anorexia binge/purge type; BED = binge eating disorder; FF/CB = fear of fatness/concern with body size and shape. (From Williamson, D. A., Gleaves, D. H., & Stewart, T. M. [2005]. Categorical versus dimensional models of eating disorders: An examination of the evidence. *International Journal of Eating Disorders, 37,* 1–10. © 2005 Wiley Periodicals, Inc. Reprinted with permission of John Wiley & Sons, Inc.)

diagnostic labels would refer to individuals who differ with regard to *severity* of drive for thinness and fear of fatness. Thus, *within* the two diagnostic categories, no qualitatively distinct groups would exist.

The TDM has implications not only for the classification of eating disorders, but also for the etiology, assessment, and treatment of them. With regard to etiology, some assume that taxonic results signify a genetic or biological basis to a disorder. Although taxonic entities may have a higher likelihood of a genetic etiology than dimensional entities (Meehl, 1992), it is conceivable that they may also result from sociocultural factors (e.g., an environmental mold taxon; Catell, 1946). Similarly, dimensional entities such as AN, restricting type may be impacted by biological factors (e.g., amount of serotonin released in the brain) and/or may result from an interaction of biological factors (e.g., genotype of the 5-HT$_{2a}$ receptor gene) and environmental factors (e.g., internalization of the thin ideal).

With regard to assessment, Gangestad and Snyder (1985) reported that mismatching the structure

(i.e., taxonic vs. dimensional) of a latent variable with a given assessment modality could result in distortion of results. For taxonic disorders, a short measure that concentrates on dichotomously classifying individuals based on a best cut can minimize misclassifications (Meehl, 1992). In contrast, measures of continuous constructs must include items that adequately assess all aspects of the latent entity and discriminate across the entire breadth of the dimension (Meehl, 1992; Ruscio & Ruscio, 2002). Finally, with regard to treatment, Williamson et al. (2005) suggest that for disorders that are dimensional in nature (e.g., AN, restricting type), progress during treatment may be relatively slow and difficult to detect at any given time. Treatment that moves someone "down" the continuum a small number of intermediate levels may result in change that is almost unperceivable in the short term. In contrast, researchers have predicted a disorder that is taxonic in nature will likely respond to treatment in an all-or-nothing fashion (Strube, 1989; Williamson et al., 2005). In this case, they have hypothesized that change may be difficult to initiate, but once initiated, should be noticeable and complete. It is important to note that these are hypotheses that have yet to be empirically examined.

As discussed by Wonderlich et al. (2007), one of the limitations of the TDM is that it relies on the results of taxometric studies that have examined the nature of existing *DSM-IV-TR* eating disorder categories. Therefore, the model's generalizability to eating disorders not currently included in the *DSM-IV-TR* (e.g., purging disorder; Keel et al., 2005b) is compromised. Further, does not consider certain variables that are integral to any classification system (e.g., what role does comorbidity play?).

Transdiagnostic Model

The transdiagnostic approach, first outlined by Fairburn and his colleagues (Fairburn & Bohn, 2005; Fairburn, Cooper, & Shafran, 2003), proposes that all eating disorders fall into a single diagnostic category called "eating disorder." Its premise is that the core psychopathology of all eating disorders is the overvaluation of control over body shape, weight, and eating. Moreover, Fairburn et al. (2003) believe that many distinctive clinical features (i.e., caloric restriction, binge eating, body checking) cut across eating disorder diagnostic categories. As evidence of their viewpoint, Fairburn et al. cite the fact that many individuals first diagnosed with a given eating disorder cross over into another eating disorder category over time.

Given the commonalities across eating disorder diagnoses, Fairburn et al. (2003) suggest that one's specific eating disorder diagnosis should not determine the treatment modality. Rather, cognitive–behavioral therapy (CBT) should be used with all eating disorder patients, and the specific techniques of CBT that are primarily employed should be based upon the psychopathological features and maintaining mechanisms of each patient. For instance, a patient presenting with high levels of clinical perfectionism should be treated with a CBT-based approach that targets the perfectionism, regardless of the *DSM-IV-TR* defined eating disorder for which she or he meets criteria. In sum, Fairburn et al. believe that regardless of a patient's diagnostic status as defined by the *DSM-IV-TR*, a similar treatment approach (CBT) should be used.

Although the transdiagnostic approach holds some intuitive appeal and addresses certain shortcomings of the *DSM-IV-TR* classification system, it is inconsistent with data from taxometric studies indicating that disorders with a binge eating and/or purging component are qualitatively distinct from those without. Further, it is apparently undermined by data that suggest genuine differences between AN and BN exist (e.g., mortality rates; Franko & Keel, 2006). Perhaps the model still offers an interesting approach to conceptualizing the dimensions that may cut across all eating disorder diagnoses. For instance, Fairburn et al. (2003) hypothesize several characteristics (i.e., maintaining mechanisms) that cut across eating disorder diagnoses such as clinical perfectionism, low self-esteem, mood lability intolerance, and interpersonal difficulties. Future taxometric studies could examine these maintaining mechanisms to determine whether they are indicators of dimensions and/or taxa relevant to eating pathology. Given that taxon members can still vary in degree on underlying dimensions (e.g., one binge eating/purging taxon member could have a higher degree of clinical perfectionism than another), the posited transdiagnostic characteristics of Fairburn et al. could help refine the results of the taxometric studies that have been conducted to date and inform future revisions of the *DSM*.

Which Classification Model Is Best?

As described in the preceding text, the *DSM-IV-TR*'s current classification system is largely a result of arbitrary, rather than empirically based, decisions. The two alternative models described in this section address some of the shortcomings of the *DSM* model. For instance, the TDM is based on empirical findings, whereas the transdiagnostic model addresses some *DSM* validity concerns (e.g., high rates of crossover between diagnoses might indicate an invalid boundary between *DSM* categories, and the transdiagnostic model minimizes the use of the arbitrary diagnostic boundaries). However, there are limitations to each of the alternative models. The TDM has focused exclusively on *DSM*-defined eating disorders, and the transdiagnostic model is not supported by some empirical findings (e.g., taxometric studies consistently show that binge eating is qualitatively distinct from other eating pathology).

Given the three models discussed in this chapter (i.e., *DSM-IV-TR*, TDM, and the transdiagnostic model) and an infinite array of other possible models, how can one discern which classification system is best? First, it is important to emphasize the importance of considering multiple variables simultaneously when evaluating a classification system's validity. Kendler (1990) suggests several validators need to be rigorously evaluated: treatment response and utility, clinical course, etiological factors, biological and genetic variables, and demographic measures. Second, it is currently unclear if either of the newly proposed systems demonstrates incremental validity or clinical utility when compared to the *DSM-IV-TR*'s system. Future researchers should consider testing alternative classification systems against one another to determine empirically which one demonstrates maximal validity, and the field should prioritize the use of empirically supported diagnostic systems.

Intra-diagnostic Heterogeneity

It is well known that there is heterogeneity in clinical presentation within each eating disorder category (Wonderlich et al., 2007), but there seems to be a limited number of personality patterns when you look across all *DSM*-based eating disorder categories (Johnson & Connors, 1987; Westen & Harden-Fischer, 2001; Wonderlich & Mitchell, 1997). Early on, most researchers focused on how multi-impulsivity and other features often associated with borderline personality disorder might be related to eating pathology (Fichter, Quadflieg, & Rief, 1994; Lacey, 1993; Steiger & Stotland, 1996; Wonderlich & Swift, 1990). More recently, however, researchers have applied statistical approaches such as cluster analysis and latent profile analysis to identify multiple personality profiles that reliably coincide with eating disturbances.

The recent empirical studies have consistently identified at least three personality clusters that are common among adults with eating disorders: impulsive/emotionally dysregulated; compulsive/emotionally constricted, and normative (e.g., Wonderlich et al., 2005). Similar results have been obtained in adolescent samples (Thompson-Brenner, Eddy, Satir, Boisseau, & Westen, 2008). The personality clusters differ from one another with regard to potential etiologic variables such as rates of childhood abuse (Steiger, Israël, Gauvin, Kin, & Young, 2003; Westen & Harden-Fischer, 2001), family history (Holliday, Landau, Collier, & Treasure, 2006), and genetic vulnerabilities (Steiger et al., 2003). Their eating disorder history and comorbidity profiles are also different (e.g., Tozzi et al., 2005; Wonderlich et al., 2005), as well as their treatment history and emotional and behavioral ratings (Wonderlich et al., 2007). These findings suggest that personality variation within a given *DSM* diagnostic construct (e.g., BN, purging type) may be associated with meaningful conceptual and clinical differences. Accordingly, a maximally effective treatment may look different when delivered to a patient

with BN, purging type who is highly impulsive versus to a patient with BN, purging type who is very compulsive. Some researchers have described modifications to treatments that account for personality variations (Fairburn et al., 2003; Wonderlich, Mitchell, Peterson, & Crow, 2001), but more research is needed.

Suggestions for Change

In this section, we address a few of the potentially practical considerations that developers of the *DSM-V* may wish to consider in the next iteration of this taxonomy. First, particular diagnostic criteria should be examined critically in terms of their validity and whether or not they are relevant when making diagnoses. In particular, amenorrhea in the AN criteria set should be examined critically in light of evidence that some individuals continue to menstruate at a very low weight and that individuals who do not meet the suggested low weight criterion (85% or less of their ideal body weight) may experience amenorrhea, particularly if they have another eating disorder (Abraham, Pettigrew, Boyd, Russell, & Taylor, 2005; Watson & Andersen, 2003). Further, amenorrhea may persist after weight restoration in patients who remit from AN (Francesca et al., 2003). Altogether, the empirical evidence suggests that amenorrhea lacks diagnostic specificity.

Second, the developers of *DSM-V* may wish to consider making the BN criteria less stringent. An empirical study on this topic was conducted by le Grange et al. (2006), who compared a group of individuals who met full criteria for BN with individuals who met criteria for subthreshold BN. The subthreshold BN group consisted of women who met for all of the criteria for BN except (1) the frequency criteria (i.e., they binged and purged an average of at least once a week, but not twice as specified by the BN criteria) or (2) they did not report consuming objectively large quantities of food during binge episodes. The two groups did not differ on measures of psychopathology including anxiety, depression, obsessive-compulsive behavior, perfectionism, and impulsivity. Thus, future developers of the *DSM-V* may want to consider the clinical utility and predictive validity of the frequency criteria in the BN set. In addition, they may want to strengthen the definition of a binge eating episode in terms of the importance of the size of the binge and the experience of loss of control. Specifically, in light of the study by le Grange et al., it may be appropriate to decrease the importance of binge size for the BN criteria.

EDNOS also should be critically examined, with concerted efforts to reduce the proportion of EDNOS diagnoses. Currently, the majority of people with eating disorders do not meet criteria for AN or BN. Rather, an estimated 60% fall into the EDNOS category, which is supposed to serve as a residual category (Fairburn & Bohn, 2005). There may be a significant reduction in EDNOS diagnoses if the symptom frequency criterion for BN is reduced, binges are defined as a loss of control of eating (rather than by their size) for BN, and/or the amenorrhea criteria for AN is removed. Also, other potentially valid diagnostic entities such as BED and purging disorder should be considered in their own right and potentially removed from the EDNOS category, where they currently reside.

It is likely that the next *DSM* classification will reflect a decision whether BED is moved from a provisional status to a full eating disorder diagnosis. Clearly, large volumes of empirical research can be considered that carefully consider the validity of this construct, especially in terms of its relationship to obesity. Important questions remain regarding whether or not it clearly predicts the onset of obesity and associated medical morbidity and also whether or not it shows treatment specificity when compared to traditional obesity treatments given to obese individuals without BED. A recent study shed some light on this issue by comparing behavioral weight loss treatment (BWL), interpersonal therapy (IPT), and guided self-help based on CBT (CBTgsh) for patients meeting *DSM-1V* criteria for BED (Wilson, Wilfley, Agras, & Bryson 2010). At the 2-year follow-up both IPT and CBTgsh were superior to BWL in terms of abstinence from binge eating. Hence, there appears to be treatment specificity in the case of BED. In addition, it is important to consider whether BED is sufficiently distinct from BN and normality to qualify as its own eating disorder category (Latner & Clyne, 2008).

Conclusion

In conclusion, the way that eating disorders are classified by the *DSM* has a significant impact on empirical research and treatment development. Therefore, it is of utmost importance that future versions of the *DSM* are guided by empirical research. In the first section of this chapter, we reviewed nosological research on eating disorders. Most latent class analysis studies found classes resembling BN, BED, and purging disorder. Meanwhile, most taxometric studies suggest that there is a bulimic taxon (consisting of BN and AN,

binge eating/purging type) that is qualitatively distinct from both AN, restricting type and normality.

Next, we reviewed diagnostic overlap among the eating disorders, and outlined a general lack of differences on certain external validators (e.g., family history, comorbid conditions), and significant differences on other validators (e.g., mortality rates and likelihood of remission or recovery; with AN generally faring worse than BN). Next, we outlined and evaluated alternative ways to classify eating disorders with the TDM (which groups people together based on findings from taxometric studies) and the transdiagnostic model (which suggests one "eating disorder" diagnosis and emphasizes the lack of differences between categories). The fourth section delineated suggestions for changing the eating disorder criteria in *DSM-V*, with a particular emphasis on reducing the number of people who are classified as EDNOS. In the final section of the chapter, we addressed the challenges that confront the classification of eating disorders, such as applicability to minority groups, children, males, and the question of whether or not clinical categories should be differentiated from research categories.

Future Directions and Controversies

Because DSM is aimed primarily at clinicians, should different classification criteria be used for research?

Although the *DSM-IV-TR* clearly states that its highest priority is to provide a helpful guide that informs clinical practice (APA, 2000, p. xxiii), the disorders and associated symptoms described in the *DSM* are often used in research endeavors as well. Unfortunately, researchers tend to adopt a rigid *DSM* definition of a given mental disorder when conducting empirical studies and this practice has likely hindered the progression of knowledge about the disorder's etiology and treatment (Grilo, Devlin, Cachelin, & Yanovski, 1997; Wilfley, Bishop, Wilson, & Agras, 2007). Specifically, when researchers study a predefined condition, they do not allow themselves to contest currently accepted conventions; therefore, the evolution of new valid diagnostic criteria, and associated etiological and treatment implications, is disrupted.

In acknowledgment of this problem, eating disorders experts have encouraged clinicians and researchers alike to stop reifying the *DSM* (Grilo et al., 1997; Kupfer, First, & Regier, 2002). Making modifications to the current diagnostic system and common research approaches may facilitate this request. One such modification may be to introduce a split-classification system in which research and clinical criteria for a given disorder are not identical. For instance, researchers may specify research criteria in need of empirical examination (e.g., frequency of binge eating that is clinically significant; personality dimensions that have clinical utility to eating pathology). If a sufficient body of empirical evidence accumulated and suggested that the research criteria were valid, subsequent changes to the clinical criteria would be warranted. This type of procedure may prevent researchers from limiting their studies to *DSM*-defined disorders, while simultaneously ensuring that only empirically supported and validated changes eventually occur in the clinically based *DSM* system.

Alternatively, the research community may adopt a new perspective on empirical studies, such that it may discourage investigators to adhere rigidly to *DSM* conventions in an effort to expedite the process of discovery. A paradigm shift of this nature would require researchers to provide clear rationales for examining alternative sets of symptoms, funding organizations to value the importance of scrutinizing existing diagnostic standards, and the peer-review system to embrace studies that examine novel diagnostic concepts.

What cultural issues should be considered for future versions of the DSM?

The majority of research on the classification of eating disorders is based upon White adolescent/young adult females from Western, industrialized nations, despite the fact that eating disorders are not restricted to this demographic group. The samples used in studies influence the description, definition, and classification of eating disorders. Therefore, a lack of diversity in study samples could limit the generalizability and utility of eating disorder classifications used to characterize eating disorders in people from non-Western cultures and from ethnic/racial minority groups.

Specifically, there are concerns about the *DSM-IV-TR* AN criteria set. Fear of weight gain as a criterion has been criticized on the grounds that it may not be present in individuals displaying apparent AN in certain cultures (e.g., Hong Kong), though this is a subject of debate (Habermas, 1989; Katzman & Lee, 1997). Attempts to examine evidence of AN across cultures have been marked by debates concerning the definition of the illness. While there is universal agreement that AN represents a disorder marked by self-starvation, some experts (Habermas, 1989) have argued that an excessive fear of weight gain is a necessary motivating force behind food

refusal while others (Katzman & Lee, 1997; Lee, 1995) have argued that it is not a core feature of AN. Cases of AN-like syndromes have been described in countries all over the world (e.g., South Africa, Nigeria, Zimbabwe, Egypt, United Arab Emirates, Iran, China, Japan, Korea, Russia, India, Pakistan, and Malaysia; Keel & Klump, 2003). Food refusal and emaciation are reported for all cases and the syndrome is found predominantly in adolescent and young adult women, but the presence of an excessive fear of weight gain as a motivating factor is not universal. In contrast, BN appears to exist mostly within the Western context (Keel & Klump, 2003).

Another challenge for cross-cultural research is the focus on *DSM* disorders, making it impossible to comment on the possible presence of other eating disorders (e.g., purging disorder, BED, or subjective binge eating disorder) outside of Western culture. Because binge episodes require large stores of readily edible food, BED, like BN, may be limited to places where food is abundant and easily obtained. In contrast, both purging disorder and subjective binge eating disorder may be relatively more common in non-Western regions because, like AN, neither requires large quantities of food.

In addition to inter-culture differences, research also supports intra-culture differences with regard to eating disorders. For example, Black women appear to be less likely to experience body dissatisfaction, disordered eating, and diagnosable eating disorders compared to White American women (Abrams, Allen, Gray, 1993; Rhea, 1999; Striegel-Moore et al., 2003). In particular, Black women appear to be protected more from AN and BN than from BED (Smith, Marcus, Lewis, Fitzgibbon, & Schreiner, 1998; Striegel-Moore et al., 2003), suggesting that Black women may not be protected from eating disorders per se, but more protected from AN and BN than White women. In contrast, no specific protection from the development of body image disturbance or disordered eating has been observed in Hispanic (Fitzgibbon et al., 1998; le Grange, Stone, & Brownell, 1998; Lester & Petrie, 1995; Robinson et al., 1996), Asian (Barnett, Keel, & Conoscenti, 2001; Robinson et al., 1996), or Native American samples (Rosen et al., 1988; Smith & Krejci, 1991; Story et al., 1994).

A strong traditional cultural identity appears to protect Black and Hispanic women from some disordered eating attitudes and behaviors (Chamorrow & Flores-Ortiz, 2000; Gowen, Hayward, Killen, Robinson, & Taylor, 1999; Lester & Petrie, 1995;

Pumariega, Gustavson, Gustavson, & Motes, 1994). In contrast, several studies have failed to find a significant association between acculturation to Western values and disordered eating among Asian women (Gowen et al., 1999; Haudeck, Rorty, & Henker, 1999; Jackson, Keel, & Lee, 2006). Instead, results suggest that cultural factors that contribute to eating disorders may be native to some Asian cultures (Jackson et al., 2006). For example, the virtues of fasting to the point of emaciation are included in the Daoist text *Sandong zhunang* (Rieger, Touyz, Swain, & Beumont, 2001). Thus, Asian women may be more likely to suffer from EDNOS characterized by fasting and very low weight in the absence of weight phobia. Native American groups appear to be at increased risk for obesity and increased body mass index. Feelings of being overweight have been associated with the use of purging among Chippewa and Native Alaskan females (Rosen et al., 1988; Story et al., 1994). Thus, AN may be underrepresented among Native American girls and women whereas purging disorder may be more common.

The failure of a diagnostic system to adequately capture disorders of eating that are experienced by members of ethnic/racial minority groups may have particularly pernicious effects for these individuals. Indeed, women from ethnic/racial minority groups are more likely to have undiagnosed and untreated eating disorders compared to White women (Cachelin, Rebeck, Veisel, & Striegel-Moore, 2001).

Given the fact that cultures change over time, it is important to recognize that eating disorder rates and symptom presentations may accordingly change over time. For instance, BN is currently observed only in societies that have plentiful access to food; however, BN rates may increase in certain societies over time if members of those societies encounter an increase in the access they have to large quantities of food. As another example, researchers have demonstrated the exposure to Western media increases the rates of eating disorder symptoms among women from cultures that are typically shielded from Western media exposure (e.g., Eddy, Hennessey, Thompson-Brenner, 2007). Therefore, it is reasonable to predict that as a society's exposure to traditional Western thin-ideals increases, the observed rates of eating disorders may increase.

Should there be separate diagnostic criteria for men and women?
Most research suggests that eating disorders in men closely resemble eating disorders in women (Keel,

Klump, Leon, & Fulkerson, 1998; Leon, Fulkerson, Perry, Keel, & Klump, 1999). Factors that appear to be more relevant for men, such as involvement in sports that require low weight (Hausenblas & Carron, 1999) and homosexuality (Carlat, Camargo, & Herzog, 1997; Russell & Keel, 2002), may increase the salience of weight control in a group that is otherwise less concerned about being thin. However, there has been speculation that men may be at risk for "reverse anorexia" (Pope, Katz, & Hudson, 1993). Instead of viewing the body as much larger than it really is, men with reverse AN are characterized by viewing their bodies as "puny" despite their efforts and success at body-building (Pope et al., 1993). This distorted perception contributes to more extreme efforts (excessive exercise, high protein diets, anabolic steroid use) to increase lean muscle mass and overall body size. Because this condition involves altered eating patterns, the use of extreme weight control behaviors, and body image disturbance, some have argued that it represents an eating disorder (e.g., Pope et al., 1993), albeit one rarely seen in women and not included in current diagnostic classifications.

Because extant research suggests that men with eating disorders present similarly to females with eating disorders, there does not appear to be sufficient evidence to justify separate *DSM* criteria at this time. The addition of "reverse anorexia" to *DSM* could potentially increase the recognition of eating disorders that are unique to males. However, it is likely premature to consider this as its own category (rather than as a type of EDNOS) until more research, particularly on the incidence and clinical validity of "reverse anorexia," is available.

Should there be separate diagnostic criteria for children and early adolescents?
Although eating disorders were initially considered Disorders Usually Diagnosed in Infancy, Childhood, and Adolescence by the *DSM* (van Son et al., 2006) and typically onset during adolescence (Hoek & Hoeken, 2003), recent editions of the *DSM* have removed eating disorders from the section focusing on childhood disorders. Despite this fact, many researchers and clinicians have raised concerns about whether the *DSM-IV-TR*'s eating disorder diagnostic criteria are as valid for youngsters as they are for later adolescents and adults. In fact, a publication by the Workgroup for Classification of Eating Disorders in Children and Adolescents (WCEDCA, 2007) argued that the *DSM-IV-TR* does not sufficiently reflect the symptomatic expression

of eating disorders that varies during the course of development.

Many specific criticisms regarding the *DSM-IV-TR*'s lack of developmental sensitivity have been raised with regard to eating disorders. For instance, AN's criterion A (a seemingly straightforward criteria stating that one's weight must be less than 85% of that which is expected) is difficult to apply to youths for many reasons. First, because children's growth rates vary widely and the age at which puberty onsets greatly impacts one's height and weight, objectively calculating a child or adolescent's ideal weight is often difficult (American Academy of Pediatrics Committee on Adolescents, American College of Obstetricians and Gynecologists Committee on Adolescent Health, 2006). Relatedly, the dynamic fluctuations in children and adolescents' growth make it challenging to quantify medically relevant changes in growth velocity over time (Berkey, Gardner, Frazier, & Colditz, 2000). For instance, a youth whose weight appears to be above the 85% cut-off at a cross-sectional glance but who has been failing to display developmentally appropriate weight *increases* over time may be showing early signs of disordered eating.

A diagnosis of AN in female patients also requires the presence of amenorrhea for at least 3 consecutive months; however, this criterion often proves irrelevant for youths (i.e., for girls or young women who develop AN before they begin menstruating, or before their menstrual periods become regular, and for boys or young men, who are over-represented in early onset groups; Peebles, Wilson, & Lock, 2006). Some have proposed alternative criteria for female youths such as a diagnosis of primary amenorrhea if menstruation has not begun by the age of 15, or within 3 years of the beginning of breast development (WCEDCA, 2007).

Another potential problem with applying the *DSM-IV-TR*'s eating disorder criteria to youths has to do with the developmentally acquired ability to observe and have insight into one's own thoughts and feelings. For instance, studies have highlighted the frequent failure of youths to endorse fear of weight gain despite the presence of behaviors that clearly contribute to harmful weight loss (Fairburn et al., 2003). Further, eating disordered youths often have difficulty articulating or conceptualizing that a large portion of their self-esteem is related to their body image. Acknowledging and conveying both fear of fatness and feelings of body dissatisfaction are processes that require cognitive and emotional sophistication, and it is well known that cognitive and emotional capacities continue developing well into adolescence (Boyer, 2006). Accordingly, youths may not be able to convey verbally their cognitively based eating disorder symptoms as effectively as adults.

Owing to the difficulty many youths have with recognizing and reporting subjective emotional experiences and thought patterns, some researchers have suggested that focusing on overt behavioral symptoms may be preferential with working with young patients. For instance, Marcus and Kalarchian (2003) suggested that behaviors such as hiding food or secretive eating may be good indicators of binge eating patterns in children, and Bryant-Waugh & Lask (1995) suggested describing a childhood eating disorder as one in which "there is an excessive preoccupation with weight or shape, *and/or food intake*..." (p. 191), at least in part because food intake can be observed by others.

Other researchers have suggested that the *DSM* authors consider adding modifiers to existing eating disorder symptoms for children and adolescents (WCEDCA, 2007). This practice has been useful for other disorders in the *DSM-IV-TR* such as major depression (e.g., irritability can be used in place of sad mood for children) and obsessive compulsive disorder (e.g., child patients are not required to recognize that the obsessions and compulsions are unreasonable; APA, 2000). WCEDCA proposed specific criteria alterations for children and adolescents with eating disorders such as coding behavioral observations by others (i.e., parents report their child engages in behaviors that indicate he/she has an intense fear of fatness) rather than self-reports of the affected youngster (i.e., instead of requiring the child to directly state that he/she is terrified of becoming fat even though he/she is underweight).

Whereas many of these suggestions for change focus on making modifications at the symptom level in an effort to better reflect eating disorders experienced by children and adolescents, some researchers have focused instead of considering the validity of eating disorder classification systems in general. To our knowledge, only one study has empirically evaluated the reliability with which existing eating disorder diagnoses are applied to youth. Nicholls, Chater, and Lask (2000) compared the classification systems set forth by the 10th edition of the International Classification of Diseases (ICD-10; World Health Organization, 2005), the *DSM-IV-TR*, and the Great Ormond Street (GOS; Lask & Bryant-Waugh, 2000) criteria. The use of the ICD-10 system resulted in the lowest inter-rater reliability of childhood eating disorder presentations. Despite the *DSM-IV-TR*'s relatively few eating disorder categories, inter-rater reliability for eating disorder diagnoses among children using the *DSM-IV-TR* was lower than reliability obtained when using the GOS criteria. These results are interesting given that the GOS criteria were designed specifically to be sensitive to developmental variables (e.g., according to this system, AN is defined as a disorder during which a child engages in determined weight loss, has abnormal cognitions regarding his/her weight or shape, and has morbid preoccupation with weight or shape); however, some have raised concerns that some of the disorders defined by the GOS criteria (e.g., pervasive refusal syndrome) should not be considered an eating disorder as defined by the *DSM-IV-TR* (WCEDCA, 2007).

Although the above-described study is the only one in which existing diagnostic systems for children have been evaluated in a head-to-head fashion, many have speculated about how other diagnostic models may address some of the limitations of the existing models. For instance, some believe that the transdiagnostic model proposed by Fairburn et al. (2003) may improve the validity of eating disorder diagnoses for all who suffer from eating pathology, including youths. In this model, a single diagnosis of eating disorder would be given to all affected individuals; however, qualifiers relevant to specific manifestations and/or clinically meaningful variables (e.g., those related to developmental differences in eating disorder presentations) would be possible. Others have suggested that a diagnostic approach be developed in which youths who present with eating pathology are required to meet some, but not all, diagnostic criteria to qualify for an eating disorder diagnosis. For instance, Hebebrand, Casper, Treasure, and Schweiger (2004) described a model in which a broad array of symptoms would be assessed (e.g., criteria could be related to age and/or menstrual status, gender-specific presentations, and medical conditions such as bradycardia, hypothermia, hypotension). Not all candidates for an eating disorder diagnosis would be evaluated on all criteria, but rather clinicians would focus on evaluating the criteria that are relevant given the individual's demographic and symptomatic presentation. Clearly, the proposed models of Fairburn et al. and Hebebrand et al. should be empirically evaluated before conclusions are reached regarding their utility in the diagnosis of eating disorders experienced by youths.

Summary

In sum, the developers of the *DSM-V* are charged with the task of creating a classification system that facilitates clinical work and scientific research, but also, as Gould (1989, p. 98) suggests in the opening quote, reflects "theories about the basis of natural order." There is much to learn about the generalizability of the *DSM* eating disorder categories with regards to relatively understudied groups (e.g., males, children, non-Western cultures). The accumulation of more empirical data on these traditionally understudied groups may lead to a greater understanding of the nature of eating disorders, and to the most valid form of classification.

References

Abraham, S. F., Pettigrew, B., Boyd, C., Russell, J., & Taylor, A. (2005). Usefulness of amenorrhea in the diagnoses of eating disorder patients. *Journal of Psychosomatic Obstetrics & Gynecology, 26*, 211–215.

Abrams, K. K., Allen, L. R., & Gray, J. J. (1993). Disordered eating attitudes and behaviors, psychological adjustment, and ethnic identity: A comparison of black and white female college students. *International Journal of Eating Disorders, 14*, 49–57.

American Academy of Pediatrics Committee on Adolescents, American College of Obstetricians and Gynecologists Committee on Adolescent Health. (2006). Menstruation in girls and adolescents: Using the menstrual cycle as a vital sign. *Pediatrics, 118*, 2245–2250.

American Psychiatric Association (APA). (2000). *Diagnostic and statistical manual of mental disorders* (4th ed., text revision). Washington, DC: Author.

Barnett, H. L., Keel, P. K., & Conoscenti, L. M. (2001). Body type preferences in Asian and Caucasian college students. *Sex Roles, 45*, 867–878.

Berkey, C., Gardner, J., Frazier, A., & Colditz, G. (2000). Relation of childhood diet and body size to menarche and adolescent growth in girls. *American Journal of Epidemiology, 152*, 446–452.

Boyer, T. (2006). The development of risk-taking: A multi-perspective review. *Developmental Review, 26*, 291–345.

Bryant-Waugh, R., & Lask, B. (1995). Eating disorders in children. *Journal of Child Psychology and Psychiatry, 36*, 191–202.

Bulik, C. M., Sullivan, P. F., & Kendler, K. S. (2000). An empirical study of the classification of eating disorders. *American Journal of Psychiatry, 157*, 886–895.

Cachelin, F. M., Rebeck, R., Veisel, C., & Striegel-Moore, R. H. (2001). Barriers to treatment for eating disorders among ethnically diverse women. *International Journal of Eating Disorders, 30*, 269–278.

Carlat, D. J., Camargo, C. A., Jr., & Herzog, D. B. (1997). Eating disorders in males: a report on 135 patients. *American Journal of Psychiatry, 154*, 1127–1132.

Catell, R. B. (1946). *Description and measurement of personality.* New York: World Book.

Chamorrow, R., & Flores-Ortiz, Y. (2000). Acculturation and disordered eating patterns among Mexican American women. *International Journal of Eating Disorders, 28*, 125–129.

Duncan, A. E., Bucholz, K. K., Neuman, R. J., Agrawal, A., Madden, P. A., & Heath, A. C. (2007). Clustering of eating disorder symptoms in a general population female twin sample: A latent class analysis. *Psychological Medicine, 37*(8), 1097–1107.

Eddy, K.T., Crosby, R.D., Keel, P.K., le Grange, D., Powers, P., Mitchell, J.E., Hill, L., Wonderlich, S.A. (2009). Empirical identification and validation of eating disorder phenotypes in a multisite clinical sample. *Journal of Nervous and Mental Disease, 197*(1), 41–49.

Eddy, K. T., Hennessey, M., & Thompson-Brenner, H. (2007). Eating pathology in East African women: The role of media exposure and globalization. *Journal of Nervous and Mental Disease, 195*, 196–202.

Eddy, K. T., Keel, P. K., Dorer, D. J., Delinsky, S. S., Franko, D. L., & Herzog, D. B. (2002). A longitudinal comparison of anorexia nervosa subtypes. *International Journal of Eating Disorders, 31*(2), 191–201.

Fairburn, C. G., & Beglin, S. J. (1994). Assessment of eating disorders: Interview or self-report questionnaire? *International Journal of Obesity, 16*, 363–370.

Fairburn, C. G., & Bohn, K. (2005). Eating disorder not otherwise specified (EDNOS): an example of the troublesome "not otherwise specified" (NOS) category in DSM-IV. *Behavior Research and Therapy, 43*, 691–701.

Fairburn, C. G., Cooper, Z., & Shafran, R. (2003). Cognitive behaviour therapy for eating disorders: A "transdiagnostic" theory and treatment. *Behaviour Research and Therapy, 41*, 509–517.

Fichter, M. M., & Quadflieg, N. (2007). Long-term stability of eating disorder diagnoses. *International Journal of Eating Disorders, Special issue on diagnosis and classification, 40* (Supplement), S61–S66.

Fichter, M. M., Quadflieg, N., & Rief, W. (1994). Course of multi-impulsive bulimia. *Psychological Medicine, 24*, 591–604.

Fitzgibbon, M. L., Spring, B., Avellone, M. E., Blackman, L. R., Pingitore, R., & Stolley, M. R. (1998). Correlates of binge eating in Hispanic, black, and white women. *International Journal of Eating Disorders, 24*, 43–52.

Francesca, B., Monteleone, P., Bortolotti, F., Grave, R. D., Todisco, P., Favaro, A., et al. (2003). Persistent amenorrhea in weight-recovered anorexics: Psychological and biological aspects. *Psychiatry Research, 118*, 249–257.

Franko, D. L., & Keel, P. K. (2006). Suicidality in eating disorders: Occurrence, correlates, and clinical implications. *Clinical Psychology Review, 26*, 769–782.

Gangestad, S., & Snyder, M. (1985). "To carve nature at its joints": On the existence of discrete classes in personality. *Psychological Review, 92*, 317–349.

Gleaves, D. H., Lowe, M. R., Green, B. A., Cororve, M. B., & Williams, T. L. (2000a). Do anorexia and bulimia nervosa occur on a continuum? A taxometric analysis. *Behavior Therapy, 31*(2), 195–219.

Gleaves, D. H., Lowe, M. R., Snow, A. C., Green, B. A., & Murphy-Eberenz, K. P. (2000b). Continuity and discontinuity models of bulimia nervosa: A taxometric investigation. *Journal of Abnormal Psychology, 109*(1), 56–68.

Gonzales, E. G. (2001). Evaluation of self-concept, body satisfaction, and social skills in anorexia and bulimia nervosa. *Clinica y Salud, 12*(3), 239–304.

Gordon, K. H., Holm-Denoma, J. M., Smith, A. R., Fink, E. L., & Joiner, T. E., Jr. (2007). Taxometric analysis: Introduction and overview. *International Journal of Eating Disorders, 40*, S35–S39.

Gould, S. J. (1989). *Wonderful life: The Burgess shale and the nature of history.* New York: W. W. Norton.

Gowen, L. K., Hayward, C., Killen, J. D., Robinson, T. N, & Taylor, C. B. (1999). Acculturation and eating disorder symptoms in adolescent girls. *Journal of Research on Adolescence, 9*, 67–83.

Grilo, C. M., Devlin, M. J., Cachelin, F. M., & Yanovski, S. Z. (1997). Report of the National Institutes of Health (NIH): Workshop on the development of research priorities in eating disorders. *Psychopharmacology Bulletin, 33*, 321–333.

Grilo, C. M., Hrabosky, J. I., White, M. A., Allison, K. C., Stunkard, A. J., & Masheb, R. M. (2008). Overvaluation of shape and weight in binge eating disorder and overweight controls: Refinement of a diagnostic construct. *Journal of Abnormal Psychology, 117*(2), 414–419.

Habermas, T. (1989). The psychiatric history of anorexia nervosa and bulimia nervosa: Weight concerns and bulimic symptoms in early case reports. *International Journal of Eating Disorders, 8*, 259–273.

Haudeck, C., Rorty, M., & Henker, B. (1999). The role of ethnicity and parental bonding in the eating and weight concerns of Asian-American and Caucasian college women. *International Journal of Eating Disorders, 25*, 425–433.

Hausenblas, H. A., & Carron, A. V. (1999). Eating disorder indices and athletes: An integration. *Journal of Sport & Exercise Psychology, 21*, 230–258.

Hebebrand, J., Casper, R., Treasure, J. L., & Schweiger, U. (2004). The need to revise the diagnostic criteria for anorexia nervosa. *Journal of Neural Transmission, 111*, 827–840.

Herzog, D. B., Sacks, N. R., Keller, M. B., Lavori, P. W., von Ranson, K.B., & Gray, H. M. (1993). Patterns and predictors of recovery in anorexia nervosa and bulimia nervosa. *Journal of the American Academy of Child & Adolescent Psychiatry, 32*, 835–842.

Hoek, H., & Hoeken, D. (2003). Review of prevalence and incidence of eating disorders. *International Journal of Eating Disorders, 34*, 383–396.

Holliday, J., Landau, S., Collier, D., & Treasure, J. (2006). Do illness characteristics and familial risk differ between women with anorexia nervosa grouped on the basis of personality pathology? *Psychological Medicine, 36*, 529–538.

Hsu, L. K. G., Mulliken, B., McDonagh, B., Das, S. K., Rand, W., Fairburn, C. G., et al. (2002). Binge eating disorder in extreme obesity. *International Journal of Obesity & Related Metabolic Disorders, 26*(10), 1398–1403.

Hudson, J. I., Hiripi, E., Pope, H. G., & Kessler, R. C. (2007). The prevalence and correlates of eating disorders in the National Comorbidity Survey Replication. *Biological Psychiatry, 61*, 348–358.

Jackson, S. C., Keel, P. K., & Lee, Y. H. (2006). Trans-cultural comparison of disordered eating in Korean women. *International Journal of Eating Disorders, 39*, 498–502.

Jimerson, D. C., Lesem, M. D., Kaye, W. H., & Brewerton, T. D. (1992). Low serotonin and dopamine metabolite concentration in cerebrospinal fluid from bulimic patients with frequent binge episodes. *Archives of General Psychiatry, 49*, 132–138.

Johnson, C., & Connors, M. E. (1987). *The etiology and treatment of bulimia nervosa: A biopsychosocial perspective.* New York: Basic Books.

Johnson, J. G., Spitzer, R. L., & Williams, B. W. (2001). Health problems, impairment, and illnesses associated with bulimia nervosa and binge eating disorder among primary care and obstetric gynecology patients. *Psychological Medicine, 31*, 1455–1466.

Katzman, M. A., & Lee, S. (1997). Beyond body image: The integration of feminist and transcultural theories in the understanding of self starvation. *International Journal of Eating Disorders, 22*, 385–394.

Keel, P., Holm-Denoma, J.M., Crosby, R., Haedt, A., Gravener, J., & Joiner, T.E. (under review). Latent structure of bulimic syndromes: An empirical approach utilizing latent profile analyses and taxometric analyses. APA Monograph.

Keel, P. K., Dorer, D. J., Eddy, K. T., Franko, D., Charatan, D. L., & Herzog, D. B. (2003). Predictors of mortality in eating disorders. *Archives of General Psychiatry, 60*, 179–183.

Keel, P. K., Dorer, D. J., Franko, D. L., Jackson, S. C., & Herzog, D. B. (2005a). Postremission predictors of relapse in women with eating disorders. *American Journal of Psychiatry, 162*(12), 2263–2268.

Keel, P. K., Fichter, M., Quadflieg, N., Bulik, C. M., Baxter, M. G., Thornton, L., et al. (2004). Application of a latent class analysis to empirically define eating disorder phenotypes. *Archives of General Psychiatry, 61*, 192–200.

Keel, P. K., Haedt, A., & Edler, C. (2005b). Purging disorder: An ominous variant of bulimia nervosa? *International Journal of Eating Disorders, 38*, 191–199.

Keel, P. K., & Klump, K. L. (2003). Are eating disorders culture-bound syndromes? Implications for conceptualizing their genetic bases. *Psychological Bulletin, 129*, 747–769.

Keel, P. K., Klump, K. L., Leon, G. R., & Fulkerson, J. A. (1998). Disordered eating in adolescent males from a school-based sample. *International Journal of Eating Disorders, 23*, 125–132.

Kendler, K. S. (1990). Toward a scientific psychiatric nosology: Strengths and limitations. *Archives of General Psychiatry, 47*, 969–973.

Kupfer, D., First, M. B., & Regier, D. (2002). *A research agenda for DSM-V.* Washington, D.C.: American Psychiatric Association.

Lacey, J. H. (1993). Self-damaging and addictive behavior in bulimia nervosa: A cachement area study. *British Journal of Psychiatry, 163*, 190–194.

Lask, B., & Bryant-Waugh, R. (2000). *Anorexia nervosa and related eating disorders in children and adolescence* (2nd ed.). Hove, UK: Psychology Press.

Latner, J. D., & Clyne, C. (2008). The diagnostic validity of the criteria for binge eating disorder. *International Journal of Eating Disorders, 41*, 1–114.

Lazarsfeld, P. F., & Henry, N. W. (1968). *Latent structure analysis.* Boston: Houghton Mifflin.

le Grange, D., Binford, R. B., Peterson, C. B., Crow, S. J., Crosby, R. D., Klein, M. H., et al. (2006). DSM-IV threshold versus subthreshold bulimia nervosa. *International Journal of Eating Disorders, 39*(6), 462–467.

le Grange, D., Stone, A. A., & Brownell, K. D. (1998). Eating disturbances in white and minority female dieters. *International Journal of Eating Disorders, 24*, 395–403.

Lee, S. (1995). Self-starvation in context: Towards a culturally sensitive understanding of anorexia nervosa. *Social Science Medicine, 41*, 25–36.

Leon, G. R., Fulkerson, J. A., Perry, C. L., Keel, P. K., & Klump, K. L. (1999). Three to four year prospective evaluation of personality and behavioral risk factors for later disordered eating in adolescent girls and boys. *Journal of Youth & Adolescence, 28*, 181–196.

Lester, R., & Petrie, T. A. (1995). Personality and physical correlates of bulimic symptomatology among Mexican American female college students. *Journal of Counseling Psychology, 42*, 199–203.

Marcus, M., & Kalarchian, M. (2003). Binge eating in children and adolescents. *International Journal of Eating Disorders, 34*(Supplement), S47–S57.

Meehl, P. E. (1992). Factors and taxa, traits and types, differences of degree and differences in kind. *Journal of Personality, 60*(1), 117–174.

Mitchell, J. E., Crosby, R. D., Wonderlich, S. A., Hill, L., le Grange, D., Powers, P., & Eddy, K. (2007). Latent profile analysis of a cohort of patients with eating disorders not otherwise specified. *International Journal of Eating Disorders, 40*, S95–S98.

Nicholls, D., Chater, R., & Lask, B. (2000). Children into DSM don't go: A comparison of classification systems for eating disorders in childhood and adolescence. *International Journal of Eating Disorders, 28*, 317–324.

Peebles, R., Wilson, J. L., & Lock, J. D. (2006). How do children with eating disorders differ from adolescents with eating disorders at initial evaluation? *Journal of Adolescent Health, 39*(6), 800–805.

Pinheiro, A. P., Bulik, C. M., Sullivan, P. F., & Machado, P. P. (2008). An empirical study of the typology of bulimic symptoms in young Portuguese women. *International Journal of Eating Disorders, 41*(3), 251–258.

Pope, H. G., Jr., Katz, D. L., & Hudson, J. I. (1993). Anorexia nervosa and "reverse anorexia" among 108 male bodybuilders. *Comprehensive Psychiatry, 34*, 406–409.

Pumariega, A. J., Gustavson, C. R., Gustavson, J. C., & Motes, P. S. (1994). Eating attitudes in African-American women: The Essence Eating Disorders Survey. *Eating Disorders: The Journal of Treatment & Prevention, 2*, 5–16.

Rhea, D. J. (1999). Eating disorder behaviors of ethnically diverse urban female adolescent athletes and non-athletes. *Journal of Adolescence, 22*, 379–388.

Rieger, E., Touyz, S. W., Swain, T., & Beumont, P. J. (2001). Cross-cultural research on anorexia nervosa: Assumptions regarding the role of body weight. *International Journal of Eating Disorders, 29*, 205–215.

Robinson, T. N., Killen, J. D., Litt, I. F., Hammer, L. D., Wilson, D.M., Haydel, K. F., et al. (1996). Ethnicity and body dissatisfaction: are Hispanic and Asian girls at increased risk for eating disorders? *Journal of Adolescent Health, 19*, 384–393.

Rosen, L., Shafer, C. L., Dummer, G. M., Cross, L. K., Deuman, G. W., & Malmberg, S. R. (1988). Prevalence of pathogenic weight-control behaviors among Native American women and girls. *International Journal of Eating Disorders, 7*, 807–811.

Ruscio, J., & Ruscio, A. M. (2002). A structure-based approach to psychological assessment: Matching measurement models to latent structure. *Assessment, 9*, 4–16.

Russell, C. J., & Keel, P. K. (2002). Homosexuality as a specific risk factor for eating disorders in men. *International Journal of Eating Disorders, 31*, 300–306.

Smith, J. E., & Krejci, J. (1991). Minorities join the majority: Eating disturbances among Hispanic and Native American youth. *International Journal of Eating Disorders, 10*, 179–186.

Smith, D. E., Marcus, M. D., Lewis, C., Fitzgibbon, M., & Schreiner, P. (1998). Prevalence of binge eating disorder, obesity, and depression in a biracial cohort of young adults. *Annals of Behavioral Medicine, 20*, 227–232.

Steiger, H., Israël, M., Gauvin, L., Kin, N., & Young, S. N. (2003). Implications of compulsive and impulsive traits for serotonin status in women with bulimia nervosa. *Psychiatry Research, 120*, 219–229.

Steiger, H., & Stotland, S. (1996). Prospective study of outcome in bulimics as a function of Axis II comorbidity: Long-term responses on eating and psychiatric symptoms. *International Journal of Eating Disorders, 20,* 149–162.

Story, M., Hauck, F. R., Broussard, B. A., White, L. L., Resnick, M. D., & Blum, R. W. (1994). Weight perceptions and weight control practices in American Indian and Alaska Native adolescents. A national survey. *Archives of Pediatrics & Adolescent Medicine, 148,* 567–571.

Striegel-Moore, R. H., Dohm, F. A., Kraemer, H. C., Taylor, C. B., Daniels, S., Crawford, P. B., & Schreiber, G. B. (2003). Eating disorders in White and Black women. *American Journal of Psychiatry, 160,* 1326–1331.

Striegel-Moore, R. H., Franko, D. L., Thompson, D., Barton, B., Schreiber, G. B., & Daniels, S. R. (2005). An empirical study of the typology of bulimia nervosa and its spectrum variants. *Psychological Medicine, 35*(11), 1563–1572.

Strober, M., Freeman, R., Lamper, C., Diamond, J., & Kaye, W. (2000). Controlled family study of anorexia nervosa and bulimia nervosa: Evidence of shared liability and transmission of partial syndromes. *American Journal of Psychiatry, 157,* 393–401.

Strube, M. J. (1989). Evidence for the type in Type A behavior: A taxometric analysis. *Journal of Personality and Social Psychology, 56,* 972–987.

Sullivan, P. F., Bulik, C. M., & Kendler, K. S. (1998). The epidemiology and classification of bulimia nervosa. *Psychological Medicine, 28*(3), 599–610.

Tauscher, J., Pirker, W., Willeit, M., de Zwaan, M., Bailer, U., Neumeister, A., et al. (2001). Beta-CIT and single photon emission computer tomography reveal reduced brain serotonin transporter availability in bulimia nervosa. *Biological Psychiatry, 49,* 326–332.

Thompson-Brenner, H., Eddy, K. T., Satir, D. A., Boisseau, C. L., & Westen, D. (2008). Personality subtypes in adolescents with eating disorders: Validation of a classification approach. *Journal of Child Psychology and Psychiatry, 49,* 170–180.

Tozzi, F., Thornton, L. M., Klump, K. L., Fichter, M. M., Halmi, K. A., Kaplan, A. S., et al. (2005). Symptom fluctuation in eating disorders: Correlates of diagnostic crossover. *American Journal of Psychiatry, 162,* 732–740.

Tylka, T. L., & Subich, L. M. (2003). Revisiting the latent structure of eating disorders: Taxometric analyses with nonbehavioral indicators. *Journal of Counseling Psychology, 50*(3), 276–286.

Uebersax, J. S. (1999). Probit latent class analysis with dichotomous or ordered category measures: Conditional independence/dependence models. *Applied Psychological Measures, 23,* 283–297.

van Son, G., van Hoeken, D., Aad, I., Bartelds, A., van Furth, E., & Hoek, E. (2006). Time trends in the incidence of eating disorders: A primary care study in the Netherlands. *International Journal of Eating Disorders, 39,* 565–569.

Wade, T. D., Crosby, R. D., & Martin, N. G. (2006). Use of latent profile analysis to identify eating disorder phenotypes in an adult Australian twin cohort. *Archives of General Psychiatry, 63*(12), 1377–1384.

Waldman, I. D., & Lilienfeld, S. O. (2001). Applications of taxometric methods to problems of comorbidity: Perspectives and challenges. *Clinical Psychology: Science and Practice, 8,* 520–527.

Waller, N. G., & Meehl, P. E. (1998). *Multivariate taxometric procedures: Distinguishing types from continua.* Newberry Park, CA: Sage.

Watson, T. L., & Andersen, A. E. (2003). A critical examination of the amenorrhea and weight criteria for diagnosing anorexia nervosa. *Acta Psychiatrica Scandinavica, 108,* 175–182.

Weizman, R., Carmi, M., Tyano, S., Apter, A., & Rehavi, M. (1986). High affinity [³H]imipramine binding and serotonin uptake to platelets of adolescent females suffering from anorexia nervosa. *Life Sciences, 38,* 1235–1242.

Westen, D., & Harden-Fischer, J. (2001). Personality profiles in eating disorders: Rethinking the distinction between Axis I and Axis II. *American Journal of Psychiatry, 158,* 547–562.

Wilfley, D. E., Bishop, M. E., Wilson, G. T., & Agras, W. S. (2007). Classification of eating disorders: Toward DSM-V. *International Journal of Eating Disorders, 40,* S123–S129.

Williamson, D. A., Gleaves, D. H., & Stewart, T. M. (2005). Categorical versus dimensional models of eating disorders: An examination of the evidence. *International Journal of Eating Disorders, 37,* 1–10.

Williamson, D. A., Womble, L. G., Smeet, M. A. M., Netemeyer, R. G., Thaw, M., Kutlesic, V., et al. (2002). The latent structure of eating disorder symptoms: A factor analytic and taxometric investigation. *The American Journal of Psychiatry, 159,* 412–418.

Wilson, G. T., Wilfley, D., Agras, W. S., & Bryson, S. W. (2010). Psychological treatments of binge eating. *Archives of General Psychiatry, 67,* 94–101.

Wonderlich, S. A., Crosby, R. D., Joiner, T. E. J., Peterson, C. B., Bardone-Cone, A. M., Klein, M. H., et al. (2005). Personality subtyping and bulimia nervosa: Psychopathological and genetic correlates. *Psychological Medicine, 35*(5), 649–657.

Wonderlich, S. A., Joiner, T. E., Jr., Keel, P. K., Williamson, D. A., & Crosby, R. D. (2007). Eating disorder diagnoses: Empirical approaches to classification. *American Psychologist, 62*(3), 167–180.

Wonderlich, S. A., & Mitchell, J. E. (1997). Eating disorders and comorbidity: Empirical, conceptual, and clinical implications. *Psychopharmacology Bulletin, 33,* 381–390.

Wonderlich, S. A., Mitchell, J. E., Peterson, C. B., & Crow, S. (2001). Integrative cognitive therapy for bulimic behavior. In R. Striegel-Moore & L. Smolak (Eds.), *Eating disorders: Innovations & directions for research and practice* (pp. 173–195). New York: American Psychological Association.

Wonderlich, S. A., & Swift, W. J. (1990). Borderline versus other personality disorders in the eating disorders. *International Journal of Eating Disorders, 9,* 629–638.

Workgroup for Classification of Eating Disorders in Children and Adolescents. (2007). Classification of child and adolescent eating disturbances. *International Journal of Eating Disorders, 40*(Supplement), S117–S122.

World Health Organization. (2005). *International classification of diseases.* Geneva, Switzerland: World Health Organization.

Epidemiology and Course of Eating Disorders

Pamela K. Keel

Abstract

The epidemiology of eating disorders holds important clues for understanding factors that may contribute to their etiology. In addition, epidemiological findings speak to the public health significance of these deleterious syndromes. Information on course and outcome are important for clinicians to understand the prognosis associated with different disorders of eating and for treatment planning. This chapter reviews information on the epidemiology and course of anorexia nervosa, bulimia nervosa, and two forms of eating disorder not otherwise specified, binge eating disorder and purging disorder.

Keywords: anorexia nervosa, binge eating disorder, bulimia nervosa, course, epidemiology, mortality, purging disorder

Introduction

Eating disorders represent a significant source of psychiatric morbidity among late adolescent and young adult women. Basic to the understanding of any mental disorder is careful description of who is affected by the disorder and disorder course and outcome. This chapter reviews information on the epidemiology and course of the major syndromes included in the category of eating disorders: anorexia nervosa (AN), bulimia nervosa (BN), and eating disorders not otherwise specified (EDNOS), including binge eating disorder (BED) and preliminary data on purging disorder (PD).

Anorexia Nervosa

The term "anorexia nervosa" was first introduced into the psychiatric nomenclature in 1874 by Sir William Gull to describe four adolescent female patients who experienced significant weight loss that could not be related to any medical condition (Gull, 1874). Given the long history of AN in the medical literature, considerable information has

been amassed on the epidemiology and course of this syndrome.

Epidemiology

Although AN is the first condition that comes to mind when most people think of eating disorders and represents a high proportion of patients encountered in inpatient settings (Dalle Grave & Calugi, 2007), AN may be less common than the other eating disorders (i.e., BN, BED, and PD) in the general population. According to the *Diagnostic and Statistical Manual of Mental Disorders* (4th ed.; *DSM-IV-TR*; American Psychiatric Association [APA], 2000), the lifetime prevalence of AN is 0.5% in adolescent and young adult women and approximately one tenth (or 0.05%) that in males. This means that approximately 1 in 200 women and 1 in 2,000 men will experience AN at some point in their lifetimes. Of note, in a population of 300 million with balanced gender representation, this does not mean that 750,000 women (150,000,000 × 0.005) and 75,000 men (150,000,000 × 0.0005) have AN because not all individuals are within the period of risk for the illness. Age at onset for AN is typically early to late adolescence, and, as discussed in the text that follows, a proportion of patients with AN eventually achieve recovery. Thus, the point prevalence, or percentage of individuals who currently meet criteria for AN, is much lower than lifetime prevalence and varies by age group and population studied. For example, Favaro, Ferrara, and Santanastaso (2003) reported a lifetime prevalence of AN of 2.0% and a point prevalence of 0.3% in women in a metropolitan area of Italy.

Four recent population-based epidemiological studies have reported higher lifetime prevalence estimates for AN in women than indicated by the *DSM-IV-TR* (APA, 2000), including a lifetime prevalence of 0.9% in the United States (Hudson, Hiripi, Pope, & Kessler, 2007), 1.9% in Australia (Wade et al., 2006), 2.0% in Italy (Favaro et al., 2003), and 2.2% in Finland (Keski-Rahkonen et al., 2007). These higher estimates may reflect detection of cases that are missed when ascertainment is based on clinical referral (Keski-Rahkonen et al., 2007). Indeed, 1-year prevalence estimates based on mental health care records are lower than estimates derived from primary care which, in turn, are lower than those obtained from the community (Hoek, 2006). In addition, results may reflect increasing prevalence of the syndrome across cohorts over time. Although the term "rate" is often used in conjunction with prevalence estimates, they are typically unsuitable[1] for determining time trends (or rates of change) for the presence of eating disorders in a population. Prevalence estimates combine new and old cases in a single value and, thus, reflect both the number of new cases in a population as well as the chronicity of an illness.

Incidence rates reflect the number of new cases ("incident cases") within a unit of population and over a unit of time (e.g., cases per 100,000 persons per year or per 100,000 person years). As such, these rates allow examination of changes over time that can address whether or not a condition has become more common in a population. A meta-analysis (Keel & Klump, 2003) and systematic review (Hoek & van Hoeken, 2003) found significant increases in AN incidence during the 20th century. Keel and Klump (2003) reported a modest effect size associated

with these changes, and Hoek and van Hoeken (2003) reported that the increase was evident until the 1970s, and then incidence rates demonstrated relative stability over time. Two recently published epidemiological studies support the stability of AN incidence rates from 1994 to 2000 in the United Kingdom (Currin, Schmidt, Treasure, & Jick, 2005) and from 1985–89 to 1995–99 in the Netherlands (van Son, van Hoeken, Bartelds, van Furth, & Hoek, 2006). However, evidence suggests increasing rates in the highest risk group of females ages 15 to 19 years, with incidence nearly doubling from 56.4 to 109.2 per 100,000 person years in the Netherlands (van Son et al., 2006). These results echo findings from the United States (Lucas, Crowson, O'Fallon, & Melton, 1999) in which incidence rates demonstrated a linear increase from 1935 to 1989 in females aged 15 to 24 years. Thus, popular media portrayals of the "epidemic" of AN have some basis in truth in that rates of the illness have increased over time, and this trend has been particularly true for adolescent and young adult females. However, sex- and age-adjusted incidence rates in the overall population are relatively low, ranging from 1.2 per 100,000 person-years for severe AN (Milos et al., 2004) to 8.3 per 100,000 person-years for broadly defined AN (Lucas et al., 1999).

Cross-Cultural Patterns

The studies reviewed in the preceding text have come from Western cultures because most research on eating disorders has been conducted in the United States, Canada, Australia, and Western European countries. Many have asserted the possibility that AN may represent a culture-bound syndrome. However, a recent review of cross-cultural data revealed evidence of AN throughout the non-Western world, including cases in individuals with no evident exposure to Western culture (Keel & Klump, 2003). Of note, several cases that emerge in a non-Western context and in the absence of exposure to Western ideals are characterized by absence of a fear of gaining weight or becoming fat. However, these features were not described by Gull (1874) when the syndrome was first introduced and may reflect culturally meaningful explanations for a syndrome for which the true causes remain unknown.

Course

AN is associated with a variable course and outcome (APA, 2000). While a minority of patients achieve remission early in the course of illness (i.e., within

---

[1] Exceptions to this occur when point prevalence estimates are taken from independent cohorts at different times from a given population (e.g., Keel, Heatherton, Dorer, Joiner, & Zalta, 2006).

1 year) and sustain recovery throughout life, most patients struggle with their illness for more than a decade. Across studies examining patients 10 to 20 years after diagnosis, just under half of patients achieved full recovery, another third remained symptomatic but demonstrated some improvement, and 20% remained chronically ill (Steinhausen, 2002). The worst prognosis has been observed in individuals diagnosed at older ages and who encounter longer delays between onset of illness and initiation of treatment (Steinhausen, 2002). Among patients demonstrating "improvement," some develop binge-purge symptoms and experience weight gain resulting in a shift in diagnosis from AN to BN. Although these individuals may be considered "improved" because they no longer meet full criteria for AN, they are not recovered. Instead, they have crossed over or migrated from one diagnosis to another. At 12-year follow-up, Fichter and Quadflieg (2007) reported that 9% of patients initially diagnosed with AN crossed over to a diagnosis of BN. Similar issues emerge for those whose illness changes over time to meet partial criteria for AN. Such individuals may be viewed as partially recovered (Herzog et al., 1999) or they may be viewed as having an EDNOS (Fichter & Quadflieg, 2007). At 12-year follow-up, Fichter and Quadflieg (2007) reported that 15.7% of patients initially diagnosed with AN crossed over to a diagnosis of EDNOS.

Mortality has been observed in approximately 1 in 20 patients (Steinhausen, 2002; Sullivan, 1995) across studies, reflecting a standardized mortality ratio (SMR) of approximately 10.0—or a 10-fold increase in risk of premature death (Keel et al., 2003; Löwe et al., 2001). Primary causes of death include starvation and suicide (Nielsen et al., 1998). Keel et al. (2003) reported an SMR due to suicide in AN of 56.9 (95% confidence interval [CI] = 15.3–145.7).

A recent study of a large AN cohort ($n = 432$) reported that 17% of individuals with lifetime diagnoses of AN reported at least one suicide attempt (Bulik et al., 2008). These findings are consistent with findings from a recent review suggesting that between 3% and 20% of AN patients endorse suicide attempts (Franko & Keel, 2006). The variability in proportions of attempts may reflect the composition of samples given that suicide attempts are more likely to occur in individuals with the binge-purge subtype of AN compared to those with the restricting subtype (Bulik et al., 2008; Franko & Keel, 2006). An examination of methods used by AN patients who completed suicide indicated the use of highly lethal methods that would be fatal regardless of the attempter's physical health (Holm-Denoma et al., 2008).

Clinical correlates of suicide attempts included purging behaviors, depression, substance abuse, and history of childhood physical or sexual abuse (Franko & Keel, 2006). Prospective predictors of fatal outcome due to any causes (suicide and non-suicide) included poor psychosocial functioning, longer duration of follow-up, and severity of alcohol use disorders (Keel et al., 2003). Thus, comorbid substance use disorders are associated with increased suicide attempts, and severity of alcohol use disorder predicts increased risk of premature death in AN.

Importantly, these course data have come predominantly from clinic-based samples and may reflect more dire outcomes than would be observed for the full population of individuals diagnosed with AN. Supporting this possibility, course data from community-based epidemiological studies suggest that a majority of individuals with lifetime diagnoses of AN do not currently meet criteria for the illness (Favaro et al., 2003; Hudson et al., 2007; Keski-Rahkonen et al., 2007; Wade et al., 2006).

Bulimia Nervosa

The term "bulimia nervosa" was introduced to the medical literature in 1979 by Dr. Gerald Russell to describe a series of 30 patients who were binge eating and purging at normal weight (Russell, 1979). In his seminal article, Russell (1979) described the illness as an "ominous variant of anorexia nervosa," and noted a history of full or partial AN in a number of his patients. Given the relatively recent delineation of BN from AN, fewer studies have examined the epidemiology and course of this syndrome.

Epidemiology

According to the *DSM-IV-TR* (APA, 2000), the lifetime prevalence of BN is 1% to 3% in adolescent and young adult women. Consistent with this range, recent population-based studies have reported that BN affects 1.5% of U.S. women (Hudson et al., 2007), 2.9% of Australian women (Wade et al., 2006), and 4.6% of Italian women (Favaro et al., 2003). Similar to findings for AN, the gender ratio of BN is approximately 10 women for every 1 man according to the *DSM-IV-TR* (APA, 2000). Onset typically occurs in late adolescence to young adulthood (APA, 2000). Thus, peak age at onset overlaps somewhat with AN but tends to fall in a slightly older age range for BN.

In a meta-analysis of studies reporting changes in BN incidence over time, Keel and Klump (2003) detected a significant increase in BN incidence over the 20th century that was associated with a large effect size. Consistent with these findings, prevalence estimates across birth cohorts in a large epidemiological sample (Hudson et al., 2007) indicate higher prevalence of BN in younger cohorts compared to older cohorts.

In contrast to these broad patterns, some recent studies have suggested the possibility of declining rates of BN in the population. Currin et al. (2005) reported an initial increase in BN incidence in women ages 10 to 39 years from less than 25 per 100,000 person-years in 1988 to greater than 50 per 100,000 person-years in 1996, this was followed by a 38.9% decline in incidence by 2000. The decline was largely attributable to changes in incidence rates for women ages 20 to 39. Incidence in this group decreased significantly from 56.7 per 100,000 person-years in 1993 to 28.6 per 100,000 person-years in 2000. In contrast, BN incidence rates were comparatively stable in women ages 10 to 19 over this period, ranging from 41.0 to 35.8 per 100,000 person-years from 1993 to 2000. van Son et al. (2006) reported a nonsignificant 29% decline in BN incidence from 1985–89 to 1995–99. Thus, although nonsignificant, the magnitude and direction of change were similar to findings reported by Currin et al. (2005). Finally, Keel, Heatherton, Dorer, Joiner, and Zalta (2006) reported a significant decline in the point prevalence of BN across three college cohorts assessed in 1982, 1992, and 2002, though this was largely explained by particularly high rates in the 1982 cohort, as no significant difference was observed between the 1992 and 2002 cohorts.

Consistent with stable point prevalence of BN from 1992 to 2002 reported by Keel et al. (2006), Crowther, Armey, Luce, Dalton, and Leahey (2008) reported no significant changes in BN point prevalence from 1990 to 2004. These trends contrast with those recently reported for population-based cohorts assessed in Australia in 1995 and 2005 (Hay, Mond, Buttner, & Darby, 2008) in which bulimic behaviors, such as binge eating and purging, increased twofold over time. Of note, this study did not examine changes in BN point prevalence over time because baseline assessments did not include all items necessary for a diagnosis. Taken together, data suggest that BN incidence and prevalence is highly variable within populations over time. Such patterns are consistent with the conclusion that BN is a culturally bound syndrome (Keel & Klump, 2003) and more likely to fluctuate in relation to immediate cultural factors.

Cross-Cultural Patterns

As with the review of epidemiological studies for AN, the aforementioned studies on BN have come from Western cultures. A recent review of cross-cultural evidence for BN (Keel & Klump, 2003) did not find any cases of BN in the absence of exposure to Western influences. Instead, evidence suggests that bulimic symptoms emerge in non-Western cultures following exposure to Western ideals (Becker, Burwell, Gilman, Herzog, & Hamburg, 2002). Thus, the emergence of BN appears to be closely linked to a combination of access to large quantities of edible food, modern plumbing to facilitate purging in private, and a modern idealization of thinness to make purging a culturally meaningful response to binge eating episodes (Keel & Klump, 2003).

Course

BN is associated with a more favorable course and outcome compared to AN (APA, 2000). Across studies examining patients 5 or more years after diagnosis, approximately 70% achieve recovery, another 20% remain symptomatic but demonstrate some improvement, and 10% remain chronically ill (Fichter & Quadflieg, 2007; Herzog et al., 1999; Keel & Mitchell, 1997; Keel, Mitchell, Miller, Davis, & Crow, 1999). The worst prognosis has been observed in individuals with comorbid alcohol use disorders (Keel et al., 1999). Among patients demonstrating "improvement," some cease to experience large binge eating episodes but continue to engage in recurrent purging to influence weight or shape (Keel, Mitchell, Miller, Davis, & Crow, 2000). Although these individuals may be considered "improved" because they no longer meet full criteria for BN, they are not recovered given the medical and psychological morbidity associated with recurrent purging. At 12-year follow-up, Fichter and Quadflieg (2007) reported that 1.8% of patients initially diagnosed with BN crossed over to a diagnosis of AN, 1.9% crossed over to BED, and 13.6% met criteria for an EDNOS. These patterns are consistent with those observed by Keel et al. (2000).

In a direct comparison of standardized mortality ratios between AN and BN in a single study using the same methods of ascertainment, Keel et al. (2003) found that BN is less likely to result in premature death compared to AN. Indeed, the standardized mortality ratio in this study did not differ significantly from 1.0, indicating no significant change in risk compared to demographically matched individuals without BN (Keel et al., 2003). Descriptively, death has been reported in 0% to 3% across follow-up studies (Keel & Mitchell, 1997). The most commonly reported cause of death across studies has been automobile accidents (Keel & Mitchell, 1997). This does not differ qualitatively from most common causes of death in demographically matched non–eating disorder individuals.

Although BN has not been associated with elevated risk of premature death in studies published thus far, suicidal attempts have been observed in 25% to 35% of patients with BN. In a study of 295 women with bulimic symptoms, drug overdose was the most common method employed for attempting suicide, at 79% (Corcos et al., 2002). Thus, the discrepancy between suicide attempts and suicide completions in BN may reflect reliance on less lethal methods. This pattern has contributed to speculation that suicide attempts may serve a different purpose in BN compared to AN. In AN, many suicide attempts may be motivated by the desire to end life whereas suicide attempts in BN may be motivated by a desire to regulate negative affect (Franko & Keel, 2006).

Eating Disorders Not Otherwise Specified

Community-based epidemiological studies have suggested that the most common eating disorder diagnosis is EDNOS (Crowther et al., 2008; Favaro et al., 2003; Hay et al., 2008; Wade et al., 2006), with lifetime prevalence estimates ranging from 5.3% (Favaro et al., 2003) to 10.6% (Wade et al., 2006) and current prevalence estimates ranging from 3.6% (Crowther et al., 2008) to 4.2% (Hay et al., 2008). Such findings are understandable given how EDNOS is defined within the DSM-IV-TR (APA, 2000). Essentially, any clinically significant disorder of eating that does not meet criteria for AN or BN receives a diagnosis of EDNOS. This creates multiple combinations of symptoms included in the EDNOS category. Given an inability to derive meaningful information on course and outcome from the hodgepodge of syndromes currently inhabiting the EDNOS category (Wilfley, Bishop, Wilson, & Agras, 2007), the following sections review epidemiology and course for two specified forms of EDNOS, BED and the recently proposed PD.

Binge Eating Disorder

Although the term "binge eating disorder" was first described by Dr. Albert Stunkard in 1959 (Stunkard,

1959), it was not included in the DSM until publication of the 4th edition in 1994. Due to limited empirical studies of the syndrome, BED was included as a provisional diagnostic category in need of further study. Data on changing incidence rates, long-term course, and outcome for BED are limited given the relatively recent inclusion of BED in the DSM.

EPIDEMIOLOGY

The recent replication of the National Comorbidity Survey suggested that the lifetime prevalence of BED was 3.5% among women and 2.0% among men in the United States (Hudson et al., 2007). Although BED is significantly more common in women than in men; gender discrepancies tend to be less robust than reported for AN or BN. Mean and median age at onset for BED were 25.4 and 21 years, respectively (Hudson et al., 2007), suggesting that BED may be associated with a slightly older age of onset compared to AN and BN. In female cohorts, Wade et al. (2006) reported a lifetime prevalence of 2.9% for BED in Australia, and Favaro et al. (2003) reported a lifetime prevalence of 0.6% for BED in Italy. Favaro et al. (2003) further reported that the current prevalence of BED was 0.1%. In contrast, Hay and colleagues (2008) reported that the current prevalence of BED in a population-based sample of Australian men and women was 2.3%, with 67% of cases occurring in women. Thus, prevalence estimates for BED vary considerably across studies. One source of discrepancy is inconsistencies in how the syndrome has been assessed (and defined) within studies. For example, Hay and colleagues (2008) defined BED as the weekly use of binge eating, the absence of regular inappropriate compensatory behaviors, and weight and shape concerns. In contrast, Favaro et al. (2003) used DSM-IV criteria to diagnose BED which require binge-eating episodes 2 days per week for 6 months, several associated characteristics of binge episodes, and marked distress over binge eating.

Incidence studies have not yet been published for BED, making it difficult to draw conclusions regarding time trends for the number of individuals affected with the syndrome in a given population. However, Hudson et al. (2007) reported that risk of BED diagnosis increased over successive birth cohorts from 1944 to 1985. This suggests that BED has become more common in the United States over recent decades.

COURSE

Given that BED was first introduced as a provisional diagnostic category in the DSM-IV (APA,

1994), it is not surprising that few long-term follow-up studies have been conducted on the illness. Fairburn, Cooper, Doll, Norman, and O'Connor (2000) described the natural course of BED over a 5-year follow-up period in a relatively small (n = 48) community-based sample. Results from this study suggested that 82% of individuals were substantially improved or recovered, 4% continued to meet full criteria for BED, and no deaths were observed. Fairburn et al. (2000) further reported no crossover from BED to AN and that 3% of individual with BED met criteria for BN during follow-up. Fichter and Quadflieg (2007) reported somewhat less favorable outcome at 6-year follow-up in their sample of 60 inpatients with BED; 78.3% were recovered, 6.7% continued to meet full criteria for BED, and 1.7% had died. Similar to findings from Fairburn et al. (2000), no crossover from BED to AN was observed; however, 8.3% met criteria for BN at follow-up and 5.0% met criteria for an EDNOS (Fichter & Quadflieg, 2007).

Comparison of data from 6- versus 12-year follow-up of the BED cohort described by Fichter and Quadflied (2007) yields some counterintuitive findings. Although recovery rates often improve as duration of follow-up increases, this was not observed for BED. Instead, at 12-year follow-up, 66.7% of patients were recovered, 6.7% continued to meet full criteria for BED, and 3.3% had died. No cases of cross-over to AN were observed at 12-year follow-up; however, crossover to EDNOS was 13.3% and crossover to BN was 10%. Collapsing across eating disorder categories, these results suggest that 20% of BED patients met criteria for an eating disorder at 6-year follow-up, whereas 30% met criteria for an eating disorder at 12-year follow-up. Overall, results suggest affected individuals may have extended periods in which they are free of BED symptoms yet be at risk for a resurgence of symptoms over an extended period of their lives. This conclusion is consistent with retrospective reports of long illness duration (e.g., more than 10 years) in epidemiological studies (Striegel-Moore & Franko, 2008).

Purging Disorder

Purging disorder is a form of EDNOS that has been recently proposed for inclusion as a provisional syndrome in need of further study in the *DSM-V* (Keel & Striegel-Moore, 2009). The syndrome can be thought of as the inverse of BED. Where BED is an EDNOS that involves recurrent binge-eating episodes in the absence of inappropriate compensatory behaviors, PD is an EDNOS that involves recurrent purging in the absence of objectively large binge episodes. Despite the very recent description of PD in the literature, several epidemiological studies have reported on the frequency of this condition, and some limited data are available on course.

EPIDEMIOLOGY

Lifetime prevalence estimates for PD in women have ranged from 1.1% in Italy (Favaro et al., 2003) to 5.3% in Australia (Wade et al., 2006). Of interest, in both studies, estimates of PD excluded individuals with lifetime diagnoses of AN, BN, or BED, thus controlling for crossover. PD is likely to be more common than suggested by these studies. Of further interest, both Favaro et al. (2003) and Wade et al. (2006) reported lifetime prevalence estimates for PD that were nearly twice as large as estimates for BED.

Current prevalence for PD has been reported in 0.5% of Australian women (Hay et al., 2008) and 0.6% of Canadian women (Gauvin, Steiger, & Brodeur, 2008) in two-stage population-based studies. Studies of college-based samples in the United States suggest that between 0.6% (Haedt & Keel, 2009) and 0.8% of women (Crowther et al., 2008) have PD. Consistency of results for point prevalence estimates (ranging only from 0.5% to 0.8%) across populations, assessment methods, and syndrome definitions is striking and may reflect the extent to which questions regarding the use of purging methods (e.g., self-induced vomiting, laxative, or diuretics) to influence weight or shape are associated with higher reliability in various methods of assessment. Age at onset for PD has been reported in late adolescence (Favaro et al., 2003), and PD is significantly more common in women than men (Haedt & Keel, 2009).

Two studies have examined point prevalence of PD in successive cohorts of college students (Crowther et al., 2008; Haedt & Keel, 2009) and reported no significant changes over time. Of note, 1982 was the earliest observation of PD point prevalence across these studies. Thus, it is possible that the syndrome became increasingly common during the 20th century in the period leading up to when estimates were first described.

COURSE

In a sample of 23 women with PD followed prospectively for approximately 8 months, 48% continued to meet full criteria for PD, 35% had a reduction in symptom frequency and met criteria for an EDNOS, 4% crossed over to a diagnosis of

BN, and 13% achieved partial or full remission (Keel, Haedt, & Edler, 2005).

Conclusion

Evidence suggests that AN, BN, and BED have affected increasing proportions of the population over the course of the 20th century. The most dramatic changes have been observed for syndromes characterized by binge eating and may reflect increased urbanization and increased access to large quantities of readily edible food (Keel & Klump, 2003). Conversely, the rise in AN incidence may reflect the increased idealization of thinness in modern, Western culture (Keel & Klump, 2003). However, the thin ideal is neither sufficient nor necessary for the emergence of a syndrome characterized by self-starvation that predominately affects adolescent and young adult females (Keel & Klump, 2003). Little is known about time trends for the incidence or prevalence of PD. Although purging as a behavior demonstrated an increase in one study (Hay et al., 2008), two other studies reported no significant change in PD point prevalence over limited period of observation towards the end of the 20th century (Crowther et al., 2008; Haedt & Keel, 2009).

Data on course and outcome suggest that AN, BN, and BED can be placed on a continuum of illness severity, with AN residing at the end with greatest chronicity and risk of premature death and BED residing at the end with lowest chronicity. However, these conclusions must be tempered by awareness of limited longitudinal data available for BN and BED. The addition of new prospective longitudinal studies with longer durations of follow-up may have a particularly profound impact on our understanding of BED course and outcome given that comparison of 6- and 12-year BED outcome suggested less favorable course as duration of follow-up increased (Fichter & Quadflied, 2007). In addition, given the significant association between BED and obesity (Hudson et al., 2007), it seems likely that increased risk of premature death will be observed in BED as studies with larger sample sizes and longer follow-up durations are conducted.

Examining information available on the epidemiology and course of different eating disorders reveals an inverse association between the prevalence of a syndrome and how much is known about the syndrome's course and outcome. Thus, we know the least about the most common syndromes. Although much of this can be addressed in upcoming revisions of the *DSM-5* by expanding criteria for AN and BN and including syndromes characterized by different symptom profiles, such as BED and PD, there will be an unavoidable lag between when revisions are made and when reliable information is obtained on course and outcome. A further complication in this process is the requirement that a proposed syndrome be associated with a distinctive course and outcome in order to be included in diagnostic systems.

Future Directions

More studies are needed to understand the epidemiology, course, and outcome associated with EDNOS. However, for these to be informative, it will be crucial for investigators to separate different forms of EDNOS in providing these descriptive data. Questions that present future directions for the field are presented below.

1. Is there a valid threshold for distinguishing AN from partial AN (i.e., EDNOS that resembles AN, except not all criteria are fully met) based on epidemiological patterns, long-term course or outcome?

2. Is there a valid threshold for distinguishing BN from partial BN (i.e., EDNOS that resembles BN, except not all criteria are fully met) based on epidemiological patterns, long-term course or outcome?

3. In both community and clinic-based populations, has the incidence of BED changed over time?

4. Is BED a culture-bound syndrome?

5. What are the long-term course and outcome associated with BED?

6. In both community and clinic-based populations, has the incidence of PD changed over time?

7. Is PD a culture-bound syndrome?

8. What are the intermediate and long-term course and outcome associated with PD?

References

American Psychiatric Association (APA). (1994). *Diagnostic and statistical manual of mental disorders* (4th ed.). Washington, DC: Author.

American Psychiatric Association (APA). (2000). *Diagnostic and statistical manual of mental disorders* (4th ed., text rev.). Washington, DC: Author.

Becker, A. E., Burwell, R. A., Gilman, S. E., Herzog, D. B., & Hamburg, P. (2002). Eating behaviours and attitudes following prolonged exposure to television among ethnic Fijian adolescent girls. *British Journal of Psychiatry, 180,* 509–514.

Bulik, C. M., Thornton, L., Pinheiro, A. P., Plotnicov, K., Klump, K. L., Brandt, H., et al. (2008). Suicide attempts in anorexia nervosa. *Psychosomatic Medicine, 70,* 378–383.

Corcos, M., Taieb, O., Benoit-Lamy, S., Paterniti, S., Jeammet, P., & Flament, M. F. (2002). Suicide attempts in women with bulimia nervosa: Frequency and characteristics. *Acta Psychiatrica Scandinavica, 106*, 381–386.

Crowther, J. H., Armey, M., Luce, K. H., Dalton, G. R., & Leahey, T. (2008). The point prevalence of bulimic disorders from 1990 to 2004. *International Journal of Eating Disorders, 41*, 491–497.

Currin, L., Schmidt, U., Treasure, J., & Jick, H. (2005). Time trends in eating disorder incidence. *British Journal of Psychiatry, 186*, 132–135.

Dalle Grave, R., & Calugi, S. (2007). Eating disorder not otherwise specified in an inpatient unit: The impact of altering the DSM-IV criteria for anorexia and bulimia nervosa. *European Eating Disorder Review, 15*, 340–349.

Fairburn, C. G., Cooper, Z., Doll, H. A., Norman, P., & O'Connor, M. (2000). The natural course of bulimia nervosa and binge eating disorder in young women. *Archives of General Psychiatry, 57*, 659–665.

Favaro, A., Ferrara, S., & Santanastaso, P. (2003). The spectrum of eating disorders in young women: A prevalence study in a general population sample. *Psychosomatic Medicine, 65*, 701–708.

Fichter, M. M., & Quadflieg, N. (2007). Long-term stability of eating disorder diagnoses. *International Journal of Eating Disorders, 40*, S61–S66.

Franko, D. L., & Keel, P. K. (2006). Suicidality in eating disorders: Occurrence, correlates, and clinical implications. *Clinical Psychology Review, 26*, 769–782.

Gauvin, L., Steiger, H., & Brodeur, J. M. (2009). Eating-disorder symptoms and syndromes in a sample of urban-dwelling Canadian women: Contributions toward a population health perspective. *International Journal of Eating Disorders. 42*, 531–536.

Gull, W. W. (1874). Anorexia nervosa (apepsia hysterica, anorexia hysterica). *Transactions of the Clinical Society of London, 7*, 22–28.

Haedt, A. A., & Keel, P. K. (in press). Comparing definitions of purging disorder on point prevalence and associations with external validators. *International Journal of Eating Disorders.*

Hay, P. J., Mond, J., Buttner, P., & Darby, A. (2008). Eating disorder behaviors are increasing: Findings from two sequential community surveys in South Australia. *PLoS ONE, 3*(2), e1541.

Herzog, D. B., Dorer, D. J., Keel, P. K., Selwyn, S. E., Ekeblad, E. R., Flores, A. T., et al. (1999). Recovery and relapse in anorexia nervosa and bulimia nervosa: A 7.5 year follow-up study. *Journal of the American Academy of Child & Adolescent Psychiatry, 38*, 829–837.

Hoek, H. W. (2006). Incidence, prevalence and mortality of anorexia nervosa and other eating disorders. *Current Opinions in Psychiatry, 19*, 389–394.

Hoek, H. W., & van Hoeken, D. (2003). Review of the prevalence and incidence of eating disorders. *International Journal of Eating Disorders, 34*, 383–396.

Holm-Denoma, J. M., Witte, T. K., Gordon, K. H., Herzog, D. B., Franko, D. L., Fichter, M., et al. (2008). Deaths by suicide among individuals with anorexia as arbiters between competing explanations of the anorexia-suicide link. *Journal of Affective Disorders, 107*, 231–236.

Hudson, J. I., Hiripi, E., Pope, Jr., H. G., & Kessler, R. C. (2007). The prevalence and correlates of eating disorders in the National Comorbidity Survey Replication. *Biological Psychiatry, 61*, 348–358.

Keel, P. K., Dorer, D. J., Eddy, K. T., Franko, D., Charatan, D. L., & Herzog, D. B. (2003). Predictors of mortality in eating disorders. *Archives of General Psychiatry, 60*, 179–183.

Keel, P. K., Haedt, A., & Edler, C. (2005). Purging disorder: An ominous variant of bulimia nervosa? *International Journal of Eating Disorders, 38*, 191–199.

Keel, P. K., Heatherton, T. F., Dorer, D. J., Joiner, T. E., & Zalta, A. K. (2006). Point prevalence of bulimia nervosa in 1982, 1992, and 2002. *Psychological Medicine, 36*, 119–127.

Keel, P. K., & Klump, K. L. (2003). Are eating disorders culture-bound syndromes? Implications for conceptualizing their etiology. *Psychological Bulletin, 129*, 747–769.

Keel, P. K., & Mitchell, J. E. (1997). Outcome in bulimia nervosa. *American Journal of Psychiatry, 154*, 313–321.

Keel, P. K., Mitchell, J. E., Miller, K. B., Davis, T. L., & Crow, S. J. (1999). Long-term outcome of bulimia nervosa. *Archives of General Psychiatry, 56*, 63–69.

Keel, P. K., Mitchell, J. E., Miller, K. B., Davis, T. L., & Crow, S. J. (2000). Predictive validity of bulimia nervosa as a diagnostic category. *American Journal of Psychiatry, 157*, 136–138.

Keel, P. K., & Striegel-Moore, R. H. (2009). *The validity and clinical utility of Purging Disorder. International Journal of Eating Disorders, 42*, 706–719.

Keski-Rahkonen, A., Hoek, H. W., Susser, E. S., Linna, M. S., Sihvola, E., Raevuori, A., et al. (2007). Epidemiology and course of anorexia nervosa in the community. *American Journal of Psychiatry, 164*, 1259–1265.

Löwe, B., Zipfel, S., Buchholz, C. Dupont, Y., Reas, D. L., & Herzog, W. (2001). Long-term outcome of anorexia nervosa in a prospective 21 year follow-up study. *Psychological Medicine, 31*, 881–90.

Lucas, A. R., Crowson, C. S., O'Fallon, W. M., & Melton, L. J. (1999). The ups and downs of anorexia nervosa. *International Journal of Eating Disorders, 26*, 397–405.

Milos, G., Spindler, A., Schnyder, U., Martz, J., Hoek, H. W., & Willi, J. (2004). Incidence of severe anorexia nervosa in Switzerland: 40 years of development. *International Journal of Eating Disorders, 35*, 250–258.

Nielsen, S., Moller-Madsen, S., Isager, T., Jorgensen, J., Pagsberg, K., & Theander, S. (1998). Standardized mortality in eating disorders—a quantitative summary of previously published and new evidence. *Journal of Psychosomatic Research, 44*, 413–434.

Russell, G. F. M. (1979). Bulimia nervosa: An ominous variant of anorexia nervosa. *Psychological Medicine, 9*, 429–448.

Steinhausen, H. C. (2002). The outcome of anorexia nervosa in the 20th century. *International Journal of Eating Disorders, 159*, 1284–1293.

Striegel-Moore, R. H., & Franko, D. L. (2008). Should Binge Eating Disorder be included in the DSM-V? A critical review of the state of the evidence. *Annual Review of Clinical Psychology, 4*, 305–324.

Stunkard, A. J. (1959). Eating patterns and obesity. *Psychiatric Quarterly, 33*, 284–295.

Sullivan, P. F. (1995). Mortality in anorexia nervosa. *American Journal of Psychiatry, 152*, 1073–1074.

van Son, G. E., van Hoeken, D., Bartelds, A. I., van Furth, E. F., & Hoek, H. W. (2006). Time trends in the incidence of eating disorders: A primary care study in the Netherlands. *International Journal of Eating Disorders, 39*, 565–569.

Wade, T. D., Bergin, J. L., Tiggemann, M., Bulik, C. M., & Fairburn, C. G. (2006). Prevalence and long-term course of lifetime eating disorders in an adult Australian twin cohort. *Australian and New Zealand Journal of Psychiatry, 40*, 121–128.

Wilfley, D. E., Bishop, M. E., Wilson, G. T., & Agras, W. S. (2007). Classification of eating disorders: Toward DSM-V. *International Journal of Eating Disorders, 40*, S123–S129.

Proposed Syndromes and the *Diagnostic and Statistical Manual V*

Kelly C. Allison *and* Jennifer D. Lundgren

Abstract

The *Diagnostic and Statistical Manual (DSM-IV-TR)* of the American Psychiatric Association (2000) is currently being revised and new disorders are being considered for inclusion in *DSM-V*. In this chapter, we evaluate three proposed eating disorders for the *DSM-V*: binge eating disorder (BED), night eating syndrome (NES), and purging disorder (PD). The history and definition for each is reviewed, relevant theoretical models are presented and compared, and evidence for the usefulness of the models is described. Empirical studies of all three disorders show their independence from other disorders, although comorbid psychopathology is common. Psychological distress is also high, but evidence for negative impact on physical health is less pronounced. Finally, remaining questions for future research are summarized.

Keywords: binge eating disorder, eating disorder not otherwise specified, night eating syndrome, nosology, purging disorder

Introduction

The *Diagnostic and Statistical Manual (DSM-IV-TR)* of the American Psychiatric Association (2000) is currently being revised. Criteria for the independently established eating disorders, anorexia nervosa (AN) and bulimia nervosa (BN), are being examined, and possible new eating disorder diagnoses are under evaluation. As generally acknowledged by experts in the field, most eating disorder diagnoses fall in the eating disorder not otherwise specified (EDNOS) category, suggesting that the current diagnostic system lacks generalizability (Wonderlich, Joiner, Keel, Williamson, & Crosby, 2007).

During the *DSM-IV* revision, Blashfield and colleagues (1990) proposed five criteria as necessary for inclusion as a psychiatric disorder:

> Criterion I: "There should be at least 50 journal articles on the proposed diagnostic category in the last 10 years, ...at least 25 of them should be empirical".... Criterion II: That there be (a) a set of diagnostic criteria which (b) include self-report measures, structured interviews, and rating scales.... Criterion III: There should be at least two empirical studies by independent research groups demonstrating high inter-clinician correlations.... Criterion IV: The proposed category represents a syndrome of frequently co-occurring symptoms, described in at least two independent studies.... Criterion V: There should be at least two independent empirical studies showing that the proposed category "can be differentiated from other categories with which it is likely to be confused" (p. 17).

These guidelines, as well as more current calls for demonstration of empirical approaches for classification (Wonderlich et al., 2007), are helpful in evaluating proposed syndromes for the *DSM-V* that are reviewed in this chapter: binge eating disorder (BED), night eating syndrome (NES), and purging disorder (PD). We review the history and definition for each, review relevant theoretical models, outline evidence for the usefulness of the models, and provide a summary of remaining questions for future research.

Binge Eating Disorder
Research Status and Description of BED
HISTORY AND PREVALENCE OF BED

Binge eating disorder was first described in Stunkard's 1959 review of eating patterns of obese mice and obese humans (Stunkard, 1959). In this initial report, binge eating was described as the consumption of "enormous amounts of food… consumed in relatively short periods." Stunkard noted that the binge eating behavior was often associated with life stress, self-condemnation, and that it had a personal or symbolic meaning to the individual (i.e., the eating behavior was a "symbolic representation or resolution of a conflict"). He contrasted this pattern of binge eating behavior to what he called night eating syndrome (reviewed later), suggesting that the primary differences between binge eating and night eating were periodicity (circadian pattern), the personal meaning of the eating episode, and the guilt or condemnation associated with the eating episode. He noted that both, however, were associated with life stress (Stunkard, 1959).

Relatively little research was conducted on BED until, in 1992, the results of a large, multisite field trial of BED were presented, and preliminary diagnostic criteria for inclusion in *DSM-IV* were presented (Spitzer et al., 1992). The goals of the field trial were to estimate the prevalence of binge eating and associated behaviors in a variety of patient populations and across gender, to assess the degree to which the symptoms of BED co-occurred with one another, and to examine the clinical utility and validity of the BED diagnosis.

The prevalence of BED differed among the patient samples: 71% in the Overeaters Anonymous sample, 30% in the weight loss-seeking samples, and 2.0% in the community samples; females were statistically more likely to be diagnosed with BED in the weight loss samples (31.9% vs. 20.8%), but the difference in the community samples was not statistically significantly different (females = 2.5% and males = 1.1%; Spitzer et al., 1992). There were moderate correlations between individual symptoms of BED (e.g., overeating, loss of control) and the number of symptoms each person experienced (up to eight BED related symptoms), ranging from 0.50 to 0.71. The internal consistency of the eight binge eating symptoms was high at 0.75 in the weight loss samples and 0.79 in the community samples. The clinical significance of BED as a predictor of excess weight was established in the weight loss sample, but not in the community samples. BED was, however, associated with weight cycling in both the weight loss and the community samples (Spitzer et al., 1992).

The result of this comprehensive field trial was not only a better understanding of the prevalence and clinical utility of the BED diagnosis, but also a standard set of research diagnostic criteria that made it possible for BED to be more reliably researched. The current criteria are quite similar to those originally proposed and are outlined and compared to the *DSM-IV-TR* criterion set in Table 4.1.

CURRENT *DSM-IV TR* DIAGNOSTIC CRITERIA

In 1994 the *DSM-IV* adopted the proposed research diagnostic criteria, with minor modifications (Table 4.1), for inclusion in Appendix B (Criteria Sets and Axes Provided for Further Study). In 2000, the *DSM-IV* Text Revision was published, and the BED criteria remained unchanged.

Models of BED

Despite the plethora of research literature on binge eating behavior and BED since Stunkard's 1959 description (a PubMed search for "binge eating disorder" in November 2008 yielded more than 5000 hits), there is still discussion about the validity, reliability, and clinical utility of BED as an eating disorder diagnosis for inclusion in *DSM-V* (Latner & Clyne, 2008; Stunkard & Allison, 2003). Below, we evaluate three proposed models of BED. These include BED as a categorically distinct disorder, BED as a continuum of other eating disorders (e.g., bulimia nervosa, obesity, and non-normative eating), and BED as a marker of psychopathology.

BED AS A DISTINCT AXIS I PSYCHIATRIC DISORDER

BED as a distinct Axis I disorder was the model suggested by Spitzer and colleagues (1992) and the *DSM-IV* Work Group on Eating Disorders when they recommended that BED be included in the *DSM-IV*. Using this model, BED is conceptualized as qualitatively and quantitatively distinct from other Axis I disorders, including AN and BN.

Very recently, Striegel-Moore and Franko (2008) reviewed the BED literature and supported this perspective, noting that BED, although it shares some features with other eating disorders, is associated with

Table 4.1   Research Diagnostic Criteria for BED Used in Spitzer and Colleagues (1992) Field Trial Compared to DSM-IV (1994) Appendix B BED Criteria

Spitzer and Colleagues (1992)	DSM-IV Appendix B Criteria
A. Recurrent episodes of binge eating, an episode being characterized by:	A. Recurrent episodes of binge eating. An episode of binge eating is characterized by both of the following:
1. Eating, in a discrete period of time (e.g., in any 2-hour period), an amount of food that is definitely larger than most people would eat during a similar period of time.	1. Eating, in a discrete period of time (e.g., within any 2-hour period), an amount of food that is definitely larger than most people would eat in a similar period of time under similar circumstances.
2. A sense of loss of control during the episodes, e.g., a feeling that one can't stop eating or control what or how much one is eating.	2. A sense of lack of control over eating during the episode (e.g., a feeling that one cannot stop eating or control what or how much one is eating).
B. During most binge episodes, at least three of the following behavioral indicators of loss of control:	B. The binge eating episodes are associated with three (or more) of the following:
1. Eating much more rapidly than usual	1. Eating much more rapidly than normal
2. Eating until feeling uncomfortably full	2. Eating until feeling uncomfortably full
3. Eating large amounts of food when not feeling physically hungry	3. Eating large amounts of food when not feeling physically hungry
4. Eating large amounts of food throughout the day with no planned mealtimes	4. Eating alone because of being embarrassed by how much one is eating
5. Eating alone because of being embarrassed by how much on is eating	5. Feeling disgusted with oneself, depressed, or very guilty after overeating
6. Feeling disgusted with oneself, depressed, or feeling very guilty after overeating	
C. Marked distress regarding binge eating.	C. Marked distress about binge eating is present.
D. The binge eating occurs, on average, at least twice a week for a 6-month period.	D. The binge eating occurs, on average, at least 2 days per week for 6 months.
E. Does not currently meet criteria for bulimia nervosa.	E. The binge eating is not associated with the regular use of inappropriate compensatory behaviors (e.g., purging, fasting, excessive exercise) and does not occur exclusively during the course of anorexia nervosa or bulimia nervosa.

a unique set of demographic correlates, treatment outcome, comorbidity, and clinical presentation.

Using the Blashfield (1990) criteria for inclusion of an Axis I disorder in *DSM-IV*, Striegel-Moore and Franko (2008) concluded that BED should be included in the *DSM-V* as a distinct eating disorder diagnosis. Specifically, they noted that (1) there were a substantial number of empirical articles on the subject of BED in the previous 10 years, (2) there were a standard diagnostic criteria set and psychometrically sound assessment measures for BED, and (3) the symptoms of BED frequently co-occur. There was mixed evidence, however, for two additional criteria. In their review of latent class analysis studies of eating disorders, Striegel-Moore and Franko (2008) noted that although BED can likely

be differentiated from other eating disorders, the methods used in this literature have been inconsistent. Similarly, they noted that little data are available to evaluate the inter-clinician reliability when making a BED diagnosis (Striegel-Moore & Franko, 2008).

BED on a continuum with other eating disorders and obesity

The perspective that BED is a distinct eating disorder diagnosis is a *categorical* one. In contrast, *dimensional* models of BED have been presented, and these include BED on a continuum with bulimia nervosa (BN) and anorexia nervosa (AN), BED on a continuum with obesity, and BED on a continuum with nondisordered, yet non-normative eating.

Statistical techniques, such as factor analysis and taxometric analysis, have been used to determine if BED is best conceptualized as independent of or on a continuum with other eating disorders. Williamson and colleagues (2005) reviewed the factor analytic and taxometric studies of eating disorder symptoms. With regard to factor analytic studies of all eating disorder symptoms (including BN, AN, and BED), they found that two factors, general psychopathology and binge eating, were the most commonly reported (each factor was found in seven of the eight studies reviewed). Taxometric analyses found that symptoms of BED could be categorically distinguished from behaviors of normal controls and of obese individuals, but not enough taxometric analyses have been conducted to determine if BED is taxonic or dimensional in relation to BN and binge/purge AN (Williamson, Gleaves, & Stewart, 2005).

Finally, Tanofsky-Kraff and Yanovski (2004) have suggested that several behavioral, cognitive/affective, and biological variables are in need of further research to distinguish a clinically useful BED diagnosis from non-normative eating among obese individuals. Such variables include the amount of food consumed during meals and snacks, hunger and satiety functioning, macronutrient content, the emotional experience of eating, neuroendocrine, hormonal, and metabolic correlates of energy intake, functional brain imaging, genetics, and gastrointestinal physiology.

BED AS A MARKER OF PSYCHOPATHOLOGY

A third model, proposed by Stunkard and Allison (2003), suggests that BED is best conceptualized as a marker of psychopathology (e.g., depression or anxiety) rather than an independent diagnostic construct. Their argument was that although standard research diagnostic criteria had been adopted, there were too many problems with the BED construct. First, they argued that there was no standard definition of a binge episode, including portion size, duration of the eating episode, and the coding of binge days versus binge episodes when making a BED diagnosis. Second, individuals with BED frequently have co-morbid psychopathology. Third, BED is responsive to many interventions, including placebo. Finally, the course of BED is highly variable (see Stunkard & Allison, 2003 for review).

Although each of these arguments against BED as a unique diagnostic construct has merit, the strongest argument for why BED should be considered a marker of psychopathology is the high rate of comorbidity between BED and other Axis I and Axis II disorders. The challenge with accepting this argument, however, is that both AN and BN are highly comorbid with mood and anxiety disorders (see Wonderlich et al., 2007). If high rates of comorbidity preclude a diagnostic construct from becoming an independent diagnosis, then all eating disorder diagnoses are in question.

The broad responsiveness of BED to treatment, including many psychotropic medications and psychotherapies, is another strong reason against the specificity of BED as an independent diagnosis. More importantly, BED has a high placebo response rate, with reductions in binge episodes ranging from 41% (Hudson et al., 1998) to 72% (Stunkard et al., 1996). In comparison, placebo response rates for reductions in binge eating in BN range from an increase of 21% (Pope, Keck, McElroy, & Hudson, 1989) to a decrease of 52% (Mitchell & Groat 1984), with most studies ranging between 2% and 30% (see Mitchell, Steffen, & Roerig, 2007 for review).

Evidence of Diagnostic Validity and Clinical Significance of Models for BED

Based on the available literature, including recent comprehensive reviews (see Striegel-Moore & Franko, 2008 and Williamson et al., 2005), there appears to be significant evidence to support the diagnostic validity and clinical significance of a BED diagnosis—at least with regard to its functional ability to communicate fairly reliable information about individuals given the diagnosis (e.g., demographic correlates, treatment outcome, comorbidity, and clinical presentation). The question of whether or not BED is distinct *enough* from other Axis I disorders, including AN, BN, Major Depressive Disorder (MDD), and anxiety disorders, and from obesity remains to be answered by future taxometric statistical approaches. Several additional research questions should be answered in order to move this research field forward; these are reviewed in the text that follows.

Research Needed to Clarify the Status of BED

Although the BED literature has grown significantly since the mid-20th century, there remain several questions about the nature and classification of BED. First, how should a binge eating episode be operationalized? Specifically, what quantity of food consumption and in what period of time constitutes a binge eating episode, and with what frequency do binge eating episodes need to occur to be considered a clinically significant psychiatric disorder?

The current criteria require an average of two binge days per week for a period of 6 months, but commonly, recent research criteria sets have used only one binge day per week.

Similarly, is a loss of control over eating behavior a pathognomonic symptom of a binge eating episode, regardless of the quantity of food consumed, and does the relationship between quantity of food and loss of control differ for a diagnosis of BED compared to binge eating that occurs in the context of BN or AN? If loss of control is an important variable in differentiating normal from abnormal eating behavior, how should it be adequately assessed and what degree of "loss of control" (perceived or objective) is considered clinically significant? Finally, how is binge eating in persons with BED related to weight and shape concern?

To address the questions of quantity, duration, and loss of control over eating, Johnson, Boutelle, Torgurd, Davig, and Turner (2000) asked non–eating disordered adults (both men and women) to evaluate the eating behavior of a female actress presented in taped vignettes. Participants were asked to rate the degree to which the eating behavior constituted a binge eating episode on several dimensions. Participants were significantly more likely to rate the eating behavior as a binge eating episode when the quantity of food was larger and when loss of control was greater. There was no main effect of time on binge eating ratings, suggesting that participants did not consider an eating episode of nine minutes, compared to three minutes, any more binge-like. There was, however, an interaction between quantity of food intake and duration, such that small quantities of food were rated similarly, regardless of the duration of the eating episode. In comparison, larger quantities of food were rated more binge-like when consumed over shorter versus longer periods of time.

In another study, Johnson, Schlundt, Barclay, Carr-Nangle, and Engler (1995) compared the subjective and objective eating behavior of patients with BED, nonclinical binge eaters, and control participants. Even after being instructed in how to evaluate and classify binge eating episodes, 12% of the control group's eating episodes were classified as a binge. Although this is significantly less than the 36% reported by BED patients, it suggests that some degree of perceived binge eating behavior is normative. Unfortunately, the criteria used to define binge eating changed during the study, such that controls were asked to rate binge eating based on quantity and duration of food intake and the two patient groups were asked to rate based on quantity, duration, and *control*.

Although loss of control might be the most difficult feature of a BED to operationalize and objectively assess, it plays a significant role in both patient conceptualizations of binge eating and in the clinical significance of binge eating. Telch, Pratt, and Niego (1998) asked obese women with BED to define binge eating in their own words. The majority of the sample (82%) used loss of control when defining binge eating, whereas only 43% used the quantity of food in their definition. With regard to the clinical significance of loss of control, Colles and colleagues (2008) found that loss of control when overeating, compared to the other behavioral features of binge eating, predicted more psychological disturbance. In particular, loss of control was associated with depression, body image distress, and poor mental health–related quality of life.

The role of loss of control in binge eating has been assessed not only among adults, but also in adolescent samples. Goldschmidt and colleagues (2008) examined the clinical significance of loss of control when overeating in overweight adolescents. Four groups were compared: (1) those whose behavior approximated BED diagnostic criteria (BED); (2) those who reported loss of control over eating, regardless of the size of eating episodes (subthreshold; SUB); (3) those who reported the consumption of an unusually large amount of food, but no loss of control over eating (OE); and (4) a healthy control group. Groups were compared on weight and shape concerns and depressive symptoms. No statistical differences were found between the BED and SUB groups for either weight and shape concerns or depressive symptoms. The BED and OE groups, however, did significantly differ on both variables. The authors concluded that in adolescents, loss of control, rather than the quantity of food intake, was associated with depression and weight and shape concerns. These results are similar to those found among adult samples (Colles, Dixon, & O'Brien, 2008).

The role of weight and shape concerns is another contentious area for further clarification in the BED diagnostic validity literature. These concerns are central to the AN and BN diagnoses, but are not currently included in the criteria for BED. Two groups have found that persons with BED who endorse overvaluation of weight and shape report more severe eating disordered psychopathology and depressed mood than those who do not report overvaluation (Grilo et al., 2008; Mond, Hay, Ridgers, &

Owen, 2007). In addition, both BED groups had more severe pathology than the comparison groups. Grilo et al. (2008) reported that a sample of 165 BED patients was fairly evenly split, with 56% categorized as having clinical levels of overvaluation and 44% with subclinical levels. Mond et al. (2007) suggested that overvaluation be included as a required criterion for BED diagnosis. Grilo et al. (2008) have suggested it be included as a specifier that may inform treatment, particularly given (1) the large number of BED patients who would be excluded if overvaluation were required and (2) that both groups showed significantly worse related pathology than the comparison group.

Night Eating Syndrome
Research Status and Description of Night Eating Syndrome
HISTORY AND PREVALENCE OF NIGHT EATING SYNDROME

Night eating syndrome (NES) was first described in 1955 as a disorder of morning anorexia, evening hyperphagia, and insomnia, usually accompanied by depressed mood and stressful life circumstances (Stunkard, Grace, & Wolf, 1955). NES did not receive much research or clinical attention until the 1990s, coinciding with increasing rates of obesity and the search for factors related to excessive weight gain. A recent PubMed search revealed almost 80 papers published on NES in the past decade (November 2008). In 1999, awakenings with ingestions (*nocturnal ingestions*) were added to those criteria originally described in 1955, and were published in a provisional set of criteria (Birketvedt et al., 1999). However, as research advanced our understanding of NES, the diagnostic criteria for NES used by researchers often changed, making comparisons across studies difficult.

Prevalence of NES in the general population has been reported at 1.5% (Rand, Macgregor, & Stunkard, 1997), 1.6% (Striegel-Moore, Franko, Thompson, Affenito, & Kraemer, 2006), and 5.7% (Colles, Dixon, & O'Brien, 2007). The variance across the studies is likely due to the different criteria and assessment methods used in each study. These rates are at least as great as the recent lifetime estimates of AN (0.9% for women and 0.3% for men) and BN (1.5% for women and 0.5% for men) (Hudson, Hiripi, Pope, & Kessler, 2007). Prevalence rates in special populations suggest ranges of 6% (Stunkard et al., 1996) to 16% (Adami, Campostano, Marinari, Ravera, & Scopinaro, 2002) in weight loss samples of class I and II obesity. Among bariatric surgery candidates, the range in prospective interview studies is 9% (Allison et al., 2006) to 27% (Rand et al., 1997). A prevalence of 3.8% has been found among older adults in a large multi-center study of type 2 diabetes (Allison et al., 2007) and 12% in two university outpatient psychiatric clinics (Lundgren et al., 2006). With the establishment of the new diagnostic criteria (see text below), new interview-based studies are needed to verify the existing estimates.

CURRENT RESEARCH DIAGNOSTIC CRITERIA

Recognizing that widely-accepted diagnostic criteria for NES were needed in order to advance our understanding and treatment of the syndrome, professionals from the eating disorder, sleep, and obesity fields convened the First International Night Eating Symposium in April, 2008. Table 4.2 shows the criteria that were established by consensus (Allison et al., 2010). They built on the two core criteria that have been used over the last decade, that is, a delayed circadian pattern of food intake manifested by evening hyperphagia and/or nocturnal ingestions. These criteria and their basis will be discussed below. Criterion II requires awareness of the eating episodes to differentiate it from somnambulistic eating typical of sleep-related eating disorder (SRED). Criterion III lists specifiers that have been consistently associated with NES, three of which are required for diagnosis. Criteria IV, V, and VI require distress or impairment in functioning, duration of the symptoms of at least 3 months, and a rule out of other primary conditions that may be causing the night eating.

Models of NES

As NES has components of eating, sleep, and mood disorders, it has been conceptualized in several different ways. These models include NES as: (1) a distinct disorder, (2) an extension of daytime eating disorders, (3) on a continuum with sleep disorders, (4) a variant of obesity, and (5) secondary to other psychopathology. We review these models in the text that follows.

NES AS A DISTINCT DISORDER

While the merits of NES as a psychiatric disorder have been questioned (Striegel-Moore et al., 2006), the evidence for its distinction as an independent construct has grown. Recent empirical studies have described the unique eating patterns and related behaviors associated with NES, including item response theory analysis, circadian analyses of eating and neuroendocrine factors, and latent class analysis.

Table 4.2   Proposed Research Diagnostic Criteria for Night Eating Syndrome

I. The daily pattern of eating demonstrates a significantly increased intake in the evening and/or nighttime, as manifested by one or both of the following:
    A. At least 25% of food intake is consumed after the evening meal
    B. At least two episodes of nocturnal eating per week

II. Awareness and recall of evening and nocturnal eating episodes are present.

III. The clinical picture is characterized by at least three of the following features:
    A. Lack of desire to eat in the morning and/or breakfast is omitted on four or more mornings per week
    B. Presence of a strong urge to eat between dinner and sleep onset and/or during the night
    C. Sleep onset and/or sleep maintenance insomnia are present four or more nights per week
    D. Presence of a belief that one must eat in order to initiate or return to sleep
    E. Mood is frequently depressed and/or mood worsens in the evening

IV. The disorder is associated with significant distress and/or impairment in functioning.

V. The disordered pattern of eating has been maintained for at least 3 months.

VI. The disorder is not secondary to substance abuse or dependence, medical disorder, medication, or another psychiatric disorder.

Reprinted with permission from Allison, K. C., Lundgren, J. D., O'Reardon, J. P., Geliebter, A., Gluck, M. E., Vinai, P. et al. Proposed diagnostic criteria for night eating syndrome. *International Journal of Eating Disorders*, 2010.

The original description of Stunkard et al. (1955) included three main symptoms: morning anorexia, insomnia, and evening hyperphagia (consumption of 25% of intake after the evening meal). Those features remained in most diagnostic sets over the years and were incorporated into the Night Eating Questionnaire (NEQ; Allison, Lundgren, et al., 2008). Over the years, the NEQ was revised, but these core features, and an assessment of nocturnal awakenings and ingestions, remained across all versions. An item response theory analysis of 1,481 NEQs gathered across six studies, including two samples of participants with night eating, one sample of control participants, and three special population samples (e.g., bariatric surgery candidates, psychiatric clinic patients, and overweight older adults with type 2 diabetes) examined six items on the NEQ for their usefulness in providing information about the construct of night eating (Allison, Engel et al., 2008). A combined item of evening hyperphagia and/or nocturnal ingestions was entered into the analysis along with morning anorexia, delayed morning meal, initial insomnia, and nighttime awakenings. Endorsement of evening hyperphagia and/or nocturnal ingestions, initial insomnia, and nighttime awakenings showed high precision in identifying the night eating construct, while reports of morning anorexia and delayed morning meal did not provide additional meaningful information. It seemed that lack of appetite in the morning were common in the two night eating

samples (71.4% and 75.5%), but were also found fairly regularly among the other four samples (24.5%, 59.2%, 58.8%, and 20%), so they were not specific to NES. This finding helped inform the decision for the new diagnostic criteria to include morning anorexia as one of five specifiers, three of which are required, but not as a required criterion (Table 4.2).

Two studies have effectively shown the delay in eating patterns experienced in NES. Boston and colleagues (2008) modeled 24-hour caloric intake using parametric deconvolution (a mathematical model examining Gaussian curves that approximate the rate and spread of food intake, in this example, over the course of time) showing that persons with NES ($n = 148$) had significantly delayed meals that were spread out over a greater period of time than those of controls ($n = 68$). Overall, there was less structure to their eating. In addition, night eaters consumed significantly more calories across the 24 hours than the controls (2555 vs. 2229 kcal, respectively, $p < 0.05$). Boston et al. (2008) showed that both breakfast and lunch were significantly smaller among the NES group than controls, suggesting that "morning anorexia" extends across the lunch period, as well.

Similarly, Goel and colleagues (2009) modeled the circadian aspects of food intake, macronutrient content, and neuroendocrine measures using cosinor analysis (a linear mixed effects model that analyzes differences in phase and amplitude, or height, of curves over time, that takes into account inter-individual differences) among a sample of 15 female night eaters and 14 control participants who underwent an extensive inpatient study. They found that energy, carbohydrate, and fat intake were significantly delayed by about 1.5 hours, and protein was non-significantly delayed by about .5 hour. In addition, phase delays for food-regulatory mechanisms of 1.0 to 2.8 hours were found for leptin and insulin and in the circadian melatonin rhythm (which regulates the sleep period). The delay in the circadian cortisol rhythm was marginally significant. Circulating levels of ghrelin were the only rhythm in the study to show a phase advance, and by quite a large margin of 5.2 hours, while the glucose rhythm showed an inverted circadian pattern (a delay of 12.4 hours). The amplitudes in the circadian rhythms of food intake, cortisol, ghrelin, and insulin were lower than those of the controls, but thyroid stimulating hormone TSH amplitude was amplified. This study highlighted the significant abnormalities in the timing and amplitude of food intake behaviors and physiological circadian markers involved in appetite and neuroendocrine regulation, suggesting that NES may result from dissociations between the central timing mechanism, that is, the suprachiasmatic nucleus (SCN, the body's "master clock" that controls the timing of many basic functions) and peripheral oscillators (e.g., the stomach or liver), which help control timing of basic bodily functions independent of the SCN.

Thus, with core features of NES identified by advanced statistical methods, a population-based analysis of the classification of putative night eaters was also reported. Latent class analysis is a statistical technique that has been used in an effort to describe BN and BED and their possible subtypes empirically (see Wonderlich et al., 2007 for review). A large community sample of 8,250 persons ages 15 to 39 was studied by Striegel-Moore and colleagues (2008) to identify the typologies of NES. In this young adult sample, 2,068 persons who reported night eating behavior were included in the analysis. Food intake patterns were assessed via 24-hour food recalls; nocturnal ingestions were not specifically assessed and, therefore, were not represented in the classifications. Night eating behaviors were based on times of food intake and not on meal markers. A four-class latent class analysis solution was identified: (1) nondepressed late night eaters (eating after 11 P.M., skipping breakfast, and consuming more than 50% of intake after 7 P.M.); (2) nondepressed evening eaters (consuming more than 50% of intake after 7 P.M. but no eating after 11 P.M.); (3) depressed late night eaters (eating after 11 P.M., with some eating more than 50% after 7 P.M., depression, disturbed sleep, tired, and loss of appetite); and (4) depressed evening eaters (same as group 2 plus depressed mood, feeling, tired and disturbed sleep). They also reported that the late night eating was associated with high energy and sodium intake and low protein intake. High body mass index (BMI) was not related to night eating in this sample, but night eaters were more likely to be male, black, and younger than non-night eaters. They also showed that evening overeating was associated with substance use, for example, marijuana and cocaine. Striegel-Moore et al. (2008) concluded that the latent class analysis showed validity for a definition of NES based on eating after 11 P.M., a cut that seemed to discriminate the syndrome better than did 7 P.M. More latent class analysis studies are needed using the new diagnostic criteria and in samples that span a larger age range to expand these findings.

CONTINUUM WITH OTHER EATING DISORDERS

The last criterion of Blashfield et al. (1990) states that a disorder should be differentiated from other categories with which it may be confused. BED and BN represent the two eating disorders with the most potential for overlap with NES.

In BED and BN, binge episodes often occur in the evening, after work or school, as this may be the most opportune time for secretive overeating. However, not much data document the percentage of intake consumed after the evening meal in these groups or whether or not there is a delay in the circadian pattern of eating in these eating disorders. Raymond, Neumeyer, Warren, Lee, and Peterson (2003) provided one of the few 24-hour dietary recall studies that examined the timing of binge episodes. They found that the BED group ($n = 12$) consumed significantly more in the evening (5 to 11 P.M.) on binge days than the control group ($n = 8$) at 1380 kcal vs. 964 kcal, respectively. While this difference was statistically significant, a difference of approximately 400 kcal certainly would not constitute an objectively large amount of food. Taken further, the explanation that binge episodes are almost exclusively happening in the evening may not be supported empirically. Energy intake from 11 P.M. to 5 A.M. did not differ between the groups. Thus, more work is needed to characterize the timing and amount of energy intake over the 24 hours among

BED and BN patients in comparison with persons with NES.

Overlap between BED and NES in most clinical studies ranges from 5% to 20% (Allison et al., 2007; Allison, Grilo, Masheb, & Stunkard, 2005, Geliebter, 2002, Striegel-Moore et al., 2005; Stunkard et al., 1996). Reports of overlap with BN are very limited. Tzischinsky and Latzer (2004) found during a three year period that 9% of BN and 16% of BED patients in an outpatient eating disorders clinic reported nocturnal ingestions. In addition, a recent pilot study (Lundgren, Shapiro & Bulik, 2008) reported that 35.5% of a BN clinical sample endorsed consuming at least 25% of their caloric intake after dinner, and 19.3% reported eating at least half of their intake after dinner. Ten (38.7%) reported at least occasional nocturnal ingestions, while 12.9% reported eating during awakenings at least half of the time. No patients reported "usually" or "always" snacking while up during the night, and only two patients reported both evening hyperphagia and nocturnal ingestions. This overlap of night eating behaviors with BN is high, and more studies are needed to understand this relationship, particularly how the concept of evening hyperphagia (consuming more than 25% of energy intake after the evening meal) fits within the diagnostic models of BED and BN where binge episodes are thought to be occurring in the evening before going to bed.

However, there are important differences in the core criteria of NES and other eating disorders that differentiate them. First, the average caloric intake consumed during nocturnal ingestions is not objectively large, but is similar to regular snacks at approximately 300 to 400 kcal (Allison, Stunkard, & Their, 2004; Birketvedt et al., 1999). Second, the circadian delay in the 24-hour pattern of eating that is core to the NES diagnosis (Boston et al., 2008; Goel et al., 2009) has not been well-documented in BED or BN.

CONTINUUM WITH SLEEP DISORDERS

The conceptual overlap between NES and sleep-related eating disorder (SRED) has been less explored than its overlap with other eating disorders. The key criterion for SRED is *involuntary* eating during the main sleep period (Sateia, 2005). One of several other qualifiers must be present. Stunkard and colleagues (2009) describe eight important differences between the disorders, as described in Table 4.3. The main difference between NES and SRED is the level of awareness during

eating episodes. Persons who sleepwalk and eat, characteristic of SRED, would obviously be more likely to ingest odd or non-food items, such as buttered cigarettes, and to injure themselves walking into obstacles or preparing foods (Schenck & Mahowald, 1994). In addition, they would be less likely to have memory or recall of nocturnal ingestions. Perhaps most importantly, treatment differs for the disorders, with dopaminergic agents in combination with codeine or clonazepam showing efficacy for SRED, as compared to selective serotonin reuptake inhibitors for NES (see Howell, Schenck, & Crow, 2009, for review). Preliminary studies for the effectiveness of topiramate for both disorders is positive (Winkelman, 2003, 2006), but randomized controlled trials for confirmation are needed. Finally, psychotherapies, such as cognitive behavioral therapy, that seem promising for NES (Allison, Lundgren, Moore, O'Reardon, & Stunkard, 2010) would not be effective for a parasomnia where the eating behavior is truly involuntary.

It is possible that SRED and NES occur along a continuum, as suggested by Howell and colleagues (2008). Clinical experience of the authors of this chapter suggests that a minority of NES patients report that they either a) began eating during the night with little to no consciousness, but over time they gained awareness of the nocturnal eating or b) they occasionally experienced nocturnal ingestions with little awareness, but for the majority of ingestions they were awake and aware. The revision of NES criteria will be helpful in future studies for further differentiating NES and SRED. While the disorders may be related, the differences, as listed in Table 4.3, certainly suggest that they are different syndromes that may sometimes co-occur.

CONTINUUM WITH OBESITY

There is mixed evidence regarding the relationship between NES and obesity. NES has been described among average weight, overweight, and obese persons (Birketvedt et al., 1999; Lundgren, Allison, O'Reardon, & Stunkard, 2008; Marshall, Allison, O'Reardon, Birketvedt, & Stunkard, et al., 2004), so it is not exclusively a disorder of overweight. Two European epidemiological studies (Andersen, Stunkard, Sorensen, Petersen, & Heitmann, 2004, Tholin et al., 2009) and three clinical studies (Aranoff, Geliebter & Zammit, 2001; Colles et al., 2007; Lundgren et al., 2006) have shown an increased risk for obesity among persons with NES, but two other studies based on American national databases did not show this increased risk (Striegel-Moore

Table 4.3 Comparison of Features Associated with Night Eating Syndrome (NES) and Sleep-Related Eating Disorder (SRED)

Sign or Symptom	NES	SRED
Consciousness during nocturnal ingestions	+	0
Memory for nocturnal ingestions	+	0
Inappropriate eating	0	+
Comorbidity with parasomnias	0	+
Prevalence	>	<
Binge eating during nocturnal ingestions	0	+
Evening hyperphagia	+	0
Delayed circadian pattern of eating	+	?
Induced by hypnotics	?	+
Pharmacological treatments	SSRI Topiramate	Topiramate Dopaminergic agents Codeine Clonazepam

Reproduced by permission from Stunkard, A. J., Allison, K. C., Geliebter, A., Lundgren, J. D., Gluck, M. E., & O'Reardon, J. P. (2009). Development of criteria for a diagnosis: lessons from the night eating syndrome. *Comprehensive Psychiatry*, *50*(5), 391–399.

et al, 2005; Striegel-Moore, Franko, Thompson et al., 2006). These latter studies were not designed to assess night eating specifically, but were based on 24-hour food records.

An early report (Birketvedt et al., 1999) suggested that carbohydrate intake was greatly increased during night eating episodes, but a more recent report has shown no difference in the proportion of macronutrient content of foods consumed during the night versus the day (Allison, Ahima et al., 2005). However, it could be assumed that the repeated and persistent nature of the disorder contributes to weight gain among its sufferers. But, counter-intuitively, Lundgren and colleagues (2008) reported that nonobese persons with night-eating reported an even higher proportion of eating after the evening meal (50%, SD = 15%), as compared with 35% (SD = 10%) reported in an overweight and obese sample of persons with NES (O'Reardon et al., 2004). Lundgren et al. (2008) also reported that the non-obese night eaters reported more excessive exercise and daytime dietary restraint in comparison to nonobese control participants. (None of the participants met current criteria for BN in that study.) The compensatory exercise and daytime restraint may help them keep their weight under control, while exaggerating the circadian delay of

their eating. Thus, overall, there is no sound evidence that NES is solely a phenotype of obesity.

NES AS SECONDARY TO OTHER PSYCHOPATHOLOGY

As in BED, high psychiatric comorbidity rates have been associated with NES. Beck Depression Inventory scores are in the mild to moderate range at 15.9 (SD = 10.6), which is comparable to scores of persons with BED (17.5, SD = 9.0; Allison, Grilo et al., 2005), BN (15, SD = 11.5), and PD (11, SD = 9.2; Keel, Haedt, & Edler, 2005); see Figure 4.1. Self-esteem is also lower in NES patients seeking weight loss than in patients without NES (Gluck, Geliebter, & Satov, 2001). Lifetime prevalence of Axis I disorders as assessed by the Structured Clinical Interview for the *DSM* (SCID) is high among those with NES at 74%, as compared with controls at 18% (Lundgren et al., 2008). This rate is similar to those found in persons with BED (70%) and BN (75%; Fink, Smith, Gordon, Holm-Denoma, & Joiner, 2009).

More specifically, NES has been related to high rates of lifetime diagnosis for major depressive disorder at 52.6% (Lundgren et al., 2008), 55.7% (de Zwaan, Roerig, Crosby, Karaz, & Mitchell, 2006) and 57.1% (Boseck et al., 2007). In addition, mood

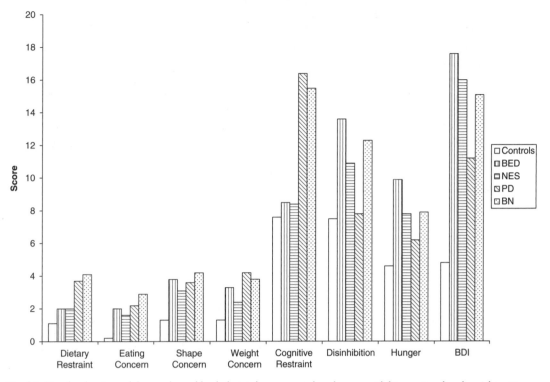

Fig. 4.1 Disordered eating and depressed mood levels depicted across controls and groups with binge eating disorder, night eating syndrome, purging disorder, and bulimia nervosa. No statistical comparisons are provided, given the numbers are generated from different studies, but the levels support the repeated findings that all of these groups experience clinical levels of disordered eating and depressed mood in comparison to control groups, and that their levels differ amongst the diagnoses in an inconsistent manner. (Data for the control, BED, and NES groups were extracted from Allison, Grilo, Masheb, & Stunkard, 2005. Data for the PD and BN groups were extracted from Keel, Haedt, & Edler, 2005.)

worsens across the day for many night eaters (Birketvedt et al., 1999, Boseck et al., 2007). With these features, one possible nosological question may be whether NES is a form of atypical depression, expressed as overeating and worsening of mood throughout the day. However, NES participants do not experience hypersomnia, a hallmark of atypical depression. Sleep onset and morning awakening times are similar to controls in both outpatient studies using actigraphy (O'Reardon et al., 2004) and inpatient studies using polysomnography, and sleep efficiency is decreased (Rogers et al., 2007). Further, improvement of NES with selective serotonin reuptake inhibitor treatment is not significantly correlated with improvement in mood, as monitored through the Beck Depression Inventory (O'Reardon et al., 2006). In sum, as argued above in the case of BED, comorbidity alone is not necessarily a reason for exclusion as an independent diagnostic construct.

Evidence of Diagnostic Validity and Clinical Significance Using Models of NES

Evidence from studies of differing methodologies supports a distinct classification for NES. NES can be discriminated from other eating disorders based on its unique circadian pattern of intake and lack of binge eating behaviors. NES may be found on a continuum with SRED, but several features discriminate the two disorders, particularly different treatment approaches. NES is found across persons of all BMIs and has not reliably been linked to obesity. Although persons with NES have high comorbidity rates with Axis I disorders, particularly mood disorders, this does not preclude NES from existing as an independent diagnosis.

Despite this evidence for NES as a distinct diagnosis, much more information is needed to clarify remaining questions associated with its specific diagnostic features and its exact relationship with other eating and sleep disorders.

Research Needed to Clarify the Status of NES

With the establishment of new, comprehensive diagnostic criteria for NES, new studies are needed to validate those criteria and to investigate the usefulness of their parameters. First, the operational definition of evening hyperphagia has been set at 25% of daily caloric intake consumed after the evening meal. The "evening meal" was chosen as a marker instead of a specific time because the dinner hour varies across cultures. The 25% figure was based on Stunkard's original definition, but this cutpoint was increased to 50% in several studies. O'Reardon et al. (2004) found that night eaters who had verbally reported consuming at least half of their intake after dinner were actually eating about 35% (SD = 10%), as reported through 7-day food logs. Control participants were consuming 10% (SD = 7%). One SD below the NES participants' and two SD's above the control participants' proportion of nighttime food intake converges at 25%, creating a useful separation point between the groups. More studies should assess the clinical utility of this cutpoint in different samples.

More research is also needed to test the clinical utility of the frequency of nocturnal ingestions, which were set at two per week to match the frequency of binges required in the diagnoses of BN and BED. Previous studies either did not specify a number (Birketvedt et al., 1999) or used three per week (Lundgren et al., 2008, O'Reardon et al., 2006). There are no data on the relationship between frequency of nocturnal ingestions and levels of clinical distress, so this should be addressed in future efforts.

As the criteria stand, only one of the core criteria is needed for diagnosis. This makes conceptual sense as both evening hyperphagia and nocturnal ingestions are expressions of a delayed circadian pattern of eating. However, more data are needed on the timing of binge episodes on BN and BED to know if an "evening hyperphagia subtype" is valid in an eating disorders population.

The presence or worsening of depressed mood across the 24-hour day is currently included as a specifier of NES. As depressed mood is common in other eating disorders but is not included in their diagnostic items, more work is needed to assess the utility of this item for the diagnosis of NES. In addition, weight and shape concerns are not included in the new criteria. These concerns are higher among persons with NES than controls, but are significantly lower than persons with BED (Allison, Grilo et al., 2005); Figure 4.1. Those with BED and NES did not differ from each other on eating concerns and dietary restraint on the Eating Disorder Examination, and both groups reported higher levels than controls. Thus, weight and shape concerns are elevated among night eaters, but how central this is to the disorder needs more investigation.

Distress and impairment in functioning are required for all psychiatric diagnoses, and it has been included in the new criteria set for NES. However, it has not been formally included in most NES studies. Items assessing distress and impairment were suggested as additions to the NEQ (Allison, Lundgren et al., 2008), and they have been added to the Night Eating Syndrome History and Inventory (NESHI; unpublished interview available by these authors), the diagnostic inventory used most frequently to diagnose NES. Thus, more data will be forthcoming.

Not only are the psychosocial correlates of a psychiatric disorder important, but increasingly, the health implications of a disorder are essential in establishing the importance of a diagnostic entity. While neuroendocrine abnormalities have been noted (Allison, Ahima, et al., 2005; Goel et al., 2009), it is not clear how these abnormalities are related to disease and mortality. However, night eating among diabetic patients has been associated with less adherence to diet, exercise, and glucose monitoring, as well as higher hemoglobin A1C levels and more diabetic complications (Morse, Katon, Ciechanowski, & Hirsch, 2006). Also, a review of the impact of night eating on bariatric surgery outcomes (Colles & Dixon, 2006) revealed that night eating behaviors often continue after surgery, and at least one study has shown that night eating after surgery is associated with greater BMIs and less treatment satisfaction (Latner, Wetzler, Goodman, & Glinski, 2004). Finally, Andersen and colleagues (2004) found that women who endorsed night eating were more likely to gain weight over six years as compared to non–night eating women. This relationship was not found in men. In general, more careful assessment of night eating behaviors is needed in relation to health outcomes, which would be aided by the development of new assessment tools based on the proposed diagnostic criteria. Longitudinal studies would also help identify the impact of NES on the development of disease and its impact on quality of life.

Similar to BED, future NES research should also focus on genetic and brain imaging methods. Lundgren and colleagues (2006) found that NES runs in families. Specifically, the first degree relatives of patient with NES were 4.9 times more likely than the first-degree relatives of controls to meet criteria for NES. Additionally, heritability for night eating behaviors has been reported at .44 among the Swedish Twin Register cohort, with a high genetic correlation of .66 between night eating and binge eating behaviors (Root et al., 2010).

Brain imaging methods could also be useful in characterizing NES. Lundgren and colleagues (2008) used single photon emission computed tomography (SPECT) to compare the serotonin transporter (SERT) uptake in persons with NES to both healthy controls and to patients with major depressive disorder. Persons with NES had significantly greater SERT uptake in the midbrain than did healthy controls (Lundgren et al., 2008). Patients with NES also had significantly greater SERT uptake ratios (effect size range 0.64 to 0.84) in the midbrain, right temporal lobe, and left temporal lobe regions compared to patients with depression (Lundgren et al., 2009). Finally, no published studies have used functional magnetic resonance imaging (fMRI) to examine response to food cues or behavioral features of night eating (e.g., impulsivity and reward dependence could be measured with delay discounting paradigms, e.g., McClure, Laibson, Lowenstein, & Cohen, 2004). Studies such as these will be important in differentiating NES from other eating and Axis I psychiatric disorders.

Purging Disorder
Research Status and Description of Purging Disorder
HISTORY AND PREVALENCE OF PURGING DISORDER
As researchers began to study BN more systematically, several groups (e.g., Mitchell, Pyle, Hatsukami, & Eckert, 1986) noted that large proportions of their cohorts were not consuming enough food in a sitting to be considered objectively large, and therefore, were not meeting criteria for binge episodes, yet they were purging (e.g., vomiting or abusing laxatives) regularly. Persistent purging behavior in the absence of binge eating has subsequently been reported among adults (Wade, 2007) and adolescents (Binford & le Grange, 2005) in community (Hay, Fairburn, & Doll, 1996), clinical (Keel, Haedt, & Edler, 2005), and undergraduate (Fink et al., 2009) samples. The name, purging disorder, was established by Keel et al. (2005) and is being increasingly used in the nomenclature. Eating disorder not otherwise specified, purging type (EDNOS-P)

has also been used to describe this group (Binford & le Grange, 2005), given that persons with these clinical features would be diagnosed in the EDNOS category in the current *DSM-IV-TR* classification system. Finally, "purging-only syndrome" has also been used in the literature (Wade, 2007).

Epidemiological studies reveal lifetime prevalence rates of 5.3% in an Australian twin cohort (Wade, 2007), 1.1% in an Italian cohort (Favaro, Ferrara, & Santonastaso, 2003), and a point prevalence of .85% in an adolescent Portuguese cohort (Machado, Machado, Goncalves, & Hoek, 2007). The relative frequency of these rates as compared to the other eating disorders has varied, likely due to the differing diagnostic criteria used in each study.

DEFINITION OF PD
In a recent review, Keel (2007) described 10 different definitions for syndromes of purging. PD is generally defined as the regular occurrence of inappropriate compensatory behaviors (e.g., vomiting, laxative use, or diuretic misuse) for the purpose of weight or shape control in the absence of objective binge eating episodes and with a body weight greater than 85% of that expected (Keel, 2007). Sufferers often feel distressed after consuming even small amounts of food that are not acceptable to them and have an overwhelming urge to purge afterwards. Aspects of the definition that have varied include (1) the frequency of purging, ranging from at least once per week to at least twice per week; (2) requirement that a loss of control over eating (i.e., subjective binge episode) precede the purging behavior; (3) the presence of undue influence of weight and shape on self-evaluation; and (4) duration of illness, ranging from 3 to 6 months.

Models of PD
Much work still remains in delineating the etiology, course, treatment, and outcome, but there is emerging evidence that PD can be differentiated from other disorders and is a clinically significant disorder. We will review the evidence for PD as (1) a distinct disorder and (2) on a continuum with other eating disorders.

PD AS A DISTINCT AXIS I PSYCHIATRIC DISORDER
PD can be damaging both physically and psychologically. The fact that it is already recognized specifically as a form of EDNOS affirms that it is a clinically significant syndrome. Keel (2007) argues that because the purging types of AN and BN have

been associated with greater medical problems (due to the effects of repeated vomiting and laxative abuse), comorbid psychopathology, and suicidality, that purging in the absence of very low body weight and binge episodes is independently quite dangerous. In addition, PD has been identified as a separate class from other eating disorders through three latent class analyses (Striegel-Moore et al., 2005; Sullivan, Bulik, & Kendler, 1998; Wade, Crosby, & Martin, 2006). Striegel-Moore, Franko, et al. (2005) further stated that the PD group was the largest of the three identified in the analysis. All members of the PD group endorsed vomiting, nearly half reported fasting, and over a third reported the use of diet pills. In addition, there was a higher proportion of persons identifying their race as white in the latent PD group than in the latent binge-eating group, who had a larger proportion of reported black racial identities (Striegel-Moore, Franko et al., 2005).

There are conflicting findings on the most prevalent purging method in PD. Vomiting has been most commonly reported, at 100% of the PD sample (Striegel-Moore, Franko et al., 2005) and 98.5% (Binford & le Grange, 2005), while Wade (2007) reported higher rates of laxative abuse (62%) than vomiting (38%), followed by diuretic abuse (21%). In their adolescent sample, Binford and le Grange (2005) reported that driven exercise was also quite common at 66%, followed by fasting at 38%, and then laxative abuse at 14%. Thus, there appears to be heterogeneity of purging and nonpurging compensatory methods within the PD classification.

Several studies have shown that persons with PD have more severe eating disordered attitudes and behaviors and general psychopathology than persons without eating disorders. Specifically, Keel et al. (2005, 2007) has shown that persons with PD have shown more severe pathology on all four scales of the EDE and all three scales of the Eating Inventory, and Wade (2007) replicated the finding on the EDE with the exception of similar levels of eating concern between those with PD and controls. Body image is more disturbed (Fink et al., 2009; Keel et al., 2005), and general psychopathology is also consistently greater in PD groups than in controls, including lifetime major depression, anxiety, and suicidality (Keel et al., 2005; Wade, 2007). Similar to comorbidity rates for lifetime diagnosis of major depressive disorder reported for BED and NES above, 54% (Binford & le Grange, 2005), and 76% of persons with PD have reported the disorder. Overall, as was shown with BED and NES, PD has

been identified through empirical methods with latent class analysis and has shown clinical greater levels of eating disordered and general psychopathology than persons without eating disorders.

PD ON A CONTINUUM WITH OTHER EATING DISORDERS

PD is most similar to BN, with both purging and non-purging compensatory behaviors being identified and normal body weight among sufferers. Binford and le Grange (2005) identified two possible theories, that PD represents (1) a prodromal state of BN or (2) a partial BN syndrome. There are various sources of evidence against PD as a precursor to BN. Binford and le Grange (2005) reported that duration of PD and BN of adolescents in their treatment sample were similar at 21 and 19 months. Keel et al. (2005) studied distinctive groups of BN, PD, and controls, requiring that their PD participants not have a previous diagnosis of BN. Remission rates from treatment for PD and BN did not differ between the groups at a 6-month follow-up, and little diagnostic cross-over was found, suggesting at least short-term stability of the diagnoses.

Perhaps, then, PD as a partial BN syndrome is more plausible. In several studies, PD groups have endorsed similar levels of disordered eating attitudes and behaviors (see Keel, 2007 for review); Figure 4.1. Differences on specific scales have sometimes differed, depending on sample characteristics and diagnostic criteria. If differences in the level of pathology were shown, the general trend was for PD to have less severe levels than the BN group. These differences on traditional eating disorder assessment tools may be contributed, at least in part, to the assessment tools, given that large portions of many of them include questions regarding binge eating behavior, which is not present in PD.

One possible avenue for differentiating PD and BN may lie in physiological functioning. A feeding study has shown that women with PD report higher levels of postprandial fullness and gastrointestinal discomfort after a standardized meal than those with BN. Most interesting, women with PD also experienced a greater release of cholecystokinin (CCK; Keel, Wolfe, Liddle, De Young, & Jimerson, 2007), suggesting that physiological cues, such as premature abdominal discomfort in response to eating, may contribute to the purging behavior.

Only one study has compared PD to AN, although the evidence for overlap between these two disorders is not very great, given the differences in body weight. Fink et al. (2009) used the Eating

Disorder Inventory to compare eating pathology among AN, BN, PD, BED, and controls, finding similarities between AN and PD for most scales, but higher purging ideation among the PD group than the AN group. In general, as discussed earlier, the BN group showed the highest scores for disordered eating and impulsivity in comparison to the other groups.

Evidence of Diagnostic Validity and Clinical Significance of Models of PD

Do these findings differentiate PD enough as an independent entity from a variant of BN? Part of the answer to this question lies in the approach that the committee for the *DSM-V* on eating disorders will ultimately take in revising the existing diagnostic schema for eating disorders. If the disorders are reconceptualized on restricting, binge-eating, and purging continua, then PD may naturally fall within that schema, as would BED. These decisions are still under consideration. If distinct, categorical disorders remain in the next *DSM*, then PD would benefit from listing as a disorder in need of further research, as BED has been, so that more information specific to PD can further characterize the psychological, medical, and physiological aspects of the disorder and its treatment.

Research Needed to Clarify the Status of PD

Research on PD as an independent construct is still in its early stages, with most studies occurring in the last decade. A literature search for the number of papers on PD was difficult to summarize, as a large number of possibilities were returned, but the vast majority of the articles were only partially concerned with PD; it often was not the main focus of the papers that were listed. A unified set of diagnostic criteria is greatly needed for our understanding of the disorder to move forward. In these criteria, clarification on the operational definition of purging must be described, including whether nonpurging compensatory behaviors are also considered (e.g., excessive exercise), as they have been in recent studies. Further, should subjective binge episodes be required, or listed as a specifier? Binford and le Grange (2005) noted that purging occurred after a subjective binge episode only half of the time in their sample, so this feature may be more appropriate as a specifier. Likewise, the duration of the signs and symptoms should be clarified at 3 or 6 months. Finally, what is the role of weight and shape concerns in the PD diagnosis? Most studies have found clinical levels of these constructs, but more work is

needed to distinguish the role of these concerns to the core pathology of the disorder, as has been done recently in BED (Grilo et al., 2008; Mond et al., 2007).

As with all psychiatric disorders, studies of PD have produced evidence of distress and impairment in functioning among its sufferers, although this should be made explicit in diagnosing PD. Empirical methods should further identify any other possible related features that would improve the utility of the diagnosis, such as personality features. Etiology is also an important factor that has yet to be explored specifically for PD. Genetics studies of eating disorders are still rare, but with new technology it is hopeful that these disorders will begin shortly for PD. Serotonin (5-hydroxytryptamine, 5-HT) transporter studies have identified dysregulation of serotonin functioning, specifically, reduced 5-HT activity among persons with BN and BED, but these studies have not been conducted specifically for PD (see Steiger & Bruce, 2007 for review). Finally, Keel et al. (2007) have provided one of the only studies of the pathophysiology of PD thus far, with informative findings regarding differential functioning of CCK in PD as compared to BN. Much more work is needed in this area as well.

Future Directions

As research on the diagnostic validity and utility of BED, NES, and PD continues, there are two primary areas that will likely make significant contributions to the literature. These include new genetic analyses and brain imaging techniques. With regard to newer genetics methods, both epigenetics (Delcuve, Rastegar, & Davie, 2009) and interspecies genetics (Kas, Kaye, Mathes, & Bulik, 2008) should be a priority in moving BED, NES, and PD research forward.

Recently, the National Institutes of Health hosted a research workshop on brain imaging and obesity (October, 2008), suggesting that brain imaging research will be a priority for NIH funding in the coming years. Several brain imaging methods are available to further research in these proposed syndromes, including functional magnetic resonance imaging (fMRI), positron emission tomography (PET), and single photon emission computed tomography (SPECT). In addition, methodological paradigms, such as the delay discounting and reward sensitivity tasks, as well as visual stimuli presentation (e.g., food cues compared to nonfood cues) are starting to be used (C. Savage, personal communication, November 6, 2008; Schienle, Schäfer, Herman, &

Vaitl, 2009). Researchers are just beginning to understand the neural mechanisms that underlie behavioral choice and the hedonic effects of food (McClure et al., 2004; Schienle et al., 2009), and these methods should help further our understanding about the independence and inter-relationships between BED, NES, PD, and other forms of disordered eating.

Summary and Conclusions

In summary, there is strong evidence for the classification of BED as a psychiatric disorder that is distinct and clinically meaningful. Evidence for NES as a disorder is growing quickly, and inclusion in the *DSM-V* would increase research efforts to discern the diagnosis' clinical utility, particularly given the delineation of its new criteria. Finally, PD seems to be associated with negative consequences similar to those found in BN, but it is lacking a widely-acknowledged criteria set and studies specific to PD (i.e., not just as part of an EDNOS sample). Thus, studies of NES and PD have provided evidence for their constructs and would benefit from inclusion as disorders in need of further research in *DSM-V* for additional consideration and careful study.

References

Adami, G. F., Campostano, A., Marinari, G. M., Ravera, G., & Scopinaro, N. (2002). Night eating in obesity: A descriptive study. *Nutrition, 18*, 587–589.

Allison, K. C., Ahima, R. S., O'Reardon, J. P., Dinges, D. F., Sharma, V., Cummings, D. E., et al. (2005). Neuroendocrine profiles associated with energy intake, sleep, and stress in the night eating syndrome. *Journal of Clinical Endocrinology and Metabolism, 90*, 6214–6217.

Allison, K. C., Crow, S., Reeves, R. R., West, D. S., Foreyt, J. P., DiLillo, V. G., et al. (2007). The prevalence of binge eating disorder and night eating syndrome in adults with type 2 diabetes mellitus. *Obesity, 15*, 1285–1291.

Allison, K. C., Engel, S. G., Crosby, R. D., de Zwaan, M., O'Reardon, J. P., Wonderlich, S. A., et al. (2008). Evaluation of diagnostic criteria for night eating syndrome using item response theory analysis. *Eating Behaviors, 9*, 398–407.

Allison, K. C., Grilo, C. M., Masheb, R. M., & Stunkard, A. J. (2005). Binge eating disorder and night eating syndrome: A comparative study of disordered eating. *Journal of Consulting and Clinical Psychology, 73*, 1107–1115.

Allison, K. C., Lundgren, J. D., O'Reardon, J. P., Geliebter, A., Gluck, M. E., Vinai, P., et al. (2010). Proposed diagnostic criteria for night eating syndrome. *International Journal of Eating Disorders, 43*, 2414–247.

Allison K. C., Lundgren, J. D., O'Reardon, J. P., Martino, N. S., Sarwer, D. B., Wadden, T. A., et al. (2008). Psychometric properties of a measure of severity of the night eating syndrome. *Eating Behaviors, 9*, 62–72.

Allison, K.C., Lundgren, J.D., Moore, R.H., O'Reardon, J.P., Stunkard, A.J. (2010). Cognitive Behavior Therapy for Night Eating Syndrome: A Pilot Study. *American Journal of Psychotherapy, 64*, 94–106.

Allison, K. C., Stunkard, A. J., & Their, S. L. (2004). *Overcoming the night eating syndrome: a step-by-step guide to breaking the cycle.* Oakland, CA: New Harbinger.

Allison, K. C., Wadden, T. A., Sarwer, D. B., Fabricatore, A. N., Crerand, C., Gibbons, L., et al. (2006). Night eating syndrome and binge eating disorder among persons seeking bariatric surgery: Prevalence and related features. *Obesity, 14* (Supplement 2), 77S–82S.

American Psychiatric Association (APA). (2000). *Diagnostic and statistical manual of mental disorders* (4th ed., text rev.) Washington, DC: Author.

Andersen, G. S., Stunkard, A. J., Sorensen, T. I. A., Pedersen, L., & Heitman, B. L. (2004). Night eating and weight change in middle-aged men and women. *International Journal of Obesity, 28*, 1138–1143.

Aronoff, N. J., Geliebter, A., & Zammit, G. (2001). Gender and body mass index as related to the night-eating syndrome in obese outpatients. *Journal of the American Dietetics Association, 101*, 102–104.

Binford, R. B., & le Grange, D. (2005). Adolescents with bulimia nervosa and eating disorder not otherwise specified-purging only. *International Journal of Eating Disorders, 38*, 157–161.

Birketvedt, G., Florholmen, J., Sundsfjord, J., Osterud, B., Dinges, D., Bilker, W., et al. (1999). Behavioral and neuroendocrine characteristics of the night-eating syndrome. *JAMA, 282*, 657–663.

Blashfield, R. K., Sprock, J., & Fuller, A. K. (1990). Suggested guidelines for including or excluding categories in the DSM-IV. *Comprehensive Psychiatry, 31*, 15–19.

Boseck, J. J., Engel, S. G., de Zwaan, M., Allison, K. C., Crosby, R. D., & Mitchell, J. E. (2007). The application of ecological momentary assessment to the study of night eating. *International Journal of Eating Disorders, 40*, 271–276.

Boston, R. C., Moate, P. J., Stunkard, A. J., Allison, K. C., & Lundgren, J. D. (2008). Modeling food intake diurnal rhythms by means of parametric deconvolution. *American Journal of Clinical Nutrition, 87*, 1672–1677.

Colles, S. L., & Dixon, J. B. (2006). Night eating syndrome: impact on bariatric surgery. *Obesity Surgery, 16*, 811–820.

Colles, S. L., Dixon, J. B., & O'Brien, P. E. (2007). Night eating syndrome and nocturnal snacking: association with obesity, binge eating and psychological distress. *International Journal of Obesity, 31*, 1722–1730.

Colles, S. L., Dixon, J. B., & O'Brien, P. E. (2008). Loss of control is central to psychological disturbance associated with binge eating disorder. *Obesity, 16*, 608–614.

Delcuve, G. P., Rastegar, M., & Davie, J. R. (2009). Epigenetic control. *Journal of Cellular Physiology*, PMID: 19127539. 219, 2, 243–250.

de Zwaan, M., Roerig, D. B., Crosby, R. D., Karaz, S., & Mitchell, J. E. (2006). Nighttime eating: A descriptive study. *International Journal of Eating Disorders, 39*, 224–232.

Favaro, A., Ferrara, S., & Santonastaso, P. (2003). The spectrum of eating disorders in young women: A prevalence study in a general population sample. *Psychosomatic Medicine, 65*, 701–708.

Fink E. L., Smith, A. R., Gordon, K. H., Holm-Denoma, J. M., & Joiner, T. E. (2009). Psychological correlates of purging disorder as compared with other eating disorders: an exploratory investigation. *International Journal of Eating Disorders, 42*, 31–39.

Geliebter, A. (2002). New developments in binge eating disorder and the night eating syndrome. *Appetite, 38*, 1–3.

Gluck, M. E., Geliebter, A., & Satov, T. (2001). Night eating syndrome is associated with depression, low self-esteem, reduced daytime hunger, and less weight loss in obese outpatients. *Obesity Research, 9*, 264–267.

Goel, N., Stunkard, A. J., Rogers, N. L., Van Dongen, H. P. A., Allison, K. C., O'Reardon, J. P., et al. (2009). Circadian rhythm profiles in women with night eating syndrome. *Journal of Biological Rhythms, 24*, 85–94.

Goldschmidt, A. B., Jones, M., Manwaring, J. L., Luce, K. H., Osborne, M. I., Cunning, D., et al. (2008). The clinical significance of loss of control over eating in overweight adolescents. *International Journal of Eating Disorders, 41*, 153–158.

Grilo, C. M., Hrabosky, J. I., White, M. A., Allison, K. C., Stunkard, A. J., & Masheb, R. M. (2008). Overvaluation of shape and weight in binge eating disorder and overweight controls: Refinement of a diagnostic construct. *Journal of Abnormal Psychology, 117*, 414–419.

Hay, P., Fairburn, C. G., & Doll, H. A. (1996). The classification of bulimic eating disorders: A community-based cluster analysis. *Psychological Medicine, 26*, 801–812.

Howell, M. J., Schenck, C. H., & Crow, S. J. (2009). A review of nighttime eating disorders. *Sleep Medicine, 13*, 23–24.

Hudson, J. I., Hiripi, E., Pope, H. G., & Kessler, R. C. (2007). The prevalence and correlates of eating disorders in the National Comorbidity Survey Replication. *Biological Psychiatry, 61*, 348–358.

Hudson, J. I., McElroy, S. L., Raymond, N. C., Crow, S., Keck, P. E., Carter, W. P., et al. (1998). Fluvoxamine in the treatment of binge eating disorder: A multicenter placebo-controlled, double-blind trial. *American Journal of Psychiatry, 155*, 1756–1762.

Johnson, W. G., Boutelle, K. N., Torgurd, L., Davig, J. P., & Turner, S. (2000). What is a binge? The influence of amount, duration, and loss of control criteria on judgments of binge eating. *International Journal of Eating Disorders, 27*, 471–479.

Johnson, W. G., Schlundt, D. G., Barclay, D. R., Carr-Nangle, R. E., & Engler, L. B. (1995). A naturalistic functional analysis of binge eating. *Behavior Therapy, 26*, 101–118.

Kas, M. J. H., Kaye, W. H., Mathes, F., & Bulik, C. M. (2008). Interspecies genetics of eating disorder traits. *American Journal of Medical Genetics, Part B* 150B(2) 318–327.

Keel, P. K. (2007). Purging disorder: subthreshold variant or full-threshold eating disorder? *International Journal of Eating Disorders, 40*, 589–594.

Keel, P. K., Haedt, A., & Edler, C. (2005). Purging disorder: an ominous variant of bulimia nervosa? *International Journal of Eating Disorders, 38*, 191–199.

Keel, P. K., Wolfe, B. E., Liddle, R. A., DeYoung, K. P., & Jimerson, D. C. (2007). Clinical features and physiological response to a test meal in purging disorder and bulimia nervosa. *Archives of General Psychiatry, 64*, 1058–1066.

Latner, J. D., & Clyne, C. (2008). The diagnostic validity of the criteria for binge eating disorder. *International Journal of Eating Disorders, 41*, 1–14.

Latner, J. D., Wetzler, S., Goodman, E. R., & Glinski, J. (2004). Gastric bypass in a low-income, inner-city population: Eating disturbances and weight loss. *Obesity Research, 12*, 956–961.

Lundgren, J. D., Allison, K. C., Crow, S., O'Reardon, J. P., Berg, K. C., Galbraith, J., et al. (2006). Prevalence of the night eating syndrome in a psychiatric population. *American Journal of Psychiatry, 163*, 156–158.

Lundgren, J. D., Allison, K. C., O'Reardon, J. P., & Stunkard, A. J. (2008). A descriptive study of non-obese persons with night eating syndrome and a weight matched comparison group. *Eating Behaviors, 9*, 343–351.

Lundgren J. L., Allison K. C., & Stunkard, A. J. (2006). Familial aggregation in the night eating syndrome. *International Journal of Eating Disorders, 39*, 516–518.

Lundgren, J. D., Amsterdam, J., Newberg, A., Allison, K. C., Wintering, N., & Stunkard, A. J. (2009). Differences in serotonin transporter binding affinity in patients with major depressive disorder and night eating syndrome. *Eating and Weight Disorders: Studies on Anorexia, Bulimia, and Obesity, 14*(1), 45–50.

Lundgren, J. D., Newberg, A., Allison, K.C., Wintering, N., Plöessl, K., & Stunkard, A. J. (2008). 123I-ADAM SPECT imaging of serotonin transporter binding in patients with night eating syndrome: A pilot study. *Psychiatry Research: Neuroimaging, 162*, 214–220.

Lundgren, J. D., Shapiro, J. R., Bulik, C. (2008). Night eating patterns of patients with bulimia nervosa: A preliminary report. *Eating and Weight Disorders: Studies on Anorexia, Bulimia, and Obesity, 13*(4), 171–175.

Machado, P. P., Machado, B. C., Goncalves, S., & Hoek, H. W. (2007). The prevalence of eating disorders not otherwise specified. *International Journal of Eating Disorders, 40*, 212– 217.

Marshall, H. M., Allison, K. C., O'Reardon, J. P., Birketvedt, G., & Stunkard, A. J. (2004). Night eating syndrome among nonobese persons. *International Journal of Eating Disorders, 35*, 217–222.

McClure, S. M., Laibson, D. I., Lowenstein, G., & Cohen, J. D. (2004). Separate neural systems value immediate and delayed monetary rewards. *Science, 306*, 503–507.

Mitchell, J. E., & Groat, R. (1984). A placebo-controlled double-blind trial of amitriptyline in bulimia. *Journal of Clinical Psychopharmacology, 4*, 186–193.

Mitchell, M. E., Pyle, R. L., Hatsukami, D., & Eckert, E. D. (1986). What are atypical eating disorders? *Psychosomatics, 27*, 21–28.

Mitchell, J. E., Steffen K. J., & Roerig, J. L. (2007). Management of bulimia nervosa. In J. Yager & P. S. Powers (Eds.) *Clinical manual of eating disorders* (pp. 171–194). Washington, DC: American Psychiatric Publishing.

Mond, J. M., Hay, P. J., Rodgers, B., & Owen, C. (2007). Recurrent binge eating with and without the "undue influence of weight or shape on self-evaluation": Implications for the diagnosis of binge eating disorder. *Behaviour Research and Therapy, 45*, 929–938.

Morse, S. A., Ciechanowski, P. S., Katon, W. J., & Hirsch, I. B. (2006). Isn't this just bedtime snacking? The potential adverse effects of night-eating symptoms on treatment adherence and outcomes in patients with diabetes. *Diabetes Care, 29*, 1800–1804.

O'Reardon, J. P., Allison, K. C., Martino, N. S., Lundgren, J. D., Heo, M., & Stunkard, A. J. (2006). A randomized placebo-controlled trial of sertraline in the treatment of the night eating syndrome. *American Journal of Psychiatry, 163*, 893–898.

O'Reardon, J. P., Ringel, B. L., Dinges, D. F., Allison, K. C., Rogers, N. L., Martino, N. S., & Stunkard, A. J. (2004). Circadian eating and sleeping patterns in the night eating syndrome. *Obesity Research, 12*, 1789–1796.

Pope H. G., Jr., Keck, P. E., Jr., McElroy, S. L., & Hudson, J. I. (1989). A placebo-controlled study of trazodone in bulimia nervosa. *Journal of Clinical Psychopharmacology*, *9*, 254–259.

Rand, C. S. W., Macgregor, A. M., & Stunkard, A. J. (1997). The night eating syndrome in the general population and among post-operative obesity surgery patients. *International Journal of Eating Disorders*, *22*, 65–69.

Raymond, N. C., Neumeyer, B., Warren, C. S., Lee S. S., & Peterson, C. B. (2003). Energy intake patters in obese women with binge eating disorder. *Obesity Research*, *11*, 869–879.

Rogers, N. L., Dinges, D. F., Allison, K. C., Maislin, G., Martino, N., O'Reardon, J. P., & Stunkard, A. J. (2006). Assessment of sleep in women with night eating syndrome. *Sleep*, *29*, 814–819.

Root, T. L., Thornton L., M., Lindroos, A. K., Stunkard, A. J., Lichtenstein P., Pederson, N. L., Rassmussin, F., Bulik, C. M. (2010). Shared and unique genetic and environmental influences on binge eating and night eating. *Eating Behaviors*, 11, 92–98.

Sateia M. J. (Ed.) (2005) *International classification of sleep disorders* (2nd ed.). Westchester, IL: American Academy of Sleep Medicine.

Schenck, C. H., & Mahowald, M. W. (1994). Review of nocturnal sleep-related eating disorders. *International Journal of Eating Disorders*, 15, 343–356.

Schienele, A., Schäfer, A., Herman, A., & Vaitl, D. (2009). Binge-eating disorder: Reward sensitivity and brain activation to images of food. *Biological Psychiatry*, *65*(8), 654–661.

Spitzer, R. L., Devlin, M., Walsh, B. T., Hasin, D., Wing, R., Marcus, M., et al. (1992). Binge eating disorder: A multisite field trial of the diagnostic criteria. *International Journal of Eating Disorders*, *11*(3), 191–203.

Steiger, H., & Bruce, K. R. (2007). Phenotypes, endophenotypes, and genotypes of bulimia spectrum eating disorders. *Canadian Journal of Psychiatry*, *52*, 220–227.

Striegel-Moore, R. H., Dohm, F. A., Hook, J. M., Schreiber, G. B., Crawford, P. B., & Daniels, S. R. (2005). Night eating syndrome in young adult women: Prevalence and correlates. *International Journal of Eating Disorders*, *37*, 200–206.

Striegel-Moore, R. H., & Franko, D. L. (2008). Should binge eating disorder be included in the DSM-V? A critical review of the state of the evidence. *Annual Review of Clinical Psychology*, *4*, 305–324.

Striegel-Moore, R. H., Franko, D. L., May, A., Ach, E., Thompson, D., & Hook, J. M. (2006). Should night eating syndrome be introduced in the DSM? *International Journal of Eating Disorders*, *39*, 544–549.

Striegel-Moore, R. H., Franko, D. L., Thompson, D., Affenito, S., & Kraemer, H. C. (2006). Night eating: Prevalence and demographic correlates. *Obesity Research*, *14*, 139–147.

Striegel-Moore, R. H., Franko, D. L., Thompson, D., Affenito, S., May, A., & Kraemer, H. C. (2008). Exploring the typology of night eating syndrome. *International Journal of Eating Disorders*, *41*, 411–418.

Striegel-Moore, R. H., Franko, D. L., Thompson, D., Barton, B., Schreiber, G. B., & Daniels, S. R. (2005). An empirical study of the typology of bulimia nervosa and its spectrum variants. *Psychological Medicine*, *35*, 1563–1572.

Stunkard, A. J. (1959). Eating patterns and obesity. *Psychiatric Quarterly*, *33*, 284–294.

Stunkard, A. J., & Allison, K. C. (2003a). Binge eating disorder: Disorder or marker? *International Journal of Eating Disorders*, *34*(Supplement), S89–S95.

Stunkard, A. J., Allison, K. C., Geliebter, A., Lundgren, J. D., Gluck, M. E., & O'Reardon, J. P. (2009). Development of criteria for a diagnosis: Lessons from the night eating syndrome. *Comprehensive Psychiatry*, *50*(5), 391–399.

Stunkard, A. J., Berkowitz, R., Wadden, T. A., Tanrikut, C., Reiss, E., & Young, L. (1996). Binge eating disorder and the night-eating syndrome. *International Journal of Obesity and Related Metabolic Disorders*, *20*, 1–6.

Stunkard, A. J., Grace, W. J., & Wolff, H.G. (1955). The night-eating syndrome: a pattern of food intake among certain obese patients. *American Journal of Medicine*, *19*, 78–86.

Sullivan, P. F., Bulik, C. M., & Kendler, K. S. (1998). The epidemiology and classification of bulimia nervosa. *Psychological Medicine*, *28*, 599–610.

Tanofsky-Kraff, M., & Yanovski, S. Z. (2004). Eating disorder or disordered eating? Non-normative eating patterns in obese individuals. *Obesity Research*, *12*(9), 1361–1366.

Telch, C. F., Pratt, E. M., & Niego, S. H. (1998). Obese women with binge eating disorder define the term binge. *International Journal of Eating Disorders*, *24*, 313–317.

Tholin, S., Lindroos, A. K., Tynelius, P., Akerstedt, T., Stunkard, A. J., Bulik, C. M., & Rassmussen, F. (2009). Prevalence of night eating in obese and non-obese twins. *Obesity*, 17, 1050–1055.

Tzischinsky, O., & Latzer, Y. (2004). Nocturnal eating: prevalence, features, and night sleep among binge eating disorder and bulimia nervosa patients in Israel. *European Eating Disorders Review*, *12*, 101–109.

Wade, T. D. (2007). A retrospective comparison of purging type disorders: Eating disorder not otherwise specified and bulimia nervosa. *International Journal of Eating Disorders*, *40*, 1–6.

Wade T. D., Crosby, R., & Martin, N. G. (2006). Use of latent profile analysis to identify eating disorder phenotypes in an adult Australian twin cohort. *Archives of General Psychiatry*, *63*, 1377–1384.

Williamson, D. A., Gleaves, D. H., & Stewart, T. M. (2005). Categorical versus dimensional models of eating disorders: An examination of the evidence. *International Journal of Eating Disorders*, *37*(1), 1–10.

Winkelman, J. W. (2003). Treatment of nocturnal eating syndrome and sleep-related eating disorder with topiramate. *Sleep Medicine*, *4*, 243–246.

Winkelman, J. W. (2006). Efficacy and tolerability of open-label topiramate in the treatment of sleep-related eating disorder: A retrospective case series. *Journal of Clinical Psychiatry*, *67*, 1729–1734.

Wonderlich, S. A., Joiner, T. E., Keel, P. K., Williamson, D. A., & Crosby, R. D. (2007). Eating disorder diagnoses: Empirical approaches to classification. American Psychologist, *62*(3), 167–180.

CHAPTER 5

Controversies and Questions in Current Evaluation, Treatment, and Research Related to Child and Adolescent Eating Disorders

James Lock

Abstract

This chapter addresses specific diagnostic, treatment, and research issues related to child and adolescent eating disorders. Current diagnostic formulations are inadequate for diagnosing eating disorders such as selective eating, food avoidance emotional disorders, and food phobias in children. Classification schemes for anorexia and bulimia nervosa are not developmentally sensitive, leading to overuse of "eating disorder not otherwise specified" as a diagnosis. Treatment studies in children and adolescents are few; however, those available suggest that certain guidelines are generally applicable. Adolescents with eating disorders should be treated as early as possible in an outpatient setting utilizing parents as resources. Medications, if used, should address comorbid conditions. Data hopefully forthcoming in the next 5 to 10 years will shed light on how best to classify and treat these disorders. Future research should integrate neuropsychological and neurofunctional findings related to brain development, cognitive functioning, and eating disorder symptom development in this age group.

Keywords: adolescents, anorexia nervosa, children, family therapy, treatment

Introduction

Anorexia nervosa (AN), bulimia nervosa (BN), and related conditions (e.g., eating disorders not otherwise specified [EDNOS]) are psychiatric disorders with onset during late childhood and adolescence (van Son et al., 2006). In addition to these classic eating disorders, a range of other eating problems such as selective eating, food phobias, and food avoidance emotional disorder also present in the childhood years (Bryant-Waugh & Lask, 1995). These disorders have potentially serious acute medical complications, including, in the case of AN, a high mortality rate (Golden et al., 2003; Sullivan, 1995). In children and adolescents, physical health problems potentially affect bone health, fertility, and growth over the life course (Golden et al., 2003). Psychiatric comorbidity is common, with affective disorders and anxiety disorders especially associated with these disorders prior to, during, and

post recovery (Bulik, Sullivan, Fear, & Joyce, 1997; Fairburn, Cooper, Doll, Norman, & O'Connor, 2000; N. Godart, Flament, Perdereau, & Jeammet, 2002; Halmi et al., 1991; Kaye et al., 2004; le Grange & Lock, 2002). At the same time, until recently, most treatment strategies and research studies have focused on adult populations. This state of affairs has led to diagnostic classification schemes and treatments designed for adults being used in many instances without significant modification with children and adolescents. This chapter focuses on the dilemmas and difficulties that have arisen as a result of this, including specifically problems in diagnosis, treatment issues, and research.

It is helpful to remember that symptoms of classic eating disorders and eating disorders proper begin during the adolescent years (Lucas, Beard, & O'Fallon, 1991). The incidence rate for adolescent AN is about 0.7% (Hoek & Hoeken, 2003).

Data suggest that the incidence rate in the adolescent age group is increasing with each generation, while the adult rates of the disorders are stable (Lucas, Beard, & O'Fallon, 1991; Lucas, Crowson, O'Fallon, & Melton, 1999; van Son et al., 2006). The average age at presentation is about 15 years. Some data have suggested a bimodal age presentation of 13 years of age and about 17 years of age (Halmi, Brodland, & Loney, 1973). Bulimic behaviors also start in the middle high school years (Stice & Agras, 1998), while rates of *DSM-IV* BN appear to be about 2% to 3% in adolescent samples (Flament, Ledoux, Jeammet, Choquet, & Simon, 1995). The most common eating disorder in children and adolescents is EDNOS with rates of 2% to 5% (Turner & Bryant-Waugh, 2004). One of the reasons for higher incidence rates of EDNOS in children and adolescents is the use of diagnostic criteria that are more applicable to adult populations than juvenile patients (Workgroup for the classification of child and Adolescent Eating Disorders, 2007; Nicholls, Chater, & Lask, 2000). In addition, because of physical maturation and increased emphasis on physical attractiveness in adolescent years, there is an increased risk for eating disorders in this age group (Lock, Reisel, & Steiner, 2001). Incidence rates for other feeding and eating problems in adolescents are unknown, though they rarely have an onset beyond the age of 14 years and begin at considerably younger ages.

Diagnostic Issues

Incidence figures illustrate that the main risk period for the onset and diagnosis of most eating and feeding problems is during the childhood and adolescent years. Current diagnostic criteria do not map well onto these epidemiological facts (Nicholls et al., 2000). However, it is interesting to note that in the original *Diagnostic and Statistical Manual*, eating disorders were included in a section entitled "Disorders Usually First Diagnosed in Infancy, Childhood, and Adolescence." Further, there was a *requirement* that onset was before age 25 years (American Psychiatric Association [APA], 1980; Feighner et al., 1972). Regardless of these historical facts, younger patients with classic eating disorders often do present differently from adults (Workgroup for the Classification of Child and Adolescent Eating Disorders, 2007). This difference in symptom presentation is not dissimilar from differences in other diagnoses, such as depression and obsessive–compulsive disorder, for example, wherein developmental, cognitive, and emotional factors are allowed

to vary by age (APA, 1994). In general, compared to adults children and adolescents have less developed verbal expression capacities, limited abstract thinking ability, and are not as aware of their emotions (Holmbeck et al., 2000; Izard & Harris, 1995; Kendall, 1993; Savin-Williams & Bernt, 1990; Sternberg, 1977; Sternberg & Nigro, 1980). As a result, the applicability of some key diagnostic criteria that depend on self report, motivation, and emotional states are challenging to apply directly to younger patients. In addition to these psychological developmental limitations in reporting symptoms, the fact that children and adolescents are in a period of growth complicates the application of physical aspects (e.g., weight and menstruation) of diagnosis as well because it is often difficult to know where these growing children are on their individual growth trajectory (Rome & Ammerman, 2003).

Childhood Eating Problems

Neither of the main diagnostic systems (*Diagnostic and Statistical Manual of Mental Disorders* or International Classification of Diseases) is an adequate classification system for common childhood eating problems that warrant clinical intervention (APA, 1994; Organization, 2005). This has contributed, in part, to a lack of systematic examination of these problems. Bryant-Waugh and Lask have perhaps been most helpful in developing systematic clinical descriptions of three of the most common presentations using the following designations: Selective Eating, Food Phobias, and Food Avoidance Emotional Disorder (Bryant-Waugh & Lask, 2007; Crist & Napier-Phillips, 2001; Nicholls et al., 2000).

Selective eating is principally characterized by extremely picky eating beyond the early childhood years (Nicholls, Randall, & Lask, 2001). The range of acceptable food is often extraordinarily limited while attempts to introduce novel foods are met with determined resistance. In some cases, the child has never eaten a normal range of foods (primary selective eating), but in other cases, food choices become limited in response to an external event (e.g., choking, gagging, or vomiting). Fear of new foods (neophobia) may be associated with enduring temperamental or other conditions such as shyness and autistic spectrum disorder (Carruth & Skinner, 2000; Pliner & Loewen, 1997; Schreck & Smith, 2004; Zucker et al., 2007). On the other hand, picky eating may result from more environmental triggers (Galloway, Lee, & Birch, 2003). Children typically come to specialist attention for these problems because of health and social concerns that arise as a result of selective eating. Children may eat only simple carbohydrates, for example, raising concerns about nutritional needs for growth and health. Other children may be willing to eat only pureed food to avoid worries about choking. Foods may be also associated with specific events, such as eating in a school cafeteria, and this may generalize to avoiding eating in associated environments. The impacts on social processes of these symptoms (e.g., teasing by peers, inability to eat at social functions) are part of the dysfunction associated with selective eating.

Food phobias are a fairly common eating problem in the school-age years. These food phobias generally develop, as in some selective eating cases, in reaction to an external event that causes the child to develop an abnormal and severe fear of food intake. Common concerns about eating in these children include fear of vomiting, choking, diarrhea, or allergic reactions to particular foods or food in general. Swallowing difficulties (sometimes called functional dysphagia) are the hallmark of food phobias though this symptom can be present in many other eating problems of early childhood. Children with food phobias can usually clearly articulate their fear as well as the specific consequences they are attempting to avoid by not eating. The clarity of the relationship between feared stimulus and fear of specific outcome distinguishes these relatively simple phobias from similar concerns that are integrated into broader eating problems in Food avoidance emotional disorder (FAED) and selective eating. Nonetheless, food phobias can become serious health problems when allowed to persist because of dehydration, malnutrition, and weight loss.

FAED (Higgs, Goodyer, & Birch, 1989), a relatively common eating problem seen in middle and late childhood, is characterized by reduced food intake, usually leading to significant weight loss and/or failure to grow. FAED is distinguished from AN because patients recognize they are underweight and claim to wish to weigh more. In addition, instead of shape and weight concerns being prominent, somatic complaints (nausea, feelings of fullness, no appetite, inability to eat) are how these children explain their food avoidance. Many young AN patients report similar complaints at times, but they also show evidence of fear of weight gain during re-feeding efforts. Thus, it may be difficult to distinguish FAED patients from young adolescents with AN until behavior change is instituted. Anxiety related to eating itself—as opposed to weight gain or body shape concerns—also distinguishes these patients from those with AN. At the same time,

children with FAED may become as malnourished and medically compromised as a result of their somatic anxieties as those with AN. It is also likely that some FAED children will develop AN over time.

Anorexia Nervosa in Children and Adolescents

There are a number of ways that a lack of developmental considerations affects *DSM-IV* criteria for AN. One criterion for AN requires an overriding fear of weight gain despite being malnourished. In studies that have included children, it has been noted that despite having behavioral evidence of a fear of weight gain (e.g., intentional restricting eating and over exercise) children themselves do not always *report* being afraid of gaining weight (Fairburn, Cooper, & Safran, 2002; Workgroup for the Classification of Child and Adolescent Eating Disorders, 2007). Although this absence of fear of weight gain has been noted in some other adult populations for cultural reasons (e.g., Chinese women; Lee, 1995), in the case of children the failure to endorse fear of weight gain may be because this type of symptomatic report requires a sophisticated cognitive capacity to identify, label, and take perspective on an emotional experience—capacities that are still emerging during usual development (Boyer, 2006).

Another challenging *DSM-IV* criterion for AN to apply to younger patients is the requirement that patients report body image distortion, or an overemphasis on body weight in evaluating self-worth or denial of the seriousness of the current behaviors on health. Body image development in itself is poorly understood; however, misperceptions of body weight, shape, and size are commonly experienced in adolescence. At the same time, however, being able to report clearly on this experience is beyond most adolescent's self-reflective and self-observing capacities. Self-worth is another highly sophisticated concept that requires perspective taking, abstract thinking, and integration of emotions with thoughts about self, values, and body that many young adolescents are not capable of achieving. Many adolescents may be able to report that being fat makes them feel bad, but the evaluative component of how this relates to self worth eludes them. Usually the interviewer *infers* that these statements represent an overvaluation of shape and weight in terms of self-esteem. This type of inference is not permitted in formal diagnostic processes in adults, but may be essential to accurate diagnosing of children and adolescents. Denial of the seriousness of the current behaviors is the most common way that younger patients meet this criterion. Because the adolescent reports no worry about malnutrition or medical problems associated with this, denial is identified by the evaluator. In addition, there is evidence that adolescents and children are not good at estimating risk in general let alone the specific risks of an eating disorder (Boyer, 2006). For these reasons, diagnosing AN shares much in common with diagnosing mental health problems in children and adolescents with other disorders; overt behaviors rather than verbal reports are often a more reliable index of psychological state and motivation.

In addition to the cognitive, reasoning, and emotional limitations of younger patients, even the medical criteria pose problems for clinicians trying to use the *DSM* to diagnose AN. For example, the first criterion for AN requires that there be weight loss or failure to gain weight during a period of growth, using a body weight less that 85% of expected by height as a clinical guideline (APA, 1994). This qualification allows AN to present differently in a younger population through this reference to a period of growth, but the practical application of this criterion is actually quite challenging. For example, the process of losing weight quickly can lead to serious medical compromise in a child or adolescent well before the suggested threshold (i.e., 85%) is reached. This is further complicated by the wide variation in adolescents in pubertal growth making it difficult to project a clinically meaningful average in a specific case. As a result, this variation may make it impossible to identify changes in previous growth patterns (American Academy of Pediatrics & American College of Obstetricians and Gynecologists, 2006; Berkey, Gardner, Frazier, & Colditz, 2000; Smith & Buschang, 2004). Although the Centers for Disease Control and Prevention (CDC) growth curves are an excellent resource, the data are drawn from cross-sectional data (CDC, 2002). Thus, any particular adolescent may not follow the mean curve, especially those who start puberty early or late or those who are particularly tall or short.

Another problematic criterion is the need for amenorrhea (defined as the absence of at least three consecutive menstrual cycles) for the diagnosis of AN in postmenarchal females. Although this is a problem even in adults with AN, in young adolescents menstrual cycles are relatively commonly inconsistent in periodicity, especially when they first begin. It has been reported that a quarter of girls

will have irregular cycles during the first year after menarche, while half of these will continue to have irregular cycles in the second postmenarchal year (van Hoof et al., 1998). At the same time, this is the age group most at risk for developing AN. It is therefore often difficult to ascertain whether menses have been missed because of normal variation or truly associated with AN. This criterion is also impossible to apply to males, who, when they present with AN, do so most commonly during adolescence. Thus, young females who are postmenarchal are held to a higher diagnostic threshold with the amenorrhea criterion than either males or premenstrual females. Recent reports suggest that this criterion is also not clinically helpful in adults with AN (Roberto, Steinglass, Mayer, Attia, & Walsh, 2008).

Bulimia Nervosa in Children and Adolescents

As is the case with AN, developmental processes and capacities have an impact on accurate diagnosis of BN in children and adolescents (APA, 1994). It had been thought that binge eating and purging behaviors was a problem of young adults, and although this older age group is the main diagnostic risk group for full syndrome BN using current criteria, it is clear that bulimic behaviors often start in middle adolescence (Stice & Agras, 1998) and have been found in children as young as 5 years old (Bryant-Waugh & Lask, 2007; Lask & Bryant-Waugh, 1992). These facts must be kept in mind when considering the cognitive criteria for BN such as the criterion that specifies that body shape and weight concerns are "unduly" influencing self-evaluation. The ability to report or describe symptoms that fit this criterion requires relatively sophisticated higher order abstract reasoning processes which are still under evolution in the adolescent years (Luna & Sweeney, 2004). For younger children who binge eat and purge, the capacity to make these assessments is even more unlikely to be able to be present. In other *DSM* diagnoses, such as obsessive–compulsive disorder (OCD), the requirement of finding OCD ego-dystonic, for example is waived in children and adolescents (APA, 1994). In addition to the problems of cognitive and self-observing limitations, because children and adolescents are younger, the durations and frequency criteria required for diagnosis should likely be lowered (Workgroup for the Classification of Child and Adolescent Eating Disorders, 2007). The precedent for this type of age related change can be found in major depression and dysthymic disorder for example (APA, 1994).

Others have suggested that because the opportunities to binge eat are limited by circumstances outside their control (parents buy food and monitor it), for children and adolescents, activities such as hiding or secretive eating may be symptomatic equivalents of binge eating in this age group (Marcus & Kalarchian, 2003). These behaviors represent a loss of control similar to that required in adults with BN during a binge episode. Others experts argue that the intent to restrain eating, binge eat, and vomit is evidence of significant psychopathology in this younger age group and may be more important that actual numbers of episodes (Bryant-Waugh, Cooper, Taylor, & Lask, 1996). Although less is known about how purging may be conceived in younger patients, it appears to be less common than in adults perhaps because younger patients have not yet learned how to purge (Peebles, Wilson, & Lock, 2006). Still, it is likely that some of the adverse effects of binge eating and purging on developing children and adolescents both psychologically and medically are greater than in adults (as also appears to be the case in adolescent AN), which supports the case for using lower diagnostic thresholds in this populations (Peebles et al., 2006).

The Problem of Eating Disorders Not Otherwise Specified

As the preceding discussion suggests, many children and adolescents with eating disorders and eating problems are classified under the diagnostic category Eating Disorder Not Otherwise Specified (EDNOS) (Turner & Bryant-Waugh, 2004). The problem of EDNOS as a diagnostic category has been highlighted recently both in adults and child and adolescent patients, because in both groups, albeit for probably somewhat different reasons, patients who are classified under this ambiguous label may not receive diagnostically specific services if they are needed, receive insurance reimbursement for care in some instances, and the severity of their problems underestimated (Fairburn & Bohn, 2005). It has been observed that there is significant symptomatic overlap and cross over among the main eating disorder diagnoses over time in adult samples (Fairburn & Bohn, 2005). Symptomatic overlap includes preoccupation with weight and shape and binge eating and purging episodes. Most migration is from adult AN to EDNOS, though some suggest up to 30% of adult AN patients move to BN (Bulik, Fear, & Pickering, 1997). A much smaller sample of adults with BN migrate to AN (Fairburn, Cooper, Doll, Norman, & O'Connor, 2000). A possible reason

for this is that it is extremely difficult to maintain the purely restricting pattern of AN over the long course. Adding other strategies for trying to lose weight and respond to the demands of extreme weight preoccupation becomes the norm. In contrast, in younger patients, there is initially a distinct profile of patients with AN, restricting type being associated with an anxious, driven, and perfectionistic temperament (Bulik, Sullivan, Fear, & Joyce, 1997; Klump et al., 2000; Woodside et al., 2002). In one recent study, only about 7% of adolescents who presented with restricting AN became BN over a 4-year follow-up period (Lock, Couturier, & Agras, 2006). There have been no longer term follow-up studies of adolescent BN samples, so it is unclear how they will ultimately progress (le Grange et al., 2008; le Grange, Crosby, Rathouz, & Leventhal, 2007). What data are available, though, do not suggest that a substantial portion are moving toward becoming AN over time.

Putting these data together, it seems that a fair proportion of EDNOS in adults is the result of more chronic eating disorders that have adopted a mixture of symptoms over time combined with some newer subthreshold cases (Fairburn & Bohn, 2005). In children and adolescents, most EDNOS is due to subthreshold cases (i.e., not meeting AN or BN criteria as discussed above) or are different types of eating problems almost exclusively presenting in this younger age group (e.g., FAED, food phobias, selective eating). The distinction is important, because the way to achieve greater clarity, at least for younger patients with AN and BN, about how to classify their eating disorders accurately would be to adopt diagnostic criteria that accurately describe AN and BN in this younger population. For children and adolescents, an ad hoc workgroup has taken on the task of making refinements to DSM to capture better the developmental issues described (Workgroup for the Classification of Child and Adolescent Eating Disorders, 2007).

In an interesting recent article, Peebles and colleagues describe the relationship between medical problems and those diagnosed with AN, BN, and EDNOS in a large adolescent sample. These authors found that AN and BN patients differed in terms of medical severity with AN patients being more physically compromised. However, the surprising finding was that EDNOS cases that resembled subthreshold AN patients were similarly medically compromised as those who met full DSM-IV criteria, while EDNOS cases that resembled subthreshold BN patients were also similarly compromised as those who met full *DSM-IV* criteria for BN. The authors suggested incorporating most of the partial (subthreshold cases) into the respective AN or BN diagnoses based on their common medical severity reclassified 86% of EDNOS cases. This could be an important additional strategy to consider when grouping similar diagnostic groups together in terms of similar clinical or social impairment.

In another recent study, Schmidt and colleagues (Schmidt et al., 2008) compared the clinical severity, comorbidity, risk factors and treatment outcomes of adolescents (mean age 17.6 years with BN (*n* = 61) or with EDNOS (subthreshold BN) (*n* = 24). Few differences were found; in fact, Eating Disorder Examination (Cooper & Fairburn, 1987) subscale scores were similar between the two groups despite the fact that full syndrome BN patients had higher rates of binge eating and purging. Response to treatment favored the EDNOS patients in terms of abstinence from binge eating and purging, but eating related psychopathology did not differ. Further, those with EDNOS had higher rates of comorbidity than full syndrome BN. Similarly, le Grange and colleagues recently reported that almost half (48%) of the adolescent patients who presented with BN symptoms for evaluation did not meet full criteria for BN (Binford & le Grange, 2005; le Grange, Crosby, Rathouz, & Leventhal, 2007). The only difference between those who had BN and those with subthreshold BN was that patients with BN reported significantly higher frequencies of binge eating and purging. However, while BN patients reported significantly more objectively large binge episodes (OBE) than subthreshold BN patients, the latter reported almost double the amount of subjectively large binge episodes (SBE) compared to their BN counterparts (21 vs. 11 episodes in 28 days; Binford & le Grange, 2005; le Grange et al., 2007).

Comorbid Psychiatric Disorders in Children and Adolescents with Eating Disorders

To complicate further the issue of assessment of children and adolescent eating disorders is the problem of comorbidity. Comorbid problems in adults with eating disorders are well known; however, in younger patients, it is sometimes more difficult to separate the primary symptoms from those of other disorders. Often there is a history of symptoms and behaviors of anxiety or depression in children who develop eating disorders (Kaye et al., 2004). Studies suggest that commonly related problems of AN include anxiety, obsessive thinking, and compulsive and driven behavior (Treasure, 2007). Data from a range of studies find that these features often antedate the onset of AN as well and may remain prominent after resolution of the specific preoccupations and behaviors of the disorder (Anderluch, Tchanturia, Rabe-Hesketh, & Treasure, 2003). Thus, it is common for young patients to present with a history consistent with having these problems and this can confuse evaluators about what to diagnose: Is this an anxiety disorder with a new focus on food? Is this OCD with specific compulsions and obsession about weight and exercise? To make these types of diagnostic distinctions requires specialized training, experience, and judgment.

At the same time, it should be expected that many children and adolescents with eating disorders will have comorbid psychiatric problems at presentation that may also need evaluation and treatment (Kaye et al., 2004; le Grange & Lock, 2002; Zucker et al., 2007). In recent studies of adolescents with bulimia, the rates of comorbidity were as high as in adult samples with rates ranging between 35% and 60% and many (20% to 35%) were on medications for such conditions (le Grange et al., 2007; J. Lock, 2005). Although adolescents with AN typically have fewer comorbid diagnoses than adults, as noted earlier, many do have anxiety symptoms that predate the onset of AN (Bulik, Sullivan, Fear, & Joyce, 1997; Godart, Flament, Perdereau, & Jeammet, 2002; Godart, Flament, Lecrubier, & Jeammet, 2000). Because of the common comorbid symptoms and conditions among children and adolescents with eating disorders, assessment procedures and treatment decisions are more complicated and require additional refinement of skills for accuracy.

Assessment Dilemmas in Children and Adolescents with Eating Disorders

The current "gold standard" for the assessment of eating psychopathology is the Eating Disorder Examination (Cooper, Cooper, & Fairburn, 1989; Cooper & Fairburn, 1987; Fairburn & Cooper, 1993). It comes in both an interview format as well as a self-report form (EDE-Q). There is no clearly accepted standard outcome assessment for child and adolescent eating disorders, though a range of assessment instruments, including a child version of the EDE are available (Bryant-Waugh, Cooper, Taylor, & Lask, 1996; Wade, Byrne, & Bryant-Waugh, 2008). Only recently have norms on the EDE for adolescent samples been published (Wade et al., 2008).

Although the EDE has been used in studies of both adolescent AN and BN, there is a suggestion that for adolescents with AN, the baseline scores on the subscales of the instrument are lower than would be expected given the clinical presentation (Couturier & Lock, 2006a, 2006b). Such minimization and denial are common in AN, but seem even more marked in adolescent AN. Some reports suggest adding a parental component to the EDE would be useful, as would be common in clinical practice and similar to other measures of childhood psychopathology for other disorders (Couturier, Lock, Forsberg, Vanderheyden, & Lee, 2007). Interestingly, these preliminary data suggest that the addition of a parental report to adolescents with eating disorders appears to lead to more clinically reliable outcomes for AN, but not BN (Couturier et al., 2007). It may be that adolescents with BN are more developmentally prepared to relate their behaviors to the kind of questions that the EDE posits. Scores on the EDE for adult and adolescent BN patients are similar to one another and are higher than scores for either adult or adolescent AN patients, for example (Binford & le Grange, 2005; Binford, le Grange, & Jellar, 2005).

In another recent report, House and colleagues suggest that an online version of the Development and Well Being Assessment (DAWBA) may be superior to the EDE (House, Eisler, Simic, & Micali, 2008). This study compared the diagnostic agreement of the EDE to the DAWBA in relation to a multidisciplinary team clinical diagnosis. The EDE was administered by an experienced evaluator, while the DAWBA included both child and parent reports. Compared to the clinical diagnosis, the EDE failed to identify an eating disorder in 35% of cases (10 with AN and 10 EDNOS), while the DAWBA failed to identify an eating disorder in 5.3% (3 cases) of clinical cases. In 35% of the cases that were correctly identified by DAWBA, parental reports were the sole basis for making the correct assessment. It is noteworthy that the sample for this study had only two subjects with a clinical diagnosis of BN and both of those did not have sufficient data to include the analysis. These authors suggest that the privacy of the online version of the DAWBA (as opposed to the face-to-face interview required in the EDE) may also have contributed to its performance. Further, they suggest that because the DAWBA was completed at home, the threat of forced treatment (in particular hospitalization) did not interfere as much with providing accurate information. Thus, although the EDE remains the gold standard assessment, there are likely ways to improve its usefulness for children and adolescents. Adding a parental component and perhaps an online version might improve the match between clinical diagnoses and those generated by the EDE (Couturier et al., 2007). Further studies of assessment of adolescents with eating disorders are warranted.

Assessment of Outcome/Recovery

Closely related to the problem of assessment, though independent of it conceptually, is the lack of clear definitions of recovery in eating disorders. Indeed, part of the problem with clear definitions rests with the lack of an agreed upon standard set of measures or assessment procedures. However, there is not substantive agreement on how recovery should be defined (Couturier & Lock, 2006c, 2006d). In the BN literature, abstinence of binge eating and purging for the last 28 days (as measured by the EDE) is commonly considered a good outcome category. However, scores on psychological measures (e.g., weight and shape concerns, dietary restraint) that are commonly elevated are not included in this type of outcome construct. In other words, behavioral improvement is often considered recovery in BN, while psychopathological variables related to weight and shape concern, though thought to be the maintaining cognitive processes for the disorder, are ignored. Although it may be reasonable to use such a standard to measure short-term treatment response, the notion of recovery conveys within it the idea of eliminating or at least reducing the risk of relapse.

Two examples of how this problem plays out in child and adolescent eating disorders can be considered. Couturier and Lock examined the impact of varying definitions of recovery on a population of adolescents treated for AN (Couturier & Lock, 2006c). They found that subsuming exactly the same data under a range of proposed definitions of good outcome or recovery resulted in short-term remission rates ranging from 4% to 90%. Most of the variation was due to varying weight thresholds, use of menstruation in the definition, and the amount of change required on psychological measures. In examining the same patients over the longer term, recovery rates also varied widely—57% to 94% (Couturier & Lock, 2006d). Most of the difference was due to varying weight thresholds used in defining recovery.

Turning to a recent study of adolescents with BN, le Grange and colleagues (2007) reported that changes in continuous variables versus categorical recovery (defined as abstinence from binge eating and purging) yielded different interpretation of treatment effectiveness. In this randomized controlled trial (RCT), family therapy was compared to individual therapy. There were no differences in outcome when using changes in continuous variables; however, when using abstinence as the categorical outcome, family therapy was clearly superior to individual therapy. These finding illustrate the potential importance of defining recovery for understanding if treatment is helpful. Depending on the study's goals, symptom reduction may be a reasonable measure of treatment response; however, if recovery is the goal, then a different measure such as abstinence may be needed. However, as noted earlier, simple behavioral change may be inadequate as measure because of the potential for relapse due to continued risks associated with eating related psychopathology. As it turns out, in the study of le Grange and colleagues there was significant relapse from abstinence in both groups over the 6-month follow-up period. Interestingly, when examining moderators and mediators of treatment outcome, both behavioral and psychopathology (as measured by the EDE) were found to significantly differentiate treatment response between the two treatments (le Grange, Crosby, & Lock, 2006). Patients with lower levels of eating-related psychopathology and behaviors experienced better outcomes in family therapy, but in patients with higher levels, there were no differences in the results for both treatments. Further, in an exploratory study of mediators of treatment, changes in psychopathology rather than behaviors were found in family therapy rather than individual therapy (Lock et al., 2008).

These studies illustrate the need to include both behavioral and eating-related psychopathological measures when defining recovery from child and adolescent eating disorders (Couturier & Lock, 2006d). Defining recovery may be particularly relevant for younger patients for whom this may be a reasonable goal. With more chronic adult patients, recovery may not be attainable in many cases, though significant abatement of clinical symptoms may still be possible. As with many disorders, early effective intervention is more likely to lead to long-lasting recovery compared to later interventions that may limit symptoms and improve quality of life in more chronic cases. It may be reasonable to consider different standards or thresholds for remission and recovery in younger patients than those who are chronically disordered. In other words, because younger patients may be more responsive to treatments for the reasons we have discussed earlier, a higher expectation for treatment might be reasonable.

On the other hand, setting the bar too high for treatment response in older and more chronic patients might undervalue treatments for this group.

The EDE and other measures of psychopathology may also not be sufficient to capture other aspects recovery that patients, families, and society value. Quality of life issues, ability to go to school, socialize, and safely leave home for college and work are important measures of recovery from this perspective. Little in the way of uniform evaluation of these types of outcomes has been systematically applied. There is currently an eating disorder specific quality of life measure being tested that may be helpful in measure some of these key variables (Engel et al., 2006). A version for younger patients with eating disorders is also being developed. Fairburn and colleagues have also recently developed and tested a measure of functional impairment related to eating disorders in adults that may be of use in this regard as well (Bohn & Fairburn, 2008). However, this latter instrument has yet to be used in younger populations and may need adjustments for this age group.

Treatment of Children and Adolescents with Eating Disorders

Treatment research in eating disorders has largely focused on adult patients with AN, BN, and BED (Mitchell, Agras, & Wonderlich, 2007). Comparatively little research has focused on child and adolescent eating disorders (Bulik, Berkman, Kimberly, Brownly, & Lohr, 2007; le Grange & Lock, 2002). This situation is similar to research in most areas of psychology and psychiatry where adult studies predominate; however, unlike that of many psychiatric disorders, the onset of these disorders, as has been discussed previously, is predominantly in the adolescent years. The focus on adult studies and clinical practice has in many ways led to treatment strategies and paradigms that are not developmentally appropriate for younger patients (APA, 2000; Lock, 2002). Often such programs remove adolescents from their parents, exclude parents from treatment, and overemphasize self-management. However, current research, mostly from treatment studies of adolescent AN, as there are few studies of adolescent BN treatment, suggest that a different strategy should be utilized with adolescent patients that encompasses the following features: (1) early intervention, (2) outpatient treatment, (3) parent involvement, (4) family therapy, (5) adjusting treatments to address the development limitations and processes of younger patients, and (6) adequate medical oversight.

Early Intervention

Considerable pessimism has been expressed about the potential for treatment to be effective in AN (Halmi et al., 2005). This has arisen to a large degree as a result of observations about the treatment response in adults with AN. Indeed, for this population, treatment study results are discouraging. Most studies of any scale have very large treatment attrition rates, averaging about 50% (Halmi et al., 2005; Walsh et al., 2006). Further, outcomes even for those who stay in treatment have not supported any specific treatment as highly effective or superior to other treatments (Fairburn, 2005). In contrast, treatment studies for adolescents with AN, especially those who receive treatment early in the course of the disorder, are more positive. Adolescents can be retained in studies where attrition rates are usually between 10% and 15% and overall outcomes are generally better than in adult samples regardless of treatment type (le Grange & Lock, 2005).

Some have suggested that these more optimistic observations are the result of adolescents being "less ill" or "easier to treat" and depending on what one means by these comments, this may well be the case. If by saying adolescents are "less ill" one means they are less medically or psychiatrically acutely compromised, then this would be mistaken. Adolescents with AN are especially vulnerable to medical complications during the acute period of onset of severe malnutrition (Golden et al., 2003). Also, adolescents with AN, though perhaps more actively denying their disorder, present with the same level of weight loss and behavioral preoccupations (dieting and exercise) associated with AN as their adult counterparts, with the exception that fewer present with the binge/purge subtype of AN (Peebles, Wilson, & Lock, 2006). On the other hand, if by being "less ill" one means that they are less entrenched in their disorder, this is likely to be often true. Because in many adolescent cases, the disorder is discovered relatively early in the course (within a year or so of onset), the impact of chronic reinforcement of the psychological and behaviors of AN may be less pronounced. Further, there is less time for integrating AN as fully into the coping style and personality of the person. In other words, AN has not yet become a fully adapted coping strategy in adolescents.

Regarding the contention that adolescents are "easier to treat"—this again may be the case,

depending on what one means. If by "easier to treat" one is suggesting that adolescents with AN engage easily and cooperatively with therapists who aim to make them gain weight, then "no" this is not true. Adolescents with AN are as reluctant to seek help, are as challenging to engage, show similar decrees of low motivation, and may be even less able to use talking therapy than adults with AN because of the stage of their cognitive development. Thus, if one means by "easier to treat" that adolescents with AN are willing, able, and insightful partners in psychological therapy, then again in most cases, this would not be accurate. However, if by "easier to treat" one means that once engaged in age-appropriate treatment, more adolescents with AN will respond, then the data on outcomes support this view. In general, based on available studies, fewer adolescents drop out of treatment, more respond to treatment, and they appear to relapse at lower rates once treated (Lock, Couturier, Bryson, & Agras, 2006).

These observations about how adolescents with AN differ from their adult counterparts also appear to be echoed, though with less substantial empirical support, in adolescents with BN as well (le Grange, Crosby, & Lock, 2008). The overall outcome data available suggest that specific treatments for adolescents with BN lead to abstinence rates of about 40% to 50% in this age group, fairly similar to that in adult samples (le Grange, Crosby, Rathouz, & Leventhal, 2007; Schmidt et al., 2007). However, in a comparison of outcomes of adolescents (mean age 17.5 years) with partial BN to those with full syndrome BN, Schmidt and colleagues found that those with a lower frequency of binge eating and purging reach abstinence faster than those with full syndrome BN (Schmidt et al., 2008). These authors noted, however, that psychological concerns about weight and shape did not differ. le Grange and colleagues, in their study of a younger sample of adolescents with BN and partial BN (mean age 16.1 years), found that abstinence was moderated by the frequency of binge eating and purging episodes, but also by the degree of eating-related psychopathology as measured by the EDE (le Grange et al., 2008). Subjects with lower rates of binge eating and purging and lower scores on the EDE were more likely to achieve abstinence. Both of these studies had a relatively narrow age range and duration of disorder in their sample, so the data about the impact of these specific factors on these variables could not be assessed. However, these preliminary data lend credence to the idea that adolescents with BN may be more responsive to treatment than adults when their symptoms are addressed while still at lower levels, which in many cases will be earlier in the course of illness.

Taken together, the studies on adolescent AN and BN support the idea that early intervention will likely lead to better outcomes. This may be the case because cognitions and behaviors are less entrenched and therefore more tractable rather than because the adolescents themselves are less acutely ill. Certainly in AN, the ability to change the trajectory of outcome in adolescents is compelling. Follow-up data from treatment studies suggest that adolescents with AN who are treated effectively are less likely to relapse than adults (Eisler et al., 1997; Eisler, Simic, Russell, & Dare, 2007; Lock, Couturier, & Agras, 2006). In other words, treatment gains for adolescent AN are maintained in these younger patients, suggesting that many are recovered. It will be important to see if these results are found in adolescents with bulimia.

It may seem self-evident to some that early intervention should lead to better outcome. Certainly, one would expect this from studies of other medical diseases wherein earlier intervention improves outcome. Unfortunately, for eating disorders, parents are too often told that their children with early symptoms of AN are going through normal developmental processes and are falsely reassured about their child's preoccupations and behaviors. Given the limitations of interventions with adults with eating disorders, early and definitive interventions during the window of opportunity before these diseases become chronic is critical. With the current lack of success of interventions for adult AN, early intervention is our only realistic strategy that has much hope for changing outcomes (Agras et al., 2004).

Outpatient Treatment

For many years, the main approach to most severe psychiatric disorders was inpatient hospitalization. However, for a range of clinical, financial, and civil liberty issues, the use of hospitalization for most psychiatric disorders has dramatically decreased. While this has not always led to beneficial outcomes in particular cases, in general, the movement toward community-based and home-based care has led to more dignified, normal, and effective treatment. For eating disorders and particularly AN, however, there continues to be an emphasis on the use of intensive treatments including hospitals, day treatment programs, and residential treatment programs (Frisch, Franko, & Herzog, 2006). There is undoubtedly a group of patients who require and benefit from these treatments and at times such programs are life-saving. Their usefulness for early-onset eating disorders and specifically adolescents with eating disorders appears to be more limited.

From a developmental perspective, removing an adolescent from his or her home and community (including the school) is a dramatic and potentially psychologically hazardous decision. Adolescents remain functionally dependent on their parents, relationally focused on family members and close peers, and socially integrated in their local communities. Hospitalization, however well intended and no matter how skilled and caring the staff of such institutions may be, cannot fully mitigate the loss of this interpersonal network of family and friends. Further, studies do not support that hospitalization for eating disorders (particularly AN) is systematically superior to outpatient care, nor is learning or behavioral change that is made in these settings generalized by the patients on discharge, and finally, the costs of these intensive interventions are extraordinarily high and may not be warranted in many instances (Byford et al., 2007; Crisp et al., 1991; Gowers et al., 2007; Gowers, Weetman, Shore, Hussain, & Elvins, 2000).

It has been noted that hospitalization is effective in weight restoration (Jenkins, 1987). However, relapse after hospitalization is very high (Lay, Jennen-Steinmetz, Reinhard, & Schmidt, 2002; Lock, 2003). These data suggest that learning in inpatient and similar settings does not generalize to the settings where the learning needs to be applied. In other words, being able to eat and gain weight and not binge or purge in a hospital setting does not lead to the ability to do this at home. This observation is not surprising, as basic learning principles are consistent with this. Thus, however hopeful we are for our professional successes in hospital and other intensive treatment settings being transplanted and utilized at home, we are working against known processes of relevancy and generalization of learning.

Two studies have compared the effectiveness of hospital treatment to outpatient treatment for AN. The first study was conducted by Crisp and colleagues (Crisp et al., 1991). These authors compared several outpatient treatments to assessment only and hospitalization treatment. The mean age of subjects in this study was about 22 years but some adolescents were included in the sample. The study experienced difficulties in recruitment to the hospital arm and solved this problem by continuing to recruit to this arm nonrandomly. Even with the biases created by this unsatisfactory solution, hospitalization failed to demonstrate systematic benefits over any of the outpatient treatments. All treatments were superior to the assessment only group. More recently, Gowers and colleagues conducted a large study of 167 adolescents with AN (Gowers et al., 2007). Subjects were randomized to either specialized outpatient treatment, treatment as usual, or specialized hospital care. This study again had difficulties maintaining randomized cohorts, as many of those randomized chose to migrate to other treatments offered in the study. This was a particular problem for those randomized to hospital, where the attrition rate was 50% compared to the overall attrition rate of 35%. As noted earlier, attrition from outpatient treatment in adolescent studies is usually much lower than this. Examining the outcomes utilizing an intent-to-treat analysis no differences between treatments were found.

In addition to being ineffective and difficult to apply, hospitalization is very costly. As Streigel-Moore observed in a recent study of insurance claims, AN was as costly as schizophrenia to treat (Streigel-Moore, Leslie, Petrill, Garvin, & Rosenheck, 2000). The largest source of these costs was the use of hospital care. Byford and colleagues (2007) examined the cost-effectiveness of the three treatments studied by Gowers described earlier. Although there were no treatment outcome differences between the groups, the costs of hospitalization greatly exceeded those of comparative treatments. In that study, the specialized outpatient treatment provided was most cost-effective. In another study, the costs of treatment in an RCT were examined (Lock, Couturier, & Agras, 2008). The majority of costs were for medical hospitalization and medical care, despite the relatively small percentage of time spent in these settings.

Because adolescents are developmentally and socially highly dependent on their families and communities, because learning in hospitals has limited generalizability, and because hospitalization is not more effective than outpatient care and is expensive, the preferred treatment is community-based treatment for adolescents with eating disorders. Long hospitalization for weight restoration, day programs that isolate children from their friends and socialize them to psychiatric setting, and residential programs for long-term care are generally to be avoided with younger nonchronic patients with eating disorders.

Parental Involvement

There was little enthusiasm for parents being involved in the care of adolescents with AN when it was first described more than 125 years ago. Parents were described as being the "worst attendants" by Gull and as "pernicious" influences by Charcot (Gull, 1874; Silverman, 1997). Parents were not viewed at this time as necessarily causing AN, but instead as ineffective agents with their children. Other later schools of psychoanalysis and psychology suggested otherwise (Thoma, 1967). Like "refrigerator mothers" in autism and "double-binding" parents in schizophrenia, parents of children with eating disorders were implicated in causing the disorder. The evidence of parental psychopathology in causation of eating disorders is not convincing. A few studies report poorer family functioning in AN (e.g., Humphrey, 1986, 1987; Strober & Humphrey, 1987b), but these are based on self-reports and involve samples of chronically ill patients. Thus it is difficult to determine precedence of cause or effect. Also, community samples (McNamara & Loveman, 1990; Råstam & Gillberg, 1991) report fewer differences (Blouin, Zuro, & Blouin, 1990). Observational studies by other authors (Kog & Vandereycken, 1989; Roijen, 1992) note statistical differences between AN families and controls, but most scores are within a "normal" range (Ravi, Forsberg, Fitzpatrick, & Lock, 2009). Parents of children with AN have been described as being overly controlling, intrusive, conflict avoidant, and enmeshed (Minuchin, Rosman, & Baker, 1978). Parents of children with BN have been described as under controlled, chaotic, and disorganized (Strober & Humphrey, 1987a). While some of these observations may have some validity, the relationship between these observations and causation, perpetuation, or maintenance of specific eating disorder symptoms is conjectural.

Treatment studies of adolescents that have included parents also contest the view that parents should not be involved in helping their children with eating disorders. Most studies of adolescents have included parents either in collateral sessions or in some form of family therapy (Lock & Gowers, 2005). It is difficult to reconcile these studies' findings with the common admonition that is made to parents "to stay out of it because eating disorders are disorders of control and you will interfere with your child's need to develop a sense of control in ways other than through food and weight." Data are now available on treatments that recommend the exact opposite of this advice—that is, treatments the encourage parents to find ways to restore weight or inhibit binge eating or purging, are those that have the most empirical support for effectiveness, particularly for adolescent AN.

Family Therapy

Family therapy for AN has been recommended as a treatment for eating disorders in children and adolescents since the 1970s (Minuchin, Rosman, & Baker, 1978). It has much less often been considered for adolescent BN (Dodge, Hodes, Eisler, & Dare, 1995). The specific types of family therapy used have varied over the past 40 years (Dare & Eisler, 1997), but most treatment studies have used a form of family-based treatment (FBT) based on a nonpathological model of families and aimed at helping parents take charge of weight restoration in AN (Dare & Eisler, 1997; Lock & le Grange, 2001; Lock, le Grange, Agras, & Dare, 2001). Many of the interventions used in this form of family therapy are derived from other schools of family therapy including structural, strategic, and narrative schools (Haley, 1973; Minuchin, Rosman, & Baker, 1978; Selvini Palazzoli, 1988; White & Epston, 1990). Despite this though, the starting point of FBT differs from these other family therapies principally because it is agnostic as to the cause of AN. Interventions in FBT address impediments to weight restoration rather than any hypothesized psychopathology in parents or the family process. Eisler (2005) has argued that the problems the parents and family are having are best considered as a response and adaptation to the problems that AN causes them rather than the other way around. This starting point shapes interventions in the direction of a solution based therapy as opposed to a process oriented or psychodynamic therapy. Such a perspective reduces blame and guilt for all family members and promotes the reemergence of confidence in the parents about their ability to help their child with AN. Enabling parents by providing guidance, support, and expert consultation while leaving decision making up to them, facilitates empowerment.

More recently, family therapy of this type has been modified to account for developmental and symptomatic differences between adolescents with AN and BN so that is applicable to adolescents with BN (le Grange & Lock, 2007). The main interventions are similar, but as adolescents with BN tend to be older and more independent than most AN patients, the therapist more actively elicits collaboration between the adolescent with BN and the parents in trying to change dysfunctional eating patterns, purging, and exercise. This is possible, because most adolescents with BN are ashamed of their symptoms and would prefer an alternative strategy to help them with their eating related problems. However, like adolescents with AN, they can still use help to from their parents to disrupt their bulimic symptoms. By helping the parents and family understand the dilemmas their child with BN is facing, there is an opportunity to reduce shame as well as increase understanding of their child's dilemmas. This permits collaboration on symptom management and control. For a time parents help their child establish a normal pattern of eating and help to reduce episodes of binge eating and purging by monitoring. Therapy provides no focus on the cognitive processes associated with BN.

FBT has systematic support for its usefulness with adolescents with AN and to a lesser extent for adolescents with BN (Eisler et al., 2000; le Grange, Crosby, Rathouz, & Leventhal, 2007; le Grange, Eisler, Dare, & Russell, 1992; Lock, Agras, Bryson, & Kraemer, 2005; Robin et al., 1999; Russell, Szmukler, Dare, & Eisler, 1987; Schmidt et al., 2007). Six randomized clinical trials focused on outpatient treatment for adolescent AN have been published. All but one of these included an examination of family therapy similar in the form to FBT (Gowers et al., 2007). When compared to supportive individual therapy or developmentally focused individual therapies, family therapy was superior in two small trials (Russell, Szmukler, Dare, & Eisler, 1987). Other studies compared various forms or doses of the same type of family therapy (Eisler et al., 2000; le Grange, Eisler, Dare, & Russell, 1992; Lock, Agras, Bryson, & Kraemer, 2005). These data support the overall effectiveness of this specific form of therapy for adolescent AN of short duration (less than 3 years). Between 60% and 80% of patients are demonstrably clinically improved (le Grange & Lock, 2005). Only two RCTs have examined this type of FBT for BN (le Grange, Crosby, Rathouz, & Leventhal, 2007; Schmidt et al., 2007). In both studies, adolescents with BN improved, achieving abstinence rates similar to those expected in adult studies for BN using CBT. However, in one study, guided self-help CBT was as effective as family therapy (Schmidt et al., 2007), while in the other family therapy was superior to an individual psychodynamic therapy (le Grange, Crosby, Rathouz, & Leventhal, 2007).

Adjusting Treatments to Address the Developmental Limitation Processes of Younger Patients

Children and adolescents differ from adults because they have different cognitive capacities, are dependent on families, are involved in developing social roles and identities, and have different abilities to process and understand their emotional states.

As suggested earlier, these differences lead to special issues in diagnosing younger patients with eating disorders. They also make it necessary to adjust treatments to better match the needs of younger patients. In addition to therapies that directly involve the family to address these differences, there are ways to create a better fit of therapy and patient for individual therapies for eating disorders as well. The two examples discussed in the text that follows are CBT for adolescents (CBT-A) and Developmentally Focused Therapy (AFT) for adolescent AN (Fitzpatrick, Moye, Hostee, le Grange, & Lock, 2010; Lock, 2005).

ADJUSTMENTS TO CBT FOR ADOLESCENT BN

A number of systematic studies support the use of CBT for adults with BN (Agras et al., 1992; Agras, Schneider, Arnow, Raeburn, & Telch, 1989; Agras, Telch, Arnow, Eldredge, & Marnell, 1997; Agras et al., 1994; Agras, Walsh, Fairburn, Wilson, & Kraemer, 2000; Barlow, Blouin, & Blouin, 1988; Cooper & Steere, 1995; Fairburn, Jones, Peveler, Hope, & O'Connor, 1993; Leitenberg et al., 1994; Mitchell, 1991; Pope, Hudson, Jonas, & Yurgelin-Todd, 1983; Walsh & Devlin, 1995; Wilfley et al., 1993). As a result, CBT is currently the treatment of choice for adult BN (National Institute for Clinical Excellence [NICE], 2004). Unfortunately, there is only one randomized clinical trial and one two small case series studies that report on the use of CBT for adolescents with BN (Lock, 2005; Schapman & Lock, 2006; Schmidt et al., 2007). These studies suggest that CBT is acceptable to and beneficial to adolescents with BN. However, to address this younger population, adjustments to CBT have been described and were used in the case series data (le Grange & Lock, 2002; le Grange & Schmidt, 2005; Lock, 2005). A manualized version of CBT for adolescents (CBT-A) has been published (Lock, 2005).

As modified for adolescents, CBT-A uses the same conceptual model as in standard CBT (Fairburn, 1981). To adjust the standard form of CBT, therapists engage the adolescent earlier in treatment than would be typical with adults. Adolescents are often reluctant participants in therapy, so the therapist tries to see them more frequently early on, including sometimes reaching out to them by telephone to demonstrate their interest in the adolescent's well-being. When working with adolescents therapists use more concrete examples to illustrate their points, and endeavor to relate the themes of therapy to concerns of adolescents (e.g., school, peer groups, early dating experience, dance, etc.). Therapists also explore the role of these age-related issues and developmental tasks as possible triggers for weight and shape concerns that are driving bulimic behaviors. Problem-solving is more often used than formal cognitive restructuring in this age group. In addition, because most adolescents live with their parents, who buy food, determine meal times, and provide the overall structure for their lives, collateral sessions are a routine part of CBT-A. In these sessions, parents are educated about BN, the goals and processes of CBT-A are described, and parents are informed about their potential role in supporting CBT-A (e.g., changing triggers in the home environment, assist with meal time structure, and provide emotional support for their child).

Even though there remains only limited empirical support for CBT for adolescents with BN, there is reason to be hopeful that a version of CBT that is appropriate for this age group will be helpful. A developmental focus that takes into consideration developmental cognitive, emotional, and social needs as well as utilizes family resources available to adolescents likely enhances standard CBT for this age group.

ADOLESCENT-FOCUSED THERAPY FOR ADOLESCENT AN

Parental involvement is necessary for all therapies provided to minors, but not all patients or families can use family therapy for AN. There are no definitive data helping therapists to identify which patient or family in particular may not be able to use family therapy, but there are some indications in the literature that family therapy may not be as good for single parent or nonintact families, for patients with severe obsessive and compulsive features, or perhaps families with high levels of criticism of one another, particularly the patient (Eisler et al., 2000; le Grange, Eisler, Dare, & Hodes, 1992; Lock, Agras, Bryson, & Kraemer, 2005). Clinically there are situations that make it difficult to use FBT (e.g., abuse, severe psychiatric disturbance in family, severe parental discord). Also, some older adolescents who are developmentally and legally independent of their parents might insist on individual treatment. For these patients, the choice of therapy might be an Adolescent Focused Therapy (AFT) that is derived from a developmentally informed individual therapy (i.e., Ego-Oriented Individual Therapy) that has been used in two randomized clinical trials and described in manual form (Fitzpatrick, Moye, Hostee, le Grange, & Lock, 2010; Robin, Siegal,

Koepke, Moye, & Tice, 1994). In contrast to a behavioral focus, AFT engages the adolescent around psychological needs that AN preoccupations and symptoms meet (e.g., feelings of accomplishment, pride, self-sufficiency, competency) and helps the adolescent develop alternative strategies to meet these needs or to replace them with other, more healthy alternatives (e.g., increased self-worth, decrease dependence on external measures of accomplishment, accepting personal limitations, interdependency with others). The primary vehicle to accomplish this is through the therapeutic relationship, which is considered as a kind of "re-parenting" aimed at providing a secure environment in which to explore these alternatives. The therapist sets limits on the most dangerous behaviors related to AN (severe dieting, over-exercise) while providing nurture and support for the adolescent. This dual role provides ongoing structure to the therapy that must sufficiently contain the dangerous behaviors of AN through limit setting, while promoting self-acceptance through modeling vulnerability, promoting increased tolerance of difficult emotions, and encouraging risk taking related to alternatives to AN. Thus, the principal aim is to help the patient develop a healthy coping style instead of the avoidant and dangerous coping processes of AN and to improve self-efficacy (Levenkron, 2001).

There is one RCT that demonstrated that a form of therapy similar to AFT was helpful for adolescents with AN (Robin, Siegal, Koepke, Moye, & Tice, 1994; Robin et al., 1999). Patients who received this form of therapy took longer to gain weight and to have a return of menstruation than adolescents who received FBT, but at follow-up there were no differences between the two treatments. The study is too small for substantive conclusions, but AFT appears helpful to some adolescents and is the subject of a larger comparison study currently underway and discussed in the section that follows.

Medication Use in Child and Adolescent Eating Disorders

The benefits of psychotropic medications for eating disorders in adults is best studied in BN (Walsh et al., 1997). Those studies support the use of a range of antidepressant medications, particularly serotonin reuptake inhibitors for BN, but psychological therapies, particularly CBT, lead to better outcomes (Mitchell, Agras, & Wonderlich, 2007). Further, the use of medications as adjunctive therapy does not appear to confer substantial benefit.

No medications have been shown to be systematically effective for adult AN either in the short or long term (Attia, Mayer, & Killory, 2001; Walsh et al., 2006). The only finding about the use of psychotropic medication in adults with AN that seems justifiable based on the limited available data is that current medication options are not generally feasible for use with adults with AN because most refuse to take them for very long (Halmi et al., 2005; Walsh et al., 2006).

The use of medications in children and adolescents with eating disorders has even less evidential support (Couturier & Lock, 2007). No systematic studies of antidepressants or other types of medications have been conducted in adolescents with either AN or BN. One small case series (10 subjects) found that fluoxetine was well tolerated in adolescents with BN in the context of psychotherapy; however, its effectiveness is unknown in this age group (Kotler, Devlin, Davies, & Walsh, 2003). For adolescents with AN, atypical antipsychotics have been used and appear to assist with weight gain and situation anxieties around eating, but no RCTs have yet been published. As concerns rise about the use of psychopharmacologic agents, selective serotonin reuptake inhibitors (SSRIs) and atypical antipsychotics in children and adolescents, the medications most likely to be used with child and adolescent eating disorder patients, appropriate caution is called for when prescribing these types of medications where there is little substantive evidence to support their use (Lock, Walker, Rickert, & Katzman, 2005). At this point, the risks may outweigh the benefits. The main caveat to this is the use of these types of medications for other psychiatric coexisting psychiatric disorders (e.g., anxiety disorders, OCD, depression). One of the complications of using medications even in this context, however, is that eating disorder symptoms often overlap those of some of these conditions (e.g., obsessions over food, anxiety about eating, depression consequent on weight loss and sadness and decreased affect after binge eating or gaining weight). For these reasons, medication use in the population should be in the hands of psychiatrists who are aware of this kind of overlap and tailor their prescribing practices to target symptoms and disorders likely to respond to them. In practice, this will often mean delaying starting a course of medication until there is some symptomatic response to psychological interventions (e.g., weight gain, more normal eating patterns, decreased binge eating or purging).

Medical Monitoring and Nutritional Counseling in Children and Adolescent Eating Disorders

Ancillary support by medical professionals including pediatric medical specialists and nutritionists is common in treatment programs for child and adolescent eating disorders. What is less common is a clear delineation of the roles and responsibilities of these professionals and how they are best integrated with specific treatment approaches. Eating disorders are primarily psychiatric disorders despite the fact that patients with eating disorders, and children and adolescents perhaps even more than adults, may develop severe medical problems as a result of their psychiatrically driven preoccupations and behaviors (Fisher, Golden, Katzman, Kreipe, RE, Rees, J, 1995). Malnutrition due to AN does not appreciably differ from malnutrition associated with nonpsychiatric conditions. Malnutrition leads to hypothermia, bradycardia, hypotension, bone loss, white and gray matter loss, and a reduction in hemopoiesis and hormone production (Golden et al., 2003). Most of these adverse health problems are completely reversible with sustained weight restoration. It is also true that malnutrition itself may help to intensify and maintain self-starvation processes (i.e., with starvation for any reason there is an increased focus on food, increased obsessional activities around eating, and with time decrease appetite and increased activity; Franklin, Schiele, Brozek, & Keys, 1948; Keys, Brozek, & Henschel, 1950). Many of these acute medical problems are more typical in adolescents than in adults. But bone loss and some brain matter loss are exceptions to this, as these persist and worsen over time (Lambe, Katzman, Mikulis, Kennedy, & Zipursky, 1997). Mortality also increases with time and is much more common in adults with AN than in adolescents (Sullivan, 1995).

Recent studies suggest that medical problems in adolescents with eating disorders are somewhat related to diagnosis, with AN patients having more acute medical problems than BN patients (Peebles, Hardy, Wilson, & Lock, in press) At the same time, so-called subthreshold groups of AN patients have as severe medical complications as those that meet full diagnostic criteria. Similarly, BN patients also have concerning medical complications that are often missed. Further, like their AN subthreshold counterparts, BN subthreshold patients have as many and as severe medical problems as those who meet full diagnostic criteria.

These observations make it clear that working with adolescents with eating disorders in an outpatient setting requires continuing medical monitoring to ensure that patients are not dangerously medically compromised. On the other hand, the role of medical providers needs to be a nuanced one that correctly cedes the main behavioral and psychological management of these patients to mental health professionals. This is not to say that the medical team should not provide medical surveillance and education and recommendations about health consequences, but they should be wary of providing other advice that might interfere with therapy. If the adolescent is working in an FBT model in which parents are responsible for weight restoration, communications with the adolescent should include parents so they are informed about current medical needs (Lock & le Grange, 2005). Parents should know if weight progress is being made. Similarly, if the adolescent is being seen by a nutritionist, designing and prescribing meal plans runs counter to the parental role in meal planning and monitoring. Such plans can set up a power struggle between the adolescent and her parents with the nutritionist or physician in the middle. This same admonition applies to medical team members working with adolescents being treated for BN whether in family therapy or CBT-A. In both situations, the medical consequences of binge eating and purging need to be monitored; however, the strategy for assisting with changing these behaviors needs to rest squarely with the family therapist or the CBT therapist.

The use of nutritional advice in eating disorders warrants some special attention. Nutritional advice has been used in a several studies as a control or comparison treatment, and in all cases outcomes have suggested that it is ineffective on its own (Hall & Crisp, 1987; Pike, Walsh, Vitousek, Wilson, & Bauer, 2004). Nonetheless, nutritional counseling is routinely mentioned as an essential component in eating disorder treatments, at least in the United States and Canada, though certainly less so in the United Kingdom, Europe, and Australia (APA, 2000). For adults with eating disorders who buy their own food, manage their own meals, and are responsible for their own weight gain or management, perhaps there is good reason for providing a professional bulwark against the distortions about these matters in eating disorder patients. It must be noted that CBT, the most effective treatment for adult BN, does not include nutritional consultants as a part of standard treatment (Fairburn, 1981). Further, the treatment studies that provide empirical support for CBT have not included nutritional counseling as part of treatment.

For adolescents with AN, though, there are reasons to be judicious in the use of professional dietary advice directly with the adolescent, especially when parents are involved in treatment. The first reason is that meal plans, with their detailed counting, measuring, portions, exchanges, calories, etc., are opportunities for increasing, not decreasing, food-related preoccupations and anxieties. Second, meal plans are artificial strategies for eating and as such are less a stepping stone toward normal eating than they are likely to perpetuate abnormal eating patterns. Third, meal plans worked out with the adolescent and dietician can become a bone of contention between the patient and her parents who are told either to let her handle it while she fails; or, an opportunity to fight over the interpretation of the meal plan if parents are asked to enforce or monitor the plan. In instances when the adolescent may be mostly in charge of her own weight restoration (e.g., in AFT), the use of nutritional advice directly to the adolescent may be beneficial. In the study that used a treatment akin to AFT, nutritional advice was allowed to patients in this arm, for example, and this advice may have contributed to their weight progress over the course of that study (Robin et al., 1999).

Future Directions

The research base guiding our understanding and treatment of eating disorders is extremely limited compared to that of psychiatric disorders of similar prevalence and seriousness. This is particularly the case for eating disorders in younger populations. Moving forward in research in eating disorders for younger patients requires attention to a range of issues, some of them shared with needs in adult eating disorders, but others specific to the needs of these younger patients. Though there are many important issues that complicate research for younger patients, we focus here on those that relate to systematic assessment and definitions of outcome relevant to younger and nonchronic cases. We also discuss some considerations for next steps in research including testing specific new treatments, integrating neuropsychological and neuroscience findings into novel treatments, and evaluating needs to examine longer term outcomes and issues of dissemination of effective treatments.

A number of important clinical trials are currently underway that will likely shed light on some of the vexing problems discussed in this chapter. A relatively large clinical trial for adolescents with AN comparing FBT-AN to AFT has recruited 121 subjects at two sites, completed treatments, and will complete follow-up assessments of those subjects within the coming year. This trial may help to clarify the relative merits of each of these therapies, identify specific populations that are better suited to one of the other therapies (moderators), as well as provide new data to examine mediators of these two treatments. This could be a significant step forward as the results of this study will provide guidance to clinicians about the relative merits of two standard treatment options, family and individual therapy, for their younger patients with AN. Another RCT is being completed in London that compares single-family FBT to a multifamily format (MFG) of this treatment. The MFG treatment is a form of FBT where four to five families meet together and is designed to invigorate families by providing additional support through these meetings as an adjunct to ongoing single family FBT (Eisler, 2005). Results of this study may suggest either general benefit to all patients who receive the booster sessions of MFG or identify subpopulations that have better outcomes if this additional support is provided. Another study of adolescent AN treatment using FBT-AN is a multisite randomized comparison of this treatment to systemic family therapy (SFT). This study is the first study to compare two different theoretical approaches to family therapy for adolescent AN. This study, which is in early recruitment, should help to clarify the specific role of families in treatment of AN as either behavioral change agents (in FBT-AN) or through examination of family processes, goals, and needs (SFT). It is also poised to establish a research network able to recruit AN subjects in sufficient numbers needed for more rigorous study design.

As noted, there are only two randomized controlled trials for adolescent BN. The U.S. National Institutes of Health (NIH) has recently funded a controlled comparison of FBT-BN to CBT-A with the primary goal of clarifying the relative efficacy of the two approaches with younger adolescents with BN. The study should also provide data about moderators and mediators of treatment outcome when the results are available about 5 years hence.

New opportunities for examining neuropsychological, neuroanatomical, and neurofunctional processes and their relationship to eating disorders are just getting started (Fischer, Nguyen, Carter, Putnam, & Kaye, 2007; Uher et al., 2005; Uher, Treasure, & Campbell, 2002; Wagner et al., 2007). Some exciting work on neuropsychological functioning in adults with AN and BN that suggests persistent difficulties in flexibility (set-shifting) and over-focus on details (weak central coherence) are also being examined in younger populations at this time to see if these are present in a nonchronic population of adolescents with AN (Holliday, Tchanturia, Landau, & Collier, 2005; Southgate, Tchanturia, & Treasure, J. 2007; Tchanturia et al., 2004; Tchanturia, Morris, Brecelj, Nikolau, & Treasure, 2004). A specific therapy to address these types of cognitive inefficiencies has been developed for adults with AN and a modified form has been manualized for use with adolescents and is being piloted (Davies & Tchanturia, 2005). The principal aims of such treatment are to increase therapeutic relevancy and acceptability, increase capacity to use psychotherapies by way of building flexibility and central coherence skills through cognitive exercises, and to promote a working relationship with a therapist that supports future more challenging work directed more specifically at changing eating disordered symptoms (Tchanturia, Whitney, & Treasure, 2006). Systematic examination of this form of treatment is just getting under way as part of an NIH-funded pilot study.

Only three studies have provided systematic data on longer term outcome after treatment in an RCT for adolescents with AN (Eisler et al., 1997; Eisler, Simic, Russell, & Dare, 2007; Lock, Couturier, & Agras, 2006). No comparable data for adolescent BN is available. Among the many reasons, studies of longer term outcomes are needed some of the most important are to determine if treatment improvements are maintained; to develop a better understanding of the natural course of the disorder; and to identify markers of chronicity, relapse, and maintenance of recovery.

Another challenge for the field of eating disorders generally, but for adolescent eating disorders specifically, is the need to disseminate effective treatments (Loeb et al., 2007). There are few successful models for dissemination, and because of the special skills needed to assess and treat younger patients with eating disorders, these need to be designed with the developmental needs of these younger patients in mind. Nonetheless, as the goal of clinical research is ultimately to change clinical outcomes on the broadest level, dissemination is essential to achieving this end. Because of the development of manualized versions of a range of treatments for child and adolescent eating disorders—FBT-AN, Family-Systems Therapy for AN, FBT-BN, CBT-A, AFT—the opportunity to use these treatments in other settings is possible (Fitzpatrick, Moye, Hostee, le Grange, & Lock, 2010; le Grange & Lock, 2007;

Lock, 2005; Lock, le Grange, Agras, & Dare, 2001). Already some evidence that FBT-AN can be disseminated has been produced, while the ongoing multisite study comparing family treatments encompasses six treatment sites and 24 therapists affords a further opportunity to explore how effectively the approach can be reproduced in diverse settings. In addition to exploring a range of strategies for dissemination effective treatments, additional studies are needed to determine if treatments can be useful in cross-cultural settings.

Concluding Comment

We have emphasized several important observations about child and adolescent eating disorders. To date, very little study of these eating problems in young childhood has been undertaken. In addition we have observed that even the AN and BN are not easily classified in child and adolescent subjects because of the developmental differences in symptom expression using current criteria. At the same time, available data on treatment provides a more optimistic view of treatment response in younger nonchronic patients with eating disorders.

Based on available studies a number of observations about how best to conduct treatment for younger patients can be made. For the most part, outpatient treatment that involves parents appears to be the best option. Early intervention is also especially effective. Medication treatments cannot yet be recommended for any child and adolescent eating disorder. However, as comorbid conditions are common, medications may be useful for this purpose. Adolescents, even those with subthreshold eating disorders, are particularly sensitive to the effects of malnutrition and purging, so supportive medical monitoring is crucial for safe care of these younger patients in the community.

There is much to anticipate from studies currently underway in AN and BN in adolescents in relation to treatment, matching patients to specific treatments, as well as potentially better understanding how some treatments work. Exciting work in neuropsychology, neuroanatomy, and neuroimaging that is underway in adults is also making its way into studies of adolescents. Studies of adults suggest that executive functioning (inhibition and disinhibition), cognitive inefficiencies (set-shifting and central coherence), and reward systems may be new targets for interventions. There are no published studies of adolescents examining these issues to date. However, when these studies are undertaken, they may help us to better understand underlying biological mechanisms of these eating disorders, to identify new targets of treatment, and to develop novel strategies to address eating problems earlier and more effectively.

References

Agras, W. S., Brandt, H., Bulik, C. M., Dolan-Sewell, R., Fairburn, C. G., Halmi, C. A., et al. (2004). Report of the National Institutes of Health Workshop on Overcoming Barriers to Treatment Research in Anorexia Nervosa. *International Journal of Eating Disorders, 35*, 509–521.

Agras, W. S., Rossiter, E. M., Arnow, B., Schneider, J. A., Telch, C. F., Raeburn, S. D., et al. (1992). Pharmacologic and cognitive-behavioral treatment for bulimia nervosa: A controlled comparison. *American Journal of Psychiatry, 149*(1), 82–87.

Agras, W. S., Schneider, J. A., Arnow, B., Raeburn, S. D., & Telch, C. F. (1989). Cognitive-behavioral and response-prevention treatments for bulimia nervosa. *Journal of Consulting & Clinical Psychology, 57*(2), 215–221.

Agras, W. S., Telch, C. F., Arnow, B., Eldredge, K., & Marnell, M. (1997). One-year follow-up of cognitive-behavioral therapy for obese individuals with binge eating disorder. *Journal of Consulting & Clinical Psychology, 65*(2), 343–347.

Agras, W. S., Telch, C. F., Arnow, B., Eldredge, K., Wilfley, D. E., Raeburn, S. D., et al. (1994). Weight loss, cognitive-behavioral, and desipramine treatments in binge eating disorder. An additive design. *Behavior Therapy, 25*, 209–238.

Agras, W. S., Walsh, B. T., Fairburn, C. G., Wilson, G. T., & Kraemer, H. C. (2000). A multicenter comparison of cognitive-behavioral therapy and interpersonal psychotherapy for bulimia nervosa. *Archives of General Psychiatry, 57*, 459–466.

American Academy of Pediatrics, & American College of Obstetricians, Gynecologists (2006). Menstruation in girls and adolescents: Using the menstrual cycle as a vital sign. *Pediatrics, 118*, 2245–2250.

American Psychiatric Association (APA). (1980). *Diagnostic and statistical manual of mental disorders* (3rd ed.). Washington, DC: Author.

American Psychiatric Association (APA). (1994). *Diagnostic and statistical manual of mental disorders* (4th ed.). Washington, DC: Author.

American Psychiatric Association (APA). (2000). Practice guideline for the treatment of patients with eating disorders (revision). American Journal of Psychiatry, *157* (Supplement).

Anderluch, M., Tchanturia, K., Rabe-Hesketh, S., & Treasure, J. L. (2003). Childhood obsessive compulsive personality traits in adult women with eating disorders: Defining a broader eating disorder phenotype. *American Journal of Psychiatry, 160*, 242–247.

Attia, E., Mayer, L., & Killory, E. (2001). Medication response in the treatment of patients with anorexia nervosa. *Journal of Psychiatric Practice, 7*, 157–162.

Barlow, J., Blouin, J., & Blouin, A. (1988). Treatment of bulimia with desipramine: A double-blind crossover study. *Canadian Journal of Psychiatry, 33*, 129–133.

Berkey, C., Gardner, J., Frazier, A., & Colditz, G. (2000). Relation of childhood diet and body size to menarche and adolescent growth in girls. *American Journal of Epidemiology, 152*, 446–452.

Binford, R., & le Grange, D. (2005). Adolescents with bulimia nervosa and eating disorder not otherwise specified-purging only. *International Journal of Eating Disorders, 38*, 157–161.

Binford, R., le Grange, D., & Jellar, C. (2005). EDE and adolescent bulimia nervosa: Interview or self-report? *International Journal of Eating Disorders, 37*, 44–49.

Blouin, A. G., Zuro, C., & Blouin, J. (1990). Family environment in bulimia nervosa: The role of depression. *International Journal of Eating Disorders, 9*, 649–658.

Bohn, K., & Fairburn, C. G. (2008). The clinical impairment assessment questionnaire. In C. G. Fairburn (Ed.), *Cognitive behavior therapy and eating disorders*. New York: Guilford Press.

Boyer, T. (2006). The development of risk-taking: A multi-perspective review. *Developmental Review, 26*, 291–345.

Bryant-Waugh, R., Cooper, P., Taylor, C., & Lask, B. (1996). The use of the Eating Disorders Examination with children: A pilot study. *International Journal of Eating Disorders, 19*, 391–397.

Bryant-Waugh, R., & Lask, B. (1995). Eating disorders in children. *Journal of Child Psychology and Psychiatry, 36*, 191–202.

Bryant-Waugh, R.,& Lask, B. (2007). Overview of eating disorders. In B. Lask & R. Bryant-Waugh (Eds.), *Eating disorders in childhood and adolescence* (3rd edition) (pp. 35–50). Hove, UK: Routledge.

Bulik, C. M., Berkman, N., Kimberly, A., Brownly, J. S., JA, & Lohr, K. (2007). Anorexia nervosa: a systematic review of randomized clinical trials. *International Journal of Eating Disorders, 40*, 310–320.

Bulik, C. M., Fear, J., & Pickering, A. (1997). Predictors of the development of bulimia nervosa in women with anorexia nervosa. *Journal of Nervous and Mental Disease, 185*, 704–707.

Bulik, C. M., Sullivan, P. F., Fear, J., & Joyce, P. R. (1997). Eating disorders and antecedent anxiety disorders: A controlled study. *Acta Psychiatrica Scandinavica, 96*, 101–107.

Byford, S., Barrett, B., Roberts, C., Clark, A., Edwards, V., Smethhurst, N., et al. (2007). Economic evaluation of a randomised controlled trial for anorexia nervosa in adolescents. *British Journal of Psychiatry, 191*, 436–440.

Carruth, B., & Skinner, J. (2000). Revisiting the picky eater phenomenon: neophobic behaviors of young children. *Journal of the American College of Nutrition, 19*, 771–780.

Centers for Disease Control and Prevention (CDC). (2002). *CDC Growth Charts for the United States: Development and Methods*. Atlanta: Author.

Cooper, P. J., & Steere, J. (1995). A comparison of two psychological treatments for bulimia nervosa: Implications for models of maintenance. *Behaviour Research and Therapy, 33*, 875–885.

Cooper, Z., Cooper, P. J., & Fairburn, C. G. (1989). The validity of the eating disorder examination and its subscales. *British Journal of Psychiatry, 154*, 807–812.

Cooper, Z., & Fairburn, C. G. (1987). The Eating Disorder Examination: A semi-structured interview for the assessment of the specific psychopathology of eating disorders. *International Journal of Eating Disorders, 6*, 1–8.

Couturier, J., & Lock, J. (2006a). Denial and minimization in adolescent anorexia nervosa. *International Journal of Eating Disorders, 39*, 175–183.

Couturier, J., & Lock, J. (2006b). Do supplementary items on the Eating Disorder Examination improve assessment of adolescent anorexia nervosa? *International Journal of Eating Disorders, 39*, 426–433.

Couturier, J., & Lock, J. (2006c). What constitutes remission in adolescent anorexia nervosa: A review of various conceptualizations and a quantitative analysis. *International Journal of Eating Disorders, 39*, 175–183.

Couturier, J., & Lock, J. (2006d). What is recovery in adolescent anorexia nervosa? *International Journal of Eating Disorders, 39*, 550–555.

Couturier, J., & Lock, J. (2007). Review of Medication Use for Children and Adolescents with Eating Disorders. *Journal of the Canadian Academy of Child and Adolescent Psychiatry, 16*, 173–176.

Couturier, J., Lock, J., Forsberg, S., Vanderheyden, D., & Lee, H. Y. (2007). The addition of a parent and clinician component to the eating disorder examination for children and adolescents. *International Journal of Eating Disorders, 40*, 472–475.

Crisp, A. H., Norton, K., Gowers, S., Halek, C., Bowyer, C., Yeldham, D., et al. (1991). A controlled study of the effect of therapies aimed at adolescent and family psychopathology in anorexia nervosa. *British Journal of Psychiatry, 159*, 325–333.

Crist, W., & Napier-Phillips, A. (2001). Mealtime behaviors of young children: A comparison of normative and clinical data. *Journal of Developmental and Behavioral Pediatrics, 22*, 279–286.

Dare, C., & Eisler, I. (1997). Family therapy for anorexia nervosa. In D. M. Garner & P. Garfinkel (Eds.), *Handbook of treatment for eating disorders* (pp. 307–324). New York: Guilford Press.

Davies, M., & Tchanturia, K. (2005). Cognitive remediation therapy as an intervention for acute anorexia nervosa: A case report. *European Eating Disorders Review, 13*, 311–316.

Dodge, E., Hodes, M., Eisler, I., & Dare, C. (1995). Family therapy for bulimia nervosa in adolescents: an exploratory study. *Journal of Family Therapy, 17*, 59–77.

Eisler, I. (2005). The empirical and theoretical base of family therapy and multiple family day therapy for adolescent anorexia nervosa. *Journal of Family Therapy, 27*, 104–131.

Eisler, I., Dare, C., Hodes, M., Russell, G., Dodge, E., & le Grange, D. (2000). Family therapy for adolescent anorexia nervosa: The results of a controlled comparison of two family interventions. *Journal of Child Psychology and Psychiatry, 41*(6), 727–736.

Eisler, I., Dare, C., Russell, G. F. M., Szmukler, G. I., le Grange, D., & Dodge, E. (1997). Family and individual therapy in anorexia nervosa: A five-year follow-up. *Archives of General Psychiatry, 54*, 1025–1030.

Eisler, I., Simic, M., Russell, G., & Dare, C. (2007). A randomized controlled treatment trial of two forms of family therapy in adolescent anorexia nervosa: A five-year follow-up. *Journal of Child Psychology and Psychiatry, 48*, 552–560.

Engel, S. G., Wittrock, D. A., Crosby, R. D., Wonderlich, S. A., Mitchell, J. E., & Kolotkin, R. L. (2006). Development and psychometric validation of an eating disorder-specific health-related quality of life instrument. *International Journal of Eating Disorders, 39*, 62–71.

Fairburn, C. (1981). A cognitive behavioural approach to the treatment of bulimia. *Psychological Medicine, 11*(4), 707–711.

Fairburn, C., & Bohn, K. (2005). Eating disorder NOS (EDNOS): An example of the troublesome eating disorder not otherwise specified(NOS) category in DSM-IV. *Behavioral Research and Therapy, 43*, 691–701.

Fairburn, C. G. (2005). Evidence-based treatment of anorexia nervosa. *International Journal of Eating Disorders, 37*, s26–30.

Fairburn, C. G., & Cooper, I. (1993). The eating disorder examination (12th ed.). In C. G. Fairburn & G. T. Wilson (Eds.), *Binge eating: Nature, Assessment, and treatment*. New York: Guilford Press.

Fairburn, C. G., Cooper, Z., Doll, H., Norman, P., & O'Connor, M. (2000). The natural course of bulimia nervosa and binge eating disorder in young women. *Archives of General Psychiatry, 57*, 659–665.

Fairburn, C. G., Cooper, Z., & Safran, R. (2002). Cognitive behavioral therapy for eating disorders: A "transdiagnostic" theory and treatment. *Behavioral Research and Therapy, 41*, 509–528.

Fairburn, C. G., Jones, R., Peveler, R. C., Hope, R. A., & O'Connor, M. (1993). Psychotherapy and bulimia nervosa. Longer-term effects of interpersonal psychotherapy, behavior therapy, and cognitive behavior therapy. *Archives of General Psychiatry, 50*(6), 419–428.

Feighner, J., Robins, E., Fuze, S., Woodruff, R., Winokur, G., & Munoz, R. (1972). Criteria for use in psychiatric research. *Archives of General Psychiatry, 26*, 57–63.

Fischer, B., Nguyen, V., Carter, C., Putnam, K., & Kaye, W. (2007). Altered reward processing in women recovered from anorexia nervosa. *American Journal of Psychiatry, 164*, 1842–1849.

Fisher, M., Golden, N., Katzman, D., Kreipe, R. E, Rees, J., Schebenclach, J., (1995). Eating disorders in adolescents: A background paper. *Journal of Adolescent Health, 16*, 420–437.

Fitzpatrick, K., Moye, A., Hostee, R., le Grange, D., & Lock, J. (2010). Adolescent focused therapy for adolescent anorexia nervosa. *Journal of Contemporary Psychotherapy, 40*, 30–39.

Flament, M., Ledoux, S., Jeammet, P., Choquet, M., & Simon, Y. (1995). A population study of bulimia nervosa and subclinical eating disorders in adolescence. In H. Steinhausen (Ed.), *Eating disorders in adolescence: Anorexia and bulimia nervosa* (pp. 21–36). New York: Brunner/Mazel.

Franklin, J., Schiele, B., Brozek, J., & Keys, A. (1948). Observations on human behavior in experimental semistarvation and rehabilitation. *Journal of Clinical Psychology, 4*, 28–45.

Frisch, J., Franko, D., & Herzog, D. B. (2006). Residential treatment for eating disorders. *International Journal of Eating Disorders, 39*, 434–439.

Galloway, A., Lee, Y., & Birch, L. (2003). Predictors and consequences of food neophobia and pickiness in young girls. *Journal of the American Dietetic Association, 103*, 692–698.

Godart, N., Flament, M., Perdereau, F., & Jeammet, P. (2002). Comorbidity between eating disorders and anxiety disorders: A review. *International Journal of Eating Disorders, 32*.

Godart, N. T., Flament, M. F., Lecrubier, Y., & Jeammet, P. (2000). Anxiety disorders in anorexia nervosa and bulimia nervosa: Comorbidity and chronology of appearance. *European Psychiatry, 15*, 38–45.

Golden, N., Katzman, D, Kreipe, Stevens, SL, Sawyer, SM, Rees, J, Nicholls, D, & Rome, E, (2003). Eating disorders in adolescents: Position paper of the Society for Adolescent Medicine: Medical Indications for Hospitalization in an Adolescent with an Eating Disorder. *Journal of Adolescent Health, 33*, 496–503.

Gowers, S., Clark, A., Roberts, C., Griffiths, A., Edwards, V., Bryan, C., et al. (2007). Clinical effectiveness of treatments for anorexia nervosa in adolescents. *British Journal of Psychiatry, 191*, 427–435.

Gowers, S., Weetman, J., Shore, R., Hussain, F., & Elvins, R. (2000). The impact of hospitalisation on the outcome of adolescent anorexia nervosa. *British Journal of Psychiatry, 45*, 138–141.

Gull, W. (1874). Anorexia nervosa (apepsia hysterica, anorexia hysterica). *Transactions of the Clinical Society of London, 7*, 222–228.

Haley, J. (1973). *Uncommon therapy: The psychiatric techniques of Milton H. Erickson*. New York: W. W. Norton.

Hall, A., & Crisp, A. H. (1987). Brief psychotherapy in the treatment of anorexia nervosa: Outcome at one year. *British Journal of Psychiatry, 151*, 185–191.

Halmi, C. A., Agras, W. S., Crow, S. J., Mitchell, J., Wilson, G. T., Bryson, S., et al. (2005). Predictors of treatment acceptance and completion in anorexia nervosa: implications for future study designs. *Archives of General Psychiatry (62)*, 776–781.

Halmi, C. A., Eckert, E. D., Marchi, M., Sampugnaro, V., Apple, R., & Cohen, J. (1991). Co-morbidity of psychiatric diagnoses in anorexia nervosa. *Archives of General Psychiatry, 48*, 712–718.

Halmi, K., Brodland, G., & Loney, J. (1973). Progress in anorexia nervosa. *Annals of Internal Medicine, 78*, 907–909.

Higgs, J., Goodyer, I., & Birch, J. (1989). Anorexia nervosa and food avoidance emotional disorder. *Archives of Diseases in Childhood, 64*, 346–351.

Hoek, H., & Hoeken, D. v. (2003). Review of prevalence and incidence of eating disorders. *International Journal of Eating Disorders, 34*, 383–396.

Holliday, J., Tchanturia, K., Landau, S., & Collier, D. (2005). Is impaired set-shifting an endophenotype of anorexia nervosa? *American Journal of Psychiatry, 162*, 2269–2275.

Holmbeck, G., Colder, C., Shapera, W., Westhoven, V., Keneally, L., & Updegrove, A. (2000). Working with adolescents: Guides from developmental psychology. In P. Kendall (Ed.), *Child and adolescent therapy*. New York: Guilford Press.

House, J., Eisler, I., Simic, M., & Micali, N. (2008). Diagnosing eating disorders in adolescent: A comparison of the Eating Disorder Examination and the Development and Well-Being Assessment. *International Journal of Eating Disorders, 41*, 535–541.

Humphrey, L. (1986). Structural analysis of parent-child relationships in eating disorders. *Journal of Abnormal Psychology, 95*, 395–402.

Humphrey, L. (1987). Comparison of bulimic-anorexic and nondistressed families using structural analysis of behavior. *Journal of the American Academy of Child and Adolescent Psychiatry, 26*, 248–255.

Izard C., & Harris, P. (Eds.). (1995). *Emotional development and developmental psychopathology*. New York: John Wiley & Sons.

Jenkins, M. (1987). An outcome study of anorexia nervosa on an adolescent unit. *Journal of Adolescence, 10*, 71–81.

Kaye, W., Bulik, C. M., Thonton, L., Barbarich, B., Masters, K., Fichter, M., et al. (2004). Anxiety disorders comorbid with bulimia and anorexia nervosa. *American Journal of Psychiatry, 161*, 2215–2221.

Kendall, P. (1993). Cognitive-behavioral therapies with youth: Guiding theory, current status, and emerging developments. *Journal of Consulting and Clinical Psychology, 61*, 235–247.

Keys, A., Brozek, J., & Henschel, A. (1950). *The biology of human starvation*. Minneapolis: University of Minnesota Press.

Klump, K., Bulik, C. M., Pollice, C., Halmi, C. A., Fichter, M., Berrettini, W., et al. (2000). Temperament and character in women with anorexia nervosa. *Journal of Nervous and Mental Diseases, 188*, 559–567.

Kog, E., & Vandereycken, W. (1989). Family interaction in eating disordered patients and normal controls. *International Journal of Eating Disorders, 8*, 11–23.

Kotler, L., Devlin, B., Davies, M., & Walsh, B. T. (2003). An open trial of fluoxetine in adolescents with bulimia nervosa. *Journal of Child and Adolescent Psychopharmacology, 13*, 329–325.

Lambe, E., Katzman, D., Mikulis, D., Kennedy, Q., & Zipursky, R. (1997). Cerebral gray matter volume deficits after weight recovery from anorexia nervosa. *Archives of General Psychiatry, 54*, 537–542.

Lask, B., & Bryant-Waugh, R. (1992). Early-onset anorexia nervosa and related eating disorders. *Journal of Child Psychology and Psychiatry, 33*, 281–300.

Lay, B., Jennen-Steinmetz, C., Reinhard, I., & Schmidt, M. (2002). Characteristics of inpatient weight gain in adolescent anorexia nervosa: Relation to speed of relapse and re-admission. *European Eating Disorders Review, 10*, 22–40.

Lee, S. (1995). Self-starvation in context: Towards a culturally sensitive understanding of anorexia nervosa. *Social Sciences and Medicine, 41*, 25–36.

le Grange, D., Binford, R., Peterson, C., Crow, S., Crosby, R., Klein, M., et al. (2006). DSM-IV Threshold versus subthreshold bulimia nervosa. *International Journal of Eating Disorders, 39*, 462–67.

le Grange, D., Crosby, R., & Lock, J. (2008). Predictors and moderators of outcome in family-based treatment for adolescent bulimia nervosa. *Journal of the American Academy of Child and Adolescent Psychiatry, 47*, 469–700.

le Grange, D., Crosby, R., Rathouz, P., & Leventhal, B. (2007). A randomized controlled comparison of family-based treatment and supportive psychotherapy for adolescent bulimia nervosa. *Archives of General Psychiatry, 64*, 1049–1056.

le Grange, D., Eisler, I., Dare, C., & Hodes, M. (1992). Family criticism and self-starvation: A study of expressed emotion. *Journal of Family Therapy, 14*, 177–192.

le Grange, D., Eisler, I., Dare, C., & Russell, G. (1992). Evaluation of family treatments in adolescent anorexia nervosa: A pilot study. *International Journal of Eating Disorders, 12*(4), 347–357.

le Grange, D., & Lock, J. (2002). Bulimia nervosa in adolescents: Treatment, eating pathology, and comorbidity. *South African Psychiatry Review*, August, 19–22.

le Grange, D., & Lock, J. (2005). The dearth of psychological treatment studies for anorexia nervosa. *International Journal of Eating Disorders, 37*, 79–81.

le Grange, D., & Lock, J. (2007). *Treating Bulimia in Adolescence*. New York: GuilfordPress.

le Grange, D., & Schmidt, U. (2005). The treatment of adolescents with bulimia nervosa. *Journal of Mental Health, 14*, 587–597.

Leitenberg, H., Rosen, J. C., Wolf, J., Vara, L. S., Detzer, M. J., & Srebnik, D. (1994). Comparison of cognitive-behavior therapy and desipramine in the treatment of bulimia nervosa. *Behaviour Research & Therapy, 32*(1), 37–45.

Levenkron, S. (2001). *Anatomy of anorexia*. New York: Guilford Press.

Lock, J. (2002). Treating adolescents with eating disorders in the family context: Empirical and theoretical considerations. *Child and Adolescent Psychiatric Clinics of North America, 11*, 331–342.

Lock, J. (2003). What predicts maintenance of weight for adolescents medically hospitalized for anorexia nervosa? *Eating Disorders, 11*, 1–7.

Lock, J. (2005). Adjusting cognitive behavioral therapy for adolescent bulimia nervosa: Results of a case series. *American Journal of Psychotherapy, 59*, 267–281.

Lock, J., Agras, W. S., Bryson, S., & Kraemer, H. (2005). A comparison of short- and long-term family therapy for adolescent anorexia nervosa. *Journal of the American Academy of Child and Adolescent Psychiatry, 44*, 632–639.

Lock, J., Couturier, J., & Agras, W. S. (2006). Comparison of long term outcomes in adolescents with anorexia nervosa treated with family therapy. *American Journal of Child and Adolescent Psychiatry, 45*, 666–672.

Lock, J., Couturier, J., & Agras, W. S. (2008). Costs of remission and recovery using family therapy for adolescent anorexia nervosa: A descriptive study. *Eating Disorders, 16*, 322–30.

Lock, J., Couturier, J., Bryson, S., & Agras, W. S. (2006). Predictors of dropout and remission family therapy for adolescent anorexia nervosa in a randomized clinical trial. *International Journal of Eating Disorders*, 639–647.

Lock, J., & Gowers, S. (2005). Effective treatments for adolescent eating disorders. *Journal of Mental Health, 14*, 599–610.

Lock, J., & le Grange, D. (2001). Can family-based treatment of anorexia nervosa be manualized? *Journal of Psychotherapy Practice and Research, 10*, 253–261.

Lock, J., & le Grange, D. (2005). *Help your child beat an eating disorder*. New York: Guilford Press.

Lock, J., le Grange, D., Agras, W. S., & Dare, C. (2001). *Treatment manual for anorexia nervosa: A family-based approach*. New York: Guilford Press.

Lock, J., le Grange, D., & Crosby, R. (2008). Exploring possible mechanisms of change in family based treatment for bulimia nervosa:. *Journal of Family Therapy*.

Lock, J., Reisel, B., & Steiner, H. (2001). Associated health risks of adolescents with disordered eating: How different are they from their peers? Results from a high school survey. *Child Psychiatry and Human Development, 31*, 249–265.

Lock, J., Walker, L., Rickert, V., & Katzman, D. (2005). Suicidality in adolescents being treated with antidepressant medications and the black box label: Position paper of the Society of Adolescent Medicine. *Journal of Adolescent Health, 36*, 92–93.

Loeb, K., Walsh, B., Lock, J., le Grange, D., Jones, J., Marcus, S., et al. (2007). Open trial of family-based treatment for adolescent anorexia nervosa: Evidence of successful dissemination. *Journal of the American Academy of Child and Adolescent Psychiatry, 46*, 792–800.

Lucas, A. R., Beard, C. M., & O'Fallon, W. M. (1991). 50–year trends in the incidence of anorexia nervosa in Rochester, Minn: A population-based study. *American Journal of Psychiatry, 148*, 917–929.

Lucas, A. R., Crowson, C., O'Fallon, W. M., & Melton, L. (1999). The ups and downs of anorexia nervosa. *International Journal of Eating Disorders, 26*, 397–405.

Luna, B., & Sweeney, J. (2004). The emergence of collaborative brain function. *Annals of the New York Academy of Sciences, 1021*, 296–309.

Marcus, M., & Kalarchian, M. (2003). Binge eating in children and adolescents. *International Journal of Eating Disorders, 34*(Supplement), S47–57.

McNamara, K., & Loveman, C. (1990). Differences in family functioning among bulimics, repeat dieters, and non-dieters. *Journal of Clinical Psychology, 46*, 516–523.

Minuchin, S., Rosman, B., & Baker, I. (1978). *Psychosomatic families: Anorexia nervosa in context*. Cambridge, MA: Harvard University Press.

Mitchell, J. (1991). A review of controlled trials of psychotherapy for bulimia nervosa. *Journal of Psychosomatic Research, 35*(Supplement.1), 23–31.

Mitchell, J., Agras, W. S., & Wonderlich, S. (2007). Treatment of bulimia nervosa: Where are we and where are we going? *International Journal of Eating Disorders, 40*, 95–101.

National Institute for Clinical Excellence (N.I.C.E.) (2004). *Core interventions in the treatment and management of anorexia nervosa, bulimia nervosa, and binge eating disorder*. London: British Psychological Society.

Nicholls, D., Chater, R., & Lask, B. (2000). Children into DSM don't go: A comparison of classification systems for eating disorders in childhood and adolescence. *International Journal of Eating Disorders, 28*, 317–324.

Nicholls, D., Randall, D., & Lask, B. (2001). Selective eating: Symptom disorder or normal variant? *Clinics in Child Psychology and Psychiatry, 6*, 257–270.

Peebles, R., Hardy, K., Wilson, J., & Lock, J. (in press). Eating disorders not otherwise specified: Are diagnostic criteria for eating disorders markers of medical severity? *Pediatrics*.

Peebles, R., Wilson, J., & Lock, J. (2006). How do children and adolescents with eating disorders differ at presentation. *Journal of Adolescent Health, 39*, 800–805.

Pike, K., Walsh, B. T., Vitousek, K., Wilson, G. T., & Bauer, J. (2004). Cognitive-behavioral therapy in the posthospitalization treatment of anorexia nervosa. *American Journal of Psychiatry, 160*, 2046–2049.

Pliner, P., & Loewen, E. (1997). Temperament and food neophobia in children and their mothers. *Appetite, 28*, 239–254.

Pope, H. G., Hudson, J. I., Jonas, J. M., & Yurgelin-Todd, D. (1983). Bulimia treated with imipramine: A placebo-controlled, double-blind study. *American Journal of Psychiatry, 140*, 554–558.

Råstam, M., & Gillberg, C. (1991). The family background in anorexia nervosa: a population based study. *Journal of the American Academy of Child and Adolescent Psychiatry, 30*, 283–289.

Ravi, S., Forsberg, S., Fitzpatrick, K., & Lock, J. (2009). Is there a relationship between parental self-reported psychopathology and symptom severity in adolescents with anorexia Nervosa. *Eating Disorders, 17*, 63–71.

Roberto, C., Steinglass, J., Mayer, L., Attia, E., & Walsh, B. T. (2008). The clinical significance of amenorrhea as a diagnostic criterion for anorexia nervosa. *International Journal of Eating Disorders, 41*, 559–563.

Robin, A., Siegal, P., Koepke, T., Moye, A., & Tice, S. (1994). Family therapy versus individual therapy for adolescent females with anorexia nervosa. *Journal of Developmental and Behavioral Pediatrics, 15*(2), 111–116.

Robin, A., Siegal, P., Moye, A., Gilroy, M., Dennis, A., & Sikand, A. (1999). A controlled comparison of family versus individual therapy for adolescents with anorexia nervosa. *Journal of the American Academy of Child and Adolescent Psychiatry, 38*(12), 1482–1489.

Roijen, S. (1992). Anorexia nervosa families a homogeneous group? A case record study. *Acta Psychiatrica Scandinavica, 85*, 196–200.

Rome, E., & Ammerman, S. (2003). Medical complications of eating disorders: An update. *Journal of Adolescent Health, 33*, 418–426.

Russell, G. F., Szmukler, G. I., Dare, C., & Eisler, I. (1987). An evaluation of family therapy in anorexia nervosa and bulimia nervosa. *Archives of General Psychiatry, 44*(12), 1047–1056.

Savin-Williams, R., & Bernt, T. (Eds.). (1990). *Friendship and peer relations*. Cambridge, MA: Harvard University Press.

Schapman, A., & Lock, J. (2006). Cognitive-behavioral therapy for adolescent bulimia. *International Journal of Eating Disorders, 39*, 252–255.

Schmidt, U., Lee, S., Beecham, J., Perkins, S., Treasure, J. L., Yi, I., et al. (2007). A randomized controlled trial of family therapy and cognitive behavior therapy guided self-care for adolescents with bulimia nervosa and related conditions. *American Journal of Psychiatry, 164,* 591–598.

Schmidt, U., Lee, S., Perkins, S., Eisler, I., Treasure, J., Beecham, J., et al. (2008). Do adolescents with eating disorder not otherwise specified or full-syndrome bulimia nervosa differ in clinical severity, co-morbidity, risk factors, treatment outcome or cost? *International Journal of Eating Disorders, 41,* 498–504.

Schreck, K. W., K, & Smith, A. (2004). A comparison of eating behaviors between children with and without autism. *Journal of Autism and Developmental Disorders, 34,* 433–438.

Selvini Palazzoli, M. (1988). *The work of Mara Selvini Palazzoli.* Lanham, MD: Jason Aronson.

Silverman, J. (1997). Charcot's comments on the therapeutic role of isolation in the treatment of anorexia nervosa. *International Journal of Eating Disorders, 21,* 295–298.

Smith, S., & Buschang, P. (2004). Variation in longitudinal diaphyseal long bone growth in children three to ten years of age. *American Journal of Human Biology, 16,* 648–657.

Southgate, L., Tchanturia, K., & Treasure, J. (2007). Neuropsychology in eating disorders. In S. Wood, N. Allen & C. Pantelis (Eds.), *Handbook of neuropsychology of mental illness.* Cambridge: Cambridge University Press.

Sternberg, R. (1977). *Intelligence, information processing, and analogical reasoning: the componential analysis of human abilities.* Hillsdale, NJ: Erlbaum.

Sternberg, R., & Nigro, G. (1980). Developmental patterns in the solution of verbal analogies. *Child Development, 51,* 27–38.

Stice, E., & Agras, W. S. (1998). Predicting onset and cessation of bulimic behaviors during adolescence. *Behavior Therapy, 29,* 257–276.

Streigel-Moore, R., Leslie, D., Petrill, S. A., Garvin, V., & Rosenheck, R. A. (2000). One-year use and cost of inpatient and outpatient services among female and male patients with an eating disorder: Evidence from a national database of health insurance claims. *International Journal of Eating Disorders, 27,* 381–389.

Strober, M., & Humphrey, L. (1987a). Family contributions to the etiology and course of anorexia and bulimia. *Journal of Clinical Psychology, 55,* 654–659.

Strober, M., & Humphrey, L. (1987b). Family contributions to the etiology and course of anorexia nervosa and bulimia nervosa. *Journal of Consulting and Clinical Psychology, 55,* 654–659.

Sullivan, P. F. (1995). Mortality in anorexia nervosa. *American Journal of Psychiatry, 152,* 1073–1074.

Tchanturia, K., Brecelj, M., Sanchez, P., Morris, R., Rabe-Hesketh, S., & Treasure, J. L. (2004). An examination of cognitive flexibility in eating disorders. *Journal of the International Neuropsychological Society, 10,* 1–8.

Tchanturia, K., Morris, R., Brecelj, M., Nikolau, V., & Treasure, J. L. (2004). Set shifting in anorexia nervosa: an examination before and after weight gain in full recovery and the relationship to childhood and adult OCDP traits. *Journal of Psychiatric Research, 38,* 545–552.

Tchanturia, K., Whitney, J., & Treasure, J. L. (2006). Can cognitive exercises help treat anorexia nervosa? *Eating and Weight Disorders, 11,* 112–117.

Thoma, H. (1967). *Anorexia nervosa.* New York: International Universities Press.

Treasure, J. (2007). Getting beneath the phenotype of anorexia nervosa: The search for viable endophenotypes and genotypes. *La revuew de psychiatrie, 52,* 212–219.

Turner, H., & Bryant-Waugh, R. (2004). Eating disorder not otherwise specified (EDNOS) profiles of clients presenting at a community eating disorder service. *European Eating Disorders Review, 12,* 18–26.

Uher, R., Murphy, D., Friederich, H., Dalgleish, T., Brammer, M., Giapietro, V., et al. (2005). Functional neuroanatomy of body shape perception in healthy and eating disordered women. *Biological Psychiatry, 12,* 990–997.

Uher, R., Treasure, J. L., & Campbell, I. (2002). Neuroanatomical bases of eating disorders. In H. D'Haenen, J. den Boer & P. Willner (Eds.), *Biological psychiatry* (pp. 1173–1180). Chichester, UK: John Wiley & Sons.

van Hoof, M., Voorhorst, F., Kaptein, M., Hirasing, R., Koppenaal, C., & Shoemaker, J. (1998). Relationship of the menstrual cycle pattern in 14–17 year old adolescents with gynecological age, body mass index and historical parameters. *Human Reproduction, 13,* 2252–2260.

van Son, G., van hoeken, D., Aad, I., Bartelds, A., van Furth, E., & Hoek, H. (2006). Time trends in the incidence of eating disorders: A primary care study in the Netherlands. *International Journal of Eating Disorders, 39,* 565–569.

Wade, T., Byrne, S., & Bryant-Waugh, R. (2008). The Eating Disorder Examination: Norms and construct validity with young and middle adolescent girls. *International Journal of Eating Disorders, 41,* 551–558.

Wagner, A., Aizenstein, H., Venkatraman, V., Fudge, J., May, J., Mazurkewicz, L., et al. (2007). Altered reward processing in women recovered from anorexia nervosa. *American Journal of Psychiatry, 164,* 1842–1849.

Walsh, B. T., & Devlin, M. J. (1995). Pharmacotherapy of bulimia nervosa and binge eating disorder. *Addictive Behaviors, 20*(6), 757–764.

Walsh, B. T., Kaplan, A. S., Attia, E., Olmsted, M., Parides, M., Carter, J., et al. (2006). Fluoxetine after weight restoration in anorexia nervosa: A randomized clinical trial. *JAMA, 295,* 2605–2612.

Walsh, B. T., Wilson, G. T., Loeb, K. L., Devlin, M. J., Pike, K. M., Roose, S. P., et al. (1997). Medication and psychotherapy in the treatment of bulimia nervosa. *American Journal of Psychiatry, 154*(4), 523–531.

White, M., & Epston, D. (1990). *Narrative means to therapeutic ends.* New York: W. W. Norton.

Wilfley, D. E., Agras, W. S., Telch, C. F., Rossiter, E. M., Schneider, J. A., Cole, A. B., et al. (1993). Group cognitive-behavioral therapy and group interpersonal psychotherapy for the non-purging bulimic: A controlled comparison. *Journal of Consulting & Clinical Psychology, 61,* 296–305.

Woodside, B., Bulik, C. M., Halmi, C. A., Fichter, M., Kaplan, A. S., Berrettini, W., et al. (2002). Personality, perfectionism, and attitudes toward eating in parents of individuals with eating disorders. *International Journal of Eating Disorders, 31,* 290–299.

World Health Organization (WHO) (2005). *International Classification of Diseases.* Geneva, Switzerland: World Health Organization.

Workgroup for the Classification of Child and Adolescent Eating Disorder (2007), *International Journal of Eating Disorders, 40,* S117–S122.

Zucker, N., Losh, M., Bulik, C. M., LaBar, K., Piven, J., & Pelphrey, K. (2007). Anorexia nervosa and autism spectrum disorders: Guided investigation of social cognitive endophenotypes. *Psychological Bulletin, 133,* 967–1006.

PART 2

Approaches to Understanding the Eating Disorders

Appetitive Regulation in Anorexia Nervosa and Bulimia Nervosa

Walter H. Kaye *and* Tyson Oberndorfer

Abstract

Anorexia and bulimia nervosa are complex disorders with dysregulated appetitive behaviors. The underlying causes of disturbed eating patterns are unknown, but in theory, could involve aberrant functioning of brain or peripheral systems. New technologies, such as positron emission tomography (PET) and functional magnetic resonance imaging (fMRI), can be used to explore whether there are perturbations of the monoamine systems and the neurocircuitry of gustatory processing in eating disorders. Together, PET and fMRI data suggest that individuals with eating disorders have disturbance of taste and reward processing regions of the brain, which may contribute to eating disorder symptoms.

Keywords: anorexia nervosa, anterior insula, bulimia nervosa, dopamine, eating disorders, functional magnetic resonance imaging, orbitofrontal cortex, positron emission tomography, serotonin

Introduction

The puzzling nature of many eating disorder (ED) symptoms has been an obstacle to identification of responsible brain regions and circuits. Consequently, the ED field lags behind other psychiatric disorders in terms of progress in understanding pathophysiology. Although anorexia nervosa (AN) and bulimia nervosa (BN) are characterized (American Psychiatric Association [APA], 2000) as EDs, it remains unknown as to whether there is a primary disturbance of appetitive function. The regulation of appetite and feeding are complex phenomena, integrating peripheral signals (gastrointestinal [GI] tract, adipose tissue, hormonal secretion, hypothalamic factors (neuropeptides), cortical and subcortical processes (reward, emotionality, cognition), and external influences (Elman, Borsook, & Lukas, 2006; Rolls, 1997; Schwartz, Woods, Porte, Seeley, & Baskin, 2000). It is possible that a disturbance could occur anywhere in this axis in AN and BN.

A number of subsystems have been investigated in AN and BN: (1) peripheral hormones such as cholecystokinin (CCK) or peripheral autonomic function; (2) neuropeptides involved in hypothalamic and lower brain center function; and (3) limbic and cortical brain circuits that contribute to appetite. We believe that the weight of evidence suggests that higher order circuits are involved because they show persistent altered function after recovery, and because they code for rewarding and emotionality properties of food, homeostatic needs, and cognitive modulation (Elman et al., 2006; Hinton, Parkinson, Holland, Arana, Roberts, & Owen, 2004; Kelley, 2004; Saper, Chou, & Elmquist, 2002).

State versus Trait Characteristics

When malnourished and emaciated, individuals with AN have widespread and severe alterations of brain and peripheral organ function; however, it is unclear whether these changes are the cause or the consequence of malnutrition and weight loss. Thus, to understand the etiology and course of illness of AN and BN, it is useful to divide the neurobiologic alterations into two categories. First, there seem to be premorbid, genetically determined trait alterations that contribute to a vulnerability to develop these ED. Second, state alterations secondary to malnutrition may sustain the illness, and perhaps accelerate the out-of-control spiral that is classically found in these disorders.

Large-scale community-based twin studies have shown that 50% to 80% of the variance in AN and BN (Berrettini, 2000; Bulik, Sullivan, Tozzi, Furberg, Lichtenstein, & Pedersen, 2006; Kendler et al., 1991) may be accounted for by genetic factors. The genetic vulnerability to EDs may be expressed as a more diffuse phenotype of continuous behavioral traits as suggested by evidence of a significant heritability of disordered eating attitudes, weight preoccupation, dissatisfaction with weight and shape, dietary restraint, binge eating and self-induced vomiting (Bulik et al., 2005; Klump, McGue, & Iacono, 2000; Rutherford, McGuffin, Katz, & Murray, 1993; Wade, Martin, & Tiggemann, 1998), and familiality of subthreshold forms of EDs (Lilenfeld et al., 1998; Strober, Freeman, Lampert, Diamond, & Kaye, 2000). Considerable evidence has suggested that childhood temperament and personality traits can create a vulnerability for developing AN and BN during adolescence. Recent studies (Anderluh, Tchanturia, Rabe-Hesketh, & Treasure, 2003; Lilenfeld, Wonderlich, Riso, Crosby, & Mitchell, 2006; Stice, 2002) describe negative emotionality, harm avoidance, perfectionism, inhibition, drive for thinness, altered interoceptive awareness, and obsessive–compulsive personality traits as childhood predisposing factors that precede the onset of an ED and that persist after recovery (see later). Studies (Bulik et al., 2007) suggest these traits are heritable, elevated in unaffected family members, and independent of body weight, providing further evidence that they confer liability to the development of AN.

Starvation and emaciation have profound effects on the function of the brain and other organ systems, lead to neurochemical disturbances that could exaggerate premorbid traits (Pollice, Kaye, Greeno, & Weltzin, 1997), and add other symptoms that maintain or accelerate the disease process. For example, AN patients have a reduced brain volume (see Ellison & Fong, 1998), altered metabolism in frontal, cingulate, temporal, and parietal regions (Kaye, Wagner, & Frank, 2006), and a regression to prepubertal gonadal function (Boyar et al., 1974).

The fact that such disturbances tend to normalize after weight restoration suggests that these alterations are a consequence and not a cause of AN.

The difficulty in distinguishing alterations due to state and trait characteristics in AN patients has been a major confound in research into this disorder. Premorbid studies are not practical given the young age of potential subjects, the rarity of the disorder, and the need to follow them for many years. An alternative strategy is to study individuals who have recovered from AN and BN, thus avoiding the confounding influence of malnutrition and weight loss on biological systems.

No agreed upon definition of recovery from AN presently exists, but in our research, we employ a definition that emphasizes stable and healthy body weight for months or years, with stable nutrition, the relative absence of dietary abnormalities, and normal menstruation. Although the process of recovery in AN and BN is poorly understood and, in most cases, protracted, approximately 50% to 70% of affected individuals will eventually have complete or moderate resolution of the illness, though this might not occur until their early to mid-20s (Steinhausen, 2002; Strober, Freeman, & Morrell, 1997; Wagner, Barbarich, et al., 2006). Studies have described temperament and character traits that persist after long-term recovery from AN, such as negative emotionality, harm avoidance and perfectionism, desire for thinness, and mild dietary preoccupation, which are similar to those described in childhood in people who will go on to develop AN and BN (Casper, 1990; Srinivasagam et al., 1995; Strober, 1980; Wagner, Barbarich, et al., 2006).

In summary, there is strong evidence supporting a genetic influence in AN and BN, as well as the persistence after recovery of personality and character traits that may predispose an individual to developing these disorders. These data support the likelihood that such persistent symptoms are not just "scars" caused by chronic malnutrition, but may reflect underlying traits that contribute to the pathogenesis of this disorder.

Studies of Altered Feeding Behaviors

Relatively little data exist on appetite regulation in EDs, despite the prominent nature of these symptoms. Laboratory studies support clinical observations that AN individuals dislike high fat foods (Drewnowski, Pierce, & Halmi, 1988; Fernstrom, Weltzin, Neuberger, Srinivasagam, & Kaye, 1994) and BN tend to binge on sweet and high fat foods (Kaye et al., 1992; Weltzin, Hsu, Pollice, & Kaye, 1991).

These patterns of responses do not change following weight regain. Other studies (Garfinkel, Moldofsky, & Garner, 1979; Garfinkel, Moldofsky, Garner, Stancer, & Coscina, 1978) reported altered interoceptive disturbances in AN in terms of the absence of satiety aversion to sucrose, and that these disturbances persisted after normalization of weight or failure to rate food as positive when hungry (Santel, Baving, Krauel, Munte, & Rotte, 2006). In addition, there is evidence (Kaye et al., 2003; Strober, 1995; Vitousek & Manke, 1994) of an anxiety-reducing character to dietary restraint in AN. For BN, negative mood states and hunger may precipitate a binge (Hilbert & Tuschen-Caffier, 2007; Smyth et al., 2007; Waters, Hill, & Waller, 2001) and overeating may relieve dysphoria and anxiety (Abraham & Beaumont, 1982; Johnson & Larson, 1982; Kaye, Gwirtsman, George, Weiss, & Jimerson, 1986).

Taken together, these studies support the possibility of an altered response to palatable foods and a dysphoria reducing aspect to pathological eating.

Neuropeptide and Neuroendocrine Alterations

The past decade has witnessed accelerating basic research on the role of neuropeptides in the regulation of feeding behavior. Indirect evidence from clinical studies suggests the possibility that altered regulation of neuropeptides may contribute to abnormal eating patterns in EDs and in obesity. The mechanisms for controlling food intake involve a complicated interplay between peripheral systems (including gustatory stimulation, GI peptide secretion, and vagal afferent nerve responses) and central nervous system (CNS) neuropeptides and/or monoamines. Thus, studies in animals show that neuropeptides such as CCK, the endogenous opioids such as beta-endorphin, and neuropeptide-Y regulate the rate, duration, and size of meals, as well as macronutrient selection (Morley & Blundell, 1988; Saper et al., 2002; Schwartz et al., 2000). In addition to regulating eating behavior, a number of CNS neuropeptides participate in the regulation of neuroendocrine pathways. Clinical studies have evaluated the possibility that CNS neuropeptide alterations may contribute to dysregulated secretion of the gonadal hormones, cortisol, thyroid hormones, and growth hormone in EDs (Jimerson & Wolfe, 2004; Stoving, Hangaard, Hansen-Nord, & Hagen, 1999).

Although there are relatively few studies to date, most of the neuroendocrine and neuropeptide alterations apparent during symptomatic episodes of AN and BN tend to normalize after recovery. This observation suggests that most of these disturbances are consequences rather than causes of malnutrition, weight loss, and/or altered meal patterns. Still, an understanding of these neuropeptide disturbances may shed light on why many people with AN or BN cannot easily "reverse" their illness. In AN, malnutrition may contribute to a downward spiral sustaining and perpetuating the desire for more weight loss and dieting. Symptoms such as increased satiety, obsessions and dysphoric mood, may be exaggerated by these neuropeptide alterations and thus contribute to this downward spiral. In addition, mutual interactions among neuropeptide, neuroendocrine, and neurotransmitter pathways may contribute to the constellation of psychiatric comorbidity often observed in these disorders. Even after weight gain and normalized eating patterns, many individuals who have recovered from AN or BN have physiological, behavioral, and psychological symptoms that persist for extended periods of time. Menstrual cycle dysregulation, for example, may persist for some months after weight restoration. The following sections provide a brief overview of studies of neuropeptides in AN and BN.

Hypothalamic–Pituitary–Adrenal Axis

When underweight, patients with AN have increased plasma cortisol secretion that is thought to be at least in part a consequence of hypersecretion of endogenous corticotropin-releasing hormone (CRH; Gold et al., 1986; Kaye et al., 1987; Licinio, Wong, & Gold, 1996; Walsh et al., 1987). In that the plasma and cerebrospinal fluid (CSF) measures return toward normal, it appears likely that activation of the hypothalamic–pituitary–adrenal (HPA) axis is precipitated by weight loss. The observation of increased CRH activity is of great theoretical interest in anorexia because intracerebroventricular CRH administration in experimental animals produces many of the physiologic and behavioral changes associated with AN, including markedly decreased eating behavior (Glowa & Gold, 1991). CRH expression in BN is less clear. CRH triggers secretion of adrenocorticotropic hormone (ACTH); CSF levels of ACTH in ill BN were reported to be similar to controls, while ACTH levels decreased when BN subjects did not engage in binge/purge behaviors (Gwirtsman et al., 1989). Given a positive correlation between ACTH and cortisol levels, these data support the hypothesis that binge/purge behaviors may relieve dysphoric mood states in BN.

Opioid Peptides

Studies in laboratory animals raise the possibility that altered endogenous opioid activity might contribute to pathological feeding behavior in EDs; opioid agonists generally increase, and opioid antagonists decrease, food intake (Morley et al., 1985). State-related reductions in concentrations of CSF beta-endorphin and related opiate concentrations have been found in both underweight AN and ill BN subjects (Brewerton, Lydiard, Laraia, Shook, & Ballenger, 1992; Kaye et al., 1987; Lesem, Berrettini, Kaye, & Jimerson, 1991). In contrast, using the T-lymphocyte as a model system, Brambilla et al. (Brambilla, Brunetta, Peirone et al., 1995) found elevated beta-endorphin levels in AN, although the levels were normal in BN (Brambilla, Brunetta, Draisci, et al., 1995). If beta-endorphin activity is a facilitator of feeding behavior, then reduced CSF concentrations could reflect decreased central activity of this system, which then maintains or facilitates inhibition of feeding behavior in the EDs.

Neuropeptide-Y and Peptide YY

Neuropeptide-Y (NPY) and peptide YY (PYY) are of considerable theoretical interest because they are among the most potent endogenous stimulants of feeding behavior within the CNS (Kalra, Dube, Sahu, Phelps, & Kalra, 1991; Morley et al., 1985; Schwartz et al., 2000). PYY is more potent than NPY in stimulating food intake; both are selective for carbohydrate rich foods. Underweight anorexics have been shown to have elevations of CSF NPY but normal PYY (Kaye, Berrettini, Gwirtsman, & George, 1990). Clearly, elevated NPY does not result in increased feeding in underweight anorexics; however, the possibility that increased NPY activity underlies the obsessive and paradoxical interest in dietary intake and food preparation is a hypothesis worth exploring. On the other hand, CSF levels of NPY and PYY have been reported to be normal in women with BN when measured while subjects were acutely ill. Although levels of PYY increased above normal when subjects were reassessed after 1 month of abstinence from binging and vomiting, levels of the peptides were similar to control values in long-term recovered individuals (Gendall, 1999).

More recently, it has been reported that the plasma concentration of NPY was lower in anorexic patients than in controls, while bulimic patients had elevated NPY levels (Baranowska, Radzikowska, Wasilewska-Dziubinska, Roguski, & Borowiec, 2000). Other data indicate that basal plasma PYY levels in AN are similar to or elevated in comparison to control values, with variability in postprandial PYY responses also noted across studies (Germain et al., 2007; Misra et al., 2006; Nakahara et al., 2007; Otto et al., 2007; Stock et al., 2005). Initial studies indicate that basal plasma PYY levels in BN are similar to control values, but that the postprandial response is significantly blunted in the patient group (Kojima et al., 2005; Monteleone et al., 2005). Additional research is needed to assess the potential behavioral correlates of these findings.

Cholecystokinin

CCK is a peptide secreted by the GI system in response to food intake. Release of CCK is thought to be one means of transmitting satiety signals to the brain by way of vagal afferents (Gibbs, Young, & Smith, 1973). In parallel to its role in satiety in rodents, exogenously administered CCK reduces food intake in humans (Kissileff, Pi-Sunyer, Thornton, & Smith, 1981). The preponderance of data suggests that patients with BN, in comparison to controls, have diminished release of CCK after ingestion of a standardized test-meal (Devlin et al., 1997; Geracioti & Liddle, 1988; Keel, Wolfe, Liddle, De Young, & Jimerson, 2007; Phillipp, Pirke, Kellner, & Krieg, 1991; Pirke et al., 1994). Measurements of basal CCK values in blood lymphocytes and in CSF also appear to be decreased in patients with BN (Brambilla, Brunetta, Draisci, et al., 1995; Lydiard et al., 1993). It has been suggested that the diminished CCK response to a meal may play a role in diminished postingestive satiety observed in BN (LaChaussee, Kissileff, Walsh, & Hadigan, 1992). The CCK response in bulimic patients was found to return toward normal after treatment (Geracioti & Liddle, 1988).

Studies of CCK in AN have yielded less consistent findings. Some studies have found elevations in basal levels of plasma CCK (Phillipp et al., 1991; Tamai et al., 1993), as well as increased peptide release after a test-meal (Harty, Pearson, Solomon, & McGuigan, 1991; Phillipp et al., 1991). One study found blunting of CCK response to an oral glucose load normalized in anorexic patients after partial restoration of body weight (Tamai et al., 1993). Other studies have found that measures of CCK function in AN were similar to or lower than control values (Baranowska et al., 2000; Brambilla, Brunetta, Peirone, et al., 1995; Geracioti, Liddle, Altemus, Demitrack, & Gold, 1992; Pirke et al., 1994). Further studies are needed to evaluate the relationship between altered CCK regulation and other indices of abnormal gastric function in symptomatic bulimic and anorexic patients (Geliebter et al., 1992).

Leptin

Leptin, the protein product of the *ob* gene, is secreted predominantly by adipose tissue cells. In the hypothalamus, leptin interacts with neuropeptide Y, serotonin, and the melanocortins to decrease food intake, thus regulating body fat stores (Friedman & Halaas, 1998; Zhang et al., 1994; Zigman & Elmquist, 2003). Defects in the leptin coding sequence resulting in leptin deficiency, or defects in leptin receptor function, are associated with obesity in rodent models. In humans, serum and CSF concentrations of leptin correlate positively with fat mass across a broad range of body weight, including obesity (Considine et al., 1996; Schwartz, Peskind, Raskind, Boyko, & Porte, 1996). Thus, obesity in humans is not thought to be a result of leptin deficiency *per se*, though rare genetic deficiencies in leptin production have been associated with familial obesity (Farooqi et al., 2001).

Underweight patients with AN have consistently been found to have significantly reduced serum leptin concentrations in comparison to normal weight controls (Baranowska, Wolinska-Witort, Wasilewska-Dziubinska, Roguski, & Chmielowska, 2001; Eckert et al., 1998; Grinspoon et al., 1996; Hebebrand et al., 1995; Mantzoros, Flier, Lesem, Brewerton, & Jimerson, 1997; Monteleone, DiLieto, Castaldo, & Maj, 2004). Based on studies in laboratory animals, it has been suggested that low leptin levels may contribute to amenorrhea and other hormonal changes in the disorder (Ahima & Osei, 2004; Ahima, Saper, Flier, & Elmquist, 2000; Holtkamp et al., 2003; Mantzoros et al., 1997). In healthy volunteers, even modest reductions in energy intake result in substantial decreases in circulating leptin levels (Wolfe, Jimerson, Orlova, & Mantzoros, 2004). Although the reduction in fasting serum leptin levels in AN correlates with reduction in body mass index, there has been some discussion of the possibility that leptin levels in anorexic patients may be higher than expected based on the extent of weight loss (Frederich, Hu, Raymond, & Pomeroy, 2002; Jimerson, 2002). Mantzoros and colleagues (1997) reported an elevated CSF to serum leptin ratio in AN compared to controls, suggesting that the proportional decrease in leptin levels with weight loss is greater in serum than in CSF. A longitudinal investigation during refeeding in AN patients has shown that CSF leptin concentrations reach normal values before full weight restoration, possibly as a consequence of the relatively rapid and disproportionate accumulation of fat during refeeding (Mantzoros et al., 1997). This finding led the authors to suggest that premature normalization of leptin concentration might contribute to difficulty in achieving and sustaining a normal weight in anorexia nervosa. Further research is needed to assess whether serum leptin levels at the time of discharge are predictive of post-hospital clinical course (Holtkamp et al., 2004; Lob et al., 2003). Plasma and CSF leptin levels appear to be similar to control values in long-term recovered AN subjects (Gendall, 1999).

As reviewed (Monteleone, DiLieto, Castaldo, & Maj, 2004), patients with bulimia nervosa, in comparison to carefully matched controls, have significantly decreased leptin concentrations in serum samples obtained after overnight fast (Baranowska et al., 2001; Brewerton, Lesem, Kennedy, & Garvey, 2000; Frederich et al., 2002; Jimerson, Mantzoros, Wolfe, & Metzger, 2000; Monteleone, Di Lieto, Tortorella, Longobardi, & Maj, 2000). Initial findings suggest that serum leptin levels remain decreased in individuals who have achieved sustained recovery from BN, compared to controls with closely matched percentage body fat. This finding may be related to evidence for a persistent decrease in activity in the hypothalamic–pituitary–thyroid axis in long-term recovered BN individuals (Wolfe et al., 2000). These alterations could be associated with decreased metabolic rate and a tendency toward weight gain, contributing to the preoccupation with body weight characteristic of bulimia nervosa.

Ghrelin

Intracerebroventricular injections of the gut-related peptide ghrelin strongly stimulated feeding in rats and increased body weight gain. When administered to healthy human volunteers, ghrelin results in increased hunger and food intake (Wren et al., 2001). In addition, it has been reported that fasting plasma ghrelin concentrations in humans are negatively correlated with body mass index (BMI; Shiiya et al., 2002; Tanaka et al., 2002), percentage body fat, and fasting leptin and insulin concentrations (Tschop et al., 2001). As recently reviewed (Jimerson & Wolfe, 2006), a number of studies have shown elevation in circulating ghrelin levels in AN, with a return to normal levels as patients regain weight (Nakahara et al., 2007). However, ghrelin has also been reported as unlikely to contribute to the array of AN symptoms (Stock et al., 2005). Further research is needed to explore the possible existence of ghrelin resistance in cachectic states related to the EDs.

Studies comparing fasting plasma ghrelin concentrations in patients with BN and healthy controls have yielded variable results (Monteleone et al., 2005; Monteleone, Martiadis, Fabrazzo, Serritella, & Maj, 2003). It is of interest, however, that the postprandial decrease in ghrelin levels appears to be blunted in patients with BN (Kojima et al., 2005; Monteleone et al., 2005), consistent with other evidence for diminished satiety responses in the disorder.

Summary of CNS Neuropeptide Alterations
Individuals with AN tend to have hypersecretion of CRH and exaggerated HPA function, lower NPY plasma concentration, lower CSF leptin concentration, and elevated ghrelin levels compared to healthy controls. However, there has been less agreement in the literature concerning other peptides, including opioid, PYY, and CCK expression in AN. In contrast, BN has been consistently described by elevated NPY levels, decreased PPY and CCK after a meal, and decreased serum leptin levels. Low CCK release recovered after treatment, but serum leptin levels remained low even after recovery. Like AN, the literature is unclear as to alterations of CSF beta-endorphin and related opiate concentrations in BN. A recent meta-analysis summarized baseline and postprandial levels of PYY, ghrelin, and CCK in AN and BN (Prince, Stahl, & Treasure, 2009).

It is likely that many of the starvation-driven endocrine and metabolic change are compensatory and attempt to conserve energy or stimulate hunger and feeding (orexigenic[Schwartz et al., 2000). For example, AN patients have increased orexigenic signals from neuropeptides such as NPY and leptin (see Inui, 2001). However, starvation in AN patients also stimulates feeding-inhibitory (anorexigenic) signaling by increasing levels of anorexigenic peptides, such as CRH, CCK, and pancreatic polypeptide. It is important to note that alterations of these and other neuropeptide systems affected in AN patients, such as beta-endorphin, are likely to result in altered mood, cognitive function, impulse control, and autonomic and hormonal systems (Jimerson & Wolfe, 2006), raising the likelihood they contribute to the behavioral symptoms associated with the ill state. For example, intracerebroventricular CRH administration in experimental animals produces many of the physiological and behavioral changes associated with AN, including hypothalamic hypogonadism, altered emotionality, decreased sexual activity, hyperactivity, and decreased feeding behavior

(Kaye et al., 1987). Thus, it can be argued that some secondary peptide changes sustain AN behaviors by driving a desire for more dieting and weight loss.

Table 6.1 summarizes CNS neuropeptide alterations in AN and BN.

Monoamine Systems
There is an abundance of evidence that individuals with AN and BN have disturbances of monoamine function in the ill state. Although less well studied, monoamine disturbances appear to persist after recovery.

Dopamine
Altered dopamine (DA) activity has been found among ill AN and BN individuals. Homovanillic acid (HVA), the major metabolite of dopamine in humans, was decreased in CSF of underweight AN subjects (Kaye, Ebert, Raleigh, & Lake, 1984). Although ill BN subjects, as a group, have normal CSF HVA, several studies have shown a significant reduction of CSF HVA in BN patients with high binge frequency (Jimerson, Lesem, Kaye, & Brewerton, 1992; Kaye et al., 1990). Individuals with AN have altered frequency of functional polymorphisms of DA D2 receptor genes that might affect receptor transcription and translation efficiency (Bergen et al., 2005). CNS dopamine metabolism may explain differences in symptoms among AN, AN-BN, and BN subjects. Our group (Kaye, Frank, & McConaha, 1999) found that recovered (REC) AN subjects had significantly reduced concentrations of CSF HVA, compared to REC AN-BN or BN women. DA neuronal function has been associated with motor activity (Kaye et al., 1999) and reward (Blum et al., 1995; Salamone, 1996). Individuals with AN have stereotyped and hyperactive motor behavior, anhedonic and restrictive personalities, and reduced novelty seeking.

Serotonin
Serotonin pathways play an important role in postprandial satiety. Treatments that increase intrasynaptic 5-hydroxytryptamine (5-HT, serotonin) or directly activate 5-HT receptors, tend to reduce food consumption whereas interventions that dampen 5-HT neurotransmission or block receptor activation reportedly increase food consumption and promote weight gain (Blundell, 1984; Leibowitz & Shor-Posner, 1986). Moreover, CNS 5-HT pathways have been implicated in the modulation of mood, impulse regulation and behavioral constraint, and obsessionality, and they affect a variety of neuroendocrine systems.

Table 6.1 Summary of Neuroendocrine/Neuropeptide Alterations in AN and BN

Measurement	References (First Author, Year)	Group	Summary
CRH	Gold, 1986; Kaye, 1987; Licinio, 1996; Walsh, 1987	Ill AN	↑
	Gwirtsman, 1989 –ACTH	Ill BN	=
		REC BN	↓
Opioid	Brambilla, 1995	Ill AN	↑
	Lesem, 1991		=
	Kaye, 1987		↓
	Brewerton, 1992	Ill BN	↓
NPY	Kaye, 1990; Baranowska, 2000	Ill AN	↑
	Baranowska, 2000		↓
	Baranowska, 2000	Ill BN	↑
PYY, basal	Germain, 2007; Misra, 2006, Nakahara, 2007	Ill AN	↑
	Baranowska, 2000; Kaye, 1990; Otto, 2007		=
	Kokima, 2005; Monteleone, 2005	Ill BN	=
PYY, postprandial	Nakahara, 2007	Ill AN	↑
	Otto, 2007, Stock, 2005		=
	Kokima, 2005; Monteleone, 2005	Ill BN	↓
CCK, basal	Phillipp, 1991; Tamai, 1993	Ill AN	↑
	Geracioti, 1992, Pirke, 1994	Ill AN	=
	Geracioti, 1992, Pirke, 1994	REC AN	=
	Brambilla, 1995; Lydiard, 1993; Pirke, 1994	Ill BN	↓
	Phillipp, 1991		=
	Geracioti, 1988	REC BN	=
CCK, postprandial	Harty, 1991; Phillipp, 1991	Ill AN	↑
	Geracioti, 1992, Pirke, 1994		=
	Baranowska, 2000; Brambilla, 1995		↓
	Geracioti, 1992, Pirke, 1994	REC AN	=
	Devlin, 1997; Geracioti, 1988; Keel, 2007; Phillipp, 1991; Pirke, 1994	Ill BN	↓
Leptin	Baranowska, 2001; Eckert, 1998; Grinspoon, 1996; Hebebrand, 1995; Mantzoros, 1997; Monteleone, 2004	Ill AN	↓
		AN, weight	↑
	Hebebrand, 1995	restored	=
	Eckert, 1998	REC AN	=
	Gendall, 1999	Ill BN	↓
	Baranowska, 2001; Brewerton, 2000;Frederich, 2002; Jimerson, 2000; Monteleone, 2000; Wolfe, 2000	REC BN	↓
	Wolfe, 2000		
Ghrelin	Nakahara, 2007	Ill AN	↑
	Stock, 2005		=
	Kojima, 2005	Ill BN	↑
	Monteleone, 2005		=
	Monteleone, 2003		↓

Increased compared to controls (↑); decreased compared to controls (↓); no difference from controls (=).

There has been considerable interest in the role that 5-HT may play in AN and BN (Brewerton, 1995; Jimerson, Lesem, Kaye, Hegg, & Brewerton, 1990; Kaye et al., 1998; Kaye & Weltzin, 1991; Steiger et al., 2005; Treasure & Campbell, 1994). In part, this is related to the fact that studies have found that AN and BN have alterations in 5-HT metabolism. When underweight, individuals with AN have a significant reduction in basal concentrations of the serotonin metabolite 5-hydroxyindoleacetic acid (5-HIAA) in the CSF compared to healthy controls, as well as blunted plasma prolactin response to drugs with 5-HT activity and reduced [3H]imipramine binding. Together, these findings suggest reduced serotonergic activity, although this may arise secondarily from reductions in dietary supplies of the 5-HT synthesizing amino acid tryptophan.

By contrast, CSF concentrations of 5-HIAA are reported to be elevated in long-term weight recovered AN individuals. These contrasting findings of reduced and heightened serotonergic activity in acutely ill and long-term recovered AN individuals, respectively, may seem counterintuitive; however, as dieting lowers plasma tryptophan levels in otherwise healthy women (Anderson, Parry-Billings, Newsholme, Fairburn, & Cowen, 1990), resumption of normal eating in individuals with AN may unmask intrinsic abnormalities in serotonergic systems that mediate certain core behavioral or temperamental underpinnings of risk and vulnerability.

Considerable evidence also exists for a dysregulation of serotonergic processes in BN. Examples includes blunted prolactin response to the 5-HT receptor agonists m-chlorophenylpiperazine (m-CPP), 5-hydroxytryptophan, and DL-fenfluramine, and enhanced migraine-like headache response to m-CPP challenge. Acute perturbation of serotonergic tone by dietary depletion of tryptophan has also been linked to increased food intake and mood irritability in individuals with BN compared to healthy controls. And, like AN, women with long-term recovery from BN have been shown to have elevated concentrations of 5-HIAA in the CSF as well as increased platelet binding of paroxetine.

There is extensive literature associating the serotonergic systems and fundamental aspects of behavioral inhibition (Geyer, 1996; Soubrie, 1986). Reduced CSF 5-HIAA levels are associated with increased impulsivity and aggression in humans and nonhuman primates, whereas increased CSF 5-HIAA levels are related to behavioral inhibition (Fairbanks, Melega, Jorgensen, Kaplan, & McGuire, 2001; Westergaard et al., 2003). Thus, it is of interest that recovered AN and BN women had elevated CSF 5-HIAA concentrations. Behaviors found after recovery from AN and BN, such as obsessionality with symmetry and exactness, anxiety, and perfectionism, tend to be opposite in character to behaviors displayed by people with low 5-HIAA levels. Together, these studies contribute to a growing literature suggesting that CSF 5-HIAA concentrations may correlate with a spectrum of behavior. Reduced CSF 5-HIAA levels appear to be related to behavioral undercontrol whereas increased CSF 5-HIAA concentrations may be related to behavioral overcontrol.

The possibility of a common vulnerability for BN and AN may seem puzzling given well-recognized differences in behavior in these disorders. However, recent studies suggest that AN and BN have a shared etiologic vulnerability. That is, there is a familial aggregation of a range of EDs in relatives of probands with either BN or AN, and these two disorders are highly comorbid in twin studies. Both disorders respond to 5-HT specific medications, and both disorders have high levels of harm avoidance (see Klump et al., 2000), a personality trait hypothesized to be related to increased 5-HT activity. These data raise the possibility that a disturbance of 5-HT activity may create a vulnerability for the expression of a cluster of symptoms that are common to both AN and BN.

Other factors that are independent of vulnerability for the development of an ED may contribute to the development of ED subgroups. For example, people with restrictor-type AN have extraordinary self-restraint and self-control. The risk for obsessive–compulsive personality disorder is elevated only in this subgroup and in their families and shows a shared transmission with restrictor-type AN (Lilenfeld et al., 1998). In other words, an additional vulnerability for behavioral overcontrol and rigid and inflexible mood states, combined with vulnerability for an ED, may result in restrictor-type AN.

The contribution of 5-HT to specific human behaviors remains uncertain. Serotonin has been postulated to contribute to temperament or personality traits such as harm avoidance (Cloninger, 1987) or behavioral inhibition (Soubrie, 1986) or to categorical dimensions such as obsessive–compulsive disorder (Barr, Goodman, Price, McDougle, & Charney, 1992), anxiety and fear (Charney, Woods, Krystal, & Heninger, 1990), or depression (Grahame-Smith, 1992), as well as satiety for food consumption. It is possible that separate components of 5-HT neuronal systems (i.e., different pathways or receptors) are coded for such specific behaviors. However, that may not be consistent with the neurophysiology of 5-HT neuronal function.

Positron Emission Tomography Studies in Eating Disorders

Positron emission tomography (PET) imaging with selective neurotransmitter radioligands has resulted in a technology permitting new insights into regional binding and specificity of 5-HT and dopamine neurotransmission in vivo in humans and their relationship to behaviors.

DA RECEPTOR RADIOLIGANDS

Little work has been done assessing neurochemical alterations involved in the feeding network. One study, using PET and the DA D2/D3 radioligand raclopride, found lower raclopride binding in the dorsal putamen and caudate nucleus in the sated state compared to hungry, suggesting DA release during or after the feeding process. In addition, the experienced meal pleasantness correlated negatively with raclopride binding, suggesting a positive correlation of pleasantness rating with DA surge (Small, Jones-Gotman, & Dagher, 2003). This is surprising because in many studies pleasantness or hedonic experiences were in relation to DA activity in the ventral striatum including the nucleus accumbens. Studying neuroreceptor networks is of particular importance since results may contribute to developing new pharmaceutical interventions. The DA system may be of special interest because it plays a role in motivation, reward, preferences, and reinforcement (Cannon & Bseikri, 2004).

DA RECEPTOR BINDING IS ALTERED IN EDS

The role of DA as a reward prediction signal is well established (Schultz, 1998; Schultz, Tremblay, & Hollerman, 1998). Several lines of evidence suggest AN have altered DA metabolism, including: (1) reduced cerebrospinal fluid DA metabolites in ill and REC AN (Kaye et al., 1999); (2) altered frequency of functional polymorphisms of DA D2 receptor genes (Bergen et al., 2005), including the A1 allele implicated in hedonic value of rewards (Cohen, Young, Baek, Kessler, & Ranganath, 2005) and feeding (Nisoli et al., 2007); (3) impaired visual discrimination learning (Lawrence, 2003), a task thought to reflect DA signaling function; (4) a generalized failure to activate the appetitive motivational system in a startle task (Friederich et al., 2006); (5) impaired set shifting (Tchanturia et al., 2004), which, in part, is related to ventral striatal DA function (Goto & Grace, 2005); and (6) REC AN had increased binding of D2/D3 receptors in the anterior ventral striatum (Frank et al., 2005), a region that contributes to optimal responses to reward stimuli (Delgado, Nystrom, Fissel, Noll, & Fiez, 2000; Montague, Hyman, & Cohen, 2004; Schultz, 2004). In addition, REC AN showed positive correlations between DA D2/D3 binding in the dorsal caudate/dorsal putamen and anxiety measures. In summary, striatal DA dysfunction in AN could contribute to altered reward and affect, decision-making, and executive control, as well as stereotypic motor activity (Yin & Knowlton, 2006)

and decreased food ingestion (Halford, Cooper, & Dovey, 2004).

5-HT RECEPTOR RADIOLIGANDS

The 5-HT$_{1A}$ autoreceptor is located presynaptically on 5-HT somatodendritic cell bodies in the raphe nucleus, where it functions to decrease 5-HT neurotransmission (Staley, Malison, & Innis, 1998). High densities of postsynaptic 5-HT$_{1A}$ exist in the hippocampus, septum, amygdala, and entorhinal and frontal cortex, where they serve to mediate the effects of released 5-HT. Studies in animals and humans implicate the 5-HT$_{1A}$ receptor in anxiety (File, Kenny, & Cheeta, 2000) and depression and/ or suicide (Mann, 1999). Pharmacological and knockout studies implicate the 5-HT$_{1A}$ receptor in the modulation of anxiety (Gross et al., 2002). Bailer (Bailer et al., 2007) reported that ill AN individuals had a 50% to 70% increase in 5-HT$_{1A}$ receptor binding potential (BP) in subgenual, mesial temporal, orbital frontal, and raphe brain regions, as well as in prefrontal, lateral temporal, anterior cingulate cortex (ACC), and parietal regions. Increased 5-HT$_{1A}$ postsynaptic activity has been reported in ill BN subjects (Tiihonen et al., 2004). REC bulimic-type AN and REC BN subjects (Bailer et al., 2005; Kaye, unpublished data) had a significant 20% to 40% increase in 5-HT$_{1A}$ receptor BP in these same regions compared to control women (CW; Bailer et al., 2005). In contrast, REC RAN women showed no difference in 5-HT$_{1A}$ receptor BP compared to controls (Bailer et al., 2005).

AN and BN are frequently comorbid with depression and anxiety disorders. However, reduced 5-HT$_{1A}$ receptor BP has been found in ill (Drevets et al., 1999; Sargent et al., 2000) and REC (Bhagwagar, Rabiner, Sargent, Grasby, & Cowen, 2004) depressed subjects, as well as in a primate model for depression (Shively et al., 2006). Parsey (Parsey et al., 2005) found no difference in carbonyl-[^{11}C]WAY100635 BP in major depressive disorder, although a subgroup of never medicated subjects had elevated carbonyl-[^{11}C]WAY100635 BP. Recent studies have found reduced [^{11}C]WAY100635 BP in social phobia (Lanzenberger et al., 2007) and panic disorder (Neumeister et al., 2004). These findings suggest AN and BN, mood, and depression share disturbances of common neuronal pathways but are etiologically different. Postsynaptic 5-HT$_{2A}$ receptors, which are in high densities in the cerebral cortex and other regions of rodents and humans (Burnet, Eastwood, & Harrison, 1997; Saudou & Hen, 1994), is of interest because it has been implicated in the modulation of feeding and mood, as well as selective serotonin reuptake inhibitor (SSRI) response (Bailer et al., 2004; Bonhomme & Esposito, 1998; De Vry & Schreiber, 2000; Simansky, 1996; Stockmeier, 1997).

5-HT RECEPTOR BINDING IS ALTERED IN EDS

Ill AN subjects have been found to have normal 5-HT$_{2A}$ receptor BP values in one study (Bailer et al., 2007) and reduced BP in another study (Audenaert et al., 2003) in the left frontal, bilateral parietal, and occipital cortex. After recovery, restricting-type AN individuals (Frank et al., 2002) had reduced 5-HT$_{2A}$ receptor BP in mesial temporal and parietal cortical areas as well as in subgenual and pregenual ACC. Similarly, REC bulimic-type AN (Bailer et al., 2004) women had reduced 5-HT$_{2A}$ receptor BP in left subgenual ACC, left parietal, and right occipital cortex. In addition, REC BN women only had reduced [^{18}F]altanserin BP relative to controls in the orbital frontal region (Kaye et al., 2001).

CORRELATIONS OF PET DATA WITH ANXIETY AND HARM AVOIDANCE

The PET imaging studies in ill and REC AN and BN subjects described above have found significant correlations between harm avoidance and binding for the 5-HT$_{1A}$, 5-HT$_{2A}$, and DA D2/D3 receptors in mesial temporal and other limbic regions. Bailer (Bailer et al., 2004) found that REC AN-BN subjects showed a positive relationship between [^{18}F] altanserin BP in the left subgenual ACC and mesial temporal cortex and harm avoidance. For ill AN subjects, [^{18}F]altanserin BP was positively related to harm avoidance in the suprapragenual ACC, frontal, and parietal regions. 5-HT$_{2A}$ receptor binding and harm avoidance were shown to be negatively correlated in the frontal cortex in healthy subjects (Moresco et al., 2002) and in the prefrontal cortex in patients who attempted suicide (van Heeringen et al., 2003).

Clinical and epidemiological studies have consistently shown that one or more anxiety disorders occur in the majority of people with AN or BN (Godart, Flament, Perdereau, & Jeammet, 2002; Kaye et al., 2004; Kendler et al., 1995; Walters & Kendler, 1995). Silberg and Bulik (2005), using twins, found a unique genetic effect that influences liability to early anxiety and ED symptoms. When a lifetime anxiety disorder is present, the anxiety most commonly occurs first in childhood, preceding the onset of AN or BN (Bulik, Sullivan, Fear, & Joyce, 1997; Deep, Nagy, Weltzin, Rao, & Kaye, 1995;

Godart, Flament, Lecrubier, & Jeammet, 2000). Anxiety and harm avoidance remain elevated after recovery from AN, AN-BN, and BN (Wagner, Barbarich, et al., 2006), even if individuals never had a lifetime anxiety disorder diagnosis (Kaye et al., 2004). Finally, anxiety (Spielberger, Gorsuch, & Lushene, 1970) and Harm Avoidance from the Cloninger (TCI; Cloninger, Przybeck, Svrakic, & Wetzel, 1994) Temperament and Character Inventory have been a robust signal in genetic studies (Bacanu et al., 2005).

Summary of PET Studies in Eating Disorders

The premorbid onset and the persistence of anxiety and harm avoidance symptoms after recovery suggest these are traits that contribute to the pathogenesis of AN and BN. The PET imaging data suggest that such behaviors are related to disturbances of 5-HT and DA neurotransmitter function in limbic and executive pathways.

This technology holds the promise of a new era of understanding the complexity of neuronal systems in human behavior. For example, postsynaptic 5-HT$_{1A}$ receptors (Celada, Puig, Casanovas, Guillazo, & Artigas, 2001; Richer, Hen, & Blier, 2002; Sibille, Pavlides, Benke, & Toth, 2000; Szabo & Blier, 2001) have "downstream" effects and interactions with other neuronal systems, such as norepinephrine, glutamate, and gama-aminobutyric acid. Enhanced 5-HT$_{1A}$ activity in AN and BN may cause or reflect an altered balance between these neuronal systems. Moreover, 5-HT$_{1A}$ receptors interact with other 5-HT receptors such as 5-HT$_{2A}$ (Martin, Kaplan, & Weir, 1997; Szabo & Blier, 2001). 5-HT$_{1A}$ post-synaptic receptors mediate locus coeruleus firing through 5-HT transmission at 5-HT$_{2A}$ receptors (Szabo & Blier, 2001). Theoretically, increased 5-HT$_{1A}$ and reduced 5-HT$_{2A}$ postsynaptic receptor activity in AN might result in an increase in noradrenergic neuron firing (Szabo & Blier, 2001). Moreover, postsynaptic 5-HT$_{1A}$ receptors hyperpolarize and 5-HT$_{2A}$ receptors depolarize layer V pyramidal neurons (Martin-Ruiz et al., 2001). In AN, synergistic effects of these receptors, which are co-localized on pyramidal neurons, may reduce pyramidal neuronal excitability.

Taken together, these PET-radioligand studies confirm that altered 5-HT neuronal pathway activity persists after recovery from AN and BN and support the possibility that these psychobiological alterations might contribute to traits such as increased anxiety, which may contribute to a vulnerability to develop an ED.

Brain Imaging Studies

Brain imaging studies in AN and BN can be divided in several categories. First, there has been a substantial literature using computerized tomography, and more recently MRI, that seeks to determine whether there are brain structural alterations in individuals with ED. Second, more recent studies have used functional magnetic resonance imaging (fMRI) or other technologies to assess blood flow responses to some stimuli, such as pictures of food or tastes of food. Third are imaging studies, such as PET, that employ a radioligand. These studies, which may use the glucose analog fluorodeoxyglucose (FDG) to study glucose metabolism, or a ligand that is specific for a serotonin receptor (such as the DA and 5-HT receptors discussed in the preceding text), provide information that is specific for the system being studied.

In general, findings from functional and radioligand studies have been relatively consistent in that most studies have positive findings within frontal, cingulate, temporal, and/or parietal regions. Thus, it can be stated that ED individuals, both when ill and after recovery, have alterations in brain activity compared to matched controls. However, it should be noted that these studies have not consistently identified regions, pathways, or behavioral correlates. Sample sizes have been small, and imaging technologies and methods vary widely. Moreover, studies have tended to assess relatively large regions of brain that vary widely between studies. Studies to date indicate gross alterations of brain function. Because brain pathways are highly complex, the neuroanatomy of AN and BN have only begun to be characterized.

It should be noted that there has been substantial progress in understanding how brain cortical regions modulate higher order functions related to appetitive behaviors in humans. Thus, this section begins first with a review of the neurocircuitry involved in appetite regulation, then with an overview of fMRI studies of taste in healthy controls, since they provide a potential baseline that can be used to determine whether individuals with AN and BN have some alteration in brain pathways devoted to the modulation of feeding.

Neurocircuitry of Appetite Regulation

In order to use fMRI to test appetitive regulation in REC EDs, we have carried out studies (Frank et al., 2006, 2008; Wagner, Aizenstein, et al., 2006, 2007) that use a pump apparatus to deliver repeat, blind gustatory stimuli, such as sucrose (Frank et al.,

2003). Although a gustatory task employing sucrose stimuli does not test the complexity of food choices (Small, 2006), it does activate appetitive pathways of interest. Sweet taste perception is peripherally mediated by tongue receptors (Chandraskekar, Hoon, Ryba, & Zuker, 2006) through cranial nerves, the nucleus tractus solitarius, and thalamic ventroposterior medial nucleus, to the primary gustatory cortex, that in humans comprise the frontal operculum and the anterior insula (AI; Faurion et al., 1999; Ogawa, 1994; Schoenfeld et al., 2004; Scott, Yaxley, Sienkiewicz, & Rolls, 1986; Yaxley, Rolls, & Sienkiewicz, 1990).

Projections from the primary taste cortex reach the central nucleus of the amygdala and from there, the lateral hypothalamus and midbrain dopaminergic regions (Simon, De Araujo, Gutierrez, & Nicolelis, 2006). The primary taste cortex also projects heavily to the striatum (Chikama, McFarland, & Amaral, 1997; Fudge, Breitbart, Danish, & Pannoni, 2005). The AI is contiguous with the posterior OFC at the operculum. This region is reciprocally connected with the medial prefrontal cortex (mPFC) and ACC (Carmichael & Price, 1996). The ventral striatum receives input from the AI and ACC (Carmichael & Price, 1996; Fudge et al., 2005; Haber, Kunishio, Mizobuhi, & Lynd-Balta, 1995).

The AI and associated gustatory cortex respond not only to the taste and physical properties of food, but also to its rewarding properties (O'Doherty, Kringelbach, Rolls, Hornak, & Andrews, 2001; Schultz, Tremblay, & Hollerman, 2000; Small, 2002; Small, Zatorre, Dagher, Evans, & Jones-Gotman, 2001). Some studies argue that the AI provide a representation of food in the mouth that is independent of hunger, and thus of reward value (Rolls, 2005), whereas the OFC computes the hedonic value of food (Kringelbach et al., 2003; O'Doherty et al., 2001; Rolls, 2005). Other studies (Small et al., 2001) suggest that the AI and OFC have overlapping representations of sensory and reward/affective processing of taste.

The AI is centrally placed to receive information about the salience (both appetitive and aversive) and relative value of the stimulus environment and integrate this information with the effect that these stimuli may have on the body state. The AI has bidirectional connections to the amygdala, nucleus accumbens (Reynolds & Zahm, 2005) and OFC (Ongur & Price, 2000). The striatum (Kelley, 2004) receives inputs from brain regions involved in reward, incentive learning, and emotional regulation, including the ACC, the ventromedial PFC, the OFC, and AI (Chikama et al., 1997; Fudge et al., 2005; Fudge, Breitbart, & McClain, 2004; Haber, Kim, Mailly, & Calzavara, 2006).

The OFC is associated with flexible responses to changing stimuli (Izquierdo, Cammarota, Medina, & Bevilaqua, 2004; Kazama & Bachevalier, 2006) such as the incentive value, e.g. whether one is hungry (Critchley & Rolls, 1996; Gottfried, O'Doherty, & Dolan, 2003; Hikosaka & Watanabe, 2000). Of note, the OFC is highly dependent on 5-HT innervation for flexible reversal learning (Clarke, Walker, Robbins, & Roberts, 2007) so that 5-HT abnormalities in ED may contribute to the disturbed inhibitory control (inability to incorporate changing incentive value of stimuli).

Information about the interoceptive state processed in the AI is relayed to the ACC, which, as part of the central executive system, can generate an error signal that is critical for conflict monitoring and the allocation of attentional resources (Carter, Botvinick, & Cohan, 1999). Thus, interoception involves monitoring the sensations that are important for the integrity of the internal body state and connecting to systems that are important for allocating attention, evaluating context and planning actions (Paulus & Stein, 2006). The role of the AI is thus focused on how the value of stimuli might affect the body state. These regions therefore play an important role in determining homeostatic appetitive needs when hungry or satiated. In addition, interoceptive sensations are often associated with intense affective and motivational components (Paulus & Stein, 2006), and the evaluative component of the signal is highly dependent on the homeostatic state of the individual.

Brain Imaging Studies of Normal Feeding Behavior in Healthy Individuals

Noninvasive brain imaging tools have stimulated new insights into how cortical brain regions are involved in the regulation of food intake in humans and primates. Before discussing findings from brain imaging studies in individuals with AN and BN, we review recent literature on feeding-related physiology in healthy controls. This system of appetite and hunger, food appetence, ingestion of food, and subsequent subjective experience, is very complex, and study methodologies and results are not homogeneous. However, those studies may help us guide research on the pathophysiology of EDs and delineate biological traits. Little work has been done in AN and BN in understanding how taste and olfaction might activate brain circuits. Perhaps the primary

question is whether individuals with AN or BN have alterations of feeding-related brain pathways and how phenomena, such as food-related anxiety plays a role in the physiology of EDs.

Recent studies have shown that it is possible to study taste and smell in conjunction with fMRI. Such studies in control individuals may help design similar taste and smell studies in the ED population (Cerf-Ducastel & Murphy, 2004; De Araujo, Rolls, Kringelbach, McGlone, & Phillips, 2003). Research from Edmund Rolls and colleagues has provided new understanding of how the brain processes taste. In brief, the insula cortex shows the primary response to taste recognition, and the orbitofrontal cortex (OFC) shows secondary response to various taste stimuli. For example, pleasant gustatory stimulation activates the OFC. This activation declines when the same food is presented repeatedly, which results in sensory specific satiety.

New studies now show that the dorsolateral prefrontal cortex (DLPFC) is responsive to gustatory activation (Kringelbach, de Araujo, & Rolls, 2004). This area is a cognitive processing center and may suggest cognitive reflection of the taste experience, perhaps on a tertiary level. In a review of their own and studies of other investigators, this group proposes that OFC activity may be separated into anterior–posterior and medial-lateral compartments with task-specific responsiveness (Kringelbach et al., 2004). With the notion that the OFC is involved in the evaluation of the reward value that a stimulus has, the medial part may then be active to reinforcing stimuli and the lateral part to aversive stimuli. This may also be the case for olfactory stimuli (Gottfried et al., 2002). The anterior part was hypothesized to be more involved in abstract stimuli such as monetary reward, as opposed to more primitive experiences including taste or pain.

Another recent study commented on the interaction between the OFC and amygdala (Arana et al., 2003). Using images of menus of varying incentive values, it was found that the amygdala responded relative to the appeal of different aspects presented on the menu, whereas the medial OFC response was activated when having to make choices between menus in relation to individual difficulty during that task. The lateral OFC was activated when the preferred menu could not be chosen, and this could be consistent with some form of aversive experience as suggested earlier.

These studies suggest testable hypotheses for understanding AN and BN. Individuals with restricting type AN may have higher lateral OFC activation to aversive and perhaps anxiety provoking food stimuli such as fat (Drewnowski, Halmi, Pierce, Gibbs, & Smith, 1987) but higher medial OFC activity in response to exercise, weight loss promoting activity or particularly "safe" foods. We also propose early sensory specific satiety in AN, such as accelerated reduction of OFC activity to food stimuli, which would be consistent with early meal termination. In contrast, BN individuals may have delayed medial OFC activation reduction (e.g., delayed sensory specific satiety) for initially lower habituation, reflecting binge eating vulnerability. Since BN may like sweeter stimuli than controls (Drewnowski, Bellisle, Aimez, & Remy, 1987), they may have increased medial OFC response but may also have increased ACC or amygdala activation reflecting heightened anxiety after binge eating episodes. It is important to note that humans have substantial variability of brain response to taste stimuli, which may limit the power and interpretability of study results (Schoenfeld et al., 2004).

Recent brain imaging studies in controls using pictures of food and similar food-related stimuli confirmed that pictures of food activate primary and secondary taste centers as well as other regions (Wang et al., 2004). In another study, both high and low calorie food images activated the amygdala and ventromedial prefrontal cortex. However, high calorie foods may stimulate more medial and dorsolateral prefrontal areas, whereas low calorie food images may activate medial OFC and temporal regions (Killgore et al., 2003). Brain imaging studies using pictures of food test motivational states and possibly the desire to approach food. The hunger state in fact seems to activate amygdala and temporal areas more than the satiation state (LaBar et al., 2001), although gender differences seem to exist. It would be of interest to determine whether there is an appetitive difference in ED subjects and if AN subjects are more resilient toward hunger. Other important questions include whether individuals with AN ignore hunger because of heightened anxiety when considering possible weight gain and if brain response such as ACC or amygdala activity associated with anxiety ratings could reflect such altered processing of hunger and a desire to eat.

Another interesting study was on taste and preconceptions about the food ingested, suggesting that what we think about a certain product may be more influential than the substance itself when we cannot distinguish the taste (McClure et al., 2004). This is a highly important issue for AN individuals, who experience aversiveness in response to food based on its presumed calorie content rather than taste itself.

A recent study showed gender differences in healthy subjects in response to a liquid meal during hunger or satiation (Del Parigi et al., 2002), which is of interest because AN and BN primarily occur in women. In particular, healthy women had higher activity in occipital and parietal sensory association cortex and in the dorsolateral prefrontal cortex, but men had greater activation in the ventromedial prefrontal cortex when sated. This study did not report on other behavioral/emotional parameters, but it is possible that there are also gender differences in terms of response to food items and taste. However, this is speculative and needs to be further tested. A design should be pursued that investigates the cognitive impact versus a more basic physiologic processing in women versus men, and then in ED subjects. Furthermore, it would be very interesting to assess similarities and differences between women versus men who all have AN or BN.

In summary, the study of normal brain activity in relation to food intake has identified cortical pathways related to the physiology of food intake, such as the insula. In particular, the medial OFC may be somewhat specific for pleasant, and the lateral OFC specific for aversive taste experiences. In addition, the prefrontal cortex may be involved in cognitive processing of the food ingestion. In this network of activation, the amygdala was confirmed to play a role and may respond relative to the incentive and emotional value of taste stimulus. The balance between learned behaviors and innate biological traits is not certain, as knowledge about the brand name of a taste stimulus may contribute to brain activation. Studies have used tastes of food and food images in controls.

However, little work has been done in determining whether brain responses are similar using different types of food-related stimuli. This may be of importance in understanding the cognitive influences of taste. Also interesting are data suggesting that men and women have different response to food: for example, the possibility that women have greater cognitive activation to food stimuli, as well as sensorimotor cortex activation in response to a liquid meal after satiation. Such studies may shed light on understanding why women are at greater risk of developing EDs. Together, these functional taste studies in healthy controls offer important new leads for the study of altered eating physiology in AN and BN.

Functional and Task Activation Studies in EDs

A number of studies have used fMRI and single photon emission computed tomography (SPECT) to investigate appetite regulation in AN and BN. In general, sample sizes have been small, and studies have used a range of methods and many different brain regions. Moreover, the resolution of SPECT is poor so that specific regions cannot be clearly identified. While many of the studies have had positive findings, there has been little in the way of attempts to replicate findings.

PET AND SPECT: REGIONAL CEREBRAL BLOOD FLOW

Nozoe measured regional cerebral blood flow (rCBF) using SPECT and detected a significant increase in response to food intake in the left inferior frontal cortex in AN compared to controls (Nozoe et al., 1993). In a later study, Nozoe (Nozoe et al. (1995) reported that individuals with AN did not have cortical laterality or activated state in any cortical area before eating. However, there was increased activity in frontal, occipital, parietal and temporal regions after eating. In contrast, BN showed the highest cortical activity in the left temporal region and the bilateral inferior frontal regions before eating compared to controls but less cortical activity in response to food intake. Naruo (Naruo et al., 2000) reported that food imagination assessed by SPECT resulted in greater activation in inferior, superior, prefrontal, and parietal regions of the right brain in binge/purge type AN in comparison to restricting type AN and healthy controls.

Gordon (Gordon et al., 2001) used PET to show a high-calorie food stimulus resulted in elevated rCBF in occipital temporal regions in individuals with AN compared to controls. Ellison et al. (1998) used fMRI and found that individuals with AN, when viewing pictures of high calorie drinks, had increased signal changes in the left insula, anterior ACC, and left amygdala/hippocampal region that were possibly anxiety related. The amygdala/hippocampus region was also activated in healthy volunteers when confronted with unpleasant words concerning body image relative to neutral words, and it negatively correlated to sub-scales of the Eating Disorder Inventory-2 (Shirao, Okamoto, Okada, Okamoto, & Yamawaki, 2003). In addition, a decrease of blood flow in the ACC was detected by Naruo using SPECT in restricting type AN compared to binge/purge type AN or controls.

In summary, the many positive findings suggest the importance of proceeding with new brain imaging studies of appetite regulation but also a need to localize regions, identify neural circuits, replicate findings, and link results to other human and animal literature.

fMRI: IMAGES OF FOOD

Uher and colleagues assessed 26 female ED patients (16 AN, 10 BN) and compared them to 19 age-matched controls using fMRI (Uher et al., 2004). During scanning, subjects were confronted with images of food and nonfood items as well as emotional aversive and neutral images. In response to food stimuli, AN subjects, in comparison to controls, had higher activation in the left medial OFC and ACC, and a lower activation in the lateral prefrontal cortex, inferior parietal lobule and cerebellum. BN showed less activation in the lateral prefrontal cortex relative to controls for this stimulus. However, the group contrast for the emotional stimuli reveals significant activation in the occipital cortex, parietal cortex, and cerebellum.

It is important to note that Uher (Uher et al., (2004) included ill subjects ($n = 8$) previously described in an earlier paper (Uher et al., 2003). In the former study, the authors found that 8 ill subjects, when compared to 9 restricting-type AN, had increased right lateral and apical prefrontal cortex and ACC activation in response to food stimuli. Still, recovered AN subjects showed increased mPFC and ACC activation as well as decreased inferior parietal lobule activation in comparison to healthy controls to food stimuli. In this study, neural processing of emotional stimuli did not differ between groups. This is an important study because it compared stimuli related to food and emotions. These findings suggest that the medial prefrontal cortex might be specifically related to food stimuli because other regions were activated by both food and emotional stimuli. Activation of the lateral prefrontal cortex might be related to good outcome as it differentiated ill and recovered subjects. In general, findings are largely compatible with previous reports in subjects with EDs, except for lack of amygdala activation in the large sample, which could be related to methodological issues.

Santel et al. (2006) explored the influence of hunger or satiety in 13 patients with AN and 10 healthy control subjects (ages 13–21). The subjects rated visual food and nonfood stimuli for pleasantness during fMRI in hungry and satiated states.

AN patients rated food as less pleasant than controls. When satiated, AN patients showed decreased activation in left inferior parietal cortex relative to controls. When hungry, AN patients displayed weaker activation of the right visual occipital cortex than healthy controls. Food stimuli during satiety compared with hunger were associated with stronger right occipital activation in patients and with stronger activation in left lateral orbitofrontal cortex, the middle portion of the right ACC, and left middle temporal gyrus in controls. The authors concluded that the observed group differences in the fMRI activation to food pictures point to decreased food-related somatosensory processing in AN during satiety and to attentional mechanisms during hunger that might facilitate restricted eating in AN.

In summary, functional neuroimaging studies that showed emaciated and malnourished AN individuals pictures of food found altered activity in the insula and OFC, as well as in mesial temporal, parietal and the ACC regions as compared to CW (Z. Ellison et al., 1998; Gordon et al., 2001; Naruo et al., 2000; Nozoe et al., 1993, 1995; Santel et al., 2006; Uher et al., 2004). Studies using SPECT, PET-O[15] or fMRI found that when ill AN ate or were exposed to food, they had activated temporal regions, and in some studies, increased anxiety (Ellison et al., 1998; Gordon et al., 2001; Naruo et al., 2000; Nozoe et al., 1993). One fMRI study (Uher et al., 2003) found that pictures of food stimulated ACC and mPFC activity in both ill and REC AN, but not CW. This suggests that hyperactivity of these regions may be a trait marker of AN.

fMRI: RESPONSE TO SUCROSE IS ALTERED IN AN

Our group (Wagner et al., 2008) found AI, ACC, and striatal abnormalities in REC AN after we administered tastes of 10% sucrose and water in a blind, controlled manner to REC AN and CW. There were two main findings: (1) Compared to CW, the REC AN had a significantly reduced blood oxygen level dependent (BOLD) response to the blind administration of sucrose or water in the AI (Fig. 6.1, left insula $p = 0.003$), ACC, and striatal regions. (2) CW, but not recovered AN, showed a positive relationship between self-ratings of pleasantness and the intensity of the signal for sugar in the AI, ventral and dorsal putamen as well as ACC.

Do AN have an AI disturbance specifically related to gustatory modulation or a more generalized disturbance related to the integration of interoceptive stimuli? Interoception has long been thought to be critical for self-awareness because it provides the link between cognitive and affective processes and the current body state (Craig, 2002; Paulus & Stein, 2006). Lack of recognition of the symptoms

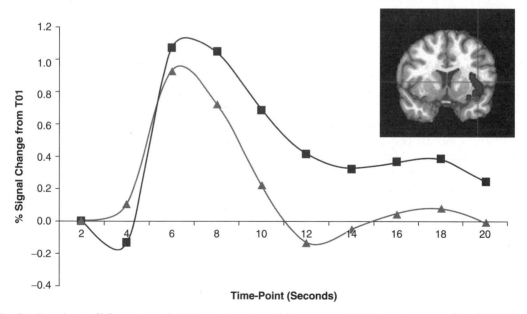

Fig. 6.1 Coronal view of left anterior insula ROI ($x = -41$, $y = 5$, $z = 5$). Time course of BOLD signal as a mean of all 16 REC AN (▲) and 16 CW (■) for taste-related (sucrose and water) response in the left insula.

of malnutrition, diminished insight and motivation to change, and altered central coherence, a measure of local versus global cognitive processing (Lopez et al., 2008), could all be related to disturbed AI function.

Appetitive dysregulation in AN and BN is poorly understood. Appetite regulation is a complex process that involves the integration of a wide variety of signals such as energy needs in the body, hedonic attraction to palatable foods, and long-term cognitive concerns about weight. The data reviewed above are the first to localize potential pathology of appetite disturbances in AN. We hypothesize that REC AN have altered incentive processing in the AI and related regions. AN fail to become appropriately hungry when starved, and are thus able to become emaciated. We think it likely that food has little rewarding value to AN, which suggests that AN may be associated with corresponding responses in the OFC or the striatum. Clinical observations suggest that AN have disturbed reward modulation that affects a wide range of appetitive behaviors, as well as behaviors not related to food.

fMRI: RESPONSE TO REWARD AND PUNISHMENT IS ALTERED IN AN

Individuals with AN have long been noted to be anhedonic and ascetic, able to sustain self-denial of food as well as most comforts and pleasures in life (Frank et al., 2005). They also tend to be highly harm avoidant and overconcerned about consequences. This temperament persists, in a more modest form, after recovery (Klump et al., 2004; Wagner, Barbarich, et al., 2006). Reward is one characteristic that differentiates AN and BN, since BN tend to be more impulsive, pleasure and stimuli seeking and less paralyzed by concerns with future consequences (Cassin & von Ranson, 2005). Positive reinforcers or rewards promote selected behaviors, induce subjective feelings of pleasure and other positive emotions, and maintain stimulus-response associations (Thut et al., 1997). Negative reinforcement also plays an essential role by encouraging avoidance or withdrawal behavior, as well as production of negative emotions. The reward circuit includes the ventral striatum, ventral tegmental area, amygdala, hippocampus, medial dorsal thalamus, ventral pallidum, and PFC (Koob, 1992).

Human neuroimaging studies show that a highly interconnected network of brain areas including OFC, mPFC, amygdala, striatum, and DA mid-brain are involved in reward processing of both primary (i.e., pleasurable tastes; Berns, McClure, Pagnoni,

& Montague, 2001; McClure, Berns, & Montague, 2003) and secondary (i.e., money) reinforcers (Breiter, Aharon, Kahneman, Dale, & Shizgal, 2001; Delgado et al., 2000; Gehring & Willoughby, 2002; Montague et al., 2004; O'Doherty, 2004). These regions code stimulus-reward value, maintain representations of predicted future reward and future behavioral choice, and may play a role in integrating and evaluating reward prediction to guide decisions. In animals, DA modulates the influence of limbic inputs on striatal activity (Goto & Grace, 2005; Montague, Hyman, & Cohen, 2004; Schultz, 2004; Yin & Knowlton, 2006) and mediates the "binding" of hedonic evaluation of stimuli to objects or acts ("wanting" response) (Berridge & Robinson, 1998). It has been postulated that dorsal striatum is engaged by real or perceived stimulus-response outcomes with DA projections modulating this behavior (O'Doherty et al., 2004; Tricomi, Delgado, & Fiez, 2004).

Because of the DA findings in REC AN (Bergen et al., 2005; Frank et al., 2005; Kaye, Frank, & McConaha, 1999), we performed an event-related fMRI study (Wagner et al., 2007) using a variation of a well-characterized "guessing-game" protocol (Delgado et al., 2000) known to activate the anteroventral striatum (AVS) with a differential response to positive and negative feedback in healthy volunteers. REC AN women had a similar response for wins and losses in the AVS ($p = 0.57$; Fig. 6.2). In contrast, REC AN showed exaggerated caudate-dorsal striatum activation in response to positive and negative feedback (Fig. 6.2) as well as greater response in the DLPFC and parietal cortex. Further, only the REC AN subjects showed a significant positive relationship between baseline trait anxiety and the percent signal change to wins or loses in the left caudate, supportive of our prior findings of dorsal caudate DA D2/D3 receptor binding being positively correlated with anxiety or harm avoidance (Frank et al., 2005).

In summary, AN individuals may have both an impaired ability to identify the emotional significance of a stimulus and an enhanced ability to plan or foresee consequences. Because of AVS pathway dysregulation, REC AN may focus on long-term consequences rather than an immediate response to salient stimuli. In fact, AN individuals tend to have an enhanced ability to pay attention to detail or use a logical/analytic approach, but exhibit worse performance for global strategies in the here and now (Lopez et al., 2007; Strupp, Weingartner, Kaye, & Gwirtsman, 1986). In particular, the most anxious

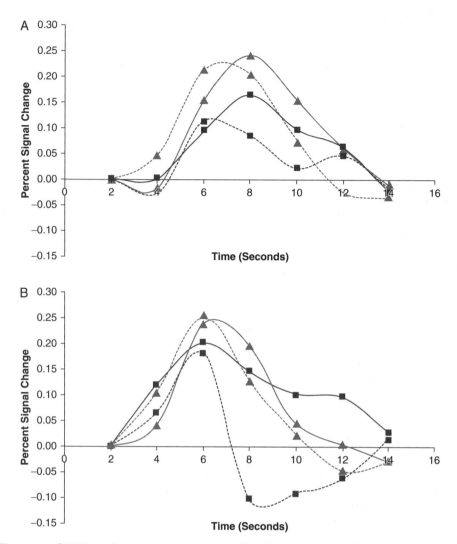

Fig. 6.2 Time course of BOLD signal as mean percent signal change (from first scan per trial) for loss (dashed line) and win (solid line) conditions, for REC AN (▲) and CW (■) corresponding to **(A)** left caudate ($x = -12$, $y = 15$, $z = 7$) and **(B)** left ventral striatum ($x = -10$, $y = 6$, $z = -5$).

AN individuals may respond in an overly "cognitive" manner to both negative and positive stimuli. Consequently, they may not be able to process information about rewarding outcomes of an action and may have impaired ability to identify emotional significance of the stimuli (Phillips, Drevets, & Lane, 2003). This may provide important new understanding of why it is so difficult to motivate AN individuals to engage in treatment since they may not be able to appreciate rewarding stimuli (Halmi et al., 2005).

fMRI STUDIES IN BN

There are a few studies that explore the functional neurobiology of appetitive control in BN. More common are studies in obesity and/or binge eating

disorder (BED; Geliebter et al., 2006; Rothemund et al., 2007; Stoeckel et al., 2008), and Prader–Willi syndrome (Holsen et al., 2006; Miller et al., 2007) of subjects responding to visual food stimuli. These patient populations are imperfect proxies to BN in that they lack one or more core characteristics of the disorder. However, functional studies in these patient populations provide insight into the neurobiological basis of appetite regulation in the absence of similar data in BN.

To parse neurobiological differences of BED and BN, Schienle et al. (Schienle, Shafer, Hermann, & Vaitl, 2008) presented images of high-calorie foods after an overnight fast to 17 BED and 14 currently ill BN subjects, comparing them to 19 normal weight controls and 17 overweight controls with no history of an ED. BED subjects demonstrated significantly greater activation in the medial and lateral OFC compared to BN and both control groups. Likewise, BN subjects demonstrated significantly greater activation in the ACC and right insula compared to BED and both control groups. Behavioral activation scale scores positively correlated with ACC and medial OFC response to food images for both BED and BN groups. In addition, insula activation in BN subjects positively correlated with behavioral activation and the binging subscale of the Eating Disorder Inventory (EDI-2), and negatively correlated with blood glucose levels. These data support the hypothesis that both BED and BN involve a primary disturbance in food-responsive neurocircuitry.

Geliebter (Geliebter et al., 2006) and colleagues compared 10 obese and 10 lean females, half of whom in each group were binge eaters. Subjects were exposed to images of binge and non-binge food items. This study examined conserved activation within these four subject groups. Activation of the secondary motor cortex was conserved only obese binge eaters, in response to binge-type foods, which may indicate past or concurrent motor planning in relation to acquiring or eating these foods. Importantly, no other group showed conserved activation to images of binge-type foods. These findings suggest that feeding behaviors might be altered at the motor planning stage in obese binge eaters.

A recent fMRI study (Marsh et al., 2009) compared 20 currently ill BN patients with 20 healthy controls during performance of the Simon Spatial Incompatibility task. Subjects pressed a button to indicate in which direction an arrow on the screen was pointing, the arrows rotated slightly left or right from vertical and shifted left or right from the middle of the screen. Congruent trials were defined by rotation and shift in the same direction and incongruent trials by rotation and shift in opposite directions. BN patients responded quicker but made more errors than control subjects, and they exhibited decreased activation in frontostriatal regions in congruent versus incongruent trials, including the inferolateral PFC, thalamus, dorsal striatum, and ACC. Error rates negatively correlated with frontostriatal activity in BN patients but positively correlated with striatal activation in healthy controls. Interestingly, BN patients with more severe symptoms were less accurate in their responses. Together, these data suggest that impaired frontostriatal activation might underlie increased impulsivity and decreased capacity for self-regulatory behaviors,

which in turn could predispose individuals to engage in binge/purge behaviors.

In summary, there are only a handful of neuroimaging studies in BN. Still, these provide interesting and provocative findings. For example, during a viewing of food images, BED showed greater activation in the OFC, a region that processes the hedonic value of food, while BN showed greater activation in the insula, which processes the physical qualities of taste and is associated with awareness of internal body state. Images of food also elicited greater ACC activation in BN, but decreased ACC response was observed during a cognitive incongruency task. These separate paradigms both point to dysregulation of the ACC, which is involved in error detection, as a component of BN neuropathology, but the nature of this dysregulation is not yet clear. Thus, despite the paucity of functional neuroimaging data in BN, the existing literature is consistent with the hypothesis that dysregulation of complex feeding behaviors in BN is associated with disturbed activity of brain regions involved in processing reward, error detection and self-regulatory cues, and food-related stimuli.

Future Directions for ED Research

Data to date raise the possibility that individuals with ED may have disturbances of circuits that modulate emotionality and reward, as well as cognition. In turn, such alterations may affect salient stimuli, such as food, and more complex behaviors, such as impulse control. One critical challenge is that it is not understood what core traits may be vulnerabilities that create a risk for developing an ED or how these traits are encoded in neuronal circuits. We do not even understand whether there is a primary disturbance of appetite regulation, or if disturbed appetite is secondary to altered reward, anxiety, obessionality, or other phenomena. Thus, it is important to construct experiments that test behaviors that basic science suggests might actually be encoded in neurocircuits.

For example, rather than try to understand the complexity of interpreting pictures of foods, which is likely to involve poorly understood pathways, we have been testing the possibility that individuals may have some aberrant response to the taste of sugar. Such circuits are relatively well understood. More specifically, our goal is to understand the effects of hunger and satiety on sensory–hedonic and homeostatic response of the insula and related brain regions to better understand the pathophysiology underlying restricted eating in AN, and overeating in BN. Thus, we have designed a series of studies that will employ a paradigm that models, in the laboratory, the naturalistic extremes of dietary intake employed by AN and BN. Another key question is whether hyperactivity of cognitive association networks compensates for the failure of limbic–striatal pathways to direct motivated responses. Alternatively, adequate limbic–striatal information may simply be too strongly inhibited by converging inputs from cognitive domains in AN.

Brain imaging studies, using a variety of methods, time courses, food substances and modalities (Kringelbach, O'Doherty, Rolls, & Andrews, 2003; Morris & Dolan, 2001; Small et al., 2001; Tataranni et al., 1999; Uher, Treasure, Heining, & Brammer, 2006) have consistently shown that food deprivation in healthy individuals activates the insula and OFC when compared to a fed state (Table 6.2) and has inconsistent effects on prefrontal, ACC, AVS, and dorsal striatum. There is one comparison of hunger and satiety in ill AN (Santel, Baving, Krauel, Munte, & Rotte, 2006) that used fMRI and pictures of food. It is important to note that food pictures, in contrast to eating food (Uher et al., 2006), tend to fail to activate the insula. When satiated, ill AN patients had, in comparison to controls, decreased activation in the left inferior parietal lobe, a region often showing altered activity in AN (Uher et al., 2004; Wagner et al., 2008), irrespective of fasting or feeding. The inferior parietal lobe is closely interconnected with the insula and receives both somatosensory and gustatory projections (Cerf-Ducastel, Van De Moortele, MacLeod, Le Bihan, & Faurion, 2001; Yoshimura et al., 2004). A decrease of activation in this area in the satiated state could be related to a decrease in gustatory perception or imagination of taste in response to visual food stimuli, which may facilitate fasting in restricting type AN. Interestingly, when satiation was compared to

hunger, the controls had stronger activation to food pictures in lateral OFC, ACC, and middle temporal gyrus regions. This pattern of activation was absent in the AN group, further supporting altered processing of food stimuli in AN.

The development of orbital and dorsolateral prefrontal regions of the cortex occurs concurrently and after the onset of puberty (Huttenlocher & Dabholkar, 1997) and may challenge vulnerable systems. Increased functional capacity of these cortical areas may be a substrate for excessive worry, perfectionism, and strategizing seen in these individuals. Taking the presumed pathological processes and involved brain areas together, top-down amplification of anticipatory signal for satiety may result in overrestrictive feeding behavior in AN. Computationally, these processes would involve generating an anticipatory body state model, which describes the neural circuitry in which a representation of the physiological condition of the body is instantiated.

Increased sensitivity toward future body states (e.g., body image distortion) that provide an increased error signal for adjustment of the behavior would provide a focus on several key neural substrates. First, the ACC is critically important for detecting conflict between a projected and observed cognitive process (Carter et al., 2000). Second, the OFC can dynamically adjust reward valuation based on the current body state of the individual (Rolls, Critchley, & Treves, 1996). Third, the DLPFC is able to switch between competing behavioral programs based on the error signal received from the cingulate (Kerns et al., 2004). We speculate that an altered sensitivity to an anticipatory prediction signal related to feeding behavior may account for some of the observed pathology.

In summary, it is important to generate overarching hypotheses about complex systems dysfunction in EDs that can be tested against new findings,

Table 6.2 Studies Showing that Food Deprivation Activates (↑) the Insula and OFC Regions When Compared to Satiety

Author	Year	Technique	Durationfasting	Insula	OFC
Small	2001	PET	4.5 hr		↑
Tataranni	1999	PET	36 hr	↑	↑
Moris	2001	PET	16 hr	↑	↑
Kringelbach	2003	fMRI	6 hr	↑	↑
Uher	2006	fMRI	24 hr	↑	

and that may be useful for stimulating new therapeutic interventions.

Summary

Individuals with AN are able to restrict their food intake everyday and maintain a low weight for many years. How are individuals with AN able to maintain a chronic diet and become emaciated when most people struggle to lose a few pounds? Likewise, individuals with BN may lose self-regulatory control by engaging in binge eating and purging behaviors. Why do these behaviors relieve dysphoric mood states in BN when most people find such behaviors aversive?

Converging receptor-binding and functional brain imaging data point to a primary disturbance of appetite regulation within taste and reward processing regions of the brain and suggest that this may be driving ED symptoms. The AI makes critical contributions toward determining the hedonic and sensory tone of food choices and interoceptive awareness. We hypothesize that a failure of the AI to respond appropriately to hunger due to altered interoceptive homeostatic mechanisms, perhaps involving disturbed sensory-hedonic tone, contributes to the ability of AN individuals to restrict food intake and become emaciated.

Numerous functional studies also implicate altered activation of the dorsal and ventral striatum, ACC, and OFC, as contributing to disturbances of feeding behaviors and appetite regulation. Behavioral correlations provide further evidence supporting a role for these brain regions in regulating taste processing, feeding behavior, and reward response to gustatory stimuli. Only recently have noninvasive neuroimaging tools such as PET, SPECT, and fMRI been available to explore the neuropathology underlying EDs, and they will likely be instrumental in identifying new therapeutic targets.

References

Abraham, S., & Beaumont, P. (1982). How patients describe bulimia or binge eating. *Psychological Medicine, 12*(3), 625–635.

Ahima, R., & Osei, S. (2004). Leptin signaling. *Physiology and Behavior, 81*, 223–241.

Ahima, R., Saper, C., Flier, J., & Elmquist, J. (2000). Leptin regulation of neuroendocrine systems. *Frontiers in Neuroendocrinology, 21*, 263–307.

American Psychiatric Association (APA). (2000). *Diagnostic & statistical manual of mental disorders: DSM:VI-TR* (4th ed.). Washington, DC: Author.

Anderluh, M. B., Tchanturia, K., Rabe-Hesketh, S., & Treasure, J. (2003). Childhood obsessive-compulsive personality traits in adult women with eating disorders: defining a broader eating disorder phenotype. *American Journal of Psychiatry, 160*(2), 242–247.

Anderson, I. M., Parry-Billings, M., Newsholme, E. A., Fairburn, C. G., & Cowen, P. J. (1990). Dieting reduces plasma tryptophan and alters brain 5-HT function in women. *Psychological Medicine, 20*(4), 785–791.

Arana, F., Parkinson, J. A., Hinton, E., Holland, A., Owen, A., & Roberts, A. (2003). Dissociable contributions of the human amygdala and orbitofrontal cortex to incentive motivation and goal selection. *Journal of Neuroscience, 23*(29), 9632–9838.

Audenaert, K., Van Laere, K., Dumont, F., Vervaet, M., Goethals, I., Slegers, G., et al. (2003). Decreased 5-HT2a receptor binding in patients with anorexia nervosa. *Journal of Nuclear Medicine, 44*(2), 163–169.

Bacanu, S., Bulik, C., Klump, K., Fichter, M., Halmi, K., Keel, P., et al. (2005). Linkage analysis of anorexia and bulimia nervosa cohorts using selected behavioral phenotypes as quantitative traits or covariates. *American Journal of Medical Genetics B, Neuropsychiatric Genetics, 139*(1), 61–68.

Bailer, U. F., Frank, G., Henry, S., Price, J., Meltzer, C., Mathis, C., et al. (2007). Exaggerated 5-HT1A but normal 5-HT2A receptor activity in individuals ill with anorexia nervosa. *Biological Psychiatry, 61*(9), 1090–1099.

Bailer, U. F., Frank, G. K., Henry, S. E., Price, J. C., Meltzer, C. C., Weissfeld, L., et al. (2005). Altered brain serotonin 5-HT1A receptor binding after recovery from anorexia nervosa measured by positron emission tomography and [^{11}C] WAY100635. *Archives of General Psychiatry, 62*(2), 1032.

Bailer, U. F., Price, J. C., Meltzer, C. C., Mathis, C. A., Frank, G. K., Weissfeld, L., et al. (2004). Altered 5–HT$_{2A}$ receptor binding after recovery from bulimia-type anorexia nervosa: relationships to harm avoidance and drive for thinness. *Neuropsychopharmacology, 29*(6), 1143–1155.

Baranowska, B., Radzikowska, M., Wasilewska-Dziubinska, E., Roguski, K., & Borowiec, M. (2000). Disturbed release of gastrointestinal peptides in anorexia nervosa and in obesity. *Diabetes and Obesity Metabolism, 2*(2), 99–103.

Baranowska, B., Wolinska-Witort, E., Wasilewska-Dziubinska, E., Roguski, K., & Chmielowska, M. (2001). Plasma leptin, neuropeptide Y (NPY) and galanin concentrations in bulimia nervosa and in anorexia nervosa. *Neuroendocrinology Letters, 22*(5), 356–358.

Barr, L. C., Goodman, W. K., Price, L. H., McDougle, C. J., & Charney, D. S. (1992). The serotonin hypothesis of obsessive compulsive disorder: implications of pharmacologic challenge studies. *Journal of Clinical Psychiatry, 53 Suppl*, 17–28.

Bergen, A., Yeager, M., Welch, R., Haque, K., Ganjei, J. K., Mazzanti, C., et al. (2005). Association of multiple DRD2 polymorphisms with anorexia nervosa. *Neuropsychopharmacology, 30*(9), 1703–1710.

Berns, G., McClure, S., Pagnoni, G., & Montague, P. (2001). Predictability modulates human brain response to reward. *Journal of Neuroscience, 21*(8), 2793–2798.

Berridge, K., & Robinson, T. (1998). What is the role of dopamine in reward: hedonic impact, reward learning, or incentive salience? *Brain Research, 28*, 309–369.

Bhagwagar, Z., Rabiner, E., Sargent, P., Grasby, P., & Cowen, P. (2004). Persistent reduction in brain serotonin$_{1A}$ receptor binding in recovered depressed men mesured by positron emission tomography with [^{11}C]WAY-100635. *Molecular Psychiatry, 9*, 386–392.

Blum, K., Sheridan, P. J., Wood, R. C., Braverman, E. R., Chen, T. J., & Comings, D. E. (1995). Dopamine D2 receptor gene variants: association and linkage studies in impulsive-addictive-compulsive behaviour. *Pharmacogenetics, 5*(3), 121–141.

Blundell, J. E. (1984). Serotonin and appetite. *Neuropharmacology, 23*(12B), 1537–1551.

Bonhomme, N., & Esposito, E. (1998). Involvement of serotonin and dopamine in the mechanism of action of novel antidepressant drugs: A review. *Journal of Clinical Psychopharmacology, 18*(6), 447–454.

Boyar, R. K., J, Finkelstein, J., Kapen, S., Weiner, H., Weitzman, E., & Hellman, L. (1974). Anorexia nervosa. Immaturity of the 24-hour luteinizing hormone secretory pattern. *New England Journal of Medicine, 291*(17), 861–865.

Brambilla, F., Brunetta, M., Draisci, A., Peirone, A., Perna, G., Sacerdote, P., et al. (1995). T-lymphocyte cholecystokinin-8 and beta-endorphin in eating disorders: II. Bulimia nervosa. *Psychiatry Research, 59*, 51–56.

Brambilla, F., Brunetta, M., Peirone, A., Perna, G., Sacerdote, P., Manfredi, B., et al. (1995). T-lymphocyte cholecystokinin-8 and beta-endorphin concentrations in eating disorders: I. Anorexia nervosa. *Psychiatry Research, 59*, 43–50.

Breiter, H. C., Aharon, I., Kahneman, D., Dale, A., & Shizgal, P. (2001). Functional imaging of neural responses to expectancy and experience of monetary gains and losses. *Neuron, 30*(2), 619–639.

Brewerton, T. D., Lesem, M. D., Kennedy, A., & Garvey, W. T. (2000). Reduced plasma leptin concentration in bulimia nervosa. *Psychoneuroendocrinology, 25*(7) Oct 2000, 649–658.

Bulik, C., Bacanu, S., Klump, K., Fichter, M., Halmi, K., Keel, P., et al. (2005). Selection of eating-disorder phenotypes for linkage analysis. *American Journal of Medical Genetics B, Neuropsychiatric Genetics, 139*(1), 81–87.

Bulik, C., Hebebrand, J., Keski-Rahkonen, A., Klump, K., Reichborn-Kjennerud, K. S., Mazzeo, S., et al. (2007). Genetic epidemiology, endophenotypes, and eating disorder classification. *International Journal of Eating Disorders, Epub ahead of print.*

Bulik, C. M., Sullivan, P. F., Fear, J. L., & Joyce, P. R. (1997). Eating disorders and antecedent anxiety disorders: A controlled study. *Acta Psychiatrica Scandinavica, 96*(2), 101–107.

Bulik, C., Sullivan, P. F., Tozzi, F., Furberg, H., Lichtenstein, P. & Pedersen, N. L. (2006). Prevalence, heritability and prospective risk factors for anorexia nervosa, *Archives of General Psychiatry, 63*, 305–312.

Burnet, P. W., Eastwood, S. L., & Harrison, P. J. (1997). [³H] WAY-100635 for 5-HT1A receptor autoradiography in human brain: a comparison with [³H]8-OH-DPAT and demonstration of increased binding in the frontal cortex in schizophrenia. *Neurochemistry International, 30*(6), 565–574.

Cannon, C., & Bseikri, M. (2004). Is dopamine required for natural reward? *Physiology and Behavior, 81*(5), 741–748.

Carmichael, S., & Price, J. (1996). Connectional networks within the orbital and medial prefrontal cortex of macaque monkeys. *Journal of Comparative Neurology, 371*, 179–207.

Carter, C., Botvinick, M., & Cohan, J. (1999). The contribution of the anterior cingulate cortex to executive processes in cognition. *Reviews in Neuroscience, 10*(1), 49–57.

Carter, C. S., Macdonald, A., Botvinick, M., Ross, L., Stenger, V., Noll, D., et al. (2000). Parsing executive processes: strategic vs. evaluative functions of the anterior cingulate cortex. *Proceedings of the National Academy of Sciences of the United States of America, 97*, 1944–1948.

Casper, R. C. (1990). Personality features of women with good outcome from restricting anorexia nervosa. *Psychosomatic Medicine, 52*(2), 156–170.

Cassin, S., & von Ranson, K. (2005). Personality and eating disorders: A decade in review. *Clinical Psychology Reviews, 25*(7), 895–916.

Cerf-Ducastel, B., & Murphy, C. (2004). Validation of a stimulation protocol suited to the investigation of odor-taste interactions with fMRI. *Physiology and Behavior, 81*(3), 389–396.

Cerf-Ducastel, B., Van De Moortele, P. F., MacLeod, P., Le Bihan, D., & Faurion, A. (2001). Interaction of gustatory and lingual somatosensory perceptions at the cortical level in the human: a functional magnetic resonance imaging study. *Chemical Senses, 26*(4), 371–383.

Chandraskekar, J., Hoon, M., Ryba, N., & Zuker, C. (2006). The receptors and cells for mammalian taste. *Nature, 444*, 288–294.

Charney, D. S., Woods, S. W., Krystal, J. H., & Heninger, G. R. (1990). Serotonin function and human anxiety disorders. *Annals of the New York Academy of Sciences, 600*, 558–572.

Chikama, M., McFarland, N. R., Amaral, D. G., & Haber, S. N. (1997). Insular cortical projections to functional regions of the striatum correlate with cortical cytoarchitectonic organization in the primate. *Journal of Neuroscience, 17*(24), 9686–9705.

Clarke, H., Walker, S. D., JW, Robbins, T., & Roberts, A. (2007). Cognitive inflexibility after prefrontal serotonin depletion is behaviorally and neurochemically specific. *Cerebral Cortex, 17*(1), 18–27.

Cloninger, C. R. (1987). A systematic method for clinical description and classification of personality variants. A proposal. *Archives of General Psychiatry, 44*(6), 573–588.

Cloninger, C. R., Przybeck, T. R., Svrakic, D. M., & Wetzel, R. D. (1994). The Temperament and Character Inventory (TCI): A guide to its development and Use. St. Louis, MO: Center for Psychobiology of Personality, Washington University.

Cohen, M., Young, J., Baek, J., Kessler, C., & Ranganath, C. (2005). Individual differences in extraversion and dopamine genetics predict neural reward responses. *Brain Research Cognitive Brain Research, 25*(3), 851–861.

Considine, R., Sinha, M., Heiman, M., Kriauciunas, A., Stephens, T., Nyce, M., et al. (1996). Serum immunoreactive-leptin concentrations in normal-weight and obese humans. *New England Journal of Medicine, 334*, 292–295.

Craig, A. D. (2002). How do you feel? Interoception: the sense of the physiological condition of the body. *Nature Reviews of Neuroscience, 3*(8), 655–666.

Critchley, H., & Rolls, E. (1996). Hunger and satiety modify the responses of olfactory and visual neurons in the primate orbitofrontal cortex. *Journal of Neurophysiology, 75*, 1673–1686.

De Araujo, I., Rolls, E., Kringelbach, M., McGlone, F., & Phillips, N. (2003). Taste-olfactory convergence, and the representation of the pleasantness of flavour, in the human brain. *European Journal of Neuroscience, 18*, 2059–2068.

——Deep, A. L., Nagy, L. M., Weltzin, T. E., Rao, R., & Kaye, W. H. (1995). Premorbid onset of psychopathology in long-term recovered anorexia nervosa. *International Journal of Eating Disorders, 17*(3), 291–297.

Del Parigi, A., Chen, K., Gautier, J., Salbe, A., Pratley, R., Ravussin, E., et al. (2002). Sex differences in the human brain's response to hunger and satiation. *American Journal of Clinical Nutrition, 75*(6), 1017–1022.

Delgado, M., Nystrom, L., Fissel, C., Noll, D., & Fiez, J. (2000). Tracking the hemodynamic responses to reward and punishment in the striatum. *Journal of Neurophysiology, 84*, 3072–3077.

Devlin, M. J., Walsh, B. T., Guss, J. L., Kissileff, H. R., Liddle, R. A., & Petkova, E. (1997). Postprandial cholecystokinin release and gastric emptying in patients with bulimia nervosa. *American Journal of Clinical Nutrition, 65*(1), 114–120.

De Vry, J., & Schreiber, R. (2000). Effects of selected serotonin 5-HT(1) and 5-HT(2) receptor agonists on feeding behavior: possible mechanisms of action. *Neuroscience and Biobehavioral Reviews, 24*(3), 341–353.

Drevets, W. C., Frank, E., Price, J. C., Kupfer, D. J., Holt, D., Greer, P. J., et al. (1999). PET imaging of serotonin 1A receptor binding in depression. *Biological Psychiatry, 46*(10), 1375–1387.

Drewnowski, A., Bellisle, F., Aimez, P., & Remy, B. (1987). Taste and bulimia. *Physiology and Behavior, 41*, 621–626.

Drewnowski, A., Halmi, K. A., Pierce, B., Gibbs, J., & Smith, G. P. (1987). Taste and eating disorders. *American Journal of Clinical Nutrition, 46*(3), 442–450.

Drewnowski, A., Pierce, B., & Halmi, K. (1988). Fat aversion in eating disorders. *Appetite, 10*, 119–131.

Eckert, E. D., Pomeroy, C., Raymond, N., Kohler, P. F., Thuras, P., & Bowers, C. Y. (1998). Leptin in anorexia nervosa. *Journal of Clinical Endocrinology and Metabolism, 83*(3), 791–795.

Ellison, A. R., & Fong, J. (1998). Neuroimaging in Eating Disorders. In H. W. Hoek, J. L. Treasure & M. A. Katzman (Eds.), *Neurobiology in the treatment of eating disorders* (pp. 255–269). Chichester: John Wiley & Sons.

Ellison, Z., Foong, J., Howard, R., Bullmore, E., Williams, S., & Treasure, J. (1998). Functional anatomy of calorie fear in anorexia nervosa. *Lancet, 352*(9135), 1192.

Elman, I., Borsook, D., & Lukas, S. (2006). Food intake and reward mechanisms in patients with schizophrenia: Implications for metabolic disturbances and treatment with second-generation antipsychotic agents. *Neuropsychopharmacology, 31*(10), 2091–2120.

Fairbanks, L., Melega, W., Jorgensen, M., Kaplan, J., & McGuire, M. (2001). Social impulsivity inversely associated with CSF 5-HIAA and fluoxetine exposure in vervet monkeys. *Neuropsychopharmacology, 24*(4), 370–378.

Farooqi, I. S., Keogh, J. M., Kamath, S., Jones, S., Gibson, W. T., Trussell, R., et al. (2001). Partial leptin deficiency and human adiposity. *Nature, 414*(6859), 34–35.

Faurion, A., Cerf, B., Van De Moortele, P. F., Lobel, E., Mac Leod, P., & Le Bihan, D. (1999). Human taste cortical areas studied with functional magnetic resonance imaging: Evidence of functional lateralization related to handedness. *Neuroscience Letters, 277*(3), 189–192.

Fernstrom, M. H., Weltzin, T. E., Neuberger, S., Srinivasagam, N., & Kaye, W. H. (1994). Twenty-four-hour food intake in patients with anorexia nervosa and in healthy control subjects. *Biological Psychiatry, 36*(10), 696–702.

File, S. E., Kenny, P. J., & Cheeta, S. (2000). The role of the dorsal hippocampal serotonergic and cholinergic systems in the modulation of anxiety. *Pharmacology and Biochemistry of Behavior, 66*(1), 65.

Frank, G., Bailer, U. F., Henry, S., Drevets, W., Meltzer, C. C., Price, J. C., et al. (2005). Increased dopamine D2/D3 receptor binding after recovery from anorexia nervosa measured by positron emission tomography and [^{11}C]raclopride. *Biological Psychiatry, 58*(11), 908–912.

Frank, G., Kaye, W., Carter, C., Brooks, S., May, C., Fissel, K., et al. (2003). The evaluation of brain activity in response to taste stimuli a pilot study and method for central taste activation as assessed by event related fMRI. *Journal of Neuroscience Methods, 131*(1–2), 99–105.

Frank, G., Oberndorfer, T., Simmons, A., Paulus, M., Fudge, J., Yang, T., et al. (2008). Sucrose activates human taste pathways differently from artificial sweetener. *NeuroImage, 39*, 1559–1569.

Frank, G., Wagner, A., Brooks-Achenbach, S., McConaha, C., Skovira, K., Aizenstein, H., et al. (2006). Altered brain activity in women recovered from bulimic type eating disorders after a glucose challenge. A pilot study. *International Journal of Eating Disorders, 39*(1), 76–79.

Frank, G. K., Kaye, W. H., Meltzer, C. C., Price, J. C., Greer, P., McConaha, C., et al. (2002). Reduced 5-HT2A receptor binding after recovery from anorexia nervosa. *Biological Psychiatry, 52*, 896–906.

Frederich, R., Hu, S., Raymond, N., & Pomeroy, C. (2002). Leptin in anorexia nervosa and bulimia nervosa: Importance of assay technique and method of interpretation. *Journal of Laboratory and Clinical Medicine, 139*(2), 72–79.

Friederich, H. C., Kumari, V., Uher, R., Riga, M., Schmidt, U., Campbell, I. C., et al. (2006). Differential motivational responses to food and pleasurable cues in anorexia and bulimia nervosa: a startle reflex paradigm. *Psychological Medicine, 36*(9), 1327–1335.

Friedman, J., & Halaas, J. (1998). Leptin and the regulation of body weight in mammals. *Nature, 395*, 763–770.

Fudge, J., Breitbart, M., Danish, M., & Pannoni, V. (2005). Insular and gustatory inputs to the caudal ventral striatum in primates. *Journal of Comparative Neurology, 490*(2), 101–118.

Fudge, J., Breitbart, M., & McClain, C. (2004). Amygdaloid inputs define a caudal component of the ventral striatum in primates. *Journal of Comparative Neurology, 476*(4), 330–347.

Garfinkel, P., Moldofsky, H., & Garner, D. M. (1979). The stability of perceptual disturbances in anorexia nervosa. *Psychological Medicine, 9*(4), 703–708.

Garfinkel, P., Moldofsky, H., Garner, D. M., Stancer, H. C., & Coscina, D. (1978). Body awareness in anorexia nervosa: Disturbances in "body image" and "satiety." *Psychosomatic Medicine, 40*(6), 487–498.

Gehring, W., & Willoughby, A. (2002). The medial frontal cortex and the rapid processing of monetary gains and losses. *Science, 295*, 2279–2282.

Geliebter, A., Ladell, T., Logan, M., Schneider, T., Sharafi, M., & Hirsch, J. (2006). Responsivity to food stimuli in obese and lean binge eaters using functional MRI. *Appetite, 26*(1), 31–35.

Geliebter, A., Melton, P. M., McCray, R. S., Gallagher, D. R., Gage, D., & Hashim, S. A. (1992). Gastric capacity, gastric emptying, and test-meal intake in normal and bulimic women. *American Journal of Clinical Nutrition, 56*(4), 656–661.

Gendall, K. (1999). Leptin, neuropeptide Y, and peptide YY in long-term recovered eating disorder patients. *Biological Psychiatry, 46*(2), 292–299.

Geracioti, T. D., Jr., & Liddle, R. A. (1988). Impaired cholecystokinin secretion in bulimia nervosa. *New England Journal of Medicine, 319*(11), 683–688.

Geracioti, T. D., Jr., Liddle, R. A., Altemus, M., Demitrack, M. A., & Gold, P. W. (1992). Regulation of appetite and cholecystokinin secretion in anorexia nervosa. *American Journal of Psychiatry, 149*(7), 958–961.

Geyer, M. A. (1996). Serotonergic functions in arousal and motor activity. *Behavioural Brain Research, 73*, 31.

Gibbs, J., Young, R. C., & Smith, G. P. (1973). Cholecystokinin decreases food intake in rats. *Journal of Comparative & Physiological Psychology, 84*(3), 488–495.

Glowa, J., & Gold, P. (1991). Corticotropin releasing hormone produces profound anorexigenic effects in the rhesus monkey. *Neuropeptides, 18*, 55–61.

Godart, N. T., Flament, M. F., Lecrubier, Y., & Jeammet, P. (2000). Anxiety disorders in anorexia nervosa and bulimia nervosa: Co-morbidity and chronology of appearance. *European Psychiatry, 15*(1), 38–45.

Godart, N. T., Flament, M. F., Perdereau, F., & Jeammet, P. (2002). Comorbidity between eating disorders and anxiety disorders: a review. *International Journal of Eating Disorders, 32*(3), 253–270.

Gold, P. W., Gwirtsman, H., Avgerinos, P. C., Nieman, L. K., Gallucci, W. T., Kaye, W., et al. (1986). Abnormal hypothalamic-pituitary-adrenal function in anorexia nervosa. Pathophysiologic mechanisms in underweight and weight-corrected patients. *New England Journal of Medicine, 314*(21), 1335–1342.

Gordon, C. M., Dougherty, D. D., Fischman, A. J., Emans, S. J., Grace, E., Lamm, R., et al. (2001). Neural substrates of anorexia nervosa: A behavioral challenge study with positron emission tomography. *Journal of Pediatrics, 139*(1), 51–57.

Goto, Y., & Grace, A. (2005). Dopaminergic modulation of limbic and cortical drive of nucleus accumbens in goal-directed behavior. *Nature Neuroscience, 386*(1), 14–17.

Gottfried, J., O'Doherty, J., & Dolan, R. (2003). Encoding predictive reward value in human amygdala and orbitofrontal cortex. *Science, 301*(5636), 1104–1107.

Gottfried, J. A., O'Doherty, J., & Dolan, R. J. (2002). Appetite and aversive olfactory learning in humans studied using event-related functional magnetic resonance imaging. *Journal of Neuroscience, 15*(22), 10829–10837.

Grahame-Smith, D. G. (1992). Serotonin in affective disorders. *International Clinical Psychopharmacology, 6*(Supplement 4), 5–13.

Grinspoon, S., Gulick, T., Askari, H., Landt, M., Lee, K., Anderson, E., et al. (1996). Serum leptin levels in women with anorexia nervosa. *Journal of Clinical Endocrinology and Metabolism, 81*(11), 3861–3863.

Gross, C., Zhuang, X., Stark, K., Ramboz, S., Oosting, R., Kirby, L., et al. (2002). Serotonin$_{1A}$ receptor acts during development to establish normal anxiety-like behaviour in the adult. *Nature, 416*, 396–400.

Gwirtsman, H. E., Kaye, W. H., George, D. T., Jimerson, D. C., Ebert, M. H., & Gold, P. W. (1989). Central and peripheral ACTH and cortisol levels in anorexia nervosa and bulimia. *Archives of General Psychiatry, 46*, 61–69.

Haber, S., Kunishio, K., Mizobuhi, M., & Lynd-Balta, E. (1995). The orbital and medial prefrontal circuit through the primate basal ganglia. *Journal of Neuroscience, 15*, 4851–4867.

Haber, S. N., Kim, K., Mailly, P., & Calzavara, R. (2006). Reward-related cortical inputs define a large striatal region in primates that interface with associative cortical connections, providing a substrate for incentive-based learning. *Journal of Neuroscience, 26*(32), 8368–8376.

Halford, J., Cooper, G., & Dovey, T. (2004). The pharmacology of human appetite expression. *Current Drug Targets, 5*, 221–240.

Halmi, K., Agras, W. S., Crow, S., Mitchell, J., Wilson, G., Bryson, S., et al. (2005). Predictors of treatment acceptance and completion in anorexia nervosa. *Archives of General Psychiatry, 62*, 776–781.

Harty, R. F., Pearson, P. H., Solomon, T. E., & McGuigan, J. E. (1991). Cholecystokinin, vasoactive intestinal peptide and peptide histidine methionine responses to feeding in anorexia nervosa. *Regulatory Peptides, 36*(1), 141–150.

Hebebrand, J., van der Heyden, J., Devos, R., Kopp, W., Herpertz, S., Remschmidt, H., et al. (1995). Plasma concentrations of obese protein in anorexia nervosa. *Lancet, 346*(8990), 1624–1625.

Hikosaka, K., & Watanabe, M. (2000). Delay activity of orbital and lateral prefrontal neurons of the monkey varying with different rewards. *Cerebral Cortex, 10*(3), 263–271.

Hilbert, A., & Tuschen-Caffier, B. (2007). Maintenance of binge eating through negative mood: a naturalistic comparison of binge eating disorder and bulimia nervosa. *International Journal of Eating Disorders, 40*(6), 521–530.

Hinton, E. C., Parkinson, J. A., Holland, A. J., Arana, F. S., Roberts, A. C., & Owen, A. M. (2004). Neural contributions to the motivational control of appetite in humans, *European Journal of Neuroscience, 20*(5), 1411–1418.

Holsen, L., Zarcone, J., Brooks, W., Butler, M., Thompson, T., Ahluwalia, J., et al. (2006). Neural mechanisms underlying hyperphagia in Prader-Willi syndrome. *Obesity (Silver Spring), 14*(6), 1028–1037.

Holtkamp, K., Hebebrand, J., Mika, C., Heer, M., Heussen, N., & Herpertz-Dahlmann, B. (2004). High serum leptin levels subsequent to weight gain predict renewed weight loss in patients with anorexia nervosa. *Psychoneuroendocrinology, 29*, 791–797.

Holtkamp, K., Mika, C., Grzella, I., Heer, M., Pak, H., Hebebrand, J., et al. (2003). Reproductive function during weight gain in anorexia nervosa. Leptin represents a metabolic gate to gonadotropin secretion. *Journal of Neural Transmission, 110*, 427–435.

Huttenlocher, P., & Dabholkar, A. (1997). Regional differences in synaptogenesis in human cerebral cortex. *Journal of Comparative Neurology, 387*, 167–178.

Inui, A. (2001). Eating behavior in anorexia nervosa an excess of both orexigenic and anorexigenic signalling? *Molecular Psychiatry, 6*(6), 620–624.

Izquierdo, I., Cammarota, M., Medina, J., & Bevilaqua, L. (2004). Pharmacological findings on the biochemical bases of memory processes: A general view. *Neural Plasticity, 11*(3–4), 159–189.

Jimerson, D., & Wolfe, B. (2006). Psychobiology of Eating Disorders. In J. Mitchell, S. Wonderlich, M. de Zwaan, & H. Steiger (Eds.), *Annual review of eating Disorders: Part 2 2006* (pp. 1–15). Oxford: Radcliffe Publishing.

Jimerson, D., & Wolfe, B. E. (2004). Neuropeptides in eating disorders. *CNS Spectroscopy, 9*, 516–522.

Jimerson, D. C. (2002). Leptin and the neurobiology of eating disorders. *Journal of Laboratory and Clinical Medicine, 139*(2), 70–71.

Jimerson, D. C., Lesem, M. D., Kaye, W. H., & Brewerton, T. D. (1992). Low serotonin and dopamine metabolite concentrations in cerebrospinal fluid from bulimic patients with frequent binge episodes. *Archives of General Psychiatry, 49*(2), 132–138.

Jimerson D. C., Lesem M.D., Kaye W. H., Hegg A. P., & Brewerton T. D. (1990). Eating disorders and depression: is there a serotonin connection? *Biological Psychiatry*, *28*(5), 443–454.

Jimerson, D. C., Mantzoros, C., Wolfe, B. E., & Metzger, E. D. (2000). Decreased serum leptin in bulimia nervosa. *Journal of Clinical Endocrinology and Metabolism*, *85*(12), 4511–4514.

Johnson, C., & Larson, R. (1982). Bulimia: An analysis of mood and behavior. *Psychosomatic Medicine*, *44*(4), 341–351.

Kalra, S. P., Dube, M. G., Sahu, A., Phelps, C. P., & Kalra, P. S. (1991). Neuropeptide Y secretion increases in the paraventricular nucleus in association with increased appetite for food. *Proceedings of the National Academy of Sciences of the United States of America*, *88*(23), 10931–10935.

Kaye, W., Bulik, C., Thornton, L., Barbarich, N., Masters, K., Fichter, M., et al. (2004). Comorbidity of anxiety disorders with anorexia and bulimia nervosa. *American Journal of Psychiatry*, *161*, 2215–2221.

Kaye, W., Wagner, A., Frank, G., & UF, B. (2006). Review of brain imaging in anorexia and bulimia nervosa. In J. Mitchell, S. Wonderlich, H. Steiger, & M. deZwaan (Eds.), *AED annual review of rating disorders, Part 2* (pp. 113–130). Abingdon, UK: Radcliffe Publishing.

Kaye, W. H., Ballenger, J. C., Lydiard, R. B., Stuart, G. W., Laraia, M. T., O'Neil, P., et al. (1990). CSF monoamine levels in normal-weight bulimia: Evidence for abnormal noradrenergic activity. *American Journal of Psychiatry*, *147*(2), 225–229.

Kaye, W. H., Barbarich, N. C., Putnam, K., Gendall, K. A., Fernstrom, J., Fernstrom, M., et al. (2003). Anxiolytic effects of acute tryptophan depletion in anorexia nervosa. *International Journal of Eating Disorders*, *33*(3), 257–267.

Kaye, W. H., Berrettini, W., Gwirtsman, H., & George, D. T. (1990). Altered cerebrospinal fluid neuropeptide Y and peptide YY immunoreactivity in anorexia and bulimia nervosa. *Archives of General Psychiatry*, *47*(6), 548–556.

Kaye, W. H., Ebert, M. H., Raleigh, M., & Lake, R. (1984). Abnormalities in CNS monoamine metabolism in anorexia nervosa. *Archives of General Psychiatry*, *41*(4), 350–355.

Kaye, W. H., Frank, G. K., & McConaha, C. (1999). Altered dopamine activity after recovery from restricting-type anorexia nervosa. *Neuropsychopharmacology*, *21*(4), 503–506.

Kaye, W. H., Frank, G. K., Meltzer, C. C., Price, J. C., McConaha, C. W., Crossan, P. J., et al. (2001). Altered serotonin 2A receptor activity in women who have recovered from bulimia nervosa. *American Journal of Psychiatry*, *158*(7), 1152–1155.

Kaye, W. H., Gwirtsman, H. E., George, D. T., Ebert, M. H., Jimerson, D. C., Tomai, T. P., et al. (1987). Elevated cerebrospinal fluid levels of immunoreactive corticotropin-releasing hormone in anorexia nervosa: relation to state of nutrition, adrenal function, and intensity of depression. *Journal of Clinical Endocrinology and Metabolism*, *64*(2), 203–208.

Kaye, W. H., Gwirtsman, H. E., George, D. T., Weiss, S. R., & Jimerson, D. C. (1986). Relationship of mood alterations to bingeing behaviour in bulimia. *British Journal of Psychiatry*, *149*, 479–485.

Kaye, W. H., Weltzin, T. E., McKee, M., McConaha, C., Hansen, D., & Hsu, L. K. (1992). Laboratory assessment of feeding behavior in bulimia nervosa and healthy women: Methods for developing a human-feeding laboratory. *American Journal of Clinical Nutrition*, *55*(2), 372–380.

Kazama, A., & Bachevalier, J. (2006). Selective aspiration of neurotoxic lesions of the orbitofrontal areas 11 and 13 spared monkeys' performance on the object reversal discrimination task. *Society for Neuroscience Abstracts*, *32*, 670.625.

Keel, P., Wolfe, B. E., Liddle, R., De Young, K., & Jimerson, D. (2007). Clinical features and physiological response to a test meal in purging disorder and bulimia nervosa. *Archives of General Psychiatry*, *64*, 1058–1066.

Kelley, A. E. (2004). Ventral striatal control of appetite motivation: role in ingestive behavior and reward-related learning. *Neuroscience and Biobehavior Reviews*, *27*, 765–776.

Kendler, K. S., Walters, E. E., Neale, M. C., Kessler, R. C., Heath, A. C., & Eaves, L. J. (1995). The structure of the genetic and environmental risk factors for six major psychiatric disorders in women. Phobia, generalized anxiety disorder, panic disorder, bulimia, major depression, and alcoholism. *Archives of General Psychiatry*, *52*(5), 374–383.

Kerns, J., Cohen, J., MacDonald, A., Cho, R., Stenger, V., & Carter, C. (2004). Anterior cingulate conflict monitoring and adjustments in control. *Science*, *303*, 1023–1026.

Killgore, W., Young, A., Femia, L., Bogorodzki, P., Rogowska, J., & Yurgelun-Todd, D. (2003). Cortical and limbic activation during viewing of high- versus low-calorie foods. *NeuroImage*, *19*(4), 1381–1394.

Kissileff, H., Pi-Sunyer, F., Thornton, J., & Smith, G. (1981). C-terminal octapeptide of cholecystokinin decreases food intake in man. *American Journal of Clinical Nutrition*, *34*, 154–160.

Klump, K., Strober, M., Johnson, C., Thornton, L., Bulik, C., Devlin, B., et al. (2004). Personality characteristics of women before and after recovery from an eating disorder. *Psychological Medicine*, *34*(8), 1407–1418.

Klump, K. L., McGue, M., & Iacono, W. G. (2000). Age differences in genetic and environmental influences on eating attitudes and behaviors in preadolescent and adolescent female twins. *Journal of Abnormal Psychology*, *109*(2), 239–251.

Kojima, S., Nakahara, T., Nagai, N., Muranaga, T., Tanaka, M., Yasuhara, D., et al. (2005). Altered ghrelin and peptide YY responses to meals in bulimia nervosa. *Clinical Endocrinology (Oxford)*, *62*, 74–78.

Koob, G. (1992). Drugs of abuse: Anatomy, pharmacology and function of reward pathways. *Trends in Pharmacological Science*, *13*, 177–184.

Kringelbach, M. L., de Araujo, I. E. T., & Rolls, E. T. (2004). Taste-related activity in the human dorsolateral prefrontal cortex. *NeuroImage*, *21*, 781–788.

Kringelbach, M. L., O'Doherty, J., Rolls, E., & Andrews, C. (2003). Activation of the human orbitofrontal cortex to a liquid food stimulus is correlated with its subjective pleasantness. *Cerebral Cortex*, *13*, 1064–1071.

LaBar, K., Gitelman, D., Parrish, T., Kim, Y., Nobre, A., & Mesulam, M. (2001). Hunger selectively modulates corticolimbic activation to food stimuli in humans. *Behavioral Neuroscience*, *115*(2), 493–500.

LaChaussee, J. L., Kissileff, H., Walsh, B., & Hadigan, C. (1992). The single-item meal as a measure of binge-eating behavior in patients with bulimia nervosa. *Physiology and Behavior*, *51*, 593–600.

Lanzenberger, R., Mitterhauser, M., Spindelegger, C., Wadsak, W., Klein, N., Mien, L., et al. (2007). Reduced serotonin-1A receptor binding in social anxiety disorder. *Biological Psychiatry*, *61*(9), 1081–1089.

Lawrence, A. (2003). Impaired visual discrimination learning in anorexia nervosa. *Appetite, 20*, 85–89.

Leibowitz, S. F., & Shor-Posner, G. (1986). Brain serotonin and eating behavior. *Appetite, 7*(Supplement), 1–14.

Licinio, J., Wong, M. L., & Gold, P. W. (1996). The hypothalamic-pituitary-adrenal axis in anorexia nervosa. *Psychiatry Research, 62*, 75–83.

Lilenfeld, L., Wonderlich, S., Riso, L. P., Crosby, R., & Mitchell, J. (2006). Eating disorders and personality: A methodological and empirical review. *Clinical Psychology Reviews, 26*(3), 299–320.

Lilenfeld, L. R., Kaye, W. H., Greeno, C. G., Merikangas, K. R., Plotnicov, K., Pollice, C., et al. (1998). A controlled family study of anorexia nervosa and bulimia nervosa: Psychiatric disorders in first-degree relatives and effects of proband comorbidity. *Archives of General Psychiatry, 55*(7), 603–610.

Lob, S., Pickel, J., Bidlingmaier, M., Schaaf, L., Backmund, H., Gerlinghoff, M., et al. (2003). Serum leptin monitoring in anorectic patients during refeeding therapy. *Experimental and Clinical Endocrinology and Diabetes, 111*, 278–282.

Lopez, C., Tchanturia, K., Stahl, D., Booth, R., Holliday, J., & Treasure, J. (2007). An examination of central coherence in women with anorexia nervosa. *International Journal of Eating Disorders, Epub ahead of print.*

Lopez, C., Tchanturia, K., Stahl, D., Booth, R., Holliday, J., & Treasure, J. (2008). An examination of the concept of central coherence in women with anorexia nervosa. *International Journal of Eating Disorders, 41*(2), 143–152.

Lydiard, R. B., Brewerton, T. D., Fossey, M. D., Laraia, M. T., Stuart, G., Beinfeld, M. C., et al. (1993). CSF cholecystokinin octapeptide in patients with bulimia nervosa and in normal comparison subjects. *American Journal of Psychiatry, 150*(7), 1099–1101.

Mann, J. J. (1999). Role of the serotonergic system in the pathogenesis of major depression and suicidal behavior. *Neuropsychopharmacology, 21*(2 Supplement), 99S-105S.

Mantzoros, C., Flier, J. S., Lesem, M. D., Brewerton, T. D., & Jimerson, D. C. (1997). Cerebrospinal fluid leptin in anorexia nervosa: Correlation with nutritional status and potential role in resistance to weight gain. *Journal of Clinical Endocrinology and Metabolism, 82*(6), 1845–1851.

Marsh, R., Steinglass, J., Gerber, A., Graziano O'Leary, K., Wang, Z., Murphy, D., et al. (2009). Deficient activity in the neural systems that mediate self-regulatory control in bulimia nervosa. *Archives of General Psychiatry, 66*(1), 51–63.

Martin-Ruiz, R., Puig, M. V., Celada, P., Shapiro, D. A., Roth, B. L., Mengod, G., et al. (2001). Control of serotonergic function in medial prefrontal cortex by serotonin-2A receptors through a glutamate-dependent mechanism. *Journal of Neuroscience, 21*(24), 9856–9866.

McClure, S., Berns, G., & Montague, P. (2003). Temporal prediction errors in a passive learning task activate human striatum. *Neuron, 38*(2), 339–346.

McClure, S., Li, J., Tomlin, D., Cypert, K., Montague, L., & Montague, P. (2004). Neural correlates of behavioral preference for culturally familiar drinks. *Neuron, 44*(2), 379–387.

Miller, J. J., Goldstone, A., Couch, J., He, G., Driscoll, D., & Liu, Y. (2007). Enhanced activation of reward mediating prefrontal regions in response to food stimuli in Prader-Wili syndrome. *Neurology and Neuroimage Psychiatry, 76*(6), 615–619.

Montague, R., Hyman, S., & Cohen, J. (2004). Computational roles for dopamine in behavioural control. *Nature, 431*, 760–767.

Monteleone, P., Di Lieto, A., Castaldo, E., & Maj, M. (2004). Leptin functioning in eating disorders. *CNS Spectroscopy, 9*, 523–529.

Monteleone, P., Di Lieto, A., Tortorella, A., Longobardi, N., & Maj, M. (2000). Circulating leptin in patients with anorexia nervosa, bulimia nervosa or binge-eating disorder: Relationship to body weight, eating patterns, psychopathology and endocrine changes. *Psychiatry Research, 94*, 121–129.

—Monteleone, P., Martiadis, V., Rigamonti, A., Fabrazzo, M., Giordani, C., Muller, e., et al. (2005). Investigation of peptide YY and ghrelin responses to a test meal in bulimia nervosa. *Biological Psychiatry, 57*, 926–931.

Monteleone, P., Martiadis, V., Fabrazzo, M., Serritella, C., & Maj, M. (2003). Ghrelin and leptin responses to food ingestion in bulimia nervosa: Implications for binge-eating and compensatory behaviours. *Psychological Medicine, 33*(8), 1387–1394.

Moresco, F. M., Dieci, M., Vita, A., Messa, C., Gobbo, C., Galli, L., et al. (2002). *In vivo* serotonin 5HT$_{2A}$ receptor binding and personality traits in healthy subjects: A positron emission tomography study. *NeuroImage, 17*, 1470–1478.

Morley J. E. & Blundell J. E. (1988). The neurobiological basis of eating disorders: some formulations, *Biological Psychiatry, 23*(1), 53–78.

Morley, J. E., Levine, A. S., Gosnell, B. A., Mitchell, J. E., Krahn, D. D., & Nizielski, S. E. (1985). Peptides and feeding. *Peptides, 6*, 181–192.

Morris, J. S., & Dolan, R. J. (2001). Involvement of human amygdala and orbitofrontal cortex in hunger-enhanced memory for food stimuli. *Journal of Neuroscience, 21*(14), 5304–5310.

Nakahara, T., Kojima, S., Tanaka, M., Yasuhara, D., Harada, T., Sagiyama, K., et al. (2007). Incomplete restoration of the secretion of ghrelin and PYY compared to insulin after food ingestion following weight gain in anorexia nervosa. *Journal of Psychiatry Research, 41*, 814–820.

Naruo, T., Nakabeppu, Y., Sagiyama, K., Munemoto, T., Homan, N., Deguchi, D., et al. (2000). Characteristic regional cerebral blood flow patterns in anorexia nervosa patients with binge/purge behavior. *American J Psychiatry, 157*(9), 1520–1522.

Neumeister, A., Brain, E., Nugent, A., Carson, R., Bonne, O., Lucnekbaugh, D., et al. (2004). Reduced serotinin type 1$_A$ receptor binding in panic disorder. *Journal of Neuroscience, 24*(3), 589–591.

Nisoli, E., Brunani, A., Borgomainerio, E., Tonello, C., Dioni, L., Briscini, L., et al. (2007). D2 dopamine receptor (DRD2) gene Taq1A polymorphism and the eating-realted psychological traits in eating disorders (anorexia nervosa and bulimia) and obesity. *Eating and Weight Disorders, 12*(2), 91–96.

Nozoe, S., Naruo, T., Nakabeppu, Y., Soejima, Y., Nakajo, M., & Tanaka, H. (1993). Changes in regional cerebral blood flow in patients with anorexia nervosa detected through single photon emission tomography imaging. *Biological Psychiatry, 34*(8), 578–580.

Nozoe, S., Naruo, T., Yonekura, R., Nakabeppu, Y., Soejima, Y., Nagai, N., et al. (1995). Comparison of regional cerebral blood flow in patients with eating disorders. *Brain Research Bulletin, 36*(3), 251–255.

O'Doherty, J. (2004). Reward representations and reward related learning in the human brain: insights from neuroimaging. *Science, 14*, 769–776.

O'Doherty, J., Dayan, P., Schultz, J., Deichmann, R., Friston, K. J., & Dolan, R. J. (2004). Dissociable roles of ventral and dorsal striatum in instrumental conditioning. *Science, 304*, 452–454.

O'Doherty, J., Kringelbach, M. L., Rolls, E. T., Hornak, J., & Andrews, C. (2001). Abstract reward and punishment representations in the human orbitofrontal cortex. *Nature Neuroscience, 4*(1), 95–102.

Ogawa, H. (1994). Gustatory cortex of primates: Anatomy and physiology. *Neuroscience Research, 20*(1), 1–13.

Ongur, D., & Price, J. L. (2000). Organization of networks within the orbital and medial prefrontal cortex of rats, monkeys, and humans. *Cerebral Cortex, 10*, 206–219.

Otto B., Cuntz U., Otto C., Heldwein W., Riepl R. L., Tschöp M. H. (2007). Peptide YY release in anorectic patients after liquid meal, *Appetite, 48*(3), 301–304.

Parsey, R. V., Oquendo, M. A., Ogden, R. T., Olvet, D., Simpson, N., Huang, Y., et al. (2005). Altered serotonin 1A binding in major depression: A [carbonyl-C-11]WAY100635 positron emission tomography study. *Biological Psychiatry, 59*(2), 106–113.

Paulus, M., & Stein, M. B. (2006). An insular view of anxiety. *Biological Psychiatry, 60*(4), 383–387.

Phillipp, E., Pirke, K. M., Kellner, M. B., & Krieg, J. C. (1991). Disturbed cholecystokinin secretion in patients with eating disorders. *Life Science, 48*(25), 2443–2450.

Phillips, M. L., Drevets, W. C., Rauch S. L., & Lane, R. (2003). Neurobiology of emotion perception I: The neural basis of normal emotion perception. *Biological Psychiatry, 54*(5), 504–514.

Pirke, K. M., Kellner, M. B., Friess, E., Krieg, J. C., & Fichter, M. M. (1994). Satiety and cholecystokinin. *International Journal of Eating Disorders, 15*(1), 63–69.

Pollice, C., Kaye, W. H., Greeno, C. G., & Weltzin, T. E. (1997). Relationship of depression, anxiety, and obsessionality to state of illness in anorexia nervosa. *International Journal of Eating Disorders, 21*(4), 367–376.

Prince, A. C., Brooks, S. J., Stahl, D., & Treasure, J. (2009). Systematic review and meta-analys is of the baseline concentrations and physiologic responses of gut hormones to food in eating disorders. *American Journal of Clinical Nutrition, 89*(3), 755–765.

Reynolds, S., & Zahm, D. (2005). Specificity in the projections of prefrontal and insular cortex to ventral striatopallidum and the extended amygdala. *Journal of Neuroscience, 25*(50), 11757–11767.

Rolls, E. T. (1997). Taste and olfactory processing in the brain and its relation to the control of eating. *Critical Reviews of Neurobiology, 11*(4), 263–287.

Rolls, E. T. (2005). Taste, olfactory, and food texture processing in the brain, and the control of food intake. *Physiology and Behavior, 85*(1), 45–56.

Rolls, E. T., Critchley, H. D., & Treves, A. (1996). Representation of olfactory information in the primate orbitofrontal cortex. *Journal of Neurophysiology, 75*(5), 1982–1996.

Rothemund, Y., Preuschhof, C., Bohner, G., Bauknecht, H., Klingebiel, R., Flor, H., et al. (2007). Differential activation of the dorsal striatum by high-calorie visual food stimuli in obese individuals. *NeuroImage, 37*(2), 410–421.

Rutherford, J., McGuffin, P., Katz, R. J., & Murray, R. M. (1993). Genetic influences on eating attitudes in a normal female twin population. *Psychological Medicine, 23*(2), 425–436.

Salamone, J. D. (1996). The behavioral neurochemistry of motivation: Methodological and conceptual issues in studies of the dynamic activity of nucleus accumbens dopamine. *Journal of Neuroscience Methods, 64*(2), 137–149.

Santel, S., Baving, L., Krauel, K., Munte, T., & Rotte, M. (2006). Hunger and satiety in anorexia nervosa: fMRI during cognitive processing of food pictures. *Brain Research, 1114*, 138–148.

Saper C.B., Chou T.C., & Elmquist J.K. (2002). The need to feed: homeostatic and hedonic control of eating, *Neuron, 36*(2), 199–211

Sargent, P. A., Kjaer, K. H., Bench, C. J., Rabiner, E. A., Messa, C., Meyer, J., et al. (2000). Brain serotonin$_{1A}$ receptor binding measured by positron emission tomography with [^{11}C]WAY-100635: effects of depression and antidepressant treatment. *Archives of General Psychiatry, 57*(2), 174–180.

Saudou, F., & Hen, R. (1994). 5-Hydroxytryptamine receptor subtypes in vertebrates and invertebrates. *Neurochemistry International, 25*(6), 503–532.

Schienle, A., Shafer, A., Hermann, A., & Vaitl, D. (2008). Binge-eating disorder: reward sensitivity and brain activation to images of food, Epub ahead of Print November 7. *Biological Psychiatry.*

Schoenfeld, M., Neuer, G., Tempelmann, C., Schussler, K., Noesselt, T., Hopf, J., et al. (2004). Functional magnetic resonance tomography correlates of taste perception in the human primary taste cortex. *Neuroscience, 127*(2), 347–353.

Schultz, W. (1998). Predictive reward signal of dopamine neurons. *Journal of Neurophysiology, 80*(1), 1–27.

Schultz, W. (2004). Neural coding of basic reward terms of animal learning theory, game theory, microeconomics and behavioural ecology. *Science, 14*, 139–147.

Schultz, W., Tremblay, L., & Hollerman, J. (1998). Reward prediction in primate basal ganglia and frontal cortex. *Neuropharmacology, 37*(4–5), 421–429.

Schultz, W., Tremblay, L., & Hollerman, J. R. (2000). Reward processing in primate orbitofrontal cortex and basal ganglia. *Cerebral Cortex, 10*(3), 272–284.

Schwartz, M. W., Peskind, E., Raskind, M., Boyko, E. J., & Porte, D., Jr. (1996). Cerebrospinal fluid leptin levels: relationship to plasma levels and to adiposity in humans. *Nature Medicine, 2*(5), 589–593.

Schwartz, M. W., Woods, S. C., Porte, D., Jr., Seeley, R. J., & Baskin, D. G. (2000). Central nervous system control of food intake. *Nature, 404*(6778), 661–671.

Scott, T. R., Yaxley, S., Sienkiewicz, Z., & Rolls, E. (1986). Gustatory responses in the frontal opercular cortex of the alert cynomolgus monkey. *Journal of Neurophysiology, 56*, 876–890.

Shiiya, T., Nakazato, M., Mizuta, M., Date, Y., Mondal, M. S., Tanaka, M., et al. (2002). Plasma ghrelin levels in lean and obese humans and the effect of glucose on ghrelin secretion. *Journal of Endocrinology and Metabolism, 87*, 240–244.

Shirao, N., Okamoto, Y., Okada, G., Okamoto, Y., & Yamawaki, S. (2003). Temporomesial activation in young females associated with unpleasant words concerning body image. *Neuropsychobiology, 48*(3), 136–142.

Shively, C., Friedman, D., Gage, H., Bounds, M., Brown-Proctor, C., Blair, J., et al. (2006). Behavioral depression and positron emission tomography-determined serotonin 1A receptor binding potential in cynomolgus monkeys. *Archives of General Psychiatry, 63*(4), 396–403.

Silberg, J., & Bulik, C. (2005). Developmental association between eating disorders symptoms and symptoms of depression and anxiety in juvenile twin girls. *Journal of Childhood Psychology and Psychiatry, 46*(12), 1317–1326.

Sibille E., Pavlides C., Benke D., & Toth M. (2000). Genetic inactivation of the Serotonin(1A) receptor in mice results in downregulation of major GABA(A) receptor alpha subunits, reduction of GABA(A) receptor binding, and benzodiazepine-resistant anxiety, *Journal of Neuroscience, 20*(8), 2758–2765.

Simansky, K. J. (1996). Serotonergic control of the organization of feeding and satiety. *Behavior and Brain Research, 73*(1–2), 37–42.

Simon, S., De Araujo, I., Gutierrez, R., & Nicolelis, M. (2006). The neural mechanisms of gustation: a distributed processing code. *Nature Reviews of Neuroscience, 7*, 890–901.

Small, D. (2002). Toward an understanding of the brain substrates of reward in humans. *Neuron, 22*, 668–671.

Small, D. (2006). Central gustatory processing in humans. *Advances in Otorhinolaryngology, 63*, 191–220.

Small, D., Jones-Gotman, M., & Dagher, A. (2003). Feeding-induced dopamine release in dorsal striatum correlates with meal pleasantness ratings in healthy human volunteers. *NeuroImage, 19*(4), 1709–1715.

Small, D., Zatorre, R., Dagher, A., Evans, A., & Jones-Gotman, M. (2001). Changes in brain activity related to eating chocolate: from pleasure to aversion. *Brain, 124*(9), 1720–1733.

Smyth, J., Wonderlich, S., Heron, K., Sliwinski, M., Crosby, R., Mitchell, J., et al. (2007). Daily and momentary mood and stress are associated with binge eating and vomiting in bulimia nervosa patients in the natural environment. *Journal of Consulting and Clinical Psychology, 75*(4), 629–638.

Soubrie, P. (1986). Reconciling the role of central serotonin neurons in human and animal behavior. *Behavioral Brain Science, 9*, 319.

Spielberger, C. D., Gorsuch, R. L., & Lushene, R. E. (1970). *STAI Manual for the State Trait Anxiety Inventory*. Palo Alto, CA: Consulting Psychologists Press.

Srinivasagam, N. M., Kaye, W. H., Plotnicov, K. H., Greeno, C., Weltzin, T. E., & Rao, R. (1995). Persistent perfectionism, symmetry, and exactness after long-term recovery from anorexia nervosa. *American Journal of Psychiatry, 152*(11), 1630–1634.

Staley, J., Malison, R., & Innis, R. (1998). Imaging of the serotonergic system: Interactions of neuroanatomical and functional abnormalities of depression. *Biological Psychiatry, 44*(7), 534–549.

Steiger H., Joober R., Israel M., Young S., Ng Ying Kin N., Gauvin L., et al. (2005). The 5HTTLPR polymorphism, psychopathologic symptoms, and platelet [(3)H-] paroxetine binding in bulimic syndromes. *International Journal of Eating Disorders, 37*, 57–60.

Steinhausen H. C. (2002). The outcome of anorexia nervosa in the 20th century, *American Journal of Psychiatry,159*(8), 1284–1293.

Stice, E. (2002). Risk and maintenance factors for eating pathology: a meta-analytic review. *Pychopharmacology Bulletin, 128*, 825–848.

Stock, S., Leichner, P., Wong, A., Ghatei, M., Kieffer, T., Bloom, S., et al. (2005). Ghrelin, peptide YY, glucose-dependent insulinotropic polypeptide, and hunger responses to a mixed meal in anorexic, obese, and control female adolescents. *Journal of Clinical Endocrinology and Metabolism, 90*, 2161–2168.

Stockmeier, C. A. (1997). Neurobiology of serotonin in depression and suicide. *Annals of the New York Academy of Sciences, 836*, 220–232.

Stoeckel, L., Weller, R., Cook, E. R., Twieg, D., Knowlton, R., & Cox, J. (2008). Widespread reward-system activation in obese women in response to pictures of high-calorie foods. *NeuroImage, 41*(2), 636–647.

Stoving, R. K., Hangaard, J., Hansen-Nord, M., & Hagen, C. (1999). A review of endocrine changes in anorexia nervosa. *Journal of Psychiatric Research, 33*, 139–152.

Strober, M. (1980). Personality and symptomatological features in young, nonchronic anorexia nervosa patients. *Journal of Psychosomatic Research, 24*(6), 353–359.

Strober, M. (1995). Family-genetic perspectives on anorexia nervosa and bulimia nervosa. In K. Brownell & C. Fairburn (Eds.), *Eating Disorders and Obesity-A Comprehensive Handbook* (pp. 212–218). New York: The Guilford Press.

Strober, M., Freeman, R., Lampert, C., Diamond, J., & Kaye, W. (2000). Controlled family study of anorexia nervosa and bulimia nervosa: Evidence of shared liability and transmission of partial syndromes. *American Journal of Psychiatry, 157*(3), 393–401.

Strober M., Freeman R., & Morrell W. (1997). The long-term course of severe anorexia nervosa in adolescents: survival analysis of recovery, relapse, and outcome predictors over 10–15 years in a prospective study, *International Journal of Eating Disorders, 22*(4), 339–360.

Strupp, B. J., Weingartner, H., Kaye, W., & Gwirtsman, H. (1986). Cognitive processing in anorexia nervosa. A disturbance in automatic information processing. *Neuropsychobiology, 15*(2), 89–94.

Szabo, S. T., & Blier, P. (2001). Serotonin (1A) receptor ligands act on norepinephrine neuron firing through excitatory amino acid and GABA(A) receptors: A microiontophoretic study in the rat locus coeruleus. *Synapse, 42*(4), 203–212.

Tamai, H., Takemura, J., Kobayashi, N., Matsubayashi, S., Matsukura, S., & Nakagawa, T. (1993). Changes in plasma cholecystokinin concentrations after oral glucose tolerance test in anorexia nervosa before and after therapy. *Metabolism: Clinical & Experimental, 42*(5), 581–584.

Tanaka, M., Naruo, T., Muranaga, T., Yasuhara, D., Shiiya, T., Nakazato, M., et al. (2002). Increased fasting plasma ghrelin levels in patients with bulimia nervosa. *European Journal of Endocrinology, 146*, R1–R3.

Tataranni, P. A., Gautier, J. F., Chen, K., Uecker, A., Bandy, D., Salbe, A. D., et al. (1999). Neuroanatomical correlates of hunger and satiation in humans using positron emission tomography. *Proceedings of the National Academy of Sciences of the United States of America, 96*(8), 4569–4574.

Tchanturia, K., Morris, R. G., Anderluh, M. B., Collier, D. A., Nikolaou, V., & Treasure, J. (2004). Set shifting in anorexia nervosa: An examination before and after weight gain, in full recovery and relationship to childhood and adult OCPD traits. *Journal of Psychiatric Research, 38*, 545–552.

Thut, G., Schultz, W., Roelcke, U., Nienhusmeier, M., Missimer, J., Maguire, R. P., et al. (1997). Activation of the human brain by monetary reward. *NeuroReport, 8*(5), 1225–1228.

Tiihonen, J., Keski-Rahkonen, A., Lopponen, M., Muhonen, M., Kajander, J., Allonen, T., et al. (2004). Brain serotonin 1A receptor binding in bulimia nervosa. *Biological Psychiatry, 55*, 871.

Tricomi, E. M., Delgado, M. R., & Fiez, J. A. (2004). Modulation of caudate activity by action contingency. *Neuron, 41*, 281–292.

Tschop, M., Wawarta, R., Reiepl, R., Friedrich, S., Bidlingmaier, M., Landgraf, R., et al. (2001). Post-prandial decrease of circulating human ghrelin levels. *Journal of Endocrinology Investigation, 24*, RC19–RC21.

Uher, R., Brammer, M., Murphy, T., Campbell, I., Ng, V., Williams, S., et al. (2003). Recovery and chronicity in anorexia nervosa: Brain activity associated with differential outcomes. *Biological Psychiatry, 54*, 934–942.

Uher, R., Murphy, T., Brammer, M., Dalgleish, T., Phillips, M., Ng, V., et al. (2004). Medial prefrontal cortex activity associated with symptom provocation in eating disorders. *American Journal of Psychiatry, 161*(7), 1238–1246.

Uher, R., Treasure, J., Heining, M., Brammer, M. J., & Campbell, I. C. (2006). Cerebral processing of food-related stimuli: Effects of fasting and gender. *Behavioral Brain Research, 169*(1), 111–119.

van Heeringen, C., Audenaert, K., Van Laere, K., Dumont, F., Slegers, G., Mertens, J., et al. (2003). Prefrontal 5-HT2a receptor binding index, hopelessness and personality characteristics in attempted suicide. *Journal of Affective Disorders, 74*, 149–158.

Vitousek, K., & Manke, F. (1994). Personality variables and disorders in anorexia nervosa and bulimia nervosa. *Journal of Abnormal Psychology, 103*(1), 137–147.

Wade, T., Martin, N. G., & Tiggemann, M. (1998). Genetic and environmental risk factors for the weight and shape concerns characteristic of bulimia nervosa. *Psychological Medicine, 28*(4), 761–771.

Wagner, A., Aizenstein, H., Frank, G. K., Figurski, J., May, J. C., Putnam, K., et al. (2006). Neural correlates of habituation to taste stimuli in healthy women. *Psychiatry Research, 147*(1), 57–67.

Wagner, A., Aizenstein, H., Frank, G. K., Figurski, J., May, J. C., Putnam, K., et al. (2008). Altered insula response to a taste stimulus in individuals recovered from restricting-type anorexia nervosa. *Neuropsychopharmacology, 33*(3), 513–523.

—Wagner, A., Aizenstein, H., Venkatraman, M., Fudge, J., May, J., Mazurkewicz, L., et al. (2007). Altered reward processing in women recovered from anorexia nervosa. *American Journal of Psychiatry, 164*(12), 1842–1849.

Wagner, A., Barbarich, N., Frank, G., Bailer, U. F., Weissfeld, L., Henry, S., et al. (2006). Personality traits after recovery from eating disorders: Do subtypes differ? *International Journal of Eating Disorders, 39*(4), 276–284.

Walsh, B. T., Roose, S. P., Katz, J. L., Dyrenfurth, I., Wright, L., Vande Wiele, R., et al. (1987). Hypothalamic-pituitary-adrenal-cortical activity in anorexia nervosa and bulimia. *Psychoneuroendocrinology, 12*, 131–140.

Walters, E. E., & Kendler, K. S. (1995). Anorexia nervosa and anorexic-like syndromes in a population-based female twin sample. *American Journal of Psychiatry, 152*(1), 64–71.

Wang, G., Volkow, N. D., Telang, F., Jayne, M., Ma, J., Rao, M., et al. (2004). Exposure to appetitive food stimuli markedly activates the human brain. *NeuroImage, 21*(4), 1790–1797.

Waters, A., Hill, A., & Waller, G. (2001). Bulimics' responses to food cravings: Is binge-eating a product of hunger or emotional state? *Behavior Research and Therapy, 39*(8), 877–886.

Weltzin, T. E., Hsu, L. K., Pollice, C., & Kaye, W. H. (1991). Feeding patterns in bulimia nervosa. *Biological Psychiatry, 30*(11), 1093–1110.

Westergaard, G., Suomi, S., Chavanne, T., Houser, L., Hurley, A., Cleveland, A., et al. (2003). Physiological correlates of aggression and impulsivity in free-ranging female primates. *Neuropsychopharmacology, 28*, 1045–1055.

Wolfe, B., Jimerson, D., Orlova, C., & Mantzoros, C. (2004). Effect of dieting on plasma leptin, soluble leptin receptor, adiponectin and resistin levels in healthy volunteers. *Clinical Endocrinology (Oxford), 61*, 332–338.

Wolfe, B., Metzger, E., Levine, J., Finkelstein, D., Cooper, T., & Jimerson, D. (2000). Serotonin function following remission from bulimia nervosa. *Neuropsychopharmacology, 22*(3), 257–263.

Wren, A., Seal, L., Cohen, M., Byrnes, A., Front, G., Murphy, K., et al. (2001). Ghrelin enhances appetite and increases foot intake in humans. *Journal of Clinical Endorinology and Metabolism, 86*, 5992–5995.

Yaxley, S., Rolls, E., & Sienkiewicz, Z. (1990). Gustatory responses of single neurons in the insula of the macaque monkey. *Journal of Neurophysiology, 63*(689–700).

Yin, H., & Knowlton, B. (2006). The role of the basal ganglia in habit formation. *Nature Neuroscience Reviews, 7*(6), 464–476.

Yoshimura, H., Kato, N., Sungai, T., Honjo, M., Sato, J., Segami, N., et al. (2004). To-and-fro optical voltage signal propagation between the insular gustatory and parietal oral somatosensory areas in rat cortex slices. *Brain Research, 1015*, 114–121.

Zhang, Y., Proenca, R., Maffei, M., Barone, M., Leopold, L., & Friedman, J. (1994). Positional cloning of the mouse obese gene and its human homologue. *Nature Genetics, 372*, 425–432.

Zigman, J., & Elmquist, J. (2003). Minireview: From anorexia to obesity–the yin and yang of body weight control. *Endocrinology, 144*, 3749–3756.

Genetic Influences on Eating and the Eating Disorders

Tracey D. Wade

Abstract

The current chapter reviews our progress in understanding how genes influence eating and eating disorders (EDs) by addressing the following areas: (1) how recognition of genetic influences on eating and EDs emerged; (2) the complex nature of genetic action; (3) what twin studies can tell us about genetic influences; and (4) the current state of linkage and association studies. It is concluded that genes are an important part of the explanatory framework for the etiology of EDs, with an important contribution of the shared environment to the development of cognition and attitudes that may initiate disordered eating practices, and a critical contribution of the environment in providing a context within which genetic risk is more likely to be expressed. We currently have a limited understanding of the specific genes that are implicated, and the ways in which genes and the environment work together to increase risk for disordered eating.

Keywords: association studies, gene × environment interactions, heritability, linkage studies, shared environment, twin studies

Introduction

It has been known for some time that eating disorders (EDs) "run in families." In 1995 a review of published family and twin studies of anorexia nervosa (AN) and bulimia nervosa (BN) (Spelt & Meyer, 1995) found that, within the context of low absolute prevalence, four of the five studies indicated elevated risk in the family members of either affected individuals (probands) with AN or BN. It was estimated that for females there was a two- to threefold risk of developing an ED if a first-degree relative was affected. More recent and larger family studies suggest a 7- to 12-fold increase in the prevalence of AN or BN in relatives of eating disordered probands compared to the families of controls (Klump, Kaye, & Strober, 2001).

The question that these findings pose is whether this increased familial risk relates to the impact of the environment that is shared in families (which does not necessarily indicate family environment but any sources of the environment that may be experienced equally in families), to genetic influences, or a combination of both. Whereas early research focused more on family environment as an explanatory framework for the development of EDs, evidence from the last 20 years of research has supported a substantial genetic contribution to the development of eating and EDs, a finding that is broadly consistent with the emerging research across a number of major psychiatric disorders and psychopathology, including emotional and behavioral disturbance (Bouchard & McGue, 2003; Paykel, 2002; Rutter & Silberg, 2002).

The acceptance of genetic influences on behavioral disturbances has been called "one of the most dramatic shifts in the modern history of the behavioral sciences" (Plomin, 2000). However, understanding the role of genetics in the development of eating and EDs is a complex task. Individual genetic contributions to risk or vulnerability may be subtle or complex and possibly of small effect. Many different individual genes are hypothesized to exert their influence through a change to the central nervous system and to receptor and metabolic pathways, in interaction with environmental variables, and with their influence likely to be mediated through psychological variables (Hewitt, 1997). Twin studies in conjunction with linkage and association studies can be used to address and understand the complexities of genetic action, but we are currently a long way from developing a coherent understanding of the causality of EDs.

Therefore the purpose of the current chapter is to review our progress in understanding how genes influence eating and EDs and to examine future directions in the area. To address these aims, the following issues are examined in turn: (1) how recognition of genetic influences on eating and EDs emerged; (2) the complex nature of genetic action; (3) what twin studies can tell us about genetic influences; and (4) linkage and association studies in terms of identifying specific genes that may influence development of EDs.

How Did Recognition of Genetic Influence on Eating and Eating Disorders Emerge?

From the work of Hilde Bruch in the 1970s (1973, 1978) through to the 1980s, there was a general consensus among eating disorder researchers that AN and BN were "disorders in which biological, familial, and sociocultural factors play important etiological roles" (Johnson & Flach, 1985). In reality, what captured the focus of most etiological research was identifying the structure of families that produced an expression of distress in the child, with the aim of delineating the specific family structure that produced an ED as opposed to other psychopathology such as depression or anxiety. This interest was fuelled by cross-sectional research that consistently showed that as the severity of eating pathology increased so too did the proband reports of family dysfunction (Wisotsky et al., 2003). Reinforcing the view that families cause EDs were the patients referred for treatment, who most commonly report the perceived causes of the eating problem as being dysfunctional families (Tozzi, Sullivan, Fear, McKenzie, & Bulik, 2003).

However, the limitations of cross-sectional associations required that the meaning of the findings be questioned. In an interesting study, Woodside and colleagues (1995) found that reports of family dysfunction were significantly worse from BN probands than from their respective family members, whose reports of family functioning were comparable to population norms. However, as treatment progressed and the influence of BN decreased, family reports of family dysfunction remained relatively unchanged but the reports of the probands became more favorable. Family members indicated that the main source of dysfunction was between the family and the person with the ED and not other dimensions of family functioning. This finding is consistent with longitudinal research that examined the direction of associations between parent–adolescent relationships and adolescent girls' unhealthy eating, and found a direct effect of unhealthy eating on parent–adolescent relationships with no direct effect in the opposite direction (Archibald, Linver, Graber, & Brooks-Gunn, 2002).

In a recent review of the 15 longitudinal studies of EDs considered to be methodologically robust (Jacobi, Hayward, de Zwaan, Kraemer, & Agras, 2004), only five included family environment measures, and of these only two found family variables to be risk factors for ED development. Specifically, this included low levels of social support from families (Ghaderi 2003), and abusive parental relationships (Johnson, Cohen, Kasen, & Brook, 2002). Hence, family environment is still viewed as a correlate rather than as a true risk factor for the development of an ED (Jacobi et al., 2004). This stance is reflected in evidence-based family therapy approaches for EDs that recognize that the family reorganize themselves around the ED in such a way as to either contribute to the maintenance of the disorder or prevent the family from being able to use their normal adaptive mechanisms to deal with change (Eisler, 2005).

Since the late 1980s a substantial body of work has been developing that indicates that genetic risk factors are an important influence in the development of EDs. The seminal paper implicating genetic risk for BN in a non-ascertained twin population (i.e., where probands were not recruited through treatment facilities but from the general population) came from the Virginia Twin Registry and the work of Kenneth Kendler and colleagues (1991), with a follow-up paper in 1995. Similarly evidence from the Virginia Twin Registry also implicated genetic risk for AN (Wade, Bulik, Neale, & Kendler, 2000; Walters & Kendler, 1995).

Twin studies are useful for delineating genetic risk as they can compare trait similarity between identical or monozygotic (MZ) twins (who share

100% of their genes) and nonidentical or dizygotic (DZ) twins (who share, on average, only 50% of their genes), where structural equation modelling approaches are used to examine the relative contribution of three latent factors: additive genetic, shared environmental, and nonshared environmental effects (Plomin, Defries, & McClearn, 1990). Additive genetic effects are the genetic factors that "add" rather than interact across genes, roughly indicated by a concordance between MZ twins for the disorder that is twice as high as that of DZ twins. Shared environmental influences are inferred when MZ and DZ twin correlations are approximately equal, as these factors are common to co-twins growing up in the same family and therefore contribute to their behavioral similarity (Plomin et al., 1990). Nonshared environmental influences are unique to each co-twin and make them different from each other. It is important to understand that nonshared environment can be either *objective*, an actual experience or event that is not shared by siblings, or *effective*, wherein the same event can be experienced uniquely by each family member, depending on a number of factors such as age and temperament, thus producing differential outcomes (Turkheimer & Waldron, 2000). It is also worth noting that nonshared environmental influences can also include a variety of prenatal events (Martin, Boomsma, & Machin, 1997), that result in MZ twins, although carrying identical DNA sequences, exhibiting numerous epigenetic differences (Petronis, 2001). In other words, there is no structural change to the DNA but gene expression is modulated by the environment in the womb.

There is a fourth source of potential variance, known as genetic dominance (Martin, Eaves, Kearsey, & Davies, 1978), that is rarely indicated as accounting for variance in phenotypes. Dominance, a term originally arising from Mendel's classical experiments, refers to the interaction between alleles at the same locus. An allele is a viable DNA coding that occupies a given position (locus) on a chromosome. Organisms have two alleles for each trait and if the same allele is present twice, the organism is said to be homozygous for this characteristic. If, however, one chromosome contains one allele and the other chromosome a contrasting allele, the organism is said to be heterozygous. In this latter case, the allele that determines the phenotype is said to be dominantly expressed, that is, it shows dominance over other alleles.

There was a rapid increase in twin studies in EDs during the 1990s that were reviewed by Cynthia Bulik and colleagues in 2000. At that time it was concluded that the limited number of studies and low power precluded definitive conclusions about the role of genes in AN, but that "there is consistent evidence to suggest that a reasonable proportion (and perhaps most) of the observed familial aggregation of BN is due to additive genetic effects" (Bulik, Sullivan, Wade, & Kendler, 2000). Similarly, evidence suggested a substantial proportion of genetic variance contributing to the etiology of traits associated with EDs such as dietary restraint, with the exception of weight concern, where the contributions of shared and nonshared environment were implicated (Wade, Martin, & Tiggemann, 1998). More recent reviews have concluded that there is a clear and possibly substantial genetic contribution to both BN and AN (Collier & Treasure, 2004; Fairburn & Harrison, 2003).

The affirmation of the importance of genetic factors in the etiology of disordered eating have fuelled a number of investigations involving molecular genetic research, which involves both linkage and association studies, in an effort to delineate specific genes that might confer risk in interaction with other factors such as the environment and temperament styles (Klump & Gobrogge, 2005). Linkage studies refer to exploratory investigations, where few if any a priori hypotheses exist about specific genes that may be involved in increasing risk for a disorder, and that examine families where typically at least more than one member has an ED. These studies examine whether these relatives share alleles at certain markers on chromosomes at a greater than chance level and thus do not focus on one particular gene but examines all identified genetic markers in the genome. In contrast, association studies adopt a case-control approach where a sample of affected probands is compared to a matched control group in terms of frequency of alleles or genotypes. Here the focus is on a specific gene (a candidate gene) and these studies are used when there are a priori hypotheses about the genes to be examined.

The Complexities of Genetic Influence

Before the extant research on genetic influences on EDs can be properly interpreted, it is important to understand the complexities of genetic action. Like any complex trait, eating and EDs are understood to be influenced by many genes and many specific environmental factors, where genetic factors are seen to operate in a probabilistic fashion like risk factors rather then predetermined programming (Plomin, 2000).

Many Different Genes Acting on Different Pathways

There is clearly no one gene that "causes" EDs, and the relevant genes are likely to be associated with at least three different biological pathways (Slof-Op 't et al., 2005), including the serotonin pathway (involved in weight regulation and eating behavior), the catecholamine pathway (including the neurotransmitters dopamine, norepinephrine, and epinephrine), and the pathway involved in neuropeptide and feeding regulation. Keeping in mind that different types of ED exist, each of which is defined by a number of different diagnostic criteria, ranging from weight to eating disordered behaviors to cognitive substrates, and that increased vulnerability to any one of these criterion can arise through a number of different pathways, it is clear that numerous genes acting on different pathways will be differentially involved in increasing a person's risk for developing an ED.

One example of this complex process is illustrated by the genetic factors likely to impact on body mass index (BMI), where low weight is just one of the diagnostic criteria of AN. We know that BMI is largely determined by genetic influence with variance estimates of 67% in adults (Maes, Neale, & Eaves, 1997), where 35% (95% confidence intervals [CI]: 29–42) and 39% (95% CI: 35–44) of the variance is due to additive genetic action in males and females respectively, of which 2% results from assortative mating (where individuals mate with those that are like themselves in some respect thus reducing the range of trait variance), and dominance accounts for the remainder of the variance. Estimates of the genetic variance of BMI are similar in younger people, with 80% (95% CI: 75–84) in adolescent females and 76% (95% CI: 70–81) in adolescent males (Slof Op et al., 2008), and 61% (95% CI: 48–76) and 64% (95% CI: 51–80) in 4-year-old girls and boys, respectively (Koeppen-Schomerus, Wardle, & Plomin, 2001). In the sample of young children there was also a significant contribution of the shared environment at around 25% for both girls and boys, with the suggestion that this influence disappears as the child gets older, resulting in increasing contributions of heritability and nonshared environment (Koeppen-Schomerus et al., 2001). However even in such a widely studied phenotype as BMI, it remains uncertain which specific genes are implicated, where a recent meta-analysis of 37 published studies examining more than 31,000 individuals from more than 10,000 families (Saunders et al., 2007) could not unequivocally implicate specific loci for BMI or obesity despite having substantial statistical power. The authors concluded that this difficulty may be caused because genes influencing adiposity are of very small effect, with substantial genetic heterogeneity and variable dependence on environmental factors. Other research has indicated that the genes that regulate BMI might differ to some degree across different ethnic groups (Guo, North, Gorden-Larsen, Bulik, & Choi, 2007). Adding to the complexity is the finding that intentional weight loss, such as that observed in AN, is moderately heritable in women (66%, 95% CI: 55–75) and less heritable in men (38%, 95% CI: 19–55) but shares few genetic risk factors with BMI (Keski-Rahkonnen, Neale, et al., 2005), with correlations ranging from 0.28 to 0.52 across males and females. The differences between BMI and intentional weight loss are also suggested by the finding that serum leptin levels differentiate between constitutionally lean females and those with AN (Köpp et al., 1997; von Prittwitz et al., 1997). Hence it is unclear whether what we do know about biology of low BMI applies to the low weight seen in AN (Bulik et al., 2007). Investigation of low BMI in ED populations using linkage analysis showed a significant association with 4q13.1 in an AN cohort (Bulik et al., 2005), indicating that the gene of interest is on the long arm of chromosome 4 at a particular band, number 3.1, in region 1. One significant [4q21.1] and three suggestive [3p23, 10p13, 5p15.3] associations were found in a BN cohort (Bacanu et al., 2005).

In addition to exploring what we know about the extant diagnostic criteria, we must also consider genetic influences on behaviors and temperaments associated with EDs that are thought to be important in determining the course of EDs but are not currently included as part of any diagnostic schemes. These continuous measures could result in useful indices of vulnerability that may not necessarily indicate the presence of a clinical disorder but may be predictive of increased risk for developing a disorder (Hewitt, 1997) and also represent quantitative risk indices that may increase reliable diagnosis (Kendler, Neale, Kessler, Heath, & Eaves, 1993) and therefore result in more focused and powerful molecular genetic investigations. For example, the importance of these types of measures in helping focus work in linkage analyses of AN has recently been shown where incorporation of two behavioral covariates, drive for thinness and obsessionality, was able to reveal several regions of interest (Devlin et al., 2002).

Using an endophenotype approach (Gershon & Goldin, 1986) where endophenotypes are seen to be expressions of biological markers for a phenotype that are associated with illness in the general population (as well as being a stable and state-independent characteristic, and found in family members at a higher rate than in the general population), four types of constructs have been identified as being worthy of further investigation as potential covariates of diagnostic criteria (Bulik et al., 2007). These include increased physical activity, dimensions of temperament (obsessionality, impulsivity, and negative emotionality), impaired set shifting (executive functioning, responsible for the supervision of such cognitive processes as setting goals, planning, and organizing), and dimensions reflecting weight concern (including drive for thinness).

Genes and Environmental Factors

One of the best ways to understand the interplay between genes and the environment is the identification of gene–environment correlations and genotype–environment interactions (Rutter & Silberg, 2002). The first of these mechanisms, genotype–environment (g–e) correlations, are correlations between genetic and environmental variables as they affect a particular trait. They describe the extent to which individuals are exposed to certain environments as a function of their genetic vulnerabilities. Three types of g–e correlations have been hypothesized to exist (Scarr & McCartney, 1983) and previously discussed in terms of their relationships to EDs (e.g., Strober, 1991; Wonderlich, 1992): passive, evocative, and active, each of which is described in the text that follows.

Passive g–e correlation occurs in reared-together biological relatives, where parents provide their children with both genes and an environment that is conducive to the development of certain traits that occur independently of the offspring's characteristics. For example, parents who are highly concerned about themselves and their children becoming overweight could transmit to their children both the genes for these traits as well as an environment that is conducive to the trait's development such as frequent weighing of the child, modeling dieting behaviors to the child, and imposing restrictive eating patterns on the child. From the research literature we know that mothers of 4-year-old children with feeding problems have a significantly higher rate of past or current ED (odds ratio = 11.1, 95% CI: 1.4–91.8) compared to the other mothers who have children with other disturbances such anxiety or mothers whose children have no disturbances (Whelan & Cooper, 2000). Videotaped interactions suggest that the child's disturbed eating may not only be caused by genetic action (i.e., inheriting the mother's risk for disturbed eating) but also through environmental action, where mothers with EDs use more verbal control in meal and play times than mothers with postnatal depression or controls (Stein et al., 2001). At meal times these mothers are also more likely to express negative emotion and to be less facilitating and more intrusive (Stein, Woolley, Cooper, & Fairburn, 1994; Stein et al., 2001; Waugh & Bulik, 1999).

By contrast, both evocative and active g–e correlations are dependent on an individual's characteristics and/or behaviors. An evocative g–e correlation occurs when genetically influenced characteristics in the child evoke an environmental response that reflects the genetic trait. For example, an adolescent with the genetically influenced trait of overweight might experience excessive teasing about body weight and shape from peers (an environmental response), and this teasing may result in dysphoric mood that triggers binge eating. From the research literature, an evocative g–e correlation is suggested by findings that people with AN are characterized by obsessionality, rigidity, low impulsivity, fear of uncertainty, and avoidance of novel situations (Cassin & von Ranson, 2005) and that increased paternal control is uniquely associated with AN in MZ twins discordant for AN compared to MZ twins discordant for BN or major depression (Wade, Gillespie, & Martin, 2007). This could suggest that a harm avoidant and timid child evokes a response of overprotection from concerned fathers, which in turn leads the child to become more timid and uncertain of their autonomy and ability to act independently and thus they start to develop an overvalued importance of control over eating and weight in order to compensate.

Active g–e correlations refer to the situation where individuals actively select or create environments that correlate with their genetic propensities. An example of this type of correlation would be the selection of weight-conscious friends by an adolescent who also places importance on physical appearance. Another example is suggested by a longitudinal study that found that regular family meals (≥5 meals a week) were associated with lower prevalence of extreme weight control behaviors in adolescents (Neumark-Sztainer, Eisenberg, Fulkerson, Story, & Larson, 2008). If adolescents who are genetically vulnerable to developing eating problems select to eat on their own and thus have less scrutiny with respect to their dietary intake, less exposure to modeling of healthy eating, as well as less experience of eating in a social realm as opposed to simply a focus on food, then this could reinforce an overvalued importance of controlling dietary intake which could lead to the development of unhealthy weight management practices.

The second mechanism that describes the interplay between genes and the environment is genotype–environment interactions (G×E) which occur when the effect of the environment depends on the genotype, such that individuals will be varyingly susceptible to the influence of high-risk environments proportional to their degree of genetic risk. Conversely, the importance of the environment in manipulating genetic expression is immense given findings from animal models that early environmental manipulation can change gene expression (Meaney et al., 1985). An example of the importance of environmental action in humans can be found in tobacco use when two historical cohorts in Sweden were compared (Kendler, Thornton, & Pedersen, 2000), one in which smoking was rare for women and one in which smoking had become widespread throughout the community. The heritability for tobacco smoking for women increased from 0% to 63%, while heritability for men stayed relatively stable at around 63%.

G×E may to some extent explain why the Western sociocultural environment and its emphasis on thinness for women and muscularity for men impacts adversely on some people but not others. For example, in an experimental study, only vulnerable adolescent girls, defined as those with elevated levels of body dissatisfaction and perceived pressure to be thin, were adversely impacted by exposure to a 15-month subscription of a fashion magazine compared to nonvulnerable girls in terms of their negative affect (Stice, Spangler, & Agras, 2001). In other words vulnerability toward body dissatisfaction can be exacerbated by an environment that further reinforces the dominance of the thin-ideal. Further candidates to examine as environmental moderators of genetic risk are indicated by research that shows an increase in negative life events predicts onset of EDs (McKnight Investigators, 2003) and that initial social support can protect vulnerable girls against the impact of fashion magazines (Stice et al., 2001). Therefore in the context of the unhelpful environment of the thin-ideal, it could be suggested that vulnerability to body dissatisfaction can be increased by negative life events or decreased by adequate social support.

Specific examples of G×E in EDs are suggested by several lines of research. The first comes from Howard Steiger's group, who has shown that, although the serotonin transporter gene promoter polymorphism (5HTTLPR) is not directly associated with bulimic behaviors, it is associated with a variety of potential endophenotypes for bulimic disorders, including affective instability and behavioral impulsivity (Steiger et al., 2005). In addition, this polymorphism in interaction with childhood abuse was associated with significant proportions of variance in stimulus seeking, insecure attachments, and borderline personality disorder in the bulimic population (Steiger et al., 2007). Intriguingly, this polymorphism was linked to reduced serotonin (5-HT) uptake activity in both women with bulimic syndromes and their unaffected first-degree relatives (Steiger et al., 2006).

A second example is informed by the work of Kelly Klump with the adolescent twin registry in Minnesota, who found that both shared and nonshared environment decrease as children become adolescents and heritability increases (Klump, Burt, McGue, & Iacono, 2007), consistent with other research that suggests that puberty moderates genetic influences on disordered eating (Klump et al., 2006). This finding has resulted in research that has implicated higher levels of prenatal circulating estrogen as increasing risk for the probability of disordered eating (Culbert, Breedlove, Burt & Klump, 2008; Procopio & Marriott, 2007), therefore posing an explanation for the observed sex differences in EDs. However, this finding was not replicated in a recent study (Raevuori et al., 2008), indicating that this hypothesis needs to be tested further.

Twin Studies
Why Are Twin Studies Useful?
Methodologies such as twin studies that investigate the interactions between genes and environments are considered to be a vital and essential companion to molecular genetics (Kendler, 2001; Lyons & Bar, 2001; Neiderhiser, 2001). Although the findings of molecular studies can identify correlations between individual genes and disorders, twin studies investigating gene–environment interplay can provide descriptive models tracing the complex causal pathway from genotype to phenotype, with a particular focus on putative environmental risk factors. Twin studies are also useful for modelling the overlap in genetic risk factors across multiple phenotypes and thus can increase power to identify potential genetic

pathways of action where the associated phenotypes are more studied than EDs.

Assessing Heritability Estimates of Phenotypes

Traditionally twin studies have also been used to develop estimates of heritability of phenotypes. However, when it comes to developing accurate estimates of heritability, twin studies can develop such estimates only commensurate with the reliability of the measured trait (Foley, Neale, & Kendler, 1998). This truism goes some way to answer the observation that "the findings of twin studies [of eating disorders] are inconsistent … with [wide] estimates for the heritability of liability" (Fairburn, Cowen, & Harrison, 1999, p. 349).

Accurate measurement of complex phenotypes, such as EDs, where the various cognitions and behaviors are likely to be impacted by different genetic risk factors, is an important endeavor. Treating an ED as a coherent whole in order to assess heritability will be at best using a very blunt instrument indeed and focus on careful definition of each component is important. Interviews rather than self-report questionnaires have been advocated as providing greater reliability of psychiatric phenotypes (Kendler et al., 1993) which hypothetically can increase estimates of heritability as measurement error, which contributes to nonshared environmental variance, is decreased. Also advocated as improving reliability are the use of multiple interview occasions and co-assessment of lifetime comorbidity (Foley et al., 1998; Rice, Rochberg, Endicott, Lavori, & Miller, 1992). Further, in the area of EDs it is particularly important to use reliable and thorough interviews that can best address the difficulties inherent in making a lifetime diagnosis (Fairburn et al., 1999), given the sometimes sporadic and ego-syntonic nature of the psychopathology.

Accurate measurement of a phenotype also speaks to an issue of general debate across psychiatric disorders and across scientific fields of enquiry, namely the validity of diagnostic criteria. Whilst there is debate in EDs as to whether a dimensional or categorical conceptualization best captures the phenotype (Rowe et al., 2002; Williamson, Gleaves, & Stewart, 2005), across psychiatric disorders it has been suggested that even the disorders seen to conform to a discontinuous model have latent dimensions that underlie the taxon (Waller & Meehl, 1998), and that there should be tandem use of categorical and dimensional assessments in order to enhance clinical practice (Kessler, 2002). In the area of depression there have been calls to adopt quantitative risk

indices, derived from depressive features that predict reliable diagnosis rather than reliance on the error-prone *DSM* diagnoses (Kendler et al., 1993). Similarly in EDs there have been calls for a reconsideration of the value of dimensional versus categorical conceptualisations of the phenotype, where "further work on dimensional scales should result in useful indices of vulnerability" (Hewitt, 1997, p. 357). A transdiagnostic approach has been suggested as a way in which to better capture the complexity of the cases that comprise the majority of clinical referrals and yet do not meet *DSM* diagnostic criteria (Fairburn, et al, 2007).

Estimates of Heritability from Twin Studies

It is within the context of the aforementioned issues that the twin studies of the heritability of eating and EDs should be interpreted. These studies have been summarized across three different tables, including only non-ascertained twin studies that are expected to give less inflated heritability estimates as opposed to studies wherein twins have been ascertained from treatment clinics.

In Table 7.1, the twin studies of AN are summarized. It can be seen that although only four studies exist, each of these is from a different twin population, albeit the Danish Twin Registry used a single self-report question to assess lifetime history of AN (Kortegaard, Hoerder, Joergensen, Gillberg, & Kyvik, 2001). Also of note are that across the three studies that used interviews, all used a slightly different definition of the phenotype. Although it is somewhat encouraging that the results from the Virginia and Swedish Twin Registries (with respect to the narrowly defined phenotype) were similar with heritability estimates between 56% and 58%, it is less encouraging to note that the 95% confidence intervals of the Swedish heritability estimates include 0, and that dropping the requirement of amenorrhea substantially decreases the estimate of heritability to 31% in the same population.

Twin studies of BN are summarized in Table 7.2. In contrast to the studies of AN, it is immediately notable that all the studies come from the Virginia Twin Registry, albeit one study (Rowe et al., 2002) does use a different (and younger) sample from the other four studies. Given this, it is particularly discouraging to note the wide variety of estimates of heritability. Selecting those studies that are likely to include the most reliable phenotype, where either BN was measured on two occasions or it was analyzed with other psychiatric disorders, two of the studies give quite low estimates of heritability

Table 7.1 Non-ascertained Twin Studies of Anorexia Nervosa

Study	Model fitting results[a]			Population[b]: How was phenotype defined?
	A (95% CI)	C (95% CI)	E (95% CI)	
Wade, Bulik, Neale, & Kendler (2000)[c]	.58 (.33–.84)	—	.42 (.16–.68)	VTR (mean age, 29.3 ± 7.7 years): SCID (first interview wave), met all *DSM-III-R* criteria except for (1) amenorrhea OR (2) feeling fat when emaciated. Bivariate analysis with major depression
Klump, Miller, Keel, McGue, & Iacono (2001)	.76 (.35–.95)	—	.24 (.05–.65)	MFTS (mean age, 17.5 ± 0.5 years): SCID, met *DSM-IV* criteria for EITHER (1) below 85% IBW and met all but one criteria for AN OR (2) <90% IBW AND at least one cognitive symptom of AN AND scored above mean on Eating Disorder Inventory for all twins in (1)
Kortegaard, Hoerder, Joergensen, Gillberg, & Kyvik (2001)	.48 (.27–.65)	—	.52 (NR)	Danish Twin Register (age 11–41 years): SRQ "Have you ever had AN?"
Bulik et al. (2006)	.56 (0–.87) .31 (0–.62)	.05 (0–.64) 0 (0–.44)	.38 (.13–.84) .68 (.37–1.0)	Swedish Twin Registry (age 49–58 years): SCID, narrow (all *DSM-IV* criteria) SCID, broad (all *DSM-IV* criteria with exception of amenorrhea)

[a]Full model or model of best fit (lowest Akaike's Information Criteria)—not necessarily significantly better fitting than the full model.
[b]All populations were female.
[c]This study can be interpreted as superseding the Walters and Kendler (1995) study of this population as the zygosities were corrected in the light of genotyping, where two DZ twin pairs were reassigned as MZ.
A = additive genetic variance; C = shared environmental variance; E = nonshared environmental variance; CI = confidence interval; VTR = Virginia Twin Registry; SCID = Structured Clinical Interview for *DSM*; MTFS = Minnesota Twin Family Study; IBW = ideal body weight; AN = anorexia nervosa; NR = not reported; SRQ = self-report questionnaire.

(Baker, Mazzeo, & Kendler, 2007; Kendler et al., 1995), at 28% and 31%, where the first of these estimated 95% CI of 7% to 62%. In contrast, the study that used a bivariate analysis of two waves of interview data estimated heritability at 83%, with 95% CI ranging from 49% to 100%. It should be noted that there was low reliability between the two waves of data, with kappa of 0.28, which may impact on the ability to develop estimates of accurate heritability. BN has previously been described as a heterogeneous disorder (Fairburn, 1991), where diagnostic features vary in severity, and the course of the disorder varies widely between patients. With heterogeneous disorders it may not be sensible to try to estimate heritability of the disorder as though it were a homogeneous entity, but rather to examine its component parts. This approach may also result in identifying phenotypes with greater genetic homogeneity and thus yield more fruitful linkage and association studies (Slof-Op 't et al., 2005).

Studies that examine the specific diagnostic criteria that currently define EDs are summarized in Table 7.3. The first three studies (Bulik, Sullivan, & Kendler, 1998, 2003; Sullivan, Bulik, & Kendler, 1998), all using the same data from the Virginia Twin Registry, examined overeating (defined as "*ever had* eating binges during which you ate a lot of food in a short period of time") which meets neither the frequency nor definition requirements for an objective binge episode which is the current diagnostic stipulation. However, the studies are included as one analysis of the data showed that results were "statistically indistinguishable" from a phenotype that included (1) loss of control and (2) an amount of food that others would consider unusual. It can be noted that all fit the criteria of methodologically stronger studies, as they include more than one measurement occasion or another phenotype, in this case self-induced vomiting and obesity, respectively. Whereas the two bivariate studies obtained

Table 7.2 Non-ascertained Twin Studies of Bulimia Nervosa

Study	Model fitting results[a]			Population[b]: How was phenotype defined?
	A (95% CI)	C (95% CI)	E (95% CI)	
Kendler et al. (1991)	.55 (0–.77) .52 (NR)	—	.45 (.23–.77) .48 (NR)	VTR (mean age, 30.1 ± 7.6 years): SCID (first interview wave) narrowmet all *DSM-III-R* criteria broad—met "most but not all" *DSM-III-R* criteria
Walters et al. (1992)	.50 (NR)	—	.50 (NR)	VTR: SCID (first interview wave) broad *DSM-III-R*. Bivariate analysis with major depression.
Kendler et al. (1995)	.28 (.07–.62)	.37 (.10–.59)	.35 (.19–.49)	VTR: SCID (first interview wave) broad *DSM-III-R*. Multivariate analysis with five other psychiatric disorders.
Bulik, Sullivan, & Kendler (1998)	.83 (.49–1.0)	0 (0–.30)	.17 (0–.36)	VTR: SCID (first and third interview waves) met all *DSM-III-R* criteria except recurrent episodes of binge eating could include less than 2× per week for - month period. Bivariate analysis of two waves with low reliability between waves (κ = .28)
Rowe et al. (2002)	.54 (.44–.62)	—	.46 (NR)	VTSABD (age 8–17 years): Child and Adolescent Psychiatric Assessment (over previous 3 months) assessing four of five *DSM-III-R* criteria (with exception of weight and shape importance). Outcome variable was number of criteria met for each individual.
Baker, Mazzeo, & Kendler (2007)	.31 (NR)	—	.59 (NR)	VTR: SCID (first and third interview waves) broad *DSM-III-R*. Bivariate analysis with drug use disorders.

[a]Full model or model of best fit (lowest Akaike's Information Criteria)—not necessarily significantly better fitting than the full model.
[b]All populations were female with the exception of the Rowe et al. (2002) study, which contained males and females.
A = additive genetic variance; C = shared environmental variance; E = nonshared environmental variance; CI = confidence interval; NR = not reported; VTR = Virginia Twin Registry; SCID = Structured Clinical Interview for *DSM*; VTSABD = Virginia Twin Study of Adolescent Behavioral Development.

similar estimates of heritability (46%–49%), the so-called measurement model approach (using two waves of interview data) estimates substantially higher heritability at 82% with 95% CI: 68% to 97%. Once again, it should be noted that there is low reliability between the two interviews (kappa = 0.34), which may impact on developing accurate heritability estimates. These results can be contrasted with two studies of objective binge episodes (Javaras et al., 2008; Wade, Treloar, & Martin, 2008), one from Norway and one from Australia, where the genetic estimates are lower (with a lower 95% CI of 5% and an upper 95% CI of 52%). It should be noted that the Norwegian study used a phenotype that occurred in the absence of purging and was required to occur only once a month for a 6-month period, whereas the Australian study, which obtained quite low estimates of heritability (17%, 95% CI: 5–28) used the *DSM* criteria of

twice a week for a 3-month period and did not exclude comorbidity with purging behaviors. The Australian study also obtained lifetime estimates by using the full Eating Disorder Examination (EDE; Fairburn & Cooper, 1993), a semistructured interview that has been described as the "gold standard" (Wilson, 1993).

There exist two studies of self-induced vomiting for weight control purposes, one from the Virginian Twin Registry (Sullivan et al., 1998) and the other from the Australian Twin Registry (Wade et al., 2008). It is clear that the heritability estimates are widely different and nonoverlapping, with the Virginian study having estimates of heritability ranging from 50% to 84% compared to the 1% to 18% estimate of the Australian study. Again the phenotypes are somewhat different, with the Virginian study requiring only that people had ever vomited, whereas the Australian study required the

Table 7.3   Non-ascertained Twin Studies of DSM Diagnostic Criteria for Eating Disorders

Study	Criterion	Model fitting results[a]			Population[b]: How was phenotype ascertained?
		A (95% CI)	C (95% CI)	E (95% CI)	
Bulik, Sullivan, & Kendler (1998)	Overeating	.82 (.68–.97)	—	.18 (.03–.32)	VTR: SCID (first and third interview waves) "Have you ever in your life had eating binges during which you ate a lot of food in a short period of time?" Bivariate analysis of two waves with low reliability between waves (κ = .34)
Sullivan, Bulik, & Kendler (1998)	Overeating	.46 (.32–.58)	—	.54 (42–.68)	VTR: SCID (first interview wave). Bivariate analysis with self-induced vomiting.
Bulik, Sullivan, & Kendler (2003)	Overeating	.49 (.38–.61)	—	.51 (.37–.64)	VTR: SCID (first and third interview waves). Bivariate analysis with lifetime history of obesity.
Javaras et al. (2008)	Objective binge episodes	.39 (.26–.52)	—	.61 (NR)	Norwegian Twin Registry (age 18–31 years): SRQ, binge eating with a feeling of loss of control in the absence of compensatory behaviors over previous 6 months at least 1× per month, females and males
Wade, Treloar, & Martin (2008)	Objective binge episodes	.17 (.05–.28)	—	83 (.72–.96)	ATR (age 28–40 years): EDE, 2× week for 3-month period ever
Sullivan, Bulik, & Kendler (1998)	Vomiting	.70 (.50–.84)	—	.30 (.16–50)	VTR (first interview wave): SCID "Have you ever vomited?" substantial genetic overlap with overeating (.74; 95% CI: .52–.95) and environment (.48; 95% CI: .16–.83)
Wade, Treloar, & Martin (2008)	Vomiting	.08 (.01–18)	—	.92 (.82–1.0)	ATR (age 28–40 years): EDE, 2× week for 3-month period ever
Keski-Rahkonen, Neale, et al. (2005)	Intentional weight loss	.66 (.55–75) .38 (.19–55)	—	.34 (.25–45) .62 (.45–81)	Finnish Twin Registry (age 16–27 years): SRQ "How many times in your life have you intentionally lost >5 kg weight?" Bivariate analysis with BMI females and *males*
Reichborn-Kjennerud et al. (2004)	Importance of weight and shape	—	.31 (.24–.38)	.69 (.68–.76)	Norwegian Twin Registry (age 18–31 years): SRQ "Is it important for your self-evaluation that you keep a certain weight? Yes, highly important; Yes, somewhat important; No, not very important." Females and males combined
Wade & Bulik (2007)	Importance of weight and shape	.25 (.14–.36)	—	.75 (.64–.87)	ATR (age 28–40 years): EDE, two items over previous 3-month period. Multivariate analysis with three measures of perfectionism
Wilksch and Wade (2009)	Importance of weight and shape	15 (0–48)	23 (0–43)	62 (52–73)	ATR (age 12–15 years): EDE, two items over previous 3-month period. Univariate analysis

[a]Full model or model of best fit (lowest Akaike's Information Criteria)—not necessarily significantly better fitting than the full model.

[b]All populations were female unless otherwise noted.

A = additive genetic variance; C = shared environmental variance; E = nonshared environmental variance; CI = confidence interval; NR = not reported; VTR = Virginia Twin Registry; SCID = Structured Clinical behavior to have occurred to a threshold of twice a week for a 3-month period, again ascertained using the EDE and analysed bivariately with objective binge episodes.

The moderate heritability of intentional weight loss has previously been discussed, as has its small overlap with the genetic risk factors for BMI. The final diagnostic criterion to be examined by three different studies is importance of weight and shape which has been described as the "core psychopathology" of EDs (Cooper & Fairburn, 1993) and is included in the current diagnostic definitions for EDs as "undue influence of body shape or weight on self-evaluation" (American Psychiatric Association [APA], 1994). A Norwegian twin study using a single self-report item for males and females (Reichborn-Kjennerud et al., 2004) found no heritability implicated in the etiology of this phenotype. Two Australian studies of two different populations, one adult (Wade & Bulik, 2007) and one a young adolescent (Wilksch & Wade, 2009) found a small contribution of heritability to the phenotype assessed by the EDE, 25% and 15% respectively, where 95% confidence intervals ranged from 0 to 48. It is of interest to note that the full model tested univariately with the adolescents also suggested the substantial presence of shared as well as nonshared environment, consistent with the Norwegian study. The shared environment was also suggested by the multi-variate twin study of BN summarized in Table 7.2 (Kendler et al., 1995). This is of significance given that the latent variable models used in twin studies have relatively low power to identify any but sizeable effects of environment that is shared by twins (Neale, Eaves, & Kendler, 1994).

Finally, Table 7.4 contains a summary of twin studies examining disordered eating: behaviors and attitudes that are not included in diagnostic criteria but include continuous measures that represent useful indices that can refine our ED categories. Within these types of measures, the subscales of the Eating Disorder Inventory (Garner, Olmsted, & Polivy, 1983) have been the most widely analysed, with five different studies across four different twin registries. Many but not all of these studies found a substantial contribution of the shared environment across these subscales (Kamakura, Ando, Ono, & Maekawa, 2003; Keski-Rahkonnen, Bulik, et al., 2005; Klump, McGue, & Iacono, 2000; Klump et al., 2007), although one of these studies only found this to be true for males and not females (Keski-Rahkonnen), and the studies from the Minnesota Twin Registry find that the contribution

of the shared environment decreases substantially from childhood to adolescence (Klump et al., 2007).

Shared environment was also a substantial contributor to the variance of weight concern (Wade et al., 1998) as well as to some measures of the Three Factor Eating Questionnaire (Neale et al., 2003; Stunkard & Messick, 1985). However, shared environment was not detected when looking at the Body Attitude Questionnaire (Ben-Tovim & Walker, 1991; Wade, Wilkinson, & Ben-Tovim, 2003), with heritability estimates ranging from 32% to 75%. Neither did two studies of disordered eating detect any shared environment, obtaining similar heritability estimates for women from the Netherlands Twin Registry of 65% (95% CI: 58–71) (Slof-Op 't et al., 2008) and 59% (95% CI: 50–68) from three waves of data from women in the Australian Twin Registry (Wade et al., 1999).

So What Can We Conclude from Twin Studies of Eating?

There are four important issues that twin studies have informed to date, and that also indicate some directions for future research. The first is that, further to the earlier conclusion that there was a clear and substantial genetic contribution to both BN and AN (Collier & Treasure, 2004; Fairburn & Harrison, 2003), twin studies suggest that the influence of the shared environment is also implicated in the etiology of EDs. Certainly it has not been implicated as strongly and consistently as genetic influences, but this is not surprising given the low power of twin studies to detect variance associated with the shared environment. Therefore, in answer to the question posed at the beginning of the chapter, namely whether increased familial risk in EDs relates to the impact of the environment that is shared in families or to genetic influences or is a result of both influences, the answer would seem to be that both are implicated, but that shared environment is most likely to influence the cognitive rather than behavioral components of disordered eating. It is also highly likely that it may influence behavioral components of eating in children but that this becomes less important as the child moves into adolescence. Future twin studies need to examine specific sources of shared environment that may be important, but differentiating direct environmental influences from genetic or environmental confounds "remains one of the fundamental problems facing the social sciences" (Turkheimer, D'Onofrio, Maes, & Eaves, 2005, p. 1229). Although the potential for extended family designs to advance

Table 7.4 Non-ascertained Twin Studies of Disordered Eating: Behaviors and/or Attitudes Not Included in DSM Criteria

Study	Outcome Measure[a]	Model fitting results[b]			Population[c]: How was phenotype defined?
		A (95% CI)	C (95% CI)	E (95% CI)	
Rutherford, McGuffin, Katz, & Murray (1993)	EAT	.41	NR	NR	Institute of Psychiatry Twin Registry (age 18–45 years)
	EDI	.44 NR	NR	NR	
Wade, Martin, & Tiggemann (1998)	Dietary restraint	.32 (.12–.48)	—	.68 (.52–.89)	ATR (age 36–51 years): EDE four subscales over last 3 months—interview
	Eating concern	.46 (.30–.58)	—	.54 (.42–.70)	
	Weight concern	—	.52 (.43–.64)	.48 (.39–.60)	
	Shape concern	.62 (.50–.71)	—	.38 (.29–.50)	
Wade et al. (1999)	Three waves of repeated measures	.59 (.50–.68)	—	.41 (.32–.51)	ATR (mean age 36.3 ± 4.7 years at first wave): First wave = eating behaviors and diagnoses ever, second wave = SCID interview for BN ever, third wave = EDE interview global score over last 3 months
Klump, McGue, & Iacono (2000)	EDI: 11 yr olds	.82 (NR)	0.11 (NR)	0.07 (NR)	MFTS
	EDI: 17 yr olds	.80 (NR)	0.00 (NR)	0.20 (NR)	
Neale, Mazzeo, & Bulik (2003)	Dietary restraint	0 (0–.30)	.31 (.04–.42)	.69 (.58–.80)	VTR (age 25–65 years): The three subscales of the Three Factor Eating Questionnaire
	Disinhibition	.45 (.32–.57)	0 0–.23	.55 (.43–.68)	
	Hunger	.08 (0–.38)	.16 (0–.34)	.76 (.62–.89)	
Kamakura, Ando, Ono, & Maekawa (2003)	Perfectionism	.37 (.23-.49)	-	.66 (.51–.77)	Keio Twin Project, Japan (age 14–29 years): Five subscales of the EDI
	Maturity fears	-	.43 (.29–.54)	.57 (.46–.71)	
	Ineffectiveness	-	.47 (.34–.57)	.53 (.43–.66)	
	Interoceptive Awareness	-	.43 (.29–.54)	.57 (.46–.71)	
	Interpersonal Distrust	-	.34 (.20–.46)	.66 (.54–.80)	
Wade, Wilkinson, & Ben-Tovim (2003)	Feeling Fat	.72 (.68–.75)	—	.28 (.25–.32)	ATR (mean age, 32.4 ± 4.2 years): Body Attitudes Questionnaire. Multivariate analysis with BMI
	Body Disparagement	.53 (.47–.59)	—	.47 (.42–.53)	
	Strength and Fitness	.39 (.32–.46)	—	.61 (.55–.68)	
	Salience of Weight & Shape	.39 (.33–.46)	—	.61 (.54–.68)	
	Attractiveness	.46 (.40–.52)	—	.54 (.48–.60)	
	Lower Body Fatness	.52 (.45–.57)	—	.48 (.43–.55)	

Study	Outcome Measure[a]	Model fitting results[b]			Population[c]: How was phenotype defined?
		A (95% CI)	C (95% CI)	E (95% CI)	
Keski-Rahkonnen, Bulik, et al. (2005)	Drive for Thinness	51 (44–58)—		49 (43–56)	Finnish Twin Registry (age 22–27 years): EDI
	Thinness	—	86 (84–88)	14 (12–16)	Females and *males*
	Body dissatisfaction	59 (53–65)		41 (35–47)	
		—	85 (83–87)	15 (13–17)	
Klump, Burt, McGue, & Iacono (2007)	EDI: 11 years	.06 (0–.26)	.40 (.21–.50)	.54 (.47–.61)	MFTS: Repeated measures EDI.
	EDI: 14 years	.46 (.24–.59)	.10 (0.31)	.44 (.38–.50)	
	EDI: 17 years	.46 (.24–.59)	.10 (0–.31)	.44 (.38–.50)	
Slof-Op 't et al. (2008)	Disordered eating	.65 (.58–.71)	—	.35 (.29–.42)	Netherlands Twin Registry (age 14–18 years): Four items: dieting, importance of weight and shape, fear of weight gain, have you ever had eating binges. Females and *males*
		.39 (.28–.49)	*—*	*.61 (NR)*	

[a]Self-report questionnaire unless otherwise noted.
[b]Full model or model of best fit (lowest Akaike's Information Criteria)—not necessarily significantly better fitting than the full model.
[c]All populations were female unless otherwise noted.
A = additive genetic variance; C = shared environmental variance; E = non-shared environmental variance; CI = confidence interval; NR = not reported; VTR = Virginia Twin Registry; SCID = Structured Clinical Interview for *DSM*; BMI = body mass index; ATR = Australian Twin Registry; EDE = Eating Disorder Examination; SRQ = self-reported questionnaire; MTFS = Minnesota Twin Family Study; EDI = Eating Disorder Inventory; EAT = Eating Attitudes Test.

the empirical science of shared environment (such as parenting) and child development is high, further progress is required for the development of accurate analytical tools.

Second, although it is clear that estimates of heritability are variable, the sources that impact on this are starting to become clearer. Across different psychiatric symptoms the use of diagnostic interviews versus self-report measures is associated with lower estimates of heritability (Burt, in press). This is highly unlikely to relate to unreliability of measurement, given the established preference for the use of interviews giving more reliable diagnoses than self-report, especially when dealing with lifetime disorders that are difficult to define such as EDs. In addition, use of the gold standard interview in EDs, the EDE, which is used in the Australian studies, can be seen to be associated with lower estimates of

heritability across ED behaviors, indicating that the most reliable measurement is associated with lower heritability. A second source of the impact on estimates of heritability may be the number of ED behaviors incorporated as part of the phenotype, as previous research has shown that the number of eating behaviors is heavily influenced by the environment (Wade, Bergin, Martin, Gillespie, & Fairburn, 2006). This finding may explain why the heritability estimates for binge-eating and vomiting that meet *DSM* threshold had much lower heritability estimates than studies that required the behavior only to have occurred at least once. Hence the definition of the phenotype is important in terms of comparability across studies. A third source of variability of heritability emerges when examining heterogeneous disorders such as BN. This seems likely to result in unstable estimates and thus the trend toward examining component behaviors and cognitions should be encouraged, including continuous measures of relevant phenotypes.

Third, overlap of genetic risk factors with other phenotypes can start to inform us of the essential nature of EDs. In this light, it is of interest to note that the genetic risk factors for BMI are consistently found to be relatively independent of disordered eating, including intentional weight loss (Keski-Rahkonnen, Neale, et al., 2005), disordered eating (Slof Op 't et al., 2008), attitudes toward one's body (Wade et al., 2003), eating attitudes and behaviors (Klump et al., 2000), and binge eating (Bulik et al., 2003). In other words, these lines of research suggest that EDs are not primarily weight disorders, given only 3% to 20% of the variance between BMI and disordered eating is shared in women.

More informative are the results of twin studies examining an overlap of genetic risk factors between EDs and a variety of psychiatric and psychological phenotypes, which emerging research would suggest are important in explaining the development of disordered eating (Cassin & von Ranson, 2005; Lilenfeld, Wonderlich, Riso, Crosby, & Mitchell, 2006). The overlap of genetic risk factors for AN and major depression has been estimated at 0.56 with 95% CI of 0.44–0.69, indicating shared genetic variance of 34% with 95% CI of 13% to 71% (Wade et al., 2000). The correlation between genetic risk factors for BN and major depression was 0.46 (Walters et al., 1992), and 0.39 (95% CI: .05–0.79) between drug use disorders and BN (Baker et al., 2007). An examination of BN in a multivariate analysis of phobia, generalized anxiety disorder, panic disorder, major depression, and alcoholism showed that there was a shared genetic factor among BN, phobia, and panic disorder (Kendler et al., 1995). Although much less work has examined shared genetic risk between eating and continuous measures, Wade and Bulik (2007) found that there was very little shared genetic risk between various dimensions of perfectionism and importance of weight and shape, where data supported an independent rather than common pathways model, and only 6% of the genetic risk factors for the importance construct overlapped with the perfectionism measures.

Although not informative with respect to differentiating between shared genetic risk and shared environmental risk, a variety of family and twin studies have implicated further variables that share risk factors with EDs using an endophenotype approach. Such studies have identified shared risk

between AN and obsessive–compulsive personality disorder (Lilenfeld et al., 1998) and obsessive–compulsive spectrum disorders (Bellodi et al., 2001), and shared risk between BN and novelty seeking and neuroticism (Wade, Bulik, Prescott, & Kendler, 2004). A further study has identified shared risk factors between AN and high personal standards (a dimension of perfectionism), a need for order, and reward dependence (Wade et al., 2008). In an adolescent sample, Wilksch and Wade (2009) found that importance of weight and shape shared risk factors with thin-ideal internalization, body dissatisfaction, ineffectiveness, and sensitivity to punishment. These phenotypes are worth further examination in twin models that can examine shared genetic risk between phenotypes.

Fourth, although most studies have not included males given the low prevalence of EDs in men compared to women, a handful of studies indicate that genetic risk works differently between males and females. Heritability for intentional weight loss and disordered eating is substantially lower in males than females, with almost half the variance (Keski-Rahkonnen, Neale et al., 2005; Slof-Op 't et al., 2008). In addition, heritability does not appear to play a role in the etiology of body dissatisfaction or drive for thinness in males, in contrast to females, where it contributes around half of the variance (Keski-Rahkonnen, Bulik et al., 2005). These findings underline the suggestion that G×E are of critical importance in the etiology of EDs. Much more work is required to investigate different specific types of environment that may increase heritability for disordered eating in females compared to males.

Linkage and Association Studies: The Current State of Play

Research in the area of linkage and association studies has already progressed to the point where reviews are being published (e.g., Collier and Treasure, 2004; Klump & Gobrogge, 2005; Slof-Op 't et al., 2005). It has been said that there has been "a virtual explosion" of association and linkage studies of AN and BN (Bulik, 2005). Despite this, strong conclusions are difficult to draw as replication of research identifying susceptibility genes is rare.

In the area of linkage analysis, there are two large studies that have been conducted in EDs. The most recent of these, funded by the National Institute of Mental Health, is the Genetics of AN (GAN) collaborative study, which has been described but results are yet to be published (Kaye et al., 2008). The other large collaborative study, funded by the

Price Foundation, has examined the genetics of AN and BN (e.g., Devlin et al., 2002; Grice et al., 2002). In the total sample of 229 affected relative pairs with AN, there were no significant associations but samples selected for particular subtypes did yield more promising results, particularly suggesting possible involvement of AN to chromosome 1. First, the sample in restrictive AN showed a linkage peak with the chromosome 1p33–36, with some evidence of a peak at 4q12–14. When behavioral covariates were incorporated into the analysis in order to select sibling pairs who were high and concordant with respect to drive for thinness and obsessionality, further suggestive linkages were identified on chromosome 1q41 with a logarithm of the odds (LOD) score of 3.46. When using drive for thinness or obessionality on their own, 13q13 (LOD = 2.50) and 2p11 (LOD = 2.22) were implicated, respectively.

This same research group examined a total sample of 154 BN affected sibling pairs, where chromosome 10 was implicated for purging types of BN (Bulik et al., 2005), a chromosome also linked to obesity (Hager et al., 1998). Three regions of linkage were reported, on chromosome 10p13, 10p14, and 14q22–23. An analysis on pairs concordant for self-induced vomiting further implicated 10p13 with a LOD score of 3.39. Selecting samples on the basis of behavioral phenotypes was found to be potentially useful for obtaining stronger signals with respect to the following: lowest BMI attained during the illness, concern over mistakes (a dimension of perfectionism), anxiety, and food-related obsessions (Kaye et al., 2008). Overall, the field of linkage analysis is rapidly expanding, and we can expect further results to become available over the next few years, which may or may not further clarify the specific genetic basis of disordered eating.

Association studies in the ED field are multiple (Slof-Op 't et al., 2005) but characterized by small samples that present contradictory findings. Three meta-analyses of association studies in this area exist (Collier, Sham, Arranz, Hu, & Treasure, 1999; Gorwood, Kipman, & Foulon, 2003; Ziegler et al., 1999): the first found a significant association between the –1438A/A genotype and AN, the second found no significant associations, and the third found the frequency of the –1438A allele in patients with AN to be significantly higher than in controls.

Two large collaborative association studies also exist between which there was no overlap in the candidate genes examined (Bergen et al., 2003; Ribases et al., 2004a, 2004b, 2005). With the first of these studies focusing on chromosome 1 for an AN sample, positive associations were obtained with serotonin receptor 1D, and three opioid receptors delta 1. However, robust associations existed only for the first of these polymorphisms. The second study found a significantly higher frequency of the Met-66-Met genotype and the Met-66 allele in both AN and BN populations along with an excess transmission of the –270C/Met66 haplotype in the brain-derived neurotrophic factor (BDNF) gene in restrictive AN. The BDNF gene has been implicated in regulating feeding behavior in the hypothalamus, including regulation of serotonin levels, where low levels are associated with depression (Collier & Treasure, 2004).

Overall, the ways in which the serotonergic pathway can increase risk for the development of AN has probably attracted most interest to date in association studies. Recent research has found evidence to suggest that reduced peripheral serotonin transporter density in AN relates to an increased dieting preoccupation, affective instability, and anxiousness–fearfulness (Bruce, Steiger, Ng Ying Kin, & Israel, 2006). Recent research has also shown that, although allelic variation of 5-HTTLPR or platelet monoamine oxidase (MAO) activity was not independently associated with increased drive for thinness in adolescent girls, this association was significant in the presence of homozygosity for the 5-HTTLPR long allele and high platelet MAO activity (Akkermann, Paaver, Nordquist, Oreland, & Harro, 2008). Finally, elevated drive for thinness has been associated with increased levels of carriers of the deletion polymorphism of the serotonin transporter promoter 5-HTTLPR (Frieling et al., 2006) and, in women recovered from a binge-purge variety of AN, [^{18}F]altanserin binding potential and drive for thinness were negatively correlated in several cortical regions, suggesting that altered 5-HT neuronal system activity persisted (Bailer et al., 2004).

Conclusion

In summary, it has been argued that genes are an important part of the explanatory framework for the etiology of EDs, along with an important contribution of the shared environment to the development of cognition and attitudes that may initiate disordered eating practices, and a critical contribution of the environment in providing a context within which genetic risk can become more likely to be expressed. We currently have a very limited understanding of the specific genes that are implicated, and the ways in which genes and the environment work together to increase risk for disordered eating.

Future Directions

Moving our understanding forward in the etiology of EDs will require: (1) further information from linkage studies, (2) larger association studies to be conducted, (3) closer attention to the way in which phenotypes are assessed and defined, (4) a focus on the components of ED diagnoses, (5) further use of family and twin studies to identify endophenotypes that can support better delineation of EDs, (6) further development of analytic techniques that can help us differentiate direct environmental influences in family and twin models such that specific sources of shared environment can be identified, and (7) an increase in the research that examines G×E. The main question that needs to guide this further work is: How can this knowledge improve the prevention and treatment of eating disorders?

References

Akkermann, K., Paaver, M., Nordquist, N., Oreland, L., & Harro, J. (2008). Association of 5-HTT gene polymorphism, platelet MAO activity, and drive for thinness in a population-based sample of adolescent girls. *International Journal of Eating Disorders, 41*, 399–404.

American Psychiatric Association. (1994). *Diagnostic and statistical manual of mental disorders* (4th ed.). Washington, DC: American Psychiatric Publishing.

Archibald, A.B., Linver, M. R., Graber, J. A., & Brooks-Gunn, J. (2002). Parent-adolescent relationships and girls' unhealthy eating: Testing reciprocal effects. *Journal of Research on Adolescence, 12*, 451–461.

Bacanu, S. A., Bulik, C. M., Klump, K. L., Fichter, M. M., Halmi, K. A., Keel, P., et al. (2005). Linkage analysis of anorexia and bulimia nervosa cohorts using selected behavioral phenotypes as quantitative traits or covariates. *American Journal of Medical Genetics. Part B, Neuropsychiatric Genetics: The official publication of the International Society of Psychiatric Genetics, 139*, 61–68.

Bailer, U. F., Price, J. C., Meltzer, C. C., Mathis, C. A., Frank, G. K., Weissfeld, L., et al. (2004). Altered 5-HT-$_{(2A)}$ Receptor binding after recovery from bulimia-type anorexia nervosa: Relationships to harm avoidance and drive for thinness. *Neuropsychopharmacology, 29*, 1143–1155.

Baker, J. H., Mazzeo, S. E., & Kendler, K. S. (2007). Association between broadly defined bulimia nervosa and drug use disorders: Common genetic and environmental influences. *International Journal of Eating Disorders, 40*, 673–678.

Bellodi, L. M. C., Cavallini, M. C., Bertelli, S., Chiapparino, D., Riboldi, C., & Smeraldi, E. (2001). Morbidity risk for obsessive-compulsive spectrum disorders in first-degree relatives of patients with eating disorders. *American Journal of Psychiatry, 158*, 563–569.

Ben-Tovim, D. I., & Walker, M. K. (1991). The development of the Ben-Tovim Walker Body Attitudes Questionnaire (BAQ), a new measure of women's attitudes towards their own bodies. *Psychological Medicine, 21*, 775–784.

Bergen, A. W., van den Bree, M. B. M., Yeager, M., Welch, R., Ganjei, J. K., Haque, K., et al. (2003). Candidate genes for anorexia nervosa in the 1p33–36 linkage region: Serotonin 1D and delta opioid receptor loci exhibit significant association to anorexia nervosa. *Molecular Psychiatry, 8*, 397–406.

Bouchard, T. J., & McGue, M. (2003). Genetic and environmental influences on human psychological differences. *Journal of Neurobiology, 54*, 4–45.

Bruce, K. R., Steiger, H., Kin, N. M. K., Ng, Y., & Israel, M. (2006). Reduced platelet [³H]paroxetine binding in anorexia nervosa: Relationship to eating symptoms and personality pathology. *Psychiatry Research, 142*, 225–232.

Bruch, H. (1973). *Eating disorders: Obesity, anorexia nervosa and the person within.* New York: Basic Books.

Bruch, H. (1978). *The golden cage. The enigma of anorexia nervosa.* Cambridge, MA: Harvard University Press.

Bulik, C. M. (2005). Exploring the gene-environment nexus in eating disorders. *Journal of Psychiatry & Neuroscience, 30*, 335–339.

Bulik, C. M., Bacanu, S. A., Klump, K. L., Fichter, M. M., Halmi, K. A., Keel, P., et al. (2005). Selection of eating disorders phenotypes for linkage analysis. *American Journal of Medical Genetics. Part B, Neuropsychiatric Genetics: The official publication of the International Society of Psychiatric Genetics, 139*, 81–87.

Bulik, C. M., Hebebrand, J., Keski-Rahkonen, A., Klump, K. L., Reichborn-Kjennerud, T., Mazzeo, S. E., & Wade, T. D. (2007). Genetic epidemiology, endophenotypes, and eating disorder classification. *International Journal of Eating Disorders, 40*, S52–S60.

Bulik, C. M., Sullivan, P. F., & Kendler, K. S. (1998). Heritability of binge-eating and broadly defined bulimia nervosa. *Biological Psychiatry, 44*, 1210–1218.

Bulik, C. M., Sullivan, P. F., & Kendler, K. S. (2003). Genetic and environmental contributions to obesity and binge eating. *International Journal of Eating Disorders, 33*, 293–298.

Bulik, C. M., Sullivan, P. F., Tozzi, F., Furberg, H., Lichtenstein, P., & Pedersen, N. L. (2006). Prevalence, heritability, and prospective risk factors for anorexia nervosa. *Archives of General Psychiatry, 63*, 305–312.

Bulik, C. M., Sullivan, P. F., Wade, T. D., & Kendler, K. S. (2000). Twin studies of eating disorders: A review. *International Journal of Eating Disorders, 27*, 1–20.

Burt, S. A. Environmental contributions to sibling similarity: Meta-analyses of shared environmental influences on child and adolescent psychopathology. Psychological Bulletin. In press.

Cassin, S. E., & von Ranson, K. M. (2005). Personality and eating disorders: A decade in review. *Clinical Psychology Review, 25*, 895–916.

Collier, D. A., Sham, P. C., Arranz, M. J., Hu, X., & Treasure, J. (1999). Understanding the genetic predisposition to anorexia nervosa. *European Eating Disorders Review, 7*, 96–102.

Collier, D. A., & Treasure, J. L. (2004). The aetiology of eating disorders. *British Journal of Psychiatry, 185*, 363–365.

Cooper, P. J., & Fairburn, C. G. (1993). Confusion over the core psychopathology of bulimia nervosa. *International Journal of Eating Disorders, 13*, 385–389.

Culbert, K. M., Breedlove, M. S., Burt, S. A., & Klump, K. L. (2008). Prenatal hormone exposure and risk for eating disorders: A comparison of opposite-sex and same-sex twins. *Archives of General Psychiatry, 65*, 329–336.

Devlin, B., Bacanu, S., Klump, K. L., Bulik, C. M., Fichter, M. M., Halmi, K., et al. (2002). Linkage analysis of anorexia nervosa incorporating behavioural covariates. *Human Molecular Genetics, 11*, 689–696.

Eisler, I. (2005). The empirical and theoretical base of family therapy and multiple family day therapy for adolescent anorexia nervosa. *Journal of Family Therapy, 27*, 104–131.

Fairburn, C. G. (1991). The heterogeneity of bulimia nervosa and its implications for treatment. *Journal of Psychosomatic Research, 35*, 3–9.

Fairburn, C. G., & Cooper, Z. (1993). The Eating Disorder Examination. In C. G. Fairburn & G. T. Wilson (Eds.), *Binge eating: Nature, assessment and treatment* (12th ed. pp. 317–360). New York: Guilford Press.

Fairburn, C. G., Cooper, Z., Bohn, K., O'Connor, M. E., Doll, H. A., & Palmer, R. L. (2007). The severity and status of eating disorder NOS: Implications for DSM-V. *Behaviour Research and Therapy, 45*, 1705–1715.

Fairburn, C. G., Cowen, P. J., & Harrison, P. J. (1999). Twin studies and the etiology of eating disorders. *International Journal of Eating Disorders, 26*, 349–358.

Fairburn, C. G., & Harrison, P. H. (2003). Eating disorders. *Lancet, 361*(9355), 407–416.

Foley, D., Neale, M. C., & Kendler, K. S. (1998). Reliability of a lifetime history of major depression: Implications for heritability and co-morbidity. *Psychological Medicine, 28*, 857–870.

Frieling, H., Römer, K. D., Wilhelm, J., Hillemacher, T., Kornhuber, J., de Zwaan, M., et al. (2006). Association of catecholamine-O-methyltransferase and 5-HTTLPR genotype with eating disorder-related behavior and attitudes in females with eating disorders. *Psychiatric Genetics, 16*, 205–208.

Garner, D. M., Olmsted, M. A., & Polivy, J. (1983). Development and validation of a multidimensional Eating Disorder Inventory for anorexia nervosa and bulimia nervosa. *International Journal of Eating Disorders, 2*, 15–34.

Gershon, E. S., & Goldin, L. R. (1986). Clinical methods in psychiatric genetics: I. Robustness of genetic marker investigative strategies. *Acta Psychiatrica Scandinavica, 74*, 113–118.

Ghaderi, A. (2003). Structural modeling analysis of prospective risk factors for eating disorder. *Eating Behaviors, 3*, 387–396.

Gorwood, P., Kipman, A., & Foulon, C. (2003). The human genetics of anorexia nervosa. *European Journal of Pharmacology, 480*, 163–170.

Grice, D. E., Halmi, K. A., Fichter, M. M., Strober, M., Woodside, D. B., Treasure, J. T., et al. (2002). Evidence for a susceptibility gene for anorexia nervosa on chromosome 1. *American Journal of Human Genetics, 70*, 787–792.

Guo, G., North, K. E., Gorden-Larsen, P., Bulik, C. M., & Choi, S. (2007). Body mass, DRD4, physical activity, sedentary behaviour, and family socio-economic status: The Add Health Study. *Obesity, 15*, 1199–1206.

Hager, J., Dina, C., Francke, S., Dubois, S., Houari, M., Vatin, V., et al. (1998). A genome-wide scan for human obesity genes reveals a major susceptibility locus on chromosome 10. *Nature Genetics, 20*, 304–308.

Hewitt, J. K. (1997). Behavior genetics and eating disorders. *Psychopharmacology Bulletin, 33*, 355–358.

Jacobi, C, Hayward, C., de Zwaan, M, Kraemer, H. C., & Agras, W. S. (2004). Coming to terms with risk factors for eating disorders: Application of risk terminology and suggestions for a general taxonomy. *Psychological Bulletin, 130*, 19–65.

Javaras, K. N., Laird, N. M., Reichborn-Kjennerud, T., Bulik, C. M., Pope, H. G., & Hudson, J. I. (2008). Familiality and heritability of binge eating disorder: Results of a case-control family study and a twin study. *International Journal of Eating Disorders, 41*, 174–179.

Johnson, C., & Flach, A. (1985). Family characteristics of 105 patients with bulimia. *American Journal of Psychiatry, 142*, 1321–1324.

Johnston, J., Cohen, P., Kasen, S., & Brook, J. (2002). Childhood adversities associated with risk for eating disorders or weight problems during adolescence or early adulthood. *American Journal of Psychiatry, 159*, 394–400.

Kamakura, T., Ando, J., Ono, Y., & Maekawa, H. (2003). A twin study of genetic and environmental influences on psychological traits of eating disorders in a Japanese female sample. *Twin Research, 6*, 292–296.

Kaye, W. H., Bulik, C. M., Plotnicov, K., Thornton, L., Devlin, B., Fichter, M. M., et al. (2008). The genetics of anorexia nervosa collaborative study: Methods and sample description. *International Journal of Eating Disorders, 41*, 289–300.

Kendler, K. S. (2001) Twin studies of psychiatric illness. *Archives of General Psychiatry, 58*, 1005–1014.

Kendler, K. S., MacLean, C., Neale, M., Kessler, R. C., Heath, A., & Eaves, L. (1991). The genetic epidemiology of bulimia nervosa. *American Journal of Psychiatry, 148*, 1627–1637.

Kendler, K. S., Neale, M., Kessler, R. C., Heath, A., & Eaves, L. (1993). The lifetime history of major depression. Reliability of diagnosis and heritability. *Archives of General Psychiatry, 50*, 863–870.

Kendler, K. S., Thornton, L. M., & Pedersen, N. L. (2000). Tobacco consumption in Swedish twins reared apart and reared together. *Archives of General Psychiatry, 57*, 886–892.

Kendler, K. S., Walters, E. E., Neale, M. C., Kessler, R. C., Heath, A. C., & Eaves, L. J. (1995). The structure of the genetic and environmental risk factors for six major psychiatric disorders in women: Phobia, generalized anxiety disorder, panic disorder, bulimia, major depression, and alcoholism. *Archives of General Psychiatry, 52*, 374–383.

Keski-Rahkonnen, A., Bulik, C. M., Neale, B. M., Rose, R. J., Rissanen, A., & Kaprio, K. (2005). Body dissatisfaction and drive for thinness in young adult twins. *International Journal of Eating Disorders, 37*, 188–199.

Keski-Rahkonnen, A., Neale, B. M., Bulik, C. M., Pietiläinen, K. H., Rose, R. J., Kaprio, K., & Rissanen, A. (2005). Intentional weight loss in young adults: Sex-specific genetic and environmental effects. *Obesity Research, 13*, 745–753.

Kessler, R. C. (2002). The categorical versus dimensional assessment controversy in the sociology of mental illness. *Journal of Health and Social Behavior, 43*, 171–188.

Klump, K. S., Burt, A., McGue, M., & Iacono, W. G. (2007). Changes in genetic and environmental influences on disordered eating across adolescence. A longitudinal twin study. *Archives of General Psychiatry, 64*, 1409–1415.

Klump, K. L., & Gobrogge, K. L. (2005). A review and primer of molecular genetics studies of anorexia nervosa. *International Journal of Eating Disorders, 37*, S43–S48.

Klump, K. L., Gobrogge, K. L., Perkins, P. S., Thorne, D., Sisk, C. L., & Breedlove, S. M. (2006). Preliminary evidence that gonadal hormones organise and activate disordered eating. *Psychological Medicine, 36*, 539–546.

Klump, K. L., Kaye, W. H., & Strober, M. (2001). The evolving genetic foundations of eating disorders. *The Psychiatric Clinics of North America, 24*, 215–225.

Klump, K. L., McGue, M., & Iacono, W. G. (2000). Age differences in genetic and environmental influences on eating attitudes and behaviors in preadolescent and adolescent twins. *Journal of Abnormal Psychology, 109*, 239–251.

Klump, K. L., Miller, K., Keel, P., McGue, M., & Iacono, W. (2001). Genetic and environmental influences on anorexia nervosa syndromes in a population-based twin sample. *Psychological Medicine, 31*, 737–740.

Koeppen-Schomerus, G., Wardle, J., & Plomin, R. (2001). A genetic analysis of weight and overweight in 4-year-old twin pairs. *International Journal of Obesity, 25*, 838–844.

Köpp, W., Blum, W., von Prittwitz, S., Ziegler, A., Lubbert, H., Emons, G., et al. (1997). Low leptin levels predict amenorrhea in underweight and eating disordered females. *Molecular Psychiatry, 2*, 335–340.

Kortegaard, L. S., Hoerder, K., Joergensen, J., Gillberg, C., & Kyvik, K. (2001). A preliminary population-based twin study of self-reported eating disorder. *Psychological Medicine, 31*, 361–365.

Lilenfield, L. R., Kaye, W. H., Greeno, C. G., Merikangas, K. R., Plotnicov, K., Pollice, C., et al. (1998). A controlled family study of anorexia nervosa and bulimia nervosa: Psychiatric disorders in first-degree relatives and effects of proband comorbidity. *Archives of General Psychiatry, 55*(7), 603–610.

Lilenfeld, L. R. R., Wonderlich, S., Riso, L. P., Crosby, R., & Mitchell, J. (2006). Eating disorders and personality: A methodological and empirical review. *Clinical Psychology Review, 26*, 299–320.

Lyons, M. J., & Bar, J. L. (2001). Is there a role for twin studies in the molecular genetics era? *Harvard Review of Psychiatry, 9*, 318–323.

Maes, H. H., Neale, M. C., & Eaves, L. J. (1997). Genetic and environmental factors in relative body weight and human adiposity. *Behavior Genetics, 27*, 325–351.

Martin, N. G., Boomsma, D., & Machin, G. (1997). A twin-pronged attack on complex traits. *Nature Genetics, 17*, 387–392.

Martin, N. G., Eaves, L. J., Kearsey, M. J., & Davies, P. (1978). The power of the classical twin study. *Heredity, 40*, 97–116.

McKnight Investigators. (2003). Risk factors for the onset of eating disorders in adolescent girls: Results of the McKnight longitudinal risk factor study. *American Journal of Psychiatry, 160*, 248–254.

Meaney, M. J., Aitken, D. H., Bodnoff, S. R., Iny, L. J., Tatarewicz, J. E., & Sapolsky, R.M. (1985). Early postnatal handling alters glucocorticoid receptor concentrations in selected brain regions. *Behavioral Neuroscience, 99*, 765–770.

Neale, B. M., Mazzeo, S. E., & Bulik, C. M. (2003). A twin study of dietary restraint, disinhibition and hunger: An examination of the Eating Inventory (Three Factor Eating Questionnaire). *Twin Research, 6*, 471–478.

Neale, M. C., Eaves, L. J., & Kendler, K. S. (1994). The power of the classical twin study to resolve variation in threshold traits. *Behavior Genetics, 24*, 239–258.

Neiderhiser, J. M. (2001) Understanding the role of genome and environment: Methods in genetic epidemiology. *British Journal of Psychiatry, 178* (Supplement. 40), s12–s17.

Neumark-Sztainer, D., Eisenberg, M. E., Fulkerson, J. A., Story, M., & Larson, N. I. (2008). Family meals and disordered eating in adolescents. *Archives of Pediatric and Adolescent Medicine, 162*, 17–22.

Paykel, E. (2002). Genetic epidemiology in a molecular age. *Psychological Medicine, 32*, 1145–1148.

Petronis, A. (2001). Human morbid genetics revisited: Relevance of epigenetics. *Trends in Genetics, 17*, 142–146.

Plomin, R. (2000). Behavioural genetics in the 21st century. *International Journal of Behavioural Development, 24*, 30–34.

Plomin, R., DeFries, J. C., & McClearn, G. E. (1990). *Behavioral Genetics: A Primer* (2nd ed.). New York: W. H. Freeman.

Procopio, M., & Marriott, P. (2007). Intrauterine hormonal environment and risk of developing anorexia nervosa. *Archives of General Psychiatry, 64*, 1402–1407.

Raevuori, A., Kaprio, J., Hoek, H., Sihvola, E., Rissanen, A., Keski-Rahkonen, A. (2008). Anorexia and Bulimia Nervosa in Same-Sex and Opposite-Sex Twins: Lack of Association With Twin Type in a Nationwide Study of Finnish Twins. *American Journal of Psychiatry. 165*(12),1604–1610.

Reichborn-Kjennerud, T., Bulik, C. M., Kendler, K. S., Roysamb, E., Tambs, K., Torgersen, S., & Harris, J. R. (2004). Undue influence of weight on self-evaluation: A population-based twin study of gender differences. *International Journal of Eating Disorders, 35*, 123–132.

Ribases, M., Gratacos, M., Fernandez-Aranda, F., Bellodi, L., Boni, C., Anderluh, M., et al. (2004a). Association of BDNF with anorexia, bulimia and age of onset of weight loss in six European populations. *Human Molecular Genetics, 13*, 1205–1212.

Ribases, M., Gratacos, M., Fernandez-Aranda, F., Bellodi, L., Boni, C., Anderluh, M., (2004b). Association of BDNF with restricting anorexia nervosa and minimum body mass index: A family-based association study of eight European populations. *European Journal of Human Genetics, 13*, 428–434.

Rice, J. P., Rochberg, N., Endicott, J., Lavori, P. W., & Miller, C. (1992). Stability of psychiatric diagnoses. An application of the affective disorders. *Archives of General Psychiatry, 49*, 824–830.

Rowe, R., Pickles, A., Simonoff, E., Foley, D., Rutter, M., & Silberg, J. (2002). Bulimic symptoms in the Virginia twin study of adolescent behavioural development. *Biological Psychiatry, 51*, 172–182.

Rutherford, J., McGuffin, P., Katz, R. J., & Murray, R. M. (1993). Genetic influences on eating attitudes in a normal female twin population. *Psychological Medicine, 23*, 425–436.

Rutter, M., & Silberg, J. (2002). Gene-environment interplay in relation to emotional and behavioural disturbance. *Annual Review of Psychology, 53*, 463–490.

Saunders, C. L., Chiodini, B. D., Sham, P., Lewis, C. M., Abkevich, V., Adeyemo, A. A., et al. (2007). Meta-analysis of genome-wide linkage studies in BMI and obesity. *Obesity, 15*, 2263–2275.

Scarr, S., & McCartney, K. (1983). How people make their own environments: A theory of genotype → environment effects. *Child Development, 54*, 424–435.

Slof-Op't, L. M. C. T., Bartels, M., van Furth, E. F., van Beijsterveldt, C. E. M., Meulenbelt, I., Slagboom, P. E., & Boomsma, D. I. (2008). Genetic influences on disordered eating are largely independent of body mass index. *Acta Psychiatrica Scandinavica, 117*, 348–356.

Slof-Op't, L. M. C. T., van Furth, E. F., Meulenbelt, I., Slagboom, P. E., Bartels, M., Boomsma, D. I., & Bulik, C. M. (2005). Eating disorders: From twin studies to candidate genes and beyond. *Twin Research and Human Genetics, 8*, 467–482.

Spelt, J., & Meyer, J. M. (1995). Genetics and eating disorders. In J. R. Turner, L. R. Cardon, & J. K. Hewitt (Eds.), *Behaviour genetic approaches in behavioural medicine* (pp. 167–185). New York: Plenum Press.

Steiger, H., Gauvin, L., Joober, R., Israel, M., Kin, N. M. K., Ng, Y., et al. (2006). Intrafamilial correspondences on platelet [³H]-paroxetine-binding indices in bulimic probands and their unaffected first-degree relatives. *Neuropsychopharmacology*, 31, 1785–1792.

Steiger, H., Joober, R., Israel, M., Young, S. N., Kin, N. M. K., Ng., Y., et al. (2005). Erratum: The 5HTTLPR polymorphism, psychopathologic symptoms, and platelet [3H-]-paroxetine binding in bulimic syndromes. *International Journal of Eating Disorders*, 37(3), 57–60

Steiger, H., Richardson, J., Joober, R., Gauvin, L., Israel, M., Bruce, K. R., et al. (2007). The 5HTTLPR polymorphism, prior maltreatment and dramatic-erratic personality manifestations in women with bulimic syndromes. *Journal of Psychiatry & Neuroscience*, 32, 354–362.

Stein, A., Woolley, H., Cooper, S. D., & Fairburn, C. G. (1994). An observational study of mothers with eating disorders and their infants. *Journal of Child Psychology & Psychiatry & Allied Disciplines*, 35, 733–748.

Stein, A., Woolley, H., Murray, L., Cooper, P., Cooper, S., Noble, F., et al. (2001). Influence of psychiatric disorder on the controlling behaviour of mothers with 1-year old infants: A study of women with maternal eating disorder, postnatal depression, and a healthy comparison group. *British Journal of Psychiatry*, 179, 157–162.

Stice, E., Spangler, D., & Agras, W. S. (2001). Exposure to media-portrayed thin-ideal images adversely affects vulnerable girls: A longitudinal experiment. *Journal of Social and Clinical Psychology*, 20, 270–288.

Strober, M. (1991). Disorders of the self in anorexia nervosa: An organismic-developmental paradigm. In C. Johnson (Ed.), *Psychoanalytic theory and treatment for eating disorders*. New York: Guilford Press.

Stunkard, A. J., & Messick, S. (1985). The Three-Factor Eating Questionnaire to measure dietary restraint and hunger. *Journal of Psychosomatic Research*, 29, 71–83.

Sullivan, P. F., Bulik, C. M., & Kendler, K. S. (1998). Genetic epidemiology of binging and vomiting. *British Journal of Psychiatry*, 173, 75–79.

Tozzi, F, Sullivan P. F., Fear, J. L., McKenzie, J., & Bulik, C. M. (2003). Causes and recovery in anorexia nervosa: The patient's perspective. *International Journal of Eating Disorders*, 33, 143–154.

Turkheimer, E., D'Onofrio, B. M., Maes, H. H., & Eaves, L. J. (2005). Analysis and interpretation of twin studies including measures of the shared environment. *Child Development*, 76, 1217–1233.

Turkheimer, E., & Waldron, M. (2000). Nonshared environment: A theoretical, methodological, and quantitative review. *Psychological Bulletin*, 126, 78–108.

von Prittwitz, S., Blum, W., Ziegler, A., Scharmann, S., Remschmidt, H., & Hebebrand, J. (1997). Restrained eating is associated with low leptin levels in underweight females. *Molecular Psychiatry*, 2, 420–422.

Wade, T. D., Bergin, J. L., Martin, N. G., Gillespie, N. A., & Fairburn, C. G. (2006). A transdiagnostic approach to understanding eating disorders: A twin study examining a dimensional model. *Journal of Nervous and Mental Disease*, 194, 510–517.

Wade, T. D., & Bulik, C. M. (2007). Shared genetic and environmental risk factors between undue influence of body shape and weight on self evaluation and dimensions of perfectionism. *Psychological Medicine*, 37, 635–644.

Wade, T. D., Bulik, C. M., Neale, M. C., & Kendler, K. S. (2000). Anorexia nervosa and major depression: An examination of shared genetic and environmental risk factors. *American Journal of Psychiatry*, 157, 469–471.

Wade, T. D., Bulik, C. M., Prescott, C., & Kendler, K. S. (2004). Sex influences on shared risk factors for bulimia nervosa and other psychiatric disorders. *Archives of General Psychiatry*, 61, 251–256.

Wade, T. D., Gillespie, N., & Martin, N. G. (2007). A comparison of early family life events amongst monozygotic twin women with lifetime anorexia nervosa, bulimia nervosa or major depression. *International Journal of Eating Disorders*, 40, 679–686.

Wade, T. D., Martin, N. G., Neale, M. C., Tiggemann, M., Treloar, S. A., Bucholz, K. K., et al. (1999). The structure of genetic and environmental risk factors for three measures of disordered eating. *Psychological Medicine*, 29, 925–934.

Wade, T. D., Martin, N. G., & Tiggemann, M. (1998). Genetic and environmental risk factors for the weight and shape concern characteristic of bulimia nervosa. *Psychological Medicine*, 28, 761–771.

Wade, T. D., Tiggemann, M., Bulik, C. M., Fairburn, C. G., Wray, N. R., & Martin, N. G. (2008). Shared temperament risk factors for anorexia nervosa: A twin study. *Psychosomatic Medicine*, 70, 239–244.

Wade, T. D., Treloar, S. A., & Martin, N. G. (2008). Shared and unique risk factors between lifetime purging and objective binge eating: A twin study. *Psychological Medicine*, 38, 1455–1464.

Wade, T. D., Wilkinson, J., & Ben-Tovim, D. (2003). The genetic epidemiology of body attitudes, the attitudinal component of body image in women. *Psychological Medicine*, 33, 1395–1405.

Waller, N. G., & Meehl, P. E. (1998). *Multivariate taxometric procedures: Distinguishing types from continua*. Newberry Park CA: Sage.

Walters, E. E., & Kendler, K. S. (1995). Anorexia nervosa and anorexic-like syndromes in a population-based female twin sample. *American Journal of Psychiatry*, 152, 64–71.

Walters, E. E., Neale, M. C., Eaves, L. J., Heath, A. C., Kessler, R. C., & Kendler, K. S. (1992). Bulimia nervosa and major depression: A study of common genetic and environmental factors. *Psychological Medicine*, 22, 617–622.

Waugh, E., & Bulik, C. M. (1999). Offspring of women with eating disorders. *International Journal of Eating Disorders*, 25, 123–133.

Whelan, E., & Cooper, P. J. (2000). The association between childhood feeding problems and maternal eating disorder: A community study. *Psychological Medicine*, 30, 69–77.

Wilksch, S. M., & Wade, T. D. (2009). An investigation of temperament endophenotype candidates for early emergence of the core cognitive component of eating disorders. *Psychological Medicine*. 39, 811–822.

Williamson, D. A., Gleaves, D. H., & Stewart, T. M. (2005). Categorical versus dimensional models of eating disorders: An examination of the evidence. *International Journal of Eating Disorders*, 31, 1–10.

Wilson, G. T. (1993). Assessment of binge eating. In C. G. Fairburn & G. T. Wilson (Eds.), *Binge eating: Nature, assessment and treatment* (pp. 227–249). New York: Guilford Press.

Wisotsky, W., Dancyger, I., Fornari, V., Katz, J., Wisotsky, W. L., & Swencionis, C. (2003). The relationship between eating pathology and perceived family functioning in eating disorder patients in a day treatment program. *Eating Disorders: The Journal of Treatment and Prevention*, 11, 89–99.

Wonderlich, S. A. (1992). Relationship of family and personality factors in bulimia nervosa. In J. Crowther, D. Tennenbaum, S.

Hobfoll, & M. Stephens (Eds.), *The etiology of bulimia nervosa: The individual and familial context*. Washington, DC: Hemisphere.

Woodside, D. B., Shekter-Wolson, L., Garfinkel, P. E., Olmsted, M. P., Kaplan, A. S. & Maddocks, S. E. (1995). Family interactions in bulimia nervosa I: Study design, comparisons to established population norms, and changes over the course of an intensive day hospital treatment program. *International Journal of Eating Disorders, 17*, 105–115.

Ziegler, A., Hebebrand, J., Gorg, T., Rosenkranz, K., Fichter, M., Herpertz-Dahlmann, B., et al. (1999). Further lack of association between the 5-HT2A gene promoter polymorphism and susceptibility to eating disorders and a meta-analysis pertaining to anorexia nervosa. *Molecular Psychiatry, 4*, 410–412.

Psychosocial Risk Factors for Eating Disorders

Corinna Jacobi *and* Eike Fittig

Abstract

The objective of this chapter is to provide an updated overview of risk factors for eating disorders on the basis of the risk factor taxonomy described by Kraemer et al. (1997). The chapter summarizes risk factors identified in longitudinal studies and markers and retrospective correlates from cross-sectional studies through April 2002 for the eating disorder syndromes anorexia nervosa, bulimia nervosa, and binge eating disorder. Limitations of these earlier studies are indicated. As part of an update of the previous analysis, results of studies identified between May 2002 and November 2008 are integrated into results of our earlier review. The updated review indicates that longitudinal evidence on risk factors is still much stronger for bulimia nervosa and binge related syndromes, whereas our knowledge of risk factors for anorexia nervosa remains limited. While recent studies were able to overcome some of the limitations of the earlier studies, results of our earlier review are mostly confirmed.

Keywords: anorexia nervosa, binge eating disorder, bulimia nervosa, Kraemer taxonomy, longitudinal studies, risk factors

Introduction

The identification of modifiable risk factors not only improves our knowledge of the etiology of a disorder but also has important public health implications, especially for chronic disorders with poor prognosis. Owing to the inconsistent use of the terms *risk* and *risk factor* and to improve communications among scientists, clinicians, and politicians in different fields, Helena Kraemer and co-workers—as part of the MacArthur Foundation Research Network on Psychopathology and Development—10 years ago proposed exact definitions and methods for risk and etiology factors (Kraemer et al., 1997). For the development of eating disorders (EDs)—comparable with other mental disorders—a wide range of variables has been claimed to be risk factors. Many of them were assessed in cross-sectional studies that do not allow for "true" risk factor identification. To separate "true" risk factors for EDs from correlates of the disorders, the methods and

definitions of the proposed theoretical framework were applied to the field of EDs. Because the results have been presented elsewhere in detail (Jacobi, 2005; Jacobi, Hayward, de Zwaan, Kraemer, & Agras, 2004), we only briefly summarize core aspects here.

In the approach of Kraemer and colleagues, precedence represents a crucial criterion for the definition of risk factors. Accordingly, the majority of risk factors can be assessed only in longitudinal studies. Exceptions are so-called fixed markers, that is, invariable risk factors documented before the onset of the ED in medical records or birth registers. These factors are usually derived from cross-sectional (case-control, family history, twin, or epidemiological studies). Variables not fulfilling precedence of the factor to the onset of the disorder are correlates. The status of variable markers and causal risk factors can be established only in randomized clinical trials (prevention or intervention studies) that confirm that the modification of the factors leads to a change in the risk of the outcome (e.g., onset of the disorder).

In our recent meta-analysis we included a separate category of factors in addition to those proposed in the Kraemer et al. typology: cross-sectional studies with retrospective (risk) factor assessment before the onset of the ED according to the subjects' self-reports. Retrospective risk factor assessment is problematic because of retrospective recall or memory bias, especially in subjects affected with the disorder. However, because longitudinal studies are difficult and expensive to conduct and thus rare, we decided to consider and include these so-called "retrospective correlates" for exploratory or hypothesis-generating reasons.

Method

The proposed taxonomy of risk factors was first applied to the field of EDs as part of a comprehensive meta-analytic review (Jacobi et al., 2004). A detailed computerized and manual literature search of potential risk factor studies published through April 2002 was conducted resulting in the screening of approximately 5000 abstracts and inclusion of about 300 (cross-sectional and longitudinal) studies. Among others, the following criteria were established for study inclusion in the original review:

1. With few exceptions (regarding epidemiological studies) only studies with a (healthy or unaffected) control group were included.

2. The sample size required in the studies was at least 10 subjects per cell.

3. For longitudinal studies, a follow-up interval of at least 1 year was needed to allow enough time for symptoms of eating disturbances or disorders to change or emerge.

4. The focus was placed on risk factors for ED *syndromes*; accordingly, longitudinal studies addressing solely (dimensional) disturbances or symptoms assessed via questionnaires (e.g., EDI) were excluded.

Summary of Risk Factors for Eating Disorders: Characteristics of Longitudinal Studies

Fifteen longitudinal studies comprising 12,776 subjects were found fulfilling our inclusion criteria (see Table 8.1).

The majority of these studies identified risk factors for a mixture of full *DSM* syndromes of anorexia nervosa (AN) and bulimia nervosa (BN) and/or partial or subclinical syndromes or eating disorders not otherwise specified (EDNOS; Ghaderi &Scott, 2001; Johnson, Cohen, Kasen, & Brook, 2002; Killen et al., 1994, 1996; Kotler, Cohen, Davies, Pine, & Walsh, 2001; Marchi & Cohen, 1990; Patton, Johnson-Sabine, Wood, Mann, & Wakeling, 1990; Patton, Selzer, Coffey, Carlin, & Wolfe, 1999; Vollrath, Koch, & Angst, 1992). In six studies, the outcome samples were high-risk samples mostly defined as scoring above the EAT-26 cutoff (Attie & Brooks-Gunn, 1989; Button, Sonuga-Barke, Davies, & Thompson, 1996; Calam & Waller, 1998; Graber, Brooks-Gunn, Paikoff, & Warren, 1994; Leon, Fulkerson, Perry, & Early-Zald, 1995; Leon, Fulkerson, Perry, Keel, & Klump, 1999). A closer examination of the outcomes reveals that the focus is on bulimic and binge eating syndromes, whereas reports of anorexic syndromes as outcomes were very rare. Taken together, of the 12,776 subjects in the 15 studies, 26 cases of AN, 88 cases of BN, 78 EDNOS cases, and 238 partial/subclinical or "binge eating" cases emerged during the follow-up periods.

Samples in the studies consisted mostly of adolescents between 12 and 15 years; three studies assessed infants or younger children (Johnson et al., 2002; Kotler et al., 2001; Marchi & Cohen, 1990), and two studies focused on young adults (Ghaderi & Scott, 2001; Vollrath et al., 1992). In eight studies the samples included females only; in seven studies the samples consisted of both males and females. The duration of follow-ups varied from 1 to 18 years. The number and breadth of included risk factors, and the definitions and assessment of risk status or caseness (symptomatic/asymptomatic; cases/non-cases; high/moderate/low risk) varied significantly: seven studies assessed ED symptoms and syndromes with structured diagnostic interviews and eight studies defined caseness on the basis of questionnaire cutoffs or score combinations.

Anorexia Nervosa

To summarize the results of our previous analysis, the following risk factors were found for AN (Jacobi, 2005): Twin studies suggest a genetic influence for anorexia present before birth. Additional fixed markers are female gender, ethnicity, season of birth (between April and June), birth-related perinatal complications (cephalhematoma), premature delivery (based on medical records), and obstetric complications. Risk factors in early and later childhood are: maternally reported health problems as well as a number of factors around childhood eating such as

Table 8.1 Characteristics of Longitudinal Studies on Risk Factors for Eating Disorders

Study	Sample (N)	Age at Baseline (years)	Follow-up Interval (years)	Cases (N)	Outcome	Predictors
1. Attie & Brooks-Gunn (1989)	193 female adolescents and their mothers; initial symptoms controlled for	13.9	2	NR	Emergence of eating problems, EAT-26 scores	Height; Weight; Body fat; Pubertal timing; Body image; Personality: Psychopathology, Emotional Tone, Impulse Control (SIQYA); Family relationships, EAT
2. Marchi & Cohen (1990)	659 children and mothers; 326 girls and 333 boys	Interviewed at three ages: 1–10 (6), 919 (14) and 11–21 (16)	10	AN = 5; BN = 9; Severe AN and BN behaviors= 65	Problematic eating behaviors and disorders (modified Diagnostic Interview Schedule for Children: DISC)	Eating behaviors (struggle over eating, amount eaten, picky eater, speed of eating, interest in food, pica, digestive problems)
3. Patton et al., (1990)	734 adolescent girls; initial symptoms controlled for by subgrouping	15	1	N = 16; BN = 4, 12 = partial syndromes	Eating disorder (risk group selected by EAT-26 cutoff: 20/21), General Health Questionnaire (GHQ) ≥ 5/6; subsequent semi-structured interview for assessment of clinical status/ caseness (categories: cases, dieters, nondieters)	EAT; GHQ; Putative risk factors: family background, reported family weight and eating pattern, personal background, weight history; perceived current social stress, personality (Cattell personality questionnaire); attitudes toward eating, weight and shape, menstrual history, current weight and shape (clinical interview)
4. Vollrath et al., (1992)	292 males and 299 females of representative young adult sample (N = 4567), divided into high- and low-risk groups according to SCL-90 scores; controlling for initial symptoms not reported	27–28	2 (out of 9 year follow-up)	BN = 4, binge eating = 28	Eating problems (binge eating, vomiting, dieting, weight, etc.) as part of the Structured Psychological Interview and Rating of the Social Consequences for Epidemiology (SPIKE); Diagnosis: computerized algorithms	Same as dependent variables
5. Killen et al., (1994)	967 adolescent girls, community sample; subjects with initial symptoms excluded from analysis	12.4	3	BN = 13, binge eating = 19	Eating disorder symptoms and partial syndromes, classification as symptomatic based on binge eating, compensatory behaviors, overconcern with weight and body shape, loss of control	Weight concerns; EDI; Dietary restraint; Pubertal development; Height; Weight; BMI, Behavior Problem Scales (Youth Self-Report Inventory)

Table 8.1 (continued) **Characteristics of Longitudinal Studies on Risk Factors for Eating Disorders**

Study	Sample (N)	Age at Baseline (years)	Follow-up Interval (years)	Cases (N)	Outcome	Predictors
6. Graber et al., (1994)	116 female adolescents, recruited from private schools); grouped into 4 groups (low to chronic risk)	14.31	8	N = 15	Subclinical or clinical eating problems (cutoff: EAT 26 ≥ 20)	EAT; Physical development (body fat, age at menarche); Body image, self-image, psychopathology, emotional tone, family relationships (SIQYA); EDI: Perfectionism, Ineffectiveness; Affective states (Youth Self-Report); Family organization and functioning (FES)
7. Leon et al., (1995)	Community sample (852 girls, 815 boys); initial symptoms controlled for	Grades 7–10	3	NR	Disordered eating (risk status: 18 items from ED checklist, BMI <17 or >30, abnormal range scores on EDI Drive for Thinness and Bulimia scales)	Demographic variables; Eating Disorders Checklist; EDI; Health Behavior Survey; Pubertal Development Scale; Personality (MMPI): Negative and Positive Emotionality, Constraint; General Behavior Inventory; Autonomy; Attitudes about sexuality
8. Killen et al., (1996)	877 high school girls, (community sample); initial symptoms controlled for	14.9	4	Partial syndromes =36	Eating disorder symptoms and partial syndromes (EDE -interview adaptation)	Weight concerns; EDI; Dietary restraint; Height; Weight; BMI; Temperament (emotionality; activity; sociability); Drinking frequency; (baseline and follow-up); EDE-adaptation
9. Button et al., (1996)	594 girls; initial symptoms not controlled for (FU: N = 394)	11–12	4	EAT+ =47	EAT 26 score; EAT score ≥ 20; "EATpath"; Eating behavior and concerns, weight variables; Self-esteem; HAMD anxiety and depression scale	Self-esteem; Perceived health status, fatness concern, family relationships, school problems, general worrying/nervousness (five questions)
10. Calam & Waller (1998)	92 girls and their mothers (part of study of family management of children's eating habits); initial symptoms not controlled for	12.8	7	NR	EAT-26, BITE-scores	EAT-26; BITE; Setting Conditions for Anorexia (SCANS)-questionnaire (including 14 self-esteem and 8 perfectionism items); BMI; Family Assessment Device (FAD)

Study	Sample	Age	Follow-up	Diagnoses	Assessment of eating disorder	Variables/measures
11. Leon et al., (1999)	726 girls, 698 boys, high-risk subjects y1 excluded from prospective analysis	Grades 7–10 to 9–12	3–4	BN = 6, AN = 1, EDNOS = 14	Eating Disorder Risk Factor Index, Kiddie-SADS: Expanded eating disorders module	Personality and temperament (MPQ;GBI), Eating Disorders Checklist, EDI; Health behaviors; Physical and pubertal development; Psychopathology (Kiddie-SADS)
12. Patton et al., (1999)	1947 male and female students, recruited in cohorts; initial symptoms controlled for	14–15	3	BN = 2, Partial BN = 27, Partial AN = 4	Branched Eating Disorders Test to assess symptoms and partial syndromes	Dieting (adolescent dieting scale); Exercise; Weight and height; Psychiatric morbidity (computerized interview)
13. Ghaderi & Scott (2001)	1157 females, random general population sample; initial symptoms controlled for by subgrouping	18–30	2	AN = 1, BN = 11, BED = 10, EDNOS = 4	Survey for Eating Disorders (SEDs), questionnaire to assess DSM-IV eating disorders	Self-Concept Questionnaire (SCQ), Body Shape Questionnaire (BSQ), Perceived social support from family (PSSFa), Ways of Coping Questionnaire (WCQ)
14. Kotler et al., (2001)	976 (t_1)–776 (t_4) children, 45%–50% female	6.1 (range 1–10.9)	17	AN = 18, BN = 29	Eating behaviors based on maternal interviews ($t_1 - t_3$); Parent (t_2, t_3) and youth ($t_2 - t_4$) versions of the Diagnostic Interview Schedule for Children (DISC)	Early childhood eating problems (unpleasant meals, struggles over eating, amount eaten, picky or choosy eating, interest in food) assessed by maternal interview
15. Johnson et al., (2002)	782 children, 397 males, 385 females; initial symptoms controlled for	6	16–18	AN = 1, BN = 10, EDNOS = 41 (atyp. AN = 9, BED = 9, others = 23)	Parent (t_2, t_3) and youth ($t_2 - t_4$) versions of the Diagnostic Interview Schedule for Children (DISC)	Childhood temperament, parental psychiatric problems, maladaptive parental behavior, childhood maltreatment, other childhood adversities (all assessed by the Disorganizing Poverty Interview)

picky eating, anorexic symptoms, digestive and other eating-related problems (e.g., eating conflicts, struggles around meals, unpleasant meals).

Surprisingly few studies identified risk factors for AN during adolescence. Apart from adolescent age and early pubertal timing (both of which are relevant for BN as well), only a factor comprising weight and shape concerns and dieting could be confirmed as a risk factor for (binge eating subtype) AN.

In addition to these longitudinally assessed risk factors, pregnancy complications and shorter gestational age were confirmed as retrospective correlates, as were feeding and gastrointestinal problems, infant sleep difficulties, and a high-concern parenting style during early childhood. Further, obsessive–compulsive personality disorders, anxiety disorders, and higher levels of feelings and experiences of loneliness, shyness, and inferiority in childhood and adolescence were also identified.

During adolescence, retrospective correlates are: a high level of exercise, dieting behavior (especially for the binge-type anorexics), the presence of body dysmorphic disorder, increased exposure to sexual abuse and other adverse life events, a higher level of perfectionism, negative self-evaluation, premorbid obsessive–compulsive disorder, and acculturation.

Bulimia Nervosa

In addition to genetic factors, gender, ethnicity, obstetric complications, and early childhood health problems, confirmed for both AN and BN, the risk factors for bulimia can be summarized as follows (Jacobi, 2005): higher body mass index (BMI), experiences of sexual abuse or physical neglect during childhood, higher levels of psychiatric morbidity or negative affectivity, negative perception of parental attitudes, low interoceptive awareness, amount of alcohol consumption over the last 30 days, temperament-related factors represented by elevations on two subscales of the YSR-Inventory (Unpopular, Aggressive), adolescent age and early pubertal timing, low self-esteem (age 13–15), as well as increased weight and shape concerns. Finally, perceived low social support from the family and an escape-avoidant style of coping with stressful events of everyday life were found in late adolescence.

Additional retrospective correlates for BN are: pregnancy complications, childhood obesity, childhood overanxious disorder, sexual abuse and adverse life events, dieting, acculturation, and social phobia.

As was the case for AN, some parental problems (alcoholism, depression, drug abuse, obesity), a number of family environmental factors (e.g., critical comments on weight and shape, low contact), other adverse family experiences, and negative self-evaluation also represent retrospective correlates. Lastly, mood- and anxiety-related prodromal symptoms including severe dieting were found during late adolescence.

Binge Eating Disorder

Because the outcome of the longitudinal studies is often a mixture of bulimic or binge eating syndromes, it can be assumed that some of the risk factors summarized in the bulimia section are equally relevant for binge eating disorder (BED). Only two risk factor studies explicitly included the proposed criteria for BED (Ghaderi & Scott, 2001; Johnson et al., 2002). On the basis of these, low self-esteem, high body concern, high use of escape-avoidance coping, low perceived social support, and childhood experiences of sexual abuse and physical neglect are risk factors for BED. Additional probable risk factors (retrospective correlates) are negative self-evaluation, major depression, marked conduct problems, deliberate self-harm, greater levels of exposure to parental criticism, high expectations, minimal affection, parental under-involvement, low maternal care and high overprotection, and greater parental neglect and rejection. In addition, BED women reported higher rates of sexual abuse; repeated severe physical abuse; bullying; critical comments by family about shape, weight, or eating; and teasing about shape, weight, eating, or appearance. In comparison to psychiatric controls the following factors turned out to be specific retrospective correlates: low parental contact; critical comments about shape, weight, or eating; and childhood obesity (Dominy, Johnson, & Koch, 2000; Fairburn, Cooper, Doll, & Welch, 1998; Striegel-Moore, Dohm, Pike, Wilfley, & Fairburn, 2002).

Limitations of Risk Factor Research

Although the improved knowledge of risk factors now allows for a clearer distinction between mostly cross-sectionally assessed correlates of EDs and "true," longitudinally assessed risk factors, the application of the rigorous risk factor methodology also made a number of limitations of previous research evident: Although the majority of longitudinal studies included sample sizes of several hundred subjects, the samples are mostly too small for consistent and meaningful risk factor detection of full syndromes of EDs, especially AN. Studies including subjects already at higher risk at study start may therefore be more promising.

Longitudinal evidence on risk factors is much stronger for BN and binge-related syndromes, whereas our knowledge on risk factors for AN is still very limited. Because of the overlap of the different full and partial syndromes in longitudinal studies, current research does not permit a valid differentiation of risk factors for BN vs. BED vs. partial syndromes. In addition, most of previous risk factor studies did not consider interactions between risk factors, necessary to improve the understanding of the etiology of the disorder and to improve the development and effectiveness of preventive interventions. Finally, the specificity of factors has been addressed for only a few retrospective correlates of AN, BN, and BED but not for risk factors from longitudinal studies, as no other outcomes than EDs were addressed.

Risk Factor Update: Method and Study Characteristics

For the update of risk factor, the same criteria for study search and inclusion as used in the original meta-analysis were applied again for studies published between May 2002 and November 2008. The literature search resulted in 5830 studies to be screened for inclusion. In addition to the aforementioned longitudinal studies, six longitudinal studies meeting our inclusion criteria were found.

Cevera et al. (2003) assessed two potential risk factors (neuroticism and low self-esteem) in a large sample (N = 2743) of young girls in Spain. During the follow-up period of 18 months, 90 incident cases of eating disorders were identified, most of which were partial syndromes (EDNOS). Moorhead et al. (2003) investigated early childhood and adolescent predictors of eating disorders in young adulthood in 21 women with lifetime diagnoses of full or partial EDs in comparison with women with no ED. Of the ED sample, 9 women met lifetime criteria for AN or BN and 12 met criteria for partial-syndrome EDs. The original sample consisted of female participants (N = 763) interviewed between ages 5 and 26 at seven time points. Because the precedence of some of the factors assessed in adolescence to the EDs is unclear, only the childhood factors are considered here. The McKnight Investigators (2003) conducted one of the most comprehensive risk factor studies for EDs. A large number of potential risk factors were examined in 1103 girls in grades 7 to 9 over a follow-up-period of 4 years. Emerging cases (N = 32) were mostly partial (BN) syndromes; no cases of AN were detected. Beato-Fernandez, Rodríguez-Cano, Belmonte-Llario,

& Martínez-Delgado (2004) assessed psychopathological, social, and family variables as predictors of ED onset 2 years later in 1076 Spanish adolescents. Probable cases of EDs (N = 159, mostly EDNOS) emerging during follow-up were compared with 150 control subjects.

The two most recent studies (Bulik et al., 2006; Fairburn, Cooper, Doll, & Davies, 2005) cannot be considered as "typical" risk factor studies in the sense that the selection of potential risk factors was restricted to very few and specific ones. However, both had large sample sizes and employed a longitudinal design: In a population-based study, Fairburn et al. (2005) examined eating habits and attitudes in a sample of 2992 young dieting women on four occasions over 2 years and compared baseline differences between those who did and did not subsequently develop an ED. One hundred and four participants were found to have a *DSM-IV* ED, most of which again were EDNOS cases. Finally, Bulik et al. (2006), in a population-based twin study explored prevalence and heritability in N = 31,406 twins. Three hundred and thirty-one narrowly and broadly defined cases of AN could be ascertained, and relations between a number of risk factors obtained 30 years earlier were assessed.

With regard to cases emerging during the follow-up, it is evident that definitions of caseness have improved. In all studies, case status was ascertained by clinical interviews or questionnaire cutoffs followed by interviews. Fewer cases of "subclinical" or partial cases can be observed, and if included at all, they are based on clear, operationalized definitions (e.g., The McKnight Investigators, 2003). The focus is on EDNOS cases. Across all studies, N = 327 (14 + 313) cases of AN, N = 34 cases of BN, N = 5 cases of BED, and N = 196 cases of EDNOS emerged. In addition, N = 38 partial cases were found. Follow-up duration varied from 18 months to 30 years.

Risk Factor Update: Results of Risk Factors and Markers

Most of the risk factors found in these more recent studies are replications of previously found factors. Two of the recent studies found higher levels of *neuroticism* to be predictive of both AN and EDNOS (Bulik et al., 2006; Cevera et al., 2003). Although none of the previous studies had explicitly examined the role of neuroticism as a risk factor for EDs, previous longitudinal studies had confirmed the role of preceding psychiatric morbidity, especially negative affect, as risk factor for BN (Leon et al., 1999;

Table 8.2 Characteristics of Risk Factor Studies (Longitudinal Studies) for Eating Disorders (2003–2008)

Study	Sample (N)	Age at baseline (years)	Follow-up interval (y)	Cases	Outcome (dependent variables)	Predictors (independent variables)	Results
1. Cevera et al., (2003)	N = 2509 girls (out of 2743)	12–21	18 months	N = 90 (EDNOS)	EAT>30, semistructured interview (psychiatrist)	Eysenck Personality Inventory, AFA (self-esteem)	Higher levels of neuroticism increased risk of ED, high levels of self-esteem were protective
2. Moorhead et al., 2003	Original sample N = 763 youth, subsample: N = 30 girls EDI DT >12 vs. N = 38 girls <10	5–26	22 years	N = 21; 9 = lifetime AN or BN, 12 = partial syndrome ED	Diagnostic Interview Schedule IV (DIS-IV); subset contacted at age 27	Health-related childhood predictors (emotional-behavioral predictors, self-concept, family history of ED, pregnancy complications	Mothers of women with ED reported more pregnancy complications, more health problems of daughters before age 5, more anxiety-depression at age 9
3. The McKnight Investigators (2003)	1103 girls	Grades 6–9	3 years	N = 32, BN: N = 1; Partial BN: N = 26; BED = 5	McKnight Eating Disorder Examination Interview; diagnoses	McKnight Risk Factor Survey variables	Arizona: Hispanic ethnicity, thin body preoccupation and social pressure, increase in life-events; California: Thin body preoccupation, social pressure to be thin
4. Beato-Fernandez et al., 2004	1076 subjects (500 males, 576 females)	12–13	2 years	N = 40; AN = 1; BN = 8; EDNOS = 31 (3 males)	EAT-40 >30; BITE+; BSQ; at 2 years SCAN interview additionally	EAT-40; BITE; BSQ; GHQ; RSE; Family APGAR	Pathological body dissatisfaction, negative perception of parental attitudes (feeling of being ignored/not loved enough by mother)
5. Fairburn et al., 2005	2992 female dieters	19.8 years	2 years	N = 104; 10 = AN; 19 = BN; 75 = EDNOS	EDE interview	EDE-Q	Low BMI (<19); objective bulimia, purging; secret eating, fear of losing control, desire to have empty stomach
6. Bulik et al., 2006	31.406 individual twins	54.6 years	30 years	N = 313 AN (narrow and broad)	SALT interview, DSM-IV criteria AN	Neuroticism, extraversion, gastric problems, physical activity, perceived life stress, height, weight	Neuroticism significantly associated with development of AN

Patton et al., 1990, 1999). In addition, in the study by Killen et al. (1996), two of the temperament scales (distress, fear) discriminated subsequent asymptomatic from symptomatic girls.

More recent support comes from the McKnight Longitudinal Risk Factor Study (The McKnight Investigators, 2003) and the study by Moorhead et al. (2003). In the McKnight Longitudinal Risk Factor Study, general psychological influences (including depressed mood) turned out to be a potential risk factor for partial BN and BED at one site (Arizona). Mothers of women with lifetime EDs in the longitudinal study by Moorhead et al. (2003) reported that their children at age 9 experienced more problems with anxiety–depression measured by the Simmons Behavior Checklist than non–eating-disordered peers. Cases were mostly partial cases of ED. Taken together, both the previous and the more recent studies confirm the role of a number of interrelated variables, that is, negative affect, neuroticism, and psychiatric morbidity, as risk factors for AN, BN, and BED.

Previous research has demonstrated the role of weight and shape concerns and body dissatisfaction as the best confirmed and most potent risk factor. The role of these factors was also confirmed by three of the newer studies. In the McKnight Longitudinal Study (The McKnight Investigators, 2003), higher scores on a factor (thin body preoccupation and social pressure) measuring concerns with weight, shape, and eating (including media modeling, social eating, dieting, and weight teasing) significantly predicted onset of EDs at both sites (Stanford and Arizona). In the study by Beato-Fernandez et al. (2004), body dissatisfaction predicted the onset on EDs (mostly EDNOS cases) 2 years later. Similarly, in the study by Fairburn et al., (2005), the desire to have an empty stomach was one of the five items predictive of (mostly) EDNOS caseness.

The remaining factors were pregnancy complications reported by mothers of women with ED, more health problems of daughters before age 5 (Moorhead et al., 2003), as well as an increase in negative life events and Hispanic ethnicity at the Arizona site (The McKnight Investigators, 2003). In the high-risk sample of dieting women, Fairburn et al. (2005) found those dieters to be at highest risk for developing an eating disorder 2 years later who—apart from the desire to have an empty stomach—initially also displayed features such as objective bulimic episodes, purging, secret eating, fear of losing control, and a low BMI (<19 kg/m²).

In addition to the longitudinal studies summarized previously, two studies were able to identify markers on the basis of medical registers. Lindberg and Hjern (2003), in a large sample of anorexic inpatients ($N = 1,122$), found that premature children with a gestational age of 23 to 32 and 33 to 36 weeks showed a higher risk of developing AN. In addition, birth traumata such as cephalhematoma (a hemorrhage of blood between the skull and the periosteum) and premature rupture of membrane were associated with a higher risk of developing AN, as were intercountry adoption and experiences of foster care before age 13. The role of perinatal factors was confirmed by the second study by Favaro, Tenconi, and Santonastaso (2006). Several obstetric complications (maternal anemia, diabetes mellitus, preeclampsia, placental infarction, neonatal cardiac problems, hyporeactivity) turned out to be predictors of the development of AN. The risk of developing AN increased with the total number of obstetric complications. Obstetric complications predictive of bulimia nervosa were placental infarction, neonatal hyporeactivity, early eating difficulties, and low birth weight for gestational age.

A third study did not confirm season of birth as fixed marker for AN (Button & Aldridge, 2007). However, although the evidence for this factor has not been quite consistent in the past, the preponderance of studies supporting it remains.

Taken together, the role of markers, such as obstetric complications and perinatal factors for both AN and BN and of season of birth for AN, has been confirmed by these previous studies.

Risk Factor Update: Results of Retrospective Correlates

Table 8.3 summarizes results of 12 recent studies on retrospective correlates for eating disorders. Two studies examined retrospective correlates in patients with AN. The first study found a maternally reported heavier weight at 6 months to be significantly predictive of developing AN (Micali et al., 2007). The second study assessed a number of retrospective correlates on the basis of the Oxford Risk Factor Interview (Fairburn et al., 1999). In accordance with results from the study by Fairburn et al. (1999), a wide range of factors from domains of the subject's mental health, quality of parenting, and parental psychopathology discriminated AN patients from the nonpsychiatric control group. In comparison with other psychiatric disorders, women with AN specifically reported greater severity and significantly higher rates of negative affectivity, perfectionism, family discord, and higher parental demands.

For BN, Micali et al. (2007) found a heavier weight at 5 and 10 years to be significantly associated

Table 8.3 Studies on Retrospective Correlates for Eating Disorders (2003–2008)

AN	Sample (N)	Results
Micali et al., 2007	Case-control study of 197 women (sister pairs), maternal reports of childhood weight and eating problems for 150 women and their sisters. Of these, AN (N = 82), BN (N = 68), mean age 19.5 and 21.8 years	Weight status at 6 months (heavier) and 1 year was significantly predictive of developing AN
Pike et al., 2008	Matched case-control study of 50 women with AN, 50 non-eating disorder psychiatric disorders and 50 with no psychiatric disorder	Women with AN specifically reported greater severity and significantly higher rates of negative affectivity, perfectionism, family discord, and higher parental demands than women with other psychiatric disorders
BN	**Sample (N)**	**Results**
Lehoux & Howe, 2007	N = 40 BN women and non-ED sisters	Childhood teasing about weight and shape and sexual abuse before age 18 more frequent in BN women
Micali et al., 2007	Case-control study of 197 women (sister pairs), maternal reports of childhood weight and eating problems for 150 women and their sisters. Of these, AN (N = 82), BN (N = 68), mean age 19.5 and 21.8 yrs.	Being heavier at 5 and 10 years was significantly associated with developing BN; women with BN ate more between ages 6 and 10 and 1 and 5; eating quickly between ages 5 and 10 was more common in BN; trend for low picky eating between ages 1 and 5 to be associated with later BN
Mixed Samples	**Sample (N)**	**Results**
Cachelin et al., 2005	ED: N = 4 AN, N = 26 BN, N = 29 BED, N = 21 EDNOS: Controls: N = 110	Cases significantly more likely to report histories of sexual abuse than controls before onset of ED
AN+BN	**Sample (N)**	**Results**
Wade et al., 2007	Twins, N = 23 lifetime AN, N = 20 lifetime BN	Both AN and BN were associated with more comments from the family about weight and shape when growing up
Sanci et al., 2008	N = 999 (out of originally 1936) females; N = 67; 35 = BN; 32 = AN	Incidence of bulimic syndrome almost 5 times higher in subjects with 2 or more episodes of CSA

BED	Sample (*N*)	Results
Striegel-Moore et al., 2002 Pike et al., 2005 Striegel-Moore et al., 2005	*N* = 162 BED women, *N* = 251 healthy controls, *N* = 107 psychiatric controls	White subjects with BED reported higher rates of sexual abuse, physical abuse, bullying by peers, and discrimination than healthy comparison subjects; Black women with BED reported more sexual abuse, physical abuse and bullying by peers; BED women reported exposure to more life-events before the onset of the ED, higher exposure to childhood obesity, family overeating or binge eating, family discord, and high parental demands.
Allison et al., 2007	*N* = 176 BED women, *N* = 57 night eating syndrome women, *N* = 38 overweight comparison women	BED women reported more childhood maltreatment than OC women, BED and NES women reported more emotional abuse, BED women more emotional neglect
Striegel-Moore et al., 2007	*N* = 45 women with a history of BED (25)/BN (20), 1515 control women	Participants with higher level of perceived stress before age 14 were more likely to develop BED/BN.

with developing BN. In addition, certain characteristics of their eating style (eating more, eating more quickly etc.) were associated with later BN. The second study confirmed the role of childhood teasing about weight and shape and of sexual abuse before age 18 as retrospective correlates for BN (Lehoux & Howe, 2007).

The role of sexual abuse as a retrospective correlate was also confirmed for a mixed group of EDs (Cachelin, Schug, Juarez, & Monreal, 2005), for bulimic syndromes (Sanci et al. 2008), and for BED (Striegel-Moore et al., 2002). In addition, physical abuse, childhood maltreatment, physical neglect, and higher exposure to life-events and levels of perceived stress were retrospectively confirmed to be more frequent in women with BED compared to controls (Allison, Grilo, Masheb, & Stunkard, 2007; Pike et al., 2005; Striegel-Moore et al., 2005, 2007).

Taken together, these studies generally confirm retrospective correlates found in the earlier review for all diagnostic groups of eating disorders.

Interactions Between Risk Factors

The lack of consideration of interactions between risk factors is one of the limitations of previous risk factor studies. Considering interactions will, however, improve the understanding of the pathways of the development of the disorder, thus enabling us to improve the effectiveness of preventive interventions. To address the different ways of interactions between risk factors (i.e., overlapping factors, proxies, mediators, moderators), Kraemer, Stice, Kazdin, Offord, and Kupfer (2001) proposed additional definitions and methodological recommendations a few years after publishing their risk factor taxonomy.

In the context of eating disorders this extended methodological approach has been applied in only three studies: The McKnight Investigators (2003) examined risk factors for EDs and their interactions in more than 1000 adolescent girls followed for 3 years. At both sites (Arizona, Stanford), thin body preoccupation and social pressure to be thin (TBPSP) were significantly related to ED onset. At the Arizona site, one proxy (general psychological influences) for TBPSP was found. Being Hispanic moderated TBPSP. In addition, change in negative life events turned out to be an independent risk factor.

In the second study, Agras and co-workers (2007) examined childhood precursors and their interactions of the most potent risk factors for eating disorders, thin body preoccupation and social pressure to be thin (TBPSP) in 11-year old children ($N = 134$).

Two moderators were found identifying different groups at risk for the development of (TBPSP). A father with high body dissatisfaction characterized the largest group in which TBPSP was elevated for girls who were concerned about and attempted to modify their weight and for children with fathers who had a high drive for thinness. A child at risk for overweight characterized the second smaller group. Parental behaviors such as overcontrol of their childᵘs eating, together with later pressure from parents and peers to be thin, were related to higher levels of TBPSP.

Our own most recent study assessed risk factors and their interactions within a college-age population of $N = 236$ women already at higher risk defined by elevated weight and shape concerns at baseline (Jacobi, Fittig, Bryson, Wilfley, & Taylor, submitted). Participants were assessed and followed over up to 3 years. At 3-year follow-up, 11.2% of subjects had developed a full or partial ED. Ten of 88 potential risk factors could be classified as independent risk factors, eight as proxies. Comments about eating, from teacher/coach/siblings and a history of depression were the most potent risk factors. The incidence for participants with either or both of these risk factors was 34.8% (16/46) compared to 4.2% % (6/144) for students without these risk factors. Although the study differed from most of the studies included in the meta-analysis with regard to risk status, age, and sample size, risk factors found in this high-risk college age sample are in accordance with factors from the meta-analysis.

Conclusions

Our risk factor update illustrates that the more recent studies were able to reduce a number of limitations of previous risk factor research: Samples sizes are larger, and diagnostic assessment of cases has been improved, resulting in the classification of clearer, well-established diagnostic categories of EDs. Further, the more recent studies seem to be aware of the terminological inaccuracy of earlier studies, retrospective assessment of potential risk factors is mostly made explicit instead of subsuming it under the category of risk factors. Although to a yet limited extend, studies do begin to address interactions between risk factors.

The most potent and best replicated risk factors for both BN and—to a lesser degree also AN—are gender, weight and shape concerns, and a cluster of variables around negative affect, neuroticism, and general psychiatric morbidity. Although most of the risk factors found in the earlier meta-analysis were confirmed by the more recent studies, the predominance of factors for BN and also for BED remains and the number of newly emerging AN cases is very small. Unfortunately, none of the newer studies included other outcomes than EDs. It therefore also remains unclear whether even well-replicated risk factors are predictors of EDs or of general psychopathology. Although that negative affect or general psychopathology has been confirmed as a risk factor for other mental disorders (e.g., Hayward, Killen, Kraemer, & Taylor, 2000; Hirshfeld-Becker, Micco, Simoes, & Henin, 2008) and it seems plausible that high weight and shape concerns and dieting is a specific risk factor for EDs, none of the longitudinal studies has compared risk factors for eating vs. other mental disorders.

Future Directions

Despite improvements in the more recent studies, a number of limitations of previous risk factor research remain and should be addressed by future studies. To address the specificity of risk factors, other outcomes need to be assessed at follow-up and even larger sample sizes may be required. To confirm interactions between factors and determine the relative strength of some factors in relation to others, it is necessary to include a range of factors instead of just a few. Again, this also requires large enough sample sizes.

Although the inclusion of high-risk samples has been suggested as one way of increasing the chance of identifying cases (Jacobi et al., 2004), to date only one study made use of such a high-risk design (Jacobi et al., submitted). Moreover, because no cases of AN could be detected, this study also demonstrates that heightened weight and shape concerns alone are not sufficient characteristics for subjects at risk for AN, but rather for BN and BED. The same would be true for negative affect, neuroticism, and general psychiatric morbidity. Based on the evidence of retrospective correlates, perfectionism seems to be one of the few confirmed factors more specific for AN. For future studies, one possibility to increase the detection of AN cases on the basis of a high-risk design could therefore be to include this factor in addition to weight and shape concerns, psychiatric morbidity or negative affect and initial weight loss.

References

Allison, K. C., Grilo, C. M., Masheb, R. M., & Stunkard, A. J. (2007). High self-reported rates of neglect and emotional abuse, by persons with binge eating disorder and night eating syndrome. *Behaviour Research and Therapy, 45,* 2874–2883.

Attie, I., & Brooks-Gunn, J. (1989). Development of eating problems in adolescent girls: A longitudinal study. *Developmental Psychology, 25,* 70–79.

Beato-Fernández, L., Rodríguez-Cano, T., Belmonte-Llario, A., & Martínez-Delgado, C. (2004). Risk factors for eating disorders in adolescents. A Spanish community-based longitudinal study. *European Journal of Child and Adolescent Psychiatry, 13,* 287–294.

Biederman, J., Ball, S. W., Monuteaux, M. C., Surman, C. B., Johnson, J. L., & Zeitlin, S. (2007). Are girls with ADHD at risk for eating disorders? Results from a controlled, five-year prospective study. *Journal of Developmental Behavioral Pediatrics, 28,* 302–307.

Bulik, C.M., Sullivan, P. F., Tozzi, F., Furberg, H., Lichtenstein, P., & Pedersen, N. L. (2006). Prevalence, heritability, and prospective risk factors for anorexia nervosa. *Archives of General Psychiatry, 63,* 305–312.

Button, E., & Aldridge, S. (2007). Season of birth and eating disorders: Patterns across diagnoses in a specialized eating disorders service. *International Journal of Eating Disorders, 40,* 468–471.

Button, E. J., Sonuga-Barke, E. J. S., Davies, J., & Thompson, M. (1996). A prospective study of self-esteem in the prediction of eating problems in adolescent schoolgirls: Questionnaire findings. *British Journal of Clinical Psychology, 35,* 193–203.

Cachelin, F. M., Schug, R. A., Juarez, L. C., & Monreal, T. K. (2005). Sexual abuse and eating disorders in a community sample of Mexican American women. *Hispanic Journal of Behavioral Sciences, 27,* 4, 533–546.

Calam, R., & Waller, G. (1998). Are eating and psychosocial characteristics in early teenage years useful predictors of eating characteristics in early adulthood? A 7-year longitudinal study. *International Journal of Eating Disorders, 24,* 351–362.

Cevera, S., Lahortiga, F., Martinez-Gonzáles, M. A., Gual, P., Irala-Estévez, & Alonso, Y. (2003). Neuroticism and low self-esteem as risk factors for incident eating disorders in a prospective cohort study. *International Journal of Eating Disorders, 33,* 271–280.

Dominy, N. L., Johnson, W. B., & Koch, C. (2000). Perception of parental acceptance in women with binge eating disorder. *Journal of Psychology, 134,* 23–36.

Fairburn, C. G., Cooper, Z., Doll, H. A., & Davies, B. A. (2005). Identifying dieters who will develop an eating disorder: A prospective, population-based study. *American Journal of Psychiatry, 162,* 2249–2255.

Fairburn, C. G., Cooper, Z., Doll, H. A., & Welch, S. L. (1999). Risk factors for anorexia nervosa. Three integrated case-control comparisons. *Archives of General Psychiatry, 56,* 468–476.

Fairburn, C. G., Doll, H. A., Welch, S. L., Hay, P. J., Davies, B. A., & O'Connor, M. E. (1998). Risk factors for binge-eating disorder: A community-based case-control study. *Archives of General Psychiatry, 55,* 425–432.

Favaro, A., Tenconi, E. & Santonastaso, P. (2006). Perinatal factors and the risk of developing anorexia nervosa and bulimia nervosa. *Archives of General Psychiatry, 63,* 82–88.

Ghaderi, A., & Scott, B. (2001). Prevalence, incidence and prospective risk factors for eating disorders. *Acta Psychiatrica Scandinavica, 104,* 122–130.

Graber, J. A., Brooks-Gunn, J., Paikoff, R. L., & Warren, M. P. (1994). Prediction of eating problems: An 8-year study of adolescent girls. *Developmental Psychology, 30,* 823–834.

Hayward, C., Killen, J. D., Kraemer, H. C., & Taylor, C. B. (2000). Predictors of panic attacks in adolescents. *Journal of the American Academy of Child and Adolescent Psychiatry, 39*, 207–214.

Hirshfeld-Becker, D. R., Micco, J. A., Simoes, N. A., & Henin, A. (2008). High risk studies and developmental antecedents of anxiety disorders. *American Journal of Medical Genetics Part C-Seminars in Medical Genetics, 148C*, 99–117.

Jacobi, C. (2005). Psychosocial risk factors for eating disorders. In S. Wonderlich, J. Mitchell, de Zwaan, M., & Steiger, H. (Eds.), *Eating disorders review* (part 1, pp. 59–85). Oxford, UK: Radcliffe.

Jacobi, C., Fittig, E., Bryson, C., Wilfley, D. E., & Taylor, C. B. (submitted). Who is really at risk: Identifying the risk factors for eating disorders in a high risk sample.

Jacobi, C., Hayward, C., de Zwaan, M., Kraemer, H., & Agras, W. S. (2004). Coming to terms with risk factors for eating disorders: Application of risk terminology and suggestions for a general taxonomy. *Psychological Bulletin, 130*, 1, 19–65.

Johnson, J. G., Cohen, P., Kasen, S., & Brook, J. S. (2002). Childhood adversities associated with risk for eating disorders or weight problems during adolescence or early adulthood. *American Journal of Psychiatry, 159*, 394–400.

Killen, J. D., Taylor, C. B., Hayward, C., Haydel, K. F., Wilson, D. M., Hammer, L. D., et al. (1996). Weight concerns influence the development of eating disorders: A 4-year prospective study. *Journal of Consulting and Clinical Psychology, 64*, 936–940.

Killen, J. D., Taylor, C. B., Hayward, C., Wilson, D. M., Haydel, K. F., Hammer, L. D., et al. (1994). Pursuit of thinness and onset of eating disorder symptoms in a community sample of adolescent girls: A three-year prospective analysis. *International Journal of Eating Disorders, 16*, 227–238.

Kotler, L. A., Cohen, P., Davies, M., Pine, D. S., & Walsh, B. T. (2001). Longitudinal relationships between childhood, adolescent, and adult eating disorders. *Journal of the American Academy of Child and Adolescent Psychiatry, 40*, 1424–1440.

Kraemer, H. C., Kazdin, A. E., Offord, D. R., Kessler, R. C., Jensen, P. S., & Kupfer, D. J. (1997). Coming to terms with the terms of risk. *Archives of General Psychiatry, 54*, 337–343.

Kraemer, H. C., Stice, E., Kazdin, A., Offord, D., & Kupfer, D. (2001). How do risk factors work together? Mediators, moderators, and independent, overlapping, and proxy risk factors. *American Journal of Psychiatry, 158*, 848–856.

Lehoux, P. M., & Howe, N. (2007). Perceived non-shared environment, personality traits, family factors and developmental experiences in bulimia nervosa. *British Journal of Clinical Psychology, 46*, 47–66.

Leon, G. R., Fulkerson, J. A., Perry, C. L., & Early-Zald, M. B. (1995). Prospective analysis of personality and behavioral influences in the later development of disordered eating. *Journal of Abnormal Psychology, 104*, 140–149.

Leon, G. R., Fulkerson, J. A., Perry, C. L., Keel, P. K., & Klump, K. L. (1999). Three to four year prospective evaluation of personality and behavioral risk factors for later disordered eating in adolescent girls and boys. *Journal of Youth and Adolescence, 28*, 181–196.

Lindberg, L., & Hjern, A. (2003). Risk factors for anorexia nervosa: A national cohort study. *International Journal of Eating Disorders, 34*, 397–408.

Marchi, M., & Cohen, P. (1990). Early childhood eating behaviors and adolescent eating disorders. *Journal of the American Academy of Child and Adolescent Psychiatry, 29*, 112–117.

Micali, N., Holliday, J., Karwautz, A., Haidvogl, M., Wagner, G., Fernandez-Aranda, F., et al. (2007). Childhood eating and weight in eating disorders: A multi-centre European study of affected women and their unaffected sisters. *Psychotherapy and Psychosomatics, 76*, 234–241.

Moorhead, D. J., Stashwick, C. K., Reinherz, H. Z., Giaconia, R. M., Striegel-Moore, R. M., & Paradis, A. D. (2003). Child and adolescent predictors for eating disorders in a community population of young adult women. *International Journal of Eating Disorders, 33*, 1–9.

Patton, G. C., Johnson-Sabine, E., Wood, K., Mann, A. H., & Wakeling, A. (1990). *Psychological Medicine, 20*, 383–394.

Patton, G. C., Selzer, R., Coffey, C., Carlin, J. B., & Wolfe, R. (1999). Onset of adolescent eating disorders: Population based cohort study over 3 years. *British Medical Journal, 318*, 765–768.

Pike, K. M., Hilbert, A., Wilfley, D., Fairburn, C. G., Dohm, F.-A., Walsh, B. T., & Striegel-Moore, R. H. (2008). Toward an understanding of risk factors for anorexia nervosa: A case-control study. *Psychological Medicine, 38*, 1143–1453.

Pike, K. M., Wilfley, D., Hilbert, A., Fairburn, C. G., Dohm, F.-A., & Striegel-Moore, R. H. (2006). Antecedent life events of binge-eating disorder. *Psychiatry Research, 142*, 19–29.

Sanci, L., Coffey, C., Olsson, C., Reid, S., Carlin, J. B., & Patton, G. (2008). Childhood sexual abuse and eating disorders in females. *Archives of Pediatrics & Adolescent Medicine, 162*(3), 261–267.

Striegel-Moore, R. H., Dohm, F.-A., Pike, K. M., Wilfley, D. E., & Fairburn, C. G. (2002). Abuse, bullying, and discrimination as risk factors for binge eating disorder. *American Journal of Psychiatry, 159*, 1902–1907.

Striegel-Moore, R-H., Dohm, F.-A., Kraemer, H. C., Schreiber, G. B., Taylor, C. B., & Daniels, S. R. (2007). Risk factors of binge-eating disorders: An exploratory study. *International Journal of Eating Disorders, 40*, 6, 481–487.

Striegel-Moore, R. H., Fairburn, C. G., Wifley, D. E., Pike, K. M., Dohm, F.-A., & Kraemer, H.C. (2005). Toward an understanding of risk factors for binge-eating disorder in black and white women: A community-based case-control study. *Psychological Medicine, 35*, 907–917.

The McKnight Investigators (2003). Risk factors for the onset of eating disorders in adolescent girls: Results of the McKnight longitudinal risk factor study. *American Journal of Psychiatry, 160*, 248–254.

Vollrath, M., Koch, R., & Angst, J. (1992). Binge eating and weight concerns among young adults. Results from the Zurich Cohort Study. *British Journal of Psychiatry, 160*, 498–503.

Wade, T. D., Gillespie, N., & Martin, N. G. (2007). A comparison of early family life events amongst monozygotic twin women with lifetime anorexia nervosa, bulimia nervosa, or major depression. *International Journal of Eating Disorders, 40*(8), 679–686.

Development of Child Taste and Food Preferences: The Role of Exposure

Myles S. Faith

Abstract

This chapter reviews factors influencing the development of child taste and food preferences. It begins with a literature review of the earliest flavor preferences for sweet, salty, and bitter tastes during infancy and the effect of early exposure to infant formulas on the later taste preferences. The effects of exposure frequency, food experience, role modeling, parenting styles, and mass media are followed by behavioral techniques to modify children's food preferences. The final section summarizes commonly used assessments of infant and child food preferences. It is concluded that *exposure* plays a critical role in shaping children's taste and food preferences.

Keywords: child development, exposure, food preferences, neophobia, parental feeding styles, taste preferences

Introduction

Individuals' food preferences are shaped early in life, possibly beginning in utero (Mennella, Jagnow, & Beauchamp, 2001; Mennella, Johnson, & Beauchamp, 1995) or during early infancy (Mennella, 1995). Children's food preferences play a critical role in determining their eating patterns, eating habits, and overall diet quality, which may persist into adulthood. Therefore, understanding children's food preferences is important for developing child-based nutrition education and intervention programs to improve children's eating habits.

The purpose of this chapter is to summarize the literature on factors influencing the development of child taste and food preferences. The chapter begins with a literature review of the earliest flavor preferences for sweet, salty, and bitter tastes during infancy and the effect of early exposure to infant formulas on the later taste preferences. The effects of exposure frequency, food experience, role modeling, parenting styles, and mass media are followed by behavioral techniques to modify children's food preferences.

The final section of the chapter summarizes commonly used assessments of infant and child food preferences. The central theme of this chapter is that of taste and food *exposure*, which, immediately from birth, plays a critical role in shaping children's taste and food preferences.

Innate Preferences for Taste

Sweet Taste

A number of studies have demonstrated a large acceptability of sucrose solutions among newborn infants (Maller & Turner, 1973; Nisbett & Gurwitz, 1970; Nowlis & Kessen, 1976), which may have evolved from the need to obtain sufficient energy from plant sources (Jacobs, Beauchamp, & Kare, 1978). Beauchamp and Moran (1982) investigated whether early dietary experiences influence sweet taste preferences in 6-month-old human infants. In this study, 199 infants were tested for sucrose preference at birth and 140 of these infants were tested again at 6 months of age. According to 7-day diet histories, infants who were regularly fed sweetened water (sweetened with table sugar, Karo syrup, or honey) ingested a significantly larger volume of sucrose solution at age 6 months compared to infants who had no prior experience with sweetened water. Beauchamp and Moran (1984) then showed that maintenance of sucrose acceptability at age 2 years was also dependent on postnatal exposure to sweetened water.

In contrast to these findings, another experiment (Beauchamp & Moran, 1984) showed greater consumption of sucrose-sweetened Kool-Aid compared to unsweetened Kool-Aid, regardless of children's prior experience with sweetened water. The fact that prior experience with sugar water was not related to consumption of plain or sweetened Kool-Aid in this study could be explained by the relatively unpalatable taste of unsweetened Kool-Aid, or infants' prior experience with other sweetened beverages such as fruit juices.

Salt Taste

While humans seem to have an innate preference for sweet tastes, their acceptance of salty tastes appears to follow a developmental shift with age. A study by Beauchamp, Cowart, and Moran (1986) investigated infants' responsiveness to sucrose and saline solutions between 2.5 and 6.7 months of age. Fifty-four infants were divided into groups based on age (Group 1 = 2.5–3.9 months, Group 2 = 4.0–5.3 months, Group 3 = 5.4–6.7 months), and were administered feedings with two different sucrose solutions (0.2 M vs. 0.4 M sucrose concentrations) and two different saline solutions (0.1 M vs. 0.2 M sodium chloride (NaCl). Infants' responses to each of the tastants was compared to their responsiveness following a control of 30 mL of sterile water. The youngest infants did not differentially consume sterile water and saline solutions. However, the two older infant groups ingested significantly more saline solution compared to sterile water. There was no significant age effect for sucrose intake. These results suggest an early developmental shift in salt taste preference, beginning at about 4 months of age, in human infants.

Beauchamp et al. (1986) reported a second developmental shift in saline solution acceptance in older children, between ages 7 to 23 months and 31 to 60 months. Children were presented with NaCl solutions (0.17 M and 0.34 M) and deionized water, and were encouraged to drink ad libitum during a 30-second time period. Infants 7 to 23 months of age consumed significantly more of the 0.17 M NaCl solution compared to water, whereas differential consumption between the 0.34 M NaCl solution and water was not significant. In contrast, children 31 to 60 months of age rejected both NaCl solutions relative to water. There are no clear explanations for the increased preference for saline solutions in early infancy or for the shift toward rejection of saline solution in older children. Beauchamp et al. conjectured that the early developmental shift may be secondary to the development of central and/or peripheral mechanisms for salt taste perception. Early experiences with salty foods in more familiar contexts also may be responsible for the rejection of saline solution in older children. Thus, context may have a critical role in determining taste preference.

Bitter Taste

Compared to the literature on children's acceptance of sweet and salty taste, research for bitter taste is more limited. To investigate young children's acceptance of bitter taste, Kajiura, Cowart, and Beauchamp (1992) compared the responses of infants to experimentally manipulated urea concentrations; infants were either 0 to 6 days old (newborns) or 14 to 180 days (older infants). Bitter taste responsiveness was measured by several outcomes including: intake of a diluent (0.07 M sucrose) vs. test solution (0.12, 0.18, and 0.24 M urea), infant sucking pressure, and hedonic responses based on infant facial expressions and body movements. Newborns tended to consume more of, and had a greater sucking response to, whichever solution was presented first. In contrast, older infants consumed more of the diluent than urea and responded with relatively more and stronger sucks for the diluent than urea, regardless of the order of presentation. Compared to newborns, a significantly greater number of older infants were classified as urea rejectors based on facial reactions and body movements. However, among those newborns who reacted differentially to diluent and urea, the majority rejected the bitter solution. This study suggests an early developmental shift in the acceptance of bitter taste.

Effect of Early Exposure on Food Preference

It has been suggested that there are sensitive periods during which infants are likely to develop flavor preferences and aversions (Beauchamp & Mennella, 1998). Mennella and Beauchamp (1996) tested these potential critical periods for flavor learning involving early exposure to the differential sensory characteristics of commercially available infant formulas. The three main classes of infant formulas include milk-based, soy-based, and protein hydrolysates.

Milk-based formulas were slightly sweet and "sour and cereal-type," while soy based formulas were slightly sweeter, more sour and bitter and with a "hay/beany" odor (Cook & Sarett, 1982). Hydrolyzed protein-based formulas are characterized by unpalatable bitter and sour tastes and an unpleasant aftertaste (Schiffman & Dackis, 1975). Previous studies had shown that infants willingly accept feedings with protein hydrolysate formula if exposed to it before, but not after, 4 months of age (Mennella & Beauchamp, 1996).

Mennella, Griffin, and Beauchamp (2004) tested whether early exposure to infant formula affects later acceptance of familiar and other formulas. Two groups of infants were exposed exclusively to either a protein hydrolysate or a milk-based formula, while the other two groups were assigned to both a protein hydrolysate and milk-based formula for specified periods of time during the intervention. When tested at the end of the 7-month exposure period, a dose-response acceptance of the protein hydrolysate formula was observed. Infants who were exposed exclusively to the protein hydrolysate formula were most accepting of this formula at 7.5 months of age, whereas infants who were exclusively fed the milk-based formula strongly rejected the protein hydrolysate at the end of the study period. Infants who were fed alternately with the protein hydrolysate and milk-based formulas were more accepting of the protein hydrolysate at 7.5 months compared to infants exclusively fed milk-based formula, but were less accepting compared to infants who were fed exclusively with the protein hydrolysate formula.

Mennella and Beauchamp (2002) further explored the hypothesis that flavor learning during infancy affects flavor preference in childhood by evaluating the responses of 4- to 5-year-old children to various flavors and odors. Children who were fed hydrolysate formula as infants were more likely to prefer sour-flavored apple juice compared to those fed milk- or soy-based formula. In contrast, children who were fed soy formula were more likely to prefer bitter-flavored apple juice compared to children who were fed milk-based formula. In addition, compared to children exposed to milk-based formula, children who were fed hydrolysate or soy formulas were more likely to rate the flavor of hydrolysate formula as pleasant. Children in the hydrolysate formula group were also more likely to rate the odor of hydrolysates as pleasant compared to those fed milk-based formulas. Interestingly, mothers whose children were fed hydrolysate or soy formula were more likely to rank broccoli as one of

their children's favorite vegetables. Thus, early exposure to differential sensory characteristics may predict children's food preferences at 4 to 5 years of age.

Liem and Mennella (2002) investigated the effects of early flavor experience on sweet and sour preferences in 4- to 5-year-old and 6- to 7-year-old children, reporting a significant interaction between age and formula group (milk vs. hydrolysate) in their preferences for sour tastes, but not sweetness. In this study, 4- to 5-year-old children who had been fed hydrolysate formula during infancy preferred higher levels of citric acid (added to increase its sourness) in their apple juice compared to older children who had been fed a similar formula. When presented with sweetened apple juice, there was no significant interaction between age or formula group in their preferences for juice with added sugar. In addition, children whose mothers reported regularly adding sugar to their children's foods were significantly more likely to prefer juice with added sugar compared to children whose mothers reported that they never added sugar to their children's foods. Thus, flavor learning during early infancy and childhood may influence taste preference in latter childhood and possibly beyond.

Effect of Frequent Exposure on Food Preference

Children's acceptance of novel foods can be enhanced by repeated exposure (Birch & Marlin, 1982; Pliner, 1982). Sullivan and Birch (1990) found that 8 to 15 exposures to an initially novel food item were necessary to achieve increased acceptance among 3- to 6-year-old children. However, it has been suggested that infants may require fewer exposures to an initially novel food before increasing their acceptance of that food, compared to older children (Birch et al., 1998). Birch and Marlin (1982) conducted one of the first studies documenting that child food preference is a function of exposure frequency. In Experiment 1, 2-year-old children received 2, 5, 10, 15, or 20 exposures to five initially novel cheeses; and in Experiment 2, children were exposed to five initially novel fruits 0, 5, 10, 15, or 20 times. The experimental foods were presented as "paired consumption trials" in which children were asked to taste and compare foods, rating which of the foods they would like to "eat more of." Child food preference was positively associated with exposure frequency in both experiments. These results are consistent with the exposure hypothesis that repeated exposures to a stimulus enhances attitudes towards it (Zajonc, 1968).

Exposure may also explain the positive correlation between parent and child food preferences, as parents may only expose their children to parent-preferred foods. For example, Borah-Giddens and Falciglia (1993) reported a strong concordance between a food that had never been offered to a child and maternal dislike for that particular food. In a study by Vereecken, Keukelier, and Maes (2004), the reported food consumption frequency by mothers was significantly associated with that of their children, ages 2.5 to 7 years. Parental food preferences may influence child food preferences by providing home exposure to those items.

Food Experience

The previous section discussed the relationship between food exposure frequency and increased liking for those foods. However, the flavors with which the food is presented, or the "food experience," is also a determinant of children's food preferences. Sullivan and Birch (1990) recruited 39 preschool children, ages 3 to 6 years, to study the effect of repeated experience with an initially novel food (tofu) on food preferences. Children were assigned to one of three varieties of tofu: salty, sweet, or plain, for a total of 15 exposures over 9 weeks. On three occasions during the exposure period, children's food preferences were assessed for the three versions of tofu as well as a sweet, salty, and plain version of a similar novel food (i.e., ricotta cheese). As a post-assessment, children tasted and rated their preferences for the three versions of tofu and the same versions of a completely novel food, jicama. Results indicated that preference for the exposed version of tofu increased over time across the three groups, confirming the exposure effect (Birch & Marlin, 1982; Pliner, 1982). However, experience with one flavor of tofu did not result in a generalized liking of the other nonexposed flavors of tofu, nor did it translate to a greater preference for ricotta cheese. Similarly, experience with one version of tofu did not transfer to a generalized preference of the corresponding version of jicama. This suggests that the flavors with which a food are exposed, or the food experience, play an important role in shaping food preferences; although flavor preferences may not necessarily transfer to similar foods.

Birch and colleagues (1998) conducted a similar study of the effect of infants' experience with a new food on their intake of similar foods. Infants were assigned to one of two target novel foods, either bananas or peas, which they consumed on 10 occasions. As a preassessment, infants were fed samples

of their *target food*, the *same food* from a different brand, a *similar* food (peaches and pears instead of bananas, or carrots and corn instead of peas), and a *different* food (i.e., peas for infants receiving bananas as their target food, and bananas or beef for those infants receiving peas). After 10 exposures to their target food, infants were given a post-assessment with the foods presented in the pre-assessment. As expected, exposure to the target food increased acceptance of that food. Acceptance for foods similar to the target foods also increased at post-exposure, while intake of the *different* foods remained constant from baseline to post-exposure. The results confirm that infants have an initial neophobic response to new foods, which can be overcome with increased exposure and that experience with certain flavors or foods can enhance acceptance for similar foods.

Effect of Role Modeling on Children's Food Preferences

Children's social environment, including role modeling by parents, siblings, teachers, and peers, as well as parenting styles, can shape children's food preferences.

Family (Parents/Siblings)

Borah-Giddens and Falciglia (1993) conducted a meta-analysis of seven child food preference studies, which specifically addressed the association between parent and child food preferences. They reported a significant correlation between the food preferences of parents and their children, ages 25 years or younger. Skinner et al. (1998) also found a positive relationship between young children's food preferences and those of other family members including the mother, father, and older sibling.

Teachers, Other Role Models

Teachers also play an important role in shaping child food preferences. Hendy and Raudenbush (2000) performed a series of studies to investigate the impact of teacher role modeling on child food preferences in a classroom setting using questionnaires and quasi-experiments. Preschool teachers reported modeling as the most effective strategy in influencing child food preferences. "Teacher silent modeling," in which teachers took bites of target foods (i.e., fresh mango and dried cranberries) without saying anything, was ineffective at increasing food acceptance for both new foods and familiar foods in the classroom setting. However, "enthusiastic teacher modeling" in which the teacher tasted the foods and proclaimed "I love (novel food)!" or "These are delicious" increased child food acceptance across the five test meals.

Not only is teacher enthusiasm important in affecting child food preference, but the social–affective context of food presentation also has a large effect. In a study by Birch, Zimmerman, and Hind (1980), teachers presented a food perceived as "neutral" to 4 year-old children in one of four conditions: reward condition (i.e., children received food reward for good behavior), non-contingent attention condition (i.e., child presented with food and adult attention, but not contingent upon completing a task), nonsocial condition (i.e., child presented with food in their locker twice a day), or the snack-time familiarity condition (i.e., control group). Foods presented in reward conditions or non-contingently paired with adult attention were associated with increased child preference of those foods. However, no changes in preference were observed in the nonsocial or control conditions.

Peers

Children's peers are also very important in the development of food preferences. A series of experiments by Hendy and Raubenbush (2000) found that teacher modeling was no longer an effective influence on preschool children's food preferences when used in competition with a peer model; peer influence was especially strong among females. In another experiment, Hendy (2002) found that same age girl models were more effective than boy models in increasing food acceptance among both sexes of children, contrary to previous research suggesting that same sex models were more effective.

Effects of General Parenting Styles

Parents play a critical role in the development of their children's food preferences beginning with infant feeding practices and parental role modeling. However, general parenting styles and parental education levels have also been identified as predictors of child food preferences. Kremers et al. (2003) explored the correlation between general parenting strategies and child eating habits (mean age = 16.5 years). Parents were defined as either "authoritative" (firm and supportive parenting), "authoritarian" (strict but less involved parenting), "indulgent" (involved but not strict parenting), and "neglectful" (low strictness and low involvement parenting) based on self-report questionnaires. Results indicated that an authoritative parenting style was associated with child fruit intake and healthy attitudes

toward eating fruits and vegetables. The authoritarian parenting style was associated with low levels of fruit consumption, while the indulgent parenting style was associated with greater fruit intake compared to the authoritarian or neglectful styles.

Vereecken et al. (2004) examined the link between maternal education level, parenting styles, and child food preferences. Highly educated mothers praised their children more, and increased verbal praise was a significant predictor of children's vegetable consumption. In contrast, lower maternal education levels were found to be more permissive, which was correlated with an increased consumption of refined sugars.

Mass Media Influences

A large percentage of commercials airing during children's programming are food advertisements. An analysis of commercials scheduled during weekend children's television showed that 37% of advertisements on American television and 49% of commercials on British television were food advertisements (Furnham, Abramsky, & Gunter, 1997). Most of these advertised products were snack foods, breakfast cereals, and fast food restaurants. Until recently, there were no studies that examined whether food advertisements directed at children had any effect on child eating preferences or behavior.

Halford et al. (2004) explored the differences between normal weight and overweight children in their ability to recognize television advertisements of food and nonfood items as well as the total amount of food consumed after viewing TV ads. A total of 42 children, ages 9 to 11 years, participated in the study and were grouped according to their obesity status. On two separate occasions, the children watched a series of food-related advertisements or advertisements that did not pertain to food followed by a 10-minute cartoon video. Next, they were given permission to eat ad libitum from an assortment of food items including a low-fat savory snack, a low-fat sweet snack, a high-fat sweet snack, and a high-fat savory snack.

When given a list of 16 food ads, from which 8 had been shown, overweight and obese children recognized significantly more food ads compared to normal weight children (Fig. 9.1a). Across all groups, the number of recognized food-related TV advertisements was directly related to the amount of food consumed after watching those ads. In addition, participants ate more of the high-fat and high-sugar snacks after viewing the food ads and more of the low-fat savory snack after viewing the non-food

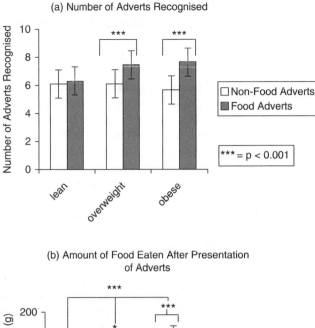

(a) Number of Adverts Recognised

*** = p < 0.001

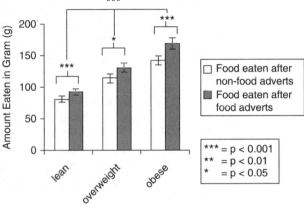

(b) Amount of Food Eaten After Presentation of Adverts

*** = p < 0.001
** = p < 0.01
* = p < 0.05

Fig. 9.1 The number of television advertisements recognized and the amount of food consumed after viewing the advertisements ***$p < 0.001$, **$p < 0.01$, *$p < 0.05$.

advertisements. These findings suggest that TV commercials can affect food preferences and eating behavior, and may especially encourage unhealthy food choices among overweight children.

Changing Children's Food Preferences
Behavior Modification

A number of studies have focused on strategies through which parents can influence and modify child food preferences. The results of a 3-year project by Hart, Bishop, and Truby (2003) on developing parent education programs suggest that behavioral techniques, rather than nutrition facts alone, have a greater impact on increasing healthy feeding behaviors in children. Similar results were found in a study by Wardle et al. (2003) investigating the effects of parent-led exposure in influencing 2- to 6-year-old children's acceptance of a target vegetable rated marginally low on a pre-intervention test.

Parents were randomized to the parent-led exposure group, the nutrition education group, or a control group which did not receive any instruction. Greater increases in liking and consumption of the target vegetable were found in the parent-led exposure group, and nutritional knowledge alone was not sufficient to influence target vegetable consumption. Wardle's results confirmed those from previous studies that repeated exposure is key to increasing child food acceptance.

Restriction

Whereas frequent exposure and role modeling have been identified as effective strategies to influence child food preferences, restrictive feeding practices may have drawbacks. Many parents believe that the most effective way to control their children's intake of high-fat and high-sugar foods is to restrict access to those foods. However, there is evidence to suggest that restricting children's food intake may be counterproductive. Liem, Mars, and De Graaf (2004) conducted a study on kindergarten-aged children's food preferences in the Netherlands and reported that children whose intake of mono and disaccharides (MDS), or simple sugars, was highly restricted by parents consume fewer MDS beverages and foods during breakfast and lunch. However, 55% of these highly restricted children preferred an "orange-ade" drink of highest sucrose concentration compared to 33% of children who were slightly restricted.

Fisher and Birch (1999) examined the behavioral effects of restricting 3- to 5-year-old children's access to palatable foods for 5 weeks. Peach and apple-flavored fruit bar cookies were chosen as the experimental foods, as these were neither highly liked nor disliked by the children. Children were randomly assigned to receive one of the experimental foods as the control and the other was restricted. Before the experimental phase, there were no differences in children's responses to the restricted food and the control food. During the restriction period, however, the restricted food received more positive comments, more requests, and more attempts to obtain it compared to the control food.

In addition to restricting children's intake of certain foods, pressuring children to consume more food may also have unintended effects on child food preferences. Fisher et al. (2002) assessed parental tendencies to pressure their 5-year-old daughters to eat more food. They found that parents who more frequently pressured their daughters to eat had children with lower fruit, vegetable, and micronutrient intakes. They also reported a negative correlation between parents' own fruit and vegetable intake and the use of pressure to eat, suggesting that role modeling may be more effective than pressuring children to eat or restricting children's intake of specific foods for changing child food preferences.

Opportune Ages to Change Food Preferences

Skinner et al. (2002) tested longitudinal changes in children's food preferences from ages 2 to 8 years. Mothers completed a 196-item Food Preference Questionnaire at T1 (2–3 years), T2 (4 years), and T3 (8 years). Mothers reported that children liked ≈60% of the listed foods at T1. The number of liked foods only increased by 3.7% at T3, whereas the number of disliked foods increased by 5.5%. Between T1 and T2, foods that were never tasted decreased from 55 to 37 foods. These results suggest that the majority of child food preferences are developed by the age of 2 to 3 years and that a critical period for increasing acceptance of novel foods may exist around age 4 years.

Barriers to Changing Food Preferences: Neophobia

Research has shown that omnivores are neophobic, or reluctant to try new foods, regardless of our need for a varied diet. This conflict has been termed the "generalist's dilemma" (Rozin, 1976). One possible mechanism responsible for the reluctance to try new foods is omnivores' self-protection against potentially poisonous substances. Individuals may learn to accept and increase their preference for initially novel food items through "learned safety," or after repeated exposure to a food item, and in the absence of accompanying gastrointestinal distress (Kalat & Rozin, 1973).

Cooke, Wardle, and Gibson (2003) sent child eating behavior questionnaires to 564 mothers of 2- to 6-year-olds, and found no association between age, gender, or parental intake and neophobia among children. High levels of neophobia were associated with lower intake of vegetables, fruits, and meats, but did not affect consumption of high-fat and high-sugar snacks, starchy food items, or eggs. These results may provide evidence for the evolutionary avoidance of potentially toxic food items, as those foods associated with neophobia are the most potentially dangerous. Toxins are found in many plants, and protein-rich foods are most likely to cause food-borne illnesses.

Assessment of Children's Food Preferences

The most significant predictor of children's food intake is their liking of particular foods (Gibson, Wardle, & Watts, 1998). For this reason, it is important to develop reliable methods for the assessment of children's food preferences.

Infants

Infant facial expressions have been used to assess acceptance or rejection of taste stimuli in some of the earliest studies on human taste development (Bergamasco & Beraldo, 1990; Rosenstein & Oster, 1988). Infant facial expressions (Fig. 9.2a-c) are fairly consistent in response to various taste stimuli such as the sweet taste of sucrose (facial relaxation and mouth gaping), the sour taste of citric acid (lip pursing and facial grimace), and the bitter taste of quinine and urea (tongue protrusion and facial grimace). There are no distinctive facial expressions associated with exposure to salty taste in infants (Mennella & Beauchamp, 1998).

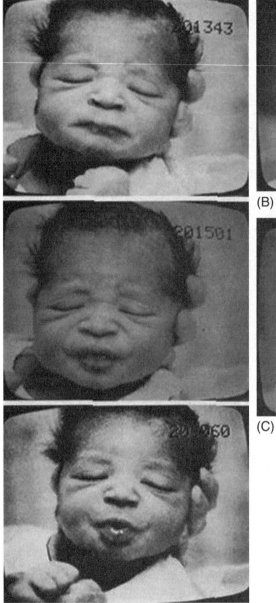

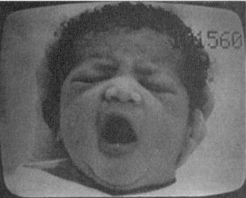

(A)

(B)

(C)

Fig. 9.2 Infant facial expressions in response to taste. **(A)** Infant facial expression in response to sweet taste; initial negative facial reaction followed by relaxation and sucking. **(B)** Infant facial expression in response to sour taste. **(C)** Infant facial expression in response to bitter taste. (From Rosenstein, D., & Oster, H. [1988]. Differential facial responses to four basic tastes in newborns. *Child Development, 59,* 1555–1568.)

Intake studies, which measure the amount of solution consumed during a brief time period, are most commonly used to assess taste preference in newborns. Intake studies typically use weaker concentrations of the taste solution compared to studies that measure facial expressions. Presumably, the volume of consumption may be indicative of the infant's preference for the taste solution (Mennella & Beauchamp, 1998).

Children

The most commonly used measure of child food preferences is a "taste and rate" procedure, in which children taste a food and describe how much they

Fig. 9.3 Three-Point Hedonic Scale.

like the food on a 3-point scale (Fig. 9.3). This method has produced reliable results in children as young as 3 years of age, but may not be practical to measure acceptance for a large number of foods. Guthrie, Rapoport, and Wardle (2000) tested whether food photographs or realistic food models could provide a reliable alternative to real foods in the evaluation of children's food preferences. Results suggest that high-quality food photographs may provide a reliable alternative to real foods in the assessment of children's food preferences.

Summary

In summary, food preferences are learned in part through early exposure, exposure frequency, and experience with foods. Given the high prevalence of fast food restaurants, convenient marts, and the wide variety of snack foods, the present environment presents children overexposure to high-fat and high-sugar foods that may become further preferred through learning. Once established, children's food preferences can be challenging to modify. Implementing behavioral techniques, such as role modeling and reinforcement for healthier food choices, in early childhood may help to establish healthier dietary choices by children that may be more sustainable. The fundamental role of exposure in the development of child taste and food preferences cannot be overstated.

Future Directions

Future research is needed to better understand the conditions under which exposure to healthier (i.e., less energy dense) foods can increase child preferences for those choices. Issues to be explored include the following:

- How can media/advertisements shape children's preferences for healthier items?
- Can cartoon and other characters be used to influence preferences in early childhood?
- To what extent can food exposures during pregnancy shape early life food preferences by infants?

The development of eating habits in early childhood and its implications for longer-term obesity prevention are also critically important issues.

Further Reading

Birch, L. L., & Marlin, D. W. (1982). I don't like it; I never tried it: Effects of exposure on two-year-old children's food preferences. *Appetite, 3,* 353–360.

Birch, L. L., et al. (1998). Infants' consumption of a new food enhances acceptance of similar foods. *Appetite, 30,* 283–295.

Fisher, J. O., & Birch, L. L. (1999). Restricting access to palatable foods affects children's behavioral response, food selection, and intake. *American Journal of Clinical Nutrition, 69,* 1264–1272.

Hendy, H. M. (2002). Effectiveness of trained peer models to encourage food acceptance in preschool children. *Appetite, 39,* 217–225.

Mennella, J. A., Griffin, C. E., & Beauchamp, G. K. (2004). Flavor programming during infancy. *Pediatrics, 113,* 840–845.

References

Beauchamp, G. K., Cowart, B.J., & Moran, M. (1986). Developmental changes in salt acceptability in human infants. *Developmental Psychobiology, 19,* 17–25.

Beauchamp, G. K., & Mennella, J. A. (1998). Sensitive periods in the development of human flavor perception and preference. In *Annales Nestle, Nestle Nutrition Workshop Series* (pp. 19–31). Vevey, Switzerland: Nestec Ltd.

Beauchamp, G. K., & Moran, M. (1982). Dietary experience and sweet taste preference in human infants. *Appetite, 3,* 139–152.

Beauchamp, G. K., & Moran, M. (1984). Acceptance of sweet and salty tastes in 2-year-old children. *Appetite, 5,* 291–305.

Bergamasco, N. H., & Beraldo, K. E. (1990). Facial expressions of neonate infants in response to gustatory stimuli. *Brazilian Journal of Medical & Biological Research, 23,* 245–249.

Birch, L. L., & Marlin, D.W. (1982). I don't like it; I never tried it: Effects of exposure on two-year-old children's food preferences. *Appetite, 3,* 353–360.

Birch, L. L., & Sullivan, S. A. (1991). Measuring children's food preferences. *Journal of School Health, 61,* 212–214.

Birch, L. L., Zimmerman, S. I., & Hind, H. (1980). The influence of social-affective context to the formation of children's food preferences. *Child Development, 51,* 856–861.

Birch, L. L., et al. (1998). Infants' consumption of a new food enhances acceptance of similar foods. *Appetite, 30,* 283–295.

Borah-Giddens, J., & Falciglia, G. A. (1993). A meta-analysis of the relationship in food preferences between parents and children. *Journal of Nutrition Education, 25,* 102–107.

Cook, D. A., & Sarett, H. P. (1982). Design of infant formulas for meeting normal and special need. In F. Lifshitz (Ed.), *Pediatric Nutrition: Infant Feeding, Deficiencies, Disease.* New York: Marcel Dekker.

Cooke, L., Wardle, J., & Gibson, E. L. (2003). Relationship between parental report of food neophobia and everyday food consumption in 2–6-year-old children. *Appetite, 41,* 205–206.

Fisher, J. O., & Birch, L. L. (1999). Restricting access to palatable foods affects children's behavioral response, food selection, and intake. *American Journal of Clinical Nutrition, 69,* 1264–1272.

Fisher, J. O., et al. (2002). Parental influences on young girls' fruit and vegetable, micronutrient, and fat intakes. *Journal of the American Dietetic Association, 102,* 58–64.

Furnham, A., Abramsky, S., & Gunter, B. (1997). A cross-cultural content analysis of children's television advertisements. *Sex Roles, 37,* 91–99.

Gibson, E. L., Wardle, J., & Watts, C. J. (1998). Fruit and vegetable consumption, nutritional knowledge and beliefs in mothers and children. *Appetite, 31,* 205–228.

Guthrie, C. A., Rapoport, L., & Wardle, J. (2000). Young children's food preferences: a comparison of three modalities of food stimuli. *Appetite, 35,* 73–77.

Halford, J. C., et al. (2004). Effect of television advertisements for foods on food consumption in children. *Appetite, 42,* 221–225.

Hart, K., Bishop, J., & Truby, H. (2003). Changing children's diets: Developing method and messages. *Journal of Human Nutrition and Dietetics, 16,* 365–366.

Hendy, H. M. (2002). Effectiveness of trained peer models to encourage food acceptance in preschool children. *Appetite, 39,* 217–225.

Hendy, H. M., & Raudenbush, B. (2000). Effectiveness of teacher modeling to encourage food acceptance in preschool children. *Appetite, 34,* 61–76.

Jacobs, W. W., Beauchamp, G. K., & Kare, M. R. (1978). Progress in animal flavor research. In R. W. Bullard (Ed.), *Flavor chemistry of animal foods* (pp. 1–20). Chicago: American Chemical Society.

Kajiura, H., Cowart, B. J., & Beauchamp, G. K. (1992). Early developmental change in bitter taste responses in human infants. *Developmental Psychobiology, 25,* 375–386.

Kalat, J. W., & Rozin, P. (1973). "Learned safety" as a mechanism in long-delay taste-aversion learning in rats. *Journal of Comparative & Physiological Psychology, 83,* 198–207.

Kremers, S. P., et al. (2003). Parenting style and adolescent fruit consumption. *Appetite, 41,* 43–50.

Liem, D. G., Mars, M., & De Graaf, C. (2004). Sweet preferences and sugar consumption of 4– and 5–year-old children: Role of parents. *Appetite, 43,* 235–245.

Liem, D. G., & Mennella, J. A. (2002). Sweet and sour preferences during childhood: Role of early experiences. *Developmental Psychobiology, 41,* 388–395.

Maller, O., & Turner, R. E. (1973). Taste in acceptance of sugars by human infants. *Journal of Comparative & Physiological Psychology, 84,* 496–501.

Mennella, J. A. (1995). Mother's milk: A medium for early flavor experiences. *Journal of Human Lactation, 11,* 39–45.

Mennella, J. A., & Beauchamp, G. K. (1996). Developmental changes in the infants' acceptance of protein-hydrolysate formula and its relation to mothers' eating habits. *Journal of Developmental and Behavioral Pediatrics, 17,* 386–391.

Mennella, J. A., & Beauchamp, G. K. (1998). Early flavor experiences: Research update. *Nutrition Reviews, 56,* 205–211.

Mennella, J. A., & Beauchamp, G. K. (2002). Flavor experiences during formula feeding are related to preferences during childhood. *Early Human Development, 68,* 71–82.

Mennella, J. A., Griffin, C. E., & Beauchamp, G. K. (2004). Flavor programming during infancy. *Pediatrics, 113,* 840–845.

Mennella, J. A., Jagnow, C. P., & Beauchamp, G. K. (2001). Prenatal and postnatal flavor learning by human infants. *Pediatrics, 107,* E88.

Mennella, J. A., Johnson, A., & Beauchamp, G. K. (1995). Garlic ingestion by pregnant women alters the odor of amniotic fluid. *Chemical Senses, 20,* 207–209.

Nisbett, R.E., & Gurwitz, S. B. (1970). Weight, sex, and the eating behavior of human newborns. *Journal of Comparative & Physiological Psychology, 73,* 245–253.

Nowlis, G. H., & Kessen, W. (1976). Human newborns differentiate differing concentrations of sucrose and glucose. *Science, 191,* 865–866.

Pliner, P. (1982). The effects of mere exposure on liking for edible substances. *Appetite, 3,* 283–290.

Rosenstein, D., & Oster, H. (1988). Differential facial responses to four basic tastes in newborns. *Child Development, 59,* 1555–1568.

Rozin, P. (1976). The selection of food by rats, humans, and other animals. In J. S. Rosenblatt, et al. (Eds.), *Advances in the Study of Behavior* (pp. 12–76). New York: Academic Press.

Schiffman, S. S., & Dackis, C. (1975). Taste of nutrients: Amino acids, vitamins, and fatty acids. *Perception Psychophysics, 17,* 140–146.

Skinner, J. D., et al. (1998). Toddler's Food Preferences: Concordance with family members' preferences. *Journal of Nutrition Education, 30*, 17–22.

Skinner, J. D., et al. (2002). Children's food preferences: A longitudinal analysis. *Journal of the American Dietetic Association, 102*, 1638–1647.

Sullivan, S. A., & Birch, L. L. (1990). Pass the sugar, pass the salt: Experience dictates preference. *Developmental Psychology, 26*, 546–551.

Vereecken, C. A., Keukelier, E., & Maes, L. (2004). Influence of mother's educational level on food parenting practices and food habits of young children. *Appetite, 43*, 93–103.

Wardle, J., et al. (2003). Increasing children's acceptance of vegetables: A randomized trial of parent-led exposure. *Appetite, 40*, 155–162.

Zajonc, R. B. (1968). Attitudinal effects of mere exposure. *Journal of Personality and Social Psychology Monograph Supplement, 9*, 1–32.

Dieting and the Eating Disorders

Eric Stice *and* Katherine Presnell

Abstract

This chapter reviews theory and empirical evidence linking dietary restraint to eating pathology. Although prospective studies suggest that dieting increases risk for future onset of eating pathology, experiments suggest that assignment to weight loss and weight maintenance diets reduces eating disorder symptoms. Because these two findings have opposing public health implications, this chapter also considers various explanations for these inconsistent findings. Our analysis suggests that dieting is not a causal risk factor for bulimic pathology, but rather may be a proxy risk factor. We posit that a tendency towards overeating may lead to both dieting and bulimic pathology, which seems to better account for the pattern of observed findings, and propose a number of studies that might help further resolve whether dietary restraint is causally related to the development of eating pathology.

Keywords: binge eating, bulimia nervosa, dietary restraint, dieting, eating disorders, obesity

Introduction

Eating disorders (EDs) are marked by chronicity and relapse, result in functional impairment, and increase the risk for future onset of obesity, depressive disorders, suicide attempts, anxiety disorders, substance abuse, and health problems (Stice & Bulik, 2008). Accordingly, numerous prospective studies have focused on identifying risk factors that predict development of eating pathology and maintenance factors that predict persistence of eating pathology in an effort to elucidate the etiologic processes that give rise to these disturbances and inform the design of effective prevention and treatment interventions (Jacobi, Hayward, Zwaan, Kraemer, & Agras, 2004).

Perhaps the most widely studied risk factor for eating pathology is dieting. Theorists posit that dieting increases risk for onset and persistence of binge eating and bulimia nervosa (Fairburn, 1997; Polivy & Herman, 1985). It is crucial to determine whether dieting increases risk for development and persistence

of bulimic pathology for three reasons. First, almost half of adolescent girls and young women report dieting for weight control purposes (Serdula et al., 1993), implying that a substantial subset of this population may be at risk for developing an ED. Second, 30% of adults in the United States and other Western countries meet criteria for obesity (Hedley et al., 2004) and the current treatment of choice for this medical condition is behaviorally based low-calorie weight loss diets (Jeffery et al., 2000). Because obesity markedly increases the risk for morbidity and mortality (Calle, Thun, Petrelli, Rodriguez, & Heath, 1999) and results in over 110,000 deaths in the United States annually (Flegal, Graubard, Williamson, & Gail, 2005), it is crucial to determine whether interventionists should promote weight control dieting as a means of reducing obesity, or whether other treatments should be used. Third, there is emerging evidence that low-calorie diets result in significant weight loss, improved health, and reduced DNA damage in humans (e.g., Heilbronn et al., 2006). Thus, the overarching goals of this chapter are to review the empirical literature that has examined the relation of dieting to eating pathology, systematically investigate factors that may account for inconsistent findings, discuss possible interpretations of the inconsistent findings, and offer suggestions for future research that may help to advance our understanding of the relation between dieting and bulimic pathology.

Dieting: Definition and Descriptive Statistics

Dieting is defined as volitional and sustained restriction of caloric intake for the purposes of weight loss or weight maintenance (Herman & Polivy, 1975; Wadden, Brownell, & Foster, 2002; Wilson, 2002). Dieting must result in a negative energy balance for weight loss (a calorie-deficit diet) and a balance between caloric intake and caloric expenditure for weight maintenance (a balanced-calorie diet).

Although the above definition is straightforward, dieting is heterogeneous because people report using various behaviors to achieve weight control. Data suggest that 60% to 75% of weight loss dieters combine reduced caloric intake with increased physical activity in an effort to enter a negative energy balance (Emmons, 1992; French, Perry, Leon, & Fulkerson, 1995; Serdula et al., 1993). However, some dieters report potentially harmful weight control behaviors, such as meal skipping, and a smaller percentage report unhealthy behaviors such as fasting, vomiting, or laxative abuse for weight control purposes (Emmons, 1992; French et al., 1995; Serdula et al., 1993). Data suggest that there is also considerable variation in the duration of self-initiated weight loss diets, ranging from less than a week to 6 months, with a mode of approximately 1 month (Emmons, 1992; French, Jeffery, & Murray, 1999; Williamson, Serdula, Anda, Levy, & Byers, 1992).

Heatherton, Herman, Polivy, King, and McGree (1988) have argued that dieting should be distinguished from dietary restraint, with the former term referring to individuals who consistently engage in caloric restriction and the latter term referring to individuals who engage in chronic dieting that is punctuated by bouts of overeating. However, because the two terms have been used synonymously for several decades (e.g., Herman & Polivy, 1975; Polivy & Herman, 1985, 1992) and because extant self-report dieting measures cannot distinguish those who consistently engage in caloric restriction from those who show intermittent bouts of overeating

(Stice, Fisher, & Lowe, 2004), we use these terms interchangeably.

Theoretical Mechanisms for the Effects of Dieting on Eating Pathology

Theorists have proposed several mechanisms by which dieting might increase risk for ED symptoms. According to Polivy and Herman (1985), "Successful dieting produces weight loss, which in turn might create a state of chronic hunger, especially if such weight loss leaves the dieter at a weight below the set-point weight that is defended physiologically" (p. 196). The chronic hunger experienced by dieters putatively increases the likelihood that they may binge eat. This account accords with evidence that caloric deprivation increases the reinforcing value of food (Bulik & Brinded, 1994; Epstein, Truesdale, Wojcik, Paluch, & Raynor, 2003). Food deprivation reduces mRNA for dopamine transporter and extracellular dopamine (Patterson et al., 1998; Pothos, Hernandez, & Hoebel, 1995), which may explain why dieting increases the reinforcing value of food. Polivy and Herman (1985) further propose that "dieting causes binging by promoting the adoption of a cognitively regulated eating style" (p. 193) and argue that a reliance on cognitive control over eating, rather than a reliance on physiological cues, leaves dieters vulnerable to uncontrolled eating when these cognitive controls are disrupted. For example, negative affect or tasks with a heavy cognitive load may distract individuals from their dietary rules and increase risk for binge eating. Violation of strict dietary rules may also result in the temporary abandonment of dietary restriction because of the abstinence violation effect (Marlatt & Gordon, 1985). Specifically, people who violate a commitment to not engage in a particular behavior (e.g., eat chocolate) may abandon the commitment and engage in that particular behavior to excess. It has also been suggested that dieting results in depletion of tryptophan, an amino acid precursor of serotonin, which may increase the likelihood of binge eating carbohydrates to restore tryptophan levels (Kaye, Gendall, & Strober, 1998). Indeed, placing individuals on short-term energy-deficit diets reduces plasma tryptophan (Attenburrow et al., 2003; Cowen, Clifford, Walsh, Williams, & Fairburn, 1996).

Researchers have also suggested that dietary restraint may serve as a maintenance factor that perpetuates binge eating and bulimic symptoms once these behaviors have emerged. Fairburn (1997) theorized that binge eating precipitates redoubled dietary efforts and use of radical weight control techniques, such as vomiting and laxative use, which may develop into the self-maintaining binge-purge cycle.

Empirical Tests of the Dieting Theory of Eating Pathology

The first objective of this chapter is to review empirical studies that have examined the relation of dieting to eating pathology. We focused on (1) prospective studies that test whether scores on self-report dieting measures predict future changes in binge eating or bulimic symptoms or predict onset or persistence of bulimic pathology and (2) controlled experiments that examined the impact of directly manipulated dietary restriction on binge eating and bulimic symptoms because these designs permit firmer inferences. Prospective studies can provide evidence of temporal precedence, which helps rule out the possibility of a reverse direction of effects and should not be influenced by demand characteristics, as participants presumably do not know how they are going to change in the future when they complete the measures of the predictors at baseline. Yet, prospective studies can suffer from systematic attrition, which may limit generalization. In addition, it is always possible that some unmeasured third variable explains any prospective effect observed in a longitudinal study. Randomized experiments provide more rigorous causal inferences because they effectively establish temporal precedence and are the most effective design available to rule out the possibility that some omitted third variable explains the observed relations. Nonetheless, experiments may not be representative of real-world processes. In addition, experiments can involve unrepresentative samples, which limits generalizability, and are vulnerable to bias created by demand characteristics and expectancies. Experimental studies can also have questionable internal validity, if the manipulation fails to change the intended variable or inadvertently changes another variable.

We did not include cross-sectional studies because there is no way to determine whether eating pathology is a precursor, concomitant, or consequence of dieting. This decision led us to omit numerous studies that have examined the eating behaviors of individuals who score high and low on self-report dieting scales because these studies are simply investigating correlates of dietary restraint scores (e.g., Polivy, Herman, & McFarlane, 1994). In addition, we focused on experiments that manipulated dietary restriction relative to some type of control group, because it is not possible to separate

the effects of the manipulation from the effects of the passage of time, regression to the mean, or measurement artifacts (pretest sensitization) without a control group. Although it would have been preferable to focus solely on experiments that included a credible placebo control condition because this would reduce the possibility that any effects on the outcomes are due to demand characteristics or expectancies, only one experiment in this area has included a placebo control condition.

It is important to acknowledge that although dietary restraint has been implicated in anorexia nervosa (AN), bulimia nervosa (BN), and binge eating disorder (BED), few studies have focused on the former ED. Most of the studies have investigated factors that impact binge eating, BN, or BED, though a few investigated predictors of any type of ED. Thus, it would be premature to draw conclusions regarding the relation of dietary restraint to AN.

Prospective Studies of the Relation of Dieting to Future Eating Pathology

Adolescent girls with elevated scores on dietary restraint scales or who report frequent weight loss dieting are at increased risk for future onset of bulimic symptoms (Field et al., 1999; Neumark-Sztainer et al., 2006; Stice & Agras, 1998; Stice, Presnell, & Spangler, 2002;), future increases in bulimic symptoms (Johnson & Wardle, 2005; Stice, 2001; Wertheim, Koerner, & Paxton, 2001), and onset of threshold and subthreshold BN (Killen et al., 1994, 1996; Stice, Davis, Miller, & Marti, 2008). However, two studies did not replicate this relation (Cooley & Toray, 2001; Spoor et al., 2006), potentially because they examined female college students who were beyond the developmental period during which bulimic symptoms typically increase and because these studies used small samples. Research has also found that adolescent girls who have elevated scores on dietary restraint scales, report frequent dieting, or self-identify as dieters are at increased risk for future onset of any ED (i.e., AN and BN; Patton, Johnson-Sabine, Wood, Mann, & Wakeling, 1990; Patton, Selzer, Coffey, Carlin, & Wolfe, 1999; Santonastaso, Friederici, & Favaro, 1999) and future increases in measures of overall ED symptoms (Leon, Fulkerson, Perry, Keel, & Klump, 1999).

Only three prospective studies have tested whether self-reported dieting is a maintenance factor that predicts persistence of bulimic symptoms among individuals who initially endorse these symptoms with nontreatment samples. Elevated dietary restraint scores predicted persistence of compensatory behaviors, but not binge eating, over a 9-month period in a study that examined female high school students (Stice & Agras, 1998). A second study that followed a community-recruited sample of women who initially met criteria for BN found that elevated dietary restriction did not predict persistence of either binge eating or compensatory behavior over a 5-year period (Fairburn, Cooper, Doll, Norman, & O'Connor, 2000). A third study that followed a community-recruited sample of young women who initially met criteria for full threshold or subthreshold BN found that elevated dietary restraint scores at baseline predicted persistence of compensatory behavior, but not binge eating over a 1-year period (Bohon, Stice, & Burton, 2008).

Engelberg, Gauvin, and Steiger (2005) used ecological momentary assessment to test whether elevated dietary restraint typically preceeded self-rated binge eating episodes among women with full and subthreshhold BN. Self-rated binge episodes were not preceded by elevations in dietary restraint relative to non-binge days.

In sum, virtually all of the prospective studies indicate that adolescent girls and young women with elevated scores on a variety of dietary restraint measures show an increased risk for future onset of binge eating and eating pathology. Most of these prospective studies were methodologically rigorous, in that many involved large representative samples, used a long follow-up period, achieved a low attrition rate, and used validated structured diagnostic interviews to assess eating pathology. There has been less support for the assertion that elevated dietary restraint increases risk for persistence of bulimic symptoms, in that dieting measures did not predict persistence of binge eating in three studies, but did predict persistence of compensatory behaviors in two of these studies.

Because self-reported dieting has emerged as a potent and consistent risk factor for eating pathology, numerous researchers and clinicians assert that dieting is causally related to BN (Fairburn, 1997; Heatherton & Polivy, 1992; Levine & Smolak, 2006; Neumark-Sztainer et al., 2006). Indeed, some have called for a moratorium on dieting because of the belief that it contributes to eating pathology and have evaluated interventions that decrease dietary restriction (Bacon, et al., 2002; Polivy & Herman, 1992). In addition, many ED prevention programs strongly discourage dieting (e.g., Smolak, Levine, & Schermer, 1998; Stewart, Carter, Drinkwater, Hainsworth, & Fairburn, 2001).

Experimental Studies of the Relation of Short-Term Caloric Restriction to Laboratory-Based Eating

Only two studies have examined the effects of experimentally manipulated acute caloric deprivation on bulimic symptoms. Because both studies focused on individuals with EDs, these experiments are considered tests of whether acute dietary restriction is a maintenance factor for binge eating. Telch and Agras (1996) found that 6-hour caloric deprivation did not result in significantly greater self-reported binge eating episodes among women with BN, BED, or obesity relative to a no-deprivation control condition during a standard multi-item buffet. Agras and Telch (1998) found that 14-hour caloric deprivation, relative to a no-deprivation control condition, produced significant increases in investigator coded binge eating, but not self-labeled binge eating, in women with BED. To date, no laboratory-based experiment has investigated the effects of caloric deprivation on all of the *Diagnostic and Statistical Manual-IV* (*DSM-IV*, American Psychiatric Association [APA], 1994) symptoms of BN.

Experiments that examined the effects of caloric deprivation on caloric intake in the lab (rather than binge eating) have also produced mixed findings. Short-term caloric deprivation (4–24 hours), relative to no deprivation control conditions, resulted in elevated ad libitum caloric intake among women and men without EDs in two experiments (Mauler, Hamm, Weike, & Tuschen-Caffier, 2006; Spiegel, Shrager, & Steller, 1989), but this effect did not emerge in three other experiments (Hetherington, Stoner, Andersen, & Rolls, 2000; Schachter, Goldman, & Gordon, 1968; Spiegel et al., 1989). Experiments have also found that short-term caloric deprivation produces significantly elevated caloric intake among women with BN (Hetherington et al., 2000; Mauler et al., 2006), but this effect did not replicate in another sample of women with BN or for individuals with binge/purge subtype of AN in the experiment conducted by Hetherington and associates (2000). Assignment to longer periods of dietary restriction (2 days to 8 weeks), versus no-diet control conditions, resulted in significantly elevated acute caloric intake in young women in one experiment in two settings chosen to represent those in which dieters have been found to overeat (e.g., after consumption of high-calorie food and during stress; Wardle & Beales, 1988), but this effect did not replicate in three other experiments (Lowe, 1992, 1994; Lowe, Foster, Kerzhnerman, Swain, & Wadden, 2001).

In sum, experiments indicate that short-term caloric deprivation did not have consistent effects on binge eating among eating disordered participants or on general caloric intake among eating disordered and nondisordered participants. These studies have generally been methodologically sound, although the moderate samples sizes may have limited the ability to detect small effects. In addition, it is possible that because participants knew that their eating behavior was being assessed in the laboratory, they altered their eating owing to social desirability biases. Moreover, because they were asked by an experimenter to diet for a specified period of time, this may have reduced dieters' internal motivation for restricting their intake.

Experimental Studies of the Relation of Longer-Term Dieting to Eating Disorder Symptoms

Randomized trials have also examined the effects of long-term weight loss diets on changes in binge eating and bulimic symptoms among in various populations. One trial found that assignment to a 20-week low-calorie weight loss intervention, which resulted in significant weight loss, produced significantly greater decreases in binge eating from pre to post among overweight women relative to an assessment-only control condition (Klem, Wing, Simkin-Silverman, & Kuller, 1997). This intervention focused on making modest changes in intake of dietary fat and cholesterol and prescribed a 1300- or 1500- calorie meal plan. However, another small experiment found that assignment to various energy-deficit diets did not result in significant changes in binge eating relative to a weight maintenance comparison condition (Redman, Martin, Williamson, & Ravussin, 2008). It is noteworthy that the weight loss interventions evaluated in this trial resulted in a 10% reduction in body mass, making it the study that has investigated the most intensive weight loss diet to date. Uncontrolled trials have also found that assignment to low-calorie diet interventions that produced weight loss were associated with significant decreases in binge eating among overweight men, women, and preadolescent girls (Epstein, Paluch, Saelens, Ernst, & Wilfley, 2001; Foster, Wadden, Kendall, Stunkard, & Vogt, 1996; Schlundt, Hill, Sbrocco, Pope-Cordle, & Sharp, 1992; Telch & Agras, 1993; Wadden, Foster, & Letizia, 1994; Wardle, Waller, & Rapoport, 2001), with one exception (Braet, Tanghe, De Bode, Franckx, & VanWinckel, 2003). It is important to note that participants in these weight loss treatments

are invited to meet regularly in groups with supportive clinicians to assist them in achieving their weight loss goals, which is unrepresentative of weight loss attempts made outside of treatment settings.

Experimental psychopathology trials have examined the effects of weight loss diet interventions on bulimic symptoms. Presnell and Stice (2003) found that young women assigned to a 6-week weight loss diet intervention, which resulted in significant weight loss, showed significantly greater reductions in bulimic symptoms and binge eating during the dieting intervention relative to waitlist controls. Groesz and Stice (2007) found that young women assigned to a 6-week weight loss diet intervention or a 6-week weight loss intervention that prescribed consuming frequent small meals, both of which produced significant weight loss, showed significantly greater reductions in bulimic symptoms and binge eating during the dieting intervention relative to assessment-only controls. The weight loss interventions examined in these trials involved group meetings in which research staff helped participants achieve the recommended 1200 calorie a day diet.

One randomized controlled prevention trial found that a weight maintenance diet intervention that promoted lasting moderate reductions in caloric intake and increases in exercise to balance caloric intake with expenditure during 4 weekly meetings, which significantly reduced risk for weight gain and onset of obesity over 3-year follow-up, produced significant reductions in ED symptoms and risk for future onset of threshold and subthreshold EDs, relative to assessment-only controls (Stice, Marti, Spoor, Presnell, & Shaw, 2008). Although there was evidence that participants in this weight maintenance intervention showed significantly lower risk for onset of obesity relative to an expressive-writing alternative intervention through 1-year follow-up, the significant reduction in eating pathology in the former group relative to the latter group only persisted through 6-month follow-up (Stice, Shaw, Burton, & Wade, 2006).

Randomized treatment trials have also examined the effects of weight loss dieting interventions among individuals with BN or binge eating disturbances. Two controlled trials found that assignment to a low-calorie weight loss diet (e.g., 1200 calories a day), relative to waitlist control conditions, resulted in significantly greater decreases in binge eating for overweight and obese women who endorsed initial binge eating (Goodrick, Poston, Kimball, Reeves & Foreyt, 1998; Reeves et al., 2001). Both interventions used behavioral self-control methods including self-monitoring, stimulus control, social support, problem solving and goal setting, and relapse prevention in weekly meetings with clinicians. However, the low-calorie interventions did not result in weight loss in these trials. Another trial found that assignment to a 6-week weight loss diet intervention, which resulted in significant weight loss that persisted through 3-month follow-up, produced significantly greater reductions in binge eating and compensatory behaviors, as well as higher remission rates, through 3-month follow-up among women with threshold or subthreshold BN than observed in wait-list controls (Burton & Stice, 2006). This trial evaluated a healthy weight intervention, in which participants met 6 times weekly in groups with a clinician who helped them make the recommended reductions in caloric intake and increases in physical activity.

Interestingly, one randomized trial that compared a group behavioral weight loss diet intervention to cognitive behavioral therapy (CBT) among overweight patients with BED found that both interventions were associated with similar statistically significant reductions in binge eating by 12-month follow-up, though CBT produced significantly larger reductions in this outcome at posttest (Munsch et al., 2007). Nauta, Hospers, Kok, and Jansen (2000) likewise found that cognitive therapy and a low-calorie weight loss intervention were similarly effective in reducing binge eating. A third randomized trial found that obese BED patients assigned to a very-low-calorie (800 kcal/day) weight loss intervention showed similar reductions in binge eating to patients assigned to a very-low-calorie weight loss intervention that included CBT to reduce binge eating (de Zwaan et al., 2005). However, Grilo and Masheb (2005) found that guided self-help CBT produced superior reductions in binge eating compared to guided self-help weight loss intervention or an assessment-only control condition, suggesting that the guided self-help modality may be more effective for CBT than for weight loss interventions. Thus, having group support during a weight loss intervention may contribute to greater reductions in binge eating, which may not generalize to individuals who diet on their own. A four-arm trial that randomized BN patients to standard CBT, a physical exercise intervention (which resulted in significant weight loss that persisted through 18-month follow-up), a nutritional counseling control group, or a waitlist control group found that participants in the CBT and exercise interventions showed significant improvements

relative to the nutritional control and waitlist control conditions by 18-month follow-up (Sundgot-Borgen, Rosenvinge, Bahr, & Schneider, 2002). Of note, the exercise intervention produced significantly greater reductions in bulimic symptoms at posttest and 18-month follow-up relative to CBT; 62% of the exercise intervention participants no longer met diagnostic criteria for BN, compared to 36% of the CBT participants at 18-month follow up.

Two additional trials evaluated interventions that sought to manipulate dieting. Bacon and associates (2002) examined the effects of assigning obese participants to a traditional low-calorie weight loss diet or to a nondiet intervention that promoted increased exercise and body acceptance, presented psychoeducational material on nutrition and healthy eating, and provided social support; participants in both interventions showed reductions in binge eating, which did not differ across groups. Those in the nondieting intervention may have shown decreases in binge eating because this intervention provided psychoeducational material on healthy eating and promoted healthy weight control behaviors (exercise) or because of regression to the mean, the passage of time, or pretest sensitization. Wadden and associates (2004) compared two low-calorie diets to a nondieting intervention that promoted increased physical activity, provided psychoeducational material on dieting, and used cognitive interventions to promote body acceptance; however, there was no evidence of differential change across conditions in binge eating for obese individuals who were initially free of binge eating. The fact that all participants were free of binge eating at baseline made it impossible to detect the decreases in bulimic symptoms, which were observed in the dieting conditions of other trials. Irrespectively, the dieting interventions in both trials resulted in significant reductions in weight relative to participants in the nondieting conditions, suggesting that the low-calorie dieting conditions resulted in a greater negative energy balance overall than the nondieting conditions, yet did not provoke the increases in binge eating that would be expected based on the dietary restraint theory. A noteworthy aspect of these null findings was that the nondieting interventions used in these trials were based on the program developed by Polivy and Herman (1992).

Animal Studies of the Effects of Caloric Deprivation on Caloric Intake

Experiments with animals have also investigated the effects of caloric deprivation on subsequent caloric intake. Rats randomized to extreme caloric deprivation conditions (in which they lost 15%–20% of their body mass) consume significantly more calories during ad libitum feeding immediately after the deprivation period than nondeprived control rats (e.g., Ogawa et al., 2005; Sterritt, 1962). Rats assigned to a moderate caloric restriction condition (in which they lost 7%–9% of their body mass) consumed significantly more calories in the 4 hours immediately after the period of deprivation but did not show significantly different caloric intake during the 24 hours after the deprivation period relative to nonrestricted rats (Hagan, Chandler, Wauford, Rybak, & Oswald, 2003). Several experiments found that rats assigned to cycles of caloric restriction and refeeding did not show significantly different ad libitum caloric intake after refeeding relative to controls (Boggiano et al., 2005; Hagan et al., 2002; Hagan et al., 2003). Thus, there is some evidence that severe caloric restriction results in elevated caloric intake immediately after the deprivation period, which is logical given that the animals did not elect to restrict their caloric intake, and therefore were compensating for the missed calories. Although experiments with animals allow greater experimental control over caloric restriction manipulations and are immune to demand characteristics, they have questionable generalizability to humans, given that the animal studies involve involuntary food restriction, which may be very different than the voluntary dietary restriction practiced by humans. In addition, these studies did not assess bulimic symptoms, so it is unclear whether these findings can provide information about whether dietary restriction is related to bulimic pathology.

Within this context, we should also comment on the Keys, Brozek, Henschel, Mickelsen, and Taylor (1950) uncontrolled laboratory study of a semistarvation diet designed to mimic the experience of prisoners of war, in which 36 healthy male conscientious objectors participated in a 6-month period of caloric deprivation during which they lost 25% of their initial body weight. Although participants reported binge eating during the refeeding phase of this study, a semistarvation diet among adult males forced to participate in an experiment may not generalize to the typical weight loss dieting voluntarily practiced by people in Western cultures. Moreover, there is no evidence that self-initiated weight loss diets practiced by adolescent girls and women results in weight loss that even approaches the degree of weight loss observed in the Keys study.

In sum, eight randomized controlled trials found that assignment to a low-calorie weight loss or weight maintenance diet resulted in significantly greater reductions in binge eating and bulimic symptoms relative to assignment to a assessment-only control condition. Assignment to a weight maintenance diet also resulted in significantly greater reductions in bulimic symptoms than assignment to a placebo control condition. Results from several noncontrolled intervention trials also indicated that assignment to weight loss diet interventions produced reductions in binge eating and bulimic symptoms, though one study did not replicate this effect. Three trials found that low-calorie weight loss diet interventions were as effective as CBT, the current treatment of choice, in reducing binge eating among obese binge eaters. However, one study that used a self-help format suggested that CBT produced superior effects and another trial found that an exercise intervention that resulted in weight loss produced greater reductions in bulimic symptoms than did CBT among patients with BN. Two trials that compared a low-calorie diet to a nondieting intervention did not produce evidence of significantly greater increases in bulimic symptoms in the former condition relative to the latter condition, as would be expected based on the dietary restraint theory. Most of these studies were methodologically rigorous, in that these trials and experiments were adequately powered, achieved a low attrition rate, and used state-of-the-art structured diagnostic interviews to assess bulimic symptoms. However, one limitation of this literature is that only one of these trials used a placebo control condition. It is noteworthy that some of these trials imply that weight loss dieting may represent an efficacious treatment for BN and that weight maintenance dieting may represent an efficacious prevention intervention for eating pathology.

Incompatible Findings

On the one hand, prospective studies have provided consistent evidence that individuals with elevated scores on various dietary restraint measures show an increased risk for future onset of and increases in binge eating, bulimic symptoms, and eating pathology. These studies seem to provide support for the dietary restraint model of eating pathology. On the other hand, the experimental studies produced findings that appear incompatible with those from the prospective studies. Although the experiments that examined the effects of acute caloric restriction on laboratory-assessed binge eating produced mixed effects that were difficult to interpret, eight controlled trials and experiments produced effects indicating that assignment to longer-term weight loss or weight maintenance diets resulted in significantly greater reductions in binge eating and bulimic symptoms than assignment to assessment-only control conditions, and one weight maintenance diet produced greater reductions in bulimic symptoms than a placebo control condition. Most of these trials and experiments verified that the participants showed weight loss or weight maintenance, providing confirmation that dietary restraint was successfully manipulated. These latter findings appear incompatible with the dietary restraint model of eating pathology. These contradictory findings from prospective and experimental studies are troubling because they have opposing public health implications. If dieting increases risk for bulimic symptoms, prevention programs and treatment interventions should attempt to decrease dieting and alternative nondieting treatments for obesity should be developed. In contrast, if dieting reduces risk for bulimic symptoms, prevention programs and treatment interventions should help individuals diet more effectively, which should yield positive effects for both eating pathology and obesity. Thus, we feel it is critical to understand why these inconsistent findings emerged.

There are several possible explanations for the contradictory findings between the prospective studies reporting that elevated dietary restraint scores predict future onset of bulimic symptoms and the experimental finding that assignment to weight loss diets result in decreased bulimic symptoms. Below, we discuss various explanations, review supporting evidence, consider the implications of each explanation, and propose studies that may help evaluate the veracity of these different explanations for the inconsistent findings.

Prospective Studies Are More Vulnerable to Confounding Variables than Experiments

One possible explanation for the contradictory findings between the prospective and experimental studies is suggested by the fact that these two types of research designs differ in their inferential power. The major weakness of prospective studies is that it is always possible that some omitted third variable accounts for any prospective effect observed in a longitudinal study. That is, some confound may actually cause both elevated dieting and elevated bulimic symptoms. In contrast, randomized experiments were developed to rule out third variable alternative explanations. The reason that researchers

randomly assign participants to conditions is to create groups that are equivalent on all potential confounds (known or unknown), which theoretically allows the investigator to isolate the effect of the one variable that is manipulated (because potential confounds should be uncorrelated with treatment condition). Although random assignment can fail in creating initially equivalent groups on all potential confounds, particularly if the cell sizes are small, this is the best available tool to rule out third variable confounds, even when these potential confounds are not identified or known by the researcher. Thus, because randomized experiments are particularly effective for ruling out third variable explanations and prospective studies are not, the positive relation of self-reported dieting to increases in eating pathology may have emerged because some third variable increases the risk for both variables.

One troubling aspect of this explanation for the inconsistent findings, however, is that the findings from the prospective and experimental studies are consistently in the *opposite direction*. Typically when prospective effects are due to an omitted confounding variable, experimental studies that manipulate the independent variable would not produce any effects on the dependent variable.

This potential explanation for the inconsistent findings has several implications for future research. First, this interpretation suggests that it will be vital to use randomized experiments to investigate the relation of dietary restraint to eating pathology because this design permits greater inferential confidence than prospective studies. It will be important for researchers to maximize the ecological validity of these experiments and to include placebo control conditions and objective measures of ED symptoms, which should reduce the risk that demand characteristics or expectancies account for the apparent intervention effects and to include manipulation checks. Second, this interpretation suggests that it will be vital to search for potential third variable confounds that explain the relation between self-reported dieting and future increases in bulimic symptoms observed in the prospective studies. We suspect it will be particularly important for this line of research to use objective measures of potential third variable confounds. We argue that it would be ideal to then manipulate potential confounds in randomized experiments to confirm their causal relation to dieting and ED symptoms. Third, this interpretation suggests that researchers should utilize randomized experiments to confirm the causal status of other putative risk factors for eating pathology because it appears that an exclusive reliance on prospective studies may produce questionable inferences. For example, experimental trials that have evaluated interventions that reduce thin-ideal internalization, body dissatisfaction, and negative affect have found that bulimic symptoms are also reduced (Bearman, Stice, & Chase, 2003; Burton, Stice, Bearman, & Rohde, 2007; Stice, Presnell, Gau, & Shaw, 2007).

Dietary Restriction Interventions May Be Unrepresentative of Real-World Dieting

Another possible explanation for the inconsistent results from the prospective and experimental studies is that the weight loss diets evaluated in the experiments involve more extreme dietary restriction than is typical of weight loss dieting as practiced in the real world. That is, perhaps real-world dietary restriction is simply less effective than most weight loss interventions, which is why the two types of studies produce different effects on change in ED symptoms.

Although this explanation holds intuitive appeal, it does not appear to be a satisfactory account for the inconsistent findings for several reasons. First, if self-initiated diets are simply less effective than the weight loss diets evaluated in the experiments, then one would predict that the effects from the prospective studies would be smaller than the effects from the experiments involving prescribed diets, but in the same direction; yet, the effects from the prospective studies are consistently in the *opposite direction* relative to those from the experimental studies. Second, both lower intensity weight maintenance interventions (Klem et al., 1997; Stice, Shaw, Burton, et al., 2006) and higher intensity weight loss interventions (Groesz & Stice, 2007; Presnell & Stice, 2003) produce significant reductions in binge eating and bulimic symptoms. This pattern of findings implies that even more modest weight control diets reduce ED symptoms. Third, the weight loss observed in the experimental trials that evaluated prescribed weight loss diets was small. These trials observed that participants lost an average of 0.14 kg per week (0.3 lbs). Fourth, the weight loss and weight maintenance diets from the experiments were similar in duration (mode = 1.5 months, range 1–18 months) to the reported duration of weight loss diets practiced in the real world (mode = 1 month, range 1 week–6 months; Emmons, 1992; French et al., 1999; Williamson et al., 1992). It is important to note that two of the weight loss interventions that produced reductions in binge eating in the

controlled experimental trials (Goodrick et al., 1998; Reeves et al., 2001) involved weight loss diets that were equal to or exceeded the length of the Keys and associates study (1950), as much interpretational weight has been placed on this latter uncontrolled trial. These considerations imply that it is unlikely that the experimental studies produced different findings from the prospective studies because the weight loss interventions evaluated in the former were more extreme than the typical weight loss diets used in the real world.

Nonetheless, we conducted an experiment that sought to provide a more ecologically valid test of whether weight loss dieting as practiced in the real world results in decreased bulimic symptoms. We focused on young women who reported at least intermittent dieting in the past year because we were only interested in generalizing the results to women who voluntarily engage in weight loss dieting. We randomly assigned participants to a condition in which they were asked to engage in their typical weight loss dieting behaviors for 1 month or to a condition in which they were asked to refrain from engaging in their usual weight loss dieting behaviors for 1 month (Presnell, Stice, & Tristan, 2007). A manipulation check confirmed that participants in the dieting as usual condition reported significantly more days of dieting during the 4-week period than those in the nondieting control condition, which corresponded to a large effect ($r = .74$). Unexpectedly, participants assigned to the usual weight loss dieting condition showed no weight loss, but participants assigned to the no dieting condition gained a significant amount of weight. These findings imply that typical weight loss dieting may not result in weight loss and further that most dieters may simply be transiently curbing an overeating tendency when they are dieting on their own in the real world. There were no significant differences in change in bulimic symptoms over time across conditions, suggesting that ineffective weight loss dieting has no impact on bulimic behaviors. This is an important point because it has been argued that it is unsuccessful dieting, rather than successful dieting, that increases risk for bulimic pathology (Heatherton et al., 1988). These results provide evidence that weight loss diets evaluated in the experimental trials may not be representative of the real-world dieting, but provide no support to the assertion that real-world dieting results in increased bulimic symptoms (despite adequate power), as suggested by the prospective studies that are ostensibly studying real-world dieting.

One other factor that limits the ecological validity of the weight loss and weight maintenance diet interventions evaluated in the experimental trials is that participants typically meet in groups with a supportive professional who help them make the recommended reductions in caloric intake and increases in physical activity. Although some interventions involved as little as 3 hours of contact, this is not something that most participants who engage in weight loss or weight maintenance diets outside of treatment settings typically do, nor are they accountable for their weight loss. The evidence that participants typically show reductions in binge eating in behavioral weight loss interventions involving group meetings with professionals (Munsch et al., 2007; Nauta et al., 2000), but not when participants use a self-help book with similar content (Grilo & Masheb, 2005), implies that these meetings may play an important role in the reductions in binge eating. In addition, the fact that participants in weight loss interventions from the experimental trials typically showed reductions in bulimic symptoms, whereas those who dieted as usual in the naturalistic dieting experiment did not, might also be interpreted as providing evidence for the importance of contact with supportive professionals.

In sum, there is preliminary evidence that the weight loss diet interventions evaluated in prior experiments are not representative of real-world weight loss dieting, in that the findings from Presnell et al. (2007) suggest that most real-world dieters may be transiently curbing an overeating tendency when they diet for weight loss purposes, but do not typically experience weight loss. However, there was no support for the assertion that this explains the inconsistent findings that have emerged from prospective and experimental studies, as ineffective real-world weight loss dieting did not result in increased bulimic symptoms. It will be vital to replicate the experimental evidence that most people engaging in weight loss dieting in the real world do not achieve the state of negative energy balance necessary for weight loss and that they may be temporarily curbing an overeating tendency because we think these two findings explain several vexing patterns of findings that have emerged in this literature. It would be useful for future experiments that manipulate real-world weight loss dieting to involve adolescent girls, as this is typically when bulimic symptoms emerge. These types of studies may also afford a unique approach for investigating whether particular dieting behaviors practiced in the real world are more effective than others in producing weight loss and whether particular dieting behaviors predict increases in bulimic symptoms.

Another factor that undermines the ecological validity of the weight loss diet interventions is that they typically involved group meetings with supportive professionals, which does not occur in dieting practiced in the real world. It would be useful for future controlled trials to investigate the impact of group meetings with professionals on change in ED symptoms among those assigned to weight loss diet interventions.

Researchers May Have Used Invalid Measures of Dietary Restraint

A third possible explanation for the conflicting findings is that the prospective studies that found dieting predicted future onset of or increases in bulimic pathology may have used invalid measures of dieting. This possibility is suggested by the fact that studies have found that people routinely under-report caloric intake and that this under-reporting is particularly acute for those with elevated scores on dieting scales and elevated body weight (Bandini, Schoeller, Cyr, & Dietz, 1990; Lichtman, Pisarska, Berman, & Pestone, 1992; Livingstone et al., 1990). It seems possible that people might also provide biased reports of dieting behaviors. In addition, several studies have found that individuals with high scores on dietary restraint scales gain more weight over time than people with low scores (Klesges, Isbell, & Klesges, 1992; Klesges, Klem, & Bene, 1989; Stice, Cameron, et al., 1999; Stice, Presnell, Shaw, & Rohde, 2005; Tanofsky-Kraff et al., 2007). Similarly, there is evidence that self-identified weight loss dieters show elevated rates of weight gain and onset of obesity relative to those who do not identify as weight loss dieters (French, Jeffery, Forster, et al., 1994; Neumark-Sztainer et al., 2006). These data also seem to suggest that these measures are not identifying individuals who are engaging in actual dietary restriction.

We conducted a series of unobtrusive observational studies that examined the validity of dietary restraint scales (Stice et al., 2004). We investigated the Restraint Scale (RS; Polivy et al. 1978), Three Factor Eating Questionnaire Restraint scale (TFEQ-R; Stunkard & Messick, 1985), Dutch Restrained Eating Scale (DRES; van Strien et al., 1986), Eating Disorder Examination-Questionnaire-Restraint scale (EDEQ-R; Fairburn & Beglin, 1994), and the Dietary Intent Scale (DIS; Stice, 1998). We used caloric intake as the criterion because the original validity studies concluded that these scales were valid measures of dietary restriction because they correlated inversely with self-reported caloric intake (French, Jeffery, & Wing, 1994; Kirkley, Burge, & Ammerman, 1988; Neumark-Sztainer, Jeffery, & French, 1997; van Strien et al., 1986; Wardle & Beales, 1987).

We conducted four studies that varied in food types consumed, settings examined, and populations studied. Commonly used dietary restraint scales were not inversely correlated with caloric intake, as was suggested by the original validity studies that relied on self-reported caloric intake. These dieting scales only showed weak correlations with caloric intake during eating episodes across four studies and virtually none of these correlations were statistically significant (mean $r = -.07$, range: $-.34$ to $.20$; Stice et al., 2004). Other independent studies have likewise found that these dietary restraint scales did not show the expected inverse correlations with objectively measured caloric intake during single eating episodes (Hetherington et al., 2000; Jansen, 1996; Ouwens, van Strien, & van der Staak, 2003; Sysko, Walsh, & Wilson, 2007; van Strien, Cleven, & Schippers, 2000).

Several studies examined multiple objective assessments of caloric intake, which should provide a more stable index of eating behaviors. Rolls and colleagues (1997) found that normal weight adults with high versus low scores on the TFEQ-R did not show significant differences in caloric intake during three meals and a snack consumed during a 20-hour monitoring period in the laboratory. Jansen and associates (2003) found the Eating Disorder Examination-Restraint scale (EDE-R, Fairburn & Cooper, 1993) did not significantly correlate with observed caloric intake during three separate taste tests involving snack foods for normal weight preadolescents. Martin and associates (2005) found that the TFEQ-restraint scale did not correlate with observed caloric intake during four healthy meals that were eaten in a laboratory setting by normal weight young women over a 1-month period. Sysko, Walsh, Schebendach, and Wilson (2005) found that the TFEQ-restraint scale, DIS, EDEQ-restraint scale, and EDE-restraint scale did not significantly correlate with observed caloric intake of a yogurt shake eaten in a laboratory setting by young women with AN or normal weight control women during two separate sessions. Stice, Cooper, Schoeller, Tappe, and Lowe (2007) found that the TFEQ-restraint scale did not correlate significantly with objectively measured caloric intake during lunch meals consumed in work cafeterias over a 3-month period.

Other studies used doubly labeled water (DLW) to assess longer-term caloric intake. DLW uses isotopic tracers to measure total carbon dioxide production, which can be used to generate accurate estimates total caloric expenditure and total caloric intake over a 2- week period. Bathalon et al. (2000) found that normal weight women with high scores on the TFEQ-restraint scale did not consume significantly fewer calories over a 2-week period than weight-matched women with low scores on this scale. Tuschl, Platte, Laessle, Stichler, and Pirke (1990) found a nonsignificant correlation between the TFEQ-restraint scale and DLW assessments of total caloric intake over a 2-week period. Stice, Cooper, et al., (2007) found that the TFEQ-restraint scale did not correlate significantly with DLW assessments of total caloric intake over a 2-week period in a sample of overweight women or in a sample of normal-weight women.

Collectively, these findings indicate that individuals with elevated scores on dietary restraint measures do not consume less food than individuals with low scores on these scales. Similar findings emerged in studies that used objective measures of caloric intake during single eating episodes, intake during multiple eating episodes, intake over a 2-week observational period, or intake at workplace cafeterias over a 3-month period. These data imply that dietary restraint scales do not assess dietary restriction as suggested by validation studies that relied on self-reported caloric intake (French et al., 1994; Kirkley et al., 1988; Neumark-Sztainer et al., 1997; van Strien et al., 1986; Wardle & Beales, 1987) and the item content of these scales. These findings are troubling because they suggest that virtually all previous studies on dietary restraint have used invalid measures of dieting and that this literature should therefore be reinterpreted in this light. Also of note, these findings provide no support for Heatherton and associates' (1988) suggestion that the Restraint Scale (Herman & Mack, 1975) assesses unsuccessful dietary restriction and that other dietary restraint measures, such as the Dutch Restrained Eating scale (van Strien et al., 1986), and the TFEQ restraint scale (Stunkard & Messick, 1985), assess successful dieting; the validity data suggest that none of these widely used measures identify successful dieters.

One explanation for the evidence that dietary restraint scales show significant inverse correlations with self-reported caloric intake, but nonsignificant relations with objectively measures caloric intake is social desirability bias. Because weight management is socially valued in Western culture and obesity is stigmatized, people may over-report dieting behaviors. This interpretation converges with evidence that under-reporting of caloric intake is greater for overweight versus lean individuals (Prentice et al., 1986).

These validity findings seem to provide a compelling explanation for why the prospective studies and experimental studies have produced inconsistent findings; although the experiments were examining the effects of confirmed calorie-deficit diets, the prospective studies were examining individuals who do not appear to be on a caloric-deficit diet necessary for weight loss. That is, the experiments appear to have been examining individuals on energy-deficit weight loss diets, whereas the prospective studies were not.

One puzzling aspect of this explanation, however, is why individuals who are either unable to achieve a true caloric-deficit diet or who want to give the impression that they are on such a diet are at increased risk for onset of binge eating and bulimic pathology. If the dietary restraint measures are invalid, such that individuals with high dietary restraint scores do not eat less than those with low dietary restraint scores, it seems that the prospective studies should simply have produced null findings with regard to the relation between dietary restraint scales and future bulimic pathology. However, the fact that the prospective studies have observed significant positive relations between initial scores on dietary restraint measures and future increases in bulimic pathology implies that these scales assess a latent construct, other than energy-deficit dieting, which increases the risk for future onset of bulimic pathology. That is, although it is tempting to dismiss the findings from the prospective studies because they appear to have used invalid measures of dietary restriction, one fact remains: These scales have strikingly consistent predictive validity for future development of bulimic pathology.

This analysis suggests that self-reported dietary restriction is a *proxy risk factor* for bulimic pathology, but that the nature of the true latent construct that is tapped by these scales has yet to be identified. A proxy risk factor is a variable that predicts a pathological outcome not because it has any causal relation to the development of pathology, but because it correlates with a true causal risk factor for the pathology (Kraemer, Stice, Kazdin, Offord, & Kupfer, 2001). Thus, we argue that a key research priority will be to elucidate the latent factor, or factors, tapped by dietary restraint scales, which increase risk for onset of bulimic pathology.

One other intriguing implication of the validity findings is that dietary restraint scales may assess *relative dietary restriction* rather than *absolute dietary restriction*. That is, these scales may be identifying people who are curbing an overeating tendency, but who are not actually achieving the negative energy balance necessary for weight loss. Because these individuals are eating less than they normally eat or less then they desire, they may perceive this relative restriction as dietary restraint despite the fact that they are not achieving the negative energy balance necessary for weight loss. This interpretation is consistent with the evidence that (1) intermittent dieters temporarily arrest a weight gain trajectory while they are attempting to engage in a weight loss diet, but do not show weight loss (Presnell et al., 2007); (2) individuals with elevated dietary restraint scores consumed significantly more calories than those with low dietary restraint scores in one study, but did not feel that they had overeaten (Jansen, 1996); and (3) dietary restraint scores often increase when individuals are placed on low-calorie diets relative to controls who are not placed on weight loss diets (Groesz & Stice, 2007; Williamson et al., 2007). Others have suggested that many dieters are eating less than they desire rather than restricting their dietary intake sufficiently to produce a negative energy balance and therefore only perceive that they are on a weight loss diet (Lowe & Levine, 2005; Timmerman & Gregg, 2003). The evidence that individuals with elevated dieting scores are more likely to gain weight over time relative to individuals with lower dietary restraint scores (French et al., 1994; Klesges et al., 1992; Stice, Cameron, et al., 1999; Tanofsky-Kraff et al., 2007) suggests that they are not only unsuccessful at reducing their caloric intake below their energy needs on a sustained basis, but are also unable to consistently avoid consumption beyond their energy needs and therefore gain weight over time (Lowe & Levine, 2005).

Only Certain Dietary Behaviors Increase Risk for Bulimic Pathology

Another possible explanation for the conflicting findings is that the weight loss interventions evaluated in the experiments promote healthy dietary behaviors, but that it is unhealthy dietary behaviors, which may be more common in weight loss diets that occur outside of weight loss interventions, that lead to bulimic pathology onset. That is, if weight loss efforts outside of treatment settings typically involve unhealthy weight control behaviors, this might explain why self-reported dietary restriction that does not occur in the context of weight loss interventions increases risk for eating pathology onset.

One way to explore this possibility is to systematically manipulate suspected unhealthy weight control behaviors experimentally because this approach would provide a rigorous test of whether these behaviors are related to bulimic symptoms. The National Task Force on the Prevention and Treatment of Obesity (2000) and others (Neumark-Sztainer, Butler, & Palti, 1995) have categorized meal skipping as an unhealthy dietary technique because it is associated with poor nutritional intake and increased consumption of higher calorie foods at subsequent feedings (de Castro & Elmore, 1988; Morgan, Zabik, & Stampley, 1986). Meal skipping may increase risk for binge eating because it results in greater reinforcement from eating (Epstein, Truesdale, et al., 2003; Raynor & Epstein, 2003) and increases attention to food (Placanica, Faunce & Job, 2002). Data indicate that 35% of adult dieters and 50% of adolescent dieters report skipping meals for weight loss purposes (Emmons, 1992; French et al., 1999; Wardle, Griffith, Johnson, & Rapoport, 2000), suggesting that this may be, the most common unhealthy weight control behavior practiced outside of formal weight loss interventions.

One study that manipulated meal skipping randomly assigned obese women to a 12-week low-calorie diet that either prescribed consumption of three meals a day or to a 12-week low-calorie diet that that prescribed consumption of two meals a day (Schlundt et al., 1992). Although a manipulation check indicated that participants in the meal skipping condition reported eating significantly fewer meals, there was no effect on change in binge eating or body mass over the 12-week study. A second study manipulated meal frequency by randomizing young women to a weight loss diet intervention that encouraged consumption of many small meals (four to five) throughout the day or to a standard weight loss intervention, in which it was assumed that many participants would skip meals based on prior findings (Groesz & Stice, 2007). Participants were told to consume 1200 calories a day in both conditions. A manipulation check indicated that participants in the many small meals condition consumed significantly more meals per day on average (3.8 meals per day) than participants in the latter condition (2.8 meals per day), which accounted for 42% of the variance in meal frequency. However, there was no significant effect on change on binge eating, bulimic symptoms, or weight over the 6-week intervention period.

Another unhealthy weight control method is fasting (skipping two or more meals in a row for weight loss purposes). It is possible that a small subset of individuals with elevated dietary restraint scales engage in fasting that produces severe weight loss and increases risk for bulimic pathology (Stice, Davis, et al., 2008). Given that full threshold BN emerges in only about 2% of young women, but that 40% to 60% of adolescent girls report engaging in weight loss dieting, it is conceivable that some particularly unhealthy weight control behavior practiced by a small subset of dieters, such as fasting, could account for the emergence of bulimic symptoms. Experiments have confirmed that enforced periods of caloric deprivation results in greater reinforcement value of food, as assessed by operant tasks that measure how hard participants will work to earn food and as assessed by caloric intake (Epstein, Truesdale et al., 2003; Raynor & Epstein, 2003). Animal studies also suggest that marked caloric restriction increases risk for subsequent overeating (e.g., Sterritt, 1962; Ogawa et al., 2005). In support of this interpretation, fasting was a more potent risk factor for future onset of binge eating and bulimic pathology relative to dietary restraint scores (Stice, Davis, et al., 2008a).

Given the importance of resolving the nature of the relation between dieting and bulimic pathology, additional prospective and experimental tests of the effects of fasting are warranted. First, researchers should test whether self-reported fasting and other unhealthy weight loss behaviors that result in documented weight loss increase risk for future increases in binge eating and bulimic symptoms using prospective studies. It may be prudent to use objective methods (e.g., doubly labeled water) to confirm that such weight loss was achieved by a reduction in caloric intake rather than an increase in caloric expenditure. Second, this account would predict that among those in the dieting as usual condition of naturalistic dieting experiments (e.g., Presnell et al., 2007), the subset of participants that showed marked weight loss should show greater pretest to posttest increases in binge eating than those who do not show weight loss. More generally, the naturalistic dieting experimental paradigm appears to offer a useful way of testing whether particular dieting behaviors practiced in the real world actually predict increases in binge eating and bulimic symptoms. It is important to acknowledge that commonly-used variable-centered analyses, such as repeated measures analysis of variance models and regression models, which focus on average effects, may not be well suited to detecting the effects of extreme fasting, which is presumably practiced by only a small subset of self-labeled dieters. Thus, it might be useful to conduct growth mixture models that test for qualitatively distinct weight change trajectory groups among self-labeled weight loss dieters, with the goal of determining whether there is a subgroup of participants who do show marked weight loss over time. However, because prospective studies are vulnerable to third-variable alternative explanations, it will be important for research to examine the effects of experimentally manipulating any potentially unhealthy weight control behaviors suggested by the prospective analyses, such as fasting (preferably by decreasing these behaviors).

In sum, there is no experimental support for the supposition that unhealthy dieting, characterized by meal skipping or frequency, increases risk for binge eating or bulimic symptoms. However, only two experiments have manipulated these behaviors, and no experiments have investigated the effects of other unhealthy weight control behaviors, such as fasting. Thus, it is premature to rule out this possible explanation for the inconsistent findings from prospective and experimental studies regarding the impact of dieting on bulimic symptoms. It will therefore be important for future research to evaluate the notion that a small subset of self-labeled weight loss dieters do show marked weight loss because of some extreme weight control behavior, and whether this results in increased ED symptoms.

Reductions in Bulimic Symptoms in Experimental Trials Are Due to Demand Characteristics

It is also possible that demand characteristics explain the inconsistency in the findings from prospective and experimental studies. Participants in the experiments evaluating weight loss and weight maintenance diets may simply report reductions in binge eating and bulimic symptoms because they feel that they are expected to show reductions in eating, including overeating. Methodologists have noted that participants in the intervention condition of randomized trials may over-report changes in the target behavior in the expected direction (Baranowski, Klesges, Cullen, & Himes, 2004). For example, one hypertension management trial found that intervention participants under-reported sodium intake relative to the underreporting of controls, as measured by biological assays of sodium intake (Espeland et al., 2001). A related explanation is that the reported reductions in bulimic symptoms are due to

participant expectancies (i.e., are a placebo response). Pearlstein and associates (2003) found a remission rate from binge eating of 50% over a 3-month period among patients assigned to a pill placebo condition of a randomized trial of a pharmacologic treatment for BED. Interestingly, one study found that patients with BN showed only a slight reduction in binge eating and compensatory behaviors in response to pill placebo treatment (Mitchell et al., 1990) and another study found that a placebo self-help intervention did not result in significantly greater reductions in binge eating or compensatory behaviors among patients with BN relative to waitlist controls (Carter et al., 2003).

Although this explanation for the inconsistent findings is important to consider, it seems untenable for several reasons. First, many of the interventions evaluated in the experiments and trials were weight loss interventions that were not portrayed as likely to have an effect on eating disordered symptoms. Second, this account does not explain why participants on many of these trials reported reductions in the compensatory behaviors (Burton & Stice, 2006; Groesz & Stice, 2007). It is our impression that these weight loss or weight maintenance interventions would not produce demand characteristics for reductions in compensatory behaviors, particularly fasting and excessive exercise. Third, most of the experiments that produced reductions in binge eating and bulimic symptoms produced reductions in objectively measured body mass, which serves to partially validate that participants showed actual reductions in binge eating since binge eating contributes to weight gain. Fourth, not all experiments in which demand characteristics would have been operating produced reductions in binge eating or bulimic symptoms (e.g., Presnell et al., 2007). Fifth, the fact that 36 of the 51 ED prevention programs evaluated to date (71%) did not result in significant reductions in ED symptoms relative to assessment-only control conditions implies that demand characteristics alone are not sufficient to produce reductions in bulimic symptoms. Sixth, one weight maintenance diet produced significantly greater reductions in bulimic symptoms than an active placebo control group (Stice, Shaw, Burton, et al., 2006). Finally, it appears that perhaps only individuals with BED show large responses to a pill placebo condition (Pearlstein et al., 2003), as there was little evidence of a placebo response among patients with BN (Carter et al., 2003; Mitchell et al., 1990). In addition, because the former trial did not include an assessment-only control condition, it is impossible to parse the effects of a placebo response from the effects of the passage of time and regression to the mean for these patients. Nonetheless, this possible alternative explanation for the inconsistent findings emerging from the prospective versus the experimental studies cannot be ruled out. It will be important for future experiments to use collateral reports of ED symptoms, objective measures of binge eating and compensatory behaviors, or placebo control conditions to provide estimates of intervention effects that are not influenced by placebo response.

Implications Regarding Possible Explanations for the Inconsistent Findings

Several interesting findings emerged from our review of studies addressing possible explanations for the inconsistent findings regarding the relation of dietary restriction to bulimic symptoms from prospective and experimental studies. First, given the evidence that the dietary restraint measures used in the literature appear to be invalid measures of dietary restriction, it is not surprising that studies using these scales find different effects relative to experiments that investigate the effects of confirmed weight loss diets. However, we do not this think this explanation can account for the fact that the prospective and experimental studies produce effects that are in the opposite direction. If self-report dietary restraint scales were simply invalid measures of actual dietary restriction and do not identify people who are engaging in calorie-deficit diets necessary for weight loss, then it follows that the prospective studies should have simply produced null effects rather than consistently observed positive relations between elevated dietary restraint scores and risk for future onset of bulimic symptoms. The fact that dietary restraint scales have predictive validity for future bulimic symptom onset suggests that these scales assess some unidentified third variable that truly increases risk for bulimic symptoms. That is, dietary restraint scales seem to identify a population at high risk for bulimic pathology because they tap some characteristic that is causally related to the development of this eating disturbance.

Second, there was evidence that weight loss dieting, as practiced in the real world, is not as effective as weight loss interventions, potentially because participants meet with weight loss professionals in the interventions. Although these findings require replication, they also seem to offer an explanation for why prospective studies examining dieting in the real world produce different effects than experiments

investigating the effects of true weight loss diet interventions; the former do not produce weight loss, whereas the latter do. Again, however, it appears that this explanation cannot account for the fact that the prospective and experimental studies produce effects that are in the opposite direction. If real-world dieting is less effective than weight loss diet interventions, the prospective studies should have produced null effects or effects that were smaller, but in the same direction, as those emerging from the experiments. The fact that prospective studies indicate that individuals who perceive themselves as engaging in weight loss dieting are at elevated risk for onset of bulimic symptoms also appears to suggest that these scales tap some third variable that is causally related to the development of eating pathology.

Third, an analysis of the inferential power of prospective and experimental studies also holds promise in explaining the inconsistent findings. Although experiments may have limited ecological validity, they are more immune to third variable alternative explanations, whereas it is always possible that relations found in prospective studies can be explained by some unmeasured third variable. Thus, it is possible that some omitted third variable that causes both dieting and eventual onset of bulimic pathology may explain the relation between initial scores on dieting measures and future increases in bulimic symptoms.

Given that the considerations discussed in the preceding text suggest that dietary restraint scales identify people with some characteristic that increases risk for bulimic symptom onset, we think it may be fruitful to search for this third variable. If we were able to identify this third variable, it would advance our understanding regarding factors that cause onset of bulimic pathology. This information could also help in the development of preventive and treatment interventions for this eating pathology.

It seems to logically follow that the only way that experimental studies of true weight loss diets can produce effects that are opposite of those observed in the prospective studies is that the weight loss diet interventions directly reduce the omitted third variable. That is, if it is necessary to reduce an overeating tendency to decrease bulimic symptoms, it suggests that the omitted third variable may be a tendency to overeat and that this could be the third variable that explains the effects emerging from prospective studies. We have posited that individuals with a tendency toward overeating may attempt to curb this overeating through dieting because of undesired weight gain and that this overeating tendency also increases risk for eventual onset of binge eating and bulimic symptoms (Stice, Cameron, et al., 1999). Others have also proposed that dietary restraint scales identify people with a tendency to overeat and that this tendency may increase risk for BN (Lowe & Kral, 2006; van Strien et al., 2000). Based on the present analysis of extant findings, we believe that this is the most logical interpretation of the results that were reviewed to explain the inconsistent findings from the prospective and experimental studies.

The working hypothesis that dietary restraint scales are a proxy risk factor for onset of bulimic pathology because these scales identify individuals with an overeating tendency appears to explain several perplexing findings in the literature. This account seems to explain why weight loss diet interventions that result in a documented energy deficit diet successfully reduce bulimic symptoms (Burton & Stice, 2006; Groesz & Stice, 2007; Klem et al., 1997; Presnell & Stice, 2003) and why individuals with elevated scores on dietary restraint scales often gain more weight over time than those with lower scores (Klesges et al., 1989, 1992; Stice, Cameron, et al., 1999; Stice et al., 2005; Tanofsky-Kraff et al., 2007). This account also seem to explain why individuals who typically engage in weight loss dieting tend to gain weight over time when they are not actively engaging in what they perceive as weight loss dieting (Presnell et al., 2007) and why individuals with high scores on dietary restraint measures typically weigh more than those with low scores on these measures (e.g., Nederkoorn & Jansen, 2002; Roefs, Herman, MacLeod, Smulders, & Jansen, 2005).

The assertion that dietary restraint scales identify people with a chronic overeating tendency also accords with several other findings in the literature. First, this may explain why such a wide variety of experimental manipulations can trigger overeating among individuals with elevated scores on these dietary restraint scales. Experiments have found that these individuals overeat in response to negative mood inductions (Baucom & Aiken, 1981; Schotte, Cools, & McNally, 1990), positive mood inductions (Cools, Schotte, & McNally, 1992), stress/threat inductions (Heatherton, Herman, & Polivy, 1991; Polivy et al., 1994), listening to the radio (Bellisle & Dalix, 2001), performing cognitively distracting tasks (Hofmann, Rauch, & Gawronski, 2007; Ward & Mann, 2000), consuming alcohol (Polivy & Herman, 1976), consumption of high-calorie foods

(Herman & Mack, 1975; Jansen, Merckelbach, Oosterlaan, Tuiten, & Van den Hout, 1988), consumption of food that is perceived to be high-calorie (Polivy, 1976; Spencer & Fremouw, 1979), the smell of foods (Fedoroff, Polivy, & Herman, 1997; Jansen & van den Hout, 1991), simply thinking of food (Fedoroff et al., 1997), or to exposure to dieting commercials (Strauss, Doyle, & Kreipe, 1994). This account is also consistent with evidence that individuals with elevated dietary restraint scores report significantly more difficulty controlling their caloric intake than individuals with lower dietary restraint scores (Jansen et al., 1988). Finally, it is consistent with evidence suggesting overlap in genetic risk factors that contribute to both obesity and binge eating (Bulik, Sullivan, & Kendler, 2003).

Origins of a Chronic Tendency Toward Overconsumption

Based on the idea that the chronic overconsumption thesis is a reasonable working hypothesis that may resolve several puzzling findings in the literature, we think it is useful to consider individual difference factors that might lead to this overeating tendency. We believe it is vital to investigate factors that may contribute to an overeating tendency because this could advance our understanding of the etiologic processes that cause development of eating pathology and obesity. In the sections that follow, we propose three potential individual difference factors that may contribute to a chronic overeating tendency, which may represent the omitted third variable that explains the relation between dietary restraint scores and bulimic pathology. We also consider research findings that are consistent or inconsistent with these individual difference factors. Finally, we propose studies that should advance our understanding of the causal risk factors for eating pathology and obesity.

Greater Consummatory Food Reward

One possibility to explore is whether individuals who experience greater reward from food intake are at elevated risk for onset of binge eating and obesity. Some individuals may experience greater activation of the meso-limbic reward system in response to the consumption of food, which might increase the odds of chronic overconsumption (Dawe & Loxton, 2004). This hypothesis is akin to the reinforcement sensitivity model of substance abuse, which also posits that there are individual differences in the sensitivity or perhaps reactivity of basic brain–behavioral systems activated by reinforcing stimuli

(Dawe & Loxton, 2004). Reinforcement from food intake is similar to the concept of "liking" invoked in Berridge's (1996) theory of food reward, which refers to the sensory pleasure experienced and subjective reward derived from food intake (i.e., hedonics).

Studies have generated findings that appear to be consistent with the thesis that individuals with BN show heightened reward sensitivity in general relative to those without this ED. Women with BN showed greater sensitivity to financial reward than healthy controls when measured by behavioral performance in some (Farmer, Nash, & Field, 2001; Kane, Loxton, Staiger, & Dawe, 2004), but not all studies (Loxton & Dawe, 2007). Women with bulimic symptoms also report greater reward sensitivity to reward in general on surveys relative to controls (Davis & Woodside, 2002; Kane et al., 2004; Loxton & Dawe, 2006, 2007; Nederkoorn, van Eijs, & Jansen, 2004). Scores on one of the reward drive scales correlated positively with activation of food reward brain regions in response to presentation of food cues in an functional magnetic resonance imaging (fMRI) study, including the right ventral striatum, left amygdala, and left orbitofrontal cortex (Beaver et al., 2006), providing evidence of convergent validity for this self-report scale.

Studies have also generated findings that appear to be consistent with the notion that individuals with BN show heightened reward from food intake relative to controls. Individuals with BN prefer sweeter tastes (Drewnowski, Bellisle, Aimez, & Remy, 1987; Franko, Wolfe, & Jimerson, 1994) and higher-fat foods (Sunday & Halmi, 1990) than do nonbulimic women. Relative to controls, individuals with BN consume more artificially sweetened solution in a modified sham-feeding paradigm and to report elevated intake of low-calorie artificially sweetened foods (Klein, Boudreau, Devlin, & Walsh, 2005, 2006) and engage in sham-feeding types of behaviors, such as chewing and spitting out food (Eckern, Stevens, & Mitchell, 1999; Guarda et al., 2004; Kovacs, Mahon, & Palmer, 2002).

Laboratory studies have found that, relative to controls, individuals with BN continue to eat after reaching satiety, report persistent urges to eat and hunger after completing meals, and often show increased rate of consumption during an eating episode (Guss, & Kissileff, 2000; Kissileff et al., 1996; Sunday & Halmi, 1996). Although people typically show a diminished preference for food that is presented repeatedly over time, including a reduction in salivary response (Epstein, Saad, et al., 2003), individuals with BN do not show sensory specific

satiety when consuming one food type (LaChaussee, Kissileff, Walsh, & Hadigan, 1992) or habituation of salivary response to tastes of palatable food relative to nondisordered controls (Wisniewski, Epstein, Marcs, & Kaye, 1997). In addition, an avid sucking style during feeding in the first month of life, which may reflect greater reinforcement from food intake, predicted future onset of overeating in childhood (Stice, Agras, & Hammer, 1999) and higher body mass by age 6 (Agras, Kraemer, Berkowitz, & Hammer, 1990).

Research has also provided evidence that obese relative to lean individuals experience greater reinforcement from eating. Obese individuals consume more high-fat and high-sugar foods than their lean counterparts (McGloin et al., 2002; Nicklas, Yang, Baranowski, Zakeri, & Berenson, 2003). Preferences for foods high in fat and sugar predicts an elevated rate of subsequent weight gain during childhood and an increased risk for onset of obesity in adulthood (Drewnowski, 1996; Stunkard, Berkowitz, Stallings, & Schoeller, 1999; Westerterp-Plantenga, Ijederma, & Wijckmans-Duijsens, 1996). Compared to children of lean parents, children of obese parents evidence a higher preference for the taste of fat foods, a greater appetitive response to food and drink (Fisher & Birch, 1995; Wardle, Guthrie, Sanderson, Birch, & Plomin, 2001), and more vigorous sucking during feeding within the first few months of birth (Stunkard et al., 1999). Yet, it is important to acknowledge that some studies have found that body mass index (BMI) does not significantly correlate with hedonic ratings of snack foods (e.g., Goldfield & Legg, 2006).

Obese individuals also self-report that food intake is more reinforcing than lean individuals (Jacobs & Wagner, 1984; Johnson, 1974; Westenhoefer & Pudel, 1993). Obese relative to lean adults work harder for food and work for more food (Johnson, 1974; Saelens & Epstein, 1996), suggesting that the former find food more reinforcing. However, two studies have found that BMI does not significantly correlate with how hard young women work for snack foods (Ahern, Field, Spoor, Bohon, & Stice, 2008) or for snack foods versus healthy fruit and vegetables (Goldfield & Legg, 2006), suggesting that the differences may only emerge when extreme groups of lean versus obese individuals are compared. Individuals who exhibit greater reinforcement value for food consume significantly more calories, as assessed by an unobtrusive observational measure, relative to those who exhibit lower food reinforcement (Epstein et al., 2004). Obese relative to lean children report a higher preference for food-related activities (Sobhany & Rogers, 1985) and more often eat in the absence of hunger (Fisher & Birch, 2002). Self-reported reward drive also correlates positively with BMI, hyperphagia, emotional eating, and self-reported food cravings (Davis, Strachan, & Berkson, 2004; Dawe & Loxton, 2004; Franken & Muris, 2005). Obese relative to lean individuals show greater activation in the gustatory cortex and somatosensory cortex when consuming palatable food, regions that encode the sensory and hedonic aspects of food intake (Stice, Spoor, Bohon, Veldhuizen, & Small, 2008). Interestingly, however, obese relative to lean individuals show blunted activation of the dorsal striatum in response to receipt of palatable food (Stice, Spoor, et al., 2008; Stice, Spoor, Bohon, & Small, 2008) and reduced dopamine receptor density in the striatum (Volkow et al., 2008; Wang et al., 2001), which is a region implicated in reward from food intake.

Although these data provide some support for the notion that individuals with BN and obese individuals may experience greater reinforcement from food intake, few studies have tested whether individuals with elevated dietary restraint scores exhibit characteristics that might be indicative of elevated reinforcement from food intake. Taste test studies found that individuals with elevated dietary restraint scores did not differ from those with lower scores on how pleasant they rated palatable foods (Ahern et al., 2008; Fedoroff et al., 1997; Goldfield & Legg, 2006; Roefs et al., 2005). In addition, individuals with elevated dietary restraint scores did not work harder for snack foods (Ahern et al., 2008) or work harder for snack foods than for healthy foods (Goldfield & Legg, 2006) relative to those with lower dietary restraint scores.

Although these studies provide little support for the notion that dieters exhibit greater food reinforcement than nondieters, it is possible that social desirability bias influenced these findings, as objective measures of taste preferences were not used (e.g., activation of reward pathways in the brain). It is also possible that these individuals experience an approach-avoidance conflict, in which they have a greater appetitive drive for food, yet feel anxious about potential weight gain from consumption of palatable foods (Ahern et al., 2008). Finally, the greater reinforcement from food may be a consequence of repeatedly engaging in binge eating or overeating.

In sum, there is support for the suggestion that elevated reinforcement from food intake is related to binge eating, bulimic symptoms, and obesity. However, there is currently little evidence that individuals with elevated dietary restraint rate food as more palatable or rewarding than those who report low dietary restraint, although only a few studies have examined this question. Future research in this area is needed before firm conclusions can be drawn. It will be particularly important to use objective techniques (e.g., brain imaging) to test whether individuals with BN or obesity and individuals with elevated dietary restraint scores show elevated reward from food intake relative to normal controls. Additional research using cognitive science paradigms that involve actual administration of food also hold the promise of advancing our understanding of this working hypothesis. Finally, prospective studies should test whether elevated reinforcement from food intake increases risk for future increases in self-reported dieting, binge eating, and weight gain.

Greater Anticipatory Food Reward

It is also possible that greater anticipated reward from food intake is what differentiates those with high versus low dietary restraint scores and increases risk for overeating and binge eating (Roefs et al., 2005). Theoretically, the elevated reward from food intake that potentially characterizes those at risk for overeating would be expected to increase anticipated reward from eating and produce craving for palatable foods (Dawe & Loxton, 2004). The conditioning model of binge eating postulates that through classical conditioning over time, cues such as the sight and smell of food eventually elicit physiological responses that are experienced as food craving, which putatively increase the risk for binge eating (Jansen, 1998). Repeating pairings of these cues (which elicit craving) and binge eating, are thought to strengthen the link between the cues and binge eating behaviors, which serves to maintain binge eating and BN.

Relative to nondisordered controls, individuals with BN or recurrent binge eating rate pictures of food as more interesting and arousing and report a greater desire to eat, even when sated (Karhunen, Lappalainen, Tammela, Turpeinen, & Uusitupa, 1997; Mauler et al., 2006). Mitchell, Hatsukami, Pyle, and Eckert (1985) found that 70% of patients with BN cite food craving as a reason for their binge eating. Interestingly, individuals with BN did not differ from dieters in terms of food craving after exposure to pictures of palatable foods (Bossert-Zaudig, Laessle, Meiller, Elllgring, & Pirke, 1991). Individuals with BN, relative to controls, report greater urges to binge and less confidence in their ability to control their food intake after exposure to the sight, smell, and taste of food (Bulik, Lawson, & Carter, 1996; Staiger, Dawe, & McCarthy, 2000). Individuals with BN report greater urges to binge eat in response to both palatable and unpalatable control foods (Staiger et al., 2000), suggesting that they may anticipate greater reward from eating any food types, rather than just palatable food. Moreover, individuals with BN, relative to controls, report persistent urges to eat and hunger after completing meals (Guss, & Kissileff, 2000).

Psychophysiology studies that have examined the salivary response to food cues of individuals with BN or recurrent binge eating versus controls have produced mixed results, with some finding that the former show more (Legenbauer, Vogele, & Ruddel, 2004; LeGoff, Leichner, & Spigelman, 1988), less (Bulik et al., 1996; Karhunen et al., 1997), or similar (Staiger et al., 2000) salivary response to food cues relative to nonbulimic controls. Salivary response to food presentation appears to reflect food craving, as it correlates positively with self-reported hunger and desire to binge eat (Legenbauer et al., 2004).

Studies that have examined other physiological measures have also produced inconsistent findings. For example, one study found that individuals with BN, relative to nondisordered controls, showed significantly reduced startle response to pictures of food and significantly increased corrugator facial muscle responses to these same images, but no significant differences with regard to skin conductance and heart rate response (Mauler et al., 2006). However, another study found that individuals with BN did not show a significantly reduced startle response while viewing pictures of food relative to controls (Friederich et al., 2006).

This pattern of findings implies that individuals with and without BN do not show reliable differences in these physiological responses to food cues, that these measures are unreliable, or that the small sample sizes produced inconsistent findings. It is also possible that individuals with BN show an approach-avoidance response to food stimuli that results from an increased drive to consume food coupled with negative feelings toward food because they often binge eat, which moves them further from the thin-ideal to which they often aspire. Such an approach–avoidance response may lead to both positive and negative emotional responses to food cues, which are being assessed by these physiological measures. Consistent with this notion, individuals

with BN often report more negative feelings while looking at, smelling, or touching food (Bulik et al., 1996; Legenbauer et al., 2004; Mauler et al., 2006; Staiger et al., 2000; Uher et al., 2004).

Research has compared obese and lean individuals using cognitive psychology paradigms to determine whether the former show a more positive attitude toward higher caloric density foods, on the basis that elevated food craving would result in positive implicit attitudes toward these foods. One study used the Implicit Association Test (IAT; Greenwald, McGhee, & Schwartz, 1998) to provide an objective test of whether obese women show more positive attitudes toward food than lean women (Roefs & Jansen, 2002). Unexpectedly, both obese and lean participants showed more negative associations with high-fat foods than with low-fat foods, with this effect being more pronounced for the obese women. A second study used the Extrinsic Affective Simon Task (EAST; De Houwer, 2003) to test whether obese youth show more positive implicit attitudes toward unhealthy foods (versus healthy foods) in relation to lean youth (Craeynest et al., 2005). Obese relative to lean youth showed a more pronounced positive implicit attitude toward food in general, though there were no differences with regard to explicit attitudes toward foods. The evidence that obese individuals have a more positive implicit attitude toward food may lead to the overconsumption of food in general, which results in the positive energy balance necessary for obesity onset. It might be useful if future studies used pictures of food or real food, rather than food words, as this may provide a more sensitive test of implicit attitudes toward food in these two groups.

Three studies have found that obese individuals show greater salivary response to food presentation than lean individuals (Johnson & Wildman 1983; Wooley, Wooley, & Dunham, 1976; Wooley, Wooley, & Woods, 1975), which may imply that they show greater food craving. However, two studies found that overweight and obese adults did not differ from lean adults in salivary reactivity to food cues (Klajner et al., 1981; LeGoff & Spigelman, 1987). Nonetheless, self-reported food cravings correlated positively with body mass (Delahanty, Meigs, Hayden, Williamson, & Nathan, 2002) and objectively measured caloric intake in the laboratory (Nederkoorn, Smulders, & Jansen, 2000). Further, obese relative to lean individuals report stronger craving of high-fat and high-sugar foods (Drewnowski, Krahn, Demitrack, Nairn, & Gosnell, 1992; Drewnowski, Kurth, Holden-Wiltse, & Saari,

1992; White, Whisenhunt, Williamson, Greenway, & Netemeyer, 2002) and show greater activation of food reward circuitry when anticipating the consumption of palatable food versus tasteless food (Stice, Spoor, et al., 2008c).

Several studies have examined the relation of dietary restraint scores to measures that may reflect food craving. Individuals with high dietary restraint scores report greater cravings for palatable foods than those with lower scores (Gendall, Joyce, Sullivan, & Bulik, 1998; Pelchat, 1997; Polivy, Coleman, & Herman, 2005), though this relation did not replicate in other studies (Fedoroff et al., 1997; Hill, Weaver, & Blundell, 1991; Rodin, Mancuso, Granger, & Nelbach, 1991; White et al., 2002). Individuals with elevated dietary restraint scores report a greater likelihood to give in to food cravings and consume the craved food (Fedoroff et al., 1997; Polivy et al., 2005). These data may imply that those with elevated dietary restraint scores only show moderately greater food craving, which is why the effects are inconsistent. It is also possible that food craving is only elicited when the individuals encounter palatable foods, which might suggest that future studies should involve presentation of real food.

There is evidence that simply smelling food (Fedoroff et al., 1997; Jansen & van den Hout, 1991; Rogers & Hill, 1989) or thinking about eating food (Fedoroff et al., 1997) leads to greater caloric intake among individuals with high but not low dietary restraint scores. These data also seem consistent with the notion that the former have elevated craving for foods that is easily triggered.

Studies have also used implicit measures to explore whether individuals with elevated dietary restraint scores show a positive emotional response to food stimuli than individuals with lower dietary restraint scores. One study used the Affective Priming Paradigm (Fazio, Sanbonmatsu, Powell, & Kardes, 1986) and the Extrinsic Affective Simon Task (EAST; De Houwer, 2003) to test whether individuals with high dietary restraint scores would show a greater automatic positive attitude toward palatable foods than to unpalatable foods relative to their lower-scoring counterparts (Roefs et al., 2005). Although both groups showed greater positive attitudes toward palatable foods relative to low-fat foods on both paradigms, there were no differences in the response between individuals with high versus low dietary restraint scores. Another study that used a version of the IAT (Greenwald et al., 1998) that presented pictures of candy found that dietary restraint scores positively correlate with implicit positive attitudes toward candy (Hofmann et al., 2007). However, another study found that individuals with high and low dietary restraint scores did not differ on implicit attitudes toward pictures of palatable foods versus unpalatable foods or control images (Ahern et al., 2008). Future studies might consider using actual food as stimuli to see if this provides a more sensitive measure of food craving.

Other studies have compared salivary reactivity in response to presentation of food and food cues among those with high and low scores on dietary restraint measures, which might be interpreted as an objective measure of food craving given that it correlates positively with self-reported hunger and desire to binge eat (Legenbauer et al., 2004). Studies found that individuals with elevated dietary restraint scores show greater salivary response to the sight and smell of real food than their lower-scoring counterparts (Klajner et al., 1981; Legenbauer et al., 2004; LeGoff & Spigelman, 1987; Sahakian, Lean, Robbins, & James, 1981), although null effects have also emerged (Bulik et al., 1996; Nederkoorn & Jansen, 2002). This pattern of findings may suggest that individuals with elevated dietary restraint scores show only moderately greater food craving that their lower-scoring counterparts, which is why the effects are not consistently observed. Alternatively, it may signal that procedural aspects of the studies, such as the duration of exposure to food, impact whether elevated salivary response is observed.

Interestingly, individuals who have been placed on weight loss low-calorie diets show lower salivary response when exposed to palatable foods relative to controls (Durrant, 1981; Rosen, 1981; Wooley, Wooley, & Williams, 1978). Given the evidence that individuals with elevated scores on dietary restraint scales do not typically achieve a negative energy balance necessary for weight loss (Presnell et al., 2007), whereas those on monitored weight loss diets do (Groesz & Stice, 2007; Presnell & Stice, 2003), the pattern of findings from the salivary response studies may imply that calorie deficit dieting reduces food craving. Indeed, noncontrolled obesity treatment trials have found that assignment to low-calorie diets that result in weight loss produce reductions in self-reported food cravings for adults (Harvey, Wing, & Mullen, 1993; Lappalainen, Sjoden, Hursti, & Vesa, 1990; Martin, Makris, et al., 2006; Martin, O'Neil, & Pawlow, 2006) and reductions in self-reported hedonics and cravings for high fat foods in children (Epstein et al., 1989). Moreover, participants on more restrictive very low-calorie diets show significantly greater reductions in self-reported food craving than those on less restrictive low-calorie diets (Lappalainen et al., 1990; Martin, O'Neil, et al., 2006). Assignment to a low-calorie diet that results in weight loss produced significantly greater reductions in self-reported hunger relative to an assessment-only control condition (Groesz & Stice, 2007). Another uncontrolled trial indicated that assignment to low-calorie diets results in reductions in hunger and food preoccupation (Wing, Marcus, Blair, & Burton, 1991).

There is also evidence that restriction from a particular food type results in reductions in craving that is specific to that particular food type (Harvey et al., 1993; Martin, Makris et al., 2006). One weight loss trial found that carbohydrate cravings decreased more for participants on a low-carbohydrate diet than for those on a low-fat diet, whereas cravings for high-fat foods decreased more for participants on the low-fat diet than for participants on the low-carbohydrate diet (Martin, Makris, et al., 2006). These findings imply that caloric deprivation reduces food craving and that deprivation of particular food types produces even greater decreases in craving for those particular foods. These data also provide another example that experiments that manipulate dietary restriction can produce findings that are opposite of studies that use self-report dietary restraint scales.

There are two theoretical accounts that may explain why low-calorie diets produce reductions in food craving. First, according to Jansen (1998), conditioned food cues will elicit food craving as long as they remain a reliable predictor of excessive food intake. According to this theory, craving will be reduced when the cues do not reliably predict excessive food intake. It is possible that low-calorie diets that involve restricted intake of high-fat and high-sugar foods effectively produce deconditioning. Perhaps individuals on low-calorie diets are still exposed to many food cues but are not engaging in excessive intake of the high-fat and high-sugar foods. A second explanation for why low-calorie diets may affect a reduction in food craving is that low-calorie diets often have a limited variety of foods (Martin, O'Neil, et al., 2006). Access to a large variety of food types, relative to a more restricted variety, promotes greater overall caloric intake (McCrory, Suen, & Roberts, 2002; Rolls, Rolls, Rowe, & Sweeney, 1981). The effect of dietary variety appears to be explained in part by sensory specific satiety, wherein participants typically show a decrease in the ratings of the hedonic value of a food

that is consumed to satiety versus foods not eaten to satiation (Rolls et al., 1981).

In sum, the evidence is mixed regarding whether individuals with obesity, bulimic pathology, or elevated dietary restraint scores show greater anticipatory reward from food than do controls, with self-report measures, implicit tests, and psychophysiology measures producing inconsistent effects. Thus, future studies that use more objective and validated measures may be warranted. Interestingly, there was consistent evidence that caloric deprivation generally reduces food craving and that deprivation of particular food types produces even greater decreases in craving for those particular foods.

Greater Impulsivity

It has also been hypothesized that impulsive individuals may be more vulnerable to the omnipresent temptation of palatable foods in the current obesogenic environment, which may increase the risk for weight gain, as well as for development of binge eating and BN (Nederkoorn et al., 2004). Among individuals with deficits in inhibitory control, impulses and immediate reward will play a more important role in determining behaviors than longer-term adverse consequences of the behavior (Nederkoorn, et al., 2004). It is possible that the elevated consummatory or anticipatory food reward may contribute to more impulsive responding to food cues.

Individuals who exhibit binge eating or BN typically have elevated scores on self-report measures of trait impulsivity (Claes, Vandereycken, & Vertommen, 2002; Fassino et al., 2002; Kane et al., 2004; Nasser, Gluck, & Geliebter, 2004; Nederkoorn et al., 2004; Vervaet, Audenaert, & Heeringen, 2003). Bulimic symptoms correlate positively with self-reported impulsivity among unselected undergraduate women (Guerrieri, Nederkoorn, & Jansen, 2007; Loxton & Dawe, 2007), particularly scales assessing a tendency to act rashly (Fischer, Smith, & Anderson, 2003). Self-reported impulsivity correlated positively with test meal caloric intake among individuals seeking weight loss treatment (Nasser et al., 2004) and individuals with BED(Galanti, Gluck, & Geliebter, 2007). Bulimic symptoms correlate positively with impulsive behaviors, including self-mutilation, suicidal ideation, and excessive substance use (Penas-Lledo & Waller, 2001; Pidcock, Fischer, Forthun, & West, 2000; Vervaet et al., 2003). Impulsive behaviors, including delinquency and substance abuse, predicted future onset of bulimic symptoms (Wonderlich, Connolly, & Stice, 2004).

Obese individuals have also shown greater impulsivity than lean individuals on self-report measures (Chalmers, Bowyer, & Olenick, 1990; Ryden et al., 2003; Williamson, Kelley, Davis, Ruggiero, & Blouin, 1985), although null findings have been reported (Nederkoorn, Smulders, Havermans, Roefs, & Jansen, 2006). Relative to lean women, obese women show more difficulties with response inhibition on a stop-signal task (Nederkoorn, Smulders, et al., 2006). Obese adults, relative to lean adults, show a preference for high immediate gain, but larger future losses in a gambling task, rather than lower immediate reward and less future loss (Davis, Levitan, Muglia, Bewell, & Kennedy, 2004). However, other studies have not found a preference for immediate rewards relative to delayed rewards between obese and lean adults (Forzano & Logue, 1992; Logue & King, 1991; Nederkoorn, Smulders, et al., 2006). Obese children more often choose a direct food reward over a larger delayed food reward relative to lean children (Bonato & Boland, 1983), although null results have also been observed (Bourget & White, 1984). Obese relative to lean children are less effective in response inhibition in a stop-signal task and are more sensitive to reward in a gambling task than lean children (Nederkoorn, Braet, van Eijs, Tanghe, & Jansen, 2006). Among obese children, response inhibition deficits on a stop-signal task correlated positively with BMI (Nederkoorn, Jansen, Mulkens, & Jansen, 2007). Overweight children consume more calories after exposure to food cues, such as smelling and tasting a palatable food, whereas lean children do not (Jansen et al., 2003), suggesting that the former are more likely to give in to cravings resulting from food cues. Initially elevated impulsivity is associated with less weight loss during obesity treatment (Jonsson, Bjorvell, Lavander, & Rossner, 1986; Nederkoorn, Braet, et al., 2006; Nederkoorn, Jansen et al., 2007). Individuals with elevated scores on self-reported impulsivity scales show greater objectively measured caloric intake than their lower-scoring peers (Guerrieri et al., 2007).

Studies that have compared individuals with high and low dietary restraint scores have also provided findings that are consonant with the impulsivity theory. Logue and King (1991) found that individuals who indicated that they were currently on a diet, relative to those who were not, exhibited significantly more impulsive responding on an immediate versus delayed food reward operant conditioning task. They also found that impulsive responding positively correlates with dietary restraint

scale scores. Nederkoorn and associates (2004) found that individuals with high dietary restraint scores exhibited significantly worse inhibition of basic non–food-related motor responses on a stop-signal task and scored higher on a self-report impulsivity scale than their lower-scoring counterparts. However, one study found that dietary restraint scores did not show a significant correlation with self-reported impulsivity (Guerrieri et al., 2007). The evidence that individuals with high versus low dietary restraint scores typically overeat in response to presentation of food cues, such as smelling a palatable food (e.g., Jansen & Van den Hout, 1991; Rogers & Hill, 1989) or even just thinking about a palatable food (Fedoroff et al., 1997), might be interpreted as suggesting that the former are more likely to yield to these tempting presentation of food cues and respond by overeating.

In sum, there is mounting evidence that individuals with BN, binge eating disturbances, obesity, and elevated dietary restraint scores show greater impulsivity in general, as well as in response to food stimuli, relative to controls. Thus, it would be useful for future studies to continue to examine the potential role of impulsivity in the etiology of binge eating, BN, and obesity. It will also be important for studies to explore factors that interact with impulsivity in the prediction of binge eating and weight gain. For instance, it has been suggested that depleted self-regulatory capacity may interact with impulsivity toward food to predict overeating (Hofmann et al., 2007). Others have suggested that a tendency toward disinhibited eating interacts with dietary restriction to increase risk for overeating (Ouwens et al., 2003).

Summary of the Review of Possible Explanations for the Inconsistent Findings

Prospective studies have found that individuals who report dietary restraint are at increased risk for future onset of binge eating, bulimic pathology, and EDs. However, experiments have found that assignment to weight loss diets results in significantly greater reductions in binge eating and bulimic symptoms and greater weight loss than assignment to assessment-only control conditions. Our analysis of potential explanations for these consistently incompatible findings identified several plausible explanations for these vexing findings.

One possibility that is suggested by a consideration of the different inferential strength of prospective versus experimental studies is that some omitted third variable explains the results from the prospective studies that suggest that individuals who report dietary restraint are at increased risk for future bulimic symptoms. Another possibility is that the prospective studies used invalid measures of dietary restraint that do not identify individuals who are in a negative energy balance, which explains why they produced different results than experiments that manipulated energy-deficit dieting. A third possibility is that the weight loss dietary interventions examined in the experiments are more extreme than weight loss dieting that is practiced in the real world and have limited ecological validity because participants meet with weight loss professionals.

However, a careful consideration of these three explanations for the inconsistent findings implies that only the first explanation can logically explain the inconsistent findings. Our analysis suggested that the only plausible explanation is that dietary restraint scales identify a subgroup at increased risk for future onset of bulimic pathology. We hypothesize, based on the evidence that true energy deficit dieting results in a reduction in bulimic symptoms, that these scales identify individuals with a chronic overeating tendency. We posit that this overeating tendency results in attempts to curb caloric intake (self-initiated dieting) and also increases risk for future onset of an ED characterized by uncontrollable bouts of overeating. This working hypothesis appears to explain the inconsistent pattern of findings, as well as several other anomalous findings. Further, we explored the available evidence that individual differences in reinforcement from food intake, anticipated reinforcement from food intake, and impulsivity may give rise to this overeating tendency.

Despite this working hypothesis, there are two other possible alternative explanations for the inconsistent findings that warrant further research. First, it is possible that the reductions in bulimic symptoms are a product of the demand characteristics of experiments in which participants are assigned to a weight loss diet condition. Although this seems unlikely, it is worth exploring this possible explanation with experiments that use confederate reports of bulimic symptoms, objective measures of these symptoms, or placebo control conditions. Second, it is conceivable that some small subset of dieters engage in a particularly unhealthy form of dieting, such as extreme fasting, which really does increase risk for bulimic symptoms for this subset of dieters. Because only a small subset of dieters eventually develop bulimic pathology, we think this is an important possibility to explore as well, though it

will be vital to use objective measures of these unhealthy weight control behaviors and to conduct randomized experiments that manipulate candidate dieting behaviors.

Conclusions

In conclusion, experiments from multiple laboratories that have evaluated weight loss and weight maintenance diet interventions suggest that neither cause eating pathology. This is key because it suggests that obesity prevention and treatment interventions that prescribe weight loss dieting do not produce iatrogenic effects. Indeed, these experiments imply that weight maintenance dieting is an efficacious prevention program for bulimic pathology, that weight loss dieting is an efficacious treatment for this ED, and that the dietary restraint model of bulimic pathology is in need of revision. One remarkable feature of this literature is the confidence that has been placed in the assertion that dieting causes bulimic pathology in the absence of any experimental evidence that actual dietary restriction increases risk for bulimic symptoms (e.g., Fairburn, 1997; Heatherton & Polivy, 1992; Polivy & Herman, 1985; Levine & Smolak, 2006; Neumark-Sztainer et al., 2006).

Nonetheless, we feel it would be useful to attempt to identify the third variable that is tapped by dietary restraint scales, which truly increases risk for future onset of bulimic pathology because we think this will advance our understanding of the etiologic processes that give rise to eating pathology. More generally, the literature reviewed here illustrates the importance of documenting the validity of measures with methods that are less subject to distortion by social desirability. Finally, this analysis underscores the hazards of relying on prospective studies when making etiologic inferences. The fact that it is impossible to rule out third-variable alternative explanations for prospective findings from longitudinal studies serves as a cogent reminder of the importance of using randomized experiments that manipulate putative etiologic factors to confirm causal relations suggested by prospective studies (Glantz, 2002; Hinshaw, 2002; Stice, 2002). Only through the use of the most rigorous research designs available, can we hope to develop valid etiologic models for psychopathology and design optimally effective prevention and treatment interventions.

Future Directions

This chapter suggests several important directions for future research. First, future research should attempt to identify the third variable that is inadvertently tapped by dietary restraint scales that truly increases risk for future onset of bulimic pathology. This will be a difficult task because it cannot be easily achieved with cross-sectional data, which is the design typically used to address a question of this nature. Thus, future studies should attempt to experimentally manipulate any potential third variables that are identified, such as a chronic tendency toward overeating, in an effort to provide more rigorous inferences about any putative causal of bulimic symptoms. It will also be vital to make these experiments as ecologically valid as possible.

Second, it will be important to investigate individual difference factors that might give rise to potential third variables under consideration. We suspect it would be useful to investigate individual differences in consummatory food reward, anticipatory food reward, and impulsivity as factors that may give rise to both efforts at curbing an overeating tendency and eventual bulimic pathology.

Third, it will also be important to conduct experiments that manipulate particular weight loss behaviors. As noted, we believe that it is possible that some subset of individuals with elevated dietary restraint scores engages in some particularly unhealthy weight loss behaviors that may increase risk for bulimic pathology, such as extreme fasting. For ethical reasons, it would be best to reduce, rather than increase, these unhealthy behaviors experimentally.

Fourth, there would be value in investigating the possibility that demand characteristics give rise to the reductions in bulimic symptoms in experiments investigating the effects of weight loss diets on this outcome. Such studies will need to use confederate reports from individuals who are blinded to the condition of the experiment, objective measures of bulimic symptoms (e.g., electrolyte abnormalities), or placebo control conditions.

Fifth, it will be important for future research to develop valid measures of dietary restriction. Without valid measures of dieting it will be virtually impossible to make accurate inferences regarding the consequences of dieting. Given the power of self-presentation biases, we suspect it may be necessary to take an empirically keyed approach when developing this measure.

Finally, given the evidence that weight loss dieting curbs bulimic symptoms in prevention and treatment trials, it will be important to develop even more effective interventions that promote weight maintenance diets for individuals at a healthy weight and weight loss diets for individuals who are overweight.

The increasing prevalence of obesity suggests that this is a particularly pressing need from a public health perspective. Prevention programs that affect two adverse outcomes (EDs and obesity) clearly have greater public health significance than programs that affect only one of these outcomes.

References

Agras, W. S., Kraemer, H., Berkowitz, R., & Hammer, L. (1990). Influence of early feeding style on adiposity by 6 years of age. *Journal of Pediatrics, 116*, 805–809.

Agras, W. S., & Telch, C. F. (1998). The effects of caloric deprivation and negative affect on binge eating in obese binge-eating disordered women. *Behavior Therapy, 29*, 491–503.

Ahern, A., Field, M., Spoor, S., Bohon, C., & Stice, E. (2008). Cognitive biases and reward sensitivity in dieters. 2010.

American Psychiatric Association (APA). (1994). *Diagnostic and statistical manual of mental disorders* (4th ed.). Washington, DC: Author.

Attenburrow, M. J., Williams, C., Odontiadis, J., Powell, J., van de Ouderaa, F., Williams, M., & Cowen, P. (2003). The effect of a nutritional source of tryptophan on dieting-induced changes in brain 5-HT function. *Psychological Medicine, 33*, 1381–1386.

Bacon, L., Keim, N. L., Van Loan, M. D., Derricote, M., Gale, B., Kazaks, A., & Stern, J. S. (2002). Evaluating a non-diet wellness intervention for improvement of metabolic fitness, psychological well-being and eating and activity behaviors. *International Journal of Obesity, 26*, 854–865.

Bandini, L. G., Schoeller, D. A., Cyr, H. N., & Dietz, W. H. (1990). Validity of reported energy-intake in obese and non-obese adolescents. *American Journal of Clinical Nutrition, 52(3)*, 421–425.

Baranowski, T., Klesges, L. M., Cullen, K. W., & Himes, J. H. (2004). Measurement of outcomes, mediators, and moderators in behavioral obesity prevention research. *Preventive Medicine, 38*, S1–S13.

Bathalon, G. P., Tucker, K. L., Hays, N. P., Vinken, A. G., Greenberg, A. S., McCrory, M. A. et al. (2000). Psychological measures of eating behavior and the accuracy of 3 common dietary assessment methods in healthy postmenopausal women. *American Journal of Clinical Nutrition, 71*, 739–745.

Baucom, D.H., & Aiken, P.A. (1981). Effect of depressed mood on eating among nonobese dieting and nondieting persons. *Journal of Personality and Social Psychology, 41*, 577–585.

Bearman, S. K., Stice, E., & Chase, A. (2003). Effects of body dissatisfaction on depressive and bulimic symptoms: A longitudinal experiment. *Behavior Therapy, 34*, 277–293.

Beaver, J. D., Lawrence, A. D., van Ditzhuijzen, J., Davis, M. H., Woods, A., & Calder, A. J. (2006). Individual differences in reward drive predict neural response to images of food. *Journal of Neuroscience, 26*, S160–S166.

Bellisle, F., & Dalix, A. (2001). Cognitive restraint can be offset by distraction, leading to increased meal intake in women. *American Journal of Clinical Nutrition, 74*, 197–200.

Berridge, K. C. (1996). Food reward, brain substrates of wanting and liking. *Neuroscience and Biobehavioral Research, 20*, 1–25.

Boggiano, M. M., Chandler, P. C., Viana, J. B., Oswald, K. D., Maldonado, C. R., & Wauford, P. K. (2005). Combined dieting and stress evoke exaggerated responses to opiods in binge-eating rats. *Behavioral Neuroscience, 119*, 1207–1214.

Bohon, C., Stice, E., & Burton, E. (2008). Maintenance factors for persistence of bulimic pathology: A community-based natural history study. *International Journal of Eating Disorders*.

Bonato, D. P., & Boland, F. J. (1983). Delay of gratification in obese children. *Addictive Behaviors, 8*, 71–74.

Bossert-Zaudig, S., Laessle, R., Meiller, C., Elllgring, H., & Pirke, K. M. (1991). Hunger and appetite during visual perception of food in eating disorders. *European Psychiatry, 6*, 237–242.

Bourget, V., & White, D. R. (1984). Performance of overweight and normal-weight girls on delay of gratification tasks. *International Journal of Eating Disorders, 3*, 63–71.

Braet, C., Tanghe, A., De Bode, P., Franckx, H., & VanWinckel, M. (2003). Inpatient treatment of obese children: A multicomponent programme without stringent calorie restriction. *European Journal of Pediatrics, 162*, 391–396.

Bulik, C. M., & Brinded, E. C. (1994). The effect of food deprivation on the reinforcing value of food and smoking in bulimic and control women. *Physiology and Behavior, 55*, 665–672.

Bulik, C. M., Lawson, R. H., & Carter, F. A. (1996). Salivary reactivity in restrained and unrestrained eaters and women with bulimia nervosa. *Appetite, 27*, 15–24.

Bulik, C. M., Sullivan, P. F., & Kendler, K. S. (2003). Genetic and environmental contributions to obesity and binge eating. *International Journal of Eating Disorders, 33*, 293–298.

Burton, E. M., & Stice, E. (2006). Evaluation of a healthy-weight treatment program for bulimia nervosa: A preliminary randomized trial. *Behaviour Research and Therapy, 44*, 1727–1738.

Burton, E. M., Stice, E., Bearman, S. K., & Rohde, P. (2007). An experimental test of the affect-regulation model of bulimic symptoms and substance use: An affective intervention. *International Journal of Eating Disorders, 40*, 27–36.

Calle, E., Thun, M., Petrelli, J., Rodriguez, C., & Heath, C. (1999). Body mass index and mortality in a prospective cohort of US adults. *New England Journal of Medicine, 341*, 1097–1105.

Carter, J. C., Olmsted, M. P., Kaplan, A. S., McCabe, R. E., Mills, J. S., & Aime, A. (2003). Self-help for bulimia nervosa: A randomized controlled trial. *American Journal of Psychiatry, 160*, 973–978.

Chalmers, D. K., Bowyer, C. A., & Olenick, N. L. (1990). Problem drinking and obesity: A comparison in personality patterns and life-style. *International Journal of Addiction, 25*, 803–817.

Claes, L., Vandereyken, W., & Vertommen, H. (2002). Impulsive and compulsive traits in eating disordered patients compared with controls. *Personality and Individual Differences, 32*, 707–714.

Cooley, E., & Toray, T. (2001). Body image and personality predictors of eating disorder symptoms during the college years. *International Journal of Eating Disorders, 30*, 28–36.

Cools, J., Schotte, D. E., & McNally, R. J. (1992). Emotional arousal and overeating in restrained eaters. *Journal of Abnormal Psychology, 101*, 348–351.

Cowen, P. J., Clifford, E. M., Walsh, A. E. S., Williams, C., & Fairburn, C. G. (1996). Moderate dieting causes 5-HT2c receptor supersensitivity. *Psychological Medicine, 26*, 1155–1159.

Craeynest, M., Crombez, G., De Houwer, J., Deforche, B., Tanghe, A., & De Bourdeaudhij, I. (2005). Explicit and implicit attitudes towards food and physical activity in childhood obesity. *Behaviour Research and Therapy, 43*, 1111–1120.

Davis, C., Levitan, R. D., Muglia, P., Bewell, C., & Kennedy, J. L. (2004). Decision-making deficits and overeating: A risk model for obesity. *Obesity Research, 12*, 929–935.

Davis, C., Strachan, S., & Berkson, M. (2004). Sensitivity to reward: Implications for overeating and obesity. *Appetite, 42*, 131–138.

Davis, C., & Woodside, D. B. (2002). Sensitivity to rewarding effects of food and exercise in the eating disorders. *Comprehensive Psychiatry, 43*, 189–194.

Dawe, S., & Loxton, N. J. (2004). The role of impulsivity in the development of substance use and eating disorders. *Neuroscience and Biobehavioral Review, 28*, 343–351.

de Castro, J. M., & Elmore, D. K. (1988). Subjective hunger relationships with meal patterns in the spontaneous feeding behavior of humans: Evidence for a causal connection. *Physiology and Behavior, 43*, 159–165.

De Houwer, J. (2003). The extrinsic affective Simon task. *Experimental Psychology, 50*, 77–85.

Delahanty, L. M., Meigs, J. B., Hayden, D., Williamson, D. A., & Nathan, D. M. (2002). Psychological and behavioral correlates of baseline BMI in the diabetes prevention program. *Diabetes Care, 25*, 1992–1998.

De Zwaan, M., Mitchell, J. E., Crosby, R. D., Mussell, M. P., Raymond, N. C., Specker, S. M., & Seim, H. C. (2005). Short-term cognitive behavioral treatment does not improve outcome in a comprehensive very-low-calorie diet program in obese woment with binge eating disorder. *Behavior Therapy, 36*, 89–99.

Drewnowski, A. (1996). The behavioral phenotype in human obesity. In E. D. Capaldi (Ed.), *Why we eat what we eat: The psychology of eating* (pp. 291–308). Washington, DC: American Psychological Association.

Drewnowski, A., Bellisle, F., Aimez, P., & Remy, B. (1987). Taste and bulimia. *Physiology and Behavior, 41*, 621–626.

Drewnowski, A., Krahn, D. D., Demitrack, M. A., Nairn, K., & Gosnell, B. A. (1992). Taste responses and preferences for sweet high-fat foods: Evidence for opioid involvement. *Physiology and Behavior, 51*, 371–379.

Drewnowski, A., Kurth, C., Holden-Wiltse, J., & Saari, J. (1992). Food preferences in human obesity: Carbohydrates versus fats. *Appetite, 18*, 207–221.

Durrant, M. (1981). Salivation: A useful research tool? *Appetite, 2*, 362–365.

Eckern, M., Stevens, W., & Mitchell, J. E. (1999). Brief report: The relationship between rumination and eating disorders. *International Journal of Eating Disorders, 26*, 414–419.

Emmons, L. (1992). Dieting and purging behavior in black and white high school students. *Journal of the American Dietetic Association, 92*, 306–312.

Engelberg, M. J., Gauvin, L., & Steiger, H. (2005). A naturalistic evaluation of the relation between dietary restraint, the urge to binge, and actual binge eating. *International Journal of Eating Disorders, 38*, 355–360.

Epstein, L. H., Paluch, R. A., Saelens, B. E., Ernst, M. M., & Wilfley, D. E. (2001). Changes in eating disorder symptoms with pediatric obesity treatment. *Journal of Pediatrics, 139*(1), 58–65.

Epstein, L. H., Saad, F. G., Handley, E. A., Roemmich, J. N., Hawk, L.W., & McSweeney, F. K. (2003). Habituation of salivation and motivated responding for food in children. *Appetite, 41*, 283–289.

Epstein, L. H., Truesdale, R., Wojcik, A. Paluch, R. A., & Raynor, H. A. (2003). Effects of deprivation on hedonics and reinforcing value of food. *Physiology and Behavior, 78,* 221–227.

Epstein, L. H., Valoski, A., Wing, R. R., Perkins, K. A., Fernstrom, M., Marks, B., & McCurley, J. (1989). Perception of eating and exercise in children as a function of child and parental weight status. *Appetite, 12,* 105–118.

Epstein, L. H., Wright, S. M., Paluch, R. A., Leddy, J. J., Hawk, L. W., Jaroni, J. L., et al. (2004). Relation between food reinforcement and dopamine genotypes and its effect on food intake in smokers. *American Journal of Clinical Nutrition, 80,* 82–88.

Espeland, M. A., Kumanyika, S., Wilson, A. C., Wilcox, S., Chao, N., Bahnson, J., et al. (2001). Lifestyle interventions influence relative errors in self-reported diet intake of sodium and potassium. *Annuals of Epidemiology, 11,* 85–93.

Fairburn, C.G. (1997). Eating disorders. In D. M. Clark & C. G. Fairburn (Eds.), *Science and practice of cognitive behaviour therapy.* (pp. 209–241). Oxford: Oxford University Press.

Fairburn, C. G., & Beglin, S. J. (1994). Assessment of eating disorders: Interview or self-report questionnaire? *International Journal of Eating Disorders, 16,* 363–370.

Fairburn, C. G., & Cooper, Z. (1993). The Eating Disorder Examination. In C. G. Fairburn & G. T. Wilson (Eds.), *Binge eating: Nature, assessment, and treatment* (pp. 317–360). New York: Guilford Press.

Fairburn, C. G., Cooper, Z., Doll, H. A., Norman, P., & O'Connor, M. (2000). The natural course of bulimia nervosa and binge eating disorder in young women. *Archives of General Psychiatry, 57*(7), 659–665.

Farmer, R. F., Nash, H. M., & Field, C. E. (2001). Disordered eating behaviors and reward sensitivity. *Journal of Behavioral Therapy and Experimental Psychiatry, 32,* 211–219.

Fassino, S., Abbate, D. G., Amianto, F., Leombruni, P., Boggio, S., & Rovera, G. G. (2002). Temperament and character profile of eating disorders: A controlled study with the temperament and character inventory. *International Journal of Eating Disorders, 32,* 412–425.

Fazio, R. H., Sanbonmatsu, D. M., Powell, M. C., & Kardes, F. R. (1986). On the automatic activation of attitudes. *Journal of Personality and Social Psychology, 50,* 229–238.

Fedoroff, I. C., Polivy, J., & Herman, C. P. (1997). The effect of pre-exposure to food cues on the eating behavior of restrained and unrestrained eaters. *Appetite, 28,* 33–47.

Field, A. E., Camargo, C. A., Taylor, C. B., Berkey, C. S., Frazier, A. L., Gillman, M. W., & Colditz, G. A. (1999). Overweight, weight concerns, and bulimic behaviors among girls and boys. *Journal of the American Academy of Child and Adolescent Psychiatry, 38*(6), 754–760.

Fischer, S., Smith, G. T., & Anderson, K. G. (2003). Clarifying the role of impulsivity in bulimia nervosa. *International Journal of Eating Disorders, 33,* 406–411.

Fisher, J. O., & Birch, L. L. (1995). Fat preferences and fat consumption of 3– to 5–year-old children are related to parental obesity. *Journal of the American Dietetic Association, 95,* 759–764.

Fisher, J. O., & Birch, L. L. (2002). Eating in the absence of hunger and overweight in girls from 5 to 7 years of age. *American Journal of Clinical Nutrition, 76,* 226–231.

Flegal, K. M., Graubard, B. I., Williamson, D. F., & Gail, M. H. (2005). Excess deaths associated with underweight, overweight, and obesity. *JAMA, 293,* 1861–1867.

Forzano, L. B., & Logue, A. W. (1992). Predictors of adult humans' self-control and impulsiveness for food reinforcers. *Appetite, 19,* 33–47.

Foster, G. D., Wadden, T. A., Kendall, P. C., Stunkard, A. J., & Vogt, R. A. (1996). Psychological effects of weight loss and regain: A prospective evaluation. *Journal of Consulting and Clinical Psychology, 64,* 752–757.

Franken, I. H., & Muris, P. (2005). Individual differences in reward sensitivity are related to food craving and relative body weight in healthy weight women. *Appetite, 45,* 198–201.

Franko, D. L., Wolfe, B. E., & Jimerson, D. C. (1994). Elevated sweet taste pleasantness ratings in bulimia nervosa. *Physiology and Behavior, 56,* 969–973.

French, S. A., Jeffery, R.W., Forster, J. L., McGovern, P. G., Kelder, S. H., & Baxter, J. E. (1994). Predictors of weight change over two years among a population of working adults: the Healthy Worker Project. *International Journal of Obesity, 18,* 145–154.

French, S., Jeffery, R. W., & Murray, D. (1999). Is dieting good for you? Prevalence, duration, and associated weight and behavior changes for specific weight loss strategies over four years in US adults. *International Journal of Obesity, 23,* 320–327.

French, S. A., Jeffery, R. W., & Wing, R. R. (1994). Food intake and physical activity: A comparison of three measures of dieting. *Addictive Behaviors, 19,* 401–409.

French, S. A., Perry, C. L., & Leon, G. R. (1995). Dieting behaviors and weight change history in female adolescents. *Health Psychology, 14*(6), 548–555.

Friederich, H. C., Kumari, V., Uher, R., Riga, M., Schmidt, U., Campbell, I. C., et al. (2006). Differential motivational responses to food and pleasurable cues in anorexia nervosa and bulimia nervosa: A startle reflex paradigm. *Psychological Medicine, 36,* 1327–1335.

Galanti, K., Gluck, M. E., & Geliebter, A. (2007). Test meal intake in obese binge eaters in relation to compulsivity and impulsivity. *International Journal of Eating Disorders, 40,* 727–732.

Gendall, K. A., Joyce, P. R., Sullivan, P. F., & Bulik, C. M. (1998). Food cravers: Characteristics of those who binge. *International Journal of Eating Disorders, 23,* 353–360.

Glantz, M. D. (2002). Introduction to the special issue on the impact of childhood psychopathology interventions on subsequent substance abuse: Pieces of the puzzle. *Journal of Consulting and Clinical Psychology, 70,* 1203–1206.

Goldfield, G. S., & Legg, C. (2006). Dietary restraint, anxiety, and the relative reinforcing value of snack food in non-obese women. *Eating Behaviors, 7,* 323–332.

Goodrick, G. K., Poston, W. S., Kimball, K. T., Reeves, R. S., & Foreyt, J. P. (1998). Nondieting versus dieting treatments for overweight binge-eating women. *Journal of Consulting and Clinical Psychology, 66,* 363–368.

Greenwald, A. G., McGhee, D. E., & Schwartz, J. L. (1998). Measuring individual differences in implicit cognition: the Implicit Association Test. *Journal of Personality and Social Psychology, 74,* 1464–1480.

Grilo, C. M., & Masheb, R. M. (2005). A randomized controlled comparison of guided self-help cognitive behavioral therapy and behavioral weight loss for binge eating disorder. *Behaviour Research and Therapy, 43,* 1509–1525.

Groesz, L. M., & Stice, E. (2007). An experimental test of the effects of dieting on bulimic symptoms: The impact of eating episode frequency. *Behaviour Research and Therapy, 45,* 49–62.

Guarda, A. S., Coughlin, J. W., Cummings, M., Marinilli, A., Haug, N., Boucher, M., & Heinberg, L. J. (2004). Chewing and spitting in eating disorders and its relationship to binge eating. *Eating Behaviors, 5*, 231–239.

Guerrieri, R., Nederkoorn, C., & Jansen, A. (2007). How impulsiveness and variety influence food intake in a sample of healthy women. *Appetite, 48*, 119–122.

Guss, J. L., & Kissileff, H. R. (2000). Microstructural analyses of human ingestive patterns: From description to mechanistic hypotheses. *Neuroscience Biobehavioral Review, 24*, 261–268.

Hagan, M. M., Chandler, P. C., Wauford, P. K., Rybak, R. J., & Oswald, K. D. (2003). The role of palatable food and hunger as trigger factors in an animal model of stress induced binge eating. *International Journal of Eating Disorders, 34*, 183–197.

Hagan, M. M., Wauford, P. K., Chandler, P. C., Jarrett, L. A., Rybak, R. J., & Blackburn, K. (2002). A new animal model of binge eating: Key synergistic role of past caloric restriction and stress. *Physiology and Behavior, 77*, 45–54.

Harvey, J., Wing, R. R., & Mullen, M. (1993). Effects on food cravings of a very low calorie diet or a balanced, low calorie diet. *Appetite, 21*, 105–115.

Heatherton, T. F., Herman, C. P., & Polivy, J. (1991). Effects of physical threat and ego threat on eating behavior. *Journal of Personality and Social Psychology, 60*, 138–143.

Heatherton, T. F., Herman, C. P., Polivy, J., King, G. A., & McGree, S. T. (1988). The (mis)measurement of restraint: An analysis of conceptual and psychometric issues. *Journal of Abnormal Psychology, 97*, 19–28.

Heatherton, T. F., & Polivy, J. (1992). Chronic dieting and eating disorders: A spiral model. In J. H. Crowther, D. L. Tennenbaum, S. E. Hobfold, M. A. Parris (Eds.), *The etiology of bulimia nervosa: The individual and familial context* (pp. 133–155). Washington, DC: Hemisphere.

Hedley, A. A., Odgen, C. L., Johnson, C. L., Carroll, M. D., Curtin, L. R., & Flegal, K. M. (2004). Prevalence of overweight and obesity among US children, adolescents, and adults, 1999–2000. *Journal of the American Medical Association, 291*, 2847–2850.

Heilbronn, L. K., Jonge, L., Frisard, M. I., DeLany, J. P., Larson-Meyer, D. E., Rood, J. et al. (2006). Effect of 6-month calorie restriction on biomarkers of longevity, metabolic adaption, and oxidative stress in overweight individuals: A randomized controlled trial. *JAMA, 295*, 1539–1548.

Herman, C.P., & Mack, D. (1975). Restrained and unrestrained eating. *Journal of Personality, 43*, 647–660.

Herman, C. P., & Polivy, J. (1975). Anxiety, restraint, and eating behavior. *Journal of Abnormal Psychology, 84*, 666–672.

Hetherington, M. M., Stoner, S. A., Andersen, A. E., & Rolls, B. J. (2000). Effects of acute food deprivation on eating behavior in eating disorders. *International Journal of Eating Disorders, 28*, 272–283.

Hill, A. J., Weaver, C. F., & Blundell, J. (1991). Food craving, dietary restraint and mood. *Appetite, 17*, 187–197.

Hinshaw, S. P. (2002). Intervention research, theoretical mechanisms, and causal processes related to externalizing behavior patterns. *Development and Psychopathology, 14*, 789–818.

Hofmann, W., Rauch, W., & Gawronski, B. (2007). And deplete us not into temptation: Automatic attitudes, dietary restraint, and self-regulatory resources as determinants of eating behavior. *Journal of Experimental Social Psychology, 43*, 497–504.

Jacobi, C., Hayward, C., Zwaan, M., Kraemer, H. C., & Agras, W. S. (2004). Coming to terms with risk factors for eating disorders: Application of risk terminology and suggestions for a general taxonomy. *Psychological Bulletin, 130*, 19–65.

Jacobs, S. B., & Wagner, M. K. (1984). Obese and nonobese individuals: Behavioral and personality characteristics. *Addictive Behaviors, 9*, 223–226.

Jansen, A. (1996). How restrained eaters perceive the amount they eat. *British Journal of Clinical Psychology, 35*, 381–392.

Jansen, A. (1998). A learning model of binge eating: Cue reactivity and cue exposure. *Behaviour Research and Therapy, 36*, 257–272.

Jansen, A., Merckelbach, H., Oosterlaan, J., Tuiten, A., & van den Hout, M. (1988). Cognitions and self-talk during food intake of restrained and unrestrained eaters. *Behaviour Research and Therapy, 26*, 393–380.

Jansen, A., Theunissen, N., Slechten, K., Nederkoorn, C., Boon, B., Mulkens, S., & Roefs, A. (2003). Overweight children overeat after exposure to food cues. *Eating Behaviors, 4*, 197–209.

Jansen, A., & van den Hout, M. (1991). On being led into temptation: 'Counterregulation' of dieters after smelling a 'preload'. *Addictive Behaviors, 5*, 247–253.

Jeffery, R., Drewnowski, A., Epstein, L. H., Stunkard, A. J., Wilson, G. T., Wing, R. R., & Hill, D. (2000). Long-term maintenance of weight loss: Current status. *Health Psychology, 19*, 5–16.

Johnson, F., & Wardle, J. (2005). Dietary restraint, body dissatisfaction, and psychological distress: A prospective analysis. *Journal of Abnormal Psychology, 114*, 119–124.

Johnson, W. G. (1974). Effect of cue prominence and subject weight on human food-directed performance. *Journal of Personality and Social Psychology, 29*, 843–848.

Johnson, W. G., & Wildman, H. E. (1983). Influence of external and covert food stimuli on insulin secretion in obese and normal persons. *Behavioral Neuroscience, 97*, 1025–1028.

Jonsson, B., Bjorvell, H., Lavander, S., & Rossner, S. (1986). Personality traits predicting weight loss outcome in obese patients. *Acta Psyciatrica Scandinavia, 74*, 384–387.

Kane, T. A., Loxton, N. J., Staiger, P. K., & Dawe, S. (2004). Does the tendency to act impulsively underlie binge eating and alcohol use problems? An empirical investigation. *Personality and Individual Differences, 36*, 83–94.

Karhunen, L. J., Lappalainen, R. I., Tammela, L., Turpeinen, A. K., & Uusitupa, M. I. (1997). Subjective and physiological cephalic phase responses to food in obese binge-eating women. *International Journal of Eating Disorders, 21*, 321–328.

Kaye, W., Gendall, K., & Strober, M. (1998). Serotonin neuronal function and selective serotonin reuptake inhibitor treatment in anorexia and bulimia nervosa. *Biological Psychiatry, 44*, 825–838.

Keys, A., Brozek, J., Henschel, A., Mickelsen, O., & Taylor, H. L. (1950). *The Biology of Human Starvation*. Minneapolis, MN: University of Minnesota Press.

Killen, J. D., Hayward, C., Wilson, D. M, & Taylor, C. B., Hammer, L. D., Litt, I. et al. (1994). Factors associated with eating disorder symptoms in a community sample of 6th and 7th grade girls. *International Journal of Eating Disorders, 15*, 357–367.

Killen, J. D., Taylor, C. B., Hayward, C., Haydel, K. F., Wilson, D. M., Hammer, L., et al. (1996). Weight concerns influence the development of eating disorders: A 4-year prospective study. *Journal of Consulting and Clinical Psychology, 64*, 936–940.

Kirkley, B. G., Burge, J. C., & Ammerman, A. (1988). Dietary restraint, binge eating, and dietary behavior patterns. *International Journal of Eating Disorders, 7*, 771–778.

Kissileff, H. R., Wantzlaff, T. H., Guss, J. L., Walsh, B. T., Devlin, M. J., & Thornton, J. C. (1996). A direct measure of satiety disturbance in patients with bulimia nervosa. *Physiology and Behavior, 60*, 1077–1085.

Klajner, F., Herman, C. P., Polivy, J., & Chhabra, R. (1981). Human obesity, dieting, and anticipatory salivation to food. *Physiology and Behavior, 27*, 195–198.

Klein, D. A., Boudreau, G. S., Devlin, M. J., & Walsh, B. T. (2005). Use of artificial sweetened products in eating disorders. *Appetite, 42*, 374.

Klein, D. A., Boudreau, G. S., Devlin, M. J., & Walsh, B. T. (2006). Artificial sweetener use among individuals with eating disorders. *International Journal of Eating Disorders, 39*, 341–345.

Klem, M. L., Wing, R. R., Simkin-Silverman, L., & Kuller, L. H. (1997). The psychological consequences of weight gain prevention in healthy, premenopausal women. *International Journal of Eating Disorders, 21*, 167–174.

Klesges, R. C., Isbell, T. R., & Klesges, L. M. (1992). Relationship between dietary restraint, energy intake, physical activity, and body weight: A prospective analysis. *Journal of Abnormal Psychology, 101*, 668–674.

Klesges, R. C., Klem, M. L., & Bene, C. R. (1989). Effects of dietary restraint, obesity, and gender on holiday eating behavior and weight gain. *Journal of Abnormal Psychology, 98*, 499–503.

Kovacs, D., Mahon, J., & Palmer, R. L. (2002). Chewing and spitting out food among eating-disordered patients. *International Journal of Eating Disorders, 32*, 112–115.

Kraemer, H. C., Stice, E., Kazdin, A., Offord, D., & Kupfer, D. (2001). How do risk factors work? Mediators, moderators, independent, overlapping, and proxy risk factors. *American Journal of Psychiatry, 158*, 848–856.

LaChaussee, J. L., Kissileff, H. R., Walsh, B. T., & Hadigan, C. M. (1992). The single item meal as a measure of binge-eating behavior in patients with bulimia nervosa. *Physiology and Behavior, 51*, 593–600.

Lappalainen, R., Sjoden, P., Hursti, T., & Vesa, V. (1990). Hunger/craving responses and reactivity to food stimuli during fasting and dieting. *International Journal of Obesity, 14*, 679–688.

Legenbauer, T., Vogele, C., & Ruddel, H. (2004). Anticipatory effects of food exposure in women diagnosed with bulimia nervosa. *Appetite, 42*, 33–40.

LeGoff, D. B., & Spigelman, M. N. (1987). Salivary responses to olfactory food stimuli as a function of dietary restraint and body weight. *Appetite, 8*, 29–35.

LeGoff, D., Leichner, P., & Spigelman, M. (1988). Salivary responses to olfactory food stimuli in anorexics and bulimics. *Appetite, 11*, 15–25.

Leon, G. R., Fulkerson, J. A., Perry, C. L., Keel, P. K., & Klump, K. L. (1999). Three to four year prospective evaluation of personality and behavioral risk factors for later disordered eating in adolescent girls and boys. *Journal of Youth and Adolescence, 28*, 181–196.

Levine, M. P., & Smolak, L. (2006). *The prevention of eating problems and eating disorders: Theory, research, and practice.* Mahwah, NJ: Lawrence Erlbaum Associates.

Lichtman, S. W., Pisarska, K., Berman, E. R., & Pestone, M. (1992). Discrepancy between self-reported and actual caloric intake and exercise in obese subjects. *New England Journal of Medicine, 327*, 1893–1898.

Livingstone, M. B., Prentice, A. M., Strain, J. J., Coward, W. A., Black, A. E., Barker, M. E., et al. (1990). Accuracy of weighed dietary records in studies of diet and health. *British Medical Journal, 300*, 708–712.

Logue, A. W., & King, G. R. (1991). Self-control and impulsiveness in adult humans when food is the reinforcer. *Appetite, 17*, 105–120.

Lowe, M. R. (1992). Staying on versus going off a diet: Effects on eating in normal weight and overweight individuals. *International Journal of Eating Disorders, 12*, 417–424.

Lowe, M. R. (1994). Putting restrained and unrestrained nondieters on short-term diets - effects on eating. *Addictive Behaviors, 19*(4), 349–356.

Lowe, M. R., Foster, G. D., Kerzhnerman, I., Swain, R. M., & Wadden, T. A. (2001). Restrictive dieting vs. 'undieting': Effects on eating regulation in obese clinic attenders. *Addictive Behaviors, 26*, 253–266.

Lowe, M. R., & Kral, T. V. E. (2006). Stress-induced eating in restrained eaters may not be caused by stress or restraint. *Appetite, 46*, 16–21.

Lowe, M. R., & Levine, A. S. (2005). Eating motives and the controversy over dieting: Eating less than needed versus less than wanted. *Obesity Research, 13*, 797–806.

Loxton, N. J., & Dawe, S. (2006). Reward and punishment sensitivity in dysfunctional eating and hazardous drinking women: Associations with family risk. *Appetite, 47*(3), 361–371.

Loxton, N. J., & Dawe, S. (2007). How do dysfunctional eating and hazardous drinking women perform on behavioural measures of reward and punishment sensitivity? *Personality and Individual Differences, 42*, 1163–1172.

Marlatt, G. A., & Gordon, J. R. (1985). *Relapse prevention: Maintenance strategies in the treatment of addictive behaviors.* New York: Guilford Press.

Martin, C. K., Makris, A., Brill, C., Stein, R., Bailer, B., Rosenbaum, D., et al. (2006). Restriction of certain types of foods during low calorie/low fat vs. low carbohydrate diets results in decreased cravings and preferences for restricted foods. *Obesity Research, 14*, A1–A318.

Martin, C. K., O'Neil, P. M., & Pawlow, L. (2006). Changes in food cravings during low-calorie and very-low-calorie diets. *Obesity, 14*, 115–121.

Martin, C. K., Williamson, D. A., Geiselman, P. J., Walden, H., Smeets, M., Morales, S., et al. (2005). Consistency of food intake over four eating sessions in the laboratory. *Eating Behaviors, 6*, 365–372.

Mauler, B. I., Hamm, A. O., Weike, A. I., & Tuschen-Caffier, B. (2006). Affect regulation and food intake in bulimia nervosa: Emotional responding to food cues after deprivation and subsequent eating. *Journal of Abnormal Psychology, 115*, 567–579.

McCrory, M. A., Suen, V. M., & Roberts, S. B. (2002). Biobehavioral influences on energy intake and adult weight gain. *Journal of Nutrition, 132*, 3830S-3834S.

McGloin, A. F., Livingstone, M. B., Greene, L. C., Webb, S. E., Gibson, J. M., Jebb, S. A., et al. (2002). Energy and fat intake in obese children and lean children at varying risk of obesity. *International Journal of Obesity, 26*, 200–207.

Mitchell, J. E., Hatsukami, D., Pyle, R. L., & Eckert, E. D. (1985). Characteristics of 275 patients with bulimia. *American Journal of Psychiatry, 142*, 482–485.

Mitchell, J. E., Pyle, R. L., Eckert, E. D., Hatsukami, D., Pomeroy, C., & Zimmerman, R. (1990). A comparison study of antidepressants and structured intensive group psychotherapy in the treatment of bulimia nervosa. *Archives of General Psychiatry, 47*, 149–157.

Morgan, K. J., Zabik, M. E., & Stampley, G. L. (1986). The role of breakfast in diet adequacy of the US adult population. *Journal of the American College of Nutrition, 5*, 551–563.

Munsch, S., Biedert, E., Meyer, A., Michael, T., Schlup, B., Tuch, A., & Margraf, J. (2007). A randomized comparison of cognitive behavioral therapy and behavioral weight loss treatment for overweight individuals with binge eating disorder. *International Journal of Eating Disorders, 40*, 102–113.

Nasser, J. A., Gluck, M. E., & Geliebter, A. (2004). Impulsivity and test meal intake in obese binge eating women. *Appetite, 43*, 303–307.

National Task Force on the Prevention and Treatment of Obesity. (2000). Dieting and the development of eating disorders in overweight and obese adults. *Archives of Internal Medicine, 160*, 2581–2589.

Nauta, H., Hospers, H., Kok, G., & Jansen, A. (2000). A comparison between a cognitive and a behavioral treatment for obese binge eaters and obese non-binge eaters. *Behavior Therapy, 31*, 441–461.

Nederkoorn, C., Braet, C., van Eijs, Y., Tanghe, A., & Jansen, A. (2006). Why obese children cannot easily resist food: The role of impulsivity. *Eating Behaviors, 7*, 315–322.

Nederkoorn, C., Jansen, E., Mulkens, S., & Jansen, A. (2007). Impulsivity predicts treatment outcome in obese children. *Behaviour Research and Therapy, 45*, 1071–1075.

Nederkoorn, C., & Jansen, A. (2002). Cue reactivity and regulation of food intake. *Eating Behaviors, 3*, 61–72.

Nederkoorn, C., Smulders, F. T., Havermans, R. C., Roefs, A., & Jansen, A. (2006). Impulsivity in obese women. *Appetite, 47*, 253–256.

Nederkoorn, C., Smulders, F. T., & Jansen, A. (2000). Cephalic phase responses, cravings and food intake in normal subjects. *Appetite, 35*, 45–55.

Nederkoorn, C., van Eijs, Y., & Jansen, A. (2004). Restrained eaters act on impulse. *Personality and Individual Differences, 37*, 1651–1658.

Neumark-Sztainer, D., Butler, R., & Palti, H. (1995). Dieting and binge eating: Which dieters are at risk? *Journal of the American Dietetic Association, 95*, 586–589.

Neumark-Sztainer, D., Jeffery, R. W., & French, S. A. (1997). Self-reported dieting: How should we ask? What does it mean? Associations between dieting and reported energy intake. *International Journal of Eating Disorders, 22*, 437–449.

Neumark-Sztainer, D., Wall, M., Guo, J., Story, M., Haines, J., & Eisenberg, M. (2006). Obesity, disordered eating, and eating disorders in a longitudinal study of adolescents: How do dieters fare 5 years later? *Journal of the American Dietetic Association, 106*, 559–568.

Nicklas, T. A., Yang, S. J., Baranowski, T., Zakeri, I., & Berenson, G. (2003). Eating patterns and obesity in children: The Bogalusa heart study. *American Journal of Preventive Medicine, 25*, 9–16.

Ogawa, R., Strader, A. D., Clegg, D. J., Sakai, R. R., Seeley, R. J., & Woods, S. C. (2005). Chronic food restriction and reduced dietary fat: Risk factors for bouts of overeating. *Physiology and Behavior, 86*, 578–585.

Ouwens, M. A., van Strien, T., & van der Staak, C. P. F. (2003). Tendency toward overeating and restraint as predictors of food consumption. *Appetite, 40*, 291–298.

Patterson, T. A., Brot, M. D., Zavish, A., Schenk, J. O., Snot, P., & Figlewicz, D. P. (1998). Food deprivation decreases mRNA and activity of the rat dopamine transporter. *Neuroendocrinology, 68*, 11–20.

Patton, G. C., Johnson-Sabine, E., Wood, K., Mann, A. H., & Wakeling, A. (1990). Abnormal eating attitudes in London schoolgirls: A prospective epidemiological study: Outcome at twelve month follow-up. *Psychological Medicine, 20*, 383–394.

Patton, G. C., Selzer, R., Coffey, C., Carlin, J. B., & Wolfe, R. (1999). Onset of adolescent eating disorders: Population based cohort study over 3 years. *British Medical Journal, 318*, 765–768.

Pearlstein, T., Spurell, E., Hohlstein, L. A., Gurney, V., Read, J., Fuchs, C., & Keller, M. B. (2003). A double-blind, placebo-controlled trial of fluvoxamine in binge eating disorder: A high placebo response. *Archives of Women's Mental Health, 6*, 147–151.

Pelchat, M. L. (1997). Food cravings in young and elderly adults. *Appetite, 28*, 103–113.

Penas-Lledo, E., & Waller, G. (2001). Bulimic psychopathology and impulsive behaviors among nonclinical women. *International Journal of Eating Disorders, 29*, 71–75.

Pidcock, B. W., Fischer, J. L., Forthun, L. F., & West, S. L. (2000). Hispanic and Anglo college women's risk factors for substance use and eating disorders. *Addictive Behavior, 25*, 705–723.

Placanica, J. L., Faunce, G. J., & Job, R. F. S. (2002). The effect of fasting on attentional biases for food and body shape/weight words in high and low eating disorder inventory scores. *International Journal of Eating Disorders, 32*, 79–90.

Polivy, J. (1976). Perception of calories and regulation of intake in restrained and unrestrained subjects. *Addictive Behaviors, 1*, 237–243.

Polivy, J., Coleman, J., & Herman, C. P. (2005). The effect of deprivation on food cravings and eating behavior in restrained and unrestrained eaters. *International Journal of Eating Disorders, 38*, 301–309.

Polivy, J., & Herman, C. P. (1976). Effects of alcohol on eating behavior: Influence of mood and perceived intoxication. *Journal of Abnormal Psychology, 85*, 601–606.

Polivy, J., & Herman, C. P. (1985). Dieting and binge eating: A causal analysis. *American Psychologist, 40*, 193–204.

Polivy, J., & Herman, C. P. (1992). Undieting: A program to help people stop dieting. *International Journal of Eating Disorders, 11*, 261–268.

Polivy, J., Herman, C. P., & McFarlane, T. (1994). Effects of anxiety on eating: Does palatability moderate distress-induced overeating in dieters? *Journal of Abnormal Psychology, 103*, 505–510.

Polivy, J., Herman, C. P., & Warsh, S. (1978). Internal and external components of emotionality in restrained and unrestrained eaters. *Journal of Abnormal Psychology, 87*, 497–504.

Pothos, E. N., Hernandez, L., & Hoebel, B. G. (1995). Chronic food deprivation decreases extracellular dopamine in the nucleus accumbens: Implications for a possible neurochemical link between weight loss and drug abuse. *Obesity Research, 3*, 525s–529s.

Prentice, A. M., Black, A. E., Coward, W. A., Davies, H. L., Goldberg, G. R., & Murgatroyd, P. R., et al. (1986). High-levels of energy-expenditure in obese women. *British Medical Journal, 292*(6526), 983–987.

Presnell, K., & Stice, E. (2003). An experimental test of the effect of weight-loss dieting on bulimic pathology: Tipping the scales in a different direction. *Journal of Abnormal Psychology, 112*, 166–170.

Presnell, K., Stice, E., & Tristan, J. (2007). An experimental investigation of the effects of naturalistic dieting on bulimic symptoms: Moderating effects of depressive symptoms. *Appetite, 50,* 91–101.

Raynor, H. A., & Epstein, L. H. (2003). The relative-reinforcing value of food under differing levels of food deprivation and restriction. *Appetite, 40,* 15–24.

Redman, L. M., Martin, C. K., Williamson, D. A., & Ravussin, E. (2008). Effect of caloric restriction in non-obese humans on physiological, psychological, and behavioral outcomes. *Physiology and Behavior, 94,* 643–648.

Reeves, R. S., McPherson, R. S., Nichaman, M. Z., Harrist, R. B., Foreyt, J. P., & Goodrick, G. K. (2001). Nutrient intake of obese female binge eaters. *Journal of the American Dietetic Association, 101,* 209–215.

Rodin, J., Mancuso, J., Granger, J., & Nelbach, E. (1991). Food cravings in relation to body mass index, restraint, and estradiol levels: A repeated measures study in healthy women. *Appetite, 17,* 177–185.

Roefs, A., Herman, C. P., MacLeod, C. M., Smulders, F. T., & Jansen, A. (2005). At first sight: How do restrained eaters evaluate high-fat palatable foods? *Appetite, 44,* 103–114.

Roefs, A., & Jansen, A. (2002). Implicit and explicit attitudes toward high-fat foods in obesity. *Journal of Abnormal Psychology, 111,* 517–521.

Rogers, P. J., & Hill, A. J. (1989). Breakdown of dietary restraint following mere exposure to food stimuli: Interrelationships between restraint, hunger, salivation, and food intake. *Addictive Behaviors, 14,* 387–397.

Rolls, B. J., Castellanos, V. H., Shide, D. J., Miller, D. L., Pelkman, C. L., Thorwart, M. L., et al. (1997). Sensory properties of a nonabsorbable fat substitute did not affect regulation of energy intake. *American Journal of Clinical Nutrition, 65,* 1375–1383.

Rolls, B. J., Rolls, E. T., Rowe, E. A., & Sweeney, K. (1981). Sensory specific satiety in man. *Physiology and Behavior, 27,* 137–142.

Rosen, J. C. (1981). Effects of low calorie dieting and exposure to diet-prohibited food on appetite and anxiety. *Appetite, 2,* 366–369.

Ryden, A., Sullivan, M., Torgerson, J. S., Karlsson, J., Lindroos, A. K., & Taft, C. (2003). Severe obesity and personality: A comparative controlled study of personality traits. *International Journal of Obesity, 27,* 1534–1540.

Saelens, B. E., & Epstein, L. H. (1996). The reinforcing value of food in obese and non-obese women. *Appetite, 27,* 41–50.

Sahakian, B. J., Lean, M. E., Robbins, T. W., & James, W. P. (1981). Salivation and insulin secretion in response to food in non-obese men and women. *Appetite, 2,* 209–216.

Santonastaso, P., Friederici, S., & Favaro, A. (1999). Full and partial syndromes in eating disorders: A 1-year prospective study of risk factors among female students. *Psychopathology, 32*(1), 50–56.

Schachter, S., Goldman, R., & Gordon, A. (1968). Effects of fear, food deprivation, and obesity on dieting. *Journal of Personality and Social Psychology, 10,* 91–97.

Schlundt, D. G., Hill, J. O., Sbrocco, T., Pope-Cordle, J., & Sharp, T. (1992). The role of breakfast in the treatment of obesity: A randomized clinical trial. *American Journal of Clinical Nutrition, 55,* 645–651.

Schotte, D.E., Cools, J., & McNally, R.J. (1990). Film-induced negative affect triggers overeating in restrained eaters. *Journal of Abnormal Psychology, 99,* 317–320.

Serdula, M. K., Collins, M. E., Williamson, D. F., Anda, R. F., Pamuk, E., & Byter, T. E. (1993). Weight control practices of United-States adolescents and adults. *Annals of Internal Medicine, 119*(7), 667–671.

Smolak, L., Levine, M., & Schermer, F. (1998). A controlled evaluation of an elementary school primary prevention program for eating problems. *Journal of Psychosomatic Research, 44,* 339–353.

Sobhany, M. S., & Rogers, C. S. (1985). External responsiveness to food and non-food cues among obese and non-obese children. *International Journal of Obesity, 9,* 99–106.

Spencer, J. A., & Fremouw, W. J. (1979). Binge eating as a function of restraint and weight classification. *Journal of Abnormal Psychology, 88,* 262–267.

Spiegel, T. A., Shrager, E. E., & Steller, E. (1989). Responses of lean and obese subjects to preloads, deprivation, and palatability. *Appetite, 13,* 45–69.

Spoor, S. T. P., Stice, E., Bekker, M. H., van Strien, T., Croon, M. A., & van Heck, G. L. (2006). Relations between dietary restraint, depressive symptoms, and binge eating: A longitudinal study. *International Journal of Eating Disorders, 39,* 700–707.

Staiger, P., Dawe, S., & McCarthy, R. (2000). Responsivity to food cues in bulimic women and controls. *Appetite, 35,* 27–33.

Sterritt, G. M. (1962). Inhibition and facilitation of eating by electric shock. *Journal of Comparative and Physiological Psychology, 55,* 226–229.

Stewart, D. A., Carter, J. C., Drinkwater, J., Hainsworth, J., & Fairburn, C. G. (2001). Modification of eating attitudes and behavior in adolescent girls: A controlled study. *International Journal of Eating Disorders, 29,* 107–118.

Stice, E. (1998). Relations of restraint and negative affect to bulimic pathology: A longitudinal test of three competing models. *International Journal of Eating Disorders, 23*(3), 243–260.

Stice, E. (2001). A prospective test of the dual pathway model of bulimic pathology: Mediating effects of dieting and negative affect. *Journal of Abnormal Psychology, 110,* 124–135.

Stice, E. (2002). Risk and maintenance factors for eating pathology: A meta-analytic review. *Psychological Bulletin, 128,* 825–848.

Stice, E., & Agras, W. S. (1998). Predicting onset and cessation of bulimic behaviors during adolescence: A longitudinal grouping analysis. *Behavior Therapy, 29,* 257–276.

Stice, E., Agras, W. S., & Hammer, L. (1999). Factors influencing the onset of childhood eating disturbances: A five-year prospective study. *International Journal of Eating Disorders, 25,* 375–387.

Stice, E., & Bulik, C. M. (2008). Eating disorders In T. P. Beauchaine, & S. P. Hinshaw (Eds.), *Child and adolescent psychopathology* (pp. 643–669). Hoboken, NJ: John Wiley & Sons.

Stice, E., Cameron, R., Killen, J. D., Hayward, C., & Taylor, C. B. (1999). Naturalistic weight reduction efforts prospectively predict growth in relative weight and onset of obesity among female adolescents. *Journal of Consulting and Clinical Psychology, 67,* 967–974.

Stice, E., Cooper, J. A., Schoeller, D. A., Tappe, K., & Lowe, M. R. (2007). Are dietary restraint scales valid measures of moderate- to long-term dietary restriction? Objective biological and behavioral data suggest not. *Psychological Assessment, 19,* 449–458.

Stice, E., Davis, K., Miller, N. P., & Marti, C. N. (2008). Fasting increases risk for onset of binge eating and bulimic pathology: A 5-year prospective study. *Journal of Abnormal Psychology, 117*, 941–946.

Stice, E., Fisher, M., & Lowe, M. R. (2004). Are dietary restraint scales valid measures of acute dietary restriction? Unobtrusive observational data suggest not. *Psychological Assessment, 16*, 51–59.

Stice, E., Marti, N., Spoor, S., Presnell, K., & Shaw, H. (2008). Dissonance and healthy weight eating disorder prevention programs: Long-term effects from a randomized efficacy trial. *Journal of Consulting and Clinical Psychology, 76*, 329–340.

Stice, E., Presnell, K., Gau, J., & Shaw, H. (2007). Testing mediators of intervention effects in randomized controlled trials: An evaluation of two eating disorder prevention programs. *Journal of Consulting and Clinical Psychology, 75*, 20–32.

Stice, E., Presnell, K., Shaw, H., & Rohde, P. (2005). Psychological and behavioral risk factors for obesity onset in adolescent girls: A prospective study. *Journal of Consulting and Clinical Psychology, 73*(2), 195–202.

Stice, E., Presnell, K., & Spangler, D. (2002). Risk factors for binge eating onset: A prospective investigation. *Health Psychology, 21*, 131–138.

Stice, E., & Shaw, H. (2004). Eating disorder prevention programs: A meta-analytic review. *Psychological Bulletin, 130*, 206–227.

Stice, E., Shaw, H., Burton, E., & Wade, E. (2006). Dissonance and healthy weight eating disorder prevention programs: A randomized efficacy trial. *Journal of Consulting and Clinical Psychology, 74*(2), 263–275.

Stice, E., Spoor, S., Bohon, C., & Small, D. (2008). Relation between obesity and blunted striatal response to food is moderated by the TaqIA1 gene. *Science, 322*, 449–452.

Stice, E., Spoor, S., Bohon, C., Veldhuizen, M., & Small, D. (2008). Relation of reward from food intake and anticipated intake to obesity: A functional magnetic resonance imaging study. *Journal of Abnormal Psychology, 117*, 924–935.

Strauss, J., Doyle, A. E., & Kreipe, R. E. (1994). The paradoxical effect of diet commercials on reinhibition of dietary restraint. *Journal of Abnormal Psychology, 103*, 441–444.

Stunkard, A. J., Berkowitz, R. I., Stallings, V. A., & Schoeller, D. A. (1999). Energy intake, not energy output, is a determinant of body size in infants. *American Journal of Clinical Nutrition, 69*, 524–530.

Stunkard, A. J., & Messick, S. (1985). The three-factor eating questionnaire to measure dietary restraint, disinhibition and hunger. *Journal of Psychosomatic Research, 29*, 71–83.

Sunday, S. R., & Halmi, K. A. (1990). Taste perceptions and hedonics in eating disorders. *Physiology and Behavior, 113*, 173.

Sunday, S. R., & Halmi, K. A. (1996). Micro- and macroanalyses of patterns within a meal in anorexia and bulimia nervosa. *Appetite, 26*, 21–36.

Sundgot-Borgen, J., Rosenvinge, J. H., Bahr, R., & Schneider, L. S. (2002). The effect of exercise, cognitive therapy, and nutritional counseling in treating bulimia nervosa. *Medicine and Science in Sports and Exercise, 34*, 190–195.

Sysko, R., Walsh, T. B., Schebendach, J., & Wilson, G. T. (2005). Eating behaviors among women with anorexia nervosa. *American Journal of Clinical Nutrition, 82*, 296–301.

Sysko, R., Walsh, B. T., & Wilson, G. T. (2007). Expectancies, dietary restraint, and test meal intake among undergraduate women. *Appetite, 49*, 30–37.

Tanofsky-Kraff, M., Cohen, M. L., Yanovski, S. Z., Cox, C., Theim, K. R., Keil, M., et al. (2007). A prospective study of psychological predictors of body fat gain among children at high risk for adult obesity. *Pediatrics, 117*, 1203–1209.

Telch, C. F., & Agras, W. S. (1993). The effect of a very-low-calorie diet on binge-eating. *Behavior Therapy, 24*, 177–193.

Telch, C. F., & Agras, W. S. (1996). The effects of short-term food deprivation on caloric intake in eating-disordered subjects. *Appetite, 26*(3), 221–233.

Timmerman, G. M., & Gregg, E. K. (2003). Dieting, perceived deprivation, and preoccupation with food. *Western Journal of Nursing Research, 25*, 405–418.

Tuschl, R. J., Platte, P., Laessle, R. G., Stichler, W., & Pirke, K. M. (1990). Energy expenditure and everyday eating behavior in healthy young women. *American Journal of Clinical Nutrition, 52*, 81–86.

Uher, R., Murphy, T., Brammer, M. J., Dalgleish, T., Ng, V. W., Andrew, C. M., et al. (2004). Medial prefrontal cortex activity associated with symptom provocation in eating disorders. *American Journal of Psychiatry, 161*, 1238–1246.

van Strien, T., Cleven, A., & Schippers, G. (2000). Restraint, tendency toward overeating, and ice cream consumption. *International Journal of Eating Disorders, 28*, 333–338.

van Strien, T., Frijters, J. E., van Staveren, W. A., Defares, P. B., & Deurenberg, P. (1986). The predictive validity of the Dutch Restrained Eating Scale. *International Journal of Eating Disorders, 5*, 747–755.

Vervaet, M., Audenaert, K., & van Heeringen, C. (2003). Cognitive and behavioural characteristics are associated with personality dimensions in patients with eating disorders. *European Eating Disorder Review, 11*, 363–378.

Volkow, N. D., Wang, G. J., Telang, F., Fowler, J. S., Thanos, P. K., Logan, J., et al., (2008). Low dopamine striatal D2 receptors are associated with prefrontal metabolism in obese subjects: Possible contributing factors. *NeuroImage, 42*, 1537.

Wadden, T. A., Brownell, K. D., & Foster, G. D. (2002). Obesity: Responding to the global epidemic. *Journal of Consulting and Clinical Psychology, 70*, 510–525.

Wadden, T. A., Foster, G. D., & Letizia, K. A. (1994). One-year behavioral treatment of obesity: Comparison of moderate and severe caloric restriction and the effects of weight maintenance therapy. *Journal of Consulting and Clinical Psychology, 62*, 165–171.

Wadden, T. A., Foster, G. D., Sarwer, D. B., Anderson, D. A., Gladis, M., Sanderson, R. S., et al. (2004). Dieting and the development of eating disorders in obese women: Results of a randomized controlled trial. *American Journal of Clinical Nutrition, 80*, 560–568.

Wang, G. J., Volkow, N. D., Logan, J., Pappas, N. R., Wong, C. T., Zhu, W., et al. (2001). Brain dopamine and obesity. *Lancet, 357*, 354–357.

Ward, A., & Mann, T. (2000). Don't mind if I do: Disinhibited eating under cognitive load. *Journal of Personality and Social Psychology, 78*, 758–763.

Wardle, J., & Beales, S. (1987). Restraint and food intake: An experimental study of eating patterns in the laboratory and in normal life. *Behaviour Research and Therapy, 25*(3), 179–185.

Wardle, J., & Beales, S. (1988). Control and loss of control over eating: An experimental investigation. *Journal of Abnormal Psychology, 97*(1), 35–40.

Wardle, J., Griffith, J., Johnson, F., & Rapoport, L. (2000). Intentional weight control and food choice habits in a national representative sample of adults in the UK. *International Journal of Obesity, 24,* 534–540.

Wardle, J., Guthrie, C., Sanderson, S., Birch, D., & Plomin, R. (2001). Food and activity preferences in children of lean and obese parents. *International Journal of Obesity, 25,* 971–977.

Wardle, J., Waller, J., & Rapoport, L. (2001). Body dissatisfaction and binge eating in obese women, the role of restraint and depression. *Obesity Research, 9,* 778–787.

Wertheim, E. H., Koerner, J., & Paxton, S. (2001). Longitudinal predictors of restrictive eating and bulimic tendencies in three different age groups of adolescent girls. *Journal of Youth and Adolescence, 30,* 69–81.

Westenhoefer, J., & Pudel, V. (1993). Pleasure from food: Importance for food choice and consequences of deliberate restriction. *Appetite, 20,* 246–249.

Westerterp-Plantenga, M. S., Ijederma, M. J., & Wijckmans-Duijsens, N. E. (1996). The role of macronutrient selection in determining patterns of food intake in obese and non-obese women. *European Journal of Clinical Nutrition, 50,* 580–591.

White, M. A., Whisenhunt, B. L., Williamson, D. A., Greenway, F. L., & Netemeyer, R. G. (2002). Development and validation of the Food-Craving Inventory. *Obesity Research, 10,* 107–114.

Williamson, D. A., Kelley, M. L., Davis, C. J., Ruggiero, L., & Blouin, D. C. (1985). Psychopathology of eating disorders: A controlled comparison of bulimics, obese, and normal subjects. *Journal of Consulting and Clinical Psychology, 53,* 161–166.

Williamson, D. A., Martin, C. K., York-Crowe, E., Anton, S. D., Redman, L. M., Han, H., et al. (2007). Measurement of dietary restraint: Validity tests of four questionnaires. *Appetite, 48,* 183–192.

Williamson, D., Serdula, M., Anda, R., Levy, A., & Byers, T. (1992). Weight loss attempts in adults: Goals, duration, and rate of weight loss. *American Journal of Public Health, 82*(9), 1251–1257.

Wilson, G. T. (2002). The controversy over dieting. In C.G. Fairburn & K.D. Brownell (Eds.), *Eating disorders and obesity: A comprehensive handbook* (2nd ed., pp. 93–97). New York: Guilford Press.

Wing, R. R., Marcus, M. D., Blair, E. H., & Burton, L. R. (1991). Psychological responses of obese type II diabetic subjects to a very-low-calorie-diet. *Diabetes Care, 14,* 596–599.

Wisniewski, L., Epstein, L. H., Marcs, M. D., & Kaye, W. (1997). Differences in salivary habituation to palatable foods in bulimia nervosa patients and controls. *Psychosomatic Medicine, 59,* 427–433.

Wonderlich, S. A., Connolly, K. M., & Stice, E. (2004). Impulsivity as a risk factor for eating disordered behavior: Assessment implications with adolescents. *International Journal of Eating Disorders, 36,* 172–182.

Wooley, O. W., Wooley, S. C., & Dunham, R. B. (1976). Deprivation, expectation, and threat: Effects on salivation in the obese and nonobese. *Physiology and Behavior, 17,* 187–193.

Wooley, O. W., Wooley, S. C., & Williams, R. S. (1978). Appetite for highly and minimally palatable foods: Effects of deprivation. *International Journal of Obesity, 2,* 380.

Wooley, O. W., Wooley, S. C., & Woods, W. A. (1975). Effect of calories on appetite for palatable food in obese and nonobese humans. *Journal of Comparative and Physiological Psychology, 89,* 619–625.

Mood, Emotions, and Eating Disorders

Claus Vögele *and* E. Leigh Gibson

Abstract

Mood and emotions are intrinsically involved with eating. The question is in what ways do these normal emotional relations with food contribute to, or shed light on, the development of abnormal relations with food that eventually become clinical eating disorders (EDs). This chapter discusses basic mechanisms, findings, and models that help our understanding of the interactions between eating and emotions, in both clinical and nonclinical populations. The finding that comorbidity with mood and anxiety disorders is the norm among patients with EDs suggests that EDs may not necessarily be restricted to domains of eating behavior and body image but may also be associated with significant difficulties in affective functioning. This chapter reviews the evidence relating to the notion that EDs are disturbances of mood regulation, in which regulatory strategies specifically related to eating and the body are used to diminish negative affect associated with food, body image, or stress.

Keywords: chocolate, disinhibition, dopamine, emotion regulation, emotional eating, negative affect, opioids, restrained eating, reward, serotonin, stress

Introduction

As with other fundamental drives that motivate us to seek pleasurable goals, eating has always been associated with mood and emotion. The questions for this chapter are: In what ways can eating and emotions be linked, and what are the implications for understanding eating disorders (EDs)? In a recent review of the links between eating and emotions, Macht (2008) has proposed a "five-way model" with the following components:

1. Emotions aroused by food stimuli affect food choice.

2. Emotions high in arousal or intensity suppress eating due to incompatible emotional responses.

3. Emotions moderate in arousal or intensity affect eating depending on motivations to eat:

    a. In restrained eating, negative and positive emotions enhance food intake due to impairment of cognitive control.

    b. In emotional eating, negative emotions elicit the tendency to be regulated by eating and, as a consequence, enhance intake of sweet and high-fat foods.

    c. In normal eating, emotions affect eating in congruence with their cognitive and motivational features (e.g., food appears more pleasing during positive moods compared to negative moods).

Macht used a flow diagram to help understand the structure and predictions from the model, which is reproduced here (Fig. 11.1). Some of these concepts are considered in more detail in the text that follows, but there are clearly several ways in which eating and emotions can interact. For example, mood could influence food choice via a change of appetite, or by changing other behavior that constrains or alters food availability. On the other hand, alteration of mood may be an outcome—perhaps

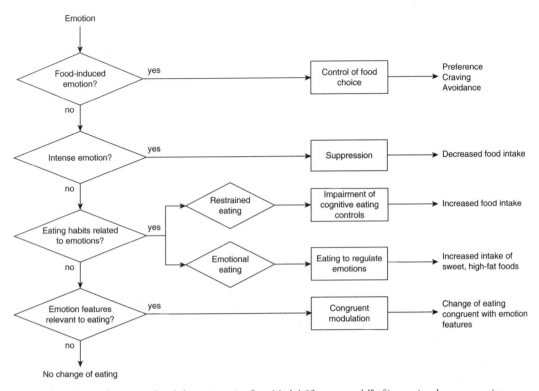

Fig. 11.1 Flow diagram showing predicted changes in eating from Macht's "five-way model" of interactions between emotions and eating.

(From Macht, M. How emotions affect eating: A five-way model. *Appetite, 50*, 1–11. © 2008. Reprinted with permission from the author and Elsevier.)

even consciously sought—of food choice. Thus, moods or emotions could provide internal stimuli or states that elicit beneficial, for example corrective, food choice. Further, eating a particular food, or combination, can alter emotions via sensory (including hedonic) effects, associated social context, cognitive expectations, changes in appetite, or nutritional modulation of brain function, for example. These possibilities are discussed in the text that follows. First, we need to consider what is meant by mood and emotion.

Mood is typically characterized as a psychological arousal state lasting at least several minutes and usually longer, with dimensions related to energy, tension, and pleasure (hedonic tone) (Matthews & Deary, 1998; Reid & Hammersley, 1999; Thayer, 1989). Moods have been distinguished from emotions, in that emotions can be defined as short-term affective responses to appraisals of particular stimuli, situations, or events having reinforcing potential, whereas moods may appear and persist in the absence of obvious stimuli, and may be more covert to observers (Matthews & Deary, 1998; Rolls, 2007). However, this distinction has been more theoretical than empirical (Fredrickson, 2004). Perhaps the

most relevant definition of emotions to this topic is that provided by Rolls (2007): "emotions are states elicited by rewards and punishers, that is, by instrumental reinforcers." Rolls then classifies different emotions on two dimensions (with intensity increasing toward the ends of the axes), one associated with delivery of reward (pleasure, elation) or punishment (fear, anxiety), and the other with the *absence* of (expected) reward (anger, frustration) or punishment (relief) (Fig. 11.2). Clearly, in the context of EDs, food may be both a reward and a punisher: an object of pleasure or fear (see the sections "Emotional Responses to Food Cues").

In this chapter, both moods and emotions are considered in relation to food, as there is evidence for involvement of both types of affect, and instances where the distinction is unclear; research on food and mood lags behind neuropsychological research on mood and emotion (Hammersley & Reid, 2008; Small, Zatorre, Dagher, Evans, & Jones-Gotman, 2001). The term "affect" is meant here to refer to either mood or emotion. Food may alter or induce emotions by rapid sensory stimulation or relief of hunger, or as a result of cognitive appraisal of the change in internal state or its expectation, but may

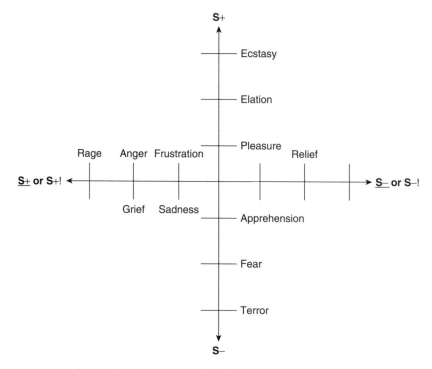

Fig. 11.2 Emotions represented on two dimensions, based on the definition of emotions as states elicited by rewards and punishers (Rolls, 2007): Intensity increases away from the center of the diagram. The vertical axis describes emotions associated with the delivery of a reward (up: S+) or punisher (down: S–). The horizontal axis describes emotions associated with the nondelivery of an expected reward (left: S+ = omission; S+! = termination) or the nondelivery of an expected punisher (right: S– = omission; S–! = termination). (Reproduced with permission from Rolls, E. T. [2007]. *Emotion explained* [Fig. 2.1., p. 14]. Oxford: Oxford University Press.)

also alter mood by slower changes in brain chemistry. In fact, for food to be maximally rewarding, all stages of processing should be intact, from expectation and initial sensory contact, via longer orosensory stimulation, to gastrointestinal and hepatic recognition (Booth, 1994).

Macht's five-way model implicates individual differences in the emotion–eating interaction. Recent theories of mood and emotion suggest that mood changes do not necessarily follow predictably from changes in neurophysiological arousal. Instead, the affective significance of a given level of arousal will depend on the person's current subjective and motivational state (Reid & Hammersley, 1999). The interaction of physiology, arousal, and emotion may also be moderated by personality factors, which have even been shown to influence effects of stress on taste perception, for example (Dess & Edelheit, 1998). In particular, the major personality traits of extraversion and neuroticism are known to moderate mood changes (Matthews & Deary, 1998), and to interact with mood and responses to emotional stimuli (Canli, Amin, Haas, Omura, & Constable, 2004). Thus, personality and cognitive factors could substantially modulate any impact of physiological

change induced by food: indeed, Macht (2008) points out that the interaction of eating and emotions can vary both between and within individuals.

One way in which cognitive factors influence emotional responses to food is via beliefs and expectations. In a laboratory study, Macht, Gerer, and Ellgring (2003) asked women to rate various emotions immediately after eating small amounts (5 g) of nine different foods, three being low in energy, three medium, and three high in energy (in counterbalanced order). Intensity of negative moods (sad, ashamed, anxious, sleepy) increased with increasing energy density of the foods, and more so for overweight than normal weight women. Moreover, medium- and high-energy foods were rated less healthy and more dangerous than low-energy foods. These effects were independent of rated pleasantness of the foods. It is most likely that these effects were psychological rather than physiological in nature, given the small amounts of food eaten, and the immediacy of the ratings. The negative effects of the high-energy foods presumably reflect concerns about their impact on health and weight gain. Interestingly, though, stronger increases in negative mood were seen for women reporting greater tendencies to eat in response to emotional state (see sections "Negative Affect, Eating Attitudes, and Comfort Eating"). This would imply that any reinforcing effect of eating such foods on prior emotional state must occur during rather than after eating.

These results are similar to the finding that self-identified chocolate "addicts" felt more guilty after eating chocolate than did a control group (Macdiarmid & Hetherington, 1995). The chocolate "addicts" also reported lower positive and higher negative affect before eating. By contrast, in healthy men, experimental induction of sadness decreased appetite, whereas when cheerful, chocolate tasted more pleasant and stimulating, and more of it was eaten (Macht, Roth, & Ellgring, 2002). The gender difference presumably reflects attitudinal differences.

Basic Mechanisms
General Effects of Hunger and Eating on Emotions: Implications for Eating Disorders

Perhaps the most reliable way in which food interacts with emotional states is the change in mood and arousal that occurs from before to after eating a meal. Many animals, including humans, tend to be aroused, alert, and even irritable when hungry: hunger is, after all, a strong motivational state aimed at encouraging the search for food. Hunger is also a powerful modulator of emotional responses (Rolls, 2007), such that the same events or stimuli may provoke quite different emotional responses in one who is hungry versus one who is sated.

In contrast to the hungry state, after eating a satiating meal, we typically become calm, lethargic, and may even sleep. Normal eaters are of course "satisfied" postprandially, and relief of hunger is typically a positive and rewarding experience, involving activation of central reward pathways (Grigson, 2002)—just as well for the survival of the species. In support of this, when mood and eating context were randomly sampled 10 times a day for a week, eating a meal was more likely to result in a positive mood than either a neutral or negative mood (Macht, Haupt, & Salewsky, 2004), at least in the short term.

VAGAL NERVE ACTIVITY, BULIMIA NERVOSA, AND DEPRESSION

A key component of this shift in arousal state is likely to be postprandial changes in autonomic neural activity. During a meal, nutrient absorption is rapidly detected by the brain, as afferent information is conveyed by the vagus (Xth cranial) nerve, from the gut and liver. Such vagal afferent activity is now known to influence higher brain centres including those involved in emotions (Zagon, 2001): even simple distension of the stomach by balloon has been shown, by brain imaging, to activate an area of the brain, the anterior cingulate, known to underlie depressive symptoms (Faris et al., 2006). Indeed, artificial vagal nerve stimulation is now used as a treatment for depression (George et al., 2002), following a successful history as a treatment for refractory epilepsy (Morris & Mueller, 1999).

A link among vagal activity, emotions, and EDs has been most extensively developed for bulimia nervosa (BN), where sufferers show increased risk of anxiety and depression (Braun, Sunday & Halmi, 1994) (see section 'Comorbidity of Affective Disorders with Eating Disorders' and Chapter 17). Faris et al. (2008) have argued that vagal activity may be elevated in BN, but with associated desensitization of the central nervous system to vagal afferent information, as a result of adaptation to frequent afferent stimulation following prolonged binging and vomiting. This is in line with recent findings on higher vagal activity in relation to dietary restriction (Vögele, Hilbert, & Tuschen-Caffier, 2009) and results on a higher threshold for satiation (Halmi & Sunday, 1991), including that mediated by the gut hormone cholecystokinin, and by evidence that bulimic symptoms are reduced by treatment with the anti-emetic 5-HT$_3$ (5-hydroxytryptamine; serotonin) antagonist, Ondansetron, which is known to inhibit vagal afferent stimulation (Faris et al., 2008). Furthermore, this treatment ameliorated the depression that otherwise tended to increase cyclically before onset of binge/vomiting episodes (Faris et al., 2006) (see section 3.3.1). Faris et al. (2008) suggest that the initially voluntary binge/purging leads to disruption of the normal regulation of vagal activity, via vago–vagal feedback, resulting in a vicious circle of depressive episodes, weak satiation, and short-term euphoria from binge/purging.

IMPACT OF MEAL SIZE, TIMING, AND HABIT ON MOOD AND EMOTIONS

Normal eaters are typically very habitual in their choice of food, and size and timing of meals: it is the essence of their normality. As a result, they have learned a set of beliefs and expectations about the impact of their habitual dietary regimen, and these are likely to mitigate any impact of physiological changes on emotions. Therefore, to some extent, dietary experiences that differ from a person's habitual eating could cause their behaviour to change through cognitive rather than, or as well as, physiological influences. For example, although there is some evidence that larger meals may reduce arousal and alertness, this effect can depend on the meal size being different from that habitually consumed (Craig, 1986). In fact, meal size per se seems to have little impact on mood unless too little is eaten (Gibson & Green, 2002), whereas Macht (1996) found that a larger meal prevented deterioration in emotion in people being stressed by noise: this may reflect competing influences of parasympathetic and sympathetic drives, with perhaps suppression of the latter by the former after a larger meal than is habitually consumed.

One implication of these findings for EDs is that initial changes in eating habits, for example, meal size, may have some impact on emotions, but this impact may soften as the disordered eating becomes more habitual. For example, short-term studies in healthy individuals show that omitting breakfast is likely to increase autonomic activity during the morning and produce cognitive effects reminiscent of increased anxiety (Conners & Blouin, 1983), such as attention to irrelevant stimuli (Dusek, Mergler, & Kermis, 1976). However, it is not known to what extent adaptation occurs to such effects when breakfast is repeatedly avoided.

Arousal levels typically peak during late morning, followed by a drop in arousal and ability to sustain attention after the midday meal that has been termed the "post-lunch dip" (Folkard & Monk, 1985). However, this dip at least partly reflects an underlying circadian rhythm that is confounded with the effect of a midday meal: thus, vigilance has also been found to decline from late morning to early afternoon in subjects not eating lunch (Smith & Miles, 1986). Moreover, susceptibility to this decline depends on anxiety level: the more anxious one is feeling before lunch, or the more neurotic the personality trait, the less one will experience any post-lunch dip (Craig, Baer, & Diekmann, 1981; Smith & Miles, 1986). Given the tendency for EDs to be associated with higher levels of anxiety, the inference is that ED patients will be less susceptible to this afternoon decline in arousal.

Neural Substrates Shared by Sensory Reward and Emotions

Brain pathways involved in food-related reward have been dissociated into two functional systems; one underlying motivational aspects of eating and food salience ('wanting'), the other involved in hedonic evaluation of food sensory stimuli (food pleasantness or "liking"). Berridge (2009) points out that this separation of "wanting" from "liking" allows for "irrational desires that could underlie

some pathologies of appetite." The dopamine, opioid, endocannabinoid, and benzodiazepine/gamma-aminobutyric acid neurotransmitter systems dominate these reward processes, with differential effects depending on the particular pathways and nuclei involved (Berridge, 2009; Berridge & Robinson, 1998). These systems are also involved in emotions and responses to stress, and findings that link some of them to both eating and emotions are considered here.

OPIOIDS, STRESS, APPETITE, AND POSITIVE MOOD

Endogenous opioid neuropeptides are released during stress, and are known to be important for adaptive effects such as resistance to pain and induction of positive mood, possibly by relief from aversive memories (Koepp, et al., 2009). They are also involved in motivational and hedonic processes in eating behavior, such as stimulation of appetite by palatable foods (Berridge, 2009; Doyle, Berridge, & Gosnell, 1993; Mercer & Holder, 1997). One might therefore expect a link between opioid action, emotions, and eating behavior. Indeed, in animals and human infants, the ingestion of sweet and fatty foods, including milk, alleviates crying and other behavioural signs of distress (Blass, Shide, & Weller, 1989; Upadhyay et al., 2004). This effect depends on sweet taste rather than calories, as non-nutritive sweeteners also reduce crying (Barr et al., 1999).

This stress-reducing effect of sweet taste can be blocked by opioid antagonists, and opioid analgesia can be enhanced by chronic intake of sucrose solutions or fat (Blass et al., 1989; D'Anci, Kanarek, & Marks-Kaufman, 1997; Kanarek, White, Biegen, & Marks-Kaufman, 1991). Opioid blockade also reduces consumption of preferred foods (Kanarek et al., 1991; Yeomans & Wright, 1991), whereas repeated intake of a sweet, fatty energy-dense food was found to downregulate an opioid pathway (ventral striatum) involved in food reward in rats (Kelley, Will, Steininger, Zhang, & Haber, 2003). Animal models of stress-related binge eating also show that the binging is dependent on opioid pathways (Boggiano et al., 2005). Intriguingly, ED patients who engage in binge–purging behavior show raised thresholds for pain, which might suggest upregulation of opioid pathways (and desensitization to vagal afferents) (Papezova, Yamamotova, & Uher, 2005), and would be in line with a drive to binge on palatable food. However, this appears to conflict with evidence above that chronic consumption of such food would downregulate reward-related opioid pathways. Also, altered opioidergic sensitivity may be an indirect consequence of other neuroendocrine disturbances in EDs, including insulin and leptin (Figlewicz & Benoit, 2009).

The ability of sweet, fatty food to alleviate pain seems to become more idiosyncratic with age (Gibson, 2006): indeed, even in infants, after a few months, sweet taste becomes less effective at calming than does pacifier sucking, which might reflect a maturational separation of taste and emotion (Blass & Camp, 2003), or a difference in opportunities to learn the instrumental emotional value of the two experiences. Thus, in adults, the ability of palatable food to alleviate aversive emotional states may depend on childhood learning opportunities, perhaps interacting with biological predispositions.

DOPAMINE, REWARD, AND OVEREATING

Dopamine was for many years considered to be a major substrate of pleasure: however, the weight of evidence now supports its role in "wanting" of rewards, or in mediating incentive salience of reward-related cues, but not the hedonics of "liking" (Berridge, 2009). One finding that may be of particular relevance to binge eating disorder (BED) is that the availability of dopamine (D_2) receptors in the striatum is inversely correlated to body mass index (BMI; Wang et al., 2001), and it was suggested that this could indicate a neurochemical predisposition to overeat palatable foods so as to enhance dopamine release (see section 'Binge Eating: Emotional Responses to Food Cues'). However, this necessitates the unpalatable (and un-evidenced) notion that the obese are eating more of foods that their brains "want" less. On the contrary, energy-dense snack food reinforced greater effort to obtain it in obese than in nonobese women (Saelens & Epstein, 1996), and young children of obese parents showed greater "enjoyment of food" as well as higher preference for high-fat, energy-dense foods than did the offspring of nonobese parents (Wardle, Guthrie, Sanderson, Birch, & Plomin, 2001). Moreover, this "enjoyment of food" measure is strongly and positively related to adiposity in young children over the entire continuum of body size (Carnell & Wardle, 2008). Therefore, it seems more probable that dopamine receptors are downregulated after chronic overconsumption of palatable energy-dense (e.g., high fat, high sugar) food, akin to downregulation seen with chronic use of addictive drugs. Alternatively, the detuned dopamine system may result from neuroendocrine feedback signals of excess adiposity, such as leptin (Figlewicz & Benoit, 2009).

Stress may also be relevant, since it reduces dopamine output in reward pathways, and moreover, this effect can be prevented in rats by training to obtain palatable sweet food (Nanni et al., 2003).

Given that EDs are associated with greater risk of substance abuse, as well as susceptibility to negative affect (Yanovski, Nelson, Dubbert, & Spitzer, 1993) (see section 'Clinical Evidence' and Chapter 17), and that dopamine is also involved in stress sensitivity and depression (Pani, Porcella, & Gessa, 2000), it seems logical to expect abnormal dopaminergic function in EDs. A range of findings from various methods including measuring dopamine metabolites in cerebrospinal fluid, genetic polymorphisms, and neuroimaging do indeed support dopamine dysfunction in anorexia nervosa (AN) and BN (Kaye, 2008; see Chapter 6).

Negative Affect, Eating Attitudes, and Comfort Eating

There is now a robust, if complex, literature on eating as a means to modify emotional states. Its origins derive from early psychosomatic and psychoanalytic clinical models of overeating and obesity, based on the notion that obese people may overeat by confusing emotional arousal with hunger and/or seeking comfort or distraction from emotional distress by eating (Bruch, 1974; Schachter et al., 1968). This concept of "comfort eating," that is, eating to reduce negative emotions, has enjoyed a resurgence of interest, for example, in its role in problematic eating and poor control of weight, perhaps inspired by the Zeitgeist of the "obesogenic environment" (Chua et al., 2004; Fulkerson, Sherwood, Perry, Neumark-Sztainer, & Story, 2004; Waters et al., 2001).

It is clear from numerous studies, including observational, survey, and experimental designs, that negative affect, for example, induced by stress, can adversely affect eating (reviewed by Gibson, 2006; Wardle & Gibson, 2002). The outcome will depend on an interaction between the nature and severity of the stressor, or cause of the negative emotions, stress-related constraints on behavior, and the individual's propensity (and perhaps learned strategies) for coping. Particularly with severe stress or anhedonia, eating of any sort may be suppressed. Nevertheless, very often the result is an increase in consumption of energy-dense, especially sweet or fatty foods, or both, and not surprisingly there is evidence to link stress eating with risk of overweight (Torres & Nowson, 2007). Moreover, animal studies suggest that selection of energy-dense foods during chronic stress, and the associated increase in (central) adiposity, together with hyperinsulinaemia, actually help to ameliorate the impact of stress by limiting activity of the limbic hypothalamic–pituitary–adrenal (LHPA) axis (Dallman et al., 2003; Peters et al., 2007). Such an effect may reduce stress-related depression and anxiety. Activation of the LHPA axis may also increase incentive salience of cues to reward (Pecina, Schulkin, & Berridge, 2006), and the over-active LHPA axis and other neuroendocrine disturbances seen in EDs (Kaye, 2008) may contribute to reinforcing the aberrant behaviors (Sodersten, Nergardh, Bergh, Zandian, & Scheurink, 2008).

RESTRAINED VERSUS EMOTIONAL EATING

Early evidence suggested a key prerequisite for over-eating during negative affect was to be a "restrained eater" (one who consciously attempts to restrict food intake and eat less than is wanted) or a dieter (Heatherton, Herman, & Polivy, 1991; Oliver & Wardle, 1999; Weinstein, Shide, & Rolls, 1997). This is consistent with a number of experimental studies, which were based on the premise that the adaptive response to stress should be reduced appetite and eating, but that the obese, overweight, or restrained eaters, may be unresponsive to their internal physiological influences on appetite (Craighead & Allen, 1995; Rodin, 1981), or normally dominant cognitive strategies for restraint may be disinhibited or overridden during negative affect or stress (Herman & Polivy, 1975; Schachter et al., 1968). However, the first measure of restrained eating (Herman & Polivy, 1980) appears to have included aspects subsequently recognized as disinhibited (uncontrolled) or emotional eating, and by definition this latter concept is probably most relevant to comfort eating (Lowe & Fisher, 1983; Oliver, Wardle, & Gibson, 2000; Williams et al., 2002). In particular, in an experimental study in which both eating attitudes were measured, Oliver et al. (2000) found that emotional eaters did not eat more food overall under stress, but instead selectively ate more sweet and fatty foods: restraint, however, did not significantly influence stress eating. Similarly, Gibson and Harris (unpublished data) have recently replicated survey findings that stress selectively increases consumption of energy dense, especially sweet and fatty foods (Gibson, 2006; Kandiah et al., 2006; Zellner et al., 2006), and extended it to show that the stress eating tendency is strongly predicted by both emotional eating ($\rho(135)$ =.59, p <.001) and uncontrolled (disinhibited) eating ($\rho(135)$ = .33, p < .001) as well as by the perception of being overweight ($\rho(135)$ = .23, p < .01), but not by

cognitive restraint ($\rho(135)$ = .07, ns) (using the revised 18-item Three Factor Eating Questionnaire; Karlsson, Persson, Sjostrom, & Sullivan, 2000).

Cognitive restraint may still be a risk factor for overeating during stress, as there is evidence that it may interact with and enhance emotional eating (Haynes, Lee, & Yeomans, 2003; Macht & Müller, 2007a; Williams et al., 2002). However, dietary restraint per se may elicit eating in response to challenging situations because of disruption to cognitive "diet monitoring," and a focus of attention on the salient food cues, with little emotional involvement (Lattimore & Caswell, 2004; Wallis & Hetherington, 2004; Ward & Mann, 2000). Moreover, Macht (2008) points out that restrained eaters can therefore be expected to show increased eating in response to both negative *and* positive emotions. These ideas would seem to be reflected in the task-based neuroimaging evidence that recovered AN women show exaggerated activation of planning areas but no dissociation of positive and negative feedback (Wagner, et al., 2007).

SUSCEPTIBILITY TO STRESS AND COMFORT EATING

Interestingly, in relation to EDs, there is accumulating evidence that emotional eaters may be particularly susceptible, both physiologically and emotionally, to the effects of stress, that is, they are high stress reactors. For example, women who ate more from a selection of snack foods after a stressful task also showed the greatest release of the stress-sensitive hormone, cortisol, and more stress-induced negative affect (Epel, Lapidus, McEwen & Brownell, 2001). These high reactors also showed a preference for sweet foods. Similarly, in an observational study of daily hassles, mood, and snacking, only women with high cortisol responses to a laboratory stressor reported eating more snacks in association with increased daily hassles (Newman, O'Connor, & Conner, 2007). This may well be relevant to binge eating: Goldfield, Adamo, Rutherford, and Legg (2008) used a computer-based food choice task to determine whether stress affected choice in binge eaters. Like the previous studies, only binge eaters who were classified as high stress reactors (based on perceived feelings of negative affect) altered food choice under stress, preferring unhealthy snacks over fruit and vegetables: non-binge eaters were unaffected in this paradigm (see section 'Binge Eating: Emotional Responses to Food Cues').

This stress susceptibility associated with binging and comfort eating may suggest another mechanism, which could encourage selection of sweet and fatty foods in an attempt to regulate emotions, that is, dietary manipulation of the brain serotonin system. Synthesis of the neurotransmitter serotonin (or 5-hydroxytryptamine; 5-HT) depends on dietary availability of the precursor essential amino acid, tryptophan (TRP): uptake into the brain of TRP in turn depends on its ratio to the large neutral, primarily branched-chain, amino acids (LNAA), with which it competes for transport from blood to brain. In brief, insulinogenic high-carbohydrate meals, with little protein, raise this ratio and can result in increased serotonin synthesis in the brain (Fernstrom & Fernstrom, 1995) (see Chapter 6).

In the context of stress susceptibility and negative emotions, there is some intriguing evidence: when participants were divided into high or low stress-prone groups, as defined by a questionnaire measure of neuroticism, carbohydrate-rich/protein-poor meals (which raised plasma TRP/LNAA ratios) before a stressful task were found to block task-induced depressive feelings and release of the glucocorticoid stress hormone cortisol, but only in the high stress-prone group (Markus et al., 1998). This finding was replicated using high- versus low-TRP-containing proteins (alpha-lactalbumin and casein, respectively) (Markus et al., 2000). It was argued that, because stress increases serotonin activity, the poor stress-coping of this sensitive group might indicate a deficit in serotonin synthesis that is improved by this dietary intervention. This is particularly relevant, because EDs are associated with anxiety, depression, impulsivity, and poor stress coping, all of which have been linked to serotonin. Further, there is now ample evidence for a dysfunctional serotonin system in brain emotional circuits in EDs, including reduced serotonin release, and postsynaptic sensitization, during food restriction (Kaye, 2008).

CHOCOLATE AND EMOTIONS: IMMEDIATE AND DELAYED EFFECTS

It is notable that chocolate, often chosen during stress, is high in sugar, which, when combined with effects of cocoa, strongly stimulates insulin release (Brand Miller Holt, de Jong & Petocz, 2003), but has only 3% to 6% of energy as protein. Thus, if eaten in sufficient amounts on an empty stomach, chocolate might increase TRP availability to the brain, and so allow improved mood via enhanced serotonin release. Macht (2008) has argued that such a TRP-dependent mechanism would be too slow acting (probably taking 1 to 2 hours after eating). However, it is still possible that a delayed

mood enhancement via increased serotonin could reinforce a learned liking for chocolate (or sweet, fatty foods), and a tendency to choose it during negative emotions: such longer-lasting effects may be particularly important in establishing disordered eating, such as binging, as Macht (2008) acknowledges. After all, Macht and Mueller (2007b) showed that the lessening of film-induced negative mood by eating chocolate, which depended on sensory palatability, lasted only a few minutes: even then, this effect was greater in emotional eaters. However, the mood-enhancing actions demonstrated for caffeine and theobromine in chocolate (Smit, Gaffan, & Rogers, 2004), together with sensory, caloric, and social reinforcement, are clearly also likely to be important mechanisms. Finally, given the conflict and ambivalence that food can create in ED patients, it is notable that images of chocolate can induce simultaneously appetitive and aversive motivational states (assessed by physiological responses) in chocolate cravers (Rodriguez, Fernandez, Cepeda-Benito, & Vila, 2005).

Clinical Evidence
Comorbidity of Affective Disorders with Eating Disorders

Comorbidity with mental disorders is reportedly the norm among patients with ED. Major Depression is the most common comorbid diagnosis in adult patients (Braun et al., 1994; Polivy & Herman, 2002), but high levels of comorbidity between depressive and eating disordered symptoms have also been reported for adolescents, both boys and girls (Santos, Richards, & Bleckley, 2007). Anxiety disorders, as a group, are the second most common comorbid diagnosis (Braun et al., 1994). General anxiety disorder and social phobia are the most prevalent anxiety diagnoses among patients with BN and AN (Godart et al., 2004; Kaye, Bulik, Thornton, Barbarich, & Masters, 2004).

Although some of these studies have recently been questioned on methodological grounds (Godart et al., 2007), these findings suggest that EDs may not be pathologies that are necessarily restricted to domains of eating behavior and body image but may also be related to significant difficulties in affective functioning. The exact nature and etiology of this comorbidity, however, is unclear. Depression and anxiety may precede, occur simultaneously, or follow the appearance of the ED (Polivy & Herman, 2002). It has also been suggested that EDs and mood disorders have common familial causal factors (Hudson et al., 2003; Mangweth et al., 2003). In addition, the presence of negative emotionality or psychiatric comorbidity in those with EDs may be associated with greater ED psychopathology (Grilo, White, & Masheb, 2009) or medical complications (Takimoto, Yoshiuchi, & Akabayashi, 2008), or both.

Negative Emotionality and Eating Disorders: Risk Factor, Retrospective Correlate, or Consequence?

It has been argued that the increased co-occurrence of ED and mood disorders (particularly depression) indicates that mood disturbances are a risk factor for EDs. In order to be ascertained as a risk factor, negative emotionality has to precede the ED and increase the likelihood of its manifestation. Negative emotionality as a predictor for EDs has been assessed in seven longitudinal studies. Leon, Fulkerson, Perry, Keel, and Klump (1999) used a composite measure of negative affectivity including negative emotionality, depression, ineffectiveness, and body dissatisfaction, and found a significant but moderate association with ED risk 3 to 4 years later. In the two studies by Patton and co-workers (1990, 1999), psychiatric morbidity predicted the onset of EDs. Nevertheless, four studies (Attie & Brooks-Gunn, 1989; Graber, Brooks-Gunn, Paikoff, & Warren, 1994; Killen et al., 1996; Leon, Fulkerson, Perry, & Early-Zald, 1995) failed to find negative emotionality or psychopathology to predict EDs in multivariate analyses. In summary, the evidence is inconclusive.

Some cross-sectional studies have investigated chronology of onset retrospectively; however, only two of those included control groups. Rastam (1992) found premorbid obsessive–compulsive personality disorder to be significantly more prevalent in patients with AN than in control participants (35% vs. 4%). Using logistic regression, Bulik, Sullivan, Fear, and Joyce (1997) showed that the risk for AN increased in the presence of obsessive–compulsive disorder and overanxious disorder relative to controls. The risk for BN was increased in the presence of social phobia and overanxious disorder relative to controls. This was true, however, also for women with major depression. The authors conclude from these findings that overanxious disorder in childhood is a nonspecific risk factor for later psychopathology, albeit the relationship with AN is particularly strong. Similarly, social phobia may precede a range of psychopathologies, but with a strong link to BN.

In their review, Jacobi, Hayward, de Zwaan, Kraemer, and Agras (2004) concluded that prior psychiatric morbidity and negative emotionality are variable risk factors of unclear potency. Results from longitudinal studies suggest that premorbid anxiety disorders and negative affectivity are risk factors for other mental disorders including affective disorders and EDs, and should, therefore, be considered as nonspecific risk factors.

Of course, negative emotionality may not cause an ED so much as to be a consequence or maintaining factor, or both. Stice, Hayward, Cameron, Killen, and Taylor (2000), for example, found ED symptoms and dietary restraint to predict subsequent depression in initially nondepressed individuals. Whichever is first, these findings suggest that negative affect can contribute to ED symptoms. Several models have been put forward for how negative affect impacts on ED symptoms, and these are discussed in the following sections.

Negative Emotionality/Mood as a Maintaining Factor for Disordered Eating Behavior

Several investigators view EDs as disturbances of mood regulation that use regulatory strategies specifically related to eating and the body (e.g., dieting, purging, exercising excessively) as techniques aimed at diminishing unpleasant affect (Taylor, Bagby, & Parker, 1997; Telch, 1997). This seems to be a unifying feature of all ED types, as the core symptoms and behaviors are shared, even if the diagnostic criteria differ. Indeed, whether or not to distinguish between different types of EDs has been debated vigorously in the literature, and some authors argue that EDs are one syndrome with different manifestations, a view that is summarized under the "spectrum hypothesis" (VanderHam, Meulman, VanStrien, & vanEngeland, 1997).

Nevertheless, differences in psychological traits and clinical symptoms exist. Impulsivity is one crucial feature that distinguishes AN on the one hand from BN and BED on the other. Increased impulsivity in those with BN or BED is reflected in their relative failure to resist food under certain circumstances, and to experience loss-of-control over eating resulting in a binge. Other examples for increased impulsivity concern sexual promiscuity, suicide attempts, drug abuse, and stealing or shoplifting, which are frequently reported for BN patients (Matsunaga, Kiriike, Iwasaki, Miyata, & Matsui, 2000). Individuals with AN (restricting type), on the other hand, are remarkably successful in maintaining restricted food intake over long periods of time, so are excessive in their capacity to control and withstand hunger signals. It has been suggested that AN is but one expression of a broader phenotype characterized by perfectionism, rigidity, and the propensity for behavioral constraint (Lilenfeld et al., 1998). Such differences in personality traits may also play a role in emotion regulation. The literature on mood, emotions and EDs emphasizes the relationship between BN or BED and affect dysregulation on the one hand, and AN and alexithymia on the other.

BULIMIA NERVOSA

The most salient feature of BN is an abnormal eating pattern characterized by alternating periods of fasting and episodes of binge eating. In addition, there is recurrent behavior to prevent weight gain including purging directly after binging (e.g., vomiting or use of laxatives) or excessive exercise. In his dual pathway model of bulimic pathology, Stice (1994, 2001) hypothesized that elevated pressure to be thin fosters body dissatisfaction in BN. This increased body dissatisfaction then promotes restrained eating and negative affect, especially depression. It is further assumed that BN use binging and purging as a means of regulating negative mood states. From the perspective of self-regulation (Hofmann, Rauch, & Gawronski, 2007; Mann & Ward, 2004) dieting or fasting can be construed as an attempt to reduce negative affect elicited by cues that are associated with food intake and the fear of gaining weight. These cues can be related to two distinct classes of stimuli: food cues and body shape. Both have been investigated in relation to emotional responses and emotion regulation in BN.

Emotional Responses to Food Cues
Emotional responses of individuals with BN to food cues differ from those of healthy study participants. When purging was rendered impossible, persons with BN responded with increased negative affect after eating compared to healthy control participants, with increased fear of gaining weight, tenseness, and feelings of being depressed and irritated (Buree, Papaeorgis, & Hare, 1990; Staiger, Dawe, & McCarthy, 2000). Legenbauer, Vögele, and Rüddel (2004) exposed women with BN and non–eating disordered participants to their favorite binge or snack foods, and gave them the opportunity to eat ad libitum after the end of the 20-minute exposure trial. BN responded with increased distress and feelings of tension and insecurity to the exposure while women in the control group showed a decrease in these ratings. In addition, women with BN ate less than women in the control group after exposure but responded with increases in feelings of guilt and shame that were positively associated with the amount of food eaten.

With a view to appetite and hunger regulation in non–eating disordered individuals these results may seem counterintuitive as food cues normally have reinforcing, appetitive qualities (see section "Comorbidity of Affective Disorders with Eating Disorders"). Indeed, predigestive physiological responses (i.e., cephalic phase responses, e.g., salivation) to food cues in BN are more marked and, therefore, seem to indicate the opposite pattern (Legenbauer et al., 2004; Tuomisto et al., 1999). BN individuals' attitude to food is, therefore, ambivalent: desired but feared, or wanted but not liked (Berridge, 2009; section "Negative Emotionality and Eating Disorders: Risk Factor, Retrospective Correlate or Consequence?"). That BN individuals perceive food cues as negative or threatening, even on a preconscious level (i.e., outside of the individual's awareness), has been demonstrated using the startle probe methodology: Mauler, Hamm, Weike, and Tuschen-Caffier (2006) found persons with BN to respond with significantly larger startle responses during viewing of food cues compared with control participants, indicating a defensive motivational state. Food deprivation for 24 hours attenuated this response, but eating before exposure to food cues augmented it. These findings show similarities to the enhanced startle response to chocolate images seen in chocolate cravers (who share with BN a struggle to control eating) compared to noncravers (Rodriguez et al., 2005; section "Anorexia Nervosa").

These results support the notion that food cues are perceived as threatening by BN individuals and that dieting or purging may be used to avoid or reduce the negative affect associated with food exposure and eating. In other words, individuals with BN make food less frightening or threatening by demonstrating control over their consumption of it. If the restrained eating pattern collapses, that is, if control fails with subsequent eating or binging, food once again becomes threatening. This pattern of results is consistent with cognitive models of bulimic pathology suggesting that core beliefs such as "control over eating" are central for BN (Cooper, Wells, & Todd, 2004). Rigid self-regulation is fundamental to the self-esteem of women with BN (Fairburn, Cooper, & Shafran, 2003), and if this self-regulation is violated the negative affect induced by food cues increases.

Emotional Responses to Body Image Exposure

Frequently, patients with BN are excessively concerned with body weight and shape, and these factors are assumed to be important for self-evaluation (*DSM-IV*) and the maintenance of disordered eating. Body dissatisfaction may arise from perceptual body size distortion or cognitive–evaluative dissatisfaction (Lautenbacher, Roscher, Strian, Pirke, & Krieg, 1993), although results on differences in accuracy of body size perception in BN are contradictory (Probst, Vandereycken, Vanderlinden, & van Coppenolle, 1998). Studies on the cognitive–evaluative aspects of body size generally find that BN are dissatisfied with their body and would like to be thinner (Cash & Deagle, 1997). Nevertheless, there is evidence that this may be true for non–eating disordered women as well (Goldfein, Walsh, & Midlarsky, 2000). Concerns about body weight and shape are widespread in adult women ranging in age from 18 to 70 years (e.g., Ricciardelli, Tate, & Williams, 1997) and also adolescent boys and girls (Vögele & Woodward, 2005).

The dual pathway model (Stice, 1994, 2001) stipulates that negative affect (and restrained eating) is the consequence of body dissatisfaction and mediates the association between body dissatisfaction and bulimic eating behaviors. Pinhas, Toner, Ali, Garfinkel, and Stuckless (1999) showed that exposure to slides of women representing the ideal of female beauty in Western culture led to an immediate negative effect on mood in a sample of nonclinical university students. These results suggest that internalized images of ideal beauty have a detrimental effect on women and may play a mediating role (e.g., through negative social comparison processes) between body image exposure and negative affect. The question whether exposure to one's own body image leads to negative affect in BN has been investigated in only a small number of studies. Tuschen-Caffier, Vögele, Bracht, and Hilbert (2003) confronted BN women and non–eating disordered female volunteers with their body shape and body related appearance using a video recording and an imagery task. In addition, they were asked to describe their physical appearance. Both groups responded with similar increases in self-reported anxiety, tension, insecurity, and sadness to both the video confrontation and imagery task. This suggests that the confrontation with body shape is a stressful and upsetting experience even for non–eating disordered women. The groups differed, however, with respect to the time taken for body description. BN individuals took less time to describe their waists, hips, and bottoms compared to non–eating disordered participants, and the authors interpreted this result as avoidance behavior.

There are an increasing number of studies employing neuroimaging techniques to investigate the brain areas that are implicated in EDs (Uher et al., 2005). Most of these studies have investigated patients diagnosed with AN or mixed groups of EDs, indicating differences in brain activation in response to visual food cues or eating. A recent study (Beato-Fernández et al., 2009) used single photon emission computed tomography to investigate the effects of body shape exposure in BN and AN on brain activation. When exposed to a video of their own figure BN individuals responded with hyperactivity in brain regions implicated in emotion processing (i.e., right temporal and occipital areas), suggesting a "fear response."

Negative Affect and Binge Eating

Continued dieting can lead to a relative state of deprivation, which increases the incentive value of food cues (Baker, Piper, McCarthy, Majeskie, & Fiore, 2004). This increased incentive value of food cues together with overall negative affective state may trigger binge eating in BN, comparable to the motivational basis of drug cues triggering relapse. In addition, body dissatisfaction may increase negative affect and thus lead to binge eating or purging, or both. There is an increasing body of evidence that such negative mood changes may precede binge-eating episodes. This has been investigated in controlled experiments (Agras & Telch, 1998; Telch & Agras, 1996), and studies monitoring food consumption in BN after mood induction have tended to find systematic associations between negative affect and caloric content or amount of food eaten (e.g., Legenbauer et al., 2004). Nevertheless, whether the amounts of food eaten would amount to an "objective" binge-episode, or whether participants' sense of loss-of-control over eating would resemble that experienced in a natural environment remains doubtful, probably because it is notoriously difficult in laboratory settings to re-create the situational context in which a binge-eating episode occurs. Researchers have, therefore, turned increasingly to investigations of binge eating in the natural environment. Using retrospective assessments some studies have found that individuals with BN report significantly more negative mood in general and prior to a binge episode compared to non–eating disordered controls (Kjelsas, Borsting, & Gudde, 2004; Mitchell et al., 1999; Waters, Hill, & Waller, 2001).

Such retrospective reports are problematic, however, as they are susceptible to memory bias, and there is evidence that retrospective reporting of binges is especially inaccurate (Bardone, Krahn, Goodman, & Searles, 2000). The concurrent assessment of mood changes and eating behavior using ecological momentary assessment (EMA) provides a method for the investigation of the temporal sequence of negative affect and binge-eating episodes (with or without subsequent purging), which is less susceptible to retrospective recall effects. Alpers and Tuschen-Caffier (2001) assessed mood, feelings of hunger and the desire to eat hourly over two consecutive days in BN patients and a clinical (panic disorder patients) and a healthy control group. Overall, both patient samples reported more negative feelings than the healthy control group. BN patients rated most feelings more negatively in the hour before binge eating compared with the rest of the day. Also, BN patients' general mood state worsened after binge eating but returned to pre-binge levels after purging. This suggests that negative mood states precede binge-eating episodes in BN, and that mood deteriorates after binge eating but is alleviated by purging. By including a clinical control group the authors were able to establish the specificity of the association of negative mood states and the desire to eat in BN. Using a similar design Hilbert and Tuschen-Caffier (2007) confirmed these findings in that negative mood increased prior to binge eating, and worsened after binge eating in both BN and BED. Results on mood after purging were not reported, however, so it remains unclear whether purging may be reinforced by mood improvement as suggested previously. A caveat for both studies is the fact that mood was assessed and analyzed in very close proximity to the binge-eating episode, so that the implied direction of negative mood leading to binge eating may have been obscured (i.e., the negative mood immediately prior to binge eating may have been a consequence of the realization of the impending binge-eating episode). Smyth et al. (2007) addressed this problem by removing mood assessments from their analyses that may have been temporally consequential to the binge event (i.e., those within 10 minutes of the event). The results confirm that decreasing positive affect and increasing negative affect including anger and hostility reliably preceded binge-eating and subsequent purging. Moreover, mood significantly improved after binging or purging, and this recovery was more rapid than the mood deterioration before the binge-eating episode. Smyth et al. (2007)

also showed that mood was significantly worse on days when binge eating and purging occurred compared with non-binge days. Even the most positive mood rating on binge days was still more negative than the average mood on a non-binge day.

In summary, these studies provide convincing evidence that mood and stress in daily life are related to binge eating in women with BN, and that purging is used to reduce the negative affect associated with food cues and eating. There is conflicting evidence as to the reinforcing effects of binging in BN: Alpers and Tuschen-Caffier (2001) and Hilbert and Tuschen-Caffier (2007) found mood to deteriorate after binging whereas Smyth et al. (2007) demonstrated a similar pattern of rapid mood recovery after both binging and vomiting. The reasons for these discrepancies in findings are not clear, although differences in research design (e.g., assessment time points, mode and frequency of assessment, length of observation period, etc.) and sample sizes may have contributed to this scenario. The former two studies involved smaller samples (40 and 20 per group, respectively) and shorter observation periods (2 consecutive days) with more frequent assessments (32 assessments over 16 hours) than the latter (131 participants, 2 weeks, 6 assessments over 13.5 hours). It is conceivable, for example, that the mood-enhancing effects of binging or vomiting follow different temporal sequences, so that results are partly determined by assessment protocols. Alternatively, binge-eating episodes may not invariably be followed by either mood improvement or mood deterioration. Rather, as yet to be identified situational or individual factors (e.g., cognitions) may determine which emotional consequences arise from binge eating in individuals with BN. For example, it could be argued that a binge-eating episode is experienced as less negative and therefore potentially mood-improving compared to pre-binge levels if the possibility for subsequent purging is given. Equally, if purging is rendered impossible, the experience of binge eating may have the described negative effect on mood (Staiger et al., 2000). Certainly, within the affective processing model of negative reinforcement (Baker et al., 2004) both binge eating and purging can be conceptualized as behaviors that allow escape or avoidance of negative affect.

BINGE EATING DISORDER
Binge eating disorder (BED) resembles BN but binge eating occurs in the absence of regular compensatory behaviors to prevent weight gain, such as

fasting or purging. Consequently, overweight and obesity are common among those diagnosed with BED (Gruzca, Przybeck, & Cloninger, 2007). BED is also associated with co-occurring physical and mental illnesses, as well as impaired quality of life and social functioning (Wilfley, Wilson, & Agras, 2003). Results from a community sample suggest that BED contributes to these comorbidities over and above those expected for obesity (Gruzca et al., 2007). Among mental illnesses mood disorders (especially depression) and anxiety disorders are the most prevalent co-morbid lifetime and current diagnoses for individuals with BED (Dingemans, Spinhoven, & Van Furth, 2007; Grilo, White, & Masheb, 2009). Those with current co-morbidity have higher levels of current ED psychopathology, negative affect and lower self-esteem compared to BED patients without lifetime or current comorbidity.

Taken together, these studies provide evidence that depressive symptoms (trait), acute negative mood (state), and binge eating behavior are related, but little is known about their causal relationships. It has been suggested that binge eating in BED reflects difficulties in regulating negative emotions (Whiteside et al., 2007), and—as for BN—that binge eating is an attempt to reduce negative affect associated with food, body shape or stress, in particular as negative emotions are reported to often precede binge eating episodes in BED (Stice, Akutagawa, Gaggar, & Agras, 2000). An important difference to BN concerns the role of dieting. Whereas in BN dieting nearly always precedes a binge-eating episode, this pattern is usually reversed in BED, in that sporadic dieting attempts follow eating binges.

Another approach follows a conditioning model of binge eating (CBE) (Jansen, 1994), in which it is postulated that through classical conditioning, certain cues such as the sight and smell of food elicit physiological responses that are experienced as craving. It is interesting in this context that the type of food seems to be important for binging in BED patients, as they prefer high-caloric food with high sugar and fat content (De Zwaan, 2001). Based on these results it has been suggested that individuals with BED differ in reward sensitivity from non–eating disordered individuals. In the following sections we review the evidence in relation to these models.

Emotional Responses to Food Cues
Emotional responses to food cues in binge eaters have mostly been investigated using experimental procedures, in both clinical and nonclinical samples.

McNamara, Hay, Katsikitis, and Chur-Hansen (2008) compared emotional responses to the presentation of food images in relation to body image concerns and ED symptoms, both assessed by self-report questionnaires. The nonclinical sample included children, adolescents, and young adults, both male and female, so that age and sex were also included in the analysis. The results show a decrease in the emotive responses (i.e., fear, disgust, happiness) to food pictures with increasing age. Males had the more positive emotive responses, but not necessarily less negative emotions toward food, whereas in adult females a fear emotive response was associated with eating concern and body dissatisfaction. The authors conclude that the more positive emotional response in males may be a protective factor that reduces their vulnerability to EDs.

Vögele and Florin (1997) examined emotional and psychophysiological responses to food exposure in self-identified female binge eaters, and found higher sympathetic arousal levels as indicated by blood pressure and electrodermal activity throughout the exposure compared to female non-binge eaters. This was accompanied by increases in ratings of hunger, desire to binge, sadness, and nervousness. Heart rate during food exposure predicted the relative amount of food eaten after exposure across all participants, but this relationship was more pronounced in binge eaters. In summary, the results indicate that binge eaters responded with greater subjective and physiological arousal to food cues than non-binge eaters, which was experienced as aversive and relieved by eating. This supports the affective processing model of negative reinforcement (Baker et al., 2004) and indicates that binge eaters use binge eating to downregulate the strong negative emotions elicited by food cues.

The foods chosen by participants in Vögele and Florin's experiment (1997) did not differ in amount or calories between binge eaters and non-binge eaters. Nevertheless, binge eaters are reported to prefer high-caloric foods with high fat and sugar content (De Zwaan, 2001), and this preference might be mediated by the reward value of these types of food. There is a literature on the neural correlates of visual food stimuli of high caloric food in normal-weight women (e.g., Killgore & Yurgelun-Todd, 2007), which indicates that activity in brain regions important for early processing of these cues can be influenced by their hedonic value as well as the affective state of the individual. Greater positive affect is associated with increased activity within the primary visual cortex during visual perception of calorie rich and highly flavorful foods, but not for less pleasurably satisfying low-calorie foods. Such findings suggest a mechanism whereby affective state may affect the early stages of sensory processing, possibly influencing subsequent perceptual experience of a stimulus.

Schienle, Schäfer, Hermann, and Vaitl (2009) used functional magnetic resonance imaging to explore the neural correlates of visual food exposure after an overnight fast in four groups of participants: overweight BED, overweight healthy control, normal-weight healthy control, and normal-weight BN. BED patients reported enhanced reward sensitivity and showed stronger activation in the medial orbitofrontal cortex (OFC) while viewing food pictures than all other groups. Activity in the OFC is assumed to reflect the hedonic value and reward relevance of food. The conclusion drawn by the Schienle et al. (2009) is that the heightened medial OFC reactivity to food cues observed for BED suggests increased reinforcement sensitivity, which may lead to binge eating. It is interesting to note in this context that the study by Schienle et al. (2009) and also the studies by Killgore and co-workers (e.g., 2007) seem to suggest a positive emotional response to visual food stimuli, even in BED (Schienle et al., 2009), although this would contradict the previous reports on negative affect in response to food cues. On closer inspection it becomes clear, however, that the positive aspects referred to in Schienle et al. (2009) and Kilgore et al. (2007) refer to appetitive characteristics of food pictures, whereas the negative emotional responses reported by McNamara et al. (2008) and Vögele and Florin (1997) refer to emotions such as fear, sadness, and nervousness. In BED these emotions seem complementary rather than mutually exclusive: food is desired (i.e., appetitive) but feared (because of its presumed consequences, i.e., fattening, etc.), as is the case for BN, and probably chocolate cravers (section "Anorexia Nervosa").

Findings related to the appetitive qualities of food cues are reported by Goldfield and co-workers (2008). This study differs from the previous investigations in that not the emotional responses to food cues per se but changes in the relative reinforcing value of snack foods were assessed in relation to participants' stress reactivity and (questionnaire-based) binge eating status. Although there were no differences between low stress-reactive binge and non-binge eaters in the way they rated the reinforcing qualities of food under stress, stress-reactive binge eaters found food more rewarding under stress as opposed to high-reactive non-binge eaters, who rated food less reinforcing. This effect was independent of BMI and dietary restraint. These findings suggest that the experience of stress has opposite effects on the relative reinforcing value of food and, therefore, food intake, depending on binge eater status (see also section "Binge Eating Disorder").

Emotional Responses to Body Image Exposure

In contrast to AN and BN, concerns about body weight and shape are currently not included in the research criteria for BED (*DSM-IV*). Nevertheless, there is increasing evidence that a negative body image is also important in BED, and that they have similar levels of overvaluation of shape and weight as those with BN and AN (Wilfley, Schwartz, Spurell, & Fairburn, 2000). Moreover, overvaluation of body weight and shape has been shown to predict the degree of eating-related psychopathology and psychological disturbance (Hrabosky, Masheb, White, & Grilo, 2007). In summary, there is accumulating evidence that overvaluation of body weight and shape and a negative body image are as important in BED as they are in AN and BN (Grilo et al., 2008).

In the studies by Hrabosky et al. (2007) and Grilo et al. (2008) overvaluation was significantly related to depression levels in BED. This points to the possibility that negative affect mediates the association between a negative body image and eating-related pathology. Further support for this notion comes from correlational studies reporting a systematic association between physical appearance-related teasing experiences and depression levels in BED (Jackson, Grilo, & Masheb, 2002). Nevertheless, to our knowledge there is only one study that examined the effects of body shape exposure on emotional responses in an experimental design. Hilbert, Tuschen-Caffier, and Vögele (2002) exposed a sample of female BED individuals to their physical appearance in a whole-body mirror using a manual to guide participants in describing their appearance. In comparison with age and weight matched non–eating disordered control participants, BED responded with more negative mood (sad, tense, insecure, anxious, disgusted), although a decrease in mood was apparent in both groups. When the exposure session was repeated 2 days later emotional responses across groups were less negative than during the first exposure. Nevertheless, the differences between BED and controls remained with BED showing more intense negative emotions. Appearance self-esteem was lower in BED during both exposure sessions than in controls, and BED described their bodies as fatter than non–eating disordered participants. Interestingly, levels of anxiety were lower and less affected by the repeated exposure than feelings of tension, sadness, insecurity, and disgust. Body image disturbance in BED may, therefore, be more related to a composite of negative mood rather than anxiety.

Negative Affect and Binge Eating

Affect models, in contrast to dietary restraint models, postulate that binge eating is triggered by negative affect (Meyer, Waller, & Waters, 1998), and that binge eating acts as a negative reinforcer as it provides short-term relief by reducing or numbing negative emotions or distraction from aversive mood states. These models are clearly more appropriate for BED than restraint models, as dieting usually follows a binge but does not precede it.

The evidence for the notion that negative affect triggers binge eating in BED is, however, mixed. Several laboratory studies have investigated this question by comparing food consumption under conditions of negative mood induction with a control condition. In Telch and Agras (1996), mood induction by tape-recorded vivid imagery did not affect food consumption in obese BED when compared to a non–eating disordered control group, although BED participants consumed more calories overall. Chua, Touyz, and Hill (2004) randomly allocated obese BED to a sad or neutral film condition before monitoring food consumption in an alleged taste test (chocolate). Participants in the sad condition ate significantly more when compared with those in the control condition. The authors' hypothesis that those with a restrained eating style in the negative mood condition would eat most failed to reach statistical significance. Munsch, Michael, Biedert, Meyer, and Margraf (2008) randomly allocated obese BED to a negative or neutral mood induction (using guided imagery). Participants also received either a balanced diet (rich in carbohydrates) or a poor diet (high in fat) over 3 consecutive days preceding laboratory testing. Although the mood induction was successful, there were no differences between experimental groups in the amount of food eaten in the alleged taste test (dessert cream). Dingemans, Martijn, Jansen, and van Furth (2009) tested the assumption that it is not the experience of negative affect per se that prompts overeating in BED, but the attempt to regulate it. Models of self-regulation provide the theoretical background for this hypothesis (e.g., Muraven & Baumeister, 2000), which stipulates that self-control is a limited resource that can be depleted. When, for example, a situation demands two consecutive acts of self-control, performance on the second act (e.g., resist eating) is usually impaired because of energy depletion. Accordingly, half of the sample was instructed to suppress their emotions while watching a sad film clip, while the other half were told to respond naturally. The main hypothesis that those in the emotion suppression condition would eat most was not confirmed. Nevertheless, individuals with BED who had severe depressive symptoms consumed more calories than those with no or mild depressive symptoms, independent of the experimental condition. Mood improved after eating to levels comparable to those before watching the film.

The notion that emotion regulation may be more important for binge eating than negative affect per se has found some support from cross-sectional studies. Whiteside et al. (2007) evaluated difficulties in regulating negative emotions in relation to binge eating in a cross-sectional study of male and female undergraduate university students. Hierarchical regression results indicated that difficulties in emotion regulation as assessed by self-report questionnaire accounted for a significant amount of the variance in binge eating, over and above sex, dietary restraint, and over-evaluation of body weight and shape. The specific types of emotion regulation difficulties most strongly associated with binge eating were limited access to emotion regulation strategies and difficulty identifying and making sense of emotional states.

The sample investigated by Whiteside et al. (2007) included predominantly young adults. Nevertheless, there is evidence that the association between emotion regulation and binge eating also applies to much younger individuals. Czaja, Rief, and Hilbert (2008) examined a community sample of 8- to 13-year-old children who had experienced at least one episode of loss of control over eating. Control participants had not experienced any loss of control over eating or other disordered eating behavior and were matched for age, sex, percentile BMI, education, and socioeconomic status of the mother. The results show that children who had experienced loss of control over eating made higher use of dysfunctional emotion regulation strategies, especially for the regulation of anxiety. The use of maladaptive strategies was associated with greater depressiveness.

In summary, there is some evidence linking negative affect or its failed regulation to overeating in BED, although results from controlled laboratory experiments are inconclusive. One reason for this may be the artificial laboratory setting, and it has been suggested that it is unclear how well laboratory eating behavior mimics naturalistic eating behavior (Walsh & Boudreau, 2003). For example, the frequently used taste tests in these investigations usually involve the presentation of only very few food items (sweets, chocolate, or dessert cream) even though typical binge foods can be quite idiosyncratic. Moreover, the negative affect experienced in a typical laboratory setting may be far less intense than that encountered in a natural setting.

As is the case for studies of binge eating in BN, the concurrent assessment of mood changes and eating behavior in the natural environment offers an attractive alternative for the investigation of antecedents and consequences of binge eating in BED. In Greeno, Wing, and Shiffman (2000) women with BED and weight- and age-matched non–eating disordered individuals monitored their eating and mood for 6 consecutive days using a hand-held computer. Poor mood, feelings of poor eating control, and craving sweets all preceded binge eating episodes in BED. Although mood was worse overall for women with BED, it was especially poor before a binge-eating episode. An unexpected finding was the relatively high percentage of women in the control group (i.e., not identified as BED) but who still reported binge eating over the observation period and who—in terms of negative affect—were between BED and those who did not experience any binge episodes.

Deaver, Miltenberger, Smyth, and Meidinger (2003) investigated a sample of self-identified female binge eaters and compared their responses on an affect grid at 2-minute intervals before, during, and after binge eating episodes and regular meals to those of individuals not reporting any binge eating. The observation period was 4 to 7 days, depending on whether at least two binge-eating episodes had occurred. The results show that negative affect preceded binge-eating episodes, which became less negative during the binge, and again increased after the binge. This pattern was the same for normal meals, but differed in level in that negative affect was less marked during normal meals. Participants in the control group experienced similar levels of negative affect before meals than did BED before meals; however, they reported significantly more pleasant affect than did binge eaters during and after eating regular meals.

Women meeting *DSM-IV* criteria for BED took part in the study of Stein et al. (2007). Over 7 consecutive days participants were prompted by hand-held

computers at six intervals during the day to answer a series of questions pertaining to eating and mood since the last data entry. As in previous studies, negative mood and hunger were significantly higher before binges compared to non-binge times. In contrast to previous results (Deaver et al., 2003), however, negative mood was even worse after binge-eating episodes, a finding that is shared by the previously mentioned study by Hilbert and Tuschen-Caffier (2007; see section 'Bulimia Nervosa: Negative Affect and Binge Eating'). An interesting finding in Hilbert and Tuschen-Caffier (2007) was that negative mood antecedent to binge eating was in part attributable to general psychopathology, suggesting that anxiety and depression predispose individuals with BED to more negative mood proximal to binge eating.

We can summarize, therefore, that there is evidence that negative affect triggers binge eating in BED and those at risk (e.g., obese individuals). The question exactly how negative affect triggers overeating, however, has not been resolved yet, and several pathways have been suggested. Affect-driven models include trade-off theory, which posits that in the face of negative mood, binge eating serves to substitute a less aversive affective condition (e.g., guilt after binge eating) for the more aversive emotional state (e.g., depression) that preceded the binge (Kenardy, Arnow, & Agras, 1996). There is the escape from self-awareness model, which proposes that the act of binge eating allows narrowing the attentional focus on the immediate stimuli (i.e., food) in order to block out negative emotions (Heatherton & Baumeister, 1991; Nolen-Hoeksema, Stice, Wade, & Bohon, 2007). The previously described self-regulation model assumes that self-regulation is a limited resource that can be depleted with a resulting loss of self-control (Muraven & Baumeister, 2000). For example, negative affect might trigger overeating because it distracts people from or depletes the resources used for their dietary vigilance (Stice, Akutagawa, et al., 2000). Another affect-related model is masking theory, according to which binge eating serves as an attribution for negative affect that masks other problems (Polivy & Herman, 1999). If negative emotions can be blamed on binge eating this could be perceived as more tolerable than other sources of distress.

These models are not mutually exclusive, but only emphasize different aspects of overeating as dysfunctional coping strategy in response to negative affect (Schachter, Goldman, & Gordon, 1968; Spoor, Bekker, Van Strien, & van Heck, 2007), with ruminative thinking probably playing a key role. Ruminative thinking can be defined as uncontrollable perseverative thinking about past or present events, in particular "dwelling on negative affect" (Nolen-Hoeksema, 1991; Thomsen, 2006). It may contribute to overeating in at least two ways: first, it might be an indicator for disinhibition, as ruminative thinking has also been linked to a general lack of behavioral inhibition (Siegle & Thayer, 2004). Second, ruminating may lead to a prolonged dwelling on negative affect, thus increasing its intensity it and possibly activating eating as a dysfunctional coping or "escapist" behavior. Kubiak, Vögele, Siering, Schiel, and Weber (2008) investigated the role of ruminative thinking for emotional eating in a sample of obese, female adolescents who reported at least one binge-eating episode over the past 12 months. Participants kept an electronic diary over 7 consecutive days and recorded daily hassles type of stress, desire to eat, negative affect, and rumination. The results of mixed regression modeling showed that daily hassles predicted the desire to eat; however, the predictive value further increased when negative affect and rumination were accounted for. This finding suggests a significant contribution of ruminative thinking to the mechanisms of negative affect induced eating. With ruminative thinking being a key feature of depression it links in with the previously reported finding (Hilbert & Tuschen-Caffier, 2007) that negative mood antecedent to binge eating is in part attributable to general psychopathology, in particular depression and anxiety.

As is the case for BN, however, there is conflicting evidence as to the reinforcement model, which for BED predicts that binging functions as at least temporary relief from negative affect experienced prior to binging. Deaver et al. (2003) found support for this notion, whereas the results of Stein et al. (2007) and Hilbert and Tuschen-Caffier (2007) suggest that BED feel even worse after a binge-eating episode. Notwithstanding methodological differences between these studies (e.g., time sampling protocols), it could be argued that these discrepancies in findings might reflect differences in situational or individual factors (e.g., subtypes of binge eaters) that determine whether mood improves after binging, or not.

ANOREXIA NERVOSA

The core feature of AN is a relentless pursuit of thinness and a refusal to maintain a body weight at a minimally acceptable standard for age and height. In the *DSM-IV* this is suggested to be 85% of the expected weight, whereas the ICD-10 recommends the criteria of a BMI equal or less than $17.5\,kg/m^2$. Individuals with AN have an essential fear of gaining weight or becoming fat, place undue value on weight, and typically show disturbed perceptions of their own body shape and size. The *DSM-IV* distinguishes two clinical subtypes: restricting AN (AN-R) accomplish weight loss primarily through fasting or excessive exercise, or both. AN of the binge eating/purging type (AN-BP) reduce weight through self-induced vomiting and use of laxatives. There is some crossover between the two subgroups, and it remains unclear as to whether these are two enduring subtypes, or different phases of the same illness (Eddy et al., 2002). Recent results from a retrospective study of a large sample of AN patients suggest that the switch from the AN-R type to the AN-BP type is associated with a large increase in the prevalence of suicide attempts (Foulon et al., 2007). The authors argue the affected patients could experience binging as a failure to control appetite, and purging as a loss of previous asceticism. Switching from AN-R to AN-BP could, therefore, be associated with higher negative affectivity or an increase in impulsivity, both of which could contribute to the observed higher rates of suicide among persons with AN-BP.

In terms of clinical symptoms and impulsivity, individuals with AN-BP, therefore, have much in common with individuals with BN, who have similar rates of suicide attempts. Both groups engage in an abnormal eating pattern characterized by alternating periods of fasting and episodes of binge eating, together with purging directly after binging (e.g., vomiting or use of laxatives) or excessive exercise. The only distinguishing feature is the abnormally low body weight in AN.

Emotional Responses to Food Cues
As previously described non–eating disordered individuals tend to assign positive emotional valence to food stimuli that is enhanced by hunger (Lozano, Crites, & Aikmann, 1999). AN patients, who are preoccupied with food irrespective of hunger, however, report negative valence of food stimuli (Vaz, Alcaina, & Guisado, 1998), and in this respect do not differ from BN or BED. Uher and co-workers (2003, 2004) have extensively studied the neural correlates of the processing of visual food stimuli in EDs and found that both, AN and BN showed decreased activation in areas that are associated with appetitive behavior (inferior parietal lobe, occipital cortex) and increased activation in areas that are associated with cognitive control (medial prefrontal

cortex), compared to non–eating disordered controls. Gordon et al. (2001) used positron emission tomographic measurements of regional cerebral blood flow (rCBF) to compare responses of AN and healthy participants while viewing pictures of high- and low-calorie foods, and nonfood items. In contrast to healthy participants who reported a desire to eat while viewing high-calorie pictures, AN responded with elevated anxiety and increased heart rates. This was associated with exaggerated responses in visual association cortexes, similar to those observed in studies of specific phobias.

To control for differences in hunger and satiety participants in these studies were required to have eaten at a specified time before the experiment started. It is not clear, therefore, in what way hunger or satiety might affect such results. This was addressed in a functional magnetic resonance imaging (fMRI) study by Santel, Baving, Krauel, Münte, and Rotte (2006) in which patients with AN and healthy controls were tested in both a hungry and a satiated state. Hunger scores of AN patients were far lower than those of healthy participants, with a trend for this effect to be more marked in the hungry condition. AN patients rated food stimuli as less pleasant than healthy controls, independent of the condition of hunger or satiety. This was accompanied by decreased somatosensory processing in the satiated state (i.e., decreased activation in the inferior parietal lobe) and decreased attention to food stimuli in the hungry state (i.e., reduced occipital activation). The authors interpret these results in terms of reduced responsiveness to the pleasant aspects of food stimuli that are highly appetizing to healthy individuals. This altered cognitive processing of visual food stimuli may facilitate fasting. For example, the decreased attention to food stimuli while hungry could be interpreted as avoidance behavior.

Such cross-sectional investigations of AN patients provide important information about abnormalities in emotional experiences and associated brain functions with this disorder. Nevertheless, the causal relationships between brain alterations and the clinical syndrome are unclear because primary neural disturbances cannot be differentiated from phenomena secondary to the disorder. In an effort to overcome this problem, Uher et al. (2003) investigated responses to food stimuli and pictures from the International Affective Picture System (IAPS) with fMRI in chronically ill AN-R and in long-term recovered AN-R and healthy controls. Instead of a prospective design, which would be difficult to realize, Uher et al. (2003) argued that by obtaining evidence from people fully recovered from AN trait factors could be identified without the confounding evidence from acute starvation, metabolic alterations, and treatment-related stress. The main finding of this study was that food-related brain activity in recovered AN-R was a combination of responses seen in currently ill AN-R (increased activity in the medial frontal and anterior cingulated cortices) and those recorded in healthy controls (increased activity in the apical and lateral prefrontal cortices). Food pictures were rated as less pleasant and more aversive by currently ill AN-R compared to either recovered AN-R or healthy controls. No differences in brain activation or subjective ratings were found for the IAPS stimuli. Although cross-sectional in research design, by comparing recovered and currently ill patients the study results suggest that the medial prefrontal response to food stimuli is present in both active illness and recovery and may, therefore, represent a trait factor of the disease.

Emotional Responses to Body Image Exposure
Individuals with AN not only perceive but actually see their bodies as being fatter than they are, especially in the abdomen, buttocks, and thighs. When compared with non–eating disordered women, they not only judge their own body size and shape much more harshly, but they are also more critical of other women's bodies (Smeets, 1999). Seeger, Braus, Ruf, Goldberger, and Schmidt (2002) used fMRI to investigate the effects of body image exposure using digital body images individually distorted by participants. In participants with AN, exposure led to an activation of the brain's "fear network," including the right amygdala, the right gyrus fusiformis, and the brain stem region. These responses are suggestive of a pattern that is otherwise seen in patients with anxiety disorders when confronted with threat-relevant stimuli.

The previously mentioned study by Beato-Fernández et al. (2009) used single photon emission computed tomography (SPECT) to investigate the effects of exposure to a video of their own body in BN and AN-R on brain activation. In contrast to BN, who showed hyperactivity in brain regions implicated in emotion processing (i.e., right temporal and occipital areas), AN-R responded with activation of the attention network and somatosensory system. This might suggest that persons with BN show higher body dissatisfaction (the cognitive–evaluative component) whereas the response of individuals with AN-R is indicative of greater perceptual distortion (the perceptual component).

This interpretation of differential brain activity was supported by results from the Silhouette Test, which showed the largest increases in the body distortion index of AN-R test after exposure compared to BN and healthy participants.

Emotional Processing Deficits

The literature on mood and emotions in AN has largely concentrated on the concept of alexithymia. This concept was initially developed by observing patients with psychosomatic disorders and hypothesizes that alexithymia is a risk factor for organic disorders (Sifneos, 1991). Alexithymia is conceptualized as a cognitive–affective deficit comprising the following impairments: (1) difficulties in identifying feelings and distinguishing emotions from physical sensations, (2) difficulties in communicating emotional states to others, (3) restricted daydreaming, and (4) a concrete/externally oriented style of thinking (Taylor, Bagby, & Parker, 1991). Alexithymia has been almost exclusively investigated using the Toronto Alexithymia Scale (TAS; Bagby, Taylor, & Parker, 1994).

Several studies suggest that alexithymia, as operationalized by the TAS, is an important factor in EDs (e.g., Beales & Dolton, 2000; Guilbaud et al., 2000; Zonnevijle-Bender, van Goozen, Cohen-Kettenis, & van Engeland, 2002), with AN-R typically reporting greater difficulties in identifying their emotions and in describing their feelings to others when compared with non–eating disordered women (Taylor, Parker, Bagby, & Bourke, 1996) and also individuals with BN (Taylor et al., 1997), although this latter result could not be replicated in a more recent study (Bydlowski et al., 2005).

As a concept alexithymia relies on a deficit model of emotional processing in that it emphasizes difficulties in identifying and describing feelings and in differentiating between feelings and physical sensations. It involves an impaired capacity to construct mental representations of emotions, which is the prerequisite for the cognitive processing of emotional experiences and their communication to others. Gilboa-Schechtmann, Avnon, Zubery, and Jeczmien (2006) compared groups of patients with AN (AN-R and AN-BP) and BN to non–eating disordered individuals. Despite some differences between the ED groups in emotional awareness, AN and BN individuals appeared to be more similar in their profile of emotional deficiencies than previously suggested. Importantly, the differences between the ED groups and non–eating disordered controls were mediated by emotional distress, a finding that

confirms a previous result by Espina Eizaguirre et al. (2004). Only a measure of rumination remained significantly correlated with a continuous measure of ED pathology when controlling for anxiety and depression (see also the previous discussion of rumination and general psychopathology in BN and BED).

As most studies investigating emotional processing deficits in ED have used the TAS, there is a preponderance of questionnaire-based, cross-sectional studies. Nevertheless, some recent psychophysiological studies have confirmed aspects of the assumption that emotional processing is impaired in AN. Pollatos, Herbert, Schandry, and Gramann (2008) found marked differences in evoked potentials and emotion recognition performance in response to emotional faces between AN and non–eating disordered controls. The authors conclude that differences in brain dynamics might contribute to difficulties in the identification of facially expressed emotions and deficits in social functioning.

Yet another approach in the study of emotional processing in AN was used by Doba et al. (2007). The authors investigated the temporal organization of emotional expression in autobiographical speech. The results show that AN expressed more negative emotions and fewer neutral states, together with negative emotional perservaration when compared with healthy participants.

In summary, individuals with AN appear to have difficulties in representing their own emotional experiences as well as that of others. This may thwart patients from seeking health care, reduce their treatment adherence, and contribute to the chronic nature of the disorder and increase the risk for potential relapse. Another consequence of these emotional processing deficits is increased negative affect, which AN may try to alleviate by starvation, hyperactivity, binging, and purging. Alternative or additional strategies to cope with increased levels of negative affect could consist of modifying access to autobiographical emotional memories by retrieving memories less specifically. Autobiographical memories are considered to represent transient mental constructions that are generated from a database of autobiographical knowledge, which is hierarchically organized from specific to general memories (Conway & Pleydell-Pearce, 2000). Previous results suggest that there is a systematic relationship between the intensity of experienced negative events and general autobiographical memory such that the more aversive the experience the lower the specificity of memories (Raes, Hermans, De Decker,

Eelen, & Williams, 2003). This was investigated in a sample of AN-R by Nandrino, Doba, Lesne, Christophe, and Pezard (2006). Patients with AN-R recalled more general memories than controls in the autobiographical memory test, but had no deficit in explicit memory. Moreover, the overgeneralization of autobiographical memories included both negative and positive memories, and this pattern increased significantly with illness duration. These results suggest a general impairment in the access to emotional memories in AN. Patients with AN may be prone to not only suppress or control negative affect but also positive affect. The positive correlation between the number of general responses and illness duration shows that this deficit in experiencing and integrating emotional events is reinforced as the disorder becomes chronic.

Conclusion

Mood and emotions are intrinsically involved with eating, as would be expected for any fundamentally rewarding behaviour: for example, the pleasure from delicious food, or the disgust from foul tasting food, are very real emotions. The question is in what ways do these normal emotional relations with food contribute to, or shed light on, the development of abnormal relations with food that eventually become clinical EDs. This chapter has first considered basic mechanisms, findings, and models that help our understanding of the interactions between eating and emotions, in both clinical and nonclinical populations. This allows consideration of normal food–emotion interactions and how these may evolve into more aberrant behavior.

Intense emotions are often incompatible with eating, at least in the short-term, although their aftermath may lead to emotion-dependent habits. Foods that are themselves capable of shifting emotional states may provide reinforcement through escape or distraction from aversive emotions. More moderate emotions can be generated by consumption of palatable foods, and in turn influence our appreciation of foods. However, even in the non-clinical population, our emotional involvement with foods is complex and conflicting. A key theme in the literature is that the nature and consequences of emotional interactions with food depends on individual predispositions.

The interaction among mood, emotions, and EDs is, however, more complex. The finding, that comorbidity with mood and anxiety disorders is the norm among patients with EDs suggests that EDs may not be necessarily restricted to domains of eating behavior and body image but also may be related to significant difficulties in affective functioning. It has been suggested that EDs are disturbances of mood regulation in which regulatory strategies specifically related to eating and the body are used to diminish negative affect associated with food, body image, or stress. In particular, three eating styles or tendencies have been identified: (1) restrained eating, (2) emotional eating, and (3) uncontrolled or disinhibited eating. In brief, restrained eating is characterized by attempts at cognitive control over how much is eaten. This strategy may be more or less successful, although in many populations it may intensify as excess weight is gained. Where the cognitive component is strong, emotional influences on eating seem to be suppressed, although intense emotions, and other distractors, may nevertheless disrupt the cognitive control through competition for attentional resources. This tendency clearly has implications for understanding AN.

By contrast, both emotional and uncontrolled eating are common tendencies that may be present in exaggerated form in BN and BED. Emotional eating is the tendency to overeat provoked by negative affect, whereas uncontrolled eating is the tendency for sensory, social, or physiological stimuli associated with food to elicit eating in excess of need. These two facets are often intercorrelated, and may share some common processes, such as altered function in opioid and dopaminergic pathways. In both cases, highly palatable sweet or fatty foods are specifically capable of inducing overeating: however, for emotional eating, stress or negative affect are prerequisites, whereas for uncontrolled eating, sensitization of hedonic and reward pathways, reflecting genetic and/or behavioral history, may be critical. This has led to the notion of EDs as one possible manifestation of behavioral addictions (Shaffer et al., 2004). The frequent co-occurrence of polysubstance abuse in EDs would further support this hypothesis.

Approaches for defining and modeling these tendencies continue to evolve: nevertheless, they are helping to understand and predict the transition from normal to abnormal eating, and the particular role that mood and emotions may play.

Future Directions

The findings reviewed here raise several key questions for future research to address:

1. What characteristics of an individual's emotion regulation lead him or her to change from

merely emotional involvement with food to the severely exaggerated and dysfunctional eating associated with a clinical diagnosis of an ED?

2. What are the implications of research on emotions and EDs for understanding the common transitions between ED diagnostic categories, and for predicting remission?

3. What is the role of brain reward systems in EDs?

4. Can improved knowledge of brain reward systems help to understand the etiology of EDs better?

5. Can successful treatments be devised based on knowledge of the role of opioidergic, dopaminergic, and serotoninergic systems in emotion regulation, normal eating, and EDs?

6. Can knowledge of the role of the vagus nerve in emotion regulation, appetite, and EDs be further developed and combined to improve treatment strategies for EDs?

References

Agras, W. S., & Telch, C. F. (1998). The effects of caloric deprivation and negative affect on binge eating in obese binge-eating disordered women. *Behavior Therapy, 29*, 491–503.

Alpers, G. W., & Tuschen-Caffier, B. (2001). Negative feelings and the desire to eat in bulimia nervosa. *Eating Behaviors, 2*, 339–352.

American Psychiatric Association (APA). (1994). *Diagnostic and statistical manual of mental disorders* (4th ed.). Washington, DC: Author.

Attie, I., & Brooks-Gunn, J. (1989). Development of eating problems in adolescent girls: A longitudinal study. *Developmental Psychology, 25*, 70–79.

Bagby, R. M., Taylor, G. J., & Parker, J. D. A. (1994). The twenty-item Toronto Alexithymia Scale—II. Convergent, discriminant, and concurrent validity. *Journal of Psychosomatic Research, 38*, 33–40.

Baker, T. B., Piper, M. E., McCarthy, D. E., Majeskie, M. R., & Fiore, M. C. (2004). Addiction motivation reformulated: An affective processing model of negative reinforcement. *Psychological Review, 111*, 35–51.

Bardone, A. M., Krahn, D. D., Goodman, B. M., & Searles, J. S. (2000). Using interactive voice response technology and timeline follow-back methodology in studying binge eating and drinking behavior: Different answers to different forms of the same question? *Addictive Behaviors, 25*, 1–11.

Barr, R. G., Pantel, M. S., Young, S. N., Wright, J. H., Hendricks, L. A., & Gravel, R. (1999). The response of crying newborns to sucrose: Is it a "sweetness" effect? *Physiology & Behavior, 66*, 409–417.

Beales, D. L., & Dolton, R. (2000). Eating disordered patients: Personality, alexithymia, and implications for primary care. *British Journal of General Practice, 50*, 21–26.

Beato-Fernández, L., Rodríguez-Cano, T., García-Vilches, I., García-Vicente, A., Poblete-García, V., Castrejon, A. S., & Toro, J. (2009). Changes in regional cerebral blood flow after body image exposure in eating disorders. *Psychiatry Research, 171*, 129–137.

Berridge, K. C. (2009). 'Liking' and 'wanting' food rewards: Brain substrates and roles in eating disorders. *Physiology & Behavior, 97*, 537–550.

Berridge, K. C., & Robinson, T. E. (1998). What is the role of dopamine in reward: hedonic impact, reward learning, or incentive salience? *Brain Research: Brain Research Reviews, 28*, 309–369.

Blass, E. M., & Camp, C. A. (2003). Changing determinants of crying termination in 6- to 12-week-old human infants. *Developmental Psychobiology, 42*, 312–316.

Blass, E. M., Shide, D. J., & Weller, A. (1989). Stress-reducing effects of ingesting milk, sugars, and fats. A developmental perspective. *Annals of the New York Academy of Sciences, 575*, 292–305.

Boggiano, M. M., Chandler, P. C., Viana, J. B., Oswald, K. D., Maldonado, C. R., & Wauford, P. K. (2005). Combined dieting and stress evoke exaggerated responses to opioids in binge-eating rats. *Behavioral Neuroscience, 119*, 1207–1214.

Booth, D. A. (1994). *Psychology of nutrition*. London: Taylor and Francis.

Brand Miller, J. C., Holt, S. H., de Jong, V & Petocz, P. (2003). Cocoa powder increases postprandial insulinemia in lean young adults. *Journal of Nutrition, 133*, 3149–3152.

Braun, D. L., Sunday, S. R., & Halmi, K. A. (1994). Psychiatric comorbidity in patients with eating disorders. *Psychological Medicine, 24*, 859–867.

Bruch, H. (1974) *Eating disorders: Anorexia, obesity and the person within*. London: Routledge and Kegan Paul.

Bulik, C. M., Sullivan, P. F., Fear, J. L., & Joyce, P. R. (1997). Eating disorders and antecedent anxiety disorders: A controlled study. *Acta Psychiatrica Scandinavica, 96*, 101–107.

Buree, B. U., Papageorgis, D., & Hare, R. D. (1990). Eating in anorexia nervosa and bulimia nervosa: An application of the tripartite model of anxiety. *Canadian Journal of Behavioural Science, 22*, 207–218.

Bydlowski, S., Corcos, M., Jeammet, P., Paterniti, S., Berthoz, S., Laurier, C., et al. (2005). Emotion-processing deficits in eating disorders. *International Journal of Eating Disorders, 37*, 321–329.

Canli, T., Amin, Z., Haas, B., Omura, K., & Constable, R. T. (2004). A double dissociation between mood states and personality traits in the anterior cingulate. *Behavioral Neuroscience, 118*, 897–904.

Carnell, S., & Wardle, J. (2008). Appetite and adiposity in children: Evidence for a behavioral susceptibility theory of obesity. *American Journal of Clinical Nutrition, 88*, 22–29.

Cash, T. F., & Deagle, E. A. (1997). The nature and extent of body-image disturbance in anorexia nervosa and bulimia nervosa: A meta-analysis. *International Journal of Eating Disorders, 22*, 107–125.

Chua, J. L., Touyz, S., & Hill, A. J. (2004). Negative mood-induced overeating in obese binge eaters: An experimental study. *International Journal of Obesity, 28*, 606–610.

Conners, C. K., & Blouin, A. G. (1983). Nutritional effects on behavior of children. *Journal of Psychiatric Research, 17*, 193–201.

Conway, M., & Pleydell-Pearce, C. (2000). The construction of autobiographical memories in the self-memory system. *Psychological Review, 107*, 261–288.

Cooper, M., Wells, A., & Todd, G. (2004). A cognitive model of bulimia nervosa. *British Journal of Clinical Psychology, 43*, 1–16.

Craig, A. (1986). Acute effects of meals on perceptual and cognitive efficiency. *Nutrition Reviews, 44*, 163–171.

Craig, A., Baer, K., & Diekmann, A. (1981). The effects of lunch on sensory-perceptual functioning in man. *International Archives of Occupational and Environmental Health*, 49, 105–114.

Craighead, L. W., & Allen, H. N. (1995). Appetite awareness training: A cognitive behavioral intervention for binge eating. *Cognitive and Behavioral Practice*, 2, 249–270.

Czaja, J., Rief, W., & Hilbert, A. (2009). Emotion regulation and binge eating in children. *International Journal of Eating Disorders*, 42, 356–362.

Dallman, M. F., Pecoraro, N., Akana, S. F., la Fleur, S. E., Gomez, F., Houshyar, H., et al. (2003). Chronic stress and obesity: A new view of "comfort food". *Proceedings of the National Academy of Sciences of the United States of America*, 100, 11696–11701.

D'Anci, K. E., Kanarek, R. B., & Marks-Kaufman, R. (1997). Beyond sweet taste: saccharin, sucrose, and polycose differ in their effects upon morphine-induced analgesia. *Pharmacology Biochemistry and Behavior*, 56, 341–345.

Deaver, C. M., Miltenberger, R. G., Smyth, J., & Crosby, R. (2003). An evaluation of affect and binge eating. *Behavior Modification*, 27, 578–599.

Dess, N. K., & Edelheit, D. (1998). The bitter with the sweet: The taste/stress/temperament nexus. *Biological Psychology*, 48, 103–119.

De Zwaan, M. (2001). Binge eating and obesity. *International Journal of Obesity*, 25, 51–55.

Dingemans, A. E., Martijn, C., Jansen, A., & van Furth, E. F. (2009). The effect of suppressing negative emotions on eating behavior in binge eating disorder. *Appetite*, 52, 51–57.

Dingemans, A. E., Spinhoven, P., & van Furth, E. F. (2007). Predictors and mediators of treatment outcome in patients with binge eating disorder. *Behaviour Research and Therapy*, 45, 2551–2562.

Doba, K., Pezard, L., Lesne, A., Vignau, J., Christophe, V., & Nandrino, J.-L. (2007). Dynamics of emotional expression in autobiographic speech of patients with anorexia nervosa. *Psychological Reports*, 101, 237–249.

Doyle, T. G., Berridge, K. C., & Gosnell, B. A. (1993). Morphine enhances hedonic taste palatability in rats. *Pharmacology Biochemistry and Behavior*, 46, 745–749.

Dusek, J. B., Mergler, M. L., & Kermis, M. D. (1976). Attention, encoding, and information processing in low- and high-test-anxious children. *Child Development*, 47, 201–207.

Eddy, K. T., Keel, P. K., Dorer, D. J., Delinsky, S. S., Franko, D. L., & Herzog, D. B. (2002). Longitudinal comparison of anorexia nervosa subtypes. *International Journal of Eating Disorders*, 31, 191–201.

Epel, E., Lapidus, R., McEwen, B., & Brownell, K. (2001). Stress may add bite to appetite in women: A laboratory study of stress- induced cortisol and eating behavior. *Psychoneuroendocrinology*, 26, 37–49.

Espina Eizaguirre, A., Saenz de Cabezón, A. O., Ochoa de Alda, I., Joaristi Olariaga, L., & Juaniz, M. (2004). Alexithymia and its relationships with anxiety and depression in eating disorders. *Personality and Individual Differences*, 36, 321–331.

Fairburn, C. G., Cooper, Z., & Shafran, R. (2003). Cognitive behaviour therapy for eating disorders: A "transdiagnostic" theory and treatment. *Behaviour Research and Therapy*, 41, 509–528.

Faris, P. L., Eckert, E. D., Kim, S. W., Meller, W. H., Pardo, J. V., Goodale, R. L., et al. (2006). Evidence for a vagal pathophysiology for bulimia nervosa and the accompanying depressive symptoms. *Journal of Affective Disorders*, 92, 79–90.

Faris, P. L., Hofbauer, R. D., Daughters, R., VandenLangenberg, E., Iversen, L., Goodale, R. L., et al. (2008). De-stabilization of the positive vago-vagal reflex in bulimia nervosa. *Physiology & Behavior*, 94, 136–153.

Fernstrom, M. H., & Fernstrom, J. D. (1995). Brain tryptophan concentrations and serotonin synthesis remain responsive to food consumption after the ingestion of sequential meals. *American Journal of Clinical Nutrition*, 61, 312–319.

Figlewicz, D. P., & Benoit, S. C. (2009). Insulin, leptin, and food reward: update 2008. *American Journal of Physiology Regulatory Integrative and Comparative Physiology*, 296, R9–R19.

Folkard, S., & Monk, T. H. (1985). *Hours of work: temporal factors in work scheduling*. Chichester: John Wiley & Sons.

Foulon, C., Guelfi, J. D., Kipman, A., Adès, J., Romo, L., Houddeyer, K., et al. (2007). Switching to the binge/purging subtype of anorexia nervosa is frequently associated with suicidal attempts. *European Psychiatry*, 22, 513–519.

Fredrickson, B. L. (2004). The broaden-and-build theory of positive emotions. *Philosophical Transactions of the Royal Society of London B: Biological Sciences*, 359, 1367–1378.

Fulkerson, J. A., Sherwood, N. E., Perry, C. L., Neumark-Sztainer, D., & Story, M. (2004). Depressive symptoms and adolescent eating and health behaviors: A multifaceted view in a population-based sample. *Preventive Medicine*, 38, 865–875.

George, M. S., Nahas, Z., Li, X. B., Kozel, F. A., Anderson, B., & Yamanaka, K. (2002). Potential new brain stimulation therapies in bipolar illness: Transcranial magnetic stimulation and vagus nerve stimulation. *Clinical Neuroscience Research*, 2, 256–265.

Gibson, E. L. (2006). Emotional influences on food choice: Sensory, physiological and psychological pathways. *Physiology & Behavior*, 89, 53–61.

Gibson, E. L., & Green, M. W. (2002). Nutritional influences on cognitive function: Mechanisms of susceptibility. *Nutrition Research Reviews*, 15, 169–206.

Gilboa-Schechtman, E., Avnon, L., Zubery, E., & Jeczmien, P. (2006). Emotional processing in eating disorders: Specific impairment or general distress related deficiency? *Depression and Anxiety*, 23, 331–339.

Godart, N. T., Perdereau, F., Curt, F., Lang, F., Venisse, J. L., Halfon, O., et al. (2004). Predictive factors of social disability in anorexic and bulimic patients. *Eating and Weight Disorders*, 9, 249–257.

Godart, N. T., Perdereau, F., Rein, Z., Berthoz, S., Wallier, J., Jeammet, P., & Flament, M. F. (2007). Comorbidity studies of eating disorders and mood disorders. Critical review of the literature. *Journal of Affective Disorders*, 97, 37–49.

Goldfein, J. A., Walsh, T., & Midlarsky, E. (2000). Influence of shape and weight on self-evaluation in bulimia nervosa. *International Journal of Eating Disorders*, 27, 435–445.

Goldfield, G. S., Adamo, K. B., Rutherford, J., & Legg, C. (2008). Stress and the relative reinforcing value of food in female binge eaters. *Physiology & Behavior*, 93, 579–587.

Gordon, C. M., Dougherty, D. D., Fischman, A. J., Emans, S. J., Grace, E., Lamm, R., et al. (2001). Neural substrates of anorexia nervosa: A behavioral challenge study with positron emission tomography. *Journal of Pediatrics*, 139, 51–57.

Graber, J. A., Brooks-Gunn, J., Paikoff, R. L., & Warren, M. P. (1994). Prediction of eating problems: An 8-year study of adolescent girls. *Developmental Psychology*, 30, 823–834.

Greeno, C. G., Wing, R. R., & Shiffman, S. (2000). Binge antecedents in obese women with and with out binge eating disorder. *Journal of Consulting and Clinical Psychology, 68*, 95–102.

Grigson, P. S. (2002). Like drugs for chocolate: Separate rewards modulated by common mechanisms? *Physiology & Behavior, 76*, 389–395.

Grilo, C. M., Hrabosky, J. I., White, M. A., Allison, K. C., Stunkard, A. J., & Masheb, R. M. (2008). Overvaluation of shape and weight in binge eating disorder and overweight controls: Refinement of a diagnostic construct. *Journal of Abnormal Psychology, 117*, 414–419.

Grilo, C. M., White, M. A., & Masheb, R. M. (2009). DSM-IV psychiatric disorder comorbidity and its correlates in binge eating disorder. *International Journal of Eating Disorders, 42*, 228–234.

Grucza, R. A., Przybeck, T. R., & Cloninger, C. R. (2007). Prevalence and correlates of binge eating disorder in a community sample. *Comprehensive Psychiatry, 48*, 124–131.

Guilbaud, O., Corcos, M., Chambry, J., Paterniti, S., Loas, G., & Jeammet, P. (2000). Alexithymie et dépression dans les troubles des conduites alimentaires. [Alexithymia and depression in eating disorders]. *Encéphale, 26*, 1–6.

Halmi, K. A., & Sunday, S. R. (1991). Temporal patterns of hunger and fullness ratings and related cognitions in anorexia and bulimia. *Appetite, 16*, 219–237.

Hammersley, R., & Reid, M. (2008). Theorising transient mood after ingestion. *Neuroscience and Biobehavioral Reviews, 33*, 213–222.

Haynes, C., Lee, M. D., & Yeomans, M. R. (2003). Interactive effects of stress, dietary restraint, and disinhibition on appetite. *Eating Behaviour, 4*, 369–383.

Heatherton, T. F., & Baumeister, R. F. (1991). Binge eating as escape from self-awareness. *Psychological Bulletin, 110*, 86–108.

Heatherton, T. F., Herman, C. P., & Polivy, J. (1991). Effects of physical threat and ego threat on eating behaviour. *Journal of Personality and Social Psychology, 60*, 138–143.

Herman, C. P., & Polivy, J. (1975). Anxiety, restraint and eating behavior. *Journal of Abnormal Psychology, 84*, 666–672.

Herman, C. P., & Polivy, J. (1980). Restrained eating. In A. J. Stunkard (Ed.), *Obesity* (pp. 208–225). Philadelphia: W. B. Saunders.

Hilbert, A., & Tuschen-Caffier, B. (2007). Maintenance of binge eating through negative mood: A naturalistic comparison of binge eating disorder and bulimia nervosa. *International Journal of Eating Disorders, 40*, 521–530.

Hilbert, A., Tuschen-Caffier, B., & Vögele, C. (2002). Effects of prolonged and repeated body image exposure in binge-eating disorder. *Journal of Psychosomatic Research, 52*, 137–144.

Hofmann, W., Rauch, W., & Gawronski, B. (2007). And deplete us not into temptation: Automatic attitudes, dietary restraint, and self-regulatory resources as determinants of eating behavior. *Journal of Experimental Social Psychology, 43*, 497–504.

Hrabosky, J. I., Masheb, R. M., White, M. A., & Grilo, C. M. (2007). Overvaluation of shape and weight in binge eating disorder. *Journal of Consulting and Clinical Psychology, 75*, 175–180.

Hudson, J. I., Mangweth, B., Pope, H. G., Jr., De Col, C., Hausmann, A., Gutweniger, S., et al. (2003). Family study of affective spectrum disorder. *Archives of General Psychiatry, 60*, 170–177.

Jackson, T. D., Grilo, C. M., & Masheb, R. M. (2002). Teasing history and eating disorder features: An age- and body mass index-matched comparison of bulimia nervosa and binge-eating disorder. *Comprehensive Psychiatry, 43*, 108–113.

Jacobi, C., Hayward, C., de Zwaan, M., Kraemer, H. C., & Agras, W.S. (2004). Coming to terms with risk factors for eating disorders: Application of risk terminology and suggestions for a general taxonomy. *Psychological Bulletin, 130*, 19–65.

Jansen, A. (1994). The learned nature of binge eating. In C. R. Legg & D. A. Booth (Eds.), *Appetite: Neural and behavioural bases* (pp. 193–211). Oxford: Oxford University Press.

Kanarek, R. B., White, E. S., Biegen, M. T., & Marks-Kaufman, R. (1991). Dietary influences on morphine-induced analgesia in rats. *Pharmacology Biochemistry and Behavior, 38*, 681–684.

Karlsson, J., Persson, L. O., Sjostrom, L., & Sullivan, M. (2000). Psychometric properties and factor structure of the Three-Factor Eating Questionnaire (TFEQ) in obese men and women. Results from the Swedish Obese Subjects (SOS) study. *International Journal of Obesity and Related Metabolic Disorders, 24*, 1715–1725.

Kaye, W. H. (2008). Neurobiology of anorexia and bulimia nervosa. *Physiology & Behavior, 94*, 121–135.

Kaye, W. H., Bulik, C. M., Thornton, L., Barbarich, N., & Masters, K. (2004). Comorbidity of anxiety disorders with anorexia and bulimia nervosa. *American Journal of Psychiatry, 161*, 2215–2221.

Kelley, A. E., Will, M. J., Steininger, T. L., Zhang, M., & Haber, S. N. (2003). Restricted daily consumption of a highly palatable food (chocolate Ensure®) alters striatal enkephalin gene expression. *European Journal of Neuroscience, 18*, 2592–2598.

Kenardy, J., Arnow, B., & Agras, W. S. (1996). The aversiveness of specific emotional states associated with binge-eating in obese subjects. *Australian and New Zealand Journal of Psychiatry, 30*, 839–844.

Killen, J. D., Taylor, C. B., Hayward, C., Haydel, K. F., Wilson, D. M., Hammer, L. D., et al. (1996). Weight concerns influence the development of eating disorders: A 4-year prospective study. *Journal of Consulting and Clinical Psychology, 64*, 936–940.

Killgore, W. D., & Yurgelun-Todd, D. A. (2007). Positive affect modulates activity in the visual cortex to images of high calorie foods. *International Journal of Neuroscience, 117*, 643–653.

Kjelsas, E., Borsting, I., & Gudde, C. B. (2004). Antecedents and consequences of binge eating episodes in women with an eating disorder. *Eating and Weight Disorders, 9*, 7–15.

Koepp, M. J., Hammers, A., Lawrence, A. D., Asselin, M. C., Grasby, P. M., & Bench, C. J. (2009). Evidence for endogenous opioid release in the amygdala during positive emotion. *Neuroimage, 44*, 252–256.

Kubiak, T., Vögele, C., Siering, M., Schiel, R., & Weber, H. (2008). Daily hassles and emotional eating in obese adolescents under restricted dietary conditions – the role of ruminative thinking. *Appetite, 51*, 206–209.

Lattimore, P., & Caswell, N. (2004). Differential effects of active and passive stress on food intake in restrained and unrestrained eaters. *Appetite, 42*, 167–173.

Lautenbacher, S., Roscher, S., Strian, F., Pirke, K. M., & Krieg, J. C. (1993). Theoretical and empirical considerations on the relation between body image, body scheme and somatosensation. *Journal of Psychosomatic Research, 37*, 447–454.

Legenbauer, T., Vögele, C., & Rüddel, H. (2004). Anticipatory effects of food exposure in women diagnosed with bulimia nervosa. *Appetite, 42*, 33–40.

Leon, G. R., Fulkerson, J. A., Perry, C. L., & Early-Zald, M. B. (1995). Prospective analysis of personality and behavioral influences in the later development of disordered eating. *Journal of Abnormal Psychology, 104,* 140–149.

Leon, G. R., Fulkerson, J. A., Perry, C. L., Keel, P. K., & Klump, K. L. (1999). Three to four year prospective evaluation of personality and behavioral risk factors for later disordered eating in adolescent girls and boys. *Journal of Youth and Adolescence, 28,* 181–196.

Lowe, M. R., & Fisher, E. B. (1983). Emotional reactivity, emotional eating and obesity: A naturalistic study. *Journal of Behavioral Medicine, 6,* 135–148.

Lozano, D. I., Crites, S. L., & Aikmann, S. N. (1999). Changes in food attitudes as a function of hunger. *Appetite, 32,* 207–218.

Macdiarmid, J. I., & Hetherington, M. M. (1995). Mood modulation by food: An exploration of affect and cravings in "chocolate addicts." *British Journal of Clinical Psychology, 34,* 129–138.

Macht, M. (1996). Effects of high- and low-energy meals on hunger, physiological processes and reactions to emotional stress. *Appetite, 26,* 71–88.

Macht, M. (2008). How emotions affect eating: a five-way model. *Appetite, 50,* 1–11.

Macht, M., Gerer, J., & Ellgring, H. (2003). Emotions in overweight and normal-weight women immediately after eating foods differing in energy. *Physiology & Behavior, 80,* 367–374.

Macht, M., Haupt, C., & Salewsky, A. (2004). Emotions and eating in everyday life: Application of the experience-sampling method. *Ecology of Food and Nutrition, 43,* 327–337.

Macht, M., & Müller, J. (2007a). Interactive effects of emotional and restrained eating on responses to chocolate and affect. *Journal of Nervous & Mental Disease, 195,* 1024–1026.

Macht, M., & Müller, J. (2007b). Immediate effects of chocolate on experimentally induced mood states. *Appetite, 49,* 667–674.

Macht, M., Roth, S., & Ellgring, H. (2002). Chocolate eating in healthy men during experimentally induced sadness and joy. *Appetite, 39,* 147–158.

Mangweth, B., Hudson, J. I., Pope, H. G., Hausmann, A., De Col, C., Laird, N. M., et al. (2003). Family study of the aggregation of eating disorders and mood disorders. *Psychological Medicine, 33,* 1319–1323.

Mann, T., & Ward, A. (2004). To eat or not to eat: Implications of the attentional myopia model for restrained eaters. *Journal of Abnormal Psychology, 113,* 90–98.

Markus, C. R., Olivier, B., Panhuysen, G. E. M., Van der Gugten, J., Alles, M. S., Tuiten, A., et al. (2000). The bovine protein alpha-lactalbumin increases the plasma ratio of tryptophan to the other large neutral amino acids, and in vulnerable subjects raises brain serotonin activity, reduces cortisol concentration, and improves mood under stress. *American Journal of Clinical Nutrition, 71,* 1536–1544.

Markus, C. R., Panhuysen, G., Tuiten, A., Koppeschaar, H., Fekkes, D., & Peters, M. L. (1998). Does carbohydrate-rich, protein-poor food prevent a deterioration of mood and cognitive performance of stress-prone subjects when subjected to a stressful task? *Appetite, 31,* 49–65.

Matsunaga, H., Kiriike, N., Iwasaki, Y., Miyata, A., & Matsui, T. (2000). Multi-impulsivity among bulimic patients in Japan. *International Journal of Eating Disorders, 27,* 348–352.

Matthews, G., & Deary, I. J. (1998). *Personality traits.* Cambridge, UK: Cambridge University Press.

Mauler, B. I., Hamm, A. O., Weike, A. I., & Tuschen-Caffier, B. (2006). Affect regulation and food intake in bulimia nervosa: Emotional responding to food cues after deprivation and subsequent eating. *Journal of Abnormal Psychology, 115,* 567–579.

McNamara, C., Hay, P., Katsikitis, M., & Chur-Hansen, A. (2008). Emotional responses to food, body dissatisfaction and other eating disorder features in children, adolescents and young adults. *Appetite, 50,* 102–109.

Mercer, M. E., & Holder, M. D. (1997). Food cravings, endogenous opioid peptides, and food intake: A review. *Appetite, 29,* 325–352.

Meyer, C., Waller, G., & Waters, A. (1998). Emotional states and bulimic psychopathology. In H. Hoek, M. Katzman, & J. Treasure (Eds.), *The neurobiological basis of eating disorders* (pp. 271–289). Chichester: John Wiley & Sons.

Mitchell, J. E., Mussell, M. P., Peterson, C. B., Crow, S., Wonderlich, S. A., Crosby, R. D., et al. (1999). Hedonics of binge eating in women with bulimia nervosa and binge eating disorder. *International Journal of Eating Disorders, 26,* 165–170.

Morris, G. L., 3rd, & Mueller, W. M. (1999). Long-term treatment with vagus nerve stimulation in patients with refractory epilepsy. The Vagus Nerve Stimulation Study Group E01–E05. *Neurology, 53,* 1731–1735.

Munsch, S., Michael, T., Biedert, E., Meyer, A. H., & Margraf, J. (2008). Negative mood induction and unbalanced nutritional style as possible triggers of binges in binge eating disorder (BED). *Eating and Weight Disorders, 13,* 22–29.

Muraven, M., & Baumeister, R. F. (2000). Self-regulation and depletion of limited resources: Does self-control resemble a muscle? *Psychological Bulletin, 126,* 247–259.

Nandrino, J.-L., Doba, K., Lesne, A., Christophe, V., & Pezard, L. (2006). Autobiographical memory deficit in anorexia nervosa: Emotion regulation and effect of duration of illness. *Journal of Psychosomatic Research, 61,* 537–543.

Nanni, G., Scheggi, S., Leggio, B., Grappi, S., Masi, F., Rauggi, R., & De Montis, M. G. (2003). Acquisition of an appetitive behavior prevents development of stress-induced neurochemical modifications in rat nucleus accumbens. *Journal of Neuroscience Research, 73,* 573–580.

Newman, E., O'Connor, D. B., & Conner, M. (2007). Daily hassles and eating behaviour: The role of cortisol reactivity status. *Psychoneuroendocrinology, 32,* 125–132.

Nolen-Hoeksema, S. (1991). Responses to depression and their effects on the duration of depressive episodes. *Journal of Abnormal Psychology, 100,* 569–582.

Nolen-Hoeksema, S., Stice, E., Wade, E., & Bohon, C. (2007). Reciprocal relations between rumination and bulimic, substance abuse, and depressive symptoms in female adolescents. *Journal of Abnormal Psychology, 116,* 198–207.

Oliver, G., & Wardle, J. (1999). Perceived effects of stress on food choice. *Physiology & Behavior, 66,* 511–515.

Oliver, G., Wardle, J., & Gibson, E. L. (2000). Stress and food choice: a laboratory study. *Psychosomatic Medicine, 62,* 853–865.

Pani, L., Porcella, A., & Gessa, G. L. (2000). The role of stress in the pathophysiology of the dopaminergic system. *Molecular Psychiatry, 5,* 14–21.

Papezova, H., Yamamotova, A., & Uher, R. (2005). Elevated pain threshold in eating disorders: Physiological and psychological factors. *Journal of Psychiatric Research, 39,* 431–438.

Patton, G. C., Johnson-Sabine, E., Wood, K., Mann, A. H., & Wakeling, A. (1990). Abnormal eating attitudes in London schoolgirls: A prospective epidemiological study: Outcome at twelve month follow-up. *Psychological Medicine, 20,* 383–394.

Patton, G. C., Selzer, R., Coffey, C., Carlin, J. B., & Wolfe, R. (1999). Onset of adolescent eating disorders: Population based cohort study over 3 years. *British Medical Journal, 318,* 765–768.

Pecina, S., Schulkin, J., & Berridge, K. C. (2006). Nucleus accumbens corticotropin-releasing factor increases cue-triggered motivation for sucrose reward: Paradoxical positive incentive effects in stress? *BMC Biology, 4,* 8 doi:10.1186/1741-7007-4-8.

Peters, A., Pellerin, L., Dallman, M. F., Oltmanns, K. M., Schweiger, U., Born, J., et al. (2007). Causes of obesity: Looking beyond the hypothalamus. *Progress in Neurobiology, 81*(2), 61.

Pinhas, L., Toner, B. B., Ali, A., Garfinkel, P. E., & Stuckless, N. (1999). The effects of the ideal of female beauty on mood and body satisfaction. *International Journal of Eating Disorders, 25,* 223–226.

Polivy, J., & Herman, C. P. (1999). Distress and eating: Why do dieters overeat? *International Journal of Eating Disorders, 26,* 153–164.

Polivy, J., & Herman, C. P. (2002). Causes of eating disorders. *Annual Review of Psychology, 53,* 187–213.

Pollatos, O., Herbert, B. M., Schandry, R., & Gramann, K. (2008). Impaired central processing of emotional faces in anorexia nervosa. *Psychosomatic Medicine, 70,* 701–708.

Probst, M., Vandereycken, W., Vanderlinden, J., & van Coppenolle, H. (1998). The significance of body size estimation in eating disorders: Its relationship with clinical and psychological variables. *International Journal of Eating Disorders, 24,* 167–174.

Raes, F., Hermans, D., De Decker, A., Eelen, P., & Williams J. (2003). Autobiographical memory specificity and affect regulation: An experimental approach. *Emotion, 3,* 201–206.

Rastam, M. (1992). Anorexia nervosa in 51 Swedish adolescents: Premorbid problems and comorbidity. *Journal of the American Academy of Child & Adolescent Psychiatry, 31,* 819–829.

Reid, M., & Hammersley, R. (1999). The effects of carbohydrates on arousal. *Nutrition Research Reviews, 12,* 3–23.

Ricciardelli, L. A., Tate, D., & Williams, R. J. (1997). Body dissatisfaction as a mediator of the relationship between dietary restraint and bulimic eating patterns. *Appetite, 29,* 43–54.

Rodin, J. (1981). Current status of the internal/external hypothesis for obesity: What went wrong? *American Psychologist, 36,* 361–372.

Rodriguez, S., Fernandez, M.C., Cepeda-Benito, A., & Vila, J. (2005). Subective and physiological reactivity to chocolate images in high and low chocolate cravers. *Biological Psychology, 70,* 9–18.

Rolls, E. T. (2007). *Emotion explained.* Oxford: Oxford University Press.

Saelens, B. E., & Epstein, L. H. (1996). Reinforcing value of food in obese and non-obese women. *Appetite, 27,* 41–50.

Santel, S., Baving, L., Krauel, K., Münte, T. F., & Rotte, M. (2006). Hunger and satiety in anorexia nervosa: fMRI during cognitive processing of food. *Brain Research, 1114,* 138–148.

Santos, M., Richards, C. S., & Bleckley, M. K. (2007). Comorbidity between depression and disordered eating in adolescents. *Eating Behaviors, 8,* 440–449.

Schachter, S., Goldman, R., & Gordon, A. (1968). Effects of fear, food deprivation, and obesity on eating. *Journal of Personality and Social Psychology, 10,* 91–97.

Schienle, A., Schäfer, A., Hermann, A., & Vaitl, D. (2009). Binge-eating disorder: reward sensitivity and brain activation to images of food. *Biological Psychiatry, 65,* 654–661.

Seeger, G., Braus, D. F., Ruf, M., Goldberger, U., & Schmidt, M. H. (2002). Body image distortion reveals amygdala activation in patients with anorexia nervosa – a functional magnetic resonance imaging study. *Neuroscience Letters, 326,* 25–28.

Shaffer, H. J., LaPlante, D. A., LaBrie, R. A., Kidman, R. C., Donato, A. N., & Stanton, M. V. (2004). Toward a syndrome model of addiction: Multiple expressions, common etiology. *Harvard Review of Psychiatry, 12,* 367–374.

Siegle, G. J., & Thayer, J. T. (2004). Physiological aspects of depressive rumination. In C. Papageorgiou & A. Wells (Eds.), *Depressive rumination nature theory and treatment* (pp. 79–104). New York: John Wiley & Sons.

Sifneos, P. E. (1991). Affect, emotional conflict, and deficit: An overview. *Psychotherapy and Psychosomatics, 56,* 116–122.

Small, D. M., Zatorre, R. J., Dagher, A., Evans, A. C., & Jones-Gotman, M. (2001). Changes in brain activity related to eating chocolate: From pleasure to aversion. *Brain, 124,* 1720–1733.

Smeets, M. A. (1999). Body size categorization in anorexia nervosa using a morphing instrument. *International Journal of Eating Disorders, 25,* 451–455.

Smit, H. J., Gaffan, E. A., & Rogers, P. J. (2004). Methylxanthines are the psychopharmacologically active constituents of chocolate. *Psychopharmacology, 176,* 412–419.

Smith, A. P., & Miles, C. (1986). Acute effects of meals, noise and nightwork. *British Journal of Psychology, 77,* 377–387.

Smyth, J. M., Wonderlich, S. A., Heron, K. E., Sliwinski, M. J., Crosby, R. D., Mitchell, J. E., & Engel, S. G. (2007). Daily and momentary mood and stress are associated with binge eating and vomiting in bulimia nervosa patients in the natural environment. *Journal of Consulting and Clinical Psychology, 75,* 629–638.

Sodersten, P., Nergardh, R., Bergh, C., Zandian, M., & Scheurink, A. (2008). Behavioral neuroendocrinology and treatment of anorexia nervosa. *Frontiers in Neuroendocrinology, 29,* 445–462.

Spoor, S. T. P., Bekker, M. H. J., van Strien, T., & van Heck, G. L. (2007). Relations between negative affect, coping, and emotional eating. *Appetite, 48,* 368–376.

Staiger, P., Dawe, S., & McCarthy, R. (2000). Responsivity to food cues in bulimic women and controls. *Appetite, 35,* 27–33.

Stein, R. I., Kenardy, J., Wiseman, C. V., Zoler Dounchis, J., Arnow, B. A., & Wilfley, D. E. (2007). What's driving the binge in binge eating disorder? A prospective examination of precursors and consequences. *International Journal of Eating Disorders, 40,* 195–203.

Stice, E. (1994). Review of the evidence for a sociocultural model of bulimia nervosa and an exploration of the mechanisms of action. *Clinical Psychology Review, 14,* 633–661.

Stice, E. (2001). A prospective test of the dual-pathway model of bulimic pathology: Mediating effects of dieting and negative affect. *Journal of Abnormal Psychology, 110,* 124–155.

Stice, E., Akutagawa, D., Gaggar, A., & Agras, W. S. (2000). Negative affect moderates the relation between dieting and binge eating. *International Journal of Eating Disorders, 27,* 218–229.

Stice, E., Hayward, C., Cameron, R. P., Killen, J. D., & Taylor, C. B. (2000). Body-image and eating disturbances predict onset of depression among female adolescents: A longitudinal study. *Journal of Abnormal Psychology, 109,* 438–444.

Takimoto, Y., Yoshiuchi, K., & Akabayashi, A. (2008). Effect of mood states on QT interval and QT dispersion in eating disorder patients. *Psychiatry and Clinical Neurosciences, 62*, 185–189.

Taylor, G. J., Bagby, R. M., & Parker, J. D. A. (1991). The alexithymia construct: A potential paradigm for psychosomatic medicine. *Psychosomatics, 32*, 153–164.

Taylor, G. J., Bagby, R. M., & Parker, J. D. A. (1997). *Disorders of affect regulation: alexithymia in medical and psychiatric illness.* Cambridge, UK: Cambridge University Press.

Taylor, G. J., Parker, J. D. A., Bagby, R. M., & Bourke, M. P. (1996). Relationships between alexithymia and psychological characteristics associated with eating disorders. *Journal of Psychosomatic Research, 41*, 561–568.

Telch, C. F. (1997). Skills training treatment for adaptive affect regulation in a woman with binge-eating disorder. *International Journal of Eating Disorders, 22*, 77–81.

Telch, C. F., & Agras, S. W. (1996). Do emotional states influence binge eating in the obese? *International Journal of Eating Disorders, 20*, 271–279.

Thayer, R. E. (1989). *The biopsychology of mood and arousal.* Oxford: Oxford University Press.

Thomsen, D. K. (2006). The association between rumination and negative affect: A review. *Cognition and Emotion, 20*, 1216–1235.

Torres, S. J., & Nowson, C. A. (2007). Relationship between stress, eating behavior, and obesity. *Nutrition, 23*, 887–894.

Tuomisto, T., Hetherington, M. M., Morris, M. F., Tuomisto, M. T., Turjanmaa, V., & Lappalainen, R. (1999). Psychological and physiological characteristics of sweet food "addiction." *International Journal of Eating Disorders, 25*, 169–175.

Tuschen-Caffier, B., Vögele, C., Bracht, S., & Hilbert, A. (2003). Psychological responses to body shape exposure in patients with bulimia nervosa. *Behaviour Research and Therapy, 41*, 573–586.

Uher, R., Brammer, M. J., Murphy, T., Campbell, I. C., Ng, V. W., Williams, S. C. R., & Treasure, J. (2003). Recovery and chronicity in anorexia nervosa: Brain activity associated with differential outcomes. *Biological Psychiatry, 54*, 934–942.

Uher, R., Murphy, T., Brammer, M. J., Dalgleish, T., Phillips, M. L., Ng, V. W., et al. (2004). Medial prefrontal cortex activity associated with symptom provocation in eating disorders. *American Journal of Psychiatry, 161*, 1238–1246.

Uher, R., Murphy, T., Friederich, H. C., Dalgsleish, T., Brammer, M. J., Giampietro, V., et al. (2005). Functional neuroanatomy of body shape perception in healthy and eating-disordered women. *Biological Psychiatry, 58*, 990–997.

Upadhyay, A., Aggarwal, R., Narayan, S., Joshi, M., Paul, V. K., & Deorari, A. K. (2004). Analgesic effect of expressed breast milk in procedural pain in term neonates: A randomized, placebo-controlled, double-blind trial. *Acta Paediatrica, 93*, 518–522.

VanderHam, T., Meulman, J. J., VanStrien, D. C., & vanEngeland, H. (1997). Empirically based subgrouping of eating disorders in adolescents: A longitudinal perspective. *British Journal of Psychiatry, 170*, 363–368.

Vaz, F. J., Alcaina, T., & Guisado, J. A. (1998). Food aversions in eating disorders. *International Journal of Food Sciences and Nutrition, 49*, 181–186.

Vögele, C., & Florin, I. (1997). Psychophysiological responses to food exposure: an experimental study in binge eaters. *International Journal of Eating Disorders, 21*, 147–157.

Vögele, C., Hilbert, A., & Tuschen-Caffier, B. (2009). Dietary restriction, cardiac autonomic regulation and stress reactivity in bulimic women. *Physiology & Behavior, 98*, 229–234.

Vögele, C., & Woodward, H. (2005). Körperbild, Diätverhalten und körperliche Aktivität bei 9–10 jährigen Kindern [Body image, dietary behaviour and physical activity in 9–10 year old children]. *Kindheit und Entwicklung (Themenheft Essstörungen bei Kindern und Jugendlichen), 14*, 229–236.

Wagner, A., Aizenstein, H., Venkatraman, V. K., Fudge, J., May, J. C., Mazurkewicz, L., et al. (2007). Altered reward processing in women recovered from anorexia nervosa. *American Journal of Psychiatry, 164*, 1842–1849.

Wallis, D. J., & Hetherington, M. M. (2004). Stress and eating: the effects of ego-threat and cognitive demand on food intake in restrained and emotional eaters. *Appetite, 43*, 39–46.

Walsh, B. T., & Boudreau, G. (2003). Laboratory studies of binge eating disorder. *International Journal of Eating Disorders, 34* (Supplement), 30–38.

Wang, G. J., Volkow, N. D., Logan, J., Pappas, N. R., Wong, C. T., Zhu, W., et al. (2001). Brain dopamine and obesity. *The Lancet, 357*, 354–357.

Ward, A., & Mann, T. (2000). Don't mind if I do: Disinhibited eating under cognitive load. *Journal of Personality and Social Psychology, 78*, 753–763.

Wardle, J., & Gibson, E. L. (2002). Impact of stress on diet: processes and implications In S. Stansfeld & M. G. Marmot (Eds.), *Stress and the heart: Psychosocial pathways to coronary heart disease* (pp. 124–149). London: BMJ Books.

Wardle, J., Guthrie, C., Sanderson, S., Birch, L., & Plomin, R. (2001). Food and activity preferences in children of lean and obese parents. *International Journal of Obesity and Related Metabolic Disorders, 25*, 971–977.

Waters, A., Hill, A., & Waller, G. (2001). Bulimic's responses to food cravings: I. Binge-eating a product of hunger or emotional state? *Behaviour Research and Therapy, 39*, 877–886.

Weinstein, S. E., Shide, D. J., & Rolls, B. J. (1997). Changes in food intake in response to stress in men and women: Psychological factors. *Appetite, 28*, 7–18.

Whiteside, U., Chen, E., Neighbors, C., Hunter, D., Lo, T., & Larimer, M. (2007). Difficulties regulating emotions: Do binge eaters have fewer strategies to modulate and tolerate negative affect? *Eating Behaviors, 8*, 162–169.

Wilfley, D. E., Schwartz, M. B., Spurrell, E. B., & Fairburn, C. G. (2000). Using the Eating Disorder Examination to identify the specific psychopathology of binge eating disorder. *International Journal of Eating Disorders, 27*, 259–269.

Wilfley, D. E., Wilson, G. T., & Agras, W. S. (2003). The clinical significance of binge eating disorder. *International Journal of Eating Disorders, 34* (Supplement), S96–S106.

Williams, J. M. G., Healy, H., Eade, J., Windle, G., Cowen, P. J., Green, M. W., & Durlach, P. (2002). Mood, eating behaviour and attention. *Psychological Medicine, 32*, 469–481.

Yanovski, S. Z., Nelson, J. E., Dubbert, B. K., & Spitzer, R. L. (1993). Association of binge eating disorder and psychiatric comorbidity in obese subjects. *American Journal of Psychiatry, 150*, 1472–1479.

Zagon, A. (2001). Does the vagus nerve mediate the sixth sense? *Trends in Neurosciences, 24*, 671–673.

Zellner, D. A., Loaiza, S., Gonzalez, Z., Pita, J., Morales, J., Pecora, D., & Wolf, A. (2006). Food selection changes under stress. *Physiology and Behavior, 87*, 789–793.

Zonnevijlle-Bender, M. J., Van Goozen, S. H., Cohen-Kettenis, P. T., & Van Engeland, H. (2002). Do adolescent anorexia nervosa patients have deficits in emotional functioning? *European Child and Adolescent Psychiatry, 11*, 38–42.

Eating and Weight Concerns in Eating Disorders

Alison E. Field *and* Nicole Kitos

Abstract

Weight and shape concerns are one of the hallmark symptoms of anorexia nervosa and bulimia nervosa, but the development of these concerns, their stability over time, and the mechanisms by which they promote the development of body image dissatisfaction and eating disorders remains unclear. Sociocultural, familial, and psychological factors are believed to be related to the development of weight and shape concerns and dissatisfaction, which in turn are thought to promote disordered eating behaviors, such as purging. In this chapter we discuss many of the risk factors for developing weight and shape concerns, as well as their consequences.

Keywords: body image, body image dissatisfaction, disordered eating, shape concerns, weight concerns

Introduction

Despite the high prevalence of overweight and obesity (Ogden, Carroll, & Flegal, 2008; Ogden et al., 2006) there are considerable social consequences of being overweight in a westernized society that values thinness and fitness. Although Phillips and Hill (1998) observed that among 313 9-year-old girls, those who were overweight were not less popular than their leaner peers, Latner and Stunkard (2003) found that among children in the 5th and 6th grades, obese children were perceived as less likable than those with disabilities. Moreover, Davison and Birch (2004) observed that negative stereotypes of overweight people were common among 178 9-year-old girls and their mothers and fathers, and large studies among adolescents have observed that overweight youth are more likely than lean adolescents to be socially isolated (Falkner et al., 2001; Strauss & Pollack, 2003). In addition, among 69 children ages 4 to 6 years, Holub (2008) found that children's attitudes about their peers' weight was related to the child's own weight, with leaner children having the most negative attitudes about

heavier peers. Given the social stigma and adverse social consequences of obesity, it is therefore not surprising that many young people are extremely concerned with their weight.

In American culture, considerable emphasis is placed on body size, weight, and appearance. Being "thin" and "in shape" are often associated with success, beauty, and being happy, whereas overweight is often viewed as lazy and undesirable (Tiggemann & Rothblum, 2004). These ideas and values are transmitted to children at young ages (Davison, Markey, & Birch, 2000) and are reinforced through family, peers, and media.

Children and adolescents, particularly girls, who are overweight are more likely than their leaner peers to be extremely concerned with their weight and to engage in bulimic behaviors (Ackard, Neumark-Sztainer, Story, & Perry, 2003; Boutelle, Neumark-Sztainer, Story, & Resnick, 2002; Field, Camargo, Taylor, Berkey, Frazier, et al., 1999; Neumark-Sztainer, Story, Hannan, Perry, & Irving, 2002). However, relatively little is known about the development of weight concerns, their stability over time, and the mechanisms through which they promote the development of eating disorders (EDs). One of complications of studying weight and shape concerns is that there is not one commonly accepted definition of concerns. Jacobi has adopted one of the broader definitions of weight concerns as a "fear of weight gain, dieting behavior, negative body image, and specific eating disorder symptoms or attitudes (e.g., bulimic behavior)" (Brewerton, 2004, p. 138). Others have conceptualized weight and shape concerns more narrowly to be the difference between perceived and desired body shape and size (Muennig, Jia, Lee, & Lubetkin, 2008), the difference between perceived and actual body shape (McCabe, Ricciardelli, Sitaram, & Mikhail, 2006), misperception of being overweight (Lowry, Galuska, Fulton, Wechsler, & Kann, 2002), dissatisfaction with weight or shape (Field, Camargo, Taylor, Berkey, & Colditz, 1999), dissatisfaction with a specific part of the body (Rief, Buhlmann, Wilhelm, Borkenhagen, & Brahler, 2006), fear of fatness (Davison et al., 2000), fear of gaining weight (Shunk & Birch, 2004), or the act of engaging in weight control behaviors (Field et al., 2001; French et al., 1997).

It is believed that weight concerns are a partial cause of starting to engage in disordered eating (i.e., binge eating, purging [i.e., laxatives, vomiting], using diet pills, fasting, and/or excessive exercise to control weight) and are a fundamental component of an ED. Therefore, understanding the risk factors for developing weight and shape concerns is a necessary step toward being able to prevent the development of unhealthy weight control practices, which are established risk factors for disordered eating. In this chapter we review the personal factors, family and peer influences, and sociocultural pressures that are thought to be associated with the development of weight concern. Although much of the research on this topic comes from cross-sectional studies, greater emphasis is given to longitudinal studies because they can address issues of temporal order of association.

Approaches to Defining Weight and Shape Concerns

One of the difficulties in understanding the development of weight concerns is that numerous approaches have been taken to assessing weight and shape concerns. Many studies have used the 9-item Body Dissatisfaction scale of the Eating Disorder Inventory (EDI), which has good reliability ($r =-.92$). An advantage of using the Body Dissatisfaction scale is that it is a self-report instrument, so it can be easily administered to large numbers of people. Moreover, it is easy to compare results to other studies that have used the measure and it is considered valid. The Weight and Shape Concern subscale of the Eating Disorder Examination (EDE) is also widely used. The validity of the scale has been documented and the EDE is considered the gold standard for ED assessment. Although a self-report version of the EDE is available, the EDE is usually administered via in-person interview, which limits the utility of the assessment for large-scale studies. The disadvantage of both approaches is that they do not take weight status into consideration. Therefore an overweight girl with a high score is considered to be similar to an underweight girl with a high score. In terms of risk of an eating disorder, this assumption may not be reasonable. This problem is not unique to the EDI and EDE subscales; it is common to most measures of weight and shape concerns.

Another validated, but less used, weight and shape concern scale is the Weight Concerns Scale from the McKnight Risk Factor Survey. It has been used in two large prospective cohort studies, the McKnight Longitudinal Risk Factor Study (Shisslak et al., 1999) and the Growing Up Today Study (Field, Camargo, Taylor, Berkey, Frazier, et al., 1999), as well as an internet-based intervention study (Taylor et al., 2006). Advantages of the scale include that it is very brief, valid, and has been used with large numbers of participants. A disadvantage of the scale is that since it is not as widely used, it is slightly more difficult to compare results to other studies which have used the EDI or EDE measures of weight concerns. However, the brevity of the instrument and the validity of the instrument in general population samples are strengths of the measure.

Unlike the scales discussed in the preceding text, the Body Shape Satisfaction Scale assesses satisfaction with weight, as well as different parts of the body (e.g., weight, stomach, hips, etc.). One advantage to using this scale is that it captures dissatisfaction with shape, as well as weight. In other words, it would be well suited for studying a girl who may be more concerned with the size of her stomach than her actual weight. However, because the scale is not that widely used, it can be difficult to compare rates of weight and shape concerns when this scale is used. Other body image assessments include the Multidimensional Body Self-Relations Questionnaire (MBSRQ; Yanover & Thompson, 2008) the Body Esteem Scale (BES; Duncan, Al-Nakeeb, & Nevill, 2004), and Social Physique

Anxiety Scale (SPAS; Motl & Conroy, 2000), all of which have been validated and used with multi-ethnic populations.

Weight and shape concerns have also been conceptualized as dissatisfaction with current weight and/or shape. Some studies have operationalized this as the difference between perceived and desired body size or weight. In these studies, investigators have presented participants with two sets of images, such as those developed by Collins (1991) and Stunkard, Sorenson, and Schulsinger (1983), and asked them to indicate their current size, as well as the size they would like to be. Participants who select a size smaller than their current perceived size are classified as dissatisfied with their weight or shape. Similarly, some studies have asked participants to report their current weight and their ideal weight. Participants who report a weight lower than their current weight are considered to be dissatisfied with their weight (Olmsted & McFarlane, 2004).

Several studies have used distorted perception of weight, namely misperceiving oneself to be overweight, as an indicator of weight concerns or body dissatisfaction. In these studies participants were asked to report whether they are underweight, normal/healthy weight, or overweight/obese. They are also measured and weighed or asked to self-report their own weight and height. Participants who report that they are overweight/obese, but are in the normal weight category according to their body mass index (BMI: wt[kg]/ht[m]^2) are considered to have a misperception of their weight. This has been considered as one type of weight concern.

Development of Weight and Shape Concerns

Weight and shape concerns are relatively common and develop at an earlier age than disordered eating (i.e., binge eating and purging). Biological, family, peer, and sociocultural factors are all believed to be involved with the development of weight and shape concerns. Although weight and shape concern are included as one of the criteria for anorexia nervosa and bulimia nervosa according to the *Diagnostic and Statistical Manual for Mental Disorders* (*DSM-IV*), it has been suggested that children and young adolescents may not have yet acquired abstract reasoning and the ability to identify and label emotions and therefore not be able to identify and describe weight and shape concerns accurately (Gowers & Shore, 2001; Nicholls & Bryant-Waugh, 2009). This complicates efforts to understand how weight and shape concerns arise and may partially explain why rela-

tively few studies have focused on identifying predictors of the development of weight and shape concerns. Further complicating our understanding of weight and shape concerns is that there are gender differences in weight concerns, but most studies have used assessment tools that have been developed and evaluated among females and therefore may miss some of the weight and shape concerns that are more common among males.

Few people have investigated whether the weight concern and body dissatisfaction scales that are commonly used perform equally well among all racial/ethnic groups. Most of the instruments were developed and tested with samples of primarily White girls, so it may not be prudent to assume that the tools work as well in other racial/ethnic groups. Franko et al. (2004) found that the positively worded items on the body dissatisfaction scale of the Children's version of the Eating Disorder Inventory loaded onto a different scale among the Black, but not the White girls. In addition, when the reliability and validity of the McKnight Risk Factor Survey (MRFS) and body silhouette ratings were assessed among 200 8- to 10-year-old African American girls participating in a pilot obesity prevention program, it was observed that although the overconcern with weight subscale, body silhouette rating, and body size discrepancy were positively associated with BMI and percent body fat, the test–retest reliabilities of the subscales were only fair (0.45–0.58) (Sherwood et al., 2004). One reason for the relatively poor performance may be that the tool is not as appropriate for African American girls as for White girls, among whom the instruments perform better. However, it is also possible that the performance was poor owing to the age range of the sample studied. Children who are 8 or 9 may not have the cognitive skills necessary to accurately complete the MRFS. In addition, Field et al. (2004) have observed race differences in accuracy of recall of childhood body size, taken together the results imply that body shape and weight assessments may not perform equally well across all ethnic/racial groups, so it remains unclear whether some of the ethnic/racial group differences that have been reported are partially due to limitations of the assessment tools.

In summary, the various weight and shape concern assessments may not perform equally well among males or across all age and racial/ethnic groups, so comparisons across these groups should be interpreted cautiously. More research is needed to refine existing assessments or develop new ones that work equally well in these various groups.

Prevalence

Prevalence estimates vary considerably, which is partially due to the wide variety of tools used to measure weight and shape concerns. For example, among 197 5-year-olds, 9% were dissatisfied with their body according to the Body Esteem Scale and 81% of their mothers and 61% of their fathers indicated that their ideal body size was smaller than their current size, thus suggesting they were dissatisfied with their body size (Davison et al., 2000). However, in a sample of 548 5th- through 12th-grade girls, 59% reported that they did not like their body shape (Field et al., 1999). Relatively modest levels of body satisfaction were observed in a cross-sectional analysis of 10,449 adolescents in the Growing Up Today Study. Only 47% of the boys and 36% of the girls were satisfied with their weight and approximately 30%, of both girls and boys reported thinking frequently about wanting more toned or defined muscles (Field et al., 2005).

Because not all people who are concerned about their weight or dissatisfied with their body shape actively engage in behaviors to lose weight, prevalence estimates of using weight control behaviors will underestimate the true prevalence of weight concerns. Unfortunately, there is no universally accepted definition of weight and shape concerns and many studies present associations of weight and shape concerns to other factors, but do not present an estimate on the prevalence of high concerns. Moreover, most of the research has been conducted with preadolescents, adolescents, and young adults; therefore it remains unclear how these concerns change throughout life. However, several studies have observed that dissatisfaction with body weight and shape decreases over time among adolescents (Bearman, Presnell, Martinez, & Stice, 2006; Eisenberg, Neumark-Sztainer, & Paxton, 2006).

Pediatric Weight and Shape Concerns

Relatively few studies have focused on weight and shape concerns of children and preadolescents. One reason for the paucity of research may be that young children may not have the cognitive abilities to understand the concept of weight and shape concerns (Bravender et al., 2007). Davison, Markey, and Birch (2003) observed that the association between BMI and weight concerns and body dissatisfaction was weak among 5-year-olds ($r = .06$, $r = .13$, respectively) and 7-year-olds ($r = 0.13$, $r = 0.15$, respectively), but moderate among 9-year-old girls ($r = .40$, $r = .27$, respectively), which supports the concern that young children may not have

the cognitive ability to accurately report on weight concerns and body dissatisfaction. Nevertheless, these authors observed that both average BMI and average body dissatisfaction at ages 5 and 7 were a significant predictor of dieting at 9 years of age.

Pubertal Development and Weight and Shape Concerns

During puberty, girls experience an increase in body fat, whereas, among boys there is an increase in lean mass, but decreases in fat mass (Rico et al., 1993). Although some weight change is a normal and healthy part of preadolescence and adolescence, for an increasing number of young people an excessive amount of body weight and body fat are gained during this period. Thus, many girls move farther away from the thin body ideal (Stice, 2003). Overweight youth enter puberty at younger ages (Lee et al., 2007), and relative timing of pubertal development has been found to be associated with weight concerns. Among girls, early puberty has been found to be associated with body dissatisfaction (Keski-Rahkonen et al., 2005) and unhealthy weight control behaviors (Field et al., 1999; McCabe & Ricciardelli, 2004b) in some, but not all (Stice & Shaw, 2002) studies.

Two of the developmental changes that occur around puberty are an increase in identification with same-gender stereotypes (Hill & Lynch, 1983) and the beginning of attraction to members of the opposite (or same) sex (Compian & Hayward, 2003). Although research is lacking on mechanism, several studies have observed that rates of weight concerns and disordered eating increase with pubertal stage (Field, Camargo, Taylor, Berkey, Frazier, et al., 1999; Killen et al., 1994; Striegel-Moore et al., 2001) and age (Cooper & Goodyer, 1997). It is plausible that the increase in weight concerns is due to a greater identification with a gender-stereotype that values physique. For females that physique is characterized by thinness (Stice, Agras, & Hammer, 1999; Wichstrom, 1999); whereas for males the desired physique is muscular or lean with well-defined muscles (McCabe & Ricciardelli, 2001; Smolak, Levine, & Thompson, 2001).

In the Growing Up Today Study, a prospective study of more than 16,000 preadolescents and adolescents throughout the United States, Field, Camargo, Taylor, Berkey, Frazier, et al. (1999) observed that the prevalence of weight loss efforts increased with age. Similar findings were observed in another large prospective epidemiologic study, Project Eating Among Teens (Project EAT).

Neumark-Sztainer, Wall, Eisenberg, Story, and Hannan (2006) found increases in unhealthy weight control behaviors from early to mid-adolescence among the more than 2500 girls studied. However, body dissatisfaction, which was related to actual weight status, decreased slightly over 5 years. Approximately 13% of the girls and 17% of the boys increased their weight status (i.e., moved from "average weight" to "moderately overweight" or "moderately overweight" to "overweight") and became more dissatisfied with their bodies, whereas for the 17% of females and 14% of males who decreased their weight status there was less body dissatisfaction, particularly among the females. Overall, the changes in body satisfaction were larger among those in high school than those who were in young adulthood at follow-up.

Gender Differences in Weight and Shape Concerns

Weight concerns and dieting are less common among males than among females (Field, Colditz, & Peterson, 1997; French, Story, Downes, Resnick, & Blum, 1995); however, recent data suggest that these concerns are becoming more prevalent (Braun, Sunday, Huang, & Halmi, 1999).

Moreover, the true prevalence among males may be underestimated because the body shape concerns of males may be slightly different from those of females and most studies use scales that were developed for use with females (Cafri & Thompson, 2004). Among females, weight dissatisfaction increases with relative weight, but among males the relationship is more complicated (Field et al., 2001; Neumark-Sztainer, Story et al., 2002).

For both males and females it is undesirable to be overweight, but for males it is also undesirable to be too lean or not sufficiently muscular (Labre, 2002; Neumark-Sztainer, Story, et al., 2002). Most of the research on weight concern and body dissatisfaction has focused on a desire to be thin and the unhealthy methods that people, mainly females, use to achieve that goal (Boutelle et al., 2002; Field, Camargo, Taylor, Berkey, Frazier, et al., 1999). The prevalence of a desire to be more muscular and correlates of using unhealthy methods to increase muscle mass or definition are less well studied (McCabe & Ricciardelli, 2001). Therefore much less is known about the prevalence or correlates of weight and shape concerns among males.

The magnitude of the gender differences appears to be moderated by age. Bearman et al. (2006) followed 428 adolescent girls and boys, ages 12 to 16 years, over 2 years. They observed that at baseline 37% of the girls and 23% of the boys where dissatisfied with their weight. Among the girls the prevalence of dissatisfaction increased to 44% over the 2 years of the study, whereas it decreased to 16% among the boys. Less is known about weight and shape concerns among young and middle-aged adults. However, Keel, Baxter, Heatherton, and Joiner (2007) followed 469 women and 189 men over 20 years (from adolescence to midlife) and observed that although body weight increased among both men and women over time, weight dissatisfaction and dieting decreased among women, but increased among men. Nevertheless, women at all ages exhibited more weight dissatisfaction, dieting, and disordered eating than the men.

Although many studies have observed that males are less likely to become eating disordered and have lower rates of weight concerns and body dissatisfaction (Gowers & Shore, 2001), a growing number of studies are finding that a nontrivial number of males are using or have used unhealthy means to obtain their body ideal (Pope et al., 2000; Ricciardelli & McCabe, 2004). It is plausible that males are becoming more concerned with their weight and shape as a result of a greater focus on body weight and the obesity epidemic or may be due to an increasing focus on male physique in the media. It is also possible that the gender difference has been overestimated due to relying on assessments that were tested among females, but may not be as appropriate for males, who tend to have greater concerns with their body shape and fatness rather than with their weight.

Race/Ethnic Differences in Weight and Shape Concerns

Although white females have been considered to be the highest risk group for developing an ED, results from population-based studies suggest that weight concerns are relatively common among non-White females, but vary by race/ethnicity (Schreiber et al., 1996; Story, French, Resnick, & Blum, 1995; Striegel-Moore et al., 2003). However, Strauss (1999) observed that among 1932 adolescents, non-overweight White adolescent females were more likely than Black females to misperceive themselves as overweight, and a recent meta-analysis by Roberts et al. (2006) found that Black females had less body dissatisfaction than Whites and that the difference was largest for women in their 20s. The differences were larger when scales on body dissatisfaction were used instead of pictograms/silhouettes to measure body dissatisfaction and there was a temporal trend toward a lessening of difference between Blacks and Whites. However, the inclusion of a large number of unpublished studies in the meta-analysis is not standard and is a cause of some concern because one cannot review each of the individual studies. Among children and adolescents, it appears that in most studies Blacks have fewer weight concerns that Whites, but those differences are not always significant. In the National Growth and Health Study, Schreiber et al. (1996) observed that among 2379 girls who were 9 to 10 years of age, although the Black girls were heavier and taller than the Whites, they were less dissatisfied with their weight, body shape, and specific body parts. However, after taking BMI into account, there was no difference between Black and White girls in the prevalence of trying to lose weight or chronic dieting.

Black males have a preference for a larger body size (Cachelin, Rebeck, Chung, & Pelayo, 2002; Ricciardelli, McCabe, Williams, & Thompson, 2007), but only one study has attempted to tease apart whether that preference is due to a desire for more muscularity, larger frame size, or more body fat (Altabe, 1998). This is an important issue because it is believed that a preference for a larger size is what has protected Black women from the pressure to achieve an unrealistically thin body ideal. Overall, studies have found that Black men are more satisfied with their body shape than are White boys and men; however, it is unclear whether Black males are more or less likely than their Black peers to be trying to lose weight or maintain their current weight (Neumark-Sztainer, Croll, et al., 2002). The lack of consistent results may partially reflect the fact that few studies have asked whether participants are trying to gain muscle; thus most are unable to separate males who are trying to change their muscle mass rather than their weight per se. Those that have assessed strategies to gain muscle mass or weight have observed that among adolescents, Black males are more likely to engage in strategies to gain weight or muscles. Unfortunately, the number of different assessment tools used and the unknown validity of some of the measures makes it difficult to compare results across studies.

Hispanic females appear to have relatively high rates of weight concerns and body dissatisfaction. In a racially diverse sample of 969 children in the 3rd grade, Robinson, Chang, Haydel, and Killen (2001) found that more than 25% of the children wanted to lose weight and 17% of boys and 24% of girls had been on a diet to lose weight. Among the girls, Latinas reported significantly more weight concerns than Whites, and white and Latina girls had greater body dissatisfaction than Asian American girls. However, among the African American and white girls, socioeconomic status (SES) modified associations such that higher SES African American girls reported significantly more overweight concerns than lower SES African American girls, whereas among the White girls, those who were lower SES had higher levels of concerns with weight. African American girls were also found to have lower body image dissatisfaction than Hispanic girls in a study of 139 African American and Hispanic girls in grades 4 and 5 from a low-income urban area (Vander Wal & Thomas, 2004). However, the effect of modification by SES was not investigated in that study.

Elevated rates of body dissatisfaction among Hispanics have also been observed among junior high and high school students. Neumark-Sztainer, Croll et al. (2002) assessed body satisfaction among 4669 children in 7th to 12th grade and observed that among both the girls and boys, the prevalence of low body satisfaction was higher in Hispanics and Asians than in Whites. However, other studies have found that Hispanic males are similar to Whites in terms of the prevalence of body dissatisfaction and weight concerns (Ricciardelli & McCabe, 2001). In terms of engaging in weight control behaviors, Hispanic females have been reported to be as likely (Field et al., 2007), or more likely (Neumark-Sztainer, Croll, et al., 2002), to engage in weight control behaviors, whereas, Hispanic males may be more likely than White males to engage in weight control behaviors (Croll, Neumark-Sztainer, Story, & Ireland, 2002; Field et al., 2007; Neumark-Sztainer, Sherwood, French, & Jeffery, 1999; Robinson et al., 2001; Story et al., 1995). The results suggest that although rates of body dissatisfaction vary by race/ethnic group, Hispanic youth are at least as likely as Whites to have low body satisfaction and engage in weight control behaviors.

It is difficult to synthesize the literature on body dissatisfaction and weight concerns among Asians because the term has been used to describe a variety of racial/ethnic groups that are quite dissimilar. Therefore it is not surprising that the results of the studies are inconsistent in regard to the prevalence of weight concerns, body dissatisfaction, and use of weight control behaviors (Cachelin et al., 2002). Nevertheless, most studies have reported fewer weight and shape concerns among Asians. For example, Cachelin et al. (2002) studied 810 women and 428 men, ages 18 to 83 years, from a variety of ethnic/

racial groups and found that among both the men and the women, Asians had less body dissatisfaction.

In summary, weight and shape concerns are relatively common among non-White males and females. Ricciardelli and colleagues (2007), in their comprehensive review on racial, ethnic, and cultural differences in body image and disordered eating among males, concluded that males from a range of ethnic and racial groups engage more often than white males in binge eating and extreme efforts to change body weight and shape, but there was no consistent pattern to differences in body image concerns. However, among both males and females, it appears that Hispanics and Whites have similar levels of body dissatisfaction and weight concerns. Most studies have found that African Americans have lower levels of weight and shape concerns, but those differences may lessen over time. However, more research is needed to understand better the preference for a larger body size among African American males and the relative validity of the weight and shape concern scales in various racial/ethnic groups.

Correlates and Predictors of Weight and Shape Concerns
Media Influences
Although the average American is overweight, males and females depicted in the media are usually extremely lean and/or fit. Many images in magazines, including advertisements, covers, and photos as part of articles, have been touched up to make the models or actors appear thinner, more toned, more muscular, and/or younger. These unrealistic images are believed to promote the development and maintenance of weight and shape concerns by encouraging viewers to internalize a thin ideal body image (Stice, 1998; Stice, Schupak-Neuberg, Shaw, & Stein, 1994) or compare their bodies to those depicted in the media (Schutz, Paxton, & Wertheim, 2002; Thompson & Heinberg, 1993), which is not attainable for most women (Brownell & Napolitano, 1995) or men (H. J. Pope, Olivardia, Gruber, & Borowiecki, 1999).

Many cross-sectional studies have reported a positive association between exposure to magazines and weight concerns and disordered eating among girls (Field et al., 1999; van den Berg, Neumark-Sztainer, Hannan, & Haines, 2007). Field et al. (1999) observed that among 548 5th to 12th grade girls in the Northeast, 69% of the girls reported that magazine pictures influence their idea of the perfect body shape and 47% reported wanting to lose weight because of magazine pictures. Similar findings

were seen by Utter, Neumark-Sztainer, Wall, and Story (2003) who observed that among the 4746 adolescents in Project EAT, even after controlling for age and BMI, the more often a boy or girl reported reading weight loss/dieting magazine articles, the lower his or her body satisfaction.

Using a modified version of the Body Shape Satisfaction Scale, van den Berg, Paxton, et al. (2007) tested whether the frequency of comparing one's body to those shown in movies, magazines, and television mediated the association between media exposure and body dissatisfaction among 1374 adolescent females and 1106 adolescent males participating in Project EAT II. Among the females they observed that media body comparisons (i.e., comparing one's body to those shown in the media) partially mediated the association between BMI and magazine messages and body dissatisfaction. However, among males, magazine message exposure was related to media body comparisons, but neither was related to body dissatisfaction. As the authors noted, the lack of association among the males may be partially due to the abbreviated assessments. In a slightly smaller study of 819 boys and 791 14- to 16-year-old adolescents, Knauss, Paxton, and Alsaker (2007) used as more detailed assessment and a less complex analytic approach than that used by van den Berg and observed that internalization of the media body ideal and perceived pressure from the media predicted increases in body dissatisfaction. Thus, the findings from cross-sectional studies are not entirely consistent. Moreover, one limitation of all cross-sectional studies is that it is unclear whether the association exists because girls or boys who are weight and shape concerned seek out magazines that reinforce these concerns. Therefore, prospective studies are needed to understand whether media images promote the development of weight and shape concerns. Studies are also needed to better elucidate the mechanism for the association.

Several studies have found that when young women and men are shown thin-ideal body images depicted in the media, there is a short-term increase in body dissatisfaction (Blond, 2008; Stice & Shaw, 2002). Studies are lacking on whether repeatedly viewing these images lead to the development of more long-term weight and shape dissatisfaction or whether individuals cease to be as influenced after multiple viewings.

There are relatively few prospective studies on media influences on weight and shape concerns, but Bearman and colleagues (2006) studied predictors of change in body dissatisfaction over 2 years among

428 adolescent boys and girls. Although dietary restraint predicted increases in body dissatisfaction, neither BMI nor thin body internalization was predictive of change in body dissatisfaction. One possible partial explanation for the lack of association may be that many of the participants may have already developed high levels of concern before they enrolled at ages 12 to 16. Among these individuals not much change may have occurred. It is unclear whether BMI or thin body internalization was related to remaining dissatisfied with body shape, but clearly that is an important topic to be studied.

To study the relationship of media exposure to increases in weight concerns it may be necessary to study preadolescents, among whom weight concerns are still developing. Unfortunately, there are few studies on the development of weight concerns or body dissatisfaction. In a longitudinal study of 257 African American and White girls, ages 7 to 12 years, Harrison and Hefner (2006) observed that time spent watching television predicted increases in disordered eating and thinner post-puberty ideal body sizes 1 year later. In addition, Field et al. (2008) prospectively assessed the association of media influences to the development of weight concerns among 6770 girls and 5287 boys, ages 9 to 14 years, in the Growing Up Today Study. They observed that both girls and boys who were trying to look like same-sex figures in the media were two times more likely than their peers to become weight concerned. The findings regarding the influence of the media on male weight concerns have not been consistent. Some (Blond, 2008; Field, Austin, Camargo, et al., 2005) studies, but not others (van den Berg, Neumark-Sztainer, Hannan, & Haines, 2007), have found that exposure to media is associated with weight and body shape concerns and dissatisfaction. Although they did not study weight or shape concerns per se, van den Berg, Neumark-Sztainer, et al. (2007) found frequent reading of magazine articles about dieting and weight-control behaviors was associated with increased frequency of healthy, unhealthy, and extreme weight control behaviors among females 5 years later. For example, when compared to females who did not read these types of magazine, those who did read them were three times more likely to engage in extreme weight loss behaviors at follow-up. Among the males, there was no evidence of an association between reading magazine articles and engaging in weight control behaviors. However, Field et al. (2005) observed that among 4237 adolescent boys, those who read men's, teen, fashion, or health and fitness magazines were more than twice as likely as their peers to have used products to increase muscle mass or definition. The discrepancy in results may reflect the ways that weight and shape concerns have been operationalized and the difference in assessment tools that have been used. Fewer males make active efforts to control their weight, thus studies relying on weight control behaviors to define weight and shape concerns may have only modest statistical power. Moreover, some of the assessment tools in the field may not capture the range of male weight and shape concerns despite working well with females. Taken together, the results suggest that media images promote increases in weight concerns and body dissatisfaction among preadolescent and adolescent girls. More research is needed on the relationship of media images to male body dissatisfaction, but it does appear that media exposure is related to boys' desire to get larger or more muscular.

Peer Influences

During preadolescence and adolescence, the acceptance of peers is important and youth may take on the perceived attitudes and behaviors of their peers to gain acceptance. Peers are known to influence teen behavior related to using tobacco products (Hall & Valente, 2007; Kobus, 2003;) and alcohol or drugs (Fergusson, Swain-Campbell, & Horwood, 2002; Sieving, Perry, & Williams, 2000); therefore it is widely assumed that peers influence the weight concerns and weight control behaviors of their friends. However, the results have been less robust than expected. Neither Bearman et al. (2006) nor Field et al. (2001, 2008) have found peer influences to independently predict disordered eating. However, both Taylor, Keil, Gold, Williams, and Goulding (1998) and Presnell, Bearman, and Stice (2004) observed that perceived pressure from peers to be thin and the importance peers placed on weight and eating predicted body dissatisfaction among adolescents. In addition, Paxton et al. (1999) examined body image and weight loss behavior among adolescent females and assessed the influences of friendship "cliques" on weight concerns and behaviors. They observed that an association between body image concerns and friend influences, including friend concern for thinness/dieting, peer teasing, pressure from peers to be thin, acceptance by peers, and body comparisons. Moreover, if friends used extreme weight control behaviors, the girls were more likely to use them herself. Further support for the influence of peers come from Hutchinson and Rapee (2007), who found that perceived peer influences in weight-related attitudes and behaviors were predictive of individual girls' level of body image concern and Eisenberg, Neumark-Sztainer, Story, and Perry, (2005) observed that among females, friends' dieting behavior has been found to increase the risk of using unhealthy weight control behaviors.

C.2.A. TEASING BY PEERS

One of the mechanisms through which peers might influence weight concerns and body dissatisfaction is through teasing. Teasing about weight is a suspected risk factor for an eating disorder and has been found to be associated with body dissatisfaction and weight concerns, two strong risk factors for EDs. Among males and females in Project EAT, teasing was found to predict increased body dissatisfaction (Paxton, Eisenberg, & Neumark-Sztainer, 2006) and risk of engaging in binge eating, and unhealthy weight-control behaviors 5 years later (Neumark-Sztainer et al., 2007).

Family Influences

Family members may influence the body dissatisfaction and weight concerns of one another. Data are lacking on the influences of spouses on each other's weight concerns and weight control behaviors, but there is a growing body of literature on how perceived importance of weight to mother, maternal weight control behaviors, and comments about weight by parents influence weight concerns and weight control behaviors in their offspring. In addition, it has been found that perceived importance of weight to father may also be related to weight concerns (Field et al., 2001) and weight control behaviors (Field et al., 2008) in children and adolescents and perceived familial pressure to be thin has been observed to predict increases in body dissatisfaction (Presnell et al., 2004).

FAMILY HISTORY

Children and adolescents, particularly girls, whose mothers are concerned with their weight, are more likely to themselves be concerned with their weight (Davison et al., 2000). Because overweight tends to cluster in families, it is unclear whether the clustering of weight concerns is due to the strong association between weight status and weight concerns. However, several studies have tried to tease apart the influence of mothers from that of weight status.

PARENTAL INFLUENCES: WEIGHT CONCERNS AND COMMENTS ABOUT WEIGHT

Maternal weight concerns and food restriction can influence weight concerns and weight control behaviors among their offspring. Davison and colleagues (2000) observed that among 197 5-year-old girls, body dissatisfaction and weight concerns were greater among the girls and mothers who were overweight or obese. In addition, maternal weight concerns predicted body dissatisfaction among the girls. Further follow-up of 173 of the girls at ages 7, 9, and 11 revealed that mothers who were preoccupied with their own weight and eating reported higher levels of restricting their daughters' intake and more encouragement of weight loss in their daughters. Maternal encouragement of weight loss was positively related to daughters' restrained eating behavior, though partially mediated by daughters' perception of maternal pressure to lose weight (Francis & Birch, 2005). Thus, these results support an independent association of maternal weight concerns and behaviors.

Direct comments made by mothers appear to have the strongest influence. For example, among 299 4th grade and 253 5th grade children, Smolak, Levine, and Schermer (1999) found that direct parental comments, especially maternal comments, had a greater impact than parental modeling on reported weight concerns and body-related attitude and shape in elementary-age children. Two main types of parental comments have been studied: negative comments about the child's weight or shape and encouragement to diet by parents. The association of negative comments about weight and weight concerns was studied among 9- to 10-year-old girls in the National Growth and Health Study. Schreiber et al. (1996) observed that approximately 40% of the Black and White 9- and 10-year-old girls were trying to lose weight and independent of her BMI, having a mother tell the daughter she was too fat was associated with the daughter trying to lose weight. This suggests that some daughters who did not have a high BMI were being told by their mother that they were too fat. Unfortunately, no information was presented on the relationship among those who were objectively overweight versus those who were not. Nevertheless, the results suggest that negative comments by mothers may have an adverse impact.

Teasing about weight or shape is one type of negative comment, and several studies have found that young women who are teased about their weight are more likely to become eating disordered (Fairburn et al., 1998; Field et al., 2008). Keery, Boutelle, van den Berg, and Thompson (2005) studied the association between teasing about weight and body dissatisfaction. They observed that among 372 middle-school girls, 23% reported being teased about their appearance by a parent and 29% reported appearance-related teasing by siblings. Even after controlling for BMI and whether they had been teased by their mother, paternal teasing was a significant predictor of body dissatisfaction. In addition, girls who reported being teased by at least one sibling had significantly higher levels of body dissatisfaction than their peers did. These results suggest that negative comments about weight by family members can promote weight and shape concerns.

PARENTAL INFLUENCES: WEIGHT CONTROL BEHAVIORS AND PERCEIVED VALUES

The relative importance of parental behaviors versus words were evaluated by Fulkerson et al. (2002), who examined the relationship between maternal dieting and dieting encouragement to the self-reported diet practices and weight-related concerns of their adolescent children. Mothers encouraging their children to diet were heavier themselves and more likely to view their child as overweight than mothers who did not encourage dieting in their children. One of the concerning findings was that more than 50% of the children who were encouraged to diet by their mothers were not objectively overweight. Among the girls, maternal dieting was associated with higher levels of weight-related concerns and behaviors. However, when the daughters' BMI was included in the model the association was attenuated and no longer significant. However, among the boys, maternal encouragement to diet was associated with an increased frequency of binge eating, dieting, and other weight control behaviors, even after controlling for BMI.

Even if not accurate, the perception by children and adolescents that their weight is important to their parents can promote weight and shape dissatisfaction. Field et al. (2005) and Keery, Eisenberg, Boutelle, Neumark-Sztainer, and Story (2006) observed that perception by preadolescents' and adolescents' of maternal weight control behaviors, such as dieting, was associated with the child's own weight concerns and weight control behaviors. Perception of the importance of weight to fathers has also been found to be associated with becoming overly concerned with weight, regardless of BMI.

Haines, Neumark-Sztainer, Hannan, and Robinson-O'Brien (2008) studied 73 parent–child dyads and observed that direct weight-related behaviors by parent (comments about weight to child, promoting child to diet) and indirect behaviors (dieting, attitude toward own weight/appearance)

were associated with weight related beliefs and behaviors among their children. It is unclear whether maternal or paternal comments and perceived weight-related values have a more deleterious effect. Dixon, Gill, and Adair (2003) studied 50 father—adolescent daughter dyads and observed that daughters who engaged in vomiting were more likely to have a father who valued attractiveness and dieting. In addition, Field et al. (2001) observed that among 12,057 preadolescents and adolescents in the Growing Up Today Study, a perception that child's thinness (for the girls) or lack of fatness (for the boys) was important to the father, was predictive of starting to engage in bulimic behaviors. However, in terms of the development of weight concerns, there was no evidence that a perception that the child's weight or fatness was important to father was a stronger risk factor than the perceived importance to the mother. Similar associations were reported by Wertheim, Martin, Prior, Sanson, and Smart (2002) who studied 587 adolescent boys and 619 girls and at least one of their parents. They observed that drive for thinness and body dissatisfaction among the girls was related to encouragement to diet by either parent. However, after controlling for the daughter's BMI, the association was attenuated and no longer significant, thus suggesting that it was the overweight youth who were being encouraged to diet.

According to Social Cognitive Theory (Bandura, 1986), observing a family member engaging in a behavior (i.e., dieting) is an important component of promoting dieting and other weight control behaviors. Both Field et al. (2005) and Keery et al. (2006) observed that preadolescents' and adolescents' perceptions of their mother's weight control behaviors and weight concerns were associated with the young person's own weight concerns and weight control behaviors. Field et al. observed that regardless of their weight and age, girls whose mothers reported thinking frequently about wanting to be thinner were significantly more likely to be concerned with their own weight. Because it has been found that independent of a child's or adolescent's BMI, those who diet gain more weight than their peers (Field et al., 2003; Tanofsky-Kraff et al., 2006; Stice, Cameron, Killen, Hayward, & Taylor, 1999), these results suggest that offspring of parents with weight concerns may be at greater risk for weight gain by modeling their behaviors of their perception of the parents' behaviors and beliefs. Thus, maternal behaviors might promote both excessive weight gain and weight concerns in their children.

Personal Characteristics

WEIGHT STATUS

Overweight children and adolescents, particularly girls, are more likely to have higher weight concerns and to engage in binge eating and purging than their average-weight peers (Ackard et al., 2003; Boutelle et al., 2002; Field, Camargo, Taylor, Berkey, Frazier, et al., 1999; Neumark-Sztainer, Story et al., 2002). It has also been found that among adults, weight status is strongly related to weight concerns and body dissatisfaction (Millstein et al., 2008). The relationship is somewhat different among males and females. Among adolescent females, even some of the leanest individuals are concerned with their weight, whereas among males weight concerns occur mainly among those who are underweight (McCabe & Ricciardelli, 2004a) or overweight (Field et al., 2001).

SEXUAL ORIENTATION

Although females have higher levels of weight and shape concerns than males, it is important to note that weight concerns and body dissatisfaction are greater among heterosexual than lesbian girls, whereas among boys, heterosexuals have lower levels of body dissatisfaction than their peers with same sex attractions (Austin et al., 2004; French, Story, Remafedi, Resnick, & Blum, 1996; Russell & Keel, 2002). In the earliest large study on sexual orientation differences in weight concerns, French et al. (1996) found among 36,320 adolescents in the 7th to 12th grades, homosexual males were more likely to report frequent dieting, poor body image, binge eating, and purging (i.e., laxatives, vomiting), when compared to their heterosexual peers. Conversely, homosexual females were more likely to report a positive body image than heterosexual females; however, dieting, binge eating, and purging behaviors were similar. More recently, Austin et al. (2004) observed that among 10,583 adolescents in GUTS, there were greater weight concern among heterosexual males and females, whereas lesbian and bisexual girls were happier with their bodies than were their heterosexual peers. Gay and bisexual males were found more likely to binge eat and were more concerned with trying to look like same-sex images in the media compared to heterosexual males.

Correlates and Consequences of Weight and Shape Concerns

Higher levels of weight concerns have been found to be related to unhealthy behaviors, including smoking, drinking, tanning, and disordered eating, as well as depressive symptoms.

Smoking

Among preadolescents and adolescents, weight concerns and dieting have been found to be associated with smoking in several studies (Pisetsky, Chao, Dierker, May, & Striegel-Moore, 2008; Potter, Pederson, Chan, Aubut, & Koval, 2004; Tomeo, Field, Berkey, Colditz, & Frazier, 1999). Lower body satisfaction predicted smoking among adolescent males in Project EAT-II, but the association was not independent of BMI (Neumark-Sztainer, Paxton, et al., 2006). Moreover, among 6956 female adolescents in the National Longitudinal Study of Adolescent Health (Add Health Study), Kaufman and Augustson (2008) did not observe an association between perceived weight status or weight loss efforts and smoking. However, among 8604 preadolescents and adolescents in the Growing Up Today Study, girls with high levels of weight concerns were two times more likely than their peers to start smoking over the following year (Field et al., 2002). The association was slightly weaker and of borderline significance among the boys. In addition, in a 10-year follow-up of the 1213 Black and 1116 White girls in the National Growth and Health Study, Voorhees, Schreiber, Schumann, Biro, and Crawford (2002) observed that drive for thinness in preadolescence predicted daily smoking in young adulthood. On reason that weight and shape concerns may be associated with smoking in several studies may be that there is a widespread belief that smoking helps to control weight (White, McKee, & O'Malley S, 2007). Although adult smokers tend to have lower BMIs than nonsmokers do (Manson et al., 1995), the association has not been established among adolescents (Potter et al., 2004).

Drinking

The association between weight and shape concerns and drinking alcohol has not been extensively studied. Striegel-Moore and Huydic (1993) found that among 234 female high school students, problem drinking was associated with a high level of weight concerns. In addition, binge drinking has been found to be associated with body dissatisfaction among college students (Nelson, Lust, Story, & Ehlinger, 2009). There are few prospective studies of the relationship, but in one of the largest prospective investigations, Field et al. observed that among 5416 girls in the Growing Up Today Study who had never been drunk, those that were highly concerned with their weight were almost two times more likely than their peers to get drunk for the first time in the next year (Field et al., 2002). No association was observed among the males.

Tanning

An understudied area is the association between use of tanning beds, a behavior that is an established risk factor for the development of skin cancer (Ting, Schultz, Cac, Peterson, & Walling, 2007) and weight concerns and body dissatisfaction. One study of 6373 females observed the weight concerns were higher among frequent users of tanning beds (O'Riordan et al., 2006). In addition, Demko, Borawski, Debanne, Cooper, and Stange (2003) found that among the 6903 non-Hispanic white adolescents in Wave II of Add Health, dieters were significantly more likely to have used a tanning bed at least three times. More studies are needed to examine these associations in greater detail.

Depressive Symptoms

Several studies have investigated the association of between depressive symptoms and weight concerns, which are both relatively common among females in the United States. Although most studies have observed a cross-sectional association between depressive symptoms and weight concerns (Fulkerson, Sherwood, Perry, Neumark-Sztainer, & Story, 2004; Gardner, Stark, Freedman, & Jackson, 2000; Rierdan & Koff, 1997), the direction of the association is unclear. Gardner et al. (2000) found low body esteem and depressive symptoms both predicted higher subsequent ED scores over a 3-year period (Gardner et al., 2000). However, among 7751 Norwegian adolescents depressed mood appeared to predict disordered eating 2 years later; the association was attenuated when baseline EAT score was included in the model (Wichstrom, 2000). There appears to be greater support for weight and shape concerns predicting depression than vice versa. For example, Paxton et al. (2006) found that dissatisfaction with body shape predicted depressive symptoms 5 years later among early adolescent girls and mid-adolescent boys, but not older adolescent girls or younger boys. However, in a review of the literature, Franko and Striegel-Moore (2002) found that there was abundant evidence that body dissatisfaction was a risk factor for depression for White girls, but the association was not observed among African American girls. These findings underscore the association of weight and shape concerns to depressive symptoms vary by race/ethnic group, gender, and age.

Weight Control Behaviors

It is of critical importance to understand the association of weight and shape concerns to weight control behaviors, as disordered eating is strongly related to weight control behaviors. Several large population-based studies have found weight concerns to be associated with unhealthy weight control behaviors, including purging, using products to improve strength and body shape, and binge eating. For example, among adolescent girls and boys in Project EAT (Neumark-Sztainer, Paxton et al., 2006) body dissatisfaction was related to the use of unhealthy weight control behaviors among both girls and boys. Moreover, Field, Austin, Camargo, et al. (2005) observed that both boys and girls who thought a lot about wanting more defined muscles were significantly more likely that their peers to use products to improve appearance or strength, such as protein powder, creatine, growth hormones, and steroids. Similar findings were observed by McCabe and Ricciardelli (2001) in a cross-sectional study of 622 males. They found that males who were not satisfied with their bodies were more likely to adopt strategies to increase weight and muscle tone.

Body dissatisfaction may also be a mediator of risk. As mentioned earlier in this chapter, it has been found that among girls, body dissatisfaction increases with BMI. Lynch, Heil, Wagner, and Havens (2008) observed that body dissatisfaction mediated the association between BMI and dieting and exercising to control weight in that BMI was only related to dieting and exercising to control weight among girls who were dissatisfied with their body.

Unfortunately, there is a paucity of prospective studies on the relationship of weight and shape concerns to use of dieting and exercise to control weight. Field et al. (2001) found that females in the Growing Up Today Study who believed thinness was important to their fathers and males who thought their body shape was important to their fathers were at an increased risk of becoming constant dieters. Females who perceived their mothers as trying to lose weight frequently were also more likely to become constant dieters.

Weight concerns and body dissatisfaction are one of the criteria for the diagnosis of an eating disorder and they have also been found to be related to the use of relatively healthy and unhealthy weight control behaviors, as well as disordered eating. Weight concerns have been found to be significantly related to the onset of disordered eating in multiple longitudinal studies. Killen et al. (1996) found that in a community-based sample of 877 adolescent girls, 4% of the girls developed a subthreshold eating disorder over the 4 years of the study. No girls in the lowest quartile of weight concerns developed a disorder, whereas 10% of the girls in the highest quartile of weight concerns became eating disordered. In addition, among 1103 girls who were followed for 3 years as part of the McKnight longitudinal Risk Factor Study, 2.9% of the girls developed a partial or full ED. Body preoccupation was one of the only risk factors for becoming eating disordered. Moreover, among 6770 girls in the Growing Up Today Study, weight concerns were significant predictors of starting to binge eat or purge at least weekly (Field et al., 2001) and in Project EAT II weight concerns predicted binge eating and extreme weight-control behaviors 5 years later (Neumark-Sztainer et al., 2007). These results underscore the important role that weight and shape concerns play in the development of disordered eating.

Conclusion

Weight and shape concerns are relatively common among Hispanic and White females and they may be becoming more common among African American females as well. Although these concerns are less frequent among males, they are most likely underestimated owing to limitations of the assessment tools that have been used. Comments, behaviors, and perceived values of peers and family members promote weight and shape concerns in females; less is known about how they influence males. The media also plays an important role in the development and promotion of weight and shape concerns by encouraging young males and females to compare themselves to the unachievable images they see depicted in the media. The thin body ideal (for females) or fit body ideal (for males) shown in movies, magazines, and television is vastly different from the body shape of the average adolescent or adult in a Westernized country. By comparing themselves to these ideals, many people become or remain concerned with their weight and dissatisfied with their body shape. These concerns are nontrivial because they are related to engaging in a variety of health-compromising behaviors, including smoking and disordered eating.

Future Directions

Although many researchers have investigated weight and shape concerns, several key questions need to be addressed to move the field forward. It is of critical importance to examine whether African American females are becoming more concerned with their weight over time, and if so, what explains this change? Another important question that needs

to be answered is what aspect of weight and shape concerns is most predictive of a person becoming eating disordered? Is it dissatisfaction with weight or dissatisfaction with body shape or size that we should try to prevent or intervene to change? Dissatisfaction with body shape or size is a more gender-neutral concern, so it is important to evaluate the relative importance of both types of dissatisfaction in order to know how best to prevent excessive weight and shape concerns, as well as prevent the development of EDs.

A variety of instruments are used to measure weight and shape concerns and dissatisfaction, but some of these tools may not work equally well for males and females, or across a variety of racial/ethnic groups. Therefore, it is important to investigate whether we need to think more about dissatisfaction or concern with body shape and body fat rather than weight per se if we are to develop a tool that works equally well for males and females. It is unclear whether body fatness or weight is more important across racial/ethnic groups; thus the question needs to be empirically tested so that appropriate tools are used to assess true racial/ethnic group differences in weight and shape concerns.

References

Ackard, D. M., Neumark-Sztainer, D., Story, M., & Perry, C. (2003). Overeating among adolescents: Prevalence and associations with weight-related characteristics and psychological health. *Pediatrics, 111*(1), 67–74.

Altabe, M. (1998). Ethnicity and body image: Quantitative and qualitative analysis. *International Journal of Eating Disorders, 23*(2), 153–159.

Austin, S. B., Ziyadeh, N., Kahn, J. A., Camargo, C. A., Jr., Colditz, G. A., & Field, A. E. (2004). Sexual orientation, weight concerns, and eating-disordered behaviors in adolescent girls and boys. *Journal of the American Academy of Child and Adolescent Psychiatry, 43*(9), 1115–1123.

Bandura, A. (1986). *Social foundations of thought and action: A social cognitive theory.* Englewood, NJ: Prentice-Hall.

Bearman, S., Presnell, K., Martinez, E., & Stice, E. (2006). The skinny on body dissatisfaction: A longitudinal study of adolescent girls and boys. *Journal of Youth and Adolescence, 35,* 229–241.

Blond, A. (2008). Impacts of exposure to images of ideal bodies on male body dissatisfaction: A review. *Body Image, 5,* 244–250.

Boutelle, K., Neumark-Sztainer, D., Story, M., & Resnick, M. (2002). Weight control behaviors among obese, overweight, and nonoverweight adolescents. *Journal of Pediatric Psychology, 27,* 531–540.

Braun, D. L., Sunday, S. R., Huang, A., & Halmi, K. A. (1999). More males seek treatment for eating disorders. *Journal of Eating Disorders, 25*(4), 415–424.

Bravender, T., Bryant-Waugh, R., Herzog, D., Katzman, D., Kreipe, R. D., Lask, B., et al. (2007). Classification of Child and Adolescent Eating Disturbances (WCEDCA). *Journal of Eating Disorders, 40,* 117–122.

Brewerton, T. (2004). *Clinical handbook of eating disorders: An integrated approach.* New York: Taylor & Francis.

Brownell, K. D., & Napolitano, M. A. (1995). Distorting reality for children: Body size proportions of Barbie and Ken dolls. *Journal of Eating Disorders*, 18(3), 295–298.

Cachelin, F. M., Rebeck, R. M., Chung, G. H., & Pelayo, E. (2002). Does ethnicity influence body-size preference? A comparison of body image and body size. *Obesity Research*, 10, 158–166.

Cafri, G. & J. K. Thompson (2004). "Measuring Male Body Image: A Review of the Current Methodology." *Psychology of Men and Masculinity* 5(1): 18–29.

Collins, M. E. (1991). Body figure perceptions and preferences among preadolescent children. *International Journal of Eating Disorders*, 10, 199–208.

Compian, L., & Hayward, C. (2003). Gender differences in opposite sex relationships: interactions with puberty. In C. Hayward (Ed.), *Gender differences at puberty* (pp. 77–92). Cambridge, UK: Cambridge University Press.

Cooper, P., & Goodyer, I. (1997). Prevalence and significance of weight and shape concerns in girls aged 11–16 years. *British Journal of Psychiatry*, 171, 542–544.

Croll, J., Neumark-Sztainer, D., Story, M., & Ireland, M. (2002). Prevalence and risk and protective factors related to disordered eating behaviors among adolescents: relationship to gender and ethnicity. *Journal of Adolescent Health*, 31(2), 166–175.

Davison, K. K., & Birch, L. L. (2004). Predictors of fat stereotypes among 9-year-old girls and their parents. *Obesity Research*, 12(1), 86–94.

Davison, K. K., Markey, C., & Birch, L. (2000). Etiology of body dissatisfaction and weight concerns among 5-year-old girls. *Appetite*, 35, 143–151.

Davison, K. K., Markey, C., & Birch, L. L. (2003). A longitudinal examination of patterns in girls' weight concerns and body dissatisfaction from ages 5 to 9 years. *International Journal of Eating Disorders*, 33, 320–332.

Demko, C. A., Borawski, E. A., Debanne, S. M., Cooper, K. D., & Stange, K. C. (2003). Use of indoor tanning facilities by white adolescents in the United States. *Archives of Pediatric and Adolescent Medicine*, 157(9), 854–860.

Dixon, R., Gill, J., & Adair, V. (2003). Exploring paternal influences on dieting behaviors of adolescent girls. *Eating Disorders*, 11, 39–50.

Duncan, M., Al-Nakeeb, Y., & Nevill, A. (2004). Body esteem and body fat in British school children from different ethnic groups. *Body Image*, 1, 311–315.

Eisenberg, M., Neumark-Sztainer, D., & Paxton, S. (2006). Five-year change in body satisfaction among adolescents. *Journal of Psychosomatic Research*, 61, 521–527.

Eisenberg, M. E., Neumark-Sztainer, D., Story, M., & Perry, C. (2005). The role of social norms and friends' influences on unhealthy weight-control behaviors among adolescent girls. *Social Science and Medicine*, 60(6), 1165–1173.

Fairburn, C. G., Doll H. A., Welch S. L., Hay P. J., Davies B. A., O'Connor M. E. (1998). "Risk factors for binge eating disorder: a community-based, case-control study." *Arch Gen Psychiatry* 55(5): 425–32.

Falkner, N. H., Neumark-Sztainer, D., Story, M., Jeffery, R. W., Beuhring, T., & Resnick, M. D. (2001). Social, educational, and psychological correlates of weight status in adolescents. *Obesity Research*, 9(1), 32–42.

Fergusson, D. M., Swain-Campbell, N. R., Horwood L. J. (2002). "Deviant peer affiliations, crime and substance use: a fixed effects regression analysis." *J Abnorm Child Psychol* 30(4):419–30.

Field, A., Cheung, L., Wolf, A., Herzog, D., Gortmaker, S., & Colditz, G. (1999). Exposure to the mass media and weight concerns among girls. *Pediatrics*, 103, E36.

Field, A. E., Aneja, P., Austin, S. B., Shrier, L. A., de Moor, C., & Gordon-Larsen, P. (2007). Race and gender differences in the association of dieting and gains in BMI among young adults. *Obesity* (Silver Spring), 15(2), 456–464.

Field, A. E., Austin, S. B., Camargo, C. A., Jr., Taylor, C. B., Striegel-Moore, R. H., Loud, K. J., et al. (2005). Exposure to the mass media, body shape concerns, and use of supplements to improve weight and shape among male and female adolescents. *Pediatrics*, 116(2), e214–220.

Field, A. E., Austin, S. B., Frazier, A. L., Gillman, M. W., Camargo, C. A., Jr., & Colditz, G. A. (2002). Smoking, getting drunk, and engaging in bulimic behaviors: In which order are the behaviors adopted? *Journal of the American Academy of Child and Adolescent Psychiatry*, 41(7), 846–853.

Field, A. E., Austin, S. B., Striegel-Moore, R., Taylor, C. B., Camargo, C. A., Jr., Laird, N., et al. (2005). Weight concerns and weight control behaviors of adolescents and their mothers. *Archives of Pediatric and Adolescent Medicine*, 159(12), 1121–1126.

Field, A. E., Camargo, C. A., Jr., Taylor, C. B., Berkey, C. S., & Colditz, G. A. (1999). Relation of peer and media influences to the development of purging behaviors among preadolescent and adolescent girls. *Archives of Pediatric and Adolescent Medicine*, 153(11), 1184–1189.

Field, A. E., Camargo, C. A., Jr., Taylor, C. B., Berkey, C. S., Frazier, A. L., Gillman, M. W., et al. (1999). Overweight, weight concerns, and bulimic behaviors among girls and boys. *Journal of the American Academy of Child and Adolescent Psychiatry*, 38(6), 754–760.

Field, A. E., Camargo, C. A., Jr., Taylor, C. B., Berkey, C. S., Roberts, S. B., & Colditz, G. A. (2001). Peer, parent, and media influences on the development of weight concerns and frequent dieting among preadolescent and adolescent girls and boys. *Pediatrics*, 107(1), 54–60.

Field, A. E., Colditz, G. A., & Peterson, K. E. (1997). Racial/ethnic and gender differences in concern with weight and in bulimic behaviors among adolescents. *Obesity Research*, 5, 447–454.

Field, A. E., Franko, D. L., Striegel-Moore, R. H., Schreiber, G. B., Crawford, P. B., & Daniels, S. R. (2004). Race differences in accuracy of self-reported childhood body size among white and black women. *Obesity Research*, 12(7), 1136–1144.

Field, A. E., Javaras, K. M., Aneja, P., Kitos, N., Camargo, C. A., Jr., Taylor, C. B., et al. (2008). Family, peer, and media predictors of becoming eating disordered. *Archives of Pediatric and Adolescent Medicine*, 162(6), 574–579.

Francis, L. A. & L. L. Birch (2005). "Maternal Influences on Daughters' Restrained Eating Behavior." *Health Psychology* 24(6): 548–554.

Franko, D., Striegel-Moore, R., Barton, B., Schumann, B., Garner, D., Daniels, S., et al. (2004). Measuring eating concerns in Black and White adolescent girls. *International Journal of Eating Disorders*, 35, 179–189.

Franko, D. L., & Striegel-Moore, R. H. (2002). The role of body dissatisfaction as a risk factor for depression in adolescent girls: Are the differences Black and White? *Journal of Psychosomatic Research*, 53(5), 975–983.

French, S. A., Story, M., Downes, B., Resnick, M. D., & Blum, R. W. (1995). Frequent dieting among adolescents: Psychosocial and health behavior correlates. *American Journal of Public Health*, 85(5), 695–701.

French, S. A., Story, M., Neumark-Sztainer, D., Downes, B., Resnick, M., & Blum, R. (1997). Ethnic differences in psychosocial and health behavior correlates of dieting, purging, and binge eating in a population-based sample of adolescent females. *International Journal of Eating Disorders*, 22(3), 315–322.

French, S. A., Story, M., Remafedi, G., Resnick, M. D., & Blum, R. W. (1996). Sexual orientation and prevalence of body dissatisfaction and eating disordered behaviors: A population-based study of adolescents. *International Journal of Eating Disorders, 19*(2), 119–126.

Fulkerson, J. A., McGuire, M. T., Neumark-Sztainer, D., Story, M., French, S. A., & Perry, C. L. (2002). Weight-related attitudes and behaviors of adolescent boys and girls who are encouraged to diet by their mothers. *International Journal of Obesity and Related Metabolic Disorders, 26*, 1579–1587.

Fulkerson, J. A., Sherwood, N. E., Perry, C. L., Neumark-Sztainer, D., & Story, M. (2004). Depressive symptoms and adolescent eating and health behaviors: A multifaceted view in a population-based sample. *Preventive Medicine, 38*(6), 865–875.

Gardner, R. M., Stark K., Freedman, B. N., & Jackson, N. A. (2000). "Predictors of eating disorder scores in children ages 6 through 14: A longitudinal study." *Journal of Psychosomatic Research 49*(3): 199–205.

Gowers, S. G., & Shore, A. (2001). Development of weight and shape concerns in the aetiology of eating disorders. *British Journal of Psychiatry, 179*, 236–242.

Haines, J., Neumark-Sztainer, D., Hannan, P., & Robinson-O'Brien, R. (2008). Child versus parent report of parental influences on children's weight-related attitudes and behaviors. *Journal of Pediatric Psychology, 33*, 783–788.

Hall, J. A. & T. W. Valente (2007). "Adolescent smoking networks: the effects of influence and selection on future smoking." *Addict Behav 32*(12): 3054–9.

Harrison, K., & Hefner, V. (2006). Media exposure, current and future body ideals, and disordered eating among preadolescent girls: A longitudinal panel study. *Journal of Youth and Adolescence, 35*(2), 153–163.

Hill, J. P., & Lynch, M. E. (1983). The intensification of gender-related role expectations during early adolescence. In Brooks-Gunn, J. & Peterson, A.C. (eds.). *Girls at puberty: Biological and psychological perspectives.* New York: Plenum.

Holub, S. C. (2008). Individual differences in the anti-fat attitudes of preschool-children: The importance of perceived body size. *Body Image, 5*(3), 317–321.

Hutchinson, D. M. & R. M. Rapee (2007). "Do friends share similar body image and eating problems? The role of social networks and peer influences in early adolescence." *Behaviour Research and Therapy 45*(7): 1557–1577.

Kaufman, A. R. & E. M. Augustson (2008). "Predictors of regular cigarette smoking among adolescent females: does body image matter?" *Nicotine Tob Res 10*(8): 1301–9.

Keel, P. K., Baxter, M. G., Heatherton, T. F., & Joiner, T. E., Jr. (2007). A 20-year longitudinal study of body weight, dieting, and eating disorder symptoms. *Journal of Abnormal Psychology, 116*(2), 422–432.

Keery, H., Boutelle, K., van den Berg, P., & Thompson, J. K. (2005). The impact of appearance-related teasing by family members. *Journal of Adolescent Health, 37*(2), 120–127.

Keery, H., Eisenberg, M. E., Boutelle, K., Neumark-Sztainer, D., & Story, M. (2006). Relationships between maternal and adolescent weight-related behaviors and concerns: the role of perception. *Journal of Psychosomatic Research, 61*(1), 105–111.

Keski-Rahkonen, A., Bulik, C. M., Neale, B. M., Rose, R. J., Rissanen, A., & Kaprio, J. (2005). Body dissatisfaction and drive for thinness in young adult twins. *International Journal of Eating Disorders, 37*, 188–199.

Killen, J. D., Hayward, C., Wilson, D. M., Taylor, C. B., Hammer, L. D., Litt, I., et al. (1994). Factors associated with eating disorder symptoms in a community sample of 6th and 7th grade girls. *International Journal of Eating Disorders, 15*(4), 357–367.

Killen, J. D., Taylor, C. B., Hayward, C., Haydel, K. F., Wilson, D. M., Hammer, L., et al. (1996). Weight concerns influence the development of eating disorders: A 4-year prospective study. *Journal of Consulting and Clinical Psychology, 64*(5), 936–940.

Knauss, C., Paxton S. J., Alsaker F. D. (2007). "Relationships amongst body dissatisfaction, internalisation of the media body ideal and perceived pressure from media in adolescent girls and boys." *Body Image 4*(4): 353–60.

Labre, M. P. (2002). Adolescent boys and the muscular male body ideal. *Journal of Adolescent Health, 30*(4), 233–242.

Latner, J. D. & Stunkard A. J. (2003). "Getting worse: the stigmatization of obese children." *Obes Res 11*(3): 452–6.

Lee, J., Appugliese, D., Kaciroti, N., Corwyn, R., Bradley, R., & Lumeng, J. (2007). Weight status in young girls and the onset of puberty. *Pediatrics, 119*, 624–630.

Lowry, R., Galuska, D. A., Fulton, J. E., Wechsler, H., & Kann, L. (2002). Weight management goals and practices among U.S. high school students: Associations with physical activity, diet, and smoking. *Journal of Adolescent Health, 31*(2), 133–144.

Lynch, W., Heil, D., Wagner, E., & Havens, M. (2008). Body dissatisfaction mediates the association between body mass index and risky weight control behaviors among White and Native American adolescent girls. *Appetite, 51*, 210–213.

Manson, J. E., Willett, W. C., Stampfer, M. J., Colditz, G. A., Hunter, D. J., Hankinson, S. E., et al. (1995). Body weight and mortality among women. *New England Journal of Medicine, 333*(11), 677–685.

McCabe, M., Ricciardelli, L., Sitaram, G., & Mikhail, K. (2006). Accuracy of body size estimation: Role of biopsychosocial variables. *Body Image, 3*, 163–171.

McCabe, M. P., & Ricciardelli, L. A. (2001). Parent, peer, and media influences on body image and strategies to both increase and decrease body size among adolescent boys and girls. *Adolescence, 36*(142), 225–240.

McCabe, M. P., & Ricciardelli, L. A. (2004a). Body image dissatisfaction among males across the lifespan: A review of past literature. *Journal of Psychosomatic Research, 56*, 675–85.

McCabe, M. P., & Ricciardelli, L. A. (2004b). A longitudinal study of pubertal timing and extreme body change behaviors among adolescent boys and girls. *Adolescence, 39*(153), 145–166.

Millstein, R., Carlson, S., Fulton, J., Galuska, D., Zhang, J., Blanck, H., et al. (2008). Relationships between body size satisfaction and weight control practices among US adults. *Medscape Journal of Medicine, 10*, 119.

Motl, R., & Conroy, D. (2000). Validity and factorial invariance of the Social Physique Anxiety Scale. *Medicine and Science in Sports and Exercise, 32*, 1007–1017.

Muennig, P., Jia, H., Lee, R., & Lubetkin, E. (2008). I think therefore I am: Perceived ideal weight as a determinant of health. *American Journal of Public Health, 98*, 501–506.

Nelson, M. C., Lust, K., Story, M., & Ehlinger, E. (2009). Alcohol use, eating patterns, and weight behaviors in a university population. *American Journal of Health Behavior, 33*(3), 227–237.

Neumark-Sztainer, D., Croll, J., Story, M., Hannan, P. J., French, S. A., & Perry, C. (2002). Ethnic/racial differences in weight-related concerns and behaviors among adolescent girls and boys: Findings from Project EAT. *Journal of Psychosomatic Research, 53*, 963–974.

Neumark-Sztainer, D., Paxton, S. J., Hannan, P. J., Haines, J., & Story, M. (2006). Does body satisfaction matter? Five-year longitudinal associations between body satisfaction and health behaviors in adolescent females and males. *Journal of Adolescent Health, 39*(2), 244–251.

Neumark-Sztainer, D., Sherwood, N. E., French, S. A., & Jeffery, R. W. (1999). Weight control behaviors among adult men and women: Cause for concern? *Obesity Research, 7*, 179–88.

Neumark-Sztainer, D., Story, M., Hannan, P. J., Perry, C. L., & Irving, L. M. (2002). Weight- related concerns and behaviors among overweight and nonoverweight adolescents: implications for preventing weight-related disorders. *Archives of Pediatric and Adolescent Medicine, 156*(2), 171–178.

Neumark-Sztainer, D., Wall, M., Eisenberg, M., Story, M., & Hannan, P. (2006). Overweight status and weight control behaviors in adolescents: Longitudinal and secular trends from 1999–2004. *Preventive Medicine, 43*, 52–59.

Neumark-Sztainer, D. R., Wall, M. M., Haines, J. I., Story, M. T., Sherwood, N. E., & van den Berg, P. A. (2007). Shared risk and protective factors for overweight and disordered eating in adolescents. *American Journal of Preventive Medicine, 33*(5), 359–369.

Nicholls, D., & Bryant-Waugh, R. (2009). Eating disorders of infancy and childhood: Definition, symptomatology, epidemiology, and comorbidity. *Child and Adolescent Psychiatric Clinics of North America, 18*, 17–30.

Ogden, C., Carroll, M., Curtin, L., McDowell, M., Tabak, C., & Flegal, K. (2006). Prevalence of overweight and obesity in the United States, 1999–2004. *JAMA, 295*(13), 1549–1555.

Ogden, C. L., Carroll, M. D., & Flegal, K. M. (2008). High body mass index for age among US children and adolescents, 2003–2006. *JAMA, 299*(20), 2401–2405.

Olmsted, M. P., & McFarlane, T. (2004). Body weight and body image. *BMC Womens Health, 4* (Supplement 1), S5.

O'Riordan, D. L., Field, A. E., Geller, A. C., Brooks, D. R., Aweh, G., Colditz, G. A., et al. (2006). Frequent tanning bed use, weight concerns, and other health risk behaviors in adolescent females (United States). *Cancer Causes and Control, 17*(5), 679–686.

Paxton, S. J., Eisenberg, M. E., & Neumark-Sztainer, D. (2006). Prospective predictors of body dissatisfaction in adolescent girls and boys: A five-year longitudinal study. *Developmental Psychology, 42*(5), 888–899.

Paxton, S. J., Schutz H. K., Wertheim E., Muir S. (1999). "Friendship clique and peer influences on body image concerns, dietary restraint, extreme weight-loss behaviors, and binge eating in adolescent girls." *J Abnorm Psychol 108*(2): 255–66.

Phillips, R. G., & Hill, A. J. (1998). Fat, plain, but not friendless: self-esteem and peer acceptance of obese pre-adolescent girls. *International Journal of Obesity and Related Metabolic Disorders, 22*(4), 287–293.

Pisetsky, E. M., Chao, Y. M., Dierker, L. C., May, A. M., & Striegel-Moore, R. H. (2008). Disordered eating and substance use in high-school students: Results from the Youth Risk Behavior Surveillance System. *International Journal of Eating Disorders, 41*(5), 464–470.

Pope, H. G., Jr., Gruber, A. J., Mangweth, B., Bureau, B., deCol, C., Jouvent, R., et al. (2000). Body image perception among men in three countries. *American Journal of Psychiatry, 157*, 1297–1301.

Pope, H. J., Olivardia, R., Gruber, A., & Borowiecki, J. (1999). Evolving ideals of male body image as seen through action toys. *International Journal of Eating Disorders, 26*, 65–72.

Potter, B. K., Pederson, L. L., Chan, S. S., Aubut, J. A., & Koval, J. J. (2004). Does a relationship exist between body weight, concerns about weight, and smoking among adolescents? An integration of the literature with an emphasis on gender. *Nicotine and Tobacco Research, 6*(3), 397–425.

Presnell, K., Bearman, S. K., & Stice, E. (2004). Risk factors for body dissatisfaction in adolescent boys and girls: A prospective study. *International Journal of Eating Disorders, 36*(4), 389–401.

Ricciardelli, L. A., & McCabe, M. P. (2001). Children's body image concerns and eating disturbance: A review of the literature. *Clinical Psychology Review, 21*(3), 325–344.

Ricciardelli, L. A., & McCabe, M. P. (2004). A biopsychosocial model of disordered eating and the pursuit of muscularity in adolescent boys. *Psychological Bulletin, 130*(2), 179–205.

Ricciardelli, L. A., McCabe, M. P., Williams, R. J., & Thompson, J. K. (2007). The role of ethnicity and culture in body image and disordered eating among males. *Clinical Psychology Review, 27*(5), 582–606.

Rico, H., Revilla, M., Villa, L. F., Hernandez, E. R., Alvarez de Buergo, M., & Villa, M. (1993). Body compostion in children and Tanner's stages. A study with dual-energy x-ray absorptiometry. *Metabolism, 42*, 967–970.

Rief, W., Buhlmann, U., Wilhelm, S., Borkenhagen, A., & Brahler, E. (2006). The prevalence of body dysmorphic disorder: A population-based survey. *Psychological Medicine, 36*(6), 877–885.

Rierdan, J., & Koff, E. (1997). Weight, weight-related aspects of body image, and depression in early adolescent girls. *Adolescence, 32*, 615–624.

Roberts, A., Cash T. F., Feingold A., Johnson B. T. (2006). "Are Black-White Differences in Females' Body Dissatisfaction Decreasing? A Meta-Analytic Review." *Journal of Consulting and Clinical Psychology 74*(6): 1121–1131.

Robinson, T. N., Chang, J. Y., Haydel, K. F., & Killen, J. D. (2001). Overweight concerns and body dissatisfaction among third-grade children: The impacts of ethnicity and socioeconomic status. *Journal of Pediatrics, 138*(2), 181–187.

Russell, C. J., & Keel, P. K. (2002). Homosexuality as a specific risk factor for eating disorders in men. *International Journal of Eating Disorders, 31*(3), 300–306.

Schreiber, G. Robins, M., Striegel-Moore, R., Obarzanek, E., Morrison, J., & Wright, D. (1996). Weight modification efforts reported by black and white preadolescent girls: National Heart, Lung, and Blood Institute Growth and Health Study. *Pediatrics, 98*, 63–70.

Schutz, H., Paxton, S., & Wertheim, E. (2002). Investigation of body comparison among adolescent girls. *Journal of Applied Social Psychology, 32*, 1906–1937.

Sherwood, N. E., Beech B. M., Klesges L. M., Story M., Killen J., McDonald T., Robinson T. N., Pratt C., Zhou A., Cullen K., Baranowski J. (2004). "Measurement characteristics of weight concern and dieting measures in 8-10-year-old African-American girls from GEMS pilot studies." *Preventive Medicine 38*(Supplement 1): 50–59.

Shisslak, C. M., Renger, R., Sharpe, T., Crago, M., McKnight, K. M., Gray, N., et al. (1999). Development and evaluation of the McKnight Risk Factor Survey for assessing potential risk and protective factors for disordered eating in preadolescent and adolescent girls. *International Journal of Eating Disorders, 25*(2), 195–214.

Shunk, J. A., & Birch, L. L. (2004). Girls at risk for overweight at age 5 are at risk for dietary restraint, disinhibited overeating, weight concerns, and greater weight gain from 5 to 9 years. *Journal of the American Dietetic Association, 104*(7), 1120–1126.

Sieving, R. E., Perry C. L., Williams C. L. (2000). "Do friend-ships change behaviors, or do behaviors change friendships? Examining paths of influence in young adolescents' alcohol use." *Journal of Adolescent Health 26*(1): 27–35.

Smolak, L., Levine, M. P., & Schermer, F. (1999). Parental input and weight concerns among elementary school children. *International Journal of Eating Disorders, 25*(3), 263–271.

Smolak, L., Levine, M. P., & Thompson, J. K. (2001). The use of the sociocultural attitudes towards appearance questionnaire with middle school boys and girls. *International Journal of Eating Disorders, 29*(2), 216–223.

Stice, E. (1998). Modeling of eating pathology and social rein-forcement of the thin-ideal predict onset of bulimic symp-toms. *Behavior Research and Therapy, 36*, 931–944.

Stice, E. (2003). Puberty and body image. In C. Hayward (Ed.), *Gender differences at puberty* (pp. 61–76). Cambridge, UK: Cambridge University Press.

Stice, E., Agras, W. S., & Hammer, L. D. (1999). Risk factors for the emergence of childhood eating disturbances: A five-year prospective study. *International Journal of Eating Disorders, 25*(4), 375–387.

Stice, E., Cameron, R. P., Killen, J. D., Hayward, C., & Taylor, C. B. (1999). Naturalistic weight-reduction efforts prospec-tively predict growth in relative weight and onset of obesity among female adolescents. *Journal of Consulting and Clinical Psychology, 67*(6), 967–974.

Stice, E., Schupak-Neuberg, E., Shaw, H., & Stein, R. (1994). Relation of media exposure to eating disorder symptomatol-ogy: An examination of mediating mechanisms. *Journal of Abnormal Psychology, 103*, 836–840.

Stice, E., & Shaw, H. E. (2002). Role of body dissatisfaction in the onset and maintenance of eating pathology: A synthesis of research findings. *Journal of Psychosomatic Research, 53*(5), 985–993.

Story, M., French, S. A., Resnick, M. D., & Blum, R. W. (1995). Ethnic/racial and socioeconomic differences in dieting behaviors and body image perceptions in adolescents. *International Journal of Eating Disorders, 18*(2), 173–179.

Strauss, R. S., & Pollack, H. A. (2003). Social marginalization of overweight children. *Archives of Pediatric and Adolescent Medicine, 157*(8), 746–752.

Striegel-Moore, R., Dohm, F., Kraemer, H., Taylor, C., Daniels, S., Crawford, P., et al. (2003). Eating disorders in white and black women. *American Journal of Psychiatry, 160*,1326– 1331.

Striegel-Moore, R. H., & Huydic, E. S. (1993). Problem drink-ing and symptoms of disordered eating in female high school students. *International Journal of Eating Disorders, 14*(4), 417–425.

Striegel-Moore, R. H., McMahon, R. P., Biro, F. M., Schreiber, G., Crawford, P. B., & Voorhees, C. (2001). Exploring the relationship between timing of menarche and eating disorder symptoms in Black and White adolescent girls. *International Journal of Eating Disorders, 30*(4), 421–433.

Stunkard, A. J., Sorensen, T., & Schulsinger, F. (1983). Use of a Danish Adoption Register for the study of obesity and thin-ness. In S. S. Kety, L. P. Rowland, R. L. Sidman, & S. W. Matthysse (Eds.), *The genetics of neurological and psychiatric disorders* (pp. 115–120). New York: Raven Press.

Tanofsky-Kraff, M., Cohen, M. L., Yanovski, S. Z., Cox, C., Theim, K. R., Keil, M., et al. (2006). A prospective study of psychological predictors of body fat gain among children at high risk for adult obesity. *Pediatrics, 117*(4), 1203–1209.

Taylor, C. B., Bryson, S., Luce, K. H., Cunning, D., Doyle, A. C., Abascal, L. B., et al. (2006). Prevention of eating disorders in at-risk college-age women. *Archives of General Psychiatry, 63*(8), 881–888.

Taylor, R. W., Keil, D., Gold, E. J., Williams, S. M., & Goulding, A. (1998). Body mass index, waist girth, and waist-to-hip ratio as indexes of total and regional adiposity in women: evaluation using receiver operating characteristic curves. *American Journal of Clinical Nutrition, 67*(1), 44–49.

Thompson, J., & Heinberg, L. (1993). Preliminary test of two hypotheses of body image disturbance. *International Journal of Eating Disorders, 14*, 59–63.

Tiggemann, M., & Rothblum, E. (2004). Gender differences in social consequences of perceived overweight in the United States and Australia. *Sex Roles, 18*, 75–86.

Ting, W., Schultz, K., Cac, N., Peterson, M., & Walling, H. (2007). Tanning bed exposure increases the risk of malignant melanoma. *International Journal of Dermatology, 46*, 1253–1257.

Tomeo, C. A., Field, A. E., Berkey, C. S., Colditz, G. A., & Frazier, A. L. (1999). Weight concerns, weight control behav-iors, and smoking initiation. *Pediatrics, 104*, 918–924.

Utter, J., Neumark-Sztainer, D., Wall, M., & Story, M. (2003). Reading magazine articles about dieting and associated weight control behaviors among adolescents. *Journal of Adolescent Health, 32*(1), 78–82.

van den Berg, P., Neumark-Sztainer, D., Hannan, P. J., & Haines, J. (2007). Is dieting advice from magazines helpful or harm-ful? Five-year associations with weight-control behaviors and psychological outcomes in adolescents. *Pediatrics, 119*(1), e30–37.

van den Berg, P., Paxton, S. J., Keery, H., Wall, M., Guo, J., & Neumark-Sztainer, D. (2007). Body dissatisfaction and body comparison with media images in males and females. *Body Image, 4*(3), 257–268.

Vander Wal, J. S. & N. Thomas (2004). "Predictors of body image dissatisfaction and disturbed eating attitudes and behaviors in African American and Hispanic girls." *Eating Behaviors 5*(4): 291–301.

Voorhees, C., Schreiber, G., Schumann, B., Biro, F., & Crawford, P. (2002). Early predictors of daily smoking in young women: The National Heart, Lung, and Blood Institute Growth and Health Study. *Preventative Medicine, 34*, 616–624.

Wertheim, E., Martin, G., Prior, M., Sanson, A., & Smart, D. (2002). Parent influences in transmission of eating and weight related values and behaviors. *Eating Disorders, 10*, 321–334.

White, M. A., McKee, S. A., & O'Malley S, S. (2007). Smoke and mirrors: Magnified beliefs that cigarette smoking sup-presses weight. *Addictive Behaviors, 32*(10), 2200–2210.

Wichstrom, L. (1999). The emergence of gender difference in depressed mood during adolescence: The role of intensified gender socialization. *Developmental Psychology, 35*(1), 232–245.

Wichstrom, L. (2000). Psychological and behavioral factors unpredictive of disordered eating: a prospective study of the general adolescent population in Norway. *International Journal of Eating Disorders, 28*(1), 33–42.

Yanover, T., & Thompson, J. (2008). Self-reported interference with academic functioning and eating disordered symptoms: Associations with multiple dimensions of body image. *Body Image, 5*, 326–328.

Cultural Influences on Body Image and the Eating Disorders

Michael P. Levine *and* Linda Smolak

Abstract

Data from different cultures and American ethnic groups help to effectively address eating problems and disorders in these groups and to elucidate sociocultural etiological factors. Research indicates that (1) eating disorders exist internationally and in all American ethnic groups; (2) indicators of disordered eating and eating disorders are similar across cultures and ethnic groups, though there are important differences; (3) among American ethnic groups, there are some etiological similarities; (4) cultural transitions (e.g., Westernization, modernization, transnational mass media) appear to increase risk of the spectrum of disordered eating; and (5), acculturation, discrimination, and racial/ethnic teasing may also be risk factors. Research concerning the etiology, course, prevention, and treatment of disordered eating in different cultural groups is urgently needed.

Keywords: body dissatisfaction; body image; cross-cultural; culture; eating disorders; ethnicity

Introduction

Models emphasizing sociocultural factors continue to dominate theoretical perspectives concerning the etiology, course, treatment, and prevention of body image dysfunction, disordered eating, and eating disorders (EDs; Levine & Smolak, 2006; Stice, 2002; Thompson & Cafri, 2007; Thompson, Heinberg, Altabe, & Tantleff-Dunn, 1999; Wertheim, Paxton, & Blaney, 2009). Sociocultural models are built on the assumption that macro-level, cultural influences shape mass media, peer interactions, and parental behaviors, variables that have received considerable empirical support as risk factors in body image disturbances and eating problems (Jacobi, Hayward, de Zwaan, Kraemer, & Agras, 2004; Stice, 2002; Smolak, 2009).

A number of reviews situate body image, disordered eating, and EDs within the context(s) of cross-cultural comparisons, ethnicity, and psychosocial issues such as media, family, and peer influences (e.g., Anderson-Fye, 2008; Anderson-Fye &

Becker, 2004; Levine & Murnen, 2009; Smolak, 2009; Wildes, Emery, & Simons, 2001). These reviews highlight different types or levels of risk and resilience (1) *within* a culture, including within the culturally defined units typically called "ethnic" groups; and (2) *across differing cultures* in other countries. Idiographic, cross-sectional, and longitudinal study of differing cultures and ethnicities are the province of multiple disciplines, such as medical anthropology, cross-cultural psychology and psychiatry, and international medicine (e.g., Anderson-Fye, 2009, 2010; Becker, Burwell, Gilman, Herzog, & Hamburg, 2002).

Goals and Key Questions

Given the definitions of culture and ethnicity we are adopting, to propose that the nature and intensity of body image, weight and shape concerns, and disordered eating are "caused" or "influenced" by "culture" is a tautology; all forms of human behavior are influenced by and reliant on culture (Canino & Alegría, 2008).

Consequently, the challenge for clinical research, including prevention science and medical anthropology, is to identify the specific values, beliefs, customs, and daily practices of a particular ethnocultural group, determine the extent to which particular individuals are exposed to and assimilate those influences, and then use various methods to establish that the process of exposure, assimilation, and enactment contributes to, in the this case, the risk of EDs (Anderson-Fye, 2009; Anderson-Fye & Becker, 2004; López & Guarnaccia, 2000).

This chapter has four sections. We begin with a discussion of what culture and ethnicity mean, how they might generally be expected to "influence" body image, disordered eating, and EDs, and what cautions are necessary in approaching these complex topics. We then discuss cross-cultural and ethnicity data separately. The final section considers lessons learned from this research as well as the ongoing debates, and then outlines some future directions for research.

One major debate that we address is the very matter of whether the psychiatric diagnoses known as anorexia nervosa (AN), bulimia nervosa (BN), and eating disorders not otherwise specified (EDNOS) are "universal." Canino and Alegría (2008) offer six criteria for determining whether a psychiatric diagnosis can be considered valid in various cultures. These criteria are summarized in Table 13.1. Research pertaining to certain criteria is extremely limited in the EDs field, so we focus on the first three criteria, including the others where possible. All six are considered in the Summary and Future Directions.

We focus on females because they are the high-risk group and because far less is known about males.

Body Image, Disordered Eating, and Eating Disorders

There remains substantial controversy over whether the EDs are best construed using dimensions and/or categories (Gleaves, Brown, & Warren, 2004). This chapter considers culture and ethnicity in relation to body image and to disordered eating, as well as the EDs AN, BN, and EDNOS (including binge eating disorder [BED]). Negative body image and disordered eating are certainly unhealthy in and of themselves, and they are risk factors for, if not precursors of, full-blown EDs as well as depression and obesity (Levine & Smolak, 2006; Smolak, 2009).

Culture, Ethnicity, and Psychopathology

Culture

Culture is a "dynamic system of rules, explicit and implicit, established by groups in order to ensure

Table 13.1 Criteria for Determining the Cross-Cultural Validity of Diagnostic Criteria for a Syndrome or Specific Disorder

1. The core, underlying problem(s) should be described in similar ways across cultures, even if the specific manifestations vary. That is, in terms of Western psychometrics, the syndrome/disorder should have face validity.
2. Risk and protective factors associated with the syndrome/disorder should be similar across cultures, although the frequency, magnitude, and pattern of such factors will likely vary.
3. The outcomes or effects of the syndrome/disorder, including those established by biological tests, should be similar and readily comparable across cultures.
4. Across cultures, there should be similar co-morbid conditions, ranging from "problems" to full-blown clinical syndromes.
5. Responses to treatments should be similar, that is, similar treatment approaches should have similar efficacy and effectiveness across cultures.
6. The reliability and validity of assessment tools is established across cultures, in accordance with accepted practices for such research.

Source: Canino, G., & Alegría, M. (2008). Psychiatric diagnosis—is it universal or relative to culture? *Journal of Child Psychology and Psychiatry*, 49, 237-250. © ACAMH. Reprinted with permission from John Wiley & Sons.

their survival, involving attitudes, values, beliefs, norms, and behaviors, shared by a group but harbored differently by each specific unit within the group, communicated across generations, relatively stable but with the potential to change across time" (Matsumoto & Juang, 2004, p. 10). "Culture" resists a focused definition because it subsumes more than 75 different aspects of life that probably cannot be reduced to fewer than 6 dimensions, such as historical traditions, sociopolitical context, ecology (e.g., how food is produced and distributed), normative cultural practices (e.g., gender and gender roles), and general psychological and behavioral tendencies (Markus & Kityama, 1991; Matsumoto & Juang, 2004). Note that culture is a dynamic set of influences that transact with individuals who, in effect, negotiate the nature and impact of culture (López & Guarnaccia, 2000).

Ethnicity

Ethnicity is a *culturally constructed* definition of a group of people who are assumed to be related in terms of values and beliefs and, often, in terms of race. Within the United States ethnicity is often associated with race and continent of origin. It is important to recognize that definitions of ethnicity, including ethnic group membership, will be determined by the broader culture. The impact of culture on both the meaning and impact of ethnicity reminds us that the two constructs should not be used interchangeably, even though our definition of ethnicity subsumes some aspects of the dimensions of culture, notably the sharing of beliefs, values, and practices that define a group and provide the basis of individual and group identity (Anderson-Fye, 2009). Within the United States the major ethnic groups are considered to be European Americans, African Americans, Hispanics, Asian Americans, and American Indians. There is considerable heterogeneity within these groups. Asian Americans may have backgrounds from China, Japan, Korea, India, or Cambodia, countries with different languages, religions, economies, and government systems. In other countries, for example, Iraq and Belize, race may be much less important than religion or language and cultural history in defining ethnicity.

Psychiatric Diagnosis: Universal or Relative to Culture?

Canino and Alegría (2008) argue that consensus in the definition of what constitutes "a disorder," formulation of diagnostic criteria for a particular disorder, translation of those criteria into methods of reliable and valid assessment, and the reliable application of assessment and diagnostic criteria have all proven extremely challenging within the United States and other single cultures in general. It is even more challenging when we attempt to apply diagnostic criteria in various cultures. For example, Bennett et al. (2004; reviewed in Becker & Fay, 2006) found that 1.5% of adolescent female students in rural Ghana reported self-starvation and had a body mass index (BMI) of less than 17.5. However, although the 1.5% figure for an anorexic condition is similar to that for AN and subthreshold AN in the West (Hoek & van Hoeken, 2003), Bennett et al. reported that all 10 saw their weight status in religious terms, without weight-related concerns.

Universalist Perspective

The American Psychiatric Association (2000) and the World Health Organization (1994) argue that there are meaningful consistencies across cultures in the core symptoms or pathological processes of psychiatric disorders, even if overt manifestations of those processes—or the threshold for conceptualizing the manifestations as a disorder—vary in accordance with cultural practices, age, and gender. Thus, Appendix I

of *DSM-IV-TR* (American Psychiatric Association [APA], 2000, pp. 897ff) encourages clinicians to supplement the standard multiaxial classification with narrative attention to the person's ethnic and/or cultural identity and traditions. According to this "universalist" perspective, cross-cultural differences in the prevalence and incidence of a disorder such as AN would reflect both (1) concomitant and systematic differences in the frequency and intensity of risk and protective factors that operate in all cultures; and (2) culture-specific variables (e.g., religious beliefs and practices) that could increase the probability and/or severity of symptoms (e.g., ascetic self-denial) that are part of a syndrome with cross-cultural applicability (APA, 2000; Paniagua, 2000). The fundamental assumption that biological substrates shape in predictable ways the core components (symptoms) of "disorder" or "disease" (syndromes) is called the assumption of "ethnotypic consistency" (Canino & Alegría, 2008).

Relativist Perspective

In contrast, those who favor a relativist rather than a universal perspective argue that it is a fallacy and an arrogant, if not dangerous, practice to ignore the ways in which different cultures shape, define, and contextualize qualitatively different meanings and expressions of disorder (Canino & Alegría, 2008). Sociocultural theorists would often argue in favor of a relativistic perspective. This perspective holds that culture is an important determinant of the very nature and type of psychological dysfunctions encountered among individuals (Canino & Alegría, 2008). Consequently, cultural values and belief systems will need to be considered up front—and not as a minor modification—in developing treatment and prevention programs (López & Guarnaccia, 2000; Paniaugua, 2000). Although the relativistic and universalistic perspectives may be integrated into a single approach, with the emphasis on biology depending on the specific disorder (Rutter & Nikota, 2002, cited in Canino & Alegría, 2008), Becker (2007) notes that assessment and treatment of cross-cultural similarities and differences in EDs "is especially difficult, given the wide variation in cultural values, practices, and norms concerning food and body experience, and by extension, symptoms related to eating disorders" (p. S111).

The Presence of Eating Disorders Across Cultures

The emergence, nature, incidence, and prevalence of EDs may well be strongly influenced by culture (including ethnicity), but EDs are definitely not "culture-bound." With the exception of Antarctica, EDs have been reported now on all the continents (Anderson-Fye & Becker, 2004; Gordon, 2000; Keel & Klump, 2003). As noted by Anderson-Fye (2009), more than 6 years ago the World Health Organization (WHO, 2003) designated EDs a "priority disorder" in its report on children and adolescents with mental disorders. This designation was based on high prevalence in the world, severity of immediate and long-term consequences, and the possibility of good primary health care making a significant difference in the lives of adolescents suffering from EDs.

By the late 1990s, Gordon (2000, 2001) had recorded the appearance of EDs in 38 countries. Moreover, as Lee (2001) has observed, AN was documented in high-income Asian countries (e.g., Singapore, Japan, Korea) and in low-income Asian countries (e.g., India, Malyasia, the Philippines). Recent work has added more countries to this list (see reviews by Anderson-Fye & Becker, 2004; Keel & Klump, 2003; Lee, 2001), bringing the total to at least 48 countries, or approximately 24.5% of the 194 or 195 countries in the world.

Cross-Cultural Comparisons of the Prevalence and Incidence of Eating Disorders
Methodology
Striegel-Moore, Franko, and Ach (2006) emphasize that methodological shortcomings mean that currently available prevalence and incidence estimates in any culture must be interpreted very cautiously. Far too many prevalence studies use convenience samples that tend to be too small and to under-represent minorities. Sample size and sampling strategy are particularly important because, given the relative rarity of full-blown AN and BN, very large sample sizes are needed to provide prevalence estimates with confidence intervals, along with information concerning basic epidemiological variables such as race, class, and gender. Further, there remains considerable variance in measures and study designs, making it difficult to compare results across cultures and over time.

Striegel-Moore et al. (2006) also point out that, for practical reasons, many studies use a two-stage process of screening via survey followed by interviews with those whose survey scores exceed a cutoff. This is a time-honored approach in epidemiology, but it raises another set of issues, ranging from participation rates at both stages, to the sensitivity and the specificity of the screening instrument, to narrow definitions of the disorders that privilege such features as dramatic weight loss over time while minimizing core features of psychopathology.

Cross-Cultural Data
Table 13.2 presents cross-cultural data pertaining to the prevalence and incidence of the spectrum of negative body image and disordered eating. The prevalence is an estimate of the percentage of people in a population at risk who suffer from the disorder at a given point in time (point prevalence), in a recent time period (e.g., the last 3 or 12 months; period prevalence), or at any point through their lives (lifetime prevalence). People who have not yet developed the disorder or who have recovered significantly would, therefore, not contribute to the point or period prevalence. The incidence of a disorder is the number of new cases occurring in the population at risk in a given time period, adjusted for changes (e.g., due to deaths).

Gender
Gender roles, gender role conflict, sexism, and other aspects of gender are extremely important and often under-appreciated elements in EDs and other psychological problems (Piran, 2001; Smolak & Murnen, 2004, 2008; Smolak & Piran, in press). Thus, it bears emphasizing that the very pronounced gender difference in the EDs, particularly AN and BN, appears to be the case cross-culturally, at least in North America, Western Europe, and Asia (Gordon, 2000). In all seven Western countries and in all nine non-Western countries reviewed by Makino et al. (2004), males on average had significantly lower prevalence of high EAT scores than did females.

Risk Factors
Dislocation
In a "dislocation" study groups of individuals who move temporarily, but for a significant amount of time, from one culture to another are compared to those from the same culture who remain at home. For example, Nasser (1997) found that 22% of a group of young Egyptian women who had emigrated to England to study at London universities had high-risk EAT scores and six were suffering from BN, as compared to (1) 12% high-risk and no cases of BN in an age-matched comparison group of women studying at the University of Cairo and (2) 11.4% high risk in a sample of 15-year-old girls in Egypt. This finding is consistent with research

Table 13.2   The Prevalence and Incidence of the Spectrum of Disordered Eating Across Cultures

Aspect of the Spectrum	Summary
AN	Rare disorder in Western countries: Point/period prevalence = 0–.5%; Lifetime prevalence = 1%–2% More prevalent in most Western, industrialized countries than in most non-Western countries, with notable exceptions (e.g., Korea) Age- and sex-adjusted incidence rates increased (effect size =. 25–.35) over 1930–1995 in countries such as United States, United Kingdom, Sweden, Denmark, Japan, the Netherlands, and New Zealand. Some evidence that in some Western countries the incidence of AN in young females continued to rise in latter part of 20th century *and* early part of the 21st
BN	Point and lifetime prevalence in Western countries such as the USA, Canada, Austria, Germany, Norway, and Hungary—and two non-Western countries (Egypt and Iran/ Tehran)—during the late 1980s and 1990s is consistently between 1% and 3%. Point/period prevalence is less (.3%–1%) in Australia and in European countries such as France, Hungary, Italy, and Spain, and in parts of Hungary. No data available on lifetime prevalence in non-Western countries. Prevalence in Hong Kong may be less than 1%, but prevalence in Japan appears to have risen from about 2% to about 3% over the 1990s. Appears to be extremely rare, if not nonexistent—and certainly less prevalent than AN—in Trinidad, Barbados, Sub-Saharan Africa (other than S. Africa), and India. Age- and sex-adjusted incidence rates increased (effect size = +.90) over 1970–1995 in countries such as United States, United Kingdom, Denmark, Japan, the Netherlands, and New Zealand. Consistent with increasing incidence, lifetime prevalence rates of BN have increased across cohorts measured during 1970–1995, whereas those for AN have not.
EDNOS	EDNOS is acknowledged as the most prevalent eating disorder, but estimated point/period prevalence varies widely (5%–15%). Prevalence of EDNOS may be higher in USA, Hong Kong, and Hungary than in Australia, Finland, and Portugal (2%–3%).
BED	Point prevalence of zero among adolescent and young adult sample in Portugal, and relatively rare in the United States, Spain, and Italy (point prevalences ranging from .40% to .80%). More prevalent among adults of varying ethnicities in the United States; lifetime prevalence ranges from 1.5% to 3.5%.
SYMPTOMS	Discrepancy between low or relatively low prevalence of diagnosable eating disorders versus relatively high rates of eating disorder symptoms has been observed in Pakistan, Hong Kong, Singapore, and Israel.
EAT Scores	In 12 studies in Western Countries (Canada, United States, United Kingdom Spain, Germany, Switzerland, and Poland) and in two recent studies in Ireland and Brazil, percentage of high-risk EAT scores (above a screening cutoff) ranged from 8.3% in Switzerland to 26% in the United States. Prevalence of high-risk eating attitudes and behaviors is probably lower in some Non-Western countries (e.g., China, Hong Kong, Japan, and Turkey) and comparable or actually *higher* in other non-Western countries (e.g., Nigeria, Oman, Pakistan, and South Africa [in both White and Black adolescents and young adults]).

Table 13.2 (continued) The Prevalence and Incidence of the Spectrum of Disordered Eating Across Cultures

Aspect of the Spectrum	Summary
EDI Scores	Non-Western clinical and community samples tend to score higher than Western samples on most of the EDI-2 subscales, even when Controlling for sample size, age, and sex.

Sources: Becker & Fay, 2006; Cummins et al. (2005); Gordon, 2000, 2001; Hoek & van Hoeken (2003); Hudson et al. (2007); Keel & Klump (2003); Kaluski, Natamba, Goldsmith, Shimony, & Berry (2008); Keski-Rahkonen et al. (2007); Levine & Smolak (2006); Machado, Machado, Goncalves, & Hoek (2007); Makino et al. (2004); Podar & Allik (2009); Striegel-Moore et al. (2006); van Son et al. (2006); Wade et al. (2006).

indicating that, as predicted by a model emphasizing the negative impact of exposure to Western values and practices, girls and young women living in Kenya and in Nigeria in the 1980s and early 1990s preferred a somewhat larger, more rounded ideal body shape than did age-matched females living in Great Britain. In fact, the Kenyan girls who had emigrated to Great Britain preferred an even thinner ideal shape than did Whites who grew up in Great Britain. In a review of the relationship between "social transition" and disordered eating, Becker (2003) found that young women from a wide variety of places in addition to Africa, including south Asia, Pakistan, and Greece, were at increased risk for disordered eating relative to age-matched comparison groups who remained in the country of origin when those going abroad went to live in countries characterized by "modernization and exposure to Western products, images, ideas, and values" (Becker & Fay, 2006, p. 39).

As with all such comparisons, there are provocative exceptions that call our attention to the limits of "factors" such as Westernization. The high level of risk for ED symptoms for Asian girls living in Great Britain, who tend to be from the Indian subcontinent, contrasts with that for Asian girls living in the United States, who tend to be from China or Japan. This strongly suggests that ethnicity interacts with other multicultural factors in complex and as yet undetermined ways (Cummins, Simmons, & Zane, 2005). In the early 1990s, Mumford and colleagues (reviewed in Nasser, 1997) found that, as expected, those girls living in Lahore, Pakistan, who were more "Westernized" were at higher risk for development of EDs. Yet the same research team found that, among Pakistani immigrant girls living in Britain, those who were more traditional—and not those who were more acculturated to Western ideas and values—had a higher prevalence of disordered eating. Yet another study (Fichter et al., 1983, cited in Anderson-Fye & Becker, 2004) found that Greek women living in Greece were more likely to

idealize slenderness and weight management behavior than similar women who had immigrated to Munich, Germany, but were also less likely to develop AN.

Acculturation and Cultural Identity

People emigrating to a new culture must decide whether to adopt the values and traditions of the new country or to maintain those of their original culture. The type and degree of balance that people opt to develop between the two cultures is known as the process of acculturation. Given the various negative influences on body image, eating, and weight management that are embedded in the dominant Western cultural influences, the simplest testable proposition is that immigrant women who are "more acculturated into Western and white culture would report greater levels of eating pathology than their non-acculturated counterparts" (Wildes et al., 2001, p. 524). The directness of this proposition is undermined, however, by lack of standardization in the conceptualization and assessment of acculturation (Wildes et al., 2001).

In a meta-analysis of dislocation and immigration studies combined, Wildes et al. (2001) located only 11 effect sizes for studies of level of eating pathology as a function of level of acculturation in non-White women in Western countries. Across all studies and over all outcome measures there was little evidence of a significant relationship, weighted mean effect size $r = 0.04$, *ns*. This may be an underestimate, given that nonsignificant F or p values were recoded as effect sizes of $r = 0$; regardless, the actual "population" effect size is very likely small at best. However, a heterogeneity statistic was not reported, and the nonzero effect sizes varied greatly from +.68 (assimilation by minorities in the U.S. to White racial identity), through 0.08 (young Arab women living in London), to −0.83 (ethnic orientation for Asian girls in Great Britain). In general, this important research area is limited by the fact that only two studies actually included a direct measure of acculturation, in keeping with the basic definition.

Although "Westernization" is a very compelling possibility for theorists and researchers concerned about, for example, the negative impact of mass media, there are two prominent alternative explanations (Cummins et al., 2005; Jackson, Keel, & Ho, 2006; Nasser & Katzman, 1999). One is acculturation stress, arising from the challenge of dealing with conflict, ambiguity, and confusion between new and old cultural values, regardless of the content of those values. It is well established that such stress is often a risk factor for serious psychosocial problems in migrant groups (Sam, 2006). Another possibility is that beliefs native to a culture (e.g., the Confucian belief still operating in Korea that proper women devote considerable attention to a pleasing physical appearance *and* to self-restriction) constitute a major contributor to risk for disordered eating. In a study of women in their late teens and early to mid-20s, Jackson et al. (2006) found that, in contrast to the Westernization hypothesis, second-generation Korean American women had a significantly *lower* mean score on the EAT-26 than did either a small sample of Korean immigrants or a large sample of native Koreans. Moreover, for both groups of Korean women now living in the United States, the correlation between scores on a valid measure of acculturation and EAT scores was virtually zero. These findings, coupled with the fact that, compared to the Korean Americans, three times as many women in the latter two samples scores in the clinical range on the EAT, supported both the Acculturation Stress and the Native Influences models (Jackson et al., 2006).

The argument of Jackson et al. (2006) is important, but one problem with their approach is that influences operating in Korea are not necessarily "native" or "indigenous" influences. Jung and Lee (2006) suggest that since the Korean War in the early 1950s the country has undergone numerous cultural transitions, including infusion of Westernized media influences. Korea is currently one of the top 10 markets in the world for the sale of cosmetics. Jung and Lee (2006) further note that the "women of South Korea … are obsessed with dieting, and Korea is the most diet-conscious of the 13 Asian countries that belong to the Organization of Economic Development and Cooperation …. Korean women, along with other Asian women, have shifted their criteria for judging the beauty of females to Western standards …" (p. 352).

Becker and colleagues point out that the relationships between acculturation, identity, and disordered eating are complex and probably culture-specific (Anderson-Fye & Becker, 2004; Becker & Fay, 2006). Anderson-Fye and Becker (2004) note that "diet-conscious" (Jung & Lee, 2006) South Koreans have a rate of disordered eating similar to that of the United States, whereas Korean Americans as an ethnic group living in the United States have a *lower* rate. Humphrey and Ricciardelli (2004) found that Chinese women residing in Australia reported greater eating pathology when they identified *more* strongly with Chinese culture *and* when they reported parental overprotection. However, when there was greater negative feedback from father or a male friend about weight and shape, then those women who identified *less* strongly with Chinese culture reported more disordered eating.

Modernization

AN was first identified as a syndrome in the 1870s, but it was considered rare, if not exotic, until the incidence in the United States and Western Europe began to increase in the 1960s, before taking off in the 1970s and 1980s. A similar situation, although possibly to a lesser extent, emerged in Japan over the second half of the 20th century (Gordon, 2001). After World War II, Japan experienced considerable growth as an industrialized nation. Extensive commerce with the West was accompanied by changes and tensions in the following areas: individualist values (vs. traditional collectivism); female roles; consumerism; the nature and impact of mass media (Gordon, 2001; Pike & Borovoy, 2004).

This type of correlation has led to speculation that increasing modernization, urbanization, industrialization, and widespread (but by no means uniform) prosperity play a role in setting the stage for EDs (Gordon, 2000). Concern has focused on specific concomitants of modernization such as an abundance of food, higher standards of living and wealth, materialism, the widespread availability and power of technology such as mass media, and changes in the roles of women. Modernization is thus linked to gender role conflict, which may be introduced and/or exacerbated by migration, media, and pressures for or against acculturation to the dominant social forms (Gordon, 2000; Nasser & Katzman, 1999).

The relevance of the modernization "factor" is supported by research across various countries indicating that urban life is associated with greater risk for EDs than rural life, and that this disparity is most pronounced in developing countries (Anderson-Fye & Becker, 2004). For example, Lee and Lee (2000) compared the eating attitudes of high school students from three different locales in China: Hong Kong (a well-established international financial center); Shenzhen (then a city of more than 3 million people, with a rapidly developing market economy); and Hunan Province, a poor, rural area with little exposure to such Western influences as television and fashion magazines. Although students in Hong Kong had the lowest mean BMI, nearly 75% wanted to weigh less. Conversely, their rural counterparts had the highest BMI, but evinced the lowest drive for weight loss.

Another important aspect of "modernization" is the possibility and indeed the "promise" of "upward mobility" via "self-improvement." Anderson-Fye and Becker (2004) note that upward mobility has been associated with EDs in Fiji, among Afro-Caribbean women in Britain, in Zimbabwe, and in Belize. The body and its shape and appearance (and adornments) become a "cultural symbol" of the new ways, of freedom from the old ways (Nasser & Katzman, 1999). During rapid transformations parents may not be able to serve as guides, so perhaps the media become transitional objects for negotiating personal development and success in new environments (Anderson-Fye & Becker, 2004).

It is probably a mistake to put too much stock in a very broad and thus overly general factor such as "modernization." Hoek et al. (2005) found that, whereas the overall incidence of AN for White and mixed race people in Curaçao of 9.1 per 100,000 person-years was similar to the incidence in the United States and in the Netherlands, the incidence of AN among the high-risk group of females ages 15 to 24 was only about a third of the incidence in the United States and the Netherlands. Coupled with the absence of AN in the majority Black population, these data led the authors to reject their original hypothesis "that socioeconomic transition had caused an emergence of anorexia nervosa" (p. 751), while emphasizing the importance of ethnic groups *within* Curaçao. Another issue is the nature of the impact of modernization. Gordon (2001) observed that in Singapore (a sovereign state of some 5 million people, located south of Johor in Malaysia and north of Indonesia) the widespread body dissatisfaction and disordered eating attitudes that have accompanied rapid, intense modernization have not translated into an increase in the incidence of EDs per se. Singaporean women may be protected, at least for a while, by the following: lack of obesity in the culture, constitutionally small body mass and size, a normative diet that is healthy, and typically cohesive families (Gordon, 2001).

Finally, it is important to remember that all potentially significant cultural change is not necessarily modernization or Westernization (Anderson-Fye, 2009; Nasser & Katzman, 1999). Recall that the Black population of South Africa is clearly at risk for EDs and disordered eating. Yet, for Blacks in modern South Africa, the social upheavals, the emergence of mobility, and the struggles for integration and assimilation into a reformulated culture resist characterization as either "modernization" or "Westernization" (see also Pike & Borovoy, 2004, for an extensive discussion of the limits of both concepts in understanding EDs in Japan).

Westernization

The well-documented finding that the rate of eating pathology in South Korea is comparable to that of the United States, Canada, and the United Kingdom may well be attributable in large part to the fact that South Korea has been enticed by marketing and other colonial forces to adopt Western ideals, attitudes, and practices, including a thin beauty ideal for females (Jung & Lee, 2006). This form of exported acculturation is typically referred to as "Westernization" (Jackson et al., 2006).

Consider a study conducted recently in the United Arab Emirates by Eapen, Mabrouk, and Bin-Othman (2006). Approximately 500 adolescent girls from various geographical areas and social classes completed various survey measures, including the EAT-40. Almost a quarter of the girls scored above the screening cutoff of 30, and a second-stage interview of 50 high scorers revealed 1 instance of AN and 24 cases of "subclinical AN." Compared to those scoring below 30 on the EAT, the total subsample of high scorers also had significantly higher scores on a number of measures that are correlated with disordered eating in Western cultures: BMI, drive for thinness, watching Western TV programs, and internalization of the slender beauty ideal.

This finding of an association between Westernization and weight and shape concerns, as well as negative body image and disordered eating, supports the conclusion reached by Anderson-Fye and Becker (2004) in their review of studies published between 1981 and 2002 in nine different countries (e.g., Hong Kong, India, Fiji, Pakistan, and Zimbabwe). The cultural values represented by Westernization go beyond the glorification of slenderness to embrace a schematic set of beliefs and values, including consumerism, the veneration of youth and beauty, the insistence that work on one's body is a very important, if not necessary pursuit, and the conviction that the body can be reshaped by those who really care and really try (see Levine & Smolak, 2006).

Not surprisingly, as was the case for the factor of modernization, the nature and impact of Westernization is far from simple. The historical record (see, e.g., Brumberg, 1988; Vandereyecken & van Deth, 1994), Lee's (2001) work on non-fat phobic AN in China, and Anderson-Fye and Becker's (2004) review all support the hypothesis that Westernization is associated with the emergence and pathogenic impact of weight concerns and body dissatisfaction. However, Westernization is probably not linked to some other aspects of AN, such as intentional but nonvolitional, "psychogenic" self-starvation. That is, Westernization is neither a necessary nor a sufficient condition for the emergence for AN (Keel & Klump, 2003).

Whereas AN emerged as a recognized syndrome in the 1860s and 1870s, BN was not officially recognized as a disorder until 1980. Keel and Klump (2003) reviewed 23 studies providing case reports or epidemiological data from four Middle Eastern-Arab countries, Malaysia (Southeast Asia), and three countries in East Asia. All reported cases of BN involved weight concerns, and in all 17 (74%) studies where it was possible to make a determination it was likely that the people suffering from BN had significant exposure to "Western influences" (Keel & Klump, 2003).

Cultures in Transition: Two Case Studies

There have been ethnographic studies of a variety of countries that appear to be undergoing Westernization and other significant changes that would affect "culture." For example, both Fiji and the Ukraine saw increases in disordered eating following the introduction of American mass media (Becker et al., 2002; Bilunka & Utermohlen, 2002). Belize and Curaçao were traditionally both relatively protected from AN and BN by the cultural roles and practices of adolescent girls (Anderson-Fye, 2004; Hoek et al., 2005; Katzman, Hermans, van Hoeken, & Hoek, 2004). In both countries, a group of young women who regularly interact with Western (American and/or Dutch) culture via tourism or education have begun to demonstrate symptoms of EDs. Although we cannot review the dynamics of all cultures in transition, we provide case studies of China and South Africa to exemplify the complex inter-related web of influences that might affect changes in the rates of EDs during modernization and Westernization.

Lee's Work in China and East Asia

The first reports of AN in China were published in the early 1990s, and this ED appears to have increased at an alarming rate during the 1990s in both Hong Kong and Beijing (more than 1300 miles [2000+ km] to the north). In a series of papers concerning clinical and nonclinical samples of Chinese living in Hong Kong, Lee (2001) made the interesting observation that, in at least half of the instances of AN, the working class girls he studied tended not to report the "fear of fat" or "drive for thinness" that are considered essential aspects of this prototypical ED. Lee also noted that nearly half of these patients were unconcerned with body image or did not have body image distortions, although their levels of general psychopathology were quite elevated.

Lee's (2001) literature review suggests that the condition he labels "non-fat phobic" AN has been documented in Europe, Canada, and the United States as well. Several reviews (e.g., Anderson-Fye & Becker, 2004; Cummins et al., 2005) point out that further work by Lee and others shows that in many parts of Asia and Malaysia "fat phobia" is not always part of full-syndrome AN, and that, similarly, in India the core features of EDs may be present without body image distortion.

Lee (2001) acknowledges "fat phobia" (fear of fat, drive for thinness, preoccupation with weight and shape as defining features of self) as a legitimate cultural "idiom of distress" (p. 46) in Hong Kong and other parts of China, noting that by the late 1990s research indicated that about 75% of young Chinese females were worried about being fat even though they are (and tend constitutionally to be) slender. Nevertheless, Lee (2001) concluded that the "voluntary self-starvation" characterizing AN has "manifold metaphorical meanings," some of which are unrelated to drive for thinness and/or irrational fear of fat, and thus are very problematic for "the biomedical claim to universalism" (p. 42). Lee contends that it would be truer to a cross-cultural perspective, a spirit of open scientific inquiry, and the existence of a wide spectrum of meaningful EDs to broaden the *DSM* criteria for Anorexia Nervosa to include a wide variety of reasons for food refusal, ranging from fear of fat to loss of interest in food, to abdominal pain, to feeling powerless, to "I really don't know." This perspective would also be consistent with the feminist argument that the pathogenic concerns of girls and women in regard to identity, control, and reconfigured relationships are much broader and deeper—and more systemic—than the venerated risk factors of idealization of the slender beauty ideal, social comparison, and body dissatisfaction (Nasser & Katzman, 1999; Piran, 2001; Smolak & Murnen, 2004, 2008).

Lee's (2001) position is an argument for a blend of the "etic," or transcultural (self-starvation, refusal to eat, resistance to help), and the "emic" (e.g., issues of familial conflict and personal agency that must be understood from the perspective of Chinese customs and of changes in China). Cummins et al. (2005) make a similar argument for the diagnosis of BN in Japan.

South Africa

EDs were well-documented in White women in South Africa in the 1970s. The first case reports of AN (bulimic subtype) in Black patients appeared in the mid-1990s (Szabo & LeGrange, 2001), following the steps taken between 1990 and 1994 that ended nearly 50 years of apartheid. The period between 1995 and 2000 was marked by the dramatic changes in South Africa; for example, schools were integrated, Blacks and other ostracized groups left designated living areas in the country and moved to the city; and many Black women were released from discriminatory, repressive policies and practices. This period saw the emergence in the literature of more reports of AN and BN in Black patients, and of data from community surveys that revealed maladaptive eating attitudes and behaviors in females from a wide variety of ethnic groups, ranging from indigenous Black peoples to mixed-race to immigrants from India. These likely represent actual changes during the 1990s, although it is possible that AN cases were previously being treated by traditional healers—and that racist assumptions about EDs as a "disease of White females" led to distortions or delays in identification of cases among non-White patients (Szabo & LeGrange, 2001).

Szabo and LeGrange (2001) note that, against this powerful and dynamic background, South African people—and, in particular, women of color—have to somehow, in their identity development (including their clothing choices), negotiate shifts in the meanings of femininity while (1) becoming more "modern" and "Western" (or, even more broadly, "global") and (2) retaining and expressing pride in a liberated (but yet traditional) status as "African" and "Black." The constellation of freedom, opportunity, choice, and potential growth available to some Black South African women is thus also a position that inevitably generates ambiguity, angst, competition, role conflicts, and a materialism that conflicts sharply with traditional rural values. In addition, predictably, Black women in general in South Africa are frequently the victims of violence, and the gap between rich and poor women increased between 1995 and 2000 (Swartz, 2001). Various researchers and clinicians from the United States (Bordo, 1993; Gordon, 2000; Silverstein & Perlick, 1995), Great Britain (Nasser, 1997; Nasser & Katzman, 1999), China (Lee, 2001), and South Africa itself (Szabo & LeGrange, 2001) have noted that such cultural identity issues are a very real source of vulnerability for the identity issues (dis)embodied in the EDs.

Body Image and Ethnicity

One significant element of the sociocultural perspective is the existence and meaning of differences in body image, disordered eating, and EDs among ethnic groups within the United States. The major U.S. ethnic groups addressed in this research are European Americans, African Americans, Hispanics, Asian Americans, and American Indians. Some studies of Hispanic and Asian heritage groups sample a particular subgroup (e.g., Puerto Ricans or Koreans) and others a broad category (e.g., Latinas or Asian Americans). Studies of Black (who may be of African or Caribbean ancestry) or American Indian people tend to sample and report data from people within the broad category.

We begin with a consideration of the research on body image.

Prevalence

It has long been argued that Black girls and women have higher body esteem and fewer weight and shape concerns than Whites do (Smolak & Striegel-Moore, 2001). A recent meta-analysis (Grabe & Hyde, 2006) confirms this difference, although the effect is relatively small ($d = 0.29$) and heterogeneous. In partial support of the argument that this body dissatisfaction difference between Black and White has decreased in recent years, Grabe and Hyde (2006) found a significantly lower d for publications between 1995 and 2000 ($d = 0.19$) than either 1990–1994 ($d = 0.40$) or 2001–2005 ($d = 0.35$). Further, in another analysis, Roberts, Cash, Feingold, and Johnson (2006) reported that, although weight-focused dissatisfaction differences showed temporal decreases, there have been increases over time in Black–White difference in more global body image measures.

It would be erroneous to conclude that being an ethnic minority in the United States is somehow "protective" against body image problems. Grabe and Hyde's (2006) meta-analysis indicated no difference between White and Asian American body dissatisfaction ($d = 0.01$) or White and Hispanic body dissatisfaction ($d = 0.09$). On the other hand, Blacks showed significantly lower body dissatisfaction than did Asian Americans ($d = -0.12$) or Hispanics ($d = -0.18$). These effects are small but homogeneous. Finally, there was no significant difference between the body dissatisfaction of Asian and Hispanic Americans ($d = -0.07$). Thus, Blacks are unique among American ethnic groups in their lower body dissatisfaction.

AGE AND GENDER

Several studies have examined ethnic group differences among children and adolescents (Franko & Edwards-George, 2009). In general, African Americans desire larger body sizes and demonstrate higher levels of body satisfaction than do other ethnic groups. Data for Hispanic and Asian-American groups are more mixed, with some studies indicating no ethnic group differences among Whites, Hispanics, and Asian Americans (e.g., Robinson et al., 1996), whereas others find differences (e.g., Neumark-Sztainer et al., 2002).

Neumark-Sztainer and colleagues (2002) provide a particularly interesting example. Their sample of 4746 male and female adolescents (M_{age} = 14.9 years) enabled them to analyze and potentially detect differences in Whites, African Americans, Hispanics, Asian Americans, and Native Americans. African American girls reported the lowest levels of body dissatisfaction, with Hispanic and Asian American girls reporting the highest. Among the boys, African Americans again reported the highest body satisfaction, while Asian Americans demonstrated the lowest levels.

It is also noteworthy that Neumark-Sztainer et al. (2002) found substantial gender differences, with girls reporting greater body dissatisfaction among all of the ethnic groups. For example, whereas 21.6% of the White boys reported low body satisfaction, 46.7% of the White girls did. Among the African Americans, 33.8% of the girls but 22.8% of the boys reported low body satisfaction. In the Hispanic group, 33.6% of the boys and 57.3% of the girls rated themselves as low on body satisfaction. Similarly, a study by Miller and her colleagues (2000) found that college men scored higher than college women on seven scales assessing body satisfaction, and there were no significant Gender × Ethnicity interactions. The gender differences in body image dimensions were consistent across African, European, and Hispanic American college students.

Indicators

Does body dissatisfaction have the same indicators or symptoms across American ethnic groups? It appears that ethnic group differences in body dissatisfaction may depend on the type of measure used. In a recent study of 1303 women and 903 men (M_{age} = 19.65 for women and 20.83 for men), Frederick, Forbes, Grigorian, and Jarcho (2007) reported that, as expected, body satisfaction scores were lower among White and Asian women than among men. They found no significant gender difference among Hispanics. Within this sample, White women had significantly higher body satisfaction than Asian Americans and marginally higher satisfaction than Hispanic women, although the latter difference appeared to be attributable to BMI differences. The Asian women were marginally more body dissatisfied than the Hispanic women. White men were more satisfied with their bodies than either Asian or Hispanic men.

Clearly, the findings of Frederick et al. (2007) are not consistent with those of the Grabe and Hyde meta-analysis (2006). This inconsistency allows us to raise an important point. The nature of the measure used to assess body dissatisfaction may be important. Roberts et al. (2006) consider the Multidimensional Body-Self-Relations Questionnaire (Brown, Cash, & Mikulka, 1990), the measure used in the Frederick et al. (2007) study, a "global" rather than "weight specific" assessment. Global scales, which Roberts et al. suggested might be more indicative of self-esteem, may yield larger ethnic group differences than scales focused exclusively on weight. This suggests that the relationships between weight esteem and more global esteem may differ by ethnic group. This, in turn, raises the possibility that the meaning of weight and shape concerns may vary by ethnicity, which seems to be the case in at least some instances cross-culturally (see, e.g., Crawford et al., 2009).

Risk and Protective Factors

A variety of biopsychosocial factors increase the risk of body dissatisfaction, including weight and shape concerns (Thompson et al., 1999). Are such factors similar across ethnic groups? The short answer to this key question is that no one knows. Very few studies have investigated risk and protective factors for development of body dissatisfaction among children or adults from ethnic minority groups, although media influences have also received some empirical attention. However, the extant studies are not limited to the "typical" variables investigated with White samples. They also include racial/ethnic discrimination and acculturation.

MEDIA

Few influences have been more strongly and consistently related to body image concerns among White girls and women than media (Grabe, Ward, & Hyde, 2008; Levine & Murnen, 2009). Black and Hispanic women may be even more negatively affected by media images than White women are (Schooler, Ward, Merriwether, & Caruthers, 2004). There are at least three reasons for this. First, Black and Hispanic girls and women watch more television (Schooler, 2008; Schooler et al., 2004). Second, Black and Hispanic girls and women are heavier than Whites and, therefore, are farther away from the generally unattainable ideal portrayed in the media (Anderson & Whitaker, 2009). Third, women from ethnic minority groups differ from the ideal, not only in terms of body shape, but also in other physical features such as skin and hair color, hair texture, and facial features. Even young adolescent girls appear to be aware of how different they are from the cultural ideal on all of these features (Piran et al., 2006).

However, there is some evidence that adolescents from ethnic minority groups are less affected by media, perhaps because they do not compare themselves to images of White women that dominate the "mainstream" media. In a small study of Asian American middle and high school girls, there was no significant correlation between either number of appearance magazines they routinely read or their investment in these magazines and EDI-body dissatisfaction scores (Jones, 2009). In a study of college students (M_{age} = 18.8 years), viewing "mainstream" television was significantly related to body dissatisfaction among White but not Black women (Schooler et al., 2004). Yet, in a 2-year longitudinal study, the more frequently Hispanic adolescent girls watched "mainstream" television, the greater the drop in body image (Schooler, 2008).

But "mainstream" media are not the only available sources of entertainment. Some magazines and television shows (and networks) feature members of ethnic minority groups, particularly Blacks and Hispanics. Though there are no content analyses of Hispanic media, there are a broader range of body shapes in Black-oriented than in "mainstream"

media (Schooler et al., 2004). Given that both Black and Hispanic girls and women who watch more Black-oriented television have higher body satisfaction, it is possible that viewing Black-oriented television is less harmful than viewing mainstream television (Schooler, 2008; Schooler et al., 2004). Among Latina adolescents, this relationship was particularly strong among girls who were more acculturated. Highly acculturated girls tend to more thoroughly internalize media messages about body image (Henrickson, 2006), so Black-oriented television viewing may serve as a protective factor under some circumstances.

ACCULTURATION AND ETHNIC IDENTITY

Many researchers have argued that girls who continue to maintain an identity rooted in their family of origin's ethnic group and who resist complete acculturation to a White middle-class U.S. culture that is more "toxic" in terms of body image should fare better. Indeed, they might show body satisfaction levels higher than both White girls and acculturated girls from their own ethnic groups. This makes sense, but data concerning the relationships among ethnic identity, acculturation, and body satisfaction are mixed. Some researchers (e.g., Schooler et al., 2004) have found that high acculturation or low ethnic identity does increase risk for body dissatisfaction, whereas others report no relationship (Iyer & Haslam, 2003; Ogden & Elder, 1998). Still others find that while the direct effects of acculturation are limited, it may serve to moderate or mediate relationships between sociocultural variables, such as media or peer pressure toward thinness, and body dissatisfaction (Henrickson, 2006; Schooler, 2008).

These more complex analyses may well be the most fruitful path for future research. First, the meaning of acculturation may vary by ethnic group. Some cultural groups may also endorse a thin ideal, thereby reducing the newness of the U.S. perspective and reducing an acculturation effect. For example, Iyer and Haslam (2003) reported no significant relationships between either ethnic identity or acculturation and body dissatisfaction in South Asian American women. They argue this is at least partly due to the substantial appearance-related pressures in South Asian cultures (see also Jung & Lee, 2006). Second, there have been difficulties in defining and measuring acculturation (Wildes et al., 2001). For example, researchers have used language spoken in the home or the type of television (Spanish language vs. English language) as indicators of acculturation (e.g., Schooler, 2008). Clearly, these are not equally applicable across ethnic groups.

DISCRIMINATION

A substantial percentage of members of ethnic minority groups in the U.S. report perceived ethnic discrimination experiences. The National Latino and Asian American Study (NLAAS) yielded a prevalence rate of 30% among Latino adults (Pérez, Fortuna, & Alegría, 2008). Younger age groups, particularly the 18- to-24-year-olds, reported higher perceived everyday discrimination, as did youth those with lower ethnic identity. Furthermore, racial teasing is common among children and adolescents, with negative effects on self-esteem and depression (Iyer & Haslam, 2003).

Given this negative impact on self-definition, and perhaps because it increases body saliency (Larkin & Rice, 2005; Piran, 2001; Piran et al., 2006), it reasonable to expect that racial teasing increases body dissatisfaction. In a study of South Asian American college women, Iyer and Haslam (2003) reported that a history of being teased about ethnic issues (including but not limited to appearance) was indeed positively correlated with body image disturbance, even after controlling for self-esteem and BMI. On the other hand, neither acculturation nor ethnic identity was associated with poor body image. It is noteworthy that 86% of this sample reported at least some experience with racial teasing.

Outcomes

Among White girls and women, body dissatisfaction and concerns about weight and shape predict the development of EDs and depression (Stice & Bearman, 2001; Wertheim et al., 2009). Research on these relationships among American ethnic groups is limited. White and Grilo (2005), using a clinical adolescent sample, found that body image dissatisfaction was significantly related to dietary restraint in Caucasian, Latina American, and African American groups. Perez and Joiner (2003) reported that body image dissatisfaction was correlated with bulimic symptoms in both Black and White undergraduate women. Weight dissatisfaction and low body pride have been associated with dieting, purging, and binge eating in White, Black, Hispanic, Asian, and American Indian adolescent girls (French et al., 1997). However, body image dissatisfaction was related to binge eating only among Caucasians in the White and Grilo (2005) study. These cross-sectional data suggest that body dissatisfaction is related to eating pathology, but prospective data examining the predictive ability of body dissatisfaction among ethnic minority groups are sorely needed.

Disordered Eating and Ethnicity
Prevalence

The most consistent finding concerning ethnic groups and disordered eating is that Blacks are less likely than other ethnic groups to engage in "dieting" or other weight control behaviors of virtually any sort (but see Franko, Becker, Thomas, & Herzog, 2007, for an exception). Chao et al. (2008) reported that, from 1995 to 2005, Black adolescent girls were less likely to report dieting or the use of dieting products than either Hispanic or White women. Croll, Neumark-Sztainer, Story, and Ireland (2002) also found that Black adolescent girls reported fewer weight control behaviors than did Hispanic, American Indian, White, or Asian American girls. In a large study of college athletes (Johnson et al., 2004), Black women ($M = 2.59$) reported a significantly lower drive for thinness than did White women ($M = 6.15$) and also reported that they restricted food intake less frequently than White women did.

These findings do not mean that Black girls and women never suffer from disordered eating. In the study by Croll et al. (2002), for example, 30.7% of the Black girls engaged in some fasting or skipping of meals to lose weight (compared to 43% of White and 40.2% of Hispanic girls). Also, compared to restrictive eating patterns, binge eating may be relatively common among Black adolescents and women (Regan & Cachelin, 2006), though studies still routinely show lower levels among Blacks than among Whites, Native Americans, Asian Americans, and Hispanics (Croll et al., 2002; Johnson et al., 2004).

Such protective advantages may not accrue for all forms of disordered eating or to all ethnic minority groups. For example, Regan and Cachelin (2006) reported that Asian American young adult women are less likely than Hispanic, White, or Black women to engage in self-induced vomiting and to use laxative, diuretic, and diet pills. Black women showed the highest levels of these purging behaviors. Interestingly, there were no ethnic group differences among the men in this study, and women's rates of both binge eating and purging behavior exceeded that of men within every ethnic group.

In addition, Wildes et al. (2001) reported in their meta-analysis that Whites demonstrated higher levels of bulimia and ED than did Blacks, while Asian Americans showed more EDs but less bulimia than Whites (though none of these effects were based on more than four studies). In general, differences were small. Franko et al. (2007) found no differences among White, Black, Hispanic, Asian, or Native American college students in terms of binge eating and purging, although their sample included both men and women. In a clinical sample, White and Grilo (2005) also uncovered no ethnic group differences in self-induced vomiting. On the other hand, Croll et al. (2002) found that disordered eating was more prevalent among Hispanic and American Indian adolescent girls than Whites, Blacks, or Asians. There were also ethnic group differences in disordered eating among the boys in this study, with American Indian males showing the highest levels and White males the lowest. Thus, ethnic group differences may vary depending on the age and gender of the sample.

Indicators

While research is very limited, it is not clear that disordered eating has the same meaning in all ethnic groups. The study by Franko et al. (2007) of college men and women indicated that correlates of binge eating, such as eating even after feeling full, were more common among Whites than Blacks. Binge eating was more strongly related to distress among Whites, Blacks, and Latinos, in contrast to Asians, who were most distressed by purging via vomiting. In the same vein, Bennett and Dodge (2007) reported ethnic group differences in feelings of embarrassment in response to binge eating. In a very large sample of young adult women, Asian and Native American women were more likely than Blacks, Whites, or Hispanics to say they would be embarrassed if others knew about their binge eating. Black women showed the lowest level of embarrassment. Hispanics were more likely than Whites or Blacks to say that they had been afraid that if they started eating they would not be able to stop. In tailoring treatments for different ethnic groups, clinicians need to be aware that women from various ethnic groups may differ in what they consider particularly problematic and in their reluctance to report certain symptoms because of embarrassment.

Risk and Protective Factors

The best predictor of disordered eating and EDs among White girls and women is body dissatisfaction, particularly weight concerns (Stice, 2002; Wertheim et al., 2009). Although there are ethnic group differences in body dissatisfaction and in disordered eating, it appears that the *relationship* between the two variables is similar across groups. This is true for Black and White women (Perez & Joiner, 2003), as well as White, Black, Hispanic, Asian, and Native American adolescent girls (French et al., 1997). Indeed, in the French et al. study, weight dissatisfaction was correlated with dieting, binge eating, and purging. It is important to note, however, that, while the relationship between body dissatisfaction and disordered eating has been investigated prospectively for White girls (see Wertheim et al., 2009, for a review), the data with girls and women from ethnic minority groups are cross-sectional.

French et al. (1997) reported other ethnic group similarities. For example, in all groups, personal emotional distress and peer appearance concerns correlated positively with binge eating, while family connectedness correlated negatively. But not all studies have found such consistency across ethnic groups. Regression analyses by White and Grilo (2005) indicated that for Caucasians binge eating was predicted by dietary restraint, body dissatisfaction, and anxiety, whereas anxiety was the only significant predictor among Latina girls, and peer insecurity the only significant factor for Black girls. Similarly, although dietary restraint was related to the likelihood of purging among Black, Hispanic, and White girls, there were unique correlates for all three groups.

ACCULTURATION AND DISCRIMINATION

As in the body dissatisfaction literature, acculturation does not show a consistent relationship to disordered eating. Again, this is at least partly due to differences in cultures of origin regarding body shape, female gender role (including investment in appearance), and disordered eating. Lake, Staiger, and Glowinski (2000) reported that Hong Kong-born women with a more traditional cultural orientation had higher EAT scores than did Hong Kong–born women who showed more acculturation to Australian culture. As noted previously, acculturation per se is too simplistic of a construct to capture the experience of being a member of an ethnic minority in the United States, the United Kingdom, Australia, and, probably, in most countries. The emphasis on acculturation fails to acknowledge the reciprocity between the individual and the culture.

Cultural acceptance of the individual, reflected in racial/ethnic discrimination, may be as important as individual acceptance of the culture (Iyer & Haslam, 2003). Recall that in the meta-analysis by Wildes et al. (2001) the mean effect size for the relationship between acculturation and eating pathology across all "non-White" ethnic groups was only +0.03, but it varied by ethnic group. Among Blacks, the mean effect size was +0.23. For Asians, the effect was −0.14, indicating that higher acculturation was associated with less eating pathology. Although all effect sizes were small, heterogeneous, and based on a small number of studies, it is noteworthy that the Asian effect size is consistent with the argument that some Asian cultures are at least as invested in female appearance as White American culture is (Cummins et al., 2005; Jung & Lee, 2006).

As discussed previously, acculturative stress refers to the pressures associated with adapting to a new culture, whereas acculturation pertains to adoption of the new culture's norms. Perez, Voelz, Pettit, and Joiner (2002) found that Black and Hispanic women who reported high levels of acculturative stress also showed significant correlations between EDI-bulimia and EDI-body dissatisfaction scores, a relationship that did not hold for women experiencing low acculturative stress. Thus, the acculturation *process* may affect the relationships between risk factors (e.g., body dissatisfaction) and eating pathology. This is an issue that requires much more research with a variety of different ethnic groups.

The Iyers and Haslam (2003) study documenting a relationship between racial teasing and body dissatisfaction in South Asian American women (see earlier) also found a significant correlation between racial teasing and EAT scores, even after controlling for BMI and self-esteem. Future research should address whether the teasing is a risk factor because it heightens increases the salience of unhealthy values and practices, heightens self-surveillance, increases negative affect, and/or decreases self-image.

Eating Disorders and Ethnicity
Prevalence
BLACKS

Two recent studies using national samples provide important information about the prevalence of EDs among Black girls and women. Using participants from the NHLBI Growth and Health Study, Striegel-Moore and colleagues (2003) surveyed and interviewed 985 White and 1061 Black young adult women. Although 0.2% of the White women met criteria for AN, none of the Black women did. This is not surprising, given the apparent lack of investment in thinness and dietary restriction that Black

women frequently demonstrate. White women (2.3%) also showed a higher rate of BN than did Black women (0.4%). Finally, Black women showed a lower rate (1.4%) of BED than White women (2.7%).

Taylor, Caldwell, Baser, Faison, and Jackson (2007) interviewed adults (*n* = 5191) and adolescents (*n* = 1170) of both genders from the National Survey of American Life (NSAL). The sample included both African-Americans and Caribbean Blacks. Among Black adults, the 12-month prevalence of AN was 0.05%, with no women and one man with AN. Similarly, there were no diagnosable cases of AN among adolescent girls and 2 among the boys, for an overall rate of 0.07%. There were fewer cases of AN than BN (12-month prevalence rates: 1.04% for adult women, 0.26% for adult men, 0.43% for adolescent girls, and 0.37% for adolescent boys). The most common disorder was BED, which was higher among adolescent girls (.57%) and adult women (1.11%) than adolescent boys (0%) and adult men (.38%). Thus, both studies indicate that AN is particularly rare among Blacks.

HISPANICS

In a study evaluating lifetime and 12-month prevalence of EDs in 2554 Hispanic men and women from the National Latino and Asian American Study (NLAAS), Alegría et al. (2007) found a relatively low rate of both AN and BN. The lifetime prevalence of AN, for example, was 0.08%, while the 12-month prevalence rate was 0.03%. Comparable rates for BN were 1.61% and 0.82%. The lifetime rate of BED was 1.92%, while the 12-month rate was 0.90%. Women exceeded men for rates of BN and BED, as well as lifetime rates of AN. The 12-month rate of AN was 0.03% for men and 0.02% for women. Surprisingly, the gender differences in AN and BN were not significant, though this may be due to the low rates of the disorders. Being born outside of the United States was associated with lower rates of BED, while the more of one's lifetime that had been spent in the United States, the higher the lifetime rate of BN. Finally, there were significant age differences, with those younger than 30 having higher rates of BN.

ASIANS

Nicdao, Hong, and Takeuchi (2007) also used data from the NLAAS, evaluating survey responses from 2095 Asian-Americans (1097 women). Rates of all EDs appear to be relatively low. For women, the lifetime prevalence rates of AN, BN, and BED were

0.12%, 1.42%, and 2.67%, while for men, these rates were 0.05%, 0.71%, and 1.35%. In contrast to Hispanics, neither place of birth nor time spent living in the United States was related to BN or BED (there were too few AN cases to calculate). Younger adults were nearly 8 times as likely to be diagnosable as having BN than those 60 or older.

Indicators

Theorists and researchers have frequently argued that there may be substantial differences in symptomatology across ethnic groups (Cummins et al., 2005; Franko, 2007; Lee, 2001; Smolak & Striegel-Moore, 2001). In general, research in the United States has not directly investigated this issue with ED clients. Among Asian Americans, 64.2% of those with BN and more than 80% with BED report substantial impairment in their personal and social lives, and 33.1% of BN and 42.9% of BED sufferers report severe impairment (Nicdao et al., 2007). Latinos seem to report lower levels of distress, although more areas are affected (Alegría et al., 2007). More than 40% of those with BN report impairment in home management, personal life, and social life. Over half of those with BED report impairment in home management, work, personal life, and social life. Severe impairment was reported in less than 10% of any of these areas by those with BN and all areas but work (where the percentage was nearly 23%) by those with BED. It is possible that a clearer, more culturally sensitive diagnostic system would better identify sources of distress among Asian and Hispanic Americans.

Risk Factors

There is little research on risk and protective factors involved in the development of ED among various ethnic groups. Research on virtually all types of variables—ranging from genetics to media to objectification—is sorely needed. Further, given ethnic group differences in gender role, body image values, stressors, and discrimination experiences, such research needs to be conducted both across and within American ethnic groups.

ACCULTURATION

One factor that has received some attention is acculturation. Although most studies find no relationship between acculturation and EDs (Cummins et al., 2005), Cachelin, Phinney, Schug, and Striegel-Moore (2006) did report that an orientation towards Anglo-American culture was significantly correlated with ED (diagnosed based on interviews) among Mexican American women. Yet neither identification with Mexican culture nor ethnic identity was associated with ED, indicating no particular protective advantage of identifying as Mexican. The previously discussed data concerning country of birth and time lived in the United States might be interpreted as providing information about acculturation. These data are mixed, indicating some effect of time spent in the United States on Hispanics but little effect on Asians (Alegría et al., 2007; Nicdao et al., 2007). Such findings have to be interpreted cautiously, because they probably reflect variables, such as familial support and conflict, that do not directly reflect acculturation.

GENDER

It is noteworthy that it is not clear at this point whether the gender differences commonly found among European Americans and in other cultures occur among all ethnic groups (e.g., Alegría et al., 2007). The possibility of a smaller or nonexistent gender difference in ED in some ethnic groups is consistent with arguments that gender differences reflect culturally constructed gender roles and gendered lived experiences (Smolak & Murnen, in press).

Treatment

The relatively low distress levels reported by Hispanics and Asian Americans suffering with ED might mean that people from these ethnic groups are less inclined to seek treatment (Franko, 2007). The lack of distress might also impact the clinician's decision to make a diagnosis of a mental disorder. Even when socioeconomic status and health insurance coverage are similar, Mexican Americans, and primarily those with BN, appear to be less likely to seek treatment than Anglo and Asian Americans are (Cachelin & Striegel-Moore, 2006; Nicdao et al., 2007). Whereas only 29.2% of the Mexican American women in the Cachelin and Striegel-Moore (2006) study who suffered from BN sought treatment, 54.6% of Asian Americans tried to obtain help (Nicdao et al., 2007). Thus, ethnic groups may differentially seek help for EDs.

Once a member of an ethnic minority group does seek therapy, she (or he) may be less likely to actually receive treatment. Cachelin and Striegel-Moore (2006) reported 51.6% of Anglo women but only 14.3% of Mexican American women who sought therapy received a diagnosis of ED. Alegría et al. (2007) found that only about 16.9% to 34.7% of Latinos (men and women) reporting lifetime symptoms of ED actually received treatment. Thus, ethnic minority members may receive treatment less frequently than European Americans. This may be at least partly due to clinicians' failure to diagnosis the minority members as having an ED, perhaps because of stereotypes about who develops ED.

Summary and Future Directions

To guide a summary and integration of this lengthy, detailed, and at times complicated review, we have organized the following sections as responses to six questions (in boldface) that have arisen in various important studies and reviews (e.g., Becker & Anderson-Fye, 2004; Gordon, 2000; Keel & Klump, 2003), in our own research, in teaching courses, and in responding to questions at conferences.

Are eating disorders culture-bound syndromes?

No. EDs are clearly *not* culture-bound syndromes, given their presence and prevalence in a large number of vastly different countries and cultures.

Are eating disorders the same throughout the world and across ethnic groups, at least in terms of the fundamental problems?

This turns out to be a very difficult question to answer. Our experience with ethnic differences strongly indicates that it is a mistake to proclaim that people in any given culture "don't develop eating disorders," especially AN (Keel & Klump, 2003; Smolak & Striegel-Moore, 2001). On the other hand, as yet we simply do not have the data necessary to determine whether Canino and Alegría's (2008) criteria (and in particular, criteria 3 through 5), as summarized in Table 13.1, apply to any aspect of the spectrum of disordered eating. Moreover, as is the case with depression, EDs function as "final common pathways" for many different types of biopsychiatric, psychological, interpersonal, and cultural issues (Smolak & Thompson, 2009).

We feel that the data warrant the following tentative conclusions. First, the sheer number of countries reporting the prototypical features of AN and (more recently) BN that meet the overlapping criteria of the American Psychiatric Association and the World Health Organization indicates that the core syndromes are strikingly similar in many cultures. This is also generally true of ethnic groups in the United States, although the specifics of which symptoms are most distressing may vary. Second, Lee's (2001) research, coupled with other studies in places such as India and Pakistan (Cummins et al., 2005),

indicates that neither fear of fat nor body image distortion are necessary or sufficient for the presence of an eating disorder. Third, as noted in the next sections, there are indeed some similarities across cultures and ethnic groups in risk and protective factors.

Finally, in relation to Canino and Alegría's (2008) criterion 6 (see Table 13.1) there is solid evidence for the cross-cultural and cross-ethnic validity of several "assessment tools," notably the EDI and EAT. The EDI subsumes three ED-related subscales (drive for thinness, body dissatisfaction, and bulimia) and measures of associated psychopathology (e.g., levels of perfectionism, interoceptive awareness, impulse regulation). Podar and Allik (2009) identified 159 clinical samples from around the world and used the pairwise–intercorrelation matrix for all 11 EDI subscales in the EDI-2 to conduct a principal components analysis. The two factors that emerged—*personality deficits* (a Western term for interpersonal distrust, maturity fears, and difficulties in impulse regulation) and *disordered eating*—were essentially replicated across nonclinical samples and across cultures.

What can epidemiological research, conducted across cultures, tell us about cultural, social, and psychological factors in the development of the spectrum of disordered eating?

Even though AN and EDNOS may not have been uncommon in the late 19th century and early 20th century in Great Britain, Western Europe, and the United States, it is almost certain that socioeconomic and other very broad social changes have led to (1) an increase in incidence of all the eating disorders in the West over the past 80 years; and (2) the emergence, after World War II of eating disorders in non-Western countries such as Korea, Japan, China, Iran, and so forth (Brumberg, 1988; Gordon, 2000; Keel & Klump, 2003; Pike & Borovoy, 2004; Silverstein & Perlick, 1995). As noted in response to the next question, the distribution of eating disorders is not uniform across cultures and within an individual culture. The significance of longitudinal changes, cross-cultural differences and similarities, and, of course, cross-sectional (e.g., ethnic or social class) differences within an individual culture, is as yet far from clear. Nevertheless, it seems very reasonable to adopt Anderson-Fye and Becker's (2004) conclusion that "the historical, cross-cultural, cross-ethnic, and subcultural differences in the prevalence of EDs and disordered eating attitudes and behaviors provide incontrovertible evidence that social and cultural contexts contribute to risk for eating disorders" (p. 574).

Keel and Klump (2003) are very specific in their support of the need to study further the nature and impact of social, ethnic, and cultural factors. They argue that the modest "secular increase" in the incidence of AN, the existence of cases of AN in numerous historical periods, and the cross-cultural distribution of cases (including those unrelated to Western ideals) all suggest the utility of the distinction between disease and illness developed by Kleinman (1977). Keel and Klump (2003) see AN as a multidetermined disease of self-starvation whose prevalence and expression as an illness may be influenced to some extent by the glorification of slenderness and the vilification of fat that has clearly increased in Western and industrialized countries over the 20th century. Lee's (2001) work in China, Anderson-Fye's (2004) work in Belize, and other analyses (see, e.g., Nasser, Katzman, & Gordon, 2001) all strongly indicate that the illnesses of AN and EDNOS are influenced by a myriad of factors affecting cultures in transition and people in transition between cultures.

With respect to BN, Keel and Klump (2003) are even more emphatic. Based on an extensive and careful review, they conclude that there is little evidence in the historical record of BN—in contrast to AN, BED, conversion disorder, or "psychogenic vomiting" (Vandereycken & Van Deth, 1994). Moreover, they emphasize in their analysis of case reports of BN from 23 studies in Middle-Eastern Arab cultures, Southeast Asia, and East Asia, that they were unable to locate a single case in which there was an absence of weight concerns. Consequently, Keel and Klump (2003) argue that BN is indeed a fairly recent development in which the syndrome of purging, binge eating, and negative body image revolves around the type of weight and shape concerns generated by the internalization of modern ideals of beauty and self-control.

Why are eating disorders prominent in some parts of the world, and why might be they spreading to or emerging in other parts?

Differences in size, age, and social status of samples, as well as significant variation in assessments and other important aspects of research design, make it impossible to draw robust conclusions from the rapidly expanding cross-cultural data. The diversity captured in the phrase "global distribution of eating disorders across diverse social contexts" (Becker & Fay, 2006, p. 56; Gordon, 2000) is both the essence of a true sociocultural approach, and its curse, because no single concept such as "Westernization" or "globalization" will come close to capturing the forces operating on people in general and females in particular (Anderson-Fye, 2009; Nasser & Katzman, 1999; Swartz, 2001).

With this caution in mind, it is still the case that the prevalence of EDs in industrialized or "post-industrialized" countries (e.g., United States, Western Europe, as well as urban China, Egypt, Israel, Japan, Korea, Eastern Europe, South Africa, and Tehran/Iran)—many of whom are profoundly influenced by Western capitalist ideals, values, and practices—is greater than in preindustrialized, more non-Western societies such as those in sub-Saharan Africa and rural China (see Table 13.2). Moreover, the connection—no matter how complex and ambiguous—between increased risk for disordered eating and "modernization" and "Westernization" as two forms of socioeconomic–cultural change cannot be ignored. Countries (or areas within countries) that are developing economically—and thus becoming more urban, modern, global, and, in some respects, "chaotic" (Nasser, 1997)—and countries whose people are coming into increasing contact with American consumerism and other Western values and practices appear to be more vulnerable (Becker & Anderson-Fye, 2004). Transitions and conflicts are two phenomena that increase the risk of negative body image and disordered eating for individual females (Levine & Smolak, 2006; Smolak & Levine, 1996); analogously, cultural transitions and cultural conflicts (e.g., the "place" and "power" of Blacks in South Africa) appear to increase the risk for peoples within a culture.

Global media purvey slender beauty ideals, fear of fat, body change technologies, and the individual "upward mobility through consumerism" fostered by many international businesses. This almost certainly contributes to the spread of negative body image and disordered eating. However, we know that individual EDs are impairments of not only eating and weight and shape concerns, but also fundamental dimensions of adaptation such as mood stability, impulse control, self-concept, interpersonal skills, and so forth (Connors, 1996; Podar & Allik, 2009). Consequently, there is a need to explore cultural influences pertaining not only to beauty ideals and the meanings of eating and not eating, but also to conflicts and problems generated by multicultural identity, cultures in transition, disenfranchisement, and gender role changes (Becker & Fay, 2006; Nasser & Katzman, 1999).

What can the study of ethnicity (within dominant cultures like that operating in the United States) really tell us at this point?

The past decade has seen both improved organization (e.g., via meta-analyses) and more sophistication in the literature that critically examines body image and disordered eating as a function of ethnic minority status in the United States. Although a good deal of research remains to be done in order to address many important, unanswered questions, we may draw three conclusions from the current literature.

First, there are meaningful differences among American ethnic groups in body image, disordered eating, and EDs. The most obvious is the lowered risk of body image and eating problems among Blacks relative to all other groups. Yet, it is noteworthy that it is not always Whites who show the highest levels of body dissatisfaction or disordered eating. We should not assume, then, that it is simply adoption of White culture that puts women from ethnic minority groups at risk (Wildes et al., 2001). Research needs to carefully consider where there are and are not differences. This includes examining within group differences since, for example, values and roles in South Asia may differ substantially from those in East Asia. A better, more detailed description of differences should facilitate identification of risk and protective factors.

Second, although various ethnic groups may share some risk and protective factors, there are also likely to be some factors that differ. Ethnic minority women face at least two issues not common among European-Americans. The first, acculturation, has received considerable attention but the results have been mixed. There are likely several reasons for this. Acculturation measures are often quite broad and are often phrased to reflect the assumption that adoption of the Anglo culture's values will lead to eating problems. Further, few studies have been careful to consider cultural differences within ethnic groups, leading to, for example, treatment of Hispanics as a unitary group. Finally, acculturation often confounds several important constructs, including ethnic identity, acculturative stress, and cultural transition.

There also continues to be considerable discrimination, including racial/ethnic teasing, directed at member of ethnic minority groups. Research examining this factor has been limited, but it has also been promising. Given the likely role of teasing overall in body image and eating problems (Menzel et al., 2009; Thompson et al., 1999), it should not be surprising that the experience of such discrimination has detrimental effects.

Third, a variety of factors may converge to make it particularly unlikely that ethnic minority members will receive appropriate treatment. Some of this reflects cultural preferences for family or other forms of private support to address problems. Clinicians' stereotypes may also affect diagnosis. The lower levels of distress reported by some ethnic minority members who suffer from ED may impede diagnosis. It should also be noted, however, that North American reliance on *DSM* standards that were developed for and with European-Americans may be reducing the recognition of clinically significant eating disorders among ethnic minority groups.

Sociocultural models of EDs argue that there are cultural values and attitudes concerning ideal body shape, gender roles, and expected discipline of the body that contribute to the development and maintenance of body image and eating problems. The research on American ethnic groups supports this argument. Closer investigation of the development of body image and eating problems among ethnic groups, particularly using longitudinal designs, will not only help provide better treatment service to ethnic minority members but will also yield clues as to risk and protective factors in etiological models of EDs.

What are the clinical and preventive implications of cross-cultural and ethnic research?

CLINICAL IMPLICATIONS

It is ethically and practically necessary for clinicians to incorporate significant aspects of culture, ethnicity, and ethnic identity into all phases of treatment, beginning with a "culturally sensitive assessment" and ending with informed and respectful understanding of culturally determined meanings of health, well-being, and resilience (Anthony & Yager, 2007). Kleinman's (1977) classic distinction between *disease* as psychopathology and *illness* as the personal and sociocultural interpretations and expressions of disease is still relevant. This reminds us that researchers and clinicians should strive "to understand the social world within mental illness" and mental illness within the social and cultural world of the sufferer (López & Guarnaccia, 2000, p. 572). It is certainly important to understand the neuropsychiatry of EDs, but it is at least as important for clinicians to be informed about the ways in which the components of disordered eating and of healthy eating and a healthy lifestyle are shaped by culture(s) and communities. Clinicians also need to be informed about and active in combating the lack of access to care that many minority populations face, and in arranging the training for themselves and others so that front-line sources of health care have the skills to speak the necessary languages and to provide culturally sensitive assessment and treatment services (Cachelin & Striegel-Moore, 2006; Franko, 2007; Smolak & Striegel-Moore, 2001).

Anthony and Yager (2007) strongly recommend that, as part of the necessary understanding of family dynamics within a cultural framework, clinicians include in their assessments such direct questions as "How do your family, extended family, family friends, and peers view issues concerning physical appearance, dieting behaviors, and weight?" (p. 398). Further, as part of an perspective that acknowledges the prominence of EDNOS in clinical work with EDs (Norring & Palmer, 2005), clinicians should be alert for and open to the likelihood that cultures and subcultures will create and shape the psychology and expression of EDs in ways that are "atypical" when compared to the rarer, prototypical disorders of full-blown AN and BN (Lee, 2001).

PREVENTION IMPLICATIONS
Along the same lines, studies of culture and ethnicity have three important implications for prevention science. First, prevention efforts should strive to integrate nomothetic scientific theories (e.g., social cognition, feminism) with a highly specific, contextualized analysis of "local" ethnic and cultural customs and practices, as embodied in and articulated by a variety of community stakeholders (Levine & Smolak, 2006; Piran, 2001). Second, some aspects of Black "culture" in the United States might well be incorporated with some aspects of multiethnic culture in Belize (Anderson-Fye, 2004, 2010) in order to further develop prevention values and practices that increase the following: appreciation of diversity in weight and shape; self-care and embodiment; and the importance of connection and friendship in resisting unhealthy influences from a dominant culture (see Nichter, Vukovic, & Parker, 1999; Piran, 2001). Finally, cross-cultural research strongly supports the need for further development in ethnographic and other qualitative methods.

What are the most important directions for future research?
It appears that efforts to understand cultural influences, including "sub"-cultures and cross-cultural factors, require a balance between regard for possible universal (etic) factors and for localized, particular

(emic) forces. This makes it necessary to think carefully about intersections among psychology, psychiatry, epidemiology/public health, medical anthropology, history, economics, and sociology, and therefore about the importance of the use of multiple methodologies in future research (Becker & Fay, 2006; Katzman et al., 2004). Certainly, further research combining ethnography, epidemiology, and clinical investigations is needed (López & Guarnaccia, 2000). Special attention should be paid to improving epidemiological research through careful attention to basic requirements such as sample size (statistical power), sampling methodology, case definition, sensitivity and specificity of screening methods, research ethics, and so forth (Hoek & van Hoeken, 2003; Striegel-Moore et al., 2006). In this process, as emphasized throughout this chapter, we need to do a much better job of distinguishing between ethnic and/or cultural groups. We need to cease, once and for all, perpetuating the mistake of assuming that Hispanics (for example) in the United States are surely different from African Americans, but within those ethnic distinctions the peoples (e.g., from Spain, Mexico, and Chile) so categorized are fairly homogeneous. Similarly, in cross-cultural psychology, we need to make a better effort, in terms of both theory and methodology, to capture the meaning and implications of heterogeneity in the construct of "Asian." Asians from Pakistan, Indian, China and Japan are quite diverse in terms of history, culture, religious influences, food practices, and so forth (Cummins et al., 2005).

In thinking about assessment via instruments that have been demonstrated to be reliable and valid in one culture, such as the EAT, the EDI, the SATAQ, and so forth, we need to draw upon theory and research that points to various "equivalences" that need to be empirically established before an instrument is validated and otherwise shown to be useful in one culture can be applied to research in another (Arnold & Matus, 2000). This work calls our attention to the importance of a respectful process of ecological validation that moves patiently and deliberately from an understanding of the culture, to development of a test (or modification of an existing instrument) that is meaningful in that culture, to an understanding of factors governing administration, to understanding how the scores can be interpreted and applied within that culture (Arnold & Matus, 2000). Translation and back translation are not adequate indices of cultural sensitivity.

What appears to be basic psychometrics is always, simultaneously, an exercise in construct development and validation. This fact is a special need and a special challenge in attempting to understand the relationship among culture, ethnicity, and the spectrum of disordered eating. If "body image" demands a multidimensional conceptualization and assessment, then surely we must begin to take the necessary, halting steps to clarify and assess "Modernization," "Westernization," and "Acculturation." And if we are to progress, we need to think of these constructs in terms of the ecology of person–environment transactions; we need "ecological" measures of social environments as well as measures of individual differences in the experience of and identification with ethnic and cultural influences. We can draw hope and inspiration from the considerable progress that has been made in understanding such important sociocultural constructs as ethnic identity (Phinney & Ong, 2007) and media influence (Levine & Murnen, 2009; Thompson et al., 1999).

As we have emphasized elsewhere (Levine & Murnen, 2009; Levine & Smolak, 2006; Smolak, 2009; Smolak & Levine, 1996), sociocultural factors are not a luxurious "add-on" to a biopsychiatric foundation of mental disease or disorder. These factors, including those illuminated in the study of ethnicity and multiple cultures, are critical to understanding the etiology, prevention, and treatment of all disorders, including the eating disorders. It is long past time to extend—and to normalize—our study and understanding of cultures, ethnopsychology, disorder, and health. In addition, this needs to be done in ways that take culture out of the final chapters and the appendices of our nosologies and other research-oriented books, including the forthcoming *DSM-V*. It is not just minorities and people who are "not from around here" who have a "culture" and an "ethnicity." All of us have a culture or cultures that shape the levels of risk and resilience to EDs, the nature and severity of EDs when they do occur, access to high-quality treatment, and the nature of effective treatment and support (López & Guarnaccia, 2000).

References

American Psychiatric Association (APA). (2000). Outline for cultural formulation and glossary of culture bound syndromes. In *Diagnostic and statistical manual of mental disorders* (4th ed., text revision, pp. 897–903). Washington, DC: Author.

Anderson, S., & Whitaker, R. (2009). Prevalence of obesity among US preschool children in different ethnic and racial groups. *Archives of Pediatrics and Adolescent Medicine, 163*, 343–348.

Anderson-Fye, E. (2004). A "Coca-cola" shape: Cultural change, body image, and eating disorders in San Andrés, Belize. *Culture, Medicine, and Psychiatry, 28*, 561–595.

Anderson-Fye, E. (2009). Cross-cultural issues in body image among children and adolescents. In L. Smolak & J. K. Thompson (Eds.), *Body image, eating disorders, and obesity in youth: Assessment, prevention, and treatment* (2nd ed., pp. 113–133). Washington, DC: American Psychological Association.

Anderson-Fye, E. (2010). The case of Maria: Culture and trauma in a Belizean adolescent girl. In C. Worthman, D. Schechter, & P. Plotsky (Eds.), *Formative experiences: The interaction of caregiving, culture, and developmental psychobiology* (pp. 331–334). New York: Cambridge University Press.

Anderson-Fye, E. P., & Becker, A. E. (2004). Sociocultural aspects of eating disorders. In J. K. Thompson (Ed.), *Handbook of eating disorders and obesity* (pp. 565–589). Hoboken, NJ: John Wiley & Sons.

Anthony, T. M., & Yager, J. ((2007). Cultural considerations in eating disorders. In J. Yager & P. S. Powers (Eds.), *Clinical manual of eating disorders* (pp. 387–405). Washington, DC: American Psychiatric Publishing.

Arnold, B. R., & Matus, Y. E. (2000). Test translation and cultural equivalence methodologies for use with diverse populations. In I. Cuéllar & F. A. Paniagua (Eds.), *Handbook of multicultural mental health: Assessment and treatment of diverse populations* (pp. 121–136). San Diego: Academic Press.

Becker, A. E. (2003). Eating disorders and social transition. *Primary Psychiatry, 10*, 75–79.

Becker, A. E. (2007). Culture and eating disorders classification. *International Journal of Eating Disorders, 40*(Supplement 1), 111–117.

Becker, A. E., Burwell, R. A., Gilman, S. E., Herzog, D. B., & Hamburg, P. (2002). Eating behaviors and attitudes following prolonged exposure to television among ethnic Fijian adolescent girls. *British Journal of Psychiatry, 180*, 509–514.

Becker, A. E., & Fay, K. (2006). Sociocultural issues and eating disorders. In S. Wonderlich, J. E. Mitchell, M. de Zwaan, & H. Steiger (Eds.), *Annual review of eating disorders: Part 2* (pp. 35–63). Oxon, UK: Radcliffe Publishing.

Bennett, S., & Dodge, T. (2007). Ethnic-racial differences in feelings of embarrassment associated with binge eating and fear of losing control. *International Journal of Eating Disorders, 40*, 454–459.

Bilunka, O. O., & Utermohlen, V. (2002). Internalization of Western standards of appearance, body dissatisfaction and dieting in urban educated Ukrainian females. *European Eating Disorders Review, 10*, 120–137.

Bordo, S. (1993). *Unbearable weight: Feminism, Western culture, and the body*. Berkeley: University of California Press.

British Medical Journal (n.d.). Quantifying disease in populations. Retrieved March 21, 2009, from http://www.bmj.com/epidem/epid.2.html.

Brown, T. A., Cash, T. F., & Mikulka, P. J. (1990). Attitudinal body image assessment: Factor analysis of the Body-Self Relations Questionnaire. *Journal of Personality Assessment, 55*, 135–144.

Brumberg, J. J. (1988). *Fasting girls: The emergence of anorexia nervosa as a modern disease*. Cambridge, MA: Harvard University Press.

Cachelin, F. M., Phinney, J., Schug, R. A., & Striegel-Moore, R. H. (2006). Acculturation and eating disorders in a Mexican American community sample. *Psychology of Women Quarterly, 30*, 340–347.

Cachelin, F. M., & Striegel-Moore, R. H. (2006). Help seeking and barriers to treatment in a community sample of Mexican American and European American women with eating disorders. *International Journal of Eating Disorders, 39*, 1544–161.

Canino, G., & Alegría, M. (2008). Psychiatric diagnosis—is it universal or relative to culture? *Journal of Child Psychology and Psychiatry, 49*, 237–250.

Chao, Y. M., Pisetsky, E. M., Dierker, L. C., Dohm, F-A, Rosselli, F., May, A. M., & Striegel-Moore, R. H. (2008). Ethnic differences in weight control practices among U.S. adolescents from 1995 to 2005. *International Journal of Eating Disorders, 41*, 124–133.

Connors, M. (1996). Developmental vulnerabilities for eating disorders. In L. Smolak, M. Levine, & R. H. Striegel-Moore (Eds.), *The developmental psychopathology of eating disorders: Implications for research, prevention, treatment* (pp. 285–310). Mahwah, NJ: Lawrence Erlbaum.

Crawford, M., Lee, I-C., Portnoy, G., Gurung, A., Khati, D., Jha, P., & Regmi, A. C. (2009). Objectified body consciousness in a developing country: A comparison of mothers and daughters in the US and Nepal. *Sex Roles, 60*, 174–185.

Croll, J., Neumark-Sztainer, D., Story, M., & Ireland, M. (2002). Prevalence and risk and protective factors related to disordered eating behaviors among adolescents: Relationship to gender and ethnicity. *Journal of Adolescent Health, 31*, 166–175.

Cummins, L. H., Simmons, A. M., & Zane, N. W. S. (2005). Eating disorders in Asian populations: A critique of current approaches to the study of culture, ethnicity, and eating disorders. *American Journal of Orthopsychiatry, 75*, 553–574.

Eapen, V., Mabrouk, A. A., & Bin-Othman, S. (2006). Disordered eating attitudes and symptomatology among adolescent girls in the United Arab Emirates. *Eating Behaviors, 7*, 53–60.

Franko, D. (2007). Race, ethnicity, and eating disorders: Considerations for DSM-V. *International Journal of Eating Disorders, 40*, S31–S34.

Franko, D., Becker, A., Thomas, J., & Herzog, D. (2007). Cross-ethnic differences in eating disorder symptoms and related distress. *International Journal of Eating Disorders, 40*, 156–164.

Franko, D., & Edwards-George, J. (2009). Overweight, eating behaviors, and body image in ethnically diverse youth. In L. Smolak & J. K. Thompson (Eds.), *Body image, eating disorders, and obesity in youth: Assessment, prevention, and treatment* (2nd ed., pp. 97–112). Washington DC: American Psychological Association.

Frederick, D., Forbes, G., Grigorian, K., & Jarcho, J. (2007). The UCLA Body Project I: Gender and ethnic differences in self-objectification and body satisfaction among 2,206 undergraduates. *Sex Roles, 57*, 317–327.

French, S., Story, M., Neumark-Sztainer, D., Downes, B., Resnick, M., & Blum, R. (1997). Ethnic differences in psychosocial and health behavior correlates of dieting, purging, and binge eating in a population-based sample of adolescent females. *International Journal of Eating Disorders, 22*, 315–322.

Gleaves, D. H., Brown, J. D., & Warren, C. S. (2004). The continuity/discontinuity models of eating disorders: A review of the literature and implications for assessment, treatment, and prevention. *Behavior Modification, 28*, 739–762.

Gordon, R. A. (2000). *Eating disorders: Anatomy of a social epidemic* (2nd ed.). Malden, MA: Blackwell.

Gordon, R. A. (2001). Eating disorders East and West: A culture-bound syndrome unbound. In M. Nasser, M. A. Katzman, & R. A. Gordon (Eds.), *Eating disorders and cultures in transition* (pp. 1–16). New York: Taylor & Francis.

Grabe, S., & Hyde, J. (2006). Ethnicity and body dissatisfaction among women in the United States: A meta-analysis. *Psychological Bulletin, 132*, 622–640.

Grabe, S., Ward, L., & Hyde, J. (2008). The role of the media in body image concerns among women: A meta-analysis of experimental and correlational studies. *Psychological Bulletin, 134*, 460–476.

Henrickson, H. (2006). *Understanding body experiences and the relationships among ethnic identity, acculturation, and international of the thinness ideal among Hispanic and Latina women.* Unpublished doctoral dissertation, Kent State University, Department of Psychology.

Hoek, H., van Harten, P. N., Hermans, K. M. E., Katzman, M. A., Matroos, G. E., & Susser, Z. S. (2005). The incidence of anorexia nervosa on Curaçao. *American Journal of Psychiatry, 162*, 748–752.

Hoek, H., & van Hoeken, D. (2003). Review of the prevalence and incidence of eating disorders. *International Journal of Eating Disorders, 34*, 383–396.

Hudson, J. I., Hiripi, E., Pope, H. G., Jr., & Kessler, R. C. (2007). The prevalence and correlates of eating disorders in the National Comorbidity Survey Replication. *Biological Psychiatry, 61*, 348–358.

Humphrey, T. A., & Ricciardelli, L. A. (2004). The development of eating pathology in Chinese-Australian women: Acculturation versus culture clash. *International Journal of Eating Disorders, 35*, 579–588.

Iyer, D., & Haslam, N. (2003). Body image and eating disturbance among South Asian-American women: The role of racial teasing. *International Journal of Eating Disorders, 34*, 142–147.

Jackson, S. C., Keel, P. K., & Lee, Y. H. (2006). Trans-cultural comparison of disordered eating in Korean women. *International Journal of Eating Disorders, 6*, 498–502.

Jacobi, C., Hayward, C., de Zwaan, M., Kraemer, H. C., & Agras, W. S. (2004). Coming to terms with risk factors for eating disorders: Application of risk terminology and suggestions for a general taxonomy. *Psychological Bulletin, 130*, 19–65.

Johnson, C., Crosby, R., Engel, S., Mitchell, J., Powers, P., Wittrock, D., & Wonderlich, S. (2004). Gender, ethnicity, self-esteem, and disordered eating among college athletes. *Eating Behaviors, 5*, 147–156.

Jones, D. (2009, April). *Appearance magazine investment among Asian-American adolescent girls.* Presented at the Biennial Meeting of the Society for Research in Child Development, Denver CO.

Jung, J., & Lee, S-H. (2006). Cross-cultural comparisons of appearance self-schema, body image, self-esteem, and dieting behavior between Korean and U.S. women. *Family and Consumer Sciences Research Journal, 34*, 350–365.

Kaluski, D. N., Natamba, B. K., Goldsmith, R., Shimony, T., & Berry, E. M. (2008). Determinants of disordered eating behaviors among Israeli adolescent girls. *Eating Disorders: The Journal of Treatment & Prevention, 16*, 146–159.

Katzman, M. A., Hermans, K. M. E., van Hoeken, D., & Hoek, H. W. (2004). Not your "typical island woman": Anorexia nervosa is reported only in subcultures in Curaçao. *Culture, Medicine, and Psychiatry, 28*, 463–492.

Keel, P. K., & Klump, K. L. (2003). Are eating disorders culture-bound syndromes? Implications for conceptualizing their etiology. *Psychological Bulletin, 129*, 747–769.

Keski-Rahkonen, A., Hoek, H. W., Susser, E. Z., Linna, M. S., & Sihvola, E., Raevuori, A., et al. (2007). Epidemiology and course of anorexia nervosa in the community. *American Journal of Psychiatry, 164,* 1259–1265.

Kleinman, A. (1977). Depression, somatization, and the "new cross-cultural psychiatry." *Social Science and Medicine, 11,* 3–10.

Lake, A., Staiger, P., & Glowinski, H. (2000). Effect of Western culture on women's attitudes to eating and perceptions of body shape. *International Journal of Eating Disorders, 27,* 83–89.

Larkin, J., & Rice, C. (2005). Beyond "healthy eating" and "healthy weights": Harassment and the health curriculum in middle schools. *Body Image,* 219–232.

Lee, S. (2001). Fat phobia in anorexia nervosa: Whose obsession is it? In M. Nasser, M. A. Katzman, & R. A. Gordon (Eds.), *Eating disorders and cultures in transition* (pp. 40–54). New York: Taylor & Francis.

Lee, S. & Lee, A. M. (2000). Disordered eating in three communities of China: A comparative study of female high school students in Honk Kong, Shenzhen, and rural Hunan. *International Journal of Eating Disorders, 27,* 317–327.

Levine, M. P., & Murnen, S. K. (2009). "Everybody knows that mass media are/are not [pick one] a cause of eating disorders": A critical review of evidence for a causal link between media, negative body image, and disordered eating in females. *Journal of Social & Clinical Psychology, 28,* 9–42.

Levine, M. P., & Smolak, L. (2006). *The prevention of eating problems and eating disorders: Theory, research, and practice.* Mahwah, NJ: Lawrence Erlbaum.

López, S. R., & Guarnaccia, P. J. (2000). Cultural psychopathology: Uncovering the social world of mental illness. *Annual Review of Psychology, 51,* 571–598.

Machado, P. P. P., Machado, B. C., Gonçalves, S., & Hoek, H. W. (2007). The prevalence of Eating Disorders Not Otherwise Specified. *International Journal of Eating Disorders, 40,* 212–217.

Makino, M., Tsuboi, K., & Dennerstein, L. (2004). Prevalence of eating disorders: A comparison of Western and non-Western countries. *Medscape General Medicine, 6*(3), 49. Retrieved March 4, 2009, from http://www.pubmedcentral.nih.gov/articlerender.fcgi?artid=1435625.

Markus, H. R., & Kitayama, S. (1991). Culture and the self: Implications for cognition, emotion, and motivation. *Psychological Review, 98,* 224–253.

Matusmoto, D., & Juang, L.(2004). *Culture and psychology* (3rd ed.). Belmont, CA: Thomson/Wadsworth.

Menzel, J. E., Mayhew, L. L., Thompson, J. K., & Brannick, M. T. (2009). *Teasing, body dissatisfaction, and restrictive eating: A meta-analysis.* Unpublished manuscript, University of South Florida, Tampa.

Miller, K., Gleaves, D., Hirsch, T., Green, B., Snow, A., & Corbett, C. (2000). Comparisons of body image dimensions by race/ethnicity and gender in a university population. *International Journal of Eating Disorders, 27,* 310–316.

Nasser, M. (1997). *Culture and weight consciousness.* London: Routledge.

Nasser, M., & Katzman, M. A. (1999). Eating disorders: Transcultural perspectives inform prevention. In N. Piran, M. P. Levine, & C. Steiner-Adair (Eds.), *Preventing eating disorders: A handbook of interventions and special challenges* (pp. 26–43). Philadelphia: Brunner/Mazel.

Nasser, M., Katzman, M. A., & Gordon, R. A. (Eds.). (2001). *Eating disorders and cultures in transition.* New York: Taylor & Francis.

Neumark-Sztainer, D., Croll, J., Story, M. Hannan, P., French, S., & Perry, C. (2002). Ethnic/racial differences in weight-related concerns and behaviors among adolescent girls and boys: Findings from Project EAT. *Journal of Psychosomatic Research, 53,* 963–974.

Nicdao, E., Hong, S., & Takeuchi, D. (2007). Prevalence and correlates of eating disorders among Asian Americans: Results from the National Latino and Asian American Study. *International Journal of Eating Disorders, 40,* S22–S26.

Nichter, M., Vukovic, N., & Parker, S. (1999). The Looking Good, Feeling Good Program: A multi-ethnic intervention for healthy body image, nutrition, and physical activity. In N. Piran, M. Levine, & C. Steiner-Adair (Eds.), *Preventing eating disorders: A handbook of interventions and special challenges* (pp. 175–193). Philadelphia PA: Brunner/Mazel.

Norring, C., & Palmer, B. (Eds.). (2005). *EDNOS—Eating disorders not otherwise specified: Scientific and clinical perspectives on the other eating disorders.* New York: Psychology Press.

Ogden, J., & Elder, C. (1998). The role of family status and ethnic group on body image and eating behavior. *International Journal of Eating Disorders, 23,* 309–315.

Paniagua, F. A. (2000). Culture-bound syndromes, cultural variations, and psychopathology. In I. Cuéllar & F. A. Paniagua (Eds.), *Handbook of multicultural mental health: Assessment and treatment of diverse populations* (pp. 139–169). San Diego: Academic Press.

Perez, D., Fortuna, L, & Alegría, M. (2008). Prevalence and correlates of everyday discrimination among U.S. Latinos. *Journal of Community Psychology, 36,* 421–433.

Perez, M., & Joiner, T. (2003). Body image dissatisfaction and disordered eating in Black and White women. *International Journal of Eating Disorders, 33,* 342–350.

Perez, M., Voelz, Z., Pettit, J., & Joiner, T. (2002). The role of acculturative stress and body dissatisfaction in predicting bulimic symptomatology across ethnic groups. *International Journal of Eating Disorders, 31,* 442–454.

Phinney, J. S., & Ong, A. D. (2007). Ethnic identity development in immigrant families. In J. E. Lansford, K. Deater-Deckard, & M. H. Bornstein (Eds.), *Immigrant families in contemporary society* (pp. 51–68). New York: Guilford Press.

Pike, K. M., & Borovoy, A. (2004). The rise of eating disorders in Japan: Issues of culture and limitations of the model of "Westernization". *Culture, Medicine, and Psychiatry, 28,* 493–531.

Piran, N. (2001). Re-inhabiting the body from the inside out: Girls transform their school environment. In D. L. Tolman & M. Brydon-Miller (Eds.), *From subjects to subjectivities: A handbook of interpretive and participatory methods* (pp. 218–238). New York: NYU Press.

Piran, N., Antoniou, M., Legge, R., McCance, N., Mizevich, J., Pesley, E., & Ross, E. (2006). *On girls' disembodiment: The complex tyranny of the 'ideal girl'.* Presented at Women, health, and education CASWE 6th Bi-annual international institute proceedings, St John's Newfoundland. Available for download at www.csse.ca/CASWE/Institute/Institute.htm.

Podar, I., & Allik, J. (2009). A cross-cultural comparison of the Eating Disorders Inventory. *International Journal of Eating Disorders, 42,* 346–355.

Regan, P., & Cachelin, F. (2006). Binge eating and purging in a multi-ethnic community sample. *International Journal of Eating Disorders, 39,* 523–526.

Roberts, A., Cash, T., Feingold, A., & Johnson, B. (2006). Are Black-White differences in females' body dissatisfaction decreasing? A meta-analytic review. *Journal of Counseling and Clinical Psychology, 74*, 1121–1131.

Robinson, T. N., Killen, J. D., Litt, I. F., Hammer, L. D., Wilson, D. M., Hayden, K. F., et al. (1996). Ethnicity and body dissatisfaction: Are Latina and Asian girls at increased risk for eating disorders? *Journal of Adolescent Health, 19*, 384–393.

Sam, D. L. (2006). Acculturation and health. In D. L. Sam & J. W. Berry (Eds.), *The Cambridge handbook of acculturation psychology* (pp. 452–468). Cambridge, UK: Cambridge University Press.

Schooler, D. (2008). Real women have curves: A longitudinal investigation of TV and the body image development of Latina Americans. *Journal of Adolescent Research, 23*, 132–153.

Schooler, D., Ward, L., Merriwether, A., & Caruthers, A. (2004). Who's that girl: Television's role in the body image development of young White and Black women. *Psychology of Women Quarterly, 28*, 38–47.

Silverstein, B., & Perlick, D. (1995). *The cost of competence: Why inequality causes depression, eating disorders, and illness in women.* New York: Oxford University Press.

Smolak, L. (2009). Risk factors in the development of body image, eating problems, and obesity. In L. Smolak & J. K. Thompson (Eds.), *Body image, eating disorders, and obesity in youth: Assessment, prevention, and treatment* (2nd ed., pp. 135–155). Washington, DC: American Psychological Association.

Smolak, L., & Levine, M. P. (1996). Developmental transitions at middle school and college. In L. Smolak, M. P. Levine, & R. H. Striegel-Moore (Eds.), *The developmental psychopathology of eating disorders: Implications for research, prevention, and treatment* (pp. 207–233). Hillsdale, NJ: Lawrence Erlbaum.

Smolak, L., & Murnen, S. (2004). A feminist approach to eating disorders. In J. K. Thompson (Ed.), *Handbook of eating disorders and obesity* (pp. 590–605). Hoboken, NJ: John Wiley & Sons.

Smolak, L., & Murnen, S. (2008). Feminism, evolution, and physical attractiveness. In A. Furman & V. Swami (Eds.), *The body beautiful: Evolutionary and sociocultural perspectives* (pp. 590–606). London: Palgrave Macmillan.

Smolak, L., & Murnen, S. (in press). The sexualization of girls and women as antecedents to objectification. In R. Calogero & J. K. Thompson (Eds.), *The objectification of women: Innovative directions in research and practice.* Washington, DC: American Psychological Association.

Smolak, L., & Piran, N. (in press). Gender and the prevention of eating disorders. In G. McVey et al. (Eds.), *Improving the prevention of eating-related disorders: Collaborative research, advocacy, and policy change.* Toronto.

Smolak, L., & Striegel-Moore, R. (2001). The myth of the golden girl: Ethnicity and eating disorders. In R. Striegel-Moore & L. Smolak (Eds.), *Eating disorders: New directions for research and practice* (pp. 111–132). Washington, DC: American Psychological Association.

Smolak, L., & Thompson, J. K. (Eds.). (2009). *Body image, eating disorders, and obesity in youth: Assessment, prevention, and treatment* (2nd ed.). Washington, DC: American Psychological Association.

Stice, E. (2002). Risk and maintenance factors for eating pathology: A meta-analytic review. *Psychological Bulletin, 128*, 825–848.

Stice, E., & Bearman, S. K. (2001). Body image and eating disturbances prospectively predict growth in depressive symptoms in adolescent girls: A growth curve analysis. *Developmental Psychology, 37*, 597–607.

Striegel-Moore, R., Dohm, F., Kraemer, H., Taylor, C. B., Daniels, S., Crawford, P., & Schreiber, G. (2003). Eating disorders in white and black women. *American Journal of Psychiatry, 160*, 1326–1331.

Striegel-Moore, R. H., Franko, D. L., & Ach, E. L. (2006). Epidemiology of eating disorders: An update. In S. Wonderlich, J. E. Mitchell, M. de Zwaan, & H. Steiger (Eds.), *Annual review of eating disorders: Part 2* (pp. 65–80). Oxon, UK: Radcliffe Publishing.

Swartz, L. (2001). Commentary [on C. P. Szabo & D. le Grange, "Eating disorders and the politics of identity: The South African experience." In M. Nasser, M. A. Katzman, & R. A. Gordon (Eds.), *Eating disorders and cultures in transition* (pp. 34–36). New York: Taylor & Francis.

Szabo, C. P., & le Grange, D. (2001). Eating disorders and the politics of identity: The South African experience. In M. Nasser, M. A. Katzman, & R. A. Gordon (Eds.), *Eating disorders and cultures in transition* (pp. 24–33). New York: Taylor & Francis.

Taylor, J. Y., Caldwell, C. H., Baser, R. E., Faison, N., & Jackson, J. S. (2007). Prevalence of eating disorders among Blacks in the National Survey of American Life. *International Journal of Eating Disorders, 40*, S10–S14.

Thompson, J. K., & Cafri, G. (Eds.). (2007). *The muscular ideal: Psychological, social, and medical perspectives.* Washington, DC: American Psychological Association.

Thompson, J. K., Heinberg, L. J., Altabe, M., & Tantleff-Dunn, S. (1999). *Exacting beauty: Theory, assessment, and treatment of body image disturbance.* Washington, DC: American Psychological Association.

Vandereycken, W., & Van Deth, R. (1994). *From fasting saints to anorexic girls: The history of self-starvation.* New York: NYU Press.

van Son, G E., van Hoeken, D., Bartelds, A. I. M., van Further, E. F., & Hoek, H. W. (2006). Time trends in the incidence of eating disorders: A primary care study in the Netherlands. *International Journal of Eating Disorders, 39*, 565–569.

Wade, T. D., Bergin, J. L., Tiggemann, M., Bulik, C. M., & Fairburn, C. G. (2006). Prevalence and long-term course of lifetime eating disorders in an adult Australian twin cohort. *Australian and New Zealand Journal of Psychiatry, 40*, 121–148.

Wertheim, E. H., Paxton, S. J., & Blaney, S. (2009). Body image in girls. In L. Smolak & J. K. Thompson (Eds.), *Body image, eating disorders, and obesity in youth: Assessment, prevention, and treatment* (2nd ed., pp. 47–76). Washington, DC: American Psychological Association.

White, M., & Grilo, C. (2005). Ethnic differences in the prediction of eating and body image disturbances among female adolescent psychiatric inpatients. *International Journal of Eating Disorders, 38*, 78–84.

Wildes, J., Emery, R., & Simons, A. (2001). The roles and ethnicity and culture in the development of eating disturbance and body dissatisfaction: A meta-analytic review. *Clinical Psychology Review, 21*, 521–551.

World Health Organization (WHO). (1994). *International statistical classification of diseases and related health problems* (10th ed., version for 2007). Geneva: Author. Retrieved April 20, 2009, from http://www.who.int/classifications/apps/icd/icd10online/.

World Health Organization (WHO). (2003). *Caring for children and adolescents with mental disorders: Setting WHO directions.* Geneva: Author. Retrieved March 1, 2009, from www.who.int/mental_health/media/en/785.pdf.

PART 3

Assessment and Comorbidities of the Eating Disorders

Psychological Assessment of the Eating Disorders

Drew A. Anderson *and* Andrea D. Murray

Abstract

The purpose of this chapter is to describe a process, based on a functional approach, that will help assessors to develop assessments for eating disorders and eating-related problems. This approach takes into account both theoretical and practical concerns, and allows assessors to individualize their assessments depending on their particular needs. This process starts with broad considerations about the context in which the assessment is to be given and ends with the choice of specific instruments to be used.

Keywords: assessment, behavioral assessment, eating disorders, functional, interview, self-report

Introduction

Discussions of assessment are often limited to reviews of particular instruments and their psychometric properties, which reduces the topic to its components. Assessment, however, is a process, and there is no one assessment instrument or test battery that is useful or appropriate in all circumstances. Instead, any choices concerning specific instruments are secondary to the function of the assessment. The purpose of this chapter is to describe a process, based on a functional approach, that will help assessors to individualize their own assessments based on their particular circumstances, taking into account both theoretical and practical concerns. Thinking in terms of the function or goals of the assessment frees the assessor to consider how to best go about achieving those goals. In this chapter we focus on assessment within the broad context of psychotherapy, but the process is applicable to other contexts.

This process starts with broad considerations about the context in which the assessment is to be given and ends with the choice of specific instruments. The steps can be summarized by the use of a few key questions: "where," "why," "what," and "how."

Step One—"Where": Understanding the Context of the Assessment

The first step is in this process is to take into account the broad context in which the assessment occurs. Context can be thought of as the "where" of assessment. Specifically, under what circumstances is the assessment taking place? For instance, is the assessment taking place in a psychiatric treatment facility as part of regular clinical practice, or is it part of a controlled research trial? This broad context shapes the larger goals of the entire assessment process. As an example, if the assessment is being conducted as part of a controlled clinical trial the assessor often will have the opportunity to use more lengthy and time-intensive instruments, including semistructured interviews, and to include more elaborate assessment batteries than he or she might do in a purely clinical setting. There are also discrete dependent variables specified in the research design that must be assessed, which will dictate to some degree the exact measures that will be used. Further, the psychometric properties of the instruments themselves will be of paramount importance. Conversely, psychologists in private practice are often faced with a number of limitations in their ability to conduct elaborate assessments, including time constraints and difficulties in obtaining reimbursement from 3rd party payers (Eisman et al., 2000; Turchik, Karpenko, Hammers, & McNamara, 2007). Thus, the assessor might not want to limit him- or herself to a semistructured interview devoted entirely to eating disorder symptomatology, but instead conduct an unstructured clinical interview that covers a broader range of topics and supports their diagnostic and treatment recommendations with a few easy to score but psychometrically sound instruments that the patient can fill out in the waiting room. (For further suggestions, see Turchik et al. (2007)). As another example, school nurses are operating in a context in which they generally do not need to conduct elaborate assessments. They may have only the need, or the time, to ask a few brief screening questions of an adolescent they suspect of an eating disorder (ED) to refer the individual for further evaluation or treatment.

The notion of context is intimately connected with the function or purpose of the assessment. The second step in designing an assessment is to examine the assessment's intended function.

Step Two—"Why:" Determining the Function of the Assessment

The function of an assessment is the "why" of the assessment process. The assessor needs to determine why exactly the assessment is being conducted.

As mentioned previously, the context of the assessment (e.g., an intake at an inpatient psychiatric facility, an outpatient treatment session, or a forensic evaluation) often dictates the function of the assessment. However, an assessment can have a number of potential functions, and the function of the assessment will dictate, in large part, the assessment measures and procedures that will be used. For example, it makes little sense to use a screening measure for EDs at an ED inpatient treatment program, since presumably the individual being assessed has already acknowledged eating-related pathology. In that context, the function of the assessment would more likely be for diagnosis and treatment planning, and a clinical interview and longer self-report instruments would be more appropriate instruments. Conversely, in the example of the school nurse given previously, in the context of a

school setting the function of the assessment would be for screening purposes. Thus, a brief screening instrument would be a more appropriate choice compared to longer and more elaborate clinical interviews. The function of the assessment also helps dictate how often assessments should occur. For example, if the function of an assessment is to track treatment progress, then periodic or even weekly administration of a brief self-report instrument would be indicated. However, in the context of screening such a schedule would clearly be excessive.

Although there are a number of different potential functions for an assessment, they can be grouped into a few common categories, including screening, diagnosis, treatment planning, and outcome. These functions can overlap; for example, a suicide screening can be embedded in a larger diagnostic interview, but we will discuss them separately.

Screening

Screening tests are quick, easy to use, and inexpensive procedures given to an entire relevant population to determine which apparently healthy individuals are actually at high risk for a particular disorder (Evans, Galen, & Britt, 2005). It is beyond the scope of this chapter to detail the statistical and mathematical principles involved in determining the efficacy of screening tests; Grimes and Schultz (2002) provide a concise overview of these issues. However, we should note one issue that is relevant for the evaluation of eating disorders screenings. The issue is that the positive predictive value (PPV) of a screening test (i.e., the proportion of individuals with a positive test who actually have the condition) varies with the prevalence rate of the condition, so even good screening tests can have poor PPV when applied to low-prevalence populations (Grimes & Schultz, 2002; Nielsen & Lang, 1999). Thus, because the rate of eating disorders is relatively low in the general population, the incidence of false positives will be relatively high. As an example, in one study of the SCOFF (Morgan, Reid, & Lacey, 2000; Parker, Lyons, & Bonner, 2005), a screening test for EDs discussed later in this chapter, had a positive predictive value of 24.4% (Luck et al., 2002). In this study, only 11 of the 45 cases in the study identified by the SCOFF actually had an ED, and the authors noted the low prevalence of EDs in their sample as an explanation for this finding. A false-positive result on a screening test can lead to potential harm (Grimes & Schultz, 2002), so individuals using screening tests for EDs should be aware of this fact.

Diagnosis

Generally, issues of diagnosis are subsumed under the function of treatment planning and outcome, discussed later in this chapter. There are some instances, however, when an assessor simply needs to verify whether or not an individual meets diagnostic criteria for an eating disorder. For example, third-party payers may require formal documentation of a diagnosis in order to reimburse for services. Also, some therapies minimize the necessity of a specific diagnosis for treatment, so diagnosis is not always a necessary part of an assessment for treatment planning purposes (e.g., Fairburn, 2008). As such, diagnosis does represent a distinct function of the assessment process.

Treatment Planning and Outcome

Treatment planning and outcome represents the broadest function for the assessment of eating disorders. This includes such things as making treatment decisions (e.g., which treatment will work best for this individual?) and evaluating treatment outcome (e.g., did this patient improve, and if so by how much?) This type of assessment can be done more or less frequently, depending on the exact circumstances of the assessment. For example, some instruments may be used only at the beginning and end of treatment, while others may be used more frequently to track treatment progress more closely.

Once the assessor determines the context and function of the assessment, he or she must determine the exact domains or constructs that are relevant to the assessment question. Determining this is the next step in the assessment process.

Step 3—"What:" Determining the Domains or Constructs of Interest

Determining the domains or constructs to be assessed can be thought of as the "what" of assessment. In this step the assessor asks what specific thoughts, attitudes, and behaviors should be assessed. For screening and diagnosis this decision can be fairly straightforward. As mentioned previously, screening measures generally ask broadly about the most common signs and symptoms of eating disorders (e.g., underweight status, compensatory behavior, binge eating, and body image disturbance). For diagnosis, the domains of interest will be the diagnostic criteria themselves. The identification of domains of interest for treatment planning and evaluation of outcome, however, can be much more complicated.

An assessment for treatment planning and outcome typically includes many of the same domains of interest that would be evaluated in screening or diagnosis functions. It goes further, however, in that it allows for the assessor to take into account process or change variables as well as more theoretical considerations about the EDs and associated psychopathology. As part of this process, the assessor should reflect on the criteria for treatment success that will be used. Some questions that are useful at this stage of the process include: What would have to change for this person to be considered to be "cured" or "improved?" What would indicate that the individual is not improving? What would be desirable but not essential for treatment to be considered a success? The answers to these questions involve considerations of the theoretical assumptions underlying treatment, discussed in the next section.

Underlying Theoretical Assumptions

It is extremely important to pay attention to the theoretical basis of the therapeutic approach being used when determining domains of interest. Therapy and therapeutic techniques do not come out of a vacuum; they are developed from theoretical assumptions about the nature of personality, psychopathology, and principles of effective change (Kanfer & Schefft, 1988; Pachankis & Goldfried, 2007). These assumptions will influence what domains will be considered to be of interest. For example, the original cognitive–behavioral account of bulimia nervosa posits that five core symptom domains are responsible for the maintenance of the disorder: low self-esteem; overconcern with body weight and shape; extreme dietary restraint; binge eating; and purgative behavior (Fairburn, Marcus, & Wilson, 1993). According to this model, an individual with bulimia nervosa being treated with cognitive behavioral therapy (CBT) should show improvement in all five of these domains to be considered a treatment success, with reductions in overconcern with body weight and shape being particularly important for long-term success (Fairburn, 1997a; Fairburn et al., 1993). Accordingly, if an individual with bulimia nervosa is being treated within a traditional CBT framework, measurement of these domains will be an essential part of the assessment of treatment progress and outcome (Anderson & Maloney, 2001). Further, the newest revision of CBT for EDs, called enhanced CBT (CBT-E), hypothesizes that additional mechanisms may be operating in some individuals with eating disorders (Fairburn, 2008; Fairburn, Cooper, & Shafran, 2003).

Thus, an assessor evaluating patients being treated with CBT-E may have to add instruments over and above what might be necessary in a traditional CBT evaluation, depending on a given individual's case formulation. As another example, interpersonal psychotherapy (IPT) posits that interpersonal problems underlie the maintenance of bulimia nervosa (Fairburn, 1997b). As such, if an individual with bulimia nervosa is being treated from within an IPT framework, measurement of interpersonal domains will be an essential part of the assessment of treatment progress and outcome.

As can be seen from these examples, some of the domains identified as essential from one therapeutic perspective might not be considered essential or even relevant from another therapeutic perspective, and even a single therapeutic modality may have variations depending on individual patient characteristics. Assessment should reflect these differences, and all the essential domains thought to be necessary for change in a given model of psychotherapy should be measured as part of the assessment process.

Secondary Domains

One must also consider not only the core domains of interest, however, but also other secondary domains that might impact the onset and course of eating disorders as well. While it is not possible to evaluate every possible factor that might be related to the EDs, certain disorders and life events have consistently been shown to be associated with eating-related problems. For example, some mood disorders, anxiety disorders, substance use disorders, Axis II disorders, and sexual abuse have repeatedly been found to be associated with EDs, and have also been hypothesized to play a causal role in their development (Cassin & von Ranson, 2005; Fichter, Quadflieg, & Hedlund, 2006, 2008; O'Brien & Vincent, 2003; Sihvola et al., 2009). Further, these comorbidities may be associated with poorer treatment outcome for EDs (Fichter et al., 2006, 2008; Keel et al., 2003).

Thresholds for Recovery

The assessor should also consider the threshold at which a change in a given domain could be considered an indicator of success. This issue can become quite difficult when evaluating EDs. For example, body image disturbance is both a common symptom and one of the diagnostic criteria for anorexia and bulimia nervosa. However, some degree of body dissatisfaction is normative in the general population

(Rodin, Silberstein, & Striegel-Moore, 1985). Given this "normative discontent," should an individual being treated for an ED have to demonstrate a total absence of body dissatisfaction to be considered a treatment success? Treatment studies suggest that this may be unlikely (Lundgren, Danoff-Burg, & Anderson, 2004), and some have argued that a return to normal functioning is an unnecessarily stringent criterion for success (Wise, 2004). Is it sufficient then to merely require them to reach a level of "normative discontent?" While more achievable, some would suggest that this represents a less-than-ideal outcome. Further, some treatment approaches do not believe any reduction in body dissatisfaction is necessary for treatment success (e.g., Acceptance and Commitment Therapy; Heffner & Eifert, 2004) and thus would see the issue as irrelevant. As another example, if an individual with bulimia nervosa, purging subtype improves from daily bulimic episodes to the point that she is only purging once a month on average, should this be considered a treatment success? These examples illustrate the complexities the assessor can face in determining thresholds for change.

There are, however, a number of conceptual and mathematical strategies for determining clinically significant change (Follette & Callaghan, 2001; Jacobson, Roberts, Berns, & McGlinchey, 1999). Perhaps the most widely known strategy for determining clinically significant change was proposed by Jacobson and colleagues (Jacobson et al., 1999; Jacobson, Follette, & Revenstorf, 1984; Jacobson & Truax, 1991). In this methodology, two criteria are necessary for clinically significant change. The first criterion is that the dependent measure showed real change (i.e., the change was not due simply to measurement error). Jacobson and colleagues proposed the reliable change index (RCI) as a statistical approach to determine if the change observed reflects more than the fluctuations of an imprecise measuring instrument (Jacobson & Truax, 1991). The RCI was originally designed to be conducted on individual-level data, but has been adapted for use on group-level data (Jacobson & Truax, 1991). The second criterion is that by the end of treatment clients should end up in a range that renders them indistinguishable from those in the normal population; a number of different cutoff points for determining when this occurs have been developed, depending on the information available and the particular needs of the researcher or clinician (Jacobson et al., 1999). Jacobson and colleagues (1999) summarized the possible outcomes using this approach. They note that patients can be considered "recovered" if the magnitude of change is statistically reliable and the client ends up within normal limits on the variable of interest or "improved but not recovered" if the patient shows statistically reliable change but ends treatment still somewhat dysfunctional. If the client ends up within normal limits by the end of therapy but the magnitude of change is not statistically reliable, then the clinical significance of the change cannot be determined. Finally, if the patient shows neither statistically reliable change nor a recovery to within normal limits, the patient would be considered "not recovered," and if he or she showed statistically reliable change in the direction opposite of recovery he or she would be classified as "deteriorated."

A similar procedure for evaluating the clinical significance of change at the group level has been developed by Kendall and colleagues (Kendall & Grove, 1988; Kendall, Marrs-Garcia, Nath, & Sheldrick, 1999), which compares data on treated individuals with that of normative individuals. A value of one standard deviation around the normative mean has often been used as the definition of clinically equivalent, although other cutoff points may be used (Kendall et al., 1999; Sheldrick, Kendall, & Heimberg, 2001; Wise, 2004).

These procedures may not be necessary for all individuals. In particular, clinicians may not have the time to calculate a RCI on every patient. Also, the use of many of these procedures requires that norms be available for the assessment instrument being used, which is not always the case. Nevertheless, these procedures provide theoretical frameworks by which assessors can help determine what constitutes "improved" or "recovered" in patients being assessed. In any event, even if these procedures are not used the assessor should think deeply about these issues when assessing treatment outcome.

Step 4—"How:" Determining the Specific Instruments to Be Used in the Assessment

Once the assessor has covered the where, why and what questions, he or she needs to answer "how." Specifically, how should he or she assess the domains identified in the previous step? One important issue to consider is the format or formats of the assessment instruments that will be used.

Interviews have traditionally been seen as the method of choice for assessment of eating-related problems, particularly when evaluating more complex constructs such as binge eating (Fairburn & Beglin, 1990, 1994). Individuals typically report

lower levels of eating-related pathology when responding via interview versus questionnaire (Anderson & Maloney, 2001; Fairburn & Beglin, 1990, 1994; French et al., 1998; Keel, Crow, Davis, & Mitchell, 2002), and this has been interpreted as evidence that individuals over-endorse symptoms on questionnaires (Fairburn & Beglin, 1990, 1994; French et al., 1998). However, a growing body of research has questioned this assumption, suggesting that individuals may respond more honestly if they feel more anonymous or do not have to directly face the person conducting the assessment. This has been shown in both clinical (Keel et al., 2002) and laboratory (Anderson, Simmons, Milnes, & Earleywine, 2007; French et al., 1998; Perry et al., 2002; Lavender & Anderson, 2008, 2009) contexts. This effect presumably occurs because eating-related pathology such as binge eating and purging are shameful and embarrassing (Hamburg, Herzog, Brotman, & Staisor, 1989; Havaki, Friedman, & Brownell, 2002; Vitousek, Daly, & Heiser, 1991) and it is therefore easier to not have to admit to these behaviors in a face-to-face setting. Thus, it is currently not clear which method of assessment produces the most valid assessment of eating-related problems. Until this issue is resolved, we suggest that assessors use both interview and self-report questionnaires in the assessment process.

A considerable number of instruments have been developed to assess eating-related constructs; in fact, entire books have been devoted to the topic (e.g., Allison, 2009; Mitchell & Peterson, 2005; Williamson, 1990). It is beyond the scope of this chapter to review all of these measures or to discuss their psychometrics in great detail. It is also beyond the scope of this chapter to discuss basic issues in psychometrics (for a brief review of psychometric issues, see Anderson & Paulosky, 2004a). We only note in passing that data collected via self-report, as is commonly-done in adult assessment, is subject to substantial error and bias, which can affect both reliability and validity (Korotitsch & Nelson-Gray, 1999). We will, however, review some of the measures specifically developed to assess eating-related pathology that are widely used in the literature or that have good psychometric properties. It is important to keep in mind, however, that assessors will likely need to supplement these measures based on their specific needs determined in the earlier other steps of the assessment process. Indeed, the use of multiple measures is common among both clinicians and researchers (Anderson & Paulosky, 2004b; Williamson, Anderson, & Gleaves, 1996).

Interview

Interviews are generally more appropriate for diagnosis, treatment planning, and evaluation than they are for screening. In the appropriate context, however, they are arguably the most important means of data collection in the entire assessment process (Groth-Marnat, 1990). Interviews vary on their degree of structure. Unstructured interviews are more flexible and can be easily adapted to a particular client and his or her unique circumstances, but they usually have poor or unknown psychometric properties (Groth-Marnat, 1990; Korotitsch & Nelson-Gray, 1999). Unstructured interviews for eating-related pathology are extremely common in clinical practice (Anderson & Paulosky, 2004b); Crowther and Sherwood (1997) and Peterson (2005) provide helpful guidelines for conducting such an interview. Semistructured interviews are more commonly used in research as opposed to clinical settings (Anderson & Paulosky, 2004a, 2004b). Although less flexible than unstructured interviews, they have more psychometric precision, and many have norms available (Groth-Marnat, 1990; Korotitsch & Nelson-Gray, 1999).

The Eating Disorder Examination (EDE; Fairburn & Cooper, 1993; Fairburn, Cooper, & O'Connor, 2008) is probably the most highly-regarded semistructured interview specific to eating-related pathology. The EDE has four subscales: Restraint, Eating Concern, Weight Concern, and Shape Concern. The most recent version, the EDE 16.0D (Fairburn et al., 2008) is a revision of the widely-used EDE 12.0D (Fairburn & Cooper, 1993). Although the 16.0D has been changed somewhat, it is still compatible with the older EDE 12.0D (Fairburn et al., 2008). The EDE 12.0D has demonstrated adequate reliability and validity, and norms are available (Anderson, De Young, & Walker, 2009; Fairburn & Cooper, 1993; Grilo, 2005). While psychometric data on the newly-released EDE 16.0D has not yet been published, given its similarity to its predecessor it should also demonstrate good psychometric properties.

The EDE is unique in that the expert interviewer, not the interviewee, decides whether a particular eating episode is a binge or not. This is particularly helpful because the *DSM-IV-TR* (American Psychiatric Association [APA], 2000) requires that a binge be objectively large and involve a loss of control, but many laypersons do not use this definition when describing an eating episode as a binge (Beglin & Fairburn, 1992; Johnson, Boutelle, Torgrud, Davig, & Turner, 2000; Telch, Pratt, & Niego, 1998).

The EDE does have some shortcomings, however. In particular, the authors note that training is essential if the EDE 16.0D is being used for research purposes (Fairburn et al., 2008), but such training does not appear to be widely available. (The training schedule, as well as a copy of the EDE 16.0D itself, is available at http://www.psychiatry.ox.ac.uk/research/researchunits/credo). A second concern is that the EDE can also be too lengthy to complete in some contexts. Nevertheless, the EDE remains a valuable tool for the assessment of eating-related pathology.

Other interviews for assessing eating-related pathology for diagnosis and treatment evaluation and planning are available, although none are as popular as the EDE. Reviews of these instruments can be found elsewhere (Anderson et al., 2009; Grilo, 2005).

The SCOFF (Morgan, Reid, & Lacey, 2000; Parker, Lyons, & Bonner, 2005), a simple, easy-to-remember instrument for EDs, can be administered orally in a brief interview format. It contains only five items and is appropriate for use by nonspecialists such as general medical practitioners. It has been shown to have good psychometric properties, although there is some disagreement about the optimal cutoff score to indicate probable eating pathology (Siervo, Boschi, Papa, Bellini, & Falconi, 2005).

The ESP (Cotton, Ball, & Robinson, 2003) is a four-item instrument developed for ED screening purposes that can be delivered orally. Like the SCOFF, it has good psychometric properties and can be delivered by nonspecialists (Cotton et al., 2003).

Self-Report Questionnaires

Self-report questionnaires can be used for every assessment-related function, from screening to diagnosis to treatment planning and evaluation. It is beyond the scope of this chapter to review all the available self-report questionnaires for EDs; readers should consult Allison (2009) and Peterson and Mitchell (2005) for more detailed discussions of a number of well-validated instruments. We do, however, provide some examples of measures that are particularly suited to each assessment function, with a focus on measures specifically designed to measure eating-related pathology.

SCREENING

For screening, the SCOFF (Morgan et al., 2000; Parker et al., 2005) has been administered in written format. Also, the Eating Attitudes Test (EAT), one of the most commonly used self-report questionnaires for eating-related pathology (Anderson & Paulosky, 2004a, 2004b), was designed to be used as a screening measure. It is available in 40-item (EAT-40; Garner & Garfinkel, 1979) and 26-item (EAT-26; Garner, Olmsted, Bohr, & Garfinkel, 1982) versions. Total scores above 30 on the EAT-40 and 20 on the EAT-26 indicate probable eating-related pathology (Garfinkel & Newman, 2001). Both versions have good psychometric properties (Anderson et al., 2009; Garfinkel & Newman, 2001).

DIAGNOSIS

One self-report questionnaire, the Eating Disorder Diagnostic Scale (EDDS; Stice, Telch, & Rizvi, 2000a, b) was developed specifically to diagnose anorexia nervosa, bulimia nervosa, and binge eating disorder according to *DSM-IV* (APA, 1994) criteria. It does not use the term "binge," which minimizes any problems with idiosyncratic definitions respondents might have for this term. It has demonstrated good psychometric properties and very good agreement with longer, more involved diagnostic interviews (i.e., the EDE and Structured Clinical Interview for *DSM-IV* Axis 1 Diagnoses (SCID; Stice et al., 2000; Stice, Fisher, & Martinez, 2004), and thus may be a good alternative where time or training considerations preclude the use of an interview.

TREATMENT PLANNING AND EVALUATION

There are a number of self-report measures that can be used throughout the therapeutic process, from initial assessment to evaluation of treatment outcome. Detailed reviews of many of these measures can be found elsewhere (Allison, 2009, Peterson & Mitchell, 2005); we will focus on some of the more widely used measures in the literature.

In addition to being used as a screening measure, the EAT (Garner & Garfinkel, 1979; Garner, Olmsted, Bohr, & Garfinkel, 1982) can also be used repeatedly to track treatment progress (Garner, 1997). The EDDS has also been used to measure changes in treatment, although in one study it was less sensitive to change than the EDE (Stice et al., 2004).

The Eating Disorders Inventory-3 (Garner, 2004), is the latest revision of this questionnaire (Garner, 1991; Garner, Olmsted, & Polivy, 1983), previous versions of which have been widely used in both clinical and research contexts (Anderson & Paulosky, 2004a, 2004b). It contains three eating-disorder-specific scales and nine psychological scales

that assess psychopathology common in eating disorder patients. It also has six composite scores; one that is ED specific and five that are general integrative psychological constructs, as well as three response style indicators. Its previous editions have shown good psychometric properties, and this latest revision appears to be no exception (Anderson et al., 2009; Garner, 2004).

The Multifactorial Assessment of Eating Disorder Symptoms scale (MAEDS; Anderson, Williamson, Duchmann, Gleaves, & Barbin, 1999) was developed as a self-report inventory to assess domains of eating disorder symptoms necessary for successful treatment (depression, binge eating, purgative behavior, fear of fatness, restrictive eating, and avoidance of forbidden foods). It was developed specifically as a treatment outcome measure and has been shown to have good psychometric properties (Anderson et al., 2009; Anderson et al., 1999).

The Eating Disorder Examination Questionnaire (EDE-Q; Fairburn & Beglin, 1994, 2008) is a self-report questionnaire derived from the EDE. As expected, individuals tend to score higher on the EDE-Q than the EDE (Anderson et al., 2009). Because the items on the EDE-Q are almost identical to the EDE and it generates the same subscales as the EDE, it can be useful for treatment planning and evaluation, particularly if the assessor or treatment team is familiar with EDE terminology.

SELF-MONITORING

Self-monitoring, broadly defined, is one of the most widely used assessment procedures in the assessment of eating pathology (Anderson & Paulosky, 2004a). Direct aspects of food intake and eating pathology (e.g., the amount of food eaten and whether a purge followed) as well as the larger context surrounding each eating episode (e.g., mood, location) can be assessed in this way. While examples of standardized forms are available (e.g., Schlundt, 1995; Williamson, 1990), self-monitoring is a very flexible procedure and can be customized to fit the specific needs of the assessor and treatment team. Self-monitoring can be used at any stage of the assessment process, but is particularly useful for tracking treatment progress; many therapies routinely have patients self-monitor their food intake (e.g., Fairburn, 2008; Garner, 1997), so these data are often readily available.

TEST MEALS

One shortcoming with both interview and questionnaire modalities is that they both rely on accurate responding from the individual being assessed. Denial and minimization are significant problems in the EDs (Anderson & Paulosky, 2004a), and it is relatively easy for individuals to minimize pathology on self-report assessment instruments. Test meals require that an individual actually eat a food or meal under controlled conditions; the amount eaten as well as the behavior of the individual being assessed can be directly measured. Some have suggested that test meals can be extremely useful in all stages of the assessment process (Andersen, 1995; Anderson & Paulosky, 2004a; Williamson, 1990), although they are probably most appropriate for evaluating treatment progress and outcome. They do not appear to be commonly used, however (Anderson & Maloney, 2001; Anderson & Paulosky, 2004b). Nevertheless, test meals represent one way to overcome some of the problems associated with self-reported food intake.

Conclusions

Although the theory-based approach outlined in this chapter represents a comprehensive and systematic approach to the assessment of EDs and related problems, it does not appear to be commonly practiced. For example, a review of controlled treatment studies of CBT for BN found that only three of the sixteen studies reviewed assessed all five of the core domains identified in the CBT model of the maintenance of that disorder (Anderson & Maloney, 2001). Improving assessment procedures can help all phases of treatment, from identification to determining long-term outcome, however, and we hope that this chapter will spur interest in developing individualized assessment batteries based on both practical needs and theoretical considerations.

References

Allison, D. B. (2009). *Handbook of assessment methods for eating behaviors and weight-related problems* (2nd ed.). Newbury Park, CA: Sage.

American Psychiatric Association (APA). (1994) *Diagnostic and statistical manual of mental disorders* (4th ed.) Washington, DC: Author.

American Psychiatric Association (APA). (2000). *Diagnostic and statistical manual of mental disorders* (4th ed., rev.). Washington, DC: Author.

Andersen, A. E. (1995). A standard test meal to assess treatment response in anorexia nervosa patients. *Eating Disorders: Journal of Treatment and Prevention, 3,* 47–55.

Anderson, D. A., De Young, K. P., & Walker, D. C. (2009). Assessment of eating disordered thoughts, feelings, and behaviors. In D. B. Allison (Ed.), *Handbook of assessment methods for eating behaviors and weight-related problems* (2nd ed.). Newbury Park, CA: Sage.

Anderson, D. A., & Maloney, K. C. (2001). The efficacy of cognitive-behavioral therapy on the core symptoms of bulimia nervosa. *Clinical Psychology Review, 21,* 971–988.

Anderson, D. A., & Paulosky, C. A. (2004a). Psychological assessment of eating disorders and related features. In J. K. Thompson (Ed.), *Handbook of eating disorders and obesity* (pp. 112–129). New York: John Wiley & Sons.

Anderson, D. A., & Paulosky, C. A. (2004b). A survey of the use of assessment instruments by eating disorder professionals in clinical practice. *Eating and Weight Disorders, 9,* 238–241.

Anderson, D. A., Simmons, A. M., Milnes, S., M., & Earleywine, M. (2007). The effect of response format on endorsement of eating disordered attitudes and behaviors. *International Journal of Eating Disorders, 40,* 90–93.

Anderson, D. A., Williamson, D. A., Duchmann, E. G., Gleaves, D. H., & Barbin, J. M. (1999). Development and validation of a multifactorial treatment outcome measure for eating disorders. *Assessment, 6,* 7–20.

Beglin, S. J., & Fairburn, C. G. (1992). What is meant by the term "binge"? *American Journal of Psychiatry, 149,* 123–124.

Cassin, S. E., & von Ranson, K. M. (2005). Personality and eating disorders: A decade in review. *Clinical Psychology Review, 25,* 895–916.

Cotton, M., Ball, C., & Robinson, P. (2003). Four simple questions can help screen for eating disorders. *Journal of General Internal Medicine, 18,* 53–56.

Crowther, J. H., & Sherwood, N. E. (1997). Assessment. In D. M. Garner & P. E. Garfinkel (Eds.), *Handbook of treatment for eating disorders* (2nd ed., pp. 34–49). New York: Guilford Press.

Eisman, E., Dies, R., Finn, S. E., Eyde, L. D., Kay, G. G., Kubiszyn, T. W., et al. (2000). Problems and limitations in the use of psychological assessment in contemporary health care delivery. *Professional Psychology: Research and Practice, 31,* 131–140.

Evans, M. I., Galen, R. S., & Britt, D. W. (2005). Principles of screening. *Seminars in Perinatology, 29,* 364–366.

Fairburn, C. G. (1997a). Eating disorders. In: D. M. Clark, & C. G. Fairburn (Eds.), *The science and practice of cognitive behaviour therapy* (pp. 209–242). Oxford: Oxford University Press.

Fairburn, C. G. (1997b). Interpersonal psychotherapy for bulimia nervosa. In: D. M. Garner & P. E. Garfinkel (Eds.), *Handbook of treatment for eating disorders.* (2nd ed., pp. 278–294). New York: Guilford Press.

Fairburn, C. G. (2008). *Cognitive behavior therapy and eating disorders.* New York: Guilford Press.

Fairburn C. G., & Beglin, S. J. (1990). Studies of the epidemiology of bulimia nervosa. *American Journal of Psychiatry, 147,* 401–408.

Fairburn C. G., & Beglin, S. J. (1994). Assessment of eating disorders: Interview or self-report questionnaire? *International Journal of Eating Disorders, 16,* 363–370.

Fairburn C. G., & Beglin, S. (2008). The eating disorder examination questionnaire 6.0. In C. G. Fairburn, *Cognitive behavior therapy and eating disorders* (pp. 309–314). New York: Guilford Press.

Fairburn, C. G., & Cooper, Z. (1993). The eating disorder examination. In C. G. Fairburn & G. T. Wilson (Eds.), *Binge eating: Nature, assessment, and treatment* (pp. 317–360). New York: Guilford Press.

Fairburn, C. G., Cooper, Z., & O'Connor, M. (2008). The eating disorder examination 16.0D. In C. G. Fairburn,

Cognitive behavior therapy and eating disorders (pp. 265–308). New York: Guilford Press.

Fairburn, C. G., Cooper, Z., & Shafran, R. (2003). Cognitive behaviour therapy for eating disorders: A "transdiagnostic" theory and treatment. *Behaviour Research and Therapy, 41,* 509–528.

Fairburn, C. G., Marcus, M. D., & Wilson, G. T. (1993). Cognitive-behavioral therapy for binge eating and bulimia nervosa: A comprehensive treatment manual. In: C. G. Fairburn, & G. T. Wilson (Eds.), *Binge eating: Nature, assessment, and treatment* (pp. 361–404). New York: Guilford Press.

Fichter, M. M., Quadflieg, N., & Hedlund, S. (2006). Twelve-year course and outcome predictors of anorexia nervosa. *International Journal of Eating Disorders, 39,* 87–100.

Fichter, M. M., Quadflieg, N., & Hedlund, S. (2008). Long-term course of binge eating disorder and bulimia nervosa: Relevance for nosology and diagnostic criteria. *International Journal of Eating Disorders, 41,* 577–586.

Follette, W. C., & Callaghan, G. M. (2001). The evolution of clinical significance. *Clinical Psychology: Science and Practice, 8,* 431–435.

French, S. A., Peterson, C. B., Story, M., Anderson, N., Mussell, M. P., & Mitchell, J. E. (1998). Agreement between survey and interview measures of weight control practices in adolescents. *International Journal of Eating Disorders, 23,* 45–56.

Garfinkel, P., & Newman, A. (2001). The Eating Attitudes Test: Twenty-five years later. *Eating and Weight Disorders, 6,* 1–24.

Garner, D. M. (1991). *Eating Disorder Inventory-2 professional manual.* Odessa, FL: Psychological Assessment Resources.

Garner, D. M. (1997). Psychoeducational principles in treatment. In D. M. Garner & P. E. Garfinkel (Eds.), *Handbook of treatment for eating disorders* (2nd ed., pp. 145–177). New York: Guilford Press.

Garner, D. M. (2004). *EDI-3 Eating Disorder Inventory-3 professional manual.* Odessa, FL: Psychological Assessment Resources.

Garner, D. M., & Garfinkel, P. E. (1979). The Eating Attitudes Test: An index of the symptoms of anorexia nervosa. *Psychological Medicine, 9,* 273–279.

Garner, D. M., Olmsted, M. P., Bohr, Y., & Garfinkel, P. E. (1982). The eating attitudes test: Psychometric features and clinical correlates. *Psychological Medicine, 12,* 871–878.

Garner, D. M., Olmstead, M. P., & Polivy, J. (1983). Development and validation of a multidimensional eating disorder inventory of anorexia nervosa and bulimia. *International Journal of Eating Disorders, 2,* 14–34.

Grilo, C. G. (2005). Structured instruments. In J. E. Mitchell & C. B. Peterson (Eds.), *Assessment of eating disorders* (pp. 79–97). New York: Guilford Press.

Grimes, D. A., & Schulz, K. F. (2002). Uses and abuses of screening tests. *Lancet, 359,* 881–884.

Groth-Marnat, G. (1990). *Handbook of psychological assessment* (2nd ed.). New York: John Wiley & Sons.

Hamburg, P., Herzog, D. B., Brotman, A. W., & Stasior, J. K. (1989). The treatment resistant eating disordered patient. *Psychiatric Annals, 19,* 494–499.

Hayaki. J., Friedman, M. A., & Brownell, K. D. (2002). Shame and severity of bulimic symptoms. *Eating Behaviors, 3,* 73–83.

Heffner, M., & Eifert, G. (2004). *The anorexia workbook: How to accept yourself, heal your suffering, and reclaim your life.* Oakland, CA: New Harbinger.

Jacobson, N. S., Follette, W. C., & Revenstorf, D. (1984). Psychotherapy outcome research: Methods for reporting variability and evaluating clinical significance. *Behavior Therapy, 15,* 336–352.

Jacobson, N. S., Roberts, L. J., Berns, S. B., & McGlinchey J. B. (1999). Methods for defining and determining the clinical significance of treatment effects: Description, application, and alternatives. *Journal of Consulting and Clinical Psychology, 67,* 300–307.

Jacobson, N. S., & Truax, P. (1991). Clinical significance: A statistical approach to defining meaningful change in psychotherapy research. *Journal of Consulting and Clinical Psychology, 59,* 12–19.

Johnson, W. G., Boutelle, K. N., Torgrud, L., Davig, J. P., & Turner, S. (2000). What is a binge? The influence of amount, duration, and loss of control criteria on judgments of binge eating. *International Journal of Eating Disorders, 27,* 471–479.

Kanfer, F. H., & Schefft, B. K. (1988). *Guiding the process of therapeutic change.* Champaign, IL: Research Press.

Keel, P. K., Crow, S., Davis, T. L., & Mitchell, J. E. (2002). Assessment of eating disorders: Comparison of interview and questionnaire data from a long-term follow-up study of bulimia nervosa. *Journal of Psychosomatic Research, 53,* 1043–1047.

Keel, P. K., Dorer, D. J., Eddy, K. T., Franko, D., Charatan, D. L., & Herzog, D. B. (2003). Predictors of mortality in eating disorders. *Archives of General Psychiatry, 60,* 179–183.

Kendall, P. C., & Grove, W. M. (1988). Normative comparisons in therapy outcome. *Behavioral Assessment, 10,* 147–158.

Kendall, P. C., Marrs-Garcia, A., Nath, S. R., & Sheldrick, R. C. (1999). Normative comparisons for the evaluation of clinical significance. *Journal of Consulting and Clinical Psychology, 67,* 285–299.

Korotitsch, W., & Nelson-Gray, R. O. (1999). Self-report and physiological measures. In S. C. Hayes, D. H. Barlow, & R. O. Nelson-Gray (Eds.), *The scientist-practitioner: Research and accountability in the age of managed care* (pp. 320–352). Boston: Allyn and Bacon.

Lavender, J. M., & Anderson, D. A. (2009). Effect of perceived anonymity in assessments of eating disordered behaviors and attitudes. *International Journal of Eating Disorders.*

Lavender, J. M., & Anderson, D. A. (2008). A novel assessment of behaviors associated with body dissatisfaction and disordered eating. *Body Image, 5,* 399–403.

Luck, A. J., Morgan, J. F., Reid, F., O'Brien, A., Brunton, J., Price, C., et al. (2002). The SCOFF questionnaire and clinical interview for eating disorders in general practice: Comparative study. *British Medical Journal, 325,* 755–756.

Lundgren, J. D., Danoff-Burg, S., & Anderson, D. A. (2004). Cognitive-behavioral therapy for bulimia nervosa: An empirical analysis of clinical significance. *International Journal of Eating Disorders, 35,* 262–274.

Mitchell, J. E., & Peterson, C. B. (2005). *Assessment of eating disorders.* New York: Guilford Press.

Morgan, J. F., Reid, F., & Lacey, J. H. (2000). The SCOFF questionnaire: A new screening tool for eating disorders. *Western Journal of Medicine, 172,* 164–165.

Nielsen, C., & Lang, R. S. (1999). Principles of screening. *Medical Clinics of North America, 83,* 1323–1337.

O'Brien, K. M., & Vincent, N. K. (2003). Psychiatric comorbidity in anorexia and bulimia nervosa: Nature, prevalence, and causal relationships. *Clinical Psychology Review, 23,* 57–74.

Pachankis, J. E., & Goldfried, M. R. (2007). An integrative, principle-based approach to psychotherapy. In S. G. Hoffman & J. Weinberger (Eds.), *The art and science of psychotherapy* (pp. 49–68). New York: Routledge.

Parker, S. C., Lyons, J., & Bonner, J. (2005). Eating disorders in graduate students: Exploring the SCOFF questionnaire as a simple screening tool. *Journal of American College Health, 54,* 103–107.

Perry, L., Morgan, J., Reid, F., Brunton, J., O'Brien, A., Luck, A., et al. (2002). Screening for symptoms of eating disorders: Reliability of the SCOFF screening tool with written compared to oral delivery. *International Journal of Eating Disorders, 32,* 466–472.

Peterson, C. B. (2005). Conducting the diagnostic interview. In J. E. Mitchell & C. B. Peterson (Eds.), *Assessment of eating disorders* (pp. 32–58). New York: Guilford Press.

Peterson, C. B., & Mitchell, J. E. (2005). Self-report measures. In J. E. Mitchell & C. B. Peterson (Eds.), *Assessment of eating disorders* (pp. 98–119). New York: Guilford Press.

Rodin, J., Silberstein, L. R., & Striegel-Moore, R. H. (1985). Women and weight: A normative discontent. In T. B. Sonderegger (Ed.), *Psychology and gender: Nebraska symposium on motivation* (pp. 267–307). Lincoln: University of Nebraska Press.

Schlundt, D. G. (1995). Assessment of specific eating behaviors and eating style. In D. B. Allison (Ed.), *Methods for the assessment of eating behaviors and weight-related problems* (pp. 142–302). Newbury Park, CA: Sage.

Sheldrick, R. C., Kendall, P. C., & Heimberg, R. G. (2001). The clinical significance of treatments: A comparison of three treatments for conduct disordered children. *Clinical Psychology: Science and Practice, 8,* 418–430.

Siervo, M., Boschi, V., Papa, A., Bellini, O., & Falconi, C. (2005). Application of the SCOFF, Eating Attitudes Test 26 (EAT 26) and Eating Inventory (TFEQ) Questionnaires in young women seeking diet-therapy. *Eating and Weight Disorders, 10,* 76–82.

Sihvola, E., Keski-Rahkonen, A., Dick, D. M., Hoek, H. W., Raevuori, A., Rose, R. J., et al. (2009). Prospective associations of early-onset Axis I disorders with developing eating disorders. *Comprehensive Psychiatry, 50,* 20–25.

Stice, E., Fisher, M., & Martinez, M. (2004). Eating Disorder Diagnostic Scale: Additional evidence of reliability and validity. *Psychological Assessment, 16,* 60–71.

Stice, E., Telch, C. F., & Rizvi, S. L. (2000a). Correction to Stice et al. (2000). *Psychological Assessment, 12,* 252.

Stice, E., Telch, C. F., & Rizvi, S. L. (2000b). Development and validation of the Eating Disorder Diagnostic Scale: A brief self-report measure of anorexia, bulimia, and binge-eating disorder. *Psychological Assessment, 12,* 123–131.

Telch, C. F., Pratt, E. M., & Niego, S. H. (1998). Obese women with binge eating disorder define the term binge. *International Journal of Eating Disorders, 24,* 313–317.

Turchik, J. A., Karpenko, V., Hammers, D., & McNamara, J. R. (2007). Practical and ethical assessment issues in rural, impoverished, and managed care settings. *Professional Psychology: Research & Practice, 38,* 158–168.

Vitousek, K. B., Daly, J., & Heiser, C. (1991). Reconstructing the internal world of the eating-disordered individual: Overcoming denial and distortion in self-report. *International Journal of Eating Disorders, 10,* 647–666.

Williamson, D. A. (1990). *Assessment of eating disorders: Obesity, anorexia, and bulimia nervosa.* Elmsford, NY: Pergamon Press.

Williamson, D. A., Anderson, D. A., & Gleaves, D. G. (1996). Anorexia and bulimia: Structured interview methodologies and psychological assessment. In K. Thompson (Ed.), *Body image, eating disorders, and obesity: An integrative guide for assessment and treatment* (pp. 205–223). Washington, DC: American Psychological Association.

Wise, E. A. (2004). Methods for analyzing psychotherapy outcomes: A review of clinical significance, reliable change, and recommendations for future directions. *Journal of Personality Assessment, 82,* 50–59.

Medical Comorbidities of Eating Disorders

James E. Mitchell *and* Scott J. Crow

Abstract

Eating disorders are frequently characterized by medical complications that at times can be severe. Because of this, the medical assessment of patients with eating disorders is an important part of the evaluation process. Frequent complications include cardiovascular problems, including a decrement in heart rate variability that is a known risk factor for cardiac arrhythmias. Skeletal system changes, particularly the risk for osteoporosis and osteopenia, are common in patients with anorexia nervosa. Gastrointestinal complications can be quite prominent. In particular, there is a risk for gastric dilatation and gastric rupture in patients who binge eat. A variety of endocrine changes have also been described and there appears to be an association with eating disorders and poor control of diabetes mellitus.

Keywords: anorexia nervosa, binge eating disorder, bulimia nervosa, medical complications

Introduction

Eating disorders (EDs) are somewhat unusual among psychiatric disorders in that they are frequently accompanied by medical complications. These complications can be severe and even lethal in extreme circumstances. Because of this the medical assessment and medical management of patients with EDs is a necessary part of the evaluation and treatment process. In this chapter, we review the major medical comorbidities of anorexia nervosa (AN) and bulimia nervosa (BN) by organ system and suggest monitoring and management strategies. We also briefly review the literature on the medical complications associated with binge eating disorder (BED), although the majority of such complications are associated with obesity in which the ED plays a part.

Signs and Symptoms

Many patients with EDs, particularly patients with AN, report no physical symptoms despite their obvious emaciation. Patients with EDs often attempt to conceal the diagnosis from clinicians even when they have complaints attributable to their ED. Many of the signs and symptoms that are seen in patients with EDs are included in Table 15.1 (Pomeroy, Mitchell, Roerig, & Crow, 2002; Williams, Goodie, & Motsinger, 2008). Some of these signs require explanation. Bradycardia is attributable to the metabolic changes and decrease in resting energy expenditure seen in patients with AN. Yellow skin, which occurs rarely, is attributable to hypercarotenemia. Lanugo is the development of fine soft body hair in places where hair is usually not seen. Edema is commonly present and often worsens during refeeding. Russell's sign refers to scar or callous formation on the dorsum of the hand from using the hand to stimulate the gag reflex to induce vomiting.

Relative to initial screening, patients with AN should undergo a variety of tests. These include a complete blood count with differential, serum electrolytes, blood urea nitrogen (BUN) and creatinine, serum glucose, calcium, and liver function determinations. Also indicated are a serum albumin or

Table 15.1 Signs and Symptoms Seen in Patients with Eating Disorders

	Anorexia Nervosa	Bulimia Nervosa
Symptoms	Amenorrhea Hyperactivity Sleep disturbance Constipation Cold intolerance Depression	Irregular menses Constipation Depression Lethargy

Signs	Sunken cheeks
	Inanition
	Low core temperature
	Yellow skin
	Lanugo
	Scalp hair loss
	Bradycardia
	Hypotension
	Acrocyanosis
	Dry skin
	Loss of dental enamel
	Edema
		Russell's sign
		Parotid gland
		  swelling
		Loss of dental
		  enamel
		Edema

transferrin (to determine nutritional status), thyroid function tests, a urinalysis, a serum magnesium (which needs to be measured and needs to be followed periodically during refeeding as well) and serum phosphorus (which also often requires monitoring). In particular, hypomagnesemia and hypophosphatemia may be overlooked, particular if patients are being refed in an environment where the staff is relatively inexperienced in such matters. Patients should also undergo an EKG. In patients with BN, the choice of laboratory work should be guided by symptoms, but at minimum should include an examination of serum electrolytes.

Cardiovascular

Cardiovascular complications are quite frequent in patients with AN and can be seen in patients with BN as well (Cooke & Chambers, 1995; Dresser, Massey, Johnson, & Bossen, 1992; Kreipe & Harris, 1992; Schocken, Holloway, & Powers, 1989; Senzaki et al., 2006; Casiero & Frishman, 2006). In patients with AN, starvation is usually associated with sinus bradycardia, at times sinus arrhythmias, and hypotension. These are considered to be adaptive to the metabolic state of starvation and the fluid restriction or loss of fluid through vomiting or laxative abuse. Several different types of rhythm disturbances and conduction abnormalities have been described (Brown & Mehler, 2000). Severe rhythm disturbances are often attributable to electrolyte

abnormalities including hypocalcemia, hypokalemia, hypophosphatemia, or hypomagnasemia (Pomeroy et al., 2001).

Electrocardiographic changes include serious abnormalities such as prolonged QT interval and marked bradycardia, which may require initial cardiac monitoring. Roche, et al. (2005) studied abnormalities of the QT interval before and after refeeding and found that the QT/RR slope was significantly enhanced in patients with AN, probably reflecting an autonomic imbalance. Some evidence suggests heart rate variability may be decreased in AN; this is a known risk factor for cardiac arrhythmia (Melanson, Donahoo, Krantz, Poirier, & Mehler, 2004). Ohwada et al. (2005) reported an ampular cardiomyopathy in young women with AN that developed post hypoglycemic coma. This condition is characterized by extensive akinesis or ballooning of the apical region of the heart seen on echocardiography. McCallum et al. (2006) provided general guidelines for the evaluation and management of cardiovascular complications. Casiero & Frishman (2006) reviewed the risk for cardiovascular complications associated with refeeding, including arrhythmia, tachycardia, congestive heart failure, and sudden death and stressed the need for careful monitoring and slow refeeding.

Related to cardiovascular risk factors, Misra et al. (2006) noted that there was an uncoupling of risk factors, with increased apolipoprotein-B (Apo-B) and interleukin-6 (IL-6) and decreased high sensitivity c-reactive protein (hsCRP) usually attributed to alterations in hormone regulation. Birmingham and Gritzner (2007) reported a case and reviewed the literature on heart failure risk in AN. They stressed that shortness of breath, particularly during re-feeding, can be a symptom of heart failure, with other possible findings including increased jugular venous pressure, shortness of breath on exertion, and pulmonary crepitations at the base of the lungs. They stressed the need in these cases for standard medical therapy for heart failure. Senzaki and colleagues (2006) describe left ventricular hypertrophy and outflow track obstruction. The patient was a 14-year-old girl with rapid weight loss and consequent rapid decrease in ventricular capacity leading to left ventricular hypertrophy and left ventricular outflow obstruction. This condition may lead to sudden death. However, in this case the condition normalized with weight gain.

In summary, patients with AN are at risk for a variety of untoward cardiovascular complications, and this risk is probably heightened during refeeding.

A careful assessment for electrolyte abnormalities as well as evidence of refeeding syndrome and heart failure needs to be routine.

Dermatologic

Patients with AN and BN can develop dermatologic complications. These were reviewed by Gupta, Gupta, and Haberman in a paper in 1987 and more recently by Strumia in 2005. These dermatological complications include acne, carotenoderma (yellowing of the skin caused by deposition of carotene, probably attributable to excessive ingestion of carotenoid-rich vegetables such as green leafy and root vegetables); acrocyanosis; circulatory problems resulting in cold, blue hands or feet; purpura (secondary to a low platelet count); nail dystrophy; and xerosis (scaly, dry skin). Patients can also develop lanugo or fine, downy body hair on the back, abdomen, and forearms and telogen effluvium (hair loss). Patients who self-induce vomiting can also evidence Russell's sign (scarring or callous formation over the dorsum of the hand secondary to trauma to the hand from using the hand to stimulate the gag reflex to vomit).

Skeletal System

It is now well established that decreased bone mineral density (BMD) is commonly seen in patients with AN, particularly with the chronic form of the illness. For example, Misra et al. (2004) compared 60 individuals presenting with AN to 58 normal controls. Bone mineral densities z scores < -1 were found in 41% of the individuals with AN and scores of -2 in 11%; while -1 scores were found in 23% of controls and -2 scores in 2%. Lean body mass, body mass index (BMI), and age at menarche were predictors of diminished bone mineral scores. Konstantynowicz, et al. (2005) reported that BMD z-scores in individuals with AN and comorbid depression were lower than those without comorbid depression, and that the overall level of depression was inversely correlated with total body mineral density. This suggests that depression may significantly increase the risk of diminished bone mineral density.

The development of osteopenia and osteoporosis is usually considered to have multiple causes (Katz & Vollenhaven, 2000), including low levels of estrogen, decreased calcium intake, low vitamin D levels, and in some cases excess growth hormone. These changes are not usually seen in patients with BN. Wolfert and Mehler (2002) underscored that the most effective treatment is still early weight restoration and the resumption of menses. This was also emphasized in a study by Dominguez et al. (2007), which concluded that the shift from the dominant resorptive state included hormonal mechanisms that require return to menses, as well as nutritional rehabilitation.

Many treatments have been used for osteoporosis including calcitonin, ipriflavone, estrogen replacement therapy, vitamin B_3, calcium, vitamin K, and most recently bisphosphonates. With the exception of several recent studies, most trials have been negative. For example, Strokosh, Friedman, Wu, and Kamin (2006) reported in a group of adolescent females with AN or eating disorder not otherwise specified (EDNOS) treatment that a triphasic oral contraceptive did not have a significant effect on mineral density in the lumbar spine or hip.

Three recent papers have examined the use of bisphosphonates. Miller et al. (2004) administered risedronate for 9 months to 10 females with AN who had osteopenia. The results were compared to control data in subjects prospectively followed for the same period. Bone density increased significantly in patients who received the active drug. Golden et al. (2005) compared alendronate to placebo in 32 adolescents with AN. All subjects also received 1200 mg of elemental calcium and 400 IU of vitamin D daily, and all received the same multidisciplinary treatment. At follow-up, body weight was the most important determinant of bone density, but after controlling for body weight assignment to the active bisphosphonate drug still had an effect on improving bone mineral density. Most recently, Nakahara et al. (2006) conducted a randomized placebo-controlled trial comparing etidronate to the combination of calcium and vitamin D and to a placebo. These researchers found that BMD in both the active treatment groups was significantly greater than in the control group, suggesting that both treatments were effective for improving BMD. The results from these studies must be tempered by the observation that bisphosphonates are not approved for this age group and cannot be used in patients who may become pregnant. Therefore, their routine use in this population cannot be recommended.

Gastrointestinal

Gastrointestinal complications are quite prominent in patients with both AN and BN (McClain, Humphries, Hill, & Nicki, 1993). These can assume a variety of forms, involving the gastrointestinal tract at various levels. First, swelling of the salivary glands, particularly the parotid or submandibular glands, is quite common in BN and may provide a useful tool in diagnosis. This may be accompanies by hyperamylasemia. This has also been described in some patients with AN (Kinzl, Biebl, & Herold, 1993).

Many of the other gastrointestinal manifestations have been reviewed by Chial, McAlpine, and Camilleri (2002). These include delayed gastric emptying, delayed small bowel transit time, and of particular prominence, constipation. Also reported, but fortunately very rare, are cases of gastric dilatation, gastric rupture, pancreatitis, and perforated ulcer.

The phenomena of gastric dilatation and the risk of gastric rupture have been well recognized in the literature, and can present as an acute, potentially lethal, complication. For example, Lunca, Rikkers, and Stanescu (2005) reported the case of a borderline mentally retarded man who developed gastric dilatation after binge eating. Lo, Yen, and Jones (2004) reported gastric dilatation and necrosis in a 26-year-old patient with anorexia nervosa. Most recently, Bravender and Story (2007) reported an acute gastric dilatation in a young woman. The patient, aged 21, had a 4 years history of BN. She presented to an emergency room with a 7-hour history of severe, sharp, constant abdominal pain. A computerized tomogram demonstrated massive gastric distention. She was treated conservatively with nasogastric decompression that provided immediate relief from her symptoms.

Gendall, Joyce, Carter, McIntosh, and Bulik (2005) looked at the history of gastrointestinal problems during childhood in women with BN. One-third of the 135 participants reported gastrointestinal complaints or constipation in childhood. These patients tended to be younger and to have an earlier onset of their ED than did other patients. In a study reported by Winstead and Willard (2001), 13 patients in an ED clinic were interviewed relative to other gastrointestinal histories. Eight (62%) had previously either seen a primary care physician or a gastroenterologist with gastric complaints. Six of these had sought treatment for these complaints before seeking treatment for their ED. This suggests that many of these patients are seen by physicians before admitting that they have an ED, and there should be high suspicion of a possible ED in young women presenting with gastrointestinal complaints.

Chronic constipation may be attributable to decreased fluid intake and dehydration consequent to purging, as well as alterations in intestinal motility. Laxative abusers generally alternate between periods of diarrhea and constipation and can develop cathartic colon wherein the colon no longer functions adequately.

Dental

Dental complications are generally seen in patients who engage in repeated episodes of self-induced vomiting (Milosevic, Brodie, & Slade, 1997; Studen-Pavlovich & Elliott, 2001). What is generally seen is decalcification of the teeth, particularly on the lingual, palatal, and posterior occlusal surfaces; this is often referred to as perimylolysis. Because the fillings or amalgams are resistant to acid they become more obvious as enamel erosion progresses, and end up looking as if they are floating on the surface on the tooth, despite the fact that when they are put in they are flush with the tooth surface. It has been mentioned that dentists need to have a good working knowledge of the behavioral management of EDs since they are often in position to identify these patients and cooperate in their treatment with other health care professionals (Ashcroft & Milosevic, 2007).

Other oral manifestations of eating disorders include, in addition to salivary gland hypertrophy previously discussed include dental mucosal erythema, and loss of papillae.

Metabolic/Endocrine

Hypercholesterolemia, perhaps reflecting accelerated cholesterol synthesis in these patients, is frequently seen in patients with AN, as is elevation in serum carotene levels (Ohwada, Hotta, Oikawa, & Takano, 2006). Changes are also seen in energy expenditure (Van Wymelbeke, Brondel, Marcel Brun, & Rigaud, 2004). Charting resting energy expenditure (REE) at baseline and at three points during the first seven weeks of treatment revealed that in patients with AN REE substantially increased by day 8, out of proportion to the change in fat free mass (FFM). The disparity between changes in REE and FFM persisted throughout treatment. This probably contributes to the large excess in calories needed to accomplish weight gain in AN patients. Misra et al. (2005) studied body composition in patients with AN compared to controls. Differences were seen in terms of percentage of trunk fat, trunk/extremity fat ratio, trunk lean mass, and trunk/extremity lean mass ratio. Nadir levels of cortisol were inversely associated with extremity lean mass and were directly correlated with the trunk lean mass. Piccoli, Codognotto, Di Pascoli, Boffo, and Caregaro (2005) looked at skinfold thickness and bioelectrical impedance in women with AN and found poor agreement between these measures, suggesting the lack of utility of skinfold thickness in individuals with a BMI less than 15.

Trace mineral deficiencies and vitamin deficiencies rarely have also been described. Caregaro, Di Pascoli, Favaro, Nardi, and Santonastaso (2005) highlighted the importance of sodium depletion and hypovolemia in patients with AN and found that with adequate hydration anemia may become apparent.

Also of concern are electrolyte abnormalities (Birmingham, Puddicombe, & Hiynsky, 2004). Of particular importance has been the development of hypomagnesemia during refeeding, but other electrolyte abnormalities including hypokalemia, hypochloremia, and metabolic alkalosis have been described in ED patients.

Prolonged purging and abuse of laxatives or diuretics can result in a hypovolemic state that can stimulate the renin–angiotensin–aldosterone system, as the body attempts to conserve fluid (Mitchell, Pomeroy, Seppala, & Huber, 1988). These patients generally retain large amounts of fluid early in the course of treatment, which can be quite upsetting for them.

Research has fairly consistently shown an increased risk for ED in patients with type 1 diabetes mellitus (Crow, Keel, & Kendall, 1998), and evidence of poor metabolic control in these individuals (Rydall, Rodin, Olmsted, Devenyi, & Daneman, 1997). Recently Takii et al. (2008) showed that the duration of insulin omission was the factor most closely associated with retinopathy and nephropathy in type 1 diabetic females with clinical eating disorders, in a study involving 109 type 1 diabetic patients.

Grylli, Hafferl-Gattermayer, Wagner, Schober, and Karwautz (2005) screened 199 adolescents with type 1 diabetes and found that those with full or subthreshhold eating disorder problems had higher mean scores on measures of harm avoidance and lower scores on self-directedness. Peveler et al. (2004) interviewed 87 patients who had been interviewed at baseline, between ages 11 to 25, who were then recontacted after 8 to 12 years. Thirteen individuals met criteria at baseline for an eating disorder, and 31 (35.6%) misused insulin for weight control purposes. Grylli, Wagner, Hafferl-Gattermayer, Schober, and Karwautz (2005) also reported that adolescents with type 1 diabetes and disordered eating reported poorer psychosocial quality of life. This literature together suggests that disordered eating and EDs present major problems in the management of patients with diabetes mellitus.

Amenorrhea is one of the diagnostic criteria for AN. Devlin et al. (1989) suggested that severe AN was associated with low levels of plasma luteinizing hormone (LH) and follicle-stimulating hormone (FSH). An immature response of LH and FSH, to corticotropin-releasing hormone has also been reported (Thomas & Rebar, 1990). Menstrual irregularities are also seen frequently in patients with BN, although frank amenorrhea is less common than in AN. The amenorrhea diagnostic criterion has been criticized because it is gender specific, and may be masked by individuals taking oral contraceptives.

Thyroid function tests are generally abnormal in patients with AN, who develop a low triiodothyronine (T3) syndrome by converting T3 to reverse T3, a less active form of the hormone (Boyar et al., 1977). Other abnormalities of the hypothalamic–pituitary axis have been described in AN including hypercortisolemia; such changes are seen less frequently in patients with BN (Laue, Gold, Richmond, & Chrousos, 1991).

Renal

Elevated BUN and creatine levels, which may partially reflect dehydration and volume depletion, also can evidence a reduction of glomerular filtration rate and problems with concentrating urine (Boag, Weerakoon, Ginsburg, Havard, & Dandonne, 1985; Lowinger, Griffiths, Beumont, Seieluna, & Touyz, 1999). It has also been noted that development of renal disease is not an uncommon outcome in patients with chronic AN (Herzog, Deter, Fiehn, & Petzold, 1997). Takakura and colleagues (2006) showed that duration of illness was a risk factor for renal function deterioration in patients with AN. This problem seemed to be particularly marked in those with laxative abuse.

Neurologic

A variety of structural abnormalities in the brains of patients with AN have been described primarily consisting of enlarged ventricles and external cerebrospinal fluid spaces (Herholz, 1996), sometimes referred to as pseudoatrophy. Wernicke's encephalopathy has also been reported in AN (Peters, Parvin, Petersen, Faircloth, & Levine, 2007).

Conclusions

Medical complications occur quite commonly in patients with AN and BN. These comorbidities can range from mild complications to life endangering conditions. An aggressive assessment for medical complications needs to be part of the assessment, particularly for patients with AN, and not uncommonly, medical follow-up will be indicated as well.

Binge Eating Disorder

Many patients with binge eating disorder (BED) are also overweight or obese and the medical complications associated with overweight and obesity have been widely studied and are well appreciated (Field et al., 2001). All major organ systems can be compromised by obesity, and the risk of premature death is substantial; hence, it is important to ascertain that patients with BED have adequate medical care. Therefore, many of the medical complications seen in patients with BED are attributable to their concomitant obesity. However, some literature suggests that BED in and of itself might increase medical risk. Johnson, Spitzer, and Williams (2001) reported a study examining psychiatric disorders, physical and mental disability, and functional status in 4651 female patients in primary care and obstetrics/gynecology clinics in the United States. Women with BN or BED reported markedly poorer functioning and much higher levels of disability and health problems after controlling for other co-occurring psychiatric disorders. Reichborn-Kjennerud, Bulik, Sullivan, Tambs, and Harris, (2004) used a series of regression models to examine data obtained on 8045 twins from a population-based Norwegian registry. Results indicated that there was substantial comorbidity between the presence of binge eating and psychiatric symptoms in men independent of BMI. Significant associations were found between binge eating and certain physical symptoms including low back pain independent of BMI. This was not shown in women. Using a separate population-based twin study Bulik, Sullivan, and Kendler (2002) found that obese women with BED reported greater health dissatisfaction and higher rates of major medical disorders than obese women without binge eating. Most recently Rieger, Wilfley, Stein, Marino, and Crow (2005) found that obese individuals with BED had impaired functioning in psychosocial aspects quality of life in addition to poorer physical functioning than were seen in non-BED obese individuals.

Taken together these results suggest the possibility that BED is associated with medical complications that are not solely attributable to the presence of overweight or obesity. Clearly further work in this area is indicated.

Future Directions

1. Can an effective preventative or treatment strategy be developed for bone loss in AN? Efforts to date have failed to show effectiveness for various strategies to prevent the development of bone loss in patients with AN, and available data suggest that bone changes may not completely reversible. Restoration of adequate nutrition and weight gain appears to be the sole method of addressing this problem at the present time.

2. Are the neuropsychological and brain imaging changes seen in patients with AN completely reversible? Although the correlation between neuropsychological dysfunction and brain imaging changes in patients with AN is not always high, some studies do suggest a lack of complete resolution of the brain imaging changes with weight recovery. This suggests that there may be permanent changes in brain tissue induced by the starvation seen in AN, if these changes are completely reversible it is not clear what neuropsychological and/or behavioral correlates might be affected, or what changes may have on psychotherapeutic treatment.

3. What is the optimal refeeding paradigm? Various treatment programs use different approaches and frequently there are marked differences in terms of weight gain goals for patients with AN. Some programs attempt to track energy expenditures as a way of deciding on calories to be administered. Some programs use tube feeding and a few use total parenteral nutrition, which can clearly be problematic in this group of patients. However, no studies to date have documented the optimal refeeding program despite the frequency of its use, and refeeding continues to be fraught with a number of potential challenges and risks.

4. What causes sudden death in AN and what are the risk factors for sudden death? It is presumed that cardiac arrhythmias might underlie some of the sudden death seen in patients with AN, although at times patients that are severely emaciated can clearly evidence multiple organ system failure that can contribute to death. While both the amount of weight loss and the rapidity of weight loss appear to be risk factors, there are patients who have been at a low body weight for a very long period of time and seem to function reasonably adequately. A more detailed analysis of the particular mechanism underlying fatalities would be useful.

References

Ashcroft, A., & Milosevic, A. (2007). The eating disorders: 2. Behavioral and dental management. *Dental Update, 34,* 619–620.

Birmingham, C. L., & Gritzner, S. (2007). Heart failure in anorexia nervosa: Case report and review of the literature. *Eating and Weight Disorders, 12,* 7–10.

Birmingham, C. L., Puddicombe, D., & Hiynsky, J. (2004). Hypomagnesemia during refeeding in anorexia nervosa. *Eating and Weight Disorders, 9,* 236–237.

Boag, F., Weerakoon, J., Ginsburg, J., Havard, C. W., & Dandonne, P. (1985). Diminished creatinine clearance in anorexia nervosa: Reversal with weight gain. *Journal of Clinical Pathology, 38,* 60–63.

Boyar, R. M., Hellman, K. L., Roffwarg, H. P., Katz, S., Sumoff, B., O'Connor, J., et al. (1977). Cortisol secretion and metabolism in anorexia nervosa. *New England Journal of Medicine, 296,* 190–193.

Bravender, T., & Story, L. (2007). Massive binge eating, gastric dilation and unsuccessful purging in a young woman with bulimia nervosa. *Journal of Adolescent Health, 41,* 516–518.

Brown, J. M., & Mehler, P. S. (2000). Medical complications occurring in adolescents with anorexia nervosa. *The Western Journal of Medicine, 172,* 189–193.

Bulik, C. M., Sullivan, P. F., & Kendler, K. S. (2002). Medical and psychiatric morbidity in obese women with and without binge eating. *The International Journal of Eating Disorders, 32,* 72–78.

Caregaro, L., Di Pascoli, L., Favaro, A., Nardi, M., & Santonastaso, P. (2005). Sodium depletion and hemoconcentration: Overlooked complications in patients with anorexia nervosa? *Nutrition, 21,* 438–445.

Casiero, D. & Frishman, W. H. (2006). Cardiovascular complications of eating disorders. *Cardiology in Review, 14,* 227–231.

Chial, H. J., McAlpine, D. E., & Camilleri, M. (2002). Anorexia nervosa: manifestations and management for the gastroenterologist. *The American Journal of Gastroenterology, 97,* 255–269.

Cooke, R. A., & Chambers, J. B. (1992). Anorexia nervosa and the heart. *British Journal of Hospital Medicine, 161,* 104–107.

Crow, S., Keel, P. K., & Kendall, D. (1998). Eating disorders and insulin dependent diabetes mellitus: A review. *Psychosomatics, 39,* 233–243.

Devlin, M. H., Walsh, B. T., Katz, J. L., Roose, S. P., Linkie, D. M., Wright, L., et al. (1989). Hypothalamic-pituitary-gonadal function in anorexia nervosa and bulimia. *Psychiatry Research, 28,* 11–24.

Dominguez, J., Goodman, L., Gupta, S. S., Mayer, L., Etu, S. F., Walsh, B. T., et al. (2007). Treatment of anorexia nervosa is associated with increases in bone mineral density, and recovery is a biphasic process involving both nutrition and return of menses. *The American Journal of Clinical Nutrition, 86,* 92–99.

Dresser, L. P., Massey, E. W., Johnson, E. E., & Bossen, E. (1992). Ipecac myopathy and cardiomyopathy. *Journal of Neurology, Neurosurgery and Psychiatry, 55,* 560–562.

Field, A. E., Coakley, E. H., Must, A., Spadano, J. L., Laird, N., Dietz, W. H., et al. (2001). Impact of overweight on the risk of developing common chronic diseases during a 10-year period. *Archives of Internal Medicine, 161,* 1581–1586.

Gendall, K. A., Joyce, P. R., Carter, F. A., McIntosh, V. V., & Bulik, C. M. (2005). Childhood gastrointestinal complaints in women with bulimia nervosa. *The International Journal of Eating Disorders, 37,* 256–260.

Golden, N. H., Iglesias, E. A., Jacobson, M. S., Carey, D., Meyer, W., Schebendach, J., et al. (2005). Alendronate for the treatment of osteopenia in anorexia nervosa: A randomized, double-blind, placebo-controlled trial. *The Journal of Clinical Endocrinology and Metabolism, 90,* 3179–3185.

Grylli, V., Hafferl-Gattermayer, A., Wagner, G., Schober, E., & Karwautz, A. (2005). Eating disorders and eating problems among adolescents with type 1 diabetes: exploring relationships with temperament and character. *Journal of Pediatric Psychology, 30,* 197–206.

Grylli, V., Wagner, G., Hafferl-Gattermayer, A., Schober, E., & Karwautz, A. (2005). Disturbed eating attitudes, coping styles, and subjective quality of life in adolescents with type 1 diabetes. *Journal of Psychosomatic Research, 59,* 65–72.

Gupta, M. A., Gupta, A. K., & Haberman, H. F. (1987). Dermatologic signs in anorexia nervosa and bulimia nervosa. *Archives of Dermatology, 123,* 1386–1390.

Herholz, K. (1996). Neuroimaging in anorexia nervosa. *Psychiatry Research, 62,* 105–110.

Herzog, W., Deter, H.C., Fiehn, W., & Petzold, E. (1997). Medical findings and predictors of long-term physical outcome in anorexia nervosa: A prospective, 12–year follow-up study. *Psychological Medicine, 27,* 269–279.

Johnson, J. G., Spitzer, R. L., & Williams, J. B. W. (2001). Health problems, impairment and illnesses associated with bulimia nervosa and binge eating disorder among primary care and obstetric gynecology patients. *Psychological Medicine, 31,* 1455–1466.

Katz, M. G., & Vollenhaven, B. (2000). The reproductive consequences of anorexia nervosa. *British Journal of Obstetrics and Gynecology, 107,* 707–713.

Kinzl, J., Biebl, W., & Herold, M. (1993). Significance of vomiting for hyperamylasemia and sialadenosis in patients with eating disorders. *The International Journal of Eating Disorders, 13,* 117–124.

Konstantynowicz, J., Kadziela-Olech, H., Kaczmarski, M., Zebaze, R. M., Iuliano-Burns, S., Piotrowska-Jastrzebska, J., & Seemon, E. (2005). Depression in anorexia nervosa: a risk factor for osteoporosis. *The Journal of Clinical Endocrinology and Metabolism, 90,* 5382–5385.

Kreipe, R. E., & Harris, J. P. (1992). Myocardial impairment resulting from eating disorders. *Pediatric Annals, 21,* 760–768.

Laue, L., Gold, P. W., Richmond, A., & Chrousos, G. P. (1991). The hypothalamic-pituitary-adrenal axis in anorexia nervosa and bulimia nervosa: Pathophysiologic implications. *Advances in Pediatrics, 38,* 287–316.

Lo, D. Y., Yen, J. L., & Jones, M. P. (2004). Massive gastric dilation and necrosis in anorexia nervosa: Cause or effect? *Nutritional Clinical Practice, 19,* 409–412.

Lowinger, K., Griffiths, R. A., Beumont, P. J., Seieluna, H., & Touyz, W. (1999). Fluid restriction in anorexia nervosa: A neglected symptom or new phenomenon? *The International Journal of Eating Disorders, 26,* 392–396.

Lunca, S., Rikkers, A., & Stanescu, A. (2005). Acute massive gastric dilatation: severe ischemia and gastric necrosis without perforation. *Romanian Journal of Gastroenterology, 14,* 279–283.

McCallum, K., Bermudez, O., Ohlemeyer, C., Tyson, E., Portilla, M., & Ferdman, B. (2006). How should the clinician evaluate and manage the cardiovascular complications of anorexia nervosa? *Eating Disorders, 14*, 73–80.

McClain, C., Humphries, L. L., Hill, K. K., & Nicki, N. S. (1993). Gastrointestinal and nutritional aspects of eating disorders. *Journal of the American College of Nutrition, 12*, 466–474.

Melanson, E., Donahoo, W. T., Krantz, M. H., Poirier, P., & Mehler, P. S. (2004). Resting and ambulatory heart rate variability in chronic anorexia nervosa. *The American Journal of Cardiology, 94*, 1217–1220.

Miller, K. K., Grieco, K. A., Mulder, J., Grinspoon, S., Mickley, D., Yehezkel, R., et al. (2004). Effects of risedronate on bone density in anorexia nervosa. *The Journal of Clinical Endocrinology and Metabolism, 89*, 3903–3906.

Milosevic, A., Brodie, D., & Slade, P. D. (1997). Dental erosion, oral hygiene, and nutrition in eating disorders. *The International Journal of Eating Disorders, 21*, 195–199.

Misra, M., Aggarwal, A., Miller, K. K., Almazan, C., Worley, M., Soyka, L. A., et al. (2004). Effects of anorexia nervosa on clinical, hematologic, biochemical, and bone density parameters in community-dwelling adolescent girls. *Pediatrics, 114*, 1574–1583.

Misra, M., Miller, K. K., Almazan, C., Worley, M., Herzog, D. B., & Klibanski, A. (2005). Hormonal determinants of regional body composition in adolescent girls with anorexia nervosa and controls. *The Journal of Clinical Endocrinology and Metabolism, 90*, 2580–2587.

Misra, M., Miller, K. K., Tsai, P., Steward, V., End, A., Freed, N., et al. (2006). Uncoupling of cardiovascular risk markers in adolescent girls with anorexia nervosa. *The Journal of Pediatrics, 149*, 763–769.

Mitchell, J. E., Pomeroy, C., Seppala, M., & Huber, M. (1988). Pseudo-Bartter's syndrome, diuretic abuse, idiopathic edema and eating disorders. *The International Journal of Eating Disorders, 7*, 225–237.

Nakahara, T., Nagai, N., Tanaka, M., Muranaga, T., Kohima, S., Nozoe, S., & Naruo, T. (2006). The effects of bone therapy on tibial bone loss in young women with anorexia nervosa. *The International Journal of Eating Disorders, 39*, 20–26.

Ohwada, R., Hotta, M., Kimura, H., Takagi, S., Matsuda, N., Nomura, K., & Takane, K. (2005). Ampulla cardiomyopathy after hypoglycemia in three young female patients with anorexia nervosa. *Internal Medicine, 44*, 228–233.

Ohwada, R., Hotta, M., Oikawa, S., & Takano, K. (2006). Etiology of hypercholesterolemia in patients with anorexia nervosa. *The International Journal of Eating Disorders, 39*, 598–601.

Peters, T. E., Parvin, M., Petersen, C., Faircloth, V. C., & Levine, R. L. (2007). A case report of Wernicke's encephalopathy in a pediatric patient with anorexia nervosa—restricting type. *Journal of Adolescent Health, 40*, 376–383.

Peveler, R. C., Bryden, K. S., Neil, H. A., Fairburn, C. G., Mayou, R. A., Dunger, D. B., & Turner, H. M. (2005). The relationship of disordered eating habits and attitudes to clinical outcomes in young adult females with type 1 diabetes. *Diabetes Care, 28*, 84–88.

Piccoli, A., Codognotto, M., Di Pascoli, L., Boffo, G., & Caregaro, L. (2005). Body mass index and agreement between bioimpedance and anthropometry estimates of body compartments in anorexia nervosa. JPEN *Journal of Parenteral and Enteral Nutrition, 29*, 148–156.

Pomeroy, C., Mitchell, J. E., & Roerig, J. (2002): *Medical complications of psychiatric disorders*. Washington, DC: American Psychiatric Association Press.

Reichborn-Kjennerud, T., Bulik, C. M., Sullivan, P. F., Tambs, K., & Harris, J. R. (2004). Psychiatric and medical symptoms in binge eating in the absence of compensatory behaviors. *Obesity Research, 12*, 1445–1454.

Rieger, E., Wilfley, D. E., Stein, R. I., Marino, V., & Crow, S. J. (2005). A comparison of quality of life in obese individuals with and without binge eating disorder. *The International Journal of Eating Disorders, 37*, 234–240.

Roche, F., Barthelemy, J. C., Mayaud, N., Pichot, V., Duverney, D., Germain, N., et al. (2005). Refeeding normalizes the QT rate dependence of female anorexic patients. *The American Journal of Cardiology, 95*, 277–280.

Rydall, A. C., Rodin, G. M., Olmsted, M. P., Devenyi, R. G., & Daneman, D. (1997). Disordered eating behavior and microvascular complications in young women with insulin-dependent diabetes mellitus. *New England Journal of Medicine, 336*, 1849–1854.

Schocken, D. D., Holloway, J. D., & Powers, P. S. (1989). Weight loss and the heart. *Archives of Internal Medicine, 149*, 877–881.

Senzaki, H., Kurihara, M., Masutani, S., Sasaki, N., Kyo, S., & Yokote, Y. (2006). Left ventricular hypertrophy and outflow tract obstruction in a patient with anorexia nervosa. *Circulation, 113*, 759–761.

Strokosch, G. R., Friedman, A. J., Wu, S., & Kamin, M. (2006). Effects of an oral contraceptive (norgestimate/ethinyl estradiol) on bone mineral density in adolescent females with anorexia nervosa: A double-blind, placebo-controlled study. *The Journal of Adolescent Health, 39*, 819–827.

Strumia, R. (2005). Dermatologic signs in patients with eating disorders. *American Journal of Clinical Dermatology, 6*, 165–173.

Studen-Pavlovich, D., & Elliott, M. A. (2001). Eating disorders in women's oral health. *Dental Clinics of North America, 45*, 491–511.

Takakura, S., Nozaki, T., Nomura, Y., Koreeda, C., Urabe, H., Kawai, K., et al. (2006). Factors related to renal dysfunction in patients with anorexia nervosa. *Eating and Weight Disorders, 11*, 73–77.

Takii, M., Uchigata, Y., Tokunaga, S., Amemiya, N., Kinukawa, N., Nozaki, T., et al. (2008). The duration of severe insulin omission is the factor most closely associated with the microvascular complications of type 1 diabetic females with clinical eating disorders. *The International Journal of Eating Disorders, 41*, 259–264.

Thomas, M. A., & Rebar, R. W. (1990). The endocrinology of anorexia nervosa and bulimia nervosa. *Current Opinion in Obstetrics and Gynecology, 2*, 831–836.

Van Wymelbeke, V., Brondel, L., Marcel Brun, J., & Rigaud, D. (2004). Factors associated with the increase in resting energy expenditure during refeeding in malnourished anorexia nervosa patients. *American Journal of Clinical Nutrition, 80*, 1469–1477.

Williams, P. M., Goodie, J., & Motsinger, C. D. (2008). Treating eating disorders in primary care. *American Family Physician, 77*, 187–195.

Winstead, N. S., & Willard, S. G. (2001). Frequency of physician visits for GI complaints by anorexic and bulimic patients. *American Journal of Gastroenterology, 96*, 1667–1668.

Wolfert, A., & Mehler, P. S. (2002). Osteoporosis: Prevention and treatment in anorexia nervosa. *Eating and Weight Disorders, 7*, 72–81.

Medical Screening and Management of Eating Disorders in Adolescents

Debra K. Katzman, Nuray O. Kanbur, *and* Cathleen M. Steinegger

Abstract

Eating disorders (EDs) in adolescents are serious illnesses that affect many aspects of their lives. The medical assessment includes a thorough history, physical exam, and targeted laboratory testing. EDs can cause serious medical complications in every organ system. Clinicians should be aware of medical conditions that may cause similar presenting symptoms and also be able to identify any medical complications that develop as consequence of the ED. Acute and long-term medical complications have been identified in adolescents with EDs. Medical management focuses on nutritional rehabilitation, weight restoration, and the prevention or reversal of medical complications. Treatment may occur in a variety of settings, but should be delivered by an interdisciplinary, experienced team and include the adolescent's family.

Keywords: adolescents, eating disorders, interdisciplinary team, medical assessment, medical complications, medical management

Introduction

For children and adolescents, eating disorders (EDs) are complex and affect many aspects of their lives. This complexity necessitates the involvement of an interdisciplinary, coordinated team of skilled professionals. An essential part of the interdisciplinary evaluation is the medical assessment, including a medical history, comprehensive physical examination, and targeted laboratory tests. The medical assessment helps establish a diagnosis, determine the medical complications, recognize comorbidities, and create an initial treatment plan. This chapter discusses the comprehensive medical assessment of adolescents with EDs and reviews the medical complications and management of this condition.

Taking a History from an Adolescent with an Eating Disorder

Assessing an adolescent with an ED is seldom straightforward. Adolescents rarely come to an assessment willingly and rarely see the need for treatment. Often their parents identify the problem and make the referral.

Characteristics unique to adolescents with EDs may explain this behavior. EDs can develop at anytime during childhood and adolescence (Nicholls, Chater, & Lask, 2000). Unique variations in the cognitive development of children and adolescents may limit their ability to understand or be aware of their body shape, weight, or size; or to understand or appreciate the meaning of their abnormal eating behaviors and thoughts (Bravender et al., 2007). Most often, adolescents with EDs do not perceive themselves as having a problem, so they see no reason to seek help or to change. Those who recognize that they have a problem may be embarrassed by their thoughts and behaviors. Regardless, they may find these issues difficult to discuss with their parents, family members, friends, or clinicians. In fact, to maintain their attitudes and behaviors, adolescents often try to keep their parents and clinicians from knowing about them, commonly minimizing or denying their symptoms. Moreover, these adolescents may be aware of the positive and negative stigma associated with EDs. Some feel a sense of pride, accomplishment, control, and satisfaction—compelling feelings they may be unwilling to give up. Others may be concerned about being judged, criticized, or labeled.

Clinicians need to be prepared that some parents may be reluctant to share with their adolescent that they are going for an ED assessment. Even those adolescents who know the purpose of the assessment may feel angry, betrayed, and ashamed, and may initially be unwilling to participate in the process. At the same time, their parents may be experiencing feelings of concern, worry, and guilt. It is often helpful for the clinician to be aware of these possible scenarios and address the issues directly if the interview with the adolescent is to be successful.

Approach to the Interview

Clinicians can approach interviewing adolescents with an ED in several ways. No one way is better than another; often the circumstances determine the approach used. One beneficial approach is to meet first with the adolescent and the parents, and then with the adolescent alone. This approach can be most productive because the adolescent may deny or downplay her or his symptoms, family members may be better able to express their concerns, and the clinician can emphasize the invaluable input of both the adolescent and the parents and the important role parents play in supporting the adolescent during recovery (Le Grange, Lock, & Dymek, 2003). With younger adolescents, in particular, having the parents take part in the assessment and treatment of their child is developmentally appropriate. Further, this approach provides a venue in which the adolescent and parents can communicate with one another and the clinician about why they have come to the assessment. This communication can be quite important to their mutual understanding and concerns, and to the clinician observing the relationship between the adolescent and parents.

At the outset, the clinician should attempt to put everyone at ease by being clear, understanding, nonjudgmental, and approachable. Providing an overview of what is going to happen during the assessment is often helpful. This initial interview and assessment establishes the foundation of the therapeutic alliance between the clinician and the adolescent and the family. This professional relationship is fundamental to the engagement of the adolescent and the family. According to one study, (Pereira, Lock, & Oggins, 2006) for adolescents with EDs and their parents, this therapeutic alliance was strongly associated with their satisfaction with their treatment and was thought to contribute to treatment retention and the positive outcome.

Having the adolescent and parents together during the first part of the interview provides an excellent opportunity for the discussion of confidentiality and its limits. Once children and adolescents understand the scope and limitations of confidentiality, they can decide how comfortable they are revealing sensitive information during the assessment. Further, educating parents about issues of confidentiality can ease their concerns about their child meeting with the clinician alone (Hutchinson & Stafford, 2005). One study showed that adolescents were more willing to disclose sensitive information to clinicians when given assurances about confidentiality (Klostermann, Slap, Nebrig, Tivorsak, & Britto, 2005).

Interviewing the Adolescent

The success of the clinician's interview with the adolescent alone, after the initial meeting with both the adolescent and the parents, is based on a number of important factors (Steinegger & Katzman, 2008). The clinician should communicate with the adolescent in a manner appropriate to her or his age and developmental stage; create an environment that is safe, nonjudgmental, and empathic; demonstrate a clear understanding of EDs in general; and convey a genuine interest in the adolescent's personal experience with the ED. Together, these factors help establish trust and rapport, and increase the adolescent's willingness to connect with the clinician in a discussion about the ED.

To begin, the clinician will want to explore why the adolescent has come for an assessment. Adolescents may acknowledge that they have come voluntarily or that they were brought reluctantly because of issues related to their weight or their parents' concern about their weight, or their attitudes or behaviors toward eating. Clinicians should encourage adolescents to express, in their own words, their perception of the problem and possible solutions. Getting a clear picture of the history and progression of the adolescent's current illness is essential. Adolescents should be asked to describe their illness in chronologic order from the onset of the first symptoms to the present. Specifically, they should be asked to identify their concerns about food and their feelings about their body weight, shape, and size. Understanding the adolescent's weight history (previous heights and weights, when available; highest and lowest weights, and their timing and duration; and the extent and rapidity of weight loss), the adolescent's reasons for trying to lose weight, precipitating events that may have triggered the changes in weight, for example, teasing, comments by others (Haines, Neumark-Sztainer, Eisenberg, & Hannan, 2006), and the adolescent's view of her or his ideal weight will all aid in making a diagnosis and creating a treatment plan.

Obtaining an accurate history of the eating behaviors can be challenging because the adolescent will often deny the symptoms or diminish the problem. Nevertheless, a detailed history is important. Adolescents with EDs use a number of disordered eating behaviors to control their weight, including food restriction; exercise; competitive sports or sports that focus on body shape, weight, and size (e.g., ballet, gymnastics, figure skating, wrestling); binging; and purging. Clinicians need to probe for these behaviors. For example, if the adolescent uses exercise to control weight, the clinician should ask about the type, amount, and frequency of the exercise, the reason for it, and its nature (group or solitary). If the adolescent binge eats, information about its frequency, duration, and precipitating events or triggers is important. For purging behaviors, collecting information about their frequency and method (e.g., self-induced vomiting, abuse of laxatives, use of diuretics or ipecac, diet pills) is essential. Self-induced vomiting, one of the more common purging methods, can occur infrequently or up to several times a day and may or may not occur after a binge. Adolescents who self-induce vomiting can use a variety of methods to elicit the gag reflex, including their fingers, a foreign body (e.g., a toothbrush, cutlery), abdominal compression, and ingestion of a large amount of fluid. The clinician should also ask adolescents about their use of medications or other substances (e.g., laxatives, diuretics, diet pills, enemas, ipecac, insulin, nutritional supplements or complementary and alternative medicines, tobacco, illegal drugs and alcohol), and the type, number taken, last use, and frequency and duration of their use of these substances (Stock, Goldberg, Corbett, & Katzman, 2002).

A detailed dietary history that includes a 24-hour dietary recall will provide insight into the adolescent's energy intake, quality of nutritional intake, and attitudes and behaviors toward eating. The clinician should determine the types of foods and beverages consumed to reduce hunger (e.g., caffeinated coffee, tea, diet soda); portion sizes; diet products used; calorie and fat intake; low-fat or fat-free foods consumed; and foods that the adolescent considers forbidden or bad, and safe or good. Some adolescents report specific food allergies or lactose intolerance. It is important to understand when, why, and how these diagnoses were made. In addition, the clinician should ask the adolescent about vegetarianism because EDs are more common among adolescents who are vegetarian than in the general adolescent population (Neumark-Sztainer, Story, Resnick, & Blum, 1997). Understanding the reasons the young person became a vegetarian is helpful: for example, determining whether becoming a vegetarian is an ethical or religious decision, or an effective way of losing weight that would not raise concern among the adults in the adolescent's life.

The clinician also needs to explore the family's beliefs about, and attitudes and behaviors toward food, weight, and health. Understanding who does the grocery shopping, who prepares meals, and who is present at meals can provide insight into these attitudes and behaviors, and a better sense of how the family functions and interacts.

Obtaining an accurate history about the adolescent's self-perception and body image can be challenging when the adolescent already feels embarrassed, guilty, and angry—with themselves and those around them—especially for younger adolescents who may be concrete thinkers. It is important to explore how adolescents feel about the way they look, whether they are trying to change the way they look, whether they are dissatisfied with any part of their bodies and why, whether their feelings about their bodies affect the way they feel about themselves, and how much they worry about eating and their weight. This information helps clinicians determine whether their self-evaluation is connected with their body image.

It is not uncommon for adolescents with EDs to weigh themselves frequently, sometimes several times a day. The weight on the scale often determines how they feel about themselves. These young people may wear baggy clothes to hide their weight loss from family and friends.

For an adolescent who binges, the family may report the disappearance of large quantities of food or the presence of empty food containers. For an adolescent who purges, the family may notice that the adolescent makes frequent trips to the bathroom, especially after meals. In addition, there may be evidence of vomit in the bathroom, or laxatives or diuretics.

Adolescents with EDs can have a number of behaviors that are confusing to their parents, family members, and friends, and to the adolescents themselves. Adolescents with EDs may engage in a variety of food rituals, including cutting food into tiny pieces and moving it around their plates, chewing food and spitting it out, taking small bites, eating foods only of a particular colour, eating the same foods at the same time every day, preparing foods in an unappealing manner or hiding food to avoid eating it, and taking a long time to complete meals. It is not uncommon for adolescents with EDs to become interested in cooking for others, but not eating any of the prepared foods themselves, reading cookbooks, and watching cooking shows on the television. Some young people restrict their fluid intake for fear of becoming fat.

Menstrual History

Clinicians should include an evaluation of the menstrual cycle in their assessment of every female adolescent. Menstrual function is an important indicator of the overall health of a female adolescent. The clinician should ask about the adolescent's age of menarche, cycle length and duration, and the date of the last normal menstrual period. If the adolescent has not reached menarche, clinicians should ask about the age of onset of thelarche (breast budding), as menarche typically occurs within 2 to 3 years after thelarche. By 15 years of age, 98% of girls should have had menarche (Diaz, Laufer, & Breech, 2006). If the adolescent has secondary amenorrhea, it is essential to know how long she has been without a menstrual period and the weight at which she lost her menstrual period or her menstrual-threshold weight. The clinician should determine whether the adolescent is using contraception, including oral contraceptive pills or other medications that may affect her menstrual period. The clinician should ask whether the adolescent has a history of bone fractures because adolescents with a current or past history of anorexia nervosa (AN) with amenorrhea are at risk for decreased bone mass and bone fractures.

Also important for all adolescents is taking a sexual history that includes information about sexual experiences; sexual orientation; sexually transmitted infections; pregnancies; pregnancy-related complications; pregnancy outcomes; and sexual, physical, and emotional abuse (Wentz, Gillberg, Gillberg, & Rastam, 2005).

Medical History

The medical history should focus on obtaining information that is helpful for formulating a diagnosis and providing the adolescent with medical care. Before diagnosing an ED, the clinician must consider other medical conditions that may cause the presenting symptoms (e.g., weight loss, amenorrhea, vomiting, or abnormal eating behaviors). The clinician must also identify any medical complications that develop as a consequence of the ED (Katzman, 2005).

Review of Systems

A thorough and directed review of systems should be completed for each adolescent. A series of questions seeking to identify common signs or symptoms that an adolescent with an ED may be experiencing or has experienced should be elicited. Table 16.1 lists common signs and symptoms associated with EDs (Steinegger & Katzman, 2008).

Family History

The clinician should get an understanding of the family background (family origin, ethnic background). The clinician should ask the adolescent and parents about other family members who may have had medical and psychiatric disorders (e.g., EDs, mental illness, or substance abuse) and the type of treatment that was provided. Causes of death in closely related family members should also be noted.

Brief Adolescent Psychiatric History

Adolescents with EDs commonly have low self-esteem and feelings of worthlessness. Parents of adolescents with EDs frequently describe the adolescent's moods as unpredictable or irritable. Many adolescents with EDs also describe themselves as moody. Although starvation alone can contribute to mood disturbances, a comorbid mental illness may also contribute to their moodiness: 50% to 60% of young people with an ED have a comorbid psychiatric disorder, most commonly depression or anxiety (Steinhausen, 2002). Over time, adolescents with EDs become increasingly isolated, withdrawing from friends and family. They spend a great deal of time on their own thinking about meals, preparing food, exercising, or planning the next binge or purge. They may become quite rigid in their thinking and behavior. For example, they may experience changes in daily routines as disastrous. Asking them about self-harm and thoughts of suicide is essential (Ruuska, Kaltiala-Heino, Rantanen, & Koivisto, 2005). These are serious problems among people with EDs; suicide attempts occur in 10% to 20% of patients with AN and in 25% to 35% of patients

Table 16.1   Physical Signs and Symptoms Associated with Eating Disorders

System	Anorexia Nervosa	Bulimia Nervosa
General	• Weight loss • Feeling cold • Dehydration • Fatigue • Irritability/mood changes • Depression • Hypothermia	• Weight fluctuations • Irritability/mood changes • Dehydration • Fatigue
Head, Eyes, Ears, Nose, and Throat	• Dry, cracked lips and tongue	• Dry lips and tongue • Palatal scratches • Sore throat • Painful teeth and gums • Dental caries/enamel erosion • Parotid gland swelling
Cardiovascular	• Dizziness • Chest pain • Palpitations • Arrhythmias (bradycardia) • Orthostatic blood pressure or heart rate changes • Cold and/or blue hands and feet • Delayed capillary refill • Ankle swelling	• Dizziness • Chest pain • Palpitations • Arrhythmias • Orthostatic blood pressure or heart rate changes • Ankle swelling
Gastrointestinal	• Early satiety • Episodes of abdominal pain and discomfort • Constipation • Bloating after meals	• Heartburn • Blood in vomitus • Epigastric tenderness • Diarrhea or constipation
Endocrine	• Absent or irregular menses • Fractures • Delay puberty	• Absent or irregular menses
Dermatologic	• Dry skin • Pallor • Lanugo • Brittle nails • Carotenoderma (Yellow-or orange discoloration of skin) • Thin, dry hair	• Calluses on the dorsum of hand - (Russell's sign) • Dry mouth
Musculoskeletal	• Fatigue, muscle weakness, and cramps	• Fatigue, muscle weakness, and cramps
Neurological	• Decreased concentration, memory, thinking ability	• Decreased concentration, memory, thinking ability

Adapted from Steinegger, C., & Katzman, D. K. (2008). Interviewing the adolescent with an eating disorder. *Adolescent Medicine: State of the Art Reviews, 19*(1), 18–40.

with bulimia nervosa (BN; Herpertz-Dahlmann, 2009).

Interviewing the Adolescent and Parents

At the conclusion of this interview, the clinician should ask whether the adolescent has any questions or additional information for the clinician. The parents are then invited back to meet with the clinician and the adolescent. This is an appropriate time to get a more detailed account of the parents' understanding of the adolescent's problem. The parents usually know that their child is suffering from an ED. However, on occasion, a parent may believe that the presenting symptoms (weight loss, loss of appetite, vomiting, or amenorrhea) may be the result of another medical problem. Meeting with the parents and the adolescent after their adolescent's solo interview lets the clinician review any unanswered questions, clarify details of the adolescent's history, and corroborate the adolescent's information. In addition, meeting with the adolescent and parents is an opportunity to provide education about the disorder and its treatment.

The clinician needs to keep in mind that having the patient and parents in the same room while gathering more history about the adolescent's complaint may be emotionally charged. Adolescents are often simultaneously angry about the assessment and worried about how their parents are feeling. Parents are often feeling both concerned and guilty about their child's health. However, having the parents and adolescent together allows the clinician to communicate the importance of having them both involved in the adolescent's treatment for the ED.

Collateral Information

Obtaining additional information from other sources may be important to making a diagnosis and treatment plan. Getting permission to speak with the adolescent's paediatrician or family physician or requesting reports, psychological tests or laboratory investigations from previous healthcare professionals can be helpful.

Concluding the Interview

At the conclusion of the interview, the clinician should inform the patient about the physical examination and laboratory investigations that are part of the comprehensive assessment for an ED. When all parts of the assessment are complete, the clinician then meets with the adolescent and the family to discuss the results, review the diagnosis, and establish a treatment plan.

Physical Examination

The physical examination should focus on the physical signs found in adolescents with EDs (see Table 16.1) (Steinegger & Katzman, 2008). The adolescent's vital signs, including orthostatic heart rate, blood pressure, and oral temperature, should be measured. Common abnormalities in vital signs include bradycardia, orthostatic hypotension, and hypothermia. Accurate measurements of weight and height should also be taken with the patient in a hospital gown, in a private area, after the patient has emptied the bladder. Some adolescents with EDs may try to hide their true weight by ingesting excessive fluids (water-loading) or by surreptitiously putting weights in their pockets or underclothing before being weighed. The body mass index (BMI; weight in kilograms divided by height in meters squared) should be calculated; then the weight, height, and BMI should be plotted on growth charts. Previous data about weight and height help establish the adolescent's premorbid growth patterns. Alterations in growth patterns may be the first indication of an ED. For instance, adolescents may have weight loss or no weight gain with normal or expected increases in height. In some cases, height will be affected and growth may stop or diminish. To monitor physical changes and normal pubertal growth and development, the sexual maturity rating (breast development and pubic hair for girls, and genital development and pubic hair for boys) should be determined.

Laboratory Evaluation

Targeted laboratory testing can help rule out other medical illnesses. When a young person is chronically starved, the results of initial laboratory tests commonly look normal. However, if an adolescent is binging and purging, the results of the laboratory testing may reveal a number of metabolic abnormalities. This section focuses on suggested laboratory tests that should be done at the time of the initial assessment; however, laboratory investigations done during nutritional rehabilitation also play an important role in revealing a variety of serious and life-threatening abnormalities.

The recommended laboratory tests done during the initial assessment include a complete blood cell count; measurements of the erythrocyte sedimentation rate (ESR) (Anyan, 1974) and electrolyte levels; glucose, renal and liver function tests; urinalysis; and measurements of the levels of thyroid-stimulating hormone (TSH), luteinizing hormone (LH), follicle-stimulating hormone (FSH), and estradiol.

A urine pregnancy test for adolescent girls who have amenorrhea should be considered. A baseline electrocardiogram (ECG) is also recommended. An x-ray examination of the hand and wrist to determine the bone age should be considered if there is evidence of growth failure. Finally, low bone mineral density (BMD) is a common complication that may occur early in the course of AN (Bachrach, Guido, Katzman, Litt, & Marcus, 1990). Therefore, the clinician should consider obtaining a dual-energy x-ray absorptiometry (DXA) scan after 6 months of amenorrhea for adolescents with AN and for those with BN who have a history of AN (Golden, 2003). An explanation of the specific laboratory abnormalities reported in adolescents with EDs is offered below.

Differential Diagnosis

The diagnosis of an ED should be suspected in any child or adolescent with unexplained weight loss, food avoidance, decreased appetite, or abnormal eating attitudes and behaviors. Occasionally, EDs may be mistaken for a medical condition or a medical condition may be misdiagnosed as an ED. However, children and adolescents with a medical condition and associated weight loss explicitly express concern over their weight loss; this is rarely, if ever, the case in adolescents with an ED. Clinicians should consider diagnoses of hyperthyroidism, Addison's disease, diabetes mellitus, malignancy, inflammatory bowel disease, immunodeficiency, malabsorption, chronic infections (tuberculosis, human immunodeficiency virus), tumors of the central nervous system, and collagen vascular disease before diagnosing an ED.

Clinicians should also consider psychiatric disorders, including mood and anxiety disorders, somatization disorder, substance abuse disorder, and psychosis in the differential diagnoses. Psychiatric comorbidity is common in children and adolescents with EDs. Up to 80% of adolescents with AN and BN have major depressive disorder during the acute stages of the illness. Between 20% and 60% of adolescents with AN have anxiety disorders (Herpertz-Dahlmann, Wewetzer, & Remschmidt, 1995; Salbach-Andrae et al., 2008). Prevalence rates for these conditions in an adolescent populations with BN are difficult to find because patients with BN are often older than those with AN. However, the prevalence of anxiety disorders in patients with BN varies between 25% and 75% (Swinbourne & Touyz, 2007). About one-third of adolescents with AN cross over to BN (Strober, Freeman, & Morrell, 1997).

Medical Complications

The clinician should be aware of the medical complications associated with EDs for adolescents who restrict, binge, or purge. EDs can be life-threatening and can cause serious medical complications in every organ system in the growing, developing body. The literature on abnormalities in cardiac structure and function, disturbances in metabolic function, impaired pubertal growth and development, decreased bone mineral accretion, and changes in brain structure and function in patients with EDs is growing (Fisher et al., 1995; Katzman, 2005). Both the acute and long-term medical complications of EDs are discussed in the following sections.

Acute Medical Complications

CARDIOVASCULAR COMPLICATIONS

Although cardiac deaths in adolescents with AN are rare, both functional and structural cardiac abnormalities have been reported early in the illness (Katzman, 2005). The most commonly reported cardiovascular complications include ECG abnormalities and arrhythmias, such as bradycardia, low voltage of P waves and QRS complexes, prolonged QTc intervals, right-axis shift of the QRS axis, nonspecific ST-T changes, presence of U waves, and conduction disturbances (Katzman, 2005).

Cardiac conduction abnormalities, most commonly sinus bradycardia, are reported in 35% to 95% of adolescents with AN (Dec, Biederman, & Hougen, 1987; Mont et al., 2003; Palla & Litt, 1988; Panagiotopoulos, McCrindle, Hick, & Katzman, 2000). A retrospective study (Vanderdokt, Lambert, Montero, Boland, & Brohet, 2001) that used 12-lead ECGs on patients with AN reported sinus bradycardia as the predominant feature and, less frequently, ectopic atrial focus, right-axis deviation, and nonspecific ST-T changes. In patients with AN, bradycardia is thought to be caused by increased vagal activity, a physiological adaptive response to the hypometabolic state caused by starvation (Nudel, Gootman, Nussbaum, & Shenker, 1984). In one study (Panagiotopoulos et al., 2000), adolescents with AN had significantly lower heart rates than matched controls, and the severity of the illness (as measured with BMI) correlated significantly with increased bradycardia.

The evidence for prolongation of the QTc interval and increased QTc dispersion in adolescents with AN is conflicting. Studies have reported QTc prolongation and dispersion (Swenne & Larsson, 1999), whereas another report exclusively done with adolescents (Panagiotopoulos et al., 2000) did not find increased QTc dispersion when patients with EDs were compared with controls. The cause for the reported QTc prolongation in some patients remains a matter of debate (Vanderdokt et al., 2001). Despite this, QTc prolongation, if present, is cause for concern because this condition is associated with ventricular arrhythmias and death (Katzman, 2005).

Changes in orthostatic heart rate and blood pressure are common in adolescents with AN (Shamim, Golden, Arden, Filiberto, & Shenker, 2003). Orthostatic changes may be the result of dehydration and hypovolemia, particularly in adolescents who restrict fluid intake, engage in self-induced vomiting, or abuse laxatives. Adolescents with AN who are dehydrated exhibit a relative tachycardia, rather than the bradycardia classically seen in patients with AN. Dizziness and fainting may occur as a result of dehydration (Fairburn & Harrison, 2003; Halmi, 2002; Pomeroy & Mitchell, 2002). Caution should be used when administering intravenous fluids because the increased cardiac work and circulating fluids can potentially precipitate acute heart failure. In the absence of dehydration, the orthostatic changes may be caused by atrophic peripheral muscles that decrease the venous return of blood to the heart. Normalization of the orthostatic heart rate occurs after adolescents with AN have had about three weeks of nutritional rehabilitation or when they reach about 80% of their ideal body weight (Shamim et al., 2003).

Many studies reported that strict caloric deprivation has significant effects on cardiac structure and myocardial mass, as well as cardiac function (Casiero & Frishman, 2006). Echocardiographic findings show a loss of cardiac muscle, which is evident from the decreased thickness of the left ventricular wall (Casiero & Frishman, 2006; Mont et al., 2003; Olivares et al., 2005). Other findings showed that patients with AN have reduced diastolic and systolic left-ventricular internal dimension, left-ventricular mass, left-ventricular mass index, and cardiac output (Olivares et al., 2005).

Mitral valve prolapse (MVP) has been reported in 20% of patients with AN. Patients with EDs seem to have an increased incidence of MVP (Casiero & Frishman, 2006; de Simone et al., 1994; Goldberg, Comerci, & Feldman, 1988; Katzman, 2005). In those with AN, MVP is believed to develop as a consequence of a relatively large and redundant mitral apparatus and a reduced left-ventricular mass (Katzman, 2005). Although this particular valvular abnormality does not seem to be clinically significant (de Simone et al., 1994), its arrhythmogenic

propensity may pose an additional risk to these adolescents (Johnson, Humphries, Shirley, Mazzoleni, & Noonan, 1986).

Pericardial effusion without clinical signs and symptoms (silent effusion) has been found in approximately 60% of patients with AN (Silvetti et al., 1998). Although the pathophysiology and the clinical significance of pericardial effusion remain unclear, the presence of a pericardial effusion is related to low BMI in patients with AN (Katzman, 2005).

Cardiovascular complications secondary to refeeding have been reported in up to 6% of hospitalized patients. The hypokalemia, hypophosphatemia, other electrolyte abnormalities, and fluid shifts caused by refeeding can result in the development of prolongation of the QTc interval, electrocardiographic changes, and other arrhythmias (Halmi, 2002; Neumarker, 1997; Pomeroy & Mitchell, 2002; Yager & Andersen, 2005). These electrolyte abnormalities and fluid shifts, in combination with decreased ventricular mass and myofibrillar atrophy, can increase cardiac workload and heart rate, causing congestive heart failure. Slow refeeding with a gradual increase in calories, and ongoing, regular cardiac and electrolyte monitoring will minimize the risk of the cardiac complications caused by refeeding.

Ipecac abuse has been reported among adolescents who use the syrup solely to self-induce emesis to control their weight (Silber, 2005). Ipecac contains the active alkaloids emetine and cephalin. Adolescents who abuse ipecac may develop cardiomyopathies that can lead to arrhythmias, T-wave abnormalities, QTc prolongation or other ECG changes, ventricular dysfunction, precordial chest pain, enlarged heart, reduced ejection fraction, and tricuspid or mitral valve insufficiency (Manno & Manno, 1977; Schneider et al., 1996). Further, ipecac causes irreversible and fatal cardiomyopathies because it accumulates in cardiac tissue (Halmi, 2002; Pomeroy & Mitchell, 2002).

PULMONARY COMPLICATIONS
Adolescents who engage in self-induced vomiting are at increased risk of primary pneumomediastinum, pneumothorax, subcutaneous emphysema, and rib fractures (McAnarney, Greydanus, Campanella, & Hoekelman, 1983). Pneumomediastinum and subcutaneous emphysema were reported in an adolescent with self-induced vomiting (Overby & Litt, 1988). Adolescents could potentially develop aspiration pneumonia as a result of inhaling gastric contents.

ORAL AND DENTAL COMPLICATIONS

In general, oral hygiene in patients with AN is satisfactory, although there seems to be an increased risk of dental caries because of poor nutrition (Lo Muzio et al., 2007). For patients with BN, oral manifestations are chiefly attributable to the practice of self-induced vomiting. The hydrochloric acid in gastric juices can affect the hard and soft tissues of the oral cavity. Perimolysis, or deterioration of the tooth enamel, specifically of the occlusal surfaces of the molars and the posterior surfaces of the maxillary incisors, and the increased sensitivity of the teeth to external stimuli are common complications in patients who vomit (Lo Muzio et al., 2007). Recurrent episodes of binging on high carbohydrate foods can also cause dental caries (Glorio et al., 2000). Since these effects are irreversible, patients with this complication need to have regular dental care. Reported changes in soft tissue include epithelial erosions, mucosal erythema, and loss of papillae on the dorsal surface of the tongue. Superficial injuries to the back of the throat or mouth are caused by the mechanical stimulation of the gag reflex (e.g., use of a finger or foreign object). Sore throat and hoarseness are not uncommon.

Bilateral, and occasionally unilateral, parotid gland swelling is an important clinical sign in adolescents who vomit or have BN. The incidence of parotid gland swelling occurs in 10% to 15% of people with BN (Brady, 1985; Ogren, Huerter, Pearson, Antonson, & Moore, 1987). The exact cause of this swelling is unknown. Glandular enlargement is typically painless and may occur within several days of excessive vomiting. Hypertrophy of parotid glands can cause elevated levels of serum amylase (Boeck; Pomeroy & Mitchell, 2002). This complication is reversible with cessation of vomiting.

GASTROINTESTINAL COMPLICATIONS

Gastrointestinal complications of EDs are common in adolescents with AN and BN. The clinical severity can range from mild discomfort to life-threatening disorders.

The exposure of the esophagus to gastric acid can cause esophagitis and esophageal spasm. Hematemesis in an adolescent with BN may be indicative of Mallory Weiss tears (Pomeroy & Mitchell, 2002), which are lacerations in the mucous membranes at the junction of the esophagus and stomach, secondary to vomiting. Making a definitive diagnosis requires endoscopy. Although rare, this condition can rupture the esophagus, causing a potentially fatal medical emergency.

Acute gastric dilatation may result from refeeding or binging (Mitchell & Crow, 2006; Pomeroy & Mitchell, 2002; Zipfel et al., 2006). Gastric dilation may manifest as spontaneous vomiting and acute abdominal pain and distention. Most cases can be managed conservatively with gastric decompression (Zipfel et al., 2006). Clinicians should be aware that although rare, gastric dilatation may result in gastric necrosis, gastric perforation and death (Zipfel et al., 2006).

Although patients with AN may frequently report dysphagia, consistent evidence for abnormal esophageal motility is lacking (Chial, McAlpine, & Camilleri, 2002; Zipfel et al., 2006). A study (Stacher et al., 1986) that investigated esophageal and gastric motility in adolescents and young adult women with AN, reported that 50% of the patients had abnormal esophageal manometry results. A subsequent study (Benini et al., 2001) of patients with AN showed normal esophageal manometry and motility, but impaired gastric and colonic motility.

Bloating, nausea, abdominal distension, and a sensation of fullness, common complaints of patients with AN, are often caused by prolonged gastrointestinal transit time (Brown, Mehler, & Harris, 2000; Woodside, 1995; Zipfel et al., 2006). Delayed gastric emptying of solids is a consistent finding in patients with AN, whereas their gastric emptying of liquids may be normal or delayed (Chial et al., 2002). One study (Holt, Ford, Grant, & Heading, 1981) showed slower gastric emptying for both the solid and liquid components of a meal in adolescents and young adults with AN than in healthy subjects. Delayed gastric emptying may be a result of increased vagal activity induced by starvation. Abnormalities in gastric emptying tend to improve with refeeding and weight restoration (Chial et al., 2002).

Constipation is a common complaint among patients with AN. Reduced food intake, dehydration, electrolyte abnormalities (e.g., hypokalemia), and slowed colonic transit time can contribute to the development of constipation (Chial et al., 2002; Pomeroy & Mitchell, 2002; Woodside, 1995; Zipfel et al., 2006). Colonic motility normalizes with consumption of a balanced diet and weight gain (Benini et al., 2001; Chial et al., 2002). Constipation is also a problem for patients with BN, secondary to dehydration, electrolyte abnormalities, and laxative abuse (Zipfel et al., 2006).

Serum protein and albumin levels are typically normal; however, mild elevation of liver enzymes secondary to fatty infiltration and focal hepatic necrosis has been reported (Sherman, Leslie, Goldberg, Rybczynski, & St. Louis, 1994). Acute pancreatitis and superior mesenteric artery syndrome have also been reported as complications for patients with EDs (Chial et al., 2002; Fisher et al., 1995; Mitchell & Crow, 2006).

The majority of gastrointestinal complications are reversible with the resumption of normal food intake, eating behaviors and body weight (Zipfel et al., 2006).

ELECTROLYTE ABNORMALITIES

Adolescents with EDs are known to have fluid and electrolyte abnormalities secondary to malnutrition or purging behaviors. Restriction of fluid intake can cause dehydration in adolescents with AN. Loss of fluids resulting from self-induced vomiting, laxative or diuretic use can cause dehydration in adolescents with BN. The resultant changes in body fluid homeostasis may lead to severe and potentially life-threatening dehydration and/or electrolyte abnormalities.

The most serious and frequently documented electrolyte abnormality is hypokalemia caused by potassium loss due to self-induced vomiting, and diuretic or laxative abuse (Coupey, 1998; Forman, 2001). Serum levels are often normal, but intracellular potassium levels may be low enough to cause symptoms. Chronic hypokalemia can cause intestinal dysmotility and constipation, muscle myopathy, and nephropathy with associated high-serum creatinine levels that result in chronic renal failure and necessitate hemodialysis (Coupey, 1998; Forman, 2001; Pomeroy & Mitchell, 2002). Severe hypokalemia can result in fatal cardiac arrhythmias.

Asymptomatic and mild hypokalemia may be treated with oral potassium supplementation. However, if the clinical picture is complicated by hypochloremic metabolic alkalosis as a result of vomiting, the alkalosis should be corrected simultaneously with intravenous fluids and potassium. Low magnesium levels may occur when total-body potassium levels are restored. Low magnesium levels have been associated with muscular weakness, cramping, paresthesias, and arrhythmias (Hall et al., 1988; Pomeroy & Mitchell, 2002).

Hyponatremia may occur in adolescents with excessive water intake or water-loading. This behavior can cause seizures or death when the serum sodium falls below 120 mEq/L. Thiazide diuretics can also cause hyponatremia.

Refeeding syndrome consists of the metabolic and physiologic consequences of shifts in fluids and electrolytes that may occur in malnourished patients who are being refed (Solomon & Kirby, 1990). The hallmark biochemical feature of refeeding syndrome is hypophosphatemia. However, abnormalities of sodium and fluid balance; changes in glucose, protein, and fat metabolism; thiamine deficiency; hypokalemia; and hypomagnesemia may all be present (Solomon & Kirby, 1990). During starvation, total-body stores of phosphorus are depleted, even though serum levels are maintained. With refeeding, a sudden increase in insulin levels may occur, leading to an increased cellular uptake of phosphate and other nutrients. If feeding is too rapid or phosphate is not replaced, phosphate levels can drop to potentially fatal levels (Kohn, Golden, & Shenker, 1998; Solomon & Kirby, 1990). Adverse effects of hypophosphatemia include cardiac arrhythmia, cardiac failure, muscle weakness, immune dysfunction, neurological complications, such as confusion, seizures, and coma, and death (Fisher, Simpser, & Schneider, 2000; Katzman, 2005; Kohn et al., 1998; Solomon & Kirby, 1990). In one study (Ornstein, Golden, Jacobson, & Shenker, 2003), 27% of adolescents with AN had documented hypophosphatemia during the first week of refeeding. Refeeding syndrome is most commonly seen in severely malnourished patients with AN who are being refed in the hospital, although it may be seen at presentation if an adolescent has eaten large amounts of food in an attempt to avoid treatment (Fisher et al., 2000).

RENAL COMPLICATIONS

Studies of patients with AN (Aperia, Broberger, & Fohlin, 1978; Banji, 1988; Boag, Weerakoon, Ginsburg, Havard, & Dandona, 1985; Mecklenburg, Loriaux, Thompson, Andersen, & Lipsett, 1974; Russell & Bruce, 1966) have reported a variety of abnormalities in renal function, including a decline in glomerular filtration rate (GFR), impaired water diuresis, decreased ability to concentrate urine, and various electrolyte abnormalities. Alterations in renal function, as manifested by elevated levels of blood urea nitrogen (BUN), decreased GFR, and low urinary specific gravity, have been described in adult patients with AN (Aperia et al., 1978; Fohlin, 1977; Silverman, 1983). Adolescents with AN have exhibited similar renal changes. In one study (Palla & Litt, 1988), 22% of adolescents with AN had mildly elevated serum BUN levels (>20 mg/dL; maximum 27 mg/dL) with associated normal serum creatinine levels. In addition, adolescents with AN had hematuria, pyuria, and proteinuria (with a negative urine culture) that subsequently resolved with rehydration and refeeding (Palla & Litt, 1988).

Abnormal osmoregulation in patients with AN has been described in several studies (Aperia et al., 1978; Evrard, da Cunha, Lambert, & Devuyst, 2004; Mecklenburg et al., 1974; Russell & Bruce, 1966). The reduced ability to concentrate urine in patients with AN has been attributed to both hypothalamic dysfunction (partial neurogenic diabetes insipidus) (Mecklenburg et al., 1974) and renal abnormalities (Aperia et al., 1978). Clinically, this can result in increased thirst (polydipsia), increased urination (polyuria), and the inability to hold urine (enuresis) (Fisher et al., 1995; Pomeroy & Mitchell, 2002). A study (Nishita et al., 1989) in patients with AN and BN found irregularities in the pattern of their secretion of plasma vasopressin (the osmoregulating hormone) in response to a hypertonic saline infusion; some showed abnormally high vasopressin secretion; others showed an abnormally low vasopressin responses. Both of these secretion abnormalities occurred in underweight and weight-recovered patients with AN. A 21-year prospective follow-up study (Zipfel, Lowe, Reas, Deter, & Herzog, 2000) reported that 5.2% of patients with AN developed chronic renal failure, which necessitated hemodialysis.

METABOLIC ABNORMALITIES
Alterations in energy metabolism are among the more common features of EDs. The basal metabolic rate (BMR), or the amount of energy expended at rest in homeostatic conditions, is reduced in low-weight patients with AN compared with the BMR in weight-recovered patients and healthy controls (Obarzanek, Lesem, & Jimerson, 1994; Platte et al., 1994). It is unclear whether the decrease in BMR is the result of a change in body composition or whether it represents a downregulation of cellular metabolism. The rise in BMR seen during refeeding is higher than that seen in normal-weight, experimentally overfed, or experimentally underfed and refed subjects (Obarzanek et al., 1994). Similar findings have been reported in normal-weight patients with BN (Devlin et al., 1990).

Energy deficits reduce the activity of the sympathetic nervous system, alter peripheral thyroid metabolism, and lower insulin secretion. Leptin, an adipocyte-secreted hormone, may play a role in the complex mechanisms that regulate energy balance (Muller, Focker, Holtkamp, Herpertz-Dahlmann, & Hebebrand, 2009). Studies (Muller et al., 2009) have shown that leptin is reduced during the acute phase of AN and increases with weight gain. The degree of hypoleptinemia in the acute phase of AN is considered an indicator of the severity of the disorder.

Mild hypoglycemia is common and usually asymptomatic in patients with AN. Severe hypoglycemia, with plasma glucose levels as low as 1.0 mmol/L, very rarely occurs in patients with AN, but when it does, it is often fatal (Mattingly & Bhanji, 1995). The observations of simultaneously low fasting–blood glucose and plasma-insulin levels in patients with AN suggest increased insulin sensitivity, despite other metabolic and hormonal changes (increased plasma concentrations of free fatty acids, cortisol, and growth hormone) that are known factors of insulin resistance (Scheen, Castillo, & Lefebvre, 1988). In a recent study (Brown et al., 2003), normal fasting glucose concentrations with significantly lower fasting insulin concentrations and a significantly higher fasting glucose/insulin ratio were reported in weight-recovered patients with AN, indicating the presence of insulin hypersensitivity. The authors concluded that a persistent alteration in pancreatic function may be a long-term pathological consequence of AN.

A trend to hyperaminoacidemia is a common feature of AN. The plasma amino acid profile of AN is different from that of other severe malnutrition states, showing a marasmic pattern of balanced protein–energy undernutrition (Moyano, Vilaseca, Artuch, & Lambruschini, 1998), which explains why almost all patients with AN and BN have normal plasma total protein and albumin levels (Palla & Litt, 1988).

Hypercholesterolemia is common in adolescents with AN (Palla & Litt, 1988). Elevated cholesterol concentrations in AN are generally the result of an increase in low-density lipoprotein cholesterol, which is mostly determined by the mobilization of body fat and cholesterol during severe weight loss (Weinbrenner et al., 2004). Increased lipolysis, decreased endogenous cholesterol synthesis, and decreased bile-acid synthesis that results in decreased cholesterol catabolism are the suggested mechanisms of hypercholesterolemia in AN.

Vitamin and mineral deficiencies are potential causes of metabolic abnormalities in adolescents with EDs since these nutrients are required for normal functioning and growth. Although overt vitamin and mineral deficiencies are rarely reported, subclinical deficiencies must be considered, in particular iron, calcium, and zinc deficiencies (Fisher et al., 1995).

ENDOCRINE ABNORMALITIES

Endocrine abnormalities are common in adolescents with EDs (Fairburn & Harrison, 2003; Fisher et al., 1995; Katzman, 2005; Pomeroy & Mitchell, 2002). Most hormonal changes are thought to represent a hypometabolic response to starvation (Lawson & Klibanski, 2008). Another hypothesis is that some of the neuroendocrine changes seen in AN play a key role in both the pathophysiology and complications of these disorders. The presence of hormonal abnormalities in every endocrine axis in patients with AN is well documented (Newman & Halmi, 1988).

The most clinically recognized endocrinologic feature of AN is amenorrhea (Fisher et al., 1995; Pomeroy & Mitchell, 2002), which is currently a diagnostic criterion of AN in *DSM-IV* (American Psychiatric Association [APA], 1994). It is well documented that a critical minimum body weight is necessary for the return and maintenance of normal menstrual function in patients with AN (Frisch & McArthur, 1974; Stoving, Hangaard, Hansen-Nord, & Hagen, 1999). Golden et al. (Golden et al., 1997) measured body weight; percent body fat, using skinfold measurements; and serum LH, FSH, and estradiol levels at baseline and every 3 months until the return of menses in a cohort of adolescent girls with AN and secondary amenorrhea. Return of menses occurred at 90% of ideal body weight (defined as the median weight for height and age, as found in the National Center for Health statistical tables) or at 2.05 kg greater than the weight at which the menstrual period ceased. These findings occurred in 86% of adolescents within six months of achieving their ideal body weight. A retrospective study by Shomento and Kreipe (Shomento & Kreipe, 1994) found similar results; the return of menses occurred at 92% of ideal body weight.

Although weight loss typically precedes amenorrhea, some patients lose their menstrual periods before significant weight loss and some may achieve an extremely low weight while maintaining regular menses (Lawson & Klibanski, 2008). Amenorrhea in patients with AN is not only a result of caloric restriction and weight loss, but may also be a result of dysfunction of the hypothalamic-pituitary-ovarian (HPO) axis (Lawson & Klibanski, 2008; Pomeroy & Mitchell, 2002; Stoving et al., 1999). The circadian pattern of gonadotropin secretion in AN resembles that seen in the prepubertal years (Stoving et al., 1999), and amenorrhea in AN is related to deficient and dysrhythmic hypothalamic gonadotropin releasing hormone release. Plasma levels of FSH, LH, and estradiol are lowered to premenarchal levels in these patients (Palla & Litt, 1988; Pomeroy & Mitchell, 2002). Weight recovery is associated with a return to adult patterns of gonadotropin secretion.

Male adolescents with AN have hormonal profiles consistent with hypogonadotrophic hypogonadism. Testosterone, LH, and FSH levels are reduced in proportion to the amount of weight lost. Clinical signs of low testosterone levels include decreased testicular volume, delayed onset of puberty, and reduced bone density in male adolescents with AN (Chial et al., 2002).

Patients with BN are also at risk of HPO dysfunction and may experience irregular menses, even if they are a normal weight (Austin et al., 2008; Pomeroy & Mitchell, 2002). Some normal-weight women with BN have low LH and FSH levels, low estradiol levels, and reduced 24-hour LH secretion patterns (Devlin et al., 1989; Naessen, Carlstrom, Garoff, Glant, & Hirschberg, 2006; Pirke et al., 1987; Pirke, Dogs, Fichter, & Tuschl, 1988; Resch, Szendei, & Haasz, 2004; Schweiger, Pirke, Laessle, & Fichter, 1992). BN is also associated with polycystic ovarian syndrome, which may contribute to the menstrual dysfunction observed in women with BN. Unfortunately, the effect of BN on menstrual function is not well studied in adolescents.

Thyroid function is commonly abnormal in patients with AN and BN (Altemus, Hetherington, Kennedy, Licinio, & Gold, 1996; Palla & Litt, 1988). The most frequently described laboratory findings are normal thyroxine (T_4) and TSH levels with decreased triiodothyronine (T_3) levels (Fisher et al., 1995; Forman, 2001; Lawson & Klibanski, 2008; Stoving et al., 1999). This pattern is called the *low T_3 syndrome* and may be due to impaired peripheral conversion of T_4 to T_3 associated with chronic malnutrition or decreased thyroidal T_3 secretion in response to endogenous TSH (Chial et al., 2002; Kiyohara, Tamai, Takaichi, Nakagawa, & Kumagai, 1989). Hypothyroidism in AN may be a physiologic response to starvation and a protective mechanism for energy conservation (Chial et al., 2002; Fairburn & Harrison, 2003; Fisher et al., 1995). These findings are associated with fatigue, hypothermia, constipation, bradycardia, and hypercholesterolemia in patients with AN (Bannai et al., 1988). This state should not be taken as an indication to treat these patients with thyroid hormone (Fairburn & Harrison, 2003; Pomeroy & Mitchell, 2002).

Sustained elevated levels of cortisol that are not suppressed with a dexamethasone suppression test have been documented in patients with AN (Chial et al., 2002; Fisher et al., 1995; Pomeroy & Mitchell, 2002). Despite the often considerable and sustained biochemical hypercortisolemia, patients with AN do not have central fat accumulation because of a lack of substrate in the starved state (Lawson & Klibanski, 2008; Stoving et al., 1999). However, during recovery, increases in trunk adiposity with limb sparing have been noted, which may be the result of elevated levels of cortisol (Mayer et al., 2005; Misra et al., 2005). Increased cortisol levels contribute to the loss of bone density (Chial et al., 2002; Fisher et al., 1995; Katzman, 2005), amenorrhea, myopathy, and neuropsychiatric comorbidities, including mood disorders, neurocognitive deficits, and hippocampal atrophy (Chial et al., 2002; Lawson & Klibanski, 2008). Cortisol abnormalities improve with weight gain in those with AN (Lawson & Klibanski, 2008; Stoving et al., 1999). A refeeding study of patients with AN found that a 10% weight gain is associated with the normalization of cortisol secretion (Fichter, Doerr, Pirke, & Lund, 1982).

Cortisol levels may also be abnormal in BN patients. A recent study (Birketvedt et al., 2006) reported that the normal diurnal pattern of cortisol secretion is altered in patients with BN, compared with that of healthy controls; other research indicates dysregulation of cortisol at the hypothalamic and pituitary levels (Birketvedt et al., 2006; Mortola, Rasmussen, & Yen, 1989). This may indicate the complex and so far poorly understood neuroendocrine dysregulation associated with BN.

Growth hormone (GH) resistance with high or normal basal levels of GH and low levels of insulin-like growth factor-1 (IGF-1) and GH-binding protein has been reported in adolescents with AN (Counts, Gwirtsman, Carlsson, Lesem, & Cutler, 1992; Golden et al., 1994; Katzman, 2005; Misra et al., 2003). Acute starvation and protein-energy malnutrition are known to block IGF-1 production by the liver; therefore, GH excess in those with AN is the result, in part, of the lack of IGF-1–mediated negative feedback on GH production (Katzman, 2005; Lawson & Klibanski, 2008). IGF-1 in the circulation is the major effector of bone growth and functions by mediating most of the physiological actions of GH. IGF-1 stimulates endochondral bone formation and rapidly activates bone turnover (Kanbur, Derman, & Kinik, 2005). Potential clinical consequences of GH resistance and low IGF-1 levels include growth failure, bone loss, or insufficient bone mineral accrual and muscle atrophy

(see below for details) (Katzman, 2005; Lawson & Klibanski, 2008).

HEMATOLOGICAL AND IMMUNE SYSTEM ABNORMALITIES

Hematological abnormalities associated with AN are thought to be the result of changes in bone marrow (Geiser et al., 2001; Mant & Faragher, 1972). Decreased bone-marrow cellularity and abnormal architecture with marrow infiltration of gelatinous acid mucopolysaccharide has been found in patients with AN (Mant & Faragher, 1972). Magnetic resonance imaging (MRI) patterns of bone marrow in patients with AN correlate with the depletion of the total-body fat mass (Lambert et al., 1997). Bone-marrow hypoplasia results in varying degrees of anemia, leukopenia (usually with neutropenia and a relative lymphocytosis (Mant & Faragher, 1972), and, less frequently, thrombocytopenia. Occasionally, pancytopenia may be observed. The marrow abnormality is rapidly reversible with nutritional rehabilitation (Abella et al., 2002; Lambert et al., 1997).

Although mild subclinical deficiency of iron and folic acid has been reported, anemia is not common in patients with AN; if present, it is relatively mild (Mant & Faragher, 1972). In a recent study (Misra et al., 2004) of adolescent girls with AN, 22% were anemic. In another study (Kennedy, Kohn, Lammi, & Clarke, 2004), iron deficiency was uncommon at initial presentation and again after nutritional rehabilitation in postmenarchal adolescent females with AN. The authors concluded that iron storage was increased, secondary to the contraction of the circulating blood volume and the reduction in iron loss from secondary amenorrhea. Decreased ferritin levels were also observed during treatment and are attributed to the increased hematopoiesis necessary to fill the increased blood volume associated with weight gain.

In adolescents with EDs, the ESR is most often decreased (ESR <4 mm/h); an elevated ESR is reason to consider another diagnosis.

Although malnutrition-induced immunodeficiency is documented in patients with AN (Allende et al., 1998), findings about the specific defects and clinical implications of this condition are controversial (Nova, Samartin, Gomez, Morande, & Marcos, 2002). Cell-mediated immunity is usually altered in AN and BN, as reflected in abnormal lymphocyte subset counts and an abnormal response to delayed hypersensitivity tests (Mustafa, Ward, Treasure, & Peakman, 1997; Nova et al., 2002). Defective bactericidal activity of granulocytes (Kay & Stricker, 1983), defective in vitro granulopoiesis (Vaisman et al., 1996), low complement levels (Kay & Stricker, 1983; Pomeroy, et al., 1997), and changes in cytokines (Schattner, Tepper, Steinbock, Hahn, & Schoenfeld, 1990) have been reported in those with AN. Despite these findings, patients with AN do not seem to have an increased propensity to infection when compared with others who are protein-malnourished (Marcos, 2000; Mustafa et al., 1997; Nova et al., 2002). Nevertheless, clinicians should be aware that the usual clinical signs (e.g., fever, increased heart rate), symptoms, and laboratory indices associated with an infection may not be present in patients with AN.

MYOPATHY

Reports (Essen, Fohlin, Thoren, & Saltin, 1981; McLoughlin et al., 1998; McLoughlin et al., 2000; Rigaud et al., 1997) have shown that protein-energy malnutrition in those with AN is an underrecognized cause of muscle dysfunction. One study (Essen et al., 1981) showed that a significant proportion of weight and lean body-mass loss in adolescents with AN could be accounted for by a loss of skeletal muscle mass. Muscle biopsies revealed that all muscle-fiber types were markedly atrophied (Essen et al., 1981). Another study (McLoughlin et al., 1998) examined muscle structure and function in patients with severe AN and found impaired muscle function on measurements of strength and exercise. Electromyography revealed myopathy and muscle-biopsy specimens consistently showed myopathic changes with severe type 2 fiber atrophy and no evidence of neuropathic changes. The effect of starvation-related malnutrition on muscle performance was studied in patients with AN during exercise (Rigaud et al., 1997). Workload performance during exercise was 49% lower in patients with AN than in healthy control subjects. On refeeding, there was improvement in muscle performance, even before the normalization of muscle mass and normal nutritional status was achieved (Rigaud et al., 1997). In another study (McLoughlin et al., 2000), the metabolic disturbance associated with skeletal myopathy in patients with AN and extreme weight loss was examined. All patients showed proximal muscular weakness, with histologically confirmed myopathy. The patients recovered from the metabolic myopathy as their nutrition improved.

DERMATOLOGIC PROBLEMS

A variety of dermatologic changes have been observed in adolescents with EDs. Starvation or malnutrition can result in dry skin, hair loss and thinning, acne, pruritis, nail dystrophy, lanugo hair, and carotenoderma (Glorio et al., 2000; Strumia, 2005). Lanugo hair, one of the most common dermatologic signs of AN, is the fine, downy hair commonly found on the back, abdomen, and forearms, and represents the body's attempt to conserve heat and save energy (Strumia, 2005; Woodside, 1995). Carotenoderma is an orange pigmentation of the skin caused by increased serum carotenoids (carotenemia) and their deposition in the outermost layer of skin. The most common cause of carotenoderma in patients with restricting EDs is the excessive dietary intake of foods rich in carotenoids such as leafy vegetables. In addition, the metabolism of carotene pigment is slowed by the starved liver, leading to decreased clearance and increased plasma levels in some of these patients (Glorio et al., 2000; Strumia, 2005).

The most characteristic cutaneous sign of vomiting is Russell's sign, a callus formation on the dorsum of the hand overlying the metacarpophalangeal or interphalangeal joints. This occurs as a result of the adolescent using the index or middle finger to stimulate the gag reflex to induce vomiting and rubbing the skin of that hand over the central incisors.

Laxative (phenolphthalein-containing nonprescription laxatives can cause fixed drug eruptions (Kanwar, Bharija, Singh, & Belhaj, 1988) and diuretic abuse can cause adverse skin eruptions. Any kind of self-induced trauma or comorbid psychiatric illness (e.g., hand dermatitis from compulsive washing) may also result in changes in the skin (Glorio et al., 2000; Strumia, 2005).

Long-Term Medical Complications

BONE MINERAL DENSITY

Forty-five percent to 60% of bone mineral accrual occurs during the second decade of life, which coincides with the timing of the highest incidence of the development of EDs (Fisher et al., 1995; Katzman, 2005). Reduced bone mineral density (BMD) occurs in about 50% of adolescent females with AN (Bachrach et al., 1990; Bachrach, Katzman, Litt, Guido, & Marcus, 1991; Golden et al., 2005; Misra et al., 2004). Loss of BMD may occur early in the course of illness (Bachrach et al., 1990). In one study (Bachrach et al., 1990), two-thirds of adolescent girls with AN had bone density values that were more than two standard deviations lower than the normal values for their age. In half of these subjects, the diagnosis of AN had been made less than one year before the measurement of BMD.

Low BMI, age at onset of AN, and duration of illness are important predictors of the reduction in BMD (Bachrach et al., 1990). A recent study (Misra et al., 2008) of adolescent boys with AN found low BMD at multiple sites that was associated with decreased bone-turnover markers. Testosterone and lean body mass predicted BMD in the population and IGF-1 was an important predictor of bone-turnover markers.

Deficits in BMD acquired during adolescence as a result of an ED may not be completely reversible (Bachrach et al., 1991). The development of an ED and prolonged starvation during adolescence is an important risk factor for the development of osteopenia and osteoporosis later in life (Soyka et al., 2002). In a large cohort study (Vestergaard et al., 2002), those with AN had a twofold increase in their risk of fracture, a risk that persisted more than 10 years after diagnosis. In the same study, those with BN and ED not otherwise specified (EDNOS) also had an increased risk of fracture.

The pathophysiology of BMD reduction in patients with AN is multifactorial and complex. Low BMD in adolescents with AN reflects bone loss combined with decreased bone accretion (Bachrach et al., 1991; Soyka et al., 2002). A number of factors have been implicated in contributing to the low BMD reported in adolescents with AN including hypoestrogenemia, low levels of IGF-1 (Soyka, Grinspoon, Levitsky, Herzog, & Klibanski, 1999), high cortisol (Lawson & Klibanski, 2008), and abnormal levels of gastrointestinal peptides (Misra et al., 2008). Further, modifiable factors such as low body mass, poor nutrition, low calcium and vitamin D intake, and excessive physical activity have also been implicated as factors contributing to low BMD (Fisher et al., 1995; Katzman, 2005).

Body weight is the most important determinant of BMD, and weight gain is associated with an increase in BMD (Bachrach et al., 1991). Research (Soyka et al., 2002) shows that normalization of bone-turnover markers is associated with nutritional and weight recovery in adolescent girls with AN, and increases in bone formation are greater in those whose BMI increased by 10% or more over a year.

Hypoestrogenemia is also an important contributing factor to low BMD in those with AN (Katzman, 2005; Lawson & Klibanski, 2008). Estrogen helps the body maintain normal calcium levels and acts directly on the bone to limit mineral resorption (Golden, 2003). Although hormone replacement therapy is commonly prescribed (Robinson, Bachrach, & Katzman, 2000), there is no evidence that this therapy effectively reverses or prevents bone loss in adolescents with AN. In a 1-year prospective observational study (Golden et al., 2002), adolescents with AN and amenorrhea for at least 6 months (92% were osteopenic, 26% met World Health Organization criteria for osteoporosis) received either estrogen–progestin therapy or no hormonal treatment. At the 1-year follow-up examination, no significant differences in BMD between the two groups were found. Body weight was the most important determinant of BMD, both at baseline and at follow-up (Golden et al., 2002). Restoration of a healthy weight and the resumption of spontaneous menstrual function (which indicates normal estrogen levels) are of central importance to bone health (Katzman, 2005; Lawson & Klibanski, 2008; Munoz & Argente, 2002). Because the use of hormonal medications masks the resumption of spontaneous menses, they should not be prescribed for this population unless necessary for contraception or other health issues (e.g., dysmenorrhea, acne, endometriosis, polycystic ovary syndrome).

Calcium is important for bone mineralization and vitamin D is crucial for the absorption of calcium. Dietary calcium requirements increase during pubertal growth and attainment of peak bone mass; however, both healthy adolescents and adolescents with AN consume less calcium than the recommended dietary intake (Bachrach et al., 1990). Adequate calcium intake alone is not sufficient to prevent deficits in BMD in adolescents with AN (Bachrach, et al., 1990, 1991).

Weight-bearing exercise is protective of bone mass in healthy children and adolescents. The intensity, frequency, and duration of activity that promotes bone mineralization in adolescents with AN are unknown. Excessive exercise can cause low body weight and suppression of the HPO axis resulting in subsequent bone loss (Golden et al., 2002; Katzman, 2005). Adolescents with AN should be encouraged to participate in weight-bearing exercise as long as they are weight-restored, medically stable, and closely monitored (Katzman, 2005).

To date, bisphosphonates have not been used for the clinical treatment of low BMD in adolescents with AN. A double-blinded, randomized trial (Golden et al., 2005) comparing alendronate to placebo in adolescents with AN reported that despite an independent positive effect at the femoral neck, body weight was the most important determinant of BMD.

The clinician should consider obtaining a DXA scan after 6 months of amenorrhea for adolescents with AN and for those with BN who have a history of AN.[12] To date, the best time to order a DXA for boys has yet to be determined. DXA is the method of choice for assessing BMD because it is quick and precise, and results in low radiation exposure. Interpretation of DXA data for growing and developing children and adolescents, however, is complex. DXA results should be compared with normative data derived from healthy children of similar age, sex, and maturity to derive a Z-score. If the results are abnormal or the adolescent continues to have amenorrhea, a DXA scan should be repeated annually (Golden, 2003).

LINEAR GROWTH

Linear growth in adolescents with AN is particularly relevant for younger adolescents who are at a stage when they should expect considerable growth. Growth impairment can be attributed to dramatic alterations in the GH–IGF axis, as well as to alterations in sex steroids, thyroid hormones, and elevated levels of cortisol. Studies (Counts et al., 1992; Golden et al., 1994; Misra et al., 2003) have shown that adolescents with AN are in a state of GH resistance; their high serum levels of GH fail to stimulate IGF-1 production. This state of resistance resolves with weight restoration.

The timing of the onset of AN in relation to pubertal development is an important determinant of linear growth. Studies of premenarchal girls with AN have reported inconsistent findings. One study (Lantzouni, Frank, Golden, & Shenker, 2002) showed that premenarchal adolescent girls with AN were at risk for growth impairment, whereas another study (Prabhakaran et al., 2008) reported that a delayed baseline bone age predicted subsequent increases in standard deviation scores for height. These findings suggest that the hypogonadism of AN may compensate for the detrimental effects of undernutrition on stature by allowing for a longer duration of growth. If this is correct, then aggressively treating the ED before the epiphyses fuse could have a positive impact on linear growth. A study of postmenarchal adolescent girls with AN showed that this cohort had either completed growth or were close to growth completion when they developed the ED, preventing growth impairment (Misra et al., 2004). Growth delay and incomplete catch-up growth has been reported for adolescent boys with AN (Modan-Moses et al., 2003). This may be explained by the fact that growth potential persists for 2 years longer in boys than in girls; therefore, boys have a longer time for their growth potential to be compromised by the ED. Further studies aimed at the onset of AN in relation to pubertal development and its impact on linear growth are needed.

An x-ray examination of the hand and wrist to determine the bone age should be considered for adolescents with evidence of growth failure. This is information, along with the child's current height and mid-parental height, can be used to determine the adolescent's growth potential and final adult height.

BRAIN STRUCTURE AND FUNCTION

The structural brain changes seen in adolescents with AN are among the earliest and most striking physical consequences. Studies (Katzman, Christensen, Young, & Zipursky, 2001; Katzman et al., 1996; Kerem & Katzman, 2003) using computed tomography and MRI have demonstrated changes in brain structure in the low-weight stages of AN. MRI studies (Katzman et al., 1996; Katzman, Zipursky, Lambe, & Mikulis, 1997) of adolescent girls with AN revealed increases in the total cerebrospinal fluid (CSF) volumes and deficits in both total gray- and white-matter volumes when compared with those of healthy controls. Severity of illness, measured with BMI, was inversely correlated with total CSF volume and positively correlated with total gray-matter volume (Katzman et al., 1996). Further evidence has shown that not all of these changes are completely reversible (Katzman et al., 2001; Kerem & Katzman, 2003). In follow-up studies (Katzman et al., 1997; Lambe, Katzman, Mikulis, Kennedy, & Zipursky, 1997), weight-recovered female patients had significantly elevated CSF volumes and deficits in gray-matter volume compared with those of age-matched controls. These studies suggest that not all of the reported structural brain changes are completely reversible.

In a recent study (Chui et al., 2008), females with adolescent-onset AN showed abnormal cognitive function and brain structure compared with that of healthy subjects. Subjects with adolescent-onset AN who remained at low weight had larger lateral ventricles than controls. In addition, subjects with adolescent-onset AN who remained amenorrheic or had irregular menstrual function had significant cognitive deficits across a broad range of neuropsychological domains.

Medical Management

The primary goals of the medical management of adolescents with EDs are nutritional rehabilitation, weight restoration (if needed), and reversal of acute medical complications. Although the focus of the behavioral treatment may be slightly different for those with restrictive rather than binge–purge EDs, the medical goals remain the same. For adolescents who have had a brief course of illness, timely intervention will often prevent long-term complications (Golden et al., 2003).

Treatment Team

Adolescents with EDs are best cared for by a skilled interdisciplinary team of medical, nutritional, mental health and nursing professionals. Regardless of the discipline, all team members should be experienced in treating adolescents with EDs and their families (Golden et al., 2003; Katzman & Golden, 2008). These specialized healthcare professionals provide a continuum of care through assessment, diagnosis, treatment, and recovery. Because it is often not the case that all the care providers for an adolescent work in the same practice, permission should be obtained from the adolescent and family for members of the team to communicate regularly about the care plan.

Although this chapter does not focus on the evidence-based psychological treatments for adolescents with EDs and their families, Chapter 21 provides a comprehensive review of this topic.

Treatment Settings

A variety of treatment settings are available for adolescents with EDs, including inpatient hospitalization, outpatient, partial-hospitalization or day treatment programs, and residential treatment centres.

INPATIENT HOSPITALIZATION

Indications for hospitalization for the adolescent with an ED are listed in Table 16.2 (Golden et al., 2003). Hospitalization is generally reserved to evaluate and treat acute or serious medical complications that result from the ED; to manage comorbid psychiatric illnesses that make outpatient treatment unsafe or ineffective; and to interrupt medical risks or complications that result from binging, vomiting, or laxative abuse. For children and young adolescents, growth or pubertal arrest is also an indication for nutritional rehabilitation and weight gain in a hospital setting.

The goals of hospitalization are weight restoration or the interruption of steady weight loss and reversal of acute medical complications, such as unstable vital signs and electrolyte abnormalities. For the patient with BN who may not need to gain

Table 16.2 Indications for Hospitalization of an Adolescent with an Eating Disorder

1. Severe malnutrition (weight ≤75% average body weight for age, sex, and height)
2. Dehydration
3. Electrolyte disturbances (hypokalemia, hyponatremia, hypophosphatemia)
4. Cardiac dysrhythmia
5. Physiological instability
   a. Severe bradycardia (heart rate <50 beats/minute daytime; <45 beats/minute at night)
   b. Hypotension (<80/50 mm Hg)
   c. Hypothermia (body temperature <96°F, or 35.6°C)
   d. Orthostatic changes in pulse (>20 beats/minute) or blood pressure (>10 mm Hg)
6. Arrested growth and development
7. Failure of outpatient treatment
8. Acute food refusal
9. Uncontrollable binging and purging
10. Acute medical complications of malnutrition (e.g., syncope, seizures, cardiac failure, pancreatitis)
11. Acute psychiatric emergencies (e.g., suicidal ideation, acute psychosis)
12. Comorbid diagnosis that interferes with the treatment of the eating disorder (e.g., severe depression, obsessive–compulsive disorder, severe family dysfunction)

Source: Golden, N. H., Katzman, K. D., Kreipe, R. E., Stevens, S. L., Sawyer, S. M., Rees, J., et al. (2003). Eating disorders in adolescents: Position paper of the Society for Adolescent Medicine. *Journal of Adolescent Health*, 33(6), 496–503. Adapted with permission from Elsevier.

weight, normalization of eating patterns and symptom interruption to correct acute medical instability should be the goal. Nutritional rehabilitation should be achieved by eating regular food, whenever possible. Some patients may initially require a liquid nutrition supplement or nasogastric feedings in the short term.

Medically unstable adolescents should be placed on bed rest until their vital signs improve. Continuous cardiac monitoring should be considered for patients with severe bradycardia or other arrhythmias. Vital signs should improve with weight restoration and reduction of physical activity.

Nutritional rehabilitation should follow the maxim "start low and go slow" to avoid refeeding syndrome. Although there is no standard protocol for the initial stages of refeeding a very starved patient, most programs start with an intake similar to what the patient reports eating at home or around 1000 kcal/day. A study (Solanto, Jacobson, Heller, Golden, & Hertz, 1994) of adolescents with AN found that an inpatient weight gain criterion of 2 lb/week ($\approx$1.0 kg/week) was safe and was not associated with the complications of refeeding. Vital signs should be closely monitored. Blood work, especially electrolytes (including phosphorus, calcium, and magnesium), and glucose should be monitored regularly. Feedings are generally increased by about 250 kcal/day, as tolerated, based on clinical evaluation and blood work, until the patient begins to gain weight. Supplemental phosphate may be required and some clinicians elect to start supplementation upon admission for all very low-weight patients (Schwartz, Mansbach, Marion, Katzman, & Forman, 2008). Potassium and magnesium supplements are also occasionally required.

PARTIAL HOSPITALIZATION OR DAY TREATMENT

Multiple models for partial hospitalization programs (also known as day hospital programs or day treatment programs) have been described (Dancyger et al., 2003; Zipfel et al., 2002). Commonly, these programs provide structure and support around mealtimes, and group treatment several days per week; patients return home at night and on weekends (although 7 day/week programs do exist). Partial hospitalization may serve as a step-down program for patients who were recently inpatients, or the program may be an intensification of treatment for outpatients. Partial hospitalization may have several advantages over inpatient care, such as decreasing costs; letting patients partially maintain social, academic, and vocational roles; and letting patients practice new skills in their home with family and friends (Zipfel et al., 2002). However, these programs may not be appropriate for those who are at acute medical or psychiatric risk or who have an unsafe home environment.

OUTPATIENT TREATMENT

The most common treatment setting for patients with EDs is outpatient care. To be treated as an outpatient, patients must be medically stable. The physician's role is to ensure continued medical and psychological stability, to monitor for acute complications (with body-weight, vital-sign, and laboratory evaluations) and chronic medical complications, and to assist the team in making ongoing treatment decisions and recommendations. Family support for adolescents with EDs is crucial in the outpatient setting because the family must ensure that the adolescent eats the prescribed diet, does not engage in inappropriate exercise, and attends therapeutic sessions.

This dynamic can lead to intense battles at home and the family may need additional support such as family counselling or support groups for parents and siblings. Family-based treatment has been found to be effective in treating adolescents with AN (Bulik, Berkman, Brownley, Sedway, & Lohr, 2007; Lock & le Grange, 2005) and this is rapidly becoming the standard treatment model. Current evidence also suggests that family-based treatment may also be an appropriate and efficacious treatment for adolescents with BN (Doyle, McLean, Washington, Hoste, & le Grange, 2009; Le Grange et al., 2003). Treatment studies in older adolescent and adult populations suggest the efficacy of cognitive-behavioral therapy (CBT) for older adolescents with BN (Keel & Haedt, 2008).

RESIDENTIAL TREATMENT

Residential treatment is generally reserved for those young people who have not responded to other forms of care. A 2004 survey (Frisch, Herzog, & Franko, 2006) of 18 residential programs in the United States found that the average length of stay was 83 days at an average cost of $956 (US dollars) per day, which is less expensive than the per-day cost of an inpatient, acute-care bed. Most programs surveyed had physicians or nursing staff who attended to the medical needs of participants. The primary therapies used were individual and group therapy, and CBT. Many programs accept only females, and the average age of those treated is 22 years, although there are programs dedicated to children and adolescents (Frisch et al., 2006).

Medications

Data about the use of pharmacotherapy for the treatment of AN are limited and mostly negative; even less are available about the use of pharmacotherapy in the adolescent population with this disorder. Initially, the use of selective serotonin reuptake inhibitors (SSRIs), such as fluoxetine, was explored (Claudino et al., 2006; Kaye et al., 2001; Walsh et al., 2006), but recent studies have found no evidence to support the use of SSRIs for the treatment of the core symptoms of AN, particularly in the pediatric population. However, SSRIs are frequently used to treat comorbid disorders, such as depression, obsessive–compulsive disorder, and anxiety disorders in the adolescent population.

Recently, the use of atypical antipsychotic medications to treat adolescents with AN has been explored. To date, published data are limited to case series and case reports in adolescents. Three case series (Boachie, Goldfield, & Spettigue, 2003; Dennis, Le Grange, & Bremer, 2006; Mehler et al., 2001) describe the therapeutic benefits and tolerability of olanzapine in children and adolescents with AN. The first study (Mehler et al., 2001) reported on five adolescents with chronic AN and described remarkable improvement: reduced negative ideation about body image or weight gain, and decreased inner tensions and phobias about food intake. The second (Boachie et al., 2003), which described four pediatric inpatients with AN, found improved weight gain and maintenance, decreased levels of agitation and premeal anxiety, and improved sleep and overall compliance with treatment. Finally, Dennis et al. (2006) published a report about the simultaneous treatment with olanzapine and psychotherapy of five adolescents with AN. All subjects increased their BMI while on olanzapine. They also had decreased anxiety about eating, improved sleep, and decreased rumination about food and body concerns. Olanzapine was well tolerated in young patients (Boachie et al., 2003), and the most common adverse effect reported was morning sedation (Dennis et al., 2006).

Two case reports (Fisman, Steele, Short, Byrne, & Lavallee, 1996; Newman-Toker, 2000) described adolescents with AN responding positively to risperidone. Although these cases are encouraging (Couturier & Lock, 2007), only placebo-controlled, blinded trials will answer the question about whether atypical antipsychotics are of use for adolescents with AN.

Unlike studies of AN, many studies of BN have confirmed the effectiveness of SSRIs, particularly fluoxetine in adults, for the treatment of BN. Treatment with fluoxetine decreased both binging and purging episodes in 55% to 65% of subjects (Nakash-Eisikovits, Dierberger, & Westen, 2002). In the one open trial (Kotler, Devlin, Davies, & Walsh, 2003) of fluoxetine for adolescents, in which subjects received fluoxetine and supportive psychotherapy, the frequency of weekly binge episodes decreased from about four to zero, and weekly purges from about six to almost none. Combining medication treatment with CBT is likely superior to either treatment alone (Nakash-Eisikovits et al., 2002).

The United States Food and Drug Administration issued a black-box warning to advise clinicians and consumers that these medications can cause increased suicidal thoughts and behaviors (but not completed suicide) (Cheung, Emslie, & Mayes, 2005, 2006) in young people prescribed SSRIs.

Clinicians should inform the patient and family about the possibility of adverse effects, provide appropriate monitoring, and work out a plan with the patient and family if the patient experiences these adverse effects (Lock, Walker, Rickert, & Katzman, 2005).

Outcomes

Numerous studies have been done on the outcome of AN with widely variable results, mostly because of different methods, definitions of recovery, and length of follow-up (Couturier & Lock, 2006a, 2006b; Lock, Couturier, & Agras, 2006). However, out of these studies has come an understanding of the clinical factors that portend a good or poor prognosis. A good prognosis is associated with a short duration of illness, early identification and intervention, early onset (<14 years old), no associated comorbid psychological diagnoses, no binging and purging, and a supportive family. Poor prognosis is associated with a longer duration of illness, binging and purging, comorbid mental illness, and a lower body weight at diagnosis (Katzman & Golden, 2008).

Strober et al. (1997) followed 95 adolescents with AN for 10 to 15 years after diagnosis. Full recovery occurred in 75.8%, partial recovery in 10.5%, and chronicity or no recovery in 13.7%. Time to full recovery ranged from 57 to 79 months and almost one-third of patients required more than one inpatient admission. Families can be reassured that full recovery does occur in adolescents with AN, but they must be prepared for a long course of illness.

The severity of AN cannot be ignored, however. A recent study (Papadopoulos, Ekbom, Brandt, & Ekselius, 2009) that retrospectively followed 6009 women who had inpatient treatment for AN with a death registry found a sixfold increase in mortality in this cohort, compared with that in the general population. The standard mortality ratio remained significantly high for 20 years or more after the first hospitalization for AN. The most frequent cause of death was suicide, followed by AN.

Long-term studies specifically of adolescents with BN are few. However, many adults with BN report that their symptoms started in adolescence. One review of the literature (Quadflieg & Fichter, 2003) found that the short-term outcome of BN was effective, but the long-term outcome was associated with relapse and chronicity. Forty-seven percent to 73% of subjects had a good outcome at 9 to 11 years of follow-up. Mortality ranges from 0% to 6%

(Steinhausen, 1999). No specific prognostic factors have been consistently identified in the literature.

Conclusion

A comprehensive medical assessment is an essential part of the overall evaluation of an adolescent with an ED and her or his family. Establishing a diagnosis; identifying and treating the medical complications; and creating an initial treatment plan with regular, transparent, and ongoing communication with the adolescent, parents, and members of the interdisciplinary team are vital to the successful treatment of the adolescent with an ED.

References

Abella, E., Feliu, E., Granada, I., Milla, F., Oriol, A., Ribera, J. M., et al. (2002). Bone marrow changes in anorexia nervosa are correlated with the amount of weight loss and not with other clinical findings. *American Journal of Clinical Pathology*, *118*(4), 582–588.

Allende, L. M., Corell, A., Manzanares, J., Madruga, D., Marcos, A., Madrono, A., et al. (1998). Immunodeficiency associated with anorexia nervosa is secondary and improves after refeeding. *Immunology*, *94*(4), 543–551.

Altemus, M., Hetherington, M., Kennedy, B., Licinio, J., & Gold, P. W. (1996). Thyroid function in bulimia nervosa. *Psychoneuroendocrinology*, *21*(3), 249–261.

American Psychiatric Association (APA). (1994). *Diagnostic and statistical manual of mental disorders* (4th ed.). Washington, DC: American Psychiatric Association.

Anyan, W. R., Jr. (1974). Changes in erythrocyte sedimentation rate and fibrinogen during anorexia nervosa. *Journal of Pediatrics*, *85*(4), 525–527.

Aperia, A., Broberger, O., & Fohlin, L. (1978). Renal function in anorexia nervosa. *Acta Paediatrica Scandinavica*, *67*(2), 219–224.

Austin, S. B., Ziyadeh, N. J., Vohra, S., Forman, S., Gordon, C. M., Prokop, L. A., et al. (2008). Irregular menses linked to vomiting in a nonclinical sample: Findings from the National EDs Screening Program in high schools. *Journal of Adolescent Health*, *42*(5), 450–457.

Bachrach, L. K., Guido, D., Katzman, D., Litt, I. F., & Marcus, R. (1990). Decreased bone density in adolescent girls with anorexia nervosa. *Pediatrics*, *86*(3), 440–447.

Bachrach, L. K., Katzman, D. K., Litt, I. F., Guido, D., & Marcus, R. (1991). Recovery from osteopenia in adolescent girls with anorexia nervosa. *Journal of Clinical Endocrinology and Metabolism*, *72*(3), 602–606.

Banji S, Mattingly D. (1988). Renal function and electrolytes. In: Banji S, Mattingly D eds. Medical Aspects of Anorexia Nervosa. Wright, London: 63–70.

Bannai, C., Kuzuya, N., Koide, Y., Fujita, T., Itakura, M., Kawai, K., et al. (1988). Assessment of the relationship between serum thyroid hormone levels and peripheral metabolism in patients with anorexia nervosa. *Endocrinology Japan*, *35*(3), 455–462.

Benini, L., Sembenini, C., Salandini, L., Dall, O. E., Bonfante, F., & Vantini, I. (2001). Gastric emptying of realistic meals with and without gluten in patients with coeliac disease. Effect of jejunal mucosal recovery. *Scandinavian Journal of Gastroenterology*, *36*(10), 1044–1048.

Birketvedt, G. S., Drivenes, E., Agledahl, I., Sundsfjord, J., Olstad, R., & Florholmen, J. R. (2006). Bulimia nervosa—a primary defect in the hypothalamic-pituitary-adrenal axis? *Appetite*, *46*(2), 164–167.

Boachie, A., Goldfield, G. S., & Spettigue, W. (2003). Olanzapine use as an adjunctive treatment for hospitalized children with anorexia nervosa: Case reports. *International Journal of Eating Disorders*, *33*(1), 98–103.

Boag, F., Weerakoon, J., Ginsburg, J., Havard, C. W., & Dandona, P. (1985). Diminished creatinine clearance in anorexia nervosa: Reversal with weight gain. *Journal of Clinical Pathology*, *38*(1), 60–63.

Boeck, M. A. Bulimia Nervosa. (1998). In: Friedman, S.B, Fisher, M, Schonberg, S. K, Alderman, E.M. (ed). Comprehensive Adolescent Health Care, 2nd edition. St Louis, MO: Mosby, 263–268.

Brady, J. P. (1985). Parotid enlargement in bulimia. *Journal of Family Practice*, *20*(5), 496–502.

Bravender, T., Bryant-Waugh, R., Herzog, D., Katzman, D., Kreipe, R. D., Lask, B., et al. (2007). Classification of child and adolescent eating disturbances. Workgroup for Classification of Eating Disorders in Children and Adolescents (WCEDCA). *International Journal of Eating Disorders*, 40 Suppl, S117–122.

Brown, J. M., Mehler, P. S., & Harris, R. H. (2000). Medical complications occurring in adolescents with anorexia nervosa. *Western Journal of Medicine*, *172*(3), 189–193.

Brown, N. W., Ward, A., Surwit, R., Tiller, J., Lightman, S., Treasure, J. L., et al. (2003). Evidence for metabolic and endocrine abnormalities in subjects recovered from anorexia nervosa. *Metabolism*, *52*(3), 296–302.

Bulik, C. M., Berkman, N. D., Brownley, K. A., Sedway, J. A., & Lohr, K. N. (2007). Anorexia nervosa treatment: A systematic review of randomized controlled trials. *International Journal of Eating Disorders*, *40*(4), 310–320.

Casiero, D., & Frishman, W. H. (2006). Cardiovascular complications of eating disorders. *Cardiology Reviews*, *14*(5), 227–231.

Cheung, A. H., Emslie, G. J., & Mayes, T. L. (2005). Review of the efficacy and safety of antidepressants in youth depression. *Journal of Child Psychology and Psychiatry*, *46*(7), 735–754.

Cheung, A. H., Emslie, G. J., & Mayes, T. L. (2006). The use of antidepressants to treat depression in children and adolescents. *CMAJ*, *174*(2), 193–200.

Chial, H. J., McAlpine, D. E., & Camilleri, M. (2002). Anorexia nervosa: Manifestations and management for the gastroenterologist. *American Journal of Gastroenterology*, *97*(2), 255–269.

Chui, H. T., Christensen, B. K., Zipursky, R. B., Richards, B. A., Hanratty, M. K., Kabani, N. J., et al. (2008). Cognitive function and brain structure in females with a history of adolescent-onset anorexia nervosa. *Pediatrics*, *122*(2), e426–437.

Claudino, A. M., Hay, P., Lima, M. S., Bacaltchuk, J., Schmidt, U., & Treasure, J. (2006). Antidepressants for anorexia nervosa. *Cochrane Database of Systematic Reviews* (1), CD004365.

Counts, D. R., Gwirtsman, H., Carlsson, L. M., Lesem, M., & Cutler, G. B., Jr. (1992). The effect of anorexia nervosa and refeeding on growth hormone-binding protein, the insulin-like growth factors (IGFs), and the IGF-binding proteins. *Journal of Clinical Endocrinology and Metabolism*, *75*(3), 762–767.

Coupey SM. Anorexia Nervosa. (1998). In: Friedman SB, Fisher M, Schonberg SK, Alderman EM. (ed). Comprehensive Adolescent Health Care, 2nd edition. St Louis, MO: Mosby, 247–262.

Couturier, J., & Lock, J. (2006a). What is recovery in adolescent anorexia nervosa? *International Journal of Eating Disorders, 39*(7), 550–555.

Couturier, J., & Lock, J. (2006b). What is remission in adolescent anorexia nervosa? A review of various conceptualizations and quantitative analysis. *International Journal of Eating Disorders, 39*(3), 175–183.

Couturier, J., & Lock, J. (2007). A review of medication use for children and adolescents with eating disorders. *Journal of Canadian Academy of Child and Adolescent Psychiatry, 16*(4), 173–176.

Dancyger, I., Fornari, V., Schneider, M., Fisher, M., Frank, S., Goodman, B., et al. (2003). Adolescents and eating disorders: An examination of a day treatment program. *Eating and Weight Disorders, 8*(3), 242–248.

Dec, G. W., Biederman, J., & Hougen, T. J. (1987). Cardiovascular findings in adolescent inpatients with anorexia nervosa. *Psychosomatic Medicine, 49*(3), 285–290.

Dennis, K., Le Grange, D., & Bremer, J. (2006). Olanzapine use in adolescent anorexia nervosa. *Eating and Weight Disorders, 11*(2), e53–56.

de Simone, G., Scalfi, L., Galderisi, M., Celentano, A., Di Biase, G., Tammaro, P., et al. (1994). Cardiac abnormalities in young women with anorexia nervosa. *British Heart Journal, 71*(3), 287–292.

Devlin, M. J., Walsh, B. T., Katz, J. L., Roose, S. P., Linkie, D. M., Wright, L., et al. (1989). Hypothalamic-pituitary-gonadal function in anorexia nervosa and bulimia. *Psychiatry Research, 28*(1), 11–24.

Devlin, M. J., Walsh, B. T., Kral, J. G., Heymsfield, S. B., Pi-Sunyer, F. X., & Dantzic, S. (1990). Metabolic abnormalities in bulimia nervosa. *Archives of General Psychiatry, 47*(2), 144–148.

Diaz, A., Laufer, M. R., & Breech, L. L. (2006). Menstruation in girls and adolescents: using the menstrual cycle as a vital sign. *Pediatrics, 118*(5), 2245–2250.

Doyle, A. C., McLean, C., Washington, B. N., Hoste, R. R., & le Grange, D. (2009). Are single-parent families different from two-parent families in the treatment of adolescent bulimia nervosa using family-based treatment? *International Journal of Eating Disorders, 42*(2), 153–157.

Essen, B., Fohlin, L., Thoren, C., & Saltin, B. (1981). Skeletal muscle fibre types and sizes in anorexia nervosa patients. *Clinical Physiology, 1*(4), 395–403.

Evrard, F., da Cunha, M. P., Lambert, M., & Devuyst, O. (2004). Impaired osmoregulation in anorexia nervosa: A case-control study. *Nephrology, Dialysis, and Transplantation, 19*(12), 3034–3039.

Fairburn, C. G., & Harrison, P. J. (2003). Eating disorders. *Lancet, 361*(9355), 407–416.

Fichter, M. M., Doerr, P., Pirke, K. M., & Lund, R. (1982). Behavior, attitude, nutrition and endocrinology in anorexia nervosa. *Acta Psychiatrica Scandinavica, 66*(6), 429–444.

Fisher, M., Golden, N. H., Katzman, D. K., Kreipe, R. E., Rees, J., Schebendach, J., et al. (1995). Eating disorders in adolescents: A background paper. *Journal of Adolescent Health, 16*(6), 420–437.

Fisher, M., Simpser, E., & Schneider, M. (2000). Hypophosphatemia secondary to oral refeeding in anorexia nervosa. *International Journal of Eating Disorders, 28*(2), 181–187.

Fisman, S., Steele, M., Short, J., Byrne, T., & Lavallee, C. (1996). Case study: Anorexia nervosa and autistic disorder in an adolescent girl. *Journal of the American Academy of Child and Adolescent Psychiatry, 35*(7), 937–940.

Fohlin, L. (1977). Body composition, cardiovascular and renal function in adolescent patients with anorexia nervosa. *Acta Paediatrica Scandinavica Suppl, (268),* 1–20.

Forman, S. (2001). The role of the primary care provider in the diagnosis and management of eating disorders: Anorexia nervosa and bulimia nervosa. Under the direction of Emans S. J., Woods E. R. , & P. M. Keenan. Postgraduate course in adolescent medicine, Harvard Medical School, Boston, Massachusetts.

Frisch, M. J., Herzog, D. B., & Franko, D. L. (2006). Residential treatment for eating disorders. *International Journal of Eating Disorders, 39*(5), 434–442.

Frisch, R. E., & McArthur, J. W. (1974). Menstrual cycles: Fatness as a determinant of minimum weight for height necessary for their maintenance or onset. *Science, 185*(4155), 949–951.

Geiser, F., Murtz, P., Lutterbey, G., Traber, F., Block, W., Imbierowicz, K., et al. (2001). Magnetic resonance spectroscopic and relaxometric determination of bone marrow changes in anorexia nervosa. *Psychosomatic Medicine, 63*(4), 631–637.

Glorio, R., Allevato, M., De Pablo, A., Abbruzzese, M., Carmona, L., Savarin, M., et al. (2000). Prevalence of cutaneous manifestations in 200 patients with eating disorders. *International Journal of Dermatology, 39*(5), 348–353.

Goldberg, S. J., Comerci, G. D., & Feldman, L. (1988). Cardiac output and regional myocardial contraction in anorexia nervosa. *Journal of Adolescent Health Care, 9*(1), 15–21.

Golden, N. H. (2003). Osteopenia and osteoporosis in anorexia nervosa. *Adolescent Medicine, 14*(1), 97–108.

Golden, N. H., Iglesias, E. A., Jacobson, M. S., Carey, D., Meyer, W., Schebendach, J., et al. (2005). Alendronate for the treatment of osteopenia in anorexia nervosa: A randomized, double-blind, placebo-controlled trial. *Journal of Clinical Endocrinology and Metabolism, 90*(6), 3179–3185.

Golden, N. H., Jacobson, M. S., Schebendach, J., Solanto, M. V., Hertz, S. M., & Shenker, I. R. (1997). Resumption of menses in anorexia nervosa. *Archives of Pediatric and Adolescent Medicine, 151*(1), 16–21.

Golden, N. H., Katzman, D. K., Kreipe, R. E., Stevens, S. L., Sawyer, S. M., Rees, J., et al. (2003). Eating disorders in adolescents: Position paper of the Society for Adolescent Medicine. *Journal of Adolescent Health, 33*(6), 496–503.

Golden, N. H., Kreitzer, P., Jacobson, M. S., Chasalow, F. I., Schebendach, J., Freedman, S. M., et al. (1994). Disturbances in growth hormone secretion and action in adolescents with anorexia nervosa. *Journal of Pediatrics, 125*(4), 655–660.

Golden, N. H., Lanzkowsky, L., Schebendach, J., Palestro, C. J., Jacobson, M. S., & Shenker, I. R. (2002). The effect of estrogen-progestin treatment on bone mineral density in anorexia nervosa. *Journal of Pediatric and Adolescent Gynecology, 15*(3), 135–143.

Haines, J., Neumark-Sztainer, D., Eisenberg, M. E., & Hannan, P. J. (2006). Weight teasing and disordered eating behaviors in adolescents: Longitudinal findings from Project EAT (Eating Among Teens). *Pediatrics, 117*(2), e209–215.

Hall, R. C., Hoffman, R. S., Beresford, T. P., Wooley, B., Tice, L., & Hall, A. K. (1988). Hypomagnesemia in patients with eating disorders. *Psychosomatics, 29*(3), 264–272.

Halmi K. A. (2002). Physiology of Anorexia Nervosa and Bulimia Nervosa. In: Fairburn CG, Brownell KD, eds. Eating disorders and obesity: a comprehensive handbook, 2nd edn. New York: Guilford Press, 267–271.

Herpertz-Dahlmann, B. (2009). Adolescent eating disorders: Definitions, symptomatology, epidemiology and comorbidity. *Child and Adolescent Psychiatric Clinics of North America*, *18*(1), 31–47.

Herpertz-Dahlmann, B. M., Wewetzer, C., & Remschmidt, H. (1995). The predictive value of depression in anorexia nervosa. Results of a seven-year follow-up study. *Acta Psychiatrica Scandinavica*, *91*(2), 114–119.

Holt, S., Ford, M. J., Grant, S., & Heading, R. C. (1981). Abnormal gastric emptying in primary anorexia nervosa. *British Journal of Psychiatry*, *139*, 550–552.

Hutchinson, J. W., & Stafford, E. M. (2005). Changing parental opinions about teen privacy through education. *Pediatrics*, *116*(4), 966–971.

Johnson, G. L., Humphries, L. L., Shirley, P. B., Mazzoleni, A., & Noonan, J. A. (1986). Mitral valve prolapse in patients with anorexia nervosa and bulimia. *Archives of Internal Medicine*, *146*(8), 1525–1529.

Kanbur, N. O., Derman, O., & Kinik, E. (2005). The relationships between pubertal development, IGF-1 axis, and bone formation in healthy adolescents. *Journal of Bone Mineral Metabolism*, *23*(1), 76–83.

Kanwar, A. J., Bharija, S. C., Singh, M., & Belhaj, M. S. (1988). Ninety-eight fixed drug eruptions with provocation tests. *Dermatologica*, *177*(5), 274–279.

Katzman, D. K. (2005). Medical complications in adolescents with anorexia nervosa: A review of the literature. *International Journal of Eating Disorders*, *37* (Supplement), S52–59; discussion S87–59.

Katzman, D. K., Christensen, B., Young, A. R., & Zipursky, R. B. (2001). Starving the brain: Structural abnormalities and cognitive impairment in adolescents with anorexia nervosa. *Seminars in Clinical Neuropsychiatry*, *6*(2), 146–152.

Katzman, D. K., & Golden, N. H. (2008). Anorexia nervosa and bulimi nervosa (pp 477–493). In L. Neinstein, C. Gordon, D. K. Katzman, D. S. Rosen & E. R. Woods (Eds.), *Adolescent health care: A practical guide* (5th ed.). Philadelphia: Lippincott, Williams & Wilkins.

Katzman, D. K., Lambe, E. K., Mikulis, D. J., Ridgley, J. N., Goldbloom, D. S., & Zipursky, R. B. (1996). Cerebral gray matter and white matter volume deficits in adolescent girls with anorexia nervosa. *Journal of Pediatrics*, *129*(6), 794–803.

Katzman, D. K., Zipursky, R. B., Lambe, E. K., & Mikulis, D. J. (1997). A longitudinal magnetic resonance imaging study of brain changes in adolescents with anorexia nervosa. *Archives of Pediatric and Adolescent Medicine*, *151*(8), 793–797.

Kay, J., & Stricker, R. B. (1983). Hematologic and immunologic abnormalities in anorexia nervosa. *Southern Medical Journal*, *76*(8), 1008–1010.

Kaye, W. H., Nagata, T., Weltzin, T. E., Hsu, L. K., Sokol, M. S., McConaha, C., et al. (2001). Double-blind placebo-controlled administration of fluoxetine in restricting- and restricting-purging-type anorexia nervosa. *Biological Psychiatry*, *49*(7), 644–652.

Keel, P. K., & Haedt, A. (2008). Evidence-based psychosocial treatments for eating problems and eating disorders. *Journal of Clinical Child and Adolescent Psychology*, *37*(1), 39–61.

Kennedy, A., Kohn, M., Lammi, A., & Clarke, S. (2004). Iron status and haematological changes in adolescent female inpatients with anorexia nervosa. *Journal of Paediatric and Child Health*, *40*(8), 430–432.

Kerem, N. C., & Katzman, D. K. (2003). Brain structure and function in adolescents with anorexia nervosa. *Adolescent Medicine*, *14*(1), 109–118.

Kiyohara, K., Tamai, H., Takaichi, Y., Nakagawa, T., & Kumagai, L. F. (1989). Decreased thyroidal triiodothyronine secretion in patients with anorexia nervosa: Influence of weight recovery. *American Journal of Clinical Nutrition*, *50*(4), 767–772.

Klostermann, B. K., Slap, G. B., Nebrig, D. M., Tivorsak, T. L., & Britto, M. T. (2005). Earning trust and losing it: Adolescents' views on trusting physicians. *Journal of Family Practice*, *54*(8), 679–687.

Kohn, M. R., Golden, N. H., & Shenker, I. R. (1998). Cardiac arrest and delirium: Presentations of the refeeding syndrome in severely malnourished adolescents with anorexia nervosa. *Journal of Adolescent Health*, *22*(3), 239–243.

Kotler, L. A., Devlin, M. J., Davies, M., & Walsh, B. T. (2003). An open trial of fluoxetine for adolescents with bulimia nervosa. *Journal of Child and Adolescent Psychopharmacology*, *13*(3), 329–335.

Lambe, E. K., Katzman, D. K., Mikulis, D. J., Kennedy, S. H., & Zipursky, R. B. (1997). Cerebral gray matter volume deficits after weight recovery from anorexia nervosa. *Archives of General Psychiatry*, *54*(6), 537–542.

Lambert, M., Hubert, C., Depresseux, G., Vande Berg, B., Thissen, J. P., Nagant de Deuxchaisnes, C., et al. (1997). Hematological changes in anorexia nervosa are correlated with total body fat mass depletion. *International Journal of Eating Disorders*, *21*(4), 329–334.

Lantzouni, E., Frank, G. R., Golden, N. H., & Shenker, R. I. (2002). Reversibility of growth stunting in early onset anorexia nervosa: A prospective study. *Journal of Adolescent Health*, *31*(2), 162–165.

Lawson, E. A., & Klibanski, A. (2008). Endocrine abnormalities in anorexia nervosa. *Nature Clinical Practice of Endocrinology and Metabolism*, *4*(7), 407–414.

Le Grange, D., Lock, J., & Dymek, M. (2003). Family-based therapy for adolescents with bulimia nervosa. *American Journal of Psychotherapy*, *57*(2), 237–251.

Lock, J., Couturier, J., & Agras, W. S. (2006). Comparison of long-term outcomes in adolescents with anorexia nervosa treated with family therapy. *Journal of the American Academy of Child and Adolescent Psychiatry*, *45*(6), 666–672.

Lock, J., & le Grange, D. (2005). Family-based treatment of eating disorders. *International Journal of Eating Disorders*, *37* (Supplement), S64–67; discussion S87–69.

Lock, J., Walker, L. R., Rickert, V. I., & Katzman, D. K. (2005). Suicidality in adolescents being treated with antidepressant medications and the black box label: position paper of the Society for Adolescent Medicine. *Journal of Adolescent Health*, *36*(1), 92–93.

Lo Muzio, L., Lo Russo, L., Massaccesi, C., Rappelli, G., Panzarella, V., Di Fede, O., et al. (2007). Eating disorders: a threat for women's health. Oral manifestations in a comprehensive overview. *Minerva Stomatologica*, *56*(5), 281–292.

Manno, B. R., & Manno, J. E. (1977). Toxicology of ipecac: A review. *Clinical Toxicology*, *10*(2), 221–242.

Mant, M. J., & Faragher, B. S. (1972). The haematology of anorexia nervosa. *British Journal of Haematology*, *23*(6), 737–749.

Marcos, A. (2000). Eating disorders: A situation of malnutrition with peculiar changes in the immune system. *European Journal of Clinical Nutrition*, *54* Suppl 1, S61–64.

Mattingly, D., & Bhanji, S. (1995). Hypoglycaemia and anorexia nervosa. *Journal of the Royal Society of Medicine, 88*(4), 191–195.

Mayer, L., Walsh, B. T., Pierson, R. N., Jr., Heymsfield, S. B., Gallagher, D., Wang, J., et al. (2005). Body fat redistribution after weight gain in women with anorexia nervosa. *American Journal of Clinical Nutrition, 81*(6), 1286–1291.

McAnarney, E. R., Greydanus, D. E., Campanella, V. A., & Hoekelman, R. A. (1983). Rib fractures and anorexia nervosa. *Journal of Adolescent Health Care, 4*(1), 40–43.

McLoughlin, D. M., Spargo, E., Wassif, W. S., Newham, D. J., Peters, T. J., Lantos, P. L., et al. (1998). Structural and functional changes in skeletal muscle in anorexia nervosa. *Acta Neuropathologica, 95*(6), 632–640.

McLoughlin, D. M., Wassif, W. S., Morton, J., Spargo, E., Peters, T. J., & Russell, G. F. (2000). Metabolic abnormalities associated with skeletal myopathy in severe anorexia nervosa. *Nutrition, 16*(3), 192–196.

Mecklenburg, R. S., Loriaux, D. L., Thompson, R. H., Andersen, A. E., & Lipsett, M. B. (1974). Hypothalamic dysfunction in patients with anorexia nervosa. *Medicine (Baltimore), 53*(2), 147–159.

Mehler, C., Wewetzer, C., Schulze, U., Warnke, A., Theisen, F., & Dittmann, R. W. (2001). Olanzapine in children and adolescents with chronic anorexia nervosa. A study of five cases. *European Child Adolescent Psychiatry, 10*(2), 151–157.

Misra, M., Aggarwal, A., Miller, K. K., Almazan, C., Worley, M., Soyka, L. A., et al. (2004). Effects of anorexia nervosa on clinical, hematologic, biochemical, and bone density parameters in community-dwelling adolescent girls. *Pediatrics, 114*(6), 1574–1583.

Misra, M., Miller, K. K., Almazan, C., Worley, M., Herzog, D. B., & Klibanski, A. (2005). Hormonal determinants of regional body composition in adolescent girls with anorexia nervosa and controls. *Journal of Clinical Endocrinology and Metabolism, 90*(5), 2580–2587.

Misra, M., Miller, K. K., Bjornson, J., Hackman, A., Aggarwal, A., Chung, J., et al. (2003). Alterations in growth hormone secretory dynamics in adolescent girls with anorexia nervosa and effects on bone metabolism. *Journal of Clinical Endocrinology and Metabolism, 88*(12), 5615–5623.

Misra, M., Prabhakaran, R., Miller, K. K., Goldstein, M. A., Mickley, D., Clauss, L., et al. (2008). Prognostic indicators of changes in bone density measures in adolescent girls with anorexia nervosa-II. *Journal of Clinical Endocrinology and Metabolism, 93*(4), 1292–1297.

Mitchell, J. E., & Crow, S. (2006). Medical complications of anorexia nervosa and bulimia nervosa. *Current Opinions in Psychiatry, 19*(4), 438–443.

Modan-Moses, D., Yaroslavsky, A., Novikov, I., Segev, S., Toledano, A., Miterany, E., et al. (2003). Stunting of growth as a major feature of anorexia nervosa in male adolescents. *Pediatrics, 111*(2), 270–276.

Mont, L., Castro, J., Herreros, B., Pare, C., Azqueta, M., Magrina, J., et al. (2003). Reversibility of cardiac abnormalities in adolescents with anorexia nervosa after weight recovery. *Journal of the American Academy of Child and Adolescent Psychiatry, 42*(7), 808–813.

Mortola, J. F., Rasmussen, D. D., & Yen, S. S. (1989). Alterations of the adrenocorticotropin-cortisol axis in normal weight bulimic women: Evidence for a central mechanism. *Journal of Clinical Endocrinology and Metabolism, 68*(3), 517–522.

Moyano, D., Vilaseca, M. A., Artuch, R., & Lambruschini, N. (1998). Plasma amino acids in anorexia nervosa. *European Journal of Clinical Nutrition, 52*(9), 684–689.

Muller, T. D., Focker, M., Holtkamp, K., Herpertz-Dahlmann, B., & Hebebrand, J. (2009). Leptin-mediated neuroendocrine alterations in anorexia nervosa: Somatic and behavioral implications. *Child and Adolescent Psychiatry Clinics of North America, 18*(1), 117–129.

Munoz, M. T., & Argente, J. (2002). Anorexia nervosa in female adolescents: endocrine and bone mineral density disturbances. *European Journal of Endocrinology, 147*(3), 275–286.

Mustafa, A., Ward, A., Treasure, J., & Peakman, M. (1997). T lymphocyte subpopulations in anorexia nervosa and refeeding. *Clinical Immunology and Immunopathology, 82*(3), 282–289.

Naessen, S., Carlstrom, K., Garoff, L., Glant, R., & Hirschberg, A. L. (2006). Polycystic ovary syndrome in bulimic women—an evaluation based on the new diagnostic criteria. *Gynecology and Endocrinology, 22*(7), 388–394.

Nakash-Eisikovits, O., Dierberger, A., & Westen, D. (2002). A multidimensional meta-analysis of pharmacotherapy for bulimia nervosa: Summarizing the range of outcomes in controlled clinical trials. *Harvard Review of Psychiatry, 10*(4), 193–211.

Neumark-Sztainer, D., Story, M., Resnick, M. D., & Blum, R. W. (1997). Adolescent vegetarians. A behavioral profile of a school-based population in Minnesota. *Archives of Pediatric and Adolescent Medicine, 151*(8), 833–838.

Neumarker, K. J. (1997). Mortality and sudden death in anorexia nervosa. *International Journal of Eating Disorders, 21*(3), 205–212.

Newman, M. M., & Halmi, K. A. (1988). The endocrinology of anorexia nervosa and bulimia nervosa. *Endocrinology and Metabolism Clinics of North America, 17*(1), 195–212.

Newman-Toker, J. (2000). Risperidone in anorexia nervosa. *Journal of the American Academy of Child and Adolescent Psychiatry, 39*(8), 941–942.

Nicholls, D., Chater, R., & Lask, B. (2000). Children into DSM don't go: A comparison of classification systems for eating disorders in childhood and early adolescence. *International Journal of Eating Disorders, 28*(3), 317–324.

Nishita, J. K., Ellinwood, E. H., Jr., Rockwell, W. J., Kuhn, C. M., Hoffman, G. W., Jr., McCall, W. V., et al. (1989). Abnormalities in the response of plasma arginine vasopressin during hypertonic saline infusion in patients with eating disorders. *Biological Psychiatry, 26*(1), 73–86.

Nova, E., Samartin, S., Gomez, S., Morande, G., & Marcos, A. (2002). The adaptive response of the immune system to the particular malnutrition of eating disorders. *European Journal of Clinical Nutrition, 56* Suppl 3, S34–37.

Nudel, D. B., Gootman, N., Nussbaum, M. P., & Shenker, I. R. (1984). Altered exercise performance and abnormal sympathetic responses to exercise in patients with anorexia nervosa. *Journal of Pediatrics, 105*(1), 34–37.

Obarzanek, E., Lesem, M. D., & Jimerson, D. C. (1994). Resting metabolic rate of anorexia nervosa patients during weight gain. *American Journal of Clinical Nutrition, 60*(5), 666–675.

Ogren, F. P., Huerter, J. V., Pearson, P. H., Antonson, C. W., & Moore, G. F. (1987). Transient salivary gland hypertrophy in bulimics. *Laryngoscope, 97*(8 Pt 1), 951–953.

Olivares, J. L., Vazquez, M., Fleta, J., Moreno, L. A., Perez-Gonzalez, J. M., & Bueno, M. (2005). Cardiac findings in adolescents with anorexia nervosa at diagnosis and after weight restoration. *European Journal of Pediatrics, 164*(6), 383–386.

Ornstein, R. M., Golden, N. H., Jacobson, M. S., & Shenker, I. R. (2003). Hypophosphatemia during nutritional rehabilitation in anorexia nervosa: Implications for refeeding and monitoring. *Journal of Adolescent Health, 32*(1), 83–88.

Overby, K. J., & Litt, I. F. (1988). Mediastinal emphysema in an adolescent with anorexia nervosa and self-induced emesis. *Pediatrics, 81*(1), 134–136.

Palla, B., & Litt, I. F. (1988). Medical complications of eating disorders in adolescents. *Pediatrics, 81*(5), 613–623.

Panagiotopoulos, C., McCrindle, B. W., Hick, K., & Katzman, D. K. (2000). Electrocardiographic findings in adolescents with eating disorders. *Pediatrics, 105*(5), 1100–1105.

Papadopoulos, F. C., Ekbom, A., Brandt, L., & Ekselius, L. (2009). Excess mortality, causes of death and prognostic factors in anorexia nervosa. *British Journal of Psychiatry, 194*(1), 10–17.

Pereira, T., Lock, J., & Oggins, J. (2006). Role of therapeutic alliance in family therapy for adolescent anorexia nervosa. *International Journal of Eating Disorders, 39*(8), 677–684.

Pirke, K., Fichter, M. M., Schweiger, U., Fruth, C., Streitmatter, A., & Wolfram, G. (1987). Gonadotropin secretion pattern in bulimia nervosa. *International Journal of Eating Disorders, 6*, 655–661.

Pirke, K. M., Dogs, M., Fichter, M. M., & Tuschl, R. J. (1988). Gonadotrophins, oestradiol and progesterone during the menstrual cycle in bulimia nervosa. *Clinical Endocrinology (Oxford), 29*(3), 265–270.

Platte, P., Pirke, K. M., Trimborn, P., Pietsch, K., Krieg, J. C., & Fichter, M. M. (1994). Resting metabolic rate and total energy expenditure in acute and weight recovered patients with anorexia nervosa and in healthy young women. *International Journal of Eating Disorders, 16*(1), 45–52.

Pomeroy, C., & Mitchell, J. E. (2002). Medical complications of Anorexia Nervosa and Bulimia Nervosa. *Eating disorders and obesity: A comprehensive handbook* (2nd ed., pp. 278–285). New York: Guilford Press.

Pomeroy, C., Mitchell, J., Eckert, E., Raymond, N., Crosby, R., & Dalmasso, A. P. (1997). Effect of body weight and caloric restriction on serum complement proteins, including Factor D/adipsin: Studies in anorexia nervosa and obesity. *Clinical and Experimental Immunology, 108*(3), 507–515.

Prabhakaran, R., Misra, M., Miller, K. K., Kruczek, K., Sundaralingam, S., Herzog, D. B., et al. (2008). Determinants of height in adolescent girls with anorexia nervosa. *Pediatrics, 121*(6), e1517–1523.

Quadflieg, N., & Fichter, M. M. (2003). The course and outcome of bulimia nervosa. *European Child and Adolescent Psychiatry, 12* (Supplement 1), I99–109.

Resch, M., Szendei, G., & Haasz, P. (2004). Bulimia from a gynecological view: hormonal changes. *Journal of Obstetrics and Gynaecology, 24*(8), 907–910.

Rigaud, D., Moukaddem, M., Cohen, B., Malon, D., Reveillard, V., & Mignon, M. (1997). Refeeding improves muscle performance without normalization of muscle mass and oxygen consumption in anorexia nervosa patients. *American Journal of Clinical Nutrition, 65*(6), 1845–1851.

Robinson, E., Bachrach, L. K., & Katzman, D. K. (2000). Use of hormone replacement therapy to reduce the risk of osteopenia in adolescent girls with anorexia nervosa. *Journal of Adolescent Health, 26*(5), 343–348.

Russell, G. F., & Bruce, J. T. (1966). Impaired water diuresis in patients with anorexia nervosa. *American Journal of Medicine, 40*(1), 38–48.

Ruuska, J., Kaltiala-Heino, R., Rantanen, P., & Koivisto, A. M. (2005). Psychopathological distress predicts suicidal ideation and self-harm in adolescent eating disorder outpatients. *European Child and Adolescent Psychiatry, 14*(5), 276–281.

Salbach-Andrae, H., Lenz, K., Simmendinger, N., Klinkowski, N., Lehmkuhl, U., & Pfeiffer, E. (2008). Psychiatric comorbidities among female adolescents with anorexia nervosa. *Child Psychiatry and Human Development, 39*(3), 261–272.

Schattner, A., Tepper, R., Steinbock, M., Hahn, T., & Schoenfeld, A. (1990). TNF, interferon-gamma and cell-mediated cytotoxicity in anorexia nervosa; Effect of refeeding. *Journal of Clinical and Laboratory Immunology, 32*(4), 183–184.

Scheen, A. J., Castillo, M., & Lefebvre, P. J. (1988). Insulin sensitivity in anorexia nervosa: A mirror image of obesity? *Diabetes and Metabolism Reviews, 4*(7), 681–690.

Schneider, D. J., Perez, A., Knilamus, T. E., Daniels, S. R., Bove, K. E., & Bonnell, H. (1996). Clinical and pathologic aspects of cardiomyopathy from ipecac administration in Munchausen's syndrome by proxy. *Pediatrics, 97*(6 Pt 1), 902–906.

Schwartz, B. I., Mansbach, J. M., Marion, J. G., Katzman, D. K., & Forman, S. F. (2008). Variations in admission practices for adolescents with anorexia nervosa: A North American sample. *Journal of Adolescent Health, 43*(5), 425–431.

Schweiger, U., Pirke, K. M., Laessle, R. G., & Fichter, M. M. (1992). Gonadotropin secretion in bulimia nervosa. *Journal of Clinical Endocrinology and Metabolism, 74*(5), 1122–1127.

Shamim, T., Golden, N. H., Arden, M., Filiberto, L., & Shenker, I. R. (2003). Resolution of vital sign instability: An objective measure of medical stability in anorexia nervosa. *Journal of Adolescent Health, 32*(1), 73–77.

Sherman, P., Leslie, K., Goldberg, E., Rybczynski, J., & St Louis, P. (1994). Hypercarotenemia and transaminitis in female adolescents with eating disorders: A prospective, controlled study. *Journal of Adolescent Health, 15*(3), 205–209.

Shomento, S. H., & Kreipe, R. E. (1994). Menstruation and fertility following anorexia nervosa. *Adolescent and Pediatric Gynecology, 7*, 142–146.

Silber, T. J. (2005). Ipecac syrup abuse, morbidity, and mortality: Isn't it time to repeal its over-the-counter status? *Journal of Adolescent Health, 37*(3), 256–260.

Silverman, J. A. (1983). Medical consequences of starvation: The malnutrition of anorexia nervosa: Caveat medicus. In *Anorexia nervosa: Recent developments in research.* New York: Alan R. Liss. Inc. 1983: 293–299.

Silvetti, M. S., Magnani, M., Santilli, A., Di Liso, G., Diamanti, A., Pompei, E., et al. (1998). [The heart of anorexic adolescents]. *Giornale italiano di cardiologia, 28*(2), 131–139.

Solanto, M. V., Jacobson, M. S., Heller, L., Golden, N. H., & Hertz, S. (1994). Rate of weight gain of inpatients with anorexia nervosa under two behavioral contracts. *Pediatrics, 93*(6 Pt 1), 989–991.

Solomon, S. M., & Kirby, D. F. (1990). The refeeding syndrome: A review. *JPEN J Parenter Enteral Nutr, 14*(1), 90–97.

Soyka, L. A., Grinspoon, S., Levitsky, L. L., Herzog, D. B., & Klibanski, A. (1999). The effects of anorexia nervosa on bone metabolism in female adolescents. *Journal of Clinical Endocrinology and Metabolism, 84*(12), 4489–4496.

Soyka, L. A., Misra, M., Frenchman, A., Miller, K. K., Grinspoon, S., Schoenfeld, D. A., et al. (2002). Abnormal bone mineral accrual in adolescent girls with anorexia nervosa. *Journal of Clinical Endocrinology and Metabolism, 87*(9), 4177–4185.

Stacher, G., Kiss, A., Wiesnagrotzki, S., Bergmann, H., Hobart, J., & Schneider, C. (1986). Oesophageal and gastric motility disorders in patients categorised as having primary anorexia nervosa. *Gut, 27*(10), 1120–1126.

Steinegger, C., & Katzman, D. K. (2008). Interviewing the adolescent with an eating disorders. *Adolescent Medicine: State of the Art Reviews, 19*(1), 18–40.

Steinhausen, H. C. (1999). Eating disorders. In V. F. Steinhausen HC, Verhulst F. C. (Eds.), *Risks and outcomes in developmental psychopathology* (pp. 210–230). Oxford, England: Oxford University Press. 210–30.

Steinhausen, H. C. (2002). The outcome of anorexia nervosa in the 20th century. *American Journal of Psychiatry, 159*(8), 1284–1293.

Stock, S. L., Goldberg, E., Corbett, S., & Katzman, D. K. (2002). Substance use in female adolescents with eating disorders. *Journal of Adolescent Health, 31*(2), 176–182.

Stoving, R. K., Hangaard, J., Hansen-Nord, M., & Hagen, C. (1999). A review of endocrine changes in anorexia nervosa. *Journal of Psychiatric Research, 33*(2), 139–152.

Strober, M., Freeman, R., & Morrell, W. (1997). The long-term course of severe anorexia nervosa in adolescents: Survival analysis of recovery, relapse, and outcome predictors over 10–15 years in a prospective study. *International Journal of Eating Disorders, 22*(4), 339–360.

Strumia, R. (2005). Dermatologic signs in patients with eating disorders. *American Journal of Clinical Dermatology, 6*(3), 165–173.

Swenne, I., & Larsson, P. T. (1999). Heart risk associated with weight loss in anorexia nervosa and eating disorders: Risk factors for QTc interval prolongation and dispersion. *Acta Paediatrica, 88*(3), 304–309.

Swinbourne, J. M., & Touyz, S. W. (2007). The co-morbidity of eating disorders and anxiety disorders: A review. *European Eating Disorders Reviews, 15*(4), 253–274.

Vaisman, N., Barak, Y., Hahn, T., Karov, Y., Malach, L., & Barak, V. (1996). Defective in vitro granulopoiesis in patients with anorexia nervosa. *Pediatric Research, 40*(1), 108–111.

Vanderdokt, O., Lambert, M., Montero, M. C., Boland, B., & Brohet, C. (2001). The 12–electrocardiogram in anorexia nervosa: A report of two cases followed by a retrospective study. *Journal of Electrocardiology, 34*, 233–242.

Vestergaard, P., Emborg, C., Stoving, R. K., Hagen, C., Mosekilde, L., & Brixen, K. (2002). Fractures in patients with anorexia nervosa, bulimia nervosa, and other eating disorders—a nationwide register study. *International Journal of Eating Disorders, 32*(3), 301–308.

Walsh, B. T., Kaplan, A. S., Attia, E., Olmsted, M., Parides, M., Carter, J. C., et al. (2006). Fluoxetine after weight restoration in anorexia nervosa: A randomized controlled trial. *JAMA, 295*(22), 2605–2612.

Weinbrenner, T., Zuger, M., Jacoby, G. E., Herpertz, S., Liedtke, R., Sudhop, T., et al. (2004). Lipoprotein metabolism in patients with anorexia nervosa: A case-control study investigating the mechanisms leading to hypercholesterolaemia. *British Journal of Nutrition, 91*(6), 959–969.

Wentz, E., Gillberg, I. C., Gillberg, C., & Rastam, M. (2005). Fertility and history of sexual abuse at 10–year follow-up of adolescent-onset anorexia nervosa. *International Journal of Eating Disorders, 37*(4), 294–298.

Woodside, D. B. (1995). A review of anorexia nervosa and bulimia nervosa. *Current Problems in Pediatrics, 25*(2), 67–89.

Yager, J., & Andersen, A. E. (2005). Clinical practice. Anorexia nervosa. *New England Journal of Medicine, 353*(14), 1481–1488.

Zipfel, S., Lowe, B., Reas, D. L., Deter, H. C., & Herzog, W. (2000). Long-term prognosis in anorexia nervosa: Lessons from a 21–year follow-up study. *Lancet, 355*(9205), 721–722.

Zipfel, S., Reas, D. L., Thornton, C., Olmsted, M. P., Williamson, D. A., Gerlinghoff, M., et al. (2002). Day hospitalization programs for eating disorders: A systematic review of the literature. *International Journal of Eating Disorders, 31*(2), 105–117.

Zipfel, S., Sammet, I., Rapps, N., Herzog, W., Herpertz, S., & Martens, U. (2006). Gastrointestinal disturbances in eating disorders: Clinical and neurobiological aspects. *Autonomic Neuroscience, 129*(1–2), 99–106.

Psychological Comorbidity of Eating Disorders

Katherine A. Halmi

Abstract

Psychological comorbidity of eating disorders may be organized most conveniently according to psychiatric diagnoses of the *Diagnostic and Statistical Manual–IV* (*DSM-IV*) and assessments of specific traits. In this chapter, further categorization of the *DSM-IV* diagnoses is made according to Axis I and Axis II diagnoses (American Psychiatric Association [APA], 1994). The most comprehensive psychological comorbidity study is from the U.S. national comorbidity survey replication (Hudson et al., 2008). In this study, at least one lifetime comorbid psychiatric *DSM-IV* disorder was present in 56.2% of anorexia nervosa participants, 94.5% of those with bulimia nervosa, 78.9% of those with binge eating disorder, 63.6% with subthreshold binge eating disorder, and 76.5% with any binge eating. Similar results were obtained with other population based studies and also from studies of clinical populations containing the diagnoses of anorexia nervosa, bulimia nervosa, and binge eating disorder (Braun, Sunday, & Halmi, 1994; Godart et al., 2002; Halmi et al., 1991; Hudson et al., 1987; Johnson et al., 2001; Kaye et al., 2004; McElroy et al., 2005).

Keywords: affective disorders, anxiety disorders, comorbidity, impulse control disorders, personality disorders, personality traits, substance abuse disorders

Comorbid Axis I Psychiatric Disorders
Affective Disorders

Affective disorders are the most prevalent of the comorbid psychiatric disorders associated with eating disorders (EDs), as indicated in Table 17.1. A study of Asians with anorexia nervosa (AN) entering an ED clinic in Singapore revealed that depression was the most common comorbid condition affecting 25.4% of that sample (Lee et al., 2005). Thus race and ethnicity do not seem to influence the predominance of depression as a comorbid condition of EDs. Table 17.1 presents data of Axis I comorbid disorders from studies that used valid structured interviews for *Diagnostic and Statistical Manual -III-R* (*DSM-III-R*) or *DSM-IV* diagnoses. Prevalence of lifetime affective disorders across population and clinical sample based studies is fairly similar. One study comparing bipolar patients with and without a lifetime history of EDs found those with EDs were heavier, rated more symptomatic on a clinical global impression severity scale, had a higher number of lifetime depressive episodes and greater psychiatric comorbidity excluding eating and mood disorders. This study suggested the ED comorbidity with bipolar disorder created an increase symptom load and illness burden in the bipolar disorder (Wildes et al., 2007).

An affective disorder was not shown to influence the response to treatment in bulimia nervosa (BN; Walsh et al., 1991) or to effect treatment acceptance or completion in AN (Halmi et al., 2005).

Anxiety Disorders

The largest number of ED individuals assessed for the presence of anxiety disorders was from a multi-site study assessing these individuals for genetic

Table 17.1 Axis I Comorbid Psychiatric Diagnoses

Authors	Comorbid Diagnosis	Anorexia Nervosa (%)	Bulimia Nervosa (%)	Binge eating Disorder (%)
	Any Mood Disorder			
Hudson et al., 2008		42.1	70.7	46.4
Hudson et al., 1987			70	
Halmi et al., 1991		80	92.9	
Braun et al., 1994		41	78	
	Major depressive disorder			
Hudson et al., 2008		39.1	50.1	32.3
Hudson et al., 1987			55	
Halmi et al., 1991		40	78.6	
Braun et al., 1994		32	45	
	Bipolar I–IIDisorders			
Hudson et al., 2008		3	17.1	12.5
Hudson et al., 1987			11	
Halmi et al., 1991		0	7.1	
Braun et al., 1994		0.33	13	
	Any Anxiety Disorder			
Hudson et al., 2008		47.9	80.6	65.1
Hudson et al., 1987			43	
Halmi, 1991		60	50	
Braun et al., 1994		41	50	
Godart et al., 2000		72	65	
Kaye et al., 2004		55	68	
	Panic Disorder			
Hudson et al., 2008		3	16.2	13.2
Halmi et al., 1991		8		
Braun et al., 1994		12	10	
Godart et al., 2000		7	15	
Kaye et al., 2004		9	11	
	Social Phobia			
Hudson et al., 2008		24.8	41.3	31.9
Halmi et al., 1991		33.9		
Braun et al., 1994		12	20	
Godart et al., 2000		55	59	
Kaye et al., 2004		22	16	

Table 17.1 (continued) Axis I Comorbid Psychiatric Diagnoses

Authors	Comorbid Diagnosis	Anorexia Nervosa (%)	Bulimia Nervosa (%)	Binge eating Disorder (%)
	Specific Phobia			
Hudson et al., 2008		26.5	50	37.1
Halmi et al., 1991		12.9		
Braun et al., 1994		14	5	
Godart et al., 2000		34	21	
Kaye et al., 2004		14	12	
	Generalized Anxiety Disorder			
Hudson et al., 2008		12	45.4	26.3
Brewerton et al., 1995			12	
Braun et al., 1994		6	0	
Godart et al., 2000		24	23	
Kaye et al., 2004		13	8	
	Posttraumatic Stress Disorder			
Hudson et al., 2008		0	17.4	8.2
Brewerton et al., 1995			3	
Kaye et al., 2004		5	13	
	Obsessive–Compulsive Disorder			
Hudson et al., 2008		7.5	3.5	12.2
Halmi et al., 1991		25.8		
Braun et al., 1994		21	17	
Godart et al., 2000		21	0	
Kaye et al., 2004		35	40	
	Any Substance Use Disorder			
Hudson et al., 2008		27	36.8	23.3
Halmi et al., 1991		18		
Braun et al., 1994		11.8	51.6	
	Alcohol Abuse or Dependence			
Hudson et al., 2008		24.5	33.7	21.4
Halmi et al., 1991		8		
Braun et al., 1994		5.9	41.9	
Bulik et al., 2004		16.8	46.1	

Table 17.1   (continued) Axis I Comorbid Psychiatric Diagnoses

Authors	Comorbid Diagnosis	Anorexia Nervosa (%)	Bulimia Nervosa (%)	Binge eating Disorder (%)
	Drug Abuse or Dependence			
Hudson et al., 2008		17.7	26.0	19.4
Halmi et al., 1991		8		
Braun et al., 1994		0	12.5	
	Impulse Control Disorder			
Hudson et al., 2008		30.8	63.8	43.3
Fernandez, 2008		1.7— Restricting AN	21.8	
	Attention-Deficit/Hyperactivity Disorder			
Hudson et al., 2008		16.2	34.9	19.8
	Oppositional Defiant Disorder			
Hudson et al., 2008		10.5	26.9	18.9
	Conduct Disorder			
Hudson et al., 2008		9.8	26.5	20.0
	Any Cluster B			
Braun et al., 1994		0	28	
	Borderline Personality Disorder	0	33	
	Histrionic	0	11	
	Antisocial	0	20	
	Any Personality Disorder			Entire Eating Disorder Sample
Powers et al., 1988				77
Woonderlich et al., 1990				62
Gartner et al., 1989				61
Schmidt & Telch 1990				43
Rossiter et al., 1993				33
Steiger et al., 1994				28
Braun et al., 1994				69
Matsunaga, 2000				26
	Any Cluster C			
Braun et al., 1994		29	50	

studies (Kaye et al., 2004). In this study, the ED subtypes had similar rates of anxiety disorders with the exception of PTSD, which was approximately three times greater in those with BN or the combination of anorexia and bulimia compared with the restricting type of AN patients. Two-thirds of the participants in this study reported one or more anxiety disorders in their lifetime with the most common diagnosis being obsessive-compulsive disorder (OCD; 41%) and social phobia (20%). In the majority of these persons the onset of OCD, social phobia, specific phobia or generalized anxiety disorder occurred in childhood before the emergence of their ED. About 42% of the participants in this study had the onset of one or more of the anxiety disorders in childhood. This figure is substantially higher than the overall anxiety disorder prevalence in childhood which ranges from 4.7% to 17.7% (Costello et al., 1995). A childhood disorder of OCD occurred in 23% of these participants compared with community samples of 2% to 3% (Piacentini and Bergman, 2000).

In another study from the same international multisite collaborative group, 39% of 249 women with a lifetime history of AN reported a history of over anxious disorder of childhood, a *DSM-III-R* diagnosis. Of these 94% met criteria for over anxious disorder of childhood before the onset of AN. Those women with both AN and the over anxious disorder self reported more extreme personality traits and attitudes and engaged in more compensatory behaviors such as purging (Raney et al., 2008) compared to AN women without over anxious disorder of childhood. The over anxious disorder was more common among the purging anorectics and anorectics with binge/purge behavior. Although the over anxious disorder of childhood does not exist in *DSM-IV*, this assessment does suggest that patterns of early onset of anxiety disorders may be a risk factor for AN. Strober (2004) suggested that AN may manifest itself as a heightened sensitivity to fear conditioning with resistance to extinction in those women who also have anxiety disorders. The anxiety symptoms may be related to altered striatal dopamine function (Frank, et al., 2005). Those individuals with a history of over anxious disorder of childhood compared to those without, engaged in more serious weight control practices and displayed greater body dissatisfaction, higher drive for thinness, more eating preoccupation and a longer duration for illness. Likewise, those who had over anxious disorder were significantly more likely to have generalized anxiety disorder, OCD, specific

phobia, social phobia, and panic disorder. The authors of this study concluded that although the observations were based on retrospective recall, they suggest the importance of early detection of over anxious disorder as a means of averting the later development of anxiety and ED symptoms.

In the study by Braun et al. (1994) social phobia most commonly preceded the ED in 52% of the patient reports. Most of these patients also had a history of major depression. In those, the social phobia preceded the depression.

Substance Abuse Disorders

The association of substance abuse and EDs with binge eating has been reported in many clinical observation studies (Holderness et al., 1994). Adolescents engaging in binge eating and purging behavior have higher rates of substance use and greater psychological distress than their nonpurging peers (Ross and Ivis, 1999). Another study found that binge eating in adolescents predicted later incidents of substance use disorders (Weiderman & Pryor, 1996). In this study about one-third of the girls with BN were engaged in smoking tobacco, using marijuana and/or drinking alcohol at least weekly. In the bulimic adolescents substance use was also related to other impulsive behaviors such as attempted suicide, stealing and sexual promiscuity.

In contrast with bulimics and binge eaters, restricting anorectics have low rates of comorbid substance abuse (Stock et al., 2002). Another study found dieting severity was positively associated with the prevalence, frequency, and intensity of substance abuse (Weiderman & Pryor, 1996).

The study with the largest ED sample size of 672 persons showed alcohol abuse and dependence was significantly lower in prevalence in individuals with AN compared with those who had BN (Bulik et al., 2004; see Table 17.1). Of those 253 persons with alcohol abuse/dependence 32% had the onset of alcoholism before the ED. Only 9% experienced the onset of both EDs and alcohol abuse in the same year. Alcohol involvement was significantly associated with increased prevalence of major depressive disorder. Eighty percent of those with major depressive disorder compared with 67% of those without it had an alcohol abuse/dependence disorder. This study also found that the alcoholism was associated with increased risk of OCD, a variety of anxiety disorders and Cluster B diagnoses, particularly borderline personality disorder.

An earlier study (Braun et al., 1994) found that the AN restricting subgroup was significantly less likely to be alcohol or drug dependent compared with the bulimic subtypes. A comparison of age of onset showed 57% developed the ED first and 27% developed alcohol dependence first. It is of interest to note that it is more typical for the onset of EDs to precede the onset of alcohol abuse/dependence disorders and more likely for anxiety disorders to predate the onset of EDs.

Impulse Control Disorders

In *DSM-IV* (American Psychiatric Association [APA], 1994) impulse control disorders (ICDs) are classified as pathological gambling, kleptomania, intermittent explosive disorder, trichotillomania, pyromania, and ICDs not otherwise specified which includes compulsive internet use, compulsive sexual behavior, and compulsive buying. ICDs are characterized by repetitive occurrence of impulsive behavior which includes core features of compulsive engagement in a behavior despite adverse consequences, failure to resist the impulse, urge or craving state before engagement in the impulsive act, and a sense of pleasure and gratification or release at the time the behavior is committed. Other than a few case studies there are only three studies with large sample size studies examining ICD in EDs. In a study by Fernandez-Aranda et al. (2006), the prevalence of lifetime ICD in 227 bulimia patients was 23.8%, with compulsive buying and intermittent explosive disorder as the most frequently reported ICD. Those individuals with BN and lifetime ICD have more extreme personality profiles, especially on novelty seeking and impulsivity and greater general psychopathology than those with BN without ICD. An analysis of data from the multisite, international Price Foundation Genetic Studies of Eating Disorders by Fernandez-Aranda et al. (2008) showed a lifetime prevalence of all ICD in this entire sample was 16.6%. Compulsive buying disorder was the most common diagnosis, 11.8%, followed by kleptomania, 4.5%, with 17 participants having both diagnoses. The remaining diagnoses were trichotillomania 1.85%, intermittent explosive disorder 0.6%, compulsive gambling 0.3% and pyromania 0.3%. In the entire sample of 118 individuals who had both ED and ICD, the impulsive control disorders were present in only 1 participant with restricting type of AN and 2 with purging AN. Thus, of the 118 cases of ED and ICD, all but 3 were associated with ED subtypes that included binge eating. This study also demonstrated the presence of ICD in EDs was significantly associated with greater severity of ED reflected in the use of maladaptive compensatory behaviors such as laxatives, diuretics, appetite suppressants and fasting. In addition there was a greater general psychiatric comorbidity and psychopathology including depression and anxiety disorders, Cluster B personality disorder, avoidant personality disorder and specific personality traits such as higher impulsivity, harm avoidance, neuroticism, cognitive impulsivity and lower self directiveness in those who had ICD as well as their ED compared with individuals who had an EDs without ICD.

It is of interest to note that in the above studies, 62% of the ICD occurred before the onset of the ED and 40% experienced the onset of both disorders within the same 3-year window. It is likely differential personality traits exist amongst the various impulse control disorders. For example, in this sample of EDs with ICD those individuals were three times more likely to have comorbid OCD compared with ED individuals without ICD. Pathological gambling one might expect to be associated with higher novelty seeking. The authors suggest that problems with removing unwanted thoughts and impaired decision-making may be a link between OCD and ICD and may partially explain the association of ICD and OCD in this ED sample. Those ED individuals with ICD were also three times more likely to have comorbid borderline personality disorder. These findings led the authors to suggest that a subtype of BN exists whose development in association with ICD, affective disturbance, substance use and personality disturbance may be an expression of genetic variance that predisposes to high levels of disinhibition and impulsivity.

The publication of prevalence and correlates of EDs in the national comorbidity survey replication (Hudson et al., 2008) showed an unusually high prevalence of total impulse control disorders in AN, 30.8%, BN 63.8% and binge ED 43.3%.

Further analyses of these impulse control disorders were not presented in that publication. It is likely that impulse control disorders are under diagnosed by clinicians who may acknowledge the behaviors but do not regard them as a specific diagnosis.

Axis II Disorders
Personality Disorders

According to *DSM-IV* (APA, 1994) personality disorders are differentiated from personality traits in that the latter are enduring patterns of perceiving the environment and are exhibited in a wide range of social and personal contexts. When these traits are inflexible and maladaptive and cause significant functional impairment or subjective distress, they then constitute a personality disorder. Thus in *DSM-IV* a personality disorder is defined as "an enduring pattern of inner experience and behavior that deviates markedly from expectation of the individual's culture, is pervasive and inflexible, has an onset in adolescence or early adulthood, is stable over time, and leads to distress or impairment" (APA, 1994). Diagnosis of personality disorders is more difficult and less accurate in that information is often necessary from other informants than the target individual who may not admit to problematic behaviors or think they are an issue. This may explain the observation that many of the studies of personality disorders and EDs are contradictory. Personality disorders are further grouped into three descriptive clusters: Cluster A individuals often appear odd or eccentric and includes the paranoid, schizoid and schizotypal personality disorder; Cluster B are individuals who often appear dramatic and emotional or erratic and this includes the antisocial, borderline, histrionic, and narcissistic personality disorders; Cluster C are individuals who often appear anxious or fearful and includes the avoidant, dependent, and obsessive– compulsive personality disorders. The *DSM-IV* classification of personality disorders are similar to the previous *DSM-III-R* classification with the exception that passive-aggressive personality disorder was deleted from *DSM-IV*. Many of the large sample structured interview personality disorder studies of EDs were conducted in the late 1980s to 1990s using *DSM-III-R* criteria. Most of those studies showed a high preponderance of Cluster B (impulsive) personality disorders associated with the bulimic subtype compared with the anorectic restrictors. Percentages of *DSM-III-R* bulimics who had at least one personality disorder ranged from 28% (Steiger et al., 1994) to 77% (Powers et al., 1988). The following intermediate percentages were studies by Wonderlich et al. (1990), 52%; Gartner, Marcus, Halmi, and Loranger (1989), 61%; Schmidt and Telch (1990), 43%; and Rossiter et al. (1993), 33%.

In a study by Braun et al. (1994) 69% of the patients had at least one personality disorder and of those 93% had an Axis I comorbidity. Thirty-one percent of the bulimic subgroups and none of the anorectic restrictors had Cluster B disorders. The most prominent of the latter was borderline personality disorder, which was present in 25% of the bulimic subgroups and the most common Cluster B condition. Cluster C personality disorders were present in 29.5% of these patients and in this category avoidant personality disorder was the most common, 14.3%, followed by dependent, 10.5%, obsessive–compulsive, 6.7%, and passive–aggressive, 4.8%. The prevalence of Cluster C personality disorders did not vary according to ED subtype.

In a study by Hertzog et al. (1992), the most commonly observed personality disorder in 210 patients with EDs was borderline personality disorder (9%). Higher rates of borderline personality disorder were found in the bulimic and anorectic–bulimic groups whereas avoidant personality disorder was the most prevalent among the anorectic and anorectic–bulimic groups. Matsunaga et al. (2000) assessed personality disorders in patients recovered from EDs and found a prevalence of at least one personality disorder in 26% with Cluster B associated with the bulimic subtypes. When Steiger et al. (2000) compared bulimics with and without borderline personality disorder they found the borderline showed elevated motor impulsivity, dissociation and higher rates of sexual abuse. In another study Steiger et al. (1994) found that personality disorder classification did not predict severity of bulimic symptoms or responsiveness to treatment.

In the Braun et al. (1994) study an attempt was made to assess personality disorders with a more sensitive dimensional measure. This was done by adding the total number of questions to which a subject made a threshold response in each of the SCID-II personality disorder modules. A weighted personality score was arbitrarily assigned to each subthreshold response within a particular module. A value of 1 was given to a subthreshold response and each threshold response was given a value of 2. Correlations were then compared across Axis I disorders and the weighted personality scores. There were significance relationships between major depression and avoidant personality scores, OCDs and weighted obsessive–compulsive scores, social phobia and avoidant personality scores, and affective disorder with borderline personality scores. There were significant correlations between alcohol abuse and antisocial personality scores as well. The dimensional profile suggested that bulimics with a history of AN and those currently ill AN bulimic subtypes may have different personality features from those patients who have always had exclusively restricting AN or exclusive BN. The groups with both ED diagnoses, the bulimics with a history of AN and the AN bulimic subtypes were high in antisocial, borderline, histrionic, and self-defeating weighted scores. The authors hypothesized that anorectic restrictors with more self-defeating and impulsive personality features may be at a greater risk of developing bulimia over time (i.e., becoming AN bulimic subtypes or normal weight BN with a history of AN).

A prospective study would be helpful to demonstrate whether specific personality disorder profiles actually predispose patients to develop particular EDs. On the other hand, it would be of interest to know whether the development of an ED during adolescent years may have a formative effect on personality.

Personality Traits

Perfectionism is one of the personality features initially identified with AN. Over a century ago, Charles Laseque described in these patients an unrelenting pursuit of unusually rigid standards of propriety (Laseque, 1873). Perfectionism may predate the onset of EDs (Fairburn, Cooper, Dell, & Welch, 1999), typify the acute phase of EDs (Halmi et al., 2000), and persist after recovery from EDs (Crostioni et al., 1995; Kaye et al., 1998; Sutandar-Pinnock et al., 2003). In an international multicenter genetic study of AN 322 women with a history of AN were assessed with the Frost Multidimensional Perfectionism Scale (Frost et al., 1997). Those with AN were distinguished from healthy comparison subjects by greater preoccupations and efforts at avoidance of mistakes in daily life, parental criticism, doubts over the correctness of actions, and more extreme adherence to personal and parental standards of excellence. This study found that AN patients who engaged in purging without binge eating had higher parental criticism scores than did those who engaged only in restricting behaviors. Greater perfectionism was associated with lower body weight and greater prominence of eating preoccupations and rituals as well as the diminished motivation to change. Thus greater severity of ED symptoms was associated with greater perfectionism (Halmi et al., 2000).

Studies on relation between perfectionism and obsessive–compulsive traits reveal a significant correlation between some perfectionism subscales and obsessive–compulsive traits (Frost & Steketee, 1997; Tozzi et al., 2004). This relationship was examined in 607 individuals with anorexia and BN participating in an international genetic study. They were assessed for perfectionism, obsessive–compulsive personality disorder and OCD (Halmi et al., 2005). There was no significant difference in comorbidity frequency among the ED subtypes; OCD 20%,

obsessive–compulsive personality disorder (OCPD) 13%, and a combination of OCD/OCPD, 16%. Perfectionism was most severe in those with OCPD or the combination of OCPD/OCD. The pairing of perfectionism with OCPD may be a relevant core behavioral feature for vulnerability to develop EDs.

Obsessions and compulsions unrelated to core ED symptomology were assessed in persons with a history of AN who were participating in an international multicenter genetic study. The obsessive–compulsive symptoms were assessed using the Y-BOCS (Goodman et al., 1989), a semistructured interview. Lifetime obsessions and compulsions occurred in 86% of the AN restricting type and in 79.1% of the AN binge/purge type. The AN subgroups did not differ from OCD controls in the frequency of obsessions in the symmetry and somatic categories or in the compulsion categories of ordering and hoarding. This finding suggests there may be some common phenotype characteristic shared by most AN and obsessive–compulsive patients and indicates there may also be some common brain behavioral pathways.

The temperament and character inventory (TCI) was used to assess personality characteristics in ED patients in the study by Klump et al. (2004). This inventory covers four temperament dimensions. Novelty seeking ranges from exploratory, curious, and impulsive nature to indifferent, frugal, orderly, and regimented. Harm avoidance ranges from the tendency to inhabit behavior to avoid punishment, fearful, shy, pessimistic, and worrying to being relaxed, optimistic, bold, and confident. Reward dependence ranges from sentimental, dedicated, attached, and dependent to practical, cold, detached, and independent. Persistence ranges from being industrious, diligent, ambitious, perfectionistic, and overachieving to being inactive, pragmatic, indolent, and underachieving. Three character dimensions assessed by the TCI are cooperativeness, self-directiveness, and self-transcendence. Cooperativeness covers the range from socially tolerant, empathetic, compassionate, and principled to critical, opportunistic, socially intolerant, and revengeful. Self-directiveness ranges from mature, responsible, reliable, self-accepted, and resourceful to immature, fragile, unreliable, self-striving, and ineffective. Self-transcendence ranges from being wise, patient, creative, and forgetful to impatient, unimaginative, and self-conscious.

All ED women scored significantly higher on harm avoidance and significantly lower on self directiveness than control women. Acutely ill AN and BN women scored significantly higher than control women on cooperativeness and acutely ill BN women and anorectics with bulimic behaviors scored significantly higher on novelty seeking compared to control women. Women who were recovered from BN and AN with binge/purge behaviors had higher harm avoidance scores than control women. They also had significantly lower self-directiveness and cooperativeness scores than control women. This study suggests consistent personality disturbances in women with BN and AN with bulimic behaviors that are present during the acute phase of the disorder and also after recovery. Other studies have also found women ill with BN to have the highest novelty seeking scores of all ED groups (Brewerton, Hand, & Bishop, 1993; Bulik, Sullivan, Joyce, & Carter, 1995; Fassino et al., 2003; Kleifield et al., 1994). These personality characteristics of women with EDs may represent enduring temperamental traits that contribute to ED pathogenesis.

Factor analysis was employed to derive phenotypes from personality and behavioral traits in a large sample of individuals with EDs (Price Foundation Collaborative Group et al., 2001). The most influential factor was one of trait and anxiety, harm avoidance, perfectionism, obsessive–compulsive behaviors and diminished self-directiveness. Further discriminant analysis showed an 80% rate of accurate classification of those individuals with a diagnosis of restricting-type AN (Klump et al., 2004).

A latent class analysis applied to the same sample of patients described above revealed a larger group characterized by greater perfectionism, obsessions, compulsions, rigidity, conscientiousness, lower levels of novelty seeking, and higher levels of harm avoidance. This group was consistent in patients with restricting type of AN Keel et al., 2004). Diagnostic crossover from BN to AN and from AN to BN in this same population was consistently associated with low self-directiveness (Tozzi et al., 2005). The authors suggested that individuals with low self-directiveness, independent of diagnosis, may be characterized by an inability to regulate behaviors and affect adequately. They suggested this instability may then lead to alternations between the cognitive and behavioral restraint common to restricting-type AN and the disinhibition present in BN. Parental criticism was a salient factor for individuals with AN who crossed over to having BN. Low scores on novelty seeking and the presence of alcohol abuse or dependence were important in the crossover from BN to AN.

In a study of binge eating disorder (BED) in a community sample, personality traits associated with BED symptomatology included high novelty seeking, high harm avoidance and low self-directiveness (Grucza, Przybeck, & Cloninger, 2007). The authors suggested a heterogeneity may exist among individuals with BED; for example there may be an impulsive novelty seeking behavior for some and others with a predominance of harm avoidance may have an underlying mood dysregulation. In a study of personality and attitudes toward food, harm avoidance predicted greater likelihood to continue eating when satiated and novelty seeking predicted lack of dietary control (VandenBree, 2006).

Negative affect as assessed by the Positive and Negative Affect Schedule (Watson & Clark, 1992) was found to moderate the relation between dieting and binge eating (Stice et al., 2000). The authors found negative affect to be an independent risk factor for binge eating.

A latent profile analysis was performed on data from two large studies of cognitive behavioral therapy for BN and revealed a 3-profile model (Willer et al., in press). The profiles were characterized as low comorbidity, anorexia/Cluster C personality disorders and substance using. Individuals in the low comorbidity profile had lower pathology on measures of ED cognitions, self-esteem and social adjustment and were significantly more likely to be abstinent from binge eating/purging at the end of treatment. A lower body mass index (BMI) and being in a substance using profile predicted greater ED symptomatology at the end of treatment and at follow-up.

Conclusions

Comorbidities of EDs with other psychiatric disorders both Axis I and Axis II disorders as well as with distinct personality traits and features are common in EDs and often typify or characterize ED subtypes. Comorbidity profiles may be associated with treatment outcome. Developing treatments for specific comorbidity ED profiles will be a meaningful focus for future research.

Future Directions

The most robust methodological technique to predict the development of comorbidities with EDs is a prospective longitudinal assessment study beginning in early childhood through the adolescent period. There are indications from a variety of retrospective studies that anxiety disorders in childhood precede the development of EDs and continue in their own path to develop comorbid anxiety disorders. For example, traits in childhood of being over anxious, perfectionistic or having excessive obsessive and compulsive tendencies with social phobias have been shown to exist before the development of EDs and then with the emergence of the ED coexist as well defined obsessive–compulsive disorder, generalized anxiety disorders, social phobias, and so forth. The relationship of the depressive symptoms in childhood and the development of EDs with substance abuse is another worthy area of attention. There are retrospective data suggesting that the depressive symptoms in childhood may lead to the comorbidity of substance abuse developing with an ED. Little information is known as to what may predict the development of impulse control disorders comorbid with EDs. Impulse control disorders are predominantly associated with the binging subtypes of EDs and it would be of significance to determine what, if any, childhood disturbance might predict this course.

Negative affect significantly influences the response to treatment and outcome in EDs. In early childhood ongoing prospective assessment studies may give some clues as to what may predict the development of a negative affect. This would be extremely useful in devising treatment strategies.

Treatment of comorbidities associated with AN predominately involves treatment of anxiety and affective disorders. These comorbidities need to be treated as well as the AN. What pharmacological interventions, for example, might be effective in treating both the comorbid conditions as well as the basic ED without incurring harmful side effects? Can psychotherapy techniques addressing both the AN and the comorbidities be effectively conducted simultaneously or do they need to be performed consecutively? Can family therapy techniques be developed to address the comorbidities as well as the basic ED?

The most common and difficult comorbidities with the binge eating subtypes of EDs are the impulse control and substance use disorders. The questions that need to be answered are many. For example, which should be treated first, the comorbid condition or the binge eating condition or should an attempt be made to treat them both simultaneously? What type of long-range treatment intervention is effective in preventing relapse of either the ED or substance abuse disorder? Are there pharmacological interventions that may be helpful for both the comorbid condition and the ED? Can family therapy for adolescents integrate techniques of treating the comorbidities with the binge subtype ED?

Treatment of the comorbidities of EDs cannot be ignored since there is a plausible likelihood that the untreated comorbidities could influence a relapse or perpetuation of a chronic condition of the ED.

References

American Psychiatric Association (APA). (1994). *Diagnostic and statistical manual of mental disorders–IV (DSM-IV)*. Washington, DC: Author.

Angst, J. (1998). The emerging epidemiology of hypomania and bipolar II disorder. *J Affective Disorders, 50*, 143–151.

Bastiani, A., Rao, R., Wiltzin, T., & Kaye, W. (1995). Perfectionism in anorexia nervosa. *International Journal of Eating Disorders, 17*, 147–152.

Braun, D. L., Sunday, S. R., & Halmi, K. A. (1994). Psychiatric comorbidity in patients with eating disorders. *Psychological Medicine, 24*, 859–867.

Brewerton, T., Hand, L., & Bishop, B. (1993). The tridimensional personality questionnaire in eating disorder patients. *International Journal of Eating Disorders, 14*, 213–218.

Bulik, C., Klump, K., Thornton, L., Kaplan, A., Devlin, B., et al. (2004). Alcohol use disorder comorbidity in eating disorders: A multicenter study. *Journal of Clinical Psychiatry, 65*, 1000–1006.

Bulik, C., Sullivan, P., Joyce, P., & Carter, F. (1995). Temperament, character, and personality disorder in bulimia nervosa. *Journal of Nervous and Mental Diseases, 183*, 593–598.

Bulik, C., Tozzi, F., Anderson, C., Mazzeo, S., et al. (2003). The relation between eating disorders and components of perfectionism. *American Journal of Psychiatry, 160*, 356–360.

Bulik, C. M., Sullivan, P. F., & Kendler, K. S. (2002). Medical and psychiatric morbidity in obese women with and without binge eating. *International Journal of Eating Disorders, 32*, 72–78.

Bushnell, J., Welles, J., McKenzie, J., Hornblow, A., Oakley-Browne, M., & Joyce, P. (1994). Bulimia comorbidity and the general population and in the clinic. *Psychological Medicine, 24*, 605–611.

Costello, E., & Angold, A. (1995). Epidemiology. In March, J. (Ed.), *Anxiety disorders in children and adolescents* (pp. 109–124). New York: Guilford Press.

Fairburn, C., Cooper, Z., Dell, H., & Welch, S. (1999). Risk factors for anorexia nervosa: Three integrated case-control comparisons. *Archives of General Psychiatry, 56*, 468–476.

Fassino, S., Amianto, F., Abbate-Daga, G., Leombruni, P., et al. (2003). Bulimic family dynamics: Role of parent's personality. A controlled study with the temperament and character inventory. *Comprehensive Psychiatry, 44*, 70–77.

Fernandez-Aranda, F., Gimenez-Murcia, S., Alvarez, E., et al., (2006). Impulse control disorders in eating disorders: Clinical and therapeutic implications. *Comprehensive Psychiatry, 47*, 482–488.

Fernandez-Aranda, F., Pinheiro, A., Thornton, L., Berrettini, W., et al. (2008). Impulse control disorders in women with eating disorders. *Psychiatry Research, 157*, 147–157.

Frank, G., Bailer, U., Henry, S., Drevets, W., et al. (2005). Increased dopamine D2/D3 receptors binding after recovery from anorexia nervosa measured by positron emission tomography and 11C Raclopride. *Biological Psychiatry, 58*, 908–912.

Frost, R. O., & Steketee, G. (1997). Perfectionism in obsessive compulsive disorder patients. *Behavior Research and Therapy*, *35*, 291–296.

Garfinkel, P. E., Goering, P., Lin, E., Spegg, C., Goldblum, D. S., Kennedy, S., et al. (1995). Bulimia nervosa in a Canadian community sample; prevalence and comparison subgroups. *American Journal of Psychiatry*, *152*, 1052–1058.

Garfinkel, P. E., Lin, E., Goering, C., Spegg, D., Goldblum, D., & Kennedy, S. (1996). Should amenorrhea be necessary for the diagnosis of anorexia nervosa? Evidence from a Canadian community sample. *British Journal of Psychiatry*, *168*, 500–506.

Gatner A, Marcus, R., Halmi, K., & Loranger, A. (1989). DSM-III-R Personality disorders in patients with eating disorders. *American Journal of Psychiatry*, *146*, 1585–1591.

Godart, N. T., Flament, M. F., Perdereau, F., & Jeammet, P. (2002). Comorbidity between eating disorder and anxiety disorders: A review. *International Journal of Eating Disorders*, *32*, 253–270.

Goodman, W., Price, L., Rasmussen, S., Mazure, C., et al. (1989). The Yale-Brown Obsessive Compulsive Scale, development, use and reliability. *Archives of General Psychiatry*, *46*, 1006–1011.

Grucza, R., Przybeck, T., & Cloninger, R. (2007). Prevalence and correlates of binge eating disorder in a community sample. *Comprehensive Psychiatry*, *48*, 124–131.

Halmi, K. A., Agras, W. S., Crow, S., Mitchell, J., Wilson, G. T., Bryson, S. W., & Kraemer, C. (2005). Predictors of treatment acceptance and completion in anorexia nervosa. *Archives of General Psychiatry*, *62*, 776–781.

Halmi, K. A., Eckert, E., Marchi, P., Sampugno, V., Apple, R., & Cohen, J. (1991). Comorbidity of psychiatric diagnoses in anorexia nervosa. *Archives of General Psychiatry*, *48*, 712–718.

Halmi, K. A., Sunday, S., Klump, K., Strober, M., Leckman, J., et al. (2003). Obsessions and compulsions in anorexia nervosa subtypes. *International Journal of Eating Disorders*, *33*, 308–319.

Halmi, K. A., Sunday, S., Strober, M., Kaplan, A., Woodside, D. B., et al. (2000). Perfectionism in anorexia nervosa: Variation by clinical subtype, obsessionality, and pathological eating behavior. *American Journal of Psychiatry*, *1157*, 1799–1805.

Halmi, K. A., Tozzi, F., Thornton, L., Crow, S., et al. (2005). The relation among perfectionism, obsessive compulsive personality disorder and obsessive compulsive disorder in individuals with eating disorders. *International Journal of Eating Disorders*, *38*, 371–374.

Herzog, D., Keller, M., Lavori, P., Kenny, G., & Sack, S. (1992). The prevalence of personality disorders in 210 women with eating disorders. *Journal of Clinical Psychiatry*, *53*, 147–152.

Holderness, C., Brook-Gunn, J., & Warren, M. (1994). Comorbidity of eating disorders in substance abuse review of the literature. *International Journal of Eating Disorders*, *16*, 1–34.

Hudson, J., Pope, H., Yurgelun-Todd, D., Johnas, J., & Frankenburg, F. (1987). A controlled study of lifetime prevalence of affective and other psychiatric disorders in bulimic outpatients. *American Journal Psychiatry*, *144*, 1283–1287.

Hudson, J. I., Hiripi, E., Pope, H., & Kessler, R. (2008). The prevalence and correlates of eating disorder in the national comorbidity survey replication. *Biological Psychiatry*, PMC February 1, 1–32.

Kaye, W., Greeno, C., Moss, H., Fernstrom, J., Fernstrom, M., et al. (1998). Alterations in serotonin activity and psychiatric symptoms after recovery from bulimia nervosa. *Archives of General Psychiatry*, *55*, 927–935.

Kaye, W. H., Bulik, C. M., Thornton, L., Barbarich, N., & Master, K. (2004). Comorbidity of anxiety disorders with anorexia and bulimia nervosa. *American Journal of Psychiatry*, *161*, 2215–2221.

Keel, P., Fichter, M., Quadflieg, N., Bulik, C., et al. (2004). Application of a latent class analysis to empirically define eating disorder phenotypes. *Archives of General Psychiatry*, *61*, 192–200.

Kendler, K. S., MacLean, C., Neale, M., Kessler, R., Heath, A., & Eaves, L. (1991). The genetic epidemiology of bulimia nervosa. *American Journal of Psychiatry*, *148*, 1627–1637.

Kleifield, E., Sunday, S., Hurt, S., & Halmi, K. (1994). The tridimensional personality questionnaire: An exploration of personality traits in eating disorders. *Journal of Psychiatric Research*, *28*, 413–423.

Klump, K., Strober, M., Bulik, C., Thornton, L., et al. (2004). Personality characteristics of women before and after recovery from an eating disorder. *Psychological Medicine*, *34*, 1407–1418.

Laseque, C. (1873). De L'Anorexie hysterique. *Archives of General Medicine*, *1*, 385–403.

Lee, H. Y., Lee, E. L., Pathy, P., & Chan, Y. H. (2005). Anorexia nervosa in Singapore: An 8 year retrospective study. *Singapore Medical Journal*, *46*, 275–282.

Matsunaga, H., Kaye, W., McConaha, C., Plotnicov, K., Pollice, S., & Rao, R. (2000). Personality disorder among subjects recovered from eating disorders. *International Journal of Eating Disorders*, *27*, 353–357.

McElroy, S., Cotwal, R., Kack, P. E., & Akiskal, H. S. (2005). Comorbidity of bipolar and eating disorders: Distinct or related disorders with shared dysregulation? *Journal of Affective Disorders*, *86*, 107–127.

Piacentini, J., & Bergman, R. (2000). Obsessive-compulsive disorder in children. *Psychiatric Clinics of North America*, *23*, 519–533.

Powers, P., Coovert, D., Brikwell, D., & Stevens, B. (1988). Other psychiatric disorders among bulimic patients. *Comprehensive Psychiatry*, *29*, 503–508.

Price Foundation Collaborative Group. (2000). Deriving behavioral phenotypes in an international, multi-center study of eating disorders. *Psychological Medicine*, *31*, 635–645.

Raney, T., Thornton, L., Berrettini, W., Brandt, H., et al. (2008). Influence of overanxious disorder of childhood on the expression of anorexia nervosa. *International Journal of Eating Disorders*, *41*, 326–332.

Ross, H., & Ivess, (1999). Binge eating and substance abuse among male and female adolescents. *International Journal of Eating Disorders*, *26*, 245–260.

Rossiter, E., Agras, W., Telch, C., & Schneider, J. (1993). Cluster B Personality disorder characteristics predict outcome in the treatment of bulimia nervosa. *International Journal of Eating Disorders*, *13*, 349–357.

Rowe, R., Pickles, A., Simonoff, E., Bulik, C. M., & Silberg, J. (2002). Bulimic symptoms in the Virginia twin study of adolescent behavioral development: Correlates, comorbidity and genetics. *Biological Psychiatry*, *51*, 172–182.

Schmidt, N., & Telch, M. (1990). Prevalence of personality disorders among bulimic, non-bulimic binge eaters, and normal controls. *Journal of Psychopathology and Behavioral Assessment*, *12*, 170–185.

Steiger, H., Lernard, S., Kim, N., Ladouceur, S. C., et al. (2007). Childhood abuse and platelet tritiated paroxetine binding in bulimia nervosa: Implications of borderline personality disorder. *Journal of Clinical Psychiatry, 61*, 428–435.

Steiger, H., Thibaudeau, J., Leung, F., Houle, L., & Ghadirian, A. (1994). Eating and psychiatric symptoms as a function of Axis II comorbidity in bulimic patients. *Psychosomatics, 35*, 41–49.

Stice, E., Akutagawa, D., Gaggar, A., & Agras, W. S. (2000). Negative affect moderates the relation between dieting and binge eating. *International Journal of Eating Disorders, 27*, 218–229.

Stock, S., Goldberg, D., Corbett, S., & Katzman, D. (2002). Substance use in female adolescents with eating disorders. *Journal of Adolescent Health, 31*, 176–182.

Strober, M. (2004). Clinical and research forum pathological fear conditioning and anorexia nervosa: On the search for novel paradigms. *International Journal of Eating Disorders, 35*, 504–508.

Sutander-Pinnock, K., Blake, W., Carter, J., Olmsted, M., & Kaplan, A. (2003). "Perfectionism in anorexia nervosa: A 6-24 month study. *International Journal of Eating Disorders, 33*, 225–229.

Tozzi, F., Thornton, L., Klump, K., Ficheter, M., Halmi, K. A., et al. (2005). Symptom fluctuation in eating disorders: Correlates of diagnostic crossover. *American Journal of Psychiatry*, 732–740.

VandenBree, M., Przybeck, T., & Cloninger, C. (2006). Diet and personality: Associations in a population-based sample. *Appetite, 46*, 177–188.

Vollrath, M., Coch, R., & Angst, J. (1992). Binge eating and weight concerns among young adults. Results from the Zurich cohort study. *British Journal of Psychiatry, 160*, 498–503.

Watson, D., & Clark, L. (1992). Affects separable and inseparable: On the hierarchical arrangement of the negative affects. *Journal of Personality and Social Psychology, 62*, 489–505.

Weiderman, M., & Pryor, T. (1996a). Substance use among women with eating disorders. *International Journal of Eating Disorders, 20*, 163–168.

Weiderman, M., & Pryor, T. (1996b). Substance use and impulsive behaviors among adolescents with eating disorders. *Addictive Behaviors, 21*, 269–272.

Wildes, J., Marcus, M., & Fagioline, A. (2007). Eating disorders and illness burden in patients with bipolar spectrum disorders. *Comprehensive Psychiatry, 48*, 516–521.

Willer, M., Crow, S., Crosby, R., Agras, W. S., Fairburn, C. G., Halmi, K. A., et al. Comorbidity–based profile of bulimia nervosa predict treatment outcome? In press.

Wonderlich, S., Swift, W., Slotnick, H., & Goodman, S. (1990). DSM-III-R Personality disorders in eating disorder subtypes. *International Journal of Eating Disorders, 9*, 607–616.

PART 4

Prevention and Treatment

Prevention: Current Status and Underlying Theory

Meghan M. Sinton *and* C. Barr Taylor

Abstract

Eating disorders (EDs) are important and common problems among adolescents and young women, and preventing them would be an important public health achievement. Fortunately, several recent studies, informed by cross-sectional, longitudinal, and clinical risk factor research, have evidenced a significant decrease in ED risk factors, with two programs also achieving a significant reduction in ED onset within at-risk females. The present chapter reviews and evaluates the state of ED prevention research, highlighting current theoretical approaches and effective programs, emphasizing emerging empirical support for cognitive dissonance, Internet, school-based, and combined ED and obesity prevention programs. Conclusions about how to enhance recent progress in the field of EDs are provided.

Keywords: cognitive dissonance, moderators and mediators, prevention psychoeducation, risk factors

Introduction

Eating disorders (EDs) are important and common problems among adolescents and young women in particular. The attitudes and behaviors associated with EDs and that may predispose young women to EDs can have serious psychological and physical consequences and are associated with loss of confidence and self-esteem, shame, and other psychological problems. There is some evidence that once EDs become established, they are more difficult to treat, at least in the case of anorexia nervosa (Guarda, 2008) and the longer the disorder lasts the more likely it is to have adverse effects. Proponents of prevention argue, then, that it is important both to reduce the prevalence of risk factors and to keep EDs from emerging and that, given the prevalence of disordered eating attitudes and behaviors in young women, this is of major public health importance. In this chapter, we review issues related to preventing EDs, with our discussion focusing almost entirely on young women, as females are

most often the focus of studies. Also, as discussed later, ED risk factors begin early, even during childhood, and the peak onset of EDs is during adolescence. For this reason, although EDs are common in adults, prevention should focus on adolescents and young women. Very little has been written about prevention in males. Discussion focuses primarily on recent progress in this field given that extensive work in the past decade has resulted in several effective preventive interventions, at least for older adolescents and college-age women (Stice, Shaw, & Marti, 2007), with two recent programs evidencing a significant reduction in ED onset among high risk women (Stice, Marti, Spoor, Presnell, & Shaw, 2008; Stice, Shaw, Burton, & Wade, 2006; Taylor et al., 2006).

Defining Prevention

There are three basic categories of prevention programs: universal, targeted (selective), and indicated. *Universal prevention programs* target the risk factors in a whole population even though most of the individuals in that population may be at no or little risk. For instance, a universal prevention program might focus on reducing the impact of media on increasing all students' desire to be very thin or on reducing unhealthy comments or pressure to be thin within schools, groups, or peers. The assumptions are that the reduction of a risk factor in a population, including those not at risk, will reduce the onset of the disorder in those at risk. The recommended intervention should be of potential benefit and little risk to the population. Ironically, one of the controversies in the ED prevention is the role of the universal public health campaign to encourage weight reduction in the U.S. population as rates of overweight and obesity have increased dramatically (Ogden, Carroll, & Flegal, 2008). Some proponents of ED prevention have argued that such campaigns may have a negative effect (O'Dea, 2005). The impact of these campaigns on the prevalence of EDs remains an important, unanswered question.

Targeted or selective prevention interventions focus on individuals or a segment of the population whose risk of developing EDs is significantly higher than average. Most of the EDs interventions have focused on populations at "high risk" of developing an ED; these programs are considered to be more effective than universal programs, as will be discussed later (Stice, Presnell, Gau, & Shaw, 2007). *Indicated prevention programs* target individuals at very high risk or even have early features of the disorder. In the ED world the distinctions among targeted and indicated interventions are often arbitrary as there may be a continuum between low-level behaviors and subclinical and clinical disorders.

Theory of Prevention

The guiding theory for prevention programs is that reduction of causative, modifiable risk factors will reduce the incidence of a disorder. Thus, the foundation of prevention is the identification of such "causative risk factors," that is risk factors that have been shown, in prospective studies, to cause the onset of the disorder (see Chapter 8 for a detailed discussion of these issues). In fact, a risk factor can only be proven to be causative if reduction in the risk factor is associated with reduction of the incidence of the disorder. Most of the modifiable risk factors for EDs are continuous measures and it is unknown how much or for how long the measure needs to be reduced to have a significant effect on reducing EDs. For instance, Taylor et al. (2006) used a score of >50 on a measure of weight and

shape concerns as an entry criterion and to characterize a group of students as being at risk. Universal preventive interventions often attempt to reduce the mean score of the risk factor in the population, but is it meaningful for instance, at least in terms of preventing EDs, to reduce a population-wise weight and shape concern (WSC) score of 35 to 32?

Following on this issue, another important consideration when considering causative issues and related prevention program development is recognition of the multiple risk factors involved in the onset of the target disorder and the required duration for reduction in risk factors to truly determine that risk is no longer present. In theory, not only should a risk factor be reduced through prevention programs but it should remain reduced over time. For instance, to the extent that elevated WSC is a common risk factor for onset of EDs, then a sustained reduction of WSC should be necessary to reduce onset in a high risk population. The *Student Bodies*™ prevention program, discussed in the text that follows, was designed with this assumption and there was a sustained reduction in WSC in the intervention sample as well as a reduction of the incidence of EDs in some subgroups (Taylor et al., 2006). However, as risk for EDs is multifactorial, with different pathways and interactions among risk factors possibly contributing to ED onset (Stice, Presnell, Gau, & Shaw, 2007), it may be that reduction of several risk factors simultaneously, may have a better effect than focusing on reducing one risk factor. For example, a young woman at risk for ED onset might have a sustained WSC of 47, the level at which she would be at risk for an ED (Jacobi, Abascal, & Taylor, 2004) but an insensitive comment from a coach or teacher about her weight at a time when she is also feeling depressed might lead to episodes of purging that elevate her to high risk for ED onset while for another young woman, having a high WSC score alone may lead to ED onset. Thus, following on the earlier statement regarding duration of risk reduction and considering the diverse array of risk factors involved in the etiology of EDs, should all relevant risk factors be reduced for prolonged periods to truly prevent EDs? This is an important consideration for both the development and evaluation of prevention programs.

Finally, it should be noted that from a public health standpoint, "harm reduction," such as reduced exposure to environmental risk factors, may be an important aspect for ED prevention. Examples of harm reduction in other fields include efforts to minimize exposure to second-hand tobacco smoke and attempts to reduce factors that promote unhealthy behaviors such as cigarette advertising. In regard to ED prevention, harm reduction efforts have focused on banning "skinny models" and, more controversially, reducing or restricting public health campaigns for "obesity prevention." However, many more adolescents and young men and women are at risk of obesity than are at risk for EDs, and from a public health standpoint, obesity poses a much more important health issue. 20062007ED prevention researchers should work to unite their efforts with those related to obesity prevention given that reduction of overweight and obesity, a critical societal need, would likely assist in reducing risk for concurrent and future eating pathology (as discussed later, programs that target multiple outcomes, such as overweight and disordered eating, are desirable from a public health and possibly a harm reduction standpoint) (Haines & Neumark-Sztainer, 2006; Neumark-Sztainer et al., 2007). There has been a concern, on the other hand, that public health messages designed to encourage weight loss might actually increase EDs. A recent review found little evidence that childhood obesity prevention programs are harmful but the researchers noted that the data are very limited (Carter & Bulik, 2008). Others have argued that ED prevention programs might benefit from the public health models developed for weight maintenance/reduction (Taylor, Franko, Neumark-Sztainer, Paxton, & Shapiro, 2007) and some evidence suggests that weight reduction may be associated with reducing weight and shape concerns, as discussed later.

Risk Factors that Inform Prevention Programs

In recent years, a number of prospective studies have been conducted to help identify risk factors for EDs. These prospective studies, along with an even larger literature on retrospective, cross-sectional, and clinical studies have identified a number of risk factors (Jacobi, Hayward, de Zwaan, Kraemer, & Agras, 2004; Stice & Shaw, 2004). Elevated perceived pressure to be thin from family, peers, and the media, internalization of the thin-ideal espoused for women by Western culture, body mass, and body dissatisfaction have predicted future eating pathology in multiple studies (Field, Camargo, Taylor, Berkey, & Colditz, 1999; Killen et al., 1996; Stice, Chase, Stormer, & Appel, 2001; Stice et al., 2007; Wertheim, Koerner, & Paxton, 2001; Wichstrom, 2000). The role of dieting as a risk factor is less clear and the results have been inconsistent, perhaps because of invalid self-report measures (Stice & Shaw, 2004) and or because it so common

as to be nonspecific. Indeed, there is evidence to suggest that children and adolescents have varied definitions of dieting, which may lead to inconsistent and inconclusive research findings (Neumark-Sztainer & Story, 1998).

In addition to the ED specific risk factors described earlier, there are additional nonspecific risk factors to consider. For example, a history of adverse childhood experiences (including sexual abuse) appears to be a risk factor for the development of a number of mental health problems, including EDs (Jacobi et al., 2004; Pike et al., 2007; Sanci et al., 2008; Speranza et al., 2003). If so, prevention of adverse childhood experiences would likely reduce the onset of EDs (and other mental health problems) but is a goal beyond ED prevention. However, in theory, one might want to ameliorate the consequences of such adverse experiences as they affect risk within a population of students already at risk for EDs. Unfortunately, these consequences have not been well specified.

Other risk factors that need to be considered include personal characteristics such as age, sex, and ethnicity as these may further identify specific groups at risk for ED onset. For example, one study provides important insight into the age of onset for anorexia nervosa (AN) and bulimia nervosa (BN) in a sample of white women with AN having the earliest onset (by age 15), with prevalence increasing throughout the early 20s (Striegel-Moore et al., 2003) (see Fig. 18.1). These data suggest that preventive programs should begin at least by age 12 for binge eating and BN and even early for AN; findings also suggest that preventive programs might be relevant into the mid-20s for Caucasian women.

Screening

Selected/targeted and indicated preventive interventions require some way in which the high risk population can be identified. Two approaches can be utilized to find target populations. In one approach, an intervention can be applied to a whole population (universal program) and then the results can be analyzed by stratified/classifying the population into high or higher risk (e.g., WSC scores above 47 or at/below 47, compensatory behaviors versus no compensatory behaviors). Alternatively, a screening measure can be included as a first step in recruiting and then identifying high risk participants. In this scenario, researchers would select items that ideally differentiate people meeting the high risk profile indicated for the study from those who are at no or low risk; this approach has also been utilized in

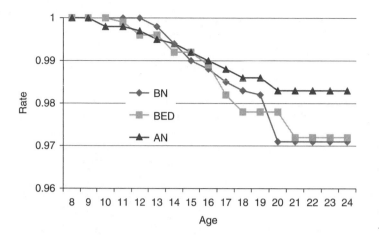

Fig. 18.1 Age at onset of eating disorders in a sample of Caucasian females. (Adapted with permission from Striegel-Moore, R. H., Dohm, F. A., Kraemer, H. C., Taylor, C. B., Daniels, S., Crawford, P. B., et al. [2003]. Eating disorders in white and black women. *American Journal of Psychiatry, 160*[7], 1326–1331.)

recent programs (Abascal, Bruning-Brown, Winzelberg, Dev, & Taylor, 2004; Luce et al., 2005; Taylor et al., 2006).

However, although much progress has been made on identifying risk factors for EDs, few studies have evaluated the psychometric properties of high-risk screens, particularly in longitudinal studies (Jacobi et al., 2004). Rathner and Messner (1993) studied the occurrence of EDs among 517 Italian school girls (ages 11–20 years). The authors used the EAT and the Anorexia Nervosa Inventory for Self Rating (ANIS) to identify groups. The study design did not permit clear analysis of the screen's sensitivity and specificity. The Weight Concerns Scale (Killen et al., 1994), consisting of five questions that assess worry about weight/shape, fear of gaining 3 lb (1.36 kg), last time student went on a diet, and the importance of weight and feelings of fatness, was derived from a principal components analysis of a set of self-report questions used to assess ED symptoms (Killen et al., 1993). In earlier studies, the investigators found that students scoring in the upper 25% were significantly more likely to develop an ED than those who score in the lower 75% range (Killen et al., 1993; Killen et al., 1994). Jacobi and colleagues (2004) reanalyzed the data from the initial sample (Killen et al., 1993) sample using a Receiver Operating Characteristic (ROC) analysis, findings that a Weight Concerns criterion of >47 had a sensitivity of 79%, a specificity of 67%, and a percent predictive value/efficiency of 13%. On the basis of a ROC analysis, the McKnight Investigators (2003) found that a four question screen had a sensitivity of 72%, a specificity of 80%, and an efficiency of 79% for identifying cases. However, this screen has never been used in a subsequent study so there is no information on how it would work in other populations. Slade and Dewey (1986) report on the development and validation of the Screening Instrument for identifying individuals at risk of developing AN and BN (SCANS). The sensitivity and specificity of case identification in known groups were relatively high. The authors concluded that very limited information is available to identify students at risk for developing an ED.

For a population-based study, a screen also needs to be able to separate out "real cases" from those at high risk or becoming a case. The ideal screen would be very sensitive and specific but no such screen exists. A sensitive screen with low specificity means that many "false positives" are identified. Unfortunately, the cost of then determining if these false positives are "true cases," through assessments such as a clinical interview can be expensive. To address this problem Jacobi et al. (2004) recommend a two-step process, with the first step focusing on sensitivity and the second on specificity. First, a test should be used to divide the sample into subgroups with different characteristics (e.g., at risk versus not at risk). Only those whose responses suggest that the person is indeed at risk (according to the proposed risk criteria) should be retested (Kraemer, 1992). For instance, among a high school population, students might be given the Weight Concerns Scale in order to determine each student's risk for ED onset, with those students with scores >47 would then be given a more specific instrument, such as the ED Diagnostic Scale (EDDS), the Eating Attitudes Test (EAT) or the BULIT, all measures shown to indicate current eating pathology to separate out those students who have might have an ED and require clinical evaluation from those who are at high risk and would merit a preventive intervention. The sequential use of these tests would balance the high sensitivity but moderate specificity and low sensitivity and high specificity issues without having to burden all students with unnecessary or time intensive testing. Thus, an example algorithm for categorizing the population would then be: Step 1, administer the Weight Concerns Scale; Step 2, administer the EDDS and/or EAT and/or BULIT to individuals with a Weight Concerns score above 47 to determine actual ED caseness and risk. Possible cases would then undergo a clinical evaluation with referrals and treatment provided as indicated. Individuals at risk for ED onset (i.e., all participants indicating some sub-clinical levels of disordered eating in Step 2 of the screen) would then be delivered a risk reduction prevention program and those individuals identified in either Step 1 or Step 2 as no or low risk being provide a universal programs focusing on issues related to healthy weight regulation and body image. Empirical examination of this proposed screening protocol is warranted; attention should be paid to not on the sensitivity and specificity of the screen but also to the percent of participants being identified as at-risk for ED onset and to the time burden associated with this screen.

Theories and Models of Preventive Interventions

As discussed in the preceding text, the overall theory of prevention is that reduction in risk factors reduces risk. Another set of theories has been used to determine the nature of the intervention itself. The risk factors chosen for a particular intervention partly determine the nature of the intervention. Five general models guiding ED preventions are summarized below.

Psychoeducation

Many preventive programs have been based on the assumption that information about EDs, including the consequences of EDs can be used to reduce risk factors. This model is widely implemented in school settings as part of universal educational programs and appears to be the most common approach to ED prevention for younger students (i.e., elementary and middle school students). It should be noted, though, that without long-term assessment of programs delivered to younger populations, it may be hard to determine the effectiveness given that onset of EDs would not be expected until mid to late adolescence. Overall, psychoeducation approaches alone, particularly those with limited interactions with participants (e.g., didactic programs)

and delivered to individuals at low risk for ED onset, may have limited effectiveness (Stice et al., 2007) and a psychoeducation only approach to the prevention of EDs does not appear effective.

Social Learning Theory

Social learning theory that assumes that behavior is affected by both external and internal processes (Bandura, 1986) following on this, disordered eating results from several processes, such as from pressure to be thin from family members and peers, exposure to maternal and peer weight and shape concerns, the individual's internalization of the thin ideal and history of disordered eating attitudes and behaviors and/or history of depression and anxiety. Thus, from a social cognitive learning theory perspective, four factors are particularly important in influencing attitudes and behavior and need to be addressed in preventive interventions: (1) modeling, (2) information, (3) instructions/persuasion from authorities, and (4) previous experience. Effective interventions incorporate each of these components. For example, social learning theory has generally been used to guide the preventive approaches used in *Student Bodies*™, an Internet based approach for at-risk college women and adolescents (see later), employs cognitive–behavioral strategies shown to be effective in reducing symptoms in individuals with clinical EDs, (Clarke et al., 2001; Fairburn & Cooper, 1993; Horowitz & Garbe, 2006; Killen et al., 1993; Lynch et al., 2005; Mann et al., 1997; Striegel-Moore et al., 2005; Wilfley & Cohen, 1997; Wilson & Fairburn, 1993). Several small controlled studies and one large scale randomized control trial support the effectiveness of this approach, suggesting that continued development and examination of programs using a social cognitive learning model are warranted.

Dissonance Theory

Stice et al. (2000) have developed interventions rooted in the theory that individuals become motivated to change their attitudes and behaviors, such as unhealthy expectations about weight and appearance and disordered eating behaviors, when faced with messages that contradict these very attitudes and behaviors (Aronson, 1980; Festinger, 1957, 1962; Leippe, 1994). Thus, dissonance programs focus on providing participants with skills to counteract the abundant weight and appearance related messages prevalent in adolescents' daily lives (Stice et al., 2001; Stice et al., 2008; Stice, Mazotti, Weibel, & Agras, 2000; Stice, Shaw, Becker, &

Rohde, 2008; Stice et al., 2007; Stice, Trost, & Chase, 2003). These programs typically involve at least two 1-hour sessions and more often three or four sessions, using trained program leaders, including endogenous staff such as peers and teachers trained to deliver the material (Stice & Presnell, 2007). A series of studies across multiple independent labs indicate that this approach is effective in reducing ED risk factors (e.g., negative affect, thin-ideal internalization, body dissatisfaction, dieting), with recent long-term follow-up studies indicating reduction of ED onset (Stice et al., 2008; Stice et al., 2006). Indeed, following on APA guidelines (1995), cognitive dissonance programs appear to be the first ED prevention program to be considered efficacious (Stice et al., 2006, 2008).

Feminist Theory

Feminist theory assumes that gender roles influence the onset of EDs and that helping young women become aware of gender role expectations may reduce weight and shape concerns. In other words, such approaches focus on providing participants with skills to critically think about and evaluate gendered issues related to body image and on teaching acceptance of and support for healthier norms for weight and appearance. Objectification theory, which states that women come to view their bodies as objects through societal pressures and tendencies to objectify the female form (Frederickson & Roberts, 1997), has also been used to inform feminist approaches to ED research in women (e.g., Cash, 1997; Peterson, Grippo, & Tantleff-Dunn, 2008; Tiggemann & Kuring, 2004). Feminist texts and theory have also informed prevention programs. For example, Springer, Winzelberg, Perkins, and Taylor (1999) developed an undergraduate course that met 2 hr each week for 10 weeks ($n = 24$). Class sessions included both structured information presentation (e.g., guest lecturers, student panels, multimedia programs) and group discussion on each of the following topics relating to body image: media, history of beauty, biological/evolutionary aspects of attractiveness, adolescent development, disability, aging, body building, cosmetic surgery, AN and BN: risk factors and consequences, obesity, and cultural difference. The readings were generally drawn from feminist texts. Results indicated a reduced frequency and severity of body dissatisfaction and disordered eating attitudes.

Media Literacy and Advocacy

Media literacy and advocacy interventions are based on the theory that the mass media plays a major role in perpetuating ED risk and that gaining both an understanding of this risk and developing strategies to resist media messages will reduce risk factors. The focus of programs adopting media literacy approaches is to develop or enhance skills to resist social persuasion (i.e., messages about thinness) with the goal of reducing heightened levels of dietary restraint and binge eating that have been linked to pressure to be thin (Stice et al., 2001) and internalization of media messages about thinness and appearance (Stice & Agras, 1998). Media literacy approaches appear to have some preliminary support in studies using pre- and early adolescent samples (Neumark-Sztainer, Sherwood, Coller, & Hannan, 2000; Sherwood, Harnack, & Story, 2000; Wade, Davidson, & O'Dea, 2003) and college women (Becker, Bull, Schaumberg, Cauble, & Franco, 2008; Becker, Smith, & Ciao, 2005; Coughlin & Kalodner, 2006) although one recent study using a mid-adolescent sample failed to find evidence for this approach (Wilksch, Durbridge, & Wade, 2008). Becker and colleagues (2008) have recently examined a media advocacy program as delivered by trained peers within an at-risk college population with results suggesting that this media advocacy program had comparable effects as those with the comparison cognitive dissonance program for a high-risk, but not mixed risk status, sample, with both programs being associated with 8-month reductions in risk factors, although effects were somewhat stronger for the cognitive dissonance program.

Effectiveness of Prevention Programs

Several recent meta-analyses (Pratt & Woolfenden, 2002; Stice et al., 2008; Stice et al., 2007) have provided evidence that some types of prevention programs are effective for reducing risk factors, at least in young women, age 15 or older. In the most recent review, Stice et al. (2008) identified 67 published and unpublished controlled studies from 1980 to 2006, using data from these studies to calculate effect sizes for changes in levels of assessed eating pathology and risk factors. Outcomes for a particular risk factor were examined in at least 15 trials to ensure that there would be sufficient power. Cohen's effect sizes were converted to rs as using a correlation coefficient (r) as an index of effect is the preferred statistical approach for these analyses as it can be used for different the combinations of interval, ordinal and nominal variables used across studies. Analyses revealed that 26 (51%) of the prevention programs resulted in significant reductions in at least one risk factor for "eating pathology."

To provide more specific insight into differences in effect sizes across studies, Stice et al. examined variables that might explain differences in effect sizes. To do this, effect sizes were tests for significant heterogeneity and, if heterogeneity was found, the potential moderators were examined in univariate analyses using random effects models (Lipsey & Wilson, 2001). Table 18.1 summarizes the main findings from this analysis for the three main risk factor variables related to body weight/shape concerns. As indicated in Table 18.1, selected interventions, programs targeted at students age ≥15, and programs with dissonance and not psychoeducation content had higher effect sizes for thin-ideal internalization, body dissatisfaction, and eating pathology. Similar patterns were found for dieting and negative affect. Surprisingly, interventions with a focus on coping and stress had less effect on thin-ideal internalization, perhaps because of a lack of material directly associated with specific ED causative risk factors such as body image concerns and/or thin-ideal internalization.

There are many limitations with this analysis that need to be considered in interpreting the data. For instance, a meta-analysis using effect sizes to compare universal and targeted interventions is questionable. Specifically, the goals and expected outcomes/change in risk would likely vary between universal and targeted programs, as no change in risk factors may be a positive outcome for universal programs but not for targeted programs. For instance, if a measure of mood was used to determine the effects of a universal depression prevention study, would we expect it to change in the normal population? Second, meta-analysis can obscure important comparisons. For example, in a study comparing dissonance theory to psychoeducation (Becker et al., 2005), the results were very similar between the two for changes in body dissatisfaction dieting and eating pathology. This controlled comparison contradicts some of the moderator analyses mentioned above in which psychoeducation programs were deemed less effective. Similarly, most universal programs focus on younger students, where rates of EDs are low and related risk factors may also be low such that it would be hard to detect, particularly in the short-term follow-up periods typical of ED prevention research, to determine if programs effectively reduced outcomes not expected to be high or even full manifest in a younger age group. A more meaningful analysis would be to look at targeted versus selected interventions within a population.

Overall, however, the results of the meta-analysis are in concordance with several long-term controlled studies, the results of which consistently suggest that programs that are feasible to deliver to populations and are effective for high-risk groups are available for older adolescents and college-age

Table 18.1 Mean Effects Sizes (r) on Three Risk Factors

	Thin-Ideal Internalization		Body Dissatisfaction		Eating Pathology	
	Post	Follow-Up	Post	Follow-Up	Post	Follow-Up
Universal vs. selected	0.10 vs. 0.24	NT*	0.06 vs. 0.22	0.05 vs. 0.19	0.06 vs. 0.21	0.07 vs. 0.19
Age ≤ 15 vs. > 15	0.11 vs. 0.23	NT	0.08 vs. 0.18	0.05 vs. 0.16	0.07 vs. 0.17	0.08 vs. 0.16
Psychoeducation content: yes vs. no	0.14 vs. 0.25	NT	0.09 vs. 0.25	NT	0.10 vs. 0.22	0.11 vs. 0.19
Focus on body acceptance: yes vs. no	0.28 vs. 0.13	NT	NT	NT	NT	NT
Focus on stress and coping: yes vs. no	0.07 vs. 0.21	NT	NT	NT	NT	NT
Dissonance content: yes vs. no	0.28 vs. 0.15	NT	0.24 vs. 0.13	NT	0.25 vs. 0.11	0.21 vs. 0.11
Didactic vs. interactive	NT	NT	.06 vs. 0.16	0.04 vs. 0.12	0.03 vs. 0.16	0.04 vs. 0.14
Interventionist vs. endogenous provider	NT	NT	0.18 vs. 0.09	0.14 vs. 0.05	NT	NT

NT = Not tested as there was no heterogeneity or insufficient data.

students and that programs are effective in reducing risk factors for subclinical, and clinical binge BED and BN.

Is Prevention Harmful?

An important aspect to address when discussing EDs prevention programs is the concern that such programs may inadvertently be harmful, as opposed to beneficial, to participants. This concern stems from two earlier prevention research studies in which results indicated an increase in ED risk factors over the course of the study. In the first, Mann et al. (1997) evaluated the effects of a single 90-minute discussion led by two students with a history of EDs to a control group receiving no discussion or ED material in a sample of 597 college women. The sessions were attended by groups of 10 to 20 participants at a time. In this study, there were no differences between the intervention and the control group at the end of the study. However, several factors reduce the strength and generalizability of these findings. Specifically, the study had a very high dropout rate: only 113/597 students were available for all follow-up time points. The authors also looked at estimates of problems for the sample available at the various time points. They found that students in the intervention reported slightly more symptoms of EDs than did students who did not attend the workshops; at the first follow-up 4 weeks later, on measures of bulimic symptoms, 23% of the intervention subjects and 22% of the control subjects report bulimic symptoms while at the second follow up 12 weeks later, 19% of the intervention subjects and 17% of the control subjects reported bulimic symptoms. Overall, the study provides no support for the benefit of such a workshop but it provides little support that the workshop was harmful. A second, small-scaled looked at the effects of primary prevention in a sample of 46 adolescents ages 13 to 14 years (Carter, Stewart, Dunn, & Fairburn, 1997). The intervention consisted of eight weekly sessions of 45-minute duration that included material related to body image, self-esteem, societal influence on appearance and dieting concerns and attitudes, weight regulation and dieting information, and information about EDs, including information on how to get help for such disorders; sessions also included cognitive behavioral skills intended to help participants become aware of and challenge unhealthy thoughts. A battery of self-report questionnaires was administered before and after the intervention and 6 months later. The authors noted an increase in knowledge about EDs at post-intervention and a decrease in target behavior and attitudes as assessed by the EDE-Q and EAT. However, there were no significant differences from baseline and at 6-month follow-up, while knowledge about EDs remained improved over time, all other outcomes returned to baseline levels, with levels of restraint being higher than they were at baseline. The authors' conclusion from this study that prevention programs may do more harm than good seems premature given the small sample size and the lack of comparison, and no apparent increase from baseline. In contrast, other controlled studies, with larger samples followed for longer periods, have not found adverse effects (Killen et al., 1993). In their meta-analysis, Pratt and Woolfenden (2002) conclude that there is no evidence that prevention programs are harmful.

There has also been some concern (e.g., from human subjects committees) that asking young adolescents about "ED behaviors" might be harmful in that it would expose adolescents to attitudes or behaviors they had previously not considered or heighten their focus on weight and shape issues. In response to this concern, Celio, Bryson, Killen, and Taylor (2003) compared results from 115 sixth-grade girls who responded to questions on risky weight control behaviors and attitudes at baseline and at 12-month follow-up with the responses of 107 girls who had not been part of the baseline assessment. Comparison of the "after-only" sample, those girls assessed at the follow-up time point only, with that from the 107 one-time assessment participants revealed no difference in scores between the two groups. Rates of unhealthy weight regulation practices behaviors decreased over time in the group assessed on two occasions. Thus, there is no empirical support suggesting that surveys of ED risk factors and behaviors increases risk for such outcomes. Further, and of critical importance to countering these concerns, the many large prevention trials conducted using older adolescents and college students have largely reduced EDs risk factors. Thus, we conclude that primary prevention programs are not harmful but that psychoeducation workshops for college students conducted by students with a history of ED have little benefit and should be replaced with programs that appear effective (see later).

Moderators and Mediators of Eating Disorder Prevention Programs

Examination of moderators and mediators in prevention studies is important for the progress and future success of prevention programs. Moderators refer to study or participant characteristics present at baseline (e.g., overweight status, risk status, age, sex, program format) that define different responses to intervention in individuals with differing characteristics. Mediators refer to process variables that should change prior to noted change in the outcome (e.g., thin-ideal internalization) that provide information on mechanisms of change. Hence examination of moderators and mediators provides critical insight into who the program is most effective for, what aspects of the program are effective and what events or changes that occur during the study predict better outcomes among participants.

As noted by Stice et al. (2007), there is consistent evidence that participant characteristics do moderate outcomes, with effects stronger for programs targeting individuals age 15 or older and programs targeting high-risk groups on several ED risk factors (i.e., thin-ideal internalization, eating pathology, dieting, negative affect, and body dissatisfaction). This is likely because the inclusion of low risk participants and/or younger participants reduces the ability to detect statistically significant and clinically meaningful changes in eating pathology due to already low levels in these groups. In addition, older adolescents likely benefit more from current prevention programs as these programs often focus on skills, such as cognitive dissonance and media literacy, that require more advanced cognitive skills and focus that younger adolescents and youth may not have fully developed. It has also been hypothesized, but not empirically examined, that individuals at risk for ED onset, which includes older adolescents, may be more motivated to participate and engage in prevention program material, leading to greater effects for targeted preventions and better outcomes for high-risk subgroups within universal programs. Stice et al. (2007) also found that programs targeting female-only populations were more effective but only for body dissatisfaction and dieting; there were no significant differences in effects between female only and mixed sex programs for body mass (BMI), thin-ideal internalization, negative affect, or overall eating pathology. Thus, while female only programs may be generally more effective, this appears to depend on the outcome assessed. As with programs focusing on high-risk and older samples, the larger effects for female only programs may be due to the greater level of eating disturbance associated with females and to higher levels of motivation to participate in ED prevention programs.

In regard to program characteristics that moderate outcomes, there is some evidence to suggest that interactive programming (as opposed to didactic) is more effective, as are programs delivered by trained interventionists. Similarly, programs that focused on specific EDs risk factors and programs that promote body acceptance and cognitive dissonance skills appear more effective than programs without such skills while programs that focus on more general risk factors without a focus on specific EDs risk factors, such as programs teaching coping skills or self-esteem promotion seem to be less effective.

However, while meta-analyses provide an overall description of moderators as they pertain to the field of ED prevention, few studies directly examine moderators, which limits our ability to determine if (and which) programs are most effective for specific populations. Even less is known about mediators. Taylor et al. (2006) did examine moderators of Student Bodies™, and found that the program was most effective for individuals with BMIs greater than 25 at baseline and, at one study site, that the program was more effective for women with baseline compensatory behaviors. Stice et al. (2008) also examined moderators of both their cognitive dissonance (CD) and healthy weight regulation programs and found support for two general program moderators (readiness to change for the healthy weight program and baseline level of risk as indicated by body image distress and bulimic symptoms for both programs) and for program specific moderators, including thin-ideal internalization for the CD program and emotional eating and body mass for the healthy weight regulation program. Overall, these findings reported by Taylor et al. and Stice et al. suggest that initial elevations in general ED risk factors, in a population motivated to change, and in heightened levels of program-specific/target risk factors moderate outcomes. These findings are of note given that both studies found moderating effects for bulimic behaviors (e.g., compensatory behaviors) and for elevated weight status, suggesting that it is possible to reduce onset of EDs in more than one high-risk group.

Stice and colleagues (2007) also recently examined mediators of the CD and healthy weight programs, finding some evidence to support thin-ideal internalization as a partial mediator for the cognitive dissonance program. Of interest, these researchers noted that in about one third of their CD participants, change in thin-ideal internalization occurred after change in the outcome measures and that change in the healthy weight mediators was inconsistently associated with outcomes, suggesting that continued examination of mediators, and elaboration on the expected change pathways/causal pathways is needed as additional mediators likely contribute to change in the ED risk factor outcomes. As noted by the researchers, examination of demand characteristics may also provide insight into the inconsistent findings. Overall, as concluded by Stice et al. (2007) these findings have important implications for prevention programs in that although both programs had program-specific mediators, both programs did result in reduction of ED risk factors in the long-term. This lends support to the notion that different pathways may be involved in the onset of EDs and that future programs may want to find ways to maximally target more than one risk pathway in order to achieve even greater reduction of risk factors and ED onset.

Examples of Effective Approaches

In the following section we discuss three programs, a cognitive dissonance program, an Internet-based program (*Student Bodies*™), and school-based prevention programs (e.g., *Healthy Schools, Healthy Kids [HS-HK]*) that have been shown, using long-term data (e.g., at least 1-year long-term follow-up data provided) from controlled clinical studies with sufficiently large samples needed to have sufficient power to detect differences. We also discuss an emerging area of prevention programming targeting both the reduction of EDs and overweight and reviews recent work supporting such programs.

Cognitive Dissonance Programs

For the past decade, Stice and colleagues have been developing, evaluating, and refining a cognitive dissonance (CD) program designed to reduce thin-ideal internalization and other ED risk factors (e.g., body dissatisfaction, negative affect) in females who indicate body image concerns. To date, 12 studies conducted by five groups of researchers have investigated either the efficacy or effectiveness of CD (for a comprehensive review of these studies see Stice et al., 2008). As previously described, cognitive dissonance programs are relatively short-term (two to four 1-hour sessions) that focus on reducing thin-ideal internalization, a robust ED risk factor, using dissonance techniques that require participants to take standpoints that are counter to their beliefs; over time participants, in order to reduce the distress associated with supporting an opinion counter to their beliefs, will indicate a change in their beliefs (e.g., less adherence to and internalization of the thin ideal).

The first CD study from Stice and colleagues evaluated a 3 1-hour sessions of CD administered to at-risk college women (e.g., endorsing body image concerns) as compared to a wait list control group with findings from this efficacy trial indicating that CD participants had greater decreases in risk factors, including body dissatisfaction, thin-ideal internalization, bulimic symptoms, and negative affect. A second study included an active control condition as well as a wait list control condition in order to verify that the previous findings were not due to demand characteristics; this active control group included healthy weight regulation materials that focused on reducing body image concerns by providing healthy weight control skills. Findings again provided support for CD with participants in the CD condition evidencing greater reductions in thin-ideal internalization and body dissatisfaction in comparison to wait list and healthy weight controls and greater reductions in dieting, bulimic symptoms, and negative affect in comparison to wait list controls. A third study was designed to replicate these findings, particularly given that healthy weight participants in the second study did show improvement on negative affect, dieting, and bulimic symptoms along with CD participants. In this study Stice and colleagues (2003) used a larger sample and longer follow-up periods; participants were also somewhat younger (mean age 17) than those in the previous studies (mean ages 18 and 19, respectively) in order to deliver the program at a time of peak ED onset. Findings again provided support for CD, with participants in CD evidencing greater short-term (post-test) reduction in thin-ideal internalization, negative affect, bulimic symptoms, and body dissatisfaction than healthy weight controls and greater long-term (6-month) reduction in body dissatisfaction and thin-ideal internalization in comparison to healthy weight controls. Both active conditions showed greater short and long-term reductions in bulimic symptoms and negative affect relative to the wait list control condition.

Stice et al. (2008) more recently completed a large scale study of cognitive dissonance with 481 adolescent females (mean age 17) who indicated body image concerns. In order to examine if CD was more effective than other active programs as well as a control group (assessment only), Stice et al. (2008) compared their programs to a healthy weight program and an expressive writing program. Findings from the 1-year, 2-year, and 3-year follow-up studies revealed support for the CD program (see Table 18.2). Post-test, 6-month, and 1-year follow-up analyses revealed greater decreases in thin-ideal internalization, bulimic symptoms,

Table 18.2 Summary of Findings and Effect Sizes from Stice and colleagues (2006, 2008)

	Post-Test	6-Month	1-Year	2-Year	3-Year
Thin-ideal internalization	CD > AO (0.38), EW (0.31), HW (0.16) HW > AO (0.22), EW (0.15)	CD > AO (0.29), HW > AO (0.21) EW > AO (0.15)	CD > AO (0.13), HW > AO (0.20), EW (0.11)	CD > AO (0.35), EW (0.20), HW > AO (0.37), EW (0.22)	HW > AO (0.23), EW (0.23)
Bulimic symptoms	CD > AO (0.17), EW (0.23), HW (0.11), HW > EW (0.14)	CD > AO (0.18), EW (0.13), HW > AO (0.16), EW (0.11)	CD > AO (0.20), HW > AO (0.15), EW > AO (0.12)	CD > AO (0.19)	CD > AO (0.19), HW > AO (0.17)
Body dissatisfaction	CD > AO (0.35), EW (0.37), HW (0.18), HW > AO (0.19), EW (0.22)	CD > AO (0.28), EW (0.24), HW > AO (0.25), EW (0.20)		CD > AO (0.28), EW (0.18), HW > AO (0.16)	CD > AO (0.43), EW (0.32), HW > AO (0.28)
Negative affect	CD > AO (0.26), HW (0.13), HW > AO (0.12), EW (0.14)	CD > AO (0.12), EW (0.12), HW (0.14)	CD > HW (0.11)	CD > AO (0.16), HW > AO (0.19)	CD > AO (0.17), HW > AO (0.16)
Dieting	CD > AO (0.27), EW (0.26), HW (0.26)	CD > AO (0.17), EW (0.15), HW > AO (0.11)	CD > AO (0.17), EW (0.12), HW > AO (0.11)		
Eating disorder onset (reduced onset)	-	-	HW > CD, AO, EW		CD > AO HW > AO
Overweight onset (reduced onset)	-	-	CD > AO, EW HW > AO, EW		HW > AO
Psychosocial impairment	-	-	-		CD > AO, EW HW > AO

Note. Findings are summarized from Stice et al. (2006, 2008); effect sizes for comparison are in parentheses (); CD = Cognitive Dissonance Condition; HW = Healthy Weight Regulation Condition; EW = Expressive Writing Condition; AO = Assessment Only Condition; Psychosocial impairment reported only for 2 and 3-year follow-up.

and dieting among CD participants than assessment-only controls; these two groups had differed on body dissatisfaction and negative affect at the post-test and 6-month follow-up but these effects appeared to fade by the 1-year follow-up. At 2-year follow-up, CD participants, in comparison to assessment-only participants, evidenced significantly less body dissatisfaction, fewer bulimic symptoms, lower levels of general psychosocial impairment (not previously assessed in the 1-year follow-up study) and continued to endorse lower negative affect and thin-ideal internalization; at 3-year follow-up these two groups continued to differ on negative affect, psychosocial impairment and body dissatisfaction. Of note was that, compared to the assessment-only group, there was a 60% reduction in ED onset for CD participants (6% onset in CD group vs. 15% in assessment only controls). Similar patterns emerged when comparing CD participants to expressive writing participants over time, although with some variation (see Table 18.2) and no noted differences in onset of EDs or obesity between these two groups. Finally, when examining differences between the CD and healthy weight participants, CD participants had greater decreases in several risk factors at 6-month and 1-year follow-up than healthy weight participants and had less psychosocial impairment at 3-year follow-up, with long-term results generally supporting a stronger effects for the CD program on ED related outcomes.

A subset of studies from Stice and colleagues (Rodriguez, Marchand, Ng, & Stice, 2008; Stice, Marti, Shaw, & O'Neil, 2008; Stice et al., 2007) also provide further elaboration on CD, with examination of moderators, mediators, and effectiveness across different racial and ethnic groups. The moderator and mediator findings were previously summarized (see section on mediators and moderators), with this work providing further elaboration on who may benefit the most from CD programs. In addition to these two studies, one additional study (Rodriguez et al., 2008), which studied the effects of a CD program on 394 adolescent girls and young women from three different ethnic groups (White $n = 311$; Hispanic/Latina $n = 61$; Asian-American/Hawaiian/Pacific Islander $n = 33$), found no differences in program effects across groups. This is an additional contribution to the literature as many studies often do not have diverse enough samples to examine race and/or ethnicity as a moderator of outcomes despite evidence that risk for EDs does exist across racial and ethnic groups.

As mentioned, other researchers have evaluated cognitive dissonance approaches to reducing EDs risk factors, with most studies supporting the findings of Stice et al.; the few studies that did not provide support for this approach did not have pre-test data and are thus limited in the conclusions offered (Green, Scott, Diyankova, Gasser, & Pederson, 2005; Matusek, Wendt, & Wiseman, 2004). In support of CD, Mitchell, Mazzeo, Rausch, and Cooke (2007) also evaluated CD programs in undergraduate women, comparing a six-session CD program to an active condition (yoga) and an assessment only control. Results revealed that, in comparison to the assessment-only condition, the CD program was associated a reduction in ED risk (e.g., drive for thinness, ED symptoms); there were no significant differences between CD and yoga, although attrition rates were much higher for the yoga group (34%) than the CD group (9%), suggesting that the CD program may have been more appealing to at-risk women. Becker and colleagues evaluated peer-led CD programs (two 2-hour sessions), which were compared to a media advocacy program which replaced dissonance activities with video clips focused on media influence on weight and shape issues, in sorority women in three studies (Becker et al., 2008; Becker et al., 2005; Becker, Smith, & Ciao, 2006). Results generally supported previous work in that participation in the CD program was associated with reductions in ED risk factors; the media advocacy program was also associated with reduction in risk at post-test assessments but not at later follow-up assessments, suggesting that only the CD program was associated with enduring effects. Further, only the CD program was associated with reductions in risk factors in both low and high-risk groups, suggesting a broader impact on risk in the general population (Becker et al., 2006). These findings are important from a dissemination stand point as this work indicates the trained peers can deliver seemingly effective programs. Thus, while findings and effect sizes vary somewhat across studies (effect sizes with the dissonance based model vary from .05 to .35), findings provide consistent support for CD programs despite some variation in study design, varied implementation of the study material (e.g., variations in the number of sessions), different modes of delivery (e.g., trained clinical psychologists versus trained teachers and peers), and variations in assessment procedures.

There are some limitations that these researchers have noted with this work. First, their studies typically rely on self-report assessments, which may introduce bias into the findings. However, as multiple programs were studied in the more recent studies from Stice and colleagues (Stice et al., 2006, 2008) and differences in risk factors were still detected, this may not be a serious limitation; future studies of CD, though, may want to include interview assessments such as the Eating Disorder Examination and/or the Structured Clinical Interview for the Diagnostic (SCID) and Statistical manual (DSM) of Mental Disorders. More concerning, though in line with all other prevention programs, are the waning effects over time, suggesting that even the most effective programs available to date still have limited long-term impact. The effect sizes, certainly compared to clinical studies are relatively small (<.40), and, as noted, waned over time such that fewer effects were found and effect sizes decreased over long-term follow-up. However, the persistence of program effects over long-term follow-ups remains noteworthy and effect sizes were in the range of other ED preventive studies, which Stice et al. (2007) noted in their meta-analysis tend to have, on average, small effects. Even though there were long-term benefits associated with CD in the most controlled, long-term study of CD, there were fewer differences in ED risk factors between CD and assessment-only and expressive writing conditions over time. This may not be a problem if programs are delivered during a period in which risk of onset would be peaking (e.g., college) but may be problematic if risk for onset of EDs remains high for an extended amount of time. Further, it remains unknown if these programs work for younger age groups and for males, both groups that are often overlooked for targeted prevention efforts. Of course, it remains a strength that this program appears to be effective for participants at risk for ED onset. The next steps for this approach to ED prevention, as well as for prevention programs in general, may be to utilize the recent mediator and moderator findings (Stice et al., 2008; Stice et al., 2007; Taylor et al., 2006) and recommendations from meta-analyses and successful programs (Berger, Sowa, Bormann, Brix, & Strauss, 2008; Stice et al., 2008; Stice et al., 2007; Taylor et al., 2006; Taylor et al., 2007), to inform and refine programs and enhance program effects.

In conclusion, across a series of independent studies, findings indicated that CD produces significant short-term reductions in ED risk factors, including thin-ideal internalization, body dissatisfaction, dietary restraint, bulimic pathology, and negative affect; long-term effects are more limited and appear to fade over time and have been studied in only one sample (Stice et al., 2008; Stice et al., 2006). Despite evidence for some waning effects, CD remains one of the most rigorously tested ED prevention programs and is one of very few programs to yield positive results that have been replicated in multiple studies and the only program to have been evaluated in independent labs. Overall, the independent and consistent findings across research labs suggest that cognitive dissonance programs are effective and efficacious; no other prevention programs are currently considered efficacious.

Stanford Student Body Studies

During the past 15 years, the Stanford group has been exploring issues related to prevention using Internet-based, psychoeducational, interactive programs. In an early study from this group, Killen et al. (1993) evaluated the effectiveness of a prevention curriculum designed to modify the eating attitudes and unhealthful weight regulation practices of young adolescent girls. Nine hundred sixty-seven sixth and seventh-grade girls were randomized to experimental healthy weight regulation curriculum or no-treatment control classes. There was a significant increase in knowledge among girls receiving the intervention but no overall effect. This study and a subsequent longitudinal prospective study in older adolescents demonstrated that students with higher scores on a measure of weight and shape were at risk for developing EDs.

The group then began to focus on targeted/selective programs. Early efforts along this line demonstrated the effectiveness of computer-based psychoeducational programs (Winzelberg et al., 2000) and evaluated an ED intervention multimedia program modeled after self-help ED treatment programs. Fifty-seven undergraduate females were randomly assigned to either the intervention or a wait-list control group. Intervention group subjects significantly improved their scores on all psychological measures over time. When compared to the control group, however, only the intervention group's improvements on the Body Shape Questionnaire were statistically significant. To establish the effectiveness of a face-to-face group for future comparisons of online programs, in an uncontrolled study, Springer et al. (1999) evaluated the effects of an undergraduate body image (BI) course, with 24 students. At posttest, subjects significantly decreased the frequency and severity of their body dissatisfaction and disordered eating. This program then served as a comparison for a study assessing the effectiveness of an

Internet-based program on reducing risk factors for EDs (Celio et al., 2000). In this study, 76 college women were randomized assigned to the BI course, a wait list control (WLC) group or an Internet based program, called *Student Bodies*™ (SB). SB had been adapted from the computer study and shown to be effective in a controlled study with 60 undergraduates (Winzelberg et al., 2000). At post-treatment, participants in SB had significant reductions in weight/shape concerns and disordered eating attitudes compared with those in the WLC condition. At 4-month follow-up, disordered behaviors were also reduced. No significant effects were found between the BT and WLC conditions.

These studies suggested that an Internet-based program can reduce risk factors in college-age women and set the stage for a more ambitious study. In the next study, 480 college-age women were randomized to SB or a wait-list group and were followed for 3 years. There was a significant reduction in Weight Concerns Scale scores in the SB group compared with the control group at post-intervention ($p < .001$), 1 year ($p < .001$), and 2 years ($p < .001$). The slope for reducing Weight Concerns Scale score was significantly greater in the treatment compared with the control group ($p = .02$). Over the course of follow-up, 43 participants developed subclinical or clinical EDs. While there was no overall significant difference in onset of EDs between the intervention and control groups, the intervention significantly reduced the onset of EDs in two subgroups identified through moderator analyses: (1) participants with an elevated body mass index (BMI) (> or = 25, calculated as weight in kilograms divided by height in meters squared) at baseline and (2) at one site, participants with baseline compensatory behaviors (e.g., self-induced vomiting, laxative use, diuretic use, diet pill use, driven exercise). No intervention participant with an elevated baseline BMI developed an ED, while the rates of onset of ED in the comparable BMI control group (based on survival analysis) were 4.7% at 1 year and 11.9% at 2 years. In the subgroup with a BMI of 25 or higher, the cumulative survival incidence was significantly lower at 2 years for the intervention compared with the control group (95% confidence interval, 0% for intervention group; 2.7% to 21.1% for control group). For the San Francisco Bay Area site sample with baseline compensatory behaviors, 4% of participants in the intervention group developed EDs at 1 year and 14.4%, by 2 years. Rates for the comparable control group were 16% and 30.4%, respectively. The study demonstrated, that, among college-age

women with high weight and shape concerns, an 8-week, Internet-based cognitive–behavioral intervention can significantly reduce weight and shape concerns for up to 2 years and decrease risk for the onset of EDs, at least in some high-risk groups. To our knowledge, this is the only study that has demonstrated that EDs can be prevented.

In other studies, the Stanford group returned to the issue of how to provide both universal and targeted interventions. The goal was to find ways to provide general healthy weight regulation programs to all high-school age students while providing targeted interventions to students at higher risk. Following a study by Abascal et al., (2004) that showed that students could be successfully allocated to various risk groups using an online program, Luce et al. (2005) provided online assessment and feedback to 174 10 grade students based on WSC and overweight risk. The algorithm identified 111 no-risk (NR), 36 ED risk (EDR), 16 overweight risk (OR), and 5 both risks. Fifty-six percent of the EDR and 50% of the OR groups elected to receive the recommended targeted curricula. Significant improvements in weight and shape concerns were observed in all groups. The program demonstrated that an Internet-delivered program can be used to assess risk and provide simultaneous universal and targeted interventions in classroom settings (see Fig. 18.2 for an example session).

The Stanford group in the meantime has expanded the protocol to include boys and to address overweight (M. Jones et al., 2008). In a pilot study, 100 eighth-grade boys and girls were sorted by an Internet-based algorithm into two groups based on risk for developing an ED. Male students participated as one general group. Participants in each group were also assigned to an online discussion group that corresponded to their group assignment and were encouraged to post messages to group members of similar risk. All three groups showed significant increases in knowledge related to the program content and reported increased physical activity levels from pre- to post-intervention. Females in the high-risk group also showed significant reductions in weight and shape concerns. Participants were enthusiastic about using the online health program; almost all reported that they would prefer an online format to a traditional classroom format. Another restudy showed that a paper-and-pencil program designed to reduce family/parental critical comments about eating and shape resulted in reduced critical comments from parents (by their report) (Bruning-Brown, Winzelberg, Abascal, & Taylor, 2004).

Fig. 18.2 Screen shot of *Student Bodies*™ Psychoeducational Page. (Reproduced with permission from the Stanford School of Medicine Behavioral Medicine Multi-Media Laboratory.)

Taken together these studies suggest that universal and targeted prevention programs can be provided simultaneously and might benefit from involvement of education programs aimed at parents/families.

In Germany, Jacobi and her group translated SB into German and adapted media more relevant to the German population (Jacobi et al., 2007). Because many of the U.S. SB programs have also been provided to German populations and examined in controlled studies, Beintner et al. (2008) undertook a meta-analysis of studies using SB done in the US and in Germany. Pre–post data from these programs across a large number of EDI and EDE-Q variables resulted in effect sizes in the moderate range for most variables. The respective controlled effect sizes for the German and U.S. studies were: drive for thinness, 0.42, 0.35; bulimia, 0.22, 0.29; restraint, 0.30, 0.26; WCS, 0.58, 0.36. This analysis suggests that programs with similar content and format, addressing similar populations in Germany and the United States have similar outcomes.

Overall, data from this group has demonstrated that an Internet-based program can reduce risk factors for high-risk individuals and even reduce onset of EDs.

Peer Support/School-Based Programs

Following on several key aspects of ecological and social systems theories, in which inclusion and targeting of critical social relationships and interactions is indicated in order to achieve enduring change on EDs risk factors, several recent studies have focused on the school and peer environments. For example, Becker and colleagues (Becker et al., 2008; Becker et al., 2005, 2006) have worked with sorority systems, which are believed to be high-risk populations, to develop and examine the effectiveness of peer-led media advocacy (MA) and cognitive dissonance programs on the risk for EDs in sorority members. The focus on peer-led programs at the college level stems from research indicating that peers contribute to body image satisfaction and, more broadly, from the notion that colleges tend to promote peer leadership, particularly in organized groups such as those in the athletic domain or in the sorority and fraternity systems. Recent findings provide support for both the CD and MA peer led programs for high-risk females and support for the peer-led CD program for both high- and low-risk females. These findings are important as they have important implications for disseminating effective programs for high-risk populations. Thus findings provide particular support for a peer-led CD program as this appears to have a positive effect on both low- and high-risk participants.

McVey and colleagues have also developed and examined a universal, school-based program that draws from several ecological approaches to reducing risk behaviors in schools using comprehensive, universal programs to reduce ED risk factors in schools. In these studies, described below, an ecological approach was utilized to address the multiple systems (e.g., teachers, peers, parents) that may influence risk for ED onset in youth. The program was implemented in a number of different classes throughout the academic year (e.g., math, drama, English, and health classes).

McVey and colleagues (2004) examined a six session life-skills programmed focused on promoting self-esteem and improving body image satisfaction and global self-esteem, with the additional goals of reducing negative attitudes shown to be associated with risk for EDs, including thoughts related to unhealthy eating and perfectionism. Participants included 258 preadolescent girls (n = 182 in prevention group; mean age 11.8). Findings revealed short term (pre–post) reductions in unhealthy dieting attitudes and improvement in self-esteem and body satisfaction; these changes were not maintained at the long-term (12-month) follow-up. This work was followed by two additional studies, again focused on young girls in grades 7 and 8, who participated in 10-session support/discussion groups facilitated by a school nurse and by trained peers. Sessions included more focused discussion related to healthy body image messages, promoting healthier norms within peer groups, and combating unhealthy appearance messages and expectations. Findings from these two studies revealed inconsistent support for this program as one study with 214 girls found decreases in dieting and improved body esteem over time for program participants but not in control participants (McVey, Davis, Tweed, & Shaw, 2004) while another similar replication study involving 282 girls failed to find differences in improvements on these outcomes between the control and intervention groups over time (McVey et al., 2003).

A more recent, large-scale study involving 982 middle school students expanded on this earlier work by including males and including a focus on teachers and parents (McVey, Tweed, & Blackmore, 2007). Materials were provided not only to students but also to teachers, and to some extent parents with the idea that it is important to address and reduce teachers' and parents' own unhealthy eating and weight attitudes and perceptions so that they may more effectively address and, over time, combat unhealthy attitudes and behaviors, including teasing, in students. Of note was that this program also included a focus on males as these researchers noted that males are indeed at growing risk for eating

disordered attitudes and behaviors and due to evidence that males are more likely than females to initiate teasing (Stein, 1999). Findings revealed that the program was associated with lower internalization of media messages for males and females, decreases in the number of students trying to lose weight, and decreased disordered eating scores for female students, although effects on weight loss behaviors did not persist at 6-month follow-up. Analyses on a high-risk group, defined as students currently trying to lose weight, revealed a significantly greater decrease in body dissatisfaction, media internalization, and disordered eating for these students in comparison to low-risk students; of note was that low-risk students did not evidence much increase in body dissatisfaction over time, which is important as such dissatisfaction may have been expected to increase as students were entering puberty. Findings, however, failed to find a reduction in weight-related teasing or improvements in body size acceptance. Additional analyses also failed to reveal no program influence on teachers' perceptions of the school environment or on their own behaviors and attitudes; a number of reasons, including time and other demands on teachers' abilities to learn and deliver program material may have contributed to the lack of findings for teachers, as well as the limited findings for student outcomes such as teasing.

Overall, despite the limited findings for some outcomes and the lack of intervention effect for teachers reported by McVey et al. and the somewhat inconsistent effects on disordered eating across studies (McVey et al., 2004; McVey, Lieberman, Voorberg, Wardrope, & Blackmore, 2003; McVey et al., 2003; McVey et al., 2007), these studies and the work from Becker and colleagues (Becker et al., 2008; Becker et al., 2005, 2006) suggest that programs that include peer based and/or school-based approaches to ED prevention may be important steps toward reducing risk for EDs in several systems that influence attitudes and behaviors (e.g., peer and school environments). These programs may be particularly appealing to institutions that want to deliver effective universal programs given that Becker et al. found equal improvements for low- and high-risk participants who received the CD program (Becker et al., 2006) and McVey et al. (2007) found equal effects on many outcomes for males and females.

Eating Disorder and Obesity Prevention

In some, but not all studies, elevated weight status has been associated with increased risk of onset of

BN and binge ED (Jacobi et al., 2004); weight status has also been linked to disordered eating attitudes and behaviors in young children and adolescents (Goldschmidt, Aspen, Sinton, Tanofsky-Kraff, & Wilfley, 2008). Despite these studies and reviews that indicate that overweight children and adolescents may already be endorsing unhealthy eating attitudes and behaviors, some have argued that the attention put on reducing and maintaining weight, particular in those in the higher BMI ranges has increased the rate of EDs. In addition others feel that the message that the majority of young people need to remain "thin" or be thinner reinforces the thin-body ideal would seem to counter the general ED prevention message that self-esteem should not be determined by body size (Neumark-Sztainer, 2003).

However, despite these concerns, it is becoming critical to comprehensively respond to the high prevalence of obesity, EDs and disordered eating behaviors among youth and researchers in both the obesity and EDs fields have proposed using an integrated approach to prevention that addresses the spectrum of weight-related disorders within interventions (Haines & Neumark-Sztainer, 2006). The identification of risk factors that are shared between these weight-related disorders is an essential step to developing effective prevention interventions. Haines and Neumark-Sztainer provide preliminary support for the existence of shared risk factors for obesity and EDs, with recent empirical research supporting this contention (Neumark-Sztainer et al., 2007). Specifically, the authors examined and found preliminary evidence that dieting, media use, body image dissatisfaction, and weight-related teasing may have relevance for the development of the spectrum of weight-related disorders. Future etiologic research designed to specifically test these and other potentially shared risk factors across different age and racial/ethnic groups remains warranted and would provide important insights into the relevant factors to be addressed in interventions aimed at preventing a broad spectrum of weight-related disorders.

Several preventive interventions have been developed based on addressing both ED and obesity prevention. Austin and colleagues (Austin, Field, Wiecha, Peterson, & Gortmaker, 2005; Austin et al., 2007) evaluated the effects of a program designed to promote healthful nutrition and physical activity on disordered weight-control behaviors in early adolescent girls and boys (*Planet Health*). In the most recent study (Austin et al., 2007) 749 girls and 702 boys in grades 6 and 7 from 13 middle schools were randomized to the intervention (5-2-1 Go!). At follow-up in girls, there was a significant effect for disordered weight-control behaviors for girls, with 3.6% (15 of 422) of girls in control schools compared with 1.2% (4 of 327) of girls in intervention schools reported engaging in disordered weight-control behaviors ($p = .04$). No intervention effect was observed in boys. Other studies also provide support for targeting both overweight and ED risk through one program. For example, Stice and colleagues (Stice et al., 2008; Stice et al., 2006) in their studies of CD also found support for their healthy weight regulation program as an effective ED prevention approach. While this program was originally intended to serve as an active control condition only, participation in the healthy weight program was found to be associated with a 55% reduction in the onset of overweight and 61% reduction of ED onset in comparison to the assessment-only control group and to be associated with reduction in other ED risk factors, such as bulimic symptoms (see Table 18.2); these findings are in concordance with earlier studies suggesting that healthy weight skills may indeed promote a reduction in ED risk (Killen et al., 1996; Matusek et al., 2004; Stice et al., 2003). Thus, a clear direction for future studies would be to evaluate a CD program that includes healthy weight regulation material. Taken together these studies suggest that interventions designed to promote healthy weight regulation and/or prevent EDs may help with weight maintenance and do not seem harmful.

Ecological/Environmental Approaches
Environment/Setting–Based

Many of the studies presented in the Stice et al. meta-analysis were delivered in schools, and as discussed, there is some emerging support that school-based and peer-based programs may be effective approaches for both low- and high-risk participants. Recently, with the goal of providing empirically supported recommendations for the continued development of such school-based and peer-based programs, Yager and O'Dea (2008) looked at 27 large, randomized, and controlled health promotion and health education programs to improve body dissatisfaction, dieting and disordered eating and exercise behaviors of male and female college students. According to their analysis, information-based, cognitive behavioral, and psychoeducational approaches have been the least effective at improving body image and eating problems among university students. Successful elements for future initiatives are identified as taking a media literacy- and dissonance-based educational approach, incorporating health education activities that build self-esteem, and using computers and the Internet as a delivery medium.

Although targeting the school environment, which may foster unhealthy attitudes about weight and shape in several different relationships (e.g., peer, student-teacher, coach-team member interactions), a subset of students may be exposed to more targeted and intense messages about weight and shape. For example, the apparent association between ED risk and certain activities such as sports has been long noted, with some programs having been developed to target the unique pressures associated with high-risk activities, such as ballet, gymnastics, and cheerleading. In response, Piran (1999) developed and evaluated a program aimed at preventing EDs in a world-class, residential ballet school for female and male students 10 to 18. The focus of the intervention was on the school environment, which was reengineered to allows students to "feel" comfortable with the processes of puberty and growth and to promote their right to fee both safe and positive in their diverse bodies. The focus of body shape was replaced with an emphasis on stamina and body condition, teachers were prohibited from making evaluative comments about body shape to students, and staff members were available to help students regarding concerns about body shape (Piran). The effectiveness of the program was examined by compared scores from two cohorts of seventh to ninth and tenth to twelfth grade students who had been in the school following implementation of the program with an earlier cohort that had not been exposed to the program. Scores on two items measuring weight and shape, the EAT and EDI, were lower in the intervention cohorts compared to the baseline cohort. The data provide evidence that a school wide intervention can be effective in reducing ED risk in a high-risk environment.

More recently, Whisenhunt, Williamson, Drab-Hudson, and Walden (2008) targeted cheerleading coaches as potential change agents by training them to recognize the symptoms of EDs and reduce the pressures for thinness among their squads. At 8 month follow-up there was self-reported improvement in coaches' behavior but no sustained knowledge about EDs. Similarly, Buchholz, Mack, McVey, Feder, and Barrowman (2008) evaluated the effectiveness of a selective prevention program designed to reduce pressures to be thin in sport, and to promote positive body image and eating behaviors in young female athletes belonging to gymnastic clubs. The intervention focused on competitive female gymnasts (ages 11– 18 years), parents, and coaches. Four clubs were randomized to receive a 3-month intervention program and three to a control group, with a total of 62 female gymnasts (intervention n = 31; control n = 31) completing the self-report post-test. The program resulted in athletes perceiving a reduction in pressure from their sports clubs to be thin, though no changes were found in body esteem, the EAT, or the SATAQ. No significant change was observed over time on mothers' measures.

Overall, findings suggest some utility in delivering programs to groups at high risk for ED onset as these the Piran (1999) and Buchholz et al. (2008) studies, although small in nature, did achieve some reduction in risk factors over time. Given that these programs focused on high-risk groups who were likely exposed to unhealthy messages and pressures about their eating and weight for an extended period of time during critical periods associated with ED onset, the finding that relatively short-term programs did achieve any reduction in risk factors is noteworthy. Continued development and examination of programs for high-risk groups is necessary; these programs may benefit from following the recommendations from Yager and O'Dea (2008) by incorporating a activity specific advocacy plan with cognitive dissonance and/or healthy weight regulation materials that appear effective for high-risk groups.

Diabetes, Eating Disorders, and Prevention

EDs are almost twice as common in adolescent females with type 1 diabetes as in their nondiabetic peers (Jones, Lawson, Daneman, Olmsted, & Rodin, 2000). In diabetic patients, EDs are associated with insulin omission for weight loss and impaired metabolic control (Jones et al., 2000) it has been suggested that binge EDs and other EDs are more common with type 2 diabetes (Crow, Kendall, Praus, & Thuras, 2000). We could find no studies that have attempted to prevent EDs in this high-risk population but such studies are needed.

Public Health/Policy and Mass Media Models

In the last few years, a number of ED prevention programs have focused on using public policy to promote higher body weight and shape. The assumption is that very thin models serve as media role models for young women and increase the risk of AN. A recent meta-analysis found a significant effect sizes between exposure to media images depicting the thin–ideal body and body image concerns in women (Grabe, Ward, & Hyde, 2008). Following the death of two South American models, one of whom had a BMI of 13.4 and another of whom died on the catwalk, and under pressure from legislators, fashion organizers in Italy, Spain, and Brazil banned models with BMIs <18.5. In addition, models will also have to carry a medical certificate to prove they are healthy. There is also a ban on "anorexic" makeup (shadows under the eyes) and postures (hunched shoulders). However, the leading fashion shows in many other places have resisted these restrictions. Israel has banned very skinny models in advertisements. The effect of these bans is unknown.

In another effort to use mass media to improve body image and resist the thin-body ideal, DOVE has undertaken a number of important activities as part of their Campaign for Real Beauty (www.campaignforrealbeauty.com). In 2004, DOVE launched an ad campaign featuring "real women" whose appearances were outside the stereotypical norms of beauty. The ads asked viewers to judge the women's looks (oversized? Outstanding? Or Wrinkle? Wonderful). In 2005, DOVE introduced a second phase which included advertising featuring six women of varying sizes and shapes. (Ironically, a recent article suggested that many of the "real women" presented in the DOVE campaign had actually been digitally altered [Collins, 2008].) The next phase, launched in 2007, addressed issues of women and aging. The latest efforts have focused on helping young girls realize that what they see in movies and magazines represents an unrealistic standard of beauty. The program includes "viral films" and an online program. The "viral" films, include *Evolution*, which depicts the transformation of a real women into a model and promotes awareness of how unrealistic perspectives of beauty are created, and *Onslaught*, a film that shows the barrage of beauty images that girls absorb ever day. The films are meant to be distributed online through sites like YouTube and MySpace. The online program follows four real girls in their struggles with self-esteem, body image, boys, and relationships. They have also developed a Self-Esteem Fund which sponsors self-esteem building workshops with "inspirational celebrities," and online tools to educate, parents, mentors and young women. In the United States, this company also sponsors ME!, a program associated with the Girl Scouts designed to build self-confidence in girls ages 8 to 17 with education resources and hands-on activities designed to promote self-esteem and self-confidence.

The impact of these programs is not known but the campaign has been associated with a 13% increase in worldwide sales of DOVE skin and hair products, suggesting some positive response to these strategies. In addition, in one small study, Oswalt and Wyatt (2007) evaluated a campaign which included defining 10 messages related to sabotaging body image and 10 ways to enhance body image. These messages were then displayed on campus buses, on billboards and magnets. Following the campaign, students were asked to evaluate the impact of these messages, with results indicating a modest impact. For instance, only 36% of the sample strongly agreeing or agreeing with the statement "The messages in this campaign positively influenced the way I think about my body." Thus, although it is important for these societal level programs to be initiated and maintained in order to achieve enduring reduction in ED risk factors, the impact of initial efforts is not yet established and remains a source for future research. Indeed, these programs provide an important opportunity for researchers to possibly disseminate effective prevention materials by working with companies and organizations whose goals and mission statements may support such programs.

Proanorexia and Bulimia Websites

The Internet hosts thousands of websites that promote AN (pro-ANA) and/or BN (pro-MIA). Such websites may include pictures of very thin women who are described as "beautiful" and also provide tips on how to hide EDs such as going to a fast food restaurant, ordering something, throwing away the food but brining the wrapper and bag home, or, at a family dinner, cutting everything into little pieces and moving them around the plate to simulate eating. Bardone-Cone and Cass (2007) constructed a prototypical pro-anorexia website, and randomly assigned 235 female undergraduates to view either the pro-anorexia website or one of two comparison websites related to female fashion (using average-sized models) or home décor. Study participants exposed to the pro-anorexia website endorsed more negative affect, lower social self-esteem, and lower appearance self-efficacy following the experimental manipulation than those who viewed a comparison website. In addition, these women perceived themselves to be heavier and reported an increased likelihood of exercising, thinking about their weight in the near future, and engaging in more image comparison. Like other Internet-based activities, pro-ANA websites have evolved into pro-ANA communities. Whatever impact these sites might have, it is not possible to remove them from the Internet.

Preventing Anorexia Nervosa

Although there has been impressive progress in preventing ED disorders, most of the studies have focused in combined onset of subclinical, clinical binge ED, BN, and/or ED not otherwise specified. The low prevalence of AN (2%–3% of the population) makes it nearly impossible to demonstrate a population-based effect, although interventions in high-risk populations may be of benefit. A focus on indicated prevention might be the most preferable approach in which adolescents with early features of AN–such as failure to gain weight in the context of other factors such as excessive exercise or perfectionism. The type of preventive intervention is also less certain for AN than for BN or binge ED. However, based on the success of family-based interventions for adolescents with AN (Keel & Haedt, 2008; Lock & le Grange, 2005; Wilson, 2005), such preventive efforts might focus on parents. An alternative approach is to focus on high-risk environments, such as was done with Piran (1999). Finally, attempts to reduce media glamorization of the thin-body ideal, as discussed above, would seem important to reducing AN, although the benefit of this tactic is difficult to demonstrate in scientific studies.

Dissemination/Implementation and Cost–Benefit Issues

Dissemination and implementation involve a number of issues which are beyond the scope of this chapter (Taylor, Taylor, & Chang, 2008). Several programs are available and involve quite different models. Stice and Presnell (2007) have published a facilitator manual to guide implementation of their dissonance manual. Packages of materials for participants can be purchased separately. It is not clear if the participant materials are necessary as the activities seem straightforward and if, not, the program would be inexpensive to implement. *Student Bodies*™ is available through a non-profit organization which provides access to *Student Bodies*™ but recommends that the program be delivered with a moderated discussion group, as was done in the outcome studies. One study found that students using *Student Bodies*™ without a discussion group did as well as those who were able to participate (Low et al., 2006)

and rate of participation is not related to outcome (Manwaring et al., 2008).

Conclusion

In conclusion, due to well-designed studies and recent meta-analytic reviews, we now know more about what does and does not appear to be effective in regard to effective ED prevention programs; these conclusions provide both guidance for future program development (e.g., cognitive-behavioral, dissonance, and/or healthy weight regulation material appear more effective than psychoeducation or life-skills alone programs) as well as highlight areas in which greater improvement is needed as discussed in the preceding text. It is critical for programs be informed by both theory and risk factor research and that these programs include skills that target and reduce risk for overweight (e.g., healthy weight regulation material) in order to ensure public health prominence for ED prevention programs. Programs that are delivered in high school environments or in schools and that target multiple systems (e.g., peers, media, teachers/coaches, and families) and the varied developmental needs of children and adolescents over time (i.e., onset of puberty, transitions to high school or college, increasing exposure to peer pressure and media messages about appearance, increased pressure to be thin or lean/muscular within competitive sports) are most needed in order to ensure that a positive social support system in which weight and eating concerns are de-emphasized is developed and strengthened over time.

Of note is the programmatic research, developed over the past decade and informed by risk factor research and theories, from two research groups has led to the development of programs and techniques that reduce risk factor scores and the onset of EDs, at least in older adolescent and college women at high risk for the development of EDs. Both programs have been designed for large-scale dissemination; *Student Bodies*™ is intended for easy distribution via the Internet with little cost and minimal staff time and training and Stice and colleagues provide a manual for their program and their program has been shown to be effectively delivered by endogenous staff (e.g., peer leaders), which is appealing as fewer external staff will have to be involved in these programs. Thus, important strides in the reduction of ED risk factors and ED onset have emerged, providing important evidence that these goals can be achieved and that prevention programs are not 'harmful' but are indeed effective and feasible. By building on the gains made in EDs prevention over the past decade and continuing to consider important issues pertaining to dissemination of materials and translation of findings to real world settings, it appears possible that researchers have the opportunity to achieve significant reductions in risk for EDs and ED onset in the coming decade.

Future Directions

In spite of the major gains associated with several of the reviewed programs (i.e., cognitive dissonance, Student Bodies™, and peer-led programs), more work must be done to increase the effectiveness of EDs prevention programs. Critical next steps appear to be (1) developing and evaluating programs that are effective for younger age groups (i.e., preadolescent and early adolescent youth) in order to reduce and ultimately prevent the emergence of early concerns about weight and shape and early signs of disordered eating that may lead to later eating pathology during adolescents; (2) enhancing individually based programs to be incorporated into environmentally focused (e.g., school-based) programs and to include a engage additional individuals who may have important and relevant developmental influences on youth, including parents, siblings, teachers, coaches, and physicians; (3) utilizing recent mediator and moderator findings and developing effective screening tools in order to ensure that the appropriate programs are delivered to individuals presenting with different risk factors and/or varied levels of risk for ED onset; (4) ensuring that programs are developed that target the issues relevant to disordered eating onset in males and in special at-risk populations, such as adolescents with type I diabetes; and (5) determining if programs that focus on a broad range of risk factors and behaviors, including problems with affect regulation, binge drinking, and excessive weight concerns, can effectively reduce ED and comorbidity onset. Recent work also suggests that EDs prevention efforts may be best paired with obesity prevention programs; this is appealing from a public health perspective and also recognizes the shared risk factors and overlap between disordered eating and overweight. Addressing these issues and building on a decade of important studies might realize the public health goal of preventing EDs.

References

Abascal, L., Bruning-Brown, J., Winzelberg, A. J., Dev, P., & Taylor, C. B. (2004). Combining universal and targeted prevention for school-based eating disorder programs. *International Journal of Eating Disorders, 35*(1), 1–9.

Aronson, E. (1980). Persuasion via self-justification: Large commitments for small rewards. In L. Festinger (Ed.), *Retrospection on Social Psychology* (pp. 3–21). Oxford: Oxford University Press.

Austin, S. B., Field, A. E., Wiecha, J., Peterson, K. E., & Gortmaker, S. L. (2005). The impact of a school-based obesity prevention trial on disordered weight-control behaviors in early adolescent girls. *Archives of Pediatrics Adolescent Medicine, 159*(3), 225–230.

Austin, S. B., Kim, J., Wiecha, J., Troped, P. J., Feldman, H. A., & Peterson, K. E. (2007). School-based overweight preventive intervention lowers incidence of disordered weight-control behaviors in early adolescent girls. *Archives of Pediatrics Adolescent Medicine, 161*(9), 865–869.

Bandura, A. (1986). *Social foundations of thought and action.* Englewood Cliffs, NJ: Prentice-Hall.

Bardone-Cone, A. M., & Cass, K. M. (2007). What does viewing a pro-anorexia website do? An experimental examination of website exposure and moderating effects. *International Journal of Eating Disorders, 40*(6), 537–548.

Becker, C. B., Bull, S., Schaumberg, K., Cauble, A., & Franco, A. (2008). Effectiveness of peer-led eating disorders prevention: A replication trial. *Journal of Consulting and Clinical Psychology, 76*(2), 347–354.

Becker, C. B., Smith, L., & Ciao, A. C. (2005). Reducing eating disorder risk factors in sorority members: A randomized trial. *Behavior Therapy, 36*, 245–254.

Becker, C. B., Smith, L. M., & Ciao, A. C. (2006). Peer facilitated eating disorders prevention: a randomized effectiveness trial of cognitive dissonance and media advocacy. *Journal of Counseling Psychology, 53*(4), 550–555.

Beintner, I., Jacobi, C., Winzelberg, A. J., & Taylor, C. B. (2008). *Wirksamkeit eines Internet-gestützten Präventionsprogrammes in Deutschland und den USA.* Unpublished manuscript.

Berger, U., Sowa, M., Bormann, B., Brix, C., & Strauss, B. (2008). Primary prevention of eating disorders: Characteristics of effective programmes and how to bring them to broader dissemination. *European Eating Disorders Review, 16*(3), 173–183.

Bruning-Brown, J., Winzelberg, A. J., Abascal, L. B., & Taylor, C. B. (2004). An evaluation of an Internet-delivered eating disorder prevention program for adolescents and their parents. *Journal of Adolescent Health, 35*(4), 290–296.

Buchholz, A., Mack, H., McVey, G., Feder, S., & Barrowman, N. (2008). BodySense: An evaluation of a positive body image intervention on sport climate for female athletes. *Eating Disorders, 16*(4), 308–321.

Carter, F. A., & Bulik, C. M. (2008). Childhood obesity prevention programs: How do they affect eating pathology and other psychological measures? *Psychosomatic Medicine, 70*(3), 363–371.

Carter, J. C., Stewart, D. A., Dunn, V. J., & Fairburn, C. G. (1997). Primary prevention of eating disorders: Might it do more harm than good? *International Journal of Eating Disorders, 22*(2), 167–172.

Cash, T. F. (1997). *The body image workbook.* Oakland, CA: New Harbinger.

Celio, A. A., Bryson, S., Killen, J. D., & Taylor, C. B. (2003). Are adolescents harmed when asked risky weight control behavior and attitude questions? Implications for consent procedures. *International Journal of Eating Disorders, 34*(2), 251–254.

Celio, A. A., Winzelberg, A. J., Wilfley, D. E., Eppstein-Herald, D., Springer, E. A., Dev, P., et al. (2000). Reducing risk factors for eating disorders: Comparison of an Internet- and a classroom-delivered psychoeducational program. *Journal of Consulting and Clinical Psychology, 68*(4), 650–657.

Clarke, G. N., Hornbrook, M., Lynch, F., Polen, M., Gale, J., Beardslee, W., et al. (2001). A randomized trial of a group cognitive intervention for preventing depression in adolescent offspring of depressed parents. *Archives of General Psychiatry, 58*, 1127–1134.

Collins, L. (2008, May 12). Pixel perfect: Pascal Dangin's virtual reality. *The New Yorker.*

Coughlin, J. W., & Kalodner, C. (2006). Media literacy as a prevention intervention for college women at low- or high-risk for eating disorders. *Body Image, 3*(1), 35–43.

Crow, S., Kendall, D., Praus, B., & Thuras, P. (2000). Binge eating and other psychopathology in patients with type II diabetes mellitus. *International Journal of Eating Disorders, 20*, 222–226.

Fairburn, C. G., & Cooper, Z. (1993). *The eating disorder examination* (12th ed.). New York: Guilford Press.

Festinger, L. (1957). *A theory of cognitive dissonance.* Palo Alto, CA: Stanford University Press.

Festinger, L. (1962). Cognitive dissonance. *Scientific American, 207*, 93–102.

Field, A. E., Camargo, C. A., Taylor, C. B., Berkey, C. S., & Colditz, G. A. (1999). Relation of peer and media influences to the development of purging behaviors among preadolescent and adolescent girls. *Archives of Pediatrics Adolescent Medicine, 153*, 1184–1189.

Frederickson, B., & Roberts, T. A. (1997). Objectification theory: Toward understanding women's lived experiences and mental health risks. *Psychology of Women Quarterly, 21*, 173–206.

Goldschmidt, A. B., Aspen, V. P., Sinton, M. M., Tanofsky-Kraff, M., & Wilfley, D. E. (2008). Disordered eating attitudes and behaviors in overweight youth. *Obesity, 16*(2), 257–264.

Grabe, S., Ward, L. M., & Hyde, J. S. (2008). Role of the media in body image concerns among women: A meta-analysis of experimental and correlational studies. *Psychological Bulletin, 134*(3), 460–476.

Green, M., Scott, N., Diyankova, I., Gasser, C., & Pederson, E. (2005). Eating disorder prevention: An experimental comparison of high level dissonance, low level dissonance, and no-treatment control. *Eating Disorders, 13*, 157–170.

Guarda, A. S. (2008). Treatment of anorexia nervosa: Insights and obstacles. *Physiology and Behavior, 94*(1), 113–120.

American Psychological Association Task force on Psychological Intervention Guidelines. (1995). *Template for developing guidelines: Interventions for mental disorders and psychological aspects of physical disorders.* Washington, D.C.: American Psychological Association.

Haines, J., & Neumark-Sztainer, D. (2006). Prevention of obesity and eating disorders: A consideration of shared risk factors. *Health Education Resource, 21*(6), 770–782.

Horowitz, J. L., & Garbe, J. (2006). The prevention of depressive symptoms in children and adolescents: A meta-analytic review. *Journal of Consulting and Clinical Psychology, 74*(3), 401–415.

Jacobi, C., Abascal, L., & Taylor, C. B. (2004). Screening for eating disorders and high-risk behavior: Caution. *International Journal of Eating Disorders, 36*(3), 280–295.

Jacobi, C., Hayward, C., de Zwaan, M., Kraemer, H. C., & Agras, W. S. (2004). Coming to terms with risk factors for eating disorders: Application of risk terminology and suggestions for a general taxonomy. *Psychological Bulletin, 130*(1), 19–65.

Jacobi, C., Morris, L., Beckers, C., Bronisch-Holtze, J., Winter, J., Winzelberg, A. J., et al. (2007). Maintenance of Internet-based prevention: A randomized controlled trial. *International Journal of Eating Disorders, 40*(2), 114–119.

Jones, J. M., Lawson, M. L., Daneman, D., Olmsted, M. P., & Rodin, G. (2000). Eating disorders in adolescent females with and without type 1 diabetes: Cross sectional study. *British Medical Journal, 320*(7249), 1563–1566.

Jones, M., Luce, K. H., Osborne, M. I., Taylor, K., Cunning, D., Doyle, A. C., et al. (2008). Randomized, controlled trial of an Internet-facilitated intervention for reducing binge eating and overweight in adolescents. *Pediatrics, 121*(3), 453–462.

Keel, P. K., & Haedt, A. (2008). Evidence-based psychosocial treatments for eating problems and eating disorders. *Journal of Clinical Child and Adolescent Psychology, 37*(1), 39–61.

Killen, J. D., Taylor, C. B., Hammer, L. D., Litt, I., Wilson, D. M., Rich, T., et al. (1993). An attempt to modify unhealthful eating attitudes and weight regulation practices of young adolescent girls. *International Journal of Eating Disorders, 13*, 369–384.

Killen, J. D., Taylor, C. B., Hayward, C., Haydel, K. F., Wilson, D. M., Hammer, L., et al. (1996). Weight concerns influence the development of eating disorders: A 4-year prospective study. *Journal of Consulting and Clinical Psychology, 64*(5), 936–940.

Killen, J. D., Taylor, C. B., Hayward, C., Wilson, D. M., Haydel, F., Hammer, L. D., et al. (1994). Pursuit of thinness and onset of eating disorder symptoms in a community sample of adolescent girls: A three-year prospective analysis. *International Journal of Eating Disorders, 16*, 227–238.

Kraemer, H. C. (1992). *Evaluating medical tests: Objective and quantitative guidelines.* Newbury Park: Sage.

Leippe, M. R. (1994). Generalization of dissonance reduction: Decreasing prejudice through induced compliance. *Journal of Personality and Social Psychology, 67*, 395–413.

Lipsey, M. W., & Wilson, D. B. (2001). The way in which intervention studies have "personality" and why it is important to meta-analysis. *Evaluation & the Health Professions, 24*(3), 236–254.

Lock, J., & le Grange, D. (2005). Family-based treatment of eating disorders. *International Journal of Eating Disorders, 37*(S1), S64–67; discussion S87–69.

Low, K. G., Charanasomboon, S., Lesser, J., Reinhalter, K., Martin, R., Jones, H., et al. (2006). Effectiveness of a computer-based interactive eating disorders prevention program at long-term follow-up. *Eating Disorders, 14*(1), 17–30.

Luce, K. H., Osborne, M. I., Winzelberg, A. J., Das, S., Abascal, L. B., Celio, A. A., et al. (2005). Application of an algorithm-driven protocol to simultaneously provide universal and targeted prevention programs. *International Journal of Eating Disorders, 37*(3), 220–226.

Lynch, F. L., Hornbrook, M., Clarke, G. N., Perrin, N., Polen, M. R., O'Connor, E., et al. (2005). Cost-effectiveness of an intervention to prevent depression in at-risk teens. *Archives of General Psychiatry, 62*, 1241–1248.

Mann, T., Nolen-Hoeksema, S., Huang, K., Burgard, D., Wright, A., & Hanson, K. (1997). Are two interventions worse than none? Joint primary and secondary prevention of eating disorders in college females. *Healthy Psychology, 16*, 215–225.

Manwaring, J. L., Bryson, S. W., Goldschmidt, A. B., Winzelberg, A. J., Luce, K. H., Cunning, D., et al. (2008). Do adherence variables predict outcome in an online program for the prevention of eating disorders? *Journal of Consulting and Clinical Psychology, 76*(2), 341–346.

Matusek, J. A., Wendt, S. J., & Wiseman, C. V. (2004). Dissonance thin-ideal and didactic healthy behavior eating disorder prevention programs: Results from a controlled trial. *International Journal of Eating Disorders, 36*(4), 376–388.

McVey, G. L., Davis, R., Tweed, S., & Shaw, B. F. (2004). Evaluation of a school-based program designed to improve body image satisfaction, global self-esteem, and eating attitudes and behaviors: A replication study. *International Journal of Eating Disorders, 36*(1), 1–11.

McVey, G. L., Lieberman, M., Voorberg, N., Wardrope, D., & Blackmore, E. (2003). School-based peer support groups: A new approach to the prevention of disordered eating. *Eating Disorders, 11*, 169–185.

McVey, G. L., Lieberman, M., Voorberg, N., Wardrope, D., Blackmore, E., & Tweed, S. (2003). Replication of a peer support program designed to prevent disordered eating: Is a life skills approach sufficient for all middle school students? *Eating Disorders, 11*(3), 187–195.

McVey, G. L., Tweed, S., & Blackmore, E. (2007). Healthy Schools-Healthy Kids: A controlled evaluation of a comprehensive universal eating disorder prevention program. *Body Image, 4*(2), 115–136.

Mitchell, K. S., Mazzeo, S. E., Rausch, S. M., & Cooke, K. L. (2007). Innovative interventions for disordered eating: Evaluating dissonance-based and yoga interventions. *International Journal of Eating Disorders, 40*(2), 120–128.

Neumark-Sztainer, D., Sherwood, N. E., Coller, T., & Hannan, P. J. (2000). Primary prevention of disordered eating among preadolescent girls: Feasibility and short-term effect of a community-based intervention. *Journal of the American Dietetic Association, 100*(12), 1466–1473.

Neumark-Sztainer, D., & Story, M. (1998). Dieting and binge eating among adolescents: What do they really mean? *Journal of the American Dietetic Association, 98*(4), 446–450.

Neumark-Sztainer, D., Wall, M. M., Haines, J. I., Story, M. T., Sherwood, N. E., & van den Berg, P. A. (2007). Shared risk and protective factors for overweight and disordered eating in adolescents. *American Journal of Preventive Medicine, 33*(5), 359–369.

O'Dea, J. A. (2005). Prevention of child obesity: 'First, do no harm.' *Health Education Resource, 20*(2), 259–265.

Ogden, C. L., Carroll, M. D., & Flegal, K. M. (2008). High body mass index for age among US children and adolescents, 2003–2006. *JAMA, 299*(20), 2401–2405.

Oswalt, S. B., & Wyatt, T. J. (2007). Mirror, mirror, help me like my body: Examining a body image media campaign. *Californian Journal of Health Promotion, 5*(2), 135–147.

Peterson, R. D., Grippo, K. P., & Tantleff-Dunn, S. (2008). Empowerment and powerlessness: A closer look at the relationship between feminism, body image and eating disturbance. *Sex Roles, 58*(9–10), 639–648.

Pike, K. M., Hilbert, A., Wilfley, D. E., Fairburn, C. G., Dohm, F. A., Walsh, B. T., et al. (2007). Toward an understanding of risk factors for anorexia nervosa: A case-control study. *Psychological Medicine, 10*, 1–11.

Piran, N. (1999). Eating disorders: A trial of prevention in a high risk school setting. *Journal of Primary Prevention, 10*(1), 75–90.

Pratt, B. M., & Woolfenden, S. R. (2002). Interventions for preventing eating disorders in children and adolescents. *Cochrane Database Systematic Reviews*, (2), CD002891.

Rathner, G., & Messner, K. (1993). Detection of eating disorders in a small rural town: An epidemiological study. *Psychological Medicine, 23*, 175–184.

Rodriguez, R., Marchand, E., Ng, J., & Stice, E. (2008). Effects of a cognitive dissonance-based eating disorder prevention program are similar for Asian American, Hispanic, and White participants. *International Journal of Eating Disorders, [ahead of print]*([ahead of print]), [ahead of print].

Sanci, L., Coffey, C., Olsson, C., Reid, S., Carlin, J. B., & Patton, G. (2008). Childhood sexual abuse and eating disorders in females: Findings from the Victorian Adolescent Health Cohort Study. *Archives of Pediatrics & Adolescent Medicine, 162*(3), 261–267.

Sherwood, N. E., Harnack, L., & Story, M. (2000). Weight-loss practices, nutrition beliefs, and weight-loss program preferences of urban American Indian women. *Journal of the American Dietetic Association, 100*(4), 442–446.

Slade, P. D., & Dewey, M. E. (1986). Development and preliminary validation of SCANS: A screening instrument for individuals at risk of developing anorexia and bulimia nervosa. *International Journal of Eating Disorders, 5*, 517–538.

Speranza, M., Atger, F., Corcos, M., Loas, G., Guilbaud, O., Stéphan, P., et al. (2003). Depressive psychopathology and adverse childhood experiences in eating disorders. *European Psychiatry, 18*(8), 377–383.

Springer, E. A., Winzelberg, A. J., Perkins, R., & Taylor, C. B. (1999). Effects of a body image curriculum for college students on improved body image. *International Journal of Eating Disorders, 26*(1), 13–20.

Stein, N. (1999). *Classrooms and courtrooms: Facing sexual harassment in K-12 schools.* New York: Teachers College Press.

Stice, E., & Agras, W. S. (1998). Predicting onset and cessation of bulimic behaviors during adolescence: A longitudinal grouping analysis. *Behavior Therapy, 29*(2), 257–276.

Stice, E., Chase, A., Stormer, S., & Appel, A. (2001). A randomized trial of a dissonance-based eating disorder prevention program. *International Journal of Eating Disorders, 29*(3), 247–262.

Stice, E., Marti, C. N., Spoor, S., Presnell, K., & Shaw, H. (2008). Dissonance and healthy weight eating disorder prevention programs: Long-term effects from a randomized efficacy trial. *Journal of Consulting and Clinical Psychology, 76*(2), 329–340.

Stice, E., Marti, N., Shaw, H., & O'Neil, K. (2008). General and program-specific moderators of two eating disorder prevention programs. *International Journal of Eating Disorders, [ahead of print]*([ahead of print]), [ahead of print].

Stice, E., Mazotti, L., Weibel, D., & Agras, W. S. (2000). Dissonance prevention program decreases thin-ideal internalization, body dissatisfaction, dieting, negative affect, and bulimic symptoms: A preliminary experiment. *International Journal of Eating Disorders, 27*(2), 206–217.

Stice, E., & Presnell, K. (2007). *The Body Project: Promoting body acceptance and preventing eating disorders: Facilitator guide.* New York: Oxford University Press.

Stice, E., Presnell, K., Gau, J., & Shaw, H. (2007). Testing mediators of intervention effects in randomized controlled trials: An evaluation of two eating disorder prevention programs. *Journal of Consulting and Clinical Psychology, 75*(1), 20–32.

Stice, E., & Shaw, H. (2004). Eating disorder prevention programs: A meta-analytic review. *Psychological Bulletin, 130*(2), 206–227.

Stice, E., Shaw, H., Becker, C. B., & Rohde, P. (2008). Dissonance-based Interventions for the prevention of eating disorders: Using persuasion principles to promote health. *Preventive Science, 9*(2), 114–128.

Stice, E., Shaw, H., Burton, E., & Wade, E. (2006). Dissonance and healthy weight eating disorder prevention programs: A randomized efficacy trial. *Journal of Consulting and Clinical Psychology, 74*(2), 263–275.

Stice, E., Shaw, H., & Marti, C. N. (2007). A meta-analytic review of eating disorder prevention programs: Encouraging findings. *Annual Review of Clinical Psychology, 3,* 207–231.

Stice, E., Trost, A., & Chase, A. (2003). Healthy weight control and dissonance-based eating disorder prevention programs: Results from a controlled trial. *International Journal of Eating Disorders, 33*(1), 10–21.

Striegel-Moore, R. H., Dohm, F. A., Kraemer, H. C., Taylor, C. B., Daniels, S., Crawford, P. B., et al. (2003). Eating disorders in white and black women. *American Journal of Psychiatry, 160*(7), 1326–1331.

Striegel-Moore, R. H., Fairburn, C. G., Wilfley, D. E., Pike, K. M., Dohm, F. A., & Kraemer, H. (2005). Toward an understanding of risk factors for binge-eating disorder in black and white women: A community-based case-control study. *Psychological Medicine, 35*(6), 907–917.

Taylor, C. B., Bryson, S., Luce, K. H., Cunning, D., Doyle, A. C., Abascal, L. B., et al. (2006). Prevention of eating disorders in at-risk college-age women. *Archives of General Psychiatry, 63*(8), 881–888.

Taylor, C. B., Franko, D. L., Neumark-Sztainer, D., Paxton, S. J., & Shapiro, J. R. (2007). Public-health approach to eating disorders. *Lancet, 369*(9577), 1928–1928.

Taylor, C. B., Taylor, K. L., & Chang, V. (2008). Issues in the dissemination of cognitive behavior therapy. *Nordic Journal of Psychiatry. 62,* 37–44.

The McKnight Investigators. (2003). Risk factors for the onset of eating disorders in adolescent girls: Results of the McKnight longitudinal risk factor study. *American Journal of Psychiatry, 160*(2), 248–254.

Tiggemann, M., & Kuring, J. K. (2004). The role of body objectification in disordered eating and depressed mood. *British Journal of Clinical Psychology, 43*(Pt. 3), 299–311.

Wade, T. D., Davidson, S., & O'Dea, J. A. (2003). A preliminary controlled evaluation of a school-based media literacy program and self-esteem program for reducing eating disorder risk factors. *International Journal of Eating Disorders, 33*(4), 371–383; discussion 384–377.

Wertheim, E. H., Koerner, J., & Paxton, S. J. (2001). Longitudinal predictors of restrictive eating and bulimic tendencies in three different age groups of adolescent girls. *Journal of Youth and Adolescence, 30*(1), 69–81.

Whisenhunt, B. L., Williamson, D. A., Drab-Hudson, D. L., & Walden, H. (2008). Intervening with coaches to promote awareness and prevention of weight pressures in cheerleaders. *Eating and Weight Disorders, 13*(2), 102-110.

Wichstrom, L. (2000). Psychological and behavioral factors unpredictive of disordered eating: A prospective study of the general adolescent population in Norway. *International Journal of Eating Disorders, 28*(1), 33–42.

Wilfley, D. E., & Cohen, L. R. (1997). Psychological treatment of bulimia nervosa and binge eating disorder. *Psychopharmacology Bulletin, 33*(3), 437–454.

Wilksch, S. M., Durbridge, M. R., & Wade, T. D. (2008). A preliminary controlled comparison of programs designed to reduce risk of eating disorders targeting perfectionism and media literacy. *Journal of the American Academy of Child and Adolescent Psychiatry, 47*(8), 939–947.

Wilson, G. T. (2005). Psychological treatment of eating disorders. *Annual Review of Clinical Psychology, 1,* 439–465.

Wilson, G. T., & Fairburn, C. G. (1993). Cognitive treatment for eating disorders. *Journal of Consulting and Clinical Psychology, 61*(2), 261–269.

Winzelberg, A. J., Eppstein, D., Eldredge, K. L., Wilfley, D., Dasmahapatra, R., Dev, P., et al. (2000). Effectiveness of an Internet-based program for reducing risk factors for eating disorders. *Journal of Consulting and Clinical Psychology, 68*(2), 346–350.

Yager, Z., & O'Dea, J. A. (2008). Prevention programs for body image and eating disorders on University campuses: A review of large, controlled interventions. *Health Promotion International, 23*(2), 173–189.

Cognitive Behavioral Therapy for Eating Disorders

G. Terence Wilson

Abstract

Cognitive behavior therapy (CBT) is the most effective treatment of bulimia nervosa (BN) and binge eating disorder (BED). Initial findings with eating disorder not otherwise specified (EDNOS) other than BED promise similar outcomes. Options for improving upon the efficacy and efficiency of CBT are discussed, primarily by incorporating an expanded range of principles and clinical strategies from CBT in general. Fairburn's (2008) enhanced CBT provides an illustration. Dissemination of CBT is poor. Guided self-help based on CBT principles is effective for a subset of patients with BN and BED and provides the means for making evidence-based treatment available to a wider range of patients. There is scant research on CBT for anorexia nervosa, and evidence of efficacy is lacking.

Keywords: bulimia nervosa, cognitive–behavioral therapy, evidence-based treatment, guided self-help

Introduction

The American Psychiatric Association's (1994) *Diagnostic and Statistical Manual of Mental Disorders (DSM-IV)* lists anorexia nervosa (AN) and bulimia nervosa (BN) as the two major eating disorders (EDs). Patients with an ED who do not meet criteria for either AN or BN can be diagnosed as "eating disorder not otherwise specified" (EDNOS) in the *DSM-IV* classification system. The Appendix of *DSM-IV* provides provisional diagnostic criteria for binge eating disorder (BED), which has been the most intensively researched disorder within the EDNOS category to date. Cognitive behavioral therapy (CBT) has been applied to the treatment of all of these EDs.

Bulimia Nervosa

The most widely used CBT approach for BN has been that derived from Fairburn's (1981) original formulation that was later formalized as a treatment manual (Fairburn, Marcus, & Wilson, 1993; Wilson, Fairburn, & Agras, 1997). This theory-driven, manual-based treatment is based on a cognitive–behavioral model of the psychopathological processes that are hypothesized to maintain the disorder. The core psychopathology is thought to be abnormal overconcern with the importance of body shape and weight that leads to dysfunctional dieting and other extreme, unhealthy weight-control behaviors such as purging. The dysfunctional dieting, in turn, predisposes the person to binge eating. Purging is also a function of the person trying to compensate for binges. The treatment consists of a series of interrelated and sequentially applied behavioral and cognitive strategies designed to enhance motivation for change: replace dysfunctional dieting with a regular and healthy pattern of eating; eliminate purging and other extreme forms of weight control; decrease overconcern with body shape and weight; and prevent relapse. Treatment typically has varied from 12 to 20 sessions of individual therapy over 4 to 5 months (Fairburn et al., 1993) although it has also been implemented effectively in a group format (Chen et al., 2003; Nevonen & Broberg, 2006).

Additional research on group CBT is warranted based on the promising preliminary findings to date and the prospect that the treatment will be more cost-effective than intensive individual therapy (Bailer et al., 2004).

Therapeutic Efficacy

The cognitive–behavioral model on which the manual-based treatment is based enjoys significant clinical and empirical support (Fairburn, 2008). The literature on treatment outcome has been repeatedly and extensively reviewed (e.g., American Psychiatric Association, 2006; National Institute for Clinical Excellence [NICE], 2004; Wilson & Fairburn, 2007; Shapiro et al., 2007; Wilson, Grilo, & Vitousek, 2007). Given the available evidence, it seems clear that manual-based CBT is currently the preferred therapy for BN. The rigorous, impartial, and comprehensive NICE guidelines concluded that manual-based CBT for BN was the treatment of choice for adults with BN. This clinical recommendation was given the grade of 'A,' reflecting strong empirical support from well-conducted randomized controlled trials (RCTs). The American Psychiatric Association practice guidelines similarly stated that CBT was "the most effective intervention" for BN (2006, p. 20).

Manual-based CBT has broad-based and enduring effects. It typically eliminates both binge eating and purging in roughly 30% to 50% of all cases in conservative intent-to-treat (ITT) statistical analyses using the state-of-the-art measure of therapeutic outcome, namely, the Eating Disorder Examination (EDE) which is a semi-structured interview with well-established reliability. Moreover, these ratings of remission using the EDE are based on a 4-week time period. This outcome measure is much more rigorous than a 1-week period based on patient self-report. Of the remaining patients, many show improvement whereas others drop out or fail to respond to treatment. CBT significantly decreases the patient's psychiatric comorbidity, enhances self-esteem, and improves social functioning. Therapeutic improvement is reasonably well maintained at 1-year follow-up. Consistent with the conceptual model on which manual-based CBT is based, reducing dietary restraint appears to be a partial mediator of treatment efficacy in eliminating binge eating and purging (Wilson, Fairburn, Agras, Walsh, & Kraemer, 2002). Importantly, manual-based CBT is more effective than treatment with antidepressant medication, which, itself, is an evidence-based treatment that is significantly superior to pill placebo

(NICE, 2004; Wilson & Fairburn, 2007). In contrast to CBT's enduring clinical effects, evidence of the long-term efficacy of antidepressant medication is still lacking. Manual-based CBT has also been shown to be significantly more effective than other psychological treatments with which it has been compared, at least in the short term (Wilson & Fairburn, 2007). For example, in the biggest and best controlled RCT of its kind, Agras et al. (2000) found that CBT was superior to interpersonal psychotherapy (IPT). Remission rates for both binge eating and purging were 29% and 6% respectively for the two treatments at post-treatment. The difference at 1-year follow-up was no longer statistically significant.

In general, robust predictors of treatment outcome in the treatment of BN have yet to be identified. A notable exception to this pattern has been early response to treatment. In the study mentioned above, Agras et al. (2000) found that early response—a significant reduction in purging by week 4—was a strong predictor of outcome at post-treatment (Fairburn, Agras, Walsh, Wilson, & Stice, 2004). a second large multisite study Agras et al. (2000) similarly showed that a 70% reduction in purging by session 6 (week 4) predicted therapeutic success or failure at post-treatment.

Problems with Dissemination

Despite the consistent evidence from research in both the United Kingdom and North America showing that manual-based CBT is the treatment of choice, this approach is relatively rarely adopted in routine clinical practice (Crow, Mussell, Peterson, Knopke, & Mitchell, 1999; Mussell et al., 2000; von Ranson & Robinson, 2006). The reasons for the failure to provide evidence-based treatments, including manual-based CBT, to patients with clinical disorders in general and EDs in particular, are many.

First, training in evidence-based treatments for BN and EDs more generally is not available in the United States for the many clinicians interested in acquiring the expertise (Wilson et al., 2007). We need to develop more efficient and effective ways of training therapists to deliver manual-based CBT. We also must ensure treatment integrity in dissemination (Perepletchikova, Treat, & Kazdin, 2007). Therapists may choose components of evidence-based treatment protocols based on their personal preferences, degree of familiarity with different techniques, or ease of implementation. The problem is that in so doing they might omit or undermine the most effective therapeutic elements (von Ranson & Robinson, 2006). Simply providing therapists with a manual is insufficient, as are 1- or 2-day workshops or training institutes. The scant research on clinical training shows that didactic introductory work needs to be followed up with supervised casework in which trainees receive feedback on how they perform specific skills.

Second, misconceptions that still abound regarding manual-based treatment may discourage some practitioners from adopting CBT. Misinformed critics erroneously allege that the findings from RCTs, which comprise the empirical foundation of manual-based CBT, do not—or cannot—generalize to clinical practice (Stirman, DeRubeis, Crits-Christoph, & Rothman, 2005). Contrary to some critics (e.g., Westen, Novotny, & Thompson-Brenner, 2004), efficacy studies of CBT have not excluded more complex, difficult-to-treat patients with high rates of psychiatric comorbidity (Fairburn, 2008; Wilson, 2007). The studies in question have more often than not included patients with severe psychopathology, high rates of psychiatric comorbidity, and histories of previously failed therapy (e.g., Agras et al., 2000). Indeed, the most common reason for screening out potential participants in RCTs is that the individual's problems are not severe enough to warrant inclusion. Moreover, the presence of psychiatric comorbidity does not necessarily predict a worse outcome as claimed by Westen et al. (2004) and others. For example, it is widely believed that personality disorders, and borderline personality disorder in particular, are associated with a worse treatment outcome (e.g., American Psychiatric Association, 2006; Westen et al., 2004). The evidence from RCTs, however, is inconsistent (NICE, 2004). In a large treatment outcome study, Rowe et al. (2008) found that borderline personality disorder had no impact on response to CBT. Moreover, a major prospective repeated-measures study of women with BN or EDNOS showed that over a time span of 5 years, the natural course of both BN and EDNOS was not "influenced significantly by the presence, severity, or time-varying changes of co-occurring PD psychopathology" (Grilo, Masheb, Brownell, & White, 2007, p. 738).

Despite these problems, there are promising indications about how manual-based CBT may be disseminated more widely. One innovation has been the demonstration that the treatment can be effectively delivered via telemedicine (Mitchell et al., 2008). Another has been the success of guided self-help programs.

Guided Self-Help

Competent administration of manual-based CBT requires therapeutic skill and training, in part because the protocol comprises multiple treatment strategies. An effective therapist must blend the focus and structure of the manual with flexibility in tailoring the treatment to the particular needs of the individual patient. The wider adoption of CBT would be advanced if the intervention were to be made briefer and less complex, thereby reducing the necessary training requirements. Guided self-help, based on the principles and procedures of CBT (CBTgsh), provides such an option; CBTgsh combines a self-help manual with a limited number of brief therapy sessions (Fairburn, 1995).

Several studies have shown that CBTgsh is effective with at least a subset of BN patients. In Australia, Banasiak, Paxton, and Hay (2005) reported that primary care physicians trained and supervised in CBTgsh obtained significantly superior results as compared with a delayed treatment control condition. The results were maintained at a 6-month follow-up, and rivalled the outcomes of more standard manual-based CBT. In Sweden Ljotsson et al. (2007) assigned BN patients the Fairburn (1995) self-help manual who, via e-mail contact with graduate clinical psychology students, received systematic guidance in completing the program. Patients were also given access to an online discussion forum. All patient contact was supervised by a clinical psychologist. The results were comparable with those obtained using formal manual-based CBT. In an analysis of a study completed in Germany, Hardy and Thiels (2009) showed that a self-help manual plus 8 biweekly sessions of CBT was as effective and 16 weekly sessions of CBT. Two findings are of note. The guided self-help showed more improvement during follow-up, and was more effective in patients with more severe problems.

Schmidt et al. (2007) compared family therapy (based on the Maudsley model) with guided self-help based on cognitive–behavioral principles using the Schmidt and Treasure (1997) manual in the treatment of adolescents (ages 13–20 years) with BN or EDNOS. The CBTgsh consisted of 10 weekly sessions, 3 monthly follow-up sessions, and 2 optional sessions with a "close other." Both treatments resulted in significant improvement in binge eating and purging at the end of treatment (6 months) and a follow-up at 12 months. Abstinence rates for binge eating and purging combined at 12 months were 36% for CBTgsh and 41% for family therapy. CBTgsh resulted in significantly more rapid reduction in binge eating. Moreover, CBTgsh was associated with greater acceptability and lower cost than family therapy. As the authors point out, the absence of a control group makes it difficult to attribute the results specifically to the treatment, although CBTgsh was more cost-effective than the comparison therapy.

Questions still remain regarding the level of training, degree of supervision, and type of setting that is needed for the effective implementation of CBTgsh (Sysko &Walsh 2007). Widely varying results have been reported across different studies. In contrast to the impressive outcomes summarized above, Bailer et al. (2004) in Germany reported that 18 sessions of CBTgsh using the Schmidt and Treasure (1997) manual resulted in a very low remission rate of 7.5% at post-treatment which improved to 22% at a 1-year follow-up. Therapists in this latter study were psychiatric residents with no previous experience in treating patients with an ED or training in psychological therapy. Walsh, Fairburn, Mickley, Sysko, and Parides (2004), employing minimally trained nurses for six to eight brief sessions of the Fairburn (1995) manual in a medical setting, found an unusually high attrition rate and little therapeutic effect.

It seems clear that inexperienced and unsupervised health care providers with minimal training in CBTgsh are ineffective. Nevertheless, even if successful CBTgsh requires specific therapist selection, training, and supervision, it would still provide a briefer, less costly, and more readily disseminable intervention to a wider range of health care providers than formal manual-based CBT. At the very least, as Perkins, Murphy, Schmidt, and Williams (2006) recommended, CBTgsh may be useful as a first intervention in a stepped-care framework. The first major study of the cost-effectiveness of CBTgsh with adults with BN within a stepped-care framework has yielded encouraging results (Crow, 2006). CBTgsh resulted in a substantially lower cost per effectively treated patient than regular manual-based CBT. Schmidt et al. (2007) similarly showed that CBTgsh for adolescents was as effective as family therapy, and was significantly less costly.

Improving the Efficacy of Treatment of Bulimia Nervosa

Manual-based CBT (Fairburn et al., 1993) is still insufficiently effective in helping the full range of BN patients who seek treatment. The immediate challenge is how to improve upon its existing efficacy. One plausible option would be to combine manual-based CBT with another evidence-based therapy—antidepressant medication, which received a methodological grade of B in the NICE (2004) guideline. However, this strategy has not proved reliably more effective in addressing specific ED psychopathology than CBT alone, although combined treatment may successfully address other comorbid psychopathology (e.g., depression; Fairburn & Wilson, 2007). An alternative approach, which has been used in other clinical disorders, would be to treat nonresponders to CBT with antidepressant medication. In a small pilot study of nonresponders to either manual-based CBT or IPT, fluoxetine proved significantly more effective than a pill placebo (Walsh et al., 2000).

A second possibility would be combining CBT with some other form of psychological treatment. "Psychotherapy integration" remains a popular notion. In the United States, this term usually denotes combining CBT with some form of psychodynamic therapy. For example, the American Psychiatric Association (2006) guidelines stated that "using psychodynamic interventions in conjunction with CBT and other psychotherapies may yield better global outcomes (e.g,. comorbidity and quality or life)" (p. 19). Research showing that some form of integrated psychotherapy is effective with BN, let alone more effective than manual-based CBT alone, is lacking. As has long been argued in the evaluation of psychotherapy (e.g., Kazdin, 1984), it would seem premature to try to integrate CBT with an empirically untested treatment. The active therapeutic elements of different treatments are largely unknown. Thus, attempts at integration might not only fail to enhance the efficacy of CBT, but might actually undermine its effects by diluting the focus on essential mechanisms and targets of change (Wilson et al., 2007).

The original Fairburn et al. (1993) treatment protocol represented a limited range of available CBT principles and procedures. Thus, it makes sense to expand the underlying cognitive behavioral model of the development and maintenance of BN, and to incorporate an expanded range of CBT techniques into the treatment protocol. These additional techniques are not only conceptually consistent with the existing manual but also have been demonstrated to be effective in the treatment of related clinical problems (e.g., anxiety, mood, and personality disorders) that are highly comorbid with BN. Accordingly, Wilson (1999) proposed "a form of manual-based CBT that included different modules that can be selectively applied to subsets of BN patients who have particular problem profiles that require more differentiated treatment. This will enhance therapeutic flexibility without sacrificing the structure and focus of manualized treatment" (p. 87).

Enhanced Cognitive Behavior Therapy

Fairburn (2008) has recently described what he calls "enhanced cognitive behaviour therapy (CBT-E) for all EDs. Essentially this is a second generation, manual-based intervention that is embedded within a transdiagnostic theory and treatment of EDs. In this approach, the focus is on the common processes that maintain different EDs as opposed to the traditional categorical diagnoses of *DSM-IV* (American Psychiatric Association, 2004). Treatment planning is guided not by matching therapy to different diagnoses, but by "personalized treatment formulations" (Fairburn, Cooper, & Shafran, 2008). This formulation underscores the importance of the functional analysis of individual cases—a seminal feature of behavior therapy since its inception.

Fairburn (2008) describes various forms of CBT-E for the full range of ED patients, including adolescents, and those who require inpatient treatment. The two main forms are a "focused" (CBT-Ef) and a "broad" treatment (CBT-Eb). The former is very similar to the earlier 1993 manual and is the default version in the current scheme. The major changes are twofold. First, a reformulated strategy and method for addressing dysfunctional body weight and shape concerns; and second, the addition of an explicit treatment module for what is called "mood intolerance" as a specific trigger of binge eating and purging. CBT-Eb is based on a broader model of the processes that are hypothesized to maintain BN, namely, perfectionism, low self-esteem, and interpersonal difficulties. It also incorporates an expanded range of strategies for treating these additional maintaining mechanisms.

A novel feature of both forms of CBT-E is the requirement that the therapist "take stock" or systematically reassess the success of the initial treatment plan early in the course of therapy (after the first seven sessions). The goal is to identity non-responders, and is based on the finding, discussed earlier in this chapter, that patients who do not show an early response to treatment are unlikely to improve. If the patient is progressing no modification in CBT-Ef need be made. However, if there is a lack of significant progress, the therapist needs to identify barriers to change and adjust treatment accordingly. For example, the focus of treatment might be shifted to one or more of the additional maintaining mechanisms included in CBT-Eb. This required early re-evaluation of the treatment plan is a distinguishing feature of CBT-E. In contrast, the evidence indicates that practitioners, including self-described behavior therapists, do not change course in the face of patient nonresponse (Kendall et al., 1992; Wilson 1998). Moreover, to the extent that practitioners change clinical strategies they tend to do so more on the basis of their personal clinical experience than available research evidence (Stewart & Chambless, 2008).

The ongoing assessment of patient progress or lack thereof in response to treatment, which is typically based on information derived from self-monitoring records, is a cardinal feature of CBT in general. One of the advantages of this assessment is that it provides an optimal means of blending the structure and focus of manual-based treatment with the flexibility needed to tailor the intervention to the particular patient's problems (Jacobson & Hollon, 1996; Wilson, 1996b). "Taking stock" and possibly revising the treatment formulation requires clinical judgment—not the unrestrained, subjective clinical judgment based primarily on the therapist's experience (von Ranson & Robinson, 2006; Wilson, 1996b)—but evidence-based judgment within the overall framework of CBT-E and in accordance with certain guidelines that are part of the treatment protocol. Nonetheless, this aspect of treatment necessarily requires specific expertise and clinical competence of the therapist—to a greater degree than in more prescriptive or less flexible manual-based interventions. Thus, therapist training and treatment integrity becomes more important than ever, and the manner in which therapists make these adjustments is worthy of future study.

Only one study to date has evaluated the efficacy of CBT-E. In a multisite RCT, Fairburn, Cooper, et al. (2009) compared CBT-Ef with CBT-Eb and a waiting list control condition in the treatment of 154 patients with BN or EDNOS. Only individuals with AN were excluded. Treatment lasted 20 weeks with a closed follow-up at 60 weeks. Several findings are of note. First, consistent with previous research on BN, the waiting list control condition showed little change. Second, both forms of CBT-E resulted in significant improvement at post-treatment and follow-up. More than half of the overall sample had a level of ED psychopathology, assessed via the EDE, less than one standard deviation above the community mean. The rate of remission from both binge eating and purging in the BN patients was 45.6% at follow-up, a figure higher than that obtained with the earlier version of CBT. Third, the response rate was very similar for both BN and EDNOS patients. The DSM-IV diagnoses were not moderators of treatment outcome. Fourth, exploratory moderator analyses indicated that CBT-Eb, as predicted, appeared to be more effective than CBT-Ef with patients characterized by at least two of the hypothesized maintaining mechanisms of mood intolerance, perfectionism, low self-esteem, and interpersonal difficulties. By contrast, the reverse pattern was obtained in the remaining patients. As the authors are quick to caution, this finding of a potential moderator should be viewed as tentative. Although the pattern was consistent over the course of the study, individual *p* values fell short of statistical significance. Whether CBT-E is more effective than the earlier version of manual-based CBT, and whether the focused versus broad form moderates treatment outcome must await replication and extension.

Ghaderi (2006) completed a preliminary study of what he called individualized CBT versus the original CBT manual (Fairburn et al., 1993). The individualized treatment was a modification of the Fairburn et al. (1993) manual based on the therapist's functional analysis of individual patients. This modified treatment focused more intensely on three particular mechanisms: interpersonal difficulties, affect regulation, and increased acceptance of emotions and thoughts. The result is some similarity to CBT-E. To use functional analysis in a manner that was replicable and less subject to criticism due to its possible idiosyncratic nature, Ghaderi (2006) adopted the guidelines of logical functional analysis as described by Hayes and Follete (1992). The results of this study showed that both treatments produced substantial improvement at post-treatment and at 6-month follow-up. The individualized treatment was significantly superior on some measures, including episodes of binge eating and body dissatisfaction.

Toward Increasing the Effectiveness of CBT
MOTIVATION

Engaging patients in therapy and enhancing motivation for change are key elements of CBT in general. They are particularly important in the treatment of patients with EDs who are commonly ambivalent about change if not actively resistant, as exemplified by AN (see later). In recent years, it has been increasingly proposed that we complement CBT with some additional approach designed to increase motivation such as motivational interviewing

(MI; Miller & Rollnick, 2002). This suggestion is based on the misconception that CBT is a somewhat narrow skills approach suitable for patients in the so-called action stage of change, but not for those in the initial precontemplation or contemplation stages who require more motivation to change (e.g., Tobin 2000). In fact, manual-based CBT explicitly focuses on engaging patients in the therapy and enhancing motivation (e.g., Vitousek Watson, & Wilson, 1998, Wilson et al., 1997), and has considerable conceptual and procedural overlap with MI (Wilson & Schlam, 2004).

Fairburn, Cooper, Shafran, Bohn, et al. (2008) declare that "*Competently* administered CBT-E is inherently motivating..." (p.49, italics added). A full analysis of this important topic is beyond the scope of this chapter. Suffice it to note briefly the core CBT strategies for enhancing motivation: (a) Case conceptualization in CBT includes providing patients with a model (understanding) of their problem and a rationale for addressing it which communicates the message that "Change is possible, and we have practical methods for achieving it" (Fennell, 2004). This includes education about the nature of the problem, conveyed not only by the therapist but also by guided reading (e.g., the Fairburn [1995] self-help book). (b) Self-monitoring can create a sense of agency (self-efficacy) that likely facilitates early symptomatic change (Wilson & Vitousek, 2000). As Fairburn, Cooper, Shafran, Bohn, et al. (2008) comment, "understanding one's problem and beginning to change" (p. 49) is especially motivating. (c) The active and collaborative therapeutic relationship that characterizes CBT which validates the patient within a framework of a commitment to change balanced by acceptance (Wilson & Schlam, 2004). It encourages and reinforces the patient. (d) Explicit and possibly repeated use of guiding the patient in exploring the pros and cons of change versus the status quo. (For details see Vitousek et al. [1998] and Wilson & Schlam [2004]). (e) "Resistance" to change becomes the focus of a functional or contextual analysis rather than a cause of confrontation. In this sense, it is similar to the MI principle of "rolling with resistance" (Wilson & Schlam, 2004). Confronted with a patient who is unwilling to adhere to treatment recommendations, "the therapist cannot resort to the client-blaming attribution that she is 'not ready' to change...the therapist's responsibility [is] to sort out why the patient is 'not ready,' and engage her in working together to resolve the problem" (Vitousek et al., 1998).

INTERPERSONAL PROBLEMS

"Interpersonal difficulties" is one of the hypothesized maintaining mechanisms of transdiagnostic CBT-Eb. The recommended treatment is IPT given that it has been shown to be effective in RCTs on BN and BED (see later) (Fairburn, 2008). The NICE guidelines assigned it a methodological grade of B. Elsewhere (Wilson, 1999) I have argued that assertion training is ideally suited to tackle many of the common interpersonal problems that patients with EDs experience. Several clinical considerations and empirical findings support its use. First, assertion training, one of the original strategies in the development of behavior therapy, is conceptually and procedurally compatible with CBT as a whole. Second, although it has not been specifically tested in a trial of ED patients, a substantial body of research dating back to the early 1970s (Franks & Wilson, 1974) has demonstrated that it is effective in reducing interpersonal conflict and self-defeating submissiveness, and increasing expressiveness and social effectiveness. There is no reason to believe that assertion training would not improve the interpersonal behavior and relationships of patients with EDs. Third, assertion training is a potent means of improving self-esteem. Self-esteem is another maintaining mechanism in CBT-Eb. Fourth, the goals of assertion training and IPT overlap extensively. Fifth, a user-friendly self-help text is readily available (Alberti & Emmons, 2001). And finally, assertion training is virtually identical to the "interpersonal effectiveness skills" training module that is a core feature of Linehan's (1993) dialectical behavior therapy (DBT) for borderline personality disorder. Dialectical behavior therapy has been shown to be a promising treatment both for BN (Safer, Telch, & Agras, 2001) and BED (Telch, Agras, & Linehan, 2001).

NEGATIVE AFFECT

"Mood intolerance" is one of the hypothesized maintaining mechanisms in CBT-E, and is therefore part of the default version (CBT-Ef) (Fairburn, Cooper, Shafran, Bohn, et al., 2008). The role of moods or emotional states as antecedants or triggers of binge eating and purging is widely recognized (e.g., Engelberg, Steiger, Gauvin, & Wonderlich, 2007; Hilbert & Tuschen-Caffier, 2007). It is suggested here that treatment should focus on the broader concept of negative affect that would include mood intolerance. Negative affect would refer to emotional states of anxiety, dysphoria or depression, anger, and frustration—and to varying mixtures of these states.

Subtyping women with BN as a function of dimensional measures of depressed mood (the Beck Depression Inventory]) and self-esteem (the Rosenberg Self-esteem Scale [Rosenberg, 1979]) on the one hand, and dietary restraint on the other, has proved to be a reliable and valid means of classification in clinical and community studies (Grilo, Masheb, & Berman, 2001; Stice & Agras, 1999; Stice, Bohon, Marti, & Fischer, 2008). The high negative affect subgroup show greater ED psychopathology, associated psychiatric problems, and functional impairment compared to those with low negative affect. Moreover, high negative affect predicts less improvement in response to treatment (Chen & le Grange, 2007; Stice & Agras, 1999) and a worse natural course (Stice et al., 2008; Stice & Fairburn, 2003). Stice et al. (2008) reported that this subtyping scheme had greater concurrent and predictive validity than using the *DSM-IV* based purging versus nonpurging distinction. The proportion of high negative affect individuals in these studies has ranged from 38% to 62%.

CBT incorporates several well-documented treatment strategies and techniques for addressing negative affect such as anxiety, anger, and depression. Among the various behavioral and cognitive methods are the strategies inherent in DBT, which is closely related to CBT (Wilson, 2004). In particular, the modules on mindfulness, distress tolerance, and emotion regulation are clearly well-matched to addressing negative affect in BN patients. Borderline personality disorder itself is a not uncommonly associated with EDs, suggesting that this intervention might have broad, transdiagnostic effects.

It is worth emphasizing that only some BN patients are characterized by high negative affect. Thus, treatments aimed at this problem would be used selectively. In contrast, in CBT-E, interventions aimed at mood intolerance would be part of the default approach.

ACCEPTANCE AND CHANGE

The potential value of DBT strategies for enhancing CBT is mentioned in the preceding text.

The relationship between behavior change and acceptance is the critical dialectic of DBT that represents an evolution from basic behavior therapy (Wilson, 2004). Acceptance is also a core concept of a related development that has been referred to as the "third wave" of behavior therapy, namely, ACT (Acceptance and Commitment Therapy; Hayes, Luoma, Bond, Masuda, & Lillis, 2006).

A focus on the balance between acceptance and change is directly applicable to treating disorders beyond the "third wave" approach to emotion regulation which proscribes experiential avoidance and emphasizes the need to experience feelings and thoughts without trying to suppress them. We have limited control over body weight, and virtually none over body shape barring cosmetic surgery. The goal of therapy is to help a patient make healthy changes in her eating patterns and nutrition, eat in moderation, and increase physical activity. The patient's resulting weight body must be accepted in lieu of engaging in extreme (unhealthy) attempts to alter body weight or shape. This guideline is captured by the Serenity Prayer: "God, give me the serenity to accept the things I cannot change, the courage to change the things I can, and the wisdom to know the difference" (Wilson, 1996a). Consider the findings from the study by Butryn, Lowe, Safer, and Agras (2006). They found that weight suppression—the discrepancy between a patient's highest adult weight ever and her present weight—predicted drop-out rate as well as remission from binge eating and purging at post-treatment. The finding held even when other potentially relevant variables (e.g., body mass index, dietary restraint, and body shape and weight concerns) were controlled. Butryn et al. (2006) concluded that patients high on weight suppression are more reluctant to abandon dietary restraint that has been shown to mediate, at least in part, the maintenance and modification of BN. Patients may be concerned that they will not lose weight, but they need to accept that their ideal weight might be unrealistic and cannot be obtained, at least not without causing severe emotional and possibly physical distress. Finally, another benefit of focusing on acceptance in relation to behavior change is that it impacts perfectionism. Greater self-acceptance is an antidote to fear of failure and biased evaluation based on rigid, self-defeating personal standards.

Scope and Focus of CBT

CBT-E "does not make much use of formal cognitive restructuring [nor]…certain widely used CBT concepts; specifically, automatic thoughts, assumptions, core beliefs and schemas." (Fairburn, Cooper, & Shafran, 2008, p. 27). In this sense, CBT-E has a different emphasis from some more cognitive approaches. The conventional cognitive restructuring method of challenging the validity of a belief by having the patient evaluate evidence for and against it works well if the belief can clearly be disconfirmed (e.g., "if I eat ice cream I will inevitably lose control and binge"). However, it is not well suited to addressing over-concern about body weight and

shape. In this case, the focus should be on the consequences of holding a particular belief or set of rigid rules. As Vitousek et al. (1998) argued, "A focus on functionality is indicated when clients' beliefs are highly valued, culturally shared, or delusional, so that evidence about their validity is unavailable or irrelevant. In these instances, a shift in focus to the utility of beliefs and associated behaviors may penetrate barriers that arguments about their correctness cannot breach…." (p. 408).

Consistent with this functional focus, recent developments within CBT ranging from behavioral activation (Addis & Martell, 2004) to mindfulness-based cognitive therapy (Segal, Teasdale, & Williams, 2005) and other "third wave" approaches have emphasized the importance of relating differently to specific thoughts rather than necessarily challenging their content. One of the key concepts in this general approach has been labeled "distancing" or "metacognitive awareness" which describes a cognitive set in which negative thoughts and feelings are seen "as passing events in the mind rather than as inherent aspects of self or as necessarily valid reflections of reality" (Teasdale et al., 2002).

Consider treating the pervasive feeling of distress among ED patients due to "feeling fat." Fairburn, Cooper, Shafran, Bohn, et al. (2008) comment that there "has been little research on feeling fat: Indeed, remarkably little has been written about it" (p. 113). The goal of training in metacognitive awareness is to help the patient see that her thoughts and feelings of "fatness" are "events of the mind" that come and go and do not reflect the reality of her body. Ideally, she would come to accept that feeling fat does not mean actually being fat; that she is a normal weight person who experiences thoughts or feelings that she is fat, and that these feelings will pass provided she thinks mindfully rather than ruminating about the thought.

Rumination is the cognitive tendency to focus repetitively on feelings of distress and the possible causes and consequences of these symptoms without engaging in active problem solving. Rumination about physical attractiveness predicts an increase in body image concerns, lack of acceptance of body shape and weight, dietary restraint, and purging over time (Clark & Wilson, 2005; Nolen-Hoeksema, Stice, Wade, & Bohon, 2007). The potential therapeutic value of focusing on rumination in ED patients is increased given the fact that rumination appears to be a common mechanism across diagnostic categories (Harvey, Watkins, Mansell, & Shafran, 2004). It is a well-established risk factor for depression (Nolen-Hoeksema, Wisco, & Lyubomirsky, 2008). Thus, treatments aimed at reducing rumination might facilitate clinical improvements in mood as well as body image concerns in patients with EDs. Addis and Martell (2004) have described behavioral treatment for overcoming rumination in which the patient monitors her thinking so as to become aware of rumination and its negative consequences, uses its occurrence to serve as a cue to action to change the context, and mindfully attends to what she is experiencing in her situation at that time. This intervention was part of the behavioral activation therapy shown to be an effective treatment for patients with severe depression (Dimidjian et al., 2006). In addition, Watkins et al. (2007) have reported promising early results using "rumination-focused cognitive behaviour therapy" in treating residual depression.

CAN LESS BE MORE?

Fairburn, Cooper, and Shafran (2008) state that in CBT-E "...simpler procedures are preferred over more complex ones; and....it is better to do a few things well than many things badly" (p. 27). Their own initial findings suggest that a simpler (more focused) intervention (CBT-Ef) may have been superior to a more expanded treatment (CBT-Eb) in "less complex" patients with BN and EDNOS (Fairburn et al., 2009). The putative superiority of a single, focused intervention should not be surprising. For example, in the treatment of anxiety disorders, Craske et al. (2007) showed that a single targeted treatment had more positive influences on co-occurring disorders than multiple targeted treatments. Ultimately, the optimal matching of the scope of treatment to specific disorders will hinge on an improved understanding of the mechanisms that maintain psychopathology and account for the success of particular therapies.

It might well be that CBT-Eb is required for patients with more complex problems as Fairburn et al. (2009) suggest. However, it should not be assumed from this that the more difficult patient necessarily requires more a broader, multimodal treatment approach. For example, based on the treatment of severe depression, Coffman, Martell, Dimidjian, Gallop, and Hollon (2007) concluded that especially difficult patients may benefit from a sustained focus on more limited goals. They propose using fewer intervention strategies and targeting fewer areas of change—the antithesis of a multimodal approach aimed at multiple maintaining mechanisms. It is entirely plausible that a "pure"

form of BN (without the additional maintaining mechanisms detailed in CBT-Eb) might prove resistant to treatment not because of co-occurring problems, but as a result of a particularly intense fear of weight gain that is the obstacle to adopting less dysfunctional eating patterns. As Coffman et al. (2007) proposed, the necessary treatment in this case might be a sustained attempt to overcome this specific fear. Instead of switching targets or tactics, therapy might most usefully implement the basic, focal treatment more systematically (Vitousek et al., 1998).

Increasing the Generalizability of CBT

The available evidence, although relatively sparse, suggests that the results from efficacy trials of manual-based CBT can generalize to different clinical service settings. Tuschen-Caffier, Pook, and Frank (2001) obtained favorable results in treating an unselected sample of adult BN patients in a clinical service setting. The Fairburn et al. (2009) study described above imposed few inclusion criteria in their clinically relevant sample of BN and EDNOS patients drawn from two catchment area clinics. Similarly, Schmidt et al. (2007) conducted their research in a catchment-area-based setting where "all comers were taken."

Encouraging also are the preliminary findings of a study of the effect of ethnicity on treatment outcome in BN (Chui, Safer, Bryson, Agras, & Wilson, 2007). In a reanalysis of the data from the Agras et al. (2000) study, across all ethnic groups, CBT showed significantly greater abstinence rates compared with IPT. Although caution must be had in interpreting these findings given the small number of minority participants, the pattern is consistent with the original Agras et al. (2000) report that manual-based CBT is the preferred treatment for BN. Replication and extension of these results with diverse patient groups in different setting remains a research priority.

It is well established that EDNOS is the most common ED encountered in clinical settings (Fairburn, Cooper, et al., 2007). EDNOS does not differ from BN in its nature, severity, or course. Yet it has been neglected in research on treatment. Hence it is of considerable importance that two major studies of CBT described above that included cases of EDNOS found that this neglected diagnostic category responded as well to CBT as traditionally defined BN. The implications of these findings are clear: manual-based CBT, especially Fairburn's (2008) CBT-E, is broadly applicable and effective with the majority of ED cases seen in outpatient clinical service settings.

Binge Eating Disorder

The standard CBT treatment for binge eating disorder (BED) has been the same as the Fairburn et al. (1993) manual described. Although the manual was developed primarily for treating BN, it contained modifications designed for application to binge eating in obese patients.

Therapeutic Efficacy

Manual-based CBT has been the most intensively studied form of psychological treatment of BED. The NICE (2004) guidelines concluded that CBT is currently the treatment of choice for BED. This clinical recommendation was assigned a methodological grade of A, indicating strong empirical support from RCTs. Research has consistently shown that manual-based CBT produces remission rates in binge eating between 60% and 70% that are generally well-maintained at a 1-year follow-up. The treatment also reliably results in reductions in specific ED and general psychopathology that are generally maintained at a 1-year follow-up. Manual-based CBT, however, does not produce clinically significant improvement in body weight (Brownley, Berkman, Sedway, Lohr, & Bulik, 2007; Wilson et al., 2007). It should be noted that the patients in these studies typically have significant comorbid psychiatric disorders and psychosocial problems.

CBT VERSUS PHARMACOTHERAPY

A recent meta-analysis shows that pharmacological treatment is significantly more effective than pill placebo in producing remission from binge eating (48.7% vs. 28.5%), although there have been no evaluations of the longer-term effects of pharmacotherapy (Reas & Grilo, 2008). Accordingly, this evidence-based treatment provides a useful standard of comparison for CBT.

Although the data are sparse, CBT to date has been shown to be superior to pharmacological therapy. Grilo, Masheb, and Wilson (2005) found that CBT was significantly more effective than either fluoxetine or pill placebo with remission rates of 61% for CBT plus pill placebo compared with 22% for fluoxetine. Critics, however, might point out that fluoxetine did not differ from pill placebo in this study. Devlin et al. (2005) reported that combining CBT with behavioral weight loss (BWL) treatment was more effective in reducing binge eating than adding fluoxetine to BWL, which had no incremental effect on outcome. Similarly, Ricca et al. (2001) showed that CBT was significantly superior to both fluoxetine and fluvoxamine in an open label study.

CBT VERSUS ALTERNATIVE PSYCHOLOGICAL THERAPIES

Two studies have compared manual-based group CBT with group IPT (Wilfley et al., 1993, 2002). In the second of these studies, one of the largest and best controlled in the literature on BED, Wilfley et al. (2002) obtained remission rates of 79% and 73% for CBT and IPT respectively at post-treatment, and 59% and 62% at a 1-year follow-up. Clinically significant reductions in body shape and weight concerns and associated psychopathology were obtained at follow-up. A striking finding of this study was that the two treatments were indistinguishable in terms of their impact on binge eating and all other outcome measures. This equivalence contrasts sharply with the findings with BN (Agras et al., 2000). Consistent with results from other studies, Wilfley et al. (2002) found that patients who had ceased binge eating had lost significantly more weight at follow-up (−2.4 kg) than those who did not (+2.1 kg).

CBT VERSUS BEHAVIORAL WEIGHT LOSS TREATMENT

Initial studies comparing CBT with behavioral weight loss (BWL) in the treatment of BED found similar effects on binge eating in the short term (Agras et al., 1994). Obesity researchers who included measures of binge eating in studies on obesity treatment concluded that BWL was effective and that there was no need for specialty psychological therapies such as CBT (Gladis et al., 1998; Stunkard & Allison, 2003). They claimed that all treatments produced roughly comparable, nonspecific outcomes in the treatment of BED. However, limitations of these studies included small sample sizes and self-report measures of binge eating rather than the more reliable and valid EDE (Wilfley, Wilson, & Agras, 2003). More recent, better controlled research has revealed treatment-specific effects of CBT.

Grilo et al. (2007) compared CBT, BWL, and a sequential CBT plus BWL treatment in obese patients with BED. At post-treatment CBT had a significantly greater binge eating remission rate (60%) than BWL (31%). At the 1-year follow-up the rates were 51% and 36% respectively. Predictably, at post-treatment weight loss in BWL (2.6%) was greater than in CBT (0.5%), but at follow-up the percentages did not differ (CBT = 0.9%; BWL = 2.1%). One of the noteworthy findings of this study was the disappointing outcome of the combined CBT+ BWL group which received 10 months of treatment as compared with 6 months for CBT and BWL alone. The post-treatment remission rate for binge eating was only 49%, which is less than that of CBT alone. Moreover, percentage weight loss was 2.6%, which is the same as BWL alone. At the 1-year follow-up, the percentage weight loss was a mere 1.5%.

In Switzerland, Munsch et al. (2007) compared 16 weekly sessions of CBT with BWL for obese patients with BED. CBT was significantly more effective than BWL in producing remission from binge eating. Similarly, BWL resulted in greater albeit modest weight loss than CBT. At a 12-month follow-up differences between the two treatments were no longer statistically significant. Finally, as noted above, Devlin et al. (2005) showed that adding CBT to BWL resulted in significantly greater reduction in binge eating than the same BWL plus antidepressant medication. The superiority of specialized CBT over BWL in these recent studies is plausibly attributable to the inclusion of more complex patients with the full BED diagnoses and with higher levels of psychiatric comorbidity than would typically be seen in obese patients seeking help for weight loss.

Predictors of Treatment Outcome

Manual-based CBT for BED results in more successful outcomes in the treatment of BED than BN. Nevertheless, there is still room for improvement. Identifying predictors and, ideally, moderators of therapeutic change would allow for the development of more targeted and possibly effective treatments.

As in the case of BN, rapid response to treatment has been found to be a clinically significant predictor of treatment outcome. Grilo, Masheb, and Wilson (2006) found that rapid response had different prognostic significance and time courses across different treatments for BED. Rapid response predicted remission rates of 73% for manual-based CBT versus 46% for fluoxetine. Rapid response to CBT predicted improvement that was sustained or even improved further during the remaining course of treatment. In contrast, when rapid response occurred in pharmacotherapy, some of the improvement tended to be lost although it was reasonably maintained during the remaining treatment course. Clinically important findings were observed for patients without a rapid response to treatment. In CBT, patients without a rapid response showed a subsequent pattern of continued improvement throughout treatment although it did not reach the very high levels of improvement achieved by the rapid responders. Clinically, these findings suggest that continuing CBT—rather than switching to another intervention—may be best. Eldredge et al. (1997) found that extending CBT for initial nonresponders was an effective option. The absence of a rapid response to antidepressant pharmacotherapy for BED suggests that the patient is quite unlikely to eventually respond to that medication and may suggest the need to try a different intervention.

In another parallel finding of BED to BN, degree of negative affect has been shown to be a reliable basis for subtyping BED patients, superior to that of subtyping based on DSM-IV diagnosis of depression (Grilo, Masheb, & Wilson, 2001). There is also evidence that patients high in negative affect fare less well in response to treatment (Stice et al., 2001).

Dissemination

Not unlike the case for BN, evidence-based treatments for BED such as CBT are rarely made available to obese patients seeking treatment from physicians (Crow, Peterson, Levine, Thuras, & Mitchell, 2004) or mental health professionals. The reasons are no doubt the same, including the lack of adequate training in manual-based CBT and commensurate shortage of professionals with appropriate expertise and experience.

Guided Self-Help

The Fairburn (1995) self-help manual described above has also been used to treat BED with CBTgsh. The NICE guidelines assigned CBTgsh a methodological grade of B, recommending that it might be a good first-step treatment for many patients. Three more recent studies suggest that CBTgsh might warrant an even higher rating.

Grilo and Masheb (2005) compared CBTgsh using the Fairburn manual with a guided-help program for weight loss based on Brownell's (2000) LEARN manual and a control condition consisting of self-monitoring of eating designed to equate for the nonspecific influences of treatment. CBTgsh resulted in a 50% remission rate compared with less than 20% in either of the comparison conditions. Aside from demonstrating the value of a brief, focal treatment for binge eating, the superiority of CBTgsh over the self-help LEARN manual provides further evidence of the treatment-specific effects of CBT in general. In a second study from the same group of investigators, Grilo, Masheb, and Salant (2005) again demonstrated the efficacy of CBTgsh in eliminating binge eating in obese BED patients (a 52% remission rate). Adding the medication Orlistat (a non-centrally acting lipase inhibitor) to CBTgsh enhanced weight loss. Patients in the CBTgsh plus Orlistat condition were significantly more likely to achieve a 5% weight loss than participants receiving CBTgsh plus pill placebo.

In a large, multisite study, Wilfley, Wilson, Agras, and Bryson (2009) evaluated the comparative effects of CBTgsh with IPT and BWL in a sample of 205 overweight and obese patients. Both IPT and BWL consisted of 20 sessions of individual treatment administered over a 6-month period. CBTgsh comprised 10 sessions over this period, nine of which had a maximum duration of 25 minutes. IPT was administered by intensively trained and supervised doctoral-level clinical psychologists, CBTgsh was provided by beginning graduate students in clinical psychology with little therapeutic experience. At post-treatment, ITT analyses revealed no differences among the three treatments on binge eating. The remission rates were as follows: IPT = 64%, BWL = 54%, and CBTgsh = 58%. Similarly, no differences were obtained on EDE subscales of eating concern, weight concern, or shape concern, as well as the BDI and self-esteem. Consistent with previous studies, BWL produced greater weight loss than either IPT or CBTgsh. Both CBTgsh and BWL had significantly greater attrition rates (30% and 28%) than IPT (7%). At the 2-year follow-up both CBTgsh and IPT not only successfully maintained their improvement but also were significantly superior to BWL which showed significant relapse. There were no differences in BMI across the three treatments. At no point did IPT differ from CBTgsh in terms of effectiveness on any of the outcome measures.

CBTgsh has also been evaluated in the treatment of patients with recurrent binge eating among a population of members of a large health Maintenance Organization in the United States (Striegel-Moore, Wilson, DeBar, et al., in press). Of the sample of 123 participants, 55 were diagnosed with BED and 56 with a frequency of binge eating once a week on average for the previous 3 months. Patients were randomly assigned to CBTgsh or Treatment-as-Usual (TAU) for eight individual sessions over a 12-week period. CBTgsh was based on the Fairburn (1995) manual supplemented by two self-help modules designed to modify excessive body-checking and body-avoidance behaviors as a means of addressing dysfunctional body shape and weight concerns. CBTgsh proved highly acceptable in this setting.

Of the full sample, 74% attended 7 or more sessions. Only 12% attended two or fewer treatment sessions. CBTgsh was significantly more effective than TAU in eliminating binge eating. Remission rates at 12 month follow-up were 64.2% and 44.6% respectively. CBTgsh was also more effective in producing greater improvement on specific measures of ED psychopathology, depression, and quality of life.

Given its brevity and advantages in disseminability to a wide range of health providers as compared with a specialty therapy that demands more extensive training and supervision, CBTgsh can be recommended as a cost-effective treatment of BED and recurrent binge eating.

PREDICTORS AND MODERATORS OF TREATMENT OUTCOME

Consistent with the evidence from full course CBT, both rapid response (Masheb & Grilo, 2007) and high negative affect (Masheb & Grilo, 2008) have been shown to be nonspecific predictors of binge eating reduction in CBTgsh. In a replication of the Masheb and Grilo (2008) findings, Wilson et al. (2010) found that whereas high negative affect predicted reduction in binge eating, it did not predict remission from binge eating.

The only evidence to date for moderators of treatment outcome comes from the Wilson et al. (2010) study. Exploratory analyses showed that both self-esteem and a composite score of the EDE subscales moderated treatment outcome at the 2-year follow-up. Low self-esteem undermined the effects of BWL in eliminating binge eating, but had no influence on IPT. CBTgsh was unaffected by low self-esteem in patients with low global EDE scores, but was substantially less effective in interaction with high EDE scores. The finding that global EDE moderated treatment outcome is consistent with a latent class analysis of the same sample of patients in which Sysko, Hildebrandt, Wilson, Wilfley, & Agras (2008) found four different latent classes within the sample. The class characterized by the most specific ED psychopathology (i.e., most severe objective and subjective bulimic episodes and highest body shape and weight concerns), which would be reflected in high global EDE scores, responded the most to IPT. CBTgsh was the most effective treatment for the "pure" binge eating class. Should these findings be replicated they would have important implications for future treatment. It may be that CBTgsh is the treatment of choice for that subset of BED patients defined mainly by binge eating. However, those patients with severe associated ED psychopathology, such as body shape and weight over-concern, would benefit from a specialty therapy like IPT or CBT. CBT-E has yet to be applied to BED patients, but as Fairburn, Cooper, and Waller (2008) propose, it might be well-suited to "those patients with obesity who have prominent ED psychopathology such as mood-triggered eating or extreme concerns about appearance" (p. 254).

Anorexia Nervosa

In contrast to BN and BED, there has been little controlled treatment research on AN. This absence of research is due to multiple factors, including the relative rarity of the disorder which makes it difficult to recruit sufficient numbers of research participants, and the challenge of treating patients who require long-term and even inpatient management (Agras et al., 2004). The different treatments that have been used with AN, including CBT, all received a methodological grade of C in the NICE guidelines with the single exception of the Maudsley method of family therapy.

In their review of the AN literature, Wilson et al. (2007) identified six controlled trials of CBT. Three of the studies failed to show greater efficacy of a CBT approach compared with alternative psychological treatments (Ball & Mitchell, 2004; Channon, de Silva, Hemsley, & Perkins, 1989; McIntosh et al., 2005). Across trials, the general pattern was for patients in most conditions to improve to some degree without achieving full recovery. Interpretation of these negative findings is complicated by the nature of the CBT treatments employed. None was consistent with the specifications of recommended treatments (e.g., Fairburn et al., 2003; Garner et al., 1997), and all comprised fewer treatment sessions than prescribed in the CBT literature. For example, McIntosh et al. (2005) compared CBT with IPT and a nonspecific supportive clinical management condition. Therapy consisted of 20 sessions over 5 months. Supportive clinical management was significantly more effective than IPT at post-treatment. CBT did not differ from either of the other treatments. Limitations of the study include not only the truncated length of therapy, but also the small sample size and high attrition rate (37%).

In the other three studies interpretation of the results is compromised by the ineffectiveness of the nonpsychological comparison treatments and relatively small sample sizes (Halmi et al., 2005; Pike, Walsh, Vitousek, Wilson, & Bauer, 2003; Serfaty, Turkington, Heap, Ledsham, & Jolley, 1999). For example, Halmi et al. (2005) compared manual-based

CBT with fluoxetine and a combined CBT/medication condition. The drop-out rate in the fluoxetine alone condition was so high that it was not possible to meaningfully evaluate the comparative effects of CBT.

The relative lack of well-controlled research on CBT for AN is surprising since a cognitive model of the maintenance and modification of the disorder has been available since the early 1980s (Garner & Bemis, 1982). Theoretically, CBT might be expected to be useful in treating AN. AN clearly shares core clinical features with BN, such as dysfunctional dietary restraint and concern with body shape and weight, which are successfully treated by manual-based CBT for BN. CBT in general has been shown to be effective in treating psychological problems that are distinctive clinical features of AN. One example is resistance to change. As discussed earlier, manual-based CBT provides well-developed strategies for enhancing motivation to change that have proved effective across a wide range of problems (Wilson & Schlam, 2004). The specific adaptation of CBT principles for overcoming resistance to change in AN has been detailed by Vitousek et al. (1998).

CBT-E remains to be evaluated. Fairburn, Cooper, Shafran, Bohn, et al. (2008) provide detailed guidelines for coping with low weight and insufficient eating, and strategies for overcoming resistance to weight gain, which is a feature that characterizes this disorder. These guidelines are to be used in conjunction with the rest of the core CBT-E protocol that is applicable to all clinical EDs.

Future Directions

The treatment of BN and EDNOS will be increasingly improved by drawing on developments in CBT in general. It is not unreasonable to predict that CBT will continue to become more effective, versatile, and applicable to a wider range of patients. A key to greater efficacy and efficiency of treatment will be a better understanding of the mechanisms of change in our current interventions (Murphy, Cooper, Hollon, & Fairburn, 2009; Wilson, 2010).

Dissemination of CBT to general clinical services has been disappointing, as summarized in the preceding text. The tide is beginning to change, however. The increased adoption of CBT by clinical practitioners in the coming years will also provide valuable feedback to researchers on the limits of efficacy studies and guidance on how existing protocols can be made more adaptable. Ultimately, it is vital to encourage a two-way street between clinical research and practice.

CBT will become increasingly available via innovative, computer-assisted applications. Internet-based CBT will feature more prominently in the future as a cost-effective means of making treatment available to individuals in areas with limited access to evidence-based psychological services (Andersson, 2009).

Developing effective treatment for AN will remain a challenge. Adequate evaluation of individual manual-based treatment for adolescents, in comparison with family-based intervention, is a priority (Wilson et al., 2007). Developmental research is needed to begin identifying effective treatments for chronic, adult cases of AN. Full-scale RCTs are ill-suited to research on this treatment-resistant population (Halmi et al., 2005).

References

Addis, M. E., & Martell, C. (2004). *Overcoming depression one step at a time.* Oakland, CA: New Harbinger.

Agras, W. S., Brandt, H. A., Bulik, C. M., Dolan-Sewell, R., Fairburn, C. G., Halmi, K. A., et al. (2004). Report of the National Institute of Health Workshop on Overcoming Barriers to Treatment Research in Anorexia Nervosa. *International Journal of Eating Disorders, 35*, 509–521.

Agras, W. S., Crow, S. J., Halmi, K. A., Mitchell, J. E., Wilson, G. T., & Kraemer, H. (2000). Outcome predictors for the cognitive-behavioral treatment of bulimia nervosa: Data from a multisite study. *American Journal of Psychiatry, 157*, 1302–1308.

Agras, W. S., Telch, C. F., Arnow, B., Eldredge, K., Wilfley, D. E., Raeburn, S. D., et al. (1994). Weight loss, cognitive-behavioral, and desipramine treatments in binge eating disorder: An additive design. *Behavior Therapy, 25*, 225–238.

Agras, W. S., Walsh, B. T., Fairburn, C. G., Wilson, G. T., & Kraemer, H. C. (2000). A multicenter comparison of cognitive-behavioral therapy and interpersonal psychotherapy for bulimia nervosa. *Archives of General Psychiatry, 57*, 459–466.

Alberti, R., & Emmons, M. (2001). *Your perfect right.* Atascadero, CA: Impact Publishers.

American Psychiatric Association (1994). *Diagnostic and statistical manual of mental disorders.* Washington, DC: American Psychiatric Association.

American Psychiatric Association (2006). Practice guideline for treatment of patients with eating disorders (third edition). *American Journal of Psychiatry, 163*, 4–54.

Andersson, G. (2009). Using the internet to provide cognitive behaviour therapy. *Behaviour Research and Therapy, 47*, 175–180.

Bailer, U., de Zwaan, M., Leisch, F., Strand, A., Lennkh-Wolfsber, C., El-Giamal, N., et al. (2004). Guided self-help versus cognitive-behavioral group therapy in the treatment of bulimia nervosa. *International Journal of Eating Disorders, 35*, 522–537.

Ball, J., & Mitchell, P. (2004). A randomized controlled study of cognitive behavior therapy and behavioral family therapy for anorexia nervosa patients. *Eating Disorders, 12*, 303–314.

Banasiak, S. J., Paxton, S. J., & Hay, P. (2005). Guided self-help for bulimia nervosa in primary care: A randomized controlled trial. *Psychological Medicine, 35*, 1283–1294.

Brownley, K. A., Berkman, N. D., Sedway, J. A., Lohr, K. N., & Bulik, C. M. (2007). Binge eating disorder treatment: A systematic review of randomized controlled trials. *International Journal of Eating Disorders, 40*, 337–348.

Burton, E., & Stice, E. (2006). Evaluation of a healthy-weight treatment program for bulimia nervosa: A preliminary randomized trial. *Behaviour Research and Therapy, 44*, 1727–1738.

Butryn, M. L., Lowe, M. R., Safer, D. L., & Agras, W. S. (2006). Weight Suppression is a robust predictor of outcome in the cognitive-behavioral treatment of bulimia nervosa. *Journal of Abnormal Psychology, 115*, 62–67.

Channon, S., de Silva, P., Hemsley, D., & Perkins, R. (1989). A controlled trial of cognitive-behavioural and behavioural treatment of anorexia nervosa. *Behaviour Research and Therapy, 27*, 529–535.

Chen, E., Touyz, S. W., Beumont, P., Fairburn, C. G., Griffiths, R., Butow, P., et al. (2003). Comparison of group and individual cognitive-behavioral therapy for patients with bulimia nervosa. *International Journal of Eating Disorders, 33*, 241–254.

Chui, W., Safer, D., Bryson, S., Agras, W. S., & Wilson, G. T. (2007). A comparison of ethnic groups in the treatment of bulimia nervosa. *Eating Behaviors, 8*, 485–491.

Coffman, S., Martell, C., Dimidjian, S., Gallop, R., & Hollon, S. (2007). Extreme non-response in cognitive therapy: Can behavioral activation succeed where cognitive therapy fails? *Journal of Consulting and Clinical Psychology, 75*, 531–541.

Craske, M., Farchione, T. J., Allen, L. B., Barrios, V., Stoyanova, M., & Rose, R. (2007). Cognitive behavioral therapy for panic disorder and comorbidity: More of the same or less of more? *Behaviour Research and Therapy, 45*, 1095–1109.

Crow, S. (2006). *Cost effectiveness of stepped care treatment for bulimia nervosa.* Paper presented at the Eating Disorders Research Society, Port Douglas, Australia, August 31.

Crow, S. J., Mussell, M. P., Peterson, C. B., Knopke, A., & Mitchell, J. E. (1999). Prior treatment received by patients with bulimia nervosa. *International Journal of Eating Disorders, 25*, 39–44.

Crow, S. J., Peterson, C., Levine, A. S., Thuras, P., & Mitchell, J. E. (2004). A survey of binge eating and obesity treatment practices among primary care providers. *International Journal of Eating Disorders, 35*, 348–353.

Devlin, M. J., Goldfein, J. A., Petkova, E., Jiang, H., Raizman, P. S., Wolk, S., Mayer, L., Carino, J., Bellace, D., Kamenetz, C., Dobrow, I., & Walsh, B. T. (2005). Cognitive behavioral therapy and fluoxetine as adjuncts to group behavioral therapy for binge eating disorder. *Obesity Research, 13*, 1077–1088.

Dimidjian, S., Hollon, S. D., Dobson, K. S., Schmaling, K. B., Kohlenberg, R. J., Addis, M. E., et al. (2006). Behavioral activation, cognitive therapy and anti-depressant medication in the acute treatment of major depression. *Journal of Consulting and Clinical Psychology, 74*, 658–670.

Eldredge, K. L., Agras, W. S., Arnow, B., Telch, C. F., Bell, S., Castonguay, L., & Marnell, M. (1997). The effects of extending cognitive-behavioral therapy for binge eating disorder among initial treatment nonresponders. *International Journal of Eating Disorders, 21*, 347–352.

Engelberg, M. J., Steiger, H., Gauvin, L., & Wonderlich, S. (2007). Binge antecedents in bulimic syndromes: An examination of dissociation and negative affect. *International Journal of Eating Disorders, 40*, 531–536.

Fairburn, C. G. (1981). A cognitive behavioural approach to the management of bulimia. *Psychological Medicine, 11,* 707–711.

Fairburn, C. G. (1995). *Overcoming binge eating.* New York: Guilford Press.

Fairburn, C. G. (2008*). Cognitive behavior therapy and eating disorders.* New York: Guilford Press.

Fairburn, C. G., Agras, W. S., Walsh, B. T., Wilson, G. T., & Stice, E. (2004). Prediction of outcome in bulimia nervosa by early change in treatment. *American Journal of Psychiatry, 161,* 2322–2324.

Fairburn, C. G., Cooper, Z., Bohn, K., O'Connor, M. E., Doll, H. A., & Palmer, R. L. (2007). The severity and status of eating disorder NOS: Implications for DSM-V. *Behaviour Research and Therapy, 45,* 1705–1715.

Fairburn C. G., Cooper Z., Doll H. A., O'Connor M. E., Bohn K., Hawker D. M., Wales J. A., & Palmer R. L. (2009). Transdiagnostic cognitive behavioral therapy for patients with eating disorders: A two-site trial with 60-week follow-up. *American Journal of Psychiatry 2009, 166,* 311–319.

Fairburn, C. G., Cooper, Z., & Shafran, R. (2008). Enhanced cognitive behavior therapy for eating disorders ("CBT-E"): An overview. In C. G. Fairburn (Ed.), *Cognitive behavior therapy and eating disorders* (pp. 23–34). New York: Guilford Press.

Fairburn, C. G., Cooper, Z., Shafran, R., Bohn, K., & Hawker, D. M. (2008). Clinical perfectionism, core low self-esteem and interpersonal problems. In C. G. Fairburn (Ed.), *Cognitive behavior therapy and eating disorders* (pp. 197–220). New York: Guilford Press.

Fairburn, C. G., Cooper, Z., Shafran, R., Bohn, K., Hawker, D. M., Murphy, R., & Straebler, S. (2008). Enhanced cognitive behavior therapy for eating disorders: The core protocol. In C. G. Fairburn (Ed.), *Cognitive behavior therapy and eating disorders* (pp. 47–193). New York: Guilford Press.

Fairburn, C. G., Cooper, Z., & Waller, D. (2008). "Complex cases" and comorbidity In C. G. Fairburn (Ed.), *Cognitive behavior therapy and eating disorders* (pp. 245–260). New York: Guilford Press.

Fairburn, C. G., Marcus, M. D., & Wilson. G. T. (1993). Cognitive behaviour therapy for binge eating and bulimia nervosa: A comprehensive treatment manual. In C. G. Fairburn & G. T. Wilson (Eds.), *Binge eating: Nature, assessment and treatment* (pp. 361–404). New York: Guilford Press.

Fennell, M. (2004). Depression, low self-esteem, and mindfulness. *Behaviour Research and Therapy, 42,* 1053–1069.

Franks, C. M., & Wilson, G. T. (1974). *Annual review of behavior therapy: Theory and practice,* (Vol. 2.) New York: Brunner/Mazel.

Garner, D. M., & Bemis, K. M. (1982). A cognitive-behavioral approach to anorexia nervosa. *Cognitive Therapy and Research, 6,* 123–150.

Garner, D. M., Vitousek, K., & Pike, K. M. (1997). Cognitive behavioral therapy for anorexia nervosa. In D. M. Garner & P. E. Garfinkel (Eds.) *Handbook of treatment for eating disorders* (2nd ed.) (pp. 91–144). Chichester: Wiley.

Ghaderi, A. (2006). Does individualization matter? A randomized trial of standardized (focused) versus individualized (broad) cognitive behavior therapy for bulimia nervosa. *Behaviour Research and Therapy, 44,* 273–288.

Gladis, M. M., Wadden, T. A., Vogt, R., Foster, G., Kuehl, R. H., & Bartlett, S. J. (1998). Behavioral treatment of obese binge eaters: Do they need different care? *Journal of Psychosomatic Research, 44,* 375–384.

Grilo, C. M., Hrabosky, J. I., White, M. A., Allison, K., Stunkard, A. J., & Masheb, R. M. (2008). Overvaluation of shape and weight in binge eating disorder and overweight controls: Refinement of BED as a diagnostic construct. *Journal of Abnormal Psychology, 117,* 414–419.

Grilo, C. M., & Masheb, R. M. (2005). A randomized controlled comparison of guided self-help cognitive behavioral therapy and behavioral weight loss for binge eating disorder. *Behaviour Research & Therapy, 43*:11, 1509–1525.

Grilo, C. M., Pagano, M. E., Skodol, A. E., Sanislow, C. A., McGlashan, T. H. Gunderson, J. G., & Stout, R. L. (2007). Natural course of bulimia nervosa and eating disorder not otherwise specified: 5-year prospective study of remissions, relapses, and the effects of personality disorder psychopathology. *Journal of Clinical Psychiatry, 68,* 738–746.

Grilo, C. M., Masheb, R., & Salant, S. (2005). CBT guided self-help and orlistat for treatment of binge eating: Randomized double-blind placebo-controlled trial. *Biological Psychiatry, 57,* 1193–1201.

Grilo, C. M., Masheb, R., & Wilson, G. T. (2001). Subtyping binge eating disorder. *Journal of Consulting and Clinical Psychology, 69,* 1066–1072.

Grilo, C. M., Masheb, R., & Wilson, G. T. (2005). Efficacy of cognitive behavioral therapy and fluoxetine for the treatment of BED: Randomized double-blind placebo-controlled trial. *Biological Psychiatry, 57,* 301–309.

Grilo, C. M., Masheb, R. M., & Wilson, G. T. (2006). Rapid response to treatment for binge eating disorder. *Journal of Consulting and Clinical Psychology, 74,* 602–613.

Grilo, C. M., Pagano, M. E., Skodol, A. E., Sanislow, C. A., McGlashan, T. H. Gunderson, J. G., & Stout, R. L. (2007). Natural course of bulimia nervosa and eating disorder not otherwise specified: 5-year prospective study of remissions, relapses, and the effects of personality disorder psychopathology. *Journal of Clinical Psychiatry, 68,* 738–746.

Halmi, K. A., Agras, W. S., Crow, S., Mitchell, J., Wilson, G. T., Bryson, S. W., & Kraemer, H. C. (2005). Predictors of treatment acceptance and completion in anorexia nervosa: Implications for future study designs. *Archives of General Psychiatry, 62,* 776–781.

Hardy, S.A., & Thiels, C. (2009). Using latent growth curve modeling in clinical treatment research: An example comparing guided self-change and cognitive behavioral therapy treatments for bulimia nervosa. *International Journal of Clinical and Health Psychology, 9,* 51–71.

Harvey, A., Watkins, E., Mansell, W. & Shafran, R. (2004). *Cognitive behavioural processes across psychological disorders: A transdiagnostic approach to research and treatment.* Oxford: Oxford University Press.

Hayes, S. C., & Follette, W. C. (1992). Can functional analysis provide a substitute for syndromal classification? *Behavioral Assessment, 14,* 345–365.

Hayes, S. C., Luoma, J. B., Bond, F. W., Masuda, A., & Lillis, J. (2006). Acceptance and commitment therapy: Model, processes and outcomes. *Behaviour Research and Therapy, 44,* 1–25.

Hilbert, A., & Tuschen-Caffier, B. (2007). Maintenance of binge eating through negative mood: A naturalistic comparison of binge eating disorder and bulimia nervosa. *International Journal of Eating Disorders, 40,* 521–530.

Jacobson, N. S., & Hollon S. D. (1996). Cognitive-behavior therapy versus pharmacotherapy: Now that the jury's returned its verdict, it's time to present the rest of the evidence. *Journal of Consulting and Clinical Psychology, 64:1*, 74–80.

Kazdin, A. E. (1984). Integration of psychodynamic and behavioral psychotherapies: Conceptual versus empirical syntheses. In H. Arkowitz & S. Messer (Eds.), *Psychoanalytic therapy and behavior therapy: Is integration possible?* (pp. 139–170). New York: Plenum Press.

Kendall, P., Kipnis, D., & Otto-Salaj, L. (1992). When clients don't progress: Influence on and explanations for lack of therapeutic progress. *Cognitive Therapy and Research, 16*, 269–282.

Linehan, M. M. (1993). *Skills training manual for treating borderline personality disorder*. New York: Guilford Press.

Ljotsson, B., Lundin, C., Mitsell, K., Carlbring, P., Ramklint, M., & Ghaderi, A. (2007). Remote treatment of bulimia nervosa and binge eating disorder: A randomized trial of Internet assisted cognitive behavioural therapy. *Behaviour Research and Therapy, 45*, 649–661.

Masheb, R. M., & Grilo, C. M. (2007). Rapid response predicts treatment outcomes in binge eating disorder: Implications for stepped care. *Journal of Consulting and Clinical Psychology, 75*, 639–644.

Masheb, R. M., & Grilo, C. M. (2008). Prognostic significance of two sub-categorization methods for the treatment of binge eating disorder: Negative affect and overvaluation predict, but do not moderate, specific outcomes. *Behaviour Research and Therapy, 46*, 428–437.

McIntosh, V. V. M., Jordan, J., Carter, F. A., Luty, S. E., Bulik, C. M., Frampton, C. M. A., & Joyce, P. R., (2005). Three psychotherapies for anorexia nervosa: A randomized, controlled trial. *American Journal of Psychiatry, 162:4*, 741–747.

Miller, W. R., & Rollnick, S. (2002). *Motivational interviewing. (2nd Ed.)* New York: Guilford Press.

Mitchell, J. E., Crosby, R. D., Wonderlich, S. A., Crow, S., Lancaster, K., Simonich, H., et al. (2008). A randomized trial comparing the efficacy of cognitive-behavioral therapy for bulimia nervosa delivered via telemedicine versus face-to-face. *Behaviour Research and Therapy, 46*, 581–592.

Munsch. S., Biedert, E., Meyer, A., et al. (2007). A randomized comparison of cognitive behavioral therapy and behavioral weight loss treatment for overweight individuals with Binge Eating Disorder. *International Journal of Eating Disorders, 40*, 02–13.

Murphy, R., Cooper, Z., Hollon, S., & Fairburn, C.G. (2009). How do psychological treatments work? Investigating mediators of change. *Behaviour Research and Therapy, 47*, 1–5.

Mussell, M. P., Crosby, R. D., Crow, S. J., Knopke, A. J., Peterson, C. B., Mitchell, J. E. (2000). Utilization of empirically supported psychotherapy treatments for individuals with eating disorders: A survey of psychologists. *International Journal of Eating Disorders, 27*, 230–237.

National Institute for Clinical Excellence (NICE). 2004. Eating Disorders—Core Interventions in the Treatment and Management of Anorexia Nervosa, Bulimia Nervosa and Related Eating Disorders. NICE Clinical. Guideline No. 9. London: NICE. www.nice.org.uk.

Nervonen, L., & Broberg, A. G. (2006). A comparison of sequenced individual and group psychotherapy for patients with bulimia nervosa. *International Journal of Eating Disorders, 39*, 117–127.

Nolen-Hoeksema, S., Stice, E., Wade, E., & Bohon, C. (2007). Reciprocal relations between rumination and bulimic, substance abuse, and depressive symptoms in female adolescents. *Journal of Abnormal Psychology, 116*, 198–207.

Nolen-Hoeksema, S., Wisco, B. E., & Lyubomirsky, S. (2008). Rethinking rumination. *Perspectives on Psychological Science, 3:5*, 400–424.

Perepletchikova, F., Treat, T., & Kazdin, A. E. (2007). Treatment integrity in psychotherapy research: Analysis of the studies and examination of the associated factors. *Journal of Consulting and Clinical Psychology, 75*, 829–841.

Perkins, S. J., Murphy, R., Schmidt, U., & Williams, C. (2006). Self-help and guided self-help for eating disorders. *Cochrane Database of Systematic Reviews, Issue 3*.

Pike, K. M., Walsh, B. T., Vitousek, K., Wilson, G. T., & Bauer, J. (2003). Cognitive behavior therapy in the posthospitalization treatment of anorexia nervosa. *American Journal of Psychiatry, 160:11*, 2046–2049.

Reas, D. L., & Grilo, C. M. (2008). Review and meta-analysis of pharmacotherapy for binge eating disorder. *Obesity, 16*, 2024–2038.

Ricca, V., Mannucci, E., Mezzani, B., Moretti, S., De Bernardo, M., Bertelli, M., et al. (2001). Fluoxetine and fluvoxamine combined with individual cognitive-behavioral therapy in binge eating disorder: A one-year follow-up study. *Psychotherapy and Psychosomatics, 70*, 298–306.

Rosenberg, M. (1979). *Conceiving of the self*. New York: Basic Books.

Rowe, S. L., Jordan, J., McIntosh, V., Carter, F. A., Bulik, C. M., & Joyce, P. R. (2008). Impact of borderline personality disorder on bulimia nervosa. *Australian and New Zealand Journal of Psychiatry, 42*, 1021–1029.

Safer, D. L., Telch, C. F., & Agras W. S. (2001). Dialectical behavior therapy for bulimia nervosa. *American Journal of Psychiatry, 158*, 632–34.

Schmidt, U., & Grover, M. (2007). Computer-based intervention for bulimia nervosa and binge eating. In: J. D. Latner & G. T. Wilson (Eds.), *Self-help approaches for obesity and eating disorders: Research and practice*. New York: Guilford Press.

Schmidt, U., Lee, S., Beecham, J., Perkins, S., Treasure, J., Yi, I., Winn, S., et al. (2007). A randomized controlled trial of family therapy and cognitive-behavioral guided self-care for adolescents with bulimia nervosa or related disorders. *American Journal of Psychiatry, 164*, 591–598.

Segal, Z. V., Teasdale, J. D., & Williams, M. (2004). Mindfulness-based cognitive therapy: Theoretical rationale and empirical status. In S. C. Hayes, V. M. Follette, & M. M. Linehan (Eds.), (pp. 45–65*). Mindfulness and acceptance: Expanding the cognitive-behavioral tradition*. New York: Guilford Press.

Serfaty, M. A., Turkington, D., Heap, M., Ledsham, L., & Jolley, E. (1999). Cognitive therapy versus dietary counselling in the outpatient treatment of anorexia nervosa: Effects of the treatment phase. *European Eating Disorders Review, 7*, 334–350.

Shapiro, J. R., Berkman, N. D., Brownley, K. A., Sedway, J. A., Lohr, K. N., & Bulik, C. M. (2007). Bulimia nervosa treatment: A systematic review of randomized controlled trials. *International Journal of Eating Disorders, 40:4*, 321–336.

Stewart, R. E., & Chambless, D. L. (2008). Treatment failures in private practice: How do psychologists proceed? *Professional Psychology: Research and Practice, 39*, 176–181.

Stice, E., & Agras, W. S. (1999). Subtyping bulimics along dietary restraint and negative affect dimensions. *Journal of Consulting and Clinical Psychology, 67*, 460–469.

Stice, E., Bohon, C., Marti, C. N., & Fischer, K. (2008). Subtyping women with bulimia nervosa along dietary and negative affect dimensions: Further evidence of reliability and validity. *Journal of Consulting and Clinical Psychology, 76*, 1023–1033.

Stice, E., & Fairburn, C. G. (2003). Dietary and dietary-depressive subtypes of bulimia nervosa show differential symptom presentation, social impairment, comorbidity and course of illness. *Journal of Consulting and Clinical Psychology, 71:6*, 1090–1094.

Stirman, S. W., DeRubeis, R. J., Crits-Christoph, P., & Rothman, A. (2005). Can the randomized controlled trial literature generalize to nonrandomized patients? *Journal of Consulting and Clinical Psychology, 73*, 127–135.

Striegel-Moore, R., Wilson, G. T., DeBar, L., Perrin, N., Lynch, F., Rosselli, F., & Kraemer, H. (in press). Guided self-help for the treatment of recurrent binge eating. *Journal of Consulting and Clinical Psychology.*

Stunkard, A.J., & Allison, K.C. (2003). Binge eating disorder: Disorder or marker? *International Journal of Eating Disorders, 34*, S107–S116.

Sysko, R., Hildebrandt, T., Wilson, G. T., Wilfley, D. E., & Agras, W.S. (2008) *An examination of the diagnostic classification and short-term course of binge eating disorder using latent class analysis.* Seattle, WA: Paper presented at the International Conference on Eating Disorders; May 16.

Sysko, R., & Walsh, B. T. (2007). Guided self-help for bulimia nervosa. In J. Latner & G. T. Wilson, (Eds.), *Self-help for obesity and binge eating* pp.92–117). New York: Guilford Press.

Teasdale, J. D., Moore, R. G., Hayhurst, H., Pope, M., Williams, S., & Segal, Z. V. (2002). Metacognitive awareness and prevention of relapse in depression: Empirical evidence. *Journal of Consulting and Clinical Psychology, 70:2*, 275–287.

Telch, C. F., Agras, W. S., & Linehan, M. M. (2001). Dialectical behavior therapy for binge eating disorder. *Journal of Consulting and Clinical Psychology, 69*, 1061–1065.

Tuschen-Caffier, B., Pook, M., & Frank, M. (2001). Evaluation of manual-based cognitive-behavioral therapy for bulimia nervosa in a service setting. *Behaviour Research Therapy, 39*, 299–308.

Vitousek, K. M., Watson, S., & Wilson, G. T. (1998). Enhancing motivation for change in treatment-resistant eating disorders. *Clinical Psychology Review, 18*, 391–420.

Von Ranson, K., & Robinson, K. (2006). Who is providing what type of psychotherapy to eating disorder clients? A survey. *International Journal of Eating Disorders, 39*, 27–34.

Walsh, B. T., Agras, W. S., Devlin, M. J., Fairburn, C. G., Wilson, G. T., Kahn, C., & Chally, M. K. (2000). Fluoxetine in bulimia nervosa following poor response to psychotherapy. *American Journal of Psychiatry, 157*, 1332–1333.

Walsh, B. T., Fairburn, C. G., Mickley, D., Sysko, R., & Parides, M. K. (2004). Treatment of bulimia nervosa in a primary care setting. *American Journal of Psychiatry, 161*, 556–561.

Watkins, E., Scott, J., Wingrove, J., Rimes, K., Bathurst, N., Steiner, H., et al. (2007). Rumination-focused cognitive behaviour therapy for residual depression: A case series. *Behaviour Research and Therapy, 45*, 2144–2154.

Westen, D., Novotny, C. M., & Thompson-Brenner, H. (2004). The empirical status of empirically supported psychotherapies: Assumptions, findings, and reporting in controlled clinical trials. *Psychological Bulletin, 130*, 631–663.

Wilfley, D. E., Agras, W. S., Telch, C. F., Rossiter, E. M., Schneider, J. A., Cole, A. G., et al. (1993). Group cognitive-behavioral therapy and group interpersonal psychotherapy for the nonpurging bulimic individual: A controlled comparison. *Journal of Consulting and Clinical Psychology, 61*, 296–305.

Wilfley, D. E., Welch, R. R., Stein, R. I., Spurrell, E. B., Cohen, L. R., Saelens, B. E., et al. (2002). A randomized comparison of group cognitive-behavioral therapy and group interpersonal psychotherapy for the treatment of overweight individuals with binge eating disorder. *Archives of General Psychiatry, 59*, 713–721.

Wilfley, D. E., Wilson, G. T., & Agras, W. S. (2003). The clinical significance of binge eating disorder. *Internationa.l Journal of Eating Disorders, 34*, 596–106.

Wilson, G. T. (1996a). Acceptance and change in the treatment of eating disorders and obesity. *Behavior Therapy, 27*, 417–439.

Wilson, G. T. (1996b). Manual-based treatments: The clinical application of research findings. *Behaviour Research and Therapy, 34*, 295–315.

Wilson, G. T. (1998). Manual-based treatment and clinical practice. *Clinical Psychology: Science and Practice, 5*, 363–375.

Wilson, G. T. (1999). Cognitive behavior therapy for eating disorders: Progress and problems. *Behaviour Research and Therapy, 37*, 579–596.

Wilson, G. T. (2004). Acceptance and change in the treatment of eating disorders: The evolution of manual-based cognitive behavioral therapy (CBT). In S. C. Hayes, V. M. Follette, & M. Linehan (Eds.), *Acceptance, mindfulness, and behavior change* (pp. 243–266). New York: Guilford Press.

Wilson, G. T. (2007). Manual-based treatment: Evolution and evaluation. In T. A. Treat, R. R. Bootzin, & T. B. Baker (Eds.), *Psychological clinical science: Papers in honor of Richard M. McFall* (pp. 105–123). Mahwah, NJ: Lawrence Erlbaum.

Wilson, G.T. (2010). What bulimia nervosa research is needed? In C. Grilo & J. Mitchell (Eds.), *The treatment of eating disorders.* New York: Guilford Press.

Wilson, G. T., & Fairburn, C. G. (2007). Eating disorders. In P. E. Nathan & J. M. Gorman (Eds.), *Treatments that work* (3rd ed., pp. 579–611). New York: Oxford University Press.

Wilson, G. T., Fairburn, C. G., & Agras, W. S. (1997). Cognitive-behavioral therapy for bulimia nervosa. In D. M. Garner & P. E. Garfinkel (Eds.), *Handbook of treatment for eating disorders*, (pp. 67–93). New York: Guilford Press.

Wilson, G. T., Fairburn, C. G., Agras, W. S., Walsh, B. T., & Kraemer, H. D. (2002). Cognitive behavior therapy for bulimia nervosa: Time course and mechanisms of change. *Journal of Consulting and Clinical Psychology, 70*, 267–274.

Wilson, G. T., Grilo, C., & Vitousek, K. (2007). Psychological treatment of eating disorders. *American Psychologist, 62*, 199–216.

Wilson, G. T., & Schlam, T. R. (2004). The transtheoretical model and motivational interviewing in the treatment of eating and weight disorders. *Clinical Psychology Review, 24*, 361–378.

Wilson, G.T., Wilfley, D.E., Agras, W.S., & Bryson, S. (2010). Psychological treatments for binge eating disorder. *Archives of General Psychiatry, 67*, 94–101.

Interpersonal Psychotherapy for the Treatment of Eating Disorders

Marian Tanofsky-Kraff *and* Denise E. Wilfley

Abstract

Interpersonal psychotherapy (IPT) is a focused, time-limited treatment that targets interpersonal problem(s) associated with the onset and/or maintenance of EDs. IPT is supported by substantial empirical evidence documenting the role of interpersonal factors in the onset and maintenance of EDs. IPT is a viable alternative to cognitive behavior therapy for the treatment of bulimia nervosa and binge eating disorder. The effectiveness of IPT for the treatment of anorexia nervosa requires further investigation. The utility of IPT for the prevention of obesity is currently being explored. Future research directions include enhancing the delivery of IPT for EDs, increasing the availability of IPT in routine clinical care settings, exploring IPT adolescent and parent–child adaptations, and developing IPT for the prevention of eating and weight-related problems that may promote full-syndrome EDs or obesity.

Keywords: eating disordered symptoms, interpersonal relationships, obesity, social functioning

Introduction

Interpersonal psychotherapy (IPT) is a brief, time-limited therapy that focuses on improving interpersonal functioning and, in turn, psychiatric symptoms, by relating symptoms to interpersonal problem areas and targeting strategies to improve these problems (Freeman & Gil, 2004; Klerman, Weissman, Rounsaville, & Chevron, 1984). Originally developed by Gerald Klerman and colleagues (Klerman et al., 1984) for the treatment of unipolar depression, IPT is an efficacious treatment for bulimia nervosa (BN) (Fairburn et al., 1991; Fairburn, Peveler, Jones, Hope, & Doll, 1993) and binge eating disorder (BED) (Wilfley et al., 1993; Wilfley, Frank, Welch, Spurrell, & Rounsaville, 1998). There are limited data from randomized-controlled trials on the effectiveness of IPT in the treatment of anorexia nervosa (AN).

The current chapter provides an overview of interpersonal theory and its foundation for IPT. Following this is a brief review of the literature supporting the central role that interpersonal functioning plays in the development, manifestation, and maintenance of eating disorders (EDs). The delivery of IPT for EDs also is explained, along with a description of the major tenets of the treatment. Empirical evidence supporting IPT's efficaciousness for the treatment of BN and BED is reviewed, as well as the limited data on the use of IPT for AN. A discussion of a novel adaptation of IPT for obesity prevention follows. Where appropriate, we provide vignettes as examples. Finally, more recent changes to the delivery of IPT are described, and future directions are proposed.

Interpersonal Theory

IPT is grounded in theories developed by Meyer, Sullivan, and Bowlby, which hypothesize that interpersonal function is recognized as a critical component of psychological adjustment and well-being. In the 1950s, Meyer postulated that psychopathology was rooted in maladjustment to one's social environment

(Frank & Spanier, 1995; Klerman et al., 1984; Meyer, 1957). During the same time period, Sullivan (who was responsible for popularizing the term "interpersonal") theorized that a patient's interpersonal relationships, rather than intrapsychic processes alone, established the relevant focus of therapeutic attention. Sullivan believed that individuals could not be understood in isolation from their interpersonal relationships and posited that enduring patterns in these relationships could either encourage self-esteem or result in anxiety, hopelessness, and psychopathology. IPT is also associated with the work of John Bowlby (1982) originator of attachment theory. Bowlby emphasized the importance of early attachment to the later development of interpersonal relationships and emotional well-being. He also hypothesized failures in attachment resulted in later psychopathology. The interpersonal roles of major interest to IPT occur within the nuclear family (as parent, child, sibling, partner); the extended family; the friendship group; the work situation (as supervisor, supervisee, or peer); and the neighborhood or community. Incorporating aspects of the theories posited by Meyer, Sullivan, and Bowlby, IPT acknowledges a two-way relationship between social functioning and psychopathology: disturbances in social roles can serve as antecedents for psychopathology and mental illness can produce impairments in the individual's capacity to perform social roles (Bowlby, 1982).

Incorporating the work of these interpersonal theorists, IPT acknowledges a two-way relationship between social functioning and psychopathology: interpersonal dysfunction heightens risk for psychopathology, and psychopathology results in deterioration of interpersonal functioning. Therefore, IPT is derived from a theory in which interpersonal functioning is recognized as a critical component of psychological adjustment and well-being. It should be noted that IPT makes no assumptions about the causes of psychiatric illness; however, IPT does assume that the development and maintenance of some psychiatric illnesses occurs in a social and interpersonal context and that the onset, response to treatment, and outcomes are influenced by the interpersonal relations between the patient and significant others. We will describe the major tenets of IPT for EDs in this chapter. However, the extensive empirical background and theoretical foundation, as well as the strategies and techniques of IPT, are fully described in a comprehensive book by Myrna Weissman and her colleagues (Weissman, Markowitz, & Klerman, 2000).

Interpersonal Functioning and EDs

A consistent relationship between poor interpersonal functioning and EDs has been identified (Wilfley, Stein, & Welch, 2005). Individuals with EDs report past difficult social experiences, problematic family histories, and specific interpersonal stressors more often than non–eating disordered individuals (Fairburn et al., 1998; Fairburn, Welch, Doll, Davies, & O'Connor, 1997). Individuals with bulimic symptoms tend to experience a wide range of social problems, including loneliness, lack of perceived social support, poor self esteem and social adjustment, and also often demonstrate difficulty with social problem-solving skills (Crow, Agras, Halmi, Mitchell, & Kraemer, 2002; Ghaderi & Scott, 1999; Grissett & Norvell, 1992; Gual et al., 2002; Johnson, Spitzer, & Williams, 2001; O'Mahony & Hollwey, 1995a; Rorty, Yager, Buckwalter, & Rossotto, 1999; Steiger, Gauvin, Jabalpurwala, Seguin, & Stotland, 1999; Troop, Holbrey, Trowler, & Treasure, 1994; Wilfley, Wilson, & Agras, 2003). Heightened sensitivity to interpersonal interactions appears to be a common component among individuals with symptoms of EDs (Evans & Wertheim, 1998; Humphrey, 1989; Steiger et al., 1999; Tasca, Taylor, Ritchie, & Balfour, 2004; Troisi, Massaroni, & Cuzzolaro, 2005). Laboratory paradigms suggest that interpersonal distress may trigger overeating (Steiger et al., 1999; Tanofsky-Kraff, Wilfley, & Spurrell, 2000) and potentially perpetuate binge eating. Further, interpersonal difficulties, low self-esteem, and negative affect are likely interconnected in a reciprocal fashion (Fairburn et al., 1997, 1998; Gual et al., 2002) and serve to perpetuate a cycle with each factor exacerbating the other and combining to precipitate and/or maintain dysfunctional bulimic or binge eating patterns (Herzog, Keller, Lavori, & Ott, 1987). Individuals with AN also report difficulties with psychosocial functioning (O'Mahony & Hollwey, 1995b; Ruuska, Koivisto, Rantanen, & Kaltiala-Heino, 2007) compared to controls and individuals at elevated risk for EDs (O'Mahony & Hollwey, 1995b). Therefore, in theory, the use of an interpersonally-focused intervention appears to be especially suitable for the treatment of EDs. IPT is designed to improve interpersonal functioning and self-esteem, reduce negative affect, and, in turn, decrease ED symptoms.

IPT for EDs
Basic IPT Concepts
IPT has been adapted for a range of clinical disorders (Weissman et al., 2000), but a number of basic concepts are common across all adaptations of IPT,

including treatment for EDs. Specifically, adaptations for IPT all focus on interpersonal problem areas and maintain a similar treatment structure. Given the time-limited nature of IPT, treatment success hinges on the therapist's rapid discernment of patterns in interpersonal relationships and the linking of these patterns to symptoms that may have precipitated and continue to maintain the disorder. Thus, in IPT for the treatment of EDs, treatment centers on facilitating clients' awareness of the links among their relationship interactions, negative affect, and disordered eating symptoms. Early identification of the problem area(s) and treatment goals by the therapist and patient is crucial. Throughout every session, interpersonal functioning is continuously linked to the onset and maintenance of the ED.

INTERPERSONAL PROBLEM AREAS

A primary aim of IPT is to help patients identify and address *current* interpersonal problems. By focusing on current as opposed to past relationships, IPT makes no assumptions about the etiology of an ED. Treatment focuses on the resolution of problems within four social domains that are associated with the onset and/or maintenance of the ED: (1) interpersonal deficits, (2) interpersonal role disputes, (3) role transitions, and (4) grief. *Interpersonal deficits* apply to those patients who are either socially isolated or who are involved in chronically unfulfilling relationships. For clients with this problem area, unsatisfying relationships and/or inadequate social support are frequently the result of poor social skills. *Interpersonal role disputes* refer to conflicts with a significant other (e.g., a partner, other family member, coworker, or close friend) that emerge from differences in expectations about the relationship. *Role transitions* include difficulties associated with a change in life status (e.g., graduation, leaving a job, moving, marriage/divorce, retirement, changes in health). The problem area of *grief* is identified when the onset of the patient's symptoms is associated with either the recent or past loss of a person or a relationship. Making use of this framework for defining one or more interpersonal problem areas, IPT for EDs focuses on identifying and changing the maladaptive interpersonal context in which the eating problem has developed and been maintained. The four problem areas are discussed in detail in the section describing the "Intermediate Phase."

TREATMENT STRUCTURE

IPT for EDs is a time-delineated treatment that typically includes 15 to 20 sessions over 4 to 5 months.

Regardless of the exact number of sessions, IPT is delivered in three phases. The *initial phase* is dedicated to identifying the problem area(s) that will be the target for treatment. The *intermediate phase* is devoted to working on the target problem area(s). The *termination phase* is devoted to consolidating gains made during treatment and preparing patients for future work on their own.

Implementing IPT for EDs

THE INITIAL PHASE

Sessions 1 to 5 typically constitute the initial phase of IPT for EDs. The patient's current ED symptoms are assessed and a history of these symptoms is obtained. The clinician provides the patient with a formal diagnosis. The ED diagnosis and expectations for treatment are discussed. An assignment of the "sick role" (described in further detail later) during this phase serves several functions, including granting the patient the permission to recover, delineating recovery as a responsibility of the patient, and allowing the patient to be relieved of other responsibilities in order to recover. The therapist explains the rationale of IPT, emphasizing that therapy will focus on identifying and altering current dysfunctional interpersonal patterns related to ED symptomatology. To determine the precise focus of treatment, the clinician conducts an "interpersonal inventory" with the patient and, in doing so, develops an interpersonal formulation that specifically relates to the patient's ED. In the interpersonal formulation, the therapist links the patient's ED to at least one of the four interpersonal problem areas. The patient's concurrence with the clinician's identification of the problem area and agreement to work on this area are essential in order to begin the intermediate phase of treatment. Indeed, a collaborative effort is promoted throughout the interpersonal inventory and all therapy sessions.

Diagnosis and Assignment of the Sick Role

After a psychiatric assessment, the patient is formally diagnosed with an ED and assigned what is termed the "sick role." The assignment of the sick role is theoretical and serves a practical purpose. Consistent with the medical model, receiving a formal diagnosis reinforces the understanding that the patient has a known condition that can be treated. Accurate diagnosis is essential to successful treatment. Providing a diagnosis also explicitly identifies the patient as being in need of help. The sick role is assigned not to demean the patient but rather to temporarily exempt the individual from other responsibilities in order to devote full attention to recovery. This is particularly important for individuals with a tendency to set aside their own needs and desires in order to care for and please others. If appropriate, the IPT therapist might explicitly highlight the patient's excessive caretaking tendencies and encourage the patient to redirect this energy from others toward self-recovery.

The Interpersonal Inventory

A primary and critical component of the initial phase of IPT is the interpersonal inventory. The interpersonal inventory involves a thorough examination of the patient's interpersonal history. Although clinicians have historically taken up to three sessions to complete the interpersonal inventory, we have found that conducting a longer (approximately 2-hour) first session to complete the entire interpersonal inventory may increase the effectiveness of the treatment. This is likely because it allows for patients to get "on board" early in terms of their understanding of IPT and how their ED fit into the IPT rationale (Tanofsky-Kraff & Wilfley, 2010; Wilfley, 2008; Wilfley, MacKenzie, Welch, Ayres., & Weissman, 2000). The interpersonal inventory is essential for adequate case formulation and development of an optimal treatment plan. The clinical importance of investing the time to conduct a comprehensive interpersonal inventory cannot be overemphasized; accurate identification of the patient's primary problem area(s) is often complicated and is crucial to success in treatment. Table 20.1 illustrates the tasks that should ideally be covered during the first session (Dounchis, Welch, & Wilfley, 1999).

The interpersonal inventory involves a review of the patient's current close relationships, social functioning, relationship patterns, and expectations of relationships. Interpersonal relationships—both patterns and changes—are explored and discussed with reference to the onset and maintenance of ED symptoms. For each significant relationship, the following information is assessed: frequency of contact, activities shared, satisfactory and unsatisfactory aspects of the relationship, and ways that the patient wishes to change the relationship. The therapist obtains a chronological history of significant life events, fluctuations in mood and self-esteem, interpersonal relationships, and ED symptoms. Throughout this process, the therapist works collaboratively with the patient to make connections between life experiences and ED development and symptoms. This exploration provides an opportunity for the patient to clearly understand the relationship between life

Table 20.1 Tasks of the Initial Session(s)

Discuss chief complaint and eating disorder symptoms.

Obtain history of symptoms.

Place patient in the sick role.

Establish whether or not there is a history of prior treatments for the eating disorder or other psychiatric problems.

Assess patient's expectations about psychotherapy.

Reassure patient about positive prognosis.

Explain IPT and its basic assumptions.

Complete an Interpersonal Inventory (detailed review of important relationships):

    I. Review *past* interpersonal functioning (e.g., family, school, social).

    II. Examine *current* interpersonal functioning (e.g., family, work, social).

    III. Identify the interpersonal precipitants of episodes of eating disorder symptoms.

Translate eating disorder symptoms into interpersonal context.

Explain IPT techniques.

Contract for administrative details (i.e., length of sessions, frequency, duration of treatment, appointment times).

Provide feedback to patient regarding general understanding of her interpersonal difficulties via IPT problem area (i.e., define *interpersonal deficits* - loneliness and social isolation).

Collaborate on a contract regarding the treatment goals.

Explain tasks in working toward treatment goals.

Adapted from Dounchis, J. Z., Welch, R. R., & Wilfley, D. E. (1999). *Using group interpersonal psychotherapy (IPT-G) for the treatment of binge eating disorders.* Workshop presented at the Academy of Eating Disorders Annual Meeting, San Diego.

events, social functioning, and the ED, and thereby clarifies the rationale behind IPT. Upon completion of the interpersonal inventory, the therapist and patient collaboratively identify a primary interpersonal problem area. In some cases, more than one problem area may be identified. Table 20.2 illustrates an example of a "Life Chart" (Fairburn, 1997) developed by an individual with BED and the therapist during the interpersonal inventory (Wilfley, 2008; Wilfley et al., 2000).

Table 20.2   Example of a Personal Historical Timeline of a Patient with BED

Age	Problems	Relationship	Events/Circumstances	Moods
5	Normal weight.		Tonsils are removed.	
6	Begins gaining weight.			
14			Grandfather died.	Feels sad at funeral but does not cry because she thinks it would be a sign of weakness.
15	Concerns about weight; first binge; prescribed amphetamines to lose weight.		Sister gets married, borrows money from parents, and files for bankruptcy with her husband.	Perceives parents as being extremely disappointed in sister.
16	Less concern about weight because "boy friend's ex-wife was a lot heavier than me" but began binge eating.	Meets boyfriend, 23, who works at a gas station.	Does not tell parents about boyfriend given father's high- profile job and position in the community.	Fearful of parents' disappointment; worries about their finding out.
18	Binge eating when alone. Loses weight.	Becomes engaged. Tells sisters, not parents. Boyfriend breaks off the engagement.	Graduates from high school; goes to technical school. Abortion Boyfriend "steals" back the ring (seen on his new girlfriend); throws herself into work as a secretary; is promoted repeatedly.	
	More comfortable about weight ("boyfriend's wife was a lot heavier than me"). Binge eating when alone ("food was my only friend when he was away"); never ate when with him.	Meets new boyfriend, who works as a salesman; he says he is separated from his wife who is pregnant. Lies to family and friends, telling them that they got married. Spouse of coworker tells her he is cheating on her.	Boyfriend's wife pickets her parents' house; parents do not make mention of this. Moves to Minnesota with boyfriend. Throws boyfriend out of the house; on his way out he takes her ring from her jewelry box.	Does not feel guilty about the relationship. Secrecy (wanting to be "perfect and not disappoint my parents"); homesick.
27	Binge eating as an outlet.	Gets pregnant, marries the father, an alcoholic, who is "cruel and verbally abusive."	Lies to mother that she got pregnant after the wedding; birth of first child.	Compliant, scared.
28		Husband occasionally shoves her.	"I channeled my energy into my son."	Hateful.
32	"Eating a lot"	Husband hits her; she stands up to husband only once, to ask him to choose between her and alcohol. Husband no longer drinks but continues being verbally abusive.	Does not tell anyone. ("Nobody had a clue that we didn't have a wonderful marriage.") Continuing Den Mother activities; very active in church.	Scared. Emotionally distant. ("I made it happy for me").

Age	Problems	Relationship	Events/Circumstances	Moods
39		Has sex with husband approximately two times a year.	Husband invests $20,000 of their joint money in real estate—all money lost; patient begins saving "every penny," sending $5,000 to her sister to open a savings account; became a workaholic.	Fearful husband will hit her; obedient; proud at holding onto her feelings; derives esteem from keeping her trouble from her children and others.
41	Eating as a way to "hold everything together".	Sexual relationship with husband ends; although she does not express anger, he yells at her, saying he can do whatever he wants with his money.		
46	260 lb., highest weight ever; blood pressure increasing with increasing weight.		Marital therapy with clergy for 3 months.	
47	Loses 60 lbs.	Patient files for divorce.		
50		Meets current boyfriend.	Mother dies.	Funeral is "a lot less stressful [than my grandfather's] because I knew it was OK to cry." Feels satisfied with their relationship.
51	Regains 30 lbs.	Moves in with current boyfriend.		
52	Binge eating at night on objectively large amounts of food at least three times per week. Begins psychotherapy	Does not tell family members she is seeking psychological help.	Works 14+ hour days, not pausing to eat or rest during the day.	

Sources: Wilfley, D. E. (2008). *Interpersonal psychotherapy for binge eating disorder (BED) therapist's manual*; Wilfley, D. E. et al., (2000). *Interpersonal psychotherapy for group*. New York: Basic Books.

The Interpersonal Formulation

After completion of the interpersonal inventory, the clinician will have developed an individualized interpersonal formulation that includes the identification of the patient's primary problem area. Although some patients may present for treatment with difficulties in several problem areas, the time-limited nature of the treatment necessitates a focused approach. Therefore, the clinician should focus treatment on the problem area(s) that appears to not only impact the patient's interpersonal functioning most, but also those most closely linked to

the ED. The therapist, with the agreement of the patient, should assign one, or at most two, problem area(s) upon which to develop a treatment plan. We recommend that therapists put the agreed-upon goals in writing and formally present this write-up to patients. The presentation of documented goals can be a very effective technique that serves as a treatment "contract" (Tanofsky-Kraff & Wilfley, 2010; Wilfley et al., 2000). The goals developed at this stage will be referenced at future sessions and will guide the day-to-day work of the treatment. If more than one problem area is identified, the patient may choose to work simultaneously on both or may decide to first address the problem area that seems most likely to respond to treatment. For example, when a patient has role disputes and interpersonal deficits, clinical attention might first be focused on role disputes, since interpersonal deficits reflect long-term patterns that may require considerably more time and effort to change. Once the role dispute has been resolved, the therapist and patient decide how to best address the more entrenched interpersonal deficits. Once the primary problem area(s) have been identified and the treatment goals have been agreed upon, the initial phase of treatment is considered complete.

THE INTERMEDIATE PHASE

The intermediate phase typically contains 8 to 10 sessions and constitutes the "work" stage of the treatment. As currently conceptualized, an essential task throughout the intermediate phase of IPT for EDs is to assist the patient in understanding the connection between difficulties in interpersonal functioning and the ED behaviors and symptoms. Therapeutic strategies and goals of this phase are shaped by the primary problem area targeted in the treatment (see Table 20.3) (Wilfley, Dounchis, & Welch, 2004). The following sections describe the implementation of specific treatment strategies based upon the identified problem area (Wilfley et al., 2005).

Problem Areas

Grief Grief is identified as the problem area when the onset of the patient's symptoms is associated with the death of a loved one, either recent or past. Grief is not limited to the physical death of a loved one. Grief can also result from the loss of a significant relationship or the loss of an important aspect of one's identity. The goals for treating complicated bereavement include facilitating mourning and helping the patient to find new activities and relationships to substitute for the loss. Reconstructing the relationship, both the positive and its negative aspects, is central to the assessment of not only what has been lost but also what is needed to counter the idealization that so commonly occurs. As patients become less focused on the past, they should be encouraged to consider new ways of becoming more involved with others and establishing new interests (Wilfley et al., 2005). The distribution of the IPT problem areas among individuals with EDs has been reviewed by Wilfley and colleagues (2003). For 12% of BN patients, grief has been identified as their primary problem area, while approximately 6% of individuals with AN and 6% with BED present with grief.

Role Transitions Role transition includes any difficulties resulting from a change in life status. Common role transitions include a career change (i.e., promotion, firing, retirement, changing jobs), a family

Table 20.3 Interpersonal Problem Areas

Main Problem Area	Description	IPT Strategies
Grief	Pathological grief stemming from fears of being unable to tolerate the painful affect associated with the loss.	Facilitate the mourning process. Help the patient reestablish interest in relationships to substitute for what has been lost.
Interpersonal role disputes	Disputes with partner, children, or other family members or coworkers.	Identify the dispute. Choose a plan of action. Modify expectations and faulty communication to bring about a satisfactory resolution.
Role transitions	Economic or family change: children leaving for college, new job, divorce, retirement, parent's caretaker.	Mourn and accept the loss of the old role Restore self-esteem by developing a sense of mastery regarding the demands of new roles.
Interpersonal deficits	A long-standing history of social isolation, low self-esteem, loneliness, and an inability to form or maintain intimate relationships.	Reduce the patient's social isolation Encourage the formation of new relationships.

Sources: Wilfley, D. E., Dounchis, J. Z., & Welch, R. R. (2004). Interpersonal psychotherapy of anorexia nervosa. In K. M. Miller, & J. S. Mizes (Eds.), *Comparative treatment of eating disorders*. New York: Springer; Dounchis, J. Z. et al. (1999). *Using group interpersonal psychotherapy (IPT-G) for the treatment of binge eating disorders.* Paper presented at the Academy of Eating Disorders Annual Meeting, San Diego.

change (marriage, divorce, birth of a child, child moving out), the beginning or end of an important relationship, a move, graduation, or diagnosis of a medical illness. The goals of therapy include mourning and accepting loss of the old role, recognizing the positive and negative aspects of both the old and new roles, and restoring the patient's self-esteem by developing a sense of mastery in the new role. Key strategies in achieving these goals will include a thorough exploration of the patient's feelings related to the role change as well as encouraging the patient to develop new skills and adequate social support for the new role (Wilfley et al., 2005). Thirty-six percent of patients with BN (Wilfley et al., 2003) and 3.7% of individuals with BED in Wilfley and colleagues' (2000) trial were identified with the problem area of role transitions. Among individuals with AN, approximately 17% present with role transitions as the primary problem area (Wilfley et al., 2003).

Interpersonal Role Disputes Such disputes are conflicts with a significant other (e.g., a partner, other family member, employer, co-worker, teacher, or close friend), which emerge from differences in expectations about the relationship. The goals of treatment include clearly identifying the nature of the dispute and exploring options to resolve it. It is important to determine the stage of the dispute; once the stage of the dispute becomes clear, it may be important to modify the patient's expectations and remedy faulty communication in order to bring about adequate resolution. It may be particularly helpful to explore how nonreciprocal role expectations relate to the dispute. If resolution is impossible, the therapist assists the patient in dissolving the relationship and in mourning its loss (Wilfley et al., 2005). This problem area is identified in approximately 64% of individuals with BN and 33% of those with AN (Wilfley et al., 2003). Interpersonal role disputes were present in 29.6% of the patients in the Wilfley et al. (2000) BED trial.

Interpersonal Deficits Interpersonal deficits include patients who are socially isolated or who are in chronically unfulfilling relationships. The goal is to reduce the patient's social isolation by helping enhance the quality of existing relationships and encouraging the formation of new relationships. To help these patients, it is necessary to determine why they have difficulty in forming or maintaining relationships. Carefully reviewing past significant relationships will be particularly useful in making this assessment. During this review, attention should be given to both the positive and negative aspects of the relationships, as well as an investigation of potentially recurrent patterns in these relationships. It may also be appropriate to examine the nature of the patient-therapist relationship, since this may be the patient's only close relationship and it is present to be observed (Wilfley et al., 2005). For patients with BN and AN, this problem area is seen in approximately 16% and 33%, respectively (Wilfley et al., 2003). Based upon one study, interpersonal deficits appeared to be the most commonly identified problem area among individuals with BED; 60.5% of patients presented with interpersonal deficits (Wilfley et al., 2000).

Therapeutic Strategies

Therapeutic Stance As with most therapies, IPT places importance on establishing a positive therapeutic alliance between therapist and patient. The IPT therapeutic stance is one of warmth, support, and empathy. Further, throughout all phases of the treatment, the clinician is active and advocates for the patient rather than remaining neutral. Issues and discussions are framed positively so that the therapist may help the patient feel at ease throughout treatment. Such an approach promotes a safe and supportive working environment. Confrontations and clarifications are offered in a gentle and timely manner, and the clinician is careful to encourage the patient's positive expectations of the therapeutic relationship. Finally, the therapist conveys a hopeful and optimistic attitude about the potential for the patient to recover.

Focusing on Goals Because IPT is a directed, goal-oriented therapy, therapists should maintain a focus each week on how the patient is working on his or her agreed-upon goals between sessions. Phrases such as "moving forward on your goals" and "making important changes" are used to encourage patients to be responsible for their treatment while also reminding them that altering interpersonal patterns requires attention and persistence. Sometimes during the course of therapy, unfocused discussions arise. The therapist should sensitively, but firmly, redirect the discussion to the key interpersonal issues. By explicitly addressing goals each week, the patient can work toward necessary changes. This goal-oriented focus has been supported by research on IPT maintenance treatment for recurrent depression, which has demonstrated that the clinician's ability to maintain focus on interpersonal themes is associated with better outcomes (Klerman et al., 1984;

Markowitz, Skodol, & Bleiberg, 2006; Weissman et al., 2000). In IPT for EDs, it is essential that the clinician facilitate and strengthen the recognition of connections between patients' problematic eating and difficulties in their interpersonal lives. The example below illustrates how the IPT therapist initiates the discussion about goals and helps a patient in treatment for BN with interpersonal deficits work on her goals.

Therapist: Ellie, I would like to check in with you to see how your work on your goals is progressing. Last week, you mentioned that you are starting to become more aware of interpersonal difficulties that trigger your binge eating and purging.

Ellie: I have been paying more attention to what is happening when I binge. It seems as though there are a lot of times that I feel the urge to binge, whether it is feeling put down at work, angry at my husband, or feeling overwhelmed about taking care of the kids. I think that I am beginning to better understand what happens with me when I get the urge to binge. I feel overwhelmed – I have so much going on in my life, I do not know how I will ever overcome the desire to binge.

Therapist: I imagine that it must feel very frightening when you have so much going on – it can seem as though gaining control over your eating might be impossible. However, you have taken a very important first step, Ellie. It is great that you have begun to identify triggers to your binge eating. From your work, it is clear that a lot of things are playing into your desire to binge. How were you able to become more aware of what was happening with you when you felt the urge to binge?

Ellie: I think that instead of just binge eating as soon as I feel the urge, I think I have become aware that something changes for me when I have the urge to binge. Lately, I have been trying hard to stop and see what is going on and what I am feeling before I binge. Even though I have still had binge episodes this week, I think that at least once or twice I seemed to have lost the desire to binge once I stopped and thought about what was going on in that moment.

Therapist: What specifically did you notice was happening with you?

Ellie: I noticed that I was feeling frustrated about my work and how angry I feel at my husband when he makes me feel like I am an inadequate wife and parent. I realized that I often do not stand up for myself and let the people in my life know what my needs are. I don't feel like I know how to do this and

end up expressing—or is it suppressing?— my frustration through food.

Therapist: This is very important work you are doing, Ellie – good job! You have identified some really important interpersonal triggers for your binge eating. As you continue to become more and more aware of the circumstances surrounding your urge to binge, we can begin to work on helping you find more effective ways to manage your feelings and relationships so that you are less likely to binge.

As this dialogue between Ellie and her therapist illustrates, a crucial component to IPT for EDs is helping to facilitate and strengthen the connections patients make between their problematic eating and difficulties they have in their interpersonal lives. Focusing on specific goals provides the structure for this to be accomplished. Ellie's ability to have insight to make links between her interactions, mood, and disordered eating is due to the therapist's persistence in emphasizing the connection between Ellie's interpersonal functioning to her eating patterns throughout all phases of the treatment.

Making Connections During the intermediate phase, it is crucial that the therapist assist patients in recognizing, and ultimately becoming more aware of, the connections between eating difficulties and interpersonal events during the week. As patients learn to make these connections, the therapist should guide them to develop strategies to alter the interpersonal context in which the disordered eating symptoms occur. As a result, the cycle of the ED is interrupted. Patients are encouraged to make connections between interpersonal functioning and eating patterns that are positive as well. For example, an individual may recognize that communication improved with a significant other and, as a result, the patient did not engage in ED behaviors. To encourage positive and negative connections, clinicians should ask the patient about his or her eating patterns between sessions and, if there were any changes, inquire about any recognized links between eating patterns and interpersonal functioning.

In the following vignette, which is also in the intermediate phase, the therapist encourages a patient with interpersonal role disputes in treatment for AN to talk about the connections she has made between her desire to restrict her food intake and difficulties she experiences with her divorced parents:

Therapist: Ashley, have you noticed any connections between your eating and how things went with your parents this past week?

Ashley: Well, my parents have been arguing a lot—mostly about where I am going to spend the summer vacation. I just can't stand it. Whenever they talk badly about the other to me, I'm not hungry at all and I just want to starve myself. Maybe this is a way to make them notice how their fighting gets to me. I don't know.

Therapist: This is terrific work Ashley! One of the things we have been working on is getting you to become more aware of what is happening when you feel the urge to restrict most intensely. You have just made an important connection between your stress and dislike related to your parents arguments and your wanting to restrict. How do you think restricting your eating affects your mood?

Ashley: Well, focusing on not eating helps me not to think about all the stuff going on between my parents. I feel kind of numb. I guess I never realized that connection until we started working together. All I cared about was how much I wanted to be thin.

Therapist: Now that you can more clearly see that connection, how would you like to start working on your relationships with your mother and father?

Redirecting Issues Related to ED Symptoms During treatment sessions, patients with EDs may raise issues relating to ED symptoms that are distressing (e.g., binge episodes, over-concern about eating, shape, and weight) or want to engage in extended discussion related to these behaviors. These issues are relevant insofar as they reflect the clinical status of the patient's ED. However, the therapist must be cognizant of how these issues are being discussed during the sessions and vigilantly keep the session focused on the patient's treatment goals by gently, but firmly, redirecting discussion to work on the treatment goals. For example, a female patient who avoids intimacy with her husband may attribute her avoidance to body dissatisfaction related to her obesity. She may wish to discuss her body concerns at great length to circumvent actual difficulties in communication with her husband, or she is not yet aware that her relationship difficulties with her husband is an important issue and that body concern is what she experiences as most distressing. Dialogue related to ED symptoms should be consistently and repeatedly linked to its functional role with regard to the identified interpersonal problem area(s).

Therapist: How are you today, Terry?

Terry: I have been busier than usual and that has made me very stressed. I was asked to cover the late shift twice this week and since we have been understaffed, I was the only nurse to cover all of the patients during my shift. I had no time to eat dinner, which was probably good for me, but then I came home both nights and had huge binges. I found myself in the kitchen eating anything and everything that I could find. I was so frantic that I didn't even bother to heat up—I ate a huge container of soup cold!

Therapist: Last week you talked about how eating is a way for you to relieve stress and to relax. Instead of allowing yourself a break or sharing your feelings with family or friends, you tend to turn to food.

Terry: That is exactly what I do—and what I did this week. It was unbelievable and I was so disgusted with how I was shoving food in by the mouthful—cookies, chips, leftover pizza. Have you ever eaten cold pizza? It does not even taste good! I just wanted…

Therapist: I am going to interrupt you for a moment, Terry, so that I can refocus you for a moment, back to your goals. How has your work in finding down time to take care of yourself been coming along?

Terry: I think it has been going somewhat better. I signed up to join a book club through my church. It hasn't started yet, but I did go buy the book we're supposed to read and I started reading a few pages. I'm hoping that my work schedule does not conflict with the nights that the club will be meeting.

Therapist: As we talked about last week, for a long time you've been feeling that you need to take care of everyone else—make everyone else happy—and, in doing so, you've put yourself last and not tended to your own needs. By not taking care of yourself, you get very stressed and use food to cope. I wonder if as you practice identifying your own needs and addressing them—like you have in joining the book club - you will feel less exhausted and more personally cared for. By taking time out for yourself, you will feel calmer and be less likely to turn to food. Joining the book club- and beginning to read—is already one way you are taking care of yourself. I have noted that you only had two overeating episodes this past week. When we first started working together, you were having binge episodes almost nightly during similarly stressful times.

By redirecting the patient away from the specifics of her binge episode, and toward her interpersonal problem area, the therapist is able to keep the patient focused on her goals.

General Therapeutic Techniques The IPT therapist differs from providers of other modalities in that throughout the course of treatment, he/she maintains a constant focus on the interpersonal context of the patient's life and its link to the ED symptoms. Although this approach is unique to IPT, a number of the therapeutic techniques utilized in IPT are similar to those used in other therapies. Such techniques include exploratory questions, encouragement of affect, clarification, communication analysis, and use of the therapeutic relationship.

1. *Exploratory questions.* Use of general, open-ended questions often facilitates the free discussion of material. This is especially useful during the beginning of a session. For example, the clinician might open a session with, "Tell me about your relationship with your husband." Once this has generated discussion, progressively more specific questioning should follow. For instance, after the patient describes an interpersonal interaction with her husband, the therapist might follow-up by asking, "what happened with (or what changes did you notice in) your eating patterns after you talked with your husband?"

2. *Encouraging affect.* The focus of IPT throughout the therapeutic process involves affect evocation and exploration (Wilfley et al., 2000). This is particularly relevant for patients with EDs because problematic eating often serves to regulate negative affect. The IPT therapist should assist patients in: (1) acknowledging and accepting painful emotions, (2) using affective experiences to facilitate desired interpersonal changes, and (3) experiencing suppressed affect (Wilfley, 2008; Wilfley et al., 2000).

   a. **Encourage acceptance of painful affects**. Patients with EDs are often emotionally constricted in situations when others would typically experience strong emotions. In the case of BN and BED, individuals use food to cope with negative affect. Therapy provides an arena to experience and express these feelings versus using food to cope with these feelings. As the feelings are expressed, it is important for the IPT therapist to validate and help the patient accept them (Wilfley, 2008).

   b. **Teach the patient how to use affect in interpersonal relationships**. While the expression of strong feelings in the session is seen as an important starting point for much therapeutic work, the expression of feelings outside the session is not a goal in and of itself.

The goal is to help the patient act more constructively (e.g., not binge eating or purging) in interpersonal relationships, and this may involve either expressing or suppressing affects, depending on the circumstances. A goal for the patient in IPT is to learn when her/his needs are met by expressing affect and when they are better met by suppressing affect. However, a primary goal is helping patients to identify, understand, and acknowledge their feelings whether or not they choose to verbalize them to others. The following is an example: "The therapist immediately noticed that Sara was silent and withdrawn at the beginning of the session. Initially, she denied any relationship between her nonverbal behavior and the therapist's observation. The therapist was persistent and she eventually acknowledged that he was feeling hurt because her father had not acknowledged her son's first birthday. She spent some time clarifying and expressing her feelings of anger and rejection with regard to her own relationship with her father. The issue that emerged in the session was "when do you stop wanting something from a parent that you can never get from them?" Even though she became aware of and expressed many painful feelings regarding her relationship with her father, Sara's goal was not to go out and express these feelings to her father directly at this time. Instead, Sara and her therapist began to discuss how she can find herself more fulfilled and satisfied by working to make other choices in terms of who to turn to for support and care" (Wilfley, 2008).

   c. **Help the patient experience suppressed affects.** Many who struggle with EDs are emotionally constricted in situations where strong emotions are normally felt. An example may be the patient who is unassertive and does not feel anger when their rights are violated. On the other hand, they may feel anger but may lack the courage to express it in an assertive manner. Sometimes patients will deny being upset, when it is clear that an upsetting interaction has just occurred. The therapists might say, "Although you said you were not upset, it appears to me that you have shut down since you talked about the situation with your husband." In this way, the therapist will attempt to draw out affect when it is suppressed (Wilfley, 2008).

3. *Clarification.* Clarification is a useful technique that can: (1) increase the patient's

awareness about what she/he has actually communicated and (2) draw awareness to contradictions that may have occurred in the patient's presentation of interactions or situations. An example might involve contradictions between the patient's affect and speech: "While you were telling me how upset you are about your father, you had a smile on your face. What do you think that's about?"

4. *Communication analysis.* The technique of communication analysis is used to: (1) identify potential communication difficulties that the patient may be experiencing and (2) assist the patient in modifying ineffective communication patterns. In using communication analysis, the therapist asks the patient to describe, in great detail, a recent interaction or argument with a significant other. As the patient describes the interactions, the therapist garners information by using probes, such as the examples below (Mufson, Dorta, Moreau, & Weissman, 2004; Young & Mufson, 2003):

"What did you specifically say?"
"What did he/she say in response?"
"Then what happened?"
"How did you feel?"
"Do you think you might be able to tell him/her how you felt?
"Thinking back to how the interaction turned out, did you send the message that you wanted to convey?"
"How do you think it made him/her feel?"

As part of communication analysis, the clinician then assists the patient in identifying ways in which the interaction could have gone differently; and how the different manifestations might impact the other person's feelings and reactions. Therapeutic queries to facilitate this process include (Mufson et al., 2004; Young & Mufson, 2003):

"How do you think this interaction might have manifested differently?"
"What could have been said differently by either your or the other person?"
"How might it have changed the way that felt and/or the interaction itself?"

The objective is for the clinician and patient to collaboratively work to identify difficulties in communication that may be impacting the process and outcome of the interaction and to find more effective strategies.

5. *Use of the therapeutic relationship.* The premise behind this technique is that all individuals have characteristic patterns of interacting with others. The technique is utilized by exploring the patient's thoughts, feelings, expectations, and behavior in the therapeutic relationship and relating these to the patient's characteristic way of behaving and/or feeling in other relationships. This technique is particularly relevant to and useful for patients with interpersonal deficits and interpersonal role disputes. Use of this technique offers the patient the opportunity to understand the nature of his/her difficulties in interacting with others and provides the patient with helpful feedback on his/her interactional style. The following is an example of using the therapeutic relationship.

> *Therapist:* Joe, I know it was hard for you last week to talk about how your girlfriend does not understand that it is important for you to have time with your friends. Did you have a chance to discuss this with her over the past week?
>
> *Joe:* No. I was really busy. She would have just argued with me if I brought it up anyway.
>
> *Therapist:* As we have talked about before, I am wondering if you approach her about the topic differently this week, she might be more open to your point of view.
>
> *Joe:* I doubt it. I am really busy this week, too.
>
> *Therapist:* It feels to me like you do not want help with this situation, so I am feeling a little frustrated right now. I am wondering if other people in your life might feel the same way. What do you think?

In a nonjudgmental and straightforward manner, the therapist not only models clear communication with Joe, but also uses the therapeutic relationship to identify a potentially dysfunctional communication pattern.

C. THE TERMINATION PHASE

By the end of the intermediate phase, patients are often acutely aware that treatment will soon be ending. The clinician should begin to discuss termination explicitly and address any anxiety the patient may be experiencing. In doing so, the patient should be prepared for emotions that may arise with termination, including grief related to the ending of treatment. At times, patients may deny any emotion with regard to the end of treatment and appear to have little reaction to termination. Nevertheless, the therapist should clearly address termination, as the patient may be unaware of or avoiding affect related to the end of treatment.

The termination phase typically lasts four to five sessions. During this phase, the patient should be encouraged to reflect on the progress that has been made during therapy—both within sessions and outside of the therapeutic milieu—and to outline goals for remaining work after the formal end of treatment. IPT does not assume that the work towards changes in interpersonal functioning is complete after the last session of the therapy. Rather, patients and therapist collaboratively summarize and draft the remaining work for the patient to continue outside of the therapeutic milieu. Patients are encouraged to identify early warning signs of relapse (e.g., binge eating, overeating and excessive dietary restriction, negative mood) and to prepare plans of action. Patients are reminded that ED symptoms tend to arise in times of interpersonal stress and are encouraged to view such symptoms as important early warning signals. The identification of potential strategies to cope with such situations is designed to increase the patient's sense of competence and security. Nevertheless, it is also essential to assist patients in identifying warning signs and symptoms that may indicate the need for professional intervention in the future.

USE OF A GROUP

The group setting frequently provides an optimal modality for conducting IPT (Wilfley et al., 2000). Data from randomized trials suggest that both individual and group milieus of IPT are equally effective in the treatment of BN (Nevonen & Broberg, 2006) and BED (Wilfley et al., 2002) (Wilfley, Wilson, & Agras, 2008). After an *individual* session to conduct a thorough interpersonal inventory, the group is an ideal milieu to work on interpersonal skills with other patients struggling with similar eating problems. It also offers the therapist an opportunity to observe and identify characteristic interpersonal patterns with other individuals. Further, when another group member recognizes and verbally identifies a dysfunctional pattern of communication in a fellow patient, it can be powerful for the patient as well as the other group members (Wilfley et al., 2000). The following vignette provides an illustration from a group of adolescents with binge eating patterns.

> *Therapist:* Sheila, you have done a great job of telling us what happened this week at school. It sounds like it was pretty upsetting when you saw Christine, your best friend, sitting with people who she knows you

do not get along with. You recognized that it was not the right time to talk to her, so you just walked away and sat with someone else. But it is still understandably upsetting to you. The rest of the group has suggested that you tell Christine what is causing you to feel upset with her. Sheila, what might you say?

> *Sheila:* I don't know. I guess I would say, "Christine, the other day you were sitting with Amy and Joyce. You know those girls talk about me behind my back. Why were you sitting with them?"

> *Therapist:* That's a good start. What do others think?

> *Becca:* I guess I would have felt bad if I was Christine.

> *Therapist:* How so?

> *Becca:* Well, Christine might have felt accused of doing something wrong. I guess she might have felt as though you think she is not allowed to hang around with whomever she wants. I think that is how I might have taken it.

> *Therapist:* Thanks, Becca. What do you think, Sheila?

> *Sheila:* I did not mean to tell her that she cannot hang out with other people. I just wanted her to know that it made me feel bad that she was spending time with girls who are not nice to me.

> *Therapist:* Does anyone have thoughts about how Sheila might better express what she really feels?

> *Lisa:* I guess you could say, "Christine, I felt upset the other day when you were sitting with…" I can't remember their names. "They talk about me behind my back. When you were sitting with them, I felt like you weren't my friend."

The group setting allows patients to experiment with different ways of communication within the safe confines of the group. Members can use the sessions to discuss problems they are having with their significant relationships and how these problems relate to their eating patterns. This often allows for patients to recognize that they are not alone in their difficulties, thereby helping to reduce feelings of isolation (Wilfley et al., 2000).

Review of Outcome Studies and Relevant Empirical Literature
IPT for BN

IPT has shown to be effective for the treatment of BN. Although cognitive behavioral therapy (CBT) is currently the most extensively researched, best-established treatment for BN (Wilson & Fairburn, 2001), IPT is the only psychological treatment for BN that has demonstrated long-term outcomes that are comparable to those of CBT (Wilson & Shafran, 2005). Currently, all *controlled* studies of IPT for BN have been compared to CBT for BN. In early studies, similar short- and long-term outcomes for binge eating reduction between CBT and IPT were reported (Fairburn et al., 1993, 1995). In a subsequent multisite study comparing CBT and IPT for BN, patients receiving CBT demonstrated higher rates of abstinence from binge eating and lower rates of purging in the shorter-term, post-treatment (Agras, Walsh, Fairburn, Wilson, & Kraemer, 2000). By 8- and 12-month follow-up, however, patients in CBT demonstrated maintenance or slight relapse while IPT participants experienced slight improvement such that rates of these behaviors were equivalent in both groups. The more impressive, immediate effect of CBT compared to IPT may be explained in part by a relative lack of focus on ED symptomatology in the research version of individual IPT for BN that was used in this study (Tanofsky-Kraff & Wilfley, 2010; Wilfley, Stein, & Welch, 2003). Despite the relatively slower response rates, IPT patients rated their treatment as more suitable and expected greater success than did CBT patients. Therefore, a potential strength of IPT may be that many patients with BN perceive the interpersonal focus of IPT as especially relevant to their ED and to their treatment needs, perhaps more so than a cognitive-behavioral focus on distortions related to weight and shape (Tanofsky-Kraff & Wilfley, 2010; Wilfley, Stein et al., 2003). Currently, IPT is considered an alternative to CBT for the treatment of BN (Wilson & Shafran, 2005). Although it has been recommended that therapists inform patients of the slower response time for improvements compared to CBT (Wilson, 2005), it is our contention that a lack of integration of BN symptoms with the interpersonal focus is likely responsible for the delayed response to IPT in the Oxford trial (Fairburn et al., 1993, 1995) and the less robust results in the multi-site study (Agras et al., 2000). Therefore, future research linking symptoms to interpersonal functioning is required.

An emerging literature has provided some insight into predictors of success with IPT for the treatment of EDs. In the multi-center trial conducted by Agras and colleagues (2000), a follow-up analysis found that while patients responded with higher abstinence rates when randomized to CBT as opposed to IPT, African American participants showed greater reductions in binge episodes when treated with IPT compared to CBT (Chui, Safer, Bryson, Agras, & Wilson, 2007). Although further investigation is clearly necessary, it is possible that IPT may be especially appropriate for African American women with BN, which speaks to the need for further study of IPT with different racial and ethnic groups. Researchers from this same study also examined the impact of therapeutic alliance on patient expectation of improvement (Constantino, Arnow, Blasey, & Agras, 2005). Expectation of improvement was positively associated with outcome for both CBT and IPT, emphasizing the important role of patient expectations in both treatments. Lastly, in a study of post-remission predictors of relapse in women with BN, the finding that worse psychosocial functioning was associated with a greater risk for relapse may support the rationale for IPT (Keel, Dorer, Franko, Jackson, & Herzog, 2005). Indeed, the authors suggested that their findings may partly help to explain the long-term effectiveness of IPT for BN.

IPT for BED
Based on the initial success of IPT in BN (Fairburn et al., 1991), IPT for BED was developed and tested in the early 1990s. Wilfley and colleagues first adapted IPT to a group format for adult patients with BED (Wilfley et al., 1993, 2000). During their work, they found that a number of patients presented with chronically unfulfilling relationships that were well-suited to be addressed in the group format. Therefore, new strategies were adapted to specifically address such interpersonal deficits. For example, in the current format of group IPT for BED, group members with interpersonal deficits are strongly encouraged to use the group as an interpersonal "laboratory"; therapists can observe, firsthand, patients interacting with one another, and patients can practice improved ways of communicating within the group. As described previously, this social milieu is designed to decrease social isolation, support the formation of new social relationships, and serve as a model for initiating and sustaining social relationships outside of the therapeutic context (Wilfley et al., 1998). In addition, self-stigmatization is common among patients with BED, and this stigmatization contributes to the maintenance of the disorder. By its very nature, group therapy offers a radically altered social environment for these individuals, who typically maintain shameful eating behaviors hidden from close others in their social network. By participating in a group with others

suffering from the same types of psychiatric and physical issues, individuals with BED are offered a unique opportunity to feel both understood and accepted in IPT.

For the treatment of BED among adults, IPT has been demonstrated to be effective in randomized-controlled studies. CBT for BED has also been shown to have specific and robust treatment effects (Devlin et al., 2005; Grilo, Masheb, & Wilson, 2005; Kenardy, Mensch, Bowen, Green, & Walton, 2002; Nauta, Hospers, Kok, & Jansen, 2000; Ricca et al., 2001; Telch, Agras, Rossiter, Wilfley, & Kenardy, 1990; Wilfley et al., 1993). In two randomized trials comparing IPT with CBT, IPT had similar effects to CBT in the treatment and management of BED. The first study, comparing group CBT and IPT, revealed that both treatments were more effective than a wait list control group at reducing binge eating and had equivalent, significant reductions in binge eating in both the short and long term (Wilfley et al., 1993). In a second substantially larger sample size, both CBT and IPT demonstrated equivalent short- and long-term efficacy in reducing binge eating and associated specific and general psychopathology, with approximately 60% of the patients remaining abstinent from binge eating at 1-year follow-up (Wilfley et al., 2002). In contrast to the literature on IPT for BN, the time course of almost all outcomes with IPT was identical to that of CBT and all participants in both groups significantly improved from baseline. In a follow-up analysis of treatment predictors for the 2002 study, patients with a greater extent of interpersonal problems at baseline and mid-treatment showed poorer treatment response to both treatments (Hilbert et al., 2007). An important caveat of this finding, however, is that not surprisingly, those individuals with greater interpersonal problems were also those who had more Axis I and Axis II psychiatric disorders and lower self-esteem than those with less severe problems. These individuals are likely in need of augmented or extended treatment. Supporting this assertion, in IPT adapted for individuals with borderline personality disorder, many of whom presented with comorbid depression, Markowitz and colleagues suggest that extending IPT effectively improves the disorder (Markowitz et al., 2006). Notably, a preliminary examination of patients in this cohort at least 5 years post-treatment indicated that individuals in IPT maintained reductions in binge eating and disordered eating cognitions (Bishop, Stein, Hilbert, Swenson, & Wilfley, 2007). These data may suggest evidence for good maintenance of change for BED patients treated with IPT.

Results from a recently completed multi-site trial that compared individual IPT to behavioral weight loss treatment or CBT guided self-help (CBTgsh) for the treatment of BED points to the importance of making a clear connection between interpersonal problems and binge eating symptoms in the delivery of IPT. Similar to the 2002 trial of Wilfley et al. (Wilfley et al., 2002), in this multisite study, the clinicians linked interpersonal functioning to disordered eating symptoms throughout the course of IPT. Findings from this study revealed that IPT was most acceptable to patients; the dropout rate was significantly lower in IPT compared to the other two interventions (Wilson et al., 2010). IPT and CBTgsh were significantly more effective than behavioral weight loss in eliminating binge eating after 2 years. Further, compared to the other two programs, IPT produced greater binge episode reductions for patients with low self-esteem and greater disordered eating behaviors and cognitions, while CBTgsh was generally effective for those with lower ED psychopathology. It is notable that in this trial, compared to the 2002 study (Hilbert et al., 2007; Wilfley et al., 2002), individuals with more psychopathology showed greater improvements in IPT than CBTgsh. This is in concert with Hilbert and colleagues' follow-up data suggesting that greater disordered eating serves as a moderator in predicting poorer outcome in CBT (Hilbert et al., 2007).

In general, compared to Caucasian participants, individuals of other ethnic minorities demonstrated less retention in the multisite study (Wilson et al., 2010). Although there was no treatment by ethnicity effects in this regard, there was very low attrition for minority participants in IPT and very high dropout rates by minorities in CBT guided self-help. The small sample size of minority participants across sites precludes definitive conclusions. Nevertheless, this pattern is in concert with the finding that IPT was particularly helpful for African American participants in the previously described multi-site study for individuals with BN (Chui et al., 2007). It is possible that the personalized nature of IPT (e.g., problem areas and goals are developed based upon each individual's social environment) is modifiable to, and thus particularly acceptable to, persons of various cultures and backgrounds.

A number of recommendations may be drawn from the research presented. It is possible, from a cost-effectiveness viewpoint, that CBTgsh could be considered the first-line treatment for the majority of individuals with BED, and that IPT is recommended for patients with low self-esteem and high ED psychopathology. Alternatively, IPT may be considered a first-line treatment for BED. This recommendation is based upon a number of factors: IPT has been shown to be effective across multiple research sites, is associated with high retention across different patient profiles (e.g., high negative affect, minority groups), and demonstrated superior outcomes to behavioral weight loss overall, and to CBTgsh among a subset of patients with high disordered eating psychopathology and low-self-esteem. Therapists and patients should consider these alternatives when deciding the best approach to treating their disorder. Finally, behavioral weight loss should not be considered as a first choice when treating individuals with BED.

In summary, the literature suggests that IPT represents an efficacious treatment alternative to CBT for BED. If delivering IPT for BED in a group format, as with all group therapies, developing member cohesion is paramount to the achievement of treatment success.

IPT for AN
In general, there are very few effective treatments for AN (Wilson, Grilo, & Vitousek, 2007). Although behavioral family therapy is considered the treatment of choice for adolescents with early onset of the disorder, these data are not especially informative when making recommendations for adults. With regard to IPT, there is a relative lack of research examining its utility for AN. Indeed, there have been no controlled studies demonstrating the efficacy of IPT for AN. To date, only one group has tested IPT for AN (McIntosh et al., 2005). Fifty-six women with AN were randomized to IPT, CBT, or a control comparison (non-specific, supportive clinical management). In contrast to the impressive effects of IPT for both BN and BED, this study found that IPT was associated with little improvement in AN symptoms compared to nonspecific, supportive clinical management (McIntosh et al., 2005). Of the three therapies, nonspecific, supportive clinical management was the most effective approach. Importantly, the authors posited that their findings may be a result of the relative lack of focus on ED symptoms in their adaptation of IPT (McIntosh, Bulik, McKenzie, Luty, & Jordan, 2000) and suggest that future studies implementing IPT for AN involve consistent connections between the interpersonal problem areas and the core symptoms

of the disorder (McIntosh et al., 2005). Particularly given the ego syntonic nature of AN, the lack of focus on ED symptoms may have blunted IPT's impact and avoided the essential work of the therapy (McIntosh et al., 2005). In summary, the short timeframe for the IPT work, a relative lack of symptom-focus, and the brief length of follow-up may have also contributed to the study outcome.

Given the importance of interpersonal functioning in etiological theories of AN (McIntosh et al., 2000), continued exploration of IPT's utility in treatment of the disorder is clearly warranted. In particular, investigation of IPT for AN that includes a focus on ED symptoms as they relate to interpersonal problems is needed. It may be that for AN, IPT is optimally delivered in the context of other adjunctive treatments (e.g., pharmacological, nutritional), rather than as a "stand alone" treatment. Staging of treatment may also be important; IPT may be more suitable for the maintenance and relapse prevention stages of treatment than for the weight regain phase (Jacobs, Welch, & Wilfley, 2004).

Choosing Treatment Modality
When determining the treatment approach for patients with EDs, the clinician and patient should together evaluate the advantages and disadvantages of utilizing IPT, CBT or another therapeutic approach, e.g. pharmacologic treatment. In making this decision, it is crucial for therapists to explore their own comfort level in terms of their expertise, theoretic knowledge, and propensity toward administering an interpersonally-focused treatment (Wilfley et al., 2000). IPT, like CBT, is a specialty treatment and should be administered only by trained practitioners. However, it has been argued that experienced therapists who have been trained in other treatment modalities tend to learn IPT quickly and are often able to implement IPT with a high degree of integrity despite minimal IPT-specific training (Birchall, 1999). Further, some therapists may consider IPT to be more acceptable than CBT. Although not specific solely to IPT, a naturalistic study of psychotherapy outcome in which 145 clinicians provided information about their ED patients found that compared to CBT, psychodynamic approaches that included IPT produced better global outcomes (Thompson-Brenner & Westen, 2005). Although there are limited data exploring the influence of therapist comfort on treatment outcome, it is possible that some clinicians are more comfortable administering treatments other than CBT, and this

is reflected in the outcome of their work (Tanofsky-Kraff & Wilfley, 2010).

To date, there are more data in support of the efficacy of CBT for EDs. Although CBT has been shown to produce more rapid effects for BN, IPT produces equivalent outcomes over the long-term for adults with this disorder. IPT for BED appears to be equally as effective as CBT. Based upon the evolving literature, IPT may be well-suited for patients presenting with or without exacerbated difficulties in social functioning. Although greater problems were associated with poorer outcomes for both CBT and IPT in the Hilbert et al. (2007) study, the moderator effect that patients presenting with greater psychopathology seem to respond well to IPT in the more recent multi-site study (Wilson et al., 2010), suggest that IPT (or another specialized treatment such as CBT) may be well suited for individuals with a broad range of disordered eating and general psychopathology. Moreover, IPT may be enhanced for individuals with exacerbated psychological problems (Markowitz et al., 2006). It is also possible that IPT may be especially fitting for some minority groups, such as African Americans. Finally, it is possible that some patients may express discomfort or difficulties with elements of CBT (e.g., keeping food diaries); IPT should be considered for these patients as well (Tanofsky-Kraff & Wilfley, 2010).

IPT for the Prevention of Excessive Weight Gain

IPT has recently been developed for the prevention of excessive weight gain in adolescents who report loss of control eating (LOC) patterns. LOC refers to the sense that one cannot control what or how much one is eating, regardless of whether the reported amount of food consumed is unambiguously large (Tanofsky-Kraff, 2008). Common among youth, LOC eating is associated with distress and overweight (Tanofsky-Kraff, 2008), predicts excessive weight gain over time (Tanofsky-Kraff et al., 2010), and in theory, is believed to be a marker of risk for the development of subsequent clinical eating pathology such as BED. This adaptation makes use of both IPT for the prevention of depression in adolescents (IPT Adolescent Skills Training, IPT-AST) (Young, Mufson, & Davies, 2006) and group IPT for BED (Wilfley et al., 2000), and evolved from the outcome data of psychotherapy trials for the treatment of BED. An unexpected finding of IPT and most psychological treatments for BED has been that individuals with BED who cease to binge

eat tend to maintain their body weight during and/or following treatment (Agras et al., 1995; Agras, Telch, Arnow, Eldredge, & Marnell, 1997; Devlin et al., 2005; Wilfley et al., 1993, 2002). Therefore, it has been hypothesized that treatment of LOC eating among youth may reduce excessive weight gain and prevent full-syndrome EDs (Tanofsky-Kraff et al., 2007).

A number of factors suggest that IPT is particularly appropriate for the prevention of obesity in high-risk adolescents with binge or LOC eating patterns. Specifically, youth frequently use peer relationships as a crucial measure of self-evaluation (Mufson et al., 2004). A recent study revealed the importance of perceived social interactions and social standing on body weight gain over time (Lemeshow et al., 2008). In this prospective cohort study, adolescent girls who rated themselves lower on a subjective social standing scale were 69% more likely to gain more weight over time, compared to girls who rated themselves higher on the scale (Lemeshow et al., 2008). Further, overweight teens are more likely to experience negative feelings about themselves, particularly regarding their body shape and weight, compared to normal weight adolescents (Fallon et al., 2005; Schwimmer, Burwinkle, & Varni, 2003; Striegel-Moore, Silberstein, & Rodin, 1986), perhaps because of their elevated rates of appearance-related teasing, rejection, and social isolation (Strauss & Pollack, 2003). The social isolation that overweight teens report may be directly targeted by IPT. Finally, IPT is posited to increase social support, which has been demonstrated to improve weight maintenance in overweight adults (Wing & Jeffery, 1999) and children (Wilfley et al., 2007). Indeed, data suggest that low social problems predict better response to weight loss treatment in children (Wilfley et al., 2007).

IPT for the prevention of excessive weight gain (IPT-WG) for adolescents at high-risk for adult obesity, delivered in a group format, maintains the key components of traditional IPT: (1) a focus on interpersonal problem areas that are related to the target behavior (e.g., LOC eating in the present adaptation); (2) the use of the interpersonal inventory at the outset of treatment to identify interpersonal problems that are contributing to the targeted behavior; and (3) the three-staged structure of the intervention (initial, middle, and termination). The primary activities of IPT-WG are to provide psychoeducation about risk factors for excessive weight gain and to teach general skill-building to improve interpersonal problems. IPT-WG was founded on

Young and Mufson's IPT-AST (Young & Mufson, 2003) and group IPT for the treatment of BED in adulthood (Wilfley et al., 2000). IPT-WG differs from other adaptations in that it was developed to specifically address the particular needs of adolescent girls at high risk for adult obesity due to their current body mass index (BMI) percentile and report of LOC eating behaviors.

Based on IPT-AST, IPT-WG is presented to teenagers as "Teen Talk" in order to be non-stigmatizing. As designed by Young (Young & Mufson, 2003), this preventive adaptation of IPT focuses on psychoeducation, communication analysis and role playing. Specific interpersonal communications skills are taught, including "strike while the iron is cold," "use 'I' statements," "be specific" (when talking about a problem), and "put yourself in their shoes" (Young & Mufson, 2003). For IPT-WG, an additional skill, "what you don't say speaks volumes," has been added to teach adolescents how their body language has the ability to impact communication regardless of their words. During the interpersonal inventory, a "closeness circle" (Mufson et al., 2004) is used to identify the close relationships of the participant. Since IPT-WG is designed for adolescents ranging from age 12 to 17 years, sessions are geared toward the adolescents' developmental level. For example, younger adolescents, who may be uncomfortable talking about themselves, may respond better to hypothetical situations and games, whereas older teenagers may more readily discuss their own interpersonal issues from the outset.

Based on IPT for BED, IPT-WG maintains focus throughout the program on linking negative affect to LOC eating, overeating, times when individuals eat in response to cues other than hunger, as well as over-concern about shape and weight. Further, a timeline of personal eating and weight-related problems and life events is discussed individually with participants prior to the group program. Similar to both programs, IPT-WG is delivered in a group format. IPT-WG is 12 weeks in duration, longer than IPT-AST (8 sessions), but shorter than group IPT for BED (typically 16–20 sessions). Similar to IPT-AST, group size is smaller than in IPT-BED (5 vs. 9 members), enabling therapists to keep adolescents engaged. As with group IPT for BED (Wilfley et al., 2000), participants meet individually with the therapist(s) for a brief mid-treatment meeting to discuss progress made on proposed therapeutic goals, areas that are particularly challenging, and plans for continued work through the second half of the group.

The following case example of "Kay" briefly illustrates the presentation and treatment of an adolescent group participant. For sample cases of adults with EDs across diagnostic categories, we recommend referring to a book by Denise Wilfley and colleagues (Wilfley et al., 2000) as well as chapters on IPT for EDs (e.g., Jacobs et al., 2004; Wilfley, Stein et al., 2003).

Presentation: Kay is a 14-year-old African American girl with a BMI at the 85th percentile for her age and sex (Ogden et al., 2006). At intake, she reported engaging in an average of five to six episodes of LOC eating per month over the 3 months before intake. She specifically recalled engaging in two such episodes in the past month, both when alone and feeling "bored." She reported feeling anger, distress, and regret following her LOC eating episodes. However, she was only able to connect her episodes to feelings of boredom. Kay endorsed some distress surrounding her shape and weight as well as feeling "fat" much of the time, but reported few attempts at dieting. She reported eating in response to a number of negative emotions, with a very strong desire to eat when feeling down, sad, stressed out, worried, or bored. Although she presented with few symptoms of depression, Kay did experience some sub-clinical threshold symptoms of anxiety. Although she reported feeling shy when meeting new people, she also endorsed having close friendships with peers in whom she could confide.

During her pre-treatment meeting, Kay reported a number of family stressors. In the months prior to intake, she had reluctantly returned to her mother's home in the Midwest to attend the local middle school, after having attended boarding school for three years on the West Coast. She reported generally poor relationships with her parents, who had divorced when she was a baby. Kay indicated that because she and her mother were "a lot alike" and both very stubborn, they argued frequently. Most often, their arguments concerned Kay's dislike of her stepfather, whom she referred to as obnoxious and racist. She reported that her mother no longer "thinks for herself," but rather just agrees with her stepfather. Fights with her mother typically involved Kay saying something hurtful in the "heat of the moment" and/or walking away without resolution. Kay reported being left with emotions of both rage and guilt. During these times, she would often overeat and experience a lack of control over how much she was eating. Following the eating episode, she reported that her negative feelings eventually "went away."

Despite living in a nearby city, her biological father had little contact with her following her parents' divorce. She had spoken with him one or two times per month for many years and up until intake. Kay reported feeling abandoned by her father and attributed his lack of availability to his own social anxiety. Nonetheless, she wished for a closer relationship, but never discussed her desire with him for fear that he would not be receptive.

Problem area: Kay's IPT problem area was conceptualized as a role dispute. Moving home from boarding school—halfway across the country—decreased her independence and exacerbated the typical changes adolescents experience during developmentally appropriate individuation from their parents. Kay struggled with being unable to communicate successfully with either parent—or her stepfather—regarding her opinions and needs. In response to such disputes, Kay would experience negative affect and eat to cope with her emotions.

Goals: The therapists and Kay generated and agreed upon the following therapy goals for the 12-week intervention. The first goal was that Kay would work on gaining perspective to feel less frustrated with her parents and work on remaining calm in the moment. Second, she would aim to express her feelings of being let down and hurt by her father. If possible, she would consider discussing these feelings with him. Kay's work in treatment would involve clarifying her role within the family, vis-à-vis her mother and stepfather, and learning how to negotiate and express herself with them in a more functional manner.

The IPT intervention is described next.

Initial phase: Kay was very engaged during the initial phase. She actively participated in the role play exercises and was open about her frustration with moving back home to live with her mother and stepfather. She also shared how she had a tendency to vacillate between speaking her mind and avoiding arguments by walking away, particularly with her mother. She reported overeating and feeling unable to stop, most often in response to avoiding arguments with her mother and feeling angry. Specifically, she shared that not only would her mother side with her stepfather during family arguments, but that her mother believed Kay was not intelligent. Her mother would often express her opinion about Kay's intelligence with her stepfather and other friends. Kay was encouraged to role play a conversation with her mother in which she dis-

cussed her feelings. However, she remained skeptical that her mother would be responsive. While the therapists encouraged Kay to practice such a conversation in the group, they also recommended that she think about how to better tolerate her mother's behavior if, in fact, she was unresponsive.

Middle phase: Kay spent more time role playing conversations that she might have with both her mother and her father. The therapists encouraged Kay to initiate a discussion with her parents during which she would be specific about her frustrations while also trying to keep in mind an understanding of their perspectives. Initially, Kay was reluctant to follow up on this work. She was therefore encouraged to examine her pattern of anger and then avoidance, particularly with her mother. During the seventh session, Kay became frustrated with the therapists' persistence and grew sullen and angered. She returned the next session to report that she was angry, confused and disappointed to have learned about some of her mother's past behaviors of which Kay did not approve. The therapists encouraged Kay to take "a leap of faith" and try talking with her mother. After in-session practicing, Kay approached her mother and talked about her feelings in a calm manner. She was very pleased with her mother's receptiveness to the discussion. By the end of the middle phase, Kay was also spending some time with her father. Moreover, she had opened up a dialogue with him regarding some of her feelings of disappointment with him. Much to her surprise, her father was more receptive to her self-expression than she had expected. Throughout this phase, Kay was frequently queried about her eating patterns. Initially, she noticed that that the frequency of her LOC eating episodes had decreased. Then, she became more cognizant of the times she would binge eat. For example, after finding out that an old friend was ill, she became very upset and was able to link her feelings to LOC eating.

Termination phase: Kay reported that not only was she sharing her feelings more often, but that she was overeating less frequently. She was supportive of other group members in taking their own "leaps of faith" by describing how overwhelmed she felt before speaking with her parents, but how much better she felt after the conversations. By the final session, Kay was quite sad about the ending of the group. She reported that she was going to miss the support of the therapists and group members and realized that she still had a great deal of work to continue. The therapists focused upon the work she had accomplished and assured her that she had achieved the skills necessary to continue making improvements. Along with the therapists and the other members, Kay outlined the future work that she would continue after the groups ended. Specifically, she planned to continue dialogues with her mother and seek to develop a closer relationship with her father, with the recognition of his emotional limitations.

After treatment, Kay reported no longer experiencing episodes of LOC while eating. Moreover, her BMI percentile had decreased 5 percentage points to the 80th percentile for her age and sex (Ogden et al., 2006).

The courses of treatment for this individual, along with two other case examples, are illustrated in Table 20.4 (Tanofsky-Kraff et al., 2007).

In a pilot study testing IPT-WG compared to a standard health education program (Bravender, 2005), IPT-WG was shown to be both feasible and acceptable to adolescent girls (Tanofsky-Kraff in press). Further, more girls in IPT than health education experienced weight stabilization or weight loss, compared to weight gain, at the last measured observation. An adequately powered controlled trial is currently underway to determine the effectiveness of IPT-WG for the prevention of excess weight gain.

Future Directions for IPT in the Treatment of EDs

Several important areas require further study. An important next step is to determine whether IPT for EDs can be translated from specialty care centers to non-research clinical practice milieus. In an effort to continually improve IPT and broaden its utility, we propose other research directions in this section (Tanofsky-Kraff & Wilfley, 2010).

Enhancing IPT for BN and BED

As efforts to more frequently and consistently link ED symptoms to interpersonal functioning has evolved in the use of IPT for BED, clinical researchers involved in developing IPT for BN should also consider stressing this link during the delivery of IPT so that it offers the utmost potency. Since IPT does appear to have specific effects in BN and good long-term maintenance of change, it seems prudent to evaluate methods for improving its efficiency and clinical effectiveness. For instance, it may be that the slower and less potent effects observed in IPT as compared to CBT were due to the manner in which IPT was implemented. Specifically, in order to minimize procedural overlap with CBT, the research application of IPT for BN has not included an ongoing focus on making links between symptomatology and interpersonal functioning, which is in stark contrast to how IPT was developed and tested for depression. In future studies, the efficacy and efficiency of IPT may be enhanced by including a specific focus on the core symptoms of BN and their connection with interpersonal issues throughout the course of treatment. Such refinements of the content and delivery of IPT may further strengthen its usefulness in the treatment of BN.

IPT, in its current form, already seamlessly incorporates aspects of other therapeutic modalities. For example, the collaborative, interpersonal formulation of the ED symptoms during the interpersonal inventory is one of the ways in which IPT may resemble the behavior therapies more so than it does the supportive or psychodynamic therapies. Therefore, some aspects of CBT may enhance the efficacy of IPT (Tanofsky-Kraff & Wilfley, 2010). For example, IPT therapists might wish to encourage self-monitoring as a method for patients to become more aware of their negative affect surrounding ED symptoms. Such an approach is already being tested in other treatment modalities. Indeed, Fairburn and colleagues have found the inclusion of an interpersonal module useful when administering a recently modified version of CBT for EDs (Enhanced CBT for EDs), (Fairburn, 2008).

Adolescent and Child/Parent Adaptations

Given the robust efficacy of IPT for adolescents with depressive disorders, and the initial promise of IPT-WG, future research should involve additional adolescent adaptations (Tanofsky-Kraff & Wilfley, 2010). Adolescence is a key developmental period for cultivating social and interpersonal patterns, which may explain why adolescents appear to relate well to IPT. From its inception, Mufson and colleagues made important adolescent-relevant adaptations to the treatment (Mufson et al., 2004). For example, IPT for adolescent depression includes a parent component and the assignment of a "*limited sick role,*" since youth are required to attend school and reducing their activities is likely to exacerbate their interpersonal difficulties. Given that this foundation has been established, the use of IPT for adolescents with BN and BED warrants investigation.

Utilizing IPT for younger children may also be a promising approach. A pilot study of family-based IPT for the treatment of depressive symptoms in 9- to 12-year-old children was found to be feasible

Table 20.4 IPT-WG Sample Case Conceptualizations and Courses of Treatment

Example Participant	LOC Eating Precipitant(s)	Interpersonal Functioning	Problem Area	Goal	Initial Phase	Middle Phase	Termination Phase
Case 1	Sadness, stress, and worry	Repeated heated arguments with mother	Role dispute	Gain perspective to decrease frustration and remain calm when communicating with mother.	Sharing feelings of frustration with mother; in group role-play of discussions with mother.	Discuss resistance to speaking with mother; with group encouragement, began productive dialogues with mother.	Emphasis on improved communication skills; discussion of transferring use of skills to other close interpersonal relationships; gaining other outside supports
Case 2	Avoiding conflict and negative affect	Does not express negative feelings or discomfort with conflict in multiple relationships.	Interpersonal deficits	Become more comfortable with conflict and work on expressing feelings.	Discuss discomfort surrounding interactions involving conflict.	Practice sharing feelings via role-playing; encouraged to communicate.< feelings with less tense relationship.	Emphasis on improved communication skills; focus on future generalizing of skills to several situations
Case 3	Boredom and frustration	Expresses emotions/needs to family (especially parents) in nonproductive manner.	Role dispute	Use more constructive communication to express self.	Communication analysis and in- group role-play of poor interactions	Continued role-playing specific situations and trying out discussions with siblings.	Emphasis on improved communication skills; focus on future sharing of deeper personal conflicts with parents

Source: Tanofsky-Kraff, M., Wilfley, D. E., Young, J. F., Mufson, L., Yanovski, S. Z., Glasofer, D. R., et al. (2007). Preventing excessive weight gain in adolescents: interpersonal psychotherapy for binge eating. *Obesity (Silver Spring), 15*(6), 1345–1355. Reprinted by permission from Nature Publishing Group/Macmillan.Obesity [*15*(6), 1345–1355]. © 2007.

and acceptable to families (Dietz, Mufson, Irvine, & Brent, 2008). Currently, an effectiveness trial is underway. The moderating influence of social problems on weight loss outcome in a family-based program (Wilfley et al., 2007) suggests that targeting interpersonal functioning in the nuclear family milieu may serve as a point of intervention for the treatment of eating and weight-related problems during middle childhood (Tanofsky-Kraff & Wilfley, 2010).

Developing IPT for the Prevention of Eating and Weight-Related Problems

Given the increasingly high rates of obesity (Ogden et al., 2006), it may be reasonably posited that the increases in disordered eating will continue as well, considering that overweight is a significant risk factor for the development of eating pathology (Fairburn et al., 1997, 1998). Therefore, the use of IPT to prevent obesity and full-syndrome EDs should be explored, by targeting other behaviors that promote both conditions (Tanofsky-Kraff & Wilfley, 2010). Since not all overweight individuals report binge or LOC eating, reducing emotional eating and eating in the absence of hunger may also be suitable for IPT modalities. Recent studies suggest that LOC eating among youth is associated with eating in response to negative affect (Goossens, Braet, & Decaluwe, 2006), including anger and frustration, depression, and anxiety (Tanofsky-Kraff et al., 2007). In studies of adolescents, emotional eating is significantly correlated with constructs of disturbed eating (van Strien, 1996; van Strien, Engels, van Leeuwe, & Snoek, 2005) and symptoms of depression and anxiety (van Strien et al., 2005). Data also suggest that emotional eating may be associated with overweight among youth (Braet & van Strien, 1997) and overeating in cross-sectional structural models (van Strien et al., 2005). Considering that in controlled trials IPT for BED effectively reduces eating in response to negative affect in adults (Wilfley et al., 1993, 2002), preventive adaptations targeting emotional eating require investigation.

Eating in the absence of hunger has been associated with overweight (Moens & Braet, 2007) and excessive weight gain over time (Shunk & Birch, 2004). Reported eating in the absence of hunger has been shown to be associated with LOC eating, emotional eating, and elevations in general psychopathology (Tanofsky-Kraff, Ranzenhofer et al., 2008). Of concern are data indicating that eating in the absence of hunger is a stable trait throughout youth (Birch, Fisher, & Davison, 2003; Fisher & Birch, 2002).

Promising findings indicate that young children may be trained to better regulate food intake (Johnson, 2000), and a number of intervention studies targeting eating in the absence of hunger are currently underway. IPT may serve as a natural extension on this work; in particular, negative affect associated with interpersonal problems might be linked to eating in absence of hunger. Then, recognition of internal physiological hunger cues may be taught so that patients learn to differentiate true hunger from when they are already sated.

Finally, there has been a growing interest in and awareness of the role that social and interpersonal factors may play in behavioral health problems (Glass & McAtee, 2006). For obesity in particular, moving away from focusing solely on individual behavioral changes (e.g., diet and exercise) and towards the greater social context has not been the norm. IPT may be particularly well-suited for developing new approaches for the prevention of obesity and EDs on a broader social level (National Institutes of Health [NIH], 2004; Tanofsky-Kraff & Wilfley, 2010).

Conclusion

Interpersonal psychotherapy for EDs is a focused, time-limited treatment that targets interpersonal problems associated with the onset and/or maintenance of the ED. The interpersonal focus is highly relevant to individuals with EDs, many of whom experience difficulties in interpersonal functioning. Depending on the individual's primary problem area, specific treatment strategies and goals are incorporated into the treatment plan. The primary problem area is determined by conducting a thorough interpersonal inventory, a unique aspect of IPT, and by devising an individualized interpersonal formulation for each patient. IPT has resulted in significant and well-maintained improvements for the treatment of BN and BED. Preliminary data support the utility of IPT for the prevention of excess weight gain in adolescent girls. Further investigation is required to determine whether IPT is suitable for and effective in the treatment of AN. Adaptations of IPT should be explored for adolescent populations and the treatment of other eating- and weight-related problems. Finally, an important next step is to disseminate IPT into routine clinical care settings.

Acknowledgments
NIDDK grant 1R01DK080906-01A1 (MTK). USUHS grant R072IC (to MTK). Disclaimer: The

opinions and assertions expressed herein are those of the authors and are not to be construed as reflecting the views of USUHS or the U.S. Department of Defense. NIMH grant 5R01MH064153-06 (DEW). NIMH grant 1K24MH070446 (DEW).

References

Agras, W. S., Telch, C. F., Arnow, B., Eldredge, K., Detzer, M. J., Henderson, J., et al. (1995). Does interpersonal therapy help patients with binge eating disorder who fail to respond to cognitive-behavioral therapy? *Journal of Consulting and Clinical Psychology*, *63*(3), 356–360.

Agras, W. S., Telch, C. F., Arnow, B., Eldredge, K., & Marnell, M. (1997). One-year follow-up of cognitive-behavioral therapy for obese individuals with binge eating disorder. *Journal of Consulting and Clinical Psychology*, *65*(2), 343–347.

Agras, W. S., Walsh, T., Fairburn, C. G., Wilson, G. T., & Kraemer, H. C. (2000). A multicenter comparison of cognitive-behavioral therapy and interpersonal psychotherapy for bulimia nervosa. *Archives of General Psychiatry*, *57*(5), 459–466.

Birch, L. L., Fisher, J. O., & Davison, K. K. (2003). Learning to overeat: Maternal use of restrictive feeding practices promotes girls' eating in the absence of hunger. *American Journal of Clinical Nutrition*, *78*(2), 215–220.

Birchall, H. (1999). Interpersonal psychotherapy in the treatment of eating disorder. *European Eating Disorders Review*, *7*, 315–320.

Bishop, M., Stein, R., Hilbert, A., Swenson, A., & Wilfley, D. E. (2007, October). *A five-year follow-up study of cognitive-behavioral therapy and interpersonal psychotherapy for the treatment of binge eating disorder*. Paper presented at the Eating Disorders Research Society.

Bowlby, J. (1982). *Attachment and loss* (2nd ed., Vol. 1). New York: Basic Books.

Braet, C., & van Strien, T. (1997). Assessment of emotional, externally induced and restrained eating behaviour in nine to twelve-year-old obese and non-obese children. *Behavior Research and Therapy*, *35*(9), 863–873.

Bravender, T. (2005). *Health, Education, and Youth in Durham: HEY-Durham Curricular Guide*, (2nd ed.). Durham, NC: Duke University.

Chui, W., Safer, D. L., Bryson, S. W., Agras, W. S., & Wilson, G. T. (2007). A comparison of ethnic groups in the treatment of bulimia nervosa. *Eating Behaviors*, *8*(4), 485–491.

Constantino, M. J., Arnow, B. A., Blasey, C., & Agras, W. S. (2005). The association between patient characteristics and the therapeutic alliance in cognitive-behavioral and interpersonal therapy for bulimia nervosa. *Journal of Consulting and Clinical Psychology*, *73*(2), 203–211.

Crow, S. J., Stewart Agras, W., Halmi, K., Mitchell, J. E., & Kraemer, H. C. (2002). Full syndromal versus subthreshold anorexia nervosa, bulimia nervosa, and binge eating disorder: A multicenter study. *International Journal of Eating Disorders*, *32*(3), 309–318.

Devlin, M. J., Goldfein, J. A., Petkova, E., Jiang, H., Raizman, P. S., Wolk, S., et al. (2005). Cognitive behavioral therapy and fluoxetine as adjuncts to group behavioral therapy for binge eating disorder. *Obesity Research*, *13*(6), 1077–1088.

Dietz, L. J., Mufson, L., Irvine, H., & Brent, D. A. (2008). Family-based Interpersonal Psychotherapy (IPT) for depressed preadolescents: An open treatment trial. *Early Intervention Psychiatry*, *2*, 154–161.

Dounchis, J. Z., Welch, R. R., & Wilfley, D. E. (1999). *Using group interpersonal psychotherapy (IPT-G) for the treatment of binge eating disorders*. Paper presented at the Academy of Eating Disorders Annual Meeting, San Diego.

Evans, L., & Wertheim, E. H. (1998). Intimacy patterns and relationship satisfaction of women with eating problems and the mediating effects of depression, trait anxiety and social anxiety. *Journal of Psychosomatic Research*, *44*(3–4), 355–365.

Fairburn, C. G. (1997). Interpersonal psychotherapy for bulimia nervosa. In D. M. Garner & P. E. Garfinkel (Eds.), *Handbook of treatment for eating disorders* (Vol. 2, pp. 278–294). New York: Guilford Press.

Fairburn, C. G. (2008). *Cognitive behavior therapy and eating disorders*. New York: Guilford Press.

Fairburn, C. G., Doll, H. A., Welch, S. L., Hay, P. J., Davies, B. A., & O'Connor, M. E. (1998). Risk factors for binge eating disorder: A community-based, case-control study. *Archives of General Psychiatry*, *55*(5), 425–432.

Fairburn, C. G., Jones, R., Peveler, R. C., Carr, S. J., Solomon, R. A., O'Connor, M. E., et al. (1991). Three psychological treatments for bulimia nervosa. A comparative trial. *Archives of General Psychiatry*, *48*(5), 463–469.

Fairburn, C. G., Norman, P. A., Welch, S. L., O'Connor, M. E., Doll, H. A., & Peveler, R. C. (1995). A prospective study of outcome in bulimia nervosa and the long-term effects of three psychological treatments. *Archives of General Psychiatry*, *52*(4), 304–312.

Fairburn, C. G., Peveler, R. C., Jones, R., Hope, R. A., & Doll, H. A. (1993). Predictors of 12-month outcome in bulimia nervosa and the influence of attitudes to shape and weight. *Journal of Consulting and Clinical Psychology*, *61*(4), 696–698.

Fairburn, C. G., Welch, S. L., Doll, H. A., Davies, B. A., & O'Connor, M. E. (1997). Risk factors for bulimia nervosa. A community-based case-control study. *Archives of General Psychiatry*, *54*(6), 509–517.

Fallon, E. M., Tanofsky-Kraff, M., Norman, A. C., McDuffie, J. R., Taylor, E. D., Cohen, M. L., et al. (2005). Health-related quality of life in overweight and nonoverweight black and white adolescents. *Journal of Pediatrics*, *147*(4), 443–450.

Fisher, J. O., & Birch, L. L. (2002). Eating in the absence of hunger and overweight in girls from 5 to 7y of age. *American Journal of Clinical Nutrition*, *76*(1), 226–231.

Frank, E., & Spanier, C. (1995). Interpersonal psychotherapy for depression: Overview, clinical efficacy, and future directions. *Clinical Psychology: Science & Practice*, *2*(4), 349–369.

Freeman, L. M. Y., & Gil, K. M. (2004). Daily stress, coping, and dietary restraint in binge eating. *International Journal of Eating Disorders*, *36*, 204–212.

Ghaderi, A., & Scott, B. (1999). Prevalence and psychological correlates of eating disorders among females aged 18–30 years in the general population. *Acta Psychiatrica Scandinavica*, *99*(4), 261–266.

Glass, T. A., & McAtee, M. J. (2006). Behavioral science at the crossroads in public health: Extending horizons, envisioning the future. *Social Science & Medicine*, *62*(7), 1650–1671.

Goossens, L., Braet, C., & Decaluwe, V. (2006). Loss of control over eating in obese youngsters. *Behaviour Research and therapy*. *45*, 1–9.

Grilo, C. M., Masheb, R. M., & Wilson, G. T. (2005). Efficacy of cognitive behavioral therapy and fluoxetine for the treatment of binge eating disorder: A randomized double-blind placebo-controlled comparison. *Biological Psychiatry*, *57*(3), 301–309.

Grissett, N. I., & Norvell, N. K. (1992). Perceived social support, social skills, and quality of relationships in bulimic women. *Journal of Consulting and Clinical Psychology, 60*(2), 293–299.

Gual, P., Perez-Gaspar, M., Martinez-Gonzalez, M. A., Lahortiga, F., de Irala-Estevez, J., & Cervera-Enguix, S. (2002). Self-esteem, personality, and eating disorders: Baseline assessment of a prospective population-based cohort. *International Journal of Eating Disorders, 31*(3), 261–273.

Herzog, D., Keller, M., Lavori, P., & Ott, I. (1987). Social impairment in bulimia. *International Journal of Eating Disorders, 6,* 741–747.

Hilbert, A., Saelens, B. E., Stein, R. I., Mockus, D. S., Welch, R. R., Matt, G. E., et al. (2007). Pretreatment and process predictors of outcome in interpersonal and cognitive behavioral psychotherapy for binge eating disorder. *Journal of Consulting and Clinical Psychology, 75*(4), 645–651.

Humphrey, L. L. (1989). Observed family interactions among subtypes of eating disorders using structural analysis of social behavior. *Journal of Consulting and Clinical Psychology, 57*(2), 206–214.

Jacobs, M. J., Welch, R. R., & Wilfley, D. E. (2004). Interpersonal psychotherapy for anorexia nervosa, bulimia nervosa, and binge eating disorder. In T. Brewerton (Ed.), *Clinical handbook of eating disorders: An integrated approach* (pp. 449–472). New York: Marcel Dekker.

Johnson, J. G., Spitzer, R. L., & Williams, J. B. (2001). Health problems, impairment and illnesses associated with bulimia nervosa and binge eating disorder among primary care and obstetric gynaecology patients. *Psychological Medicine, 31*(8), 1455–1466.

Johnson, S. L. (2000). Improving preschoolers' self-regulation of energy intake. *Pediatrics, 106*(6), 1429–1435.

Keel, P. K., Dorer, D. J., Franko, D. L., Jackson, S. C., & Herzog, D. B. (2005). Postremission predictors of relapse in women with eating disorders. *American Journal of Psychiatry, 162*(12), 2263–2268.

Kenardy, J., Mensch, M., Bowen, K., Green, B., & Walton, J. (2002). Group therapy for binge eating in type 2 diabetes: A randomized trial. *Diabetic Medicine, 19*(3), 234–239.

Klerman, G. L., Weissman, M. M., Rounsaville, B. J., & Chevron, E. S. (1984). *Interpersonal psychotherapy of depression.* New York: Basic Books.

Lemeshow, A. R., Fisher, L., Goodman, E., Kawachi, I., Berkey, C. S., & Colditz, G. A. (2008). Subjective social status in the school and change in adiposity in female adolescents: Findings from a prospective cohort study. *Archives of Pediatric and Adolescent Medicine, 162*(1), 23–28.

Markowitz, J. C., Skodol, A. E., & Bleiberg, K. (2006). Interpersonal psychotherapy for borderline personality disorder: Possible mechanisms of change. *Journal of Clinical Psychology, 62*(4), 431–444.

McIntosh, V. V., Bulik, C. M., McKenzie, J. M., Luty, S. E., & Jordan, J. (2000). Interpersonal psychotherapy for anorexia nervosa. *International Journal of Eating Disorders, 27*(2), 125–139.

McIntosh, V. V., Jordan, J., Carter, F. A., Luty, S. E., McKenzie, J. M., Bulik, C. M., et al. (2005). Three psychotherapies for anorexia nervosa: A randomized, controlled trial. *American Journal of Psychiatry, 162*(4), 741–747.

Meyer, A. (1957). *Psychobiology: A science of man.* Springfield, IL: Charles C Thomas.

Moens, E., & Braet, C. (2007). Predictors of disinhibited eating in children with and without overweight. *Behavior Research and Therapy, 45*(6), 1357–1368.

Mufson, L., Dorta, K. P., Moreau, D., & Weissman, M. M. (2004). *Interpersonal psychotherapy for depressed adolescents,* (2nd ed.) New York: Guilford Press.

Nauta, H., Hospers, H., Kok, G., & Jansen, A. (2000). A comparison between a cognitive and a behavioral treatment for obese binge eaters and obese non-binge eaters. *Behavior Therapy, 21,* 441–461.

Nevonen, L., & Broberg, A. G. (2006). A comparison of sequenced individual and group psychotherapy for patients with bulimia nervosa. *International Journal of Eating Disorders, 39*(2), 117–127.

National Institutes of Health (NIH), O. R. T. F. (2004). *Strategic plan for NIH obesity research.* Bethesda, MD: NIDDK, NIH, DHHS.

O'Mahony, J. F., & Hollwey, S. (1995a). The correlates of binge eating in two nonpatient samples. *Addictive Behaviors, 20*(4), 471–480.

O'Mahony, J. F., & Hollwey, S. (1995b). Eating problems and interpersonal functioning among several groups of women. *Journal of Clinical Psychology, 51*(3), 345–351.

Ogden, C. L., Carroll, M. D., Curtin, L. R., McDowell, M. A., Tabak, C. J., & Flegal, K. M. (2006). Prevalence of overweight and obesity in the United States, 1999–2004. *JAMA, 295*(13), 1549–1555.

Ricca, V., Mannucci, E., Mezzani, B., Moretti, S., Di Bernardo, M., Bertelli, M., et al. (2001). Fluoxetine and fluvoxamine combined with individual cognitive-behaviour therapy in binge eating disorder: A one-year follow-up study. *Psychotherapy and Psychosomatics, 70*(6), 298–306.

Rorty, M., Yager, J., Buckwalter, J. G., & Rossotto, E. (1999). Social support, social adjustment, and recovery status in bulimia nervosa. *International Journal of Eating Disorders, 26*(1), 1–12.

Ruuska, J., Koivisto, A. M., Rantanen, P., & Kaltiala-Heino, R. (2007). Psychosocial functioning needs attention in adolescent eating disorders. *Nordic Journal of Psychiatry, 61*(6), 452–458.

Schwimmer, J. B., Burwinkle, T. M., & Varni, J. W. (2003). Health-related quality of life of severely obese children and adolescents. *JAMA, 289*(14), 1813–1819.

Shunk, J. A., & Birch, L. L. (2004). Girls at risk for overweight at age 5 are at risk for dietary restraint, disinhibited overeating, weight concerns, and greater weight gain from 5 to 9 years. *Journal of the American Dietetic Association, 104*(7), 1120–1126.

Steiger, H., Gauvin, L., Jabalpurwala, S., Seguin, J. R., & Stotland, S. (1999). Hypersensitivity to social interactions in bulimic syndromes: Relationship to binge eating. *Journal of Consulting and Clinical Psychology, 67*(5), 765–775.

Strauss, R. S., & Pollack, H. A. (2003). Social marginalization of overweight children. *Archives of Pediatric and Adolescent Medicine, 157*(8), 746–752.

Striegel-Moore, R. H., Silberstein, L. R., & Rodin, J. (1986). Toward an understanding of risk factors for bulimia. *American Psychologist, 41*(3), 246–263.

Tanofsky-Kraff, M. (2008). Binge eating among children and adolescents. In E. Jelalian & R. Steele (Eds.), *Handbook of child and adolescent obesity* (pp. 41–57). New York: Springer.

Tanofsky-Kraff, M., Ranzenhofer, L. M., Yanovski, S. Z., Schvey, N. A., Faith, M., Gustafson, J., et al. (2008). Psychometric properties of a new questionnaire to assess eating in the absence of hunger in children and adolescents. *Appetite, 51*(1), 148–155.

Tanofsky-Kraff, M., & Wilfley, D. E. (2010). Interpersonal psychotherapy for bulimia nervosa and binge eating disorder. In C. M. Grilo & J. Mitchell (Eds.), *The treatment of eating disorders*. New York: Guilford Press. 271–293.

Tanofsky-Kraff, M., Wilfley, D. E., & Spurrell, E. (2000). Impact of interpersonal and ego-related stress on restrained eaters. *International Journal of Eating Disorders, 27*(4), 411–418.

Tanofsky-Kraff, M., Wilfley, D. E., Young, J. F., Mufson, L., Yanovski, S. Z., Glasofer, D. R., Salaita, C. G., Schvey, N. A. In press. A pilot study of interpersonal psychotherapy for preventing excess weight gain in adolescent girls at-risk for obesity. *International Journal of Eating Disorders*.

Tanofsky-Kraff, M., Wilfley, D. E., Young, J. F., Mufson, L., Yanovski, S. Z., Glasofer, D. R., et al. (2007). Preventing excessive weight gain in adolescents: interpersonal psychotherapy for binge eating. *Obesity (Silver Spring), 15*(6), 1345–1355.

Tanofsky-Kraff, M., Yanovski, S. Z., Schvey, N. A., Olsen, C., Gustafson, J., & Yanovski, J. A. (In press). A prospective study of loss of control eating for body weight gain in children at high-risk for adult obesity. *International Journal of Eating Disorders*.

Tasca, G. A., Taylor, D., Ritchie, K., & Balfour, L. (2004). Attachment predicts treatment completion in an eating disorders partial hospital program among women with anorexia nervosa. *Journal of Personality Assessment, 83*(3), 201–212.

Telch, C. F., Agras, W. S., Rossiter, E. M., Wilfley, D., & Kenardy, J. (1990). Group cognitive-behavioral treatment for the nonpurging bulimic: An initial evaluation. *Journal of Consulting and Clinical Psychology, 58*(5), 629–635.

Thompson-Brenner, H., & Westen, D. (2005). A naturalistic study of psychotherapy for bulimia nervosa, part 2: Therapeutic interventions in the community. *Journal of Nervous and Mental Disorders, 193*(9), 585–595.

Troisi, A., Massaroni, P., & Cuzzolaro, M. (2005). Early separation anxiety and adult attachment style in women with eating disorders. *British Journal of Clinical Psychology, 44*(Pt 1), 89–97.

Troop, N. A., Holbrey, A., Trowler, R., & Treasure, J. L. (1994). Ways of coping in women with eating disorders. *Journal of Nervous and Mental Disease, 182*(10), 535–540.

van Strien, T. (1996). On the relationship between dieting and "obese" and bulimic eating patterns. *International Journal of Eating Disorders, 19*(1), 83–92.

van Strien, T., Engels, R. C., van Leeuwe, J., & Snoek, H. M. (2005). The Stice model of overeating: Tests in clinical and non-clinical samples. *Appetite, 45*(3), 205–213.

Weissman, M. M., Markowitz, J., & Klerman, G. L. (2000). *Comprehensive guide to Interpersonal psychotherapy*. New York: Basic Behavioral Science Books.

Wilfley, D. E. (2008). *Interpersonal psychotherapy for binge eating disorder (BED) Therapist's Manual*. Unpublished manuscript.

Wilfley, D. E., Agras, W. S., Telch, C. F., Rossiter, E. M., Schneider, J. A., Cole, A. G., et al. (1993). Group cognitive-behavioral therapy and group interpersonal psychotherapy for the nonpurging bulimic individual: A controlled comparison. *Journal of Consulting and Clinical Psychology, 61*(2), 296–305.

Wilfley, D. E., Dounchis, J. Z., & Welch, R. R. (2004). Interpersonal psychotherapy of anorexia nervosa. In K. M. Miller & J. S. Mizes (Eds.), *Comparative treatment of eating disorders*. New York: Springer.

Wilfley, D. E., Frank, M. A., Welch, R., Spurrell, E., & Rounsaville, B. J. (1998). Adapting interpersonal psychotherapy to a group format (IPT-G) for binge eating disorder: Toward a model for adapting empirically supported treatments. *Psychotherapy Research, 8,* 379–391.

Wilfley, D. E., MacKenzie, K. R., Welch, R. R., Ayres., V. E., & Weissman, M. M. (2000). *Interpersonal psychotherapy for group*. New York: Basic Books.

Wilfley, D. E., Stein, R., & Welch, R. R. (2003). Interpersonal psychotherapy. In U. S. J. Treasure, & E. van Furth (Ed.), *Handbook of eating disorders*. London: John Wiley & Sons.

Wilfley, D. E., Stein, R. I., Saelens, B. E., Mockus, D. S., Matt, G. E., Hayden-Wade, H. A., et al. (2007). Efficacy of maintenance treatment approaches for childhood overweight: A randomized controlled trial. *JAMA, 298*(14), 1661–1673.

Wilfley, D. E., Stein, R. I., & Welch, R. R. (2005). Interpersonal Psychotherapy. In J. Treasure, U. Schmidt & E. van Furth (Eds.), *The essential handbook of eating disorders* (pp. 137–154). West Sussex: John Wiley & Sons.

Wilfley, D. E., Welch, R. R., Stein, R. I., Spurrell, E. B., Cohen, L. R., Saelens, B. E., et al. (2002). A randomized comparison of group cognitive-behavioral therapy and group interpersonal psychotherapy for the treatment of overweight individuals with binge-eating disorder. *Archives of General Psychiatry, 59*(8), 713–721.

Wilfley, D. E., Wilson, G. T., & Agras, W. S. (2003). The clinical significance of binge eating disorder. *International Journal of Eating Disorders, 34* (Supplement), S96–106.

Wilson, G. T., Wilfley, D. E., Agras, W. S., Bryson, S. W. (2010). Psychological treatments of binge eating disorder. *Archives of General Psychiatry, 67*(1), 94–101.

Wilson, G. T. (2005). Psychological treatment of eating disorders. *Annual Review of Clinical Psychology, 1,* 439–465.

Wilson, G. T., & Fairburn, C. G. (2001). Eating Disorders. In P. N. J. Gorman (Ed.), *Treatments that work*. New York: Oxford University Press.

Wilson, G. T., Grilo, C. M., & Vitousek, K. M. (2007). Psychological treatment of eating disorders. *American Psychologist, 62*(3), 199–216.

Wilson, G. T., & Shafran, R. (2005). Eating disorders guidelines from NICE. *Lancet, 365*(9453), 79–81.

Wing, R. R., & Jeffery, R. W. (1999). Benefits of recruiting participants with friends and increasing social support for weight loss and maintenance. *Journal of Consulting and Clinical Psychology, 67*(1), 132–138.

Young, J. F., & Mufson, L. (2003). *Manual for Interpersonal Psychotherapy-Adolescent Skills Training (IPT-AST)*. Columbia University, New York.

Young, J. F., Mufson, L., & Davies, M. (2006). Efficacy of Interpersonal Psychotherapy-Adolescent Skills Training: An indicated preventive intervention for depression. *Journal of Child Psychology and Psychiatry, 47*(12), 1254–1262.

Daniel le Grange *and* Renee Rienecke Hoste

Abstract

Family therapy is increasingly recommended as the treatment of choice for eating disorders (EDs) among adolescents. The shift from blaming parents for causing an ED to seeing them as a necessary part of the recovery process was set in motion by Salvador Minuchin and colleagues and has been reinforced and expanded upon by researchers at the Maudsley Hospital in London and in the United States. Data supporting the efficacy of family-based treatment for adolescent anorexia nervosa (AN) continues to accumulate, while family-based approaches are beginning to be tested in the treatment of adolescents with bulimia nervosa (BN). Further research is needed to replicate the findings of existing studies and to further clarify the utility of parental involvement in the treatment of older adolescents and young adults with AN and BN.

Keywords: adolescents, anorexia nervosa, bulimia nervosa, family-based treatment

History of Family Therapy in Eating Disorders

More than 125 years ago the family was first considered to be at the center of eating disordered behavior. Views regarding the role of parents in anorexia nervosa (AN) varied from the outset. On the one hand, the British physician William Gull (1874) considered parents as "*generally the worst attendants*," while the French physician Charles Lasegue (1883) took a more inclusive stance in emphasizing that the "*preoccupations of relatives*" are important. Another colleague in France, Jean-Martin Charcot (1889), described the influence of parents as "*particularly pernicious.*" These early reflections suggest that parents were not seen as playing a positive role in their child's illness. In fact, some clinicians went one step further by blaming parents for the eating disorder (ED).

The turn of the century did not alter the outlook regarding parents' role in ED treatment and/or development. In fact, the emergence of the term "parentectomy" as a popular concept in the 1940s solidified the exclusion of parents from treatment for the next several decades. This sentiment was in vogue until the 1960s, at which time the role of the family was revisited in a more positive light by Salvador Minuchin and his colleagues at the Child Guidance Center in Philadelphia (Minuchin et al., 1975; Minuchin, Rosman, & Baker, 1978). This group developed what is referred to as the psychosomatic family model, a model that exerted considerable influence on subsequent treatment efforts for AN. This model hypothesized that an adolescent will develop an ED only when a very specific family context is in place. The psychosomatic model characterizes this family context as rigid, enmeshed, overinvolved, and conflict avoidant. These processes fluctuate in concert with the adolescent's symptomatic behavior. For AN to develop, the adolescent should also present with a situational vulnerability, such as being given the role as a go-between in cross-generational alliances. Markedly distinct from previously established ideology, Minuchin and colleagues did not simply ascribe responsibility or blame for the ED to the parents. Instead, the psychosomatic model highlighted the evolving, interactive nature of the development of the illness. However, the authors did believe that the psychosomatic family was a necessary component for the development of an ED, and that treatment should aim to change the way the family functions. This view still falls short of completely absolving the parents of any blame.

Researchers at the Institute of Psychiatry and the Maudsley Hospital in London (Dare, 1983; Dare & Eisler, 1997) furthered this shift in thinking about the role of families in EDs. Whereas the psychosomatic model described dysfunctional family characteristics that were thought to be necessary for the development of an ED, Dare and Eisler were more interested in the family dynamics that arise in the midst of, or as a result of, an ED. Rather than focusing on families' missteps and transgressions, this team of researchers developed a family therapy approach that considers the parents as a resource and does not place emphasis on the etiology of the ED (Eisler et al., 2000; Le Grange, Eisler, Dare, & Russell, 1992; Russell, Szmukler, Dare, & Eisler, 1987; Eisler et al., 1997). The body of work put forth by the Maudsley group has changed the emphasis in treatment from pathologizing families to absolving them from being blamed for causing their child's ED. The approach still requires families to change, however, because steps initially taken by parents to address their child's ED may have been ineffective or may require revision.

Theoretical Model of Family Therapy in Adolescent EDs

It is fair to say that over the past 40 years family therapy has gradually established itself as one of the most prominent treatment approaches for adolescents with AN. The clinical and theoretical accounts of some of the pioneers of the family therapy field, such as Minuchin and his colleagues (1975) and Selvini Palazzoli (1974), have been enhanced as increasing empirical support for the efficacy of family therapy for adolescents becomes available. Le Grange and Eisler (2009) would argue that this development has undoubtedly been one of the most significant changes in the treatment of EDs that the field has witnessed in the past 10 to 15 years.

Eisler (2005), however, points out that although data for the efficacy of family therapy are mounting, quite ironically there has also been growing evidence

of fundamental flaws in the theoretical models on which the treatment approach is based. For instance, the influential psychosomatic family model of Minuchin et al. (1978) postulates a prerequisite interactive family context within which the ED develops. A modest number of studies (e.g., Dare, Le Grange, Eisler, & Rutherford, 1994; Humphrey, 1989) have embarked on a course to systematically test Minuchin's claim of a psychosomatic family. Researchers have attempted to determine whether certain characteristics are specific to families of a child with AN, and, therefore, whether these families can be considered "typical" AN families. These studies were unable to confirm any particular pattern that typifies families with eating disordered offspring. In addition, it remains unclear whether such characteristics, if they do exist, are present prior to the onset of the ED, or if they are instead more indicative of the family's response to the illness.

Thus, our current state of knowledge does not provide sufficient evidence for the existence of the psychosomatic family. Instead, there is growing evidence that families with an ED offspring are a heterogeneous group with respect to sociodemographic characteristics, the emotional climate of intrafamilial relationships, and the patterns of interactions within the family (Eisler, 1995). Moreover, families in which there is a member suffering with an ED do not change or respond to the ED in predictable ways. Thus, there is a need for further investigation to identify what the specific targets of effective family interventions should be, how these targets may differ between families, and what processes accompany any changes that may occur.

The role of family environment in the etiology of EDs is also unclear. However, there is little doubt that the presence of an ED has an important effect on family life (Bara-Carrill & Nielsen, 2003). As time passes, food, eating, and related concerns begin to saturate family life, resulting in compromised family routines, coping, and problem-solving behaviors (Eisler, 2005). A similar process is described for families with an alcoholic member (Steinglass, Horan et al., 1987) and for families coping with a wide range of chronic illnesses (Steinglass, 1998). According to the model of Steinglass et al., families reorganize themselves in a stepwise fashion in response to the challenges brought about by the illness. This alters the family's routines and decision-making processes until such time that the illness becomes the central organizing principle of the family's life. Typically, families in this position will attempt to minimize the impact of the illness on either the sufferer or on other family members, and as a consequence increasingly focus their attention on the present moment while losing sight of the larger familial context. When this occurs, it becomes difficult for the family to meet their changing developmental needs. Steinglass and colleagues' model can easily be applied to EDs. It is common for families dealing with an ED to comment that it feels as if time has come to a standstill because they have had to focus all their attention on the ED. However, although there may be similarities in the way families respond to an ED, it is quite difficult, if not impossible, to disentangle which family processes are cause or effect, or just incidental to the development of the ED.

Uncontrolled Studies of Family Therapy for Adolescent AN

The most influential of the uncontrolled studies was the seminal work by Minuchin and his colleagues (1975, 1978) in Philadelphia. They were the first to involve families in the treatment of adolescents with AN, utilizing a structural family therapy approach to reorganize relationships within the family system. Using this approach, the team reported a remarkably high recovery rate of 86% in a series of 53 cases diagnosed with AN. The age range of these cases was quite wide (9–21 years old), although the majority were adolescents with a short duration of illness (mean duration = 8 months). Before the publication of this work, most accounts of treatment outcome with children and adolescents suffering from AN were more pessimistic in their outlook (e.g., Blitzer, Rollins, & Blackwell, 1961; Lesser et al., 1960; Warren, 1968). The positive results achieved by Minuchin and his colleagues, coupled with the persuasive theoretical model that underpinned their treatment approach, elevated the Philadelphia team's efforts to among the most important treatments for this patient population. This comes despite the methodological weaknesses for which the study has been criticized (Eisler et al., 2003).

Since Minuchin's work, at least two similar case series for adolescents with AN have been conducted. In Toronto, Martin (1984) reported a 5-year follow-up of 25 adolescent patients (mean age = 14.9 years) with a short duration of illness (mean = 8.1 months). While family therapy was the primary treatment, a combination of individual and inpatient treatment was employed, showing significant improvements at post-treatment. Utilizing the Morgan/Russell outcome criteria, which is a structured interview allowing for a composite of biological (weight and menses) and psychological (mental

status, and psychosocial and psychosexual development) markers, only a modest 23% of patients would have met criteria for a good outcome, while 45% would have met criteria for an intermediate outcome and 32% would have met criteria for a poor outcome. Five-year follow-up data were promising and comparable to Minuchin's results, with 80% of patients having a good outcome, 4% having an intermediate outcome, and the remainder still in treatment (12%), or relapsed (4%). In Buenos Aires, Herscovici and Bay (1996) conducted a follow-up study of 30 adolescent patients (mean age = 14.7 years; mean duration of illness = 10.3 months) between 4 and 8 years after their first presentation. Forty percent of the cohort were admitted to the hospital during the study; nevertheless, 60% met criteria for a good outcome, 30% for an intermediate outcome, and 10% for a poor outcome.

A small number of additional uncontrolled studies have utilized family therapy as the only treatment. At the Maudsley Hospital in London, Dare (1983) treated 12 adolescent patients in outpatient family therapy, and Mayer (1994) reported on the treatment of 11 adolescents at a general practice–based family therapy clinic in North London. For both studies, treatment was brief (<6 months), and the majority of patients (90%) were reported as having recovered or having made significant improvements at the time of follow-up. In a larger study, Stierlin and Weber (1987, 1989) reported on 42 female patients with AN who were seen at the Heidelberg Center over a follow-up period of 10 years. This study differed from the two studies mentioned above in that patients were older (mean age at first presentation = 18.2 years), had been ill longer (>3 years), and the majority had undergone previous treatment, with 56% having had prior inpatient stays. Family therapy was relatively brief (<9 months) and not intensive (mean number of treatment sessions = 6). At 4½-year follow-up, just under 50% were within a normal weight range and were menstruating. However, this study failed to distinguish between adolescents and adults, consequently rendering their findings not directly comparable to the other studies described.

At least half a dozen larger uncontrolled studies of family interventions for adolescents have been reported recently (Le Grange & Gelman, 1998; Le Grange, Binford, & Loeb, 2005; Lock & Le Grange, 2001; Lock, Couturier, & Agras, 2006; Loeb et al., 2007; Wallin & Kronwall, 2002). All of these studies utilized the family therapy modality developed by the Maudsley group, and further add to the evidence that children and adolescents do well in treatment when their parents are utilized in this process.

Controlled Studies of Family Therapy for Adolescent AN

Controlled treatment studies for adolescents with AN have been limited, and only a handful of randomized controlled trials (RCTs) have been published.

The Seminal Study of Family Therapy

The first and perhaps most influential RCT of family therapy for EDs was conducted by Russell and colleagues at the Maudsley Hospital in London (Russell et al., 1987). In this study, the relative efficacy of family therapy versus individual supportive therapy was tested. Eighty female participants (ages 14–55 years) were first admitted for weight restoration to the inpatient program. Admission lasted an average of 10 weeks, after which patients were discharged and randomly allocated to 1 year of either family therapy or the control individual supportive therapy. Participants were divided into four subgroups based on diagnosis and/or age, while outcome was defined by the Morgan/Russell outcome criteria (see Russell et al., 1987, p. 8). Findings were inconclusive for those participants with AN whose illness had lasted more than 3 years, or for patients with a diagnosis of bulimia nervosa (BN). However, findings for patients in one subgroup favored family therapy. This subgroup comprised 21 adolescents with AN who had a relatively young age at onset (on or before 18 years) and a short duration of illness (<3 years). At 5-year follow-up adolescents in this same subgroup continued to do well, with 90% of those who had received family therapy meeting criteria for a good outcome (Eisler et al., 1997). Adolescents who had received the individual control treatment did not do as well, with almost half of this group still presenting with significant ED symptoms after 5 years. This was the first long-term follow-up study to demonstrate that the benefits of a psychosocial treatment for AN could be maintained 5 years after the end of treatment.

Building on this RCT from Russell and his group (1987), three subsequent studies compared different forms of family interventions. An important difference from the original work is that the following studies tested outpatient family therapy without prior hospitalization.

Outpatient Treatment: Family Therapy Without Prior Hospitalization

The first of these three studies was also conducted at the Maudsley Hospital. Le Grange et al. (1992) and

Eisler et al. (2000) compared two forms of outpatient family treatment—conjoint family therapy (CFT) and separated family therapy (SFT)—among a total of 58 adolescents with AN. Both CFT and SFT shared the same goals, and the treatment principles were similar to the family therapy utilized in the original Russell et al. (1987) study. The two forms of treatment differed in their structure: in SFT the same therapist meets first with the adolescent on her own and then meets separately with the parents, whereas in CFT the adolescent and the parents are seen together. Also, unlike CFT, SFT did not include a family meal as part of the treatment protocol. Overall, results were similar in that significant improvements were reported for patients whether they were assigned to the conjoint or separated forms of family therapy. Utilizing Morgan/Russell outcome criteria, the majority of participants (>60%) were classified as having a good or intermediate outcome at the end of treatment. The authors found that CFT was superior to SFT in that significantly more change was demonstrated in terms of individual psychological and family functioning for participants in this treatment modality (Eisler et al., 2000). One important difference found between the treatment groups was that families with high levels of parental criticism toward their affected offspring (as defined by Expressed Emotion), did worse in CFT. Similar to the follow-up in the first RCT (Eisler et al., 1997), participants in this trial continued to improve after treatment ended. At 5-year follow-up, irrespective of type of family therapy received, the majority of participants had either a good (75%) or intermediate outcome (15%), while only 10% failed to respond to treatment (Eisler, Simic, Russell, & Dare, 2007).

The First Family Therapy RCT Outside the United Kingdom

The first family therapy treatment trial outside the United Kingdom was conducted by Robin and his colleagues (1999) in Detroit. In this study, 38 adolescents with AN were randomly assigned to either behavioral family systems therapy (BFST), a treatment that shares several similarities with the Maudsley conjoint family therapy, or to ego-oriented individual therapy (EOIT). The latter was comprised of weekly individual sessions for the adolescent and bimonthly collateral sessions with the parents. The main goal of this treatment is to support the adolescent's ability to resolve challenges through strengthening ego development rather than resorting to self-starvation as an option. At post-treatment patients in both BFST and EOIT demonstrated significant improvements, in that the majority (67%) reached their target weight and 80% regained menstruation. Patients continued to improve after the conclusion of treatment. At 1-year follow-up three quarters of patients reached their target weight, and 85% reported regular periods (Robin et al., 1999). The authors found that BFST was superior to EOIT in terms of physiological improvements, that is, changes in weight and menses, at both post-treatment and follow-up, but that changes were similar for patients in BFST and EOIT in terms of psychological improvements, that is, eating attitudes, mood, and eating-related family conflict. Robin and colleagues (1995) also reported results of observational ratings of family interaction in a subsample of this study. In this investigation they demonstrated significant reductions in maternal negative communication and a corresponding increase in positive communication for families in BFST but not for those in EOIT.

Some differences between the Detroit and Maudsley family therapy studies warrant comment as these could have had some impact on outcome. First, patients in the Detroit study were hospitalized at the outset of treatment if percentage of ideal body weight (% IBW) was below 75 (≈50% of the sample). Such patients remained in inpatient treatment until they reached 80% IBW. Patients in the Maudsley studies (Eisler et al., 2000; Le Grange et al., 1992) were treated on an outpatient basis from the outset and were only admitted to the inpatient unit if they were unresponsive to outpatient efforts to gain weight (4 out of 58 patients were admitted to the inpatient service during the study). Second, in the Detroit study, patients received an average number of 30 treatment sessions over a period of 12 to 18 months. The duration and intensity of treatment were lower in the Maudsley studies, with patients receiving an average number of 10 sessions over a period of 6 to 12 months. Finally, patients in the Maudsley studies appeared to have been ill for longer, received more prior treatment, and had higher rates of comorbid depression.

Family Therapy and Inpatient Treatment
With the exclusion of the second generation Maudsley studies (Eisler et al., 2000; Le Grange et al., 1992), the studies presented so far all combined inpatient with outpatient family therapy in some format. The specific role of family therapy within inpatient settings is poorly understood. Only one published study has attempted to compare family therapy, aimed at family dynamic and structural issues, with family group psychoeducation for patients in an inpatient setting (Geist, Heineman, Stephens, Davis & Katzman, 2000). Most of the weight gain (76%) reported for these patients occurred prior to discharge from the hospital, with equivalent treatment effects observed for family therapy and family group psychoeducation. Consequently, it is difficult to tease apart any differential effects of the family interventions versus inpatient treatment.

Development of a Treatment Manual for Family Therapy
Other than the RCT of Robin et al. (1999) for adolescent AN, family therapy treatment studies have been limited to the Maudsley group. One main reason for the limited use of this helpful treatment approach has been the fact that the London researchers did not employ a treatment manual. The recent development of a treatment manual for the Maudsley family therapy approach (Lock, Le Grange, Agras, & Dare, 2001) has not only made dissemination of this treatment approach possible, but it has also allowed for improvements in the design of subsequent treatment studies. The authors of the manual refer to this form of treatment as family-based treatment for AN (FBT-AN) and provide details of the goals and techniques of this treatment in the clinician's manual (Lock et al., 2001).

Briefly, FBT-AN consists of three treatment phases. The first phase focuses entirely on weight restoration, and control over this process is given to the parents. The second phase commences when the patient is approaching a healthy weight and the parents feel reassured that handing control over eating back to the adolescent will not result in renewed weight loss. The third phase is shorter in duration and consists of a brief overview of adolescent developmental issues and a discussion of how the adolescent can meet these developmental challenges without reverting to self-starvation as a coping mechanism.

This family therapy approach has changed the therapeutic focus from the traditional exploration of the etiology of the disorder to exploring how and where a family has become stymied by the ED. The therapist also helps the family to identify their strengths in order to extricate themselves from the problem and explore potential solutions. Emphasizing that the family is a resource, and part of the solution rather than the problem, is the most crucial element of this family therapy. More traditional therapies place the emphasis on making changes within the family. While this is not the primary objective of the Maudsley group's treatment, families may indeed learn during the course of therapy that there are ways in which they function as a family that they want to change. This change, however, is secondary to the primary goal, which is to help the child overcome the ED (Eisler, 2005).

All of the studies described in the text that follows have employed this manualized version of family therapy.

The Stanford Dosage Study

The first study to utilize FBT-AN was conducted by Lock and his colleagues (2005) at Stanford University in California. These authors examined the treatment dose of FBT-AN and randomly assigned 86 adolescents to either a 6-month, 10-session version of this treatment, or to a 12-month, 20-session version. At the 1-year mark there were no differences in weight gain between these two doses of FBT-AN. However, some moderators of treatment were identified. The longer version of this treatment was more efficacious for those patients who came from single-parent families, and for patients who presented with higher levels of eating related obsessions and compulsions. In what is now the third long-term follow-up study for this patient sample, Lock and his colleagues (2006) found that FBT-AN was equally effective regardless of treatment dose 4 years after the end of the study. That is, 66% of patients achieved healthy body weights (mean body mass index >20.5) and had Eating Disorder Examination scores within the normal range.

Utilizing the Treatment Manual in Clinical Practice

As a result of the development of the clinician's manual for FBT-AN, three groups in the United States have utilized case series data to demonstrate that (1) manualized FBT-AN is feasible and effective for consecutive patients referred to a specialist ED clinic (Le Grange et al., 2005), (2) FBT-AN can be disseminated and administered by investigators other than its developers (Loeb et al., 2007), and (3) the treatment approach appears to be as effective for children as it is for adolescents (Lock et al., 2007). Additional projects currently underway, all utilizing the manualized version of FBT-AN, include a large multisite RCT of FBT-AN versus ego-oriented individual therapy (EOIT) (Chicago and Stanford), a six-site clinical comparison of FBT-AN versus systemic family therapy, an adaptation of FBT for early intervention in subsyndromal AN (Mt Sinai, New York), and a parent group format of FBT for adolescent AN (Duke).

Family Therapy for Adolescent BN

Until recently treatment development for adolescents with BN had received almost no attention, and in contrast to adolescent AN, the utilization of families in the treatment of adolescents with BN has been much more limited. A recent advance has allowed for the development of family-based treatment for bulimia nervosa (FBT-BN) (Le Grange & Lock, 2007). This treatment was adapted from FBT-AN (Lock et al., 2001), and like its precursor, FBT-BN was designed for adolescents. Arguments in favor of parental involvement in treatment for adolescents with BN are both theoretically and clinically persuasive. As reviewed earlier in this chapter, a convincing body of evidence now supports mobilizing parents to take charge of weight restoration in the treatment of adolescents with AN. Further, researchers have found that the binge-purge subtype of AN responds favorably to family therapy. In treatment studies for adolescent AN, where the binge-purge subtype typically comprises about 20% of cases, family therapy has been found to be equally effective for weight gain as for curtailing binge and purge episodes (Eisler, Dare, Hodes, et al., 2000; Lock, Agras, Bryson, & Kraemer, 2005). These data seemed to suggest that parents are able to both alleviate bulimic symptoms in their children and reverse severe dieting.

Although modified from the approach for adolescents with AN, FBT-BN shares many key characteristics with FBT-AN. Most prominently, both treatments emphasize parents' love and understanding of their child and encourage the family to promote behavioral change around eating. While BN in adolescence may be experienced as ego-dystonic, patients nevertheless tend to deny the alarming nature of their symptoms and are therefore mostly unable to appreciate the seriousness of BN. Unlike a sense of pride that often accompanies starvation in AN, binge and purge symptoms in BN can lead to heightened feelings of shame and guilt. Such feelings tend to isolate these adolescents from parental support, which in turn can reinforce the symptomatic behavior. However, FBT-BN regards the parents as a resource for resolving the ED, and attempts to alleviate misplaced blame that may be directed toward either the parents or the adolescent. In most instances the adolescent suffering from BN is unable to recognize or effectively manage their dysfunctional eating behaviors. Consequently, the parents are encouraged to assist their adolescent in bringing about the necessary behavioral changes that will lead to recovery. Robin and colleagues (1999) conceptualize the teenager with AN as "unable to take care of herself." If the adolescent with BN is defined in the same way, then the parents should be coached to work as a team with their offspring to develop ways to restore healthy eating. This collaborative effort between the adolescent and her parents shows respect and regard for the adolescent's point of view and experience. Because of this collaborative stance, information about ED symptoms is shared between the parents and the adolescent in order to address struggles around eating and to understand the impact of the disorder on family relationships.

FBT-BN does not delve into the possible causes of BN and is instead primarily focused on the ED symptoms. In other words, this treatment focuses on what can be done to resolve the disorder. FBT-BN makes the assumption that parental guilt about having possibly caused the illness, along with anxiety about how best to address the symptomatic behavior, both serve to disable parents in their efforts. Consequently, a primary goal of treatment is to empower the parents and the adolescent in their collaborative attempts to disrupt the ED behaviors. Another important goal of treatment is to externalize the disordered behaviors from the affected adolescent. This separation of the adolescent from the disorder serves to promote parental action and decrease adolescent resistance to their assistance. Once these goals have been accomplished, the parents' next task is to return control over eating to the adolescent in a way that is age appropriate, that is, control over eating may be different for a 12-year-old versus an 18-year-old. Siblings are encouraged to play a supportive role only, and are therefore sheltered from the job assigned to the parents. Once the ED symptoms have resolved and the patient is eating on her own in an age-appropriate way, parents will then assist her in negotiating predictable adolescent developmental tasks. The therapist aims to take a nondirective stance throughout treatment and in doing so joins the family as a consultant and sounding board, while decision-making is left to the parents. This strategy facilitates parental ownership of decisions made in treatment and further promotes their empowerment.

FBT-BN differs from FBT-AN in a number of key ways. In family treatment for BN, (1) the emphasis is on regulating eating and curtailing purging as opposed to weight restoration; (2) treatment follows an approach that supports a collaborative effort between the adolescent and her/his parents in addressing the ED, whereas in AN parents take charge of weight restoration; (3) the secretive nature, guilt, and shame typically associated with BN may make it more of a challenge for the family and therapist to remain symptom focused, whereas the emaciation experienced in AN makes it relatively easier to keep treatment focused on weight restoration; and (4) the therapist and parents have to confront the challenges of comorbid illnesses in BN, which can more readily derail treatment than is usually the case in AN.

Studies of Family-Based Treatment for Adolescent BN

As noted earlier, data in support of treatments for adolescents with BN are sparse. Family therapy was first applied to adolescents with BN in a small case series that was conducted by the Maudsley group (Dodge, Hodes, Eisler, & Dare, 1995). This study demonstrated significant reductions in bulimic behaviors through educating the family about the ED and helping the parents to disrupt binge eating and purging episodes. Following the case series by Dodge and her colleagues (1995), Le Grange and his colleagues (2003) provided a detailed description of an adolescent progressing in FBT-BN. Both of these studies concluded that families can play a positive role in the recovery of adolescent BN, and that this is a promising avenue to pursue in the treatment for this population. These preliminary findings were recently extended with the publication of the first RCTs for adolescents with BN, both studies utilizing family treatments in their design (Le Grange, Crosby, Rathouz, & Leventhal, 2007; Schmidt et al., 2007).

In the Le Grange et al. (2007) study, 80 patients with *DSM-IV* BN and partial BN, ranging in age from 12 to 19 years (mean age = 16.1 years; mean duration of illness = 20.6 months), were assigned to either FBT-BN ($n = 41$) or to individual supportive psychotherapy (SPT) ($n = 39$). Both treatments provided 20 therapy sessions over a 6-month period with assessments at four time points: baseline, mid-treatment, end of treatment, and 6-month follow-up. There was no difference in adherence to treatment across FBT-BN and SPT with only 11% of patients dropping out of therapy prematurely.

In terms of categorical outcomes, FBT-BN demonstrated a clinical and statistical advantage over SPT at the end of treatment as well as at 6-month follow-up. At the end of treatment, significantly more patients in FBT-BN (39%) than in SPT (18%) were binge and purge abstinent. Abstinence rates were not as high at 6-month follow-up; however, significantly more patients in FBT-BN (29%) were binge and purge free compared to SPT (10%). Using random regression models, secondary analyses of continuous outcome variables showed greater improvements for FBT-BN on behavioral and attitudinal measures of ED psychopathology. Core bulimic symptoms also showed a more rapid rate of improvement for FBT-BN. Taken together, these findings support the superiority of FBT-BN over SPT in terms of the behavioral as well as attitudinal aspects of BN.

The Le Grange RCT also explored nonspecific predictors, moderators, and mediators of outcome (Le Grange, Crosby, & Lock, 2008; Lock, Le Grange, & Crosby, 2008). The clearest predictor to emerge from these analyses was level of eating concern as measured by the Eating Disorder Examination (EDE). That is, patients with lower scores on the EDE Eating Concern subscale at baseline were more likely to have remitted (abstinence from both binge eating and purging) at the end of treatment and at follow-up, regardless of which treatment they received. Four EDE variables (Weight Concern, Shape Concern, Eating Concern, and Global Score) significantly moderated the effects of treatment on partial remission status (no longer meeting study entry criteria). That is, partial remission rates were much higher for FBT-BN participants with low EDE scores. For participants receiving SPT, rates of partial remission were similar regardless of EDE scores. As for mediators, changes in the EDE Restraint subscale score at mid-treatment may mediate outcome for FBT-BN, but not for SPT (Lock et al., 2008), suggesting that FBT-BN may exert its effects in part by changing disordered thinking. These findings remain exploratory and a more detailed examination of these constructs awaits further testing in future controlled studies. Collectively these results support the use of FBT-BN as an effective intervention for adolescents who are identified early in the course of their illness, before the degree of psychopathology reaches levels that might be less responsive to treatment.

In the Schmidt and colleagues (2007) RCT, family therapy ($n = 41$) was compared to cognitive–behavior therapy guided self-care ($n = 44$) (CBT-GSC). Participants included adolescents and young adults ages 12 to 20 years (mean age = 17.6 years) meeting *DSM-IV* criteria for BN or ED not otherwise specified (ED-NOS). In terms of categorical outcomes,

significantly more patients in CBT-GSC were abstinent from binge eating at the end of treatment compared to patients receiving family therapy; however, this difference was no longer significant at 6-month follow-up. There were no differences in vomiting between the two treatment groups. Combining abstinence from binge eating *and* vomiting, there were no significant differences between family therapy (12.5%) and CBT-GSC (19.4%) at the end of treatment or at 6-month follow-up (family therapy = 41.4% vs. CBT-GSC = 36%). The only other differences reported were the direct cost of treatment, which was lower for CBT-GSC. Schmidt and colleagues acknowledge that their sample size might have been too modest to detect differences between two active treatments. Further, they state that without a waiting-list or attention placebo-control group it would be difficult to rule out that improvement was simply due to nonspecific effects or the passage of time.

Although no published manual is available for the family therapy utilized by Schmidt and her colleagues (2007), it appears to closely resemble FBT-BN. One key difference is that "family" was defined in family therapy as *any* "close other," rather than restricting this definition to a parent or legal guardian. Twenty-five percent of all participants utilized a "close other" in their treatment. The rationale for defining family in this way was likely due to the fact that the mean age of participants was at the upper end of adolescence (17.6 years), well above the age of consent in the United Kingdom (16 years of age). However, this definition of family might not be the most effective way to approach family-based treatments with younger adolescents who are still legally dependent on parents. Notwithstanding these uncertainties, the abstinence rate for family therapy in Schmidt's study was comparable to that achieved using FBT-BN in Le Grange's study.

Some questions require consideration when we examine issues pertaining to the dissemination of family-based treatments for this patient population. A treatment that involves the family may not always be suitable, especially in older adolescents. Twenty-eight percent of eligible participants in Schmidt's study refused participation because they did not want their families involved in treatment. CBT-GSC appeared to present fewer barriers, as fewer patients refused to participate. Further, patients faired as well in CBT-GSC as they did in family therapy (Schmidt's study) or FBT-BN (Le Grange's study). Delivering CBT-GSC was also more cost efficient than was the case for family therapy, which only serves to underscore the need for further evaluation of effective treatments given that treatment studies for adolescents with BN are still in their infancy.

Acceptability of Family Therapy

Two studies have examined the acceptability of family therapy for adolescents with AN (Krautter & Lock, 2004; Le Grange & Gelman, 1998), and one study has been published regarding adolescents with BN (Zaitsoff et al., 2008). Family therapy that empowers parents to play a significant role in addressing their offspring's ED is highly demanding, in part because the adolescent is initially not allowed to make independent decisions about her eating and weight related behaviors, and may be quite resistant to her parents' efforts. Therefore, the question of how acceptable this treatment is for both adolescents and parents is particularly salient. The initial report, a qualitative description of family therapy in a modest sample of adolescents with AN (Le Grange & Gelman, 1998), supported the notion that this form of treatment was ultimately acceptable for adolescents and their families. A larger study of patient satisfaction in family therapy for AN, employing both quantitative and qualitative evaluations, provided additional empirical support for this notion (Krautter & Lock, 2004). These authors found that adolescents and their parents rated treatment effectiveness as well as therapeutic alliance quite highly. However, it should be noted that almost a third (30%) expressed a desire for individual therapy in addition to the family therapy they received. In adolescents with BN, therapeutic alliance and treatment acceptability were high for both FBT-BN and SPT and did not differ between the two treatments (Zaitsoff et al., 2008).

Multiple-Family Day Treatment for Adolescent AN

Given the success of family-based treatments for adolescents with EDs, in conjunction with the need for more concentrated forms of interventions for those cases who do not respond to outpatient work, multiple-family day treatment programs have been developed in Dresden, Germany (Scholz & Asen, 2001) and in London, UK (Dare & Eisler, 2000). Multiple-family day treatment for EDs builds on the effectiveness of treatment formats for family intervention with other serious disorders (e.g., schizophrenia). It utilizes the same general principles of parental empowerment while focusing only on the specific problems related to AN as used in the approach for single families described in the preceding text. Doing multiple-family day treatment requires families to meet together for an extended weekend. During this time, a supportive community is created that aims to absolve families of any blame and provide opportunities to experiment with behavioral change. Not only are expert consultants available, but this treatment format is also an opportunity to share experiences with other families that are confronted with similar challenges. Realizing that one's struggles are quite similar to that of other families allows for an intensive learning environment under relatively controlled and supportive conditions. After the initial extended weekend, meetings over the ensuing months occur in a group format for a single day. The goal of these meetings is for families to help each other with the dilemmas that AN presents to their families. In practice, single family sessions are also provided for families who participate in multiple-family day treatment. Providing treatment in this way, multiple-family day treatment may best be considered an attempt to boost the efficacy of single family therapy for more resistant or challenging cases (Le Grange & Eisler, 2009).

Work from the research groups in London and Dresden are in a developmental stage and only preliminary findings can be offered here. Noteworthy symptomatic improvements such as increased weight, return of menstruation, stabilization of eating, reduction of bulimic symptoms, and decreased laxative abuse have been reported for several cases. As has been the case in the studies of family therapy for both AN and BN, treatment retention has been high for both sites. Feedback from parents and a majority of patients (80%) in Dresden indicated that working together with other families in a day hospital setting was experienced as helpful and desirable (Scholz & Asen, 2001). In particular, parents reported that the experience was helpful because of the collaborative nature of the program and the opportunity to share ideas with other families about how to cope with their common predicament. These results suggest that multiple-family day treatment is acceptable to families and a feasible treatment for further study. In fact, researchers at the Maudsley Hospital in London are about to complete a systematic evaluation of the effectiveness of a multiple-family day treatment program (Ivan Eisler, personal communication).

Family Therapy for Adults with EDs
Family Therapy for Adults with AN
Compared to the adolescent literature, family therapy for adults with AN has received much less attention.

Only two published studies have tested the efficacy of family therapy, both conducted at the Maudsley Hospital (Dare et al., 2001; Russell et al., 1987). Russell and colleagues' (1987) study was the first to investigate family therapy for adults with AN and was described in some detail earlier in this chapter. This was the first RCT of family therapy involving adult AN patients (*n* = 36, mean age at start of treatment = 20.6 years). Participants were randomly assigned to either family therapy or a control individual therapy at the time that they were discharged from the hospital. Unlike the findings for adolescents with AN, family therapy showed no benefit over individual therapy for adults. In fact, in terms of weight gain, there was a trend in favor of individual therapy for those patients with an adult onset (mean age at onset = 24.6 years) as opposed to those with an early onset (mean age at onset = 14.3 years), although this trend had dissipated at 5-year follow-up. However, at follow-up adult patients in individual therapy scored higher in terms of psychological adjustment (based on Morgan/Russell outcome criteria) compared to patients in family therapy (Eisler et al., 1997).

The second study of family therapy for adults with AN was administered on an outpatient basis only (Dare et al., 2001). This RCT of 84 adult patients was designed to assess the relative effectiveness of three specific psychotherapies—family therapy, focal psychoanalytic psychotherapy, and cognitive analytic therapy—versus routine care. At the end of treatment, no differences in outcome were reported for the three specific treatments. However, patients in family therapy and focal psychotherapy showed modest symptomatic improvements that were superior to the control treatment. Findings from this study were inconclusive perhaps in part because it was insufficiently powered to detect differential therapeutic effects. Moreover, no treatment manuals were utilized. Taking these two studies together, it would be difficult to draw a definitive conclusion about the efficacy of family therapy for this age group. Further studies are clearly required to establish whether family therapy can be helpful for this patient population. To this end, an adaptation of FBT-AN for young adults with AN is currently underway in Chicago and Sydney.

Family Therapy for Adults with BN

Family therapy has received the least amount of attention among adults with BN. A few studies have described single cases of family therapy for this age group (Madanas 1981; Roberto 1986; Root, Fallon, & Friedrich, 1986; Wynne 1980), and two larger studies have provided clear accounts of this treatment (Russell et al., 1987; Schwartz et al., 1985). Findings from these studies were inconclusive and it remains unclear whether family therapy is helpful for this patient population.

Conclusion

Despite a historical bias against the involvement of parents in the treatment of adolescents with EDs (Silverman, 1997), evidence in support of family interventions for AN has continued to mount over the past 40 years (Le Grange & Eisler, 2009). The published controlled studies involving adolescents with AN suggest that outpatient family therapy can be quite effective. Based on the data currently available, more than two thirds of adolescent patients are successful in reaching a healthy weight by the end of treatment, and 80% will have further improved or remained recovered five years later (Eisler et al., 1997, 2007; Lock et al., 2006). Although data have accumulated on the efficacy of FBT-AN, the state of research on the treatment for adolescents with BN has lagged behind. However, results from the first two published RCTs suggest that parents can be helpful not only in restoring their child's weight, but also in helping their child decrease binge eating and purging (Le Grange et al., 2007; Schmidt et al., 2007). Taken together, these results for adolescents with EDs are encouraging but must be interpreted cautiously as replication is needed with larger sample sizes; this task may now be more readily accomplished with the manualization of both FBT-AN (Lock et al., 2001) and FBT-BN (Le Grange & Lock, 2007).

Another reason for cautious interpretation is due to the fact that the same form of family therapy was not consistently used across the studies described in this chapter. Nevertheless, treatments that encourage parents to take an active role in helping their child recover from an ED, rather than observing from the sidelines, appear to be promising interventions for young adolescents with a short duration of illness who are medically suitable for outpatient treatment. Treatment studies for older adolescents and adults with AN are sorely needed, as the disorder seems to become more resistant to treatment over time. The lack of effective treatments for older age groups is especially alarming given the severe consequences of chronicity and the high mortality rate associated with AN (Powers & Bannon, 2004).

Despite the still significant gaps in our knowledge, FBT is one exciting example of the enormous strides made in the field of ED treatment in the last 20 years.

Future Directions

Enthusiasm for FBT ought to be tempered by the fact that there is a dearth of research on other treatment approaches for adolescents with an ED. For example, in AN there is only one published study comparing EOIT with FBT, while cognitive, interpersonal, and psychodynamic treatment approaches have not been systematically evaluated. Nor do we know whether promising outcomes with FBT are due to the active involvement of parents in *this* type of family treatment, or whether similar results can be obtained by more generic family therapies.

The utility of individual procedural elements of FBT has not been examined. Dismantling studies can highlight which part(s) of FBT are necessary and which part(s) can be removed. For instance, the therapeutic value of the family meal that is typically implemented early on in this treatment has not been determined. Likewise, the relative usefulness of phases two and three of FBT as opposed to the first phase of this treatment is not known.

Matching patients and treatment modality is another challenge that requires attention. Other than the finding that SFT may be more appropriate than CFT in families with highly critical parents, there is little to guide clinicians who are attempting to determine the appropriateness of FBT for one family compared to another.

The uptake and implementation of manualized treatments among many clinicians in the community are often less than satisfactory. Consequently, the development of published clinician manuals for both FBT-AN and FBT-BN provides an opportunity for the examination of effective dissemination of these treatment modalities.

Finally, no study has been able to demonstrate an efficacious treatment for adults with AN, including family therapy. This treatment, in its current format, is of limited use for adult patients. However, adapting FBT for a subset of young adult patients who agree to have their families (parents or partners) involved in treatment and work collaboratively toward weight recovery is a promising avenue to pursue.

Acknowledgments

The authors wish to thank Blaine Washington, BA, and Kristen Hewell, LSW, for their help with an earlier version of the manuscript.

References

Bara-Carril, N., & Nielsen, S. (2003). Family, burden of care and social Consequences. In J. L. Treasure, U. Schmidt, & E. van Furth (Eds.), *Handbook of eating disorders* (pp. 191–206). Chichester: John Wiley and Sons.

Blitzer, J. R., Rollins, N., & Blackwell, A. (1961). Children who starve themselves: Anorexia nervosa. *Psychosomatic Medicine, 23*, 369–383.

Charcot, J. M., & Savill, T. (trans.) (1889). Lecture XVII: Isolation in the treatment of hysteria. *Clinical Lectures on the diseases of the nervous system delivered at the infirmary of la Salpetriere by Professor J.M. Charcot*. London: The New Sydenham Society.

Dare, C. (1983). Family therapy for families containing an anorectic youngster. Columbus, OH, IVth Ross Conference on Medical Research, Ross Laboratories: 28–37.

Dare, C., & Eisler, I. (1997). Family therapy for anorexia nervosa. In D. M. Garner & P. Garfinkel (Eds.), *Handbook of treatment for eating disorders* (pp. 307–324). New York: Guilford Press.

Dare, C., & Eisler, I. (2000). A multi-family group day treatment programme for adolescent eating disorders. *European Eating Disorders Review, 8*, 4–18.

Dare, C., Eisler, I., Russell, G., Treasure, J., Dodge, L. (2001). Psychological therapies for adults with anorexia nervosa: Randomized controlled trial of outpatient treatments. *British Journal of Psychiatry, 178*, 216–221.

Dare, C., Le Grange, D., Eisler, I., & Rutherford, J. (1994). Redefining the psychosomatic family: Family process of 26 eating disorder families. *International Journal of Eating Disorders, 16*, 211–226.

Dodge, E., Hodes, M., Eisler, I., & Dare, C. (1995). Family therapy for bulimia nervosa in adolescents: An exploratory study. *Journal of Family Therapy, 17*, 59–77.

Eisler, I. (2005). The empirical and theoretical base of family therapy and multiple family day therapy for adolescent anorexia nervosa. *Journal of Family Therapy, 27*, 104–131.

Eisler, I., Dare, C., Russell, G. F. M., Szmukler, G. I., Le Grange, D., & Dodge, E. (1997). Family and individual therapy in anorexia nervosa: A five-year follow-up. *Archives of General Psychiatry, 54*, 1025–1030.

Eisler, I., Dare, C., Hodes, M., Russell, G., Dodge, E., & Le Grange, D. (2000). Family therapy for adolescent anorexia nervosa: The results of a controlled comparison of two family interventions. *Journal of Child Psychology and Psychiatry, 41*, 727–736.

Eisler, I., Le Grange, D. Asen, E. (2003). Family Interventions. In J. L. Treasure, U. Schmidt, & E. van Furth (Eds.), *Handbook of eating disorders* (pp. 291–310). Chichester: John Wiley & Sons.

Eisler, I., Simic, M., Russell, G. F. M., & Dare, C. (2007). A randomized controlled treatment trial of two forms of family therapy in adolescent anorexia nervosa: A five-year follow-up. *Journal of Child Psychology and Psychiatry, 48*, 552–560.

Geist, R., Heineman, M., Stephens, D., Davis, R., Katzmanm, D. K. (2000). Comparisons of family therapy and family group psychoeducation in adolescents with anorexia nervosa. *Canadian Journal of Psychiatry, 45*, 173–178.

Gowers, S., Clark, A., Roberts, C., Griffiths, A., Edwards, V., Bryan, C., et al. (2007). Clinical effectiveness of treatment for anorexia nervosa in adolescents: Randomised controlled trial. *British Journal of Psychiatry, 191*, 427–435.

Gull, W. (1874). Anorexia nervosa (apepsia hysterica, anorexia hysterica). *Transactions of the Clinical Society of London, 7,* 222–228.

Herscovici, C., & Bay, L. (1996). Favorable outcome for anorexia nervosa patient treated in Argentina with a family approach. *Eating Disorders, 4,* 59–66.

Humphrey, L. (1989). Observed family interactions among subtypes of eating disorders using structural analysis of social behavior. *Journal of Consulting and Clinical Psychology, 57,* 206–214.

Krautter, T., & Lock, J. (2004). Is manualized family-based treatment for adolescent anorexia nervosa acceptable to patients? Patient satisfaction at end of treatment. *Journal of Family Therapy, 26,* 65–81.

Lasegue, C. (1883). De l'anorexie hysterique. *Archives Generales de Medecine, 21,* 384–403.

Le Grange, D., & Eisler, I. (2009). Family interventions in adolescent anorexia nervosa. *Child and Adolescent Psychiatric Clinics of North America, 18,* 159–173.

Le Grange, D., Eisler, I., Dare, C., & Russell, G. F. (1992). Evaluation of family treatments in adolescent anorexia nervosa: A pilot study. *International Journal of Eating Disorders, 12,* 347–357.

Le Grange, D., & Lock, J. (2005). The dearth of psychological treatment studies for anorexia nervosa. *International Journal of Eating Disorders, 37,* 79–81.

Le Grange, D., & Lock, J. (2007). *Treating bulimia in adolescents: A family-based approach.* New York: Guilford Press.

Le Grange, D., Lock, J., Dymek, M. (2003). Family-based therapy for adolescents with bulimia nervosa. *American Journal of Psychotherapy, 67,* 237–251.

Le Grange, D., Binford, R., Loeb, K. L. (2005). Manualized family-based treatment for anorexia nervosa: A case series. *Journal of the American Academy of Child and Adolescent Psychiatry, 44,* 41–46.

Le Grange, D., Crosby, R. D., Rathouz, P. J., & Leventhal, B. L. (2007). A randomized controlled comparison of family-based treatment and supportive psychotherapy for adolescent bulimia nervosa. *Archives of General Psychiatry, 64,* 1049–1056.

Le Grange, D., Crosby, R., Lock, J. (2008). Predictors and moderators of outcome in family-based treatment for adolescent bulimia nervosa. *Journal of the American Academy of Child & Adolescent Psychiatry, 47,* 464–470.

Le Grange, D., & Gelman, T. (1998). The patient's perspective of treatment in eating disorders: A preliminary study. *South African Journal of Psychology, 28,* 182–186.

Lesser, L., Ashenden, B., Debunskey, M, Eisenberg, L. (1960). Anorexia nervosa in children. *American Journal of Orthopsychiatry, 30,* 572–580.

Lock, J., & Le Grange, D. (2001). Can family-based treatment of anorexia nervosa be manualized? *Journal of Psychotherapy Practice and Research, 10,* 253–261.

Lock, J., Le Grange, D., Agras, W. S., & Dare, C. (2001). *Treatment manual for anorexia nervosa: A family-based approach.* New York: Guilford Press.

Lock, J., Le Grange, D., Crosby, R. (2008). Exploring mechanisms of change in family-based treatment for adolescent bulimia nervosa. *Journal of Family Therapy, 30,* 260–271.

Lock, J., Couturier, J., & Agras, W. S. (2006). Comparison of long term outcomes in adolescents treated with family therapy. *Journal of the American Academy of Child and Adolescent Psychiatry, 45,* 666–672.

Lock, J., Agras, W. S., Bryson, S., Kraemer, H. C. (2005). A comparison of short- and long-term family therapy for adolescent anorexia nervosa. *Journal of the American Academy of Child and Adolescent Psychiatry, 44,* 632–639.

Loeb, K., Walsh, T., Lock, J., Le Grange, D. Jones, J., Marws, S., et al. (2007). Open trial of family-based treatment for full and partial anorexia nervosa in adolescence: Evidence of successful dissemination. *Journal of the American Academy of Child & Adolescent Psychiatry, 46,* 792–800.

Madanas, C. (1981). *Strategic family therapy.* San Francisco: Jossey-Bass.

Martin, A. (1984). A revised measure of approval motivation and its relationship to social desirability. *Journal of Personality Assessment, 48,* 508–519.

Mayer, R. (1994). *Family therapy in the treatment of eating disorders in general practice.* London: Birkbeck College, University of London.

Minuchin, S., Baker, B. L., Rosman, B. L., Liebman, R., Milman, L., & Todd, T. C. (1975). A conceptual model of psychosomatic illness in children: Family organization and family therapy. *Archives of General Psychiatry, 32,* 1031–1038.

Minuchin, S., Rosman, B. L., & Baker, B. L. (1978). *Psychosomatic families: Anorexia nervosa in context.* Cambridge, MA: Harvard University Press.

Powers, P. S., & Bannon, Y. (2004). Medical comorbidity of anorexia nervosa, bulimia nervosa, and binge eating disorder. In T. D. Brewerton (Ed.), *Clinical handbook of eating disorders: An integrated approach* (pp. 231–255). New York: Marcel Dekker.

Roberto, L. (1986). Bulimia: The transgenerational view. *Journal of Marital and Family Therapy, 12,* 231–240.

Robin, A., Siegal, P., Moye, A. (1995). Family versus individual therapy for anorexia: Impact on family conflict. *International Journal of Eating Disorders, 17,* 313–322.

Robin, A., Siegal, P., Gilroy, M., Dennis, A., Sikand, A. (1999). A controlled comparison of family versus individual therapy for adolescents with anorexia nervosa. *Journal of the American Academy of Child and Adolescent Psychiatry, 38,* 1482–1489.

Root, M. P. P., Fallon, P., & Friedrich, W. N. (1986). *Bulimia: A systems approach to treatment.* New York: W. W. Norton.

Russell, G. F., Szmukler, G. I., Dare, C., & Eisler, I. (1987). An evaluation of family therapy in anorexia nervosa and bulimia nervosa. *Archives of General Psychiatry, 44,* 1047–1056.

Schmidt, U., Lee, S., Beecham, J., Perkins, S., Treasure, J., Yi, I., et al. (2007). A randomized controlled trial of family therapy and cognitive behavior therapy guided self-care for adolescents with bulimia nervosa and related disorders. *American Journal of Psychiatry, 164,* 591–598.

Scholz, M., & Asen, K. E. (2001). Multiple family therapy with eating disordered adolescents. *European Eating Disorders Review, 9,* 33–42.

Schwartz, R., Barrett, M., Saba, G. (1985). Family therapy for bulimia. *Handbook of psychotherapy for anorexia nervosa and bulimia.* New York: Guilford Press, 280–310.

Selvini Palazzoli, M. (1974). *Self-starvation: From the intrapsychic to the transpersonal approach.* Oxford: Chaucer.

Silverman, J. (1997). Anorexia nervosa: Historical perspective on treatment. In D. Garner & P. Garfinkel (Eds.), *Handbook of treatment for eating disorders* (2nd ed.) (pp. 3–10). New York: Guilford Press.

Steinglass, P. (1998). Multiple family discussion groups for patients with chronic medical illness. *Families, Systems, and Health, 16,* 55–70.

Steinglass, P., & Horan, M. (1987). Families and chronic medical illness. *Journal of Psychotherapy and the Family, 3,* 127–142.

Stierlin, H., & Weber, G. (1987). Anorexia nervosa: Lessons from a follow-up study. *Family Systems Medicine, 7,* 120–157.

Stierlin, H., & Weber, G. (1989). *Unlocking the family door: A systemic approach to the understanding and treatment of anorexia nervosa.* New York: Brunner/Mazel.

Wallin, U., & Kronwall, P. (2002). Anorexia nervosa in teenagers: Changes in family function after family therapy at 2 year follow-up. *Nordic Journal of Psychiatry, 56,* 363–369.

Warren, W. (1968). A study of anorexia nervosa in young girls. *Journal of Child Psychology and Psychiatry, 9,* 27–40.

Wynne, L. (1980). Paradoxical interventions: Leverage for therapeutic change in individual and family systems. *The Psychotherapy of Schizophrenia.* In T. Strauss, S. Bowers, S. Downey, S. Fleck, & I. Levin. New York: Plenum Press.

Zaitsoff, S, Doyle, A. C., Hoste, R. R., et al. (2008). How do adolescents with bulimia nervosa rate the acceptability and therapeutic relationship in family-based treatment? *International Journal of Eating Disorders, 41,* 390–398.

CHAPTER

22

Self-Help and Stepped Care in Eating Disorders

Peter Musiat *and* Ulrike Schmidt

Abstract

This chapter reviews the utility of self-help interventions in the treatment of eating disorders. It describes the origins, rationale, and theoretical considerations for the development and use of self-help interventions. Different forms of self-help and modes of delivery are described. The existing research evidence on self-help in eating disorders (EDs) is detailed, including an overview of what is known about predictors and moderators of outcome. The chapter also considers clinical and practical factors in the use of such interventions. Finally, the limitations in our knowledge of self-help in EDs are discussed as well as implications for future research.

Keywords: anorexia, binge eating, bulimia, CD-ROM, eating disorders, guided self-help, Internet-based treatment, pure self help, self-help, stepped care

Introduction

The eating disorders (EDs) [anorexia nervosa (AN), bulimia nervosa (BN), binge eating disorder (BED), and eating disorder not otherwise specified (EDNOS)] cover a broad range of clinical severity. At the most severe end of the spectrum EDs (EDs) pose a serious threat to the short- and long-term psychological and physical health of those affected, but there are also many milder cases, which transiently flare up at times of stress and, whilst distressing to the sufferer, do not pose a major risk to life or limb. Studies examining time trends in ED epidemiology suggest that the incidence and prevalence of the classical EDs, anorexia nervosa and bulimia nervosa, is now stabilizing in Western countries (Currin et al., 2005), whereas EDNOS and BED continue to increase (Hay, Mond, Buttner, & Darby, 2008).

Effective psychological therapies exist for the EDs (e.g., Fairburn et al., 2008), and demand for such treatments is rising. However, treatment capacities in primary and secondary care are limited and specialized units are rare and tend to focus resources

on the needs of the most severely ill. Rigid organizational structures in services, for example, where all patients irrespective of level of severity or complexity get offered the same type or intensity of treatment, may get in the way optimally addressing patients needs and prevent best use of scarce resources (Lovell & Richards, 2000).

Those presenting for treatment are only the "tip of the iceberg" and for many people with EDs, in particular those with BN, there are significant delays in seeking and obtaining help, because of the embarrassment and stigma associated with the disorder and its treatment (de la Rie, Noordenbos, Donker, & van Furth, 2006).

Self-help interventions may provide an answer to some of these problems. First, such interventions can provide those reluctant to seek professional help with independent and early access to specialist help and give them tools for overcoming their problems on their own. When used with support from health professionals such interventions can help to improve patient care in nonspecialist settings (e.g., primary care) or make best use of specialist resources by reducing demands on therapist time.

The aims of this chapter are to give an overview on the development of such treatments in the field of EDs and to discuss the rationale for using self-help. Further, different modes of delivery are discussed and existing evidence is summarized. At the end of the chapter, predictors and moderators, use of self-help in different settings and research implications are discussed.

The History of Self-Help in EDs

The idea that people with mental health problems can be empowered to overcome their own difficulties dates back to the 1970s. It has its origins in the psychiatric consumer/survivor movement and the idea that there needs to be more choice, greater service user involvement and self-determination in care. It is also linked to the concept of Expert Patients and the idea of disease self-management, which has gained prominence in recent years based on research in the United States (Lorig & Holman, 2003) and the United Kingdom (Department of Health, 2001). In the world of psychological therapies, there has been a parallel shift from an emphasis on the central role of a powerful, charismatic psychotherapist who induces change through clever therapeutic maneuvers on the patient's unconscious difficulties to more collaborative treatments, such as cognitive–behavioral therapies where patients are seen as partners and therapists impart knowledge and skills based on explicit, transparent, and shared models of what is wrong.

A further impetus for the development of ED self-help interventions came from the epidemic rise of BN cases following its first description by Gerald Russell in 1979 and the early successes of cognitive behavioral treatment in the treatment of this condition. In 1986, Lindsey Hall and Leigh Cohn published *Bulimia—A Guide to Recovery*, probably the first self-help book for people with this condition. This book includes a great deal of information from recovered sufferers and gives advice on how to reduce binges. In comparison, however, with the more recent self-help literature, the book offers a less structured approach on how to get better. Instead sufferers are given advice on where to get help.

Since these early days, a number of cognitive–behavioral self-help manuals for the treatment of BN and related conditions such as BED have become available, including *Getting Better Bit(e) by Bit(e): A Survival Kit for Sufferers of Bulimia Nervosa and Binge Eating Disorders* by Schmidt and Treasure (1993), *Bulimia Nervosa—A Guide to Recovery*, by Cooper (1993) and *Overcoming Binge Eating* (Fairburn, 1995). More recent examples, such as *Overcoming Eating Disorders* by Apple and Agras (1997), are presented in a larger format and appear more workbook like, incorporating multiple structured tasks. Finally, the self-help book by Cooper, Todd, and Wells (2000), in addition to addressing ED symptoms, also addresses underlying schemata. Most of these manuals have been evaluated in case series or randomized controlled trials, with the majority of trials using either Fairburn's (1995) book or that by Schmidt and Treasure (1993).

In contrast to the number of self-help manuals available for BN and BED, self-help material for AN is still rare. This is unsurprising given that patients with AN often value their disorder highly and are reluctant to change (Schmidt & Treasure, 2007). Moreover, the medical risks involved make unsupervised treatment less attractive. *Overcoming Anorexia* (Freeman, 2002) is the first attempt to provide a self-help intervention for sufferers from AN using a cognitive–behavioral approach.

With the advent of new technologies, cognitive–behavioral treatments for EDs have been translated into interactive computerized programs available on CD-ROM or via the internet as stand-alone self-help interventions. Examples include Overcoming Bulimia, a CD-ROM–based self-help intervention for patients with BN (Williams, Aubin, Cottrell, & Harkin, 1998), POWER (Preventing Overweight with Exercise and Reasoning), a CD-ROM–based intervention for people with binge eating disorder (Shapiro et al., 2007), and the European Salut-programme (Fernández-Aranda et al., 2008).

The latest trend in the development of self-help materials focuses on the caregivers of people with EDs. This acknowledges that caregivers of people with EDs are often highly distressed by their close other's disorder and may inadvertently contribute to keeping this going through desperate, but ultimately unhelpful actions (Kyriacou, Treasure, & Schmidt, 2008a, 2008b; Perkins, Winn, Murray, Murphy, & Schmidt, 2004; Winn, Perkins, Murray, Murphy, & Schmidt; Winn et al., 2007). Caregivers are usually highly motivated to effect change in their loved ones, yet do not have appropriate information as to how to best support their loved one. Given high levels of caregiver anxiety and depression and the often chronic nature of EDs, caregivers may also benefit from being taught strategies for reducing and managing their own levels of distress. A self-help book for caregivers of people with EDs (Treasure,

Smith, & Crane, 2007) and an Internet program (Schmidt et al., 2008) using a systemic cognitive–behavioral approach have been developed and are being tested (Grover et al., submitted). In this latest generation of self-help interventions there is also recognition that there is a need to involve patients and caregivers in the intervention development, whereas earlier examples of self-help interventions were developed entirely by experts.

Theoretical Models
What Is Self-Help?
Several attempts have been made to define what constitutes self-help interventions. A broad definition was given by Jorm et al. (2002) who includes under self-help any treatment that can be used by a person without necessarily consulting a health professional, including over-the-counter medicines, exercise and bibliotherapy. Other definitions focus more specifically on psychological self-help interventions. For example, Marrs (1995) defined self-help as "the use of written materials or computer programs or the listening/viewing of audio/video tapes for the purpose of gaining understanding or solving problems relevant to a person's developmental or therapeutic needs." Cuijpers (1997) emphasized that any psychological self-help intervention has to describe the treatment in a way that allows the patient to work independently. Hence, the provision of one-off information or advice about the disorder in itself is not enough to qualify for inclusion as a self-help intervention. A recent review of self-help interventions for mental health (Lewis et al., 2003) proposed that a self-help approach needs to "utilise a clear model and structure of treatment which focus on problems of relevance to the patient." The review emphasized the longitudinal and program-led nature of any psychological self-help intervention with the aim to teach users relevant skills to manage or overcome their health problems. This latter definition excludes self-help groups that meet mainly with the aim to give people peer support rather than following a particular treatment program.

Translating Effective Treatments into Self-Help Interventions
Self-help interventions ideally should be translations of tried and tested specific psychological treatments for a given condition into a written, audio–visual, or computerized format. For BN and BED, the treatment of choice with the best underlying evidence base is a specific form of cognitive–behavioral therapy that addresses key maintaining factors

(National Institute for Clinical Excellence, 2004). Most of the available self-help interventions for these disorders are indeed based on this type of cognitive–behavioral approach (Lewis et al., 2003). By their very nature, cognitive–behavioral approaches in general lend themselves very well for a translation into self-help programs. These therapies are based on adult learning models and the therapist has the function of a teacher or coach who imparts important information to the patient and teaches them a set of reproducible skills. Cognitive–behavioral therapies have an "built-in" self-help element, that is, they underline the importance of regular homework in between treatment sessions, to allow patients to put their newly learned skills into practice.

However, there is no reason why other therapies with different underlying theoretical models should not be usefully translated into self-help treatments for EDs. For example, in our self-help interventions for caregivers we teach them the principles and practice of motivational interviewing (Treasure & Schmidt, 2008) as a way of communicating with their loved one about anorexia with the aim to reduce conflict and high expressed emotion in the family.

Other potential candidates include, for example, therapeutic writing, as developed and tested by Pennebaker and colleagues which has been translated into a stand-alone self-help format (Pennebaker, 2004) and has shown promise in the treatment of EDs (e.g., Robinson & Serfaty, 2008; Schmidt et al., 2000).

With increasing availability of computerized neurocognitive tests, approaches such as cognitive remediation (Tchanturia et al., 2008), which has shown preliminary efficacy in the treatment of EDs, may also be a potential candidate for translation into self-help.

Finally, self-help treatments for problems that frequently co-occur with EDs and may contribute to maintaining these, such as perfectionism or low assertiveness, may also be of use in treating EDs even though they are not designed to specifically target the ED. Such interventions may complement and be integrated with other components of treatment.

Rationale for Use of Self-Help in EDs
Discussions of the rationale for the use of self-help treatments in mental health often point to economic arguments and these undoubtedly play a role. The demand for psychological therapies in general by far outstrips available resources and in many countries there are long waiting lists for psychological services

or huge inequalities in access to specialist services. The use of self-help interventions undoubtedly is helpful in cutting down waiting lists for treatment, by reducing the number of patients who need to see a therapist or by reducing therapist time spent with patients.

However, there are other advantages, too. For example, therapists working in primary or secondary care or private practice often do not have particular expertise in the specifics of treatment of EDs, and may find that a good self-help manual can also double up as a training tool for them and allow them to provide a much more specialist intervention to their patients.

Although therapists often voice concerns or criticisms of self-help interventions (Waller & Gilbody, 2008), it is of note that the view of the general public is much more positive and that self-help treatments for EDs are seen as more acceptable than face-to-face therapy (Mond, Hay, Rodgers, Owen, & Beumont, 2004). A number of advantages of self-help treatments for service users have been identified by experts (Williams, 2001) and confirmed by qualitative studies of patients' views (Murray et al., 2003; Pretorius et al., 2009, submitted;). For example, self-help treatment can be accessed with minimum delay and patients can work in their own time, at their own pace without having to travel to appointments. This is of relevance to ED sufferers who are a young, mobile population, many of whom are students or work full-time. They may therefore find it hard to make time for attending regular appointments and if they receive face-to-face care this may be disrupted, for example, by frequent moves between home and university (Treasure, Schmidt, & Hugo, 2005). The privacy and confidentiality afforded by self-help treatments is also especially relevant to EDs as patients can avoid the embarrassment or stigma often associated with conventional psychotherapy. Further, starvation or binge/purging can affect attention and concentration, or be associated with high levels of anxiety or depression, making it difficult to benefit from face-to-face therapy. With a self-help treatment, patients can go over parts of the treatment as often as they need to and refer back to it at times of setbacks without extra costs or inconvenience.

Description of Treatment

In the self-help literature there is a distinction between pure self-help and guided self-help. Pure self-help (PSH) means that patients work through the material completely on their own. One of the difficulties with this is that it requires high levels of self-directedness and sustained motivation to change. EDs patients can be extremely self-critical, making it difficult for them to perceive and acknowledge progress. With pure self-help it is less easy to provide patients with encouragement and feedback about their progress, although newer, interactive computerized programs may be able to overcome this problem to some extent. ED patients are also often fearful of trying new strategies or of making mistakes or may invalidate their efforts by exaggerated expectations of themselves. Although pure self-help programs can name some of these issues and build in some strategies to circumvent these problems, there is a limit to how well these barriers to successful use of pure self-help can be overcome.

In contrast, guided self-help (GSH) includes support from another person, who can be a specialist therapist, a health professional with more basic training, a lay person, or an ex-sufferer. This additional support can be delivered face-to-face, via telephone, or electronically via e-mail, chat, or discussion forums. The main aim of such guidance is to "monitor progress, clarify procedures, answer general questions, or to provide general support or encouragement" (Gould, 1993). Further, supporters can also point the patients to certain aspects of the self-help manual that are particularly relevant for the patient or discuss difficulties with them. Thus guided self-help is on a continuum with therapist delivered treatment, and differs from this in terms of the more strongly program-led nature of the therapeutic interaction, the briefer therapist contact and often (though not necessarily) the lesser training of the supporter.

Psychological treatment services often offer the same treatment package in terms of intensity, duration, and type of treatment to all comers, for example, 16 to 20 once weekly sessions of CBT, without taking into account the complexity of the patient's problem or the patient's preferences (Lovell & Richards, 2000). This leads to some patients being under- and others being overtreated and is not an optimal use of resources. Stepped care models have been suggested (Haaga, 2000) to circumvent this problem, starting with the least intensive intervention, and stepping up to more intensive ones. This model of care is based on two assumptions. First, different patients will benefit from different intensities of treatment. Second, the level of intensity needed by a particular patient cannot be predicted beforehand (Lewis et al., 2003). In this model, self-help treatments with or without guidance could be the first step in the treatment of patients with BN, BED, or EDNOS presenting to services, and only if patients do not respond adequately are they offered more intensive and more expensive treatments. Findings from two randomized controlled trials (RCTs) in BED support this approach: These studies found that a rapid response to guided self help treatment predicted better outcomes (Grilo & Masheb, 2007; Masheb & Grilo 2007). In these studies, pretreatment patient characteristics differed little between patients with or without a rapid response to GSH (i.e., it was not merely the "easy" patients who got better quickly with GSH).

Modes of Delivery

As with self-help for other disorders, different modes of delivery are possible. Although the general advantages of self-help as discussed in the previous section probably apply to all forms of self-help, each mode of delivery has its specific advantages and disadvantages. The pros and cons of the most common modes of delivery are discussed in the following section.

Self-Help Books

Most of the existing self-help programs for EDs are available as books. Although books might seem a little bit old-fashioned now that new media are available, one should not underestimate the advantages of a self-help book. First, they are widely available and can be anonymously obtained. In fact, a large number of patients prefer books and very often such manuals are best sellers (Williams, 2003). Second, they can be read anywhere and no computer or other technical equipment is needed. The disadvantages of printed material, on the other hand, are obvious, too. Only text and pictures can be included, limiting the possibilities of creating attractive and user-friendly self-help. As a large amount of information has to be delivered in the course of the intervention, books can soon loose their appeal to the patients or be demotivating. Further, there is only little room for interactivity, flexibility, or feedback. Patients can skip certain steps of the treatment if they are not relevant to them, but beyond this, individual tailoring of the intervention to the patient's problems is not possible. Books also allow unstructured browsing, without a systematic step-by-step working through of the intervention. This may lead to users going through the whole book quickly without allowing sufficient time for practice.

Computerized Self-Help

Another way of delivering self-help interventions is via CD-ROM. In this mode of delivery, multimedia components such as sounds, animations or videos can be included. Even more important is the potential for including interactive components or feedback. This can, for example, include the option for the patient of designing their own individual "vicious circle," self-assessment questionnaires or knowledge quizzes. With such computerized interventions, treatment can also be adapted to the patient's needs by cascading only modules that are relevant to them. An example of feedback would be visual analogue scales where users can indicate their degree of well-being or impairment. Such information can be summarized by the program and presented visually or even submitted to a guiding person. However, the disadvantages of such an intervention have to be considered. On the side of the providers of the treatment, the development of a CD-ROM–based treatment is very difficult. Multimedia components have to be produced and the program interface needs to be designed, programmed and carefully tested. This is labour intensive and with increasing degree of complexity, the costs of development increase, too. Further, technical support has to be offered. On the users' side, patients need access to a personal computer that meets the hardware requirements of the program and sufficient knowledge of using it. In comparison with books, only very few CD-ROM–based interventions are commercially available. Usually, such treatments are delivered in the context of an efficacy study or provided by specialized ED services. Hence, patients have to contact the service provider and, in some cases, also attend an initial assessment. This is important, as the patient's motivation might be different compared to a patient looking to find help in a book. In qualitative studies on computerized self-help, patients report that they sometimes experience the intervention as impersonal (Murray et al., 2003; Pretorius et al., 2009, submitted). Considering the fact that these patients contacted the service providers to get personal help, this is not surprising. Such factors have to be considered in the decision whether a self-help intervention might be beneficial for a particular patient.

Most of the advantages and disadvantages for CD-ROM–based treatments also apply to Internet-based treatments. There are, however, important differences. Interventions delivered via the Internet allow higher levels of interactivity and feedback. Additional support can be provided via e-mail, chat rooms, or discussion boards, where patients can also get in contact with each other. Further, the intervention can be evaluated much more easily, as patients can be assessed within the treatment interface. Making an Internet-based intervention for EDs available via the Internet also diminishes the problem of limited availability of CD-ROM treatments. In theory, any patient could access the package without having to contact professionals. On top of the hardware requirements as discussed in the preceding text, patients also need an Internet connection at sufficient speed to access such treatments. Providers of a Web-based package need to make sure that patient data are treated confidentially and have to administer chats or discussion boards.

In summary, it is clear that there is no perfect way of delivering self-help interventions. Each method has its advantages and disadvantages. Further, patients prefer different modes of self-help and such preferences have to be considered when offering treatment to a patient.

Different Modes of Supporting Self-Help Interventions

Very little is known about what distinguishes different modes of support and whether they are associated with different levels of treatment retention and efficacy. In a comparison of face-to-face versus telephone guidance of manual-based self-help treatment little difference was seen in outcome (Palmer, Birchall, McGrain, & Sullivan, 2002). In a recent pilot study of a self-help intervention for caregivers (Grover et al., submitted), these were offered either support by e-mail or over the phone. About half chose one or the other. The only pretreatment difference between the sub-groups was that those choosing e-mail support had a more avoidant coping style (Grover et al., submitted). Although on the face of it support by e-mail is a more impoverished medium because of the absence of any contextual cues (voice, facial expressions, body posture), among the specific advantages of e-mail support participants cited that they were able to reflect beforehand on what they wanted to ask/say to their supporter and also the fact that they had a record of what was discussed.

A recent RCT of Internet-based self-help with guidance from trained CBT therapists by e-mail examined the nature of the therapists' comments. The overwhelming majority of comments were supportive in nature, rather than specifically cognitive–behavioral. Patients uniformly liked the e-mail support. Perhaps this suggests that it is not necessary

for trained CBT therapists to provide the support and that less highly trained personnel may be able to deliver this (Sánchez-Ortiz, unpublished PhD thesis).

Evidence Base for Effectiveness
Manual-Based Self-Help
EVIDENCE FROM SYSTEMATIC REVIEWS

Two systematic reviews investigated the effectiveness and efficacy of manual-based self-help treatments in EDs. In the following section, the main findings of these reviews are summarized.

A systematic review by Perkins, Murphy, Schmidt, and Williams (2006) investigated the results of RCTs and controlled clinical trials (CCTs) of pure self-help (PSH) and guided self-help (GSH) in people with EDs. The primary aim was to evaluate the effectiveness and efficacy of self-help compared with waiting list or placebo/attention control and other psychological or pharmacological treatments. The secondary objective of this review was to evaluate evidence for the efficacy of PSH or GSH regarding comorbid symptomatology and costs.

A total of 13 RCTs and three CCTs was identified and included in the analyses. The studies focused on adults with BN, BED, EDNOS, or a combination of the three disorders and manual based PSH or GSH in different settings. Six studies included at least one arm with PSH and the others evaluated GSH. The people giving the self-help interventions differed markedly in their degree of experience and training (e.g., lay persons, psychology students, general nurses, junior psychiatrists, doctoral level psychologists, research clinicians, psychotherapists, specialist ED therapists, general practitioners, and people recovered from an ED). A variable amount of guidance was provided, ranging from 90 minutes to 8 hours. Studies were conducted in diverse settings including primary care, university and community settings and secondary or tertiary ED services. Most of the studies were from Europe (n = 7), the United States, or Canada (n = 6) and Australia (n = 2). A number of comparisons and meta-analyses were conducted. These are summarized below:

1. Four studies compared PSH or GSH with a waiting list control (Banasiak, Paxton, & Hay, 2005; Carter & Fairburn, 1998; Carter et al., 2003; Palmer et al., 2002). These did not find any difference in abstinence from binge eating or purging at the end of treatment (average abstinence from binging after PSH or GSH was 35.2% and

after waiting list was 11.2%; average abstinence from purging after PSH or GHS was 21.8% and 10.4% after waiting list). However, self-help treatments produced greater improvement than waiting list on ED symptoms, psychiatric symptomatology, and interpersonal functioning.

2. One study compared GSH to a placebo/attention control treatment in BED (Grilo & Masheb, 2005). GSH produced greater improvements in abstinence rates from binge eating (46% vs. 13.4% in the control group) and ED symptoms, but not on depression.

3. Four studies compared self-help treatments (with or without guidance) to other psychological therapies (Bailer et al., 2004; Durand & King, 2003; Thiels, Schmidt, Treasure, Garthe, & Troop, 1998; Treasure et al., 1996). There was no difference in terms of abstinence rates from binge eating and purging, improvement on ED symptomatology, interpersonal functioning, or depression at the end of treatment or at follow-up In PSH or GSH, average abstinence rates from binging or purging at the end of treatment were 11% and 15.5% respectively and at follow-up were 35% and 42%. In other psychological treatments, abstinence rates were 33% for binging and 31% for purging at the end of treatment and 32% and 32% at follow-up.

4. Five studies compared PSH to GSH (Carter & Fairburn, 1998; Ghaderi & Scott, 2003; Huon et al., 1985; Loeb, Wilson, Gilbert, & Labouvie, 2000; Palmer et al., 2002). There were no differences between groups on any of the outcome measures at end of treatment or follow-up. Abstinence rates were as follows: end of treatment: binging: PSH (35.7%) vs. GSH (42.9%); purging: PSH (53.4 %) vs. GSH (68%); follow-up: Binging: PSH (40%) and GSH (50%). One study reported adherence to self-help treatment and this was 6% in PSH and 50% in GSH (Carter & Fairburn, 1998).

5. Two studies compared different types of self-help (Carter et al., 2003; Grilo & Masheb, 2005). There were no differences on abstinence rates from binge eating and purging, depression scores and body mass index (BMI), but some differences on ED symptoms and interpersonal functioning. Average abstinence from binge eating at the end of treatment was 29% in those using a CBT-based self-help treatment compared with 17% in those using another type of self-help treatment [behavioral weight loss control treatment (Grilo & Masheb, 2005) or self-help for

self-assertion (Carter et al., 2003)]. In the study by Carter et al. (2003), abstinence from purging at the end of treatment was 7% for CBT self-help and 18% for the other form of self-help.

6. Three studies compared self-help with pharmacological interventions (Grilo, Masheb, & Salant, 2005; Mitchell et al., 2001; Walsh, Fairburn, Mickley, Sysko, & Parides, 2004). One of these compared GSH combined with orlistat to GSH combined with placebo in BED. People receiving GSH with added orlistat achieved a larger post-treatment weight reduction and were more likely to maintain this at 3-month follow-up (Grilo et al., 2005). The addition of orlistat was also associated with a greater reduction of binge eating episodes at post-treatment but not at follow-up. Two other studies compared fluoxetine only, placebo only, fluoxetine and PSH or GSH and placebo and PSH or GSH in patients with BN (Mitchell et al., 2001; Walsh et al., 2004). The Walsh et al. (2004) study had very high drop out rates, making it impossible to draw any conclusions from this study. The Mitchell et al. (2001) study suggested that both fluoxetine and PSH were effective in reducing the frequency of self-induced vomiting episodes at the end of treatment and both interventions acted additively on the outcome measures in this study.

None of the studies included in this review provided information on patients' satisfaction with the self-help treatment in comparison with conventional therapist-aided intervention. Little is know about the characteristics of people who engage in and complete a self-help intervention.

A second systematic review was conducted by Stefano, Bacaltchuk, Blay, and Hay (2006). This review was more limited in scope and included self-help studies on BN and binge eating disorder (BED). Abstinence from episodes of binge eating was considered the primary outcome criterion and secondary outcome criteria were bulimic symptoms; the proportion of nonresponders, noncompleters, or dropouts; and BMI at the end of treatment. Nine studies were included and the authors conducted several meta-analyses. In the comparison of any form of self-help against waiting list, 26.5% of the patients, who received self-help were abstinent from binging in contrast to only 6.5% in the waiting list group. No differences were found for the rate of noncompleters or dropouts. There were similar nonsignificant trends on the other comparisons (PSH vs. WL; GSH vs. WL), that is, participants offered self-help intervention had higher rates of abstinence than waiting list control groups, but the number of studies and participants included was probably too low to reach significance. In the last meta-analysis, the authors compared any form of self-help with CBT. Interestingly, patients in both groups showed similar abstinence rates (self-help: 15%, CBT: 17.5%), rates of noncompleters (self-help: 28%, CBT: 27.5%), and a comparable average number of binge eating episodes after treatment.

Both reviews were limited by the heterogeneity of the studies (in terms of methodological details, for example, type of participant, setting, amount and type of guidance, type of self-help), the small size of the studies, their varying quality, and the low number of studies included in the meta-analyses. Nonetheless one can conclude that self-help interventions have some utility as a first step in treatment or might be considered as an alternative for specialist care depending on the patients' needs and resources.

ADDITIONAL STUDIES ON MANUALIZED SELF-HELP NOT INCLUDED IN THE SYSTEMATIC REVIEWS

Since the publication of these reviews several other studies have been published that contribute to the evidence in this area. These are listed below.

Comparison of Self-Help versus Wait List

One CCT investigated the efficacy of guided self-help for patients with AN of binge/purge subtype before in-patient treatment (Fichter, Cebulla, Quadflieg, & Naab, 2008). The self-help treatment included a 6-week manual-based program that focused on healthy eating behavior, alternatives to binge eating and purging behaviors, coping strategies for negative thoughts, body image, and dealing with emotions. Patients also received a maximum of 30 minutes telephone guidance per week. Patients were consecutively assigned to either the self-help treatment or a waiting list group prior to commencing in-patient treatment. The primary outcome was the number of days patients spent in impatient treatment afterwards. The number of in-patient days was significantly lower (by 5.2 days) for patients who received the self-help program compared to those who remained on the waiting list. In addition, body image and general psychopathology improved during the intervention. Eleven of 68 patients in the manual group either did not fully complete the self-help manual ($n = 6$) or did not start with the manual at all ($n = 5$). Although the study has limitations (e.g., lack of randomisation) this is nonetheless an important one, as it is the first ever attempt to deliver guided self-help for patients with anorexia; moreover, it was performed in the context of a stepped care treatment model.

Comparison of GSH Against Another Psychological Therapy

One recent RCT examined the efficacy and cost-effectiveness of guided self-help compared to family therapy in adolescents with BN or EDNOS (Schmidt et al., 2007). In this study, GSH led to improvements in ED symptoms at 1 year similar to those of family therapy. Changes on binge eating outcomes occurred faster in the guided self-help group, with GSH producing a greater reduction of binge eating at 6 months than family therapy. Further, GSH was perceived as more acceptable by the patients and direct treatment costs were lower.

Comparison of GSH and PSH

One very small RCT compared 12-week CBT-based PSH and GSH among 29 patients with BN, BED, or EDNOS-BN. The study replicated an earlier study by the same author (Ghaderi & Scott, 2003) and found no significant differences in outcome between the pure and guided self-help treatments. Post-treatment abstinence rates from binging or purging were 31% for PSH and 44% for GSH. The study was almost certainly underpowered to detect any differences.

Comparison of Different Types of Self-Help and Placebo

An interesting small RCT (Steele & Wade, 2008) of BN or EDNOS BN patients compared three different forms of eight sessions of guided self-help over 6 weeks, one based on Cooper's (1993) CBT manual for bulimia and binge eating, a second based on a CBT–self-help manual addressing perfectionism (Antony & Swinson, 1998), and a third designed as a placebo intervention drawing from the book *Mindfulness-Based Cognitive Therapy for Depression* (Segal, Williams, & Teasdale, 2002). Before treatment, patients underwent two baseline assessments 6 weeks apart. There was no significant change in any of the outcome variables over the 6 weeks no treatment period, in line with previous studies. There were also no significant differences between groups, but at post-treatment and 6-month follow-up there were significant within group improvements in bulimic symptoms and related psychopathology. This is of interest as it suggests that focusing treatment on relevant maintaining factors for BN, such as perfectionism, appears to be an effective treatment. The placebo treatment also led to significant improvements, but given that it was based on a Mindfulness intervention, it may also have been relevant to BN.

Increasing Motivation for Self-Help

Three studies focused on how to increase ED patients' motivation to take up and adhere to self-help treatments (Cassin, von Ranson, Heng, Brar, & Wojtowicz, 2008; Dunn, Neighbors, & Larimer, 2006; Schmidt et al., 2006). In the first of these studies (Dunn et al., 2006), the effect of adding one session of Motivational Enhancement Therapy (MET) before self-help treatment was examined in people with BN or BED. Participants were randomly assigned either to have a 1-hour MET session before PSH with a manual or to PSH only. Participants in the MET group showed increased readiness to change binge eating compared to those in the PSH-only group. Few other differences were found between groups, in terms of eating attitudes, frequency of binge eating, and compensatory behaviors and treatment adherence.

A second trial in 108 women with BED also compared guided self-help for BED with or without the addition of one Motivational Interviewing session (Cassin et al., 2008). Both groups showed improvement in binge eating, affective symptoms, and quality of life, but significantly more women in the group with the added motivational Interviewing were abstinent from binge eating after treatment than in the comparison group (27.8% vs. 11.1%).

A third trial compared GSH with or without repeated personalized feedback (Schmidt et al., 2006) in adults with BN or EDNOS. The study found that added feedback did not have an effect on take-up or dropout from treatment. However, it did lead to greater improvements in self-induced vomiting and dietary restriction than GSH without feedback.

Computerized Self-Help

Several computerized interventions for BN, EDNOS, and BED have been developed and tested. As the evidence supporting them has not been included in the reviews described in the preceding text we will discuss them here separately.

OVERCOMING BULIMIA

A CBT multimedia self-help treatment for BN (Overcoming Bulimia; Williams et al., 1998, 2002) was developed initially as a stand-alone CD-ROM

and later adapted for use over the internet. The CD-ROM version was tested in two uncontrolled pilot studies and one RCT. In the first pilot study, BN patients used the CD-ROM in the clinic without any therapist guidance. There were significant pre–post treatment reductions in binging and self-induced vomiting (Bara-Carril et al., 2004). The second pilot study compared data from the first cohort with data from a second cohort from the same Centre, in which patients were offered three brief guidance sessions with a trainee psychologist (Murray et al., 2007), to examine whether the addition of therapist support to the CD-ROM intervention would improve treatment uptake, adherence or outcome. Patients in both cohorts improved significantly in their bulimic symptoms without any differences between the groups in treatment uptake, adherence or outcome.

The RCT of the CD-ROM intervention tested its effectiveness in 97 patients with BN or EDNOS referred to a specialist ED service (Schmidt et al., 2008). Patients were randomly assigned to two groups. The first group accessed the CD-ROM intervention in the clinic over 3 months with no clinician guidance, followed by a flexible number of therapist sessions. The second group was on a waiting list for 3 months, followed by 15 sessions of face-to-face CBT. Treatment uptake in both groups was low, with only two thirds of patients starting treatment. Although there were significant group by time interactions for binge eating and vomiting, favoring CD-ROM at 3 months and the other group at 7 months, post hoc group comparisons at 3 and 7 months found no significant differences on binge eating or vomiting frequency. This study was conducted in a routine clinical setting where patients had lengthy waiting periods before being assessed by the specialist service and prior to inclusion in the study. The authors concluded that accessing the CD-ROM in clinic without support from a clinician may not be the best way of exploiting the benefits of this intervention.

More recently, two further studies have used an Internet-based version of the same program, that is, Overcoming Bulimia Online. The first of these was conducted in a cohort of 101 adolescents with BN or EDNOS. The intervention consisted of the interactive CBT Web program together with weekly e-mail support from a therapist and a message board for participants and their parents (Pretorius et al., 2009, submitted). There were significant pre–post intervention improvements in binge eating episodes, vomiting episodes and in most ED symptoms.

These changes were maintained at 6 months follow-up.

The second study was an RCT comparing Overcoming Bulimia Online with a delayed treatment control group who were on a waiting list for 3 months before accessing online treatment, in students with BN or EDNOS, recruited via their University networks (Sánchez-Ortiz et al., submitted). At 3 months, the group receiving immediate Internet-based CBT had greater improvements in binge eating episodes, other EDs symptomatology, depression, anxiety, and quality of life compared to participants in the delayed treatment group (who by then had not as yet received any treatment). Improvements in the immediate treatment group were maintained at 6 months. At 6 months, participants in the delayed treatment group had not caught up with those who received immediate treatment.

OTHER TECHNOLOGY-BASED INTERVENTIONS

Two other RCTs and a clinically controlled trial have used other technology-based interventions. The first of these compared face-to-face group CBT to a CD-ROM–based CBT program (POWER [Preventing Overweight with Exercise and Reasoning]) and to a waiting list control group in 66 adults with BED, recruited via advertisements (Shapiro et al., 2007). Participants in the group CBT condition had a significantly higher dropout rate than those receiving the CD-ROM intervention or waiting list controls. At the end of treatment, both the CD-ROM and the group CBT participants had a significantly greater reduction in the number of binge eating days compared to the waiting list group.

A European Multi-Centre project (the Salut project) developed an Internet-based CBT with e-mail guidance for the treatment of BN. Treatment consisted of seven lessons and it lasted for 4 months. Cohort studies evaluating the efficacy and acceptability of the intervention were conducted in Switzerland, Germany, and Sweden (Carrard et al., 2006; Liwowsky, Cebulla, & Fichter 2006; Nevonen, Mark, Levin, Lindstroüm, & Paulson-Karlsson, 2008; Rouget et al., 2005). A CCT was conducted in Spain in 62 women with BN comparing the computerized self-help program against a waiting list. At the end of treatment patients receiving GSH had significantly higher abstinence rates from binging and purging than the control group (22.6% vs. 0%) (Fernández-Aranda et al., 2008).

An RCT including BN and BED sufferers assessed the efficacy of a manual-based CBT self-help intervention combined with email support and an online discussion forum for participants (Ljotsson et al, 2007). The treatment lasted for 12 weeks and was compared to waiting list. A significant improvement was found in the treatment group, compared to the waiting list group in the number of binge eating episodes and in ED symptoms such as eating, shape and weight concern, and dietary restraint.

Taken together these studies suggest that computerized self-help treatments hold considerable promise as first-step interventions in the treatment of people with BN, EDNOS and BED; however, further studies are needed comparing technology-based treatments against manual-based self-care and face-to-face treatments in different populations and settings.

Predictors and Moderators
Treatment Uptake

Two studies assessed the characteristics of patients who were offered the CD-ROM package Overcoming Bulimia (Bara-Carril et al., 2004; Murray et al., 2003). There were few differences between those who did or did not take up the package, although Bara-Carril et al. (2004) found that those who did not take up the intervention had more severe bulimic symptoms.

The study by Murray et al. (2003) which included quantitative and qualitative elements, found no differences between those who did or did not take up the intervention in terms of previous experience with self-help, participants' views on previous self-help, views on the usefulness of self-help in general, computer literacy or knowledge about BN. However, those who took up the package thought that self-help would be more useful for themselves than those who did not take it up. They were also more willing to try this treatment and understood that additional treatment would be available to them if self-help did not lead to improvements. Those who did not take up the treatment felt that they were being short-changed by being offered a computer treatment rather than seeing a therapist.

Outcome

Only a handful of studies have assessed predictors or moderators of outcome in self-help studies. In studies of self-help for BN, pretreatment characteristics predicting poor outcome were binge-frequency (Thiels, Schmidt, Troop, Treasure, & Garthe, 2000; Turnbull et al., 1997) and those predicting good outcome were duration of illness (Turnbull et al., 1997), lower baseline knowledge about EDs, more problems with intimacy, and higher compulsivity scores (Carter et al., 2003), higher scores on the EDI perfectionism scale and EAT and a higher minimum BMI (Fernández-Aranda et al., 2008). In an RCT of Internet-based self-help for BN and EDNOS 45% of the variance of the EDE global score at the end of treatment was predicted by a regression model including global EDE at baseline, current major depression and multiple purging methods (Sánchez-Ortiz, unpublished PhD thesis). In a study of self-help for BEDs, predictors and moderators of outcomes were examined (Masheb & Grilo, 2008). Current age and age of onset did not predict outcomes. Pretreatment binge frequency and eating psychopathology predicted the post-treatment levels of these outcomes. Personality disorders, in particular Cluster C, and negative affect predicted post-treatment ED psychopathology. None of the variables tested were predictive of binge remission (i.e., a categorical outcome). No moderator effects were found.

Within-treatment predictors of outcome have included rapid response to treatment that predicted remission from binge eating, greater improvements in ED psychopathology, and greater weight loss in two studies of guided self-help in BED (Grilo et al., 2006; Grilo & Masheb, 2007; Masheb & Grilo, 2007).

Moreover, several studies have found that good adherence to self-care (e.g., in terms of proportion of manual read, number of homework exercises done, computer modules worked through, etc.) is a predictor of positive outcome (Ghaderi et al., 2008; Schmidt et al., 2008; Thiels et al., 2000; Troop et al., 1996).

In summary, prediction of outcome from self-help interventions remains problematic with limited numbers of studies addressing this and inconsistent findings.

Use and Effectiveness of Self-Help in Different Settings

Several questions arise in relation to the delivery of optimal delivery of self-help and these are discussed in the text that follows.

Which Self-Help Intervention to Use?

The content covered by different available self-help interventions for bulimia, BED, and EDNOS significantly overlaps, so how to choose between them and what to recommend to patients? One could argue that perhaps one should settle for those self-help interventions that have been evaluated in RCTs, but it is unlikely that all available self-help interventions

will be tested in this rigorous way and would not be a good use of research money and time. To some extent which manual or computer intervention is a matter of patients' personal taste, level of education, and learning and life style. With self-help manuals, factors such as font size; length of text; and whether text is broken up by illustrations, figures, or tables may matter in terms of its attractiveness and user-friendliness. Another important factor in judging the appropriateness of different interventions is the complexity of the language in which they are written. Table 22.1 summarizes the readability scores of commercially available treatment manuals for EDs, suggesting that some might be most appropriate for people with high levels of education, whereas others may be appropriate to a broader range of users.

How to Get Patients Interested and Keep Them Going with Self-Help?

A recent systematic review of the uptake of computerized cognitive–behavioral therapy noted that there were widespread barriers to this (Waller & Gilbody, 2008) and that "personal circumstances" seemed to be the most common cause of dropout.

In our own research we found that being able to access the intervention immediately once the patient had made up their mind to utilize self-help appeared to be an important factor in terms of optimizing uptake and outcomes (Sánchez-Ortiz et al., submitted) and that having to wait for treatment (whether this was self-help or therapist aided, lead to low uptake and adherence (Schmidt et al., 2008). Interventions designed to increase motivation and self-efficacy (e.g., Cassin et al., 2008; Dunn et al., 2006; Schmidt et al., 2006) also seem promising in improving outcomes from self-help.

Expertise of the Supporter

One of the intriguing findings in the AN treatment literature is that Specialist Supportive Clinical Management, a pragmatic no-frills treatment given by experts, produced better outcomes than specialist therapies such as CBT or IPT (McIntosh et al., 2005). In the context of self-help treatments one question is whether support from ED experts may produce better outcomes than support from lay people or therapists with little expertise in the field of EDs. To date no studies exist that can answer this question.

Settings

Very little is known about what is the optimal setting and service context for using self-help interventions.

Table 22.1 Readability Scores of Popular Self-Help Manuals

Author	Title of Manual	Year	Flesch Reading Ease Score[a]	Flesch–Kincaid Grade Level[b]
Apple & Agras	*Overcoming Eating Disorders. A Cognitive-Behavioral Treatment for Bulimia Nervosa and Binge-Eating Disorder*	1997	43.4	13.8
Cooper	*Bulimia Nervosa: A Guide to Recovery*	1993	48.2	11.4
Cooper et al.	*Bulimia Nervosa: A Cognitive Therapy Programme for Clients: A Cognitive Manual*	2000	68.0	7.6
Fairburn	*Overcoming Binge Eating*	1995	53.8	10.8
Freeman	*Overcoming Anorexia Nervosa*	1995	53.6	11.7
Schmidt & Treasure	*Getting Better Bit(e) by Bit(e): A Survival Kit for Sufferers of Bulimia Nervosa and Binge*	1993	64.3	8.5

Scores were calculated by choosing two random passages of text of about 100 to 150 words from each manual.
[a]The Flesh Reading Ease Score rates text on a 100-point scale; the higher the score, the easier it is to understand the document. For most standard documents, aim for a score of approximately 60 to 70.
[b]The Flesh–Kincaid Grade level rates text on a U.S. school grade level. For example, a score of 8.0 means that an eighth grader can understand the document. For most documents, aim for a score of approximately 7.0 to 8.0.

In many ways one would think that less specialized settings (e.g., primary care, university health services) are more appropriate than specialist settings where people have the expectation that they will be seeing an expert. However, one of the few studies done in a primary care setting (Walsh et al., 2004) had exceptionally high dropout rates, and some studies using self-help in more specialist settings (e.g., Schmidt et al., 2007) have produced good outcomes. So perhaps the issue is not so much about which setting per se, but about how in a given setting self-help is presented to the patient, how it is supported and how well it is integrated into an overall care plan. Patients may be perfectly willing to try self-help in any setting, provided there is clarity about what will happen if they do need additional care thereafter. As yet very little is known about how best to sequence self-help interventions with other psychological and pharmacological interventions.

Medication and Self-Help Interventions

An important clinical question of relevance in particular in settings where psychological therapies are not readily available is about the relative merits of medication and self-help in the treatment of EDs and whether to consider combining these approaches. The evidence available in this area is limited but suggests that combining self-help with medication may improve outcomes.

Limitations in Our Knowledge and Future Research

Despite a growing literature on self-help interventions and some encouraging findings there are as yet many gaps in our knowledge. In part these are to do with the heterogeneous nature and methodological limitations of the available studies. There seems to be a suggestion that self-help with guidance is superior to pure self-help, but whether this is true for all relevant outcomes and in the longer term is not certain. It is also as yet not clear how well guided self-help compares with traditional face-to-face treatments and whether different modes of delivery (manual or electronic) are superior. We do not really know much about who benefits most from self-help interventions. Further, little is known about the cost-effectiveness of such interventions. It is also not clear what the effective ingredients and best settings are for such interventions.

In line with a general trend toward brief psychotherapies, there has been much enthusiasm for self-help, but one needs to remember that many patients do not make a full recovery with self-help interventions and need additional treatment thereafter. As yet practically nothing is known about the optimal sequencing of self-help and other interventions in stepped care models.

The potential of self-help interventions to harm patients is generally considered very low. However, it is possible that patients who do not benefit from this kind of intervention get demoralized and may perceive the lack of improvement as their failure, leading them to disengage from any type of therapy. In EDs, such a scenario is not unlikely, as most patients suffer from low self-esteem and want to "do things right." Very few studies explicitly assess harm from self-help.

To answer some of the preceding questions, and in particular to learn more about moderators of outcome, large well-designed multicenter studies of different types of self-help interventions compared against other effective treatments and using stepped care models need to be conducted.

Further research is also needed on self-help interventions for AN. As described in the beginning of this chapter, such manuals are now available for patients or their caregivers.

As yet, all available self-help interventions for EDs have been designed for adults. However, given the typical onset of AN and BN in mid-adolescence, self-help materials for younger patients need to be developed and evaluated.

Conclusion

The field of self-help is rapidly growing and developing. A number of self-help approaches for EDs have been developed including books, CD-ROMs, or Internet-based solutions. Although large effectiveness studies are not as yet available, the existing results are promising and encourage mental health service providers to have a closer look into such treatments.

Self-help interventions have the potential of bridging the gap between the high and increasing demands for treatment of EDs and the limited resources and inequalities in access to specialist care in most health care systems. Especially for BN, BED, and EDNOS, self-help is a feasible alternative to specialized treatment.

For many people with EDs, self-help interventions may be an attractive option for overcoming their own problems. As many people with EDs do not actively seek help, self-help interventions could be one way to address this problem and improve their situation.

Future research needs to focus on large well-designed effectiveness studies that also allow exploration of moderators and of the cost/cost-effectiveness of these approaches.

References

Apple, R. F., & Agras, W. S. (1997). *Overcoming eating disorders: A cognitive-behavioral treatment for bulimia nervosa and binge-eating disorder*. San Antonio, California: Graywind Publications.

Bailer, U., De Zwaan, M., Leisch, F., Strnad, A., Lennkh-Wolfsberg, C., El-Giamal, N., et al. (2004). Guided self-help versus cognitive-behavioral group therapy in the treatment of bulimia nervosa. *International Journal of Eating Disorders, 35*(4), 522–537.

Banasiak, S. J., Paxton, S. J., & Hay, P. J. (2007). Perceptions of cognitive behavioural guided self-help treatment for bulimia nervosa in primary care. *Eating Disorders, 15*(1), 23–40.

Bara-Carril, N., Williams, C. J., Pombo-Carril, M. G., Reid, Y., Murray, K., Aubin, S., et al. (2004). A preliminary investigation into the feasibility and efficacy of a CD-ROM-based cognitive-behavioral self-help intervention for bulimia nervosa. *International Journal of Eating Disorders, 35*(4), 538–548.

Carrard, I., Rouget, P., Fernaĭndez-Aranda, F., Volkart, A., Damoiseau, M., & Lam, T. (2006). Evaluation and deployment of evidence based patient self-management support program for bulimia nervosa. *International Journal of Medical Informatics, 75*(1), 101–109.

Carter, J. C., & Fairburn, C. G. (1998). Cognitive-behavioral self-help for binge eating disorder: A controlled effectiveness study. *Journal of Consulting and Clinical Psychology, 66*(4), 616–623.

Carter, J. C., Olmsted, M. P., Kaplan, A. S., McCabe, R. E., Mills, J. S., & Aimeĭ, A. (2003). Self-help for bulimia nervosa: A randomized controlled trial. *American Journal of Psychiatry, 160*(5), 973–978.

Cassin, S. E., von Ranson, K. M., Heng, K., Brar, J., & Wojtowicz, A. E. (2008). Adapted motivational interviewing for women with binge eating disorder: A randomized controlled trial. *Psychology of Addictive Behaviors, 22*(3), 417–425.

Cooper, M., Todd, G., & Wells, A. (2000). *Bulimia nervosa: A cognitive therapy programme for clients*. London: Jessica Kingsley Publishers.

Cooper, P. (1995). *Bulimia nervosa: A guide to recovery*. London: Robinson Publishing.

Cuijpers, P. (1997). Bibliotherapy in unipolar depression: A meta-analysis. *Journal of Behavior Therapy and Experimental Psychiatry, 28*(2), 139–147.

Currin, L., Schmidt, U., Treasure, J., & Jick, H. (2005). Time trends in eating disorder incidence. *British Journal of Psychiatry, 186*(Feb.), 132–135.

de la Rie, S., Noordenbos, G., Donker, M., & van Furth, E. (2006). Evaluating the treatment of eating disorders from the patient's perspective. *International Journal of Eating Disorders, 39*(8), 667–676.

Department of Health. (2001). *The expert patient: A new approach to chronic disease management in the 21st century*. London: Department of Health.

Dunn, E. C., Neighbors, C., & Larimer, M. E. (2006). Motivational enhancement therapy and self-help treatment for binge eaters. *Psychology of Addictive Behaviors, 20*(1), 44–52.

Durand, M. A., & King, M. (2003). Specialist treatment versus self-help for bulimia nervosa: A randomised controlled trial in general practice. *British Journal of General Practice, 53*(490), 371–377.

Fairburn, C. G., Cooper, Z., Doll, H. A., O'Connor, M. E., Bohn, K., Hawker, D. M., et al. (2008). Transdiagnostic cognitive-behavioral therapy for patients with eating disorders: A two-site trial with 60–week follow-up. *Am J Psychiatry*, appi.ajp.2008.08040608.

Fernández-Aranada, F., Santamaria, J., Nunez, A., Martinez, C., Krug, I., Cappozzo, M., et al. (2008). Internet-based cognitive-behavioral therapy for bulimia nervosa: A controlled study. *European Psychiatry, 23*(Supplement 2), S186–S186.

Fichter, M., Cebulla, M., Quadflieg, N., & Naab, S. (2008). Guided self-help for binge eating/purging anorexia nervosa before inpatient treatment. *Psychotherapy Research, 18*(5), 594–603.

Freeman, C. (2002). *Overcoming anorexia.* New York: New York University Press.

Ghaderi, A. (2006). Attrition and outcome in self-help treatment for bulimia nervosa and binge eating disorder: A constructive replication. *Eating Behaviors, 7*(4), 300–308.

Ghaderi, A., & Scott, B. (2003). Pure and guided self-help for full and sub-threshold bulimia nervosa and binge eating disorder. *British Journal of Clinical Psychology, 42*(3), 257–269.

Grilo, C. M., & Masheb, R. M. (2005). A randomized controlled comparison of guided self-help cognitive behavioral therapy and behavioral weight loss for binge eating disorder. *Behaviour Research and Therapy, 43*(11), 1509–1525.

Grilo, C. M., & Masheb, R. M. (2007). Rapid response predicts binge eating and weight loss in binge eating disorder: Findings from a controlled trial of orlistat with guided self-help cognitive behavioral therapy. *Behaviour Research and Therapy, 45*(11), 2537–2550.

Grilo, C. M., Masheb, R. M., & Salant, S. L. (2005). Cognitive behavioral therapy guided self-help and orlistat for the treatment of binge eating disorder: A randomized, double-blind, placebo-controlled trial. *Biological Psychiatry, 57*(10), 1193–1201.

Grover, M., Williams, C., Eisler, I., Treasure, J., Smith G., McCloskey, C., Fairburn, P., Schmidt, U. (2009). *An off-line pilot evaluation of a web-based systemic cognitive-behavioural intervention for carers of people with anorexia nervosa.* Manuscript sumbitted for publication.

Haaga, D. A. F. (2000). Introduction to the special section on stepped care models in psychotherapy. *Journal of Consulting and Clinical Psychology, 68*(4), 547–548.

Hall, L., & Cohn, L. (1986). *Bulimia: A guide to recovery.* Carlsbad, CA: Gurze Books.

Hay, P. J., Mond, J., Buttner, P., & Darby, A. (2008). Eating disorder behaviors are increasing: Findings from two sequential community surveys in south Australia. *PLoS ONE, 3*(2).

Huon, G. F. (1985). An initial validation of a self-help program for bulimia. *International Journal of Eating Disorders, 4*(4), 573–588.

Kyriacou, O., Treasure, J., & Schmidt, U. (2008a). Expressed emotion in eating disorders assessed via self-report: An examination of factors associated with expressed emotion in carers of people with anorexia nervosa in comparison to control families. *International Journal of Eating Disorders, 41*(1), 37–46.

Kyriacou, O., Treasure, J., & Schmidt, U. (2008b). Understanding how parents cope with living with someone with anorexia nervosa: Modelling the factors that are associated with carer distress. *International Journal of Eating Disorders, 41*(3), 233–242.

Lewis, G., Anderson, L., Araya, R., Elgie, R., Harrison, G., Proudfoot, J., et al. (2003). Self-help interventions for mental health problems. *Report to the Department of Health R&D Programme,*

Liwowsky, I., Cebulla, M., & Fichter, M. (2006). New ways to combat eating disorders - evaluation of an Internet-based self-help program in bulimia nervosa. [Virtuelle esstagebuücher und motivation per E-mail: Neue wege bei der behandlung von bulimia nervosa] *MMW-Fortschritte Der Medizin, 148*(31–32), 31–33.

Ljotsson, B., Lundin, C., Mitsell, K., Carlbring, P., Ramklint, M., & Ghaderi, A. (2007). Remote treatment of bulimia nervosa and binge eating disorder: A randomized trial of internet-assisted cognitive behavioural therapy. *Behaviour Research and Therapy, 45*(4), 649–661.

Loeb, K. L., Wilson, G. T., Gilbert, J. S., & Labouvie, E. (2000). Guided and unguided self-help for binge eating. *Behaviour Research and Therapy, 38*(3), 259–272.

Lorig, K. R., & Holman, H. R. (2003). Self-management education: History, definition, outcomes, and mechanisms. *Annals of Behavioral Medicine, 26*(1), 1–7.

Lovell, K., & Richards, D. (2000). Multiple access points and levels of entry (maple): Ensuring choice, accessibility and equity for cbt services. *Behavioural and Cognitive Psychotherapy, 28*(4), 379–391.

Marrs, R. W. (1995). A meta-analysis of bibliotherapy studies. *American Journal of Community Psychology, 23*(6), 843–870.

Masheb, R. M., & Grilo, C. M. (2007). Rapid response predicts treatment outcomes in binge eating disorder: Implications for stepped care. *Journal of Consulting and Clinical Psychology, 75*(4), 639–644.

Masheb, R. M., & Grilo, C. M. (2008). Examination of predictors and moderators for self-help treatments of binge-eating disorder. *Journal of Consulting and Clinical Psychology, 76*(5), 900–904.

McIntosh, V. V. W., Jordan, J., Carter, F. A., Luty, S. E., McKenzie, J. M., Bulik, C. M., et al. (2005). Three psychotherapies for anorexia nervosa: A randomized, controlled trial. *American Journal of Psychiatry, 162*(4), 741–747.

Mitchell, J. E., Fletcher, L., Hanson, K., Mussell, M. P., Seim, H., Crosby, R., et al. (2001). The relative efficacy of fluoxetine and manual-based self-help in the treatment of outpatients with bulimia nervosa. *Journal of Clinical Psychopharmacology, 21*(3), 298–304.

Mond, J. M., Hay, P. J., Rodgers, B., Owen, C., & Beumont, P. J. V. (2004). Beliefs of the public concerning the helpfulness of interventions for bulimia nervosa. *International Journal of Eating Disorders, 36*(1), 62–68.

Murray, K., Pombo-Carril, M. G., Bara-Carril, N., Grover, M., Reid, Y., Langham, C., et al. (2003). Factors determining uptake of a CD-ROM-based CBT self-help treatment for bulimia: Patient characteristics and subjective appraisals of self-help treatment. *European Eating Disorders Review, 11*(3), 243–260.

Murray, K., Schmidt, U., Pombo-Carril, M., Grover, M., Alenya, J., Treasure, J., et al. (2007). Does therapist guidance improve uptake, adherence and outcome from a CD-ROM based cognitive-behavioral intervention for the treatment of bulimia nervosa? *Computers in Human Behavior, 23*(1), 850–859.

National Institute for Clinical Excellence. (2004). *Eating disorders: Core interventions in the treatment and management of anorexia nervosa, bulimia nervosa and related eating disorders.* London: National Institute for Clinical Excellence.

Nevonen, L., Mark, M., Levin, B., Lindstroüm, M., & Paulson-Karlsson, G. (2006). Evaluation of a new Internet-based self-help guide for patients with bulimic symptoms in Sweden. *Nordic Journal of Psychiatry, 60*(6), 463–468.

Palmer, R. L., Birchall, H., McGrain, L., & Sullivan, V. (2002). Self-help for bulimic disorders: A randomised controlled trial comparing minimal guidance with face-to-face or telephone guidance. *British Journal of Psychiatry*, *181*(SEPT.), 230–235.

Perkins, S., Winn, S., Murray, J., Murphy, R., & Schmidt, U. (2004). A qualitative study of the experience of caring for a person with bulimia nervosa. part 1: The emotional impact of caring. *International Journal of Eating Disorders*, *36*(3), 256–268.

Perkins, S. J., Murphy, R., Schmidt, U., & Williams, C. (2006). Self-help and guided self-help for eating disorders. *Cochrane Database of Systematic Reviews (Online)*, 3.

Pretorius, N., Arcelus, J., Beecham, J., Dawson, H., Doherty, F., Eisler, I., et al. (2009a). *The feasibility, acceptability, and efficacy of a web-based CBT intervention for adolescents with bulimia nervosa.* Manuscript submitted for publication.

Pretorius, N., Arcelus, J., Beecham, J., Dawson, H., Doherty, F., Eisler, I., et al.(2009b).*Perceptions of web-based CBT for bulimia nervosa.* Manuscript submitted for publication.

Robinson, P., & Serfaty, M. (2008). Getting better byte by byte: A pilot randomised controlled trial of email therapy for bulimia nervosa and binge eating disorder. *European Eating Disorders Review*, *16*(2), 84–93.

Russell, G. (1979). Bulimia nervosa: An ominous variant of anorexia nervosa. *Psychological Medicine*, *9*(3), 429–448.

Sánchez-Ortiz, V.C., Munro, C., Stahl, D., House, J., Startup, H., Treasure, J., Williams, C., Schmidt, U. (2008) *A randomised controlled trial of Internet-based Cognitive-Behavioural Therapy for Bulimia Nervosa in a student.* Manuscript submitted for publication.

Schmidt, U., Andiappan, M., Graver, M., Robinson, S., Perkins, S., Dugmore, O., et al. (2008). Randomised controlled trial of CD-ROM-based cognitive-behavioural self-care for bulimia nervosa. *British Journal of Psychiatry*, *193*(6), 493–500.

Schmidt, U., Bone, G., Hems, S., Lessem, J., & Treasure, J. (2002). Structured therapeutic writing tasks as an adjunct to treatment in eating disorders. *European Eating Disorders Review*, *10*(5), 299–315.

Schmidt, U., Landau, S., Pombo-Carril, M. G., Bara-Carril, N., Reid, Y., Murray, K., et al. (2006). Does personalized feedback improve the outcome of cognitive-behavioural guided self-care in bulimia nervosa? A preliminary randomized controlled trial. *British Journal of Clinical Psychology*, *45*(1), 111–121.

Schmidt, U., Lee, S., Beecham, J., Perkins, S., Treasure, J., Yi, I., et al. (2007). A randomized controlled trial of family therapy and cognitive behavior therapy guided self-care for adolescents with bulimia nervosa and related disorders. *American Journal of Psychiatry*, *164*(4), 591–598.

Schmidt, U., & Treasure, J. (1993). *Getting better bit(e) by bit(e).* Hove: Psychology Press.

Schmidt, U., & Treasure, J. (2006). Anorexia nervosa: Valued and visible. A cognitive-interpersonal maintenance model and its implications for research and practice. *British Journal of Clinical Psychology*, *45*(3), 343–366.

Schmidt, U., Williams, C., Eisler, I., Fairbairn, P., McCloskey, C., Smith, G., &Treasure, J. (2007 unpublished) *Overcoming Anorexia: Effective Caring.* Web-programme. Media Innovations, Leeds, UK

Shapiro, J. R., Reba-Harrelson, L., Dymek-Valentine, M., Woolson, S. L., Hamer, R. M., & Bulik, C. M. (2007). Feasibility and acceptability of CD-ROM-based cognitive-behavioural treatment for binge-eating disorder. *European Eating Disorders Review*, *15*(3), 175–184.

Steele, A. L., & Wade, T. D. (2008). A randomised trial investigating guided self-help to reduce perfectionism and its impact on bulimia nervosa: A pilot study. *Behaviour Research and Therapy*, *46*(12), 1316–1323.

Stefano, S. C., Bacaltchuk, J., Blay, S. L., & Hay, P. (2006). Self-help treatments for disorders of recurrent binge eating: A systematic review. *Acta Psychiatrica Scandinavica*, *113*(6), 452–459.

Tchanturia, K., Davies, H., Lopez, C., Schmidt, U., Treasure, J., & Wykes, T. (2008). Letter to the editor: Neuropsychological task performance before and after cognitive remediation in anorexia nervosa: A pilot case-series. *Psychological Medicine*, *38*(9), 1371–1373.

Thiels, C., Schmidt, U., Treasure, J., Garthe, R., & Troop, N. (1998). Guided self-change for bulimia nervosa incorporating use of a self-care manual. *American Journal of Psychiatry*, *155*(7), 947–953.

Thiels, C., Schmidt, U., Troop, N., Treasure, J., & Garthe, R. (2000). Binge frequency predicts outcome in guided self-care treatment of bulimia nervosa. *European Eating Disorders Review*, *8*(4), 272–278.

Thiels, C., Schmidt, U., Troop, N., Treasure, J., & Garthe, R. (2001). Compliance with a self-care manual in guided self-change for bulimia nervosa. *European Eating Disorders Review*, *9*(2), 115–122.

Treasure, J. & Schmidt, U. (2007). In: H. Arkowitz, H. Westra, W. Miller, & S. Rollnick (Eds.). *Eating disorders. Motivational interviewing in psychotherapy and mental health.*, New York: Guilford Press.

Treasure, J., Schmidt, U., & Hugo, P. (2005). Mind the gap: Service transition and interface problems for patients with eating disorders. *British Journal of Psychiatry*, *187*(NOV.), 398–400.

Treasure, J., Schmidt, U., Troop, N., Tiller, J., Todd, G., & Turnbull, S. (1996). Sequential treatment for bulimia nervosa incorporating a self-care manual. *British Journal of Psychiatry*, *168*(Jan.), 94–98.

Treasure, J., Smith, G., & Crane, A. (2007). *Skills-based learning for caring for a loved one with an eating disorder: The new maudsley method.* Hove: Routledge.

Troop, N., Schmidt, U., Tiller, J., Todd, G., Keilen, M., & Treasure, J. (1996). Compliance with a self-care manual for bulimia nervosa: Predictors and outcome. *British Journal of Clinical Psychology*, *35*(3), 435–438.

Turnbull, S. J., Schmidt, U., Troop, N. A., Tiller, J., Todd, G., & Treasure, J. L. (1997). Predictors of outcome for two treatments for bulimia nervosa: Short and long term. *International Journal of Eating Disorders*, *21*(1), 17–22.

Waller, R., & Gilbody, S. (2008). Barriers to the uptake of computerized cognitive behavioural therapy: A systematic review of the quantitative and qualitative evidence. *Psychological Medicine*, 1–8.

Walsh, B. T., Fairburn, C. G., Mickley, D., Sysko, R., & Parides, M. K. (2004). Treatment of bulimia nervosa in a primary care setting. *American Journal of Psychiatry*, *161*(3), 556–561.

Williams, C. (2001). Use of written cognitive-behavioural therapy self-help materials to treat depression. *Advances in Psychiatric Treatment*, *7*(3), 233–240.

Williams, C. (2003). New technologies in self-help: Another effective way to get better? *European Eating Disorders Review*, *11*(3), 170–182.

Williams, C., Schmidt, U., & Aubin, S. (2005). *Overcoming bulimia Internet version* Media Innovations.

Winn, S., Perkins, S., Murray, J., Murphy, R., & Schmidt, U. (2004). A qualitative study of the experience of caring for a person with bulimia nervosa. part 2: Caregivers' needs and experiences of services and other support. *International Journal of Eating Disorders, 36*(3), 269–279.

Winn, S., Perkins, S., Walwyn, R., Schmidt, U., Eisler, I., Treasure, J., et al. (2007). Predictors of mental health problems and negative caregiving experiences in carers of adolescents with bulimia nervosa. *International Journal of Eating Disorders, 40*(2), 171–178.

CHAPTER

23 | Dialectical Behavior Therapy

Eunice Y. Chen *and* Debra Safer

Abstract

This chapter provides a description and reviews the research evidence for the adaptation of Dialectical Behavior Therapy (DBT) for eating disorders (EDs). First, the chapter briefly describes the standard DBT program as originally developed for women with borderline personality disorder (BPD). Second, the rationale for the adaptation of DBT for EDs is reviewed. Third, the DBT model of maintenance and etiology of EDs is discussed. Fourth, the randomized controlled trial evidence for DBT for BPD is reviewed as well as that for DBT for EDs. Finally, the DBT program for EDs is outlined. It is concluded that DBT is a promising treatment for EDs, worthy of further investigation with this population.

Keywords: borderline personality disorder, dialectical behavior therapy, eating disorders, trials

Introduction

Standard dialectical behavior therapy (DBT) is an outpatient cognitive–behavioral therapy originally developed for women with extreme emotion dysregulation and recurrent suicidal behavior, that is, borderline personality disorder (BPD). A comprehensive skills-based treatment, DBT integrates strategies derived from behavior change principles (such as problem-solving, skills training, contingency management, exposure-based procedures, cognitive modification) with strategies derived from acceptance-based practices such as Zen and contemplation practice (such as mindfulness and validation). These strategies are integrated within a framework derived from dialectical philosophy, a view of reality that emphasizes wholeness, interrelatedness, and process and is also a method of persuasive dialogue and relationship. Over time, standard DBT has been adapted to address a variety of problematic behaviors associated with emotion dysregulation, including eating disorders (EDs).

The aims of this chapter are (1) to briefly review standard DBT as originally developed for women

with BPD, including its biosocial theory; (2) to present the rationale for the adaptation of DBT for EDs; (3) to describe the DBT model of maintenance and etiology of EDs; (4) to review the randomized controlled trial evidence for DBT for BPD; (5) to present the available research on DBT for EDs; (6) to outline the DBT program as adapted for binge eating disorder (BED) and bulimia nervosa (BN); and (7) to offer conclusions and future directions for research.

In standard DBT, BPD is conceptualized as a disorder of pervasive emotion dysregulation and the biosocial theory is utilized to describe its etiology and maintenance. According to this biosocial theory, BPD behaviors develop as a result of a transaction over time between a biological vulnerability to emotion dysregulation and the experience of an emotionally invalidating environment. Emotional vulnerability refers to a heightened sensitivity to emotional stimuli, intense emotional responses, and a slow return to emotional baseline. An environment is labeled invalidating if it (1) indiscriminately rejects an individual's communication of personal experience, particularly emotions; (2) intermittently reinforces an escalation of emotions; and (3) oversimplifies problem-solving and meeting goals. These characteristics lead individuals to have difficulties validating their own internal experiences and to search the environment for ways to respond, often reacting with extreme oscillations between emotional inhibition and intense responses in order to communicate private experience, as well as forming unrealistic goals. The pervasive emotion dysregulation that results includes several difficulties: inhibiting mood-dependent behaviors; organizing behavior in the service of goals, independent of current mood; up- or down-regulating physiological arousal as needed; diverting attention from emotionally evocative stimuli; and/or experiencing emotion without avoidance or an extreme secondary negative emotion.

The biosocial theory incorporates an affect dysregulation model to explain the maintenance of suicidal and self-injurious behavior. These behaviors are the result of intolerable emotions and function to reduce painful emotional states in individuals who lack other adaptive skills to modulate their emotions. While engaging in suicidal and self-injurious behavior may bring relief temporarily, such behavior typically leads to more distressing emotions or other negative consequences. For example, secondary emotions (e.g., shame) arise from engaging in the suicidal or self injurious behavior and these intolerable emotions cause the cycle of suicidal of self-injurious behavior to repeat itself or engagement in other dysfunctional ways of escape.

Standard DBT treatment is organized around the client's level of severity and chronicity, with each level of disorder associated with a different treatment stage and each stage associated with particular treatment goals. DBT stages involve (1) *Pretreatment*, orientation and commitment to treatment; (2) *Stage I*, stopping out-of-control behaviors, (3) *Stage II*, replacing "quiet desperation" with nontraumatic emotional experiencing, (4) *Stage III*, reducing ongoing disorders and problems in living, and (5) *Stage IV*, resolving a sense of incompleteness to achieve freedom. Each stage of treatment is associated with a target hierarchy. DBT is unique in that the content of an individual session is dictated by an overall target hierarchy rather than a prescribed agenda for each session. The Stage I target hierarchy (for BPD) is to (1) cease life- threatening behaviors (e.g., suicide attempts, increase in suicide ideation, nonsuicidal self-injurious behaviors, homicidal threats and behaviors); (2) cease therapy-interfering behaviors (e.g., missed sessions); (3) cease quality-of-life-interfering behaviors (e.g., EDs or other Axis I disorders, homelessness); and (4) increase behavioral skills.

Stage I DBT functions to enhance client and therapist's behavioral capabilities and motivation. This is accomplished for clients by reducing reinforcement for dysfunctional or ineffective behavior (which may include restructuring the environment), and generalizing behavior from the therapy setting to the natural environment. To fulfill these functions, the modes of treatment in Stage I DBT involve (1) weekly individual psychotherapy, (2) weekly group skills training, (3) 24-hour telephone consultation, and (4) a weekly therapist consultation team. Each mode involves a different hierarchy of targets. The individual psychotherapist is responsible for the assessment and problem solving of skill deficit and motivational problems and organizing other treatment modes in service of these. Group skills training targets the acquisition of new behavioral skills in a structured psychoeducational format and includes four modules: Mindfulness, Distress Tolerance, Emotion Regulation, and Interpersonal Effectiveness skills. Telephone consultation provides emergency crisis intervention, disrupts potential reinforcement of suicidal behavior by therapists, provides skills coaching, promotes skills generalization and repairs client–therapist relationships. Finally, the therapist consultation team enhances the therapist's motivation and skills and manages problems arising in the delivery of DBT.

The treatment strategies in standard DBT (e.g., dialectical strategies, core strategies, stylistic strategies, and case management strategies) balance change and acceptance.

Dialectical strategies highlight dichotomous relationships and assist clients in finding balanced and synthesized responses. Dialectical strategies include the use of metaphors, stories, paradox, playing devil's advocate, fluctuating between ambiguity and certainty, using cognitive restructuring, highlighting continual change, and validating a client's intuitive wisdom.

The *core strategies* balance acceptance and behavioral change strategies. The latter include chain analyses, the meticulous examination of the topography, intensity, frequency, duration, situation, antecedents, and consequences of a problem behavior. In standard DBT, chains are typically conducted during individual psychotherapy. Repeated chain analyses of a problem behavior allow determination of the cues, maintaining factors and function of the behavior. This enables the client and therapist to identify what prevented the client from being effective in a situation and then to teach, role-play, and rehearse new skills (e.g., emotion regulation skills) or use cognitive modification or mindfulness to address faulty cognitions or clarify environmental contingencies. Having established a solution with the client and a plan to prevent future problem behavior, the therapist assesses the client's commitment using a variety of commitment strategies such as evaluating pros and cons, playing devil's advocate, and using '"foot in the door/door in the face" strategies. The therapist then troubleshoots this plan, and searches for commitment to the revised plan.

In every DBT encounter with a client, change strategies are balanced with acceptance strategies (e.g., validation) to build and maintain a strong therapeutic relationship. Validation strategies range on a continuum from listening in an interested fashion to being radically genuine, that is, treating the client as one would treat an equal, a sister, or a friend.

Stylistic strategies also balance acceptance and change. Reciprocal communication, on the one hand, involves interpersonal warmth, responsiveness to a client's concerns and strategic self-disclosure to model a coping model. On the other hand, irreverent communication involves an outrageous, humorous, or blunt style and is utilized when therapy becomes polarized and a therapist and client become deadlocked.

Case management strategies include "consultation-to-the-client," "environmental interventions," and "consultation-to-the-therapist." The first teaches clients how to skillfully interact with the environment rather than organizing the environment to meet their needs. Environmental interventions are used when a client is in immediate danger or is powerless, with the therapist acting directly on the client's behalf. Consultation-to-the-therapist strategy involves individual therapists seeking consultation within their team for support and assistance in delivering DBT effectively.

The preceding is a brief description of the standard DBT program for women with BPD. A more exhaustive description of Stage I DBT for BPD can be found in Linehan's manuals (Linehan, 1993a, 1993b). As discussed later, standard DBT has been adapted to address a variety of problem behaviors associated with emotion dysregulation, including eating disorder behavior, as described in the text that follows.

Rationale for the Adaptation of DBT for EDs

DBT offers an alternative for difficult-to-treat clients for whom existing treatments have failed.

Currently the most empirically tested treatments for eating disorders, cognitive–behavior therapy (CBT) and interpersonal psychotherapy (IPT) result in about 50% of BN and BED patients (Fairburn & Brownell, 2001) remaining symptomatic after treatment. Predictors of poor outcome in CBT for eating disorders may include co-occurring Axis I and II disorders or symptoms such as BPD and depressive symptoms (Grilo, Masheb, & Wilson, 2001; Stice & Agras, 1999; Wilfley et al., 2000). Standard DBT represents a viable option for ED clients with co-occurring psychopathology or for whom existing treatments have failed because it has efficacy for and was originally designed for individuals with multiple and "difficult-to-treat" disorders.

As described briefly, DBT is uniquely based upon a broad affect regulation model. In other words, the precursors of binge eating are understood to be the result of affect rather than due directly to dietary restraint and weight and shape concerns (as in CBT) or as a result of difficulties with resolving interpersonal problems (as in IPT). Although this affect regulation model does not preclude weight and shape concerns, interpersonal difficulties, thoughts about food or the self, or perfectionistic thinking playing a role in triggering an affective state, this model parsimoniously focuses upon affect as the important cue leading to problematic ED behavior. The affect regulation model views binge eating and other types of eating disordered behavior (e.g., vomiting) as the means (albeit maladaptive) by which individuals regulate emotions. Because standard DBT treatment is specifically designed to teach adaptive affect regulation skills and to target behaviors resulting from emotional dysregulation, a theoretical rationale exists for applying DBT to treating EDs.

By utilizing the biosocial theory, DBT also offers an etiological theory for the development of ED behaviors over time. This theory describes the areas needed for change but also encourages an attitude of effective compassion in the therapist. This theory is also validating to clients and serves to reduce some of the self-judgment and blame these individuals have with regard to their disorder. Dysfunctional behaviors such as ED behaviors are seen as developing over time from a transaction between a biologically emotionally vulnerable individual poorly matched with an environment experienced as invalidating.

As noted, DBT is a protocol-driven treatment in which sessions are organized by the highest ranking (or highest risk) target behavior that took place that day or over the last week. In addition, there are special protocols designed for addressing life-threatening and therapy-interfering behavior. DBT provides detailed guidance for therapists in managing crisis behaviors, which may be particularly valuable as suicidal and nonsuicidal self-injurious behaviors are often found in individuals with EDs (e.g., Franko & Keel, 2006; Svirko & Hawton, 2007). In addition, multiple co-occurring Axis I and II disorders (e.g., obsessive–compulsive disorder, obsessive–compulsive personality disorder, major depression, and alcohol use disorders) are found in individuals with EDs (e.g., Berkman, Lohr, & Bulik, 2007). The protocol-driven nature of DBT offers flexibility within a session, allowing multiple problems besides the eating disorder to be addressed. In addition, DBT uniquely targets therapy-interfering behavior (e.g., the client/therapist missing sessions or being late to sessions, not completing homework).

DBT fuses behavior change strategies and novel acceptance-based strategies such as mindfulness skills. Mindfulness-based approaches to thoughts and emotions contrast with older style cognitive restructuring techniques. Clients are taught to learn to observe and describe their thoughts and feelings, to watch them come and go, to note this constant passage, and to learn that thoughts and feelings are just thoughts and feelings, phenomena that can be sat with and observed but do not need to be acted upon. DBT is thus unique among ED treatments by balancing acceptance-based strategies with behavior change.

The nonjudgmental component of mindfulness is important for both clients and therapists. For example, clients with EDs are often judgmental about their appearance and themselves. Therapists also may become judgmental of client's thoughts and behaviors, as ED behaviors are often trivialized or judged to be scheming, deceitful, or superficial. This can lead to invalidation of clients, a lack of motivation for treatment, and burnout of both clients and therapists. DBT's nonjudgmental standpoint allows ED behaviors to be viewed nonpejoratively and thus usefully defined as responses that are within a client's current skill repertoire but that can be replaced by more helpful responses.

DBT Model of Maintenance and Etiology of EDs
Affect Regulation Model for EDs
Stress and negative mood are the most frequently cited precipitants of binge eating (Polivy & Herman, 1993). In DBT for EDs, binge eating is viewed as analogous to that of self-injury in standard DBT treatment for individuals with BPD. Binge eating or bulimic behaviors are understood as the result of attempts to escape from primary or secondary aversive emotions that may be triggered by thoughts regarding food, body image, perfectionism, negative thoughts about the self, or interpersonal situations (Linehan & Chen, 2005). Binge eating and bulimic behavior function to quickly narrow attention and cognitive focus from these thoughts and to provide immediate escape from physiological responses and feelings. Over time, binging as an escape behavior becomes reinforced (Heatherton & Baumeister, 1991), especially if no other adaptive emotion regulation skills are present. The longer-term effects of binging or bulimic behaviors are secondary emotions such as shame that in turn promote the eating disordered behavior (e.g., Sanftner & Crowther, 1998). Eventually binge-eating becomes an over-learned dysfunctional response to dysregulated emotions.

Research evidence supports the role of negative emotions and emotion regulation in binge eating. Self-report studies of weight loss participants show, for example, that independent of degree of overweight, individuals with BED report higher urges to binge in response to negative emotions (emotional eating) than non-binge eaters (Eldredge & Agras, 1996). The most frequently cited emotion triggering binge eating is anxiety followed by sadness, loneliness, and anger. Happiness is the least frequently cited (Masheb & Grilo, 2006).

When caloric deprivation and mood were experimentally manipulated Agras and Telch (1998) found that self-defined binges in obese women with BED were significantly more associated with negative mood rather than caloric deprivation. In a study utilizing experience sampling, in which subjects' mood and eating behaviors were tracked over 6 days, more aversive mood preceded binge-eating in a BED group compared to a weight-matched non-BED group (Greeno, Wing, & Shiffman, 2000). Further, BED subjects reported significantly worse mood on average than non-BED subjects. Using a similar methodology, greater diurnal fluctuation in depression and anxiety and higher frequency of these moods during eating and binge eating was reported in BED subjects compared to non-BED subjects (Lingswiler, Crowther, & Stephens, 1987).

In addition to eating in response to negative moods, individuals who binge eat also appear to evaluate situations as more stressful than non–eating disordered individuals (Hansel & Wittrock, 1997). This may be due to difficulties in identifying and making sense of emotional states, along with limited access to emotion regulation strategies (Whiteside et al., 2007).

Adaptation of the Biosocial Theory for EDs

In DBT, ED behaviors, just like BPD behaviors, are understood as resulting from a transaction over time between an individual biologically predisposed to be more emotionally vulnerable and a mismatch with an environment experienced (but not necessarily intended) as invalidating. This invalidating environment may punish emotional displays, leading individuals to engage in ED behaviors to manage their emotions and the secondary emotions of shame that may result. Sometimes, the invalidation may be in respect to specific ED behaviors (e.g., "Why can't you just stop eating?"), or take the form of weight-related teasing or over concern with weight by peers and family. The invalidating environment may also be broader, including typical Western societal messages idealizing thinness and disparaging overweight such that each is associated with polar moral values. The difficulties of weight loss may also be minimized by the media.

Over time, the results of this transaction may include (1) difficulties in identifying and regulating emotional arousal; (2) difficulties in tolerating emotional distress without engaging in ED behavior; (3) difficulties in trusting one's own emotional responses as valid, that is, engaging in self-invalidation; and (4) learning to form unrealistic goals and expectations resulting from oversimplification of problem-solving and goal-setting by the invalidating environment. Self-invalidation may make individuals particularly vulnerable to turning to body image focused environments as sources of information about what the self "should" look like. This may increase the likelihood of establishing unrealistic expectations among overweight or normal-weight clients regarding weight loss.

Efficacy of DBT with BPD

Standard DBT is currently the most empirically validated of treatments for BPD and is generally considered the treatment-of-choice for individuals with BPD (Lieb, Zanarini, Schmahl, Linehan, & Bohus, 2004). Seven randomized controlled trials provide evidence for its efficacy ([1] Linehan, Armstrong, Suarez, Allmon, & Heard, 1991, with follow-up reported in Linehan, Tutek, Heard, & Armstrong 1994; Linehan, Heard, & Armstrong, 1993; [2] Linehan et al., 1999; [3] Linehan et al., 2002; [4] Turner, 2000; [5] Koons et al., 2001; [6] Verheul et al., 2003, with the study description

reported in van den Bosch, Verheul, Schippers, & van de Brink, 2002; [7] Linehan et al., 2006). These data include three research teams independent from that of the original developer (Koons et al., 2001; Turner, 2000; van den Bosch et al., 2002) and is based on trials conducted not only in the United states but in the Netherlands as well (van den Bosch et al., 2002).

Standard DBT has been compared to Treatment-as-Usual (Koons et al, 2001; Linehan et al., 1991, 1999; Verheul et al., 2003), Treatment-by-Experts (Linehan et al., 2006), Comprehensive Validation (Linehan et al., 2002), and Client-Centered Therapy (Turner, 2000). Compared to its control condition, DBT showed significantly greater reductions in suicide attempts, intentional self-injury, and suicidal ideation (Koons et al., 2001; Linehan et al., 1991, 1999, 2002, 2006; Turner, 2000; Verheul et al., 2003). Even after controlling for number of hours of psychotherapy and telephone contact in control conditions where clients received stable psychotherapy, DBT maintained greater efficacy (Linehan et al., 1993, 1999). Standard DBT also resulted in significantly less treatment dropout than control treatments (Linehan et al., 1991, 1999, 2006; Verheul et al., 2003). Clients receiving DBT were less likely to utilize inpatient (Linehan et al., 1991, 2006; Turner, 2000) or emergency room services (Linehan et al., 2006). Treatment with DBT resulted in improvement of depressed mood (Linehan et al., 2006) general mood (Linehan et al., 2002) and psychosocial or global functioning (Linehan et al., 2002), with certain studies showing that DBT significantly improved these variables compared to control (Koons et al., 2001; Linehan et al., 1991, 1999; Turner, 2000).

The largest of these trials ($n = 101$) which included the longest follow-up (12 month) compared DBT with Treatment-by-Experts (TBE) among suicidal BPD participants (Linehan et al., 2006). By utilizing a TBE control, therapist availability, expertise, allegiance, gender, training and experience, consultation availability, and institutional prestige could be controlled. After treatment and 1 year of follow-up, DBT clients were half as likely to make a suicide attempt (23% vs. 46% of clients), less likely to be to be hospitalized for suicidal ideation, were less likely to drop out (25% vs. 59%), and had lower medical risk across all suicide attempts and self-injurious acts. DBT clients were also less likely to drop out of treatment, had utilized psychiatric crisis services less, and had fewer psychiatric hospitalizations.

DBT has also been adapted for variety of populations not specifically selected for BPD (Dimeff &

Koerner, 2007), including randomized controlled trials for depressed older adults (Lynch, Morse, Mendelson, & Robins, 2003; Lynch et al., 2007) and for treatment-resistant depressed individuals (Harley, Sprich, Safren, Jacobo, & Fava, 2008). Controlled trials utilizing DBT have also been conducted, such as with suicidal adolescents with BPD features (Rathus & Miller, 2002).

Research Evidence for DBT with EDs

There are currently two published small open trials for individuals with both BPD and ED, both utilizing minimal adaptations of standard DBT Chen (Matthews, Allen, Kuo, & Linehan, 2008; Palmer et al., 2003). The former, employing minimally adapted standard DBT for women with BED or BN and BPD (n = 8), found large reductions from pretreatment to the 6-month follow-up in suicidal behavior and non-suicidal self-injury, binge eating, secondary ED concerns, the number of comorbid Axis I disorders, and social functioning. The same large reductions were also found from pre- to post-treatment with smaller reductions in the number of comorbid Axis I disorders and suicidal behavior, and self-injury. The latter study (n = 7), which added five to six sessions of a psychoeducational skills module addressing ED behavior, showed a substantial reduction in hospital days and self-injury.

Currently, the only adaptation of DBT for EDs that has been supported through randomized controlled trials is the Stanford DBT Model for BED and BN. The Stanford DBT Model for BED and BN differs from the standard DBT program for BPD in key ways affecting treatment structure and content. For example, the adapted Stanford version employs a single modality of treatment delivery (weekly 2-hour group DBT for BED and or weekly 50- to 60-minute individual DBT for BN) versus standard DBT's weekly individual therapy (50–60 minutes) plus 2-hour group skills training.

The Stanford DBT Model for BED and BN was originally developed for adult women 18 to 65 years old. Exclusion criteria included: (1) current use of psychotropic medications, (2) psychotic or bipolar affective disorders diagnoses; (3) current involvement in psychotherapy or weight loss treatments; (4) current suicidality; (5) current substance abuse or dependence; or (6) pregnancy. Clients with BPD were not specifically excluded.

The Stanford DBT Model has been researched in three randomized-controlled trials, two for BED (Telch, Agras, & Linehan, 2001) and one for BN

(Safer, Telch, & Agras, 2001), as well as through an uncontrolled trial (Telch, Agras and Linehan, 2000) and two case reports (Safer et al., 2001; Telch, 1997a).

The preliminary results are promising. For example, in the first randomized controlled trial of DBT for BED, 16 of the 18 women (89%) who received DBT were abstinent from binge-eating at the end of the 20-week treatment compared to 2 of 16 (12.5%) wait-list controls (Telch et al., 2001). The drop-out rate was low, with only 9% (2 of 22) of the sample dropping out after initially beginning DBT. At post-treatment, clients in DBT reported significantly improved weight and shape concerns, eating concerns and, on the Emotional Eating Scale (Arnow, Kenardy, & Agras, 1995), demonstrated reduced urges to eat, especially when angry. At the 3-month follow-up, 67% of the 18 participants in DBT were abstinent from binge eating and 56% of the 18 at the six-month follow-up. DBT participants reported practicing on average 3.6 different skills per week an average of 4 days per week at the final assessment. The high abstinence rates were consistent with those of the smaller uncontrolled trial of DBT for BED where 82% of the participants were abstinent from binge eating after 20 group sessions, with none dropping out after commencing treatment (Telch, Agras, & Linehan, 2000). Similar findings were found as part of a replication/extension study of the Stanford DBT Model for BED in which the client population was expanded to include both men and women and individuals on stable psychotropic medication (Safer, Robinson & Jo, 2010). Using a conservative statistical analysis that involved all participants, even those who dropped from treatment (i.e., the intent-to-treat sample) versus analyzing only those who completed treatment (i.e., completer sample), the binge abstinence results for those receiving DBT for BED were 64% after 20 sessions which was maintained at the 12-month follow-up (Safer, Robinson & Jo, 2010). These rates are similar to abstinence rates found in CBT and IPT for BED (Wilfley et al., 1993, 2002). Although these require further replication, these initial findings for DBT for BED show potential.

In the randomized controlled trial of group DBT for BN, 20 weeks of individually delivered DBT for bulimic symptoms was compared to a wait-list control. Abstinence from binge eating/purging behaviors at the end of 20 weeks of treatment was 28.6% (4 of 14) for DBT and 0% (0 of 15) for the wait-list control (Safer et al., 2001). These findings were similar to post-treatment abstinence rates from the largest multisite CBT for BN trial (Agras, Walsh, Fairburn, Wilson, & Kraemer, 2000). DBT resulted in moderate to large effect size changes on the Emotional Eating Scale (Arnow et al., 1995), in terms of reducing urges to eat when angry or frustrated, anxious, or depressed. In addition, the Positive and Negative Affect Scale (Watson, Clark, & Tellegen, 1988) showed significant decreases in participant's experience of negative affect. At post-treatment the dropout rate in DBT was 0% (0 of 14).

Stanford DBT Model for BED or BN

The Stanford Model of DBT was developed to target clients whose primary focus of treatment is BED or BN symptoms that interfere with their quality of life. It was not intended for individuals with active suicidal or self-injurious behaviors, who should be offered the full program of standard DBT. In this section, the Stanford Model of DBT as adapted for BED (in a group format) and for BN (in an individual format) is described. As briefly noted above, the Stanford adaptation of DBT for BED or BN differs in three important ways from standard DBT for BPD. First, it differs in its structure. The Stanford DBT model combines two modalities in standard DBT (individual treatment and group skills treatment) into one modality, either a 2-hour group treatment for BED or a 50- to 60-minute individual session for BN. As opposed to what is typically a year-long treatment in standard DBT, the Stanford DBT model utilizes 20 sessions of treatment and covers three (e.g., Core Mindfulness, Emotion Regulation, and Distress Tolerance) as opposed to the four skills training modules. Second, the Stanford DBT model differs from standard DBT in the use of specific eating disordered behavior targets, resulting in adaptations to the treatment hierarchy, diary card, and behavioral chain analysis. Third, the Stanford model involves the addition of particular concepts and skills specific to eating disordered clients (e.g., the concept of dialectical abstinence, use of skills such as mindful eating, urge surfing, alternate rebellion, etc.).

These adaptations were made primarily for research purposes. For instance, other efficacious treatments for BED and BN, such as CBT and IPT, have been researched using 20 sessions and so as to compare DBT to these in the future, a similar number of sessions are required. The Interpersonal Effectiveness module was removed due to time constraints and because of a potential theoretical overlap with IPT. For clinicians and programs that are not limited by the constraints of time, resources, or research, there is no research-based reason not to include the Interpersonal Effectiveness module—particularly given the data on IPT's efficacy with BED.

Structure of Treatment (Session Structure, Number of Sessions, Modules Covered)

DBT for BED/BN combines elements of individual psychotherapy and group skills training from standard DBT. DBT for BED/BN incorporates chain analysis strategies, typically conducted in individual psychotherapy in standard DBT, with skills training, typically offered in a group format in standard DBT.

The format of each session is divided evenly. The first half, consisting of 50 to 60 minutes if treatment is carried out in a 2-hour group format or 25 to 30 minutes if treatment is carried out in a 50- to 60-minute individual format, is devoted to homework review and includes discussion of client diary cards and chain analyses (motivation and skills strengthening). During this review, each group member has between 5 and 10 minutes to report on his or her use of new skills in the past week and to describe specific successes or difficulties in applying the skills to replace the targeted problem eating behaviors. The length of time each member has for homework review varies given the total duration of the session (which may be 2 hours or 2 ½ hours) and the number in attendance so that sufficient time is available for everyone to share. Group members are encouraged to help one another identify solutions to problems encountered in using the skills and to "cheerlead" efforts made. Separated by a 5- to 10-minute break when using a group format, the second half of each session is devoted to teaching new content and practice of new skills (e.g., skills acquisition).

Like skills training groups in standard DBT, groups in the Stanford DBT Model for eating disorders are composed of eight to ten members and are taught by two skills trainers—a leader and a co-leader. As described, the Stanford DBT Model for BED utilized a group format and the Stanford DBT Model for BN/partial BN was carried out in an individual format. In the Stanford model, DBT for BN was administered individually because of difficulties in recruiting sufficient numbers to start a group in a timely fashion (as needed in a research study) and because most treatments for BN are individually delivered.

Sequence of Treatment

The Stanford Model begins with a pretreatment interview. During this session, each participant meets individually with one of the co-therapists (or, for BN, the individual therapist) for 30 to 45 minutes before beginning therapy. The major goals of this pre-treatment visit involves orienting the participant to the DBT program (e.g., dates of treatment), assessing prior group experience, introducing the emotion regulation model of binge eating and the targets of treatment, describing the expectations for participants (e.g., regular timely attendance, listening to tapes of any missed sessions, completing homework assignments) and therapists, and orienting individuals to the goals of treatment.

The pretreatment interview, as well as sessions 1 and 2, comprise of the pretreatment stage of treatment. In session 1, a major goal is to obtain each group member's commitment to stop binge eating (or for BN, the individual client's commitment to stop binge eating and purging). Standard DBT commitment strategies are used, such as having therapists play devil's advocate in order to have clients to consider and argue why they cannot have the quality of life they seek and continue binge eating. Other tasks of this session are to explain the biosocial theory, review and sign formal therapist and client agreements, and introduce the diary card and chain analysis.

In session 2, after conducting homework review for the first half of the session, therapists introduce clients to the concept of dialectical abstinence, a concept originally developed in DBT for substance use disorders (Linehan & Dimeff, 1997). This concept is described in greater detail below.

After the introductory sessions, the modules covered, in sequence, are: the Core Mindfulness module (sessions 3–5), the Emotion Regulation module (sessions 6–12), and the Distress Tolerance module (sessions 14–18).

Sessions 19 and 20 are devoted to a review of the different skills modules and relapse prevention. Clients are asked to detail their plans for continuing to practice the skills taught, to outline their specific plans for skillfully managing emotions that triggered binge eating in the future and to consider what they need to do next to continue to build a satisfying and rewarding quality of life. Clients say their final goodbyes and perhaps conduct a goodbye ritual (e.g., writing cards) to mark the ending of treatment.

Adaptations to Treatment Hierarchy, Diary Card, and Behavioral Chain Analysis

Adaptations from standard DBT were made to the treatment hierarchy and related tools to reflect the needs of the population for whom the Stanford

DBT model was developed—clients whose ED symptoms (e.g., binge eating and/or purging) are the primary treatment focus. For most clients with primary BN or BED, the highest treatment target is to prevent any behavior(s) that interfere with the successful delivery of treatment, followed by the Path to Mindful Eating—an additional target hierarchy adapted specifically for individuals with BED or BN (see Table 23.1). However, as per the standard DBT hierarchy, if suicidal or nonsuicidal self-injurious behaviors emerge during treatment, the focus of therapy is first and foremost on stopping Life-Threatening Behaviors before either treatment interfering behaviors or those outlined in the Path to Mindful Eating.

Mindless eating refers to not attending to eating e.g., watching TV with popcorn but finding it is gone without being aware of how this happened. Mindless eating is defined as occurring without experiencing a loss of control (as opposed to binge eating). Food preoccupation is when one's thoughts or attention are absorbed or focused on food to the point of interference with functioning (e.g., work). Capitulating involves giving one's goals to stop binge eating and to use skilful attempts to cope with emotions. When capitulating, one acts as if there is no other option or way to cope than with food. Finally, Apparently Irrelevant behaviors are those that do not seem relevant to binge eating and purging or that a client convinces themselves do not matter but that, actually, are important in the chain analysis, e.g., purchasing extra dessert "for company" may not seem to matter but may actually be linked to a client's binge eating.

The Stanford model of DBT for BED/BN also involves adaptations to the standard DBT diary card to allow clients to track any dysfunctional eating behaviors as outlined on the Path to Mindful Eating (Table 23.1). A sample diary card can be found in Table 23.2. Finally, the chain analysis used in DBT for BED or BN is the same as that of standard DBT. Clients are directed to fill them out each week on the highest disordered eating behavior since the previous session as listed in the Path to Mindful Eating.

Table 23.1 Path to Mindful Eating

1. Stop binge eating (and purging—for BN clients).
2. Eliminate mindless eating.
3. Decrease cravings, urges, preoccupation with food.
4. Decrease capitulating.
5. Decrease apparently irrelevant behaviors.

Table 23.2 Stanford DBT Model Diary Card: Explanations Only for the Nonexplanatory

Instructions for Completing Your Diary Card

Urge to Binge: Refer to the legend and choose the number from the scale (0–6) that best represents your highest rating for the day. The key characteristics of the urge to consider when making your rating are intensity (how strongly you felt the urge) and duration (how long the urge lasted).

Binge Episodes: Write the number of binge episodes you had each day. A binge refers to an eating episode in which you felt a loss of control during the eating.

Mindless eating: Write in the number of "mindless" eating episodes that you had each day. Mindless eating refers to not paying attention to what you are eating, although you do not feel the sense of loss of control that you do during binge episodes. A typical example of mindless eating would be sitting in front of the TV and eating a bag of microwave popcorn without any awareness of the eating (i.e., somehow, the popcorn was gone and you were only vaguely aware of having eaten it). Again, however, you didn't feel a sense of being out of control during the eating.

Apparently Irrelevant Behaviors (AIB): Circle either "yes" or "no" depending on whether you did or did not have any AIBs that day. If you did, briefly describe the AIB in the place provided or on another sheet of paper. An AIB refers to behaviors that, upon first glance, do not seem relevant to binge eating and purging but which actually are important in the behavior chain leading to these behaviors. You may convince yourself that the behavior doesn't matter or really won't affect your goal to stop bingeing and purging when, in fact, the behavior matters a great deal. A typical AIB might be buying several boxes of your favorite Girl Scout cookies because you wanted to help out a neighbor's daughter (of course, you could buy the cookies and donate them to the neighbor).

Capitulating: Refer to the legend and choose the number from the scale (0–6) that best represents your highest rating for the day. The key characteristics to consider when making your rating are intensity (strength of the capitulating) and duration (how long it lasted). Capitulating refers to giving up on your goals to stop binge eating and to skillfully cope with emotions. Instead, you capitulate or surrender to bingeing, acting as if there is no other option or way to cope than with food.

Food Preoccupation: Refer to the legend and choose the number from the scale (0–6) that best represents your highest rating for the day. Food preoccupation refers to your thoughts or attention being absorbed or focused on food. For example, your thoughts of a dinner party and the presence of your favorite foods may absorb your attention so much that you have trouble concentrating at work.

Emotion Columns: Refer to the legend and choose the number from the scale (0–6) that best represents your highest rating for the day. The key characteristics to consider when making your rating are intensity (strength of the emotion) and duration (how long it lasted).

Used Skills: Refer to the legend and choose the number from the scale (0–6) that best represents your attempts to use the skills each day. When making your rating, consider whether or not you thought about using any of the skills that day, whether or not you actually used any of the skills, and whether or not the skills helped.

Weight: Weigh yourself once each week and record your weight in pounds in the space provided. Please write in the date you weighed. It is best if you choose the same day each week to weigh. Many women find that arriving a few minutes early to the session and weighing at the clinic is a good way to remember to weigh.

Urge to Quit Therapy: Indicate your urge to quit therapy before the session and after the session each week. Both of these ratings should be made for the same session as the one in which you received the diary card. It is best to make both of these ratings as soon as possible following that day's session. Use a 0 to 6 scale of intensity of the urge, with 0 indicating no urge to quit and a 6 indicating the strongest urge to quit.

Completing the Skills Side of the Diary Card:

How Often Did You Fill Out This Side? Place a check mark to indicate how frequently you filled out the skills side of the diary card during the week.

Skills Practice: Go down the column for each day of the week and circle each skill that you practiced/used that day. If you did not practice or use any of the skills that particular day, then circle that day on the last line, which states, "Did not practice/use any skills."

Diary Card

Initials _____ ID _____

How often did you fill out this side? Daily _____ 4–6× _____ 2–3× _____ Once _____

Day And Date	Urge to Binge[a] (0–6)	Binge Episodes # OBE lg	# SBE sm	Mindless Eating # episodes	AIB[b] Circle one	Capitulating[a] (0–6)	Food[a] Craving (0–6)	Food[a] Preoccupation (0–6)	Anger[a] (0–6)	Sadness[a] (0–6)	Fear[a] (0–6)	Shame[a] (0–6)	Pride[a] (0–6)	Happiness[a] (0–6)	Used[c] Skills (0–7)
Mon					yes/no										
Tues					yes/no										
Wed					yes/no										
Thurs					yes/no										
Fri					yes/no										
Sat					yes/no										
Sun					yes/no										

[a]Use the following scale to indicate the highest rating for the day:
0 = urge/thought/feeling not experienced
1 = urge/thought/feeling experienced slightly and briefly
2 = urge/thought/feeling experienced moderately and briefly
3 = urge/thought/feeling experienced intensely and briefly
4 = urge/thought/feeling experienced slightly and endured
5 = urge/thought/feeling experienced moderately and endured
6 = urge/thought/feeling experienced intensely and endured

[b]Describe Apparently Irrelevant Behaviors (AIB): _____

[c]Used Skills:
0 = Not thought about or used
1 = Thought about, not used, didn't want to
2 = Thought about, not used, wanted to
3 = Tried but couldn't use them
4 = Tried, could do them but they didn't help
5 = Tried, could use them, helped
6 = Didn't try, used them, didn't help
7 = Didn't try, used them, helped

Weight _____ Date Weighed _____
Urge to quit therapy (0–5): Before therapy session: _____ After therapy session: _____

NIMH 1997–2000
ER BED TELCH

SKILLS DIARY CARD

Instructions: Circle the days you worked on each skill.

How often did you fill out this side?
___ Daily ___ 4–6× ___ 2–3× ____ Once

1. Diaphragmatic Breathing	Mon	Tues	Wed	Thurs	Fri	Sat	Sun
2. Wise mind	Mon	Tues	Wed	Thurs	Fri	Sat	Sun
3. Observe: just notice	Mon	Tues	Wed	Thurs	Fri	Sat	Sun
4. Describe: put words on	Mon	Tues	Wed	Thurs	Fri	Sat	Sun
5. Participate: enter into the experience	Mon	Tues	Wed	Thurs	Fri	Sat	Sun
6. Mindful eating	Mon	Tues	Wed	Thurs	Fri	Sat	Sun
7. Nonjudgmental stance	Mon	Tues	Wed	Thurs	Fri	Sat	Sun
8. One-mindfully: in-the-moment	Mon	Tues	Wed	Thurs	Fri	Sat	Sun
9. Effectiveness: focus on what works	Mon	Tues	Wed	Thurs	Fri	Sat	Sun
10. Urge surfing	Mon	Tues	Wed	Thurs	Fri	Sat	Sun
11. Alternate rebellion	Mon	Tues	Wed	Thurs	Fri	Sat	Sun
12. Mindful of current emotion	Mon	Tues	Wed	Thurs	Fri	Sat	Sun
13. Loving your emotions	Mon	Tues	Wed	Thurs	Fri	Sat	Sun
14. Reduce vulnerability: PLEASE	Mon	Tues	Wed	Thurs	Fri	Sat	Sun
15. Build MASTERy	Mon	Tues	Wed	Thurs	Fri	Sat	Sun
16. Build positive experiences	Mon	Tues	Wed	Thurs	Fri	Sat	Sun
17. Mindful of positive experiences	Mon	Tues	Wed	Thurs	Fri	Sat	Sun
18. Opposite-to-emotion action	Mon	Tues	Wed	Thurs	Fri	Sat	Sun
19. Observing-your-breath	Mon	Tues	Wed	Thurs	Fri	Sat	Sun
20. Half-smiling	Mon	Tues	Wed	Thurs	Fri	Sat	Sun
21. Awareness exercises	Mon	Tues	Wed	Thurs	Fri	Sat	Sun
22. Radical acceptance	Mon	Tues	Wed	Thurs	Fri	Sat	Sun
23. Turning the mind	Mon	Tues	Wed	Thurs	Fri	Sat	Sun
24. Willingness	Mon	Tues	Wed	Thurs	Fri	Sat	Sun
25. Burning your bridges	Mon	Tues	Wed	Thurs	Fri	Sat	Sun
26. Distract	Mon	Tues	Wed	Thurs	Fri	Sat	Sun
27. Self-soothe	Mon	Tues	Wed	Thurs	Fri	Sat	Sun
28. Improve the moment	Mon	Tues	Wed	Thurs	Fri	Sat	Sun
29. Pros and cons	Mon	Tues	Wed	Thurs	Fri	Sat	Sun
30. Commitment	Mon	Tues	Wed	Thurs	Fri	Sat	Sun
30. Did not practice any skills	Mon	Tues	Wed	Thurs	Fri	Sat	Sun

NIMH 1997–2000 ER BED TELCH

Use of DBT Concepts and Skills Specifically Adapted for Binge Eating and/or Purging

A number of DBT concepts and skills were added in DBT for BED/BN to specifically address the needs of clients who binge eat and/or purge. As noted, many of these were originally developed for DBT for substance abuse (see Linehan & Dimeff, 1997; Marlatt & Gordon, 1985). Included are the concept of Dialectical Abstinence as well as ED specific skills such as Mindful Eating, Urge Surfing, Alternate Rebellion, and Burning Bridges. Each is reviewed in turn.

Dialectical abstinence, introduced in session 2, is a synthesis of a 100% commitment to abstinence and a 100% commitment to relapse prevention strategies. Before a client engages in binge eating, there is an unrelenting insistence on total abstinence. After a client has binged, however, the emphasis is on radical acceptance, nonjudgmental problem solving and effective relapse prevention, followed by a speedy return to an unrelenting insistence on abstinence. Therapists liken clients to Olympic athletes (Telch, 1997b; Safer, Telch, & Chen, 2009) with therapists as their coaches. As an Olympian, one only focuses on "going for the gold" as opposed to focusing on what might happen if one were to fall or telling oneself before the race that "Maybe a bronze would be okay." Similarly, clients must focus only on binge abstinence. Yet athletes and clients must be prepared for the possibility of failure, of course. The key is to be prepared to fail well. The dialectical dilemma is that both success and failure exist. The dialectical abstinence solution involves 100% certainty that binge eating is out of the question and 100% confidence that one will never binge again. However simultaneously, one keeps in mind ("Way, way back in the very farthest part so that it never interferes with your resolve") that if one slips, one will deal with it effectively by accepting the behavior nonjudgmentally and picking oneself back up, knowing one will never slip again.

ED specific Mindfulness skills include Mindful Eating, Urge Surfing, and Alternate Rebellion, and are taught over sessions 3 to 5.

Mindful eating, as opposed to mindless eating, is the experience of full participation in eating, that is, observing and describing in one's mind the experience. It is eating with full awareness and attention (one-mindfully) but without self-consciousness or judgment.

Urge surfing involves mindful, nonattached observation of urges to binge or eat mindlessly. Clients are educated about how urges and cravings are classically conditioned responses that have been associated with a particular cue. Mindful urge surfing involves awareness without engaging in impulsive mood-dependent behavior. One learns to "let go" or "detach" from the object of the urge, being fully in the moment, "riding the wave" of the urge and noticing its ebb and flow. Although similar to mindfulness of the current emotion, urge surfing is a mindfulness skill that involves nonjudgmental observing and describing of urges, cravings, and food preoccupation.

Alternate Rebellion involves using the mindfulness skill of being effective to satisfy a wish to rebel without destroying one's overriding objective of stopping binge eating. The purpose is not to suppress or judge the rebellion but to find creative ways to rebel that do not involve "cutting off your nose to spite your face." Many clients with BED have described the desire to "get back" at society, friends, and/or family perceived to be judgmental about their weight. For these clients, "getting back" often involves rebelling by consuming even more food. However, this is not effective as it runs contrary to achieving the goal of binge abstinence and an improved quality of life. Therapists can encourage clients to observe the need to rebel, label it as such, and then, if the decision is to act upon the wish, to do so effectively. Clients can be creative in thinking up alternate rebellion strategies. For example, a client who feels judged by society for being obese might "rebel" by buying attractive lingerie that makes her feel beautiful or mindfully sitting in a well-regarded restaurant and openly, unselfconsciously treating herself to a healthy and delicious bowl of soup.

Burning Bridges is a radical acceptance skill that involves accepting at the deepest and most radical level the idea that one is really not going to binge eat, mindlessly eat, or abuse oneself with food ever again, thus burning the bridge to those behaviors. One accepts that one will no longer block, deny, or avoid reality with binge eating. Instead, one makes a covenant from deep within to accept reality and one's experiences.

Conclusion

In summary, this chapter briefly describes the Dialectical Behavior Therapy program originally developed for individuals with borderline personality disorder. DBT is uniquely based on an affect regulation model, and offers an alternative approach for EDs that have failed to respond to existing therapies. In addition, DBT fuses behavior change strategies with novel acceptance-based strategies such as mindfulness. DBT also includes distinctive protocols for addressing life-threatening and therapy-interfering behavior.

Standard DBT is an efficacious evidence-based treatment for BPD, with promising treatment development data for use with individuals with BPD and EDs. For individuals with binge eating disorder or bulimia that primarily affects quality-of-life, an adaptation of standard DBT for individuals with BED and bulimia by researchers at Stanford University has been found to be efficacious in randomized controlled trials. The Stanford University DBT model involves 20 group (for BED) or individual (for BN) sessions. These sessions teach Mindfulness, Emotion Regulation and Distress Tolerance skills, integrating these with the use of chain analyses (careful step-by-step behavioral analyses) for problem behaviors. This model utilizes a unique target hierarchy of ED behaviors (the "path to mindful eating") to target (1) stopping binge eating (and purging, for clients with bulimia); (2) eliminating mindless eating (eating without awareness); (3) decreasing cravings, urges, preoccupation with food; (4) decreasing capitulating (i.e., giving into binge eating); and (5) decreasing apparently irrelevant behaviors (i.e., behaviors that appear not to matter but really do in leading to a binge). Finally, the Stanford DBT model for BED and bulimia adds eating disorder specific concepts and skills to the standard treatment. Eating disorder specific DBT concepts include Dialectical Abstinence, which teaches clients to focus on attaining binge abstinence while simultaneously being aware that if one slips, this can be addressed effectively. Additional ED-specific DBT skills include Mindful Eating, Urge Surfing (i.e., surfing urges to binge eat), Alternative Rebellion (effectively managing urges to rebel without binge eating), and Burning Bridges (radical acceptance of a commitment to cease ED behavior).

Future Directions

• For individuals with BED or BN, how does DBT fare compared to other active psychotherapies for these disorders?
• Are there ways to combine elements of DBT with CBT and/or IPT?
• How can maintenance of treatment gains in DBT be improved for individuals with BN or BED?
• What client or therapist or combinations of these features are associated with better or worse outcome in DBT for BED or BN?

• Given the original use of DBT for individuals with difficult-to-treat disorders, can DBT be adapted for adults with chronic anorexia nervosa?
• What components of the Stanford DBT model are particularly helpful for individuals with BED or BN?
• Can the Stanford DBT model be efficacious for adolescents with BED/BN?
• Does DBT specifically change vulnerability to emotions in individuals with BED or BN?

References

Agras, W. S., & Telch, C. F. (1998). The effects of caloric deprivation and negative affect on binge eating in obese binge-eating disordered women. *Behavior Therapy, 29*(3), 491–503.

Agras, W. S., Walsh, T., Fairburn, C. G., Wilson, G. T., & Kraemer, H. C. (2000). A multicenter comparison of cognitive-behavioral therapy and interpersonal psychotherapy for bulimia nervosa. *Archives of General Psychiatry, 57,* 459–466.

Arnow, B., Kenardy, J., & Agras, W. S. (1995). The Emotional Eating Scale: the development of a measure to assess coping with negative affect by eating. *International Journal of Eating Disorders, 18,* 79–90.

Berkman, N. D., Lohr, K. N., & Bulik, C. M. (2007). Outcomes of eating disorders: A systematic review of the literature. *International Journal of Eating Disorders, 40*(4), 293–309.

Chen, E. Y., Matthews L., Allen C., Kuo J., & Linehan, M. M. (2008). Dialectical Behavior Therapy for clients with binge-eating disorder or bulimia nervosa and borderline personality disorder. *International Journal of Eating Disorders, 41*(6), 505–512.

Dimeff, L. A., & Koerner, K. (2007). *Dialectical behavior therapy in clinical practice: Applications across disorders and settings*: New York: Guilford Press.

Eldredge, K. L., & Agras, W. S. (1996). Weight and shape overconcern and emotional eating in binge eating disorder. *International Journal of Eating Disorders, 19*(1), 73–82.

Fairburn, G., & Brownell, K. (2001). *Eating disorders and obesity*. New York: Guilford Press.

Franko, D. L., & Keel, P. K. (2006). Suicidality in eating disorders: Occurrence, correlates, and clinical implications. *Clinical Psychology Review, 26*(6), 769–782.

Greeno, C. G., Wing, R. R., & Shiffman, S. (2000). Binge antecedents in obese women with and without binge eating disorder. *Journal of Consulting and Clinical Psychology, 68,* 95–102.

Grilo, C. M., Masheb, R. M., & Wilson, G. (2001). Subtyping binge eating disorder. *Journal of Consulting and Clinical Psychology, 69*(6), 1066–1072.

Hansel, S. L., & Wittrock, D. A. (1997). Appraisal and coping strategies in stressful situations: A comparison of individuals who binge eat and controls. *International Journal of Eating Disorders, 21*(1), 89–93.

Harley, R., Sprich, S., Safren, S., Jacobo, M., & Fava, M. (2008). Adaptation of dialectical behavior therapy skills training group for treatment-resistant depression. *Journal of Nervous and Mental Disorders, 196*(2), 136–143.

Heatherton, T. F., & Baumeister, R. F. (1991). Binge eating as escape from self-awareness. *Psychological Bulletin, 110,* 86–108.

Koons, C. R., Robins, C. J., Tweed, J. L., Lynch, T. R., Gonzalez, A. M., Morse, J. Q., et al. (2001). Efficacy of Dialectical Behavior Therapy in women veterans with borderline personality disorder. *Behavior Therapy*, *32*, 371–390.

Lieb, K., Zanarini, M. C., Schmahl, C., Linehan, M. M., & Bohus, M. (2004). Borderline personality disorder. *Lancet*, *364*(9432) 453–461.

Linehan, M. M. (1993a). *Cognitive-behavioral treatment of borderline personality disorder*. New York: Guilford Press.

Linehan, M. M. (1993b). *Skills training manual for treating borderline personality disorder*. New York: Guilford Press.

Linehan, M. M., Armstrong, H. E., Suarez, A., Allmon, D., & Heard, H. L. (1991). Cognitive-behavioral treatment of chronically parasuicidal borderline patients. *Archives of General Psychiatry*, *48*, 1060–1064.

Linehan, M. M., & Chen, E. Y. (2005). Dialectical Behavior Therapy for eating disorders. In: S. Felgoise, A.M. Nezu, C. M. Nezu, M. A. Reinecke, & A. Freeman (Eds.), *The encyclopedia for cognitive-behavioral therapy*. Mew York: Springer.

Linehan, M. M., Comtois, K. A., Murray, A. M., Brown, M. Z., Gallop, R. J., Heard, H. L., et al. (2006). Two-year randomized controlled trial and follow-up of dialectical behavior therapy vs. therapy by experts for suicidal behaviors and borderline personality disorder. *Archives of General Psychiatry*, *63*(7), 757–766.

Linehan, M. M., & Dimeff, L. A. (1997). *Dialectical Behavior Therapy manual of treatment interventions for drug abusers with borderline personality disorder*. Unpublished Manuscript, University of Washington Seattle, WA.

Linehan, M. M., Dimeff, L. A., Reynolds, S. K., Comtois, K. A., Welch, S. S., Heagerty, P., & Kivlahan, D. R. (2002). Dialectical behavior therapy versus comprehensive validation therapy plus 12-step for the treatment of opioid dependent women meeting criteria for borderline personality disorder. *Drug and Alcohol Dependence*, *67*(1), 13–26.

Linehan, M. M., Heard, H. L., & Armstrong, H. E. (1993). Naturalistic follow-up of a behavioral treatment for chronically parasuicidal borderline patients. *Archives of General Psychiatry*, *50*, 971–974.

Linehan, M. M., Schmidt, H., III, Dimeff, L. A., Craft, J. C., Kanter, J., & Comtois, K. A. (1999). Dialectical behavior therapy for patients with borderline personality disorder and drug-dependence. *American Journal of Addiction*, *8*, 279–292.

Linehan, M. M., Tutek, D.A., Heard, H. L., & Armstrong, H. E. (1994). Interpersonal outcome of cognitive behavioral treatment for chronically suicidal borderline patients. *American Journal of Psychiatry*, *151*, 1771–1776.

Lingswiler, V. M., Crowther, J. H., & Stephens, M. A. (1987). Emotional reactivity and eating in binge eating and obesity. *Journal of Behavioral Medicine*, *10*(3), 287–299.

Lynch, T. R., Cheavens, J. S., Cukrowicz, K. C., Thorp, S. R., Bronner, L., & Beyer, J. (2007). Treatment of older adults with co-morbid personality disorder and depression: A dialectical behavior therapy approach. *International Journal of Geriatric Psychiatry*, *22*(2), 131–143.

Lynch, T. R., Morse, J. Q., Mendelson, T., & Robins, C. J. (2003). Dialectical behavior therapy for depressed older adults: A randomized pilot study. *American Journal of Geriatric Psychiatry*, *11*, 33–45.

Marlatt, G., & Gordon, J. R. (1985). *Relapse prevention and maintenance strategies in the treatment of addictive behaviours*. New York: Guilford Press.

Masheb, R. M., & Grilo, C. M. (2006). Emotional overeating and its associations with eating disorder psychopathology among overweight patients with binge eating disorder. *International Journal of Eating Disorders*, *39*(2), 141–146.

Palmer, R. L., Birchall, H., Damani, S., Gatward, N., McGrain, L., & Parker, L. (2003). A dialectical behavior therapy program for people with an eating disorder and borderline personality disorder—description and outcome. *International Journal of Eating Disorders*, *33*(3), 281–286.

Polivy, J., & Herman, C. P. (1993). Etiology of binge eating: Psychological mechanisms. In: C. G. Fairburn & G. T. Wilson (Eds.), *Binge eating: Nature, assessment, and treatment* (pp. 173–205). New York: Guilford Press.

Rathus, J. H., & Miller, A. L. (2002). Dialectical behavior therapy adapted for suicidal adolescents. *Suicide and Life Threatening Behaviors*, *32*, 146–157.

Safer, D. L., Robinson, A. H., Jo, B., (2010). Dialectical behavior therapy versus supportive group therapy for binge eating disorder: Results of a randomized controlled trial. *Behavior Therapy*, *41*, 106–120.

Safer, D. L., Telch, C. F., & Agras, W. (2001). Dialectical behavior therapy adapted for bulimia: A case report. *International Journal of Eating Disorders*, *30*(1), 101–106.

Safer, D. L., Telch, C. F., & Chen, E. Y. (2009). *Dialectical Behavior Therapy as adapted for binge eating disorder and bulimia*. New York: Guilford Press.

Safer, D. L., Telch, C. F., & Agras, W. S. (2001). Dialectical behavior therapy for bulimia nervosa. *American Journal of Psychiatry*, *158*, 632–634.

Sanftner, J. L., & Crowther, J. H. (1998). Variability in self-esteem, moods, shame, and guilt in women who binge. *International Journal of Eating Disorders*, *23*(4), 391–397.

Stice, E., & Agras, W. S. (1999). Subtyping bulimic women along dietary restraint and negative affect dimensions. *Journal of Consulting and Clinical Psychology*, *67*, 460–469.

Svirko, E., & Hawton, K. (2007). Self-injurious behavior and eating disorders: The extent and nature of the association. *Suicide and Life-Threatening Behavior*, *37*(4), 409–421.

Telch, C. F. (1997a). *Emotion regulation skills training treatment for binge eating disorder: Therapist manual*. Unpublished Manuscript, Stanford University.

Telch, C. F. (1997b). Skills training treatment for adaptive affect regulation in a woman with binge-eating disorder. *International Journal of Eating Disorders*, *22*(1), 77–81.

Telch, C. F., Agras, W. S., & Linehan, M. M. (2000). Group dialectical behavior therapy for binge-eating disorder: A preliminary, uncontrolled trial. *Behavior Therapy*, *31*, 569–582.

Telch, C. F., Agras, W. S., & Linehan, M. M. (2001). Dialectical behavior therapy for binge eating disorder. *Journal of Consulting and Clinical Psychology*, *69*(6), 1061–1065.

Turner, R. M. (2000). Naturalistic evaluation of dialectical behavior therapy-oriented treatment for borderline-personality disorder. *Cognitive Behavioral Practice*, *7*, 413–419.

van den Bosch, L. M., Verheul, R., Schippers, G. M., & van den Brink, W. (2002). Dialectical Behavior Therapy of borderline patients with and without substance use problems. Implementation and long-term effects. *Addictive Behaviors*, *27*(6), 911–923.

Verheul, R., Van Den Bosch, L.M., Koeter, M. W., De Ridder, M. A., Stijnen, T., & Van Den Brink, W. (2003). Dialectical behavior therapy for women with borderline personality disorder: 12-month, randomised clinical trial in The Netherlands. *British Journal of Psychiatry*, *182*, 135–140.

Watson, D., Clark, L. A., & Tellegen, A. (1988). Development and validation of brief measures of positive and negative affect: The PANAS scales. *Journal of Personality and Social Psychology*, *54*, 1063–1070.

Whiteside, U., Chen, E. Y., Neighbors, C., Hunter, D., Lo, T., & Larimer, M. E. (2007). Binge eating and emotion regulation: Do binge eaters have fewer skills to modulate and tolerate negative affect? *Eating Behaviors*, *8*, 162–169.

Wilfley, D. E., Agras, W., Telch, C. F., Rossiter, E. M., Schneider, J. A., Cole, A. G., et al. (1993). Group cognitive-behavioral therapy and group interpersonal psychotherapy for the nonpurging bulimic individual: A controlled comparison. *Journal of Consulting and Clinical Psychology*, *61*(2), 296–305.

Wilfley, D. E., Friedman, M. A., Dounchis, J. Z., Stein, R. I., Welch, R. R., & Ball, S. A. (2000). Comorbid psychopathology in binge eating disorder: Relation to eating disorder severity at baseline and following treatment. *Journal of Consulting and Clinical Psychology*, *68*, 641–649.

Wilfley, D. E., Welch, R., Stein, R. I., Spurrell, E. B., Cohen, L. R., Saelens, B. E., et al. (2002). A randomized comparison of group cognitive-behavioral therapy and group interpersonal psychotherapy for the treatment of overweight individuals with binge-eating disorder. *Archives of General Psychiatry*, *59*(8), 713–721.

Pharmacotherapy of the Eating Disorders

Susan L. McElroy, Anna I. Guerdjikova, Anne M. O'Melia, Nicole Mori, *and* Paul E. Keck, Jr.

Abstract

Many persons with eating disorders (EDs) receive pharmacotherapy, but pharmacotherapy research for EDs has lagged behind that for other major mental disorders. In this chapter, we first provide a brief rationale for using medications in the treatment of EDs. We then review the data supporting the effectiveness of specific medications or medication classes in treating patients with anorexia nervosa (AN), bulimia nervosa, binge eating disorder (BED), and other potentially important EDs, such as night eating syndrome (NES) and sleep-related eating disorder (SRED). We conclude by summarizing these data and suggesting future areas for research in the pharmacotherapy of EDs.

Keywords: antidepressants, antiepileptic drugs, antipsychotics, eating disorders, mood stabilizers, pharmacotherapy

Introduction

Many persons with eating disorders (EDs) receive pharmacotherapy (Grigoriadis, Kaplan, Carter, & Woodside, 2001; Mond, Hay, Rodgers, & Owen, 2007; Walsh et al., 2006). A number of reviews (Berkman et al., 2006; Mauri et al., 1996; Ramoz, Versini, & Gorwood, 2007; Steffen, Roerig, Mitchell, & Uppala, 2006; Yager & Powers, 2007; Zhu & Walsh, 2002) and guidelines (American Psychiatric Association [APA], 2006; National Institute for Clinical Excellence, 2004) have recently emerged summarizing the role pharmacotherapy might play in treating patients with EDs. However, only one drug has been approved by the United States Food and Drug Administration (FDA) for the treatment of an ED (fluoxetine for bulimia nervosa [BN]), and pharmacotherapy research for EDs lags behind that for other major mental disorders. Indeed, no drug has been specifically developed to treat an ED.

In this chapter, we first provide a brief rationale for using medications in the treatment of EDs. We then review the data supporting the effectiveness of specific medications or medication classes in treating patients with anorexia nervosa (AN), BN, binge eating disorder (BED), and other potentially important EDs, such as night eating syndrome (NES) and sleep-related eating disorder (SRED). We conclude by summarizing these data and suggesting future areas for research in the pharmacotherapy of EDs.

Rationale for Using Pharmacotherapy in Treating EDs

There are several rationales for using pharmacotherapy to treat EDs. First is that EDs are major mental disorders with genetic contributions and neurobiological abnormalities that do not always respond adequately to available psychological interventions (Bulik et al., 2007b; Bulik, Slof-Op't Landt, van Furth, & Sullivan, 2007c; Kaye, 2008; Slof-Op't Landt et al., 2005). Some patients, including those with chronic or intractable illness, may need medication for optimal outcomes (Yager, 2007).

Second is that individual pharmacologic agents with diverse molecular targets and mechanisms of action have been found efficacious in a variety of neuropsychiatric and metabolic conditions that are likely related to EDs. Thus, the overlap of BN with depressive and anxiety disorders, all of which respond to antidepressants, is well established (Hudson et al., 2003). In addition, there are conditions for which medications have regulatory approval, but whose co-occurrence with EDs may be under-recognized, such as bipolar disorder, migraine, and delayed gastric emptying (Brewerton & George, 1993; McElroy, Kotwal, Keck, & Akiskal, 2005; Stacher et al, 1993a). Conversely, there are conditions whose co-occurrence with EDs is well established and for which emerging placebo-controlled data suggest medications have efficacy, such as antiepileptic drugs (AEDs) for substance use disorders, personality disorders, and obesity (Johnson et al., 2007; McElroy, Keck, & Post, 2008b). Medications that are effective in conditions related to EDs might be effective in EDs themselves, or be useful in managing co-occurring conditions in ED patients (Woodside & Staab, 2006).

A third reason for treating EDs with pharmacotherapy is that many medications have effects on appetite and weight as well as the central or peripheral systems important in regulating eating behavior and weight control. Thus, appetite stimulants (e.g., cyproheptadine), many antipsychotics (e.g., clozapine, olanzapine, and chlorpromazine), some antidepressants (e.g., tricyclics), and some AEDs (e.g., valproate and pregabalin) are associated with increased appetite and weight gain, whereas antiobesity agents (e.g., sibutramine and orlistat), some antidepressants, and some AEDs (e.g., topiramate, zonisamide, and felbamate) are associated with decreased appetite and/or weight loss (Biton, 2003; Powers & Cloak, 2007). Examples of neurotransmitter systems involved in the regulation of feeding behavior and weight control affected by these drugs include the biogenic amines serotonin (5-hydroxytryptamine, 5-HT), norepinephrine (NE), and dopamine (DA) (e.g., by antidepressants, antipsychotics, and some AEDs); the major inhibitory transmitter gamma-aminobutyric acid (GABA; e.g., by many AEDs); and the major excitatory transmitter glutamate (e.g., by topiramate; Biton, 2007; Clifton & Kennett, 2006). Affected neuropeptides involved in controlling feeding and body weight include neuropeptide Y (NPY; e.g., by valproate, topiramate, and zonisamide) and extracellular-signal regulated kinase (ERK; e.g., by valproate) (Brill, Lee, Zhao, Fernald, & Huguenard, 2006; Gao & Horvath, 2008; Husum, van Kammen, Termeer, Bolwig, &

Mathé, 2003; Kwak et al., 2005; Meister, 2007; Rosenberg, 2007). Although some of the effects of medication on appetite and weight are problematic in certain clinical situations (e.g., weight gain from antipsychotics or valproate in obese patients), they might be therapeutic in EDs. For example, the second-generation antipsychotic olanzapine may be helpful for weight restoration in AN (Bissada, Tasca, Barber, & Bradwejn, 2008), whereas medications with anorectic or weight loss effects may be helpful for ED patients with binge eating and overweight or obesity (McElroy et al., 2007b; Wilfley et al., 2008).

Yet another rationale for understanding the potential utility of currently available medications in EDs is that a number of novel pharmaceutical compounds in development will likely come to market. These include drugs being developed for mood, psychotic, and other mental disorders; cachexia and obesity; and epilepsy (Chen, Yang, & Tobak, 2008; Fong, 2008; Johannessen Landmark & Johannessen, 2008; Kushner, 2008; Lieberman, Javitch, & Moore, 2008; Strasser, 2007; Zarate & Manji, 2008b). Some of these agents may prove to have beneficial psychotropic properties and/or useful effects on appetite or weight regulation, and might therefore have therapeutic effects in ED patients, including the substantial portion who are inadequately responsive to current treatments.

Pharmacotherapy of Anorexia Nervosa

Two primary randomized controlled trial (RCT) designs have been utilized to evaluate medications in AN: studies aimed to restore weight in acutely ill underweight patients (weight restoration trials) and those aimed to maintain weight gain in patients whose weight has been restored to some degree (relapse prevention or weight maintenance trials). The primary outcome in the former has usually been either a measure of weight gain or time to a certain amount of weight gain; in the latter, it often has been time to or rate of relapse. However, varied primary outcome measures have been used in both types of trials (Bulik, Berkman, Brownley, Sedway, & Lohr, 2007a). Secondary outcomes have included measures of ED pathology, depressive and/or anxiety symptoms, overall clinical improvement, and treatment acceptability. Various biomarkers in addition to weight have also been assessed, such as vital signs, endocrine parameters, menstrual function, and bone density. In most studies, consistent with treatment guidelines, pharmacotherapy was given in conjunction with inpatient, supportive, and/or specialist psychotherapeutic treatment.

The most common medications evaluated in AN for weight restoration in RCTs have been antidepressants, antipsychotics, and appetite stimulants (Table 24.1). The only medications evaluated in AN for weight maintenance in RCTs have been fluoxetine and recombinant human growth hormone (rhGH). Other medications evaluated in RCTs include prokinetics, zinc, hormonal agents, lithium, opiate antagonists, and D-cycloserine.

Antidepressants

Findings of elevated rates of depressive symptoms and depressive disorders in acutely ill and recovered patients with AN and their families led to studies of antidepressants in AN. High rates of obsessive–compulsive symptoms and obsessive–compulsive disorder in patients with AN and their families, and the hypothesis that AN might be a form of obsessive–compulsive spectrum disorder, led to studies of serotonin reuptake inhibitor antidepressants in particular (Crisp, Lacey, & Crutchfield, 1987; Kaye, Weltzin, Hsu, & Bulik, 1991).

At least four randomized, placebo-controlled trials of antidepressants have been published in acutely ill, underweight patients with AN (Bulik et al., 2007a; Claudino et al., 2006). In the first

Table 24.1   Medications Studied for Anorexia Nervosa in Randomized, Placebo-Controlled Trials: Qualitative Results

Medication	Maximum Dosage Studied (mg/day)	Effect on Weight Restoration	Effect on Weight Maintenance
Antidepressants			
Amitriptyline	175	−	NDA
Clomipramine	50	−	NDA
Fluoxetine	60	−	+/−
Antipsychotics			
Olanzapine	15	++	NDA
Pimozide	6	+/−	NDA
Sulpiride	400	−	NDA
Appetite Stimulants			
Cyproheptadine	32	+	NDA
Prokinetics			
Cisapride	30	+/−	NDA
Hormonal Agents			
rhGH	.33	+−	NDA
Testosterone	300μg	−	NDA
Other Agents			
Lithium	NDA[a]	+	NDA
Zinc	100	+	+/−

NDA = no data available; SSRI = selective serotonin reuptake inhibitor; rhGH = recombinant human growth hormone.
[a]Mean plasma lithium level = 1.0 mEq/L.

trial, amitriptyline, up to 175 mg/day, did not differ from placebo in 25 youth, ages 11 to 17 years, on weight, eating, or mood outcomes (Biederman et al., 1985). There were no dropouts. In the second trial, 72 female inpatients with AN, ages 13 to 26 years, were randomized to amitriptyline (*n* = 23), cyproheptadine (*n* = 24), or placebo (*n* = 25) (Halmi, Eckert, LaDu, & Cohen, 1986). Seventeen (74%) amitriptyline-treated patients and 16 (64%) placebo-treated patients achieved target weight. Among patients who achieved target weight, excluding noncompleters, the daily rate of weight increase was numerically, but not statistically significantly, higher in the amitriptyline group. Significantly fewer days were needed to achieve target weight with amitriptyline than placebo. Attrition was 30% for amitriptyline and 20% for placebo. In the third trial, clomipramine 50 mg/day was not associated with greater weight gain than placebo in 16 female inpatients with AN after an 11-week acute phase of treatment, after which medication was discontinued, or at 1-year and 4-year follow-up evaluations (Crisp et al., 1987). In the most recent trial, 31 female inpatients with AN (ages 16–45 years) who had achieved 65% of ideal body weight were randomly assigned to fluoxetine, up to 60 mg/day, or placebo for 7 weeks on a clinical research unit (Attia, Haiman, Walsh, & Flater, 1998). Average (SD) body mass index (BMI) at randomization was 15 mg/kg (4.2). Mean (SD) fluoxetine dose at termination was 56.0 (11.2) mg/day. There were no significant differences between fluoxetine and placebo on weight gain, ED psychopathology, obsessive–compulsive symptoms, measures of depression or anxiety, or clinical global improvement.

In 2006, Claudino et al. published a Cochrane Review evaluating evidence of efficacy and acceptability of antidepressant treatment for weight restoration in AN from seven RCTs: the four above-noted studies which compared antidepressants to placebo (Attia et al., 1998; Biederman et al., 1985; Halmi et al., 1986; Lacey et al., 1980) and three studies that compared different antidepressant drugs with one another (Brambilla et al., 1995a, 1995b; Ruggiero et al., 2001). Due to methodological limitations, aggregation of data for meta-analysis was not possible for most outcomes. However, it was concluded that the studies were not able to show any effect of antidepressants compared to placebo in the majority of outcomes, including weight gain, ED symptoms, associated anxious and depressive symptoms, or clinical global improvement. In the three comparative studies, the only findings were a greater effect for amineptine (an atypical tricyclic that selectively inhibits DA, and to a lesser extent NE, reuptake) compared to fluoxetine in reducing end-of-treatment Eating Disorder Inventory (EDI) scores, and a greater effect of nortriptyline compared to fluoxetine in decreasing mean Hamilton Anxiety Scale (HAM-A) scores. These isolated findings were of unclear significance.

Two randomized, placebo-controlled relapse prevention studies have been conducted with fluoxetine in AN. In the first trial, 35 patients (34 inpatients) with restricting-type AN (none had binged during their lifetime) who had been restored to 76% to 100% of average body weight (with most above 90%) were randomized prior to discharge to fluoxetine (*n* = 16) or placebo (*n* = 19) for 52 weeks (Kaye et al., 2001). Only patients with restricting-type AN were included based upon prior open-label data suggesting this subtype might respond better to fluoxetine than bulimic and/or purging-type patients with AN (Kaye et al., 1991). Fluoxetine was initiated at 20 mg/day and adjusted to a maximum of 60 mg/day. Adjunctive outpatient psychotherapy was allowed but not required; the number of participants who received psychotherapy was not provided. Fluoxetine-recipients were more likely to complete the trial: 10 (63%) patients remained on fluoxetine for a year, whereas only 3 (16%) patients remained on placebo for that period of time (*p* =.006). At the endpoint for the entire group, however, patients receiving fluoxetine did not differ significantly from those receiving placebo on measures of weight, obsessive–compulsive symptoms, anxiety, or depression.

In the second trial, 93 patients with AN who had regained weight to a minimum BMI of 19.0 mg/kg^2 after intensive inpatient or day program treatment were randomized to outpatient fluoxetine (*n* = 49) or placebo (*n* = 44) for up to 1 year (Walsh et al., 2006). All patients also received individual cognitive behavior therapy (CBT) specifically designed to prevent relapse. Similar percentages of fluoxetine-recipients and placebo-recipients maintained a BMI ≥ 18.5 and stayed in the study for 1 year (fluoxetine, 26.5%; placebo, 31.5%; *p* = .57). In addition, there was no significant difference between fluoxetine and placebo in time-to-relapse (hazard ratio (HR) 1.12; 95% confidence interval [CI] 0.65, 2.01; *p* = .64). The authors concluded that their study failed to demonstrate any benefit from fluoxetine in the treatment of patients with AN after weight restoration.

In an uncontrolled but randomized and prospective 1-year study evaluating treatment acceptance of medication versus psychotherapy, 122 outpatients with AN who were within 75% of their target weight received fluoxetine 60 mg/day alone, CBT alone, or the combination (Halmi et al., 2005). Similar percentages (17%–18%) of patients were withdrawn (primarily for treatment failure) from the three conditions. However, among the remaining patients, there were more noncompleters in the fluoxetine alone group (56%) than the CBT alone (40%) or the combination (41%) groups. The authors concluded that fluoxetine given alone had a very low treatment acceptance rate.

In sum, taken together, these studies have led some to conclude that antidepressants are ineffective for promotion of weight gain or prevention of weight loss in AN. However, it has also been noted that these trials have methodological shortcomings that limit their interpretation. These include the use of small sample sizes leading to decreased power to detect differences in effects; use of patients in various stages of illness; use of narrow entry criteria that limit generalizability of findings; and use of antidepressants in combination with other interventions designed specifically to promote weight gain or prevent weight loss (Walsh et al., 2006). Thus, the possibility that fluoxetine might be effective for relapse prevention if given at a different stage of illness (i.e., after a longer period of weight restoration) or as a sole intervention (i.e., not as an adjunct to a structured psychotherapy designed to prevent relapse) cannot be excluded.

Another consideration is that findings with one class of antidepressant (e.g., selective serotonin reuptake inhibitors [SSRIs]) may not generalize to other classes (e.g., selective serotonin norepinephrine reuptake inhibitors [SNRIs]). For example, there are reports of AN patients responding to the unique antidepressant mirtazapine, which enhances NE and 5-HT release, stimulates $5-HT_1$ receptors, blocks $5-HT_2$, $5-HT_3$, and histamine H_1 receptors, and is associated with increased appetite and weight gain (Hrdlicka, Beranova, Zamecnikova, & Urbanek, 2008; Jaafar, Daud, Rahman, & Baharudin, 2007). There are also reports of patients with treatment-resistant AN responding to antidepressants when given in conjunction with other agents, such as antipsychotics, mood stabilizers, and other antidepressants (Fountoulakis, Iacovides, Siamouli, Koumaris, & Kaprinis, 2006; Newman-Toker, 2000; Reilly, 1977; Wang et al., 2006) (see later).

Antipsychotics

Several rationales have prompted studies of antipsychotics in AN. First is the hypothesis that AN may be a psychotic disorder or have a psychotic subtype, because it is often associated with psychotic features, including delusional beliefs about body image and food, poor insight, and denial of illness (Steinglass et al., 2007a). Second is that antipsychotics may have direct beneficial effects on appetite and weight in AN through their appetite-stimulating, weight gaining, or metabolic properties. Third is data suggesting AN might be associated with central dopaminergic dysfunction (Brambilla, Bellodi, Arancio, Ronchi, & Limonta, 2001; Kaye, 2008).

Reports on the use of antipsychotics to treat AN first appeared in the late 1950s. Dally and Sargant (1960) described success with chlorpromazine, up to 1000 mg/day, in combination with insulin, for weight restoration. These and other positive open-label reports led to two randomized, placebo-controlled, crossover trials of first-generation antipsychotics in patients with AN. In the first, 18 female inpatients with *DSM-III* AN were randomized to a single dose of pimozide (4 or 6 mg) or placebo in alternating 3-week periods (Vandereycken & Pierloot, 1982). All patients received concomitant behavior therapy. Mean changes in weight were positive with pimozide but negative with placebo. A crossover analysis showed a trend for the pimozide group to be associated with more weight gain ($p = .067$). After the first 3-week period, for example, patients receiving pimozide ($n = 8$) had a mean daily weight gain of 135 grams whereas those receiving placebo ($n = 10$) had a mean daily weight gain of 80 grams. In the second study, 18 female inpatients with *DSM-III* AN were randomized to sulpiride (300 or 400 mg/day) or placebo in alternating 3 week periods (Vandercycken, 1984). Crossover analyses showed no direct effects of sulpiride on weight change, clinical scales, or self-report questionnaires. However, individual analysis of the data showed numerically greater weight gain in both periods with sulpiride than placebo, suggesting that, as in the first trial, negative findings could be due to small sample size and inadequate power.

Second-generation (atypical) antipsychotics have been reported effective for AN in open-label reports in children, adolescents, and treatment-resistant patients (Barbarich et al., 2004a; Dunican & DelDotto, 2007; Mehler-Wex, Romanos, Kirchheiner, & Schulze, 2008). Olanzapine has been the most commonly used drug but positive reports of aripiprazole, quetiapine, and risperidone have also appeared (Bosanac et al., 2007; Newman-Toker, 2000; Powers, Bannon, Eubanks, & McCormick, 2007). These drugs have been described as helpful for weight restoration; for many of the core psychological symptoms of AN, such as fear of fatness, difficulty eating, distorted body image, and poor insight; and for many of the associated symptoms of AN, including binge eating, purging, hyperactivity, delusionality, depression, anxiety, and mood instability.

These observations led to three randomized studies of olanzapine in AN. In the first study, 15 inpatients with AN received olanzapine (n = 8) or chlorpromazine (n = 7) in addition to standard care until the time of discharge (Mondraty et al., 2005). However, the treatment arms were not blinded. Average (range) olanzapine dose was 10 (5–15) mg/day; average chlorpromazine dose was 50 (25–100) mg/day. The two treatment groups did not differ in weight gain, but olanzapine recipients showed a significantly greater reduction in anorexic rumination. A limitation of this study is that five olanzapine patients and one chlorpromazine patient were receiving concomitant antidepressants. One patient on olanzapine and three on chlorpromazine reported sedation; one patient on chlorpromazine had postural hypotension.

In the second RCT, 30 female outpatients with *DSM-IV* AN (18 with restricting-type AN and 12 with binge eating-purging type AN) received olanzapine (2.5 mg/day for 1 month, then 5 mg/day for 2 months) or placebo, in addition to CBT (Brambilla et al., 2007a; Brambilla, Monteleone, & Maj, 2007b). BMI increased significantly but similarly in both groups. There were also no differences between groups in improvements in Eating Disorder Inventory-2 (EDI-2) individual item or total values, Yale-Brown-Cornell Eating Disorder Scale (YBC-EDS) obsessiveness or total values, or Buss-Durkee scale (BDS) total values for aggressiveness. However, measures of rituals (on the YBC-EDS), direct aggressiveness (on the BDS), depression (on the HAM-D), and persistence (on the Temperament and Character Inventory [TCI]) improved significantly with olanzapine compared with placebo. Olanzapine was well tolerated, with mild sleepiness as the only side effect. When stratifying for AN subtype, changes in BMI, depression, and direct aggression were significant among binge eating-purging type patients, whereas change in persistence was significant among restricting-type patients. It was concluded that olanzapine might improve different aspects in different subtypes of AN.

In the third study, 34 patients with AN receiving day treatment were randomized to receive flexible dose olanzapine (n = 16) or placebo (n = 18) for 10 weeks (Bissada et al., 2008). Twenty-eight patients (14 in each group) completed the trial. Compared with placebo, olanzapine was associated with a greater rate of increase in BMI (p = .03), an earlier achievement of target BMI, and a greater rate of decrease in obsessive symptoms (as evaluated by the YBOCS; p = .02). Of the total sample, 87.5% of olanzapine recipients achieved weight restoration compared with 55.6% of placebo recipients (p = .02). There were no differences in reductions between the groups on measures of anxiety, depression, or compulsions. The mean (SD) olanzapine dose over the 10-week treatment period for study completers was 6.61 (2.32) mg/day. No differences in adverse effects were observed between the two treatment conditions. There were no serious adverse effects; in particular, there was no evidence of impaired glucose tolerance or *de novo* development of diabetes mellitus in any participant. However, because olanzapine may cause glucose intolerance in AN (possibly by inducing insulin resistance), it has been recommended that AN patients receiving treatment with olanzapine have their glucose metabolism closely monitored (Yasuhara, Nakahara, Harada, & Inui, 2007).

No controlled studies of antipsychotics for weight maintenance in AN have yet been published, but there are open-label reports. For example, Cassano et al., (2003) treated 13 outpatients with treatment-resistant restricting-type AN for 6 months with haloperidol in addition to standard therapy. BMI increased significantly from baseline (15.7 ± 1.9) to endpoint (18.1 ± 2.5; p = .03). Significant improvement was also observed on the EDI (p = .02), Eating Attitude Test (EAT; p = .009), and CGI-I scale (p = .001) scores. There are also reports of antipsychotics being helpful in AN patients with serious comorbid neuropsychiatric and medical disorders, including schizotypal personality disorder (Nagata, Ono, & Nakayama, 2007), autism (Fisman, Steele, Short, Byrne, & Lavallee, 1996), and epilepsy with chronic renal failure (Aragona, 2007).

Antidepressant–Antipsychotic Combinations

AN has similarities with psychotic depression including depressive symptoms, delusional thinking, and hypercortisolism (Klein, Kennedy, Piran, & Garfinkel,2007; Steinglass et al., 2007a). Psychotic depression is characterized by better response to antidepressant–antipsychotic combination therapy than to antipsychotic monotherapy (Wijkstra, Lijmer, Balk, Geddes, & Nolen, 2006). No controlled studies of antidepressant–antipsychotic combinations have been published in AN, but there are open-label reports of patients reporting to such regimens.

These include descriptions of treatment-resistant AN patients responding to the addition of a second generation antipsychotic to an antidepressant, such as risperidone to an SSRI (Newman-Toker, 2000). There are also reports of AN patients with depressive symptoms responding to the combination of olanzapine and mirtazapine (Fountoulakis et al., 2006; Wang et al., 2006).

Appetite Stimulants

Cyproheptadine is an anti-allergy and appetite-stimulating drug with high affinity for various serotonin, histamine, dopamine, adrenergic, and muscarinic receptors (Goudie, Cooper, Cole, & Sumnall, 2007). It has a benign side effect profile and is available over the counter in some countries. Several positive case reports, along with the rationale that it might facilitate weight gain in AN, led to two randomized, placebo-controlled trials published in the English-language literature for weight restoration.

In the first study, 81 female inpatients with AN were randomized to one of four treatment combinations of cyproheptadine (12–32 mg/day) or placebo with or without behavior therapy (Goldberg, Halmi, Eckert, Casper, & Davis, 1979). Mean weight gain did not differ between the groups receiving cyproheptadine (5.11 kg) versus placebo (4.32 kg). However, in a subgroup analysis, cyproheptadine was superior to placebo for weight gain in patients with a history of two or more birth delivery complications compared to those with none.

In the second study, 72 female inpatients with AN were randomized to cyproheptadine ($n = 24$), amitriptyline ($n = 23$), or placebo ($n = 25$) (Halmi et al., 1986). As noted earlier, 83% of cyproheptadine versus 64% of placebo-treated patients achieved their target weights. Among these patients, significantly fewer days were required to achieve target weight with cyproheptadine (mean ± SD = 36.5 ± 19.5) than placebo (mean ± SD = 45.0 ± 18.3; $p < .05$). In addition, cyproheptadine significantly increased treatment efficiency in the nonbulimic patients and significantly decreased treatment efficiency in the bulimic patients. (Treatment efficacy was the reciprocal of the number of days to target weight times the constant 90, the maximal length of treatment.) Attrition was 25% for cyproheptadine and 20% for placebo.

Prokinetics

Findings of delayed gastric emptying and associated symptoms (e.g., epigastric fullness and pain, belching, bloating, and early satiety) in AN prompted two randomized, placebo-controlled trials of the prokinetic drug cisapride. In the first, 12 outpatients with DSM-III-R AN received cisapride 10 mg administered orally three times daily ($n = 6$) or placebo ($n = 6$) for 6 weeks after completing an 8-week inpatient program (Stacher et al., 1993a). All patients then received 6 weeks of open-label cisapride. Gastric emptying was accelerated in all six patients receiving cisapride; gastric emptying was accelerated in three patients receiving placebo and slowed in the other three. Symptoms of gastric retention and constipation were numerically improved in the cisapride group versus the placebo group. Mean weight (SD) gain with cisapride was greater than with placebo (7.3% [7.1] versus 1.7% [3.1] of ideal body weight, respectively). After the 6 weeks of cisapride treatment during the second period, gastric retention symptoms stayed reduced in the cisapride-first patients and decreased in the placebo-first patients. Five of the 6 placebo-first patients gained weight. However, after their second 6 weeks of cisapride, only 1 of the 6 cisapride-first patients gained more weight; the other five lost weight (mean change, −3.0%).

In the second study, 29 inpatients with AN were randomized to cisapride 10 mg three times daily or placebo for 8 weeks (Szmukler, Young, Miller, Lichtenstein, & Binns, 1995). Both scintigraphic-assessed gastric emptying and weight improved significantly but equally in both groups. However, patients receiving cisapride rated themselves as hungrier ($p = .02$) and more improved on a global measure of symptom change ($p = .02$). The correlation between gastric emptying and weight gain was modest ($r = .30$; $p = .11$). There were no correlations between gastric emptying and symptomatic measures.

Cisapride's access has since been restricted because of an association with potentially fatal cardiac arrhythmias (Tooley, Vervaet, & Wager, 1999). Except for one small placebo-controlled crossover study showing erythromycin 200 mg accelerated gastric emptying in 10 patients with AN (Stacher et al., 1993b), no controlled studies of other prokinetic agents in AN have been done. Open reports describe successful use of domperidone and metoclopramide to decrease symptoms and promote weight gain (Russell et al., 1983; Saleh & Lebwohl, 1980). In one case, excessive weight gain was described (Sansone & Sansone, 2003). Of note, if either domperidone or metoclopramide are used, patients should be monitored for extrapyramidal side effects.

Zinc

Clinical similarities between zinc deficiency and AN (e.g., appetite and weight loss, impaired sexual development, amenorrhea, and skin abnormalities) led to two randomized, placebo-controlled trials of zinc supplementation in patients with AN (Su & Birmingham, 2002). In the first study, six adolescents with AN who received elemental zinc 50 mg/day for 6 months ($n = 6$) showed decreased depression and anxiety on the Zung Depression Scale ($p < .05$) and the State-Trait Anxiety Inventory ($p < .05$) compared with seven adolescents who received placebo (Katz et al., 1987). The zinc-supported group also showed a greater weight gain and increase in height, improved taste function, greater advancement in sexual maturation, and better resolution of skin abnormalities, but these differences did not reach statistical significance. A fourteenth patient who dropped out of the trial was excluded from analysis. In the second trial, 35 female inpatients with AN who were considered completers had been randomized to zinc gluconate 100 mg/day ($n = 16$) or placebo ($n = 19$) until they achieved a 10% increase in BMI (Birmingham, Goldner, & Bakan, 1994). The rate of BMI increase in the zinc supplemented group was twice that of the placebo group ($p = .03$). However, 19 patients who did not complete the study ($n = 10$ receiving zinc) did not appear to be included in the efficacy analysis. In addition, antidepressants and major tranquilizers were utilized but their amount of use was not quantitatively presented. Zinc was not associated with any harmful effects.

Another study was a 12-week crossover trial with 6 weeks of oral zinc sulphate 50 mg/day alternating with 6 weeks of placebo to be given to children with AN (Lask, Fosson, Rolfe, & Thomas, 1993). Though described as double-blind, this trial was unlikely to be randomized because of 26 patients enrolled, 7 children received zinc supplementation whereas 19 received standard treatment. Moreover, only three of seven trials of zinc supplementation were completed. Thus, no conclusions about zinc supplementation could be drawn from this study.

Based on the above preliminary data, along with zinc's low cost and benign side effect profile, some have argued that oral zinc administration during weight restoration should be routinely considered (Birmingham & Gritzner, 2006). However, further randomized, placebo-controlled studies appear needed to better establish zinc's efficacy, adverse event profile, and optimal dosing and treatment duration.

Hormonal Treatments

Hypothesizing that androgen deficiency in AN may be related to depressive symptoms, cognitive function deficits, and bone loss, Miller, Grieco, and Klibanski (2005) randomized 33 women with AN and relative testosterone deficiency to transdermal testosterone (150 or 300 µg) or placebo for 3 weeks. Serum total and free testosterone levels increased significantly in patients receiving testosterone. Significant improvement in depression was seen in depressed patients receiving testosterone, whereas there was no change in depressed patients receiving placebo ($p = .02$). Testosterone recipients showed improved spatial cognition ($p = .0015$). Weight, however, did not change over the 3 weeks in either group. Attrition rate was 13%.

One randomized, placebo-controlled study of recombinant human growth hormone (rhGH) in AN has been published to date, prompted by the possibility that insufficient GH action contributes to the progression of AN and to the successful use of rhGH in several malnourished populations (Chu et al., 2001; Gelato et al., 2007; Lawson & Klibanski, 2008). Fifteen inpatients with AN, ages 12 to 18 years, received rhGH .05 mg/kg subcutaneously ($n = 8$) or an equivalent volume of placebo ($n = 7$) daily for 28 days in addition to a standard refeeding protocol (Hill et al., 2000). Patients given rhGH reached medical/cardiovascular stability (defined as normal orthostatic heart rate response to a standing challenge) significantly sooner than those receiving placebo (median 17 versus 37 days, $p = .02$). Numerical improvements were also seen in weight gain and hospitalization length in the rhGH group. There were no dropouts.

A treatment currently being evaluated in psychotic depression, the glucocorticoid antagonist mifepristone, has been hypothesized as possibly being effective in AN (Klein et al., 2007). No treatment studies with this compound, or any other antiglucocorticoid agents, however, have yet been published in AN (Kling et al., 1993).

Mood Stabilizers

Lithium's association with weight gain, AN's association with depressive and manic symptoms, and reports of patients with long-standing AN responding to lithium (Barcai, 1977; McElroy et al., 2005; Wildes, Marcus, Gaskill, & Ringham, 2007) prompted a 4-week placebo-controlled trial of lithium in 16 female inpatients with AN (Gross et al., 1981). All patients received behavior modification therapy, which included tube findings. The 8 patients receiving lithium showed significantly greater weight gain after 3 (p = .04) and 4 weeks (p = .03) of treatment than the 8 patients receiving placebo. After 4 weeks, lithium-treated patients also showed significantly more improvement on an item measuring "denial and minimization of illness" and ingested more fat per day. The mean (SD) plasma lithium level over the 4 weeks of treatment was 1.0 (0.1) mEq/L. Importantly, lithium was tolerated well and there were no serious adverse events.

Some authorities are extremely reluctant to consider lithium for AN, given the drug's low therapeutic index and need for monitoring, and AN's association with dehydration, electrolyte abnormalities, and cardiac arrhythmias (Kolata, 1980). It should be noted, however, that case reports describe patients with AN and comorbid bipolar disorder responding to lithium alone or in combination with carbamazepine (Hudson, Pope, Jonas, & Yurgelun-Todd, 1985). There are also case reports of patients with treatment-resistant AN responding to lithium (Reilly, 1977; Stein, Hartshorn, Jones, & Steinberg, 1982). Use of lithium in AN requires careful monitoring of patients' fluid, electrolyte, renal, cardiac, and thyroid status.

Opiate-Related Medications

Involvement of the opiate system in regulating eating behavior led to two placebo-controlled studies of opiate antagonists in AN. In the first study, 12 inpatients with AN receiving behavioral treatment and antidepressants gained significantly more weight during naloxone infusion, up to 3.2 to 6.4 mg/day for a mean of 4.9 weeks, compared with the 4 weeks post-infusion (p < .01) (Moore, Mills, & Forster, 1981). In the second study, 6 AN patients treated with naltrexone, up to 200 mg/day, or placebo in individual randomized crossover trials, showed significant reductions in binges and purges, but not a significant increase in daily food intake, on naltrexone compared with placebo (Marrazzi, Bacon, Kinzie, & Lubu, 1995a, et al., 1995). Although quantitative weight data were not provided, no patients lost weight on naltrexone. Naltrexone 25 to 75 mg/day has also been used for successful weight restoration in hospitalized patients with chronic AN (Luby, Marrazzi, & Kinzie, 1987). Finally, tramadol, a synthetic opiate that binds μ-opioid receptors and weakly inhibits the uptake of serotonin and norepinephrine, was reported to be helpful for a patient with intractable AN (Mendelson, 2001).

D-Cycloserine

D-Cycloserine is a partial agonist at the N-methyl-D-aspartate (NMDA) glutamatergic receptor that may facilitate extinction of conditioned fear and may be helpful as a short term adjunctive intervention to exposure therapy for anxiety disorders, including phobias (Hofmann et al., 2006). AN is associated with food avoidance and anxiety related to eating. Eleven patients with AN were randomly assigned to either D-cycloserine 50 mg or placebo before each of four exposure therapy interventions (e.g., training meals) aimed to increase meal intake (Steinglass et al., 2007b). A trend (p = .06) with a large effect size (d = −1.33) was seen for D-cycloserine-recipients to experience a greater decrease in Beck Depression Inventory (BDI) scores than placebo recipients from the baseline test meal to the final test meal (a mean [SD] of 27.8 ± 5.8 days), but there were no other outcome differences between the groups. There were no adverse events with D-cycloserine. This study was limited by small sample size. Also, patients assigned to D-cycloserine had significantly lower post-meal anxiety than those assigned to placebo at the baseline meal.

Antiepileptic Drugs

A potential overlap of AN with epilepsy and various brain lesions prompted open-label reports of antiepileptic drugs (AEDs) in patients with AN (Uher & Treasure, 2005). A 16-year-old girl with "classical" AN beginning simultaneously with partial complex seizures showed both weight gain and seizure control with phenytoin treatment (Szyper & Mann, 1978). In another report of phenytoin, a subset of 42 patients also receiving psychotherapy and other medications showed improvement in attitude towards food, eating behavior, hostility, and fear, but quantitative results were not provided (Parsons & Sapse, 1985). A 13-year-old girl with AN and epilepsy responded to the combination of valproate and clonazepam (Tachibana, Sugita, Teshima, & Hishikawa, 1989).

Case reports of topiramate use in AN have mixed results. Topiramate possibly "triggered" a recurrent episode of AN in a woman with an extensive psychiatric history receiving the drug for epilepsy (Rosenow, Knake, & Hebebrand, 2002), whereas it improved the concurrent AN of a patient with bipolar disorder (Guille & Sachs, 2002). ED patients have misused topiramate to lose weight (Chung & Reed, 2004; Colom et al., 2001).

Nutritional Supplements

A study of nutritional supplementation of fluoxetine aimed to enhance serotonergic neurotransmission was ineffective in promoting weight gain in AN (Barbarich et al., 2004b). Twenty-six patients with AN receiving fluoxetine were randomized to receive a nutritional supplement containing tryptophan, vitamins, minerals, and essential fatty acids, or a nutritional placebo. There were no significant differences in weight gain or in mean changes in anxiety or obsessive and compulsive symptoms between the two groups.

Other Somatic Treatments

There are case reports of patients with intractable AN and comorbid major depressive disorder in which both conditions responded to electroconvulsive therapy (ECT) (Ferguson, 1993; Hill, Haslett, & Kumar, 2001). Controlled trials found no effects with tetrahydrocannabinol (Gross et al., 1983) and clonidine (Casper, Schlemmer, & Javaid, 1987), but were limited by small sample sizes.

Pharmacotherapy of Bulimia Nervosa

Two primary pharmacotherapy RCT designs have been utilized to evaluate medications in BN: short-term acute studies of patients who are actively bingeing and purging and long-term maintenance studies of patients whose bulimic symptoms have responded to an acute intervention. In addition, pharmacotherapy studies in BN have been done as monotherapy trials, in which medication alone is compared with placebo, another medication, or a psychological treatment, and as combination therapy trials, where medication plus a psychological treatment is compared with the psychological treatment alone and/or the medication alone. Primary outcomes in the acute trials have usually been measures of the frequency of binge eating episodes and/or inappropriate compensatory behaviors (e.g., vomiting), or rates of remission or response of bulimic symptoms. Primary outcomes in the maintenance trials have usually been time to relapse or rate of relapse. Secondary outcomes have been measures of ED pathology, mood symptoms, global clinical improvement, and treatment adherence. The two major classes of drugs studied thus far in BN in randomized, placebo-controlled trials have been antidepressants and AEDs (Table 24.2). Drug classes that have received less study include 5-HT$_3$ antagonists, opiate antagonists, hormonal agents, and stimulants.

Antidepressants

As with AN, studies of antidepressants in BN were prompted by the high rates of depressive symptoms and depressive disorders found in patients with BN and their families (Pope, Hudson, Jonas, & Yurgelun-Todd, 1983). Unlike AN, however, many different antidepressant classes have been evaluated in BN in randomized, placebo-controlled trials; these include SSRIs, tricyclics, monoamine oxidase inhibitors (MAOIs), and atypical agents. Drugs from each of these classes have been shown superior to placebo for reducing the frequency of both binge eating and purging episodes in BN (Shapiro et al., 2007; Yager & Powers, 2007) (Table 24.2). As noted earlier, an antidepressant, fluoxetine, is the only medication with an FDA approval for the treatment of an ED, that being BN.

In August, 2003, Bacaltchuk and Hay published a Cochrane Review of randomized, placebo-controlled trials of antidepressants in patients with BN. Nineteen studies were included: six trials with tricyclics (imipramine, desipramine, and amitriptyline; Agras, Dorian, Kirkley, Arnow, & Bachman, 1987; McCann et al., 1990; Mitchell & Groat, 1984; Mitchell et al., 1990; Pope et al., 1983; Walsh et al., 1991); five with MAOIs (phenelzine, isocarboxazid, moclobemide, and brofaromine; (Carruba et al., 2001; Kennedy et al., 1988, 1993; Rothschild et al., 1994; Walsh et al., 1984), five with the SSRI fluoxetine (FBNCSG, 1992; Kanerva et al., 1994; Mitchell et al., 2001; Walsh et al., 2000; Wheadon et al., 1992), and three with atypical drugs (mianserin, trazodone, and bupropion; Horne et al., 1998; Pope, Keck, McElroy, & Hudson,1989; Sabine, Yonace, Farrington, Barrant, & Wakeling, 1983). Study durations ranged from 6 to 16 weeks. Meta-analysis showed that the pooled relative risk (RR) for remission of binge episodes was 0.87 (95% CI = 0.81, 0.93; p < 0.001), favoring antidepressants. The number needed to treat (NNT) for a mean treatment duration of 8 weeks, taking the 92% non-remission rate in the placebo controls as a measure of the baseline risk, was 9 (95% CI = 6, 16). The RR for clinical improvement, defined as a 50% or greater reduction in binge episodes, was 0.63 (95% CI = 0.55, 0.74). The NNT for a mean duration of 9 weeks was 4 (95% CI = 3, 6), with 67% unimproved in the placebo group. There was no evidence of statistically significant differences in efficacy among the different classes of antidepressants. However, remission rates were low and a considerable fraction of patients did not show a reduction of at least 50%

Table 24.2 Medications Studied for Bulimia Nervosa in Randomized, Placebo-Controlled trials: Qualitative Results

Medication	Maximum Dosage Studied (mg/day)	Effect on Binge Reduction	Effect on Purge Reduction
Tricyclic Antidepressants Amitriptyline	150	+++	+++
Desipramine	300	+++	+++
Imipramine	300	+++	+++
Monamine Oxidase Inhibitors			
Brofaromine	200	–	+++
Isocarboxazid	60	+++	+++
Moclobemide	600	–	–
Phenelzine	90	+++	+++
SSRIs			
Fluoxetine	60	+++	+++
Fluvoxamine	300	++	++
Other Antidepressants			
Mianserin	60	–	–
Bupropion	450	+++	+++
Trazodone	400	+++	+++
Antiepileptics			
Carbamazepine	NDA[a]	–	–
Topiramate	400	+++	+++
Other Agents			
Dexfenfluramine	60	++	++
Flutamide	500	++	–
Lithium	600-1200[b]	–	–
Naltrexone	200	++	++
Ondansetron	24	+++	+++
Spironolactone	150	–	–

SSRI = selective serotonin reuptake inhibitor; NDA = no data available.
[a]Plasma carbamazepine levels = 6–10 μg/mL
[b]Mean plasma lithium level =. 62 mEq/L.

in bulimic symptoms. Moreover, patients treated with antidepressants were more likely to discontinue prematurely due to adverse events. Patients receiving tricyclics dropped out due to any cause more frequently than those receiving placebo, though the opposite was found for fluoxetine. The authors concluded that, in general, a single antidepressant agent is clinically effective for the treatment of BN when compared to placebo, but that the effect is modest.

Importantly, among the studies reviewed was the first pivotal RCT of fluoxetine in 387 women with BN in which 60 mg/day was shown to be superior to placebo for reducing binge eating and vomiting episodes, while 20 mg/day was shown to have an intermediate effect (FBNCSG et al., 1992). Fluoxetine 60 mg/day was also superior to placebo in reducing depression, carbohydrate craving, and pathological eating attitudes and behaviors. Also reviewed was the single study of bupropion showing that although effective in reducing binging and purging, this agent was associated with an increased risk for seizures (Horne et al., 1998). It is therefore contraindicated for the treatment of BN and AN.

Antidepressants have been studied both against and in combination with a variety of psychological interventions in BN, most commonly CBT but also intensive inpatient psychotherapy and nutritional counseling (Bacaltchuck, Hay, & Trefiglio, 2001; Shapiro et al., 2007). Designs and results have varied, making firm conclusions difficult to make. In 2001, Bacaltchuk et al., published a Cochrane Review of RCTs in which antidepressants were compared with psychological treatments or the combination of antidepressants with psychological treatments was compared to each treatment alone for reducing symptoms in BN. The main efficacy outcome was remission of bulimic symptoms. Three comparisons were made. In the first, which included 5 trials and 237 patients, antidepressants alone were compared with psychological treatments alone (Agras et al., 1992; Goldbloom et al., 1997; Leitenberg et al., 1994; Mitchell et al., 1990; Walsh et al., 1997). In the second, which included 5 trials and 247 patients, antidepressants alone were compared with antidepressant-psychological treatment combinations (Agras et al., 1992; Goldbloom et al., 1997; Leitenberg et al., 1994; Mitchell et al., 1990; Walsh et al., 1997). In the third, which included 7 trials and 343 patients, psychological treatments alone were compared with combination treatment (Agras et al., 1992; Beaumont et al., 1997; Fichter et al., 1991; Goldbloom et al., 1997; Leitenberg

et al., 1994; Mitchell et al., 1990; Walsh et al., 1997). Comparison 1 found remission rates for antidepressant treatment alone were 20% versus 39% for psychological treatment alone (RR = 1.28; 95% CI = 0.98, 1.67). Dropout rates were higher for antidepressants alone than psychological treatments alone (RR = 2.18; 95% CI = 1.09, 4.35). The number needed to harm (NNH) for a mean treatment duration of 17.5 weeks was 4 (95% CI = 3, 11). Comparison 2 found remission rates for the combination of 42% versus 23% for antidepressants alone (RR = 1.38; 95% CI = 0.98, 1.93). Comparison 3 found remission rates of 36% for psychological treatments alone versus 49% for the combination (RR = 1.21; 95% CI = 1.02, 1.45. Dropout rates were higher for the combination compared with psychological treatments alone (RR = .57; 95% CI = .38, .88). The NNH was 7 (95% CI = 4, 21). Using a conservative approach, the only statistically significant difference between groups was that combination therapy was superior to psychological treatment alone. The authors concluded that the effectiveness of combined antidepressant-psychological approaches was superior to psychotherapy alone, but that the number of trials might be insufficient to show combination therapy or psychotherapy alone superior to antidepressants alone. They also concluded that psychotherapy was more acceptable to patients and that the addition of antidepressants to psychotherapy reduced its acceptability.

At least two randomized, controlled relapse-prevention trials have been done with antidepressants in BN. In the first, 72 patients with *DSM-III-R* BN successfully treated with intensive inpatient psychotherapy were randomized to receive fluvoxamine (*n* = 33) or placebo (*n* = 39) as outpatients for 12 weeks (Fichter, Krüger, Rief, Holland, & Döhne, 1996). Fluvoxamine was begun 3 weeks before hospital discharge, for a total of 15 weeks of treatment. The relapse rate was significantly lower for fluvoxamine than placebo, as shown by: (1) 10% versus 46% deterioration on the Psychiatric Status Rating Scale for Bulimia Nervosa; (2) 111% versus 270% increase in self-reported binges in the last week; and 3) 50% versus 175% increase on the Structured Interview for Anorexia and Bulimia Nervosa (SIAB) subscale of bulimic behavior. In addition, at the end of relapse-prevention, the fluvoxamine group had significantly more patients reporting no binges in the past week than the placebo group (*p* < .05). However, the dropout rate was high (33%), with 14 (38%) fluvoxamine recipients stopping prematurely compared with 5 (14%) placebo recipients.

In the second study, 232 outpatients with *DSM-IV* BN, purging type received single-blind treatment with fluoxetine 60 mg/day for 8 weeks; 150 (65%) met response criteria (a ≥50% decrease from baseline in vomiting episode frequency during 1 of the 2 preceding weeks) and were randomly assigned to continue fluoxetine 60 mg/day (*n* = 76) or switch to placebo (*n* = 74) for 52 weeks (Romano et al., 2002). Fluoxetine-treated patients exhibited a significantly longer time to relapse (defined as a return to baseline vomiting frequency that persisted for 2 weeks) than placebo-treated patients (χ^2 = 5.79, f = 1, *p* < 0.02). Endpoint analysis showed statistically significant differences favoring fluoxetine for vomiting episodes, binge eating episodes, obsessive–compulsive symptoms, and clinical global outcome. However, relapse rates and efficacy measures increased over the trial in both treatment groups. In addition, the attrition rate was very high, with 63 (83%) fluoxetine recipients and 68 (92%) placebo recipients discontinuing the study prematurely.

Of note, several antidepressant classes have not yet been evaluated in randomized, placebo-controlled trials in BN. These include serotonin norepinephrine reuptake inhibitors (SNRIs; e.g., desvenlafaxine, duloxetine, milnacipran, and venlafaxine), and norepinephrine reuptake inhibitors (NRIs; e.g., reboxetine). Open-label data, however, suggest milnacipran, reboxetine, and to a lesser extent, duloxetine, may be effective in BN, including in treatment resistant cases (Castilho & Costa, 2003; El-Giamal et al., 2000 & 2003; Fassino et al., 2004; Hazen & Fava, 2006; Noma, Uwatoko, Yamamoto, & Hayashi, 2008).

Antiepileptic Drugs

Several rationales led to three randomized, placebo-controlled studies of AEDs in BN—one with carbamazepine and two with topiramate. First is the phenomenological similarity between the binge eating episodes of BN and partial complex seizures (Hudson & Pope, 1988). Second is the comorbidity between BN and mood disorders, and that mood disorders may respond to AEDs (e.g., carbamazepine, divalproex, and lamotrigine are all FDA approved for bipolar disorder). Third is that some AEDs are associated with anorexia (e.g., felbamate, topiramate, and zonisamide) and the possibility that compounds that suppress appetite may reduce binge eating.

In the first RCT of an AED in BN, 16 patients with DSM-III BN and at least one binge per week and no binge-free internals of longer than three weeks during the previous year received carbamazepine in a crossover design (Hudson & Pope, 1988; Kaplan, 1987; Kaplan, Garfinkel, Darby, & Garner, 1983). The first six patients received 6-week intervals of placebo–carbamazepine–placebo or carbamazepine–placebo–carbamazepine over 18 weeks. The next 10 patients received two 6-week intervals of placebo–carbamazepine or carbamazepine–placebo over 12 weeks. There was no significant difference in response between carbamazepine and placebo. One patient had a complete remission of binge eating, one patient had a marked response, and three additional patients improved on carbamazepine compared with baseline but did not show a difference on drug compared with placebo. Of note, the patient who had a remission had comorbid cyclothymic disorder; she showed marked improvement in both her mood and her bulimic symptoms while receiving carbamazepine.

The first study of topiramate in BN was a 10-week trial in 69 patients (Hedges et al., 2003; Hoopes et al., 2003). Twenty-two (63%) of 35 topiramate recipients and 18 (53%) of 34 placebo recipients completed the trial. Topiramate (median dose 100 mg/day; range, 25 to 400 mg/day) was superior to placebo in reducing the frequency of binge and purge days (days during which at least one binge eating or purging episode occurred; *p* = .004); the bulimia/uncontrollable overeating (*p* = .005), body dissatisfaction (*p* = .007), and drive for thinness (*p* = .002) subscales of the EDI; the bulimia/food preoccupation (*p* = .019) and dieting (*p* = .031) subscales of the EAT; the mean HAM-A score (*p* = .046), and body weight (mean decrease of 1.8 kg for topiramate versus 0.2 kg increase for placebo; *p* = .004). Significantly more topiramate recipients than placebo recipients reported improvement on the Patient Global Improvement scale (*p* = .004). The percentage of patients who achieved ≥50% reduction in the number of binge and/or purge days was significantly greater for the topiramate group (52%) than the placebo group (24%; *p* = .012). Remission rates from binge eating and purging were numerically, but not significantly, higher for topiramate (23%) than placebo (6%); attrition rates were numerically lower for topiramate (34%) than placebo (47%). One patient discontinued topiramate for an adverse event (nausea). The most common side effects associated with topiramate were fatigue, flu-like symptoms, and paresthesia.

In the second study, 60 patients who had BN for at least 12 months received topiramate (*n* = 30; titrated to 250 mg/d by the sixth week with the dosage, then held constant) or placebo (*n* = 30) for

10 weeks (Nickel et al., 2005). Topiramate was associated with significant decreases in the frequency of binging/purging (defined as a > 50% reduction; 37% for topiramate and 3% for placebo); body weight (difference in weight loss between the two groups = 3.8 kg); and all scales on the SF 36 Health Survey (all p's < .001). Five (17%) patients on topiramate and six (20%) patients on placebo were considered dropouts. All patients tolerated topiramate well.

In addition, topiramate has been reported to reduce binge eating and/or purging in BN patients with treatment-resistant illness, those with comorbid depressive or bipolar disorders, and those receiving the drug as adjunctive therapy in combination with antidepressants and/or mood stabilizers (Barbee, 2003; Felstrom & Blackshaw, 2002). There is also a report of topiramate decreasing binge eating in a woman with BN and epilepsy (Knable, 2001). Her BN antedated her epilepsy and had not responded to five years of treatment with phenytoin, which had been effective in preventing her seizures.

5-HT$_3$ Antagonists

Ondansetron is a potent and selective antagonist of the 5-HT$_3$ receptor. Like several other 5-HT$_3$ antagonists, it is marketed for the treatment of nausea and vomiting associated with chemotherapy, radiation therapy, and surgery, which, in turn, is caused by serotonin release from gastric enterochromaffin cells (Haus, Späth, & Färber, 2004). Hypothesizing that vagal nerve dysfunction plays a role in BN and that ondansetron might exert therapeutic effects by blocking overactive 5-HT$_3$ receptors on afferent vagal fibers in the gastric mucosa, Faris et al., (2000) conducted a 4-week randomized, placebo-controlled trial of the drug in 26 women with severe BN. To be enrolled, patients had a minimum frequency of 7 coupled episodes of binge eating followed by self-induced vomiting per week for at least 6 months. Ondansetron (n = 14), which was self-administered in 4-mg capsules up to 6/day upon the urge to binge or vomit, was associated with a significantly greater decrease in binge/vomit frequencies (p < .001) and with a significant increase in normal meals consumed (p < .03) compared with placebo (n = 12). It was also associated with a significant improvement in the time spent engaging in bulimic behaviors (p < .05). There was no difference in weight change between groups. One patient receiving ondansetron discontinued due to accidental injury.

Hormonal Treatments

In women with BN, binge eating fluctuates with the menstrual cycle, increasing with decreases in estradiol and increases in progesterone (Edler, Lipson, & Keel, 2007). In addition, BN in women may be associated with high androgen levels and hyperandrogenic symptoms (Cotrufo et al., 2000; Monteleone et al., 2001), and may be related to polycystic ovary syndrome (Naessén, Carlström, Garoff, Glant, & Hirschberg, 2006). These observations, along with two positive case reports with the testosterone receptor antagonist flutamide (Bergman & Eriksson, 1996), led to two controlled studies of antiandrogenic compounds in women with BN.

In the first study, 46 women meeting the DSM-IV criteria for BN, purging type were randomized to flutamide (n = 9), citalopram (n = 15), flutamide plus citalopram (n = 10), or placebo (n = 12) for 3 months (Sundblad, Landén, Eriksson, Bergman, & Eriksson, 2005). Final flutamide and citalopram doses were 500 mg/day and 40 mg/day, respectively. Ten patients did not complete the trial. On a self-rated global assessment of symptom intensity, all three active treatment groups were superior to placebo. A comparison of all flutamide-recipients versus placebo-recipients showed significant reductions in global ratings (p = .03) and binge eating (p = .02) but not vomiting. Binge eating was significantly reduced only in the group given the combination of flutamide and citalopram (p = .04); vomiting was not significantly decreased in any group. Dry skin was the most common side effect with flutamide. Two patients discontinued flutamide for moderate but reversible increases in serum transaminase levels.

In the second study, the effects of an antiandrogenic oral contraceptive (30 µg ethinyl estradiol plus 3 mg drospirenone; Yasmin®) were evaluated in 21 women with BN and 17 age and BMI-matched controls (Naessén, Carlström, Byström, Pierre, & Hirschberg, 2007). Before treatment, women with BN had a higher frequency of menstrual disturbances, higher acne and hirsutism scores, and higher levels of testosterone, but lower meal related cholecystokinin (CCK) secretion than controls. After 3 months of treatment, meal-related hunger and gastric distention were decreased in BN women. Meal-real CCK secretion was unchanged in BN women but decreased in control women. Testosterone and free testosterone were decreased in patients and controls. Frequency of self-induced vomiting decreased during treatment (p = .05), but binge eating and weight phobia were not significantly changed. Compared with nonresponders, the six (29%) responders had significantly higher levels of total and free testosterone and significantly higher scores of binge eating and self-induced vomiting, but lower scores of weight phobia, at baseline. Reduced frequency of vomiting correlated with reduced testosterone levels (r_s =.50, p < .05). The authors suggested that antiandrogenic oral contraceptives might be a new treatment strategy for women with BN and hyperandrogenic symptoms.

Opiate Antagonists
Involvement of the endogenous opioid system in eating behavior, reward, and addiction prompted a number of studies of opiate antagonists in the treatment of BN. In the first, 16 normal weight women with *DSM-III* BN completed a 6-week, placebo-controlled, crossover trial of naltrexone (50 mg/day), a competitive opioid receptor antagonist approved by the FDA for treating opiate and alcohol dependence (Mitchell et al., 1989). No significant differences in binge eating or vomiting episodes between active drug and placebo were found. In a subsequent study, 28 women with *DSM-III-R* BN and 33 obese patients with binge eating received naltrexone (100–150 mg/d), imipramine, or placebo as (Alger Schwalberg, Bigaouette, Michalek, & Howard, 1991). Among all patients, there was no change in binge frequency or binge duration. Among the 22 bulimics who completed, naltrexone was associated with a significant reduction in binge duration (p = .02), but not binge frequency. In a study of 13 patients with BN receiving naltrexone up to 200 mg/day or placebo in individualized crossover 6-week trials, significant reductions in binges, purges, urges to binge, and urges to purge were seen with active drug (Marrazzi et al., 1995a). In a study of 41 women, intravenous administration of the opioid antagonist naloxone selectively suppressed the consumption of sweet high-fat foods in obese and lean subjects with BN (n = 20), but not in controls (n = 21; Drewnowski, Krahn, Demitrack, Nairn, & Gosnell, 1995).

Open studies suggest some BN patients, including those resistant to antidepressants and psychotherapy and those with type 1 diabetes, may respond when treated with doses of naltrexone up to 400 mg/day (Raingeard, Courtet, Renard, & Bringer, 2004). In a comparison of standard dose (50–100 mg/day) versus high-dose (200 to 300 mg/day) naltrexone in 16 patients with antidepressant-resistant BN,

participants in the standard-dose group had no significant change in frequency of binge eating or purging after 6 weeks of treatment, whereas participants in the high-dose group had significant reductions in both behaviors (Jonas & Gold, 1988).

Stimulants
In a double-blind, randomized, crossover trial, eight patients with BN were given methylamphetamine or placebo intravenously followed by a test meal and separated by a 1-week interval (Ong, Checkley, & Russell, 1983). Significantly fewer mean (SD) calories were consumed after methylamphetamine (224 ± 111) than after placebo (943 ± 222; p < .02). In addition, "the frequency of bulimia" was significantly lower after methylamphetamine (zero of eight patients) than after placebo (four of eight patients; p < .05). Importantly, case reports have described the successful use of methylphenidate in treating patients with BN, including those resistant to psychotherapy and antidepressants and those with comorbid cluster B personality and attention-deficit hyperactivity disorders (Drimmer, 2003; Dukarm, 2005; Schweickert, Strober, & Moskowitz, 1997; Sokol, Gray, Goldstein, & Kaye, 1999).

Mood Stabilizers
Observations of bipolar-like affective instability and two positive open-label trials of lithium in BN (Hsu 1984, 1987) prompted a placebo-controlled trial of lithium in 91 patients with BN (Hsu, Clement, Sandhouse, & Ju, 1991). Lithium (mean level, .62 mEq/L) was not superior to placebo in decreasing binge eating episodes, except possibly in depressed patients. Importantly, there were no serious adverse events.

Case reports have described the successful treatment with mood stabilizers of patients with BN and comorbid bipolar disorder (McElroy et al., 2005). Lithium was effective for eating and mood disorder symptoms in a woman with BN who became manic on imipramine (Shisslak, Perse, & Crago, 1991). In another report, one of two women with BN and rapid cycling bipolar disorder responded to lithium with imipramine; the other woman failed lithium alone (Leyba & Gold, 1988). In yet another report, two of three men with BN and bipolar (n = 2) or cyclothymic (n = 1) disorders responded to lithium alone (n = 1) or lithium plus imipramine (n = 1); one patient failed lithium alone (Pope, Hudson, & Jonas, 1986). Valproate was effective in three hospitalized young women with BN and comorbid rapid-cycling bipolar disorder who were previously inadequately unresponsive to lithium and antipsychotics (Herridge & Pope, 1985; Hudson & Pope, 1988; McElroy, Keck, & Pope, 1987). Two patients received valproate alone, and one received valproate in combination with lithium. All three patients showed marked improvement of both bulimic and mood symptoms. Finally, as noted earlier, carbamazepine was reported effective in a patient with BN and comorbid cyclothymic disorder (Hudson & Pope, 1988; Kaplan, 1987; Kaplan et al., 1983).

Antiobesity Agents

Fenfluramine and its isomer dexfenfluramine are efficacious weight loss drugs with strong pro-serotonergic properties. Serotonin's role in enhancing satiety and findings of central serotonergic abnormalities in BN (Kaye, 2008) led to three RCTs of fenfluramine in BN before the drug was removed from the worldwide market in 1997 because of concerns it caused cardiac valvular abnormalities (Colman, 2005; Gardin et al., 2000). In one study, fenfluramine was compared with desipramine in a 15-week randomized, placebo-controlled crossover trial in 22 outpatients with BN (Blouin et al., 1988). Both drugs reduced bingeing and vomiting frequency. A greater proportion of patients responded to fenfluramine than to desipramine. In the other study, 42 patients with BN were randomized to dexfenfluramine or placebo for 12 weeks (Russell, Checkley, Feldman, & Eisler, 1988). Dexfenfluramine was associated with significantly greater decreases in binge eating and self-induced vomiting, but not in measures of depressive symptoms. In the third trial, however, dexfenfluramine plus CBT was not superior to placebo plus CBT in reducing bulimic or depressive symptoms in 43 women with BN (Fahy, Eisler, & Russell, 1993).

No other RCTs of antiobesity agents in BN have been published. However, orlistat misuse by patients with BN has been reported (Fernández-Aranda et al., 2001; Malhotra & McElroy, 2002).

Antipsychotics

In contrast to AN, there are no published controlled studies of antipsychotics in BN. Second-generation antipsychotics have been reported to induce or exacerbate binge eating in patients with binge eating–related disorders, including BN (Brewerton & Shannon, 1992; Crockford et al., 1997; Gebhardt et al, 2007).

Light Therapy

Seasonal variation in binge eating behavior in persons with BN prompted two RCTs of light therapy, but results were mixed. In one study in 18 women with BN by DSM-III-R criteria, 2500 lux of bright light significantly improved depressed mood compared with <500 lux of dim light, but had no effect on the frequency, size, or content of binge-eating episodes (Blouin et al., 1996). In the other study, which used a counterbalanced, crossover design in 17 women with DSM-III-R BN, reductions in binge eating, purging, and depression were seen after 2 weeks of bright white light exposure (10,000 lux for 30 min/day), but not after 2 weeks of dim red light exposure (500 lux for 30 min/day; Lam, Goldner, Solyom, & Remick, 1994).

Other Treatments

In an open-label trial, the gaba-B agonist bacolofen, given at 60 mg/day for 10 weeks, reduced binge eating in two of three patients with BN (Broft et al., 2007). In addition, an open-label study of vagal nerve stimulation in 10 patients with chronic, unremitting BN showed good results, with 5 patients attaining remission (Faris et al., 2008).

By contrast, a randomized, placebo-controlled trial in 93 women with DSM-IV BN found no effect with spironolactone, a diuretic with mineralocorticoid and aldosterone antagonistic properties (von Wietersheim et al., 2008). A randomized, placebo-controlled study also found no effect for repetitive transcranial magnetic stimulation in 14 women with DSM-IV BN, but was limited by its small sample size (Walpoth et al., 2008).

Pharmacotherapy of Binge Eating Disorder

Randomized, placebo-controlled studies of BED have been conducted primarily with three drug classes: antidepressants, antiobesity agents, and AEDs (Appolinario & McElroy, 2004) (Table 24.3). In some studies, medication was used as monotherapy; in others it was used adjunctively with psychological interventions. To date, BED trials have been short term (6–16 weeks) and conducted in patients who were actively binge eating; no placebo-controlled maintenance monotherapy trial in a group of patients whose binge eating was in remission has yet been published. The primary outcome has usually been a measure of binge eating episode frequency or rate of remission or response of binge eating behavior. Secondary outcomes have included measures of ED pathology; mood, anxiety,

Table 24.3 Medications Studied for Binge Eating Disorder in Randomized, Placebo-Controlled Trials: Qualitative Results

Medication	Maximum Dosage Studied (mg/day)	Effect on Binge Reduction	Effect on Weight Loss
Tricyclic Antidepressants			
Desipramine	200	+++	−
Imipramine	200	+++	−
SSRI Antidepressants			
Citalopram	60	+++	+
Escitalopram	30	+	++
Fluoxetine	80	+++	+
Fluvoxamine	300	+++	+
Sertraline	200	+++	++
Antiobesity Agents			
Dexfenfluramine	30	+++	−
Orlistat	360	++	+++
Sibutramine	15	+++	+++
Antiepileptics			
Topiramate	400	+++	+++
Zonisamide	600	+++	+++
Other Agents			
Atomoxetine	120	+++	+++

SSRI = selective serotonin reuptake inhibitor; TCA = tricyclic antidepressant.

obsessive-compulsive, and impulsive symptoms; weight; global clinical improvement; metabolic parameters; and adherence.

Antidepressants

Several rationales led to studies of antidepressants in BED. First is that BED is related to BN, and antidepressants are efficacious in BN (Bacaltchuk & Hay 2003). Second is that, like BN, BED co-occurs with other disorders that are responsive to antidepressants, including major depressive disorder, panic disorder, generalized anxiety disorder, and obsessive–compulsive disorder (Hudson, Hiripi, Pope, & Kessler, 2007). Third is that, like BN, BED may also be associated with abnormalities in serotonin, which is targeted by several antidepressant classes (Monteleone, Tortorella, Castaldo, & Maj, 2006).

To date, at least 8 randomized, placebo-controlled studies of antidepressants have been published in patients with BED as defined by all of most of the *DSM-IV* criteria (Arnold et al., 2002; Grilo Masheb, & Wilson, 2005b; Guerdjikova et al., 2008; Hudson et al., 1998; Laederach-Hofmann et al., 1999; McElroy et al., 2000, 2003; Pearlstein et al., 2003). Six studies evaluated antidepressant monotherapy and two compared antidepressants in combination with weight loss therapy (Laederach-Hofmann et al., 1999) or CBT (Grillo et al., 2005). All studies were small, consisting of 15 to 85 patients, of short duration, ranging from 6 to 16 weeks, and associated with substantial dropout rates (7%–40%). Tricyclic doses were low compared to those used in depression; SSRI doses were higher, comparable to those used in BN. A study of fluoxetine used doses up to 80 mg/day (Arnold et al., 2002) and a study of escitalopram used supratherapeutic doses (up to 30 mg/day; Guerdjikova et al., 2008).

When viewed collectively, SSRIs led to greater rates of reduction in target binge eating, psychiatric, and weight symptoms than placebo, but were associated with substantial dropout rates (16%–57%; Brownley, Berkman, Sedway, Lohr, & Bulik, 2007). Also, most weight reductions would not be considered clinically significant. TCAs led to reductions in binge eating without weight loss.

A meta-analysis of seven of these studies (one with a TCA, six with SSRIs) showed significantly higher binge eating remission rates for the antidepressant group compared with the placebo group: 40.5% versus 22.2% (RR = 0.77 [95% CI = 0.65, 0.92; p = .003]) (Stefano, Bacaltchuk, Blay, & Appolinario, 2008). Evaluating studies that used the HAM-D to evaluate change in depressive symptoms, a statistically significant difference between groups was also seen favoring antidepressants (SMD = –0.38 [95% CI = –74, –0.03; p = 0.03]). However, no differences between groups were found in the mean frequency of binge-eating episodes at the end of treatment (SMD = –0.36 [95% CI = –0.74, 0.01; p = 0.06]), in BMI (SMD = 0.03 [95% CI = –0.49, 0.55]), or in treatment discontinuation for any reason (RR = 1.35 [95% CI = 0.61, 3.00]). In light of the frequent chronicity of BED, it was concluded that the data were not sufficient to formally recommend antidepressants as a single first-line therapy for short-term remission of binge eating episodes and weight reduction in BED patients.

Controlled combination therapy studies had contrasting results. In one, diet counseling with psychological support plus imipramine was superior to diet counseling and psychological support plus placebo for 8 weeks in decreasing binge eating (p < .01) and weight (p < .001; Laederach-Hofmann et al., 1999). In the other, a 16-week trial, CBT with placebo and CBT with fluoxetine were both superior to fluoxetine alone and placebo alone for decreasing binge eating (Grillo et al., 2005). There was no difference between fluoxetine and placebo. No treatment was effective for weight loss.

Open-label data has suggested some patients who initially respond with decreased binge eating and weight loss may maintain these beneficial effects for up to 6 months (Leombruni et al., 2006, 2008b). The only randomized, placebo-controlled maintenance trial of an antidepressant published in BED, however, suggested these results may not be maintained over longer periods of time. In that study, 116 BED patients who achieved a 75% or greater reduction in binge frequency after a 5-month initial phase of group behavioral weight control therapy received maintenance weight control treatment for up to 24 months. Patients were randomized twice: to fluoxetine or placebo, and to CBT or no CBT. Results showed fluoxetine appeared to be effective for depressive symptoms, but not for binge eating or weight reduction (Devlin et al., 2005; Devlin, Goldfein, Petkova, Liu, & Walsh, 2007).

Of note, several promising types of antidepressants have not yet been studied in BED in randomized, placebo-controlled trials. These include bupropion and SNRIs. A retrospective chart review, however, found that the SNRI venlafaxine was effective for reducing binge eating and body weight in 33 patients with BED and obesity (Malhotra, King, Welge, Brunsman-Lovins, & McElroy, 2002).

Antiobesity Agents

At least two rationales led to studies of several antiobesity agents in BED. First is that BED is associated with obesity and antiobesity agents cause weight loss. Second is that antiobesity agents may have anti-binge eating properties—either directly through appetite suppressant or satiety enhancing properties or indirectly through metabolic effects. The antiobesity agents studied thus far in BED in RCTs have been sibutramine, orlistat, and dexfenfluramine.

Three placebo-controlled studies, including one large multicenter trial, have shown that sibutramine, a reuptake inhibitor of NE, 5HT, and, to a lesser extent, DA (Padwal & Majumdar, 2007), reduces both binge eating and excessive body weight in BED. In the first study, 60 patients with DSM-IV BED and obesity were randomly assigned to sibutramine 15 mg/day (n = 30) or placebo (n = 30) for 12 weeks at two centers (Appolinario et al., 2003). The number of binge days was significantly reduced in the sibutramine group compared with the placebo group (p = .03). In addition, sibutramine was associated with a significant weight loss (–7.4 kg) compared with a small weight gain (1.4 kg) for placebo (p < .001), as well as significantly greater decreases in Binge Eating Scale (BES) and BDI scores. Seven (23%) sibutramine patients and 5 (17%) placebo patients did not complete the trial. Dry mouth and constipation were more common with sibutramine than placebo. In the second study, 20 women with BED by *DSM-IV* criteria were randomized to sibutramine 10 mg/day (n = 10) or placebo ($n = 10$) for 12 weeks (Milano et al., 2005). At study end, average (SD) binge frequency was significantly decreased among women receiving sibutramine (from 4.4 [1.0] days/week to 1.0 [1.0] day/week; $p < .001$) but unchanged among those receiving placebo (from 4.7 [1.3] days/week to 4.4 [0.5] days/week). Similarly, BES scale scores decreased significantly among sibutramine-treated patients but not those given placebo. The average (SD) weight loss among sibutramine recipients was 4.5 (2.1) kg compared with 0.6 (.05) kg among placebo recipients ($p < .001$). All 20 patients completed the trial. The most common adverse events with sibutramine were dry mouth and constipation.

The third study was a multisite trial in which 304 participants with DSM-IV BED were randomized to sibutramine (15 mg/day; $n = 152$) or placebo ($n = 152$) for 24 weeks. Compared with placebo-treated patients, sibutramine-treated patients had significantly greater reductions in weekly binge frequency (the primary outcome; sibutramine group mean = 2.7, placebo group mean = 2.0), binge days, weight, BMI, and measures of eating pathology assessed by the Three Factor Eating Questionnaire (TFEQ; cognitive restraint, disinhibition, and hunger). Sibutramine-treated patients also showed significantly greater global improvement and level of response, including remission of binge eating (59% for sibutramine versus 43% for placebo). Fifty (33%) sibutramine recipients and 65 (43%) placebo recipients did not complete the study. Ten sibutramine patients versus six placebo patients discontinued for adverse events. Headache, dry mouth, constipation, insomnia, and dizziness were significantly more common with sibutramine.

Two randomized, placebo-controlled studies have been conducted with orlistat, a gastrointestinal lipase inhibitor (Padwal & Majumdar, 2007). In one study, 50 patients with BED and obesity were randomized to 12 weeks of guided self help CBT (CBTgsh) with orlistat 120 mg three times daily or placebo (Grilo, Masheb, & Salent, et al., 2005a). Remission rates were significantly higher for orlistat plus CBTgsh (64% vs. 36%) at post-treatment but not at 3-month follow-up (52% in both groups). Rates for achieving at least 5% weight loss were significantly higher for orlistat plus CBTgsh than placebo + CBTgsh at both post-treatment (36% vs. 8%) and 3-month follow-up (32% vs. 8%).

In the other study, 89 patients with BED and obesity were randomized to orlistat 120 mg three times daily ($n = 44$) or placebo ($n = 45$), in combination with a mildly reduced calorie diet, for

24 weeks (Golay et al., 2005). At endpoint, the mean percentage weight loss (the primary outcome measure) for orlistat-treated patients was significantly greater than for placebo-treated patients (-7.4% vs. -2.3%; $p = .0001$). Waist circumference, hip circumference, total percentage body fat, total cholesterol level, diastolic blood pressure, and insulin level were also significantly improved with orlistat. Effectiveness of orlistat in binge eating per se was less clear. At 24 weeks, the mean number of binge eating episodes per week was numerically but not significantly decreased (1.0 for orlistat-treated patients vs. 1.7 for placebo-treated patients). Also, similar rates of patients in both groups who completed the study continued to suffer from BED (23% for orlistat vs. 29% for placebo). However, the Eating Disorder Inventory 12 score at week 24 was significantly lower for orlistat than placebo ($p = .011$). In addition, fat intake was significantly lower in orlistat-treated patients at week 12; total caloric intake was significantly lower at week 24. Eighteen patients discontinued the study prematurely, 5 (11%) in the orlistat group and 13 (29%) in the placebo group. No patient discontinued orlistat because of an adverse event. Data on side effects were otherwise not reported.

In the only RCT of dexfenfluramine, 28 women with BED and obesity received active drug, up to 30 mg/day, or placebo for 8 weeks (Stunkard, Berkowitz, Tanrikut, Reis, & Young, 1996). The rate of binge eating fell three times more rapidly in the dexfenfluramine group than the placebo group. However, no significant weight changes were observed. In addition, binge eating increased to pretreatment levels 4 months after discontinuation of dexfenfluramine.

Two open-label studies evaluated phentermine in combination with other treatments in patients with BED. In a 6-month of study of phentermine, 15 mg/day, plus fenfluramine, 60 mg/day, in 22 severe binge eaters, 17 moderate binge eaters, and 16 non-binge eaters, binge eating and BDI scores improved in all three groups (Alger, Malone, Cerulli, Fein, & Howard, 1999). In addition, 73% of the severe binge eaters, 59% of moderate binge eaters, and 69% of non-binge eaters experienced a greater than 10% weight loss. However, of 35 patients receiving echocardiograms, 20 had evidence of valvular insufficiency in one or more valves (Colman, 2005; Gardin et al., 2000). In the second study, phentermine, up to 30 mg/day, in combination with fluoxetine, up to 60 mg/day, and CBT was assessed in 16 obese women, 14 of whom met DSM-IV criteria for BED (Devlin, Goldfein, Carino, & Wolk, 2000). During the 20-week active treatment phase, mean weekly binge frequency declined by 95% from baseline, with 12 (75%) patients showing complete remission. In addition, mean body weight and BMI declined by 8.6% and 8.7%, respectively, from baseline. After 6 months of maintenance treatment, 10 patients were still taking both medications (two patients were taking fluoxetine alone), binge frequency was 63% lower than at the start of treatment, but only 5 (42%) of 12 patients were binge free. Only six patients completed 18 months of maintenance therapy, and only two were taking both medications; four were taking fluoxetine alone. Four of four BED patients were in remission from binge eating, but patients had regained most of the weight they had lost at the end of active treatment. On average, at the end of active treatment, these patients had regained most of the weight they had lost.

Antiepileptic Drugs

Several rationales, similar to those for BN, prompted studies of AEDs in BED. First, as noted earlier, is the phenomenological similarity between binge eating episodes and complex partial seizures. Second is the comorbidity between BED and a number of conditions that respond to AEDs, including mood, alcohol use, and borderline personality disorders (McElroy et al., 2008b). Third is that some AEDs are efficacious as weight loss agents in obesity (e.g., topiramate and zonisamide; Gadde, Franciscy, Wagner, & Krishnan, 2003; McElroy, Guerdjikova, Keck, Pope, & Hudson, 2008a). These observations led to four randomized, placebo-controlled studies of AEDs (three for topiramate and one for zonisamide) in *DSM-IV* defined BED and to two small crossover studies of phenytoin in the similar condition compulsive or binge eating (McElroy et al., 2009).

The three RCTs of topiramate, which include one large multicenter trial, have all shown that topiramate reduces binge eating and excessive body weight in BED. In the first study, 61 BED patients with obesity received topiramate (n = 30) or placebo (n = 31) for 14 weeks (McElroy et al., 2003). Topiramate was significantly superior to placebo in reducing binge frequency, as well as obsessive–compulsive features of binge eating symptoms as assessed with the Yale Brown Obsessive–Compulsive Scale Modified for Binge Eating (YBOCS-BE), global severity of illness, body weight, and BMI. Topiramate-treated patients experienced a 94%

reduction in binge frequency and a mean weight loss of 5.9 kg, whereas placebo-treated patients experienced a 46% reduction in binge frequency and a mean weight loss of 1.2 kg. Dropout rate, however, was high: 14 (47%) topiramate recipients and 12 (39%) placebo recipients failed to complete the trial. The most common side effects associated with topiramate were paresthesias, dry mouth, headache, and dyspepsia.

The second controlled study was a multicenter trial in which 407 patients with BED and ≥3 binge eating days/week, a BMI between 30 and 52 kg/m², and no current psychiatric disorders or substance abuse were randomized to receive topiramate or placebo for 16 weeks (McElroy et al., 2007b). Thirteen subjects failed to meet inclusion criteria, resulting in 195 topiramate and 199 placebo subjects who were evaluated for efficacy. Compared with placebo, topiramate significantly reduced binge eating days/week (-3.5 ± 1.9 vs. -2.5 ± 2.1), binge episodes/week ($- 5.0 \pm 4.3$ vs. -3.4 ± 3.8), weight (-4.5 ± 5.1 kg vs. 0.2 ± 3.2 kg), and BMI (-1.6 ± 1.8 kg/m² vs. 0.1 ± 1.2 kg/m²) (all p's < 0.001). Topiramate also significantly decreased obsession, compulsion, and total scores of the YBOCS-BE; overall, motor, and nonplanning impulsiveness scores of the Barratt Impulsiveness Scale, Version II; cognitive restraint, disinhibition, and hunger subscores of the TFEQ; and overall, social, and family life disability scores of the Sheehan Disability Scale. Significantly more topiramate-treated subjects (58%) achieved remission compared with placebo-treated subjects (29%; p < 0.001). Discontinuation rates were 30% in each group; adverse events were the most common reason for topiramate discontinuation (16%; placebo, 8%). Paresthesias, upper respiratory tract infection, somnolence, and nausea were the most frequent topiramate side effects.

The third controlled study of topiramate in BED was another multicenter trial in which 73 patients with BED and obesity were randomized to 19 sessions of CBT in conjunction with topiramate (n = 37) or placebo (n = 36) for 21 weeks (Claudino et al., 2007). Compared with patients receiving placebo, patients receiving topiramate showed a significantly greater rate of reduction in weight, the primary outcome measure, over the course of treatment (p < .001). Topiramate recipients also showed a significant weight loss (-6.8 kg) compared with placebo recipients (-0.9 kg). Rates of reduction of binge frequencies and BES and BDI scores did not differ between the groups, but a greater number of topiramate-treated patients (31/37) attained remission of binge eating as compared to placebo-treated patients (22/36; *p* = .03). There was no difference between groups in completion rates, though one topiramate recipient withdrew for an adverse effect. Paresthesias and taste perversion were more frequent with topiramate, whereas insomnia was more frequent with placebo.

In the fourth controlled study, 60 outpatients with *DSM-IV* BED and obesity received flexible dose (100–600 mg/day) zonisamide (*n* = 30) or placebo (*n* = 30) for 16 weeks (McElroy et al., 2006). Compared with placebo, zonisamide was associated with a significantly greater rate of reduction in binge-eating episode frequency (*p* = .021), body weight (*p* < .0001), BMI (*p* = .0001), and scores on the CGI-Severity (*p* < .0001), YBOCS-BE (*p* < .0001), and TFEQ disinhibition (*p* < .0001) scales. The mean (SD) zonisamide daily dose at endpoint evaluation was 436 (159) mg/day. Plasma ghrelin concentrations (which may be decreased in obesity and BED) increased with zonisamide but decreased with placebo (*p* = .0001). Attrition rate, however, was high, with 18 (60%) zonisamide patients and 12 (40%) placebo patients not completing the 12-week treatment period. Eight zonisamide recipients discontinued for adverse events. The most common reasons for stopping zonisamide were cognitive complaints (*n* = 2), psychological complaints (*n* = 2), and bone fracture (*n* = 2). The most common side effects associated with zonisamide were dry mouth, somnolence, headache, nausea, nervousness, and altered taste. This trial was consistent with an earlier open-label study in which zonisamide was associated with reduced binge eating and body weight but also with a high discontinuation rate (McElroy, Kotwal, Hudson, Nelson, & Keck, 2004a).

The two small placebo-controlled crossover trials of phenytoin in patients with compulsive or binge eating had contrasting results (Hudson & Pope, 1988). In the negative trial, four obese patients with compulsive eating showed no significant differences between phenytoin and placebo on any outcome measure and no patient had a marked response to phenytoin (Greenway, Dahms, & Bray, 1977). In the positive study, 19 of 20 women with "binge eating syndrome" completed 12 weeks wherein they received phenytoin and placebo for 6 weeks each in a counterbalanced design (Wermuth, Davis, Hollister, & Stunkard, 1977). Twelve patients had final serum phenytoin levels of 10 to 20 µg/ml; 5 had levels of 5 to 10 µg/ml. Patients given phenytoin first experienced a 37% decrease in binge frequency

(*p* < .01), but when administered placebo, they experienced no change in binge frequency. Patients given placebo first experienced no change in binge frequency, and they did experience a 39% decrease after switching to phenytoin (*p* < .01). Eight (42%) patients displayed a moderate or better response (≥50% reduction in binge episode frequency) on phenytoin, but only one patient experienced a remission of binge eating. When the two groups were compared, there were significantly fewer binges in the phenytoin–placebo group than in the placebo–phenytoin group (*p* < .02), indicating a carryover effect for the phenytoin-first sequence.

Although there are no controlled relapse prevention studies of AEDs in BED, an open-label extension trial has suggested that the anti-binge eating and weight loss effects of topiramate may be maintained long term. BED patients who completed the first RCT of topiramate (*n* = 35) were offered participation in a 42-week open-label extension study of the drug (McElroy et al., 2004b). Forty-four patients (31 who received topiramate in the open-label trial plus 13 who received topiramate in the double-blind study only) received at least one dose of topiramate; 43 patients provided outcome measures at a median final dose of 250 mg/day. Mean weekly binge frequency declined significantly from baseline to final visit for all 43 patients (–3.2; *p* < .001), for the 15 patients who received topiramate during the controlled and open-label studies (–4.0; *p* < .001), and for the 15 patients who received topiramate only during the open-label trial (–2.5; *p* = .044). Patients also exhibited a statistically significant reduction in body weight. However, only 10 (32%) of the 31 patients entering the extension trial completed the 42 weeks of open-label treatment; the most common reasons for topiramate discontinuation were protocol nonadherence (*n* = 11) and adverse events (*n* = 8).

There are also open-label descriptions of AEDs being helpful in difficult-to-treat patients with BED. Thus, topiramate has been reported to reduce binge eating and/or overweight in BED patients with treatment-resistant illness, comorbid depressive or bipolar disorders, traumatic brain injury, and those receiving the drug adjunctively with antidepressants and/or mood stabilizers (De Bernardi, Ferraris, D'Innella, Do, & Torre, 2005; Dolberg, Barkai, Gross, & Schreiber, 2005; Kotwal, Guerdjikova, McElroy, & Keck, 2006; Schmidt do Prado-Lima & Bacaltchuck 2002; Shapira, Goldsmith, & McElroy, 2000). Topiramate has also been successfully used to reduce binge eating and weight loss difficulties after adjustable gastric banding or gastric bypass surgery (Guerdjikova, Kotwal, & McElroy, 2005; Zilberstein et al., 2004).

By contrast, valproate has been reported to worsen binge eating and enhance weight gain in patients with BED and comorbid bipolar disorder (Shapira et al., 2000). In addition, a case series of 9 obese patients with BED treated with oxcarbazepine had inconsistent findings (Leombruni et al., 2008a). Four showed a decrease in binge eating and three lost weight. However, three reported no change in binge eating, 2 showed no weight change, and five gained weight. Five patients discontinued the drug and seven reported side effects. The authors noted that the drug appeared beneficial for patients with impulsive eating behaviors and depressive symptoms.

Norepinephrine Reuptake Inhibitors

In the only controlled study of an NRI in BED, 40 patients were randomized to receive atomoxetine, a highly selective NRI approved by the FDA for the treatment of attention-deficit/hyperactivity disorder, or placebo for 10 weeks at a single center (McElroy et al., 2007a). Atomoxetine was flexibly dosed from 40 to 120 mg/day; the mean (SD) dose at endpoint evaluation was 106 (21) mg/day. Compared with placebo-treated patients (n = 20), atomoxetine-treated patients (n = 20) showed a significantly greater rate of reduction in binge eating episode frequency (the primary outcome measure), as well as in binge day frequency, weight, BMI, and scores on the CGI-Severity scale, YBOCS-BE obsession subscale, and TFEQ hunger subscale. Fifteen patients (six receiving atomoxetine) did not complete the 10-week trial. The most common side effects associated with atomoxetine were dry mouth, nausea, nervousness, insomnia, headache, constipation, and sweating. Three atomoxetine recipients discontinued because of increased depressive symptoms, constipation, and nervousness (n = 1 each, respectively).

The only other selective NRI studied in BED has been reboxetine. In a 12-week open-label trial in nine patients, significant reductions were seen in binge eating frequency and BMI (Silveira, Zanatto, Appolinário, & Kapezinski, 2005).

Opiate Antagonists

The rationale for the use of opiate antagonists in the treatment of BED is similar to that for their use in BN; that is, like BN, BED resembles an addictive disorder, and medications that interfere with addiction may be effective in BED. In a RCT, 33 obese bingers and 22 normal weight bulimics were treated for 8 weeks with naltrexone, 100-150 mg/day, imipramine, or placebo (Alger, et al., 1991). Naltrexone did not significantly reduce binge duration or binge frequency in the obese bingers. However, two favorable case reports of naltrexone in BED have been published. One was a positive on-off-on case of naltrexone monotherapy using doses of 200 and 400 mg/day (Marrazzi et al., 1995b). The other was the successful augmentation of fluoxetine using naltrexone 100 mg/day (Neumeister, Winkler, & Wöber-Bingöl, 1999).

Stimulants

A double-blind, placebo-controlled crossover study in 32 patients with BED and 46 healthy age-matched controls showed that BED patients with at least one copy of the 9-repeat allele of the dopamine transporter showed significant appetite suppression in response to methylphenidate compared with controls with this allele or BED patients with the 10/10 genotype, whose methylphenidate response was indistinguishable from placebo (Davis et al., 2007). The authors hypothesized that a currently unknown genetic variant, which is overrepresented in BED, interacts with the DA transporter to suppress appetite in response to stimulant administration.

Antipsychotics

As with BN, there are no published controlled studies of antipsychotics in BED. Moreover, second-generation antipsychotics have been reported to induce or exacerbate binge eating, including BED, in patients receiving the drugs for psychotic disorders (Theisen et al., 2003).

Other Agents

The glutamate modulating agent memantine has been reported to reduce binge eating in BED in two open-label trials. In the first, five women with BED and obesity received memantine 10 mg in the morning and 10 to 20 mg in the late afternoon. As a group, they also lost weight; on average, 1.2 kg per week (Hermanussen & Tresguerres, 2005). In the second, 16 patients received a mean endpoint memantine dose of 18.3 mg/day. Although they did not lose weight as a group, weight loss was seen in the four patients who had a remission of binge eating (Brennan et al., 2008).

The gaba-B agonist baclofen, given at 60 mg/day for 10 weeks, has also been reported to reduce binge eating frequency in BED; however, two of the four women in the trial with BED gained weight at trial endpoint despite reporting reduced binge eating (Broft et al., 2007).

Pharmacotherapy of Night Eating Syndrome

In the only randomized, placebo-controlled pharmacotherapy study published to date in NES, 34 outpatients with NES were randomly assigned to receive sertraline (n = 17) or placebo (n = 17) for 8 weeks (O'Reardon et al., 2006). Sertraline was flexibly dosed at 50 to 200 mg/day. On the primary outcome measure, the CGI-Improvement scale (a clinician-administered measure of global symptomatic improvement), sertraline was significantly superior to placebo: 12 (71%) sertraline-treated patients were classified as responding (CGI-Improvement scale rating ≤2, indicating much or very much improved) compared with 3 (18%) placebo-treated patients. There was also significant improvement with sertraline in night eating symptoms, CGI Severity scale ratings, frequency of nocturnal ingestions and awakenings, caloric intake after the evening meal, and quality of life ratings. In addition, overweight and obese patients receiving sertraline (n = 14) lost a significant amount of weight by week 8 (mean = –2.9 kg) compared with overweight and obese patients receiving placebo (n = 14) (mean = –0.3 kg).

There are open-label reports of topiramate successfully reducing nighttime eating in patients with NES (Tucker, Masters, & Nawar, 2004; Winkelman, 2003). Improvements in weight and sleep were also described.

Pharmacotherapy of Sleep-Related Eating Disorder

A small placebo-controlled pilot study suggested beneficial results for the DA D_3-receptor agonist pramipexole in SRED (Provini et al., 2005). Eleven patients with SRED underwent actigraphic recording and subjective sleep diary evaluation for 1 week before and every week for 2 weeks of treatment with pramipexole 0.18 to 0.36 mg/day or placebo in a randomized, crossover trial. Pramipexole decreased median night-time activity (p = .02). However, the number and duration of wake episodes related to eating behavior was not significantly improved. The drug was well tolerated with no patients withdrawing from the study.

Clinical reports have suggested topiramate may decrease nocturnal eating episodes in SRED (Martinez-Salio, Soler-Algarra, Calvo-Garcia, &

Sanchez-Martin, 2007; Winkelman, 2003; Winkelman, 2006). One of these reports was a retrospective chart review of 30 patients with SRED receiving topiramate at a sleep disorders clinic (Winkelman, 2006). Of the 25 patients with at least one post-baseline follow-up appointment, 17 (68%) were considered topiramate responders, receiving a CGI-Improvement rating of "much" or "very much improved." Seven (28%) patients lost more than 10% of their baseline body weight. The mean dose of topiramate was 135 mg/d (range, 25–300 mg) over a mean period of 12 months (range, 1–42 months). Seven (41%) patients discontinued topiramate after a mean of 12 months.

There are also isolated reports of clonazepam, given as monotherapy and adjunctively with DA agonists, for SRED with mixed results (Schenck, Hurwitz, O'Connor, & Mahowald, 1993; Yeh & Schenck, 2007).

Conclusions

Research into the pharmacotherapeutic treatment of EDs has lagged behind that into most other serious mental disorders. Only one medication (fluoxetine) has regulatory approval for use in an ED (BN). No drug has been specifically developed to treat an ED. Many of the available pharmacotherapy studies in EDs are plagued by limitations, such as small sample size and inadequate power to detect effects, and unclear generalizability of findings to real world clinical situations. Moreover, some treatments may have been prematurely dismissed as ineffective or unsafe despite studies having these limitations (e.g., first generation antipsychotics and mood stabilizers in AN) (Gross et al., 1981; Vandereycken, 1984; Vandereycken & Pierloot, 1982).

Some preliminary conclusions and suggestions for the future can nonetheless be made. Regarding AN, neither tricyclics nor the SSRI fluoxetine appear to be effective in promoting weight gain when used adjunctively with hospital care (Claudino et al., 2006). In addition, one well designed study showed that fluoxetine does not appear to be effective in maintaining weight gain in weight-restored patients with AN when used in conjunction with CBT (Walsh et al., 2006). However, a smaller study showed fluoxetine might be helpful for weight maintenance in restricting AN when CBT is not a required treatment component (Kaye et al., 2001). Whether these findings can be generalized from tricyclics and SSRIs to antidepressants from other classes is presently unknown. Questions also remain as to the efficacy of antidepressants in weight restoration and weight maintenance in AN when used in combination with other classes of compounds (e.g., antipsychotics; see below); in AN with comorbid depressive, anxiety, or obsessive-compulsive disorders; and/or in treatment–refractory, intractable, or chronic AN.

By contrast, emerging placebo-controlled evidence shows olanzapine may be effective for weight restoration in AN, as well as some of the core and associated symptoms of AN (Bissada et al., 2008). Further controlled trials of olanzapine and other antipsychotics, both first and second generation, for weight restoration in AN are needed, as are RCTs of these agents for weight maintenance. Other compounds that hold promise for AN and need further study include cyproheptadine, recombinant human growth hormone (rhGH), prokinetics, zinc, and D-cycloserine.

In contrast with AN, substantial evidence indicates SSRIs and antidepressants from several other classes are efficacious for BN (Bacaltchuk & Hay, 2003). Indeed, although the therapeutic effects of antidepressants in general on binge eating and purging are moderate, RCTs have shown fluoxetine may be useful in the primary care setting, may be effective when psychotherapy is inadequate, and may work over the long term (Romano et al., 2002; Walsh et al., 1999; Walsh, Fairburn, Mickley, Sysko, & Parides, 2004). Other available treatments that show promise for BN and merit further study are the AED topiramate and the $5\text{-}HT_3$ antagonist ondansetron (Faris et al., 2000; Hedges et al., 2003; Nickel et al., 2005). Antiandrogen agents in women with hyperandrogenism and naltrexone, at doses higher than used for substance abuse, also warrant further evaluation.

Similar to BN, SSRIs and TCAs appear to have a modest beneficial effect on binge eating in BED (Stefano et al., 2008). They do not, however, appear to have clinically significant benefits on body weight and their long term effects are unknown. Also similar to BN, a considerable amount of double-blind, placebo-controlled data show that topiramate is effective for binge eating in BED with obesity; these data further show that topiramate is effective for weight loss in this patient population (McElroy et al., 2007b). One small open-label study suggests topiramate's anti-binge-eating and weight loss effects in BED may persist for up to one year, but that drug discontinuation rates are high, in part due to adverse events (McElroy et al., 2004). A comparable amount of controlled data show sibutramine is effective for reduction of binge eating and weight

loss in BED with obesity (Wilfley et al., 2008). Orlistat, when used in combination with CBT or dietary therapy, also leads to weight loss and possibly reduced binge eating (Golay et al.; Grillo et al., 2005). Other available compounds that show promise for BED and merit further evaluation are zonisamide, naltrexone (especially at higher doses than used for substance abuse), stimulants, and glutamate modulating agents (e.g., memantine).

Pharmacotherapy research into NES and SRED has been extremely limited. One small controlled study has provided support for sertraline in NES and for pramipexole in SRED. Open-label data suggests topiramate may be helpful for both conditions and merits further study.

Future Directions

Further pharmacotherapy research into AN, BN, BED, and other EDs is greatly needed at many levels. Randomized, placebo-controlled maintenance trials would be useful for olanzapine in AN, for topiramate in both BN and BED, for ondansetron in BN, and for sibutramine and orlistat in BED. RCTs in which a novel medication strategy (e.g., maintenance olanzapine treatment of AN or maintenance topiramate treatment of BN or BED) is combined with a specific psychological treatment would be useful. There have been no RCTs devoted to ED patients who have had partial or inadequate responses to pharmacotherapy or who have treatment-resistant illness (Walsh et al., 1997). As has been done in other major mental disorders, trials are needed which explore strategies where medications are optimized, switched, augmented, or combined (Berlim, Fleck, & Turecki, 2008; McGrath et al., 2006). For example, antipsychotics in combination with other promising agents, such as antidepressants, zinc, or rhGH, should be explored in randomized, placebo-controlled trials in treatment-resistant, intractable, or chronic AN. Similarly, studies of topiramate or ondansetron in combination with antidepressants would be important in patients with treatment-resistant or chronic forms of BN and BED. In addition, studies are needed in ED patients who have clinically important comorbidities, such as major depressive disorder, bipolar disorder, anxiety disorders, substance use disorders, borderline personality disorder, and diabetes (Woodside & Staab, 2006). For BED, further trials in patients with co-occurring obesity are needed.

Studies with new compounds are also greatly needed in AN, BN, and BED. Novel drugs in development for psychotic and bipolar disorders and diseases characterized by cachexia might be considered as potential candidates for study in the treatment of AN. The former includes agents targeting dopaminergic, serotoninergic, cholinergic, and/or glutamatergic systems (Gonzalez-Maeso et al., 2008; Jones & McCreary, 2008; Lieberman et al., 2008; Patil et al., 2007; Zarate & Manji, 2008b). The latter includes orexigenic compounds such as ghrelin-mimetic agents and melanocortin receptor antagonists (Strasser, 2007). Because hypercortisolemia usually accompanies AN, antiglucocorticoid agents might also represent potential therapeutic candidates (Klein et al., 2007; Zarate & Manji, 2008b).

Available drugs that may hold promise for BN and BED and merit evaluation in RCTs include the SNRIs desvenlafaxine, duloxetine, milnacipran, and venlafaxine; 5-HT$_3$ antagonists besides ondansetron; and memantine and other glutamate modulating agents such as riluzole (Chen et al., 2008; Haus et al., 2004; Zarate & Manji; 2008b). RCTs of atomoxetine and zonisamide in BN, and of new long-acting stimulant preparations, such as oros-methylphenidate and lisdexamfetamine, and the cannabinoid receptor antagonist rimonabant in BED would also be informative (Padwal & Majumdar, 2007; Price, 2006). (However, rimonabant, an anti-obesity agent, was not been approved by the FDA and was removed from the European market in 10/2008—in both cases because of psychiatric side effects [European Medicines Agency, 2008]). Randomized, placebo-controlled trials of topiramate are probably warranted for NES and SRED. Novel compounds that might hold promise for both BN and BED include some of those in development for mood disorders and obesity. Examples of such agents being developed for depression include serotonin-norepinephrine-dopamine (triple) reuptake inhibitors, serotonin-melatonin agents, and corticotropin-releasing hormone antagonists (Chen et al., 2008; Zarate &Manji, 2008a). Examples of such compounds being developed for obesity include triple reuptake inhibitors (e.g., tesofensine); selective 5-HT$_{2C}$ receptor agonists (e.g., lorcaserin); cannabinoid receptor antagonists beyond rimonabant; melanin-concentrating hormone receptor 1 antagonists; combination therapies (e.g., bupropion sustained release [SR] with naltrexone SR, bupropion with zonisamide, and topiramate with phentermine), and agents that target gut hormones that control appetite (Astrup et al., 2008; Field, Wren, Cooke, & Bloom, 2008; Fong, 2008; Heal, Smith, Fisas, Codony, & Buschmann, 2008; Kushner, 2008; Rivera et al., 2008). Drugs with potential for both depression and obesity (e.g., triple reuptake inhibitors) might be especially promising candidates for BED. Some of the many drugs in development for epilepsy might also be considered as potential therapeutic agents for EDs (Johannessen Landmark & Johannessen, 2008).

Pharmacotherapy research for EDs will need to be informed by advances in both clinical trial design and molecular genetics. Regarding the former, there is presently a lack of consensus about what constitutes ideal clinical trial design in ED pharmacotherapy research. This includes lack of agreement on assessment instruments; definitions of primary outcome and of response, remission, recovery, and relapse; stages of illness to be studied; metrics for reporting outcome; and how best to manage low completion rates (Brownley et al., 2007; Bulik et al., 2007; Halmi et al., 2005; Shapiro et al., 2007; Walsh et al., 2006). Regarding the latter, intensive research is needed to identify genes and endophenotypes that will predict response to treatment and facilitate novel drug discovery (Bulik 2007b; Ramoz et al., 2007).

Finally, for pharmacotherapy research in EDs to truly advance, it will need to be made a national priority. Such an advance will require collaborations among academia, the pharmaceutical industry, and governmental agencies. For example, one goal would be to form a network of sites devoted to conducting RCTs in EDs similar to the networks that have been successful in conducting RCTs in mood, psychotic, and substance use disorders (Anton et al., 2006; Lieberman et al., 2005; Rush et al., 2006; Sachs et al., 2007; Trivedi et al, 2006). Another goal would be to foster public-private partnership programs devoted to developing potential therapeutic compounds specifically targeting EDs, as has been done by the National Institute of Mental Health for mood, anxiety, and psychotic disorders (Brady, Winsky, Goodman, Oliveri, & Stover, 2008).

In sum, pharmacotherapy has an important role in the management of EDs, especially in patients resistant to psychotherapy, patients with comorbid serious mental or medical disorders, and those with chronic or intractable EDs. Further study is needed to clarify which specific agents might be most useful for which patient subgroups. However, the available pharmacotherapeutic armamentarium and its supporting evidence base for EDs is still far from adequate. Novel medical treatments for EDs are needed. In particular, rational drug discovery devoted to

EDs needs to occur. In the meantime, current and future medications with psychotropic benefits and/or effects on appetite and weight might be considered as potential therapeutic agents for these conditions.

References

Agras, W. S., Dorian, B., Kirkley, B. G., Arnow, B., & Bachman, J. (1987). Imipramine in the treatment of bulimia: A double-blind controlled study. *International Journal of Eating Disorders, 6,* 29–38.

Agras, W. S., Rossiter, E. M., Arnow, B., Schneider, J. A., Telch, C. F., Raeburn, S. D., et al. (1992). Pharmacologic and cognitive-behavioral treatment for bulimia nervosa: A controlled comparison. *American Journal of Psychiatry, 149,* 82–87.

Alger, S. A., Malone, M., Cerulli, J., Fein, S., & Howard L. (1999). Beneficial effects of pharmacotherapy on weight loss, depressive symptoms, and eating patterns in obese binge eaters and non-binge eaters. *Obesity Research, 7,* 469–476.

Alger, S. A., Schwalberg, M. D., Bigaouette, J. M., Michalek, A. V., & Howard, L. J. (1991). Effect of a tricyclic antidepressant and opiate antagonist on binge eating behavior in normo-weight bulimic and obese, binge-eating subjects. *American Journal of Clinical Nutrition, 53,* 865–871.

American Psychiatric Association. (2006). Treatment of patients with eating disorders. (3rd ed.). American Psychiatric Association. *American Journal of Psychiatry, 163,* (Supplement 7), 4–54.

Anton, R. F., O'Malley, S. S., Ciraulo, D. A., Cisler, R. A., Couper, D., Donovan, D. M., et al. (2006). Combined pharmacotherapies and behavioral interventions for alcohol dependence: The COMBINE study: A randomized controlled trial. *JAMA, 295,* 2003–2017.

Appolinario, J. C., Bacaltchuk, J., Sichieri, R., Claudino, A. M., Godoy-Matos, A., Morgan, C., et al. (2003). A randomized, double-blind, placebo-controlled study of sibutramine in the treatment of binge-eating disorder. *Archives of General Psychiatry, 60,* 1109–1116.

Aragona, M., (2007). Tolerability and efficacy of aripiprazole in a case of psychotic anorexia nervosa comorbid with epilepsy and chronic renal failure. *Eating and Weight Disorders, 12,* e54–e57.

Arnold, L. M., McElroy, S. L., Hudson, J. E., Welge, J. A., Bennett, A. J., & Keck, P. E. (2002). A placebo-controlled, randomized trial of fluoxetine in the treatment of binge-eating disorder. *Journal of Clinical Psychiatry, 63,* 1028–1033.

Astrup, A., Madsbad, S., Breum, L., Jensen, T. J., Kroustrup, J. P., & Larsen, T. M. (2008). Effect of tesofensine on body weight loss, body composition, and quality of life in obese patients: A randomized, double-blind, placebo-controlled trial. *Lancet,* [Epub ahead of print].

Attia, E., Haiman, C., Walsh, B. T., & Flater, S. R. (1998). Does fluoxetine augment the inpatient treatment of anorexia nervosa? *American Journal of Psychiatry, 155,* 548–551.

Bacaltchuk, J., & Hay, P. (2003). Antidepressants versus placebo for people with bulimia nervosa. *Cochrane Database of Systematic Reviews,* Issue 4, CD003391.

Bacaltchuk, J., Hay, P., & Trefiglio, R. (2001). Antidepressants versus psychological treatments and their combination for bulimia nervosa. *Cochrane Database of Systematic Reviews,* Issue 4, CD003385.

Barbarich, N. C., McConaha, C. W., Gaskill, J., La Via, M., Frank, G. K., Achenbach, S., et al. (2004a). An open trial of olanzapine in anorexia nervosa. *Journal of Clinical Psychiatry, 65,* 1480–1482.

Barbarich, N. C., McConaha, C. W., Halmi, K. A., Gendall, K., Sunday, S. R., Gaskill, J., et al. (2004b). Use of nutritional supplements to increase the efficacy of fluoxetine in the treatment of anorexia nervosa. *International Journal of Eating Disorders, 35,* 10–15.

Barbee, J. G. (2003). Topiramate in the treatment of severe bulimia nervosa with comorbid mood disorders: A case series. *International Journal of Eating Disorders, 33,* 456–472.

Barcai, A. (1977). Lithium in adult anorexia nervosa. A pilot report on two patients. *Acta Psychiatrica Scandinavica, 55,* 97–101.

Beaumont, P. J., Russell, J. D., Touyz, S. W., Buckley, C., Lowinger, K., Talbot, P., & Johnson, G. F. (1997). Intensive nutritional counselling in bulimia nervosa: A role for supplementation with fluoxetine? *The Australian and New Zealand Journal of Psychiatry, 31,* 514–524.

Bergman, L., & Eriksson, E. (1996). Marked symptom reduction in two women with bulimia nervosa treated with the testosterone receptor antagonist flutamide. *Acta Psychiatrica Scandinavica, 94,* 137–139.

Berkman, N. D., Bulik, C. M., Brownley, K. A., Lohr, K. N., Sedway, J. A., Rooks, A., et al. (2006). Management of eating disorders. *Evidence Report Technology Assessment, 135,* 1–166.

Berlim, M. T., Fleck, M. P., & Turecki, G. (2008). Current trends in the assessment and somatic treatment of resistant/refractory major depression: An overview. *Annals of Medicine, 40,* 149–159.

Biederman, J., Herzog, D. B., Rivinus, T. M., Harper, G. P., Ferber, R. A., Rosenbaum, J. F., et al. (1985). Amitriptyline in the treatment of anorexia nervosa: A double-blind, placebo-controlled study. *Journal of Clinical Psychopharmacology, 5,* 10–16.

Birmingham, C. L., Goldner, E. M., & Bakan, R. (1994). Controlled trial of zinc supplementation in anorexia nervosa. *International Journal of Eating Disorders, 15,* 251–255.

Birmingham, C. L., & Gritzner, S. (2006). How does zinc supplementation benefit anorexia nervosa? *Eating and Weight Disorders, 11,* 109–111.

Bissada, H., Tasca, G. A., Barber, A. M., & Bradwejn, J. (2008). Olanzapine in the treatment of low body weight and obsessive thinking in women with anorexia nervosa: A randomized, double-blind, placebo-controlled trial. *American Journal of Psychiatry,* June 16. [Epub ahead of print].

Biton, V. (2003). Effect of antiepileptic drugs on body weight: Overview and clinical implications for the treatment of epilepsy. *CNS Drugs, 17,* 781–791.

Biton, V. (2007). Clinical pharmacology and mechanism of action of zonisamide. *Clinical Neuropharmacology, 30,* 230–240.

Blouin, A. G., Blouin, J. H., Iversen, H., Carter, J., Goldstein, C., Goldfield, G., et al. (1996). Light therapy in bulimia nervosa: A double-blind, placebo-controlled study. *Psychiatry Research, 60,* 1–9.

Blouin, A. G., Blouin, J. H., Perez, E. L., Bushnik, T., Zuro, C., & Mulder, E. (1988). Treatment of bulimia with fenfluramine and desipramine. *Journal of Clinical Psychopharmacology, 8,* 261–269.

Bosanac, P., Kurlender, S., Norman, T., Hallum, K., Wesnes, K., Manktelow, T., et al. (2007). An open-label study of quetiapine in anorexia nervosa. *Human Psychopharmacology, 22,* 223–230.

Brady, L. S., Winsky, L., Goodman, W., Oliveri, M. E., & Stover, E. (2008). NIMH initiatives to facilitate collaborations among industry, academia, and government for the discovery and clinical testing of novel models and drugs for psychiatric disorders. *Neuropsychopharmacology*, [Epub ahead of print].

Brambilla, F., Bellodi, L., Arancio, C., Ronchi, P., & Limonta, D. (2001). Central dopaminergic function in anorexia and bulimia nervosa: A psychoneuroendocrine approach. *Psychoneuroendocrinology*, 26, 393–409.

Brambilla, F., Draisci, A., Peirone, A., & Brunetta, M. (1995a). Combined cognitive-behavioral, psychopharmacological and nutritional therapy in eating disorders. 2. Anorexia nervosa-binge-eating/purging type. *Neuropsychobiology*, 32, 64–7.

Brambilla, F., Draisci, A., Peirone, A., & Brunetta, M. (1995b). Combined cognitive-behavioral, psychopharmacological and nutritional therapy in eating disorders. 1. Anorexia nervosa-restricted type. *Neuropsychobiology*, 32, 59–63.

Brambilla, F., Garcia, C. S., Fassino, S., Daga, G. A., Favara, A., Santonastaso, P., et al. (2007a). Olanzapine therapy in anorexia nervosa: Psychobiological effects. *International Clinical Psychopharmacology*, 22, 197–204.

Brambilla, F., Monteleone, P., & Maj, M. (2007b). Olanzapine-induced weight gain in anorexia nervosa: Involvement of leptin and ghrelin secretion? *Psychoneuroendocrinology*, 32, 402–406.

Brennan, B. P., Roberts, J. I., Fogarty, K. V., Reynolds, K. A., Jonas, J. M., & Hudson, J. I. (2008). Memantine in the treatment of binge eating disorder: An open-label, prospective trial. *International Journal of Eating Disorders*, 41, 520–526.

Brewerton, T. D., & George, M. S. (1993). Is migraine related to the eating disorders? *International Journal of Eating Disorders*, 14, 75–79.

Brewerton, T. D., & Shannon, M. (1992). Possible clozapine exacerbation of bulimia nervosa. *American Journal of Psychiatry*, 149, 1408–1409.

Brill, J., Lee, M., Zhao, S., Fernald, R. D., & Huguenard, J. R. (2006). Chronic valproic acid treatment triggers increased neuropeptide Y expression and signaling in rat nucleus reticularis thalami. *Journal of Neuroscience*, 26, 6813–6822.

Broft, A. I., Spanos, A., Corwin, R. L., Mayer, L., Steinglass, J., Devlin, M. J., et al. (2007). Baclofen for binge eating: An open-label trial. *International Journal of Eating Disorders*, 40, 687–691.

Brownley, K. A., Berkman, N. D., Sedway, J. A., Lohr, K. N., & Bulik, C. M. (2007). Binge eating disorder treatment: A systematic review of randomized controlled trials. *International Journal of Eating Disorders*, 40, 337–348.

Bulik, C. M., Berkman, N. D., Brownley, K. A., Sedway, J. A., & Lohr, K. N. (2007a). Anorexia nervosa treatment: A systematic review of randomized controlled trials. *International Journal of Eating Disorders*, 40, 310–320.

Bulik, C. M., Hebebrand, J., Keski-Rahkonen, A., Klump, K. L., Reichborn-Kjennerud, T., Mazzeo, S. E., et al. (2007b). Genetic epidemiology, endophenotypes, and eating disorder classification. *International Journal of Eating Disorders*, 40, Suppl., S52–60.

Bulik, C. M., Slof-Op't Landt, M. C., van Furth, E. F., & Sullivan, P. F. (2007c). The genetics of anorexia nervosa. *Annual Review of Nutrition*, 27, 263–275.

Carruba, M. O., Cuzzolaro, M., Riva, L., Bosello, O., Liberti, S., Castra, R., et al. (2001). Efficacy and tolerability of moclobemide in bulimia nervosa: A placebo-controlled trial. *International Journal of Psychopharmacology*, 16, 27–32.

Casper, R. C., Schlemmer, R. F., & Javaid, J. I. (1987). A placebo-controlled crossover study of oral clonidine in acute anorexia nervosa. *Psychiatry Research*, 20, 249–260.

Cassano, G. B., Miniati, M., Pini, S., Rotondo, A., Banti, S., Borri, C., et al. (2003). Six-month open trial of haloperidol as an adjunctive treatment for anorexia nervosa: A preliminary report. *International Journal of Eating Disorders*, 33, 172–177.

Castiho, S. M., Costa, L. H. (2003). Reboxetine in the treatment of bulimia nervosa. *Rev Bras Psiquiatr*, 25, 100–2.

Chen, Z., Yang, J., & Tobak, A. (2008). Designing new treatments for depression and anxiety. *IDrugs: The Investigational Drugs Journal*, 11, 189–197.

Chu, L. W., Lam, K. S., Tam, S. C., Hu, W. J., Hui, S. L., Chiu, A., Chiu, K. C., & Ng, P. (2001). A randomized controlled trial of low-dose recombinant human growth hormone in the treatment of malnourished elderly medical patients. *Journal of Clinical Endocrinology and Metabolism*, 86, 1913–1920.

Chung, A. M., & Reed, M. D. (2004). Intentional topiramate ingestion in an adolescent female. *Annals of Pharmacotherapy*, 38, 1439–1442.

Claudino, A. M., de Oliveira, I. R., Appolinario, J. C., Cordás, T. A., Duchesne, M., Sichiere, R., et al. (2007). Double-blind, randomized, placebo-controlled trial of topiramate plus cognitive-behavior therapy in binge-eating disorder. *Journal of Clinical Psychiatry*, 68, 1324–1332.

Claudino, A. M., Hay, P., Lima, M. S., Bacaltchuk, J., Schmidt, U., & Treasure, J. (2006). Antidepressants for anorexia nervosa. *Cochrane Database Systematic Reviews*, Issue 1, CD004365.

Clifton, P. G., & Kennett, G. A. (2006). Monoamine receptors in the regulation of feeding behaviour and energy balance. *CNS & Neurological Disorders - Drug Targets*, 5, 293–312.

Colman, E. (2005). Anorectics on trial: A half century of federal regulation of prescription appetite suppressants. *Annals of Internal Medicine*, 143, 380–385.

Collaborative Study Group (1992). Fluoxetine in the treatment of bulimia nervosa: a multicenter, placebo-controlled, double blind trial. *Archives of General Psychiatry*, 49, 139–147.

Colom, F., Vieta, E., Benabarre, A., Martinez-Arán, A., Reinares, M., Corbella, B., et al. (2001). Topiramate abuse in a bipolar patient with an eating disorder. *Journal of Clinical Psychiatry*, 62, 475–476.

Cotrufo, P., Monteleone, P., d'Istria, M., Fuschino, A., Serino, I., & Maj, M. (2000). Aggressive behavioral characteristics and endogenous hormones in women with bulimia nervosa. *Neuropsychobiology*, 42, 58–61.

Crisp, A. H., Lacey, J. H., & Crutchfield, M. (1987). Clomipramine and "drive" in people with anorexia nervosa: An inpatient study. *British Journal of Psychiatry*, 150, 355–358.

Crockford, D. N., Fisher, G., & Barker, P. (1997). Risperidone, weight gain, and bulimia nervosa. *Canadian Journal of Psychiatry*, 42, 326–327.

Dally, P. J., & Sargant, W. (1960). A new treatment of anorexia nervosa. *British Medical Journal*, 1, 1770–1773.

Davis, C., Levitan, R. D., Kaplan, A. S., Carter, J., Reid, C., Curtis, C., et al. (2007). Dopamine transporter gene (*DAT1*) associated with appetite suppression to methylphenidate in a case-control study of binge eating disorder. *Neuropsychopharmacology*, 32, 2199–2206.

De Bernardi, C., Ferraris, S., D'Innella, P., Do, F., & Torre, E. (2005). Topiramate for binge eating disorder. *Progress in Neuro-Psychopharmacology & Biological Psychiatry*, 29, 339–341.

Devlin, J. J., Goldfein, J. A., Carino, J. S., & Wolk, S. L. (2000). Open treatment of overweight binge eaters with phentermine and fluoxetine as an adjunct to cognitive-behavioral therapy. *International Journal of Eating Disorders*, 28, 325–332.

Devlin, M. J., Goldfein, J. A., Petkova, E., Jiang, H., Raizman, P. S., Wolk, S., et al. (2005). Cognitive behavioral therapy and fluoxetine as adjuncts to group behavioral therapy for binge eating disorder. *Obesity Research*, 13, 1077–1088.

Devlin, M. J., Goldfein, J. A., Petkova, E., Liu, L., & Walsh, B. T. (2007). Cognitive behavioral therapy and fluoxetine for binge eating disorder: two-year follow-up. *Obesity (Silver Spring)*, 15, 1702–1709.

Dolberg, O. T., Barkai, G., Gross, Y., & Schreiber, S. (2005). Differential effects of topiramate in patients with traumatic brain injury and obesity—a case series. *Psychopharmacology (Berl.)*, 179, 838–845.

Drewnowski, A., Krahn, D. D., Demitrack, M. A., Nairn, K., & Gosnell, B. A. (1995). Naloxone, an opiate blocker, reduces the consumption of sweet high-fat foods in obese and lean female binge eaters. *American Journal of Clinical Nutrition*, 61, 1206–1212.

Drimmer, E. J. (2003). Stimulant treatment of bulimia nervosa with and without attention-deficit disorder: Three case reports. *Nutrition*, 19, 76–77.

Dukarm, C. P. (2005). Bulimia nervosa and attention deficit hyperactivity disorder: A possible role for stimulant medication. *Journal of Women's Health*, 14, 345–350.

Dunican, K. C., & DelBotto, D. (2007). The role of olanzapine in the treatment of anorexia nervosa. *Annals of Pharmacotherapy*, 41, 111–115.

Edler, C., Lipson, S. F., & Keel, P. K. (2007). Ovarian hormones and binge eating in bulimia nervosa. *Psychological Medicine*, 37, 131–141.

El-Giamal, N., deZwaan, M., Bailer, U., Strnad, A., Schüssler, P., & Kasper, S. (2003). Milnacipran in the treatment of bulimia nervosa: A report of 16 cases. *European Neuropsychopharmacology*, 123, 73–79.

European Medicines Agency. (2008). The European Medicines Agency recommends suspension of the marketing authorisation of Acomplia. London, 23 October 2008, http://www.emea.europa.eu, accessed 10/31/08.

Fahy, T. A., Eisler, I., & Russell, G. F. (1993). A placebo-controlled trial of d-fenfluramine in bulimia nervosa. *British Journal of Psychiatry*, 162, 597–603.

Faris, P. L., Hofbauer, R. D., Daughters, R., Vandenlangenberg, E., Iversen, L., Goodale, R. L., et al. (2008). De-stabilization of the positive vago-vagal reflex in bulimia nervosa. *Physiology and Behavior*, 94, 136–153.

Faris, P. L., Kim, S. W., Meller, W. H., Goodale, R. L., Oakman, S. A., Hofbauer, R. D., et al. (2000). Effect of decreasing afferent vagal activity with ondansetron on symptoms of bulimia nervosa: A randomized, double-blind trial. *Lancet*, 35, 792–797.

Fassino, S., Daga, G. A., Boggio, S., Garzaro, L., Piero, A. (2004). Use of reboxetine in bulimia nervosa: a pilot study. *J Psychopharmacol*, 18, 423–8.

Felstrom, A., & Blackshaw, S. (2002). Topiramate for bulimia nervosa with bipolar II disorders. *American Journal of Psychiatry*, 159, 1246–1247.

Ferguson, J. M. (1993). The use of electroconvulsive therapy in patients with intractable anorexia nervosa. *International Journal of Eating Disorders*, 13, 195–201.

Fernández-Aranda, F., Amor, A., Jiménez-Murcia, S., Giménez-Martínez, L., Turón-Gil, V., & Vallejo-Ruiloba, J. (2001). Bulimia nervosa and misuse of orlistat: two case reports. *International Journal of Eating Disorders*, 30, 458–461.

Fichter, M. M., Krüger, R., Rief, W., Holland, R., & Döhne, J. (1996). Fluvoxamine in prevention of relapse in bulimia nervosa: Effects on eating-specific psychopathology. *Pharmacopsychiatry*, 30, 85–92.

Fichter, M. M., Leibl, K., Rief, W., Brunner, E., Schmidt-Auberger, S., & Engel, R. R. (1991). Fluoxetine versus placebo: A double-blind study with bulimic inpatients undergoing intensive psychotherapy. *Pharmacopsychiatry*, 24, 1–7.

Field, B. C., Wren, A. M., Cooke, D., & Bloom, S. R. (2008). Gut hormones as potential new targets for appetite regulation and the treatment of obesity. *Drugs*, 68, 147–163.

Fisman, S., Steele, M., Short, J., Byrne, T., & Lavallee, C. (1996). Case study: Anorexia nervosa and autistic disorder in an adolescent girl. *Journal of the American Academy of Child and Adolescent Psychiatry*, 35, 937–940.

Fluoxetine Bulimia Nervosa Collaborative Study Group (FBNCSG). (1992). Fluoxetine in the treatment of bulimia nervosa. A multicenter, placebo-controlled, double-blind trial. *Archives of General Psychiatry*, 49, 139–147.

Fong, T. M. (2008). Development of anti-obesity agents: drugs that target neuropeptide and neurotransmitter systems. *Expert Opinion on Investigational Drugs*, 17, 321–325.

Fountoulakis, K. N., Iacovides, A., Siamouli, M., Koumaris, V., & Kaprinis, G. S. (2006). Successful treatment of anorexia with a combination of high-dose olanzapine, fluoxetine, and mirtazapine. *International Journal of Clinical Pharmacology Therapy*, 44, 452–453.

Gadde, K. M., Franciscy, D. M., Wagner, H. R., 2nd, & Krishnan, K. R. (2003). Zonisamide for weight loss in obese adults: A randomized controlled trial. *JAMA*, 289, 1820–1825.

Gao, Q., & Horvath, T. L. (2008). Neuronal control of energy homeostasis. *FEBS Letters*, 582, 132–141.

Gardin, J. M., Schumacher, D., Constantine, G., Davis, K. D., Leung, C., & Reid, C. L. (2000). Valvular abnormalities and cardiovascular status following exposure to dexfenfluramine or phentermine/fenfluramine. *JAMA*, 283, 1703–1709.

Gebhardt, S., Haberhausen, M., Krieg, J. C., Remschmidt, H., Heinzel-Gutenbrunner, M., Hebebrand, J., et al. (2007). Clozapine/olanzapine-induced recurrence or deterioration of binge eating-related eating disorders. *Journal of Neural Transmission*, 114, 1091–1095.

Gelato, M., McNurlan, M., & Freedland, E. (2007). Role of recombinant human growth hormone in HIV-associated wasting and cachexia: pathophysiology and rationale for treatment. Clin Ther, 29, 2269–88.

Golay, A., Laurent-Jaccard, A., Habicht, F., Gachoud, J. P., Chabloz, M., Kammer, A., et al. (2005). Effect of orlistat in obese patients with binge eating disorder. *Obesity Research*, 13, 1701–1708.

Goldberg, S. C., Halmi, K. A., Eckert, E. D., Casper, R. C., & Davis, J. M. (1979). Cyproheptadine in anorexia nervosa. *British Journal of Psychiatry*, 134, 67–70.

Goldbloom, D. S., Olmsted, M., Davis, R., Clewes, J., Heinmaa, M., Rockert, W., et al. (1997). A randomized controlled trial of fluoxetine and cognitive behavioral therapy for bulimia nervosa: Short-term outcome. *Behavioral Research and Therapy*, 35, 803–811.

González-Maeso, J., Ang, R. L., Yuen, T., Chan, P., Weisstaub, N. V., López-Giménez, J. F., et al. (2008). Identification of a serotonin/glutamate receptor complex implicated in psychosis. *Nature, 452,* 93–97.

Goudie, A. J., Cooper, G. D., Cole, J. C., & Sumnall, H. R. (2007). Cyproheptadine resembles clozapine in vivo following both acute and chronic administration in rats. *Journal of Psychopharmacology, 21,* 179–190.

Greenway, F. L., Dahms, W. T., & Bray, G. A. (1977). Phenytoin as a treatment of obesity associated with compulsive eating. *Current Therapeutic Research, 21,* 338–342.

Grigoriadis, S., Kaplan, A., Carter, J., & Woodside, B. (2001). What treatments patients seek after inpatient care: A follow-up of 24 patients with anorexia nervosa. *Eating and Weight Disorders, 6,* 115–120.

Grilo, C. M., Masheb, R. M., & Salant, S. L. (2005a). Cognitive behavioral therapy guided self-help and orlistat for the treatment of binge eating disorder: A randomized, double-blind, placebo-controlled trial. *Biological Psychiatry, 57,* 1193–1201.

Grilo, C. M., Masheb, R. M., & Wilson, G. T. (2005b). Efficacy of cognitive behavioral therapy and fluoxetine for the treatment of binge eating disorder: A randomized double-blind placebo-controlled comparison. *Biological Psychiatry, 57,* 301–309.

Gross, H., Ebert, M. H., Faden, V. B., Goldberg, S. C., Kaye, W. H., Caine, E. D., et al. (1983). A double-blind trial of delta 9-tetrahydrocannabinol in primary anorexia nervosa. *Journal of Clinical Psychopharmacology, 3,* 165–171.

Gross, H. A., Ebert, M. H., Faden, V. B., Goldberg, S. C., Nee, L. E., & Kaye, W. H. (1981). A double-blind controlled study of lithium carbonate in primary anorexia nervosa. *Journal of Clinical Psychopharmacology, 1,* 376–381.

Guerdjikova, A. I., Kotwal, R., & McElroy, S. L. (2005). Response of recurrent binge eating and weight gain to topiramate in patients with binge eating disorder after bariatric surgery. *Obesity Surgery, 15,* 273–277.

Guerdjikova, A. I., McElroy, S. L., Kotwal, R., Welge, J. A., Nelson, E., Lake, K., et al. (2008). High-dose escitalopram in the treatment of binge-eating disorder with obesity: A placebo-controlled monotherapy trial. *Human Psychopharmacology, 23,* 1–11.

Guille, C., & Sachs, G. (2002). Clinical outcome of adjunctive topiramate treatment in a sample of refractory bipolar patients with comorbid conditions. *Progress in Neuro-Psychopharmacology and Biological Psychiatry, 26,* 1035–1039.

Halmi, K. A., Agras, W. S., Crow, S., Mitchell, J., Wilson, G. T., Bryson, S. W., et al. (2005). Predictors of treatment acceptance and completion in anorexia nervosa: implications for future study designs. *Archives of General Psychiatry, 62,* 776–781.

Halmi, K. A., Eckert, E., LaDu, T. J., & Cohen, J. (1986). Anorexia nervosa: Treatment efficacy of cyproheptadine and amitriptyline. *Archives of General Psychiatry, 43,* 177–181.

Haus, U., Späth, M., & Färber, L. (2004). Spectrum of use and tolerability of 5-HT3 receptor antagonists. *Scandinavian Journal of Rheumatology* (Supplement), *119,* 2–8.

Hazen, E., & Fava, M. (2006). Successful treatment with duloxetine in a case of treatment refractory bulimia nervosa: A case report. *Journal of Psychopharmacology, 20,* 723–724.

Heal, D. J., Smith, S. L., Fisas, A., Codony, X., & Buschmann, H. (2008). Selective 5-HT6 receptor ligands: Progress in the development of a novel pharmacological approach to the treatment of obesity and related metabolic disorders. *Pharmacology & Therapeutics, 117,* 207–231.

Hedges, D. W., Reimherr, F. W., Hoopes, S. P., Rosenthal, N. R., Kamin, R., & Capace, J. A. (2003). Treatment of bulimia nervosa with topiramate in a randomized, double-blind, placebo-controlled trial, part 2: improvement in psychiatric measures. *Journal of Clinical Psychiatry, 64,* 1449–1454.

Hermanussen, M., & Tresguerres, J. A. (2005). A new anti-obesity drug treatment: first clinical evidence that, antagonizing glutamate-gated Ca2+ ion channels with memantine normalizes binge-eating disorders. *Economics & Human Biology, 3,* 329–337.

Herridge, P. L., & Pope, H. G., Jr. (1985). Treatment of bulimia and rapid-cycling bipolar disorder with sodium valproate: A case report. *Journal of Clinical Psychopharmacology, 5,* 229–230.

Hill, K., Bucuvalas, J., McClain, C., Kryscio, R., Martini, R.T., Alfaro, M. P., et al. (2000). Pilot study of growth hormone administration during the refeeding of malnourished anorexia nervosa patients. *Journal of Child and Adolescent Psychopharmacology, 10,* 3–8.

Hill, R., Haslett, C., & Kumar, S. (2001). Anorexia nervosa in an elderly woman. *Australian and New Zealand Journal of Psychiatry, 35,* 246–248.

Hofmann, S. G., Meuret, A. E., Smits, J. A., Simon, N. M., Pollack, M. H., Eisenmenger, K., et al. (2006). Augmentation of exposure therapy with D-cycloserine for social anxiety disorder. *Archives of General Psychiatry, 63,* 298–304.

Hoopes, S. P., Reimherr, F. W., Hedges, D. W., Rosenthal, N. R., Kamin, R., Karim, R., et al. (2003). Treatment of bulimia nervosa with topiramate in a randomized, double-blind, placebo-controlled trial, part 1: Improvement in binge and purge measures. *Journal of Clinical Psychiatry, 64,* 1335–1341.

Horne, R. L., Ferguson, J. M., Pope, H. G., Jr, Hudson, J. I., Lineberry, C. G., Ascher, J., et al. (1988). Treatment of bulimia with bupropion: A multicenter controlled trial. *Journal of Clinical Psychiatry, 49,* 262–266.

Hrdlicka, M., Beranova, I., Zamecnikova, R., & Urbanek, T. (2008). Mirtazapine in the treatment of adolescent anorexia nervosa. Case-control study. *European Child and Adolescent Psychiatry, 17,* 187–189.

Hsu, L. K. (1984). Treatment of bulimia with lithium. *American Journal of Psychiatry, 141,* 1260–1262.

Hsu, L. K. (1987). Lithium in the treatment of eating disorders. In P. E. Garfinkel & D. M. Garner (Eds.), *The role of drug treatments for eating disorders* (pp. 90–95). New York: Brunner/Mazel.

Hsu, L. K., Clement, L., Sandhouse, R., & Ju, E. S. (1991). Treatment of bulimia nervosa with lithium carbonate. A controlled study. *Journal of Mental and Nervous Disease, 179,* 351–355.

Hudson, J. I., Hiripi, E., Pope, H. G., Jr., & Kessler, R. C. (2007). The prevalence and correlates of eating disorders in the National Comorbidity Survey Replication. *Biological Psychiatry, 61,* 348–358.

Hudson, J. I., Mangweth, B., Pope, H. G., Jr., DeCol, C., Hausmann, A., Gutweniger, S., et al. (2003). Family study of affective spectrum disorder. *Archives of General Psychiatry, 60,* 170–177.

Hudson, J. I., McElroy, S. L., Raymond, N. C., Crow, S., Keck, P. E., Jr., Carter, W. P., et al. (1998). Fluvoxamine in the treatment of binge-eating disorder: A multicenter placebo-controlled, double-blind trial. *American Journal of Psychiatry, 155,* 1756–1762.

Hudson, J. I., Pope, H. G., Jr., Jonas, J. M., & Yurgelun-Todd, D. (1985). Treatment of anorexia nervosa with antidepressants. *Journal of Clinical Psychopharmacology, 5,* 17–23.

Hudson, J. I., & Pope, H. G., Jr. (1988). The role of anticonvulsants in the treatment of bulimia. In S. L. McElroy, & H. G. Pope, Jr., (Eds.), *Use of anticonvulsants in psychiatry* (pp 141–153). Clifton, NJ: Oxford Health Care.

Husum, H., Van Kammen, D., Termeer, E., Bolwig, G., & Mathé, A. (2003). Topiramate normalizes hippocampal NPY-LI in flinders sensitive line 'depressed' rats and upregulates NPY, galanin, and CRH-LI in the hypothalamus: Implications for mood-stabilizing and weight loss-inducing effects. *Neuropsychopharmacology, 28,* 1292–1299.

Jaafar, N. R., Daud, T. I., Rahman, F. N., & Baharudin, A. (2007). Mirtazapine for anorexia nervosa with depression. *Australia and New Zealand Journal of Psychiatry, 41,* 768–769.

Johannessen Landmark, C., & Johannessen, S. I. (2008). Pharmacological management of epilepsy: Recent advances and future prospects. *Drugs, 68,* 1925–1939.

Johnson, B. A., Rosenthal, N., Capece, J., Wiegard, F., Mao, L., Beyers, K., et al. (2007). Topiramate for treating alcohol dependence: A randomized controlled trial. *JAMA, 298,* 1641–1651.

Jonas, J. M., & Gold, M. S. (1988). The use of opiate antagonists in treating bulimia: A study of low dose versus high dose naltrexone. *Psychiatry Research, 24,* 195–199.

Jones, C. A., McCreary, A. C. (2008). Serotonergic approaches in the development of novel antipsychotics. *Neuropharmacology,* [Epub ahead of print].

Kaplan, A. S. (1987). Anticonvulsant treatment of eating disorders. In P. E. Garfinkel & D. M. Garner (Eds.), *The role of drug treatments for eating disorders* (pp. 96–123). New York: Brunner/Mazel.

Kaplan, A. S., Garfinkel, P. E., Darby, P. L., & Garner, D. M. (1983). Carbamazepine in the treatment of bulimia. *American Journal of Psychiatry, 140,* 1225–1226.

Katz, R. L., Keen, C. L., Litt, I. F., Hurley, L. S., Kellams-Harrison, K. M., & Glader, L. J. (1987). Zinc deficiency in anorexia nervosa. *Journal of Adolescent Health Care, 8,* 400–406.

Kaye, W. (2008). Neurobiology of anorexia and bulimia nervosa. *Physiology & Behavior, 94,* 121–135.

Kaye, W. H., Nagata, T., Weltzin, T. E., Hsu, L. K., Sokol, M. S., McConaha, C., et al., (2001). Double-blind placebo-controlled administration of fluoxetine in restricting and restricting-purging-type anorexia nervosa. *Biological Psychiatry, 49,* 644–652.

Kaye, W. H., Weltzin, T. E., Hsu, L. K., & Bulik, C. M. (1991). An open trial of fluoxetine in patients with anorexia nervosa. *Journal of Clinical Psychiatry, 52,* 464–471.

Kennedy, S. H., Piran, N., Warsh, J. J., Prendergast, P., Mainprize, E., Whynot, C., et al. (1988). A trial of isocarboxazid in the treatment of bulimia nervosa. *Journal of Clinical Psychopharmacology, 8,* 391–396.

Kennedy, S. H., Goldbloom, D. S., Ralevski, E., Davis, C., Disouza, J. D., & Lofchy, J. (1993). Is there a role for selective monoamine oxidase inhibitor therapy in bulimia nervosa? A placebo-controlled trial of brofaromine. *Journal of Clinical Psychopharmacology, 13,* 415–422.

Klein, D. A., Mayer, L. E., Schebendach, J. E., & Walsh, B. T. (2007). Physical activity and cortisol in anorexia nervosa. *Psychoneuroendocrinology, 32,* 539–547.

Kling, M. A., Demitrack, M. S., Whitfield, H. J. Jr., Kalogeral, K. T., Listwak, S. J., DeBellis, M. D., et al. (1993). Effects of the glucocorticoid antagonist RU 486 on pituitary-adrenal function in patients with anorexia nervosa and healthy volunteers: Enhancement of plasma ACTH and cortisol secretion in underweight patients. *Neuroendocrinology, 57,* 1082–1091.

Knable, M. (2001). Topiramate for bulimia nervosa in epilepsy. *American Journal of Psychiatry, 158,* 322–323.

Kolata, G. G. (1980). NIH shaken by death of research volunteer. *Science, 209,* 475–476, 478–479.

Kotwal, R., Guerdjikova, A., McElroy, S. L., & Keck, P. E., Jr. (2006). Lithium augmentation of topiramate for bipolar disorder with comorbid binge eating disorder and obesity. *Human Psychopharmacology, 21,* 425–431.

Kushner, R. F. (2008). Anti-obesity drugs. *Expert Opinion on Pharmacotherapy, 9,* 1339–1350.

Kwak, S. E., Kim, J. E., Kim, D. S., Won, M. H., Choi, H. C., Kim, Y. I., et al. (2005). Differential effects of vigabatrin and zonisamide on the neuropeptide Y system in the hippocampus of seizure prone gerbil. *Neuropeptides, 39,* 507–513.

Lacey, J. H., & Crisp, A. H. (1980). Hunger, food intake and weight: the impact of clomipramine on a refeeding anorexia nervosa population. *Postgrad Med J, 56* (Supplement 1), 79–85.

Laederach-Hofmann, K., Graf, C., Horber, F., Lippuner, K., Lederer, S., Michel, R., et al. (1999). Imipramine and diet counseling with psychological support in the treatment of obese binge eaters: A randomized, placebo-controlled double-blind study. *International Journal of Eating Disorders, 26,* 231–244.

Lam, R. W., Goldner, E. M., Solyom, L., & Remick, R. A. (1994). A controlled study of light therapy for bulimia nervosa. *American Journal of Psychiatry, 151,* 744–750.

Lask, B., Fosson, A., Rolfe, U., & Thomas, S. (1993). Zinc deficiency and childhood-onset anorexia nervosa. *Journal of Clinical Psychiatry, 54,* 63–66.

Lawson, E. A., & Klibanski, A. (2008). Endocrine abnormalities in anorexia nervosa. *Nature Clinical Practice Endocrinology and Metabolism, 4,* 407–414.

Leitenberg, H., Rosen, J. C., Wolf, J., Vara, L. S., Detzer, M. J., Srebnik, D. (1994). Comparison of cognitive-behavior therapy and desipramine in the treatment of bulimia nervosa. *Behav Res Ther, 32,* 37–45.

Leombruni, P., Gastaldi, F., Lavagnino, L., & Fassino, S. (2008a). Oxcarbazepine for the treatment of binge eating disorder: A case series. *Advances in Therapy, 25,* 718–724.

Leombruni, P., Pierò, A., Brustolin, A., Mondelli, V., Levi, M., Campisi, S., et al. (2006). A 12 to 24 weeks pilot study of sertraline treatment in obese women binge eaters. *Human Psychopharmacology, 21,* 181–188.

Leombruni, P., Pierò, A., Lavagnino, L., Brustolin, A., Campisi, S., & Fassino, S. (2008b). A randomized, double-blind trial comparing sertraline and fluoxetine 6-month treatment in obese patients with binge eating disorder. *Progress in Neuropsychopharmacology and Biological Psychiatry, 32,* 1599–1605.

Leyba, C. M., & Gold, D. D. (1988). The relation between rapid-cycling cyclothymia and bulimia; Case reports of two women. *South Dakota Journal of Medicine, 41,* 21–22.

Lieberman, J. A., Javitch, J. A., & Moore, H. (2008). Cholinergic agonists as novel treatments for schizophrenia: The promise of rational drug development for psychiatry. *American Journal of Psychiatry, 165,* 931–936.

Lieberman, J. A., Stroup, T. S., McEvoy, J. P., Swartz, M. S., Rosenheck, R. A., Perkins, D. O., et al. (2005). Effectiveness of antipsychotic drugs in patients with chronic schizophrenia. *New England Journal of Medicine, 353,* 1209–1223.

Luby, E. D., Marrazzi, M. A., & Kinzie, J. (1987). Treatment of chronic anorexia nervosa with opiate blockade. *Journal of Clinical Psychopharmacology, 7,* 52–53.

Malhotra, S., King, K. H., Welge, J. A., Brunsman-Lovins, L., & McElroy, S. L. (2002). Venlafaxine treatment of binge-eating disorder associated with obesity: A series of 35 patients. *Journal of Clinical Psychiatry, 63,* 802–806.

Marazzi, M. A., Bacon, J. P., Kinzie, J., & Luby, E. D. (1995a). Naltrexone use in the treatment of anorexia nervosa and bulimia nervosa. *International Clinical Psychopharmacology, 10,* 163–172.

Marrazzi, M. A., Markham, K. M., Kinzie, J., & Luby, E. D. (1995b). Binge eating disorder: response to naltrexone. *International Journal of Obesity Related Metabolic Disorders, 19,* 143–145.

Martinez-Salio, A., Soler-Algarra, S., Calvo-Garcia, I., & Sanchez-Martin, M. (2007). [Nocturnal sleep-related eating disorder that responds to topiramate]. *Revue Neurologique, 45,* 276–279.

Mauri, M. C., Rudelli, R., Somaschini, E., Roncoroni, L., Papa, R., Mantero, M., et al. (1996). Neurobiological and psychopharmacological basis in the therapy of bulimia and anorexia. *Progress in Neuropsychopharmacology and Biological Psychiatry, 20,* 207–240.

McCann, U. D., & Agras, W. S. (1990). Successful treatment of nonpurging bulimia nervosa with desipramine: A double-blind, placebo-controlled study. *American Journal of Psychiatry, 147,* 1509–1513.

McElroy, S. L., Arnold, L. M., Shapira, N. A., Keck, P. E., Jr., Rosenthal, N. R., Karim, M., et al. (2003). Topiramate in the treatment of binge eating disorder associated with obesity: A randomized, placebo-controlled trial [published erratum appears in *American Journal of Psychiatry* 2003; 160:612]. *American Journal of Psychiatry, 160,* 255–261.

McElroy, S. L., Casuto, L. S., Nelson, E. B., Lake, K. A., Soutullo, C. A., Keck, P. E., Jr., et al. (2000). Placebo-controlled trial of sertraline in the treatment of binge eating disorder. *American Journal of Psychiatry, 157,* 1004–1006.

McElroy, S. L., Guerdjikova, A. I., Keck, P. E., Jr., Pope, H. G., Jr., & Hudson, J. I. (2008a). Antiepileptic drugs in obesity, psychotropic-associated weight gain, and eating disorders. In S. L. McElroy, Keck, P. E., Jr., & Post, R. M. (Eds.), *Antiepileptic drugs to treat psychiatric disorders* (pp. 283–309). New York: Informa Healthcare.

McElroy, S. L., Guerdjikova, A., Kotwal, R., Welge, J. A., Nelson, E. B., Lake, K. A., et al. (2007a). Atomoxetine in the treatment of binge-eating disorder: A randomized placebo-controlled trial. *Journal of Clinical Psychiatry, 68,* 390–398.

McElroy, S. L., Guerdjikova, A. I., Martens, B., Keck, P. E., Jr., Pope, H. G., Jr., & Hudson, J. I. (2009). Role of antiepileptic drugs in the management of eating disorders. *CNS Drugs. 23,* 139–156.

McElroy, S. L., Hudson, J. I., Capece, J. A., Beyers, K., Fisher, A. C., Rosenthal, N. R., et al. (2007b). Topiramate for the treatment of binge eating disorder associated with obesity: A placebo-controlled study. *Biological Psychiatry, 61,* 1039–1048.

McElroy, S. L., Hudson, J. I., Malhotra, S., Welge, J. A., Nelson, E. B., Keck, P. E., Jr. (2003). Citalopram in the treatment of binge-eating disorder: A placebo-controlled trial. *Journal of Clinical Psychiatry, 64,* 807–813.

McElroy, S. L., Keck, P. E., Jr., & Pope, H. G., Jr. (1987). Sodium valproate: Its use in primary psychiatric disorders. *Journal of Clinical Psychopharmacology, 7,* 16–24.

McElroy, S. L., Keck, P. E., Jr., & Post, R. M. (Eds.) (2008b). *Antiepileptic drugs to treat psychiatric disorders.* New York: Informa Healthcare.

McElroy, S. L., Kotwal, R., Guerdjikova, A. I., Welge, J. A., Nelson, E. B., Lake, K. A., et al. (2006). Zonisamide in the treatment of binge eating disorder with obesity: A randomized controlled trial. *Journal of Clinical Psychiatry, 67,* 1897–1906.

McElroy, S. L., Kotwal, R., Hudson, J. I., Nelson, E. B., & Keck, P. E., Jr. (2004a). Zonisamide in the treatment of binge eating disorder: An open-label, prospective trial. *Journal of Clinical Psychiatry, 65,* 50–56.

McElroy, S. L., Kotwal, R., Keck, P. E., Jr., & Akiskal, J. S. (2005). Comorbidity of bipolar and eating disorders: Distinct or related disorders with shared dysregulations? *Journal of Affective Disorders, 86,* 107–127.

McElroy, S. L., Shapira, N. A., Arnold, L. M., Keck, P. E., Jr., Rosenthal, N. R., Wu, S. C., et al. (2004b). Topiramate in the long-term treatment of binge-eating disorder associated with obesity [published erratum appears in *Journal of Clinical Psychiatry* 2005; 66:138]. *Journal of Clinical Psychiatry, 65,* 1463–1469.

McGrath, P. J., Stewart, J. W., Fava, M., Trivedi, M. H., Wisniewski, S. R., Nierenberg, A. A., et al. (2006). Tranylcypromine versus venlafaxine plus mirtazapine following three failed antidepressant medication trials for depression: A STAR*D report. *American Journal of Psychiatry, 163,* 1531–1541.

Mehler-Wex, C., Romanos, M., Kirchheiner, J., & Schulze, U. M. (2008). Atypical antipsychotics in severe anorexia nervosa in children and adolescents—review and case reports. *European Eating Disorders Review, 16,* 100–108.

Meister, B. (2007). Neurotransmitters in key neurons of the hypothalamus that regulate feeding behavior and body weight. *Physiology & Behavior, 92,* 263–271.

Mendelson, S. D. (2001). Treatment of anorexia nervosa with tramadol. *American Journal of Psychiatry, 158,* 963–964.

Milano, W., Petrella, C., Casella, A., Capasso, A., Carrino, S., & Milano, L. (2005). Use of sibutramine, an inhibitor of the reuptake of serotonin and noradrenalin, in the treatment of binge eating disorder: A placebo-controlled study. *Advances in Therapy, 22,* 5–31.

Miller, K. K., Grieco, K. A., & Klibanski, A. (2005). Testosterone administration in women with anorexia nervosa. *Journal of Clinical Endocrinology and Metabolism, 90,* 1428–1433.

Mitchell, J. E., Christenson, G., Jennings, J., Huber, M., Thomas, B., Pomeroy, C., et al. (1989). A placebo-controlled, double-blind crossover study of naltrexone hydrochloride in outpatients with normal weight bulimia. *Journal of Clinical Psychopharmacology, 9,* 94–97.

Mitchell, J. E., Fletcher, L., Hanson, K., Mussell, M. P., Seim, H., Crosby, R., et al. (2001). The relative efficacy of fluoxetine and manual-based self-help in the treatment of outpatients with bulimia nervosa. *Journal of Clinical Psychopharmacology, 21,* 298–304.

Mitchell, J. E., & Groat, R. (1984). A placebo-controlled double-blind trial of amitriptyline in bulimia. *Journal of Clinical Psychopharmacology, 4*, 186–193.

Mitchell, J. E., Pyle, R. L., Eckert, E. D., Hatsukami, D., Pomeroy, C., & Zimmerman, R. (1990). A comparison study of antidepressants and structured intensive group psychotherapy in the treatment of bulimia nervosa. *Archives of General Psychiatry, 47*, 149–157.

Mond, J. M., Hay, P. J., Rodgers, B., & Owen, C. (2007). Health service utilization for eating disorders: Findings from a community-based study. *International Journal of Eating Disorders, 40*, 399–408.

Mondraty, N., Birmingham, C. L., Touyz, S., Sundakov, V., Chapman, L., & Beaumont, P. (2005). Randomized controlled trial of olanzapine in the treatment of cognitions in anorexia nervosa. *Australasian Psychiatry, 13*, 72–75.

Monteleone, P., Luisi, M., Colurcio, B., Casarosa, E., Monteleone, P., Ioime, R., et al. (2001). Plasma levels of neuroactive steroids are increased in untreated women with anorexia nervosa or bulimia nervosa. *Psychosomatic Medicine, 63*, 62–68.

Monteleone, P., Tortorella, A., Castaldo, E., & Maj, M. (2006). Association of a functional serotonin transporter gene polymorphism with binge eating disorder. *American Journal of Medical Genetics. Part B, Neuropsychiatric Genetics, 141B*, 7–9.

Moore, R., Mills, I. H., & Forster, A. (1981). Naloxone in the treatment of anorexia nervosa: Effect on weight gain and lipolysis. *Journal of the Royal Society of Medicine, 74*, 129–135.

Naessén, S., Carlström, K., Byström, B., Pierre, Y., & Hirschberg, A. L. (2007). Effects of an antiandrogenic oral contraceptive on appetite and eating behavior in bulimic women. *Psychoneuroendocrinology, 32*, 548–554.

Naessén, S., Carlström, K., Garoff, L., Glant, R., & Hirschberg, A. L. (2006). Polycystic ovary syndrome in bulimic women—an evaluation based on the new diagnostic criteria. *Gynecological Endocrinology, 22*, 388–394.

Nagata, T., Ono, K., & Nakayama, K. (2007). Anorexia nervosa with chronic episodes for more than 30 years in a patient with a comorbid schizotypal personality disorder. *Psychiatry and Clinical Neurosciences, 61*, 434–436.

National Institute for Clinical Excellence (NICE). (2004). Eating disorders. Core interventions in the treatment and management of anorexia nervosa, bulimia nervosa and related eating disorders. Clinical guideline no 9. London.

Neumeister, A., Winkler, A., & Wöber-Bingöl, C. (1999). Addition of naltrexone to fluoxetine in the treatment of binge eating disorder. *American Journal of Psychiatry, 156*, 797.

Newman-Toker, J. (2000). Risperidone in anorexia nervosa. *Journal of the American Academy of Child and Adolescent Psychiatry, 39*, 941–942.

Nickel, C., Tritt, K., Muehlbacher, M., Pedrosa Gil, F., Mitterlehner, F. O., Kaplan, P., et al. (2005). Topiramate treatment in bulimia nervosa patients: A randomized, double-blind, placebo-controlled trial. *International Journal of Eating Disorders, 38*, 295–300.

Noma, S., Uwatoko, T., Yamamoto, H., & Hayashi, T. (2008). Effects of milnacipran on binge eating—a pilot study. *Neuropsychiatric Disease and Treatment, 4*, 295–300.

O'Reardon, J. P., Allison, K. C., Martino, N. S., Lundgren, J. D., Moonseong, H., & Stunkard, A. J. (2006). A randomized, placebo-controlled trial of sertraline in the treatment of night eating syndrome. *American Journal of Psychiatry, 163*, 893–898.

Ong, Y. L., Checkley, S. A., & Russell, G. F. (1983). Suppression of bulimic symptoms with methylamphetamine. *British Journal of Psychiatry, 143*, 288–293.

Padwal, R. S., & Majumdar, S. R. (2007). Drug treatments for obesity: Orlistat, sibutramine, and rimonabant. *Lancet, 369*, 71–77.

Parsons, J. M., & Sapse, A. T. (1985). Significance of hypercortisolism in anorexia nervosa. *Journal of Orthomolecular Psychiatry, 14*, 13–18.

Patil, S. T., Zhang, L., Martenyi, F., Lowe, S. L., Jackson, K. A., Andreev, B. V., et al. (2007). Activation of mGlu2/3 receptors as a new approach to treat schizophrenia: A randomized Phase 2 clinical trial. *Nature Medicine, 13*, 102–1107.

Pearlstein, T., Spurell, E., Hohlstein, L. A., Gurney, V., Read, J., Fuchs, C., et al. (2003). A double-blind, placebo-controlled trial of fluvoxamine in binge eating disorder: A high placebo response. *Archives of Women's Mental Health, 6*, 147–151.

Plante, D. T., & Winkelman, J. W. (2006). Parasomnias. *Psychiatric Clinics of North America, 29*, 969–987.

Pope, H. G., Hudson, J. I., & Jonas, J. M. (1986). Bulimia in men: A series of fifteen cases. *Journal of Nervous and Mental Disease, 174*, 117–119.

Pope, H. G., Jr., Hudson, J. I., Jonas, J. M., & Yurgelun-Todd, D. (1983). Bulimia treated with imipramine: Placebo-controlled, double-blind study. *Amercian Journal of Psychiatry, 140*, 554–558.

Pope, H. G., Jr., Keck, P. E., Jr., McElroy, S. L., & Hudson, J. I. (1989). A placebo-controlled study of trazodone in bulimia nervosa. *Journal of Clinical Psychopharmacology, 9*, 254–259.

Powers, P. S., Bannon, Y., Eubanks, R., & McCormick, T. (2007). Quetiapine in anorexia nervosa patients: An open label outpatient pilot study. *International Journal of Eating Disorders, 40*, 21–26.

Powers, P. S., & Cloak, N. L. (2007). Medication-related weight changes. Impact on treatment of eating disorder patients. In J. Yager, & P. S. Powers (Eds.), *Clinical manual of eating disorders* (pp. 255–285). Washington, DC: American Psychiatric Publishing.

Prince, J. B. (2006). Pharmacotherapy of attention-deficit hyperactivity disorder in children and adolescents: Update on new stimulant preparations, atomoxetine, and novel treatments. *Child and Adolescent Psychiatry Clinics in North America, 15*, 13–50.

Provini, F., Albani, F., Vetrugno, R., Vignatelli, L., Lombardi, C., Plazzi, G., et al. (2005). A pilot double-blind placebo-controlled trial of low-dose pramipexole in sleep-related eating disorder. *European Journal of Neurology, 12*, 432–436.

Raingeard, I., Courtet, P., Renard, E., & Bringer, J. (2004). Naltrexone improves blood glucose control in type 1 diabetic women with severe and chronic eating disorders. *Diabetes Care, 27*, 847–848.

Ramoz, N., Versini, A., & Gorwood, P. (2007). Eating disorders: An overview of treatment responses and the potential impact of vulnerability genes and endophenotypes. *Expert Opinion on Pharmacotherapy, 8*, 2029–2044.

Reilly, P. P. (1977). Anorexia nervosa. Lithium administration has contributed to the management of anorexia nervosa. *Rhode Island Medical Journal, 60*, 419–456.

Rivera, G., Bocanegra-García, V., Galiano, S., Cirauqui, N., Ceras, J., Pérez, S., et al. (2008). Melanin-concentrating hormone receptor 1 antagonists: A new perspective for the pharmacologic treatment of obesity. *Current Medicinal Chemistry, 15,* 1025–1043.

Romano, S. J., Halmi, K. A., Sarkar, N. P., Koke, S. C., Lee, J. S. (2002). A placebo-controlled study of fluoxetine in continued treatment of bulimia nervosa after successful acute fluoxetine treatment. *Am J Psychiatry, 159,* 96–102.

Rosenberg, G. (2007). The mechanisms of action of valproate in neuropsychiatric disorders: Can we see the forest for the trees? *Cellular and Molecular Life Sciences, 64,* 090–103.

Rosenow, F., Knake, S., & Hebebrand, J. (2002). Topiramate and anorexia nervosa. *American Journal of Psychiatry, 159,* 2112–2113.

Rothschild, R., Quitkin, H. M., Quitkin, F. M., Stewart, J. W., Ocepek-Welikson, K., McGrath, P. J., et al. (1994). A double-blind placebo-controlled comparison of phenelzine and imipramine in the treatment of bulimia in atypical depressives. *International Journal of Eating Disorders, 15,* 1–9.

Ruggiero, G. M., Laini, V., Mauri, M. C., Ferrari, V. M., Clemente, A., Lugo, F., et al. (2001). A single blind comparison of amisulpride, fluoxetine and clomipramine in the treatment of restricting anorectics. *Progress in Neuropsychopharmacology and Biological Psychiatry, 25,* 1049–1059.

Rush, A. J., Trivedi, M. H., Wisniewski, S. R., Stewart, J. W., Nierenberg, A. A., Thase, M. E., et al. (2006). Bupropion-SR, sertraline, or venlafaxine-XR after failure of SSRIs for depression. *New England Journal of Medicine, 354,* 1231–1242.

Russell, G. F. M., Checkley, S. A., Feldman, J., & Eisler, I. (1988). A controlled trial of *d*-fenfluramine in bulimia nervosa. *Clinical Neuropharmacology, 11* (Supplement 1), S146–S159.

Russell, D. M., Freedman, M. L., Feiglin, D. H., Jeejeebhoy, K. N., Swinson, R. P., & Garfinkel, P. E. (1983). Delayed gastric emptying and improvement with domperidone in a patient with anorexia nervosa. *American Journal of Psychiatry, 140,* 1235–1236.

Sabine, E. J., Yonace, A., Farrington, A. J., Barrant, K. H., & Wakeling, A. (1983). Bulimia nervosa: A placebo-controlled double-blind therapeutic trial of mianserin. *British Journal of Clinical Pharmacology, 15,* 195–202.

Sachs, G. S., Nierenberg, A. A., Calabrese, J. R., Marangell, L. B., Wisniewski, S. R., Gvulai, L., et al. (2007). Effectiveness of adjunctive antidepressant treatment for bipolar depression. *New England Journal of Medicine, 356,* 1711–1722.

Saleh, J. W., & Lebwohl, P. (1980). Metoclopramide-induced gastric emptying in patients with anorexia nervosa. *American Journal of Gastroenterology, 74,* 127–132.

Sansone, R. A., & Sansone, L. A. (2003). Metoclopramide and unintended weight gain. *International Journal of Eating Disorders, 34,* 265–268.

Schenck, C. H., Hurwitz, T. D., O'Connor, K. A., & Mahowald, M. W. (1993). Additional categories of sleep-related eating disorders and the current status of treatment. *Sleep, 16,* 457–466.

Schmidt, do Prado-Lima P. A., & Bacaltchuck, J. (2002). Topiramate in treatment-resistant depression and binge eating disorder. *Bipolar Disorders, 4,* 271–273.

Schweickert, L. A., Strober, M., & Moskowitz, A. (1997). Efficacy of methylphenidate in bulimia nervosa comorbid with attention-deficit hyperactivity disorder: A case report. *International Journal of Eating Disorders, 21,* 299–301.

Shapira, N. A., Goldsmith, T. D., & McElroy, S. L. (2000). Treatment of binge-eating disorder with topiramate: A clinical case series. *Journal of Clinical Psychiatry, 61,* 368–372.

Shapiro, J. R., Berkman, N. D., Brownley, K. A., Sedway, J. S., Lohr, K. N., & Bulik, C. M. (2007). Bulimia nervosa treatment: A systematic review of randomized controlled trials. *International Journal of Eating Disorders, 40,* 321–336.

Shisslak, C. M., Perse, T., & Crago, M. (1991). Coexistence of bulimia nervosa and mania: A literature review and case report. *Comprehensive Psychiatry, 32,* 181–184.

Silveira, R. O., Zanatto, V., Appolinário, J. C., & Kapezinski, F. (2005). An open trial of reboxetine in obese patients with binge eating disorder. *Eating and Weight Disorders, 10,* e93–e96.

Slof-Op't Landt, M. C., van Furth, E. F., Meulenbelt, I., Slagbloom, P. E., Bartels, M., Boomsma, D. I., et al. (2005). Eating disorders: From twin studies to candidate genes and beyond. *Twin Research and Human Genetics, 8,* 467–482.

Sokol, M. S., Gray, N. S., Goldstein, A., & Kaye, W. H. (1999). Methylphenidate treatment for bulimia nervosa associated with a cluster B personality disorder. *International Journal of Eating Disorders, 25,* 233–237.

Stacher, G., Abatzi-Wenzel, T. A., Wiesnagrotzki, S., Bergmann, H., Schneider, C., & Gaupmann, G. (1993a). Gastric emptying, body weight and symptoms in primary anorexia nervosa. Long-term effects of cisapride. *British Journal of Psychiatry, 162,* 398–402.

Stacher, G., Peters, T. L., Bergmann, H., Wiesnagrotzki, S., Schneider, C., Granser-Vacariu, G. V., et al. (1993b). Erythromycin effects on gastric emptying, antral motility and plasma motilin and pancreatic polypeptide concentrations in anorexia nervosa. *Gut, 34,* 166–172.

Stefano, S. C., Bacaltchuk, J., Blay, S. L., & Appolinario, J. C. (2008). Antidepressants in short-term treatment of binge eating disorder: Systematic review and meta-analysis. *Eating Behaviors, 9,* 129–136.

Steffen, K. J., Roerig, J. L., Mitchell, J. E., & Uppala, S. (2006). Emerging drugs for eating disorder treatment. *Expert Opinion on Emerging Drugs, 11,* 315–336.

Stein, G. S., Hartshorn, S., Jones, J., & Steinberg, D. (1982). Lithium in a case of severe anorexia nervosa. *British Journal of Psychiatry, 140,* 526–528.

Steinglass, J. E., Eisen, J. L., Attia, E., Mayer, L., & Walsh, B.T. (2007a). Is anorexia a delusional disorder? An assessment of eating beliefs in anorexia nervosa. *Journal of Psychiatric Practice, 13,* 65–71.

Steinglass, J., Sysko, R., Schebendach, J., Broft, A., Strober, M., & Walsh, B. T. (2007b). The application of exposure therapy and D-cycloserine to the treatment of anorexia nervosa: A preliminary trial. *Journal of Psychiatric Practice, 13,* 238–245.

Strasser, F. (2007). Appraisal of current and experimental approaches to the treatment of cachexia. *Current Opinion in Supportive and Palliative Care, 1,* 312–316.

Stunkard, A., Berkowitz, R., Tanrikut, C., Reis, E., & Young, L. (1996). D-Fenfluramine treatment of binge eating disorder. *American Journal of Psychiatry, 153,* 1455–1459.

Su, J. C., & Birmingham, C. L. (2002). Zinc supplementation in the treatment of anorexia nervosa. *Eating and Weight Disorders, 7,* 20–22.

Sundblad, C., Landén, M., Eriksson, T., Bergman, L., & Eriksson, E. (2005). Effects of the androgen antagonist flutamide and the serotonin reuptake inhibitor citalopram in bulimia nervosa: A placebo-controlled pilot study. *Journal of Clinical Psychopharmacology, 25*, 85–88.

Szmukler, G. I., Young, G. P., Miller, G., Lichtenstein, M., & Binns, D. S. (1995). A controlled trial of cisapride in anorexia nervosa. *International Journal of Eating Disorders, 17*, 347–357.

Szyper, M. S., & Mann, J. D. (1978). Anorexia nervosa as an interictal symptom of partial complex seizures. *Neurology, 28*, 335.

Tachibana, N., Sugita, Y., Teshima, Y., & Hishikawa, Y. (1989). A case of anorexia nervosa associated with epileptic seizures showing favorable responses to sodium valproate and clonazepam. *Japanese Journal of Psychiatry and Neurology, 43*, 77–84.

Theisen, F. M., Linden, A., König, I. R., Martin, M., Remschmidt, H., & Hebebrand, J. (2003). Spectrum of binge eating symptomatology in patients treated with clozapine and olanzapine. *Journal of Neural Transmission, 110*, 111–121.

Tooley, P. J., Vervaet, P., & Wager, E. (1999). Cardiac arrhythmias reported during treatment with cisapride. *Pharmacoepidemiology and Drug Safety, 8*, 57–58.

Trivedi, M. H., Fava, M., Wisniewski, S. R., Thase, M. E., Ouitkin, F., Warden, D., et al. (2006). Medication augmentation after the failure of SSRIs for depression. *New England Journal of Medicine, 354*, 1243–1252.

Tucker, P., Masters, B., & Nawar, O. (2004). Topiramate in the treatment of comorbid night eating syndrome and PTSD: A case study. *Eating Disorders, 12*, 75–78.

Uher, R., & Treasure, J. (2005). Brain lesions and eating disorders. *Journal of Neurology, Neurosurgery, and Psychiatry, 76*, 852–857.

Vandereycken, W. (1984). Neuroleptics in the short-term treatment of anorexia nervosa. A double-blind placebo-controlled study with sulpiride. *British Journal of Psychiatry, 144*, 288–292.

Vandereycken, W., & Pierloot, R. (1982). Pimozide combined with behavior therapy in the short-term treatment of anorexia nervosa: A double-blind, placebo-controlled, cross-over study. *Acta Psychiatrica Scandinavica, 60*, 446–451.

von Wietersheim, J., Müler-Bock, V., Rauh, S., Danner, B., Chrenko, K., & Bühler, G. (2008). No effect on spironolactone on bulimia nervosa symptoms. *Journal of Clinical Psychopharmacology, 28*, 258–260.

Walpoth, M., Hoertnagl, C., Mangweth-Matzek, B., Kemmler, G., Hinterhölzl, J., Conca, A., et al. (2008). Repetitive transcranial magnetic stimulation in bulimia nervosa: Preliminary results of a single-centre, randomised, double-blind, sham-controlled trial in female outpatients. *Psychotherapy and Psychosomatics, 77*, 57–60.

Walsh, B. T., Agras, W. S., Devlin, M. J., Fairburn, C. G., Wilson, G. T., Kahn, C. M., et al. (2000). Fluoxetine for bulimia nervosa following poor response to psychotherapy. *American Journal of Psychiatry, 157*, 1332–1334.

Walsh, B. T., Fairburn, C. G., Mickley, D., Sysko, R., & Parides, M. K. (2004). Treatment of bulimia nervosa in a primary care setting. *American Journal of Psychiatry, 161*, 556–561.

Walsh, B. T., Gladis, M., Roose, S. P., Stewart, J. W., & Glassman, A. H. (1988). Phenelzine vs placebo in 50 patients with bulimia. *Archives of General Psychiatry, 45*, 471–475.

Walsh, B. T., Hadigan, C. M., Devlin, M. J., Gladis, M., Roose, S. P. (1991). Long-term outcome of antidepressant treatment for bulimia nervosa. *Am J Psychiatry, 148*, 1206–12.

Walsh, B. T., Kaplan, A. S., Attia, E., Olmsted, M., Parides, M., Carter, O. C., et al. (2006). Fluoxetine after weight restoration in anorexia nervosa: A randomized controlled trial [published erratum appears in *JAMA*, 2006; *296*, 934 and *JAMA* 2007; *298*, 2008]. *JAMA, 295*, 2605–2612.

Walsh, B. T., Stewart, J. W., Roose, S. P., Gladis, M., & Glassman, A. H. (1984) Treatment of bulimia with phenelzine. A double-blind, placebo-controlled study. *Arch Gen Psychiatry, 41*, 1105–9.

Walsh, B. T., Wilson, G. T., Loeb, K. L. Devlin, M. J., Pike, K. M., Roose, S. P., et al. (1997). Medication and psychotherapy in the treatment of bulimia nervosa. *Am J Psychiatry, 154*, 523–31.

Wang, T. S., Chou, Y. H., & Shiah, I. S. (2006). Combined treatment of olanzapine and mirtazapine in anorexia nervosa associated with major depression. *Progress in Neuropsychopharmacology and Biological Psychiatry, 30*, 306–309.

Wermuth, B. M., Davis, K. L., Hollister, L. E., & Stunkard, A. J. (1977). Phenytoin treatment of the binge eating syndrome. *American Journal of Psychiatry, 134*, 1249–1253.

Wheadon, D. E., Rampey, A. H. Jr., Thompson, V. L., Potvin, J. H., Masica, D. N., Beasley, C. M. Jr. (1992). Lack of association between fluoxetine and suicidality in bulimia nervosa. *J Clin Psychiatry, 53*, 235–41.

Wijkstra, J., Lijmer, J., Balk, F. J., Geddes, J. R., & Nolen, W. A. (2006). Pharmacological treatment for unipolar psychotic depression: Systematic review and meta-analysis. *British Journal of Psychiatry, 188*, 410–415.

Wildes, J. E., Marcus, M. D., Gaskill, J. A., & Ringham, R. (2007). Depressive and manic-hypomanic spectrum psychopathology in patients with anorexia nervosa. *Comprehensive Psychiatry, 48*, 413–418.

Wilfley, D. E., Crow, S. J., Hudson, J. I., Mitchell, J. E., Berkowitz, R. I., Blakesley, V., et al. (2008). Efficacy of sibutramine for the treatment of binge eating disorder: A randomized multicenter placebo-controlled double-blind study. *American Journal of Psychiatry, 165*, 51–58.

Winkelman, J. W. (2003). Treatment of nocturnal eating syndrome and sleep-related eating disorder with topiramate. *Sleep Medicine, 4*, 243–246.

Winkelman, J. W. (2006). Efficacy and tolerability of open-label topiramate in the treatment of sleep-related eating disorder: A retrospective case series. *Journal of Clinical Psychiatry, 67*, 1729–1734.

Woodside, B. D., & Staab, R. (2006). Management of psychiatric comorbidity in anorexia nervosa and bulimia nervosa. *CNS Drugs, 20*, 655–663.

Yager, J. (2007). Management of patients with chronic, intractable eating disorders. In J. Yager & P. S. Powers (Eds.), *Clinical manual of eating disorders* (pp. 407–439). Washington, DC: American Psychiatric Publishing.

Yager, J., & Powers, P. S. (Eds.). (2007). *Clinical manual of eating disorders*. Washington, DC: American Psychiatric Publishing.

Yasuhara, D., Nakahara, T., Harada, T., & Inui, A. ((2007). Olanzapine-induced hyperglycemia in anorexia nervosa. *American Journal of Psychiatry, 164*, 528–529.

Yeh, S. B., & Schenck, C. H. (2007). Sleep-related eating disorder in a 29 year-old man: A case report with diagnostic polysomnographic findings. *Acta Neurologica Taiwanica, 16,* 106–110.

Zarate, C. A., & Manji, H. K. (2008a). Riluzole in psychiatry: A systematic review of the literature. *Expert Opinion on Drug Metabolism and Toxicology, 4,* 1223–1234.

Zarate, C. A., Jr., & Manji, H. K. (2008b). Bipolar disorder: candidate drug targets. *Mt. Sinai Journal of Medicine, 75,* 226–247.

Zhu, A. J., & Walsh, B. T. (2002). Pharmacologic treatment of eating disorders. *Canadian Journal of Psychiatry, 47,* 227–234.

Zilberstein, B., Pajecki, D., Garcia de Brito, A. C., Gallafrio, S. T., Eshkenazy, R., & Andrade, C. G. (2004). Topiramate after adjustable gastric banding in patients with binge eating and difficulty losing weight. *Obesity Surgery, 14,* 802–805.

Evidence-Based Treatment for the Eating Disorders

Phillipa J. Hay *and* Angelica de M. Claudino

Abstract

This chapter comprises a focused review of the best available evidence for psychological and pharmacological treatments of choice for anorexia nervosa (AN), bulimia nervosa (BN), binge eating disorder (BED), and eating disorder not otherwise specified (EDNOS), and discusses the role of primary care and presents treatment algorithms. In AN, although there is consensus on the need for specialist care that includes nutritional rehabilitation in addition to psychotherapy, no single approach has been found to offer a distinct advantage. In contrast, manualized cognitive behavior therapy (CBT) for BN has attained "first-line" treatment status with a stronger evidence base than other psychotherapies. Although more trials are needed in BED and EDNOS, less intensive and nonspecialist CBT is likely to be efficacious, combined where appropriate with weight management strategies, either behavioral or pharmacological. Primary care practitioners are in a key role, both with regard to providing care as with co-ordination and initiation of specialist care.

Keywords: anorexia nervosa, binge eating disorder, bulimia nervosa, cognitive behavior therapy, pharmacological treatment, psychological treatment

Introduction

"It is the best of times and the worst of times."

This well-known quote (from the novel *A Tale of Two Cities* by Charles Dickens) perhaps best epitomizes where the evidence base for treatments in eating disorders (EDs) stands today. Although there has been a substantive body of research into efficacy of psychological and pharmacological therapies, these have largely been in bulimia nervosa (BN) and to a lesser degree binge eating disorder (BED), leaving knowledge into how to best treat anorexia nervosa (AN) and eating disorder not otherwise specified (EDNOS) impoverished. However, there are a number of promising new approaches being tested.

This chapter presents a distillation of best available evidence for psychological and pharmacological treatments of choice for AN, BN, BED, and EDNOS. This is followed by specific information for treatment in primary care and non-specialist settings and then a discussion of existing evidence based recommendations and treatment algorithms of each of the EDs.

This chapter's focus is on where the evidence is most relevant to and most informs clinical practice and choice of treatments. Treatments are discussed where they are either recommended by reputable professional or other guidelines (indicating at least Level IV evidence; see later) and/or supported by at least one randomized controlled trial of moderate quality. Treatments that have not been taken up widely and/or are yet regarded as experimental (e.g., transcranial magnetic stimulation and bright light therapy) have not been included. Evidence is drawn from systematic reviews, which are also sources to identify trials, and an additional data base search for papers published since the reviews. Features of the therapies are described, particularly pertaining to their testing in controlled trials, with reference where relevant to more detailed accounts are found in other chapters of this book addressing specific therapies. Treatments for which there is support (or not) from at least one randomized controlled trial are summarized in Table 25.1.

Methods of Literature Searching

The authors (PH and AC) conducted extensive searches of the literature in 2007 (Claudino, Bacaltchuk, & Hay, 2009, search date 2007; Hay, 2008, search date 2006; Hay & Bacaltchuk, 2008, search date 2007; Hay, Bacaltchuk, Kashyap, & Stefano, 2009, search date 2007; Hay, et al., 2003, search date 2007) and have further updated these searches for the present chapter. Additional systematic reviews consulted were Brownley, Berkman, Sedway, Lohr, & Bulik (2007, search date 2005); Bulik, Berkman, Brownley, Sedway, & Lohr (2007, search date 2005); Shapiro et al. (2007, search date 2005); and Treasure & Schmidt (2007, search date 2005). The additional PUBMED and PsychINFO search was dated January 2007 to August 2008 and it used the terms "eating disorders" and "randomized controlled trial." It identified 73 studies, of which 19 were primary reports of randomized controlled trials (RCTs, 9 of which had not been previously identified), 1 was an RCT in progress, 6 were prevention trials, 2 were of obesity, 2 were for alcohol dependence, and the remainder were not RCTs.

In assessing level of evidence, this chapter follows the hierarchy of the National Institute for Clinical Evidence guidelines (NICE, 2004):

Level I. Evidence from at least one RCT or meta-analysis of controlled trials

Level IIa. Evidence from at least one well-designed controlled trial without randomization

Level IIb. Evidence from at least one other well designed quasi-experimental study

Level III. Evidence obtained from well-designed nonexperimental descriptive studies, such as comparative studies, correlation studies, and case-control studies

Level IV. Evidence obtained from expert opinions or committee reports and/or clinical experiences of respected authorities

The quality of the evidence, both in regards to systematic reviews and trials, was considered and in formulating treatment algorithms most weight was given where consistency was found.

In this chapter, evidence for therapies is presented for the EDs as defined according to the *Diagnostic and Statistical Manual of Mental Disorders* (4th ed.), the *DSM-IV-Text Revision* (*DSM-IV-TR*; American Psychiatric Association [APA], 2000). For AN and BN these are consistent with (although not equivalent to) the World Health Organization (WHO; 1992) International Classification of Diseases and Related Health Problems, 10th Revision (ICD-10). The ICD-10 provides additional subcategories of atypical AN and atypical BN as well as an ED unspecified category. These would be subsumed within EDNOS and BED of the *DSM-IV*.

Treatments of Choice: Anorexia Nervosa
Psychological Therapy

AN is the "oldest" of the EDs and early attempts with psychotherapies utilized a psychoanalytic or psychodynamic framework. Bruch was a key figure in the expansion of psychological therapy in AN treatment. She (Bruch, 1973) described the core therapeutic elements to change in AN as being through the understanding of the meaning of food for the patient, and helping them find alternatives to anorexic self-experience and self-expression. Self-psychology for EDs (Goodsitt, 1997) has developed out of the older psychodynamic traditions. These therapies by their nature are long-term and therapist time intensive. They also require specific training that may often not be readily accessible or available. Although still in common use worldwide there is little evidence of efficacy and modified forms of dynamic therapy (e.g., cognitive analytic therapy and focal psychoanalytic psychotherapy; see later) that integrate active symptom management have been proposed as viable alternatives to cognitive–behavioral therapy (Garner, 1997). However, treatment of AN is by its nature long term, and therapists may benefit from an appreciation of psychodynamic processes such as transference that may occur during intensive therapy, albeit not the focus of therapy.

There is currently no agreed first-line psychological therapy for AN but there are some with Level I evidence of efficacy when compared to "treatment as usual" or a nonspecialist treatment. These include cognitive behavioral therapy (CBT; see also Chapter 19 of this Handbook), behavior therapy (BT; diary keeping and exposure), focal psychoanalytic psychotherapy (FPT), cognitive analytical therapy (CAT), family therapy with and without individual therapy including dietary counseling (see Chapter 21), and

Table 25.1 Support of Treatments in Eating Disorders from Randomized Controlled Trials or Level I[a] Evidence

	Grading of Support[b]		
	Anorexia Nervosa	Bulimia Nervosa	Binge Eating Disorder
Psychological therapy			
Behavioral weight loss therapy	n.a.	n.a.	A[c]
Cognitive behavior therapy	A	A	A
Dialectical behavior therapy	n.a.	A	A
Family therapy	A[d]	C[d]	n.a.
Guided self-help	n.a.	A	A
Interpersonal psychotherapy	B	A	A
Modified dynamic therapies (CAT/FPT)	A	n.a.	n.a.
Pure self-help	n.a.	B	A
Specialist supportive clinical management	A	n.a.	n.a.
Pharmacological therapy			
Antidepressants	C	A	A
Antipsychotics	A	n.a.	n.a.
Antiobesity agents (sibutramine, orlistat)	n.a.	n.a.	A
Bisphosphonate(s)	C	n.a.	n.a.
Cyproheptadine	C	n.a.	n.a.
Flutamide	C	n.a.	n.a.
Hormone replacement	B	n.a.	n.a.
Naltrexone	n.a.	C	n.a.
Ondansetron	n.a.	C	n.a.
Topiramate	n.a.	A	A[c]
Zinc	C	n.a.	n.a.
Zonisamide	n.a.	n.a.	A[c]
Exercise	n.a.	A	A

[a]Level 1 evidence has at least one well conducted randomized controlled trial.
[b]Grading of support:
    A. At least one well conducted randomized controlled trial is supportive.
    B. Randomized controlled trial(s) found to be not supportive or less supportive than other approaches.
    C. Mixed or inconsistent results from trials.
[c]In overweight/obese participants.
[d]In adolescent participants.
n.a. = not applicable to this eating disorder diagnostic group—either not well studied, no randomized controlled trials, or not an indicated therapy.
CAT = cognitive analytic therapy; FPT = focal psychoanalytic psychotherapy.

group therapy with dietary counseling. In addition, CBT has been compared to interpersonal psychotherapy (IPT) and to specialist supportive clinical management (SSCM; see Chapter 20), and various forms of family therapy have been compared to each other. Complicating the picture is the problem that the therapies have been trialed at varying time points in treatment, from the initial acute phase to following weight restoration. Some therapies have also been evaluated only in either child/adolescent or adult (that may include older adolescent) samples. Finally, trials have used a range of differing outcome measures and, with the exception of family therapy in younger patients, there is little evidence for superiority of any one approach on the most fundamental of outcomes, namely weight gain.

In adults, trials have been mostly of individual or group psychotherapy. Channon, de Silva, Hemsley, & Perkins (1989), in a nonblinded randomized trial, compared CBT (with a cognitive focus) to behavior therapy (diary keeping and exposure) and to a control "eclectic" therapy in 24 of 34 outpatients referred to a specialist service. Treatments comprised 18 intensive sessions over 6 months with 6 booster sessions over 6 months follow-up. Mean ages ranged from 21.6 to 25.75 years. Overall participants in all treatment groups improved and there were no differences in the number of participants not completing treatment. Serfaty (1999) compared a form of CBT over 20 weekly sessions with dietary advice in 35 patients followed to 6 months. On post-randomization group comparisons, those in the dietary counseling alone group had significantly shorter duration of illness (2.2 years SD 4.5 vs. 5 years SD 5.5, $p = 0.048$). The small numbers randomized may have contributed to this difference and it was likely that the study was under-powered. No patients in the dietary advice group completed therapy. CBT subjects showed significant improvements in ED and depressive symptom severity, and body mass index (BMI), although the mean BMI in those receiving CBT at end of treatment (<18) was not yet in a normal range.

Dare, Eisler, Russell, Treasure, and Dodge (2001) conducted a RCT of three "active" outpatient treatments compared to "routine" outpatient treatment in 84 adults with AN presenting sequentially to a specialist outpatient service. Participants were randomly allocated to focal psychoanalytic psychotherapy (FPT), cognitive analytic therapy (CAT), family therapy, and low contact routine care from a supervised psychiatry trainee. All therapies were conducted over 1 year except the CAT which comprised 20 weekly sessions followed by less frequent "booster" sessions over 3 months. Significantly more patients in FPT or family therapy "recovered" or "significantly improved" and in a secondary analysis relative risk (RR) was significantly in favor of FPT versus treatment as usual (RR 0.70, 95% confidence interval [CI] 0.51–0.97) and just failed to reach significance for CAT versus treatment as usual (RR 0.77, 95% CI 0.58–1.01; Hay et al., 2003). Of the 84 participants randomized, 54 (64%) completed treatment, 12 (14%) required admission to hospital, one died, and outcome was categorized as "poor" in 52 participants (62%). In an earlier study Treasure et al. (1995) compared two forms of outpatient treatment, educational behavior treatment (EBT) and CAT for adults with AN. Information from the author (Treasure, personal communication) was that the CAT in Dare, Eisler, Russell, Treasure & Dodge, et al. (2001) was the same or closely similar to the CAT in Treasure et al. (1995) and EBT was similar to 'treatment as usual' in Dare Eisler et al. (2001). Thirty patients were randomly allocated to the two treatments. At 1 year, all had gained 6.8 kg and 19 (63%) had a good or intermediate recovery in terms of nutritional outcome. The group given CAT reported significantly greater subjective improvement, but there were no between group differences reported in other outcome parameters. End of treatment data were not reported. Therapists were supervised and treatment was conducted over 20 weekly 50-minute sessions.

Crisp et al. (1991) and Gowers, Norton, Halek, & Crisp (1994) conducted a RCT of individual and group (both including family therapy) versus inpatient treatment versus assessment only in adults older than 20 years. In this study outpatient individual and family psychotherapy (20 subjects, up to 12 sessions, up to 5 of which were family sessions, over about 10 months) was compared to outpatient group psychotherapy (10 sessions) in-patient treatment (see later) and assessment only (20 subjects) for new adult referrals (age range 20–23 years, mean 22) to a specialist unit. At 2-year follow-up (Gowers et al., 1994) outcome in the individual and family psychotherapy was compared to assessment only. There was significantly better weight maintenance and psychological and social adjustment at 2 years in the psychotherapy groups. Prognosis was associated with prior low weight, treatment noncompliance and self- induced vomiting. Small numbers and nonblinding of groups limited conclusions from this study. Those in the assessment only group had significantly less weight gain than those in active therapy groups ($p < 0.01$).

McIntosh et al. (2005) have reported the results of their trial of 56 women (ages 17–40 years) with AN broadly defined (BMI 15.5–19 kg/m^2), who were randomized to CBT, IPT, or a control treatment of specialist supportive care, later termed specialist supportive clinical management (SSCM; McIntosh et al., 2006). CBT included self-monitoring and homework, assessment of motivation for engagement in treatment, prescription of normal eating, and negotiation of a goal weight range in Phase 1. Phase 2 incorporated CBT skills of challenging dysfunctional thoughts and thought restructuring with psychoeducational material. Phase 3 prepared the patient for termination and included relapse prevention strategies. IPT was based on the model developed both for depression and BN, and used the patient's presentation of ED symptoms to facilitate work on the agreed interpersonal problem. SSCM included psychoeducation, "care" and supportive psychotherapy, with focus on resumption of normal eating and weight gain, strategies for weight maintenance, information about energy requirements, and relearning to eat normally. Thus it incorporated elements of nutritional counseling and some behavioral weight restoration strategies. All therapies were delivered by therapists who were experienced in treating EDs. Treatment was relatively short, with 20 one-hour manual-based sessions over a minimum of 20 weeks. McIntosh et al. (2005) found that CBT was associated with a greater number of people rated as significantly improved (1 or 2 on their global scale) than those in the IPT group and EDE Restraint subscale scores also favored CBT, but differences were not significant for weight, Global Assessment of Function (GAF) scores or Hamilton Depression Rating Scale (HDRS) scores. In addition, CBT was not associated with a greater number of people rated as significantly improved (1 or 2 on their global scale) than those in the SSCM group, or with lower EDE Restraint subscale scores, greater weight, greater GAF or lower HDRS scores. SSCM was significantly favored over IPT for improved global outcome, EDE Restraint scores and GAF scores, but not for weight or HDRS scores. There were no significant differences in the number of people not completing treatment in the three arms but attrition was high, 38% (7/19 in the CBT arm, 9/21 in the IPT arm, and 5/16 in the SSCM arm, respectively).

PSYCHOTHERAPY STUDIES POST WEIGHT RESTORATION

Russell (1987) and Eisler, et al., Russell, Szmulker, Dare, & Eisler (1997) compared a 1-year family therapy with individual supportive therapy in an RCT of 80 outpatients (mean age 21.8 years). Therapy began on discharge from a specialist inpatient hospital program after weight restoration. Fifty-seven patients had AN, and 23 had BN with a past history of AN. The 80 patients had been subdivided into four prognostically homogeneous groups, of which two turned out to be the most important: patients with early onset and short history of AN, and patients with late-onset AN. At the 5-year follow-up, the efficacy of the outpatient therapies were assessed by the maintenance of weight, and the categories of general outcome and dimensions of clinical functioning defined by the Morgan-Russell scales. Analyses were by completers only and only subgroup results were presented. Significant improvements were found in the group of 80 patients as a whole, mainly attributable to the natural outcome of AN, and most evident in the early onset and short history group, as expected. Within two of the prognostic groups, significant benefits attributable to previous psychological treatments were still evident, favoring family therapy for patients with early onset and short history of AN, and favoring individual supportive therapy for patients with late-onset AN.

Pike, Walsh, Vitousek, Wilson, and Bauer (2003) found CBT had a better outcome and longer time to relapse when compared to nutritional counseling therapy after their hospitalization and attaining weight gain to within 90% of ideal body weight. However, numbers were small (n = 33).

FAMILY THERAPY AND STUDIES IN CHILDREN AND ADOLESCENTS

In addition to the study by Dare Eisler, Russell, Treasure & Dodge (2001) and Russell et al. (1987) described in the preceding text there have been three studies of family therapy incorporating weight restoration in children and adolescents comparing different modalities and/or intensity of family therapy. Eisler et al. (2000) compared a Maudsley model conjoint family therapy (CFT) to Maudsley model separated family therapy (SFT). Noncompletion rates were low (4/40, 10%) and similar between groups. At follow-up there was a trend toward better improvement in the SFT group (76% good/intermediate global outcome ratings) compared to the CFT group (47% good/intermediate outcome). Small numbers may have explained the failure of this difference to reach statistical significance. On other secondary analyses CFT was favored, and a 5-year follow-up did not favor either approach excepting that where maternal criticism was high SFT was favored (Eisler, Simic, Russell, & Dare, 2007).

Geist, Heinmaa, Stephens, Davis, and Katzman (2000) conducted an RCT of two forms of family "therapy," one where the families were seen for eight sessions attended by the patient and her parents and siblings, and "family group psycho-education" where families were seen together in a class or workshop format for eight times. Participants were 25 female adolescents with AN with a modification to the DSM-IV criteria to include those with less than 90% ideal body weight. No significant differences between groups were found. Third, Lock, Agras, Bryson, and Kraemer (2005) compared a short- and a longer-term Maudsley model family therapy with no differences found at end of treatment, and longer term family therapy being slightly favored at follow-up in those with intact families.

Robin et al. (1999) have compared behavioral family systems therapy to ego-orientated individual psychotherapy in 37 adolescents (11–20 years) with *DSM-III R* AN, who all also received common medical treatment and dietary advice. Although family therapy was found to be associated with greater weight gain at 1-year follow-up there were no differences at end of treatment and no differences in attenuation of ED attitudes, depression or family conflict. Finally, Gowers et al. (2007), in a large RCT trial of inpatient care versus specialist outpatient care (manualized CBT and parental counseling) versus general psychiatric outpatient care (nonmanualized family and supportive care), found no differences between groups (see also below under *Treatment Setting*).

Pharmacotherapy in AN Treatment

Shared inheritance (Strober, Freeman, Lampert, Diamond, & Kaye, 2000; Wade, Bulik, Neale, & Kendler, 2000); neurobiological, most notably serotonergic dysfunction (Kaye et al., 2005); and depressive psychopathology have supported the use of antidepressant treatment in AN, particularly where is there is comorbidity such as mood disorders, and obsessive–compulsive disorder or obsessive–compulsive personality disorder (Godart et al., 2007; Kaye, Bulik, Thornton, Barbarich, & Masters, 2004). A recent systematic review of the use of antidepressants in AN (Claudino et al., 2006) evaluated the efficacy of antidepressants in the acute phase. Only four small RCTs were found. Three of these tested the tricyclic antidepressants (TCA) amitriptyline (Biederman, Herzog, & Rivinus, 1985; Halmi, Eckert, LaDu, & Cohen, 1986) and clomipramine (Lacey & Crisp, 1980). One trial tested the SSRI fluoxetine (Attia, Haiman, Walsh, & Flater, 1998) in comparison with placebo. Only one trial (Halmi, Eckert, LaDu & Cohen, 1986), with 72 inpatients randomized to amitriptyline, cyproheptadine or placebo treatment groups, reported a mild but statistically significant effect in decreasing the time to achieve target weight, for both drug groups. However, tricyclic drugs are more often associated with adverse effects and cardiovascular risk (Biederman et al., 1985; Halmi Eckert, LaDu & Cohen, 1986).Overall, the results of trials of antidepressant efficacy did not reveal statistically significant or clinically relevant differences from placebo. The doses of antidepressant used in these trials were usually low and the duration of treatment was short, but the consistency of negative findings seems to indicate that antidepressants may have a limited role in improving the overall symptomatology during the acute phase of AN.

The lack of efficacy of serotonergic drugs in the acute phase of the disease may be related to low levels of serotonin (5-hydroxytryptamine [5-HT]) metabolites in the cerebrospinal fluid (5-hydroxyindoleacetic acid [5-HIAA]) due to malnourishment and poor dietary intake of tryptophan, the precursor of serotonin. However, a small RCT that compared fluoxetine plus nutritional supplements against fluoxetine plus "placebo nutritional supplements" found that the addition of nutritional supplements with tryptophan to selective serotonin reuptake inhibitors (SSRIs) did not improve the physiological effects of chronic undernutrition or enhance the efficacy of drugs (Barbarich et al., 2003).

Two recent double-blind RCTs tested the use of fluoxetine for patients to prevent relapse after weight restoration (Kaye, Nagata, Weltzin, Hsu, & Sokol., 2001; Walsh et al., 2006). In the first study, with 35 patients with restricting-type AN, Kaye Nagata, Weltzin, Hsu & Solcol (2001) found significantly more patients on fluoxetine had reduced relapse, namely maintained an adequate weight and symptom reduction during the 1-year follow-up after hospital discharge but attrition was high in the placebo group (84% vs. 37% in treatment group). For the majority of the patients, the decision to terminate the study was based on symptoms indicating a relapse. However, the more recent and larger (93 AN patients) trial (Walsh et al., 2006) did not find an added effect of fluoxetine to CBT in preventing relapse (defined as BMI falling to or below 16.5 kg/m² and/or worsening of AN symptoms, development of major clinical problems, or suicidal ideation).

ANTIPSYCHOTICS

The use of antipsychotic drugs in AN is for a putative reduction of the "psychotic-like" symptoms, such as extreme body image distortion, pseudo hallucinations and psychomotor agitation, and the potential for weight-gain as a "side-effect" (Powers & Santana, 2004; Taylor & McAskill, 2000). There is speculation that antipsychotics may target dopaminergic dysregulation in AN and comorbid disorders. If an antipsychotic drug can help lessen the intensity of disturbed cognitions and heightened arousal it is thought anxiety and resistance to gaining weight may decrease and thereby patients improve.

Use of older antipsychotics, for example, chlorpromazine, has largely ceased because of adverse effects such as convulsions and Parkinsonian symptoms. In addition, the findings of earlier RCTs supporting the efficacy of pimozide and sulpiride over placebo were not replicated and there was a lack of clear evidence of the benefits of antipsychotics in AN (Vandereycken, 1984; Vandereycken & Pierloot, 1982). In recent years, second-generation antipsychotics that have a broader range of targeted symptoms and a different spectrum of side effects (mainly olanzapine, risperidone, and quetiapine) have been used in case reports and open trials (Bosanac, Norman, Burrows, & Beumont, 2005; Powers, Bannon, Eubanks, & McCormick, 2007). Patients in these trials were usually severely underweight, with treatment-resistant EDs, important comorbid psychopathologies and histories of previous unsuccessful treatments. Despite methodological limitations, these studies found clinical improvements in weight gain over baseline weight, and reductions in core ED symptoms, compulsive activity, pre-meal anxiety, comorbid symptoms and social withdrawal, as well as greater adherence to treatment (Bosanac, Norman, Burrows & Beaumont, 2005; Duncan & Del Dotto, 2007; Powers, Bannon, Eubanks & McCormick, 2007).

Olanzapine has been compared to chlorpromazine (added to standard care) in an unblinded RCT of 15 AN patients (Mondraty et al., 2005) and to placebo and CBT in two double-blind randomized trials (Brambilla et al., 2007; Bissada, Tasco, Barber & Brodwejn, 2008). In the first trial, olanzapine (mean dose 10 mg/day) showed greater efficacy in reducing "anorexic ruminations" when compared with chlorpromazine (50 mg/day) (Mondraty et al., 2005). The second trial compared olanzapine to placebo as an adjunctive treatment to CBT (Brambilla et al, 2007) in 30 outpatients enrolled for a 3-month treatment. Olanzapine was found to increase weight gain, and reduce depressive symptoms and aggressive-

ness when compared to placebo, but only for patients of the binge-purge type. A third trial that included 34 AN subjects showed better results when olanzapine was combined with a day-hospital treatment for 10 weeks (Bissada et al, 2008); compared to placebo, subjects taking olanzapine showed a greater rate of increase in weight (achieving target BMI earlier) and improvement of obsessive symptoms. Although completion rates were high (82%) in the third trial, 55% of eligible patients declined to be randomized, indicating a potential problem of low acceptance of olanzapine treatment in this patient group. The level of evidence is insufficient to strongly support use of antipsychotics, however they do warrant further research and in particular larger trials of olanzapine and other atypical antipsychotics.

ZINC

Zinc deficiency from nutritional insufficiency and extreme exercise is found in about 50% of AN patients, and it itself may cause many physical symptoms found in AN, including weight loss, appetite and taste changes, amenorrhea, skin abnormalities, depression and hormone changes (Birmingham & Gritzner, 2006). Birmingham and colleagues have argued that zinc deficiency may be a maintaining factor in AN through dysregulation of serotonergic and GABAergic neurotransmission (Birmingham & Gritzner, 2006; Birmingham, Goldner, & Bakan, 1994).

Three double-blind RCTs (Birmingham, Goldner & Bakan, 1994; Katz et al., 1987; Lask, Fosson, Rolfe, & Thomas, 1993) investigated the efficacy of zinc supplementation in comparison with placebo in underweight AN patients. In the largest trial (with 35 female inpatients), zinc supplementation significantly increased the weight gain rate (twofold increase) during the treatment (Birmingham, Goldner & Bakan, 1994). The two other trials did not show an effect in weight increase, but one of them (with 15 adolescent outpatients) reported a greater decrease in depression and anxiety scores in patients taking zinc supplementation than in those on placebo (Katz et al., 1987). The results of the third trial were compromised by a high dropout rate (Lask et al., 1993).

CYPROHEPTADINE

Cyproheptadine is a histamine and serotonin antagonist that has been found to increase hunger and weight gain in the treatment of physical illnesses. Its efficacy in RCTs has been inconsistent. Halmi, Eckert, LoDu & Cohen (1986) reported that when cyproheptadine was compared with amitriptyline and placebo, both treatment groups reached target weights an average 10 days earlier than placebo. However, this was only in the restricting AN participants and weight gain was impeded in the bulimic form. Cyproheptadine, with vitamins, has been found to increase weight gain compared to placebo, but produced hypersomnia and stomatitis in 60% of participants (Toledo, 1970). Three other studies (Goldberg, Casper & Eckert, 1980; Goldberg, Halmi, Eckert, Casper, & Davis, 1979; Vigersky & Loriaux, 1977) offer only limited support for a role for cyproheptadine and it has not been recommended in clinical practice guidelines (APA, 2006, NICE, 2004).

OTHER AGENTS

The use of several other agents in AN has been studied (deZwann & Roerig, 2003; Treasure & Schmidt, 2005), but no proof of beneficial effects was found for agents such as lithium or growth hormone. In addition, some negative effects were identified in studies with, for example, tetrahydrocannabinol and clonidine. One double-blind RCT tested the opiate antagonist naltrexone (Marrazzi, Bacon, Kinzie, & Luby, 1995) based on the premise that some ED behaviors (specially binge eating) could be seen as "addictive" behaviors. This trial enrolled 19 patients with bulimic symptoms, 6 of who had bulimic-type AN. Positive findings regarding reduction of these symptoms were reported but too few had AN for any meaningful conclusions.

Prokinetic agents, namely cisapride, metoclopramide and domperidone have been found to improve gastric emptying time in patients with AN but there was no effect on their weight gain (Abatzi-Wenzel, Wiesnagrotzki, Bergmann, Schneider, & Gaupmann, 1993; Szmukler, Young, Miller, Lichtenstein, & Binns, 1995). Of these agents, only cisapride has been studied in RCTs, but this drug was recalled from the market in the United States and other countries because of lethal cardiac effects. Its use in Australia is restricted to gastroparesis diagnosed by a consultant physician.

Finally, anxiolytic drugs such as benzodiazepines are sometimes used in AN but there are no RCTs (deZwann & Roerig, 2003). Steinglass et al. (2007) have examined the effects of D-cycloserine (a glutamate partial agonist) in a very small study of 14 (9 with AN) patients which was part of evaluating an exposure (to food) therapy. Results were mixed and food intake was not enhanced.

DRUGS TO TREAT OSTEOPENIA AND OSTEOPOROSIS

More than 50% of patients with AN develop osteoporosis related to the state of estrogen deficiency and other metabolic effects of low weight and starvation (Biller et al., 1989; see also Chapters 15 and 16 of this Handbook). A very few small studies have investigated drugs that could potentially improve bone mineral density in AN. Two small RCTs compared hormone replacement therapy (with oestrogens) with no treatment (Klibanski, Biller, Shoenfeld, Herzog, & Saxe, 1995) or placebo (Grinspoon, Thomas, Miller, Herzog, & Klibanski, 2002). Patients were followed up to 3 years in the first trial or 9 months in the second trial and all patients in both trials also received oral calcium supplementation. There was no difference in bone mineral density at follow up in both trials and treatment effect was reported to be highly dependent on patient's initial percent of ideal body weight in the first study. The second trial also included two other arms where patients were treated with recombinant human insulin-like growth factor I (rnIGF-1) alone or combined with oral contraceptives (oestradiol). Patients in these two arms showed significant changes in bone density compared to the placebo group, with the combined treatment showing the greatest effect.

A more recent RCT compared the effects of the bisphosphonate alendronate (10 mg daily)—a bone antiresorptive drug—with placebo. Thirty-two adolescents were enrolled in the trial and all received calcium and vitamin D oral supplementation and the same multidisciplinary treatment for one year (Golden et al., 2005). Although groups did not differ in final measurements, patients treated with alendronate showed significant increase in bone mineral density from baseline to follow-up, which was not observed in patients taking placebo. However, the most important determinant of bone mass density at follow-up was body weight and this finding needs to be replicated in larger trials to establish the efficacy and long-term safety of alendronate in adolescents. In addition, a recent meta-analysis of bisphosphonate therapy for children and adolescents with secondary osteopenia (including from AN) similarly did not support bisphosphonates as standard therapy (Ward et al., 2007).

TREATMENT REGIMENS AND SETTINGS

Meads, Gold, and Burls (2001) completed a systematic review of inpatient versus outpatient care in AN. They identified one properly conducted RCT (Crisp et al., 1991) and a second unpublished RCT (Freeman, 1992) and also reviewed a body of evidence from clinical cohort studies. They concluded that for the group of people with AN which is severe enough to consider in-patient care but not severe enough for this to be essential, outpatient treatment is at least as effective (if not more effective) than inpatient treatment. The benefits of both treatments appear to increase over time. Out-patient treatment is also considerably cheaper. Caveats include the non-blinding of the single published trial (Crisp et al., 1991) and the imprecision of the cost-evaluation. It is of note that adherence was higher in the outpatient groups and that there were two deaths in the trial, one in the outpatient group and one randomized to the inpatient group.

Since this review there has been a further (Gowers et al., 2007) well conducted large (n = 170) RCT of inpatient care versus specialist outpatient care (manualized CBT and parental counseling) versus general psychiatric outpatient care (nonmanualized family and supportive care) in young (mean age nearly 15 years) AN patients. Attrition was, however, moderately high (35%) especially in the inpatient group, where it was 51%. Analyses were by intention-to-treat. At 1 year, there were no statistically significant differences between groups in outcomes but only 18% overall had a good outcome at one year and 31% a good outcome at 2 years. Adherence to treatment improved outcomes.

In contrast, Kong (2005), in a RCT, compared a combined psychological (CBT and IPT) and pharmacological (SSRIs and benzodiazepines) regime delivered in a day versus an outpatient setting and found the day hospital setting was associated with both significantly better weight recovery and improved psychological symptoms. In an earlier RCT, Bergh, Brodin, Lindberg, and Sodersten (2002) compared a comprehensive inpatient followed by partial hospitalization treatment over a median of 14 months to a waitlist control in 19 patients with AN and 13 with BN from 47 treatment referrals. The median age of the 19 AN patients was 16 years. The treatment approach was predominantly nutritional and behavioral and incorporated computer supported feedback to participants on satiety ratings. After eating they rested in a warm room. There was a graded reduction in restriction of physical activity until remission. In addition participants had two other daily meals (with supplements) and between meal snacks provided in the program. Ten of 11 patients in the treatment group were in remission after a median of 14.4 months of treatment, and none of the eight patients in the delayed treatment control group went into remission during 21.6 month observation period (RR 15.75, 95% CI 1.06–234.88; Hay et al., 2003). Rigaud, Brondel, Poupard, Talonneau, and Brun (2007) compared two refeeding 70-day inpatient regimes in a quasi-randomized trial, one regime including nasogastric feeding in 81 adult patients with a very high (nearly 100%) completion rate and one that did not have enteral feeding. Follow-up was at 12 months post-discharge. Patients were treated in two sequential groups. The results favored the enteral feeding regime, with significantly earlier behavioral change (at 1 week), improved weight gain and longer time to relapse post-discharge.

Although treatment regimens have traditionally limited or severely restricted exercise a systematic review of five controlled studies of well supervised moderate exercise regimens indicated positive psychological benefits without detracting from weight gain (Hausenblas, Cook, & Chittester, 2008). Three of the five studies were however tiny (with fewer than 20 participants). Adequately powered randomized controlled studies are needed to further explore the cautious use of exercise in treatment of AN.

Taken together, these findings support consensus guidelines that indicate a need for a continuum of care ranging from comprehensive multidisciplinary inpatient and partial hospital regimes to less intensive outpatient individual or family therapy (APA, 2006; NICE, 2004; RANZCP, 2004). Medical risk (see Chapter 15), psychiatric (suicide) risk, and motivation are all important in the assessment and decision for treatment setting. No treatment is associated with very poor outcomes but for many the outcome remains poor even with treatment, and attrition in trials is problematic (Halmi et al., 2005) in this most ego-syntonic of mental illnesses. When also considering predictors of a favorable outcome (Table 25.2) it is also important that treatment regimes, particularly hospital based programs, aim to achieve weight restoration prior to discharge (Barren, Weltzin, & Kaye, 1995, Fichter & Quadfleig, 2004; Gross et al., 2000).

Treatments of Choice: Bulimia Nervosa
CBT and Other Psychotherapies for BN
The CBT model for bulimia is based on a theoretical understanding of the origin of disordered eating and weight and shape concern emanating from a cycle of binge eating followed by extreme dieting and/or weight-control behaviors which exacerbate extreme weight concern and reinforce in turn the ED behaviors. Although this model has since been refined, extended, and adapted, the core dieting/binge eating/extreme weight-control behaviors cycle is invariably found. The rationale for CBT in BN is

Table 25.2 Factors Most Consistently Associated with an unfavorable outcome with treatment

	Pre-treatment	Post-treatment
Anorexia Nervosa	Low BMI[a]	Poor weight gain
	Medical compromise/emergency	Psychiatric comorbidity[a]
	Binge/purge subtype[a]	High drive for thinness
	Interpersonal difficulties/	and/or exercise
	personality disorder	Poor social adjustment
	Previous treatment	Treatment <1 year
	Family disturbance	
	Older age at presentation[a]	
	Longer illness duration	
	Body image disturbance severe	
Bulimia Nervosa	Borderline personality structure	Poor social adjustment
	Comorbid substance misuse	Depression
	Low motivation	Continued high level ED
	History of obesity	symptoms
	Higher levels binge eating and/or	Higher cognitive disturbance
	purging[a]	Non abstinent at end
	Impulsivity	treatment
	Longer duration illness	Lower social class/income
		Purging
		Psychiatric comorbidity

Sources: Berkman, Lohr, & Bulik (2007); NICE (2004).
[a]More than one study has also found a negative result.

to first address the dieting/binge eating/extreme weight control behavior(s) cycle by use of behavioral experiments and specific strategies, such as proscribing restrictive dieting that reduce the frequency of the behaviors. Second, a range of cognitive techniques are employed, that address the ED ideation, such as fear of weight gain after binging, that underpins and drives the behavioral cycle. The goal is a "normalization" of both eating patterns and an individual's thoughts (and subsequently feelings) about food and body image issues (Fairburn, 2002, 2008). This specific CBT for BN (CBT-BN) takes place over 19 to 20 usually weekly individual hourly sessions. It has been modified to be less intensive, with either fewer and/or briefer sessions, and to be delivered in self-help, guided nonspecialist self-help formats and group formats. CBT-BN in full and

modified forms has been tested in a number of RCTs.

Systematic reviews and subsequent randomized controlled trials identified for the purposes of this chapter consistently supported CBT as having a high level of evidence for efficacy. In the NICE (2004) guidelines it reached Level I (see earlier), in Clinical Evidence (Hay & Bacaltchuk, 2008) it was listed as "likely to be beneficial," and in the RTI International University of North Carolina Evidence-based Practice Center (RTI-UNC EPC; Shapiro et al., 2007) review it received a rating of "strong" evidence. In all these CBT for BN was noted for being the only psychotherapy to be endorsed with the highest ranking of evidence. This is an important consistency noting that these reviews were conducted independently with each applying similar but individual methodologies including inclusion and exclusion criteria for trials.

In meta-analyses (Hay, Bacaltchuk, & Stefano, 2007; NICE, 2004,) of trials CBT is favored over wait-list and other psychotherapies for a range of outcome measures including binge eating abstinence rates, bulimia symptom (usually binge frequency) severity, depression, general psychiatric symptom severity and function. Table 25.3 summarizes findings from the recent update to the Cochrane Library Review (Hay, Bacaltchuk, Kashyap, & Stefano, 2009). Compared to no treatment, CBT achieved a superior outcome with 37% cumulative binge eating abstinence versus a rate of almost zero (3%) in the cumulative wait-list trials. Abstinence rates were very similar for CBT in the trials comparing with other psychotherapies, 34% versus 22% for cumulative other therapies. It is also important to note that no significant differences were found in treatment noncompletion rates for either meta-analyses or for body weight in the CBT versus other psychotherapy analysis and noncompletion rates were moderate to low: 24% and 23% for CBT and 24% for other psychotherapies.

However, heterogeneity, as reflected by the I^2 statistic, is high in these meta-analyses, and is particularly high in the analyses comparing a symptom severity outcome score as there was little consistency in trials in tools and methods of measurement of bulimic symptom severity, binge frequency, depression, or other outcomes. Heterogeneity may have been expected to be even higher mindful that the CBT tested in trials is not consistently the manualized 19 to 20 session therapy as developed by Fairburn, Marcus, and Wilson (1993). In addition a range of control therapies have been tested, namely focal psychotherapy (one trial), interpersonal psychotherapy (three trials), hypnobehavioral therapy (one trial), exposure and response prevention (one trial), supportive psychotherapy and pill placebo (one trial), support group (one trial), and psychoeducation (one trial). When the efficacy of manual-based CBT for BN (CBT-BN, Fairburn et al., 1993) with outcome assessed over a 4-week period by interview (using the Eating Disorder Examination) was examined there are insufficient trials for meta-analyses of CBT-BN versus wait-list control groups. Only four trials to date (listed in Table 25.4) have

Table 25.3 Results of Meta-analyses of Randomized Controlled Trials of CBT for Bulimia Nervosa

Outcome	*n* trials	*n* participants	I^2%	Effect size	95% CI
CBT vs. wait list					
Binge abstinence	5	204	0	RR 0.67	0.58, 0.78*
Binge/bulimic symptoms	9	323	45.8	SMD −1.01	−1.33, −0.68*
Non-completion rate	9	331	45.2	RR 1.89	0.83, 4.30
Depression score	6	223	55.9	SMD -0.80	−1.22, −0.37*
CBT vs. alternate psychotherapy					
Binge abstinence	7	484	22.1	RR 0.83	0.71, 0.97*
Binge/bulimic symptoms	8	514	27.4	SMD −0.15	−0.38, 0.07
Noncompletion rate	8	523	34.2	RR 1.00	0.63, 1.58
Body weight/BMI	5	190	0	SMD 0.13	−0.15, 0.42
Depression score	7	242	71.3	SMD −0.48	−0.98, 0.02
Psychiatric symptoms	5	165	0	SMD −0.14	−0.45, 0.17
Psychosocial function	4	330	0	SMD −0.09	−0.31, 0.13

Source: Hay, Bacaltchuk, Kashyap, and Stefano (2009).
*SMD = Standardized mean difference, <0 on the upper 95% confidence interval (CI) is significant and favors the active (CBT) therapy.
*RR = Relative risk, <1 on the upper 95% CI is significant and favors the active (CBT) therapy.
I^2% Test of heterogeneity; It provides an estimate of the percentage of variability due to heterogeneity rather than chance alone and a value >50% is considered substantial heterogeneity.

compared the full manualized treatment to any other psychotherapy (Agras, Walsh, Fairburn, Wilson, & Kraemer, 2000; Fairburn, Kirk, O'Connor, & Cooper, 1986; Fairburn et al., 1991; Walsh et al., 1997). Heterogeneity fell in the meta-analyses and CBT-BN retained significantly greater improvements in binge frequency or other bulimic symptoms (n = 4 trials, n = 338 participants, I^2 = 0%, SMD = -0.17, 95% CI –0.60; –0.17) and binge eating abstinence rates (n = 3 trials, I^2 = 16.1%, RR 0.81, 95% CI 0.69; 0.95) but not greater reduction in depression scores (n = 3 trials; I^2 = 0%, SMD = –0.33, 95% CI –0.70; 0.05) compared to another psychotherapy. CBT also consistently has better outcomes when compared with "dismantled" CBT, usually with behavior therapy alone (Hay, Bacaltchuk, & Stefano, 2004). In addition, improvements are generally sustained or increased at follow-up (Hay, 2008).

Where access to therapists is precluded by distance and/or cost CBT has been found efficacious in RCTs when delivered in other modalities such as by teleconference or e-mail. Mitchell et al. (2008) compared manualized CBT-BN delivered face-to-face or by tele-medicine link and found no differences in abstinence rates at end of treatment (50% on intention-to-treat analyses) or 12-month follow-up. Although face-to-face delivery was slightly favored on some secondary outcomes the study supports telemedicine delivery of CBT-BN where face-to-face is not feasible. The study was blinded and well conducted but had a moderately high attrition rate (38%).

Robinson and Serfaty (2008) compared a non-manualized CBT to a control therapeutic writing therapy both delivered by e-mail to a wait list control in an RCT of 97 students with BN, BED, or EDNOS identified by self-report. Attrition was 37%. Active therapy was favored but attrition was high (37%) limiting conclusions. Ljotsson et al. (2007) reported similarly favorable outcomes (significant differences in binge eating and other ED psychopathology excepting purging by intention to treat analyses) of an internet supported guided self-help CBT versus wait-list control in an RCT of community participants with either BN (n = 33) or BED (n = 36). Attrition was, however, 31% in the treatment group.

OTHER PSYCHOTHERAPIES

Two psychotherapies appear to have moved into wider use with yet a small Level I evidence base for efficacy. These are interpersonal psychotherapy and dialectical behavior therapy (DBT; Hay & Bacaltchuk, 2008, see also Chapters 20 and 23 of this Handbook). Interpersonal psychotherapy has been compared in head-to-head RCTs with CBT (see earlier) and found to have lower (or similar; Wilfley et al., 2002) abstinence rates at end of treatment, but not at one year follow-up (Agras, Walth, Fairburn, Wilson & Kraemen, 2000; Fairburn, Jones, Peveler, Hope, & O'Connor, 1993). There has been one RCT of dialectical behavior therapy compared to a wait list control (Safer, Telch, & Agras, 2001a, 2001b) that significantly favored active therapy for binge eating purging abstinence (29% vs. 0%) and other ED features but not depression.

In addition, other psychotherapeutic approaches addressing predisposing and perpetuating factors have been incorporated into an extended CBT-BN. In this, modules are added with foci on mood intolerance, interpersonal relationships, clinical perfectionism, and self-esteem (Fairburn, 2008). Preliminary unpublished findings of the efficacy of this extended therapy indicate it may offer advantages and, for example, increase abstinence rates to well over sixty to seventy percent (Fairburn, oral presentation to the London International Meeting of Eating Disorders in 2007). However, CBT-BN also performed very well. Subgroup analyses may reveal particular efficacy for the extended CBT for patients with the particular problems that are addressed in the additional modules.

Family Therapy and Adolescent Therapy

There has been one RCT of manualized Maudsley type family therapy, finding it more efficacious than individual nondirective supportive therapy in 80 adolescents with BN (Doyle, McLean, Washington, Rienecke Hoste, & le Grange, 2009; Le Grange, Crosby, Rathouz, & Leventhal 2007,). Abstinence from binging and purging was 39% in the family therapy group versus 18% in the supportive therapy group, and still significantly different at 6 months although abstinence reduced over time (29% vs. 10%). Other middle, end therapy and 6-month ED outcomes favored family therapy and there were no differences in improvements in depression or self-esteem. Although antidepressants were used by 32% to 42% of participants at various phases, their use did not differ between groups or impact on remission status. The trial is also noted for the low attrition rates (11% active treatment phase, 15% at 6 months) and high comorbidity rates.

In contrast, Schmidt et al. (2007) have compared manualized (Treasure & Schmidt, 1997) CBT

Table 25.4 Randomized Controlled Trials of Manualized Cognitive Behavior Therapy (CBT-BN) versus Control Psychological Therapy for Bulimia Nervosa with Outcome Assessment over 4 Weeks

Study	Trial Quality	Participants per Group and Settings	Intervention(s)	Outcome at End active Rx[a]	Outcome at 1-year[a]
Agras (2000)	Multisite Adequate allocation concealment Assessors blinded ITT analysis done	$n = 220$, 61 (28%) dropouts Gender: not specified Adults Diagnosis: BN purging type Recruitment: Media advertising and referrals Setting: specialist Country: USA	CBT-BN vs. IPT Other: no significant effects on psychosocial function or dropouts	29% vs. 6 % abstinence	31% vs. 19%
Fairburn (1991)	Unclear allocation concealment ITT not done Assessors blinded Follow-up 5 years	$n = 73$, 13 (18%) dropouts All female Adults BN (*DSM-IIIR*) Recruitment: Primary and secondary care Setting: tertiary Country: UK	CBT-BN vs. IPT: CBT-BN vs. BT:	60% vs. 54% abstinence BT 46% abstinent No significant differential effects on dropouts depression, psychosocial function or weight	Outcome poor in BT group & attrition high (48%) 20% BT, 36% CBT & 44% IPT abstinent CBT superior to BT Effects maintained at 5 years
Fairburn (1986)	Unclear allocation concealment ITT not done but supplied by authors[a] Assessors blinded	$n = 24$, 2 (8%) dropouts All female Adults BN-P (Russell, 1979) Recruitment primary care Setting: Tertiary Country: UK	CBT-BN vs. focal psychotherapy	Reduced bulimic symptoms CBT-BN No difference: dropouts, depression, psychosocial function, general psychiatric symptoms or weight	SMD 0.42 NS Effects maintained over time
Walsh (1997)	Unclear allocation concealment ITT done Assessors blinded	$n = 120$, 47 to non medication group Adults, all female *DSM-III-R* BN Recruitment community Setting: Tertiary Country: US	Group CBT-BN vs. supportive therapy (also vs. placebo vs. CBT plus antidepressant)	24% vs 23% abstinence No significant effects on dropouts, depression, psychosocial function, general psychiatric symptoms or weight	n.a.

NS = not significant, IPT = interpersonal psychotherapy, BT = behaviour therapy, ITT = intention to tract analysis.
[a]Data reported in Hay et al. (2007)

guided self-help (GSH), conducted over 10 weekly sessions by experienced therapists, to manualized Maudsley family therapy up to 15 sessions in 85 adolescents with BN. Attrition was 29% and 27.8% of those eligible were not randomized as they did not want their families involved. However, all analyses were by intention to treat and 89% completed at least one follow-up assessment. The results did not confirm the hypothesis that family therapy would be favored. Those in GSH showed a significantly earlier improvement in binging than the clients who received family therapy, and there were no differences between groups at 12-month follow-up. The authors speculated that the earlier change in the

GSH group may have been because of its focus on key symptoms such as binge eating as a key symptom in GSH. It should also be noted that GSH was more acceptable to patients than family therapy and more cost-effective.

Exercise

Sundgot-Borgen, Rosenvinge, Bahr, and Schneider (2002), in a nonblinded RCT of 64 BN participants, compared CBT to nutritional counseling to an exercise program to a wait-list group. Follow-up was for 18 months and attrition was very low (8%). Exercise and CBT had similar efficacy at end of treatment (and were favored over wait-list) and at follow-up "recovery" was greatest in the exercise group (53% vs. 31% in the CBT group vs. 24% in the nutritional counselling group). Although there were problems with this study, it supports more research into the judicious use of a "healthy" exercise program for patients who would benefit, particularly the overweight and those with low physical fitness.

Antidepressants

Although many patients with BN have a comorbid depression (Hudson, Hiripi, Pope, & Kessler, 2007) the efficacy of antidepressants appears to be independent of current or preexisting depression (Goldstein, Wilson, Ascroft, & al-Banna, 1999; Walsh et al., 2000). Efficacy does not seem to differ between classes of antidepressants, such as tricyclic antidepressants, SSRIs, and monoamine oxidase inhibitors (MAOIs), when compared with placebo and all classes of agents studied lead to reductions in binge eating and vomiting and improved comorbid mood and anxiety symptoms (Bacaltchuk & Hay, 2003).

A systematic review which collected data from 24 RCTs found that severe bulimic behaviors decreased up to 70% in the short-term (mean 8 weeks). However, pooled abstinence rates were less than 20% when drugs are used without any concurrent psychosocial intervention (Bacaltchuk & Hay, 2003). Moreover, reported relapse rates are high. For example, Agras et al. (1992) found that one-third of the 25% of patients who were abstinent at the end of treatment relapsed over time. Published relapse prevention studies, although limited in number, have reported an effect of continuing pharmacotherapy (Fichter, Kruger, Rief, Holland, & Dohne, 1996; Romano, Halmi, & Sarkar, Koke, & Lee, 2002). Dropout rates were substantially high in most trials (around 40%) that evaluated single pharmacological treatments, in part because of side effects and in part because of the negative attitude of patients with BN toward medication use.

There appears to be a better acceptability of SSRIs, which may be associated with their short-term effects on reduction in appetite and weight (Fichter, Kruger, Rief, Holland & Dohne, 1996; Fluoxetine Bulimia Nervosa Collaborative Study Group, 1992; Goldstein et al., 1999, Romano et al., 2002). The SSRI antidepressant fluoxetine is the only medication approved by leading guidelines and the FDA for the treatment of BN (at a dose of 60 mg/day). It is also the most extensively studied agent for this condition (Fluoxetine Bulimia Nervosa Collaborative Study Group, 1992; Goldstein, Wilson, Ascroft, & al-Banna, 1999).

Strong evidence of the efficacy of other SSRI agents is still lacking. In clinical practice, however, they may be alternatives for patients that do not respond well to fluoxetine. There are three similar and very small randomized placebo controlled trials of citalopram (Milano, Petrella, & Capasso, 2005), sertraline (Milano, Petrella, Sabatino, & Capasso, 2004), and fluvoxamine (Milano, Siano, Petrella, Sabatino, & Capasso 2005), supporting the efficacy of all these three SSRIs. However, a later study from the same group (Giaquinto, Capasso, Petrella, & Milano, 2006) compared the three SSRIs in the treatment of BN and found sertraline was (100 mg daily) associated with a very small reduction in binge eating and purging when compared to fluvoxamine or fluoxetine. In addition, a small (n = 27) single-blinded trial comparing fluoxetine and citalopram found no differences in outcomes but the attrition rate was moderately high (Leombruni et al., 2006).

Bupropion, an antidepressant that blocks reuptake of noradrenaline and dopamine, has been found superior to placebo at reducing binge eating and purging episodes in BN participants (Horne et al., 1988). However, it is contraindicated for subjects with BN due to the high rates of generalized tonic–clonic seizures found in this single clinical trial (4 out of 55 participants).

Topiramate

Anticonvulsant drugs such as topiramate are thought to be useful in BN for their anti-impulsivity and appetite effects. In a preliminary open-label case series, almost complete resolution of binging and purging was observed in three of the five patients with BN (Barbee, 2003). This effect was sustained throughout an 18-month follow-up (Barbee, 2003). Subsequently, a double-blind, placebo-controlled study published in two parts also supported the efficacy of topiramate (Hedges et al., 2003; Hoopes, Reimherr, & Hedges, 2003). Patients treated with topiramate had significantly greater reductions in mean weekly binge and/or purge days than those on placebo (44.8% vs. 10.7% for placebo), besides an also greater decrease in mean body weight with topiramate (1.8 kg, whereas the placebo group had a mean increase of 0.2 kg).

A second 10-week, double-blind RCT (Nickel et al., 2005) found effects of topiramate (250 mg/day) significantly reduced binge/purge frequency compared to placebo (n = 60). Topiramate also resulted in a significant reduction in body weight when compared with placebo, with a difference in weight loss between the two groups of 3.8 kg, and was associated with significant improvement of health-related quality of life.

Although topiramate was reportedly well tolerated in these trials, many patients experienced cognitive impairment and neurological symptoms such as paresthesia. In addition, the safety profile of this drug in patients with BN has not been established yet and there has been a recent report of very high congenital malformation rates in women taking topiramate for epilepsy which may limit its use in young women (Hunt et al., 2008).

Ondansetron
Ondansetron, a peripheral 5-HT$_3$ antagonist administered to prevent nausea and vomiting due to such vagal overactivity caused by cancer chemotherapeutic agents, has been evaluated as a potential treatment for BN (Faris et al., 2000; Hartman et al., 1997). After a small open trial with positive results (Hartman et al., 1997), the same research group completed a double-blind RCT to assess the effects of ondansetron administered to 25 patients with severe BN (Faris et al., 2000). During the 4-week study, participants were instructed to take a 4-mg capsule of ondansetron or matching placebo whenever they felt an urge to binge eat or vomit (24 mg/day dose), and then to try to restrain themselves for 30 minutes. During treatment, mean binge and vomit frequencies were significantly lower in the ondansetron group (6.5 per week [SD 3.9] vs. 13.2 per week [SD 11.6] in the placebo group). The ondansetron group also showed significant improvement in reduction in time spent engaging in bulimic behaviors and an increase in the number of normal meals and snacks without vomiting compared with the placebo group.

Despite these initial encouraging results, no further studies have replicated these findings in long-term treatments. Therefore, the feasibility of prescribing ondansetron for the maintenance treatment of BN in regular clinical settings remains unclear.

Other Agents
Results of clinical trials with naltrexone are conflicting. Mitchell et al. (1989) reported negative results in their low-dose naltrexone crossover study with 16 normal-weight women with BN, whereas Marrazzi, Bacon & Kinzie (1995) found significant reductions in binge/purge symptoms during naltrexone treatment in all patients (n = 19) with bulimic symptoms (AN of the bulimic subtype or BN) during a double-blind placebo crossover study.

To test the hypothesis that women with BN may have elevated serum levels of androgens due to polycystic ovaries, and that androgens may promote bulimic behavior by stimulating food craving or affecting impulse control, a placebo-controlled, double-blind pilot study on the efficacy of the androgen antagonist flutamide in BN was conducted recently in 46 patients (Sundblat, Landen, Eriksson, Bergman, & Eriksson, 2005). Results from this trial suggested that flutamide significantly decreased binge eating in both groups that were given the drug (flutamide only and flutamide plus citalopram), but its effect on purging was not significant.

Combination Treatment: CBT and Pharmacotherapy
Results of combination medications and CBT or other psychotherapies vary considerably across these trials. When results from different studies are pooled in meta-analyses (Bacaltchuk, Hay, & Trefiglio, 2001; NICE, 2004) some preliminary findings are that: (1) drug-alone treatments have consistently less efficacious abstinence rates than CBT, and (2) dropout rates in the antidepressant arms of such trials are always very high (more than 50% in some studies). Combinations of antidepressants with CBT may increase remission rates of either single approach (NICE, 2004), but may also increase dropout rates when compared with CBT alone (Bacaltchuk, Hay & Trefiglio, 2001).

Treatments of Choice: Binge Eating Disorder
CBT and Other Psychotherapies for BED and EDNOS
It is perhaps not surprising given the similarities in symptomatology that CBT-BN has been modified

for use in BED. CBT developed for BED and EDNOS has, however, not reached the levels of evidence as for BN. This is simply because there is yet an insufficient number of good quality randomized controlled trials of individual manualized CBT.

Peterson et al. (1998) randomized 61 *DSM-IV* female adults with BED to group-based CBT (therapist was a PhD psychologist trained in CBT), partial self-help with specialist guidance, structured self-help with groups lead by participants, or to a wait list group. Only 8 (13%) did not complete therapy. Outcome was not blind to assessor and randomization was by group with the wait list group formed at the end of other groups. Remission rates were significantly higher in the CBT group than wait list (11/16 vs. 1/11) but were highest in the structured self-help group. Gorin, Le Grange, and Stone (2003) randomized 94 (32, 34%, noncompletion rate) adult women with *DSM-IV* BED to standard group CBT or group CBT with spouse involvement or a wait list control. CBT with or without spousal involvement was superior to wait list in binge eating abstinence with less clear advantages for reduction in depression and function (as like Peterson et al., (1998) and there was no clear advantage as regards weight loss.

A meta-analysis of four trials that compared CBT with behavioral weight loss therapy in the overweight with BED found and clear advantage for CBT little a tendency for greater weight loss in those treated with BWLT (see Table 25.5). In addition, CBT has been compared with interpersonal psychotherapy without clear advantage (Wilfley et al., 2002).

There has been one wait list RCT of dialectical behavior therapy in 44 women with BED (Telch, Agras, & Linehan, 2001) with 23% attrition. Assessors were not blind and data were not analyzed by intention-to-treat. Nevertheless, dialectical behavior therapy was found significantly superior to wait list on a range of ED and other outcomes.

Exercise

Pendleton, Goodrick, Poston, Reeves, and Foreyt (2002) in an RCT of 114 BED patients compared a 45-minute three times weekly aerobic exercise regime combined to CBT with and without a maintenance program, versus CBT with or without maintenance. The study was not blinded, intention-to-treat analyses were not done and attrition was 26%. Abstinence rates were greater in the groups that included exercise and at 16 months follow-up were 47% in either exercise group versus 19% in the no exercise group. Like the study by Sundgot-Borgen, Rosenvinge Bahr & Schneider (2002) above in BN, this provides support for further research into the role of promoting healthy levels of exercise in patients with BED.

Antidepressants and BED and EDNOS

Studies of the role of antidepressants in the treatment of BED are based on their efficacy in reducing binge-eating in patients with BN (Bacaltchuk & Hay, 2003) and on the high rate of comorbid major depressive disorder in patients with BED (Fontenelle et al., 2003). SSRIs, such as fluvoxamine, sertraline, fluoxetine, and citalopram, are the most extensively tested antidepressants in RCTs of pharmacological treatment for BED. Most studies, however, had small samples (up to 85 patients) and examined short-term treatments (mean duration of 8 weeks) although the doses used were in accord with those recommended in the literature (Carter, Hudson et al., 2003; Devlin et al., 2005; Grilo, Masheb, & Wilson, 2005a; Pearlstein et al., 2003).

Table 25.5 Meta-analysis Randomized Controlled Trials of Therapies for Binge Eating Disorder: Cognitive Behavior Therapy versus Behavioral Weight Loss Therapy

Outcome	*n* Trials	*n* Participants	I^2 %	Effect size	95% CI
Bulimic symptom scores	4	189	3.0	SMD -0.31	−.61, −.02*
Depression scores	4	167	0	SMD -0.03	−.33, 0.28
Weight/BMI	4	190	0	SMD 0.24	−.05, 0.53
Non-completion rate	3	193	57.8	RR 0.68	0.24, 1.95

Source: Hay et al. (2009).
Trials included in the analyses were Agras *et al.* (1994); Munsch *et al.* (2007); Nauta, H., Hospers, H., Kok, G., & Jansen, A. (2000); and Porzaslius, Houston, Smith, Arfken, & Fisher (1995).
SMD = Standardized mean difference, <0 on the upper 95% confidence interval (CI) is significant and favors the active (CBT) therapy.
RR = Relative risk, <1 on the upper 95% CI is significant and favors the active (CBT) therapy
I^2%—Test of heterogeneity, it provides an estimate of the percentage of variability due to heterogeneity rather than chance alone and a value >50% is considered substantial heterogeneity.

These studies of SSRIs have reported, in general, a greater efficacy of drugs compared with placebo in reducing frequency of binge eating episodes and weight. However, the longest trials (4–24 months) do not confirm this greater effect for fluoxetine (Devlin, Goldfein, Petkova Lia & Walsh, 2005a, 2007; Grilo et al., 2005). With regard to weight, except for sertraline (50–200 mg/day), which promoted a clinically significant weight loss (mean 5.4 kg in 6 weeks) (McElroy, Casuto, et al., 2000), weight loss was modest in most studies. Another trial (Devlin et al., 2005) described greater weight loss with the use of fluoxetine by patients who achieved binge abstinence. Analyses of effects on depressive symptoms found that only citalopram (McElroy, Hudson, Malhotra, et al., 2003) had a greater efficacy than placebo in studies, and fluoxetine showed just a trend toward a greater efficacy (Arnold et al., 2002), possibly because most of the studies included patients with low baseline scores in depression scales (Appolinario & McElroy, 2004). Guerdjikova et al. (2008) found high (mean 26.5 mg) dose escitalopram was effective compared to placebo in reducing weight but did not consistently reduce binge eating and other psychological symptoms in 44 obese (mean BMI 40) women with BED. Attrition was 22% and data were analyzed by intention-to-treat.

A recent systematic review of RCTs that tested antidepressants versus placebo to treat BED (Stefano, Bacaltchuk, Blay, & Appolinario, 2008) found, in a meta-analysis, a greater remission of binge eating episodes at the end of trials in the groups that received the drug compared with the placebo groups (40.5% vs. 22.2%). This review analyzed the results of seven studies, six with SSRIs and one with imipramine involving a total of 300 patients and no differences in weight loss were found between conditions. Venlafaxine, a selective serotonin and noradrenaline reuptake inhibitor, has been tested only in one uncontrolled open trial that included 35 obese or overweight patients with BED. Results showed a significant reduction in binge-eating episodes and weight (Malhotra, King, Welge, Brusman-Lovins, & McElroy, 2002).

In sum, as with most psychological treatments, SSRIs show promise in consistently reducing binge eating but not weight in people with BED.

Antiobesity Agents

The use of antiobesity agents in the treatment of BED is supported by two main factors: their effects on the reduction of appetite or increase in satiety thus their possible effects on binge eating behaviors, and their promotion of weight loss, as BED is frequently associated with obesity or overweight (Appolinario & McElroy, 2004).

Sibutramine is a selective serotonin and noradrenaline inhibitor that is thought to induce weight loss by enhancing satiety and preventing the fall in energy expenditure that usually follows weight loss. Sibutramine at a dose of 15 mg/day was tested against placebo in two 12-week RCTs (Appolinario et al., 2003; Milano et al., 2005) and one 24-week trial (Wilfley et al., 2008). In the first trial (Appolinario et al., 2003), with 60 patients, sibutramine was associated with greater reduction in binge-eating episodes and depression, and a clinically significant weight loss when compared with placebo (–7.4 kg vs. +1.4 kg). Milano et al. (2005) found similar results in a smaller trial. Most recently Wilfley et al. (2008) in 304 adults with BED found sibutramine to be associated with significantly reduced binge eating and weight loss compared to placebo (effect size 0.46, 58.7% abstinence versus 42.8%). Attrition was high, 37%, and data were analyzed by intention-to-treat. The high placebo response (also found by, e.g., Pearlstein et al., 2003) was of note and in a secondary analysis the authors reported that those more likely to have a placebo response had less severe symptoms at baseline (Jacobs-Pilipski et al., 2007).

One RCT has tested the use of orlistat, a lipase inhibitor, against placebo, in combination with a mildly reduced-calorie diet in 89 obese patients with BED (Golay et al., 2005). After 24 weeks, patients taking orlistat showed clinically important and significantly greater percentages of mean weight loss (–7.4% vs. –2.3%), as well as a greater reduction of ED symptoms, compared to those taking placebo.

Anticonvulsants

Anticonvulsant drugs have been thought to be useful in BED for associated mood intolerance and impulsivity (Carter, Hudson et al., 2003). Moreover, some agents in this drug class, such as topiramate and zonisamide, have been found to be associated with reductions in appetite and weight loss (Ben-Menachem, Axelsen, Johanson, Stagge, & Smith, 2003; Li et al., 2005; McElroy, Hudson, Capece, et al., 2007). Topiramate is a broad-spectrum neurotherapeutic agent approved for epilepsy that has also been studied in many other psychiatric conditions (Arnone, 2005). Two double-blind RCTs have tested topiramate against placebo in obese patients with BED. One initial study enrolled 61 subjects for a 14-week treatment and used a median topiramate dose of 213 mg/day (McElroy, Arnold, et al., 2003). The second, a larger multicenter trial (McElroy, Hudson, Capece, et al., 2007) with 394 patients, lasted 16 weeks and used a median dose of 300 mg/day. In these two trials, topiramate was associated with substantial decreases in binge frequency, greater binge remission and weight loss, as well as greater improvement of associated comorbidity. The long-term efficacy of topiramate has also been addressed in a 42-week, open-label (i.e., no longer blinded or controlled) extension (McElroy et al., 2004) of the first trial with 35 patients. Patients on topiramate during the double-blind phase maintained the reduction in binge eating frequency and weight loss in the subsequent open phase, and patients on placebo during the double-blind phase also showed a reduction of these parameters when given topiramate in the open phase. However, attrition and adverse effects were high (McElroy, Arnold, et al., 2003; McElroy et al., 2004).

Finally, one RCT compared zonisamide at a mean endpoint dose of 436 mg/day with placebo (McElroy et al., 2006) for 16 weeks in 60 obese women with BED. Although zonisamide was more effective than placebo in reducing binge eating frequency and weight, it had considerable side effects and was not well tolerated.

Other Agents

Recently, a short, placebo controlled double-blind trial tested atomoxetine, a highly selective norepinephrine reuptake inhibitor with weight loss properties, in 40 obese patients with BED. The drug was associated with greater improvement in binge eating behaviors and weight loss in this trial, and was fairly well tolerated (McElroy, Guerdjikova, et al., 2007).

Combination Treatment

Combination treatments have not been widely investigated and results of RCTs generally do not support combining antidepressants and CBT to reduce binge eating (Agras et al., 1994; Devlin et al., 2005; Grilo, Masheb & Wilson, 2005). However, there may be effects on weight loss beyond the effects of psychotherapy (Agras et al., 1994; Laederach-Hofmann et al., 1999) or antidepressants alone (Ricca et al., 2001). Two recent combination trials, which lasted 16 (Grilo, Masheb & Wilson, 2005) and 20 (Devlin et al., 2005) weeks, used a four-cell design to make these comparisons (CBT plus fluoxetine, CBT plus placebo, fluoxetine, and placebo). These studies did not report any increase of treatment efficacy when

fluoxetine was added to CBT. However, when eating psychopathologies were analyzed, results were better in the groups treated with CBT than in the groups treated only with drugs. Greater binge remission (but not greater weight loss) was also found in the group treated with fluoxetine and CBT than in the one treated with medication alone (Grilo, Masheb & Wilson, 2005).

Two RCTs compared combination treatments of BED using CBT and an antiobesity agent orlistat (Grilo, Masheb, & Salant, 2005a) or CBT and an anticonvulsant drug, topiramate (Claudino et al., 2007). When administered with guided self-help CBT for 12 weeks, orlistat was associated with greater weight loss than placebo (36% vs. 8% of patients with ≥5% of baseline weight loss), and greater binge remission rates (64% vs. 36%), but only increased weight loss was found at the 3-month follow-up after treatment discontinuation. A double-blind, multicenter RCT in 73 patients found topiramate, at a mean dose of 206 mg/day, improved the efficacy of CBT by increasing binge remission (83.8% vs. 61.1%) and weight loss (–6.8 kg vs. –0.9 kg) in the short term (21 weeks) (Claudino et al., 2007). In this trial, a greater number of patients in the topiramate group (33% vs. 11%) lost more than 10% of baseline weight, a clinically significant weight loss. Adverse effects were more frequently reported in the topiramate group, but were fairly well tolerated. However, BED may have an intermittent course, with relapses and remissions. Therefore, although these initial findings seem encouraging, the long-term effects of combined interventions remain unknown.

Treatment in Primary Care
Primary or Targeted Prevention

Compared with other health professionals family doctors and dietitians are more likely to be consulted for help by a person with an ED (Mond, Hay, Rodgers, Owen, & Beumont, 2003). Thus, they are in a key position to promote healthy attitudes toward shape and weight and good nutrition. She or he may do this in consultation(s) with patients and their families, in community-based educational programs, and in waiting rooms with handouts and other information. Primary practitioners can also help prevent EDs by identifying and (where appropriate) intervening to reduce behaviors that increase risk of an ED, for example, discouraging restrictive dieting in young women of normal weight, and giving appropriate advice and help to those struggling with obesity.

Indicative or Secondary Prevention

Although the evidence base is not large, there are a number of RCTs that support the premise that EDs, particularly BN and BED, can be treated successfully by nonspecialist primary care practitioners, particularly when utilizing guided CBT self-help manuals or similar tools (see also Chapter 22 of this Handbook). These include the study of Banasiak, Paxton, and Hay (2005) comparing guided self-help CBT delivered by family doctors to a wait-list control. More compelling are the trials by Bailer et al. (2003) and Durand and King (2003) where guided self-help has been compared to specialist therapy (group CBT-BN and group CBT/IPT) and few difference in outcome have been found. In addition one RCT of pure self-help versus wait-list for BED (Carter & Fairburn, 1998) was supportive of the efficacy of pure self-help, although a similar study in BN was less supportive of pure self-help (Carter, Olmsted, et al., 2003).

Of note as well, critical reviews such as Sysko and Walsh (2008) and meta-analyses such as Stefano, Bacaltchuk, Blay, and Hay (2006) and Perkins, Murphy, Schmidt, and Williams (2006) support self-help approaches for bulimic EDs. However, both these meta-analyses conflate diagnostic groups and the latter also conflates types of self-help in all but one meta-analysis, which limits information in regards to specific diagnostic groups or type of self-help.

With appropriate training family doctors may thus provide modified cognitive-behavioral psychotherapy programs to those with BN and EDNOS syndromes. These can be supplemented by "self-help" programs outlined in books such as *Bulimia Nervosa and Binge Eating: A Guide to Recovery* (Cooper, 1993, 2007) Such approaches follow a manual outline of the treatment and can be broken up into steps that can be applied in the shorter consultation times of primary care. However, many find that in practice such psychological therapies may require extended sessions.

Medicine is an inexact science and there are few "absolutes" for when secondary referral is appropriate in EDs. People with AN should almost always have a specialist opinion, urgently if there are physical or laboratory signs of serious medical complications. For people with BN and EDNOS syndromes, referral will be modulated by the prior experience and skills of the general practitioner. Referral would be appropriate in any instance where there is failure to make progress, where the patient's physical and/or mental health is of concern, or where there are complicating factors such as pregnancy or severe depression with risk of suicide, and where there is need for clarification of diagnosis or treatment advice.

For patients who are referred to specialist care there is, however, much that doctors or primary care practitioners can do. As described in the preceding text, education about normal nutrition, EDs and their consequences is very important. Many doctors have a central role in the coordination of care, providing ongoing supportive psychotherapy, often coupled with nutritional counseling and monitoring of patient's physical health and medical complications. They may also be involved in the prescription of medication such as a SSRI, which can be effective in treatment of BN, in addition to and separate from their efficacy in depression (see earlier). Primary care practitioners may also help families and patients connect with appropriate consumer and caregiver groups to provide additional support. These provide educational material, information about local medical and psychological services, and support meetings that may have an additional educational focus.

As a profession dietitians provide special expertise in the management of EDs and are invaluable in the nutritional care of people with AN. In addition, some work in collaboration with the family doctor at the primary care level, or with a psychologist/psychiatrist, to provide care to people with BN or similar disorders.

Existing Evidence-Based Recommendations
Quality of the Evidence Base

Recommendations necessarily need to be considered in light of the evidence base. As noted at the beginning of this chapter, the evidence base for treatments in EDs is highly variable. Trials in AN have been most problematic in being under-powered and lacking blinded outcome assessments and consistently has had low ratings on quality across published systematic reviews (e.g., Bulik, Berkman, Brownley, Sedway & Lohr, 2007; Hay, et al., 2003; NICE, 2004;) with one review concluding there was no evidence for any treatment likely to be beneficial excepting refeeding (Treasure & Schmidt, 2008)—for which it would be unethical and unnecessary to conduct a RCT. Generally family therapy in adolescents with AN has been endorsed by guidelines as having better evidence than other approaches but this is relative to the very poor quality of evidence base of other psychotherapies and pharmacotherapies.

Even for BN, where evidence is better, independent quality appraisals have rated all but one outcome in treatments (that for combination CBT-BN versus CBT-alone) as having low or very low quality trials—with most problems being in incomplete reporting of results and lack of intention-to-treat data (Hay & Bacaltchuk, 2008). However, in other respects RCTs (particularly those more recent) of CBT and CBT versus other psychotherapies, for bulimic EDs have low risk of bias with adequate randomization and allocation concealment, and they are inclusive at recruitment, enhancing generalizability (Hay, Balcaltchuk, & Stefano, 2004). Shapiro et al. (2007) ranked the evidence for behavioral and for pharmacological therapies in BN as "strong" regarding outcomes, and like others, noted that RCTs of psychotherapies invariably fail to report adverse effects. In contrast, Brownley, Berkman, Sedway, Lohr, and Bulik (2007) ranked the evidence for behavioral and for pharmacological therapies in binge ED as "moderate" regarding outcomes—with under powering of RCTs a particular problem.

An important problem has been the variation in outcomes that are used across trials. In AN there is lack of agreement on "recovery" with differing definitions applied. In BN and BED, the most common outcome is abstinence from binge-eating or binge frequency, and this is measured in different ways and over variable time periods. For example, some trials combine abstinence data from both binge eating and purging behaviors, whereas others report abstinence from binge-eating and separately abstinence from purging behaviors. More contemporary studies are using the Eating Disorder Examination (EDE; Fairburn & Cooper, 1993; Fairburn, 2008) interview which is the gold standard method of assessment of outcome in EDs and which measures binge eating and other behaviors over a three month window, but again, use of the EDE is not universal. Finally, but not least, a difficult issue, and one yet to be addressed across psychotherapy research is the lack of, and feasibility of, blinding of participants to treatment group.

Predictors of Outcomes: How This Informs Treatment

There is much inconsistency in evaluating factors associated with a favorable or unfavorable outcome. Table 25.2 is a collation of the factors that have been found most consistently predict a better outcome in AN and bulimia from two systematic reviews (Berkman, Lohr, & Bulik, 2007; NICE, 2004). Insufficient evidence was found for EDNOS or binge ED excepting that Cluster B *DSM-IV* personality traits may predict a poorer outcome for

the latter. Berkman et al. (2007) particularly noted that there also has been only one prospective cohort community study in AN (Gillberg, Rastram, & Gillberg, 1994) and none in BN—although they described a community based study by Fairburn et al. (2000) as a case series. In addition, early change within treatment has been found to predict a better outcome in therapy for BN (Fairburn, Agras, Walsh, Wilson, & Stice, 2004) and for BED (Grilo, Masheb & Wilson, 2006).

Taken together, the body of outcome research supports early intervention in treatment, sustaining treatments in AN over time (and probably until there is at least full weight recovery), avoiding where possible medical compromise, and treating actively comorbidities. Engaging the patient early in psychotherapy (e.g., by more frequent sessions at the beginning of therapy) for BN also appears important.

Figures 25.1, 25.2, and 25.3 present algorithms for the management of AN, BN and BED, based on the best available evidence and in accordance with international guidelines.

Conclusion

In AN, although there is consensus on the need for specialist care that includes nutritional rehabilitation and weight restoration in addition to psychotherapy, no single approach has been found to offer a distinct advantage. Pharmacotherapy beyond replacement of essential nutrients has little evidence-base, however in practice the newer antipsychotics and antidepressants are being used and, as for psychological therapies, more trials are urgent. Treatment is medium to longer-term and may be provided in outpatient and day patient settings depending on medical and psychiatric state.

In contrast, manualized cognitive behavior therapy (CBT) for BN has attained "first-line" treatment status and has a stronger evidence base than other psychotherapies. Fluoxetine (or an alternate SSRI antidepressant) at high dose may be used as an adjunctive agent but, despite efficacy, is unlikely to be acceptable as a first line treatment. Extended forms of CBT await completion and publication of clinical trials.

More trials are needed in BED and EDNOS, the placebo response may be higher than other EDs, and management of the former is often complicated by weight disorder. However, less intensive and nonspecialist CBT is likely to be efficacious, combined where appropriate with weight management strategies, either behavioral or pharmacologic.

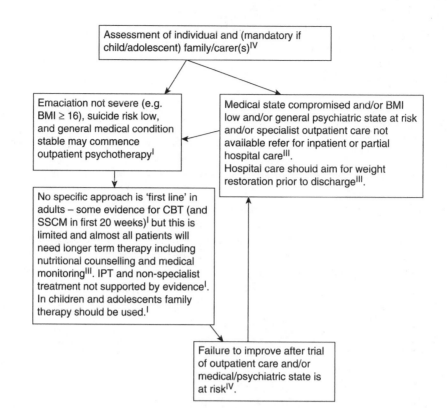

Fig. 25.1 Algorithm for evidence based treatment of anorexia nervosa. Level I, IIa, IIb, III, IV; see text pp. 453 and 453–460.

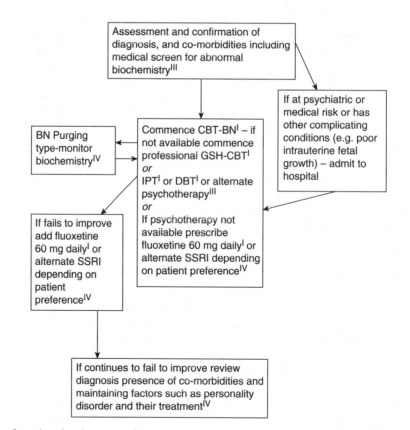

Fig. 25.2 Algorithm for evidence based treatment of Bulimia Nervosa. Level I, IIa, IIb, III, IV; see text pp. 453 and 460–466.

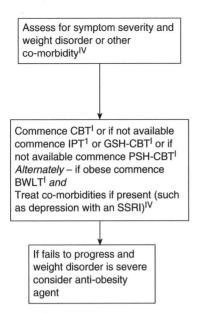

Assess for symptom severity and
weight disorder or other
co-morbidity[IV]

Commence CBT[I] or if not available
commence IPT[1] or GSH-CBT[I] or if
not available commence PSH-CBT[I]
Alternately – if obese commence
BWLT[I] *and*
Treat co-morbidities if present (such
as depression with an SSRI)[IV]

If fails to progress and
weight disorder is severe
consider anti-obesity
agent

Fig. 25.3 Algorithm for evidence based treatment of Binge Eating Disorder. Level I, IIa, IIb, III, IV; see text pp. 453 and 466–469.

Primary care professionals have a central treatment role. This is both with regards to directly providing care as well as coordination and initiation of specialist care. They are also in a key position to promote health behaviors and strategies to decrease the risk of people developing EDs.

Future Directions

The most important research needed is larger and higher quality trials in AN. Such trials in AN require much more coordination and collaboration with targeted national and international funding to support multisite studies. Research needs to investigate how can services best be developed to provide appropriate levels of care for patients who have variable needs for intensity and duration of treatment? Should all care be provided in a stepped approach starting with pure self-help for BED, guided self-help for BN and a trial of outpatient care for AN?

In BED with associated obesity treatment regimes should be developed to address both the goals of reducing ED symptoms and that of reducing weight, or at least minimizing harm from the weight disorder. Trials need to assess the efficacy of treatment combinations, particularly pharmacological with psychological.

For all EDs, there is a need to better match treatment to features in the patient. Studies that examine how prognostic factors, as found in Table 25.2, may mediate and moderate outcome are needed to answer the question of who responds best to what

treatment and inform the development of more comprehensive protocols and algorithms. For example, it is not known which of the many putative features of borderline personality disorder (e.g., impulsivity, mood intolerance) may mediate poorer outcome in BN. How does previous exposure to treatment moderate outcome in later treatment for AN? (See Kramer, Stice, Kazdin, Offord, & Kupfer [2001] for a discussion of the role of moderators, mediators and other risk factors in outcome.)

Finally, the optimal role of exercise—as both an approach that may enhance psychotherapy for BN and BED and how best to help patients move from "disordered eating" extreme exercise to normative and "healthy" exercise—has yet to be elucidated.

References

Agras, S. W., Telch, C. F., Arnow, B., Eldregde, K., Wilfley, D. E., Raeburn, S. D., Henderson, J., & Marnell, M. (1994). Weight loss, cognitive-behavioral, and desipramine treatments in binge eating disorder – An addictive design. *Behavioural Therapy, 25,* 225–238.

Agras, S., Walsh, T., Fairburn, C., Wilson, G.T., & Kraemer, H. (2000). A multicentre comparison of cognitive-behavioural therapy and interpersonal psychotherapy for bulimia nervosa. *Archives of General Psychiatry, 57,* 459–466.

Agras, W. S., Rossiter, E. M., Arnow, B., Schneider, J. A., Telch, C. F., Raeburn, S. D., et al. (1992). Pharmacologic and cognitive-behavioral treatment for bulimia nervosa: A controlled comparison. *American Journal of Psychiatry, 149,* 82–87.

American Dietetic Association (ADA). (2001). Position of the American Dietetic Association: Nutrition intervention in the treatment of anorexia nervosa, bulimia nervosa, and eating disorders not otherwise specified (EDNOS). *Journal of the American Dietetic Association, 101,* 810 – 819.

American Psychiatric Association (APA). (2000). *Diagnostic and statistical manual of mental disorders* (4th ed., Text Revision). Arlington, VA: American Psychiatric Publishing.

American Psychiatric Association (APA). (2006). Practice guidelines for the treatment of patients with eating disorders. In *Practice guidelines for the treatment of psychiatric disorders* (3rd ed., pp. 1097–1222). Arlington, VA: American Psychiatric Publishing.

Appolinario, J. C., & McElroy, S. L. (2004). Pharmacological approaches in the treatment of binge eating disorder. *Current Drug Targets, 5*(3), 301–307.

Appolinario, J. C., Bacaltchuk, J., Sichieri, R., Claudino, A. M., Godoy-Matos, A., Morgan, C., et al. (2003). A randomized, double-blind, placebo-controlled study of sibutramine in the treatment of binge eating disorder. *Archives of General Psychiatry, 60,* 1109–1116.

Appolinario, J. C., Bueno, J. R., & Coutinho, W. (2004). Psychotropic drugs in the treatment of obesity: What promise? *CNS Drugs, 18*(10), 629–51.

Arnold, L. M., McElroy, S. L., Hudson, J. I., Welge, J. A., Bennett, A. J., & Keck, P. E. (2002). A placebo-controlled, randomized trial of fluoxetine in the treatment of binge-eating disorder. *Journal of Clinical Psychiatry, 63*(11), 1028–1033.

Arnone, D. (2005). Review of the use of topiramate for treatment of psychiatric disorders. *Annals of General Psychiatry*, *4*(1), 5.

Attia, E., Haiman, C., Walsh, B. T., & Flater, S. R. (1998). Does fluoxetine augment the inpatient treatment of anorexia nervosa? *American Journal of Psychiatry*, *155*, 548–551.

Bacaltchuk, J., & Hay, P. (2003). Antidepressants versus placebo for people with bulimia nervosa. *Cochrane Database of Systematic Reviews*, (4). CD 003391.

Bacaltchuk. J., Hay, P., & Trefiglio, R. (2001). Antidepressants versus psychological treatments and their combination for bulimia nervosa. *Cochrane Database of Systematic Reviews*, *4*, CD003385.

Bailer, U., de Zwaan, M., Leisch, F., Strnad, A., Lennkh-Wolfsberg, C., El-Giamal, et al. (2004). Guided self-help versus cognitive-behavioral group therapy in the treatment of bulimia nervosa. *International Journal of Eating Disorders*, *35*, 522–537.

Banasiak, S. J., Paxton, S. J., & Hay, P. J. (2005). Guided self-help for bulimia nervosa in primary care: A randomized controlled trial. *Psychological Medicine*, *35*, 1283–1294.

Barbarich, N. C., McConaha, C. W., Halmi, K.A., Gendall, K., Sunday, S. R., Gaskill, J., et al. (2003). Use of nutritional supplements to increase the efficacy of fluoxetine in the treatment of anorexia nervosa. *International Journal of Eating Disorders*, *35*(1), 10–15.

Barbee, J. G. (2003). Topiramate in the treatment of bulimia nervosa with comorbid mood disorders: A case series. *International Journal of Eating Disorders*, *33*, 468–472.

Barren, S. A., Weltzin, T. E., & Kaye, W. H. (1995). Low discharge weight and outcome in anorexia nervosa. *American Journal of Psychiatry*, *152*, 1070–1072.

Ben-Menachem, E., Axelsen, M., Johanson, E. H., Stagge, A., & Smith, U. (2003). Predictors of weight loss in adults with topiramate-treated epilepsy. *Obesity Research*, *11*(4), 556–562.

Bergh, C., Brodin, U., Lindberg, G., & Sodersten, P. (2002). Randomized controlled trial of a treatment for anorexia and bulimia nervosa. *Proceedings of the National Academy of Sciences of the USA*, *99*, 9486–9491.

Berkman, N. D., Lohr, K. N., & Bulik, C. M. (2007). Outcomes of eating disorders: A systematic review of the evidence. *International Journal of Eating Disorders*, *40*, 293–309.

Biederman, J., Herzog, D. B., Rivinus, T. M., Harper, G. P., Ferber, R. A., Rosenbaum, J. F., et al. (1985). Amitriptyline in the treatment of anorexia nervosa. *Journal of Clinical Psychopharmacology*, *5*, 10–6.

Biller, B. M. K., Saxe, V., Herzog, D. B., Rosenthal, D. I., Holzman, S., & Klibanski, A. (1989). Mechanisms of osteoporosis in adult and adolescent women with anorexia nervosa. *Journal of Clinical Endocrinology and Metabolism*, *68*, 548–54.

Birmingham, C. L., & Gritzner, S. (2006). How does zinc supplementation benefit anorexia nervosa? *Eating and Weight Disorders*, *11*, e109–111.

Birmingham, C. L., Goldner, E. M., & Bakan, R. (1994). Controlled trial of zinc supplementation in anorexia nervosa. *International Journal of Eating Disorders*, *15*(3), 251–255.

Bissada, H., Tasca, G. A., Barber, A. M., & Bradwejn, J. (2008). Olanzapine in the treatment of low body weight and obsessive thinking in women with anorexia nervosa: A randomized, double-blind, placebo-controlled trial. *American Journal of Psychiatry*, 2008 June 16. (Epub ahead of print).

Bosanac, P., Norman, T., Burrows, G., & Beumont, P. (2005). Serotonergic and dopaminergic systems in anorexia nervosa: A role for atypical antipsychotics? *Australian and New Zealand Journal of Psychiatry*, *39*, 146–153.

Brambilla, F., Garcia, C. S., Fassino, S., Daga, G. A., Favaro, A., Santonastaso, P., et al. (2007). Olanzapine therapy in anorexia nervosa: Psychobiological effects. *International Clinical Psychopharmacology*, *22*(4), 197–204.

Brownley, K. A., Berkman, N. D., Sedway, J. A., Lohr, K. N., & Bulik, C. M. (2007). Binge eating disorder treatment: A systematic review of randomized controlled trials. *International Journal of Eating Disorders*, *40*, 337–348.

Bruch, H. (1973). *Eating disorders: Obesity, anorexia nervosa and the person within*. New York: Basic Books.

Bulik, C. M., Berkman, N. D., Brownley, K. A., Sedway, J. A., & Lohr, K. N. (2007). Anorexia nervosa treatment: A systematic review of randomized controlled trials. *International Journal of Eating Disorders*, *40*(4), 310–320.

Carter, J., & Fairburn, C. (1998). Cognitive-behavioral self-help for binge eating disorder. *Journal of Consulting and Clinical Psychology*, *1998*, 616–623.

Carter, J. C., Olmsted, M. P., Kaplan, A. S., McCabe, R. E., Mills, J. S., & Aime, A. (2003). Self-help for bulimia nervosa: A randomized controlled trial. *American Journal of Psychiatry*, *160*, 973–978.

Carter, W. P., Hudson, J. I., Lalonde, J. K., Pindyck, L., McElroy, S. L., & Pope, H. G. (2003). Pharmacologic treatment of binge eating disorder. *International Journal of Eating Disorders*, *34* (Supplement), S74–88.

Channon, S., de Silva, P., Hemsley, D., & Perkins, R. (1989). A controlled trial of cognitive-behavioural and behavioural treatment of anorexia nervosa. *Behavior Research and Therapy*, *27*, 529–535.

Claudino, A. M, Bacaltchuk, J., & Hay, P. J. (2009). Pharmacotherapy for eating disorders. In S. Paxton & P. Hay (Eds.), *Treatment approaches for body dissatisfaction and eating disorders; Evidence and practice*. IP Communications. pp 184–216.

Claudino, A. M., de Oliveira, I. R., Appolinario, J. C., Cordás, T. A., Duchesne, M., Sichieri, R., & Bacaltchuk, J. (2007). Randomized, double-blind, placebo-controlled trial of topiramate plus cognitive-behavior therapy in binge eating disorder. *Journal of Clinical Psychiatry*, *68* (9), 1324–1332.

Claudino, A., Hay, P., Lima, M. S., Bacaltchuk, J., Schmidt, U., & Treasure, J. (2006,). Antidepressants for anorexia nervosa. *Cochrane Database of Systematic Reviews*, *25*(1), CD004365.

Cooper, P. J. (1993). *Bulimia nervosa and binge-eating: A guide to recovery*. London: Robinson.

Cooper, P. J. (2007). *Overcoming bulimia and binge-eating self-help course: A 3–part programme based on cognitive behavioural techniques*. London: Robinson.

Crisp, A. H., Norton, K., Gowers, S., Halek, C., Bowyer, C., Yeldham, D., et al. (1991). A controlled study of the effect of therapies aimed at adolescent and family psychopathology in anorexia nervosa. *British Journal of Psychiatry*, *159*, 325–333.

Dare, C., Eisler, I., Russell, G., Treaure, J., & Dodge, L. (2001). Psychological therapies for adults with anorexia nervosa. *British Journal of Psychiatry*, *178*, 216–221.

Dare, C., Dodge, E., Eisler, I., LeGrange, D., Russell, G. F. M., & Szmukler, G.I. (1997). Family and individual therapy in anorexia nervosa: A five year follow-up. *Archives of General Psychiatry*, *54*, 1025–1030.

Dare, C., Eisler, I., Russell, G. F. M., & Szmukler, G. I. (1987). An evaluation of family therapy in anorexia nervosa and bulimia nervosa. *Archives of General Psychiatry, 44*, 1047–1056.

Dennis, A., Gilroy, M., Moye, A., Robin, A., Siegal, P., Sikand, A. (1999). A controlled comparison of family versus individual therapy for adolescents with anorexia nervosa. *Journal of the American Academy of Child and Adolescent Psychiatry, 38*, 1482–1489.

Devlin, M. J., Goldfein, J. A., Jiang, H., Raizman, P. S., Wolk, S., Mayer, L., et al. (2005). Cognitive behavioral therapy and fluoxetine as adjunct to group behavioral therapy for binge eating disorder. *Obesity Research, 13*(6), 1077–1088.

Devlin, M. J., Goldfein, J. A., Petkova, E., Liu L., Walsh, B. T. (2007) Cognitive behavioral therapy and fluoxetine for binge eating disorder: two-year follow-up. Obesity (Silver Spring). Jul;*15*(7):1702–9.

De Zwaan, M., & Roerig, J. (2003). Pharmacological treatment of eating disorders: A review. In M. Maj, K. A. Halmi, J. J. López-Ibor, & N. Sartorius (Eds.), *Eating disorders* (pp. 223–285). Chichester, UK, Wiley.

Doyle, A. C., McLean, C., Washington, B. N., Rienecke Hoste, R. R., le Grange, D. (2009). Are single-parent families different from two-parent families in the treatment of adolescent bulimia nervosa using family-based treatment? *International Journal of Eating Disorders. 42*(2), 153–157.

Faris, P. L., Kim, S.W., Meller, W. H., Goodale, R. L., Oakman, S. A., Hofbauer, R. D., Marshall, A. M., Daughters, R. S., Banerjee-Stevens, D., Eckert, E. D., Hartman, B.K. (2000). Effect of decreasing afferent vagal activity with ondansetron on symptoms of bulimia nervosa: a randomised, double-blind trial. Lancet. Mar 4; *355*(9206): 792–7.

Dunican, K. C., & Del Dotto, D. (2007). The role of olanzapine in the treatment of anorexia nervosa. *Annals of Pharmacotherapy, 41*(1), 111–115.

Durand, M. A., & King, M. (2003). Specialist treatment versus self-help for bulimia nervosa: A randomised controlled trial in general practice. *British Journal of General Practice, 53*, 371–377.

Eisler, I., Dare, C., Hodes, M., Russell, G., Dodge, E., & Le Grange, D. (2000). Family therapy for adolescent anorexia nervosa: The results of a controlled comparison of two family interventions. *Journal of Child Psychology and Psychiatry, 41*, 727–736.

Eisler, I., Dare, C., Russell, G., Szmukler, G., le Grange, D., & Dodge, E. (1997). Family and individual therapy in anorexia nervosa: A 5–year follow-up. *Archives of General Psychiatry, 54*, 1025–1030.

Eisler, I., Simic, M., Russell, G. F. M., & Dare C. (2007). A randomised controlled treatment trial of two forms of family therapy in adolescent anorexia nervosa: a five-year follow-up. *Journal of Child Psychology and Psychiatry, 48*, 552–560.

Fairburn, C. (1997). Interpersonal psychotherapy for bulimia nervosa. In D. Garner & P. Garfinkel (Eds.), *Handbook of treatment for eating disorders* (pp. 278–294). New York: Guilford Press.

Fairburn, C., Jones, R., Peveler, R., Hope, R., & O'Connor, M. (1993). Psychotherapy and bulimia nervosa: Longer-term effects of interpersonal psychotherapy, behaviour therapy, and cognitive behaviour therapy. *Archives of General Psychiatry, 50*, 419–428.

Fairburn, C. G. (2002). Cognitive-behavioral therapy for bulimia nervosa. In C. G. Fairburn & K. D. Brownell (Eds.), *Eating disorders and obesity: A comprehensive handbook* (2nd edi., pp. 302–307). New York: Guilford Press.

Fairburn, C. G. (2008). Cognitive behavior therapy and eating disorders. New York: Guilford Press.

Fairburn, C. G., Agras, W. S., Walsh, B. T., Wilson, G. T., & Stice, E. (2004). Prediction of outcome in bulimia nervosa by early change in treatment. *American Journal of Psychiatry, 16*, 2322–2324.

Fairburn, C. G., & Cooper, Z. (1993). The eating disorder examination (12th ed.). In C. G. Fairburn & G. T. Wilson (Eds.) *Binge eating: Nature, assessment and treatment* (pp. 317–360). New York: Guilford Press.

Fairburn, C. G., Cooper, Z., Doll, H. A., Norman, P., & O'Connor, M. (2000). The natural course of bulimia nervosa and BED in young women. *Archives of General Psychiatry, 57*, 659–665.

Fairburn, C. G., Jones, R., Peveler, R., Carr, S. J., Solomon, R. A., O'Connor, M. E., et al. (1991). Three psychological treatments for bulimia nervosa: A comparative trial. *Archives of General Psychiatry, 48*, 463–469.

Fairburn, C. G., Kirk, J., O'Connor, M., & Cooper, P. J. (1986). A comparison of two psychological treatments for bulimia nervosa. *Behavior Research and Therapy, 24*, 629–43.

Fairburn, C. G., Marcus, M. D., & Wilson, G. T. (1993). Cognitive behavior therapy for binge eating and bulimia nervosa: A comprehensive treatment manual. In C. G. Fairburn & G. T. Wilson (Eds.), *Binge eating: Nature, assessment, and treatment* (pp. 361–404). New York: Guilford Press.

Fichter, M. M., Kruger, R., Rief, W., Holland, R., & Dohne, J. (1996). Fluvoxamine in prevention of relapse in bulimia nervosa: Effects on eating specific psychopathology. *Journal of Clinical Psychopharmacology, 16*, 9–18.

Fichter, M. M., Leibl, K., Rief, W., Brunner, E., Schmidt-Auberger, S., & Engel, R. R. (1991). Fluoxetine versus placebo: A double blind study with bulimic inpatients undergoing intensive psychotherapy. *Pharmacopsychiatry, 24*, 1–7.

Fichter, M. M., & Quadflieg, N. (2004). Twelve year course and outcome of bulimia nervosa. *Psychological Medicine, 34*, 1394–1406.

Fluoxetine Bulimia Nervosa Collaborative Study Group. (1992). Fluoxetine in the treatment of bulimia nervosa: A multicenter, placebo-controlled, double-blind trial. *Archives of General Psychiatry, 49*, 139–147.

Fontenelle, L. F., Vltor Mendlowicz, M., de Menezes, G. B., Papelbaum, M., Freitas, S. R., Godoy-Matos, A., et al. (2003). Psychiatric comorbidity in a Brazilian sample of patients with binge-eating disorder. *Psychiatry Research, 119*(1–2), 189–94.

Freeman, C. (1992). Day patient treatment for anorexia nervosa. *British Review of Bulimia and Anorexia Nervosa, 6*, 3–8.

Garner, D. M., & Needleman, L. D. (1997). Sequencing and integration of treatments. In D. M. Garner & P. E. Garfinkel (Eds.), *Handbook of treatment for eating disorders.* (2nd ed., pp. 50–66). New York: Guilford Press.

Geist, R., Heinmaa, M., Stephens, D., Davis, R., & Katzman, D. K. (2000). Comparison of family therapy and family group psychoeducation in adolescents with anorexia nervosa. *Canadian Journal of Psychiatry – Revue Canadienne de Psychiatrie, 45*(2), 173–178.

Giaquinto, K., Capasso, A., Petrella, C., & Milano, W. (2006). Comparative study between three different SSRIs in the treatment of bulimia nervosa. *Pharmacology Online, 1*, 11–14.

Gillberg, I., Råstam, M., & Gillberg, C. (1994). Anorexia nervosa outcome: Six-year longitudinal study of 51 cases including a population cohort. *Journal of the American Academy of Child and Adolescent Psychiatry, 33*, 729–739.

Godart, N., Perdereau, F., Rein, Z., Berthoz, S., Wallier, J., Jeammet, P., & Flament, M. F. (2007). Comorbidity studies of eating disorders and mood disorders. Critical review of the literature. *Journal of Affective Disorders, 97*(1–3), 37–49.

Golay, A., Laurent-Jaccard, A., Habicht, F., Gachoud, J. P., Chabloz, M., Kammer, A., & Schutz, Y. (2005). Effect of orlistat in obese patients with binge eating disorder. *Obesity Research, 3*(10), 1701–1708.

Goldberg, S. C., Casper, R., & Eckert, E. D. (1980). Effects of cyproheptadine in anorexia nervosa. *Psychopharmacology Bulletin, 16*, 29–30.

Goldberg, S. C., Halmi, K., Eckert, E. D., Casper, R., & Davis J. M. (1979). Cyproheptadine in anorexia nervosa. *British Journal of Psychiatry, 134*, 67–70.

Golden, N. H., Iglesias, E. A., Jacobson, M. S., Carey, D., Meyer, W., Schebendach, J., et al. (2005). Alendronate for the treatment of osteopenia in anorexia nervosa: a randomized, double-blind, placebo-controlled trial. *Journal of Clinical Endocrinology and Metabolism, 90* (6), 3179–85.

Goldstein, D. J., Wilson, M. G., Ascroft, R. C., & al-Banna, M. (1999). Effectiveness of fluoxetine therapy in bulimia nervosa regardless of comorbid depression. *International Journal of Eating Disorders, 25*, 19–27.

Goldstein, D. J., Wilson, M. G., Thomson, V. L., Potvin, J. H., Rampey, A. H. Jr. (1995). Long-term fluoxetine treatment of bulimia nervosa. *British Journal of Psychiatry, 166*, 660–666.

Goodsitt. A. (1997). Eating Disorders: A self-psychological perspective. In D. M. Garner& P. E. Garfinkel (Eds.), *Handbook of treatments for eating disorders* (2nd ed., pp. 205–228). New York: Guilford Press.

Gorin, A. A., Le Grange, D., & Stone, A. A. (2003). Effectiveness of spouse involvement in cognitive behavioral therapy for binge eating disorder. *International Journal of Eating Disorders, 33*, 421–433.

Gowers, S., Norton, K., Halek, C., & Crisp, A. H. (1994). Outcome of outpatient psychotherapy in a random allocation treatment study of anorexia nervosa. *International Journal of Eating Disorders, 15*, 165–177.

Gowers, S. G., Clark, A., Roberts, C., Griffiths, A., Edwards, V., Bryan, C., et al. (2007). Clinical effectiveness of treatments for anorexia nervosa in adolescents. *British Journal of Psychiatry, 191*, 427–435.

Grilo, M. C., Masheb, R. M., & Salant, S. L. (2005). Cognitive behavioral therapy guided self-help and orlistat for the treatment of binge eating disorder: A randomized, double-blind, placebo-controlled trial. *Biological Psychiatry, 57*(10), 1193–1204.

Grilo, M. C., Masheb, R., & Wilson, T. (2005). Efficacy of cognitive behavioral therapy and fluoxetine for the treatment of binge eating disorder: A randomized double-blind placebo-controlled comparison. *Biological Psychiatry, 57*(3), 301–309.

Grilo, M. C., Masheb, R., & Wilson, T. (2006). Rapid response to treatment for binge eating disorder. *Journal of Consulting and Clinical Psychology, 74*, 602–613.

Grinspoon, S., Thomas, L., Miller, K., Herzog, D., & Klibanski, A. (2002). Effects of recombinant human IGF-I and oral contraceptive administration on bone density in anorexia nervosa. *Journal of Clinical Endocrinology and Metabolism, 87* (6), 2883–91.

Gross, G., Russell, J. D., Beumont, P. J. V., Touyz, S. W., Roach, P., Aslani, A., et al. (2000). Longitudinal study of patients with anorexia nervosa 6 to 10 years after treatment. Impact of adequate weight restoration on outcome. *Annals of the New York Academy of Science, 904*, 614–616.

Guerdjikova, A. I., McElroy, S. L., Kotwal, R., Welge, J. A., Nelson, E., & Katie Lake, K. (2008). High-dose escitalopram in the treatment of binge-eating disorder with obesity: A placebo-controlled monotherapy trial. *Human Psychopharmacology, 23*, 1–11.

Halmi, K. A., Agras, W., Crow, S., Mitchell, J., Wilson, G., Bryson, S. W., et al. (2005). Predictors of treatment acceptance and completion in anorexia nervosa: Implications for future study designs. *Archives of General Psychiatry, 62*, 776–781.

Halmi, K. A., Eckert, E., LaDu, T. J., & Cohen, J. (1986). Anorexia nervosa: Treatment efficacy of cyproheptadine and amitriptyline. *Archives of General Psychiatry, 43*, 177–181.

Hartman, B. K., Faris, P. L., Kim, S. W., Raymond N. C., Goodale, R. L., Meller, W. H., & Eckert, E. D. (1997). Treatment of bulimia nervosa with ondansetron. *Archives of General Psychiatry, 54*, 969–970.

Hausenblas, H. H., Cook, B. J., & Chittester, N. I. (2008). Can exercise treat eating disorders? *Ecercise, Sport and Science Review, 36*, 43–47.

Hay, P. (2008). Treating eating disorders. In J. A. Trafton & W. Gordon, (Eds.), *Best practices in behavioral management of health from preconception to adolescence.* Vol III. Chapter 8. Los Altos, CA: The Institute for Brain Potential.

Hay, P. J., & Bacaltchuk, J. (2008). Bulimia nervosa. *Clinical Evidence, 6*, 1009.

Hay, P. J., Bacaltchuk, J., & Stefano, S. (2007). Psychotherapy for bulimia nervosa and binge eating. *Cochrane Database of Systematic Reviews, 3*, CD000562.

Hay, P. J., Bacaltchuk, J., Byrnes, R. T., Claudino, A. M., Ekmejian, A. A., Yong, P. Y. (2003). *Individual psychotherapy in the outpatient treatment of adults with anorexia nervosa. Cochrane Database of Systematic Reviews* 2003, 4. Art. No.: CD003909. DOI: 10.1002/14651858.CD003909. IF 4.6 UPDATED 2008

Hay, P. J., Bacaltchuk, J., Kashyap, P., & Stefano, S. (2009). Pschological treatment for bulimia nervosa and binge eating. *Cochrane Database of Systematic Reviews, 4*, CD000562.

Hedges, D. W., Reimherr, F. W., Hoopes, S. P., Rosenthal, N. R., Kamin, M., Karim, R., & Capece, J. A. (2003). Treatment of bulimia nervosa with topiramate in a randomized, double-blind, placebo-controlled trial, part 2: Improvement in psychiatric measures. *Journal of Clinical Psychiatry, 64*, 1449–1454.

Hoopes, S. P., Reimherr, F. W., Hedges, D. W., Rosenthal, N. R., Kamin, M., Karim, R., et al. (2003). Treatment of bulimia nervosa with topiramate in a randomized, double-blind, placebo-controlled trial, part 1: Improvement in binge and purge measures. *Journal of Clinical Psychiatry, 64*, 1335–1341.

Horne, R. L., Ferguson, J. M., Pope, H. G. Jr., Hudson, J. I., Lineberry, C. G., Ascher, J., & Cato, A. (1988). Treatment of bulimia with bupropion: A multicenter controlled trial. *Journal of Clinical Psychiatry, 49*, 262–266.

Hughes, P. L., Wells, L. A., Cunningham, C. J., & Ilstrup, D. M. (1986). Treating bulimia with desipramine: A double-blind, placebo-controlled study. *Archives of General Psychiatry, 43*, 82–86.

Hunt, S., Russell, A., Smithson, W. H., Parsons, L., Robertson, I., Waddell, R., et al. (2008). Topiramate in pregnancy. *Neurology, 71*, 272–276.

Jacobs-Pilipski, M. J., Wilfley, D. E., Crow, S., & Walsh, B. T., Lilenfeld, L. R., West, D. S., et al. (2007). Placebo response in binge eating disorder. *International Journal of Eating Disorders, 40,* 204–211.

Katz, R. L., Kern, C. L., Litt, I. F., Hurley, L. S., Kellams-Harrison, K. M., & Glader, L. J. (1987). Zinc deficiency in anorexia nervosa. *Journal of Adolescent Health Care, 8,* 400–406.

Kaye, W., Bulik, C., Thornton, L., Barbarich, N. & Masters, K. (2004). Comorbidity of anxiety disorders with anorexia and bulimia nervosa. *American Journal of Psychiatry, 161*(12), 2215–21.

Kaye, W., Gendall, K., & Strober, M. (1998). Serotonin neuronal function and selective serotonin reuptake inhibitor treatment in anorexia and bulimia nervosa. *Journal of Biological Psychiatry, 44,* 825–838.

Kaye, W. H., Frank, G. K., Bailer, U. F., Henry, S. E., Meltzer, C. C., Price, J. C., et al. (2005). Serotonin alterations in anorexia and bulimia nervosa: New insights from imaging studies. *Physiology and Behavior, 85,* 73–81.

Kaye, W. H., Frank, G. K., & McConaha, C. (1999). Altered dopamine activity after recovery from restricting-type anorexia nervosa. *Neuropsychopharmacology, 21,* 503–506.

Kaye, W. H., Gwirtsman, H. E., Obarzanek, E., & George, D. T. (1988). Relative importance of calorie intake needed to gain weight and level of physical activity in anorexia nervosa. *American Journal of Clinical Nutrition, 47,* 989–994.

Kaye, W. H., Nagata, T., Weltzin, T. E., Hsu, L. K., & Sokol, M. S. (2001). Double-blind placebo-controlled administration of fluoxetine in restricting- and purging-type anorexia nervosa. *Biological Psychiatry, 49,* 644–652.

Keys, A. J., Henschel, A., Mickelsen, O., & Taylor, H.L. (1950). *The biology of human starvation.* Minneapolis, MN: University of Minnesota Press.

Klibanski, A., Biller, B.M.K., Shoenfeld, D.A., Herzog, D.B. & Saxe, V.C. (1995). The effects of estrogen administration on trabecular bone loss in young women with anorexia nervosa. *Journal of Clinical Endocrinology and Metabolism, 80* (3), 898–904.

Kong, S. (2005). Day treatment programme for patients with eating disorders: Randomized controlled trial. *Journal of Advanced Nursing, 51,* 5–14.

Kramer, H., Stice, E., Kazdin, A., Offord, D., & Kupfer, D. (2001). How do risk factors work together? Mediators, moderators, and independent, overlapping, and proxy risk factors. *American Journal of Psychiatry, 158,* 848–856.

Laederach-Hofmann, K., Graf, C., Horber, F., Lippuner, K., Lederer, S., Michel, R., & Schneider, M. (1999). Imipramine and diet counseling with psychological support in the treatment of obese binge eaters: A randomized, placebo-controlled double-blind study. *International Journal of Eating Disorders, 26,* 231–244.

Lask, B., Fosson, A., Rolfe, U., & Thomas, S. (1993). Zinc deficiency and childhood-onset anorexia nervosa. *Journal of Clinical Psychiatry, 54*(2), 63–66.

Le Grange, D., Crosby, R. D., Rathouz, P. J., & Leventhal, B. L. (2007). A randomized controlled comparison of family-based treatment and supportive psychotherapy for adolescent bulimia nervosa. *Archives of General Psychiatry, 64,* 1049–1056.

Leombruni, P., Amianto, F., Delsedime, N., Gramaglia, C., Bbate-Daga, G., & Fassino, S. (2006). Citalopram versus fluoxetine for the treatment of patients with bulimia nervosa. *Advances in Therapy, 23,* 481–484.

Li, Z., Maglione, M., Tu, W., Mojica, W., Arterburn, D., Shugarman, L. R., et al. (2005). Meta-Analysis: Pharmacologic treatment of obesity. *Annals of Internal Medicine, 142,* 532–546.

Ljotsson B., Lundin C., Mitsell K., Carlbring P., Ramklint M., & Ghaderi A. (2007). Remote treatment of bulimia nervosa and binge eating disorder: A randomised trial of Internet-assisted cognitive behavioural therapy. *Behaviour Research and Therapy, 45,* 649–661.

Lock, J., Agras, S., Bryson, S., & Kraemer, H. (2005). A comparison of short and long term family therapy for adolescent anorexia nervosa. *Journal of the American Academy of Child and Adolescent Psychiatry, 47,* 632–638.

Malhotra, S., King, K. H., Welge, J. A., Brusman-Lovins, L., & McElroy, S. L. (2002). Venlafaxine treatment of binge-eating disorder associated with obesity: A series of 35 patients. *Journal of Clinical Psychiatry, 63*(9), 802–826.

Marrazzi, M. A., Bacon, J. P., & Kinzie, J. (1995). Naltrexone use in the treatment of anorexia nervosa and bulimia nervosa. *International Journal of Clinical Psychopharmacology, 10,* 163–172.

Masheb, R. M., & Grilo, C. M. (2007). Rapid response predicts treatment outcomes in binge eating disorder: Implications for stepped care. *Journal of Consulting and Clinical Psychology, 75*(4), 639–644.

McElroy, S. L., Arnold, L. M., Shapira, N. A., Keck, P. E., Rosenthal, N. R., Karim, M. R., et al. (2003). Topiramate in the treatment of binge-eating disorder associated with obesity: A randomized, placebo-controlled trial. *American Journal of Psychiatry, 160*(2), 255–261.

McElroy, S. L., Casuto, L. S., Nelson, E. B., Lake, K. A., Soutullo, C. A., Keck, P. E., & Hudson, J. I. (2000). Placebo-controlled trial of sertraline in the treatment of binge eating disorder. *American Journal of Psychiatry, 157*(6), 1004–1006.

McElroy, S. L., Guerdjikova, A., Kotwal, R., Welge, J. A., Nelson, E. B., Lake, K. A., et al. (2007). Atomoxetine in the treatment of binge-eating disorder: A randomized placebo-controlled trial. *Journal of Clinical Psychiatry, 68,* 390–398.

McElroy, S. L., Hudson, J. I., Capece, J. A., Beyers, K., Fisher, A. C., & Rosenthal, N. R; Topiramate Binge Eating Disorder Research Group. (2007). Topiramate for the treatment of binge eating disorder associated with obesity: A placebo-controlled study. *Biological Psychiatry, 61,* 1039–1048.

McElroy, S. L., Hudson, J. I., Malhotra, S., Weldge, J. A., Nelson, E. B., & Keck, P. E. (2003). Citalopram in the treatment of binge-eating disorder: A placebo-controlled trial. *Journal of Clinical Psychiatry, 64*(7), 807–813.

McElroy, S. L., Kotwal, R., Guerdjikova, A. I., Welge, J. A., Nelson, E. B., Lake, K. A., et al. (2006). Zonisamide in the treatment of binge eating disorder with obesity: A randomized controlled trial. *Journal of Clinical Psychiatry. 67*(12), 1897–906. Erratum in: *Journal of Clinical Psychiatry* (2007). *68,* 172.

McElroy, S. L., Shapira, N. A., Arnold, L. M., Keck, P. E., Rosenthal, N. R., Wu, S. C., et al. (2004). Topiramate in the long-term treatment of binge eating disorder associated with obesity. *Journal of Clinical Psychiatry, 65*(11), 1463–1469.

McIntosh, V. V. W., Jordan, J., Carter, F. A., Luty, S. E., McKenzie, J. M., Bulik, C. M., et al. (2005). Three psychotherapies for anorexia nervosa: A randomized controlled trial. *American Journal of Psychiatry, 162*(4), 741–747.

McIntosh, V. V. W., Jordan, J., Luty, S. E., Carter, F. A., McKenzie, J. M., Bulik, C. M., et al. (2006). Specialist supportive clinical management for anorexia nervosa. *International Journal of Eating Disorders, 39*(8), 625–632.

Meads, C., Gold, L., & Burls, A. (2001). How effective is outpatient care compared to inpatient care for the treatment of anorexia nervosa. A systematic review. *European Eating Disorder Reviews, 9*, 229–241.

Milano, W., Petrella, C., & Capasso, A. (2005). Treatment of bulimia nervosa with citalopram: A randomized controlled trial. *Biomedical Research, 16*, 85–87.

Milano, W., Petrella, C., Casella, A., Capasso, A., Carrino, S., & Milano, L. (2005). Use of sibutramine, an inhibitor of the reuptake of serotonin and noradrenaline, in the treatment of binge-eating disorder: A placebo-controlled study. *Advances in Therapy, 22*(1), 25–31.

Milano, W., Petrella, C., Sabatino, C., & Capasso, A. (2004). Treatment of bulimia nervosa with sertraline: A randomized controlled trial. *Advances in Therapy, 21*, 232–237.

Milano, W., Siano,C., Petrella, C., Sabatino, C., & Capasso, A. (2005). Treatment of bulimia nervosa with fluvoxamine: A randomized controlled trial. *Advances in Therapy, 23*, 278–283.

Mitchell, J. E., Christenson, G., Jennings, J., Huber, M., Thomas, B., Pomeroy, C., & Morley, J. (1989). A placebo-controlled, double-blind crossover study of naltrexone hydrochloride in outpatients with normal weight bulimia. *Journal of Clinical Psychopharmacology, 9*, 94–97.

Mitchell, J. E., Crosby, R. D., Wonderlich, S. A., Crow, S., Lancaster, K., & Simonich, H., et al. (2008). A randomized trial comparing the efficacy of cognitive–behavioral therapy for bulimia nervosa delivered via telemedicine versus face-to-face. *Behavior Research and Therapy, 46*, 581–592.

Mondraty, N., Birmingham, C. L., Touyz, S., Sundakov, V., Chapman, L., & Beaumont, P. (2005). Randomized controlled trial of olanzapine in the treatment of cognitions in anorexia nervosa. *Australasian Psychiatry, 13*(1), 72–75.

Munsch, S., Biedert, E., Meyer, A., Michael, T., Schlup, B., Tuch, A., & Margraf, J. (2007). A randomised comparison of cognitive behavioral therapy and behavioral weight loss treatment for overweight individuals with binge eating disorder. *International Journal of Eating Disorders, 40*, 102–113.

National Institute for Clinical Excellence (NICE). (2004). *Eating disorders: Core interventions in the treatment and management of anorexia nervosa, bulimia nervosa and related disorders.* Clinical Guideline Number 9. London: NICE.

Nauta, H., Hospers, H., Kok, G., & Jansen, A. (2000). A comparison between a cognitive and a behavioral treatment for obese binge eaters and obese non-binge eaters. *Behavior Therapy, 3*, 441–61.

Nickel, C., Tritt, K., Muehlbacher, M., Pedrosa, G. F., Mitterlehner, F. O., Kaplan, P., et al. (2005). Topiramate treatment in bulimia nervosa patients: A randomized, double-blind placebo-controlled trial. *International Journal of Eating Disorders, 38*, 295–300.

Pearlstein, T., Spurrell, E., Holstein, L. A., Gurney, V., Read, J., Fuchs, C., & Keller, M. B. (2003). A double-blind, placebo-controlled trial of fluvoxamine in binge eating disorder: A high placebo response. *Archives of Womens Mental Health, 6*, 147–451.

Pendleton, V. R., Goodrick, G. K., Poston, W. S. C., Reeves, R. S., & Foreyt, J. P. (2002). Exercise augments the effects of cognitive-behavioral therapy in the treatment of bulimia nervosa. *International Journal of Eating Disorders, 31*, 172–184.

Perkins, S. J., Murphy, R., Schmidt, U., & Williams, C. (2006). Self-help and guided self-help for eating disorders. *Cochrane Database of Systematic Reviews, 3*, CD004191.

Peterson, C. B., Mitchell, J. E., Engbloom, S., Nugent, S., Mussell, M. P., & Miller, J. P. (1998). Group cognitive-behavioral treatment of binge-eating disorder: A comparison of therapist-led versus self-help formats. *International Journal of Eating Disorders, 24*, 125–36.

Pike, K. M., Walsh, B. T., Vitousek, K., Wilson, G. T., & Bauer J. (2003). Cognitive behavior therapy in the posthospitalization treatment of anorexia nervosa. *American Journal of Psychiatry, 160*, 2046–2049.

Porzelius, L. K., Houston, C., Smith, M., Arfken, C., & Fisher, E. (1995). Comparison of a standard behavioral weight loss treatment and a binge eating weight loss treatment. *Behavior Therapy, 26*, 119–134.

Powers, P. S., & Santana, C. (2004). Available pharmacological treatments for anorexia nervosa. *Expert Opinion in Pharmacotherapy, 5*(11), 2287–2292.

Powers, P. S., Bannon, Y., Eubanks, R., & McCormick, T. (2007). Quetiapine in anorexia nervosa patients: An open label outpatient pilot study. *International Journal of Eating Disorders, 40*(1), 21–26.

Ricca, V., Mannucci, E., Mezzani, B., Moretti, S., Di Bernardo, M., Bertelli, M., et al. (2001). Fluoxetine and fluvoxamine combined with individual cognitive-behaviour therapy in binge eating disorder: A one-year follow-up study. *Psychotherapy and Psychosomatics, 70*, 298–306.

Rigaud, D., Brondel, L., Poupard, A. T., Talonneau, I., & Brun, J. M. (2007). A randomized trial on the efficacy of a 2-month tube feeding regimen in anorexia nervosa: A 1–year follow-up study. *Clinical Nutrition, 26*, 421–429.

Robin, A., Siegel, P., Moye, A., Gilroy, M., Dennis, A., & Sikand, A. (1999). A controlled comparison of family versus individual therapy for adolescents with anorexia nervosa. *Journal of the American Academy of Child & Adolescent Psychiatry, 38*, 1482–1489.

Robinson, P. H, & Serfaty, M. (2008). Getting better byte by byte: A pilot, randomized controlled trial of email therapy for bulimia nervosa, binge eating disorder and EDNOS. *European Eating Disorders Review, 16*, 84–93.

Romano, S. J., Halmi, K. A., Sarkar, N. P., Koke, S. C., & Lee, J. S. (2002). A placebo-controlled study of fluoxetine in continued treatment of bulimia nervosa after successful acute fluoxetine treatment. *American Journal of Psychiatry, 159*, 96–102.

Royal Australian and New Zealand College of Psychiatrists Clinical Practice (RANZCP) Guidelines Team for Anorexia Nervosa. (2004). Australian and New Zealand clinical practice guidelines for the treatment of anorexia nervosa. *Australian and New Zealand Journal of Psychiatry, 38*, 659–670.

Russell, G., Szmulker, G., Dare, C., & Eisler, I. (1987). An evaluation of family therapy in anorexia nervosa and bulimia nervosa. *Archives of General Psychiatry, 44*, 1047–1056.

Safer, D. L., Telch, C. F., & Agras, W. S. (2001). Dialectical behavior therapy for bulimia nervosa. *American Journal of Psychiatry, 158*, 632–634.

Schmidt, U., Lee, S., Beecham, J., Perkins, S., Treasure, J., Irene, Y., et al. (2007). A randomized controlled trial of family therapy and cognitive behaviour therapy guided self-care for adolescents with bulimia nervosa and related disorders. *American Journal of Psychiatry, 164*, 591–598.

Shapiro, J. R., Berkman, N. D., Brownley, K. A., Sedway, J. A., Lohr, K. N., & Bulik, C. M. (2007). Bulimia nervosa treatment. A systematic review of randomised controlled trials. *International Journal of Eating Disorders, 40*, 321–336.

Sundgot-Borgen, J., Rosenvinge, J. H., Bahr, R., & Schneider, L. (2002). The effect of exercise, cognitive therapy, and nutritional counselling in treating bulimia nervosa. *Medicine and Science in Sports and Exercise, 34*, 190–195.

Stacher, G., Abatzi-Wenzel, T. A., Wiesnagrotzki, S., Bergmann, H., Schneider, C., & Gaupmann, G. (1993). *British Journal of Psychiatry, 162*, 398–402.

Stefano, S. C., Bacaltchuk, J., Blay, S. L., & Appolinário, J. C. (2008). Antidepressants in short-term treatment of binge eating disorder: Systematic review and meta-analysis. *Eating Behaviours, 9*, 129–136.

Stefano, S. C., Bacaltchuk, J., Blay, S. L., & Hay, P. (2006). Self-help treatments for disorders of recurrent binge eating: A systematic review. *Acta Psychiatrica Scandinavica, 113*, 452–459.

Steinglass, J., Sysko, R., Schebendach, J., Broft, A., Strober, M., & Walsh, B. T. (2007). The application of exposure therapy and D-cycloserine to the treatment of anorexia nervosa: A preliminary trial. *Journal of Psychiatric Practice, 13*, 238–245.

Strober, M., Freeman, R., Lampert, C., Diamond, J., & Kaye, W. (2000). Controlled family study of anorexia nervosa and bulimia nervosa: Evidence of shared liability and transmission of partial syndromes. *American Journal of Psychiatry, 157*(3), 393–401.

Sundblat, C., Landen, M., Eriksson, T., Bergman, L., & Eriksson, E. (2005). Effects of the androgen antagonist flutamide and the serotonin reuptake inhibitor citalopram in bulimia nervosa. *Journal of Clinical Psychopharmacology, 25*, 85–88.

Sundgot-Borgen, J., Rosenvinge, J.H., Bahr, R., Schneider, L. S. (2002) The effect of exercise, cognitive therapy, and nutritional counseling in treating bulimia nervosa. *Med Sci Sports Exerc.* Feb; *34*(2):190–5.

Sysko, R., & Walsh, B. T. (2008). A critical evaluation of the efficacy of self-help interventions for the treatment of bulimia nervosa and binge-eating disorder. *International Journal of Eating Disorders, 41*, 97–112.

Szmulker, G. I., Young, G. P., Miller, G., Lichtenstein, M., & Binns, D. S. (1995). A controlled trial of cisapride in anorexia nervosa. *International Journal of Eating Disorders, 17*, 347–357.

Taylor, D. M., & McAskill, R. (2000). Atypical antipsychotics and weight gain—a systematic review. *Acta Psychiatrica Scandinavica, 101*, 416–432.

Telch, C. F., Agras, W. S., & Linehan, M. M. (2001). Dialectical behavior therapy for binge eating disorder. *Journal of Consulting and Clinical Psychology, 69*(6), 1061–1065.

Toledo, M. Z. (1970). Tratamiento de la anorexia nervsoa cno una asociacon ciproheptadina-vitamins. *Revista medica caja nacional de segura social*, 147–153.

Treasure, J., & Schmidt, U. (1997). *Clinician's Guide to Getting Better Bit(e) by Bit(e): A survival kit for sufferers of bulimia nervosa and binge eating disorders*. London: Routledge

Treasure, J., & Schmidt, U. (2008). Anorexia nervosa. *BMJ Clinical Evidence, 1*, 1001.

Treasure, J., Todd, G., Brolly, M., Tiller, J., Nehmed, A., & Denman, F. (1995). A pilot study of a randomised trial of cognitive analytical therapy vs. educational behavioral therapy for adult anorexia nervosa. *Behaviour Research and Therapy, 33*(4), 363–367.

Vandereycken, W. (1984). Neuroleptics in the short-term treatment of anorexia nervosa, a double-blind placebo-controlled study with sulpiride. *British Journal of Psychiatry, 144*, 288–292.

Vandereycken, W., & Pierloot, R. (1982). Pimozide combined with behavior therapy in the short-term treatment of anorexia nervosa. *Acta Psychiatrica Scandinavica, 66*, 445–450.

Vigersky, R. A., & Loriaux, D. L. (1977). The effect of cyproheptadine in anorexia nervosa: A double blind trial. In Vigersky R. A. (Ed.). *Anorexia nervosa*, (pp. 349–356). New York: Raven Press.

Wade, T. D., Bulik, C. M., Neale, M., & Kendler, K. S. (2000). Anorexia nervosa and major depression: Shared genetic and environmental risk factors. *American Journal of Psychiatry, 157*(3), 469–471.

Walsh, B. T., Agras, W. S., Devlin, M. J., Fairburn, C. G., Wilson, G. T., Kahn, C. M. A., & Chally, M. K. (2000). Fluoxetine for bulimia nervosa following poor response to psychotherapy. *American Journal of Psychiatry, 157*, 523–531.

Walsh, B. T., Wilson, G. T., Loeb, K. L., Devlin, M. J., Pike, K. M., Roose, S. P., et al. (1997). Medication and psychotherapy in the treatment of bulimia nervosa. *American Journal of Psychiatry, 154*, 523–531.

Walsh T., Kaplan, A. S., Attia, E., Olmsted, M., Parides, M., Carter, J. C., et al. (2006). Fluoxetine after weight restoration in anorexia nervosa. *Journal of the American Medical Association, 295*(22), 2605–2612.

Ward, L., Tricco, A. C., Phuong, P., Cranney, A., Barrowman, N., Gaboury, I., et al. (2007). Bisphosphonate therapy for children and adolescents with secondary osteopaenia. *Cochrane Database of Systematic Reviews, 4*, Art. No.: CD005324.

Wilfley, D., Welch, R., Stein, R., Spurrell, E. B., Cohen, L., & Salens, B., et al. (2002). A randomised comparison of group cognitive-behavioural therapy and group interpersonal psychotherapy for the treatment of overweight individuals with binge eating disorder. *Archives of General Psychiatry, 59*, 713–721.

Wilfley, D. E., Crow, S., Hudson, J. I., Mitchell, J. E., Berkowitz, R. I., Blakesley, V., & Walsh, B. T. (2008). Efficacy of sibutramine for the treatment of binge eating disorder: a randomized multicenter placebo-controlled double-blind study. *American Journal of Psychiatry, 165*, 51–58.

World Health Organization. (1992). *The ICD-10 Classification of Mental and Behavior Disorders*. Geneva, Switzerland: World Health Organization.

Costs and Cost-Effectiveness in Eating Disorders

Scott J. Crow *and* Nicholas Smiley

Abstract

Costs and cost-effectiveness are now well recognized as important aspects of the burdens of and treatment for eating disorders. Ample evidence indicates that the cost burdens associated with eating disorders are high; this is true whether viewed from the perspective of a health care payer or from a national perspective. On the other hand, it is important to note that studies involving cost modeling and direct cost collection in treatment have shown that eating disorders treatment is quite cost-effective. This is an area of great need for further research.

Keywords: anorexia nervosa, bulimia nervosa, burden, cost, cost-effectiveness, eating disorders, treatment

Introduction

Cost is increasingly recognized as an important aspect of health care provision. The issue of cost has received particular attention in health care systems with hybrid payment patterns, such as that found in the United States. However, costs are equally important in any system in which health care has attendant costs (that is to say, every health care system) and decisions about health care based on cost might be most readily implemented in single-payer systems.

Costs and cost-effectiveness are also increasingly recognized to be important in eating disorder (EDs; Agras, 2001; Crow & Peterson, 2003; Kaye, Kaplan, & Zucker, 1996). The EDs are often viewed as expensive and difficult to treat, and at least partly for that reason, EDs have been an area of focus for cost containment efforts in some systems, including many third-party payer systems in the United States (Sigman, 1996; Silber, 1994). The fact that they have been targeted for cost containment in some settings suggests that the same may eventually occur in others as well, particularly until treatments with a

reliably high degree of effectiveness and reasonable cost are identified.

In spite of the widely acknowledged important of costs, costs and cost-effectiveness have been relatively little studied within the field of EDs. This chapter will examine what is known about the overall costs burden associated with EDs and their treatment. It will also examine the limited existing data on the cost-effectiveness of specific treatments. Finally, directions for future study in this area will be examined.

Estimates of the Individual Costs of EDs

Having an ED may carry costs for the specific individual affected, and these may be a fairly large part of the overall cost burden associated with EDs. Potential costs include the direct financial costs associated with treatment; direct financial costs associated with symptoms of the illness, such as food for binge eating or substances used for purging; and time costs associated with symptoms of these illnesses or their treatment. These aspects of costs have been virtually unstudied until recently.

One study to date has attempted to estimate the financial costs associated with bulimia nervosa (BN) symptoms (Crow et al., in press). This study estimated yearly food and purging-related costs of having bulimia symptoms in 10 subjects based on completion of 1-week food records. Subjects in this study reported 2.5 objective binge episodes, 2.4 subjective binge episodes and 3.6 purging episodes per week on average, and spent an average of $5,582.00 US dollars per year on food. Food and purging related costs represented 32.7% of all food costs, about $1,600 per year. However, these figures might be viewed as underestimates, as frequency of binge eating and purging was somewhat lower than average for many studies of BN.

A second study has made a limited attempt to measure time costs associated with BN (Crow et al., submitted). In this large multicenter bulimia trial (described later in this chapter) time costs to family members related to participants with BN were measured in a subset of participants. A family member or significant other was asked to complete time monitoring records at entry into treatment and after the first 18 weeks of treatment. The results showed that a substantial amount of time was lost to BN symptoms and their treatment by family member/ significant others (about 4 hours per week) and that this amount dropped by about 75% over the first 18 weeks of treatment.

One study has examined cost per patient from a third party payer perspective using health plan data. Striegel-Moore, Leslie, Petrill, Garvin, and Rosenheck (2000) accessed data through U.S. insurance database (MarketScan®) containing annual inpatient and outpatient health care service use data of individuals insured through large employers. The above database is composed from privately insured paid medical and prescription drug claims. A data sample of 4 million was used in 1995 and diagnosed according to the *International Classification of Disease*, 9th ed. Treatment costs and out-of-pocket patient expenses were assessed from insurance claims. Group differences in annual treatment costs of EDs (anorexia nervosa [AN], BN, and binge eating disorder [BED]) were compared against schizophrenia and obsessive–compulsive disorder [OCD]).

A total of 21,567 insurance claims, compromising a total of 1932 patients, were reported for EDs; this number accounted for 1.1% of all mental health claims. Inpatient treatment occurred much less frequently than outpatient treatment for all EDs. The average cost of inpatient treatment collapsed across EDs was $12,432 for female patients and $10,126 for male patients. The groups did not differ significantly in inpatient treatment costs. Outpatient treatment costs for female patients were $2,344 for AN, $1,882 for BN, and $1,582 for eating disorder not otherwise specified (EDNOS). Male outpatient treatment costs were $1,154 for AN, $1,206 for BN, and $1,150 for EDNOS.

Using analysis of variance (ANOVA), treatment rates of EDs were compared against schizophrenia and OCD. Mean treatment costs for AN were significantly higher than for both schizophrenia and OCD. Treatment costs of BN were found to be significantly lower than schizophrenia, but significantly higher than OCD. EDNOS treatment costs were significantly lower than schizophrenia, and did not differ significantly from OCD. The above findings suggest that EDs (especially AN) compare to and even exceed treatment costs of other severe psychiatric disorders.

Estimates of the National Cost of EDs

Currently, few cost-of-illness studies exist within the scientific literature examining the cost implications of EDs. This is striking given the common view of EDs as expensive. Further, evidence suggests that utilization of health care in those with EDs is higher than in those without EDs and elevated to a degree similar to comparison subjects with other psychiatric disorders (Sansone, Wiederman, & Sansone, 1997; Striegel-Moore et al., 2005). Only five formal cost-of-illness studies examining the cost implication of EDs exist; these are reviewed in the text that follows.

The Office of Health Economics (1994) used national surveys to assess both primary and tertiary care costs of EDs. For primary care, cost of AN was estimated through the use of the 3rd National Survey of Morbidity in General Practice (OPCS, 1986). Using the above survey, the number of individuals who sought general practitioner consultation was used, along with the average unit cost of consultation, to assess primary care cost. For tertiary care, the OHE used the UK Hospital Inpatient Enquiry in 1985 to estimate the prevalence of in-patient treatment of AN patients using the same calculation technique.

The authors concluded that in 1990, 46,806 patients in the United Kingdom sought general practitioner consultation with AN. The average unit cost per consultation was used (9.85 euros) to calculate the annual primary care cost in the United Kingdom of 580,000 euros. For tertiary care cost, the total number of in-patient treatment bed days were used to assess the cost of AN. A total of 25,748 annual bed days occurred in 1990, with an average in-patient length of stay of 21.5 days for AN, for a total cost of 3.5 million euros. However, the authors highlighted that the data was from 1985 which would likely have doubled, citing the mean length of hospital stay in 2004 at 51 days (UK Hospital Episode Statistics, 2004). Therefore, the overall cost of AN in the United Kingdom is likely to be grossly underestimated at 4.2 million euros. In addition, this method may not have identified other medical utilization, further underestimating cost burden.

Krauth, Buser, and Vogel (2002) examined both direct and indirect costs accrued from EDs in Germany. The study remains the only cost-of-illness research including indirect cost estimates for EDs. Data was accessed through statutory health insurance (SHI), statutory pension insurance (SPI), and epidemiological literature on anorexia and bulimia. Direct cost was assessed through inpatient treatment costs, as well as rehabilitation measures (time spent in convalescent centers). Indirect costs were assessed through mortality and morbidity costs. Outpatient care, psychotherapy, and pharmaceuticals were not examined by this study. The estimated costs of EDs are thus underrepresented and reflect a low estimate.

A prevalence study by Hsu (1996) was used with the 1998 German population (roughly 82 million) to establish an estimated national prevalence of AN and BN. Mortality rates were also examined (Sullivan, 1995), and the mortality rates associated with AN and BN were projected to equate their representative proportion in the German population in 1998.

Direct costs were assessed by using aggregated costs of inpatient bed days in psychosomatic wards and the number of cases to yield the overall direct cost of hospitalization and rehabilitation stays in Germany. Indirect mortality and morbidity costs were assessed using the human capital approach. Average yearly labor cost of persons with full and part-time employment in 1998 was examined. The average duration of inability to work was then assessed in ED patients and this number was multiplied by the number of relevant cases to come up with an overall cost of inability to work. With the use of the estimated mortality rates by Sullivan, annual death rates were estimated for the overall German population. Average life expectancy rates were then used and potential labor capital from employment was averaged across age groups to assess the amount of capital lost due to premature death. Limitations to this study include not including

primary care costs, as well as out-patient care, pharmaceutical costs, and psychosocial costs due to illness.

The direct and indirect cost of anorexia nervosa was estimated to be 195 million Euros in Germany (range of 115–298). Direct cost of illness estimates were 59 million for inpatient expenses and 6 million for both rehabilitation and convalescence costs, totaling 65 million Euros for direct treatment costs. Interestingly, indirect treatment costs were estimated to be vastly greater, totaling 130 million euros (67% of total). Mortality costs were estimated at 123 million euros, using the human capital approach. Finally, according to the prevalence data on AN used in the study, the annual cost per anorexic patient was estimated at roughly 5300 euros per year (range of 2600–12,300).

Bulimia nervosa was estimated at a cost of 124 million euros to the German economy (range of 39–264). Direct treatment costs were approximately 7 million for inpatient treatment costs and 3 million for rehabilitation and convalescent costs, totaling 10 million euros. Indirect costs were estimated at being 92% of the overall cost of BN, totaling 112 million euros. The estimated annual cost, according to the prevalence data used, was 1300 euros per bulimia patient. Overall, AN and BN in Germany combined to equate a total estimated cost of 319 million euros (for a population of roughly 82 million).

The publication by Matthers, Vos, and Stevenson (1999) is currently the most comprehensive cost-of-illness study for EDs. Data were accessed from National Mental Health Surveys (1994–1997) to assess years lost due to disability, public and private health care costs, pharmaceutical costs, as well as research and prevention funding. Annual cost of EDs in Australia (1994) was estimated at 22 million (Aus). In addition, expenses on research, administration and prevention were estimated at 4 million (Aus) in 1994. Primary and in-patient care costs were estimated at 3 and 14 million, respectively. A limitation to the above study is that methodological procedures were not included within the study, so it is not certain which methods were employed to ascertain their data estimates.

Two additional studies have been conducted to assess the costs of EDs. An Austrian study by Rathner and Rainer (1997) assessed the in-patient treatment cost of anorexia and bulimia which was estimated at 140 million Austrian schillings in 1994. Furthermore, Nielsen et al. (1996) published a study in Denmark assessing the in-patient treatment costs of EDs. The researchers found the annual treatment cost for in-patients with EDs equated €6.4 million in 1993, 4.7 million of which was specifically incurred by AN.

Overall, current cost-of-illness literature on EDs is limited in scope, and the methodological inconsistencies used within the studies provide vastly differing cost estimates. An additional limitation that is strikingly apparent within the existing literature is the limited estimate of indirect costs associated with EDs. With limited evidence suggesting indirect costs are almost triple direct costs accrued from EDs (Krauth et al., 2002), research including indirect costs of EDs would likely drastically increase cost estimates as well as improve the validity and accuracy of cost-of-illness studies. Following the recommendation of the Institute of Medicine (1981), indirect costs should be assessed using both the human cost and willingness-to-pay methods for a more thorough and accurate cost estimate. For now, cost-of-illness research findings for EDs likely remains gross underestimates.

Cost-Effectiveness of ED Treatments

Only a handful of studies have specifically examined the cost-effectiveness of various treatments. In conducting such a study, the first question to be answered is: Will the analysis involve direct data collection or modeling based on existing literature? Modeling studies are more readily conducted and can be quite valuable, but introduce a greater number of uncertainties with regard to the assumptions made in the model. Thus, direct data collection is preferable. However, most ED treatment studies to date have only collected data primarily examining clinical effectiveness; only a few studies (Byford et al., 2007; Crow et al., in press) have been designed for prospective examination of cost-effectiveness. In a few other instances, studies have been designed to examine clinical effectiveness only and examinations of cost-effectiveness have only followed thereafter.

One study has attempted to model cost outcomes in AN treatment (Crow & Nyman, 2004) This study made a number of assumptions regarding course of illness and mortality. In addition, assumptions were made about an integrated treatment approach versus a more typical "community" approach with regard to treatments provided, unit costs, and effectiveness. The unit of analysis (given the high mortality rate associated with AN) was the cost per year of life saved. This modeling analysis yielded an overall cost per year of life saved of $30,180. The authors concluded that this cost fell well within the typically accepted norms for the cost of a year of life in other areas of medicine.

Another study has reported attempts to assign unit costs to a BN treatment trial (Koran et al., 1995). In this study, costs were assigned to the utilization observed in participants in a trial examining various lengths of cognitive–behavioral therapy treatment or desipramine treatment, either alone or in combination, in the treatment of bulimia nervosa. The effectiveness metric came from the data collected in the original trial. Cost-effectiveness ratios were calculated to yield a cost per abstinent patient at 32-week follow up; these suggested that medication treatment was more cost-effective than psychotherapy alone or combination treatment.

Two studies to date have prospectively set out to measure both cost and effectiveness in EDs treatment. The first of these (Byford et al., 2007) reported on the cost-effectiveness for different treatment strategies for AN. This multicentered trial with 167 participants examined cost-effectiveness of inpatient, specialist outpatient, or generalist outpatient treatment over 2 years of follow-up. Utilization and unit costs came from National Health Service data, while effectiveness results were generated by the trial. Numerically, specialist outpatient treatment dominated (i.e., was more effective and cost less than) the alternative treatment.

Second, Lock and colleagues examined the cost-effectiveness of family-based therapy for AN (Lock, Couturier, & Agras, 2008). This study estimated costs for 81 participants in the trial; avenge cost per subject was $33,015. The cost-effectiveness index (the costs for all subjects divided by the number of remitted subjects) was calculated using several remission definitions, and this ranged from approximately $34,000 to nearly $84,000, depending on the definition used.

A third study examined the cost-effectiveness of cognitive–behavioral therapy versus a stepped series of interventions in the treatment of BN (Crow et al., submitted). In this study involving 293 subjects, utilization was determined from study participation records as well as the completion of health care diaries. Unit costs came from the Center for Medicare Services, as well as the Red Book, in the case of drug prices (Thompson Healthcare, 2005). Effectiveness was defined as abstinence, generated from study records. The results of the trial showed that stepped care approaches were more effective and cost less than beginning with cognitive–behavioral therapy (CBT; mean costs of $12,146/abstinent subject for stepped vs. $20,317 for CBT). Of note, these costs per abstinent subject substantially exceeded the cost of treating a given subject (since only a fraction of subjects become abstinent).

Finally, one paper has reported on the results a cost-effectiveness analysis of an integrated treatment program for EDs in a hospital setting (Williamson, Thaw, & Varnado-Sullivan, 2001). This study compared two strategies for treatment: beginning with inpatient treatment, or using a "systematic, decision-tree approach to treatment." This study involved 51 subjects with either anorexia or bulimia who were assigned to one of those two treatment strategies. Costs came directly from hospital records. The results of this study showed that overall costs were nearly $10,000 less per case in the decision-tree treatment approach. Of note, however, since the costs were hospital-based only, it seems certain that not all health care costs were captured; a fuller accounting of outpatient and other medical costs might have resulted in a smaller or even larger advantage for the decision-tree approach.

Future Opportunities

The foregoing suggests several areas for future research efforts. First, up to date estimates of the national costs associated with EDs from a wide variety of countries would be useful. Such estimates would help to emphasize the importance of EDs; this in turn would be potentially useful to advocacy groups seeking funding her treatment and research and would aid policy makers in allocation of scare resources. Such estimates would ideally cover a broader range of cost than studied in the past, including both direct and indirect costs. As noted before, time cost associated with EDs may be particularly important. Developing methodologies to measure individual indirect costs would help to provide a more accurate picture of the total illness associated burden and may help to form part of a stronger rationale for treatment.

The second broad area in which further research is needed involves the cost-effectiveness of treatments. Several studies have examined this topic thus far, but the number of studies examining clinical effectiveness greatly outweighs the number examining cost-effectiveness. At present, extensive work is examining new treatments and another large body of work has begun to examine multiple methods of treatment delivery including group versus individual treatment, the use of guided and unsupervised self-help, the use of medications, and increasingly various methods of media-based treatment delivery (including telemedicine, Internet-based delivery,

and text messaging approaches). As clinical effective new methods of treatment delivery become available, and as a wider variety of more successful treatments become available, then the stage will be set for a greater role for cost in treatment selection.

References

Agras, W. S. (2001). The consequences and costs of the eating disorders. *Psychiatric Clinics of North America, 24*(2), 371–379.

Byford, S., Barrett, B., Roberts, C., Clark, A., Edwards, V., Smethurst, N., et al. (2007). Economic evaluation of a randomised controlled trial for anorexia nervosa in adolescents. *British Journal of Psychiatry, 191,* 436–440.

Crow, S. J., Agras, W. S., Halmi, K. A., Fairburn, C. G., Mitchell, J. E., & Nyman, J. A. (submitted). A cost effective analysis of stepped care treatment for bulimia nervosa.

Crow, S. J., Frisch, M. J., Peterson, C. B., Croll, J., Raatz, S. K., & Nyman, J. A. (2009). Monetary costs associated with bulimia. *International Journal of Eating Disorders, 42,* 81–83.

Crow, S. J., & Nyman, J. A. (2004). The cost-effectiveness of anorexia nervosa treatment. *International Journal of Eating Disorders, 35*(2), 155–160.

Crow, S. J., & Peterson, C. B. (Eds.). (2003). *The economic and social burden of eating disorders* (Vol. 6). New York: John Wiley & Sons.

Hsu, L. K. (1996). Epidemiology of the eating disorders. *Psychiatric Clinics of North America, 19*(4), 681–700.

Kaye, W. H., Kaplan, A. S., & Zucker, M. L. (1996). Treating eating-disorder patients in a managed care environment. Contemporary American issues and Canadian response. *Psychiatric Clinics of North America, 19*(4), 793–810.

Koran, L. M., Agras, W. S., Rossiter, E. M., Arnow, B., Schneider, J. A., Telch, C. F., et al. (1995). Comparing the cost effectiveness of psychiatric treatments: Bulimia nervosa. *Psychiatry Research, 58*(1), 13–21.

Krauth, C., Buser, K., & Vogel, H. (2002). How high are the costs of eating disorders – anorexia nervosa and bulimia nervosa – for German society? *European Journal of Health Economics, 3*(4), 244–250.

Lock, J., Couturier, J., & Agras, W. S. (2008). Costs of remission and recovery using family therapy for adolescent anorexia nervosa: A descriptive report. *Eating Disorders, 16*(4), 322–330.

Matthers, C. D., Vos, E. T., & Stevenson, C. E. (1999). *The burden of disease and injury in Australia.* Canberra: Australian Institute of Health and Welfare.

Nielsen, S., Moller-Madsen, S., Isager, T., Jorgensen, J., Pagsberg, K., & Theander, S. (1996). *Utilization of psychiatric beds in the treatment of icd-8 eating disorders in denmark 1970–1993.* Paper presented at the AEP Conference, London.

Office of Health Economics, Eating Disorders: Anorexia Nervosa & Bulimia Nervosa, Author: Richard West, Published January 1994.

Rathner, G., & Rainer, B. (1997). [annual treatment rates and estimated incidence of eating disorders in Austria]. *Wiener Klinishche Wochenschrift, 109*(8), 275–280.

Sansone, R. A., Wiederman, M. W., & Sansone, L. A. (1997). Healthcare utilization among women with eating disordered behavior. *American Journal of Managed Care, 3*(11), 1721–1723.

Sigman, G. (1996). How has the care of eating disorder patients been altered and upset by payment and insurance issues? Let me count the ways. *Journal of Adolescent Health, 19*(5), 317–318.

Silber, T. J. (1994). Eating disorders and health insurance. *Archives of Pediatric and Adolescent Medicine, 148*(8), 785–788.

Striegel-Moore, R. H., Dohm, F.-A., Kraemer, H. C., Schreiber, G. B., Crawford, P. B., & Daniels, S. R. (2005). Health services use in women with a history of bulimia nervosa or binge eating disorder. *International Journal of Eating Disorders, 37*(1), 11–18.

Striegel-Moore, R. H., Leslie, D., Petrill, S. A., Garvin, V., & Rosenheck, R. A. (2000). One-year use and cost of inpatient and outpatient services among female and male patients with an eating disorder: Evidence from a national database of health insurance claims. *International Journal of Eating Disorders, 27*(4), 381–389.

Sullivan, P. F. (1995). Mortality in anorexia nervosa. *American Journal of Psychiatry, 152*(7), 1073–1074. Ann Arbor, Michigan

Thompson Healthcare. (2005). *The red book.*

Williamson, D. A., Thaw, J. M., & Varnado-Sullivan, P. J. (2001). Cost effectiveness analysis of a hospital-based cognitive-behavioral treatment program for eating disorders. *Behavior Therapy, 32*, 459–477.

W. Stewart Agras

Abstract

This chapter briefly summarizes some of the research issues raised in this volume and highlights some of the potential areas for further research. Among the areas examined are the contributions of genetics, environmental factors, developmental issues, treatment, and prevention. The role of other areas of research that impinge on these topics is also examined.

Keywords: developmental stages; genetics; pharmacogenetics; prevention; research; treatment

Introduction

Research in the field of eating disorders (EDs) is ultimately aimed at improving the prevention and treatment of these disorders thus reducing the overall impact of EDs on individuals and society. Hence, these aims need to guide studies in the very different research arenas described in this volume. Moreover, we should be able to define the relation of research in any one area to the enhancement of prevention and treatment.

Genetics

Genetic research is one of the most fundamental areas of endeavor, although whether or not genetic studies will provide useful information leading to improved prevention and treatment of the EDs is at the moment questionable. Because there are many variables impinging on eating, the disorders of eating are complex problems likely to involve many genes interacting with one another and with the environment. Hence each gene related to the EDs will probably account for only a small portion of the variance in the disorder, which in turn may not much illuminate either causation or treatment. Ultimately, genetic findings that point to the biological mechanisms involved in the EDs may lead to

more targeted treatments or prevention strategies, either pharmacological or psychotherapeutic, for these disorders. Hence, this is a research topic worth investigating over the long-term, particularly the interaction between genes and environmental risk factors. More precise delineation of the ED syndromes may be necessary to enhance genetic studies and this in turn requires more exact assessment and classification of the disorders in order to deal with the heterogeneity within the existing syndromes. Moreover, it is unclear at present whether genetic research should concentrate on the already defined syndromes, or on sub-syndromes as defined in some classification studies, or on eating behaviors such as binge eating, purging, or dieting. Characterization of potential phenotypes is also likely to be helpful in furthering genetic research (Lopez, Tchanturia, & Treasure, 2009). One potential phenotype involves anorectic individuals characterized by the symptom complex of anxiety, depression, and obsessive–compulsive behaviors. The second involves the cognitive processes underlying the rigid thinking found in many anorectic individuals. In addition, the field of pharmacogenetics is rapidly developing with the potential of identifying groups of individuals who do and do not respond to a particular pharmacological agent, possibly allowing for a more targeted use of medication in the EDs (Drago, De Ronchi, & Serreti, 2009).

Environmental Influences

The characterization of environmental variables that either cause or maintain the EDs has shown progress in identifying risk factors, and to a lesser extent, causal risk factors. The identification of modifiable, preferably causal, risk factors leads directly to the formulation of prevention studies. Prospective studies large enough to investigate the contribution of many hypothesized risk factors combined with laboratory studies or clinical trials modifying a risk factor in order to identify causal risk factors are needed. The interaction between causal risk factors and specific genes at particular developmental stages may eventually be a useful research area to pursue, as noted previously.

One putative risk factor, dieting, requires further investigation because of the conflicting evidence regarding its role in the EDs. Although it is widely accepted that dieting is an important precipitating and maintaining factor for all the EDs, some research has raised doubts about this proposition (Stice, Cameron, Killen, Hayward, & Taylor, 1999; Stice, Cooper, Schoeller, Tappe, & Lowe, 2008). The alternative view is that our present methods of assessing of dieting status is identifying an unknown variable that is a hidden risk factor for EDs. Candidates for the third variable include a tendency toward overeating, possibly biological in origin, that would lead to dieting to overcome the changes in weight and shape that such eating would induce. Unraveling this mystery may well lead to the identification of different targets for prevention and treatment.

Preventing EDs is likely to be difficult given the current societal pressures for women to attain a thin body shape in many countries, cultures, and subcultures, inevitably leading to increases in dieting and other weight control measures. Moreover, such pressures are unlikely to abate soon given the spreading problem of obesity and associated calls for weight reduction. At present, most ED prevention programs are aimed at adolescents or young adults—an appropriate group given the rates of EDs in these individuals. However, it is clear that the roots of the EDs are to be found further back in childhood, often fostered by family attitudes and behaviors. Preoccupation with weight and shape and dieting begin in childhood. Hence, a focus on identifying modifiable risk factors at earlier ages may be valuable in leading to earlier prevention efforts (Agras, Bryson, Hammer, & Kraemer, 2007).

Prevention of some of the medical consequences of severe dieting would also seem useful. For example, the only treatment of any promise for osteopenia and osteoporosis, both of which are common in anorexia nervosa (AN), is enhanced nutrition and weight gain (Mehler & MacKenzie, 2009). Because of the long-term consequences of unresolved osteoporosis it would seem important to prevent this consequential disorder very early in the illness. This requires identification and treatment as early as possible in the course of the disorder.

Culture and Ethnicity

Another factor contributing to the EDs, possibly both genetic and environmental, involves the specific effects of culture and ethnicity on eating habits in general and the EDs in particular. Although the situation has improved in the last few years, we still know too little about the relative distribution of the EDs in minority populations in the United States or the causes for the observed variations in frequencies among different populations. AN, for example, appears to be rare in black women but further studies are needed to confirm this tentative opinion and to provide information about beliefs, attitudes, and behaviors relevant to dieting, weight and shape concerns, and so forth that may be specific to the black population (Striegel-Moore et al., 2003). Individuals from different cultures are likely to interact differently with different risk factors to produce EDs. There is also little information available on responses to different treatments across different ethnicities (Chui, Safer, Bryson, Agras, & Wilson, 2007). Such treatment studies are difficult because they require oversampling of minority populations. However, combining data sets may lead to sufficient minority representation to allow comparisons between some ethnic minority groups and Caucasians. Such information may be useful both for the prevention and treatment of ED in minority populations as well as the broader population.

Epidemiology

Epidemiologic studies combined with longitudinal, family, and twin studies can shed light on the frequency, cultural and ethnic variation, transmission, and classification of EDs. One problem that needs to be resolved is the classification of cases in the eating disorders not otherwise specified (EDNOS) group, namely which classes of EDNOS belong within one of the full syndromes (including binge eating disorder). It is likely that the majority of EDNOS cases will fit into a major syndrome. At that point, the question becomes how to separate cases from non-cases, that is, how to define the lower threshold of severity and what measure to use to do this. A measure of the effect of the disorders on everyday living may prove more useful than symptomatology to distinguish cases from non-cases at the lower boundary. Statistical methods such as latent class analysis and taxometric analysis may, in the context of large enough studies, shed further light on classification. Correct classification is important because it may provide more accurate information on the course and treatment of disorders and, as noted previously, provide more tightly defined classes likely to be useful in genetic studies.

The incidence, prevalence, and variations of newly described syndromes such as vomiting disorder and night eating syndrome also need further study to ascertain their importance from a public health viewpoint and their distinction from existing syndromes. Finally, epidemiologic information on infant, childhood, and adolescent EDs as well as the nature of EDs in other cultures are needed.

Developmental Issues

The study of EDs across the lifespan reveals some relatively neglected areas including infancy, childhood, adolescence, and the elderly. Relatively little is known about disorders such as "picky eating" or "overeating" that are common, cause much worry and sometimes strife for parents, and may confer later health problems. Little is known about the persistence of these behaviors or their health consequences, although early overeating may be related to overweight and picky eating to underweight later in childhood. Some data suggest that both picky eating and overeating persist at least through early childhood (Dubois, Farmer, Girard, Peterson, & Tatone-Tokuda, 2007). Larger and longer studies, more exact assessment methods, and better classification of these and other disorders of eating in infancy and childhood are needed (Lewinsohn, Holm-Denoma, Gau, Joiner, & Striegel-Moore, 2005). Such studies would help to delineate the childhood syndromes more accurately, possibly identifying new syndromes as well as assessing the health consequences of these disorders in later childhood and adolescence and eventually in adults. Further study of the relationship between childhood and adolescent eating problems and adult EDs, an area about which relatively little is known, also requires further research. Studies suggest that the adolescent ED tends to ameliorate

although associated general psychopathology such as anxiety, depression, and personality disorders may worsen in adult life (Patton, Coffey, Carlin, Sanci, & Sawyer, 2008; Wentz, Gillberg, Anckarsater, Gillberg, & Rastam, 2009). Such knowledge would allow assessment of the need for the treatment of EDs in adolescence and perhaps lead to prevention of later health problems whether EDs or other psychiatric or medical disorders.

The status of EDs in adolescence is somewhat better defined than in early childhood partly because the definitions for EDs in adult life fit the observed ED syndromes fairly well, although developmental differences across adolescence and childhood may require different criteria, which do not presently exist, for diagnosis. Treatment studies for this age group have lagged far behind those in adult populations, with a handful of controlled studies for the treatment of AN and even fewer studies of the treatment of bulimia nervosa (BN). Because the incidence and prevalence of EDs in adolescence are similar to those of adults this is clearly an area for accelerated research, although, as noted previously, it would be useful to know more about the relation between adolescent and adult EDs. The majority of cases of AN onset in late childhood and adolescence making identification and treatment of AN in adolescence a high priority, with the aim of reducing the number of chronic cases of the disorder for which there are no evidence-based treatments at this point.

There is also remarkably little research into the type, prevalence, incidence, and health consequences of EDs in geriatric populations although there are case reports of the classical EDs in the elderly (Miller, Morley, Rubenstein, & Pietruszka, 1991). Given the importance of nutritional disturbances in the elderly, this again is an area in which more research is needed.

Treatment

At this point there are no evidence-based first-line treatments for AN, although a specific family therapy for adolescents, in which parents take temporary control of their adolescent's feeding, is promising (Agras & Robinson, 2008; Keel & Haedt, 2008). No pharmacological agent has been adequately tested in adolescents with AN and there is no effective medication for adults (Reinblatt, Redgrave, & Guarda, 2008). Given the rarity of the disorder, almost all the studies in adults or adolescents have had an inadequate sample size or the dropout rates (mostly in adults) have been so large as to preclude firm conclusions being drawn from the studies. It has been argued that high dropout rates, particularly if unequal between treatment groups, essentially preclude statistical analysis because individuals with different characteristics may drop out of different treatments in which case randomization has broken down (Halmi et al., 2005). Moreover, recruitment of participants with AN is very difficult, partly because the disorder is relatively uncommon and partly because potential participants with AN resist treatment and hence do not volunteer for treatment studies. Because of these problems, multisite studies are needed to enable recruitment of an adequate sample size although small-scale single-site studies are useful to indicate fruitful pathways to pursue in larger trials. Similar to research in a number of medical conditions, it is necessary to identify several sites that have shown the ability to recruit participants with AN that can work together to pursue treatment research.

Treatment research in BN is more advanced, with both medication (most antidepressants, although only fluoxetine is FDA approved) and cognitive–behavioral therapy (CBT) as first line treatments, although CBT is probably more effective than antidepressants. However, recovery rates with CBT of about 25% to 40% are lower than desirable. Other treatments such as interpersonal psychotherapy (IPT) fare no better, and IPT is less effective than CBT at the end of treatment but not at follow-up. This relatively low rate of recovery needs to be enhanced, but so far no treatment has been found superior to CBT. This is an area requiring more intensive treatment development.

In the treatment of binge eating disorder (BED), IPT is equivalent to CBT at both end of treatment and follow-up and a larger proportion of patients are recovered than is the case with BN. Again, however, more treatment research is needed to enhance recovery rates of 50% to 60%. Moreover, neither IPT nor CBT lead to much weight loss in this largely overweight population. Antiepileptic drugs such as topiramate appear promising in reducing both binge eating and weight. Further trials of these medications in combination with CBT or IPT are warranted. Urgently needed are newer medications that may affect both binge eating and weight. Finally, shortened versions of CBT (guided self-help) appear promising both for BN and BED.

Because larger studies are needed to answer questions of differential effectiveness of treatment, multisite studies have become more common for treatment outcome studies of BN and BED. Such studies also allow for examination of moderators and mediators of treatment. Identifying moderators, that is, groups of individuals who do better in one treatment and worse in another, points the way to the development of treatment algorithms, whereas identifying mediators allows for a better understanding as to how treatments work. Treatment algorithms based either on cost considerations, that is, using the least costly treatment as a first step, or on moderator analyses, that is, differentially assigning individuals to treatments based on an individual characteristic, are likely to be important in the future.

Dissemination

Once effective treatments have been identified, it is necessary to consider methods to achieve dissemination of these therapies from effectiveness or efficacy studies to other milieus, for example, medical settings such as HMOs, community clinics, college campuses, and so forth. Such studies have not yet been attempted for EDs but are likely needed if treatment is to become more widely available. It is evident that apart from AN, EDs – the majority of which are EDNOS – will be treated outside specialty ED centers. Hence there is a need for effective and cost-effective methods of dissemination.

Evidence-Based Treatment

Given the relatively early state of development of treatments in the ED field, the evidence base is incomplete. This is particularly the case for AN, paradoxically the first ED to be described, for the reasons outlined previously. Specific forms of family therapy for children or adolescents appear promising, and it is clear that a continuum of care is needed in many cases including hospitalization, day care, outpatient psychotherapy, and rehabilitation services. From an evidence-based perspective, the most urgent need is for large-scale well-coordinated studies to identify effective treatments for AN, with a particular focus on adolescent AN. At the other end of the ED spectrum, the question of how to effectively treat both the ED symptoms and overweight that are features of BED is important, given the prevalence of BED and the disease consequences associated with overweight and obesity. Finally, the role of nonspecialist care for the EDs needs better definition based on controlled outcome studies. The latter is an aspect of the dissemination of research findings to the wider community of practitioners including family physicians.

Cost-Effectiveness

It could be argued that all large-scale treatment studies should include the needed assessments to calculate the cost-effectiveness of treatment. This is a much neglected research area and one of growing importance given the need to contain treatment costs. For example, the relative effectiveness and cost-effectiveness of guided self-help and CBT or IPT need to be determined. Hence, future treatment research designs should take into account the costs associated with different treatments.

References

Agras, W. S., Bryson, S., Hammer, L. D., & Kraemer, H. C. (2007). Childhood risk factors for thin body preoccupation and social pressure to be thin. *Journal of the American Academy of Child & Adolescent Psychiatry, 46*, 171–178.

Agras, W. S., & Robinson, A. H. (2008). Fory years of progress in the treatment of the eating disorders. *Nordic Journal of Psychiatry, S47*, 19–24.

Chui, W., Safer, D. L., Bryson, S., Agras, W. S., & Wilson, G. T. (2007). A comparison of ethnic groups in the treatment of bulimia nervosa. *Eating Behavior, 8*, 485–491.

Drago, A., De Ronchi, D., & Serreti, A. (2009). Pharmacogenetics of antidepressant response: An update. *Human Genomics, 3*, 257–274.

Dubois, L., Farmer, A., Girard, M., Peterson, K., & Tatone-Tokuda, F. (2007). Problem eating behaviors related to social factors and body weight in preschool children: A longitudinal study. *International Journal of Behavioral Nutrition and Physical Activity, 4*, 9.

Halmi, K. A., Agras, W. S., Crow, S., Mitchell, J. E., Wilson, G. T., Bryson, S., et al. (2005). Predictors of treatment acceptance and completion in anorexia nervosa: Implications for future study designs. *Archives of General Psychiatry, 62*, 776–781.

Keel, P. K., & Haedt, A. (2008). Evidence-based psychosocial treatments for eating problems and eating disorders. *Journal of Clinical Child and Adolescent Psychology, 37*, 39–61.

Lewinsohn, P. M., Holm-Denoma, J. M., Gau, J. M., Joiner, T. E., & Striegel-Moore, R. H. (2005). Problematic eating and feeding behaviors of 36-month-old children. *International Journal of Eating Disorders, 38*, 208–219.

Lopez, C., Tchanturia, K., & Treasure, J. (2009). Weak central coherence in eating disorders: A step toward looking for an endophenotype of eating disorders. *Clinical Experimental Neuropsychology, 1*, 117–125. Epub.

Mehler, P. S., & MacKenzie, T. D. (2009). Treatment of osteopenia and osteoporosis in anorexia nervosa: A systematic review of the literature. *International Journal of Eating Disorders, 42*, 195–201.

Miller, D. K., Morley, J. E., Rubenstein, L. Z., & Pietruszka, F. M. (1991). Abnormal eating attitudes and body image in older undernourished individuals. *Journal of the American Geriatric Society, 39*, 462–466.

Patton, G. C., Coffey, C., Carlin, J. B., Sanci, L., & Sawyer, S. (2008). Prognosis of adolescent partial syndromes of eating disorder. *British Journal of Psychiatry, 192*, 294–299.

Reinblatt, S. P., Redgrave, G. W., & Guarda, A. S. (2008). Medication management of pediatric eating disorders. *International Review of Psychiatry, 20*, 183–188.

Stice, E., Cameron, R., Killen, J. D., Hayward, C., & Taylor, C. B. (1999). Naturalistic weight reduction efforts prospectively predict growth in relative weight and onset of obesity among female adolescents. *Journal of Consulting and Clinical Psychology, 67*, 967–974.

Stice, E., Cooper, J. A., Schoeller, D. A., Tappe, K., & Lowe, M. R. (2008). Are dietary restraint scales valid measures of moderate- to long-term dietary restriction? Objective biological and behavioral data suggest not. *Psychological Assessment, 19*, 449–458.

Striegel-Moore, R. H., Dohm, F. A., Kraemer, H. C., Taylor, C. B., Daniels, S., Crawford, P. B., et al. (2003). Eating disorders in white and black women. *American Journal of Psychiatry, 160*, 1326–1331.

Wentz, E., Gillberg, I. C., Anckarsater, H., Gillberg, C., & Rastam, M. (2009). Adolescent-onset anorexia nervosa: 18-year outcome. *British Journal of Psychiatry, 194*, 168–174.

INDEX

Note: Page numbers followed by "*f*" and "*t*" denote figures and tables, respectively.

A

Abdominal distension, 275
Abstinence violation effect, 149
Acculturation, 128. *See also* Culture and
    disordered eating
    process of, 228–29
    relationship to disordered eating,
        236–37
    in terms of body image, 234–35
Acrocyanosis, 261
Active genotype environment (g-e)
    correlations, 107–8
Adjunctive outpatient psychotherapy, 420
Adolescent, eating disturbances and
    disorders, 4
    incidence rate for AN, 25–26
    incidence rate for EDNOS, 26
    indications for hospitalization, 283*t*
Adolescent focused therapy (AFT), 37–38
Adolescents with AN
    atypical antipsychotics, 38
    developmentally focused therapy
        (AFT) for, 37
    dietary advice, 40
    family therapy, 36
    outpatient treatment for, 35
    parental involvement, 35
    treatment, 33–34
Adolescents with an ED, assessment
    approach to interview, 268
    bone mineral density (BMD)
        complications, 280–82
    brief adolescent psychiatric history,
        270–72
    cardiovascular complications, 273–74
    clinician's interview, 268–70
    conclusion of the interview, 272
    dermatologic changes, 280
    differential diagnoses, 273
    electrolyte abnormalities, 276
    endocrine abnormalities, 278–79
    evaluation of menstrual cycle, 270
    family history, 270
    gastrointestinal complications,
        275–76
    hematological and immune system
        abnormalities, 279–80
    interviewing parents, 272
    laboratory evaluation, 272–73
    linear growth, 282

medical history, 270
medical management, 282–86
metabolic abnormalities, 277
myopathic changes, 280
oral and dental complications, 275
physical examination, 272
pulmonary complications, 274
QTc EKG abnormalities, 273–74
renal complications, 276–77
review of systems, 270
structural brain changes, 282
unique characteristics, 267
Adolescents with BN
    developmentally focused therapy
        (AFT) for, 37
    family therapy, 36
    parental involvement, 35
    treatment, 33–34
Adrenocorticotropic hormone
    (ACTH), 77
Adverse health problems, 39
Adverse life events, 128
Advocacy interventions, 312
Aerobic exercise, 467
Affective disorders, 25, 292
African Americans and body image
    concerns, 210–12
Age of onset, for ED, 309, 310*f*
Alcoholism, 116
Alexithymia, 198
Altered feeding behaviors, 76–77
Amenorrhea, 10, 16
Amenorrhea, primary, 20
Amenorrhea diagnostic criterion, 263
American culture. *See* Body image
Amitriptyline, 420, 457–58
Ampular cardiomyopathy, 260
Amygdala, 87–88
Anemia, 278
Anglo-American culture, 238
Anorectics with binge/purge behavior, 296
Anorexia nervosa (AN), 1, 47, 150. *See*
    also Weight and shape concerns
    actual diagnostic criteria, 12
    altered interoceptive disturbances
        in, 77
    appetitive dysregulation in, 90
    assessment dilemma in children and
        adolescents, 30–31
    BED on a continuum with, 49

beta-endorphin levels in, 78
binge eating/purging type, 10–11, 13,
    196
binge-purge subtype of, 67
binge/purge subtype of, 33
bone mineral density (BMD),
    decreased, 261
CCK function in, 78
CNS neuropeptide alterations, 80–81
criterion A, 20
criterion for in children and
    adolescents, 27–28
cross-cultural patterns, 66
diagnosis in female patients, 20
dopamine (DA) activity, 80
emotions and mood states, 196–99
epidemiology, 65–66
family therapy for, 36
fat phobia, 231
fMRI studies in, 89–91
genetic influences, 75–76
5-HT_{1A} activities, 83–84
5-hydroxytryptamine (5-HT) activity,
    80–82
incidence rate for adolescent, 25–26
leptin concentrations, 79
malnutrition due to, 39
neuroendocrine/neuropeptide
    alterations in, 81*t*
neurotransmitter functioning in, 13
non-ascertained twin studies of, 110*t*
"non-fat phobic," 231
outpatient treatment for, 34
popular media portrayals of, 66
prognosis, 66–67
psychotropic medication in adults
    with, 38
REC bulimic-type, 84
response to reward and punishment,
    90–91
restricting type, 10–11, 13
subthreshold patients of, 39
suicide attempts, 67
treatment, 4
Anorexia Nervosa Inventory for Self
    Rating (ANIS), 310
Anterior cingulate cortex (ACC), 83, 85,
    87–89, 91–92
Anterior insula (AI), 85–86
Anticonvulsant drugs, 468–69

Antidepressant–antipsychotic combination therapy, 422–23
Antidepressants, 38, 419–21, 426–29, 433–34, 467–68
Antiepileptic drugs (AEDs), 425–26, 429–30, 436–38
Antiobesity agents, 432, 434–36, 468
Antipsychotics, 421–22, 438, 458
Anxiety, 60, 77, 84
Anxiety disorders, 2, 12, 16, 25, 38, 50, 84, 128, 292–96
Anxiety-related prodromal symptoms, 128
Apolipoprotein-B (Apo-B), 260
Appetite-stimulating drugs, 423, 431
Appetitive dysregulation, 90
Arrhythmias, 273
Asian Americans, 238
Aspiration pneumonia, 274
Assessment, 14
    broad context of, 249–50
    determining the domains or constructs, 251–53
    diagnostic criteria for an eating disorder, 251, 255
    function of, 250–51
    instruments used, 253–56
    interviews, 254
    screening tests, 250, 254–55
    secondary domains, 252
    self-report questionnaires, 254–56
    test meals, 255–56
    theoretical assumptions, 251–52
    thresholds of change, 252–53
    treatment planning and outcome, 251, 255
Attrition rate, from outpatient treatment, 35
Atypical antipsychotics, 38
Autism, 35
Axis I disorder in DSM-IV, 48–50, 292–97
    Axis I comorbid psychiatric diagnoses, 293–95t
Axis II disorders, 50, 297–300

B

Baclofen, 439, 432
Balanced-calorie diet, 149
Behavioral weight loss treatment (BWL), 5, 17
Behavior modification impact, on child taste and food preferences, 142
Behavior therapy (BT), 453
Benzodiazepines, 459
Beta-endorphin activity, 78
Binge eating disorder (BED), 1–4, 13, 47, 91–92, 150, 153, 168, 300, 331, 386
    CBT, 340–43
    on a continuum with other eating disorders and obesity, 49–50
    current DSM-IV TR diagnostic criteria, 48

diagnostic criteria, 12
    as a distinct Axis I disorder, 48–49
    emotions and mood states, 191–96
    epidemiology, 69
    evidence of diagnostic validity and clinical significance of models for, 50
    history and prevalence of, 48
    as a marker of psychopathology, 50
    medical comorbidities in, 264
    models, 48–50
    multisite field trial of, 48–49
    prevalence of, 48
    prognosis, 69–70
    research criteria, 50–52
    research diagnostic criteria for, 49t
    research needed to clarify the status of, 50–52
    role of weight and shape concerns, 51
    symptoms of, 48
    treatments, 4–5
Binge-eating episodes, 69–70, 189, 190–92, 195–96, 432, 434, 437, 468
Binge eating patterns in children, 20
Binge eating syndromes, 124
Binge episodes, 50–51
Biological factors, 14
Biological underpinnings, of eating disorders, 2
Bitter taste preferences, 138
Bloating, 275
Blood oxygen level dependent (BOLD) response, 89
Blood urea nitrogen (BUN), 259, 276
Body Attitude Questionnaire, 113
Body Dissatisfaction scale of the Eating Disorder Inventory (EDI), 207
Body Esteem Scale (BES), 207, 209
Body image
    acculturation in terms of, 234–35
    in AN patients, emotional responses, 197–98
    in BED patients, emotional responses, 193–94
    biopsychosocial factors and, 233–35
    in BN patients, emotional responses, 190
    and development of EDs and depression, 235
    and ethnic discrimination experiences, 235
    as a function of ethnic minority status in the United States, 241
    indicators across ethnic groups, 233
    media concerns, 234
    in Western culture, 3, 206
Body mass index (BMI), 79, 106, 128, 208, 225, 230, 320, 455
Bone loss, 39
Bone-marrow hypoplasia, 278
Bone mineral density (BMD), decreased, 261, 280–82
Boundary problem, in eating disorders, 2–3

Bradycardia, 21, 259, 273
Brain imaging studies, in AN and BN
    neurocircuitry of appetite regulation, 85–86
    of normal feeding behavior in healthy individuals, 86–87
Brain matter loss, 39
Bulimia nervosa (BN), 1–2, 4, 47, 150, 183. See also Weight and shape concerns
    actual diagnostic criteria, 12
    appetitive dysregulation in, 90
    assessment dilemma in children and adolescents, 30–31
    BED on a continuum with, 49
    beta-endorphin levels in, 78
    CNS neuropeptide alterations, 80–81
    criteria, in DSM-V, 16
    cross-cultural patterns, 68
    CSF levels, 78
    dopamine (DA) activity, 80
    emotions and mood states, 189–91
    epidemiology, 67–68
    fMRI studies, 91–92
    genetic influences, 75–76
    5-HT_{1A} activities, 83–84
    5-hydroxytryptamine (5-HT) activity, 80–82
    neuroendocrine/neuropeptide alterations in, 81t
    neurotransmitter functioning in, 13
    non-ascertained twin studies of, 111t
    nonpurging type, 10–11, 13
    peptide YY (PYY) levels, 78
    postprandial decrease in ghrelin levels, 80
    prognosis, 68–69
    purging type, 10–11
    retrospective correlates for, 128, 132–33t
    risk factors, 3
    subthreshold patients, 39
Bulimic behaviors, 26
Bulimic pathology, 159–63
Bulimic syndromes, 124, 134
BULIT, 310–11
Bupropion, 465

C

Calcium, 259
Caloric deprivation, effects of, 151–52
Calorie-deficit diet, 149
Carbonyl-[^{11} C]WAY100635 BP, 83
Catecholamine pathway, 106
Cathartic colon, 262
Causal risk factor, 3
CGI-Improvement scale, 439
Childhood, eating disturbances and disorders, 4. See also Child taste and food preferences, influencing factors
    obesity, 128
    overanxious disorder, 128

Children facial expressions, to taste, 144–45
Child taste and food preferences, influencing factors
  assessment, 143–45
  barriers to changing food preferences, 143
  behavior modification impact, 142
  bitter, 138
  early exposure, effect of, 138–39
  and food experience, 140
  frequent exposure, effect of, 139–40
  longitudinal changes according to age, 143
  mass media influences, 141–42
  parental role models, 140
  parental styles, effects of, 141
  peer influences, 141
  and restrictive feeding practices, 142–43
  salt, 138
  sweet, 137–38
  teacher influences, 140–41
Chinese culture and disordered eating, 229, 231–32
Chlorpromazine, 421
Cholecystokinin (CCK), 60, 78–79
Chromosome linkage peaks, 117
Chronic hunger, state of, 149
Chronic overconsumption thesis, 163
Cisapride, 423, 459
Classifications, 9
Clinical perfectionism, 15
Clonazepam, 439
CNS neuropeptide alterations, 80–81
Cognitive–affective deficit, 198
Cognitive analytical therapy (CAT), 453, 455
Cognitive–behavioral therapy (CBT), 4–5, 15, 153–54, 420
  AN, 343
  BED, 340–43
  BN, 331–39
  CBT for adolescents (CBT-A), 37
  CBT for BN (CBT-BN), 461–63
  efficacy studies, 332–33, 341
  and evidence-based treatments, 332–33
  expanded treatment (CBT-Eb), 339
  with fluoxetine, 343
  generalizability of, 339
  guided self-help (CBTgsh), 5, 333–34, 341–43
  interpersonal problems, 337
  motivation for change, 336
  negative affects in, 337
  predictors and moderators of treatment outcomes, 341–43
  relationship between behavior change and acceptance, 337–38
  scope and focus, 338–39

therapeutic efficacy, 332, 334–36, 340–41
Cognitive dissonance (CD) programs, 315–19
Cognitive impairment, 58
Comorbid conditions, 2
Compulsive/emotionally constricted personality, 16
Conditioning model of binge eating (CBE), 192
Confucian belief, 229
Conjoint family therapy (CFT), 456
Constipation, 262, 275
Cooperativeness, 299
Coping behavior, 38
Corticotropin-releasing hormone (CRH), 77
Costs and cost-effectiveness
  of ED treatments, 483–84
  individual, 480–81
  national, 481–83
Creatinine, 259
CSF concentrations, 78
Cultural changes, in dieting, 2
Cultural identity, 228–29
Culture and disordered eating, 224, 487
  case studies of China and South Africa, 231–32
  Chinese culture, 229
  clinical and preventive implications of research, 241–42
  cross-cultural comparisons and prevalence, 225–28
  cross-cultural validity of diagnostic criteria, 224t
  directions for future research, 242–43
  Korean culture, 229
  prevalence and incidence of the spectrum, 227–28t
  psychiatric diagnosis relative to, 225
  risk factors and eating pathology, 226–31
Culture-bound syndromes, 239
  AN, 66
  BN, 68
Cyproheptadine, 423, 458–59

D
Day treatment programs, 34
D-cycloserine, 425, 459
Decalcification of the teeth, 262
Dehydration, 263
Delayed gastric emptying, 275
Deliberate self-harm, 128
Dental care, 2
Depressed mood, 58
Depression, 2, 16, 26, 38, 109, 183
Depressive symptoms and weight concerns, association between, 217
Developmental issues, of ED, 488
Developmentally focused therapy (AFT) for adolescents, 37–38, 40–41

Development and Well Being Assessment (DAWBA), 31
Dexfenfluramine, 432
Diabetes, 58
Diagnostic and Statistical Manual -III-R (DSM-III-R), 292
Diagnostic and Statistical Manual of Mental Disorders DSM-IV-Text Revision (DSM-IV-TR), 10, 47, 65, 69, 208, 453
  classification system, 15–17, 331
  criteria, 47
  eating disorder criteria to youths, 20
  eating disorder symptom criteria, 12–13
Diagnostic dilemmas, in children and adolescents
  accurate diagnosis of BN, 28–29
  changes in psychopathology, 32
  childhood eating problems, 26–27
  criterion for AN, 27–28
  diagnostic category eating disorder not otherwise specified (EDNOS), 29–30
  due to varying weight thresholds, 31
  problem of assessment, 30–31
  problem of comorbidity, 30
  psychological developmental limitations in reporting symptoms, 26
  use of menstruation in definition, 31
  varying definitions of recovery or outcome, 31–32
  younger patients, 32
Diagnostic models
  three-dimensional model (TDM), 13–15, 14f
  transdiagnostic model (TDM), 15
Diagnostic overlaps, among the eating disorders, 12–13
Dialectical behavior therapy (DBT)
  adaptation of the biosocial theory for, 406
  adaptation of treatment, 409
  affect regulation model for, 405–6
  efficacy of, 406–7
  model of maintenance and etiology of, 405–6
  rationale for use, 404–5
  research evidence, 407–8
  sequence of treatment, 408–9
  standard treatment, 402–3
  Stanford Model of, 408, 410–12t
  structure of treatment, 408
  treatment strategies, 403–4
  use of concepts and skills specifically adapted for binge eating and/or purging, 413
Dietary advice, 40
Dietary calcium requirements, 281
Dietary Intent Scale (DIS), 157
Dietary restraint, 76, 105

Dieting, 128
   and bulimic pathology, 159–63
   chronic overconsumption thesis, 163
   confounding variables, prospective
      effects due to, 155–56
   definition and descriptive
      statistics, 149
   dietary restraints, measures of, 157–59
   effects on caloric deprivation on
      caloric intake, 153–54
   effects on eating pathology, 149–51
   greater anticipated reward from food
      intake, 165–68
   greater consummatory food reward,
      163–65
   incompatible findings in prospective
      studies, 154–55
   lean versus obese individuals, 164–65,
      169
   real-world, 156–57
   relation of long-term dieting to eating
      disorder syndrome, 152–53
   relation of short-term caloric
      restriction to laboratory-based
      eating, 151–52
   relative dietary restriction versus
      absolute dietary restriction, 159
   and self-reported impulsivity, 168–69
Disordered eating attitudes, 76
Dissatisfaction with weight and shape, 76
Dissemination, of effective treatments, 41
Dissonance programs, 311–12
Dissonance theory, 311–12
Distress, 58
Diuretic abuse, 60
Diuretics, 10
DL-fenfluramine, 82
Dominance, genetic, 105
Domperidone, 423, 459
Dopamine (DA) activity, in ED, 80
Dorsal striatum, 92
Dorsolateral prefrontal cortex
   (DLPFC), 86
Doubly labeled water (DLW), 158
DOVE campaign, 325
Drinking behavior and body image
   concerns, 216–17
Dropout rates, 4
DSM-III AN, 421
DSM-IV Work Group on Eating
   Disorders, 48
DSM's classification system
   controversies with, 17–20
   criteria for children and early
      adolescents, 19–20
   gender-based criteria, 18
DSM's classification system, 9–12
DSM-V, BN criteria, 16
DSM-1V criteria for BED, 17
Dutch Restrained Eating Scale
   (DRES), 157
Dysphagia, 275
Dysphoria, 77

E

Early intervention, 33–34
EAT-26 cutoff, 124
Eating and emotions, links between
   comfort eating, concept of, 185–87
   comorbidity of affective disorders with
      eating disorders, 187–88
   emotions and dimensions,
      181–82, 182*f*
   general effects of hunger on, 183–84
   impact of meal size, timing, and habit,
      183–84
   Macht's "five-way model" of
      interactions, 180–81, 181*f*
   moods, 181
   motivational aspects, 184–85
   negative affect and eating attitude,
      185–87
   negative emotionality and eating
      disorders, 188–99
Eating Attitudes Test (EAT), 310, 422
Eating Disorder Examination (EDE), 30,
   33, 58, 60, 207
   EDE 12.0D, 254
   EDE 16.0D, 254
Eating Disorder Examination-
   Questionnaire-Restraint scale
   (EDEQ-R), 157
Eating Disorder Examination-Restraint
   scale (EDE-R), 158
Eating Disorder Inventory (EDI),
   60–61, 420
Eating Disorder Inventory (EDI-2), 91
Eating disorder not otherwise specified
   (EDNOS), 2–3, 17, 47, 59, 68,
   124, 129, 240, 261, 331, 339,
   386
   DSM-IV-TR classification, 10
   incidence rate in children and
      adolescents, 26
   prevalence estimates, 69
Eating Disorders Examination-
   Questionnaire, 11
ED Diagnostic Scale (EDDS), 310
Edema, 259
Ego-oriented individual therapy, 37
Electroconvulsive therapy (ECT), 426
Electrolyte abnormalities, 263
Elevated dietary restraint scores, 150–51
Energy-deficit diets, 149, 152
Enhanced CBT (CBT-E), 251
Environmental factors, 14, 487
Environmental variables, 3
Epidemiologic studies, 1, 487–88
Epigenetics, 61
Escape-avoidance coping, 128
Esophageal motility, 275
Ethnicity, 224–25, 487
   acculturation and relationship to
      disordered eating, 236–37
   among Asians, 237–38
   among Blacks, 237
   among Hispanics, 237

   clinical and preventive implications of
      research, 241–42
   development of ED, 238
   directions for future research, 242–43
   and inclination to treatment, 238–39
   and indicators of disordered eating
      behavior, 236
   and prevalence of disordered eating
      behavior, 235–36
Etiology, 14
Evening hyperphagia subtype, 58
Evidence-based treatments, 5
   algorithm, 472–73*f*
   CBT guided self-help (GSH), 464–65
   CBT model for bulimia, 460–63
   of combination medications, 466, 469
   exercise and CBT, 465
   factors associated with unfavourable
      outcome with treatment, 461*t*
   family therapy, 456–57
   level I evidence, 454*t*
   methods of literature searching, 453
   ondansetron, 466
   pharmacotherapy, 457–60
   predictors of outcomes, 471
   psychological therapy, 453–56
   recommendations, 470–71
   supportive therapy, 463
   topiramate, 465–66
   treatment choice in BED, 466–69
   treatment in primary care, 469–70
   use of antidepressants, 465
Evocative genotype environment (g-e)
   correlation, 107
Exercise, 465, 467
External validators, 12–13
Extrinsic Affective Simon Task (EAST), 166

F

[18 F]altanserin BP, 84
Family-based approach for adolescents, 4
Family-based treatment (FBT). *See*
   Family therapy
Family history studies, 12
Family therapy, 4, 36
   acceptability of, 381
   for adolescent BN, 378–81
   for adults, 381–82
   for AN, 36, 40
   for BN, 40
   development of manual, 377–78
   future directions, 382
   history, 373–74
   and inpatient treatment, 377
   multiple-family day treatment for
      adolescent AN, 381
   outpatient treatment, 376
   seminal study of, 376
   Stanford Dosage Study, 377
   theoretical model for adolescents with
      AN, 374–77
   treatment trial outside the United
      Kingdom, 376–77

Fasting, 160, 297
Fat free mass (FFM), 262
Fear of fatness, 13–14
Feminist theory, 312
Fenfluramine, 432
Fluorodeoxyglucose (FDG), 85
Fluoxetine, 4, 38, 284, 420–21, 426, 468–69
Flutamide, 466
Fluvoxamine, 465
Focal psychoanalytic psychotherapy (FPT), 453
Follicle-stimulating hormone (FSH), 263
Food avoidance emotional disorder, 25
Food cues, 61
    emotional responses
        of individuals with AN, 196–97
        of individuals with BED, 192–93
        of individuals with BN, 189
Food phobias, 25
Food test motivational states, 87
Full syndrome BN, 33
Full-syndrome eating disorders, 11
Functional magnetic resonance imaging (fMRI), 59, 61, 85, 197
    BOLD signal, 89, 91f
    food deprivation studies, 93t
    images of food, 88–89
    response to reward and punishment in AN, 90–91
    studies in BN, 91–92
    sucrose response in AN, 89–90, 89f

G
Gastric dilatation, 262
Gastric rupture, 262
Generalized anxiety disorder, 116
Genetic factors, of eating disorders, 3
    additive genetic effects, 105
    in AN and BN, 75–76
    complexities, 105
    endophenotype analysis, 107, 116
    gene–environment correlations and genotype–environment interactions, 107–8
    genes acting on different pathways, 106–7
    genetic dominance, 105
    genetic markers, 105
    genetic variance of BMI, 106
    heritability estimates, 109–16
    linkage and association studies, 116–17
    nonshared environmental influences, 105
    overlap of genetic risk factors, 116
    rationale for research, 104–5
    shared environmental influences, 105
    twins studies. *See* Twin studies
Genetic research, 486–87
Genotype–environment interactions (G×E), 108
Ghrelin concentrations in ED, 79–80

Glandular enlargement, 275
Global Assessment of Function (GAF), 456
Global distribution of eating disorders, 240
Glomerular filtration rate, reduced, 263
Glomerular filtration rate (GFR), 276
Granulopoiesis, 279
Greater anticipated reward from food intake, 165–68
Greater consummatory food reward, 163–65
Great Ormond Street (GOS) criteria, 20–21
Grief, 354
Guided self-help based on CBT (CBTgsh), 17
Guided self-help (CBTgsh) for BED, 5

H
Hamilton Anxiety Scale (HAM-A), 420
Hamilton Depression Rating Scale (HDRS), 456
Health promotion program, 324–25
Heterogeneity, in clinical presentation, 16
High-energy foods, 182
High sensitivity c-reaction protein (hsCRP), 260
[³H]imipramine binding, 82
Hispanic females and body image concerns, 211–12
Hispanics, 237–38
Histamine H_1 receptors, 421
Historical continuity of eating disorders, 2
Homovanillic acid (HVA), 80
Hormone replacement therapy, 281, 424–25, 430–31
Hospitalization, 34, 283–84, 283t
5-HT$_3$ antagonists, 430
5-HT$_{1A}$ receptor BP, 83
5-HT$_{2A}$ receptor BP, 84
Hunger state, 87
Hydrolyzed protein-based formulas, 139
5-hydroxyindoleacetic acid (5-HIAA), 81–82, 457
5-hydroxytryptamine (5-HT) activity, in ED, 80–82, 457
5-hydroxytryptamine (5-HT) neurotransmission system, 13
5-hydroxytryptophan, 82
Hyperaminoacidemia, 277
Hyperamylasemia, 262
Hypercholesterolemia, 262, 277
Hypercortisolemia, 263
Hypertrophy, 275
Hypochloremia, 263
Hypoestrogenemia, 281
Hypoglycemia, 277
Hypokalemia, 263, 276
Hypomagnesemia, 260
Hypophosphatemia, 260, 276
Hypotension, 21
Hypothalamic–pituitary–adrenal axis, 77

Hypothalamic–pituitary–thyroid axis, 79
Hypothermia, 21
Hypovolemia, 263

I
ICD-10, 453
Impaired interpersonal functioning, 12
Implicit Association Test (IAT), 166–67
Impulse control disorders (ICDs), 297
Impulsive behaviors, 16, 168–69
Impulsive/emotionally dysregulated personality, 16
Incidence
    AN in children and adolescents, 25–26
    eating disorder not otherwise specified (EDNOS) in children and adolescents, 26
    rate for AN, 25–26
    rate for EDNOS, 26
Indicated prevention programs, 308
Indicators, of disordered eating behavior, 236
    across ethnic groups, 233
Individual psychotherapy, 4
Infant facial expressions, to taste, 143–45f
Infant formulas, 138–39
Inpatient hospitalization, 34
Insulin-like growth factor-1 (IGF-1), 278
Interleukin-6 (IL-6), 260
International Affective Picture System (IAPS), 197
International Classification of Diseases (ICD-10), 20–21
Internet-based cognitive–behavioral intervention, 320
Internet-based program, 320
Interoception, 86, 89
Interoceptive awareness, 128
Interpersonal deficits, 355
Interpersonal psychotherapy (IPT), 4–5, 17, 252, 343, 454
    adolescent and child/parent adaptations, 367–68
    for AN, 363
    assessment of ED symptoms, 350
    basic concepts, 349–50
    for BED, 361–63
    for BN, 360–61
    development of individualized interpersonal formulation, 353–54
    diagnosis and assignment of the sick role, 350–51
    future directions, 367–69
    general therapeutic techniques, 358
    implementation for EDs, 350–60
    interpersonal inventory, 351
    interpersonal problem areas, 350, 354–59, 354t
    interpersonal theory, 348–49
    IPT-WG case sample, 368t
    personal historical timeline of a patient with BED, 352–53t

Interpersonal psychotherapy (*cont.*)
  for the prevention of eating and
    weight-related problems, 369
  for the prevention of excessive weight
    gain, 364–67
  redirecting of issues relating to ED
    symptoms, 357
  relationship between poor
    interpersonal functioning and
    EDs, 349
  tasks of initial session, 351*t*
  therapist-patients relations, 356–57
Interpersonal role disputes, 355
Interspecies genetics, 61
Ipecac abuse, 274

K

Kool-Aid, 138

L

Lanugo, 259
Latent class analysis, 10–11
Latent profile analysis, 300
Lateral prefrontal cortex, 88
Latinos, 238
Laxative abuse, 60
Laxatives, 10
Left ventricular hypertrophy, 260
Leptin, 277
Leptin concentrations, in ED, 79
Leukopenia, 278
Life-Threatening Behaviors, 409
Light therapy, 432
Linear growth in adolescents with
    AN, 282
Linkage and association studies, 105,
    116–17
Lithium, 431–32
Liver function determinations, 259
Longitudinal studies, characteristics of,
    124–28, 130*t*
Loss of control in binge eating, 51
Loss of control over eating behavior, 51
Low-calorie diets, 148, 153, 159, 167–68
Luteinizing hormone (LH), 263
Lymphocytosis, 278

M

Major depression, 20, 50, 60, 83, 116,
    128
Mallory Weiss tears, 275
Malnutrition, 39, 75–76
Malnutrition-induced
    immunodeficiency, 278
Marked conduct problems, 128
Mass media influences, on child taste and
    food preferences, 141–42, 142*f*
Maternal influences, in meal and play
    times, 107
M-chlorophenylpiperazine (*m* -CPP), 82
McKnight Risk Factor Survey (MRFS),
    208
Meal plans, 40

Meal skipping, 160
Media literacy, 312
Medial orbitofrontal cortex (OFC), 193
Medial prefrontal cortex (mPFC), 85
Mediators, 315
Medical comorbidities of ED
  cardiovascular complications, 260–61
  dental complications, 262
  dermatological complications, 261
  gastrointestinal complications,
    261–62
  metabolic/endocrine complications,
    262–63
  neurologic complications, 263
  renal complications, 263
  signs and symptoms, 259–60,
    260*t*, 271*t*
  skeletal systems, 261
Memantine, 438
Men. *See also* Weight and shape concerns
  genetic variance of BMI, 106
  heritability issues, 116
  prevalence of AN, 65
  prevalence of BED, 69
  prevalence of PD, 70
Mendeleev's periodic table of elements, 9
Menstrual cycle dysregulation, 77
Mental disorders, 2
Mental health-related quality of life, 51
ME! program, 325
Metabolic alkalosis, 263
Metoclopramide, 423, 459
Mexican Americans, 238
Milk-based formulas, 139
Mineral deficiencies, 277
Mitral valve prolapse (MVP), 274
Moderators, 314–15
Modernization and weight and shape
    concerns, 229–30
Monoamine functions, in ED, 80
Mood disorders, 12, 50
Mood lability intolerance, 15
Mood-related prodromal symptoms, 128
Moods, 181
Mood stabilizers, 425, 431–32
Mortality rates, 13, 25, 39
    AN, 67
Motor cortex, 91
Mucosal erythema, 275
Multidimensional Body Self-Relations
    Questionnaire (MBSRQ), 207
Multifamily format (MFG) treatment, 40
Myopathy, 280

N

NaCl solution, 138
Nail dystrophy, 261
Naltrexone, 438, 459
Nausea, 275
Necrosis, 262
Negative affect and eating attitude, 185–87
  binge eating in BED, 194–96
  binge eating in BN, 190–91

Negative body image, 224
Negative emotionality and eating
    disorders, 188. *See also* Impulsive
    behaviors
Neophobia, 143
Neurobiologic alterations, 76
Neurocircuitry of appetite regulation,
    85–86
Neuroendocrine abnormalities, 58, 77
Neuropeptides, 77
Neuropeptide-Y (NPY), 78
Neurotransmitter functioning, 13
Neurotransmitter pathways, 77
Night eating on bariatric surgery
    outcomes, 58
Night Eating Syndrome History and
    Inventory (NESHI), 58
Night eating syndrome (NES), 47
  current research diagnostic criteria, 52
  as a distinct disorder, 52–54
  evidence of diagnostic validity and
    clinical significance, 57
  future research for, 58–59
  history and prevalence, 52
  models, 52–57
  with obesity, 55–56
  with other eating disorders, 54–55
  proposed research diagnostic criteria
    for, 53*t*
  as secondary to other
    psychopathology, 56–57
  with sleep-related eating disorder
    (SRED), 55, 56*t*
Non-ascertained twin studies of
    anorexia nervosa (AN), 110*t*
  behaviors and/or attitudes not
    included in DSM criteria,
    114–15*t*
  bulimia nervosa (BN), 111*t*
  of DSM diagnostic criteria for eating
    disorders, 112*t*
Nonclinical binge eaters, 51
Nonfood cues, 61
Norepinephrine reuptake inhibitors, 438
Normal feeding behavior in healthy
    individuals, 86–87
Normative personality, 16
Nutritional advice in eating disorders,
    39–40
Nutritional supplementation, 426

O

Obesity, 2–3, 17, 91, 206
  prevention program, 322–23
Objectification theory, 312
Obsessions, 77
Obsessive-compulsive disorder (OCD),
    16, 20, 38, 296, 299, 457
Obsessive–compulsive personality
    disorders, 128
Obsessive–compulsive traits, 299
Occipital cortex, 89
Oestradiol, 459

Olanzapine, 422, 458
Ondansetron, 466
Opiate antagonists, 425, 431, 438
Opioid activity, 78
Opportune ages, and food
    preferences, 143
Oral manifestations, of eating disorders, 262
Orbitofrontal cortex, 89
Orbitofrontal cortex (OFC), 85–94
Osmoregulation abnormalities, 277
Osteopenia, 261
Osteoporosis, 261
Outpatient treatment, 34–35
Overweight, 2, 206
Oxford Risk Factor Interview, 131

P

Pairwise taxometric analyses, 12
Pancreatitis, 262
Pancytopenia, 278
Panic disorder, 116
Parental attitudes, perception of, 128
Parental involvement, 35
Parental styles, effects of, 141
Parietal cortex, 89
Partial BN syndrome, 60
Passive g–e correlation, 107
Path to Mindful Eating, 409t
Peer-led CD program, 321–22
Peptide YY (PYY), 78
Perfectionism, 16, 128
Perforated ulcer, 262
Perimolysis, 275
Personality clusters, 16, 298
Personality disorders, 12, 297–99
Personality traits and ED, 75–76
Pharmacotherapy, 419t, 427t, 433t
    for AN, 418–26
    for BED, 432–39
    for BN, 426–32
    for NES, 439
    rationale for use, 417–18
    of sleep-related eating disorder, 439
Phobia, 116
Physiologic indices, 2
Planet Health, 323
Pneumomediastinum, 274
Positive and Negative Affect Schedule, 300
Positron emission tomography (PET), 61
Positron emission tomography (PET)
    studies
        correlation with anxiety and harm
            avoidance, 84
        and the DA D2/D3 radioligand
            raclopride, 83
        effects of released 5-HT, 83–84
        5-HT 2A receptor BP values, 84
        regional cerebral blood flow
            (rCBF), 88
        role of DA as a reward prediction
            signal, 83
Post-lunch dip, 184
Posttraumatic stress disorder (PTSD), 296

Potassium levels, 2
Pramipexole, 439
Pregnancy complications, 128
Prevention, 3–4
    and benefits, 314
    definition, 307–8
    ecological/environmental approaches,
        323–26
    effective program for, 312–14
    examples of effective approaches,
        316–23, 317t
    and identifying risk factors, 309
    models, 311–12
    moderators and mediators of success
        of prevention programs, 314–16
    screening measures for, 309–11
    theory of, 308–9
Primary taste cortex, 85
Project Eating Among Teens (Project
    EAT), 210, 212, 214
Prokinetic drugs, 423
Proxy risk factor, 159
Psychiatric comorbidity, 25
Psychoeducation, 311
Psychological therapies, 386
Psychopathology marker, BED as, 50
Psychotherapies, 41, 463
Psychotropic medications, use of, 38
Purging anorectics, 296
Purging disorder (PD), 47–48
    as axis I psychiatric disorder, 59–60
    on a continuum with other eating
        disorders, 60–61
    definition, 59
    epidemiology, 70
    evidence of diagnostic validity and
        clinical significance of models, 61
    future research for, 61
    history and prevalence, 59
    models, 59–61
    prognosis, 70–71
Purpura, 261

Q

Quetiapine, 458

R

Race/ethnicity differences, in weight and
    shape concerns, 210–12
Randomized clinical trials (RCT), 36, 38,
    40, 150, 152, 420, 432, 454t,
    458–59, 462t, 464t, 467t
Real-world dietary restrictions,
    156–57
Receiver Operating Characteristic (ROC)
    analysis, 310
Recombinant human growth hormone
    (rhGH) in AN, 424
Recombinant human insulin-like growth
    factor I (rnIGF-1), 459
Refeeding syndrome, 276
Regional cerebral blood flow (rCBF)
    studies, 88, 197

Relativist perspective, of diagnosis of
    ED, 225
Reliable change index (RCI), 252
Remission, likelihood of, 13
Rennin–angiotensin–aldosterone
    system, 263
Repeated binge eating episodes, 10
Residential treatment programs, 34, 284
Resting energy expenditure (REE), 262
Restraint Scale (RS), 157
Restrictive anorexic syndrome, 13
Restrictive feeding practices, 142–43
Retrospective correlates, for eating
    disorders, 132–33
Retrospective (risk) factor assessment, 124
Reward, 90–91
Risk factors, 3–4, 123
    for AN, 124, 128
    for AN during adolescence, 128
    for BED, 128
    for BN, 128
    for cardiac arrhythmia, 260
    consideration of interactions, 134
    in early and later childhood, 124, 128
    limitations of research, 128–29
    longitudinal evidence on, 129
    McKnight Longitudinal Risk Factor
        Study, 131
    meta-analytic review, 124–28
    retrospective, 124
    taxonomy of risk, 124
    update of, 129–34
Risk of death, 2
Risperidone, 458
Role transitions, 354–55
Ruminative thinking, 195–96
Russell's sign, 259, 261

S

Salt taste preferences, 138
Satiation state, 77, 87
SCANS screening tool, 310
Schizophrenia, 2, 35
SCID-II personality disorder, 298
SCOFF screening tool, 254
Selective eating, 25
Selective serotonin norepinephrine
    reuptake inhibitors (SNRIs), 421
Selective serotonin reuptake inhibitors
    (SSRIs), 38, 84, 284–85, 421, 457
Self-directiveness, 299
Self-esteem, 15, 128, 322
Self-Esteem Fund, 325
Self-help interventions, 386
    definition, 388
    distinction between pure self-help and
        guided self-help, 389–90
    factors in terms of optimizing uptake
        and outcomes, 396
    history, 387–88
    limitations, 397–98
    medications and, 397
    modes of delivery, 390–91

Self-help interventions (*cont.*)
outcome, 395–96
rationale for use of, 388–89
self-help books, 390
self-help manuals, 397*t*
support by e-mail, 391
supporter expertise, 396
systematic reviews of, 391–95
translating effective treatments
into, 388
use and effectiveness of, 396–97
via CD-ROM, 390–91, 394–95
Self-identified chocolate "addicts," 183
Self-induced vomiting, 2, 76, 111, 259,
261, 274
Self-initiated weight loss diets, 149
Self-labeled dieters, 161
Self-rated binge episodes, 151
Self-reported impulsivity, 168–69
Self-starvation, 2
Self-starvation processes, 39
Self-transcendence, 299
Separated family therapy (SFT), 456
Serotonin (5-hydroxytryptamine,
5-HT), 61
Serotonin reuptake inhibitor
antidepressants, 419
Serotonin reuptake inhibitors, 38
Serotonin transporter gene promoter
polymorphism (5HTTLPR), 108
Serotonin transporter (SERT), 59
Sertraline, 439, 468
Serum glucose, 259
Sexual abuse, 128
Sexual abuse, as risk factor, 134
Sexual orientation differences in weight
concerns, 216
Sheehan Disability Scale, 436
Sibutramine, 468
Simon Spatial Incompatibility task, 91
Single photon emission computed
tomography (SPECT), 59, 61,
88, 197
Sinus arrhythmias, 260
Sinus bradycardia, 260
Sleep-related eating disorder (SRED), 55,
56*t*, 439
Smoking behavior and body image
concerns, 216
Social cognitive theory, 215–16
Social learning theory, 311
Social phobia, 128, 296
Social Physique Anxiety Scale (SPAS), 208
Social support, 128
Sore throat and hoarseness, 275
South African culture and disordered
eating, 231–32
Soy based formulas, 139
Specialist supportive clinical management
(SSCM), 454, 456
Spectrum of disordered eating, 239–40
Spironolactone, 432
Split-classification system, 17

Starvation, 260
State alterations, 76
Statistical approaches, to the classification.
See Latent class analysis;
Taxometric analysis
Statistical comparisons, of eating
disorders, 57*f*
Stress-reactive binge eaters, 193
Striatum, 85
Structural brain changes, in adolescents
with AN, 282
Student Bodies™, 311, 315–16, 320,
321*f*, 326
Subcutaneous emphysema, 274
Substance abuse disorders, 296–97
Substance use disorders, 12
Subthreshold BED, 51
Suicidality, 60
Suicide attempts, 67, 84
Sweet taste perception, 85
Sweet taste preferences, 137–38
Systematic study of the eating disorders, 1
Systemic family therapy (SFT), 40

T
Tanning beds usage and body image
concerns, 217
Targeted or selective prevention
interventions, 308
Taxometric analysis, 10–12
of BED, 50
Taxonic disorders, 14
Taxonomy, 9
Teacher influences, on child taste and
food preferences, 140–41
Telogen effluvium, 261
Temperament and Character Inventory
(TCI), 422
Test meals, 255–56
Thalamus, 92
Therapeutic Stance, 355
Thiazide diuretics, 276
Thin body preoccupation and social
pressure to be thin (TBPSP), 134
Thinness, drive for, 13–14
Three-dimensional model (TDM) of
eating disorders, 13–15
Three Factor Eating Questionnaire
Restraint scale (TFEQR), 157
Thyroid functions, 263
T-lymphocyte, 78
Topiramate, 426, 439, 468–69
Toronto Alexithymia Scale (TAS), 198
Transdiagnostic model (TDM) of eating
disorders, 15, 21
Treatment, of eating disorders, 4–5,
488–90
in children and adolescents, 32–40
determining the treatment
approach for patients with EDs,
363–64
Tricyclic antidepressants (TCA), 457
Tryptophan, 149

TV commercials, influence on child
taste and food preferences,
141–42, 142*f*
Twin studies, 76
American twins, 11
of AN, 110
Australian twins, 11, 59
of BN, 111
of disordered eating, behaviors and/or
attitudes, 114–15
of DSM diagnostic criteria for eating
disorders, 112
female Caucasian, 10
heritability of phenotypes, 109–13
important issues, 113–16
uses, 104–5, 108–9
Type 1 diabetes, 263, 324

U
Universalist perspective, of diagnosis of
ED, 225
Universal prevention programs, 307–8
U.S. National Institutes of Health
(NIH), 40

V
Vagal afferent activity, 183
Valproate, 432
Venlafaxine, 468
Ventromedial prefrontal cortex, 87
Viral films, 325
Vitamin deficiencies, 277
Vitamin D oral supplementation, 459
Vomiting, 10, 60, 149. *See also* Self-
induced vomiting

W
Weight and shape concerns
among heterosexuals, 216
approaches to defining, 207–8
association between BMI and, 209
of children and preadolescents, 209
correlates and predictors of, 212–15
development of, 208–12
family influences, 214–15
gender differences, 210
media influences, 212–13
peer influences, 213–14
and personal characteristics, 216
during puberty, 209–10
race/ethnicity differences, 210–12
sexual orientation differences in
weight concerns, 216
unhealthy behaviors related to,
216–18
Weight and Shape Concern subscale of
the Eating Disorder Examination
(EDE), 207
Weight-bearing exercise, 281
Weight Concerns Scale, 207, 311, 320
Weight control behaviors, 217–18
Weight criteria, for AN and BN, 2–3
Weight loss, 75–76

Weight maintenance diet, 155
Weight preoccupation, 76
Westernization and weight and shape concerns, 230–31
Western sociocultural environment, 109
Women. *See also* Weight and shape concerns
  BN, abuse reporting, 128
  brain imaging studies, 87
  gastrointestinal problems during childhood in BN patients, 262
  genetic variance of BMI, 106
  heritability for tobacco smoking, 108
  prevalence of AN, 65–66
  prevalence of BED, 69
  prevalence of BN, 67–68
  prevalence of PD, 70
Workgroup for Classification of Eating Disorders in Children and Adolescents (WCEDCA), 19–20

X

Xerosis, 261

Y

Yale-Brown-Cornell Eating Disorder Scale (YBCEDS), 422
Yellow skin, 259
Yoga, 318
YSR-Inventory, 128

Z

Zinc, 424
Zinc deficiency, 458
Zonisamide, 437